ing jurisdiction. In the event that .... shall be required to divest itself of its interest in the Venture, Section 6.03 hereof shall be applicable to such sale and Sections 4.03 and 6.04 hereof shall not be applicable until .... shall have completed such divestitute.

Section 10.09. *Captions: Partial Invalidity.* The captions, section numbers, article numbers, and index appearing in this Joint Venture Agreement are inserted only as a matter of convenience and in no way define, limit, construe, or describe the scope or intent of such sections or articles of this Joint Venture Agreement, nor in any way affect this Joint Venture Agreement. If any term, covenant, or condition of this Joint Venture Agreement or the application thereof to any person or circumstance shall, to any extent, be invalid or unenforceable, the remainder of this Joint Venture Agreement, or the application of such term, covenant, or condition to persons or circumstances other than those as to which it is held invalid or unenforceable, shall not be affected thereby and each term, covenant, or condition of this Joint Venture Agreement shall be valid and be enforced to the fullest extent permitted by law.

Section 10.10. *Entire Agreement.* This Joint Venture Agreement shall constitute the entire agreement of the Venturers; all prior agreements between the Venturers, whether written or oral, are merged herein and shall be of no force and effect. This Joint Venture Agreement cannot be changed, modified, or discharged orally but only by an agreement in writing signed by the Venturer against whom enforcement of the change, modification, or discharge is sought.

Section 10.11. *Applicable Law.* This Joint Venture Agreement shall be interpreted and construed under and governed by the laws of the State of ....

Section 10.12. *Counterparts, Complete Agreement.* This Joint Venture Agreement is being executed in two (2) original counterparts, each of which shall for all purposes be deemed an original, and all of such counterpart shall together constitute but one and the same agreement.

Section 10.13. *Successors.* All of the provisions of this Joint Venture Agreement shall inure to the benefit of and be binding upon the successors and assigns of the Venturers hereto. Any Venturer who makes a transfer or assignment permitted by the terms of this Joint Venture Agreement shall have no further liability or obligation to the Venture.

COMMENT: See discussion of joint venture agreement at ¶ 11.02[5].

tax returns, nothing contained in this Joint Venture Agreement shall constitute the Venturers as partners with one another or agents for one another to render any Venturer liable for any debts or obligations of the other, which is granted by this Joint Venture Agreement.

Section 10.06. *Brokerage.* Developer represents to .... that .... is entitled to a brokerage fee in connection with the creation of the Venture. Developer shall pay the fee of .... and defend, indemnify, and hold .... and the Venture harmless from any claim for such fee. Developer shall be entitled to reimbursement for such fee to the extent provided in Section 3.02 (3)(o).

Except as hereinabove provided, each Venturer represents to the other that no person, firm, or corporation is entitled to any brokerage fee or commission or other compensation in connection with the creation of the Venture, and each Venturer shall defend, indemnify, and hold the other harmless from any claim for such commission or compensation based on the alleged employment of such person, firm, or corporation by the party so agreeing to defend.

Section 10.07. *Indemnities.* Each Venturer shall indemnify and hold the other harmless against and from all claims, demands, actions, and rights of action which shall or may arise by virtue of anything done or omitted to be done by the other (through or by its agents, employees, or other representatives) outside the scope of, or in breach of the terms of, this Joint Venture Agreement, provided the other shall be notified promptly of the existence of the claim, demand, action, or right of action and shall be given reasonable opportunity to participate in the defense thereof. In the event that one Venturer shall be held severally liable for the debts of the Venture, such Venturer shall be entitled to contribution from the other Venturer so that each Venturer shall only be obligated to pay that portion of such liability as shall be proportionate to such Venturer's interest in the profits and losses of the Venture.

Section 10.08. *Legal Disabilities.* Developer recognizes that .... is subject to certain limitations and restrictions imposed by the .... and agrees that as long as .... or an affiliate or subsidiary of .... continues to own an interest in the Venture, the Venture cannot operate and manage the Project in any manner or engage in or conduct any business if such Venturer would be prohibited from doing so by such law or by the regulations or requirements of the Superintendent of Insurance of the State of .... and other regulatory bodies hav-

Section 9.03. *Distribution of Project.* In the event that the Venturers shall not be able to dispose of the Project in the manner provided in Section 9.01 hereof, title to the Project shall be placed in the names of the Venturers as tenants in common and the undivided interest of each in the Project shall be equal to the interests of such Venturers in the profits and loss of the Ventures as of the time of liquidation.

ARTICLE 10
Miscellaneous

Section 10.01. *Further Assurance.* Each Venturer hereto agrees to execute and deliver all such other and additional instruments and documents and do all such other acts and things as may be necessary to more fully effectuate this Joint Venture Agreement and carry on the business contemplated herein.

Section 10.01. *Notices.* Any notice, request, demand, report, offer, acceptance, certificate, or other instrument which may be required or permitted to be delivered to or served upon the Venturers or any other entity or person succeeding to the interest of a Venturer hereto shall be deemed sufficiently given or furnished to or served upon any such party if in writing, addressed to any such party at the business address set forth on the first page hereof, or at such other address of which any party may notify the other party, and such notice or instrument shall be received by any such party.

Section 10.03. *Equitable Remedies.* In the event of a breach or threatened breach of this Joint Venture Agreement by either Venturer, the remedy at law in favor of the other Venturer will be inadequate and such shall accordingly have the right of specific performance in the event of any breach or injunction or in the event of any threatened breach of this Joint Venture Agreement by the other Venturer.

Section 10.04. *Remedies Cumulative.* Each right, power, and remedy provided for herein or now or hereafter existing at law, in equity, by statute or otherwise, shall be cumulative and concurrent and shall be in addition to every other right, power, or remedy provided for herein or now or hereafter existing at law, in equity, by statute or otherwise, and the exercise or beginning of the exercise or the forebearance of exercise by any party of any one or more of such rights, powers, or remedies shall not preclude the simultaneous or later exercise by such party of any or all of such other rights, powers, or remedies.

Section 10.05. *No Partnership.* Except to the extent expressly provided in this Joint Venture Agreement with respect to the filing of

preparation of annual financial statements for the Venture to prepare a complete and final certified audit of the books, records, and accounts of the Venture, and all adjustments between the Venturers shall be made upon the basis of such certified audit.

Section 9.02. *Liquidation Distribution.* Upon the completion of the winding up of the affairs and business of the Venture, and after payment or making provision for payment of all liabilities of the Venture other than liabilities to the Venturers, the net assets of the Venture shall be distributed as follows:

(1) If the proportion of the capital account of any Venturer to the capital accounts of both Venturers exceeds the proportion of the interest in profits and losses of that Venturer to the interests in the profits and losses of both Venturers, the amount of any such excess capital account shall be repaid to the other Venturer out of the first available assets.

(2) The remaining net assets, if any, shall be distributed to the Venturers in proportion to their respective interest in the profits and losses of the Venture.

(3) In the event any part of the net assets distributed hereunder consists of notes receivable or noncash assets, the cash shall be distributed first, and such notes and any noncash assets shall be distributed later.

(4) No Venturer shall have any claim or recourse against the other in the event the assets of the Venture are insufficient to repay any capital contribution or interest, except for the failure by such other Venturer to perform its obligations hereunder.

(5) In the event that upon such dissolution the assets of the Venture are insufficient to pay and discharge all unsecured obligations and liabilities of the Venture authorized in accordance with this Joint Venture Agreement and upon which recourse may be had against either Venturer personally by persons other than a Venturer, each Venturer shall (i) contribute to the capital of the Venture the amount required to make the capital account of such Venturer the same proportion of the aggregate capital accounts of both Venturers which the interest in profits and losses of that Venturer bears to the aggregate interests in profits and losses of both Venturers; and after such contribution if the assets of the Venture remain insufficient, (ii) contribute to the capital of the Venture a percentage of the aggregate amount required by the Venture to pay and discharge in full and in cash all of such obligations and liabilities of the Venture equal to its interest in profits and losses of the Venture.

the required capital contibution on behalf of the Defaulting Venturer shall each execute and deliver to the other a written memorandum evidencing the revised interests of such Venturers in the profits and losses of the Venture.

(4) The nondefaulting Venturer shall have the option, exercisable by delivery of notice in writing to the Defaulting Venturer within forty-five (45) days after the expiration of the period for the curing of such default (unless such default shall have been cured prior to the expiration of the period for the curing of such default) to purchase the Defaulting Venturer's entire interest in the Venture, the Project, and the other property and assets of the Venture, for a price equal to the total of the Defaulting Venturer's capital contributions to the Venture, less any distribution of capital made to the Defaulting Venturer. If the nondefaulting Venturer shall exercise such option within the time and in the manner hereinbefore provided, (i) the sale shall be consummated within ninety (90) days after the exercise of such option, (ii) the purchase price shall be paid in cash or by certified or cashier's check, and (iii) the Defaulting Venturer shall execute and deliver such deeds, assignments, and other documents as shall be necessary to convey the interest being purchased with all required transfer tax stamps affixed. In the event the Defaulting Venturer shall fail or refuse to execute any instrument to consummate such purchase, the nondefaulting Venturer is hereby granted the irrevocable power of attorney, which shall be binding on the Defaulting Venturer as to all third parties, to execute and deliver on behalf of the Defaulting Venturer all instruments required to consummate such transfer.

(5) The Defaulting Venturer shall become an Inactive Venturer as defined in Article VII hereof and shall remain an Inactive Venturer unless and until such default is cured.

ARTICLE 9
Winding Up: Liquidation Distribution

Section 9.01. *Winding Up.* Upon the expiration or earlier termination of this Joint Venture Agreement and the failure of the Venture to be reconstituted by the Venturers, the Venturers shall proceed promptly to wind up the affairs and business of the Venture, including the sale or other disposition of the Project and other property and assets of the Venture, if such sale or disposition can be made within the discretion of the Venturers on a commercially feasible basis. The Venturers shall cause the certified public accountant charged with responsibility for the

constitute a debt to the Venture and may be collected through the institution of appropriate legal proceedings initiated by the other Venturer.

(2) The Defaulting Venturer's interest in the Venture, the Project, and any other property and assets of the Venture shall be subject to a lien securing the payment of the debt referred to in subparagraph (1) above and securing the other Venturer against any loss, cost, or expense resulting from the default of the Defaulting Venturer, and the nondefaulting Venturer may foreclose such lien in the manner provided by law for the foreclosing of mortgages on real property by advertisement or by court proceedings.

(3) If the default consists of the failure to make a required capital contribution or other payment, the nondefaulting Venturer shall have the option, exercisable by delivery of notice in writing to the Defaulting Venturer within forty-five (45) days after the date of such default (unless such default shall have been cured during the period for curing such default) to make the capital contribution or other payment which the Defaulting Venturer should have made. By making such capital contribution or other payment on behalf of the Defaulting Venturer, the nondefaulting Venturers shall be deemed to have purchased a portion of the Defaulting Venturer's interest in the Venture, the Project, and any other property and assets of the Venture. The portion purchased shall be determined by dividing the amount of such capital contribution by the then current agreed net value of the Venture. The resulting quotient shall be the percentage of the interest in the profits and losses of the Venture purchased by the Venturer making such capital contribution. As used in this subparagraph (3) of Section 8.02 only and for no other purpose, the term "current agreed net value of the Venture" shall be the amount agreed upon by the Venturers as representing the difference between the value of the assets of the Venture and the liabilities of the Venture at the time such agreement is reached. The Venturers shall establish the current annually agreed net value of the Venture within thirty (30) days after receipt of the annual statements of the Venture referred to in Section 3.09. If the Venturers cannot agree upon the current agreed net value of the Venture for any annual period within the aforesaid thirty-day period, the current agreed net value of the Venture for such annual period shall be the amount which is the average of the values proposed in good faith by each of the Venturers. The Defaulting Venturer and the Venturer making

certified check at the time of the consummation of the sale. The sale should be consummated within ninety (90) days after the Active Venturer shall have exercised its option to purchase the interest of the Inactive Venturer. The Inactive Venturer shall execute and deliver such deeds, assignments, and other documents as shall be necessary to convey the interest of the Inactive Venturer in the Venture, the Project, and any other property and assets of the Venture to the Active Venturer, with all required transfer tax stamps affixed. In the event such Inactive Venturer shall fail or refuse to execute any instrument required to consummate this purchase, the Active Venturer is hereby granted the irrevocable power of attorney, which shall be binding on the Inactive Venturer as to all third parties, to execute and deliver on behalf of the Inactive Venturer all instruments required to consummate such purchase.

Any determination by the appraisers under the terms of this Article shall be enforceable in accordance with the statutes of the State of .... governing arbitration.

ARTICLE 8
Events of Default: Remedies

Section 8.01. *Events of Default.* Either Venturer (hereinafter referred to as the "Defaulting Venturer") shall be in default hereunder if such Venturer shall fail to make any initial capital contribution; shall fail to pay its share of any expenses or other moneys required to be paid by it; shall fail to perform any obligation imposed upon it by any agreement by which the Venture or the Venturers (in their capacity as such) may be bound; or shall fail to comply with any laws applicable to joint ventures generally or in connection with the interest of the Venturers in the Project and other property and assets of the Venture, and shall fail to cure such failure to pay, perform, or comply within ten (10) days after receiving written notice thereof from the other Venturer, or if such failure (other than a failure to make a required initial capital contribution or other payment) shall be curable, but of a nature requiring more ten (10) days and less than ninety (90) days within which to cure, the Defaulting Venturer shall fail to commence to cure such failure within such ten-day period and thereafter, to continue to correct such failure with due diligence until the same has been corrected.

Section 8.02. *Remedies.* If any of the events of default provided in Section 8.01 hereof shall occur, the nondefaulting Venturer shall have the following remedies available to it in addition to all other remedies provided herein or by law against the Defaulting Venturer:

(1) The default in the payment of money by either Venturer shall

a going concern basis, taking into account all debts of the Venture and encumbrances on the Project and any other property and assets of the Venture.

The Active Venturer shall have the right, within sixty (60) days after the date on which the Inactive Venturer shall have become an Inactive Venturer to have an appraisal made of the value of the Venture, the Project, and any other property and assets of the Venture. At the time that the Active Venturer exercises such right it shall designate, in writing, a person to act as its appraiser for the purpose of establishing the appraised value of the Venture, the Project, and designation to the Inactive Venturer. Within ten (10) days after the Active Venturer gives such notice, the Inactive Venturer shall designate, in writing, a person to act as a second appraiser for establishing the appraised value and shall give notice thereof to the Active Venturer. If the Inactive Venturer shall fail to designate an appraiser in the manner and within the time hereinbefore provided, the Active Venturer shall make such designation on behalf of the Inactive Venturer. If any appraiser so designated by the Inactive Venturer or by the Active Venturer shall die, be disqualifed, become incapacitated, or shall fail or refuse to act before the appraised value shall have been determined, the Venturer so designating such appraiser shall designate a new appraiser. The appraisers so designated shall be members of the American Institute of Real Estate Appraisers or such successor body hereinafter constituted exercising similar functions; shall have not less than ten (10) years active experience as a real estate appraiser in the appraisal of property similar to the Property and the Project, and shall never have been in the employ of either Venturer. The two (2) appraisers shall meet promptly to determine the appraised value. If, within thirty (30) days following the designation of the second appraiser, the appraisers shall fail to agree upon the appraised value, the appraisers shall designate, in writing, within ten (10) days thereafter, a third appraiser. If the appraisers shall fail to designate the third appraiser in the manner and at the time hereinbefore provided, the appraisers or the Active Venturer shall request the American Institute of Real Estate Appraisers or its successor organization to designate the third appraiser. If within thirty (30) days following the designation of the third appraiser, the appraisers are unable to agree on the appraised value, the determination of the appraised value by the third appraiser shall be conclusive. During the course of their deliberations, the appraisers appointed in the manner set forth above shall be required to consult with ...., or another national accounting firm selected by them. The fees and expenses of the appraisers and the accounting firm shall be borne by the Venture.

The purchase price shall be payable in cash or by cashier's or

ity to act on behalf of the Venturer or the other Venturer (hereinafter referred to as the "Active Venturer"), nor have any voice in the management and operations of the Venture or the Project, nor have any rights which it otherwise would have under the terms of this Joint Venture Agreement to sell, assign, convey, encumber, or alienate in any way part of its interest in the Venture, the Project, or in any other property and assets of the Venture, except as otherwise expressly provided under the terms of Article 7. The Active Venturer shall then have the right to make all of the management decisions for the Venture and (unless otherwise provided in this Joint Venture Agreement) shall have the power and authority to enter into agreements and incur obligations in connection with the Venture or the Project on behalf of the Venture and the Venturers, including the Inactive Venturer, without first having to obtain the consent or concurrence of the Inactive Venturer. Anything herein contained to the contrary notwithstanding, the Inactive Venturer shall continue to be obligated to make the capital contributions required to be made under the terms of Section 3.03 and shall be liable for the costs, expenses, and obligations of the Venture in accordance with the provisions contained in Section 3.03, including the costs, expenses, and obligations of the Venture which are incurred subsequent to the date on which such Venturer shall have become an Inactive Venturer. The Inactive Venturer shall also continue to bear its share of any losses and be entitled to receive its share of any profits or distributions from the Venturer.

Section 7.02. *Right to Purchase the Interest of an Inactive Venturer.* The Active Venturer shall have the right and option to purchase all (but not part) of the interest of the Inactive Venturer in the Venture, the Project, and in any other property and assets of the Venture at a price equal to the amount obtained by multiplying the Inactive Venturer's percentage interest in the profits and losses of the Venture by the appraised value of the Venture, the Project, and the other property and assets of the Venture. The amount by which the capital account of the Inactive Venturer exceeds (or is less than, as the case may be) the amount obtained by multiplying the total of the capital accounts of both Venturers by the Inactive Venturer's percentage interest in the profits and losses of the Venture shall be added to (or deducted from, as the case may be) the purchase price so determined. Such option to purchase shall be exercisable by delivery of notice in writing to the Inactive Venturer within sixty (60) days after the determination of the appraised value, as hereinafter provided in this Section 7.02. As used herein, the term "appraised value" shall mean the value of the Venture, the Project, and any other property and assets of the Venture appraised on

Section 6.04. *Buy-Sell.* Any Venturer shall have the right to exercise the rights and privileges set forth in Section 4.03, whether or not a dispute between the Venturers shall then exist, to purchase the interest of the Venturer or to cause a sale of the other Venturer's interest to it; provided, however, no Venturer shall exercise its rights and privileges under this Section 6.04 more than once during any period of twelve (12) consecutive calendar months.

Section 6.05. *Indemnification of Selling Venturer.* Any Venturer purchasing the interest of the other Venturer under the terms of this Article VI shall indemnify and hold the Selling Venturer harmless from all liabilities of the Selling Venturer accruing thereafter under any then existing agreements or other obligations arising with respect to the Venture and the Project.

Section 6.06. *Sale in Violation of Joint Venture Agreement.* In the event that either Venturer shall attempt to sell, assign, transfer, hypothecate, pledge, encumber, or alienate, in any way, all or any part of its interest in the Venture, the Project, or in any property or assets of the Venture, in violation of any of the provisions contained in this Joint Venture Agreement, including, but not limited to, the provisions contained in this Article 6, such Venturer shall become, effective as of the date of such attempted sale, assignment, transfer, hypothecation, pledge, encumbrance, or alienation, an Inactive Venturer within the meanings of Section 7.01 hereof. Any such attempted sale or transfer shall not be effective to transfer any interest in the Venture, the Project, or any other property or assets of the Venture to any proposed transferee.

ARTICLE 7
Bankruptcy

Section 7.01. *Bankruptcy or Insolvency of a Venturer.* If either Venturer shall be adjudicated bankrupt or insolvent or shall petition for an arrangement or reorganization pursuant to the provisions of any state or federal bankruptcy or insolvency act; or if a receiver or trustee shall be appointed for all or any part of such Venturer's property; or if any assignment of such Venturer's property shall be made for the benefit of creditors; or if any execution or other process shall issue against any Venturer's interest in the Venture, the Project, or in any other property or assets of the Venture and shall not be vacated within ninety (90) days thereafter, then, effective as of the date of the occurrence of any of the foregoing events, such Venturer shall become an "Inactive Venturer." An Inactive Venturer shall not have any author-

not part) of their respective interests in the Venture, the Project, and any other property and assets of the Venture, to any purchaser from whom such Venturer had received a bona fide offer to purchase all (but not part) of its interest in the Venture, the Project, and any other property and assets to the Venture; provided, however, that in the event that any Selling Venturer shall receive a bona fide offer to purchase all (but not part) of its interest in the Venture, the Project and any other property and assets of the Venture which it desires to accept, it shall promptly give written notice to the other Venturer, which notice shall contain the name and address of the proposed purchaser and all material terms and conditions of the offer. The notice shall be accompanied by an offer to sell the Selling Venturer's interest to the other Venturer upon the terms and conditions contained in the offer tendered by the proposed purchaser.

The Venturer receiving such offer shall have the right, exercisable by delivery of notice in writing to the Selling Venturer within sixty (60) days after receipt of such notice and offer, to elect to purchase the interest of the Selling Venturer at the price and upon the same terms and conditions contained in the offer tendered by the proposed purchaser.

In the event that such offeree shall fail to exercise its rights to purchase within the time and in the manner hereinbefore provided, the Selling Venturer shall be free to complete the sale to the proposed purchaser upon the terms and conditions contained in the offer submitted to the offeree, within sixty (60) days after the expiration of the initial sixty (60) day period. If the sale is concluded with the proposed purchaser, the proposed purchaser shall be bound by all of the terms and conditions of this Joint Venture Agreement with the same force and effect as if the proposed purchaser had been a signatory and an original party to this Joint Venture Agreement. The proposed purchaser shall, by written instrument delivered to the other Venturer, expressly assume all obligations of the Selling Venturer, but only by forclosure of a lien or encumbrance on the Project or on the property or assets of the Venture.

In the event of any change in the identity of the proposed purchaser, or in the price, terms, or conditions of the offer, or in the event the sale to the proposed purchaser is not completed in the manner and within the time hereinbefore provided, the Selling Venturer may not sell or otherwise alienate his interest to anyone unless and until a new offering notice shall be given by the Selling Venturer to the other Venturer, in accordance with the procedure hereinbefore provided in this Section 6.03. The provisions of Section 4.03 and 6.04 shall be inapplicable during the period any offer to sell under this Section 6.03 remains outstanding.

the Project, whether or not the lease or occupancy agreement shall refer to such sums as "additional rental."

ARTICLE 6
Transferability Restrictions on Transfer

Section 6.01. *Right of Transfer Restricted*. Except as otherwise expressly provided in this Joint Venture Agreement, neither Venturer shall sell, assign, transfer, encumber, hypothecate, pledge, or alienate in any way, all or any part of its interest in the Venture. The sale or other transfer of any of the capital stock of any corporate Venturer which is not publicly traded, or the issuance by such corporate Venturer of additional shares of capital stock, shall be deemed to be a sale or transfer of all, or a part, as the case may be, of the interest of such corporate Venturer in the Venture, the Project, and the other property and assets of the Venture.

Section 6.02. *Permissable Transfers*. Any Venturer may sell or transfer all (but not part) of its interest in the Venture, the Project, and in any other property and assets of the Venture to any affiliated corporation, as hereinafter defined. Such transferee shall be bound by all of the terms and conditions of this Joint Venture Agreement with the same force and effect as if such transferee had been a signatory and an original party to this Joint Venture Agreement. Such transferee shall by written instrument, delivered to the other Venturer, expressly assume all obligations of the transferor, except those obligations which are enforceable against the transfer only by foreclosure of a lien or encumbrance on the Project or the other property or assets of the Venture. As used herein, the term "affiliated corporation" shall mean a corporation which owns all of the issued and outstanding stock of the Venturer (its parent corporation) or a corporation the stock of which is wholly owned by the Venturer or its parent corporation. Notwithstanding anything herein contained to the contrary, ... may transfer all of its interest in the Venture, the Project, and in any other property and assets of the Venture to a wholly owned subsidiary of ....or to .... a .... corporation, or to any corporation a majority of the voting stock of which is owned by .... either directly or indirectly, and in such event .... shall be relieved from any further liability hereunder.

Section 6.03. *Right of First Refusal*. Any Venturer shall have the right exercisable only after the completion of the Project, to sell all (but

tionments customarily made in the closing of real estate transactions in the City of .... The selling Venturer shall execute and deliver such deeds, assignments and other documents as shall be necessary to convey its interest in the Venture, the Project and all other property and assets of the Venture to the purchasing Venturer with all required transfer tax stamps affixed. In the event such selling Venturer shall fail or refuse to execute any of such instrument, the purchasing Venturer is hereby granted an irrevocable power of attorney which shall be binding on the selling Venturer as to all third parties, to execute and deliver on behalf of the selling Venturer all such required instruments of transfer.

ARTICLE 5
MANAGEMENT OF PROJECT

Section 5.01. *Developer as Manager.* The Project shall be managed by Developer pursuant to a Management Agreement entered into contemporaneously herewith. As manager, Developer shall keep accurate and complete books of account and records in accordance with sound and generally accepted accounting principles applied on an accrual basis. .... and its representatives shall be permitted to examine and make copies of such books of account and records at all times during reasonable business hours. Upon the expiration of the aforesaid Management Agreement the renewal thereof or the appointment of a successor manager shall be made only upon the concurrence of both the Venturers and upon such terms and conditions as shall be approved by both of the Venturers. All books and records shall be the property of the Venture.

Section 5.02. *Compensation of Project Manager.* Developer shall be entitled to receive as compensation for the services to be rendered by it pursuant to the aforesaid Management Agreement, an annual fee equal to .... percent of the gross rentals of the Project, as hereinafter defined. Such fee shall be paid quarterly within fifteen (15) days after the end of each calendar quarter. In the event the services of Developer as manager shall be terminated during any quarterly payment period, Developer shall be entitled to receive only that portion computed on a per diem basis of the Project Manager's fee as shall have been earned prior to the effective date of termination. The term "gross rentals" as used in this Section 5.02 shall mean the gross rentals received from all occupants of the Project, less all commissions paid thereon and any sums received which represent reimbursement to the Venture for payment of taxes, maintenance, utilities, insurance, and any other services of any kind or nature whatsoever furnished to the occupants of

Section 4.03. *Dispute.* In the event that a decision with respect to an action to be taken by the Venture in accordance with this Joint Venture Agreement shall require the consent or approval of both of the Venturers, and if both the Venturers shall not agree, then in such event, either of the Venturers shall have the right to tender to the other a combined offer to sell the entire interest of the offer or in the Venture, the Project, and the other property and assets of the Venture to the offeree, and offer to purchase the entire interest of the offeree in the Venture, the Project, and the other property and assets of the Venture.

Such offer must provide that the purchase price shall be paid in cash or by cash or by cashier's or certified check (except to the extent that any portion thereof shall consist of the assumption of indebtedness secured by an interest in the Property or of the discharge or assumption of the purchase). In addition to the foregoing, the price in the offer to sell must bear the same proportion to the interest covered by such offer as the price in the offer to purchase bears to the interest covered by the offer to purchase, i.e., the price in the offer to sell, for each percent interest in the profits and losses of the Venture and the capital of the Venture covered by the offer to sell must equal the price in the offer to purchase for each percent interest in the profits and losses of the Venture and the capital of the Venture covered by the offer to purchase.

Such offer shall be irrevocable for a period of sixty (60) days from and after the delivery of such offer and the offeree may, on or before the sixtieth (60th) day after the exercise of such offer, accept either the offer to sell or the offer to purchase, and upon acceptance, the offeror shall be required to sell or to purchase, as the case may be. If the offeree shall fail, within the sixty-day period, to accept either the offer to sell or the offer to purchase, the offeror shall thereupon have the right on or before the fifteenth (15th) day after the expiration of such sixty-day period, to purchase the interest of the offeree, at the price and on the terms provided in the original offer to purchase. If the offeror exercises such right, the offeree shall be required to sell the interest covered by the offer to the offeror. If the offeror does not exercise such right within the fifteen-day period, the offer to sell and the offer to purchase shall both expire and be of no further force and effect.

Section 4.04. *Consummation of Sale.* In the event of the sale of the interest of either Venturer in the Venture, the Project and any other property or assets of the Venture, such sale shall be consummated within thirty (30) days following the election of the other Venturer of an offer to sell, and each Venturer to purchase or the acceptance by the other Venturer of an offer to sell, and each Venturer shall pay its own expenses in connection with such purchase and sale, including appor-

the results of the operations of the Venture for the period indicated. Such statements shall reflect the depository accounts referred to in Section 3.04.

ARTICLE 4
Decisions Regarding Venture

Section 4.01. *Decisions Regarding Venture.* All managerial and policy decisions with respect to the Venture shall be made by the unanimous action of the Venturers or their designated representatives. Notwithstanding the foregoing, however, the day-to-day management of the Project shall be conducted by Developer. Except as hereinafter provided, Developer shall have the authority, acting alone, to bind the Venture in connection with the day to day management of the Project.

Section 4.02. *Limitations on Authority of Venturers.* No Venturer shall take any of the following actions without first obtaining the written consent of the other:
(1) Sell, assign, transfer, exchange, grant leasehold estates, or otherwise dispose of the Project, any portion thereof, or any interest therein.
(2) Apply for, execute, or modify any mortgage, pledge, encumbrance, or other hypothecation or security agreement affecting the Project or any interest therein, or execute any financing statement in connection therewith.
(3) Incur any indebtedness on behalf of the Venture other than for meeting current obligations incurred in the ordinary course of business and due within twelve (12) months.
(4) Make any capital improvements or incur any debt or obligation, the cost or amount of which shall exceed .... Dollars ($.......) or embark upon any program of capital improvement or incur any series of debts or obligations related to a unified improvement or program which involves in the aggregate expenditures exceeding ....Dollars ($.......).
(5) Execute or enter into any contract, agreement, or undertaking to borrow money on behalf of the Venture.
(6) Change or permit to be changed in any substantial way the accounting process and procedures employed in keeping the books of account or preparing financial statements with respect to operation or management of the Project.
(7) Settle any claim for insurance proceeds if the loss thereunder exceeds .... Dollars ($.......).

showing the assets, liabilities, costs, expenditures, receipts, profits, and losses of the Venture, which books and records shall include provisions for separate capital and profit and loss accounts for each of the Venturers, the computation of depreciation on a straight line basis, and shall provide for such other matters as the independent certified public accountants selected by .... for the Venture shall deem reasonably necessary. To the extent the accumulated losses of the Venture shall exceed the accumulated profits therefrom, such net loss shall be allocated to the Venturers in accordance with Section 3.06 hereof and shall be charged against their respective capital accounts. Future net profits so allocable to the Venture shall be first used to restore any such impairment of the Venturer's capital accounts and thereafter to the Venturer's separate profit and loss accounts. Such books and records shall be kept and maintained at the principal office of the Venture or at such places as the Venturers shall determine in accordance with sound and generally accepted accounting practice on an accrual basis. Such books and records shall be made available for examination by .... or its representatives during normal business hours and .... or its representatives shall have the right to make copies of such books and records or to extract therefrom such information as .... or its representatives may desire.

The Venture shall file partnership returns as provided in Section 6031 of the Internal Revenue Code of 1954 and shall avail itself of the right to file partnership afforded by it and similar provisions of any other taxing authority having jurisdiction over the Venture or the Property. The Venture shall make an election pursuant to the provisions of Section 754 of the Internal Revenue Code of 1954 for the first taxable year to which such election applies.

Section 3.05. *Auditors: Reports.* .... shall select a firm of independent certified public accountants who, at the cost of the Venture, shall within thirty (30) days after the end of each calendar quarter prepare and deliver to each Venturer a profit and loss statement showing the operating results of the Venture during the preceding calendar quarter and a balance sheet as of the end of such calendar quarter. As soon as possible following the end of such calendar year and in any event within sixty (60) days thereafter, the Venture shall cause such certified public accountants to prepare and deliver to each Venturer a profit and loss statement for such calendar year and a balance sheet as of the end of such calendar year, together with a certificate that such profit and loss statements, balance sheets, and any related statements, including any notes thereto, are complete and correct and fairly represent the financial condition of the Venture as of the date indicated and

upon the books and records of the Venture and shall not be treated as a capital contribution to the Venture for any purpose whatsoever, nor shall Developer be entitled to the repayment of such initial capital contribution from the net cash flow of the Venture.

Section 3.03. *Liabilities of Venturers: Additional Capital Contributions.* All obligations, expenses, and losses incurred, and all payments made by the Venturers in connection with the Venture, the Property, and the Project (except obligations, expenses, or losses incurred or payments made in connection with the construction of the Project), including without limitation, payments due on indebtedness incurred in connection with the permanent mortgage financing of the Project and any liability for damages arising out of claims or actions against any of the Venturers on account of the ownership or operation of the Project, shall be obligations of the Venture (such obligations are hereinafter referred to as "Venture Obligations"). Each Venturer shall be liable only for that portion of Venture Obligations which is equal to its interest in the profits and losses of the Venture as of the date such Venture Obligations shall have been incurred. Each Venturer shall, to the extent the Venture is unable to borrow funds to meet such Venture Obligations, contribute to the capital of the Venture in addition to the contributions made pursuant to Section 3.02 hereof, a sum equal to the amount necessary to meet such Venture Obligations, multiplied by such Venturer's percentage interest in the profits and losses of the Venture. Any indebtedness which is secured by a mortgage, security interest, or other lien or encumbrance of the Property, the Project, or the interests of the Venturers in the Venture, its assets, profits, and distributions, and any mortgages, security interests or other liens or encumbrances executed or granted in connection therewith shall expressly provide that the obligee shall look solely to its security interest in the Project or the interests of the Venturers in the Venture, its assets, profits, and distributions for the payment of any and all amounts due under the terms of such instrument and of the Venture, except such funds as shall reasonably be required to meet the cash requirements of the Venture during the succeeding six (6) month period shall be distributed at not less than quarterly intervals. Such distributions shall be applied to the repayment to the Venturers of the capital contributions made by them pursuant to the repayment of such capital contributions and shall be charged against the separate profit and loss accounts to be maintained as part of the books and records of the Venture.

Section 3.04. *Accounting Procedures.* Developer shall keep complete and accurate books of account and other records of the Venture,

(m) A fee to Developer of ....
Dollars ($.......) to cover general conditions, supervision, overhead, and profit.
(n) Interest on construction loans and real estate taxes during the period of construction.
(o) Miscellaneous costs such as the cost of land, leasing commissions, promotion and advertising expenses, commitment and mortgage brokerage fees, not to exceed the sum of .... Dollars ($.......).

The term "audited cost of construction" shall *not* include any of the following items:

(aa) Salaries or other compensation of officers, executives, general managers, estimators, auditory, accountants, purchasing and contracting agents, or other employees of Developer or the general contractor located at principal office and branch offices.
(bb) Expenses of the general contractor's principal and branch offices other than the field office.
(cc) Any part of the capital expenses of Developer or the general contractor employed in the construction of the Project, including interest thereon.
(dd) Any allowance for general conditions, supervision, overhead on profit of any kind, except as provided in item (m) above.
(ee) Costs due to the negligence of the general contractor, any subcontractor, anyone directly or indirectly employed by any of them, or for whose acts any of them may be liable, including but not limited to, the cost of correction of defective work, disposal of materials and equipment wrongly supplied, or making good any damage to property.
(ff) Leasing commissions, promotion and advertising expenses, and mortgage brokerage fees, except as provided in item (o) above.
(gg) Cost of land, including legal fees and other expenses incurred in the acquisition thereof except as provided in item (o) above.

Regardless of the actual amount contributed by Developer pursuant to Subparagraph 2 above, Developer shall receive credit on the books and records of the Venture for an initial capital contribution equal to that made by ...., pursuant to subparagraph 1 above. Any amount contributed by Developer in excess thereof shall not be included

(b) Salaries of the general contractor's manual employees and its superintendent and assistant superintendent while actually engaged in the construction of the Project, together with such welfare or other benefits, if any, as may be payable with respect, thereto.

(c) Cost of contributions, assessments, or taxes for such items as unemployment compensation and social security, insofar as such cost is based on wages, salaries, or other remuneration paid to employees of the general contractor.

(d) Cost of all materials, supplies, and equipment incorporated in the work, including costs of transportation thereof and storage as necessary.

(e) Payments made by the general contractor to bona fide subcontractors for work performed on the Project.

(f) All costs, including transportation and maintenance, of all materials, supplies, equipment, and hand tools not owned by the workmen, which are consumed in the performance of the work on the Project; provided, however, that a credit shall be made for the salvage value of any materials, supplies, equipment, or tools for which the general contractor has paid the full cost and which have not been wholly consumed.

(g) Rental charges of all necessary machinery and equipment, exclusive of hand tools, used in the performance of the work on the Project, including installation, minor repairs and replacements, dismantling removal, transportation and delivery costs thereof, at rental charges consistent with those prevailing in..........

(h) Cost of premiums for all bonds and casualty insurance which the general contractor is required to purchase and maintain.

(i) Sales, use, or similar taxes paid by the general contractor.

(j) Permit fees and inspection fees, water, sewer, power and other utility service fees, and connection costs.

(k) Fees of architects, engineers, and surveyors.

(l) Losses and expenses, not compensated by .... insurance or otherwise, sustained in connection with the work, provided they have resulted from causes other than the fault or neglect of the general contractor and subcontractor or any agent or employee of either. Losses due to theft and vandalism shall be included as a part of cost.

($......), such excess shall not be reimbursed or paid to Developer, and in lieu thereof, such excess shall be the intitial capital contribution of Developer to the Venture.

ARTICLE 3
SOURCE AND APPLICATION OF JOINT VENTURE FUNDS
DEPOSITORIES: ACCOUNTING PROCEDURES AND AUDITS

Section 3.01. *Permanent Financing of Project.* Simultaneously herewith the Venture has received a permanent loan commitment from ...., providing not less than .... Dollars ($.......) of permanent financing, a copy of which is attached hereto as Exhibit C. The proceeds of such permanent loan shall be used to the extent possible to reimburse the Venture for the cost incurred by it in connection with the acquisition of the Project.

Section 3.02. *Initial Capital Contributions.* To the extent that the permanent loan commitment shall not provide sufficient funds to fully reimburse the Venture for the cost of acquiring the Project, the Venturers shall make the following initial capital contributions to the Venture, the proceeds of which shall be used to pay the balance of such costs:

(1) .... shall make an initial capital contribution to the Venture equal to the lesser of:
   (a) The difference between the amount of the permanent financing described in Section 3.01 hereof and the audited cost of the Project (as hereinafter defined); or
   (b) The sum of .... Dollars ($.......).
(2) Developer shall make an initial capital contribution to the Venture in an amount equal to the difference between the audited cost of the Project and the sum of .... Dollars ($.......), the sum of the funds available from the proceeds of the permanent loan and the initial capital contribution of ....
(3) As used herein, the audited cost of the Project shall include the following:
   (a) Wages paid for labor in the direct employ of the general contractor in the performance of the work calculated under applicable collective bargaining agreements or under an agreed salary or wage, together with such welfare or other benefits, if any, as may be payable with respect thereto.

of .... Dollars ($........) shall not be deemed a defect in title and the same shall be in fact discharged out of the proceeds payable to Developer by the Venture as provided in Section 2.04 hereof.

(4) ....shall have received a commitment for title insurance from a title insurance company approved by .... in an amount equal to the audited cost of the Project (as such term is defined in Section 3.02 hereof) guaranteeing title to the Property in the condition required by Section 2.02 hereof.

(5) .... shall have received the opinion of counsel acceptable to it, to the effect that the Project as completed complies with all applicable zoning laws and all other land use and development control regulations and ordinances applicable to the Project as of the date of the acquisition of the Project by the Venturers and as to such other matters as .... may request, which opinion shall be obtained at the expense of the Developer.

(6) .... shall have received copies of a survey prepared and certified to it by a licensed surveyor approved by ...., which survey shall depict the boundaries of the Property and the adjacent public roadways, access between the Property and such roadways, the location of all improvements constructed thereon, and the nature and location of all easements (public utility and otherwise) affecting the Property or used in connection therewith. Such survey shall also indicate that the improvements have been erected completely within the boundaries of the Property and are not in violation of any setback restrictions affecting the Property and that no improvements which are not part of the Project encroach upon the Property.

(7) This Joint Venture Agreement shall in all respects be in full force and effect and there shall exist no default hereunder.

Section 2.04. *Payment for the Project.* Simultaneously with the acquisition of the Project by the Venturers, the Venture shall pay to Developer an amount equal to the proceeds of the permanent financing for the Project, as described in Section 3.01 hereof, together with the initial capital contribution to be made to the Venture by ...., pursuant to Section 3.02 hereof, but in no event shall the amount to be paid exceed the audited cost of the Project, as defined in Section 3.02 hereof. In the event the audited cost of the Project shall exceed the sum of .... Dollars

writing to .... that the Project has been fully completed in accordance with the approved plans and specifications and as such is ready for occupancy.
(2) The building department or other agency of the City of .... shall have issued a certificate of occupancy for the Project.
(3) The Venture shall have received a certificate of compliance in accordance with the provisions of the urban renewal development agreement covering the Property.
(4) .... shall have received a certificate from an architect or engineer employed by it, stating that the Project has been fully completed in accordance with the approved plans and specifications. Should .... elect to use an independent architect or engineer for the purpose of determining whether or not the Project has been constructed and completed in accordance with the approved plans and specifications, the fee of such architect or engineer shall be paid by Developer and shall not have been completed by .... may, at at its option, terminate this Joint Venture Agreement upon written notice to Developer.

Section 2.02. *Acquisition of the Project.* Upon the completion of the Project as determined in accordance with Section 2.01 hereof, and upon the satisfaction of each and every condition precedent set forth in section 2.03 hereof, Developer shall cause the Property and the Project to be conveyed by general warranty deed to the Venture, free and clear of all leases, liens, restrictions, and encumbrances, except as may have been previously provided in writing by ....

Section 2.03. *Conditions Precedent to the Acquisition of the Project.* The Venture shall have no obligation to acquire the Property or the Project or to pay for the same until all of the following conditions precedent have been fulfilled:
(1) The Project shall have been fully completed and evidence thereof, as provided in Section 2.01, shall have been delivered to and approved by..............
(2) The Project shall not have been materially damaged or destroyed by fire or other casualty.
(3) Title to the Property and the Project shall be in such condition that the same may be conveyed in the manner specifically required by Section 2.02 hereof; provided, however, a lien or encumbrance upon the Property which can be discharged by the payment to the lien holder of a sum of money not in excess

.... and thereafter at such place as the Venturers may from time to time determine.

Section 1.06. *Duration.* The term of this Joint Venture Agreement shall expire upon the first to occur of the following events:
(1) December 31, 2001.
(2) The sale of the interest of both of the Venturers in the Project, or the sale of the entire interest of one Venturer in the Project to the other.
(3) The termination of this Joint Venture Agreement in accordance with the terms hereof or by the mutual agreement of both of the Venturers.

Notwithstanding the expiration or any termination of this Joint Venture Agreement, the Venture may be reconstituted when provided for herein or by the agreement of the Venturers then having an interest in the Project, and the successor to any former Venturer, unless such successor would be an Inactive Venturer as hereinafter defined, in which event this Joint Venture Agreement shall apply to the Venture as reconstituted, except that the Venturers may select a new expiration date which shall not be earlier than December 31, 2001.

Section 1.07. *Memorandum of Joint Venture Agreement.* Simultaneously with the execution hereof, the parties shall execute a Memorandum of Joint Venture Agreement in such form as shall be approved by the Venturers, which Memorandum of Joint Venture Agreement may be recorded with the consent of ...., with the Register of Deeds for .... County, ... This Joint Venture Agreement shall not be recorded except upon the agreement of both of the Venturers or upon the receipt by either Venturer of any opinion of its counsel that such recording is required in order for the rights and privileges of such Venturer to be fully protected.

ARTICLE 2
Acquisition of the Project

Section 2.01. *Completion of the Project.* Developer shall cause the Project to be completed, strictly in accordance with plans and specifications which shall have been submitted to and been approved by .... prior to the commencement of construction. The Project shall be deemed to have been completed upon the concurrence of all of the following events:
(1) The architect selected for the Project shall have certified in

The Property and the improvements to be constructed thereon are sometimes hereinafter referred to as the "Project."

Section 1.02. *Opinions of Counsel: Corporate Authorizations.* Simultaneously with the execution of this Joint Venture Agreement, such Venturer shall deliver to the other the opinion of its counsel, satisfactory in scope and form to it and the other Venture, to the effect that the execution of this Joint Venture Agreement has been duly authorized by the Board of Directors of such Venturer and is not in violation of or in conflict with the Articles of Incorporation and Bylaws of such Venturer or any agreement by which such Venturer may be bound; that this Joint Venture Agreement constitutes the legal, valid, and binding obligation of such Venturer, enforceable in accordance with its terms, except as may be limited by bankruptcy or other laws generally affecting creditors' rights, and such opinion shall at the reasonable request of any Venturer to whom it is addressed cover such other matters as may be incidental to the transactions contemplated by this Joint Venture Agreement. Each Venturer shall, prior to or simultaneously with the execution of this Joint Venture Agreement, deliver to the other a copy of the resolutions adopted by its Board of Directors authorizing the execution of this Joint Venture Agreement and appointing the representative referred to in Section 1.03 hereof, duly certified by the Secretary of such Venturer to be in full force and effect.

Section 1.03. *Designation of Representatives.* Simultaneously with the execution hereof, each Venturer shall deliver to the other a written designation of the person authorized to speak and act on behalf of such Venturer, upon which the Venturer and the other Venturer shall be entitled to rely until such designation shall be revoked or altered. No designation by any Venturer shall be effectively revoked or altered until such time as such Venturer shall have delivered to the other Venturer a written designation of a successor representative.

Section 1.04. *Assumed Names; Name of Project.* The business of the Venturer shall be conducted under the name of................. ...., and the Venturers shall cause such assumed name to be registered or filed with the County Clerk of the County within the State of ...., in which the Venturer shall maintain its principal office from time to time and if no such office shall be located within the State of ...., such assumed name shall be registered with the County Clerk of ....County.

Section 1.05. *Principal Place of Business.* The principal place of business for the Venture shall be initially located at ....

hereto must be in writing and shall be effective only to the extent specifically set forth therein.

(6) All remedies under this Agreement, or by law or otherwise, afforded to Lender shall be cumulative and not alternate. Nothing in this Agreement shall be deemed any waiver or prohibition of Lender's right of lien or setoff.

(7) This Agreement shall be governed by and construed in accordance with the laws of the State of ....

IN WITNESS WHEREOF, Lender, a national banking association, and ....
....Borrower,

Form 11.4

JOINT VENTURE AGREEMENT

This JOINT VENTURE AGREEMENT made this.............
.... day of ...., 19...., by and between .... (hereinafter referred to as "Institution") and ...., a corporation with offices at......................................
....
(hereinafter referred to as "Developer").

WITNESSETH:

IN CONSIDERATION OF THE MUTUAL COVENANTS HEREIN CONTAINED, THE PARTIES HERETO AGREE AS FOLLOWS:

ARTICLE 1
CREATION AND PURPOSE: DURATION

Section 1.01. *Creation and Purpose.* The parties hereto (the "Venturers") hereby associate themselves as a Joint Venture (the "Venture") for the purpose of acquiring, owning, and operating certain real property located at..,
more particularly described on Exhibit A attached hereto (the "Property"), together with certain improvements to be constructed thereon, consisting of ....

rower or the right of Lender to the collateral security theretofore assigned to it, or its right to enforce and use the provisions of this Agreement in respect of the enforcement and collection of such collateral security.

J. *Miscellaneous Provisions.*
   (1) Any and all communications between the parties hereto or notices provided herein to be given may be given by mailing the same to Lender at .... , and to Borrower at .... , or to such addresses as either party may in writing indicate to the other from time to time.
   (2) The terms and provisions of this Agreement shall be binding upon and inure to the benefit of the parties hereto and their respective successors and assigns. All representations, warranties and agreements herein contained on the part of Borrower shall be effective as long as any sum is owed to Lender hereunder, including principal, interest accrued thereon, or other charges outstanding in connection therewith.
   (3) This Agreement, the Master Note, and any collateral security assigned to Lender hereunder, may at any time be transferred or assigned by Lender, in whole or in part, and any assignee thereof from Lender may enforce this Agreement, the Master Note, and such collateral security so assigned in accordance with the terms of the assignment; provided, however, that no deed of trust note may be separately sold or assigned unless the Borrower shall have failed or refused for a period of ten (10) days to comply with a written demand to pay the respective sums advanced for which said note was pledged as collateral security, pursuant to Section D. (4) hereinabove.
   (4) No delay in exercising, or failure to exercise any right, power or remedy accruing to Lender through any breach or default of Borrower under this Agreement, or any acquiescence to any such breach or default, or to any similar breach or default thereafter occurring, shall impair any such right, power or remedy of Lender, nor shall any waiver of any single breach or default be deemed a waiver of any breach or default thereafter occurring.
   (5) No amendment, modification or waiver of any of the terms of this Agreement shall be valid unless in writing and executed with the same formality as this Agreement. Any permit, consent or approval on the part of Lender pursuant

make such payment or deposit such additional collateral as shall be satisfactory to Lender; or,
   (d) Determination by Lender that a material adverse change in the financial condition of Borrower or any endorser or guarantor of Borrower's obligations to Lender hereunder or under the Master Note has occurred since the date hereof.
(2) In addition to all other rights and remedies provided hereunder and by law to Lender, in the event of any default as set forth hereinabove, Lender may, at its option and at its sole discretion, until the Loan is paid in full,
   (a) Communicate with and notify the debtors of Borrower's assignments hereunder, and note any such assignments hereunder and note any such assignment on Borrower's records; or,
   (b) Take over the exclusive right to collect any collateral security hereunder at the sole expense of Borrower. For any acts done or not done incident to such collection or liquidation, Lender shall not be liable in any manner; Lender shall have the right to settle, compromise, or adjust collateral and the claims or rights of Borrower thereunder and accept return of the real estate involved, and in turn sell and dispose of all said real estate without notice to or approval of Borrower. Lender may employ agents and attorneys to collect or liquidate any collateral security hereunder, and Lender shall not be liable for such collateral security, or defaults of any such agents and attorneys; and,
   (c) Open any mail addressed to Borrower in connection with any real estate loan or any sums advanced hereunder, and as attorney in fact for Borrower, sign the Borrower's name to any receipts, checks, notes, agreements, or other instruments or letters in order to collect or liquidate collateral security hereunder; and,
   (d) Enter the office of Borrower and take possession of any records that pertain to collateral security hereunder.
I. *Termination.* Either party hereto may terminate this Agreement at any time upon giving the other ten (10) days written notice by certified mail. Such termination of this Agreement will not alter or affect any of the rights or obligations of the parties hereto in respect of any transactions then pending hereunder, particularly the indebtedness or obligation of Bor-

such terms as Lender, in its sole discretion, may deem to be appropriate.
(3) Upon deposit of the proceeds of the sale of such deed of trust note or notes to the said special account, Borrower authorizes and directs Lender to apply all or any part of such proceeds to payment in full of the sums advanced by Lender in connection with such note or notes, including principal, interest accrued thereon, and other charges outstanding in connection therewith, in the manner more particularly set forth hereinabove.
(4) Upon payment in full of all sums advanced for which a deed of trust note was pledged as security, together with all interest accrued thereon and all other charges outstanding in connection therewith, and provided no default exists with respect to any provisions hereof, Borrower may withdraw from such special account the aggregate amount of all payments made on account of the respective deed of trust note or notes and deposited by Borrower in such special account less the aggregate amount theretofore paid to Lender from such special account to satisfy such sums advanced, interest accrued, and other charges.

H. *Default by Borrower.*
(1) The entire amount of the Loan, including principal, interest accrued thereon, and other charges outstanding in connection therewith, shall, at the option of Lender and at its sole discretion, at once become due and payable upon the occurrence of any of the following events, each of which constitutes a default hereunder.
(a) The breach of, or default under, any term, condition, provision, representation or warranty contained in this Agreement, or in the Master Note, or in any other obligation of Borrower to Lender or in any obligation to Lender of the endorsers or guarantors of Borrower's obligations hereunder or under the Master Note; or,
(b) The death, dissolution or insolvency of Borrower or of any endorser or guarantor of Borrower's obligations to Lender hereunder or under the Master Note, or application for the appointment of a receiver for any of them, or filing of a petition in bankruptcy by or against any of them; or,
(c) At any time the collateral security hereunder shall decline in value or become unsatisfactory to Lender and Borrower shall not immediately upon demand

books of all endorsements to Lender hereunder, and to give such notice thereof as Lender may from time to time require.
(6) That Borrower will execute such additional instruments of assignment of the collateral security hereunder as Lender may from time to time require, including assignment of all rights to which Borrower is now or may hereafter become entitled by virtue of owning such collateral security.
(7) That Borrower will provide to Lender, on a monthly basis, a written statement in full detail of all outstanding commitments to purchase deed of trust notes which it has obtained together with a report of all outstanding deed of trust notes financed by Borrower, indicating
(8) That Borrower will comply with such reasonable administrative directions as Lender may give in order to provide proper servicing of the advances hereunder.

G. *Sale of Deed of Trust Notes.*
(1) Lender covenants and agrees that, except in cases where a default as defined hereunder has occurred, Lender, on behalf of Borrower, will deliver or cause to be delivered to an insured bank or S&L to be held in escrow for an acceptable purchaser of a deed of trust note or notes, such note or notes, together with all supporting documents transferred and endorsed to Lender by Borrower, upon receipt of written orders from Borrower to deliver the same together with a cover letter in a form satisfactory to Lender on the stationery of Borrower executed with due authority which directs that payment to Borrower for such deed of trust note or notes be made in care of Lender for deposit to the special account established pursuant hereto.
(2) Borrower shall maintain a special account in its name at Lender for transactions pursuant hereto. Borrower expressly authorizes and impowers Lender to endorse its name upon any check, draft, transfer or other instrument due to Borrower, and to deposit amounts due to Borrower in such special account for and on behalf of Borrower. Any such amounts deposited thereto shall be held by Lender as collateral security for the payment of any sums advanced to or on behalf of Borrower by Lender. Lender may, from time to time, at its sole discretion, apply all or any part of such special account to the payment of the Loan, including principal, interest accrued thereon, and other charges outstanding in connection therewith, in such priority and upon

rights and obligations held by Borrower are negotiable and assignable to Lender.

F. *General Covenants by Borrower.* Borrower covenants and agrees as follows:

(1) That the amount of the Loan, the interest accrued thereon, and any charges outstanding in connection therewith, shall be determined in accordance with the records maintained by Lender and Borrower hereby accepts the said records as maintained from time to time hereafter as correct, complete and conclusive of the aggregate unpaid amount of principal, interest and other charges due and owing to Lender. Lender may provide, but shall not be required to provide, a statement of transactions pursuant hereto to Borrower at such interval as Lender may deem appropriate. Borrower shall notify Lender in writing within ten (10) days of receipt of any such statement of any discrepancies between the statement and the records of the Borrower. In the event Borrower should fail to provide such written notice to Lender within ten (10) days of its receipt thereof, such statement shall be deemed to be conclusive evidence of the amount of the Loan and all transactions pursuant hereto, including the amount of principal, interest and other charges owing to Lender, and Borrower hereby waives any objection as to the accuracy of such statement in any action or proceeding to enforce the obligations of Borrower to Lender hereunder in any court of competent jurisdiction.

(2) That Borrower, in addition to all other sums which it may be called upon to pay hereunder, will pay to Lender a reasonable sum for its attorney's fee in the event that the Master Note is turned over to an attorney for collection or in the event of any action at law or suit in equity in relation to or to enforce this Agreement, the Master Note, or any deed of trust note or notes endorsed hereunder.

(3) That Borrower will furnish and supply such financial statements, audited by a certified public accountant, and other financial information concerning the Borrower and any investor as Lender may from time to time require.

(4) That Borrower will maintain adequate books, accounts and records in accordance with good accounting standards and practice, and permit Lender or its representatives at any reasonable time to inspect or examine or audit the books, accounts and records of Borrower.

(5) That Borrower will make appropriate notations on its

E. *Warranties of Borrower.* In order to induce Lender to enter into this Agreement and to make each separate advance, Borrower warrants and represents to Lender as follows:
   (1) That Borrower is legally and properly organized and existing and is in good standing under the laws of .... ; and,
   (2) That Borrower has the power and authority to own its properties, to carry on its business in the manner it conducts such business and to execute and deliver this Agreement and the Master Note; and,
   (3) That each deed of trust note tendered to Lender pursuant hereto shall evidence a loan to an individual who will occupy the single-family residential improvements completed upon the property securing such loan; and,
   (4) That the deed of trust notes tendered to Lender evidence loans that are insured by the FHA, or guaranteed by the VA, or that such notes evidence conventional loans, and that prior to making any loans evidenced by deed of trust note intended to be FHA-insured or VA-guaranteed, Borrower will obtain from the FHA or the VA a firm commitment to insure or guarantee such deed of trust note; and, in the event that Borrower has been given the authority to close loans on an automatic basis in Washington, D.C., Maryland and Virginia, it will be necessary for the Borrower to furnish Lender a copy of the letter from the VA naming each underwriter and alternate underwriter; and in addition Borrower is to furnish with each loan package Notice of Underwriting Action completed in full and signed by authorized Underwriter; and,
   (5) That, Borrower customarily sells such deed of trust note to responsible investors and that there will be, at the time of endorsement to Lender of each of such deed of trust notes hereunder, a commitment, in writing, to purchase the same by a responsible investor; and,
   (6) That Borrower has done no act to impair or encumber the deed of trust notes and security therefore tendered to Lender and that Lender shall have quiet possession of the same, free from all liens, claims or encumbrances whatsoever; and,
   (7) That each deed of trust note tendered to Lender pursuant hereto is in full force and effect and is not in default; and,
   (8) That each deed of trust note, the deed of trust securing such note, and all such insurance, guarantees, bonds and other

such insurance satisfactory to Lender, Lender may obtain such insurance at the Borrower's expense, and such expense shall be added to the amount of the Loan.

(3) Borrower will forward a copy to Lender of all original policies of insurance, including title insurance, each and every original deed of trust, and copies of such other original documents not previously provided to Lender in connection with each deed of trust note or notes endorsed to Lender, immediately upon receipt thereof.

(4) Borrower will pay in full on demand of Lender, any sums advanced by Lender in connection with any deed of trust note or notes, plus accrued interest thereon, if such deed of trust note or notes transferred to Lender as collateral security for such sums advanced:
 (a) shall be rejected as unsatisfactory for purchase by a responsible investor, or
 (b) has not been purchased within ...... months after its delivery and endorsement to Lender, or
 (c) remains in default for a period in excess of ninety (90) days.
 (d) has not been paid within ...... days after shipment to investor.

(5) Borrower shall act, until Lender gives Borrower notice in writing otherwise, as the representative of and in trust for Lender in receiving and collecting all moneys payable pursuant to any deed of trust note held as collateral security by Lender under this Agreement.

(6) Borrower will notify Lender in writing within thirty (30) days of any default which occurs relative to any deed of trust note or notes delivered and endorsed to Lender.

(7) Borrower will enforce payment and collection, at its own expense, of all deed of trust notes delivered and endorsed to Lender hereunder as collateral security, or, in the event of default and Lender, in its sole discretion, elects to undertake the collection of enforcement of such note or notes, Borrower will pay the cost of collection thereof, including attorney's fees.

(8) Borrower will not, without prior written consent of Lender, make any compromise, adjustment or settlement in respect of any collateral security endorsed to Lender, take any actions to impair the value of such collateral security, or accept other than cash in payment or liquidation of such collateral security.

percent (80%) of the appraised value of the real estate securing such loan, shall be insured by Borrower with an approved private mortgage insurance company in accordance with the terms of the investor's commitment, such insurance to be evidenced by appropriate documents delivered to Lender.
- (3) Lender reserves the right to refuse to make advances to Borrower with respect to any deed of trust note if Lender, in its sole discretion, deems such deed of trust note or the supporting documents relative thereto to be unsatisfactory or inadequate.
- (4) Lender covenants and agrees, except in cases where a default as defined hereunder has occurred, that, with respect to each separate advance,
  - (a) Lender will forward, upon written request of Borrower, to the FHA or the VA for the purpose of obtaining the insurance or guarantee thereof, any item of collateral security and its supporting documents; and,
  - (b) Lender will reassign to Borrower any deed of trust note endorsed to it pursuant hereto, and deliver such note and all supporting documents to the Borrower, upon payment in full to Lender of all sums advanced for which said note was delivered to Lender as collateral security together with accrued interest thereon and all other charges in connection therewith.

D. *Obligations of Borrower with Respect to Each Advance.*
  - (1) Borrower will endorse and transfer to Lender at the time of making each separate advance, as collateral security for the Loan, all its right, title and interest in the deed of trust note or notes tendered to Lender, in the deed of trust securing said Deed of Trust note or notes, and in all policies of insurance, guarantees, bonds and other rights and obligations held by Borrower in connection with such transaction. Borrower agrees to do such further acts, execute such further documents and assist Lender in such a manner as Lender may require in order that Lender may fully and completely receive the benefit of and exercise the rights and obligations transferred to it pursuant hereto.
  - (2) Borrower will maintain, or cause to be maintained, such fire and extended coverage insurance on all real property forming the basis of the collateral security hereunder as may be required by the ultimate investor or by Lender; provided, however, that should Borrower fail to maintain

deed of trust note, or of the Veterans Administration to guarantee a sufficient percentage of the loan so that the loan to value ratio is at least 80 percent (80%), together with such other documents as are customarily required in the processing of FHA-insured or VA-guaranteed loans; and,

(e) A certified true copy of the original commitment in writing, of a responsible investor to purchase such deed of trust note or notes; and,

(f) A copy of the survey, when it is a requirement of the ultimate investor or of the title insurance company; and.

(g) An appraisal of the real estate securing the deed of trust note or notes, either performed by the agency insuring or guaranteeing such loan, or, in the case of conventional loans, performed by an appraiser acceptable to Lender; and,

(h) Satisfactory evidence of fire and hazard insurance in an amount not less than the principal amount of the deed of trust note or notes together with an endorsement to such insurance providing for payment thereof to Borrower as mortgagee; and,

(i) Satisfactory evidence of flood insurance under the National Flood Insurance Program or of an exemption from the requirements of such program; and,

(j) Satisfactory evidence of compliance with the requirements of the Truth-In-Lending Act and the Real Estate Settlement Procedures Act, including disclosures executed by the individual mortgagors in a form satisfactory to Lender; and,

(k) A copy of settlement sheets relative to the closing of the loan evidenced by such deed of trust note or notes, including summaries of the transactions of the individual borrowers and of the seller, if any;

(l) Satisfactory evidence of compliance with the requirements of such other federal, state or local laws and regulations as may, from time to time, become applicable to the said deed of trust notes or to the underlying real estate transactions.

(m) Evidence of clean termite inspection/certificate.

(2) Each conventional loan shall, in addition, when applicable, be subject to Federal Home Loan Bank regulations, and in the case of loans in a principal amount in excess of 80

of all persons holding an interest in said partnership, the extent of such interest, and whether such interest is held as general or limited partner; or,
  (iii) If Borrower is conducting business under a trade name or fictitious name, a copy of all documents filed by Borrower to qualify to do business under such trade name or fictitious name in any state or district; and,
 (b) A copy of each and every policy maintained by Borrower insuring against errors and omissions and a copy of each and every blanket bond maintained by Borrower, together with endorsements thereto requiring written notice to Lender of any claim or action seeking recovery under any such policy or bond within ten (10) days thereof and further requiring written notice to Lender at least ten (10) days prior to cancellation of any such policy or a reduction in the limits of liability thereunder.
C. *Conditions for Each Advance.* Lender shall not be required to make any advance to Borrower pursuant hereto until the following conditions precedent have been performed to the satisfaction of Lender as to each separate advance:
(1) The delivery to Lender of the following documentation:
 (a) The deed of trust note or notes evidencing a real estate loan acceptable as collateral security to Lender, which said deed of trust note or notes shall be duly endorsed and assigned to Lender without recourse by Borrower; and,
 (b) An interim binder for title insurance or a preliminary letter of title issued by a title insurance company acceptable to Lender, together with any attachments thereto, indicating that the permanent policy of title insurance, when issued, will insure the deed of trust securing the deed of trust note or notes to be the first lien on the subject property with no prior lien or encumbrance; and,
 (c) A certified copy of the deed of trust securing the deed of trust note or notes together with copy of receipt, for the recordation thereof among the appropriate land records; and,
 (d) In the case of each FHA-insured or VA-guaranteed deed of trust note, a certified copy of the commitment of the Federal Housing Administration to insure the

(ii) That, if a partnership, Borrower is empowered and authorized under the Partnership Agreement to execute this Agreement and the Master Note, endorsements and assignments referred to herein, and that the partner or partners who execute this Agreement, Master Note, endorsements and assignments herein referred to on behalf of the partnership are empowered by law and by the Partnership Agreement to bind Borrower, the general partners thereof, and the limited partners, if any, to the extent of their interest in Borrower; or,

(iii) That, if conducting a business under a trade name or fictitious name, Borrower has filed with the appropriate official all documents required under the laws of any state or district in which it does business to conduct such business under such trade name or fictitious name; and,

(c) That this Agreement is a valid and binding obligation of Borrower, and that the Master Note and any endorsements or assignments hereunder will be valid and binding obligations of Borrower and any endorsers thereto.

(2) The delivery to Lender of documentation, satisfactory for Lender, that Borrower is empowered to borrow the sums provided for herein, to execute this Agreement and the Master Note provided for hereunder, and endorse and assign to Lender the collateral security provided herein, such documentation to include, but not to be limited to, the following:

(a) (i) If Borrower is a corporation, a certified copy of a resolution passed by the Borrower's Board of Directors authorizing the borrowing herein provided for, the execution and delivery of this Agreement and of the Master Note provided for hereunder, and endorsement and assignment to Lender of the collateral security herein provided; or

(ii) If Borrower is a partnership, a copy of the Partnership Agreement under which the partnership was created together with copies of all the modifications, amendments or changes thereto, a copy of any certificate of partnership filed together with modifications, amendments or changes thereto, and a statement reflecting the names and addresses

and acceptable as collateral security to Lender, an amount of money equal to .... percent (.... %) of the committed purchase price of such deed of trust note as evidenced by a certified copy of the investor's commitment to purchase under which the loan will be sold; provided, however, that the aggregate unpaid principal amount, at a given time, of all sums advanced pursuant to this Agreement (hereinafter referred to as "Loan") does not exceed the maximum amount which Lender has agreed to advance to Borrower hereunder.

(2) The Loan shall be evidenced by a demand, secured promissory note (hereinafter referred to as "Master Note") executed by the Borrower, in a principal amount equal to the maximum amount which Lender has agreed to advance to Borrower hereunder, and bearing interest on the principal balance outstanding at the rate of .... percent (.... %) of the prime commercial lending rate of Lender, as established by the Lender from time to time, to be adjusted without prior notice upon any change in such prime rate. Interest due shall be computed daily on the basis of a 360-day year by applying the rate, as adjusted, from its effective date to the date of any subsequent change.

(3) Borrower will pay interest accrued upon the Loan on the first day of each month, which interest may, at the discretion of Lender, be charged to and paid from any account maintained by Borrower with Lender without notice to the Borrower, including the special account established hereinafter.

B. *General Conditions.* Lender shall not be required to make any advance to Borrower pursuant hereto until the following conditions precedent have been performed to the satisfaction of Lender

(1) The delivery to Lender of an opinion of counsel satisfactory to Lender stating in the opinion of such counsel:

   (a) That Borrower is legally and properly organized and in existence and has the power and authority to own its properties and to carry on its business in the manner it conducts such business; and,

   (b) (i) That, if a corporation, Borrower is empowered and authorized under the charter and bylaws of Borrower to execute this Agreement and the Master Note, endorsements and assignments referred to herein; or,

company located in the Commonwealth of .... selected by any Noteholder.

9. This Agreement shall be binding on the assigns and successors in interest of the Noteholder.

IN WITNESS WHEREOF, the parties have executed this Noteholder's Agreement the day and year stated above.

The Trustee, by executing this Agreement, acknowledges that it has read the terms and conditions and agrees to be bound thereto.

COMMENT: See discussion of separate noteholder's agreement at ¶ 11.01[8].

Form 11.3

MASTER MORTGAGE WAREHOUSE SECURITY AGREEMENT AND FINANCING STATEMENT

This Agreement is made and entered into on this ...... day of ...., 19 .... by and between .... , a national banking association (hereinafter referred to as "Lender") and .... (hereinafter referred to as "Borrower").

WHEREAS, Borrower, from time to time, makes loans to individuals, which loans are secured by first deeds of trust conveying certain properties and the improvements thereon; and,

WHEREAS, Borrower customarily sells and transfers such loans and the security therefor to certain investors within a reasonable time after making such loans; and,

WHEREAS, Borrower desires to borrow funds for the purpose of making such loans, to be repaid upon the sale of such loans; and,

WHEREAS, Lender is willing, upon the execution of this Agreement, to make advances to Borrower, in a maximum amount which shall be determined from time to time by Lender, for purposes of making such loans to be secured by an assignment of the loans and the security therefor, subject to the terms, provisions, conditions and warranties herein.

Now, THEREFORE, this Agreement, WITNESSETH, that for and in consideration of the premises and the mutual agreements herein contained, the parties hereto agree as follows:

A. *Advances to the Borrower.*
    (1) Lender will, upon demand, advance and lend to Borrower, in connection with any note secured by a first deed of trust

2. If either Noteholder is desirous of selling or assigning its Note other than to a family member, said Noteholder desiring of selling shall first offer to sell said Note to the other Noteholder. The other Noteholder will have a two-week period to accept or reject said offer. If said offer is rejected and the Noteholder desirous of selling receives a bonafide offer to purchase from a third party which is less than the price offered to the Noteholder on the first right of refusal, the Noteholder desiring to sell must first offer to sell to the other Noteholder at the price offered by the third party. Said Noteholder shall have a one-week period to accept or reject said offer.

3. No Noteholder will enter into any modification of the Note with the Maker of the Note without the prior written consent of the other Noteholder.

4. If the occasion arises where the Maker defaults under one Note, but not the other, the Noteholder of the Note which is in default has full authority to request the Trustee under the Deed of Trust to commence foreclosure.

5. If the occasion arises where the Maker is in default under both Notes, but one Noteholder desires to institute foreclosing proceedings and the other Noteholder does not, no foreclosure shall be commenced for a thirty-day period. If a Noteholder still does not want to commence foreclosure, no foreclosure shall take place if the Noteholder not desiring to foreclose brings the other Noteholder current in its payments. The Noteholder being brought current in payments shall simultaneously execute an assignment of its claim for delinquent interest to the other Noteholder.

6. If prior to the actual day of foreclosure sale, the Maker tenders the full amount of cash necessary to cure the default, if one Noteholder moves to reinstate, the loan shall be so reinstated provided the Maker pays for the expenses incurred in foreclosure through the date of reinstatement.

7. Notwithstanding any terms of this Agreement limiting the right of the Noteholder to request the Trustee to foreclose on the Deed of Trust, if a default arises under any of the Notes held by the Noteholders, any Noteholder with a Note so in default can at any time bring an action at law on the Note against the Maker of said Note, and it is expressly understood that the right of any Noteholder to receive payment of principal and interest on such Note as and when the same shall become due and payable as therein expressed or to institute suit of enforcement of such payment on or after such date upon the Note shall not be impaired or affected by any term or condition of this Agreement.

8. At any time and from time-to-time, any Noteholder can request a substitution of Trustee, and said successor Trustee shall be any title

WITNESS the signatures and seals of the parties hereto as of the day and year first hereinbefore written.

COMMENT: See discussion of loan participation agreement at ¶ 11.01[7].

Form 11.2

SEPARATE NOTEHOLDER'S AGREEMENT

This Agreement made this .... day of........................, 19...., by and between ....
of ....
and ....
of ....

WITNESSETH:

WHEREAS, ... and .... being the former owners of the office building located at..
.... have each received a Promissory Note from .... in the amount of .... Dollars ($..........).

WHEREAS, each Note is in pari passu with the other and secured by a certain Deed of Trust, executed by .... in favor of Trustee for...
.... and ...., the Noteholders.

WHEREAS, in light of the equality between the Noteholders, it is necessary to agree beforehand to certain conditions governing the authorization of the Trustee to act and the ability of each Noteholder to deal separately with the Maker of the Notes.

NOW, THEREFORE, in consideration of Ten Dollars ($10.00), each in hand paid unto the other, receipt of which is hereby acknowledged, it is agreed as follows:

1. If either of the Noteholders receives actual or constructive notice of default by the Maker of the Deed of Trust and Promissory Notes, said Noteholder with such knowledge, will so inform the other Noteholder of the default by registered mail.

the party receiving such payment shall share the same ratably with the other party a portion of the Loan, so that, following such purchase, the total outstanding indebtedness of the Borrower to both parties shall be in the same proportions as existed immediately prior to such setoff. In case any payment received by way of such setoff is subsequently recovered by the Borrower, in whole or in part, appropriate further adjustment shall be made between the parties hereto so as to maintain the aforesaid proportion of holdings of indebtedness of the Borrower.

9. *Standards of Care.* In making advances to Borrower, servicing, administering, and enforcing the Loan, and in exercising any other right or duty hereunder, Principal shall be obligated to exercise reasonable care.

10. *Loan Documents and Their Approval.* Principal represents that the only documents pertinent to this Loan (the Loan Documents) consist of the following:

- Principal's Commitment
- Promissory Note
- Guarantee Agreement
- Mortgage or Deed of Trust
- Building Loan Agreement
- Title Insurance Policy
- Survey
- Hazard Insurance Policy
- MAI Appraisal
- Final Plans and Specifications

Unless all of said Documents (and any other loan documents Participant shall deem pertinent hereto) shall have been exhibited to and approved by Participant, true copies thereof will be furnished to Participant no later than ten (10) days following the execution hereof. If, upon examination, any of said Documents are objectionable to Participant, Participant may require Principal to repurchase Participant's interest in said Loan for the total amount which Participant shall have advanced, together with interest thereon to the date of repurchase. Such right to require repurchase shall be conditioned upon Participant giving Principal written notice of such requirement no later than twenty (20) days following the receipt by Participant of all of the Loan Documents.

11. Commitment Agreement dated ...., between Principal and Participant is hereby incorporated herein and made a part hereof.

3. *Collections and Servicing of the Loan.* Principal shall do all normal servicing of the Loan and receive all payments in connection therewith. Principal shall promptly remit to Participant its share of all payments of principal and interest received on the Loan.

4. *Sharing Expenses.* Principal and Participant shall share all expenses in connection with the Loan in proportion to their respective shares of the principal of the Loan. Said expenses shall include, but not be limited to, disbursement for the protection of the property or enforcement of the Loan but shall not include Principal's ordinary overhead expenses.

5. *Defaults.* In event of a default continuing for more than ten (10) days, Principal will notify Paticipant. Principal will not, without Participant's consent, institute foreclosure proceedings. In event either Principal or Participant wishes to institute foreclosure proceedings and the other will not consent, then the party desiring to institute foreclosure proceedings may purchase the interest of the other for the total of the unrepaid advances, which such other party shall have made with interest thereon to the date of purchase.

6. *Bookkeeping and Accounting.* The Principal shall at all times keep proper books of account and records reflecting all disbursements on, and out-of-pocket expenses in connection with, the Loan and shall from time to time, as Participant may reasonably request, give a report thereof to the Participant. In recording its interest in the Loan in its own books and records, the Principal shall clearly reflect the partial ownership interest of the Participant in the Loan. The Principal will, upon reasonable requests made by the Participant from time to time, permit the Participant or its representatives to examine and make copies of or extracts from all books, records, and documents held by the Principal in connection with the Loan.

7. *Sale of Participation.* The Participant represents that it is purchasing its interest in the Loan for investment and not with a view to subsequent sale or distribution, and that it will not sell or otherwise transfer its participation in the Loan without giving the Principal thirty (30) days advance written notice thereof, during which period the Principal shall have the right to purchase such participation and to cancel this Agreement by paying to the Participant its share of the principal of the note with interest to date, or such lesser amount as Participant may have agreed or be willing to agree to accept therefor from any other purchaser.

8. *Sharing Setoffs.* If either the Principal or the Participant shall, by enforcement of any right of setoff, obtain a payment on the Loan,

(the "Borrower"), said Commitment consisting of .... Dollars ($. . . . .); and .... and ....

WHEREAS, said Loan is for the purpose of financing construction of .... Shopping Center on a tract of land containing approximately 11.6 acres located on the southeast corner of ...., said land and improvements being herein referred to as the Project; and

WHEREAS, Participant desires to join with Principal in the making of the construction portion only of said Loan under the terms and conditions hereinafter set forth;

NOW, THEREFORE, in consideration of their mutual promises, Principal and Participant represent and agree as follows:

1. *Participation.* Principal and Participant each agree to make advances to Borrower in accordance with the Loan Documents with Principal advancing...................................... percent (.....%), which participation shall amount to................... ....percent (.....%), which participation shall amount to .... Dollars ($................). Principal will determine when advances are required under the loan documents and will give Participant reasonable notice on behalf of Participant and call upon Participant for its share. In event that either party shall advance, in share, the other party shall, upon demand, pay to the party making such excess advancement such amount as shall cause the investment of the parties to be equal to the above percentages. In the event Principal shall have sold or shall hereafter sell to others participations in the Loan, all references to the Principal's share in the Loan shall be deemed to include the shares held by such others; and all reference to advances by Principal shall be deemed to mean advances by Principal and such others, it being agreed that Principal will make all advances required of such other participants in event they do not do so. All Loan Documents shall be deemed to mean advances by Principal and such others, it being agreed that Principal will make all advances required of such other participants in event they do not do so. All Loan Documents shall be in the name of Principal for convenience of administration. All such documents shall be held by Principal for the benefit of both parties.

2. *Participation Certificate.* Upon each advance by Participant, pursuant to Paragraph 1 above, the Principal shall deliver to Participant a Participation Certificate in the form annexed hereto as Exhibit A.

to reduce the proposed sale prices on the units to a level which will permit sale of that number of units sufficient to pay out the Loan prior to its stated maturity.

9. Subject to any presale requirement established by any end loan lender and provided the Borrower is not in default under the Loan, the Lender will release individual units within the condominium regime upon payment of a sum equal to 85 percent (85%) of the units sales price or 135 percent of the Loan amount allocated to such unit, whichever is greater, plus Ten Dollars and Fifty Cents ($10.50) per release. The release fee shall be applied at Lender's option, either to unpaid interest on the Loan or to principal.

A release schedule setting forth specific release prices for each unit approved by Lender will be appended to the loan documents at the time of the Loan Closing. Borrower shall submit to Lender a schedule of proposed sale prices for each unit and following approval by Lender, Borrower shall make no change in the proposed sales prices without the prior written consent of Lender.

10. The opinion of Borrower's counsel required pursuant to General Condition 3(1) hereof shall also contain a statement that the planned conversion of the Improvements conforms in all respects to all applicable District of Columbia rules, regulations, and building codes.

11. The Borrower shall not execute any leases for the units within the Improvements that would have a lease maturity later than twelve (12) months from the date of the Loan Closing.

Borrower's Acknowledgment........................

COMMENT: See discussion of construction lender's requirements with respect to condominium financing at ¶ 10.02[2]

Form 11.1

LOAN PARTICIPATION AGREEMENT

THIS IS AN AGREEMENT, made as of the .... day of ...., 19....., between ...., herein called Principal, and ...., herein called Participant.

WHEREAS, Principal has issued a Commitment to make a construction and permanent loan (herein called the Loan) to ....,

5. The Borrower's interest in the contracts of sale for the units within the Improvements shall be assigned to the Lender together with any security deposits or down payment thereunder as the contracts are executed, and the moneys shall be held by the Lender in an interest-bearing trust account for the benefit of the Borrower. The Borrower shall have the right to have any such security deposits or down payments released for distribution to any purchasers of such units at the time of release of such units or to the Borrower in the event of the cancellation of any such units or to the Borrower in the event of the cancellation of any of the contracts of sale; provided, however, that Lender, subject to any superior rights enjoyed by the contract purchasers, may, upon default by Borrower under the Loan, apply all such deposits to the interest or principal due on the Loan.

6. A condominium regime covering the Real Property shall be established in accordance with the provisions of the laws of the District of Columbia when and as the presale requirements of the end loan lender have been met (but not prior to the sale of 51 percent (51%) of the condominium units within the Improvements) and all aspects of the condominium regime shall have been approved by the Bank, FHLMC, and the lender providing the end loans. The condominium declaration and bylaws, plat of condominium subdivisions, and the building plans shall conform to FHLMC requirements, and must be submitted for the approval of the Lender, the end loan lender, and FHLMC as soon as available and in any event prior to the establishment of the regime and each must be recorded when required by the Lender. It shall constitute an event of default under the Deed of Trust should the condominium regime be thereafter terminated during the term of the Loan without the prior written consent of the Lender.

7. The proposed condominium regime covering the Real Property must be registered as required under applicable law within three months after the Loan Closing. All documents applicable to the formation and qualification of the condominium regime required on the part of the Borrower shall be prepared by an attorney acceptable to Lender.

8. The Loan documents will provide that the Borrower shall have achieved not less than fifty (50) "reservations" for purchase of units within the Improvements prior to the expiration of six (6) months from the expiration of twelve (12) months from the Loan Closing. The Borrower shall have achieved not less than fifty (50) sales (meeting the requirements of the Loan Closing and not less than one hundred (100) sales prior to the expiration of fourteen (14) months from the Loan Closing. Failure to comply with the foregoing provisions shall constitute an event of default under the loan documents; upon the occurrence of such event of default, Lender will have the right to request the Borrower

Bank to purchasers of the units within the Improvements, which commitment shall be for a term not less than twelve (12) months from the date of the Loan Closing (with an option exercisable by Borrower to extend for two additional terms of six (6) months each), shall include all 195 units within the Improvements and shall be for a minimum of Five Million Five Hundred Thousand Dollars ($5,500,000). The commitment will conform in all respects to the regulations promulgated by FHLMC, and Borrower shall apply for a waiver to permit acceptance of end loans upon sale of 51 percent (51%) of the units within the Improvements. Loans for individual units shall be made up to 90 percent (90%) of their sales prices, with loans exceeding 80 percent (80%) of sales price required to be insured by a private mortgage insurer. The interest rate payable by the purchasers of the units shall be not greater than 9 $7/8$ percent (9 $7/8$) per annum.

(d) A copy of the legislation enacted in the state of .... establishing the maximum rate of interest for end loans such as those proposed in subparagraph C above at not less than 10 percent (10%) per annum. The opinion required of Borrower's counsel shall contain an affirmative statement as to the maximum permissable rate of interest.

(e) A copy of the Certificate of Eligibility issued by the Department of Housing and Community Development of the state of ....

(f) A copy of the exclusive sales agency contract with .... Lender reserves the right to approve any party proposed to be substituted as exclusive sales agent for the Improvements. Borrower shall, with the consent of .... assign such contract to Lender.

4. Borrower shall accept and execute contracts covering individual condominium units only if they and the contract purchasers conform to FHLMC guidelines for permanent financing and if the contract purchaser meets the credit underwriting requirements of the end loan lender providing financing for such units. Each contract of sale covering a condominium unit shall also:

(a) Be in form approved by Lender;

(b) Unless the purchase is for cash, be accompanied by a loan commitment addressed to the purchaser from a lender and in form, amount, and substance acceptable to Lender, with a commitment maturity date satisfactory to Lender;

(c) Be accompanied by a deposit of not less than Five Hundred Dollars ($500) with the total deposit to be escrowed with Lender, if possible under applicable law; and

(d) Be assigned to Lender as provided in Special Condition 5 below.

14. The Borrower, Guarantors and Indemnitors agree that this commitment and the loan documents shall be governed by and construed under the laws of the State of .... or such other state as Lender may designate and shall consent to be sued in any court in the State of .... or such state as is designated by Lender having jurisdiction in any action to enforce the provisions of this commitment and/or the loan documents. If the Borrower, the Guarantor or Indemnitor are not residents or corporations of the state under whose laws the loan documents shall be construed, the Borrower, Guarantors and Indemnitors shall irrevocably appoint a resident of such state satisfactory to Lender as their true and lawful attorney-in-fact to accept service of process for them and on their behalf in any proceeding to enforce the provisions of the loan documents.

15. The terms and conditions of this commitment shall survive the closing of the Loan; provided, however, that if any of the terms and conditions of this commitment shall conflict with any of the terms and conditions of the Loan documents, the terms and conditions of the Loan documents shall prevail. Time is of the essence hereof.

SPECIAL CONDITIONS

1. Lender's Supervising Engineers shall provide the Lender with a report covering the structural soundness and mechanical integrity of the Improvements, which report shall be in form and substance in all respects satisfactory to Lender. Additionally, not later than nine (9) months after the Loan Closing, Borrower shall provide Lender with evidence of approval of the Improvements by the Federal Home Loan Mortgage Corporation (FHLMC) for the purpose of purchasing loans on individual units within the Improvements.

2. Conversion of the Improvements contemplates painting of the units and common areas, some carpentry work, and some modification of the central utility system. Lender understands no structural work is intended by Borrower.

3. Receipt and approval by Lender of each of the following shall be a condition precedent to Lender's obligation to make the Loan:

(a) A fully executed copy of Borrower's contract to purchase the Real Property.

(b) A copy of the notice to be given to each tenant of the Improvements advising them of Borrower's intention to convert the Improvements to a condominium regime, advising of the right to purchase and/or notice to vacate.

(c) Commitment for end loans from a lender approved by the

examination of title to the date of each advance, which must be satisfactory to Lender and show title vested in Borrower.

7. The Deed of Trust shall contain a provision whereby the entire principal sum and interest will become due and payable at the option of the Mortgagee upon the sale, transfer, conveyance or other encumbrance of the Real Property, without the prior written consent of Lender, except as provided in Special Condition 9 hereof.

8. If an appraisal is required by the terms of the letter portion of this commitment, the appraised value shall be determined by an appraiser designated by Lender. The appraiser may be a member of Lender's in-house staff. The basis of the appraisal calculation shown in the appraisal report and all other aspects of the appraisal report must be satisfactory to Lender.

9. At Lender's request, Borrower shall place a sign at a location on the Premises satisfactory to Lender, which sign shall recite, among other things, that Lender is financing construction of the project. Borrower expressly authorizes Lender to prepare and to furnish to the news media for publication from time to time news releases with respect to the Real Property, specifically to include but not limited to releases detailing Lender's involvement with the financing of the Real Property.

10. Any leases affecting the Premises shall be assigned to Lender as additional collateral for the Loan. Any such leases and assignments to Lender shall be in form and substance satisfactory in all respects to Lender and its counsel.

11. The Loan Closing shall be held at such location in ....as is designated by Lender.

12. No statements, agreements or representations, oral or written, which have been made to you or Borrower or to any employee or agent of yours or Borrower's, either by Lender or by any employee, agent, or broker acting on Lender's behalf, with respect to the Loan, shall be of any force or effect, except to the extent stated in this commitment, and all prior agreements and representations in respect of the Loan are merged herein. This commitment may not be (i) changed except by written agreement signed by Borrower, Lender, and the Guarantors and Indemnitors, if any, or (ii) assigned by Borrower by operation of law or otherwise, unless Lender shall consent in writing to such assignment.

13. If the Real Property is located in a special flood hazard area, Lender must be furnished with a flood insurance policy at closing of the Loan in the amount of the Loan or the maximum limit of coverage available on the Real Property, whichever is less. If the Real Property is not located in a special flood hazard area, Borrower shall furnish to Lender at or prior to settlement a signed statement to that effect from its insurance agent or broker.

(m) A projection of the progress of conversion of the Improvements by months.

(n) If an advance is requested at settlement, a requisition on Lender's form detailing the purpose for and application of the proceeds of the advance.

(o) Such other documents, instruments, opinions, and assurances as Lender and its counsel may request.

4. Lender may terminate this commitment if, except as may be otherwise provided herein, the Loan, or any other feature of the transaction has or is misrepresented by Borrower in the mortgage loan application, or otherwise, or if any adverse change, in the sole judgment of Lender, shall have occurred with respect to the Premises at time of closing or if any part of the Premises shall have been taken in condemnation or other like proceedings, or if such proceeding is pending at the time of closing, or if the Borrower or any person who is defined in the term Guarantor or Indemnitor shall be involved in any arrangement, bankruptcy, reorganization, or insolvency proceeding, or shall have suffered any adverse change in his, its, or their financial condition.

5. All instruments and documents required hereby or affecting the Premises, securing the Loan or relating to Borrower's capacity and authority to make the Loan and to execute the Loan documents and such other documents, instruments, opinions, assurances, consents, and approvals as Lender may request, and all procedures connected herewith shall be subject to the approval, as to form and substance, of Lender, Lender's state counsel and Lender's local counsel, if any.

6. Advances under the Building Loan Agreement shall be made not more frequently than monthly and shall be based upon inspections and certifications by the Supervising Engineers. All requisitions shall be made on forms furnished by the Lender. The Borrower shall furnish the Lender with lien waivers signed by all major subcontractors and suppliers for all work done and materials supplied that were included in the preceding requisition, which waivers shall be furnished prior to the twentieth (20th) day after the date of disbursement of the preceding requisition or prior to disbursement of the next requisition, whichever date shall first occur. All requisitions for conversion costs shall be approved by the Supervising Engineers and all requirements for indirect costs and expenses shall be approved by Lender. The Lender shall disburse not more than 90 percent (90%) of each requisition for conversion costs until (a) conversion is completed and approved by the Supervising Engineer, and (b) final mechanics' lien waivers have been furnished to Lender. Advances will also be contingent upon a current

information regarding the subcontractors as Lender may request.

(e) The undertaking of subcontractors designated by Lender to continue performance on Lender's behalf under any of the Loan documents and not to permit nor execute any change order increasing the price of the Improvements or materially altering the scope of the Improvements.

(f) The Guarantys and the Indemnification Agreement.

(g) Current certified financial statements (to include balance sheet, profit and loss statement, and cash flow projection) of Borrower, Guarantors, and Indemnitors, and in form as Lender may request.

(h) All required building and other governmental permits and evidence of compliance with all zoning and other laws, ordinances, rules, regulations, and restrictions affecting the Premises, and the conversion to the operation and occupancy of the Improvements as a condominium project.

(i) Fire, extended coverage insurance, collapse and vandalism and malicious mischief insurance coverage of the Improvements in the form of "all risk," 100 percent (100%) nonreporting policy and containing such other extended coverage as may be required by Lender in an amount to be designated by the Lender as to insurable value of the Real Property. The policy shall indicate Lender's value of the mortgage and shall be in form and issued by companies acceptable to Lender.

(j) Copies of workman's compensation and public liability (minimum $500,000/$1,000,000) and property damage (minimum $250,000) policies.

(k) Opinion of local counsel for Lender in transactions where the Premises are not located in Maryland that neither the making nor the servicing of the Loan will subject the Lender to any requirements with respect to qualifying to do business or taxation (except ad valorem taxes on the Premises) in the state in which the Premises are located and that the Loan is not usurious. The opinion must also inform us (i) of the cost of foreclosing and time necessary to complete the foreclosure process as well as any particular limitation on our right to foreclose, (ii) any limitations on our right to obtain or the amount of a deficiency judgment, (iii) any unusual difficulties in enforcing the loan documents or in delivering possession to a purchaser at foreclosure, and (iv) the existence of and details surrounding any redemption period enjoyed by the borrower following a sale at foreclosure.

(l) An opinion of counsel for Borrower as to Borrower's form, powers, and authority and as to the validity, binding effect, and enforceability of the Loan documents and a copy of the agreement creating the entity and any recorded certificate or agreement relating thereto.

fined), fees and charges for surveys, examination of title to the Premises and mortgage title insurance thereon, hazard insurance, mortgage taxes, transfer taxes, and all recording fees and charges.

2. Lender shall not be required to pay any brokerage fees or commission arising from this transaction, and Borrower and Guarantor agree to defend, indemnify, and hold Lender harmless against any and all expenses, liabilities, and losses arising from such claims in connection therewith, to include payment of reasonable attorney's fees.

3. Prior to the Loan Closing, Lender shall have received and approved the following:

(a) A current survey of the Premises satisfactory to Lender and its counsel, which survey shall be certified to the title company and to Lender. The survey shall show dimensions and locations of any improvements, easements, rights of way, adjoining sites, encroachments and the extent thereof, established building lines and street lines, the distance to, and names of the nearest intersecting streets, and such other details as Lender may request.

(b) A mortgage title insurance binder with a commitment to issue a title insurance policy in approved ALTA form in the amount of the Loan insuring the lien of the Deed of Trust, subject only to those exceptions to title as are approved by Lender and its counsel, and with affirmative insurance on such matters as Lender may require. The title binder shall be issued by a company acceptable to Lender, and shall contain such terms and coverage as Lender and its counsel shall deem acceptable. In lieu of the title binder, Lender will accept a title report or certificate of title signed by the title company with an agreement to issue a title insurance policy in approved ALTA form.

(c) A detailed trade breakdown on Lender's forms of the cost of the renovation of the Improvements verified in writing by the Supervising Engineers and an itemization on Lender's forms of non-construction costs and cost of the Premises, verified by Lender. If the renovation costs, in the sole judgment of the Supervising Engineers, plus the cost of the Premises and the estimated non-construction costs, in the sole judgment of Lender, exceed the amount of the Loan, Borrower shall be required to invest the excess in the project or deposit such excess with the Lender in an account pledged in a manner satisfactory to Lender prior to any advance by Lender of the Loan proceeds. In no event, however, shall the amount of the Loan exceed the aggregate amount of the estimated costs as determined above. It is estimated that the Borrower's cash equity requirement shall be a minimum of $1,000,000; the Borrower's Equity shall be invested at the Loan Closing.

(d) All subcontracts as required by Lender, as well as the identity of the subcontractors. Borrower shall furnish Lender with such

Exhibit A, which together constitute the commitment, to Lender together with the commitment fee, within fifteen (15) days of the date hereof or this commitment shall be deemed null and void. The Loan Closing shall be held within thirty (30) days from the date of your acceptance of this commitment or this commitment will expire.

Very truly yours,

By:........................

THE FOREGOING TERMS AND CONDITIONS ARE HEREBY ACCEPTED AND AGREED TO THIS .... DAY OF........................ ENCLOSED IS OUR CHECK IN THE AMOUNT OF SIX THOUSAND FIVE HUNDRED DOLLARS ($6,500) COVERING THE COMMITMENT AND APPRAISAL FEES.

By:........................
(Guarantors) (Indemnitors)

....

....

....

EXHIBIT A

General Conditions

Borrower's Name....................   Date..................

The commitment for a construction loan to which this Exhibit A is attached and is a part, unless otherwise indicated therein, is subject to the following terms and conditions:

1. Borrower's acceptance of the commitment shall constitute its unconditional agreement to pay all fees, commissions, costs, charges, taxes, and other expenses incurred in connection with this commitment and the making of the Loan, whether or not the Loan closes, including but not limited to fees of Lender's state counsel and local counsel, if any, appraisal fees, fees of Supervising Engineers (as hereinafter de-

from the date of each advance, calculated on the basis of a 360-day year. Upon default in any payment of the monthly installments of interest, such installment of interest and the Loan shall bear interest at a rate of one percent per annum in excess of the Loan interest rate until the default is cured. A late charge of 5 percent of the payment shall be imposed on any payment made more than fifteen (15) days after it is due.

Conversion of the Improvements shall commence not later than ninety (90) days prior to settlement of the first unit and shall be completed within sixteen (16) months from the Loan Closing, time being of the essence.

Lender's obligation to make the Loan is subject to the terms and conditions contained in this letter and in Exhibit A attached hereto and made a part hereof and to the receipt by Lender of (a) a joint and several guaranty of payment of the Note and completion of the Borrower's obligations under the Building Loan Agreement (the Guarantys) and a joint and several indemnification against losses to Lender resulting from the sale of the note and mortgage after default (the indemnification) executed by .... (the Guarantors and Indebitors) and (b) an appraisal from an appraiser designated by Lender, indicating a sellout value in the Real Property equal to not less than Eight Million One Hundred Twenty-Seven Thousand Dollars ($8,127,000), and including a feasibility analysis concluding that the Improvements can be fully sold within twenty four (24) months of the Loan Closing. If the sellout appraisal value is less than Eight Million One Hundred Twenty-Seven Thousand Dollars ($8,127,000), the Loan shall be reduced to 66 percent of such lesser appraised value. You shall enclose with your acceptance of this commitment an appraisal fee in the sum of One Thousand Five Hundred Dollars ($1,500).

Lender's obligation to make the Loan is further subject to Borrower's payment of a nonrefundable construction loan fee of Twenty-Six Thousand Six Hundred Sixty Five Dollars ($26,665), as follows: Five Thousand Dollars ($5,000) upon acceptance of this commitment and Twenty-One Thousand Six Hundred Sixty-Four Dollars ($21,664) at the Loan Closing. The payment of this fee in no way lessens the Borrower's obligation to close the Loan in accordance with the terms of this commitment.

If the foregoing is satisfactory to you, kindly indicate your acceptance thereof and your agreement to borrow the proceeds of the Loan upon the terms and conditions contained herein and in Exhibit A hereto by signing and returning the enclosed copy of this letter and initialling each page of Exhibit A and returning one fully executed letter and

Form 10.2

CONSTRUCTION LOAN COMMITMENT LETTER FOR CONDOMINIUM FINANCING

Gentlemen:

Lender is pleased to inform you that its Real Estate Committee has approved your request for a construction loan (the Loan) in the amount of $.......... to be made to ...., a .... general partnership (Borrower). The Loan is to be evidenced by a note (the Note) of Borrower and is to be secured by a first lien mortgage or deed of trust (the Deed of Trust) on Borrower's fee interest in the above described land (the Premises), and the improvements thereon consisting of a .... to be converted to a condominium project (the Improvements) (the Premises and the Improvements hereinafter collectively referred to as the Real Property), and by a first perfected lien on all fixtures, chattels, building materials, and personalty which Lender believes is necessary or desirable in connection with the maintenance or operation of the Improvements. Following an advance at the loan closing against the purchase price of the Premises, the remainder of the Loan shall be advanced pursuant to a Building Loan Agreement to be executed by and between Lender and Borrower.

Interest only on the outstanding balance of the Loan at a rate equal to 2 percent per annum in excess of the Lender's commercial prime rate of interest in effect at the close of the first day of each and every month shall be payable monthly until repayment of the Loan. However, the rate of interest hereunder shall never be less than 9 percent per annum nor greater than 12 percent per annum. The Loan shall mature eighteen (18) months from the date of the Loan Closing. Provided the "end loan commitment" described in Special Condition 3(c) hereof shall have been extended so as to be coterminous with the extended loan maturity, the Borrower shall have the option to extend the maturity of the Loan for a period of six (6) months upon sixty (60) days prior written notice to Lender and payment therewith of a fee in the amount equal to the sum of ½ of 1 percent of the then outstanding principal balance of the Loan plus any Loan funds remaining to be advanced. It is also a condition precedent to the exercise of such extension that the Borrower not be in default under any of the Loan documents. During the extension period, the 12 percent "ceiling" interest rate shall not be applicable. Interest shall be computed for the actual number of days which have elapsed

.... } ss:
....

I HEREBY CERTIFY that on this .... day of ...., before me, the subscriber, a Notary Public in and for the State of ...., personally appeared ...., who, being duly sworn, did depose and say that he is the President of and attorney-in-fact for ...., the corporation named in the foregoing Declaration, and that by virtue of authority conferred upon him, acknowledged such instrument to be the act and deed of ....

WITNESS my hand and notarial seal.

....
Notary Public

My Commission expires:........................

EXHIBIT A

LEGAL DESCRIPTION OF PROPERTY

Description of property appears here.

COMMENT: See discussion of condominium master deed at ¶ 10.02[2][d].

Section 7. *Right to Lease or Sell Units.* Declarant shall retain title to each Unit not sold to any purchaser. Declarant retains the right to enter into leases with any third parties for the occupancy of any of the Units so retained by Declarant and not be exercised in its sole discretion to offer Parking Units on a priority basis in the following order: (a) to purchasers of Apartment Units who, as tenants, have occupied the Building and, in the event of any unsold Units after such offers, to (b) other purchasers of Apartment Units.

Section 8. *Conflicts and Construction.* In the event of any conflict between the Condominium Instruments, this Declaration shall control; but particular provisions shall control more general provisions, except that a construction conformable with the Condominium Act shall in all cases control over any construction inconsistent therewith.

IN WITNESS WHEREOF, the said .... has caused these presents to be signed with its corporate name by ...., its President, attested by ...., its Secretary, and its corporate seal to be hereto attached, and does hereby appoint .... its attorney-in-fact to acknowledge and deliver these presents as its act and deed, this ..... day of ...., for the purposes herein expressed.

ATTEST:

....
.... Corporation

By:......................
Secretary
(CORPORATE SEAL)

By:........................
President

CERTIFICATE

This is to certify that the foregoing and annexed Declaration was duly executed and delivered pursuant to, and in strict conformity with, the provisions of a Resolution of the Board of Directors and of the Stockholders of ...., passed at a regularly called meeting of said Board of Directors and of the Stockholders, and that a quorum was present at said meeting.

....
Secretary

Sections 216, 221, and 222 of the Condominium Act, the following easements are hereby granted:

(a) *Easement to Facilitate Sales.* All Units shall be subject to the statutory easement in favor of Declarant provided in Section 222 of the Condominium Act. The Declarant and its duly authorized agents, representatives, and employees shall have the right, exercisable in the Declarant's sole discretion, to use any Units owned by Declarant as models, management offices, or sales offices until such time as Declarant conveys title thereto to Unit Owners. Each Unit so utilized shall be a Unit within the meaning of this Declaration and the Condominium Act and not part of the Common Elements. Declarant reserves the right to relocate the same from time to time within the Property. Upon relocation or sale of a model, management office, or sales office, the furnishings thereof may be removed. Declarant further reserves the right to enter into certain agreement with other Unit Owners to lease their Units to the Declarant for use by the Declarant as model units, management offices, and/or sales offices. Declarant further reserves the right to maintain on the Property such advertising signs as may comply with applicable governmental regulations, which may be placed in any location on the Property and may be relocated or removed, all at the sole discretion of Declarant.

(b) *Easement for Ingress and Egress Through Common Elements and Access to Units.*
> (i) Each Unit Owner is hereby granted an easement in common with each other Unit Owner for ingress and egress through, the use and enjoyment of, all Common Elements. Each Condominium Unit is hereby burdened with and subjected to an easement for ingress and egress through, and use and enjoyment of, all Common Elements by persons lawfully using or entitled to the same.
> (ii) Declarant reserves in favor of Declarant and the Managing Agent and/or any other person authorized by the Board of Directors the right of access to any Unit as provided in Section 307(a) of the Condominium Act and Article V, Section 9 of the Bylaws. In case of emergency, such entry shall be immediate, whether the Unit Owner is present at the time or not.

Section 6. *Amendment of Declaration.* No amendment of this Declaration may be made without the prior written approval of the Mortgagees where such approval is provided for in Article VIII, Section 5 of the Bylaws, or where such approval is required elsewhere in the Condominium Instruments or by the Condominium Act.

and with the upper and lower boundaries. If a wall rather than a stripe or other floor marking delineates a vertical boundary of such Parking Unit, such boundary shall be the vertical plane of the finished surface of such wall extended to intersections with each other and with the upper and lower boundaries.

(b) The Parking Units located outside the garage as shown on the Condominium Plat shall consist of the space within the following boundaries:

>> (1) The lower boundary shall be the horizontal plane of the top unfinished surface of the parking lot or other facility extended to an intersection with the vertical boundaries.
>> (2) The vertical boundaries shall be the vertical plane perpendicular to the center line of the stripe or other ground marking delineating each such Parking Unit boundary. If a wall rather than a stripe or other floor marking delineates a vertical boundary of such Parking Unit, such boundary shall be the vertical plane of the finished surface of such wall extended to intersections with each other and with the upper and lower boundaries.

> (iii) To the extent that walls, floors, or ceilings are designated as the boundaries of any Units, all lath, wallboard, plastering, and other materials constituting any part of the unfinished surfaces thereof shall be deemed a part of such Units, while all other portions of such walls, floors, or ceilings shall be deemed a part of the Common Elements.
> (iv) If any chutes, flues, ducts, conduits, wires, bearing walls, bearing columns, or any other apparatus lies partially within and partially outside of the designated boundaries of any Unit, any portions thereof serving only that Unit shall be deemed as part of that Unit, while any portions thereof serving more than one Unit or any portion of the Common Elements shall be deemed a part of the Common Elements.

(c) *Relocation of Unit Boundaries and Subdivision of Units.* Relocation of boundaries between the Units and subdivision of Units will be permitted subject to compliance with the provisions therefor in Article V, Section 7 of the Bylaws and in Sections 225 and 226 of the Condominium Act.

Section 5. *Easements.* In addition to the easements created by

assigned as a Parking Unit shall be part of the Common Elements.

(c) *Storage and Trash Disposal Areas.* Storage and trash disposal areas within or adjacent to the Building shall be Common Elements except such areas that are within the boundaries of a Unit and shall be subject to such rules as the Board of Directors may establish for their use and maintenance; provided, however, that each Apartment Unit shall be entitled to the use of one below-ground level storage area as assigned by the Board of Directors.

Section 4. *Units.*

(a) *Units.* Annexed hereto as Exhibit C is a list of all Units, their Identifying Numbers, location, all as shown more fully on the Condominium Plat, type and the Ownership Interest appurtenant to each Unit determined on the basis of par value. The locations of the Common Elements to which each unit has direct access are shown on the Condominium Plat.

(b) *Dimensions of Units.*

> (i) *Apartment Units.* Each Apartment Unit consists of the space bounded by the walls, floors, and ceilings, if any, of such Unit as shown on the Condominium Plat, *provided,* however, that the wall, floor, and ceiling materials, other than the finished surface thereof (such as paint, wallcoverings, ceramic, vinyl tile, decorative plaster, and wood floors) shall be Common Elements. Doors and windows in Apartment Units leading onto or into Common Elements shall be Common Elements.
>
> (ii) *Parking Units*

(a) The Parking Units located in the multi-space parking garage as shown on the Condominium Plat shall consist of the space within the following boundaries:

> (1) The upper boundary of such Parking Unit shall be the horizontal plane of the outermost unfinished surface of the ceiling of the garage, extended to an intersection with the vertical boundaries.
>
> (2) The lower boundary of such Parking Unit shall be the horizontal plane of the top surface of the floor slab extended to an intersection with the vertical boundaries.
>
> (3) The vertical boundaries of such Parking Unit shall be a vertical plane perpendicular to the center line of the stripe or other floor marking delineating each such Parking Unit extended to intersections with each other

Unit Owner in the Common Elements, Common Expenses, and Common Profits as set forth in Exhibit C annexed hereto.

(m) *Property.* The Land, Building, all other improvements and structures thereon (including the Units and the Common Elements), all easements, rights and appurtenances thereunto belonging, and all other property, personal or mixed, intended for use in connection therewith, owned by the Declarant in fee simple and submitted to the Condominium Act. References in the Condominium Instruments to "Property" shall at all times be deemed to refer to such portions of the Property as have been submitted to the Condominium Act at the time in question.

(n) *Rules and Regulations.* Those rules and regulations governing the conduct of occupants of Units adopted from time to time by the Board of Directors and deemed necessary for the enjoyment of the Property; provided, however, that the same do not conflict with the Condominium Act or the Condominium Instruments.

(o) *Unit Owners Association.* All of the Unit Owners, acting as a group in accordance with the Condominium Act, the Declaration, and the Bylaws, shall constitute the Unit Owners' Association.

(p) *Units.* The Condominium shall consist of two types of Units:
  (i) Apartment Units are those units located in the Building other than those in the garage as shown on the Condominium Plat.
  (ii) Parking Units are those units located in the parking garage of the Building and outside the garage as shown on the Condominium Plat.

Reference in the Condominium Instruments to "Units" without specific reference to Apartment Units or Parking Units as such shall refer to both types of Units.

Section 3. *Building, Parking Spaces, Storage Areas.*

(a) *Building.* The location, dimensions, and area of the Building is shown on the Condominium Plat. The Building has nine (9) stories, including a ground (first) floor and eight (8) above ground floors, and a below-ground level consisting of a parking garage and various boiler, mechanical, maintenance, laundry, and storage rooms.

(b) *Parking Spaces.* There are located below the ground floor of the Building forty (40) parking spaces, apportioned into a multi-space garage area; and there are located twelve (12) parking spaces outside the garage. The aforesaid parking spaces are designated by number on the Condominium Plat and are further designated as Parking Units pursuant to Section 4 of this Declaration. Such Parking Units shall be reserved for the exclusive use of the owners of such Parking Units. All paved areas necessary and appurtenant to such Parking Units and not

conditioning equipment and storage rooms, entrances and exits of the Building;

(v) Those pumps, pipes, wires, cables, conduits, and other apparatus relating to the water distribution, power, light, telephone, sewer, heating and air-conditioning and plumbing systems serving more than one Unit and/or any portion of the Common Elements, regardless of the actual location thereof;

(vi) All apparatus and installations existing in the Building or on the Property for common use or necessary or convenient to the existence, the common maintenance, or the safety of the Property;

(vii) All surface driveway and walkway areas and exterior landscaping, subject to the provisions of Section 3b. of this Declaration.

(e) *Condominium Act.* The State of .... Condominium Act of 1976 as the same may be amended from time to time.

(f) *Condominium Plat.* The plats and plans described in Section 214 of the Condominium Act and recorded in the Office of the Surveyor of the District of Columbia on .... 1978, in Condominium Book ..... Page ..... The term "General Common" on the Condominium Plat indicates Common Elements that are not Limited Common Elements.

(g) *Land.* The real property, exclusive of the Building thereon, at the time submitted to the Condominium Act, being the real property described in Exhibit A.

(h) *Majority of the Unit Owners.* Except as otherwise specifically provided in the Condominium Instruments, the owners of more than 50 percent of the aggregate Ownership Interests in the Condominium voting in person or by proxy at one time at a duly convened meeting at which a quorum is present. Any specified percentage of the owners means the Unit Owners owning such Ownership Interests in the aggregate.

(i) *Managing Agent.* A professional managing agent employed by the Unit Owners' Association to perform such duties as the Board of Directors shall authorize in accordance with the Condominium Instruments.

(j) *Mortgage.* Any recorded first deed of trust or first mortgage encumbering a Condominium Unit.

(k) *Mortgagee.* Any mortgagee under a first Mortgage, or trustee or beneficiary under a first deed of trust.

(l) *Ownership Interest.* The undivided ownership interest in each

Section 1. *Submission of Property.* ...., a .... corporation ("Declarant"), owner of the land located at ...., ..., and more particularly described in Exhibit A annexed hereto ("Land"), hereby submits the Land, together with the buildings and improvements erected thereon and all easements, rights and appurtenances thereunto belonging and all other property, personal or mixed, intended for use in connection therewith owned by the Declarant in fee simple ("Property"), to the provisions of the State of .... Condominium Act of 1976 (the "Condominium Act") and hereby creates with respect to the Property a plan of condominium ownership to be known as the .... Condominium ("Condominium").

Section 2. *Definitions.* As provided in Section 206 of the Condominium Act as in effect on the date of recordation of this Declaration, capitalized terms not otherwise defined herein or in the other Condominium Instruments shall have the meanings specified in Section 102 of the Condominium Act. The following terms as used herein and in the other Condominium Instruments shall have the following meanings:

(a) *Board of Directors.* The Executive Organ as defined in Section 102(m) of the Condominium Act.

(b) *Building.* The building and other improvements erected on the Land.

(c) *Bylaws.* The rules for the governance of the Condominium attached hereto as Exhibit B, as the same may be amended from time to time.

(d) *Common Elements.* The Common Elements consist of the entire Property, other than the Units, and include, without limitation unless otherwise provided herein, the following:

 (i) The Land;
 (ii) All foundations, columns, girders, beams, and supports of the Building;
 (iii) All exterior walls of the Building, all walls, floors, and ceilings enclosing a Unit (except those portions of such walls, floors, and ceilings included as part of the Unit pursuant to the provisions of Section 4 of this Declaration), and all walls and partitions separating Units from hallways, lobbies, corridors, and stairways (except those portions of such walls included as part of a Unit pursuant to the provisions of Section 4 of this Declaration);
 (iv) The roof, halls, lobbies, corridors, stairs, stairways, elevator shafts, elevators, laundry, meter, incinerator, boiler, mechanical, telephone, maintenance, trash disposal, air

correspond with the number and gender of the individuals, partnerships, corporations, or other legal entities or persons executing this Agreement as Borrower. The terms used to designate Lender and Borrower shall be deemed to include the respective heirs, legal representatives, successors, and assigns of such parties.

27. The parties do not intend to create a partnership or joint venture, rather, they are hereby creating the relationship of debtor and creditor. Neither party is authorized to act as agent for the other, to act on behalf of the other, to do or omit to do any act which will be binding on the other, nor to incur or authorize any expenditures for or on behalf of the other, except as set forth in the third paragraph of Section 3 or 4 and Paragraph 20.

IN WITNESS WHEREOF, the parties have hereunto set their hands and seals the day and year first above written.

BORROWER:
.... CORPORATION

ATTEST:

By:........................
President

....

LENDER:
.... BANK

By:........................

COMMENT: See Discussion at ¶ 9.01[4].

LEGAL DESCRIPTION

[*Description of property appears here.*]

Together with and subject to all riparian rights, covenants, easements, rights of way, and conditions of record.

Form 10.1

MASTER DEED FOR CONDOMINIUM

DECLARATION

ESTABLISHING A PLAN FOR CONDOMINIUM OWNERSHIP FOR PREMISES LOCATED AT
....
PURSUANT TO ....
CONDOMINIUM ACT OF 1976

M. In the event ...., by reason of disability or otherwise, ceases to be the person actively in charge of the development of the property;

N. In the event the proceeds of the loan are insufficient to complete the contemplated improvements to the property, Borrower, at Lender's request, will deposit funds with Lender to guarantee completion of the improvements, and to further guarantee payment of other obligations which may be incurred during construction of said improvements, such as interest, taxes, and the like.

23. If Borrower is not in default under any of the terms and conditions of the loan documents, Lender will release from its lien a lot upon the following release schedule.

Lot Description	Release Price
House	$100,000
Waterfront	60,000
Waterview-First Tier (9 lots)	45,000
Waterview-Marina Side (15 lots)	40,000
Interior	35,000

24. All moneys received by Borrower for Lender are to be used only for paying bills, expenses, and indebtedness incurred in the development of the property.

25. All notices, elections, and other communications hereunder shall be in writing, signed by the party making the same, and shall be sent certified or registered mail, postage prepaid, addressed

To Lender: ....
....
....

To Borrower: ....
....
....

or at such other address as may be hereafter designated in writing by either party hereto. The time and date on which mail is postmarked shall be the time and date on which such communication is deemed to have been given.

26. The term "Borrower," as used herein shall mean and include all and each of the individuals, partnerships, corporations, or other legal entities or persons executing this Agreement. The number and gender or pronouns used in referring to Borrower shall be construed to mean and

Borrower or violate restrictive covenants of record or local zoning ordinances;

C. If Borrower does not accept loan advances within thirty (30) days after they are made payable;

D. If Borrower fails to keep, observe, perform, carry out, and execute in every particular the covenants, agreements, obligations, and conditions contained in the Note, the Deed of Trust, or any other instrument now or hereafter evidencing or securing the loan;

E. If Borrower is a corporation, then the sale or transfer of stock except intrastock transfers with existing stockholders;

F. If Borrower is unable to satisfy any condition of the right to receipt of an advance hereunder for a period in excess of thirty (30) days;

G. If Borrower fails to keep, observe, perform, carry out, and execute in every particular the covenants, agreements, obligations, and conditions contained in this Agreement between Lender and Borrower pertaining to the acquisition and development of property located in .... County, ...;

H. If any materials or articles used in the construction of the improvements and appurtenant thereto not be so purchased by Borrower that the ownership thereof vests in Borrower free from encumbrances on delivery of the property;

I. If Borrower does not construct said improvements in accordance with plans and specifications which are satisfactory to Lender and which have been approved by .... County and all other governmental authorities having jurisdiction;

J. If Borrower does not permit a representative of Lender to enter upon the property and inspect the same at reasonable times;

K. If there should be filed any voluntary or involuntary bankruptcy proceedings by or against Borrower or any guarantor;

L. If there shall be asserted with regard to the property any violation of any regulation or ordinance of any local, state, or federal agency having jurisdiction over the property (unless such violation is diligently and promptly remedied by Borrower);

and all sums advanced for such purposes over and above the total of the funds placed in escrow and the balance of loan proceeds, including reasonable attorney's fees incurred by the Lender incident to such default and completion of such construction or incident to the enforcement of any provision hereof, shall be an indebtedness of the Borrower to the Lender even though they may, when added to the monies advanced and disbursed under this Agreement, exceed the amount of the Note and Deed of Trust, and shall be secured by the lien of the Deed of Trust, as though same was part of the debt originally described and secured thereby, all of which are due and payable to Lender immediately, although the amount advanced in excess of the original principal sum of this loan shall not exceed 125 percent (125%) of the principal amount of the Note, and all such advances shall bear interest at the rate specified in the Note.

21. In the event that the Borrower shall default in any manner under the terms, provisions, and conditions of the Note, Deed of Trust, or this Agreement, the Lender shall have all the rights, privileges, options, and remedies reserved to it under said Note, Deed of Trust, and this Agreement, and in addition, shall be entitled to cancel this Agreement by notice to Borrower, and/or by appropriate action to enforce such performance and correction of such defaults, and/or declare the amount of principal and interest secured by the Note, Deed of Trust, and this Agreement due and payable and in default, and proceed to collect the same foreclosure or other remedy.

22. In addition to the foregoing, if any of the following events occur, all obligations on the part of the Lender to make the loan or to make any further advances shall, if Lender so elects, cease and terminate, and the loan, plus all accrued interest thereon, shall become due and payable at the option of Lender or Holder of the Deed of Trust, but Lender may make advances without becoming liable to make any other advances:

    A. If Borrower assigns this Agreement, or said advances or interest therein, or if the property is conveyed or encumbered in any way without consent of Lender before completion of the improvements to be erected thereon;

    B. If the Land Improvements or the marina on the Mortgaged Property shall encroach upon any street or upon adjoining property or property not owned by

or if the Borrower shall fail, neglect, or refuse to perform either or any of the Borrower's promises or agreements hereunder or breach any promises, covenants, warrants, or agreements made hereby or made under the Note hereinabove mentioned or the Deed of Trust securing the same, or under any other collateral loan documents, or if it becomes apparent in the sole judgment of the Lender that the Borrower's Contractor will not complete said buildings and improvements with the time specified herein, or if construction shall cease before completion and remain abandoned for a period of ten (10) days, or if the Borrower or any endorser or guarantor of the Note should become insolvent or make an assignment for the benefit of creditors, or if an involuntary petition in bankruptcy is filed against, or a voluntary petition in bankruptcy is filed by the Borrower or any endorser or guarantor of the Note, or if a conservator or trustee is appointed for the assets of the Borrower or any endorser or guarantor of the Note, then in any of such events, the Borrower shall be considered in default hereunder and the Lender may, at its option, without benefit of any notice or grace period, withhold further disbursements hereunder, and in addition to all other remedies provided by the Mortgage Loan Documents and by law, either:

A. Declare all sums evidenced by the Note hereinabove mentioned and secured by said Deed of Trust and all sums hereunder to be immediately due and payable and unless the same are paid on demand, foreclose said Deed of Trust; or

B. Enter into and upon the Mortgaged Property and complete construction of the improvements, employing Borrower's Contractor or such other Contractor as Lender may deem appropriate and in its own best interest to complete the improvements, and Borrower hereby gives Lender full power and authority to make such entry and to enter into such contract arrangements as may be necessary to complete the improvements, and in this event, the Lender shall be entitled to have any of the remaining undisbursed funds, whether cash deposited by Borrower or undisbursed loan proceeds (Construction and Nonconstruction) disbursed to it or under its direction in the payment of bills theretofore or thereafter contracted in connection with the construction, it is hereby expressly agreed between the parties hereto that all work remaining to be done and material still to be furnished shall be considered as work necessary for the conservation and preservation of the Mortgaged Property,

consent shall not be unreasonably withheld where Borrower desires to sell stock to raise additional equity capital for the project and expects further that this covenant shall not be applicable where any transfer of stock is between parties already stockholders of Borrower or tranfers of stock by reason of the death of any individual stockholder.

16. Nothing herein shall be construed to waive or diminish any right or security of the Lender under the Note and Deed of Trust hereinabove described. It is the purpose and intent hereof to provide safeguards, protection, and rights to the Lender in addition to those provided in said Note and Deed of Trust and to better secure said Lender for and on account of said construction loan.

17. Where any disbursing agent is utilized, whether title company or other party, such party shall procure and deliver an Insured Closing Letter to Lender in form and content required by Lender and such other instrument as Lender may require whereby the disbursing agent agrees to receive and handle the funds in compliance with the provisions of this Master Development Loan Agreement and acknowledges that it will not commingle any funds received with its own funds, and that the same will be disbursed in account or accounts used as a fiduciary for escrow or loan disbursement purposes.

18. In the event the Borrower fails to construct and complete said Land Improvements and/or the marina in accordance with the terms and provisions of this Agreement, the Borrower hereby assigns to the Lender the right to possess and use the Plans and Specifications for the purpose of completing said Improvements.

19. Borrower shall cause its architect, at Borrower's expense, to make regular inspections of the site as construction progresses and at all critical times during construction, to determine that the work is progressing in a timely manner and in compliance with the Plans and Specifications and to certify with each requisition of loan proceeds that all construction to date of requisition has been completed to the extent indicated in the Contractor's Requisition and if such be the case, indicating any variances where the amount approved may be less than that requisitioned by the Contractor, and that the work to the extent so indicated is in accordance with the Plans and Specifications and to furnish Lender with full and complete reports on construction, for all of which Architect shall look solely to Borrower for payment of any fees and not to Lender or Project.

20. In addition to any other right hereinbefore reserved unto the Lender for default of Borrower, without benefit of notice or grace period, if the Borrower's Contractor shall fail to perform according to the terms of this Agreement or permits conditions to arise or exist so that performance will be rendered difficult or hazardous for the Lender,

9. Borrower agrees that it must proceed with reasonable diligence with the development of the property.

10. Borrower agrees to provide or cause to be provided workmen's compensation insurance and public liability and other insurance as may be required in such amounts and with such companies as shall be approved by Lender. Borrower agrees to employ such contractors, subcontractors, and agents as shall be required for the construction of the improvements and agrees to either pay, bond off, or otherwise take care of satisfactory to the title company claims which may become liens against the property with respect to such work.

11. If Borrower, during the progress of the work, neglects to employ a watchman for the protection of the Mortgaged Property, Lender may employ a watchman or watchmen for this purpose, and any amount thus expended shall be deemed to be secured by the Note and Deed of Trust, and may be charged, at the option of Lender, to any advance thereafter becoming due.

12. Borrower will furnish to Lender, whenever requested to do so, satisfactory evidence showing that all moneys theretofore advanced or paid by Lender on account of the Loan have actually been paid or applied for the construction of the Land Improvements and marina by Borrower, and until such evidence is produced, at the option of Lender, no other or further advances or payments need be made by it hereunder.

13. The Borrower shall not assign this Master Development Loan Agreement nor any part of any advance to be made hereunder, nor convey, nor further encumber said premises, nor change title company, architect, or contractor without the Lender's written consent.

14. The Borrower shall not make any conveyance of the Mortgaged Property without the written consent of the Lender, and without assumption of the obligation created hereunder by the grantee of the Borrower, and if any conveyance is made without such written consent and/or without such assumption, then and in that event and at option of the Lender and without notice to the Borrower, all sums of money due on the Note and secured by the Deed of Trust and hereunder shall immediately and concurrently with such conveyance become due and payable and in default whether or not the same are so due and payable and in default by the specific terms hereof, in which event Lender shall have no further obligation to make any disbursements hereunder.

15. If Borrower is a corporation, then the sale or transfer of stock in Borrower of interests aggregating 20 percent (20%) or more of the present outstanding capital stock of Borrower shall be classified as a transfer made in the same manner as though Borrower had conveyed its interest in the mortgaged premises without Lender's consent, which

3. Borrower will deliver to Lender on demand any contracts, bills of sale, statements, receipted vouchers or agreements, under which Borrower claims title to any materials, fixtures, or articles used in the construction of the Land Improvements and the marina.

4. Borrower agrees that all improvements to the Mortgaged Property shall be constructed strictly in accordance with all applicable ordinances and statutes and in accordance with the requirements of regulatory authorities having jurisdiction; that all said improvements shall be constructed entirely on the property and will not encroach upon any easement of right-of-way, nor upon land of others; and Borrower will furnish from time to time satisfactory evidence with respect to the foregoing.

5. Borrower agrees to employ such contractors, sub-contractors, and agents as shall be required for the construction of the improvements and agrees to either pay, bond off, or otherwise take care of satisfactory to the title company claims which may become liens against the Mortgaged Property with respect to such work.

6. Borrower agrees that no extra work nor materials nor changes in the nature and scope of said improvements, more being particularly described in plans and specifications approved in writing by Lender, shall be ordered or authorized by the Borrower without the prior written consent of Lender. If the Lender shall consent to any such extra work or materials or change in plans and specifications, the Borrower shall immediately deposit with Lender the amount of the costs thereof, such additional deposit shall be disbursed upon the completion of such extras or changes, subject to applicable 10 percent (10%) holdback to be disbursed at time of final payment after completion of the Land Improvements and construction of the marina.

7. Borrower agrees that Lender and its agents shall at all times have the right of entry and free access to the Mortgaged Property and improvements and the right to inspect all work, labor performed, and materials furnished in and about the Mortgaged Property and to inspect all books, sub-contracts, and records of Borrower with respect to the property. Prior to any advance for improving in any way the Mortgaged Property, Lender's inspecting engineer or inspecting architect must review the work completed and certify that said work is of first class construction and will conform to all governmental regulations.

8. Borrower represents that there are satisfactory means of ingress and egress over improved and dedicated public roads, storm and sanitary sewer service, water, electricity, and other utilities are currently available to serve the property, and that all of said utilities can be connected to any improvements constructed on the property at the time when such connections would normally be made during construction.

content of all such Certificates and/or Certifications are to be as specified by the Lender. The Lender shall be entitled to such evidence and proof as it deems appropriate from Borrower and Contractor to establish that upon final disbursement, the entire cost of completing the Improvements will have been fully paid.

10. Advances of the Land Improvements and Construction Funds shall be made monthly during progress of construction in a sum not to exceed 90 percent (90%) of the value of all labor and materials incorporated in the construction since the date of the last previous advance of funds therefor. The amount requested by the Contractor shall be set forth in a Contractor's Requisition and shall relate to the Cost Breakdown previously approved by Lender, which Contractor's Requisition will be accompanied by the Borrower's Requisition for Disbursement. Such documents shall further be accompanied by the following:

(A) Certificate of Borrower's Architect in form acceptable to Lender;

(B) Contractor's receipt and partial Release of Liens for all funds previously disbursed on account of construction of the Land Improvements and the marina and evidence from the Borrower or Contractor, or both, of the payment of bills for work, labor, material, supplies, and equipment for all sums advanced through the last prior request for disbursement and Contractor's Requisition. Final payment shall be not less than 10 percent (10%) of the original construction fund for Land Improvement and construction of the marina.

11. All payments may be made by Lender at its discretion to Borrower, or Contractor, or to Borrower and Contractor jointly, or to the Borrower, Contractor, and its subcontracts and material suppliers where circumstances so warrant in the sole judgment of the Lender.

ARTICLE 5
Representations of Borrower

By execution of this Agreement, Borrower represents to Lender and agrees as follows:

1. Borrower shall make no contract or arrangement of any kind the performance of which by the other party would give rise to the lien on the property and improvements.

2. Borrower will indemnify the Lender from claims of brokers arising by reason of the execution hereof or the consummation or transaction contemplated hereby.

and accompanying Contractor's Requisition, Borrower shall furnish Lender with improvement surveys of land Improvements and the marina, where and when required by Lender, reflecting that all construction by Borrower is within the boundary lines of the Mortgaged Property and is not in violation of any building setback lines or restrictions, and as a condition to the final advance shall furnish Lender with a Final Survey reflecting all Improvements in place; including all walkways and paved parking areas, all existing easements, and the location of all utility lines, both underground and overhead, all surveys to be duly certified to and prepared by a licensed and registered Surveyor authorized to do business in the Commonwealth of..........

6. Notwithstanding provision for inspection and approval of construction by Borrower's Architect and for his certifications, in no event will the amount to be paid out of the Construction Fund be in excess of the amount approved by Lender's independent inspecting Architect or Construction Inspector.

7. If Lender utilized Title Company as a Disbursing Agent, all costs and fees of the Title Company incurred therefor shall be paid by the Borrower.

8. Prior to payment under each request for disbursement and accompanying Contractor's Requisition, the Borrower shall cause its Contractor to prepare and submit to Lender a written schedule, in Affidavit form where required by Lender, setting forth the name and address of each party employed as a subcontractor and/or material supplier in connection with construction of the Improvements, the amount of such subcontract or material purchase order, and the status of performance and payment under each subcontract and material purchase order, and where requested by Lender, the Borrower shall cause Contractor to furnish to Lender and Contractor shall furnish to Lender, signed copies of each and every subcontract and/or material purchase order. And, the Lender is hereby given the right by Borrower and Contractor to make inquiry of all subcontractors and material suppliers to verify and determine the status of all matters pertaining to subcontracts and material purchase orders.

9. As a condition to final advance of the Construction Fund, which will include final advance to Contractor under the Construction Contract, the Lender shall be furnished by Contractor with Final Contractor's Affidavit as required under the Mechanic's Lien Law of the Commonwealth of .... and Contractor's final release of Lien. In addition to the Lender being furnished with certificates of substantial completion by Borrower's architect, Lender's independent architect or construction inspector and certificate of useability for the marina issued by the appropriate governmental agency, the form and

Lender evidence satisfactory to Lender that Borrower and Contractor have obtained or can obtain all necessary materials as and when required for completion of construction in accordance with the Plans and Specifications, and this shall be a condition precedent to making any disbursement from the Loan Funds.

    3. Prior to payment under each request for disbursement and accompanying Contractor's Requisition, should it appear that the loan proceeds of either the Land Improvements or the loan proceeds for the construction of the marina remaining undisbursed will be insufficient to complete all of the Improvements in accordance with the Plans and Specifications and to pay for all labor, material, and costs in the premises, Borrower shall, upon demand of Lender, deposit with Lender additional moneys in a non-interest-bearing account which shall, when added to the undisbursed proceeds of either of the loan funds, be sufficient to complete and pay for the Land Improvements and/or the cost of construction of this marina, costs and expenses in connection therewith, and the amount so deposited by Borrower shall be disbursed to pay for the Improvements before any additional advance will be paid out from either of the funds.

    4. Prior to payment under each request for disbursement and accompanying Contractor's Requisition, the Title Company issuing the title policy to Lender insuring its examination of the title current will certify to Lender in writing that there have been no instruments filed of record to the date of each advance which in any way disturbs the priority of the first mortgage lien of Lender, and that there have not been filed any liens against the Mortgaged Property and that upon making of such advance by Lender the amount so advanced, and all prior advances made under the Mortgage, are insured as being secured by Lender's first mortgage lien, to be confirmed by endorsement to the title policy to be forthwith issued after receipt of advice of the making of each such advance by the Lender, or Lender shall furnish the funds to be advanced to Title Company with instructions for it to examine title and disburse proceeds in each instance when it is assured that the advance can be made with the foregoing assurance of full coverage therefor, and for prior advances, as secured by the first mortgage lien of Lender's Deed of Trust, with appropriate title endorsements to be issued and delivered to Lender. Borrower, in order that title company can issue such written certification and Endorsement as is required from time to time agrees to fully observe and comply with any regulations and requirements which the Title Company may make with respect to the title, disbursement of advances, and proof of payment as to construction bills, partial releases of lien, waivers, inspections, and surveys.

    5. Prior to making payment under each request for disbursement

8. A Conditional Assignment of all permits and licenses set forth in Article 3 to be activated in the event of Borrower's default and said Assignment to be consented to by all governmental authorities that have issued the applicable permits and licenses.

9. Lender reserves the right at its option of not disbursing construction funds for the marina until .... County has released all rights that it has to certain loan funds allocated for Land Improvements pursuant to a certain set-aside letter set forth in Article 2 of this Agreement.

10. Lender reserves the right of requiring the Borrower, in the event condition No. 1, above, shall not have been satisfied, to provide funds from nonloan sources for construction of that portion of the marina on land owned by the Commonwealth of ...., with Lender disbursing loan funds only on that portion of the marina to be built on property owned by Borrower.

11. After Lender has received all the foregoing requirements, Lender will disburse to Borrower from time to time in accordance with Article 4.

ARTICLE 4
Method of Loan Disbursement

When all of the foregoing prerequisites entitling Borrower to the advance of Land Improvement Funds and Construction Funds for the marina have been met, and Borrower continues to be in good standing and not in default hereunder, loan funds from these categories shall be advanced in payment for construction of the improvements in the time and manner hereinafter provided. Said funds for construction of Land Improvements and the marina may be comprised of loan proceeds and funds of or from Borrower. For purposes of this section, the general contractor for the Land Improvements and the general contractor for the construction of the marina are referred to as "Contractor."

1. The Contractor's Requisition and Borrower's request for disbursement shall be on forms designated by Borrower and/or prepared and furnished by the Borrower, containing such certifications required of, and signed by, Contractor and/or Borrower, respectively, under oath as Lender may require, and may be accompanied by all such other documents which may be called for herein to substantiate entitlement of Borrower and/or its Contractor as the case may be, to the funds requisitioned.

2. Prior to payment under each request for disbursement and accompanying Contractor's Requisition, Borrower and/or Contractor shall furnish to Lender from time to time as and when required by

receives the written approval of .... County to do so. Accordingly, Borrower must at all times, when called upon by Lender, prove to the satisfaction of Lender that it has other nonloan sources to draw upon while waiting for .... County to approve disbursement of set-aside funds to complete development of Land Improvements. In the event the Lender is required to disburse on this set-aside letter, Borrower agrees that all funds disbursed shall be automatically added to Borrower's indebtedness owing to Lender as evidenced by this Note.

When all of the foregoing prerequisites entitling Borrower to the advance of land improvement funds has been met and Borrower continues to be in good standing and not in default hereunder, the land improvement funds shall be advanced in payment for development of the land improvements in the time and manner provided in Article 4.

ARTICLE 3
Construction of Marina Stage

As part of the total development plan, Borrower is required to construct a private marina and Lender has agreed to lend One Hundred Eighty Thousand Dollars ($180,000) of loan funds to Borrower for the purpose of constructing said marina, subject to the following conditions:

Prior to disbursement of loan funds for the purpose of constructing the marina, Borrower shall furnish to Lender the following:

1. A satisfactory endorsement to title insurance policy whereby the title company insures the marina can lawfully be built and that Lender's lien is valid and subsisting on funds disbursed for construction of the marina.

2. A detailed breakdown of costs for construction to take place in that portion of the submerged land owned by the Commonwealth of ....

3. Execution of a construction contract with the contractor satisfactory to Lender.

4. Copy of the plans and specifications.

5. Payment and performance bonds, or at the option of Lender, a completion guaranty agreement from the contractor.

6. Evidence satisfactory to Lender that Borrower has received all necessary governmental permits of a local, state, and federal nature to allow construction of said marina.

7. An original special multi-peril builder's risk insurance policy, naming Lender as an insured Mortgagee on a standard mortgagee endorsement clause. Said policy and its amount to be in form and content satisfactory to Lender.

5. Curbs & Gutter 25,000
6. Water 46,000
7. Siltration Controls 40,000
8. General Conditions 46,000
9. Contingencies 70,000

Reduction or use of the Contingency Code and General Conditions may be accomplished by allocation funds from the Contingency Code or General Conditions to some specific Construction Code contained in the Cost Breakdown by virtue of a changeorder (AIA Form G701) which results in a cost increase within such specific Construction Code.

Prior to the initial advance of any loan funds designated for Land Improvements, the Borrower shall furnish Lender, at Borrower's expense, the following:

1. A fully executed copy of the development contract with Lender, reserving the right to review, approve, and require changes in said development contract, including a substitution of the general contractor.

2. All grading and improvement permits from applicable government authorities having jurisdiction necessary to authorize said permits.

3. Deposit with Lender cash funds, if any may be required, which when added to the then remaining undisbursed balance of the loan proceeds allocated to pay for costs of Land Improvements, will aggregate the amount or value of the work under the development contract, together with deposit of such other funds, if any may be required by the Lender, to guarantee payment of other obligations which may be incurred during construction, such as interest, taxes, and the like.

If the Borrower on or before ...., 19...., has not complied with the conditions necessary to authorize disbursement of funds for Land Improvement and has not caused such improvements to be actually commenced, then the Lender, at its option, shall have and is hereby given the right at any time, on or after ...., 19...., to accelerate and declare entirely due and payable the indebtedness due on the Note in the same manner as though the loan had been fully disbursed and said date was the final maturity date for payment hereunder, and said Lender may enforce the Note, Deed of Trust, and this Master Development Loan Agreement against the Borrower and/or the security of both in addition to having the right to proceed under the Guaranty.

Pursuant to a certain set-aside letter executed by Lender in favor of .... County (said set-aside letter attached as Exhibit B), Lender has agreed to set aside Four Hundred Twenty-Nine Thousand Nine Hundred Dollars ($429,900) from the funds allocated for land improvements. Lender will only disburse this amount from time to time when it

land, establishing that the improvements may be constructed upon the land without violating said zoning.

5. Evidence of the existence of workmen's compensation, public liability, and property damage insurance coverage.

6. A satisfactory agreement with .... Service Corporation whereby .... Service Corporation, during the term of this loan, makes available to Lender an amount not to exceed Two Hundred Thousand Dollars ($200,000) to be drawn down by Lender from time to time in the event Borrower fails to pay interest.

7. Evidence satisfactory to Lender that the subject loan is duly authorized by the shareholders and board of directors of the Borrower, that the execution of the loan is not in violation of the corporate bylaws, and a satisfactory corporate resolution of Borrower authorizing said loan.

8. Receipt of an unconditional Guaranty executed by .... and ...., individually and unconditionally, jointly and severally guaranteeing payment of the indebtedness of Borrower to the Lender.

9. Evidence satisfactory to the Lender that Borrower has paid for all costs incidental to this Mortgage Loan, including, without limiting the generality of the foregoing, title insurance premium, survey, recording fees, state and documentary stamps, and Lender's attorney fees. (Where any of the foregoing costs, are included within the initial disbursement to be made hereunder and are not required to be paid as a condition to recording of the Deed of Trust, the foregoing shall not be construed as requiring prepayment of such costs, and they may be paid simultaneously with the initial disbursement.)

10. Satisfactory soils report.

11. Collateral Assignment to Lender of Joint Venture Agreement dated ...., 19...... between ...., Inc., a corporation, ... and ...., to acquire the finished lots.

ARTICLE 2
Construction of Land Improvements

Six Hundred Ninety-Five Thousand Dollars ($695,000) is allocated for the following land improvements:

Cost Breakdown

1. Storm Sewer	$ 74,000
2. Sanitary Sewer	123,000
3. Gravel & Paving Streets	125,000
4. Clearing & Grading	146,000

46 acres all of which will be subdivided for 73 lots, described in Exhibit A hereto (the "Property"), and (2) for improving the Property by installing certain roads and utilities and land improvements to serve the same, the nature and scope of said Improvements as hereinafter set forth, and (3) for the construction of a private marina.

NOW, THEREFORE, in consideration of the mutual promises hereinafter contained, the parties hereto agree as follows:

Borrower agrees to take and Lender agrees to make (subject to this Agreement), a loan in the principal sum of Two Million Five Hundred Seventy-Five Thousand Dollars ($2,575,000) (hereinafter called the "Loan"), to be advanced as hereinafter provided. The Loan is evidenced by one Promissory Note (hereinafter called the "Note") of even date herewith, executed by Borrower and payable to Lender, on order, bearing interest on the outstanding balance at the rate specified in the Note, interest only on the principal sum for time-to-time advanced being due and payable monthly, as provided in the Note. The Note is secured by a Deed of Trust of even date which conveys a valid and subsisting security title to the Property, subject openly to taxes and assessments not yet payable. Borrower and Lender agree for the convenience of monitoring disbursement and development that the loan shall be divided into three stages: (1) Land Disbursement; (2) Construction of Land Improvements, and (3) Construction of the Marina.

ARTICLE 1
Land Disbursement Stage

As a condition of the intitial land acquisition advance of One Million Seven Hundred Thousand Dollars ($1,700,000), receipt of said funds acknowledged by Borrower, Borrower shall have furnished Lender with the following:

1. Original title insurance policy of .... Land Title Insurance Company, insuring the Deed of Trust to be a first lien upon the Mortgaged Property, with affirmative mechanics' and materialmen's lien protection, the form of which policy shall be satisfactory at all times to Lender, subject only to such exceptions as Lender may approve. The policy is to be for the full amount of the loan, although it may contain a pending disbursement clause in form satisfactory to Lender, provided the policy will be endorsed from time to time to cover the loan amount disbursed on account of the Note and Deed of Trust.

2. A copy of the recorded subdivision plat.

3. A satisfactory set-aside letter from Lender to .... County.

4. Evidence satisfactory to Lender as to the present zoning of the

which the Board or its designee might grant.

The undersigned warrant that this set-aside letter is made and executed pursuant to authority properly granted by the charter, and by laws and action of the Board of Directors of the respective undersigned corporations.

Sincerely yours,

....
(Signature)
(Type Name & Title)

.... Company
....
BY: ....
(Signature)
(Type Name & Title)

COMMENT: See discussion at ¶ 9.01[2].

Form 9.3

MASTER DEVELOPMENT LOAN AGREEMENT

THIS AGREEMENT made as of this .... day of ...., 19...., by and between .... Corporation, a .... Corporation, hereinafter called "Borrower," and .... Bank, hereinafter called "Lender."

WITNESSETH:

Borrower desires to obtain a loan in the principal sum of Two Million Five Hundred Seventy-Five Thousand Dollars ($2,575,000) for the purpose of (1) paying off existing liens encumbering the property, located at the intersection of .... and .... in .... County, ..., containing

Form 9.2

SET-ASIDE LETTER

(ISSUING AGENCY LETTERHEAD)

We have committed to make a development loan covering .... No. ....: to .... Company. In consideration of the acceptance of this set-aside letter by the Board of Supervisors of .... County, ..., through its designee, in lieu of surety for the bond, to secure the Agreement dated ...., 19...., between .... Company and the Board, we agree to set aside from the development funds, a sum in the amount of .... Dollars ($........), which is to be used in paying for the construction of the improvements and facilities shown on the approved plans and profiles pertaining to said tract, in accordance with the terms of the Agreement, dated ...., 19...., between .... Company and the Board, a copy of which is attached hereto and made a part hereof.

The commitment covering this project provides that as work progresses, the amount of the set-side may be reduced and only after .... Bank .... and .... County have satisfied themselves that the work paid for has actually been done, provided, however, that the sum set aside shall at all times (prior to release of the bond by .... County) be at least equal to the cost to complete the construction of the improvements and facilities as estimated by the Director of Design Review or 50 percent (50%) of the bond amount, whichever is greater.

In the event that .... Company fails to complete the said improvements and facilities, all funds remaining in said set-aside shall be immediately available to the Board to complete the said improvements and facilities in accordance with the terms of the Agreement. The Board shall not in any way be obliged to repay said funds so used.

This is an irrevocable commitment of funds which is not subject to recall by .... Bank provided that in no event shall the liability of .... Bank exceed .... Dollars ($. . . . .). .... Bank by execution hereof, expressly waives any right it may have to review and approve any revisions to the plans, profiles, and specifications referred to in the Agreement or to any extensions of time to complete the aforesaid improvements and facilities

four months, the Department of Environmental Management actively monitors the developer's progress.

If the Department of Environmental Management evaluation indicates that the developer is uncooperative and it is unlikely that the public improvements will be completed within three or four months, the Department requests legal assistance from the County Attorney. In response, the County Attorney sends a letter to the developer informing him of the default condition and asks that he contact the Department of Environmental Management and make arrangements for the completion of the improvements.

In most instances, developers respond to the letter from the County Attorney because of the threat of legal action. The developer is directed by the County Attorney to contact the Department of Environmental Management to correct the default status.

PHASE V: ABANDONMENT AND LEGAL ACTION*

The first action the County Attorney takes with respect to a defaulted agreement is to write a letter to the developer. This is done when the Department of Environmental Management has not been able to receive a response and when it seems the developer is not making an attempt to abide by the terms of the agreement. If the County Attorney does not receive a response from the developer within a specified amount of time, permission to file suit is requested from the County Executive.

When litigation becomes necessary, the Department of Public Works is requested to provide an estimate of the costs necessary to complete the public improvements. Funds, if any, recovered from the lawsuit are either turned into General Funds, or turned over to the homeowner's association for completion of unfinished improvements.

Projects which are to be completed by the County become the responsibility of the Department of Public Works. Scheduling for completion of these projects depends on the availability of funds as appropriated in the fiscal year budget.

COMMENT: See discussion at ¶ 9.01[2]

---

*It should be noted that procedures for insuring *prompt* completion of default projects are being developed pursuant to resolution adopted by the Board of Supervisors on ...., 19..... These phases (IV and V) will be modified when new procedures have been approved.

that other code requirements have been satisfied in compliance with the agreement. A copy of the letter to the developer stating that his bond and escrow has been released is circulated to other agencies to ensure that:
- All appropriate code enforcement complaints are satisfied;
- All sanitary sewer lines and as-built plans have been accepted by the County;
- All fees have been collected;
- All contributions for off-site drainage improvements have been paid;
- All as-built plans have been approved;
- All tree ordinance provisions have been met (residential projects);
- All physical improvements covered by the agreement have been approved and accepted;
- All water agreements have been satisfied;
- All necessary maintenance bonds have been received and approved;
- All conditions of litigation have been met;

After all of the above reviews, where appropriate, have been performed, the Director of Design Review authorizes the release of the agreement and bond.

PHASE IV: DEFAULT AND EVALUATION PROCEDURES*

If the developer does not complete the necessary site improvements in the period of time specified in the agreement or extension, the agreement is in default.

In these events where the developer is still active on the project but the agreement has defaulted, the Department of Environmental Management determines whether any further action is required.

Some of the elements taken into consideration in the evaluation process include:
- The amount of the original bond;
- The inspector's report of percent completion;
- The weather conditions prevailing during the construction period;
- The anticipated date of completion at the present rate of activity;
- The local housing market conditions;
- The health, safety, and welfare of the County citizens.

If it is determined that, given the circumstances, the developer can or is at least trying to complete the project within the following three or

- Percent of project already completed;
- Complaints lodged against the developer, if any;
- Number of homes already completed, occupied, and served by public facilities;
- Rate of construction activity;
- Developer's history in the County;
- Market conditions and developer's ability to sell homes to provide cash flow;

Following their review, the Bonding Committee makes its recommendations to the County Executive.

In situations where there is a possibility that the developer will complete the physical improvements in less than three or four months of the expiration of the agreement date, the Department of Environmental Management takes no further action. However, the project is continuously monitored to insure that progress is being made. This action does not decrease the ability of the County to pursue completion of improvement by legal action at a later date because the statute of limitation for bonds which guarantee completion of the project extend for ten (10) years beyond the agreement expiration date.

In the event the developer does not respond to the letter sent by the Department of Environmental Management cautioning him of potential default, the matter is referred to the County Attorney for guidance. The appropriate action by the County Attorney depends on the inspection report, which indicates how much of the work has already been completed and whether the developer is still active on the site.

PHASE III: BOND AND AGREEMENT RELEASE

Upon the completion of 100 percent (100%) of the physical site improvements and acceptance of streets where applicable, the developer can be released from his bond and agreement by the Department of Environmental Management. The actual release process can be initiated upon receipt of a letter from the developer stating that the work has been completed and requesting release from his agreement or upon receipt by the Bonds and Permits Branch of a "100 Percent Complete Report" from the Public Utilities Branch.

Upon receipt of a 100 Percent Completion Report form from the Public Utility inspector, a memorandum is sent to the appropriate District Supervisor advising that the project is being considered for release. If a response is not received within two weeks, it is assumed that the Supervisor has no objections to the release.

Before the bond is released certain reviews are performed to ensure

pleted in a specified period of time. If all the noted improvements are not completed within this time period, and no extension has been obtained, or a replacement agreement and bond have not been submitted and approved with a new expiration date, the agreement is considered to be in default.

Approximately sixty (60) days prior to the expiration of an agreement, the County prepares a report which provides the completion status of the physical improvements as noted on the approved plans. If the inspection of the site indicates that the balance of work cannot be completed within the remaining sixty (60) days, then the developer is notified in writing. The letter cautions the developer that unless the work is completed by the expiration date of the agreement, he will be in default.

The developer can make a formal request to the Director of Environmental Management for an initial extension of the expiration date for a maximum period of six (6) months. The developer must indicate the reasons and conditions which have inhibited him from completing required physical improvements. The developer must also have all sureties consent to the request, including corporate surety companies. All signatures must be notarized. If the developer feels subsequent extensions are required, an extension request may be submitted and approved by the Board of Supervisors, subject to the developer demonstrating that the extension would be in the best interests of the County. Each extension shall be subject to the "Extension Fee."

Where appropriate, the developer may make application for a replacement agreement and bond. A new bond amount, which cannot be less than 50 percent (50%) of the face amount of the original bond, will be estimated by the Department of Environmental Management. A new bond package is then prepared and forwarded to the developer for his review and execution. This bond package is handled in the same manner as the original agreement and bond except that final approval must be granted by the Board of Supervisors. The original agreement and bond can be released to the developer when the new bond has been approved. The reduction of the bond amount will be permitted once in the life of a project.

The developer will be required to pay a fee for processing the replacement bond.

In situations where developers have requested an extension or a new agreement and bond, the Bonding Committee reviews the County's inspector's report on the project and the reasons supplied by the developer. The factors considered by the Bonding Committee include the following:

the developer. These letters cannot be drawn below 50 percent (50%) of the original bond amount.

After the County staff has completed the review of the subdivision or site plan, established the estimated cost of constructing bonded improvements, and reviewed the amount of time estimated by the developer to complete these improvements, a package of documents is forwarded to the developer for his review and execution. The package includes copies of the agreement and bond, County estimates of the cost of the physical improvements, and a statement of the amount of bond required of him.

The County is responsible for researching the developer's background on past development performance in the County, and where possible, in other jurisdictions. The findings of the County staff along with the signed documents returned by the developer, are forwarded to the Bonding Committee.

Bonding Committee/County Executive Approval

The Bonding Committee consists of members from the Office of Finance, the Department of Environmental Management, and the Office of the County Attorney. The County Executive, as an ex-officio member, serves as an arbitrator when necessary. The Bonding Committee is an advisory body formed for the purpose of reviewing all agreements and any subsequent revisions to these agreements entered into by the County. The Bonding Committee also reviews and makes recommendations on all extensions which have been requested by developers. The final approval is executed by the County Executive or his designee on behalf of the Board of Supervisors.

Upon approval of the agreement between the developer and the County, a file is established which is continually updated until all construction is completed. A monthly "tickler" file is also established which notifies the County staff that sixty (60) days remains prior to the expiration of the agreement date.

If, in researching the developer/developers' performance background it is revealed that he/they is/are associated with any prior agreement that has expired, the new agreement will not be approved without notification of the Board of Supervisors.

PHASE II: EXTENSIONS AND REBONDING OF AGREEMENTS

When a developer enters into an agreement with the County, it is understood that all the necessary physical improvements must be com-

bond will be required. An agreement *not supported by a bond* will be obtained for required, nonpublic improvements.

THE BOND

The County requires developers to provide a guarantee (bond) which assures compliance with terms of the agreement for the performance of certain physical improvements. The amount of bond required is based on the estimated cost of the improvements covered by the agreement which is established by County Staff's review of the plans. The amount of the bond itself is equivalent to approximately 115 percent (115%) of the estimated cost of improvements. The additional 15 percent (15%) is for engineering costs, contingencies, and inflationary factors which may be necessary should the improvements not be completed by the developer in a timely manner.

The following types of bonds will be accepted as surety by .... County:

- *Corporate Bonds.* This surety will be furnished by an insurance company with an Attorney-in-Fact recorded in the land records of .... County, and will guarantee the full amount of the bond.
- *Noncorporate Bonds.* These bonds are supported by a security in one of the following forms:
  - ☐ *Cash Escrow.* The face amount of the bond will be submitted to the Department of Environmental Management and deposited in the .... County Office of Finance. (Escrows held previously by bank or savings institutions will no longer be acceptable.) The Office of Finance will pay 5 percent (5%) interest or prevailing passbook savings rate, whichever is lower, on all escrows deposited with .... County. Interest will be forfeited if needed for completion of project by .... County.
  - ☐ *Letters of Credit.* This security is furnished by a bank or savings institution and will be written in such a manner as to extend six (6) months beyond the agreement expiration date. The letters of credit *must* contain the condition of automatic renewal, providing that the letter of credit will automatically be extended for additional periods of six (6) months unless the County is notified in writing at least thirty (30) days in advance of the letter of credit expiration date that the bank does not intend to extend such letter of credit.
  - ☐ *Set-Aside Letters.* This security will be furnished by the Mortgagor of the development and executed and agreed to by

apply to cash escrows, set aside letters, and letters of credit, although a new agreement need not be approved for these.

• No new bonds and agreements will be approved for developers who have other agreements in default without prior notification of the Board of Supervisors.

Staff work is continuing on the following:

• Procedures are being developed which recognize the urgency of preventing defaults and preventing the deterioration of streets and other improvements. We will also attempt to propose policies and procedures that will enforce project completion immediately upon default either by the developer or the Department of Public Works. The development of these procedures will require additional time.

• Reporting procedures concerning the status of developer default projects will also be developed in the near future.

• A proposal for charging fees for all extensions and rebonds will be developed and presented to the Board at the time the Public Facilities Manual is considered.

• An amendment to the County Code in accordance with Recommendation #12 of the committee concerning new approvals for developers in default will be prepared as soon as possible.

Enclosed Documents: "Bond and Agreement Procedures."

Staff: ...., Acting Director, Department of Environmental Management.

BOND AND AGREEMENT PROCEDURES

PHASE I: AGREEMENT AND BOND ESTABLISHMENT

THE AGREEMENT

The agreement is a legal, bonding contract between the developer and .... County. The agreement specifies the manner and the time frame in which the physical site improvements will be made according to the plans approved.

Agreements for Residential Developers

An agreement supported by a bond will be required on all projects which will obligate the developer to construct required improvements in approved subdivisions or site plans (townhouse, condominium, and apartment developments) in a timely manner.

Agreements for Commercial & Industrial Developments

An agreement providing for the timely construction of public improvements located in easements and rights-of-way supported by a

BONDING POLICIES AND PROCEDURES

Issue: Board confirmation of bonding policies and procedures as outlined in enclosed, "Bond and Agreement Procedures."

Timing: As soon as possible.

Background: On ...., 19..... the Board of Supervisors approved new bonding policies and procedures. The enclosed procedures, "Bond and Agreement Procedures," were prepared in accordance with Board action and are transmitted to ensure that staff has properly interpreted the intent of the Board's action. The significant changes to the past policy and procedures are delineated below:

- Personal bonds are now precluded from consideration.
- Required improvements on private property for commercial/industrial projects such as screening, parking lot landscaping, and paving will not be bonded. Only public improvements included within the dedicated rights-of-way or easements will be included in the bond and agreement.
- *All* required improvements will be included in the bond and agreement for residential projects (townhouses, condominiums, multi-family apartments,* etc.), including paving of private streets and parking areas, parking lot landscaping, screening, public improvements in dedicated rights-of-way, and easements, etc.
- All cash escrows supporting bonds will be posted with the county and not with attorneys, banks, etc. This will include escrows posted for Conservation agreements, pro rata share agreements, future completion and public improvements.
- One extension of the original agreement for a period not to exceed six (6) months may be approved by the County Executive. Subsequent extensions will be approved by the Board of Supervisors, after review and recommendations by the Bonding Committee and the County Executive, where it is clearly demonstrated that it is in the County's interest to approve such an extension.
- A single reduction in the bond amount may be approved upon request of the developer. The amount of the reduced bond must be sufficient to complete all incomplete improvements and ensure correction of any defects that may develop in work that has been completed but not yet accepted. The minimum of such bond will be 50 percent (50%) of the original bond amount. This reduction procedure will also

---

*Board action to require bonding of *only* public improvements on multifamily rental projects, to be considered Monday, May 9, would modify this provision.

REAL ESTATE BROKER:

....
Realty Associates, Inc.

....
....
ESCROW AGENT:

.... Title Insurance Co.

By: ....

COMMENT: See discussion of three-cornered tax free exchanges at ¶ 8.02[4].

Form 9.1

BOND AND AGREEMENT PROCEDURES FOR RESIDENTIAL DEVELOPMENT

COUNTY OF ....
STATE OF ....

Purpose: The purpose of this memorandum is to transmit the procedures used for processing bonds and agreements which have been updated pursuant to action taken by the Board of Supervisors on ......, ..., 19.....

Recommendation: It is recommended that the attached Consideration Item be included in the Board package for their review at the earliest possible date.

Discussion: The Board's action on ...., 19....., replaced the moratorium on personal bonds with new procedures which preclude approval of personal bonds for developer projects. In addition, certain changes to current procedures were approved and these have been incorporated into the attached.

C. *Governing Law*—This Agreement shall be construed and enforced in accordance with the laws of the state of ....
....

D. *Escrow Agent*—Escrow Agent's signature hereto constitutes receipt of Deposit only, and the Association and the Company agree that the Escrow Agent assumes no responsibility for the performance of this Agreement by the parties hereto.

E. *Headings*—The captions and headings herein are for convenience and reference only and in no way define or limit the scope or content of this Agreement or in any way affect its provisions.

F. *Effective Date*—This Agreement shall be effective as of the last date upon which the parties hereto have executed this Agreement, as demonstrated by the date beside the signatures on the signature page.

G. *Counterpart Copies*—This Agreement may be executed in two or more counterpart copies, all of which counterparts shall have the same force and effect as if all parties hereto had executed a single copy of this Agreement.

H. *Survival of Provisions*—The provisions of this Agreement and the representations and warranties herein shall survive settlement hereunder and the execution and delivery of the Deed of Conveyance of the Property and shall not be merged therein, except as otherwise provided herein.

I. *Binding Effect*—This Agreement shall be binding upon and inure to the benefit of the parties hereto and their respective legal representatives, heirs, executors, administrators, successors, and assigns.

J. *Entire Agreement*—This Agreement and the exhibits attached hereto contain the final and entire agreement between the parties hereto with respect to the sale and purchase of the property and are intended to be an integration of all prior negotiations and understandings. The Association, the Company, and their agents shall not be bound by any terms, conditions, statements, warranties, or representations, oral or written, not contained herein. No change or modification of this Agreement shall be valid unless the same is in writing and is signed by the party against whom it is sought to be enforced.

IN WITNESS WHEREOF, the parties hereto have executed this Agreement under seal on this .... day of ...., 19....

.... COMPANY
By: ....
    ....

the Association in substantially its present condition, normal wear and tear expected.

8. *Conditions of Premises.* The Association acknowledges that the Company has not made and does not make any representations as to the physical condition, layout, leases, footage, rents, income, expenses, operation, or any other matter or thing affecting or related to the property and to this Agreement, except as herein specifically set forth or provided by the Company to the Association under this Agreement, and that neither party is relying upon any statement or representation made by the other not embodied in this Agreement. The Association hereby expressly acknowledges that no such representation has been made. The Company is not liable or bound in any manner by any verbal or written statements, representations, real estate brokers' "set-ups" or information pertaining to the property or its physical condition, layout, leases, footage, rents, income, expenses, operation, or any other matter or thing furnished by any real estate broker, agent, employee, servant, or any other person, unless specifically set forth herein, embodied by this Agreement or provided pursuant to the terms of this Agreement.

9. *Other Provisions.*
   A. *Broker*—The Company recognizes ....
.... Realty Association, Inc. as its Broker in this transaction and agrees to pay said Broker in accordance with the terms of a separate agreement between the Company and Broker. Except as aforesaid, The Company and the Association each represent and warrant to the other that they have not authorized any other Broker, Agent, or Finder to act on their behalf nor do they have any knowledge of any Broker, Agent, or Finder purporting to act on their behalf in respect to this transaction.

   B. *Notices*—Any and all notices, requests, and other communications hereunder shall be deemed to have been duly given if in writing and if transmitted by hand delivery with receipt therefor, or by registered or certified mail, return receipt requested, and first class postage prepaid as follows:

   To the Company: ....
                      ....
                      ....
                      ...., ...

   To the Association: ....
                        ....
                        ....
                        ...., ...

Notice shall be deemed effective when received.

materialmen's liens (whether or not perfected) on or affecting the property at the date of settlement.

(5) the Company warrants, as of settlement date, that to its knowledge all elevators, plumbing equipment, heating, ventilating and air-conditioning equipment, the electrical wiring and fixtures, the water and sewage systems, and the fire sprinkler system presently in the property will be in good working order and condition.

E. *Access to the Property*—The Association and the Association's agents and representatives shall have full access to the property during normal business hours throughout the period prior to settlement.

6. *Casualty Loss and Condemnation.* In the event that the property or any part thereof is damaged or destroyed by fire or other casualty, or in the event condemnation or eminent domain proceedings (or private purchase in lieu thereof) shall be commenced by any public or quasi-public authority having jurisdiction against all or any part of the property, then the Company shall promptly notify the Association. The Association may, at its option, by giving written notice the Company within thirty (30) days after receipt of notice of such casualty or condemnation proceedings, terminate this Agreement. In such event, the Association shall be entitled to the return of the Deposit and, thereafter, neither the Association nor the Company shall have any liability to the other hereunder except for the Company's obligation to indemnify the Association arising out of any contract for the Designated Exchange Property. In the event the Association does not elect to terminate this Agreement, then all insurance proceeds and/or any awards in condemnation, as the case may be, will be assigned to the Association at the time of settlement hereunder, or, if paid to the Company thereto, shall be credited against the unpaid balance of the purchase price due at settlement. The Company shall not adjust or settle any insurance claims or condemnation awards whatsoever without the prior written approval of the Association; further, the Association and its counsel shall have the right (prior to settlement) to participate in all negotiations relating to any such insurance claims or condemnation awards.

7. *Risk of Loss and Maintenance of the Property.* The risk of loss or damage to the property by fire or other casualty until recordation of the Deed of Conveyance is assumed by the Company. The existing insurance policies shall be kept in effect by the Company through to the time of recordation of the Deed of Conveyance. The Company agrees to maintain the property in at least its present condition and repair and to make any and all repairs until settlement so as to deliver the property to

The Company represents that the Wraparound Deed of Trust can be prepaid at any time without penalty by the Association or Assigns. Before ...., 19...., the Company shall receive a letter from Realty, Inc. (hereinafter referred to as Realty, Inc.) setting forth a payoff amount without penalty.

C. *Power and Authority to Exchange—*
    (1) Seller has the full and entire right, power, and authority to transfer and convey to the Association full legal and beneficial ownership of the property and the persons executing this Agreement on behalf of the Company have executed and delivered this Agreement under full authority duly given to them by the proper representatives of the Company. Where events necessitate the election of the option to purchase, the Company acknowledges that it has the proper authority to sell the subject property.

    (2) The execution and delivery of this Agreement and the performance by the Company of its obligation hereunder are binding and enforceable obligations of the Company.

D. *The Property—*
    (1) The property shall be conveyed except for the Deeds of Trust in favor of .... Life and Realty, Inc., and those exceptions set forth in .... Title Policy No. ......, which deeds of trust can be assumed without penalty, free and clear of all liens, debts, charges, and encumbrances.

    (2) All public utility connections located at or on the Property have been paid for, and all sewer, water, and other utilities required for the operation of the property enter through adjoining private lands. Any parking areas located within the perimeter of the property are private and have not been dedicated to any public authority.

    (3) This Agreement includes the exchange of all of the fixtures, furnishings, equipment, machinery, supplies, and articles of personal property located in, attached to, or used in connection with the management, operation and maintenance of the Property now owned by the Company. The Company agrees not to remove any of the fixtures, furnishings, equipment, machinery, supplies, or articles of personal property from the property prior to the date of settlement (except for repairs) and agrees to deliver all such fixtures, furnishings, equipment, machinery, supplies and articles of personal property to the Association at settlement.

    (4) All bills and claims for labor performed and materials furnished to or for the benefit of the property during the period preceding the date of settlement have been (or will be prior to at settlement) paid in full, and there shall be no mechanic's or

the then owner of the property and which must be obtained by the Association.

E. *Period of Inspection and Review*—Purchaser shall have until ...., 19...., to physically inspect the building, including the structural, mechanical, and electrical systems, and to review the leases, financing documents, operating expenses, prior operating statements, and other legal documents affecting the property. The Association shall have the right, at its option, by said date, to terminate this Agreement by giving written notice to the Company (in the manner specified in Paragraph 8-B hereof) and the Deposit shall be returned to the Association and all parties shall thereupon be released from any further liability or obligation hereunder. If said notice is not received, the Association shall deposit an additional Seventy-Five Thousand Dollars ($75,000) with the Escrow Agent to insure compliance with this Agreement.

F. *Remedies of the Association*—If any condition in this Paragraph 4 is not satisfied, the Association shall have the right (to be exercised not later than the time scheduled for settlement) with (1) notwithstanding such fact to proceed to settlement or (2) to terminate this Agreement and recover the Deposit, whereupon all parties shall be released from any further liability or obligation hereunder. Notwithstanding the foregoing, if the condition as to title is of such character that they may be remedied by legal action or payment, then, if the Association does not elect to terminate this Agreement, such legal action or payment must be taken or paid promptly by the Company at its own expense, whereupon the time for settlement hereunder will be extended for the period necessary for such action or payment but in no event for more than six (6) months, unless the Association, by written notice to the Company, extends the time period for such reasonable additional time needed.

5. *Representations and Warranties of the Company.* Each of the following representations and warranties by the Company is true and correct and shall be true and correct on the date of settlement hereunder.

A. *No Material Omissions*—Neither this Agreement nor any other certificate, statement, documents of other information furnished, or to be furnished, to the Association, by or on behalf of the Company, pursuant to or in connection with the transaction contemplated in this Agreement, contains or will contain any misstatement of a material fact, or omits or will omit to state a material fact necessary in order to make the representations and warranties and other statements hereon or therein contained not misleading, in the circumstances in which made.

B. *Prepayment of the Realty, Inc. Wraparound Deed of Trust—*

A. *Representations and Warranties*—The representations and warranties made by the Company in Paragraphs 3D and 5 hereof shall be true and correct on and as of the date of settlement as fully as if made at that time.

B. *Specified Conditions Not Present*—At the time of settlement, the Company shall have no knowledge of and there shall be no:

(1) Proceedings pending to change or redefine the zoning classification of all or any portion of the Property.

(2) Pending annexation or condemnation proceeding or private purchase in lieu thereof affecting or which may affect the property or any part thereof;

(3) Pending special assessments affecting the Property or any part thereof;

(4) Notices, suits, or judgments pending or threatened relating to violations of any governmental regulations, ordinances or requirements affecting the property which have not been satisfactorily corrected;

(5) Penalties or interest due with respect to real estate taxes;

(6) Liens, choate or unchoate, against the property, except as referred to herein.

C. *Title*—the Company is the owner of record and in fact, legally and beneficially, of the property, has the right to sell the property without the agreement of any other person, has title to the property that is good and marketable, and such title is fully insurable under a full coverage owner's title insurance policy without material exceptions at standard rates. The property shall be conveyed free of any encumbrances, easements, or restrictions, except as herein stated. The Association shall, after acceptance of this contract by the Company, cause an examination of title to the property to be made and shall, within thirty (30) days after the effective date hereof notify the Company in writing of the Association's acceptance of title as shown on such title examination report or of all title defects disclosed on such title examination report which adversely affect title. Should any such title defects exist, the Association's remedies shall be those set forth in Paragraph 4F hereof.

D. *Licenses and Permits*—All licenses and permits necessary or required under the laws, ordinances, rules and regulations of .... County in the State of.................... for the occupancy and use of the building or other facilities of the property have been obtained and paid for by the the Company, and will be currently in effect and valid on the date of settlement, except for those licenses and permits which are personal to the Company and/or

1978, and said settlement on or before July 31, 1978, is not contingent on the foregoing designated space becoming vacant.

E. *The Association's Obligations—*

(1) Upon execution of this Agreement, the Association will deposit, to be placed at interest, with the Escrow Agent, ... Title Insurance Company, a .... Dollar ($........) deposit, which will be increased to .... Dollars ($.........) pursuant to Paragraph 4E, with all interest on the entire deposit accrued to the Association.

(2) At settlement hereunder, the Company shall receive by Special Warranty Deed (without recourse to the Association) the Designated Exchange Property, or in the event said contemplated exchange is not possible to consummate, the Association shall pay the price specified in Paragraph 2F above, whereupon the deposit required herein shall be returned to the Association by the Escrow Agent, or, at the option of the Association, shall be applied against the cash payment for the net equity at settlement described in paragraph 1B hereof.

F. *The Company's Default—*If the Company shall fail to perform its obligations hereunder to make full settlement in accordance with the terms hereof, the Escrow Agent shall be required to return the deposit to the Association and the Association may avail itself of any legal or equitable rights (including, without limitation, the right of specific performance), which purchaser may have at law or in equity or under this Agreement.

G. *The Association's Default—*If, prior to the selection of the Designated Exchange Property set forth in Paragraph 2C, the Association shall be obligated to proceed to settlement under the provisions of this Agreement and shall fail to do so for any reason whatsoever, the One Hundred Thousand Dollar ($100,000) Deposit shall be paid to the Company as agreed upon liquidated damages, whereupon this Agreement shall terminate and the parties hereto shall be released from any further liability or obligation to each other, it being expressly understood that the payment of the Association's deposit to the Company shall be the sole and exclusive right and remedy of the Company. But, if after the execution of a firm contract on the Designated Exchange Property, the Association shall fail to proceed to settlement, the Company could elect to either accept the One Hundred Thousand Dollar ($100,000) Deposit as liquidated damages or at its option require specific performance.

4. *Conditions of the Association's Obligation to Settle.*

It shall be a condition of the Association's obligation to make settlement hereunder that at the time of settlement:

(1) A good and sufficient Special Warranty Deed, duly executed and acknowledged by the Company (and by any other persons, e.g., trustees, required by the Association's title insurer);

(2) A Bill of Sale for all personal property owned and used by the Company in connection with the management, operation, and maintenance of the property, which Bill of Sale shall convey good title to such personal property to the Association, subject only to the existing Deeds of Trust of record referred to in 2(B) above.

(3) Duplicate copies of all books, records, operating reports, files, and other material necessary to complete continuity of operation of the property; and

(4) The original executed copy of the existing leases, to be furnished by the Company, together with a valid Assignment of each lease.

The property is to be conveyed in the name of the Association or Assigns. At settlement, the Company shall give full and complete possession of the property to the Association, subject only to the occupancy of the tenants under the said leases. The Association prior to closing is desirous of having free of tenancies 18,226 square feet on the fourth, fifth, and sixth floors. Seller represents that the existing written leases which have not been validly modified by other writings or oral agreements known to Seller contain clauses which provide that such leases are cancellable on ninety (90) days written notice except those leases listed on Schedule B. Based upon the expiration and cancellation clauses contained in such leases, the Company at the request of the Association will promptly in writing inform the tenants designated by the Association (on any floor) that their leases are canceled or terminated under the terms of their leases. "Promptly" means within ten (10) days after the expiration of the period described in Paragraph 4E. The Company will cooperate fully with the Association for the purpose of vacating the above-mentioned spaces prior to settlement, but the Association will bear the costs incurred in removing said Tenants from the specified spaces. The Company agrees that it shall not execute any new leases, or extend or modify any existing leases, without consent of the Association, which consent shall not be unreasonably withheld, prior to settlement, except expiring leases may be extended on a month-to-month basis when not inconsistent with the foregoing. If on the date scheduled for settlement, ..., 19...., the fourth, fifth, and sixth floors have not been vacated to the extent of 18,226 square feet, then the settlement date shall be extended until said 18,226 square feet become vacant but not later than ...., 19..... It is understood and agreed that settlement will take place on or before July 31,

according to the certificate of taxes issued by the appropriate authorities); but assessments for improvements, if any, completed prior to the date of settlement hereunder, whether assessment therefor has been levied or not, shall be paid by the Company or allowance made therefor at the time of settlement.

(2) (a) Insurance premiums, if any; (b) annual front foot benefit charges applicable to the property, if any; (c) water and sewer payments; (d) salaries, including vacation pay and other fringe benefits of employees to be retained by the Association; (e) charges under the service contracts or agreements, to be furnished by the Company; (f) any or all other apportionable operating costs, charges, and expenses; (g) rents for the month of settlement collected by the Company prior to settlement; (h) rents and operating expenses; (i) security deposits, if any. Subsequent to settlement, the Association shall deliver to the Company any and all rents accrued but uncollected as of the date of settlement to the extent subsequently collected by the Association, less the Association's collection costs, including attorney's fees; provided, however, the Association shall hold any monies collected after settlement date from such tenant in arrears as trust fund for the benefit of the Company (but not to the extent of more than one month's arrearages), to be applied first to the payment of such tenant's rent in arrears and upon receipt of such money shall promptly remit the same to the Company. The Association shall not be liable for the collection of any rent due to the Company prior to settlement. Utilities shall be read on the date of settlement and the bills to such date paid by the Company.

C. *Settlement Charges* —

(1) Recordation and transfer taxes, including Grantor's tax, in connection with the sale and purchase of the Property shall be divided equally between the Association and the Company. The Company shall pay the costs for preparation of the Deed. All other costs and expenses attendant to settlement hereunder, including, without limitation, title company and settlement charges, title insurance premiums, title examination, survey costs, and notary fees shall be at the cost of the Association; provided, however, that if upon examination of title to the property, it should be found not good and marketable, the Company shall pay the title examination and survey charges.

(2) At settlement, the Company shall be credited with the following: (a) assignable tax and utility company deposits, if any; (b) fuel on hand, if any, at last invoice price and based upon the supplier's measurement; and (c) inventories and supplies in unbroken cartons or packages, at the Company's cost.

D. *The Company Obligations*—At settlement hereunder, the Company shall deliver to the Association:

shall be on or before June 1, 1978, except as extended pursuant to Paragraph 3D(4) below.

E. *Net Cost of Designated Exchange Property*—The Net Cost of the Designated Exchange Property to the Association shall equal its purchase price plus all costs of acquisition, less the outstanding balance of every Deed of Trust, mortgage, or other encumbrance to be assumed by the Company, or subject to which it will take the Designated Exchange Property. If the Association's net cost of acquiring the Designated Exchange Property exceeds the Company's equity in the subject property, then the Company shall pay the excess to the Association at the Closing, by certified or bank check. If the Association's net cost is less than the Company's equity in the subject property, then the Association shall pay the difference to the Company at the Closing by certified or bank check. The Association agrees to abide by these exchange provisions, provided the Association incurs no cost or liability of any kind in the acquisition of the Designated Exhange Property in excess of what it would have incurred if it had purchased the Subject Property without exchange and is satisfactorily indemnified by the Company against any such cost or liability.

F. *Option to Purchase Subject Property*—If the Company shall fail to designate suitable property, as described in subparagraph C, or if the Association, after said cooperation, shall for reasons beyond its control be unable to acquire the designated exchange property on the terms and in the manner specified by the Company prior to the settlement date, the Company hereby agrees to sell to the Association and the Association hereby agrees to buy from the Company the subject property on the terms and conditions set forth in this Agreement, without the necessity of any further agreement, for an amount, at the Closing by certified or bank check (after applying the deposit to the purchase price) equal to the equity of the Company, computed under Paragraph 2B, in the subject property at the day of Closing, and shall take the subject property subject to the existing financing.

3. *Settlement.*

A. *Time and Place*—Settlement hereunder shall be held on or before ...., 19...., at the office of ...., ..., ..., ... except as may be extended pursuant to Paragraph 3D(4) below.

B. *Adjustments*—The following items shall be apportioned between the Company and the Association as of the date of settlement:

(1) Real estate and personal property taxes for the tax year in which settlement is held (with such real estate taxes to be adjusted

WHEREAS, the Company desires to exchange the subject property for other property to be held for investment in an exchange that will qualify for nonrecognition of gain under Section 1031 of the United State Internal Revenue Code,

NOW, THEREFORE, for and in consideration of the premises and the mutual covenants and agreements herein contained and other good and valuable consideration, the receipt and sufficiency of which are hereby acknowledged, the parties hereto agree as follows:

1. *Property to Be Transferred.* The Association agrees to acquire and the Company agrees to exchange and convey all of the Company's right, title and interest in and to the subject property pursuant to the terms and conditions set forth herein.

2. *Conditions of Transfer.*

A. *Market Value of Subject Property*—The Association and the Company agree that the market value of the subject property is .... Dollars ($.........).

B. *Equity in Subject Property*—The "equity" of the Company in the subject property shall equal its market value less the outstanding balance under the senior note held by .... Life Insurance Company (hereinafter referred to as "Life") and less the outstanding balance or discount amount, whichever is the smaller amount of the wraparound note held by .... Realty, Inc. (hereinafter referred to as "Realty, Inc."), is not computed from the face amount of the note but rather from .... Dollars ($ ....), which was the actual amount of the purchase money financing taken back by Realty, Inc.

C. *The Selection of Designated Exchange Property*—Prior to settlement, the Company will (i) use its best efforts to designate a suitable investment property (the "Designated Exchange Property"), that is of a like kind as the subject property within the meaning of Section 1031 of the Internal Revenue Code; and (ii) negotiate for the acquisition of the Designated Exchange Property including the establishment of the purchase price and the financing under the terms of the contract. Upon the request of the Company, the Association shall promptly approve the proposed acquisition terms and conditions.

D. *Acquisition and Exchange of Designated Exchange Property*—The Association shall cooperate with the Company to acquire the Designated Exchange Property on those terms and conditions after its designation by the Company. If the Association is thus able to acquire the Designated Exchange Property, then the Association and the Company shall exchange the Designated Exchange Property for the subject property on the same day and immediately after the Association acquires the Designated Exchange Property in its own name; which day

closing, but said obligations, warranties and representations under this contract shall survive the closing and the passing of the deed hereunder.

Signed, sealed and delivered in the presence of:

SELLER:

....
Witness

....

....
Notary Public

....

Signed, sealed and delivered in the presence of:

PURCHASER:

.... By: ....
Witness

....
Notary Public

COMMENT: See discussion of sale-and-leaseback financing at ¶ 6.04.

Form 8.1

THREE-CORNERED EXCHANGE AGREEMENT

THIS REAL ESTATE TRANSFER AGREEMENT ("Agreement") is made between .... Company (hereinafter referred to as the "Company") and .... Association or Assigns (hereinafter referred to as the "Association").

WITNESSETH:

WHEREAS, the Company is the owner of record and in fact, legally and beneficially, of a certain parcel of land with improvements thereon, known as .... Building, at ...., legally described in the attached Exhibit A.

WHEREAS, the Association desires to acquire from the Company the land, improvements, and personal property, together with all appurtenances, rights, easements, right-of-way, tenements, and hereditaments incident thereto (collectively the "Subject Property");

19. Seller agrees to pay Purchaser, upon execution of this contract, a fee which shall be nonrefundable in the amount of .... Dollars ($...............) for the first year or any part thereof and .... Dollars ($...............) on each anniversary of execution of this contract by Purchaser until the settlement date as described in paragraph 7.

Also, in addition to the nonrefundable fee, Seller is to give Purchaser, at the date of execution .... Dollars ($...........), which sum represents a Good Faith Deposit. In the event Seller fails to comply with any of the covenants and conditions of this agreement, and without failure on the part of Purchaser the transaction is not consummated, then the Good Faith Deposit shall be retained by Purchaser for entering in good faith this agreement and holding itself ready and willing to complete the transaction during such period. Such retaining of the Good Faith Deposit shall in no way preclude Purchaser from exercising any other remedy that it might have under law, including but not limited to, damages and specific performance.

20. Purchaser, prior to settlement date, will be furnished a copy of the permanent loan documents and occupancy leases for its review and approval.

21. At the option of Purchaser, this contract shall be void and no longer binding on Purchaser unless settlement of this land sale for the initial payment in the amount of .... Dollars ($...............) shall have been consummated within .... (   ) months of execution of this contract.

22. It is further understood that, at the option of the purchaser, this contract shall be null and void upon the happening prior to the settlement date of one or more of the following: (a) The filing of a voluntary or involuntary petition of bankruptcy by or against the Seller if such petition remains undischarged for an aggregate period of sixty (60) days, (b) if Seller shall be a corporation, the transferring, selling or disposing of the controlling interest of the Seller, (c) if Seller shall be an individual or partnership, upon the death or incapacitation of that individual or upon the death or incapacitation of one of the general partners, or (d) if the Property has been materially adversely affected in any way as the result of any legislative or regulatory change or in any fire, explosion, flood, drought, windstorm, earthquake, accident, casualty, condemnation, requisition, Act of God, or of public enemy, or of the Armed Forces of the United States of America, or otherwise, whether or not insured against.

23. Seller agrees that none of the obligations of the warranties and representations shall be merged into the warranty deed at the time of

ground lease, become liable for the condition of the Property, the cost of any labor or materials furnished in connection with the improvements thereon, noncompliance with any laws, requirements, or regulations, or taxes, assessments, or other charges now or hereafter due to governmental authorities, or for any other charges or expenses whatsoever pertaining to the construction or the ownership, title, possession, use, or occupancy of the Property or the building thereon, and Seller hereby indemnifies the Purchaser and will save the Purchaser harmless from any such liability and all costs and expenses relating thereto.

13. If, at the time of closing, the Property shall be or shall have been affected by any assessment which is or may become payable in installments, then for purposes of this agreement all unpaid installments of any such assessments becoming due and payable prior to or at the time of the closing shall be paid by Seller prior to or at the closing, and all unpaid installments of any such assessments becoming due and payable after the time of the closing shall be paid by Seller pursuant to the terms of the ground lease.

14. The parties hereto agree that a short form memorandum of this Sales Contract shall be filed among the land records of ....
....

15. The provisions hereof shall be binding upon and shall inure to the benefit of .... and its personal representatives, successors, and assigns, subject to the provisions of paragraph ..... The provisions hereof shall also be binding upon and shall inure to the benefits of the Seller hereto and its respective heirs, personal representatives, and successors. This contract cannot be assigned by the Seller.

16. The parties hereto shall have the right to mutually amend in writing any of the terms and conditions hereof in any manner whatsoever or to mutually terminate same without liability or obligation to any broker or any third party.

17. This agreement is delivered and is intended to be performed in the State of .... and shall be construed in accordance with the laws of said state, except that as to the form of conveyance the laws of the state of the situs of said property shall govern.

18. All notices provided herein shall be deemed to have been given on the date when the notice is mailed by certified or registered mail, postage prepaid, and addressed as follows:

    If addressed to
      Purchaser: If addressed to Seller:
      ....
      ....
      ....

to Purchaser a copy of the current rent schedule for the Property, including names of the tenants, their rental payments, and the terms of their leases.

9. Commencing with the execution hereof by Seller and continuing until settlement hereunder, Purchaser and its representatives shall have reasonable rights of access to the Property to determine whether the Property is in compliance with representations and warranties contained herein and whether any defects exist in the Property, its equipment, or appurtenances. Purchaser shall have access, among other things, to all leases and rental agreements affecting the Property and all records showing security deposits from tenants.

10. Consummation of this transaction is further contingent upon (a) the execution and delivery by Purchaser and Seller of a Ground Lease in form and substance satisfactory to Purchaser as lessor containing the general terms set forth in Exhibit C attached hereto, (b) review and approval of final plans and specifications, and (c) execution of an instrument satisfactory to Purchaser agreeing that in event of termination arising from Lessee's default, Purchaser-Lessor will be indemnified for any mortgage payments, taxes, and bills due and owing by Seller-Lessee, but not paid at the date of termination, as well as indemnification for any security deposits or rents unjustly collected and retained by Lessee at the date of termination. Said document is to be executed at date of closing by ....

COMMENT: Needless to say, counsel for the developer should review and approve the ground lease prior to executing the sales contract. As for the condition contained in item (c), it would appear under this sales contract that the developer as lessee is not personally liable for rental payments under the terms and conditions of the ground lease. This anti-milking clause attempts to make the developer-lessee liable for any diversion of funds. Counsel for the developer-lessee would perhaps wish to clarify this provision that liability would ensue only to the extent cash flow was derived from the property.

11. Whether or not the transactions contemplated by this agreement are consummated, Seller shall pay or cause to be paid all costs and expenses connected with the transactions contemplated herein, including, but not limited to, brokerage commissions, the fee and expenses of Purchaser's counsel, title company's premiums and charges, printing costs, survey costs, and all other expenses of Purchaser incurred or paid by it in connection with said transactions.

12. Purchaser shall not, by entering into this agreement or the

quitclaim shall survive the settlement until said contingent contractual right has been satisfied or terminated as provided in this Sales Contract.

3. Seller will execute and deliver a General Warranty Deed in the form generally accepted in commercial transactions in the jurisdiction in which the Property is located as determined by the title insurance company insuring title to the Property.

COMMENT: Purchaser is not obligated to fund the holdback amount if there has been a default in either the Ground Lease or under the terms of the mortgage described in Exhibit B by the Seller. Counsel for the developer should strenuously object to this provision and demand that technical default should be eliminated as a disqualifying condition; moreover, the developer should be entitled to the holdback amount as long as any material default has been cured prior to the termination of the time in which the developer's right to the holdback amount expires.

4. All notices of violations of any applicable laws or regulations issued by any governmental agency or prosecutions in any court on account thereof against or affecting the Property or the buildings or improvements thereon at the date of settlement of this contract shall be complied with by the Seller and the Property conveyed free thereof.

5. Settlement is to be made at the office of .... The deposit with said title company of the payment as aforesaid, and the deed of conveyance and such other papers as are required of either party by the terms of this contract shall be a good and sufficient tender of performance of the terms hereof. Payment of the purchase price at settlement may be made by check of Purchaser provided said check is good when presented for payment. Title shall be conveyed in such name or names as shall be designated by Purchaser at settlement.

6. Seller shall pay for examination of title, owner's title insurance, conveyancing, notary fees, Purchaser's inspecting architect's fees, transfer, recordation and intangible taxes, and the like, all costs of settlement and transfer of title, legal fees and all costs involved with the preparation, execution, and recording of the Ground Lease.

7. Seller and Purchaser shall make settlement as described in Paragraph 5 above within thirty (30) days after accomplishment of the following: (a) closing of the permanent mortgage as described in Exhibit B, (b) receipt of occupancy permits from the local governing authority, and (c) completion of improvements in accordance with plans and specifications that shall have been approved by Purchaser.

8. At least thirty (30) days prior to settlement, Seller shall deliver

7. That, as of the date of closing, no condemnation or eminent domain proceeding shall have been threatened or shall have been commenced against the property or any part thereof.

8. That Seller has had no dealings with respect to this transaction with any real estate broker, firm, or salesman other than .... In the event that any suit arises for such commission, Seller further agrees to defend, indemnify, and hold harmless Purchaser against any claim. This warranty and representation shall survive the delivery of the deed hereunder. Counsel for the developer should insist that this warranty be mutual.

IT IS FURTHER AGREED THAT

1. The purchase price of the Property shall be .... Dollars ($................), which sum shall be payable in cash at settlement.

_____ or _____.

2. The purchase price of the Property will be .... Dollars ($............), which sum shall be payable .... Dollars ($............) in cash at settlement and .... Dollars ($............) in cash, which latter sum shall hereinafter be called the Holdback Amount, at such time as the Purchaser is assured that .... Dollars ($..............) rental requirement shall have been achieved and that this rate: (a) shall have been collected for at least .... consecutive months, (b) is currently being collected, (c) is based on a Gross Annual Rent Schedule on a fully rented basis of .... Dollars ($..............), (d) is being collected from actual occupants of the realty as described herein, (e) is based on leases satisfactory to the Purchaser, (f) is on an unfurnished basis, and (g) is without rental concessions.

The agreement to fund the Holdback Amount shall be null and void and no longer binding on the Purchaser .... (   )months after project has been satisfactorily completed as certified by the inspecting architect for the Purchaser.

Purchaser is not obligated to fund the Holdback Amount if there has been a default in either the Ground Lease or under the terms of the mortgage described in Exhibit B by the Seller.

Seller acknowledges that the agreement of purchase set forth in this section to pay the Holdback Amount is a contingent right of Seller as provided for in the Sales Contract and is contractual only, Seller hereby waiving, releasing, and quitclaiming unto Purchaser any lien or any right to a lien against the Property, which might arise by reason of such contingent contractual right. Seller agrees that this waiver, release, and

violate any state or local laws. If Purchaser concludes that the consummation of this transaction based on the above opinion or any other independent facts would violate any state or local laws and/or regulations, then the contract will be cancelled without expense or liability. (d) The construction and completion of the ...., to be built satisfactorily to the Purchaser. Purchaser is to receive monthly inspection reports during the construction period from an architect satisfactory to Purchaser. Purchaser shall receive an architect's certification that all improvements have been completed in accordance with the plans and specifications approved by Purchaser (including any grading, seeding, landscaping, and all other on-site and off-site improvements); that direct connection has been made to abutting public water, sewer, gas and electricity facilities, and that the improvements are ready for occupancy. (e) An opinion from Seller's counsel that the consummation of this purchase-leaseback is a valid transaction, that the ground lease documents are valid and conform to state law and that this purchase-leaseback will not violate or come within the parameters of any state usury statute. (f) No unpaid federal or state inheritance and transfer taxes, or, with respect to the Seller or any other corporation in the chain of title, unpaid state or local franchise and/or income taxes, unless, based upon a reasonable deposit by Seller with Purchaser's title insurance company, said insurance company agrees, at the closing of title, to issue to Purchaser a policy of title insuring Purchaser against the collection of any such taxes out of the premises.

SELLER REPRESENTS AND WARRANTS

1. That it is or will be the owner of record of the fee simple title to the Property at the time of settlement.

2. That neither now nor at the time of settlement is the Property subject to any liens or encumbrances other than a permanent mortgage upon the terms set forth in Exhibit B.

3. That at the time of settlement, the land and improvements thereon will be in conformity with all applicable federal, state and local laws and regulations including, but not limited to, zoning ordinances.

4. That Seller assumes risk of loss or damage to the Property by fire or other casualty, that the improvements remain unimpaired and not reduced and will be undamaged and free from settling or other structural defects. Seller will further maintain the Property and the buildings or improvements thereon in good condition.

5. That none of the subtenants are entitled to concession or free rent, rebate, or allowance for any period.

6. That all of Seller's obligations as landlord under the various leases shall have been complied with at the date of settlement.

Owner's Policy Form B-1970 at ordinary rates without any exceptions other than those to be approved by Purchaser. At least ninety (90) days prior to settlement, Purchaser, at Seller's expense, will receive an updated preliminary title report. If any defects, exceptions, objections, or other restrictions are found to impair substantially the value or marketability of the property and cannot be cured within sixty (60) days after the settlement date of closing, Purchaser, if it so elects, can cancel this contract without expense or liability. Title Policy will insure that title is marketable and will insure in the amount of the land purchase price plus the amount of any prior mortgage loan to which the land is subject, and will further include, but not be limited to, protection of purchaser against any filed or unfiled mechanic's liens for labor and/or materials supplied prior to the date of settlement hereunder.

> **COMMENT: The owner and the title company will often object to the provision that the title policy will be in the amount of the land purchased, plus the amount of any prior mortgage loan to which the land is subject. The argument is made that this increases the premiums and that the actual purchase price is limited to the price paid for the land. The problem is that in the Standard Owner's ALTA Policy there is a condition termed "liability noncumulative" that states, "it is expressly understood that the amount of insurance under this policy shall be reduced by any amount the company may pay under any policy insuring either (1) a mortgage shown or referred to in Schedule B hereof, which is a lien on the estate or interest covered by this policy, or (2) a mortgage hereafter executed by an insured, which is a charge or lien on the estate or interest described or referred to in Schedule A, and the amount so paid shall be deemed the payment under this policy. The company shall have the option to apply to the payment of any such mortgages any amount that otherwise will be payable hereunder to the insured owner of the estate or interest insured by this policy, and the amount so paid shall be deemed payment under this policy to said insured owner." Where the premiums are excessive, counsel for the developer should pursue two alternatives: one is to have the title company delete this condition; the second alternative is to obtain an owner's title policy from the title company other than the company that insured the prior mortgage lien.**

(c) An opinion from Purchaser's legal counsel assuring that the consummation of this purchase of property by .... will not

E. Inclusion in Ground Lease of normal leasehold provisions satisfactory to Mortgagee.

F. Developer agrees that during construction, Payment and Performance Bonds will be obtained in the amount of the construction price.

.... Associates

By: ....

COMMENTS: See discussion at ¶ 6.03.

Form 6.4

LAND PURCHASE-LEASEBACK TRANSACTION SALES CONTRACT

This agreement of sale and purchase made as of this .... day of ...., 19...., by and between ...., having its principal place of business at .... ("Seller"), and .... (with the right in either to act for both), having its principal place of business at .... ("Purchaser").

WITNESSETH:

I. Seller agrees to sell and Purchaser agrees to purchase and lease back under all of the terms and conditions of this agreement, a tract of ground (herein called "the Property"), but not the buildings or improvements thereon, together with all rights and interests of Seller appurtenant thereto, consisting of approximately .... acres located in .... and more particularly described in Exhibit A hereto attached and made a part hereof.

COMMENT: This contract is silent as to the purchaser's right to acquire the buildings or improvements at the expiration of the lease term, or sooner in the event of default. It is the author's suggestion that this valuable future interest should be included in the description of the property to be sold.

II. THE SAID PROPERTY IS SOLD AND IS TO BE CONVEYED SUBJECT TO: (a) A current certified survey of the completed project disclosing no encroachments, deficiencies, or other objectional matters unless approved in writing by the Purchaser. (b) Standard ALTA

B. During demolition and construction rent will be 50 percent of rental due upon issuance of Certificate of Occupancy or actual occupancy of the building by space tenants.
C. Upon the earlier of (1) Issuance of Certificate of Occupancy or (2) actual occupancy of building by space tenants, the rent will be $95,000 per annum, assuming that the leased land includes one-half of the abutting private alleyway to be closed, subject to a proportionate decrease in rent in the event the alleyway is not closed. If Developer incurs any expenses arising from the closing of the alleyway, said expenses shall be deducted from the rental due for the additional square footage achieved by the closing of the alley.

Percentage Rental: Owner will receive 15 percent (15%) of net income in excess of a $110,000 "net income base" per annum. Net income is defined as gross rents received from the office building less operating expenses, repairs, debt service, ground rent, expenditure for improvements, real estate taxes, business and franchise taxes, and insurance premiums. This percentage rental will be due within ninety (90) days after the close of each lease year. It is understood that this percentage rental will be subordinate to the lien of the First Trust Holder.

Adjustment of Base Rent: The base rent is to be adjusted on the fifteenth anniversary of the execution of the Lease and at the end of 10-year increments thereafter, so that the base rent shall be equal to 8 percent (8%) of the fair market value of the land subject to the leasehold estate. Said fair market value is to be determined by an MAI appraisor satisfactory to Developer and Owner. All costs and expenses of such appraisals are to be borne by Owner.

4. *Other Terms.*
   A. Tenant has no personal liability under the Lease.
   B. Owner does not share in any refinancing proceeds of any leasehold mortgage financing or equity syndication.
   C. During the term of the Lease, Owner will not mortgage its fee.
   D. Developer has first right of refusal to purchase land.

Form 6.3

GROUND LEASE OPTION AND DEVELOPMENT AGREEMENT: INVOLVING GROUND LEASE ON UNSUBORDINATED FEE

1. *Option to Lease.* .... Associates (the "Developer") will be given a 15-month option in recordable form to lease the above-captioned property upon payment of a $10,000 good faith rental deposit. At any time within ninety (90) days from the date of the execution of the Option to Lease, if Developer determines that the proposed Development is not feasible, the $10,000 good faith rental deposit will be returned to Developer and the Option to Lease will be canceled. If the Option is not canceled during the 90-day period to arrange for plans and specifications, building permits, financing, etc., the good faith rental deposit will be applied against the rental due on the ground lease. Owner agrees that Developer can make all applications for permits and licenses to further development on behalf of Owner. Provided that Developer has made substantial progress toward leasing and financing, the initial 12-month option period prior to construction, at Developer's request, will be extended an additional six (6) months upon payment of an additional $5,000 good faith deposit to be credited against the first year's rent due on the ground lease. During this 12-month period and any 6-month extension, Owner will be entitled to all of the rent received from existing occupancy tenants. However, Owner will not rent additional space after commencement of the option period. If Owner is unable to lease the property to Developer free and clear of all space leases within the 15-month option period, the option period will automatically be extended without any additional good faith rental payment.

2. *Commencement of Construction.* Construction shall commence no later than fifteen (15) months from the date of the execution of the Option to Lease, unless the 6-month extension is exercised or the option to lease period is extended because of existing space leases.

3. *Unsubordinated Ground Lease.* Within forty-five (45) days after the initial 90-day feasibility period, Developer and Owner will enter into a Ground Lease on the following terms and conditions:
Term: 60 years
Renewal Option: 39 years (Same terms and conditions of original term.)
Base Rent: A. No rent prior to demolition and construction.

1. The state of facts shown by Survey Plat of ...., No. ...., dated........., 19...., and revised ...., 19....;
2. Taxes and assessments not yet due or payable and special assessments not yet certified to the Treasurer's office;
3. Easement for construction and maintenance of sewer line as granted to the City of .... by instrument recorded ...., 19...., in Book ..... at Page .....;
4. Easement granted to .... Power Company by instrument recorded ...., 19...., in Book ..... at Page .....;
5. Restriction as contained in Deed recorded ...., 19...., in Book ..... at Page .....;
6. Reservation in ...., Ltd. of the right, title, and interest in certain leases, agreements to lease, tenancies, and other occupancy arrangements, all as reserved in Deed dated ...., 19...., from ...., Ltd. to Partner A, recorded on ...., 19...., in Book ..... at Page .....;
7. Right of the public over and across Lots ....;
8. Agreement dated ...., 19......, between ...., Ltd. as Seller and .... as Purchaser, recorded on ...., 19...., at Reception No. .... Tenant, by acceptance of this Lease, assumes the obligaiton thereunder to join with Landlord in a conveyance to Purchaser of the six parcels, each 10' x 10' in size, referred to therein (which conveyance will among other things impose certain restrictions on the Demised Premises), without any reduction in rent under this lease;
9. Rights of ....Club Swimming Pool, Inc., and ....Golf Club, Inc. to remove certain improvements from the premises conveyed by each to ...., Ltd. for various periods of time, none of which extend beyond ...., 19....;
10. Right of .... to remain in possession through ...., 19...., of the premises conveyed to them by ...., Ltd.

COMMENT: See discussion of lender's requirements with respect to groundlease (where underlying fee is not subordinated to the lien of the leasehold mortgage) at ¶ 6.03.

My Commission Expires ....

....
Notary Public
My commission expires:

(NOTARIAL SEAL)

SCHEDULE A

Attached to and forming a part of the Indenture of Lease dated as of ...., 19.... between .... Company as Landlord and ...., Ltd. as Tenant.

The Demised Premises

The following described land in the County of ...., State of ....:

[Description of Demised Premises appears here]

TOGETHER with all the right, title, and interest, if any, of Landlord in and to all strips and gores of land separating the above described land from nearby adjacent land or lands or streets, roads, railway rights of way, avenues, and alleys; and in and to vacated streets, alleys, avenues, and public ways adjacent to such parcels.

TOGETHER with all and singular the hereditaments and appurtenances thereunto belonging or in anywise appertaining, and all the estate, right, title, interest, claim, and demand whatsoever of Landlord, either in law or in equity, of, in, and to the above described premises, with the hereditaments and appurtenances.

TOGETHER, ALSO, with all fixtures and articles of personal property at any time owned by Landlord and installed in or used in connection with the operation of the Project.

SCHEDULE B

Attached to and forming a part of that Indenture of Lease dated as of ...., 19...., between .... Company as Landlord and ...., Ltd. as Tenant.

Matters to Which the Demised Premises are Taken Subject

The Demised Premises shall be subject to the following matters, but only insofar as they affect the Demised Premises:

Section 33.09. This lease may be executed in any number of counterparts, each of which shall be deemed to be an original and all of which shall be considered equally valid and binding.

IN WITNESS WHEREOF, Landlord and Tenant have duly executed this instrument the day and year first above written.

                                 .... Company

                     By: ....
                                         Partner

                                 ...., Ltd.

                     By: ....,
                                        General Partner

                     By: ....
                                              President

ATTEST:
....
Asst. Secretary

STATE OF ....
                                      ss.:
COUNTY OF ....

The foregoing instrument was acknowledged before me this .... day of ...., 19...., by ...., as a general partner of the partnership known as .... Company.

Witness my hand and seal.

                                      ....
                                                Notary Public

STATE OF ....
                                      ss.:
COUNTY OF ....

The foregoing instrument was acknowledged before me this .... day of ...., 19...., by ...., as President of ....Company, a .... State corporation, which is a general partner in the limited partnership known as ...., Ltd.

Witness my hand and seal.

ably declining to express such satisfaction where similar consent or approval or expression of satisfaction is required from the holder of any mortgage to which this lease is subject and subordinate and such holder fails, refuses, or delays the giving of such consent or approval or expression of satisfaction nor shall any such request or requirement by Landlord be deemed to be unreasonable where any such holder may request or require similar action by the mortgagor. All disputes as to the reasonableness of any such disapproval, consent, expression of satisfaction, consent, or otherwise shall be settled by agreement, if possible, and otherwise by arbitration as provided in Article 24 hereof.

Section 33.06. Neither Landlord nor Tenant nor any person, partnerships, or other entities affiliated in any way with either of them shall, without the prior written approval of the other, have the right during the period commencing on the date hereof and ending five (5) years after the Compliance Date, to purchase, sell, exchange, lease, or develop any parcel of land or interest therein which is located within one-half (½) mile of the Demised Premises and which is not part of the Demised Premises or the lands covered by a mortgage of even date with this lease made by Tenant to Landlord as security for the performance of certain obligations of Tenant. Such approval need not be obtained if the party desiring to make such purchase, sale, exchange, lease, or development offers to the other, in the manner provided in Section 4.02(b) hereof, an opportunity to acquire an undivided one-half (½) interest in the property in question at a purchase price equal to one-half (½) of the offering party's cost of acquiring such property and the other party declines such offer. This provision shall not prevent the sale or other disposition by Management Associates, Inc. or Tenant of the land in the City and County of ...., subject, however, to the provisions affecting the proceeds of any such sale contained in the First Supplement hereto but in no event shall Tenant or said Management Associates, Inc. or any person, firm, or corporation affiliated with either of them develop said land as a shopping center.

Section 33.07. The captions of the various articles of this lease and the table of contents preceding this lease but under the same cover are inserted only as a matter of convenience and for reference and in no way define, limit, or describe the scope or intent of this lease, nor in any way affect this lease.

Section 33.08. The agreements, terms, covenants, and conditions herein shall bind and inure to the benefit of Landlord and Tenant and their respective heirs, legal representatives, successors and, except as otherwise provided herein, their assigns.

this lease shall control in the event of any conflict between such short form or memorandum and this lease.

Section 33.02. This lease contains the entire agreement between the parties and cannot be changed or terminated orally, but only by an instrument in writing executed by the parties.

Section 33.03. This agreement shall be governed by and construed in accordance with the laws of the State of .... except so far as the laws of the State of .... may apply and govern the provisions of Section 24.01.

Section 33.04. It is mutually agreed by and between Landlord and Tenant that the respective parties hereto shall and do hereby waive trial by jury in any action, proceeding, or counterclaim brought by either of the parties hereto against the other on any matters whatsoever arising out of or in any way connected with this lease, tenant's use or occupancy of the Demised Premises, and/or claim of injury or damage, unless the action relates to personal injury or property damage.

Section 33.05. In every case where this lease provides that the approval or consent of one party is necessary before the other party may act, a failure to disapprove in writing, within ten (10) days after a written request for a desired approval or consent specifying in reasonable detail the facts and circumstances on which such approval or consent would be based, shall be construed as approval or consent unless a longer period is specifically elsewhere provided in this lease; provided, however, that actual written consent must always be obtained with respect to an assignment, mortgage, pledge, or encumbrance of this lease, a sublease of all or substantially all of the Demised Premises or a management contract where such consent is required by any provision of Article 4 hereof. No such approvals or consents may be withheld unreasonably nor will any approval or consent required by either party be unreasonably withheld or delayed. In any case where anything is required to be done to the satisfaction of or satisfactory to either party or which either party may request or require, such party shall not unreasonably request or require such action by the other party or decline to express its satisfaction therewith. In any case where the judgment of a party is specified as the required standard, such judgment shall be reasonably exercised. In any case where provision is made for the payment of expenses or attorneys' fees of either party, the same will be reasonable. In no event, however, shall landlord be deemed to be unreasonably withholding or delaying consent or approval or unreason-

become part of the Demised Premises and shall be subject to all of the terms, covenants, provisions, and conditions of this lease. On and after the date of the closing of the repurchase, the monthly net rent hereunder, as the same may have theretofore been increased or reduced pursuant to any provision of this lease, shall from time to time be increased by three-quarters of one percent (.75%) of any part of the repurchase price paid to Optionee by Landlord by other than regular payments of amortization under the mortgages hereinafter referred to, each such increase to be effective on the date of the repurchase or of the making of each such payment, as the case may be (Landlord hereby reserving the right at any time to pay or prepay all or any part of such repurchase price in cash, whether or not such cash payment shall be required). Whether or not the monthly net rent shall be increased as provided in the preceding sentence, it shall also be increased by an amount equal to one-twelfth ($^1/_{12}$) of the aggregate annual amounts payable (i) to the holder of any mortgage subject to which said premises shall have been repurchased, and (ii) to Optionee with respect to any purchase money mortgage, the increase under this sentence to be effective in such manner that Landlord shall be put in funds by such increased rent payments to make any such mortgage payment at least thirty (30) days prior to the due date thereof, such further increase to continue so long as said mortgages of either of them shall be outstanding. Upon the final payment of any such mortgage at its maturity, the increase in net rent, theretofore in effect with respect to the payments on such mortgage, shall be reduced by one-half ($^1/_{12}$) thereof. If in lieu of any such repurchase, Landlord shall acquire any leasehold estate in said premises that may be held by Optionee or its successor in interest, then Tenant shall observe and perform all of the lessee's obligations under the lease creating such leasehold estate and shall also pay to Landlord, as additional rent hereunder, amounts equal to all rent and additional rent payable thereunder at least thirty (30) days prior to the due date thereof.

ARTICLE 33
Miscellaneous

Section 33.01. On the date hereof Partner A (for and on behalf of Landlord) and Tenant executed, acknowledged, and delivered a short form or memorandum of this lease which was recorded in the Office of the Recorder of ...., ..., on ...., in Book ..., at Page .... Such short form or memorandum was recorded for the purpose of giving constructive notice of Tenant's rights hereunder, but the parties agree that the terms, covenants, and conditions of

inafter called "Optionee," dated ...., 19...., and recorded in the office of the Recorder of .... County, ... State on ...., 19...., in Book .... at Page ...., under which Optionee was granted an option to purchase a portion of the Demised Premises, and it was provided that if such option were exercised, Optionee would, at the time of its purchase, enter into a reciprocal easement agreement with respect to the operation by Optionee of a department store on the premises so acquired by it, the continuing operation of a shopping center on the balance of the Demised Premises, and the maintenance in connection with such operations of all parking and other common areas in the shopping center. Landlord agrees to perform such obligations of Tenant under said agreement, as the same may be modified and amended, not requiring the payment of money, which are necessary in order to convey title to the optioned premises to Optionee in the event that it shall exercise such option. Tenant agrees to observe and perform all other obligations of Tenant under said agreement as so modified and amended, including, without limitation, the paying to Optionee of any closing adjustment for taxes, insurance, and like items to which Optionee may become entitled thereunder, and further to observe and perform each and every covenant, condition, and agreement on Landlord's part to be observed or performed under any such reciprocal easement agreement that may be entered into between Landlord and Optionee.

Section 32.02. Upon the conveyance to Optionee of a portion of the Demised Premises pursuant to Optionee's exercise of the option referred to in the foregoing Section 32.01, the premises so conveyed shall thereafter no longer be part of the Demised Premises, and the monthly net rent hereunder shall be reduced by three-quarters of one percent (.75%) of so much of the price paid by Optionee to Landlord for said premises as shall be applied to reduce Landlord's Unrecovered Costs. Thereafter, on request of either, the parties hereto will enter into an agreement further supplementing this lease and the recorded short form or memorandum thereof to delete from the description contained in Schedule A hereto the premises so conveyed to Optionee and fixing exactly the amount of the monthly net rent thereafter payable under Section 2.01(c) hereof. Tenant shall be entitled to all common area charges which Optionee may become obligated to pay under the terms of said reciprocal easement agreement.

Section 32.03. In the event that, pursuant to any provision of the said reciprocal easement agreement, Landlord shall repurchase the premises so conveyed to Optionee, the same shall thereafter again

perform any of the lessee's obligations under said lease, then Landlord, after ten (10) days notice to Tenant (or without notice in case of emergency) and without waiving or releasing Tenant from any obligation of Tenant contained in this Article 31, may (but shall be under no obligation to do so) pay any amount or perform any act on Tenant's part to be paid or performed as in said lease provided and may enter upon the premises covered by said lease for the purposes of curing any default or performing any obligations contained therein. All sums so paid by Landlord and all costs and expenses incurred by Landlord in connection with the performance of any such acts, together with interest thereon at the rate of 6 percent (6%) per annum from the respective dates of Landlord's making any such payments or incurring any such costs or expenses, shall constitute additional rent hereunder and shall be paid by Tenant to Landlord on demand. Landlord may, at any time that Tenant shall be in default in the performance of any of the terms, covenants, and conditions of this lease on Tenant's part to be performed, make demand upon Tenant for, and Tenant will deliver, a full and complete assignment to Landlord of said lease and Tenant's leasehold estate thereunder. At the time of making such assignment, Tenant shall also perform any and all acts on the assignor's part to be performed. No sale, assignment, transfer, mortgage (except as hereinafter provided), pledge, or other disposition of this lease shall be made if the assignee of mortgagee in any such transaction will not contemporaneously therewith become the owner or mortgagee, as the case may be, of said lease and the leasehold estate created thereby.

Lands demised by said lease and all structures thereon shall be considered as part of the Demised Premises for the purposes of determining whether the two and a half to one parking ratio (2½: 1) is being or can be maintained wherever such ratio shall be pertinent under the provisions of this lease.

If necessary, in order to procure either the Interim Mortgage or the Long-Term Mortgage, Tenant shall execute, acknowledge, and deliver, or join in the execution, acknowledgment, and delivery of, such mortgage or other instrument as may be required to subject said lease to the lien of the Interim Mortgage or the Long-Term Mortgage, or to mortgage said lease as additional collateral security for the indebtedness secured thereby, without, however, assuming personal liability to pay said indebtedness or the interest thereon.

ARTICLE 32
OPTION AGREEMENT ON PORTION OF DEMISED PREMISES

Section 32.01. The Demised Premises are affected by a certain agreement between Tenant and .... Company, here-

The term "Noncredit Subtenant" shall mean a subtenant who does not hold such a Dun & Bradstreet rating.

The term "commencement of construction of the Project" or any variation thereof shall mean the time when a permit for such construction has been issued by the municipal authorities having jurisdiction and the pouring of footings and foundations has been commenced.

ARTICLE 30
Land to Be Conveyed to the City

Upon completion of the Project, Landlord will convey to the City of .... the portion of the Demised Premises that has been heretofore agreed on by the parties as the portion thereof to be conveyed to such City pursuant to Paragraph 9 of the Contract of Sale dated ...., 19...., between Tenant and said City. Following such conveyance, the premises so conveyed shall no longer constitute a portion of the Demised Premises, and the parties hereto will enter into an agreement further supplementing this lease and the recorded short form or memorandum thereof to revise the description contained in Schedule A hereto to conform to the remainder of the Demised Premises not so conveyed. Thereafter, however, Tenant shall continue to maintain and keep in repair the premises so conveyed with the same force and with like effect as if they were still a part of the provisions of said Paragraph 9 of said Contract of Sale. Tenant shall be entitled to all income, proceeds from use, or other benefits of the 5 percent (5%) of the premises to be so conveyed in which Landlord is entitled under said Paragraph 9 to retain an interest. The selection of such 5 percent (5%) shall be made by Tenant and subject to Landlord's approval.

ARTICLE 31
Lease of Adjacent Land

Tenant represents that it is the lessee under, and the owner and holder of the leasehold estate created by, that certain lease dated ...., 19...., made to it by ..... Company, also known as ...., a partnership, as lessor, which was recorded in the office of Recorder of .... County on ...., 19...., in Book .... at Page .... Tenant shall perform all of the lessee's obligations under said lease, shall not assign, mortgage, or otherwise transfer or encumber said lease or make any modification or amendment thereof, or enter into any cancellation agreement with respect thereto, without the prior written consent of Landlord first had and received, and shall forthwith furnish Landlord with a copy of each notice, demand, or communication served or given by said lessor under said lease. If Tenant shall at any time fail to

by Landlord as being in charge of the work certifying that the Project has been so completed;

(b) There are then no defaults hereunder;

(c) The Long-Term Mortgage shall have been placed on the Demised Premises or in lieu thereof the full credit leasing requirements of the prospective holder of such Long-Term Mortgage shall have been satisfied; and

(d) Subleases approved by Landlord have been executed and have become effective providing aggregate gross minimum annual subrents, including the common area subcharges, of at least Four Hundred Forty-Three Thousand Dollars ($443,000) per annum for Noncredit Subtenants and of at least Two Million Four Hundred Seven Thousand Dollars ($2,407,000) per annum for Credit Subtenants, plus additional gross minimum annual subrents, from either Credit or Noncredit Subtenants, at least equal to the amount (if any) by which the real estate taxes on the Demised Premises for the first full year after the Project is fully assessed exceed Three Hundred Sixty-one Thousand Two Hundred Dollars ($361,200). If such amount has not been determined by any date on which Tenant claims that all of the other conditions contained in this definition have been met, then the amounts shall be agreed upon between Landlord and Tenant, or if they cannot agree, it shall be determined by arbitration pursuant to Section 24.01 hereof.

The term "Long-Term Mortgage" shall mean the mortgage procured by Landlord with the approval of Tenant for at least Twenty-Two Million Five Hundred Thousand Dollars ($22,500,000) for a term of at least twenty-five (25) years pursuant to a commitment therefor issued by an Institution. The "prospective holder of the Long-Term Mortgage" shall mean the issuer of such commitment.

The term "Interim Mortgage" as used herein shall mean the building loan mortgage provided by Landlord in order to pay the costs of constructing the Project which shall be for a term of eighteen (18) months or until ...., 19..., whichever is the longer, and shall be in an amount equal to the amount of the said commitment for the Long-Term Mortgage.

The term "mortgage" as used herein shall include a deed of trust and the term "mortgagee" or "holder of such mortgage" or any variation thereof shall include the trustee under such deed of trust or the beneficiary thereof, as the context may require.

The term "Credit Subtenant" shall mean either (a) a subtenant with a Dun & Bradstreet rating of AAA-1 or better or whose obligations under its sublease are guaranteed by a guarantor having such a rating or (b) a subtenant who is approved as a "Credit Tenant" by the prospective holder of the Long-Term Mortgage for the purposes of the commitment for such mortgage.

and after any valid assignment of the whole of Tenant's interest in this lease pursuant to the provisions hereof, shall mean only the assignee thereof.

The term "subtenant" shall mean any tenant or licensee of any space in less than the whole of the Demised Premises; the term "sublease" shall mean any lease or other agreement to or with any subtenant for the use and occupancy of any such space; the term "subrent" shall mean any rent or other charge, including without limitation common area maintenance charges, for such use or occupancy under a sublease.

The term "term of this lease," or words of similar import, shall mean the initial term and any renewal term of this lease that has become effective.

The terms "Leasehold Mortgage" and "Leasehold Mortgagee" shall have the meaning specified in section 27.01.

The term "Institution" shall have the meaning specified in Section 4.03.

The term "Insurance Trustee" shall have the meaning specified in Section 9.03(b).

The word "equipment" as used herein shall, among other things, include, but shall not be limited to, all machinery, engines, dynamos, boilers, elevators, electrical refrigerators, air-conditioning compressors, ducts, units, and equipment, heating and hot water systems, pipes, plumbing, wiring, gas, steam, water, and electrical fittings, ranges and radiators, and snow removal equipment used in the operation of the Demised Premises.

The words "reenter" and "reentry" as used herein shall not be restricted to their technical legal meaning.

The use herein of the neuter pronoun in any reference to Landlord or Tenant shall be deemed to include any individual Landlord or Tenant, and the use herein of the words "successors and assigns" or "successors or assigns" of Landlord or Tenant shall be deemed to include the heirs, legal representatives, and assigns of any individual Landlord or Tenant.

The term "Project" shall have the meaning specified in the first recital paragraph of this lease.

The term "Compliance Date" as used herein shall mean the time when the following conditions have been satisfied:

(a) The Project has been substantially completed in accordance with plans and specifications approved by the parties hereto and the prospective holder of the Long-Term Mortgage as evidenced by the issuance of (i) a Certificate of Occupancy by the municipal authorities having jurisdiction certifying to the substantial completion of such construction and (ii) a certificate by the architect theretofore designated

ARTICLE 28
Shoring

Section 28.01. In the event that an excavation shall be made for building or other purposes upon land (including land in the bed of a street) adjacent to the Demised Premises or shall be contemplated to be so made, Tenant shall afford, to the person or persons causing or authorized to cause such excavation, license to enter upon the Demised Premises for the purpose of doing such work as said person or persons shall deem to be necessary to preserve the wall or walls, structure or structures, of any building which is a part of the Demised Premises from injury or damage and to support the same by proper foundations. Tenant shall, at its own expense, repair or cause to be repaired any damage caused to any part of the Demised Premises because of any excavation, construction work, or other work of a similar nature which may be done on any such adjacent lands, and Landlord hereby assigns to Tenant any and all rights to sue for or recover against the adjoining owners, or the parties causing such damage, the amounts expended or injuries sustained by Tenant because of the provisons of this Article 28 requiring the Tenant to repair any damage sustained by such excavations, construction work, or other work.

ARTICLE 29
Definitions

The term "Landlord" as used herein shall mean only the owner for the time being in fee of the Demised Premises, or the owner of the leasehold estate created by an underlying lease, or the mortgagee of the fee or of such underlying lease, in possession for the time being of the Demised Premises, so that in the event of any sale or sales of the Demised Premises, or of the making of any such underlying lease, or of any transfer or assignment or other conveyance of such underlying lease and the leasehold estate thereby created, the seller, lessor, transferor, or assignor shall be and hereby is entirely freed and relieved of all agreements, covenants, and obligations of Landlord herein, except that the obligations of Partner A and his legal representatives under the First Supplement hereto shall continue as therein provided, and it shall be deemed and construed without further agreement between the parties or their successors in interest or between the parties and the purchaser, lessee, transferee, or assignee on any such sale, leasing, transfer, or assignment that such purchaser, lessee, transferee, or assignee has assumed and agreed to carry out any and all agreements, covenants, and obligations of Landlord hereunder.

The term "Tenant" shall mean the Tenant named herein, and from

hereof, which notice shall be addressed to such Leasehold Mortgagee at the address last furnished to Landlord as above provided. Landlord shall, on written request of such Leasehold Mortgagee made any time within thirty (30) days after the mailing of such notice, execute and deliver a new lease of the Demised Premises to such Leasehold Mortgagee, or its designee or nominee, for the remainder of the term of this lease, at the annual net rent and additional rent and upon the covenants, conditions, limitations, and agreements herein contained, including the covenants in respect to renewals, provided that such Leasehold Mortgagee shall have paid to Landlord all monthly installments of net rent, additional rent, and other charges due under this lease at the date of termination and which thereafter would have been due hereunder, if the same had not been terminated, up to and including the date of the commencement of the term of such new lease, together with all expenses, including reasonable attorney's fees, incident to the termination of this lease and the execution and delivery of such new lease, less all net amounts received by Landlord from subtenants up to the said date of the commencement of such new lease, but nothing herein contained shall be deemed to impose any obligation on the part of Landlord to remove Tenant or any subtenants from physical possession of the Demised Premises.

Section 27.04. In the event that Tenant shall fail to exercise any option to renew the term of this lease within the applicable period prescribed in Article 23 hereof, Landlord shall give notice thereof to any Leasehold Mortgagee entitled to notice under Section 27.02 hereof, and any such Leasehold Mortgagee may, within thirty (30) days after the giving of such notice, elect that this lease be renewed for the relevant renewal term upon the same terms, covenants, and conditions and with the same effect as though such option had been exercised by Tenant as in said Article 23 provided, except that Tenant shall not be the lessee in the renewal lease and shall have no obligations thereunder and the Leasehold Mortgagee shall deliver to Landlord an assumption agreement, executed in recordable form, wherein and whereby such Leasehold Mortgagee or its designee shall assume the performance of all the terms, covenants, and conditions of this lease as so renewed.

Section 27.05. If more than one Leasehold Mortgagee shall make written request upon Landlord pursuant to Section 27.03 or shall elect to renew this lease pursuant to Section 27.04, the Leasehold Mortgagee whose Leasehold Mortgage shall be prior in lien of record shall be entitled to the new lease or the renewal of this lease, as the case may be, and the requests or elections of all other Leasehold Mortgagees shall be and be deemed to be null and void and of no force or effect.

............., ..., ..., except that Landlord may from time to time designate one or more other addresses by notice given to Tenant by registered mail, in which case the same shall be sent to such other address or addresses.

Every notice, demand, request, or other communication hereunder shall be deemed to have been given or served at the time that the same shall be deposited in the United States mail, postage prepaid, in the manner aforesaid. Nothing herein contained, however, shall be construed to preclude personal service of any notice, demand, request, or other communication in the same manner that personal service of a summons or other legal process may be made.

ARTICLE 27
RIGHTS OF LEASEHOLD MORTGAGEE

Section 27.01. The term "Leasehold Mortgage" as used in Article 4 hereof and elsewhere in this lease refers to a mortgage or deed of trust permitted by the provisions of Section 4.03 or made with Landlord's express written consent. The holder of such a Leasehold Mortgage or of any bonds or notes issued thereunder and the trustee, if any, thereof is hereinafter and elsewhere in this lease referred to as "Leasehold Mortgagee."

Section 27.02. If a Leasehold Mortgagee shall have given to Landlord, before any notice of default under this lease shall have been given, a written notice, specifying the name and address of such mortgagee, Landlord shall give to such Leasehold Mortgagee a copy of each notice of default by Tenant at the same time as and whenever any such notice of default shall thereafter be given by Landlord to Tenant, addressed to such Leasehold Mortgagee at the address last furnished to Landlord. No such notice by Landlord shall be effective as to such Leasehold Mortgagee unless and until a copy thereof shall have been so given to such Leasehold Mortgagee. Landlord will accept performance by any such Leasehold Mortgagee of any covenant, condition, or agreement on Tenant's part to be performed hereunder with the same force and effect as though performed by Tenant, if, at the time of such performance, Landlord shall be furnished with evidence reasonably satisfactory to Landlord of the interest in this lease claimed by the person tendering such performance.

Section 27.03. In case of termination of this lease by reason of the happening of any event of default described in Section 19.01, Landlord shall give notice thereof to any Leasehold Mortgagee who shall have notified Landlord of its name and address pursuant to Section 27.02

The expenses of such appraisal shall be borne equally by the parties.

In the event of the failure, refusal, or inability of any appraiser to act, a new appraiser shall be appointed in his stead, which appointment shall be made in the same manner as hereinbefore provided for the appointment of the appraiser so failing, refusing, or unable to act.

ARTICLE 25
Estoppel Certificate

Section 25.01. Either party shall, without charge, at any time and from time to time hereafter, within ten (10) days after request by the other, certify by a written instrument duly executed and acknowledged to any mortgagee or purchaser, or proposed mortgagee or proposed purchaser, or any other person, firm, or corporation specified in such request, as to the validity and force and effect of this lease, in accordance with its tenor as then constituted, as to the existence of any default on the part of any party thereunder, as to the existence of any offsets, counterclaims, or defenses thereto, and as to any other matters which may be reasonably requested.

ARTICLE 26
Notices

Whenever it is provided herein that notice, demand, request, or other communication shall or may be given to or served upon either of the parties by the other, and whenever either of the parties shall desire to give or serve upon the other any notice, demand, request, or other communication with respect hereto or to the Demised Premises, each such notice, demand, request, or other communication shall be in writing and, any law or statute to the contrary notwithstanding, shall be effective for any purpose if given or served as follows:

(a) If by Landlord, by mailing the same to Tenant by registered mail, postage prepaid, return receipt requested, addressed to Tenant at , ..., with a copy to ...., at ...., ..., ..., except that Tenant may from time to time designate one or more other addresses by notice given to Landlord by registered mail, in which case the same shall be sent to such other address or addresses.

(b) If by Tenant, by mailing the same to Landlord by registered mail, postage prepaid, return receipt requested, addressed to Landlord at ...., ..., ..., with a copy to .... at

manner provided by the .... State Rules of Civil Procedure, if applicable. All awards made in any arbitration may be made the basis of declaratory or other judgment and of the issuance of execution, on filing the same with the clerk of one or more courts, state or federal, having jurisdiction over the party against whom such an award is rendered, or its property. No party shall be considered in default hereunder during the pendency of arbitration proceedings relating to such default.

Section 24.02. If it shall become necessary, for purposes of Section 11.03 hereof, to fix the value of the interest of either Landlord or Tenant in the Demised Premises by appraisal, such appraisal shall be made in accordance with the provisions of this Section 24.02.

At any time after either party shall have received notice or been otherwise advised that the Demised Premises have been or are about to be taken, either party may, by notice to the other, appoint a disinterested person of recognized competence in the field as one of the appraisers. Within ten (10) days thereafter the other party shall, by written notice to the party appointing the first appraiser, appoint another disinterested person of recognized competence in such field as a second appraiser. If the appraisers thus appointed cannot agree on such value, they shall appoint a third disinterested person of recognized competence in such field, and such three appraisers shall as promptly as possible determine such value, provided, however, that:

(a) If the second appraiser shall not have been appointed as aforesaid, the first appraiser shall proceed to determine such value; and

(b) If, within five (5) days after the appointment of the second appraiser, the two appraisers appointed by the parties shall be unable to agree upon such value and upon the appointment of a third appraiser, they shall give written notice of such failure to agree to the parties, and, if the parties fail to agree upon the selection of such third appraiser within five (5) days after the appraisers appointed by the parties gave notice as aforesaid, then within five (5) days thereafter either of the parties upon written notice to the other party hereto may apply for such appointment to The American Institute of Appraisers. Landlord and Tenant shall each be entitled to present evidence and argument to the appraisers.

The determination of the majority of the appraisers or of the sole appraiser, as the case may be, shall be conclusive upon the parties and judgment upon the same may be entered in any court having jurisdiction thereof. The appraisers shall give written notice to the parties stating their determination and shall furnish to each party a copy of such determination signed by them.

after the expiration of the fifth and last renewal term. Tenant may, at any time or times, exercise such renewal options in a single instance with respect to more than one of said renewal terms, or separately with respect to any one such renewal term; provided, that each exercise by Tenant of any such renewal option or options shall be evidenced and effected by Tenant giving to Landlord, not less than fifteen (15) months prior to the expiration of the then current term, written notice of Tenant's intention to renew this lease for the renewal term or terms specified in such notice; and provided further, that at the date of expiration of the then current term this lease shall be in full force and effect and none of the events of default referred to in Section 19.01 shall have occurred and be continuing. Such notices of renewal shall be effective without the necessity of any other act or instrument, but either party will at any time on request of the other execute, acknowledge, and deliver an instrument evidencing such renewal.

ARTICLE 24
Arbitration

Section 24.01. All controversies, claims, or matters of difference arising hereunder shall be settled and determined by arbitration, except that claims for nonpayment of rent or additional rent, where the amount of computation thereof is not in dispute, need not be arbitrated. Such arbitrations shall be held in the City, County, and State of .... until the Compliance Date and thereafter in the City and County of ...., State of .... In either case, the arbitration shall be conducted according to the rules and practices of the American Arbitration Association from time to time in force, except that if such arbitration shall be held in the City of .... and shall conflict with the .... State Rules of Civil Procedure or any other provisions of .... State law then in force, such .... State rules and provisions shall govern. This submission and agreement to arbitrate shall be specifically enforceable. Without limiting the generality of the foregoing, the following shall be considered controversies for this purpose: (a) all questions relating to the breach of any obligation, warranty, or condition hereunder; (b) all questions relating to representation, negotiation, and other proceedings leading to the execution hereof; (c) failure of either party to deny or reject a claim or demand of the other party; and (d) all questions as to whether the right to arbitrate any question exists. Arbitration may proceed in the absence of either party if notice of the proceedings has been given to such party. The parties agree to abide by all awards rendered in such proceedings. Such awards shall be final and binding on all parties to the extent and in the

Landlord shall not so elect, Landlord may remove such fixtures or property from the Demised Premises and store them at Tenant's risk and expense. Tenant shall repair and restore and save Landlord harmless from all damage to the Demised Premises caused by the removal therefrom, whether by Tenant or by Landlord, of all such trade fixtures and personal property.

Section 21.03. Upon surrendering the Demised Premises to Landlord as provided in Section 21.01 hereof, Tenant will pay to Landlord all deposits or other security and all prepaid rents received from subtenants and other occupants whose tenancies may continue beyond the last day of the term of this lease or the sooner termination thereof and will deliver to Landlord all original subleases and modifications thereof, lease files, plans, records, registers and all other papers, and documents which may be required for the proper operation and management of the Demised Premises and are then in Tenant's possession. It is agreed that Landlord will suffer irreparable injury if such records, papers, and documents are not so delivered and that Landlord shall be entitled to a mandatory injunction (including a temporary mandatory injunction *pendente lite*) to enforce such delivery. Tenant shall have access to any records, papers, and documents so delivered to such extent and at such times as the same may be reasonably required after the last day of the term of this lease or such sooner termination thereof.

Section 21.04. The provisions of this Article 21 shall survive the expiration or sooner termination of this lease.

ARTICLE 22
Quiet Enjoyment

Section 22.01. Landlord covenants that, so long as Tenant shall faithfully perform the agreements, terms, covenants, and conditions hereof, Tenant shall and may peaceably and quietly have, hold, and enjoy the Demised Premises for the term hereby granted without molestation or disturbance by or from Landlord and free of any encumbrance created or suffered by Landlord, except those to which this lease is made subject and subordinate as herein provided.

ARTICLE 23
Renewal Privileges

Section 23.01. Tenant shall have the option to renew this lease for five (5) successive renewal terms of thirty-five (35) years each. Each of such renewal terms shall be upon all of the agreements, terms, covenants, and conditions hereof. There shall be no further renewal right

any and all such moneys so collected shall be deemed to be payments on account of the use and occupation of the Demised Premises or, at the election of Landlord, on account of Tenant's liability hereunder.

Section 19.15. The failure of Landlord to insist upon a strict performance of any of the agreements, terms, covenants, and conditions hereof shall not be deemed a waiver of any rights or remedies that Landlord may have and shall not be deemed a waiver of any subsequent breach or default in any of such agreements, terms, covenants, and conditions.

ARTICLE 20
No Representations by Landlord

Section 20.01. At the commencement of the term, tenant shall accept the buildings and improvements and any equipment on or in the Demised Premises in their existing condition and state of repair, and Tenant covenants that no representations, statements, or warranties, express or implied, have been made by or on behalf of Landlord in respect thereof in respect of their condition, or the use or occupation that may be made thereof, and that Landlord shall in no event whatsoever be liable for any latent defects therein.

ARTICLE 21
End of Term

Section 21.01. Tenant shall, on the last day of the term, or upon the sooner termination of the term, peaceably and quietly surrender and deliver the Demised Premises to Landlord free of subtenancies (unless Landlord shall consent to the continuance thereof), broom-clean, including all buildings, replacements, changes, additions, and improvements constructed, erected, added, or placed by Tenant thereon, with all equipment in or appurtenant thereto (except for movable trade fixtures and equipment installed by any subtenant which such subtenant is entitled to remove under the terms of its sublease) in good condition and repair, reasonable wear and tear excepted.

Section 21.02. Any trade fixtures or personal property not used in connection with the operation of the Demised Premises and belonging to any subtenant, if not removed at such termination and if Landlord shall so elect, shall be deemed abandoned and become the property of Landlord without any payment or offset therefor unless the sublease shall continue as a direct lease from Landlord to the subtenant. If

Section 19.11. In the event payment of any sums required to be paid by Tenant to Landlord under this lease shall become overdue for ten (10) days beyond the date on which they are due and payable as in this lease provided, a late payment charge, computed at the rate of 10 percent (10%) per annum on the sums so overdue from the due date thereof, shall become due and payable to Landlord as liquidated damages for Tenant's failure to make prompt payment and said late charges shall be payable five (5) days after notice from Landlord specifying the amount of the late payment charge. In the event of nonpayment of any late payment charges, Landlord shall have, in addition to all other rights and remedies, all the rights and remedies provided for herein and by law in the case of nonpayment of the net rent. No failure by Landlord to insist upon the strict performance by Tenant of Tenant's obligations to pay late payment charges shall constitute a waiver by Landlord of its rights to enforce the provisions of this section in any instance thereafter occurring.

Section 19.12. The rights and remedies given to Landlord in this lease are distinct, separate, and cumulative, and no one of them, whether or not exercised by Landlord, shall be deemed to be in exclusion of any of the others herein or by law or in equity provided.

Section 19.13. In all cases hereunder, and in any suit, action, or proceeding of any kind between the parties, it shall be presumptive evidence of the fact of the existence of a charge being due, if Landlord shall produce a bill, notice, or certificate of any public official entitled to give the same to the effect that such charge appears of record on the books in his office and has not been paid.

Section 19.14. No receipt of moneys by Landlord from Tenant, after the cancellation or termination hereof in any lawful manner, shall reinstate, continue, or extend the term, or affect any notice theretofore given to Tenant, or operate as a waiver of the right of Landlord to enforce the payment of rent and additional rent then due or thereafter falling due, or operate as a waiver of the right of Landlord to recover possession of the Demised Premises by proper suit, action, proceeding, or other remedy; it being agreed that, after the service of notice to cancel or terminate as herein provided and the expiration of the time therein specified, after the commencement of any suit, action, proceeding, or other remedy, or after a final order or judgment for possession of the Demised Premises, Landlord may demand, receive, and collect any moneys due, or thereafter falling due, without in any manner affecting such notice, suit, action, proceeding, order, or judgment; and

provided by or under any statute, law, or decision now or hereafter in force and effect.

Section 19.08. If this lease shall be canceled and terminated as provided in Section 19.01, or if there shall be any breach of this lease referred to in Paragraphs (a) or (b) of said Section 19.01, Tenant covenants and agrees, any other covenant in this lease to the contrary notwithstanding:

(a) That the Demised Premises shall be then in the same condition as that in which Tenant has agreed to surrender them to Landlord at the expiration of the term hereof;

(b) That Tenant, on or before the occurrence of any such event, shall perform any covenant contained in this lease for the making of any improvement, alteration, or betterment to the Demised Premises, or for restoring any part thereof; and

(c) That, for the breach of any covenant above-stated in this Section 19.08, Landlord shall be entitled *ipso facto* without notice or without action by Landlord to recover, and Tenant shall pay as and for liquidated damages therefor, the then cost for performing such covenant.

Each and every covenant contained in this Section 19.08 shall be deemed separate and independent and not dependent upon other provisions of this lease, and the performance of any such covenant shall not be considered to be rent or other payment for the use of the Demised Premises. The damages for failure to perform the same shall be deemed in addition to and separate and independent of the damages accruing by reason of the breach of any other covenant contained in this lease.

Section 19.09. Nothing contained in this Article 19 shall limit or prejudice the right of Landlord to prove and obtain as liquidated damages in any bankruptcy, insolvency, receivership, reorganization, or dissolution proceeding an amount equal to the maximum allowed by any statute or rule of law governing such proceeding and in effect at the time when such damages are to be proved, whether or not such amount be greater, equal to, or less than the amount of the damages referred to in any of the preceding sections.

Section 19.10. In the event of a breach or a threatened breach by Tenant of any of the agreements, terms, covenants, or conditions hereof, Landlord shall have the right of injunction to restrain the same and the right to invoke any remedy allowed by law or in equity, as if specific remedies, indemnity, or reimbursement were not herein provided.

days Tenant shall pay to Landlord the amount of the deficiency then existing; and Tenant shall be and remain liable for any such deficiency, and the right of Landlord to recover from Tenant the amount thereof, or a sum equal to all such net rent, additional rent, and other charges payable hereunder, if there shall be no reletting, shall survive the issuance of any dispossessory warrant or other cancellation or termination hereof, and Landlord shall be entitled to retain any overplus; and Tenant hereby expressly waives any defense that might be predicated upon the issuance of such dispossessory warrant or other cancellation or termination hereof.

Section 19.05. In any of the circumstances mentioned in Section 19.04 in which Landlord shall have the right to hold Tenant liable upon the several rent days as therein provided, Landlord shall have the election, in place and instead of holding Tenant so liable, forthwith to recover against Tenant as damages for loss of the bargain and not as a penalty, in addition to any other damages becoming due under Section 19.08, an aggregate sum which, at the time of the termination of this lease or of the recovery of possession of the Demised Premises by Landlord, as the case may be, represents the then present worth of the excess, if any, of the aggregate of the net rent and additional rent and all other charges payable by Tenant hereunder that would have accrued for balance of the term over the aggregate rental value of the Demised Premises (such rental value to be computed on the basis of a tenant paying not only a rent to the Landlord for the use and occupation of the Demised Premises, but also such additional rent and other charges as are required to be paid by Tenant under the terms of this lease) for the balance of such terms.

Section 19.06. Suit or suits for the recovery of the deficiency or damages referred to in Sections 19.04 and 19.05, or for any installment or installments of net rent and additional rent hereunder, or for a sum equal to any such installment or installments may be brought by Landlord from time to time, at Landlord's election, and nothing in this lease contained shall be deemed to require Landlord to await the date whereon this lease or the term hereof would have expired by limitation had there been no such default by Tenant or no such cancellation or termination.

Section 19.07. Tenant hereby expressly waives service of any notice of intention to reenter. Tenant hereby waives any and all rights to recover or to retain possession of the Demised Premises or to reinstate or to redeem this lease or other right of redemption as permitted or

succeeding monthly installment of rent. Landlord shall have the right to enter the Demised Premises for the purpose of correcting or remedying any such default and to remain therein until the same shall have been corrected or remedied, but neither any such expenditure nor any such performance by Landlord shall be deemed to waive or release Tenant's default or the right of Landlord to take such action as may be otherwise permissible hereunder in the case of such default.

Section 19.03. In the event of cancellation or termination of this lease, either by operation of law, by issuance of a dispossessory warrant, by service of notice or cancellation or termination as herein provided, or otherwise, except as provided in Article 11 hereof, or in the event of a default referred to in Paragraphs (c) or (e) of Section 19.01, Landlord may reenter and repossess the Demised Premises, using such force for that purpose as may be necessary without being liable to prosecution therefor, and Tenant shall nevertheless remain and continue liable to Landlord in a sum equal to all net rent, additional rent, and other charges payable hereunder for the remainder of the term of this lease. If Landlord shall so reenter, Landlord may repair and alter the Demised Premises in such manner as to Landlord may seem necessary or advisable, and/or let or relet the Demised Premises or any parts thereof for the whole or any part of the remainder of the term of this lease or for a longer period, in Landlord's name or as the agent of Tenant, and out of any rent collected or received from subtenants or as a result of such letting or reletting Landlord shall first pay to itself the cost and expense of retaking, repossessing, repairing, and/or altering the Demised Premises, and the cost and expense of removing all persons and property therefrom; second, pay to itself the cost and expense sustained in securing any new tenant and, if Landlord shall maintain and operate the Demised Premises, the cost and expense of operating and maintaining the Demised Premises; and, third, pay to itself any balance remaining on account of the liability of Tenant to Landlord for the sum equal to all net rent, additional rent, and other charges payable hereunder and unpaid by Tenant for the remainder of the term of this lease. No reentry by Landlord, whether had or taken under summary proceedings or otherwise, shall absolve or discharge Tenant from liability hereunder.

Section 19.04. Should any rent collected by Landlord as provided in Section 19.03 after the payments therein mentioned be insufficient to fully pay to Landlord a sum equal to all net rent, additional rent reserved herein, and other charges payable hereunder for the remainder of the term of this lease, the balance or deficiency shall be paid by Tenant on the rent days herein specified, that is, upon each of such rent

(d) If Tenant shall fail to perform any of the other agreements, terms, covenants, or conditions hereof on Tenant's part to be performed and such nonperformance shall continue after notice for the period within which performance is required to be made by specific provision of this lease, or if no such period is so provided for a period of thirty (30) days after notice thereof by Landlord to Tenant, or if such performance cannot be reasonably had within such thirty-day period, Tenant shall not in good faith have commenced such performance within such thirty-day period and shall not diligently proceed therewith to completion.

(e) If Tenant shall vacate or abandon the Demised Premises.

(f) If this lease or the estate of Tenant hereunder shall be transferred to or shall pass to or devolve upon any other person or party, except in a manner permitted under Article 4 hereof.

If this lease shall be held by a permitted assignee or successor of Tenant, the provisions of Subparagraphs (a) and (b) above shall apply only to such assignee or successor while in possession of the Demised Premises. The events specified in said Subparagraphs (a) and (b) shall not, however, constitute a default hereunder or a breach of this lease after the Compliance Date so long as net rent and additional rent hereunder is paid and all of the other agreements, terms, covenants, and conditions herein on Tenant's part to be observed and performed are observed and performed.

If any such event shall occur and be continuing, Landlord shall have the right to cancel and terminate this lease, as well as all of the right, title, and interest of Tenant hereunder, by giving to Tenant not less than five (5) days notice of such cancellation and termination, and upon the expiration of the time fixed in such notice this lease and the term hereof, as well as all of the right, title, and interest of Tenant hereunder, shall expire in the same manner and with the same force and effect, except as to Tenant's liability, as if the expiration of the time fixed in such notice of cancellation and termination were the end of the term of this lease.

Section 19.02. After expiration of the applicable period of notice specified in Paragraphs (c) or (d) of Section 19.01, or, without notice in the event of any emergency, Landlord at its option may, but shall not be obligated to, make any payment required of Tenant herein or comply with any agreement, term, covenant, or condition required hereby to be performed by Tenant, and the amount so paid, together with interest thereon at the rate of 6 percent (6%) per annum from the date of such payment by Landlord, shall be deemed to be additional rent hereunder payable by Tenant and collectible as such by Landlord with the next

actions, fines, penalties, claims, and demands of every kind or nature, including reasonable counsel fees, by or on behalf of any person, party, or governmental authority whatsoever arising out of (a) any failure by Tenant to perform any of the agreements, terms, covenants, or conditions of this lease on Tenant's part to be performed, (b) any accident, injury, or damage that shall happen in or about the Demised Premises or appurtenances or on or under the streets, sidewalks, curbs, or vaults in front of or adjacent thereto, however occurring, and any matter or thing growing out of the condition, occupation, maintenance, alteration, repair, use, or operation of the Demised Premises, or any part thereof, and/or of the streets, sidewalks, curbs, or vaults adjacent thereto during the term, (c) failure to comply with any laws, ordinances, requirements, orders, directions, rules, or regulations of any federal, state, county, or municipal governmental authority, (d) any contest permitted by the provisions of Sections 3.03 and 8.02 hereof, (e) any mechanic's lien, conditional bill of sale, or chattel mortgage filed against the Demised Premises or any equipment therein or any materials used in the construction or alteration of any building or improvement thereon, (f) any tax attributable to the execution, delivery, or recording of this lease or any modification thereof, agreement supplemental thereto, or any short form or memorandum of this lease or of any such modification or agreement.

ARTICLE 19
Default

Section 19.01. Each of the following events shall be a default hereunder by Tenant and a breach of this lease:

(a) If Tenant shall file a petition in bankruptcy or insolvency or for reorganization or arrangement under the bankruptcy laws of the United States or any insolvency act of any state or shall voluntarily take advantage of any such law or act by answer or otherwise or shall be dissolved or shall make an assignment for the benefit of creditors.

(b) If involuntary proceedings under any such bankruptcy law or insolvency act or for the dissolution of a corporation shall be instituted against Tenant or if a receiver or trustee shall be appointed for all or substantially all of the property of Tenant and such proceedings shall not be dismissed or such receivership or trusteeship vacated within thirty (30) days after such institution or appointment.

(c) If Tenant shall fail to pay Landlord any rent or additional rent or any deposit under Section 2.04 hereof within ten (10) days after the same shall become due and payable; provided that with respect only to the first such nonpayment in any one period of twelve (12) consecutive months, such ten (10) day period shall not commence to run until Landlord shall have given to Tenant written notice of such failure.

making repairs that Tenant may neglect or refuse to make in accordance with the agreements, terms, covenants, and conditions hereof, and also for the purpose of showing the Demised Premises to persons wishing to purchase the same or to make a mortgage loan on the same and, at any time within one (1) year prior to the expiration of the term, to persons wishing to rent the same.

ARTICLE 16
Vaults

In case any vault or basement in front of or adjoining the Demised Premises, or any portico, stoop, window, or other projection or erection of any kind beyond the building lines, as the same shall be authorized and fixed by law from time to time during the term, shall be ordered removed or shall be removed as the result or by virtue of any present or future laws, ordinances, requirements, orders, directions, rules, or regulations of any federal, state, county, or municipal government or other governmental authority, such removal, whether entire or partial, shall not constitute nor be deemed to be a violation or breach of any covenant hereof on the part of Landlord to be kept, observed, and performed, an eviction, actual or constructive, or a ground for any claim for the abatement, diminution, or reduction of rent or other charges; and such removal and incidental alteration and repair shall be made by and at the expense of Tenant.

ARTICLE 17
No Unlawful Occupancy

Tenant shall not use or occupy, nor permit or suffer, the Demised Premises or any part thereof to be used or occupied for any unlawful or illegal business, use, or purpose, nor for any business, use, or purpose deemed by Landlord disreputable or extra hazardous, nor in such manner as to constitute a nuisance of any kind, nor for any purpose or in any way in violation of any present or future governmental laws, ordinances, requirements, orders, directions, rules, or regulations. Tenant shall immediately, upon the discovery of any such unlawful, illegal, disreputable, or extra-hazardous use, take all necessary steps, legal and equitable, to compel the discontinuance of such use and to oust and remove any subtenants, occupants, or other persons guilty of such unlawful, illegal, disreputable, or extra-hazardous use.

ARTICLE 18
Indemnity

Tenant shall indemnify and save harmless Landlord against and from all costs, expenses, liabilities, losses, damages, injunctions, suits,

.... County, ...State. Tenant will accept performance by the holder of any such mortgage of any covenant, condition, or agreement on Landlord's part to be performed hereunder with the same force and effect as though performed by Landlord.

ARTICLE 13
Landlord Not Liable For Injury Or Damage

Tenant is and shall be in exclusive control and possession of the Demised Premises as provided herein, and Landlord shall not in any event whatsoever be liable for any injury or damage to any property or to any person happening on or about the Demised Premises, nor for any injury or damage to any property of Tenant, or of any other person contained therein. The provisions hereof permitting Landlord to enter and inspect the Demised Premises are made for the purpose of enabling Landlord to be informed as to whether Tenant is complying with the agreements, terms, covenants, and conditions hereof, and to do such acts as Tenant shall fail to do.

ARTICLE 14
No Rent Abatement

No abatement, diminution, or reduction of rent, charges, or other compensation shall be claimed by or allowed to Tenant or any persons claiming under it, under any circumstances, whether for inconvenience, discomfort, interruption of business, or otherwise, arising from the making of alterations, changes, additions, improvements, or repairs to any buildings now on or which may hereafter be erected on the Demised Premises, by virtue or because of any present or future governmental laws, ordinances, requirements, orders, directions, rules, or regulations or by virtue or arising from, and during, the restoration of the Demised Premises after the destruction or damage thereof by fire or other cause (except to the extent that Landlord shall apply the proceeds of rent insurance pursuant to Section 9.02) or the taking or condemnation of a portion only of the Demised Premises (except as provided in Article 11) or arising from any other cause or reason.

ARTICLE 15
Access To Premises

Tenant shall permit Landlord or its agents to enter the Demised Premises at all reasonable hours for the purpose of inspection or of

refinancing thereof whether or not this lease and Tenant's rights hereunder shall be subordinated thereto as provided in said Section 12.01.

Section 12.03. In the event of a default on the part of Landlord (not cured by Landlord at least three (3) days prior to the expiration of the grace period with respect to any matter requiring only the payment of money, but at least ten (10) days prior to the expiration of the grace period for any other matters) under any mortgage affecting the Demised Premises to which this lease is or shall be subject and subordinate, Tenant may itself on notice to Landlord cure such default. Tenant shall be entitled to collect from Landlord all reasonable sums expended by Tenant in curing each such default under any such mortgage, including reasonable counsel fees, and interest on all such expenditures at the rate of 6 percent (6%) per annum, by any available remedy or, if the default so cured shall be with respect to a first mortgage, by deducting the same from any rent payments thereafter becoming due hereunder. If, in connection with the curing of any such default, Tenant shall acquire and become the holder of any mortgage affecting the Demised Premises and thereafter shall deduct the full cost and expense of acquiring such mortgage from rents, the said mortgage shall be satisfied, released, and discharged of record when Tenant shall have recouped the full actual cost and expense of acquiring the same, including interest.

Section 12.04. Tenant shall upon demand at any time or times execute, acknowledge, and deliver to Landlord, without expense to Landlord, any and all instruments that may be necessary or proper to subordinate this lease and all rights hereunder to any mortgage, renewal, modification, consolidation, replacement, or extension to which this is required to be subordinated under Section 12.01 hereof. If Tenant shall fail at any time to execute, acknowledge, and deliver any such subordination agreement, Landlord, in addition to any other remedies available to it in consequence thereof, may execute, acknowledge, and deliver the same as the attorney in fact of Tenant and in Tenant's name, place, and stead, and Tenant hereby irrevocably makes, constitutes, and appoints Landlord, and its successors and assigns, such attorney in fact for that purpose.

Section 12.05. Tenant shall give to the holder of any mortgage to which this lease is or shall be subject and subordinate a copy of each notice of default by Landlord at the same time as and whenever any such notice of default shall be given by Tenant to Landlord. Such copy of such notice shall be addressed to such holder at the address last furnished by such holder or Landlord to Tenant or, if no such address has been so furnished, at the address of such holder indicated in the record of such mortgage in the Office of the Recorder of

the Long-Term Mortgage to be hereinafter placed by Landlord on the Demised Premises, and Tenant shall observe and perform all of the terms, provisions, conditions, and covenants of said mortgages except as otherwise expressly provided in this lease. This lease and all rights of Tenant hereunder shall also be subject and subordinate to any and all extensions, modifications, or replacements of the Long-Term Mortgage and to any and all mortgage or mortgages or consolidated mortgage or mortgages which may, subsequent to the release and discharge of the Long-Term Mortgage, be placed on the Demised Premises or any part thereof or the Demised Premises and other premises and to any and all renewals, modifications, consolidations, replacements, and extensions of any such subsequent mortgage or mortgages, but only if (a) the mortgagee under each such mortgage other than the Interim Mortgage shall be an Institution (as defined in Section 4.03) without any participation in the loan secured thereby by any investor which is not an Institution, and (b) there shall be included in each mortgage to which this lease is subordinate (except the Interim Mortgage and the Long-Term Mortgage) and in each extension, modification, replacement, renewal, or consolidation of any mortgage (including the Interim Mortgage and the Long-Term Mortgage), or in a written instrument in recordable form executed by the mortgagee in connection therewith, provisions to the effect that, so long as there shall not be outstanding beyond the applicable period of grace provided in Section 19.01 hereof any default in any of the terms, covenants, and conditions of this lease on the part of Tenant to be performed, the leasehold estate of Tenant created hereby, Tenant's peaceable and quiet possession of the Demised Premises and all its other rights hereunder, including those relating to insurance proceeds and condemnation awards, shall remain undisturbed by any foreclosure of such mortgage and shall be recognized by the mortgagee, all receivers, purchasers on foreclosure, their successors in title, and other persons claiming by, through, or under the mortgagee. Landlord will use his best efforts to include in any such mortgage (including the Interim and Long-Term Mortgages), or other instrument above referred to, the mortgagee's agreement to give Tenant a copy of each notice of default by the mortgagor at the same time as and whenever any such notice of default shall be given by the mortgagee to the mortgagor and to accept performance from Tenant of any provision of the mortgage on the mortgagor's part to be performed, with the same force and effect as though performed by the mortgagor.

Section 12.02. Tenant will have no interest in the proceeds of any replacement of the Long-Term Mortgage or other refinancing thereof, or in any subsequent mortgage referred to in Section 12.01 or any reduction of the constant monthly or quarterly payments under such Mortgage in case such holder shall apply any condemnation awards in reduction of the indebtedness secured by such Mortgage, in such manner that the maturity of such Mortgage will remain unchanged.

Section 11.05. In the case of any governmental action not resulting in the taking or condemnation of any portion of the Demised Premises, but creating a right to compensation therefor, such as, without limitation, the changing of the grade of any street upon which the Demised Premises abut, or if less than a fee title to all or any portion of the Demised Premises shall be taken or condemned by any federal, state, municipal, or governmental authority for temporary use or occupancy, this lease shall continue in full force and effect without reduction or abatement of rent, and the rights of Landlord and Tenant shall be unaffected by the other provisions of this Article 11 and shall be governed by applicable law; provided, however, that:

(a) If any such temporary taking for a period not extending beyond the term of this lease results in changes or alterations in any building, improvement, or equipment on the Demised Premises which would necessitate an expenditure to restore the same to their former condition, or if any other such governmental action shall require alteration to be made in any such building, improvement, or equipment to adapt the same to the change of grade or other result of such action, then any award or payment made to cover the expenses of such restoration or alterations shall be received by the Condemnation Trustee and disbursed substantially in the same manner and subject to the same conditions as those provided in Section 10.02 hereof with respect to insurance and other monies, or

(b) If any such temporary taking is for a period extending beyond the term of this lease, the amount of any award or payment allowed or retained for restoration of any building, improvement, or equipment on the Demised Premises shall remain the property of Landlord if this lease shall expire prior to the restoration of the same to their former condition.

Section 11.06. In the case of any taking covered by provisions of this Article, Landlord and Tenant shall be entitled to reimbursement from any award or awards for all reasonable costs, fees, and expenses incurred in the determination and collection of any such awards.

ARTICLE 12
Subordination

Section 12.01. This lease and all rights of Tenant hereunder are and shall be subject and subordinate to the lien of the Interim Mortgage and

original maturity date of the Long-Term Mortgage and the maturity date of the Long-Term Mortgage resulting from any reduction of the principal thereof by such application of a condemnation award. For the purpose of this Subparagraph (b), if the taking shall occur prior to the expiration of the first thirty (30) years after the placing of the Long-Term Mortgage, and if either the Interim or Long-Term Mortgage shall have been prepaid in whole or in part prior to the taking, no part of the award which would have been paid to the holder of such mortgage, if it had not been so prepaid, shall be deemed to have been received and retained by Landlord, the amount under the foregoing clause (i) shall be computed on the basis of the reduction in the payments on the Long-Term Mortgage that would have been made if it had been in effect on the date of the taking, and the shortening of the thirty-year period referred to in the preceding sentence shall be computed as therein provided, also as if the Long-Term Mortgage had been in effect on the date of the taking.

(c) If, after completion of the work and acquisitions described in Subparagraph (a) of this Section 11.04, Tenant's prospective net income from the Demised Premises shall be materially diminished as a result of such taking (but not to such extent that a termination of this lease shall be thereby effected) or if Tenant shall have been required to invest substantial sums not available to it from the condemnation award, then the provisions of the foregoing Subparagraph (b) shall likewise be applicable, except that where reference is made therein to one-half ($^1/_2$) of an amount or number of days, the same shall be deemed to refer to the full amount or the total number of days, as the case may be.

(d) If Landlord and Tenant shall not be able to agree as to whether Tenant's prospective net income from the Demised Premises shall have been materially diminished as a result of such taking, or whether the sums required to be invested by Tenant as aforesaid are substantial, then such dispute shall be resolved by arbitration as provided in Section 24.01 hereof. The arbitrators thereunder shall have the power and authority to resolve such dispute by rendering an award fixing the amount of the reduction in Tenant's monthly rent at any amount which is not less than the amount computed under the foregoing Subparagraph (b) and not more than the amount computed under Subparagraph (c) hereof and/or if the maturity date of the Long-Term Mortgage has been or would have been accelerated, fixing the shortening of the period of thirty (30) years referred to in Section 2.01(e) hereof at a number of days not less than the number of days specified in said Subparagraph (b) and not more than the number specified in Subparagraph (c).

(e) The parties will use their best efforts to persuade the holder or prospective holder of the Long-Term Mortgage to reduce or agree to the

this lease or by any sublease. Any deficiency will be paid by Tenant. Such work and the performance thereof shall be subject to and shall be performed in accordance with the provisions of Section 5.01 respecting alterations, except that the surety company bond provided for in Subparagraph (g) thereof shall be in the amount, if any, by which the estimated cost of the work exceeds the portion of the award available to Tenant for such purpose. The part of the award not so used shall be distributed as provided in Section 11.03.

(b) If, after completion of the work and acquisitions described in Subparagraph (a) of this Section 11.04, Tenant's prospective net income from the Demised Premises shall not be materially diminished as a result of such taking, and if Tenant shall not have been required to invest substantial sums not available to it out of the condemnation award, the monthly net rent after the date of taking shall be the monthly net rent payable by Tenant immediately prior to the taking, reduced by one-twelfth ($^1/_{12}$) of the aggregate of (i) one-half ($^1/_2$) of the amount of the reduction in the aggregate annual payments of principal and interest on the Long-Term Mortgage which results from the payment to the holder of such mortgage in reduction thereof of any part of the award, plus (ii) 9 percent (9%) of any remaining portion of the net award up to the then amount of Landlord's Unrecovered Costs which is not applied to the reduction of the Interim or Long-Term Mortgage, but is received and retained by Landlord as his own property and not used for any repair or restoration of the Demised Pemises, and (iii) 6 percent (6%) of any further portion of such award in excess of said amount of Landlord's Unrecovered Costs, which is received and retained by Landlord as aforesaid. Such net rent shall not, in any event, be reduced below Sixty-seven Thousand Five Hundred Dollars ($67,500) per month, plus or minus, as the case may be, 50 percent (50%) of the adjustment made pursuant to Section 2.01(d)(ii). Pending final determination, the reduction in such net rent shall be based upon estimates of the amount of any award, and the cost of demolition, repair, and restoration, and the amount likely to be retained by the holder of the Interim or Long-Term Mortgage. Such estimates shall be fixed by agreement of the parties, or in the absence of such agreement, by arbitration pursuant to Section 24.01. In the circumstances described in this Subparagraph (b), if the holder of the Long-Term Mortgage shall not agree to reduce the aggregate annual payments of principal and interest under the Long-Term Mortgage as a result of the payment to it of any such awards in reduction thereof and shall apply the same to reduce the indebtedness secured by such mortgage in such manner that the maturity thereof is accelerated, the period of thirty (30) years referred to in Section 2.01(e) shall be shortened by one-half ($^1/_2$) of the number of days between the

or the Long-Term Mortgage, as the case may be, the unpaid balance of principal and interest due on such mortgage.

(b) Landlord shall then be paid the fair market value of Landlord's interest in the Demised Pemises based on the then capitalized value of the net rent payable hereunder, determined immediately prior to such taking without regard to any mortgage that may affect the Demised Premises and as if this lease had not provided for termination and as if Tenant had the credit rating of a Credit Subtenant. Such value shall be fixed by agreement between Landlord and Tenant or, if they shall not agree, then by appraisal pursuant to the provision of Section 24.02 hereof. The amount computed under this Subparagraph (b) shall be reduced by the amount paid under Subparagraph (a).

(c) Tenant shall then be entitled to receive the fair market value of Tenant's leasehold estate hereunder determined immediately prior to such taking and as if this lease had not provided for termination. Such value shall be determined by the method described in Subparagraph (b).

(d) The balance, if any, of said award shall be divided equally between Landlord and Tenant.

(e) In the event of a partial taking that shall result in the termination of this lease, the value of the portion of the Demised Premises not taken (hereafter called the "Remainder") after such taking shall be determined by agreement between Landlord and Tenant, or by arbitration as herein provided. Upon such determination of value, Landlord may, within thirty (30) days thereafter, elect to convey the Remainder to Tenant. If Landlord shall so elect, upon conveyance of the Remainder to Tenant, Landlord shall receive its full share of the award as hereinbefore provided, and there shall be deducted from Tenant's share thereof the value of the Remainder as so determined. If Landlord shall not so elect, but shall retain the Remainder, the value thereof, as so determined, shall be deducted from Landlord's share of the award.

Section 11.04. (a) In the event of a partial taking, which shall not result in termination of this lease, Tenant shall promptly proceed to rebuild, repair, and restore the remainder of any building or parking area on the Demised Premises affected thereby to a complete architectural or operating unit, for the purposes in use before the taking. The entire award, except for such portion thereof as may be payable to the holder of the Interim Mortgage or the Long-Term Mortgage, as the case may be, shall be disbursed by the Condemnation Trustee subject to the same provisions and limitations specified in Sections 10.02 and 10.03 respecting insurance proceeds, to pay the cost of restoration and to acquire, by purchase or lease, any adjacent or nearby lands designated by Tenant, for the purpose of maintaining the parking ratios required by

ARTICLE 11
Condemnation

Section 11.01. In the event that the Demised Premises or any part thereof shall be taken in condemnation proceedings or by exercise of any right of eminent domain or by agreement between Landlord, Tenant, and those authorized to exercise such right, the entire award made in any such proceeding shall be deposited with a Condemnation Trustee, selected and compensated in the same manner as the Insurance Trustee provided for in Section 9.03(b) hereof, for disbursement as hereinafter provided in this Article 11. Landlord and Tenant agree to execute any and all further documents that may be required in order to facilitate collection by the Condemnation Trustee of any and all such awards. Tenant and any person or entity having an interest in Tenant's share of the award, in cooperation with Landlord, shall have the right to participate in any condemnation proceedings or agreement as aforesaid for the purpose of protecting Tenant's interest hereunder.

Section 11.02. If at any time during the term of this lease the whole or substantially all of the Demised Premises shall be so taken or condemned, this lease shall terminate and expire on the date upon which title shall vest in the condemning authority and the net rent provided to be paid by Tenant shall be apportioned and paid to such date. For the purposes of this Section "substantially all of the Demised Premises" shall be deemed to have been taken if the portion of the Demised Premises not so taken, together with the land referred to in Article 31 hereof and any adjacent or nearby land which Tenant shall propose to acquire, whether by purchase or by lease, cannot be repaired, reconstructed, or augmented by any such additional land, taking into consideration the amount of the net award available for such repair, reconstruction, or acquisition, so as to constitute a complete shopping center providing parking facilities having an area of at least two and one-half (2½) square feet for each square foot of rentable store space and capable of producing a proportionately fair and reasonable net annual income after payment of all operating expenses thereof, the net rent, as the same may be reduced as a result of such taking, additional rent, and all other charges hereunder payable, and after performance of all covenants, agreements, terms, and provisions herein and by law provided to be performed and paid by Tenant.

Section 11.03. In the event of a taking which shall result in the termination of this lease, the rights of Landlord and Tenant in any award shall be as follows, and in the following order of priority:

(a) There shall first be paid to the holder of the Interim Mortgage

the restoration has been completed and paid for in full and that there are no liens of the character referred to therein, any balance of the insurance money held by the Insurance Trustee shall be paid to Tenant.

Section 10.03. If insurance proceeds received by the holder of a mortgage to which this lease is or shall be subject and subordinate, other than the Long-Term Mortgage, shall not be made available by such holder to pay for the work as provided in Section 10.02, Landlord shall, nevertheless, be obligated to supply funds equivalent to such insurance proceeds, which shall be held by Landlord or deposited with the Insurance Trustee, as the case may be, and disbursed as provided in said Section 10.02. Landlord shall be afforded a reasonable opportunity to procure such funds by refinancing such mortgage or by placing an additional mortgage, but if thereafter Landlord shall fail to make such funds available, Tenant may supply the same and in such event shall be entitled to deduct the amount thereof from any net rent thereafter becoming due hereunder.

Section 10.04. Such work and the performance thereof shall be subject to and shall be performed in accordance with the provisions of Section 5.01 hereof except that the surety company bond provided for in Subparagraph (e) of said Section 5.01 shall be in the amount, if any, by which the estimated cost of the work exceeds the insurance proceeds.

Section 10.05. At least ten (10) days before the commencement of such repairs, replacement, or rebuilding, Tenant shall notify Landlord of its intention to commence the same.

Section 10.06. Except as provided in this Section 10.06, this lease shall not terminate or be affected in any manner by reason of damage to or total, substantial, or partial destruction of the buildings, improvements, or equipment on, in, or appurtenant to the Demised Premises at the commencement of the term or thereafter erected thereon or therein, or by reason of the untenantability of the Demised Premises, or any part thereof, for or due to any reason or cause whatsoever. If during the last five years of the term the buildings and other improvements shall be damaged to an extent exceeding Five Million Dollars ($5,000,000), either party may by ninety (90) days prior written notice to the other elect to terminate this lease, but Tenant may avoid the effect of any notice so given by Landlord by exercising its right to renew (if such right shall then exist) during such ninety (90) day period.

basis, in any previous or then pending request, for the withdrawal of insurance money or has been made out of the proceeds of insurance received by Tenant, and that the sum then requested does not exceed the value of the services and materials described in the certificate.

(b) That, except for the amount, if any, stated pursuant to the foregoing subclause (1)(a) in such certificate to be due for services or materials, there is no outstanding indebtedness known to the persons signing such certificate, after due inquiry, which is then due for labor, wages, materials, supplies, or services in connection with such restoration.

(c) That the cost, as estimated by the person signing such certificate, of the restoration required to be done subsequent to the date of such certificate in order to complete the same does not exceed the insurance money, plus any funds deposited by Landlord or Tenant pursuant to Section 10.03 hereof to defray such cost and remaining in the hands of the Insurance Trustee after payment of the sum requested in such certificate.

(2) An opinion of counsel (who may be selected by Tenant) or a title company or official search or other evidence, satisfactory to Landlord, showing that there has not been filed with respect to the Demised Premises or any part thereof or upon Tenant's leasehold interest therein any vendor's, mechanic's, laborer's, materialman's, or other similar lien which will not be discharged by payment of the amount then requested or which have not been bonded as provided in Section 7.02 hereof.

(3) Waivers of lien as described in Section 5.01(h) with respect to each person referred to in the foregoing Subclause (1)(a) or, in lieu of any such waiver, proof that the right of the person in question to file a lien has expired.

Upon the compliance with the foregoing provisions of this Section 10.02, the Insurance Trustee shall, out of such insurance money and such other funds, pay or cause to be paid to Tenant or the persons named (pursuant to Subclause (1)(a) of this Section 10.02) in such certificate the respective amounts stated therein to have been paid by Tenant or to be due to them, as the case may be.

If the insurance money and other funds deposited pursuant to Section 10.03 at the time available for the purpose, less the actual cost, fees, and expenses, if any, incurred in connection with the adjustment of the loss, shall be insufficient to pay the entire cost of such restoration, Tenant will pay the deficiency.

Upon receipt by the Insurance Trustee of satisfactory evidence of the character required by clauses (1) and (2) of this Section 10.02 that

commencement of the term or thereafter erected thereon or therein shall be destroyed or damaged in whole or in part by fire or other cause, Tenant shall give to Landlord immediate notice thereof, and Tenant, acting for and on behalf of Landlord, but at Tenant's own cost and expense, shall promptly repair, replace, and rebuild the same, at least to the extent of the value and as nearly as possible to the character of the buildings and improvements and the equipment therein existing immediately prior to such occurrence; and Landlord shall in no event be called upon to repair, replace, or rebuild any such buildings, improvements, or equipment, nor to pay any of the costs or expenses thereof beyond or in excess of the insurance proceeds as herein provided. In the event that, at the time of such destruction or damage, the Project shall contain more than 1,200,000 square feet of rentable space, Tenant shall be obligated only to repair, replace, or rebuild the same to contain at least 1,200,000 square feet of rentable space and to put the balance of the Project in good order and condition with no visible evidence of such damage or destruction remaining.

Section 10.02. All insurance proceeds received by the Insurance Trustee on account of such damage or destruction, less the actual cost, fees, and expenses, if any, incurred in connection with adjustment of the loss, shall be applied by the Insurance Trustee to pay or reimburse Tenant for the payment of the cost of the aforesaid restoration repairs, replacement, rebuilding, or alterations, including the cost of temporary repairs or for the protection of property pending the completion of permanent restoration, repairs, replacements, rebuilding, or alterations (all of which temporary repairs, protection of property, and permanent restoration, repairs, replacement, rebuilding, or alterations are hereinafter collectively referred to as the "restoration"), and shall be paid out from time to time as such restoration progresses upon the written request of Tenant which shall be accompanied by the following:

(1) A certificate signed by Tenant or an authorized representative of Tenant and by the architect or engineer in charge of the restoration (selected by Tenant and approved by Landlord), dated not more than thirty (30) days prior to such request, setting forth the following:

(a) That the sum then requested either has been paid by Tenant, or is justly due to contractors, subcontractors, materialmen, engineers, architects, or other persons who have rendered services or furnished materials for the restoration therein specified, the names and addresses of such persons, a brief description of such services and materials, the several amounts so paid or due to each of said persons in respect thereof, that no part of such expenditures has been or is being made the

(a) With respect to any loss not exceeding Twenty-five Thousand Dollars ($25,000) in the aggregate, such loss shall be paid to Tenant, who shall hold the proceeds in trust for the purpose of paying the costs of repair and restoration; and

(b) With respect to losses exceeding Twenty-five Thousand Dollars ($25,000) in the aggregate, the loss shall be paid to a commercial bank or trust company selected by Tenant, having a banking office in the City of ......, having a capital of not less than Five Million Dollars ($5,000,000), and supervised by the Comptroller of Currency of the United States or the Banking Department of the State of .... (such bank or trust company being hereinafter called the "Insurance Trustee"). Tenant shall be responsible for the fees and charges of the Insurance Trustee. All insurance proceeds, less any cost of recovery, shall be held by the Insurance Trustee and shall be applied by the Insurance Trustee to pay the costs of repair and restoration in accordance with the provisions of Article 10 hereof.

Section 9.04. Tenant shall procure policies for all such insurance for periods of not less than one (1) year and shall deliver to Landlord such policies or certificates thereof with evidence of the payment of premiums thereon, and shall procure renewals thereof from time to time at least twenty (20) days before the expiration thereof.

Section 9.05. Tenant shall not violate or permit to be violated any of the conditions or provisions of any such policy, and Tenant shall so perform and satisfy the requirements of the companies writing such policies that at all times companies of good standing, satisfactory to Landlord or any mortgagee designated by Landlord, shall be willing to write and/or continue such insurance.

Section 9.06. Tenant and Landlord shall cooperate in connection with the collection of any insurance moneys that may be due in the event of loss and shall execute and deliver such proofs of loss and other instruments as may be required for the purpose of obtaining the recovery of any such insurance moneys.

Section 9.07. Upon the expiration of the term of this lease, Landlord shall pay to Tenant the pro rata amount of the prepaid premiums on all transferable insurance then carried by Tenant as required by this Article 9.

ARTICLE 10
Destruction—Fire or Other Causes

Section 10.01. If, during the term, the buildings, improvements, or the equipment on, in, or appurtenant to the Demised Premises at the

amounts as may from time to time be required by Landlord against such other insurable hazards as at the time are commonly insured against in the case of premises similarly situated.

Section 9.02. All insurance provided by Tenant as required by this Article 9 shall be carried in favor of Landlord and Tenant, as their respective interests may appear. If requested by Landlord, such insurance against fire or other casualty shall include the interest of the holder of any mortgage on the fee to which this lease is or shall be subject and subordinate. The interest of any such holder may be covered by a so-called New York Standard Mortgagee Clause or a clause providing such holder with equivalent protection, provided that in any event the loss under such insurance shall always be payable as provided in Section 9.03 hereof. Rent insurance and use and occupancy insurance may be carried in favor of Tenant, but the proceeds thereof are hereby assigned to Landlord to be applied, as and when received by Landlord, to the payment of the rent and additional rent hereunder. All such insurance shall be taken in such responsible companies, licensed to do business in the State of ...., as Landlord shall approve and the policies therefor shall at all times be held by Landlord or, when appropriate, by the holder of any such mortgage, in which case copies of the policies or certificates of such insurance shall be delivered by Tenant to Landlord. So long as Partner A or any person or entity affiliated with him or a charitable institution shall be Landlord herein, such insurance shall be placed through ...., or such other insurance broker as may be designated by Landlord and an insurance broker designated by Tenant acting as co-brokers, who shall share equally in all commissions payable for placing such insurance. The insurance shall be serviced in ....,........., by the insurance broker designated by Tenant. All such policies shall be nonassessable and shall require fifteen (15) days notice by registered mail to Landlord of any cancellation thereof or change affecting Landlord's coverage thereunder.

Section 9.03. The loss, if any, under any policies provided for in paragraphs (a), (d), and (h) of Section 9.01 shall be adjusted with the insurance companies (a) by Tenant in the case of any particular casualty resulting in damage or destruction not exceeding Twenty-five Thousand Dollars ($25,000) in the aggregate, or (b) by Landlord and Tenant, in the case of any particular casualty resulting in damage or destruction exceeding Twenty-five Thousand Dollars ($25,000) in the aggregate. Subject to the rights of the holder of the Long-Term Mortgage, the proceeds of any such insurance, as so adjusted, shall be payable as follows:

without any deduction for depreciation), excluding the cost of excavation and of foundations below the level of the lowest basement floor or, if there is no basement, below the level of the ground. Such replacement value shall be determined from time to time, but not more frequently than once in any twenty-four (24) consecutive calendar months, at the request of Landlord, by one of the insurers or, at the option of Landlord, by an appraiser, architect, or contractor who shall be mutually and reasonably acceptable to Landlord and Tenant;

(b) Provide and keep in force comprehensive general public liability insurance against claims for personal injury, death, or property damage occurring on, in, or about the Demised Premises or any elevators or escalator therein and on, in, or about the adjoining streets, property, and passageways, such insurance to afford minimum protection, during the term of this lease, of not less than Five Hundred Thousand Dollars ($500,000) in respect of personal injury or death to any one person, and of not less than Two Million Dollars ($2,000,000) in respect of any one occurrence, and of not less than One Hundred Fifty Thousand Dollars ($150,000) for property damage;

(c) Provide and keep in force boiler and machinery insurance, provided any building on the Demised Premises contains equipment of the nature ordinarily covered by such a policy which subtenants are not required to maintain under their subleases, in such amounts as may from time to time be required by Landlord;

(d) Keep all buildings and improvements on the Demised Premises insured against loss or damage due to war or nuclear action as and when such insurance is obtainable from the United States of America, or any agency or instrumentality thereof, in an amount equal to the lesser of the full replacement value thereof or the maximum amount of such insurance obtainable;

(e) Provide and keep in force plate glass insurance covering the glass in the Demised Premises which subtenants are not required to maintain and replace under their subleases;

(f) Provide and keep in force rent insurance (and/or, as the case may require, use and occupancy insurance) in an amount not less than the annual net rent plus the estimated annual taxes, water charges, sewer rents, and installments of assessments and the annual premiums for the insurance required by this Article 9;

(g) If a sprinkler system shall be located in any building or portion thereof on the Demised Premises, provide and keep in force sprinkler leakage insurance in amounts and forms satisfactory to Landlord, except in cases where neither Landlord nor Tenant would have any liability to subtenants for sprinkler leakage damage;

(h) Provide and keep in force such other insurance and in such

or to any vaults, passageways, franchises, or privileges appurtenant thereto or connected with the enjoyment thereof, or to alterations, changes, additions, improvements, replacements, or repairs incident to or as a result of any use or occupation thereof, or otherwise, including, without limitation, the removal of any encroachment on the street or on adjoining premises by any building on the Demised Premises and whether the same are in force at the commencement of the term or may in the future be passed, enacted, or directed.

Section 8.02. Tenant, after notice to Landlord, may by appropriate proceedings conducted promptly at Tenant's own expense, in Tenant's name and/or (whenever necessary) Landlord's name, contest in good faith the validity or enforcement of any such law, ordinance, requirement, order, direction, rule, or regulation. So long as (a) such deferment shall not subject Landlord to a fine or other criminal liability, (b) Tenant shall be diligently prosecuting such contest to a final determination by a court, department, or governmental authority or body having jurisdiction thereof, and (c) Tenant shall have furnished Landlord with such security, by bond or otherwise, as Landlord may request in connection with such contest, Tenant may defer compliance with such law, ordinance, requirement, order, direction, rule, or regulation.

ARTICLE 9
Insurance

Section 9.01. Commencing on the first day of the month on which net rent shall first become payable as provided in Subparagraph (b) of Section 2.01 hereof, or on such earlier date when Landlord shall have paid since the date hereof an aggregate of Fifty-Seven Thousand Four Hundred Thirty-nine and 78/100 Dollars ($57,439.78) for real estate taxes and insurance premiums on the Demised Premises, and thereafter during the term, Tenant, at its own cost and expense, shall:

(a) Keep all buildings and improvements and equipment on, in, or appurtenant to the Demised Premises at the commencement of the term and thereafter erected thereon or therein, including all alterations, rebuildings, replacements, changes, additions, and improvements insured against loss or damage by fire and such other risks as may be included in the standard form of extended coverage from time to time available, in an amount sufficient to prevent Landlord or Tenant from becoming co-insurers under provisions of applicable policies of insurance, but in any event in an amount not less than the greater of (i) the amount required to be carried by the Long-Term Mortgage, or (ii) 80 percent (80%) of the full insurable value thereof (replacement value

Premises or in the buildings or improvements thereon; it being agreed that should Tenant cause any alterations, rebuildings, replacements, changes, additions, improvements, or repairs to be made to the Demised Premises, or cause any labor to be performed or material to be furnished therein, thereon, or thereto, neither Landlord nor the Demised Premises shall under any circumstances be liable for the payment of any expenses incurred or for the value of any work done or material furnished, but all such alterations, rebuildings, replacements, changes, additions, improvements, and repairs, and labor and material, shall be made, furnished, and performed at Tenant's expense, and Tenant shall be solely and wholly responsible to contractors, laborers, and materialmen furnishing and performing such labor and material.

Section 7.02. If, because of any act or omission (or alleged act or omission) of Tenant, any mechanic's or other lien, charge, or order for the payment of money shall be filed against the Demised Premises or any building or improvements thereon, or against Landlord or any conditional bill of sale, chattel mortgage, or security agreement shall be filed for or affecting any equipment or any materials used in the construction or alteration of, or installed by Tenant in, any such building or improvement, whether or not such lien, charge, or order, conditional bill of sale, chattel mortgage, or security agreement is valid (or enforceable as such), Tenant shall, at its own cost and expense, cause the same to be cancelled and discharged of record or bonded within ten (10) days after notice of filing thereof.

ARTICLE 8
Requirements of Law

Section 8.01. During the term, Tenant shall, at its own cost and expense, promptly observe and comply with all present and future laws, ordinances, requirements, orders, directions, rules, and regulations of the federal, state, county, and municipal governments and of all other governmental authorities having or claiming jurisdiction over the Demised Premises or appurtenances or any part thereof, and of all their respective departments, bureaus, and officials, and of the insurance underwriting board or insurance inspection bureau having or claiming jurisdiction, or any other body exercising similar functions, and of all insurance companies writing policies covering the Demised Premises or any part thereof, whether such laws, ordinances, requirements, orders, directions, rules, or regulations relate to structural alterations, changes, additions, improvements, replacements, or repairs, either inside or outside, extraordinary or ordinary, foreseen or unforeseen, or otherwise, to or in and about the Demised Premises, or any building thereon,

and may be disposed of by Tenant without accountability to Landlord, except that any such property remaining on the Demised Premises after the expiration or sooner termination of this lease shall be deemed abandoned and may be disposed of by Landlord without accountability to Tenant.

ARTICLE 6
Repairs

Section 6.01. Tenant shall, at all times during the term, and at its own cost and expense, keep and maintain in good order and condition, ordinary wear and tear excepted, all buildings and improvements on the Demised Premises at the commencement of the term and thereafter erected on the Demised Premises, or forming part thereof, and their full equipment and appurtenances, and make all repairs thereto and restorations, replacements, and renewals thereof, both inside and outside, structural and nonstructural, extraordinary and ordinary, foreseen or unforeseen, howsoever the necessity or desirability for repairs may occur, and whether or not necessitated by latent defects or otherwise; and shall use all reasonable precaution to prevent waste, damage, or injury.

Section 6.02. Tenant shall also, at its own cost and expense, put, keep, replace, and maintain in thorough repair and in good, safe, and substantial order and condition, and free from dirt, snow, ice, rubbish, and other obstructions or encumbrances, parking areas, the sidewalks, areas, coalchutes, sidewalk hoists, railings, gutters, and curbs within, in front of, and adjacent to the Demised Premises.

Section 6.03. Landlord shall not be required to furnish to Tenant any facilities or services of any kind whatsoever during the term, such as, but not limited to, water, steam, heat, gas, hot water, electricity, light, and power. Landlord shall in no event be required to make any alterations, rebuildings, replacements, changes, additions, improvements, or repairs during the term.

ARTICLE 7
Mechanics' and Other Liens

Section 7.01. Tenant shall have no power to do any act or make any contract that may create or be the foundation for any lien, mortgage, or other encumbrance (other than subleases) upon the reversion or other estate of Landlord, or upon any interest of Landlord in the Demised

compensation insurance covering all persons employed in connection with the work and with respect to whom death or bodily injury claims could be asserted against Landlord, or the Demised Premises shall be maintained by Tenant at its sole cost and expense at all times when any such work is in progress.

(g) If the estimated cost of such work shall exceed Twenty-five Thousand Dollars ($25,000), Tenant shall at Tenant's expense furnish to Landlord a performance and payment bond issued by a surety company acceptable to Landlord, in an amount equal to the estimated cost of such work, or other security satisfactory to Landlord, guaranteeing the completion of such work, free and clear of all liens, encumbrances, chattel mortgages, and conditional bills of sale, according to said plans and specifications therefor, and

(h) In any case where such a bond is not so required, or, if required, in lieu of such bond, with respect to each contract or agreement (oral or written) for labor, services, materials, or supplies in connection with any such alteration, rebuilding, replacement, change, addition, or improvement at a price in excess of Two Thousand Five Hundred Dollars ($2,500), before the commencement of any such work, Tenant shall deliver to Landlord a written waiver by the architect, engineer, contractor, subcontractor, materialman, mechanic, or other person or corporation contracting to furnish such labor, services, materials, or supplies, of all right of lien that he or it might otherwise have upon or against the Demised Premises, or the buildings or improvements to be altered, repaired, improved, or constructed, or the interest of Landlord therein, but Tenant shall not be required to furnish such waivers from individual workmen, foremen, draftsmen, and other employees of such persons.

Section 5.02. All buildings, alterations, rebuildings, replacements, changes, additions, improvements, equipment, and appurtenances on or in the Demised Premises at the commencement of the term, and which may be erected, installed, or affixed on or in the Demised Premises during the term, are and shall be deemed to be and immediately become part of the realty and the sole and absolute property of Landlord and shall be deemed to be part of the Demised Premises, except that all movable trade fixtures and equipment installed by any subtenant, which such subtenant is entitled to remove under the terms of its sublease, shall be and remain the property of such subtenant.

Section 5.03. All salvage arising out of work that Tenant is permitted or required to carry out under any provision of this lease, including the provisions of Articles 5, 6, 10, and 11 hereof, shall upon detachment from the Demised Premises become Tenant's sole property

able for inspection in ....,......, by Landlord and his authorized agents and representatives during Tenant's regular business hours until three (3) years after the closing of the Long-Term Mortgage.

ARTICLE 5
Alterations

Section 5.01. No substantial portion of any building on the Demised Premises shall be demolished or removed by Tenant, and Tenant shall not at any time during the term make any alteration, rebuilding, replacement, change, addition, or improvement in or to the Demised Premises or to any building thereon, unless:

(a) In the case of demolition of a building the demolished structures shall be replaced by others having a value, upon completion, at least equal to those demolished, and Tenant shall, before commencing the work of demolition, furnish Landlord with a bond or other reasonably satisfactory evidence that such replacement structures will be completed and paid for, and

(b) In the case of any work other than demolition of a building, the buildings upon the Demised Premises shall be at least equal in value, after such work, as before.

(c) Such work shall be performed in a first class workmanlike manner, at Tenant's sole cost and expense, and shall not weaken or impair the structural strength, or lessen the value, of such buildings as shall be on the Demised Premises at the time, but no such work performed during the first sixty (60) years of the term shall change the principal use of the Demised Premises as a retail shopping center without the prior written consent of Landlord.

(d) The same shall be made according to plans and specifications therefore, which, provided the estimated cost thereof is more than Twenty-five Thousand Dollars ($25,000), shall be first submitted to and approved in writing by Landlord.

(e) Before the commencement of any such work, such plans and specifications shall be filed with and approved by all governmental departments or authorities having jurisdiction and all public utility companies whose installations shall be affected thereby, and all such work shall be done subject to and in accordance with the requirements of law and local regulations of all governmental departments or authorities having jurisdiction and of such public utility companies.

(f) Before the commencement of any such work, Tenant shall pay the amount of any increase in premiums on insurance policies provided for under Section 9.01 on account of endorsements to be made thereon covering the risk during the course of such work and workmen's

hereby expressly consents and agrees that it will not, without Landlord's prior written consent, take any action in conflict with the rights so assigned. Landlord, however, hereby authorizes Tenant to permit the cancellation or accept the surrender of a sublease (a) if made in connection with the making of a new sublease complying with the provisions of Section 4.04 hereof and (b) in case the subtenant shall remain in default after lapse of any applicable grace period in the sublease.

Section 4.08. So long as the assignment of subleases and subrents to Landlord provided in Section 4.06 shall not be in effect on or before the fifteenth day of each month, Tenant, at Tenant's sole cost and expense, shall prepare or cause to be prepared and transmit to Landlord an operating statement with respect to the Demised Premises for the preceding calendar month, which shall reflect the following: (a) the actual cash flow; (b) a schedule of aged rents and other receivables; (c) a schedule of prepaid expenses and other assets; (d) a schedule of current and long-term liabilities; (e) a statement of income and expenses on an accrual basis, which shall set forth the type of income and expenses, e.g., in the case of income, rent, parking and electricity charges, etc., and in the case of expenses, payroll, heat, electricity, repairs, supplies, telephone, water, sewer, etc., as well as the names of the payors and payees; (f) a schedule of the commissions earned by the managing agent; and (g) a schedule of vacancies. In such case, Tenant will also furnish Landlord, within thirty (30) days after the end of each calendar quarter and within ninety (90) days after the end of each period of twelve (12) months ending December 31 during the term of this lease and after the termination thereof, an operating statement containing all of the information required by the preceding sentence for such quarter or twelve-month period, as the case may be. Each annual statement shall be audited and shall be accompanied by (a) the statement required by the next to the last sentence of Section 4.02 (b), and (b) a rent schedule showing, as to each sublease, the subtenant, space, rent, and expiration date.

Until the Compliance Date, the monthly statements provided for in the preceding paragraph shall also contain a report of Tenant's progress in the construction of the Project and the annual audited statements shall be certified by .... or such other accountants as may be designated by Landlord. After the Compliance Date, such certifications may be made by any national firm of accountants selected by Tenant.

Tenant shall cause all of the books and records of Tenant and Management Associates, Inc. relating to the Project to be made avail-

subtenant and, in the case of any advance rent, the month for which the same was paid shall have ended, in which event or events the same shall be applied by Landlord to the net rent or additional rent next becoming due and payable hereunder. Such right of Tenant to collect subrents may be revoked by Landlord at any time by giving five (5) days notice thereof to Tenant; provided that if Partner A or any person or entity affiliated with him or an Institution shall not be Landlord hereunder, then such right may only be revoked upon the occurrence of an event of default by Tenant under this lease. So long as Landlord shall collect subrents pursuant to such assignment and until the occurrence of such a default, Tenant shall be furnished with monthly reports of collections and photographic copies of subtenant's statements relating to percentage rents and shall be paid any excess in such collections after the application of the same to the net rent and additional rent currently due hereunder. In any event, Tenant may pursue all remedies against defaulting subtenants and may audit their percentage rents, but if Tenant fails to use diligent efforts to collect delinquent subrents, Landlord may do so. In the event of the failure of any subtenant to pay subrent to Landlord pursuant to the foregoing assignment after the giving of such notice of revocation, or to pay advance rent or a security deposit to Landlord at any time when Landlord is entitled to the same under such assignment, any such subrent, advance rent, or security deposit thereafter collected by Tenant shall be deemed to constitute a trust fund for the benefit of Landlord.

Section 4.07. Tenant shall not directly or indirectly collect or accept any payment of advance rent (other than additional rent) under any sublease, except that, in case of a sublease where Tenant, as the sublessor thereunder, is required to make Tenant changes or alterations at Tenant's expense, Tenant may collect advance rent for an amount not in excess of one year's subrent or the estimated cost of the work, whichever is less. Any sublease may require the subtenant thereunder to make a rent security deposit in an amount not exceeding 10 percent (10%) of the aggregate subrent reserved for the term of such sublease.

Tenant shall fully observe and perform all of the obligations and provisions under any sublease on the sublessor's part to be observed and performed.

Included in the rights assigned to Landlord by Section 4.06 hereof are Tenant's right to modify any sublease so as to reduce the rent, shorten the term, or adversely affect in any other respect to any material extent the rights of the lessor thereunder, or to permit cancellation or to accept the surrender of any sublease, or to surrender any security deposited thereunder, or to release any guarantor thereof, and Tenant

hold its approval, where required, it shall apprise Tenant in writing of the reason in sufficient detail to enable Tenant to comply with Landlord's requirements. In any event, even where Landlord's approval shall not be required, tenant shall furnish Landlord with fully executed duplicate originals of all subleases of space in the Demised Premises within ten (10) days after the execution and delivery thereof.

Section 4.05. Landlord will, on request of any subtenant under a sublease approved by Landlord, execute and deliver to such subtenant an agreement to the effect that, so long as such subtenant is not in default under its sublease, after the expiration or other termination of this lease (except by reason of fire or other casualty or condemnation), if the term of the sublease shall have commenced, Landlord will accept attornment to Landlord and thereby become the lessor under such sublease; provided, however, that no modification or amendment of such sublease made without the prior written consent of Landlord, nor any prepayment of rent prior to such attornment for more than one month in advance of its due date, shall be binding on Landlord. In any such case, the last sentence of the provision set forth in clause (g) of Section 4.04 hereof may be omitted or deleted therefrom.

Section 4.06. Subject to the rights of the holder of any mortgage to which this lease is or shall be subject and subordinate and as security for the prompt payment of the net rent and additional rent hereunder, Tenant hereby assigns to Landlord all of its right, title, and interest in and to all existing and future subleases and all subrents due and to become due thereunder and grants to Landlord the right to collect said subrents, applying any net amount collected from subtenants to the net rent or additional rent due hereunder. If an event of default or breach of this lease as described in Section 19.01 hereof shall occur, then Landlord shall be entitled to deduct from any collections under the foregoing assignment Landlord's expenses in making such collections and in accounting therefor before applying the same to the net rent and additional rent due hereunder.

Landlord hereby waives such right to collect rents and agrees that until notice to Tenant revoking the waiver, Tenant shall be entitled to collect and receive such subrents, except that this waiver shall not be effective as to any subrents paid more than one month in advance of the date when the same would otherwise become due (hereinafter called "advance rents") or as to any rent security deposits, all of which unless deposited by Tenant in a special trust account shall be paid to and held by Landlord until Tenant, as lessor under the sublease in question, shall be entitled to retain the same without accountability therefor to the

full compliance with any and all requirements hereunder shall be invalid and of no effect against Landlord.

No instrument entered into under the provisions of this Section 4.03 shall be deemed to be an assignment of this lease so as to require, in order to be effective, the assumption of the obligations on assignor's part to be performed under this lease, as provided in Section 4.02(d) hereof.

Section 4.04. Tenant shall also have the right, without Landlord's consent, to sublet portions (constituting less than all or substantially all) of the Demised Premises where the sublease meets the following requirements:

(a) It is prepared on a form which has been agreed upon between Landlord and Tenant;

(b) The subtenant has a credit standing meeting a standard which has been agreed upon between Landlord and Tenant;

(c) The subrent is at least the amount set forth in a schedule agreed upon between Landlord and Tenant;

(d) The term is not less than that set forth on said schedule;

(e) The subtenant is granted no exclusive selling privileges and is not subjected to any restrictive covenants not provided in said agreed-upon form, or if exclusive selling privileges or restrictive covenants are contained in such sublease, the same meet objective standards which have been agreed upon between Landlord and Tenant;

(f) The sublease is subject and subordinate to the rights of Landlord hereunder; and

(g) Except as provided in Section 4.05 hereof, the sublease contains substantially the following provisions:

> "Tenant understands that Landlord is the lessee under an underlying lease of the entire shopping center of which the leased premises form a part. In the event that such underlying lease is terminated, this lease shall not terminate or be terminable by Tenant, and Tenant shall attorn to the lessor thereunder or to the purchaser at the sale on any foreclosure of a mortgage or deed of trust to which this lease or such underlying lease is subordinate. This provision shall not be construed to deprive the lessor under such underlying lease from specifically naming and joining Tenant in any proceeding for the termination of such underlying lease and from thereby obtaining a judgment, final order, warrant, or other legal process in such proceeding against Tenant to terminate this lease."

Unless a sublease shall meet all of the foregoing requirements, Landlord's approval thereof must be obtained. If Landlord shall with-

with respect to any other proposal made at any time or from time to time except as hereinafter otherwise provided.

(d) No assignment made with Landlord's consent or as hereinabove or hereinafter permitted shall be effective until there shall have been delivered to Landlord an executed counterpart of such assignment containing an agreement, in recordable form, executed by the assignor and the proposed assignee, wherein and whereby such assignee assumes due performance of the obligations on the assignor's part to be performed under this lease to the end of the term hereof.

Upon the making of an effective assignment hereunder and the delivery by the assignor to Landlord of an executed counterpart of such assignment containing the agreement of the assignee to assume the obligations of this lease as aforesaid, all liabilities and obligations on the part of the assignor accruing after such assignment shall terminate.

Section 4.03. Tenant shall have the right, without Landlord's consent, to mortgage this lease to an Institution and to execute and deliver to a trustee a deed of trust of this lease securing bonds or notes issued by Tenant to one or more Institutions, provided that any investor not an Institution shall in no way participate in any such mortgage or be the holder of any such bonds or notes. The term "Institution" as used herein shall mean a savings bank, bank, trust or insurance company, savings and loan association, college, university, pension fund, employees' profit-sharing trust, or any other monetary or lending institution primarily engaged in the making of first mortgage loans. No Leasehold Mortgage shall be binding upon Landlord in the enforcement of its rights and remedies herein and by law provided, unless and until an executed counterpart thereof or a copy thereof certified by the recording officer shall have been delivered to Landlord, notwithstanding any other form of notice, actual or constructive. Any Leasehold Mortgage shall be specifically subject and subordinate to the rights of Landlord hereunder.

Any Leasehold Mortgage shall provide that in the event of a foreclosure of such mortgage or of any other action or proceeding for the enforcement thereof or of any sale thereunder, if the subtenant under any existing or future sublease shall not then be in default in the payment of rent or additional rent for which a proceeding is then pending brought by such subtenant's lessor, any provision in such sublease to the contrary notwithstanding, such sublease will not be barred, terminated, cut off, or foreclosed nor will said subtenant be named a defendant in such foreclosure action or proceeding, nor will the rights and possession of said subtenant thereunder be disturbed. Any mortgage on this lease or the interest of Tenant hereunder without

Compliance Date, a bona fide written proposal to purchase this lease or to sublease all or substantially all of the Demised Premises shall be received by Tenant and if Tenant shall desire to accept such proposal, or in the event a bona fide written proposal to purchase 51 percent (51%) or more of any proprietary interest in the firm then constituting Tenant or 51 percent (51%) or more of the issued and outstanding stock of any corporation then constituting Tenant shall be received by any of the proprietors or stockholders of such firm, or corporation, as the case may be, and if the prospective seller shall desire to accept such proposal, then and in any such event, unless Landlord's consent to the assignment or transfer contemplated by such proposal shall not be required under Subparagraph (b) hereof, Tenant shall, or shall cause such seller to, give written notice to Landlord of the receipt of such proposal, which notice shall be accompanied by a photostatic or similar copy of such proposal with the name and address of the person, firm, or corporation making such proposal. Landlord shall thereupon have an exclusive option to purchase said proprietary interest or said stock or to sublease all or substantially all of the Demised Premises, as the case may be, for the same price or consideration and upon the same terms as contained in such proposal, which option shall be exercised by written notice given by Landlord to Tenant and to such seller within thirty (30) days next after the giving to Landlord of such notice of such proposal. If Landlord shall exercise such option within said time limit, Tenant shall, or shall cause said proprietors or stockholders to, sell this lease or said proprietary interest or said issued and outstanding stock, or shall sublet all or substantially all of the Demised Premises, as the case may be, to Landlord, and Landlord shall purchase the same for the same price or consideration and upon the same terms as contained in such proposal. Such transaction shall be closed on the first business day following the expiration of sixty (60) days next after the giving by Landlord to Tenant of such notice of the exercise of such option, or shall be closed on the date, if any, provided in the proposal, whichever is later.

If Landlord shall not exercise such option within said thirty (30) day time limit, Tenant, said proprietors, or said stockholders, as the case may be, shall be free to sell, pursuant to such proposal, without Landlord's consent but subject to the requirements of Subparagraph (d) hereof, to the person, firm, or corporation making such proposal, or its successors in interest or designees, for a price upon the terms contained in such proposal.

If any purchase should not be consummated with the person, firm, or corporation making the proposal to his or its successors in interest or designees and pursuant to the proposal, Landlord shall have the option

(b) If the sale, assignment, transfer, management contract, or other disposition of any of the issued and outstanding capital stock of Tenant (or of any successor or assignee of Tenant which is a corporation), or of the interest of any general partner in a partnership owning the leasehold estate created hereby, or of the interest of any member of a joint venture, syndicate, or other group which may collectively own such leasehold estate, shall result in changing the control of Tenant or such other corporation or such partnership, joint venture, syndicate, or other group, such sale, assignment, transfer, or other disposition shall be deemed an assignment of this lease and shall be subject to all of the provisions of this lease with respect to assignments. The consent of Landlord shall not, however, be required, and the right of first refusal hereinafter created shall not apply to an assignment or transfer which does not have the effect of removing control of Tenant from Management Associates, its executors or administrators. For the purpose of this Section 4.02, "control" of any corporation shall be deemed to be vested in the person or persons owning more than 50 percent (50%) of the voting power for the election of the Board of Directors of such corporation and "control" of a partnership, joint venture, syndicate, or other group shall be deemed to be vested in the person or persons owning more than 50 percent (50%) of the general partners' interest in such partnership or of the total interest in such joint venture, syndicate, or other group, and members of the family or any assignor or transferor shall include his spouse, grandparents, parents, brothers and sisters, nephews and nieces, and issue, a legally adopted child being treated as a child by blood. The annual statement to be furnished by Tenant to Landlord pursuant to Section 4.08 shall be accompanied by a statement of the names and addresses of all stockholders in any corporation or general partners in any partnership holding this lease, showing the number of shares of stock owned by each stockholder of such corporation, or the respective interests of the partners in such partnership, as the case may be; provided, however, that, if at any time during the term of this lease any corporation holding this lease is an Institution (as defined in Section 4.03) or if the stock of any corporation holding this lease is listed on any recognized Stock Exchange, then a list of its stockholders shall not be required. Such statement shall be signed by an officer of each corporation and by a general partner of each partnership holding this lease.

(c) Any partnership, joint venture, syndicate, or other group collectively owning the leasehold estate created hereby is hereinafter referred to as a "firm" and the general partners of such partnership and members of such joint venture, syndicate, or other group are hereinafter referred to as "proprietors". In the event that, subsequent to the

ARTICLE 4
Assignments, Leasehold Mortgages, and Subleases; Operating Statements

Section 4.01. Except as otherwise provided in this Article 4, neither Tenant, nor Tenant's successors or assigns, shall assign, mortgage, pledge, or encumber this lease, in whole or in part, or sublet the Demised Premises, in whole or in part, or permit the same or any portion thereof to be used or occupied by others, or enter into a management contract or other arrangement whereby the Demised Premises shall be managed and operated by anyone other than Management Associates, Inc., or the then owner of Tenant's leasehold estate hereunder, nor shall this lease be assigned or transferred by operation of law without the prior consent in writing of Landlord in each instance. If this lease be assigned or transferred, or if all or any part of the Demised Premises be sublet or occupied by anybody other than Tenant, Landlord may, after default by Tenant, collect rent from the assignee, transferee, subtenant, or occupant, and apply the net amount collected to the rent reserved herein, but no such assignment, subletting, occupancy, or collection shall be deemed a waiver of any agreement, term, covenant, or condition hereof, or the acceptance of the assignee, transferee, subtenant, or occupant as Tenant. Except as provided in Section 4.02(d) hereof, Tenant shall not thereby be released from the performance or further performance by Tenant of the agreements, terms, covenants, and conditions hereof, and shall continue liable hereunder in accordance with the agreements, terms, covenants, and conditions hereof. The consent by Landlord to an assignment, mortgage, pledge, encumbrance, transfer, management contract, or subletting shall not in any wise be construed to relieve Tenant from obtaining the express consent in writing of Landlord, if required hereunder, to any further assignment, mortgage, pledge, encumbrance, transfer, management contract, or subletting. Notwithstanding the foregoing, Landlord's consent shall not be required on a management contract with a person, firm, or corporation experienced in and engaged in the business of the management and operation of shopping centers which shall be compensated thereunder at a fixed rate not in excess of 5 percent (5%) of the gross annual collections of subrents and which agent shall be subject to the general direction and control of Tenant.

Section 4.02. (a) Until the Compliance Date, Tenant may not assign its leasehold interest or sublet substantially all the Demised Premises without Landlord's prior written consent. Thereafter, Tenant may sell or enter into such subleases without such consent, but subject to the following portions of this Section 4.02.

such mortgagee, sufficient to cover the amount of the contested item or items, with interest and penalties, for the period which such proceedings may be expected to take, securing payment of such contested items, interest, and penalties, and all costs in connection therewith. Notwithstanding the furnishing of any such bond or security other than a cash deposit, Tenant shall promptly pay such contested item or items if at any time the Demised Premises or any part thereof shall be in danger of being forfeited or otherwise lost or Landlord shall be subjected to criminal liability for such nonpayment. If, however, Tenant shall have made a cash deposit, in any such event Landlord or such mortgagee, as the case may be, may pay such contested item or items out of such deposit. When any such contested item or items shall have been paid or cancelled, any balance of any such cash deposit not so applied shall be repaid to Tenant without interest. The legal proceedings herein referred to shall include appropriate proceedings to review tax assessments and appeals from orders therein and appeals from any judgments, decrees, or orders, but all such proceedings shall be begun as soon as possible after the imposition or assessment of any contested item and shall be prosecuted to final adjudication with dispatch. If there shall be any refund with respect to any contested item based on a payment by Tenant, Tenant shall be entitled to the same to the extent of such payment, subject to apportionment as provided in Section 3.02.

Section 3.04. Nothing herein contained shall require or be construed to require Tenant to pay any inheritance, estate, succession, transfer, gift, franchise, corporation, income, excess profits tax, or capital levy that is or may be imposed upon Landlord, provided, however, that if at any time during the term of this lease the methods of taxation prevailing at the commencement of the term hereof shall be altered so that in lieu of or as a substitute for the whole or any part of the taxes, assessments, levies, impositions, or charges now levied, assessed, or imposed on real estate and the improvements thereon, there shall be levied, assessed, and imposed (a) a tax, assessment, levy, imposition, or charge, wholly or partially as a capital levy or otherwise, on the rents received therefrom, or (b) a tax, assessment, levy (including but not limited to any municipal, state, or federal levy), imposition, or charge measured by or based in whole or in part upon the Demised Premises and imposed upon Landlord, or (c) a license fee measured by the rent payable by Tenant under this lease, then to the extent that such taxes, assessments, levies, impositions, charges, or license fees or the part thereof so measured or based, would be payable if the Demised Premises were the only property of Landlord subject thereto, Tenant shall pay and discharge the same as herein provided.

Tenant, such franchises, if any, as may be appurtenant to the use of the Demised Premises, this transaction, or all stamp or like taxes on any document to which Tenant is a party, creating or transferring an interest or estate in the Demised Premises, and all taxes charged, laid, levied, assessed, or imposed in lieu of or in addition to the foregoing under or by virtue of all present or future laws, ordinances, requirements, orders, directions, rules, or regulations of the federal, state, county, and municipal governments, and of all other governmental authorities whatsoever, and all fees and charges of public and governmental authorities for construction, maintenance, occupation, or use during the term of any vault, passageway, or space in, over, or under any sidewalk or street on or adjacent to the Demised Premises, or for construction, maintenance, or use during the term of any part of any building covered hereby within the limits of any street. To the extent that the same may be permitted by law and shall not be inconsistent with any existing or future mortgage or mortgages affecting the Demised Premises, Tenant shall have the right to take advantage of any provision of law or ordinance permitting any special assessment for local improvements to be paid in installments, and Tenant shall thereafter be obligated to pay and discharge punctually only such of said installments as shall become due and payable during the term. Tenant shall within twenty (20) days after the time above provided for the payment by Tenant of any such tax, assessment, water rent, rate, or charge, sewer rent, or other governmental levy, imposition, or charge, produce and exhibit to Landlord satisfactory evidence of such payment.

Section 3.02. All such taxes, water rents, rates, and charges, sewer rents, and other governmental levies, impositions, and charges which shall be charged, laid, levied, assessed, or imposed for the fiscal period in which the term of this lease terminates shall be apportioned pro rata between Landlord and Tenant in accordance with the portion of such fiscal period during which such term shall be in effect.

Section 3.03. Tenant shall have the right to contest or review by legal proceedings, or in such other manner as it may deem suitable (which, if instituted, Tenant shall conduct promptly at its own expense, and free of any expense to Landlord, and, if necessary, in the name of Landlord), any tax, assessment, water rent, rate, or charge, sewer rent, or other governmental levy, imposition, or charge aforementioned. Tenant may defer payment of a contested item upon condition that, before instituting any such proceedings, Tenant shall furnish to Landlord, or to any mortgagee Landlord may designate, a surety company bond, a cash deposit, or other security satisfactory to Landlord and

or mortgage payments which Landlord shall have so failed to pay, together with interest, penalties, or late charges thereon, if any, and deduct the amount so paid, with interest thereon at six percent (6%) per annum from the date of such payment, from the next succeeding installments of net rent and/or from any deposits under Section 2.04 that would otherwise be due and payable by Tenant to Landlord.

Section 2.06. All taxes, charges, costs, and expenses which Tenant assumes or agrees to pay under any provisions of this lease, together with all interest and penalties that may accrue thereon in the event of Tenant's failure to pay the same as herein provided, all other damages, costs, and expenses which Landlord may suffer or incur, and any and all other sums which may become due by reason of any default of Tenant or failure on Tenant's part to comply with the agreements, terms, covenants, and conditions of this lease on Tenant's part to be performed, and each or any of them, shall be deemed to be additional rent and, in the event of nonpayment, Landlord shall have all the rights and remedies herein provided in the case of nonpayment of rent.

ARTICLE 3
Taxes and Other Charges

Section 3.01. Tenant shall, in the manner described in Section 2.04 hereof, but whether or not the deposits therein provided are sufficient therefor, bear, pay, and discharge, on or before the last day on which payment may be made without penalty or interest, all taxes, assessments, water rents, rates and charges, sewer rents, transit taxes, charges for public utilities, excises, levies, license and permit fees, and other governmental impositions and charges of every kind and nature whatsoever, extraordinary as well as ordinary, foreseen or unforeseen, and each and every installment thereof, which shall or may, on the first day of the month on which net rent shall first become payable as provided in Subparagraph (b) of Section 2.01 hereof or on such earlier date when Landlord shall have paid since the date hereof an aggregate of Fifty-Seven Thousand Four Hundred Thirty-Nine and $^{78}/_{100}$ Dollars ($57,439.78) for real estate taxes and insurance premiums on the Demised Premises, and thereafter during the term, be charged, laid, levied, assessed, imposed, become due and payable, or liens upon, or arise in connection with the use, occupancy, or possession of, or grow due or payable out of or for the Demised Premises or any part thereof, or any buildings, appurtenances, or equipment thereon or therein or any part thereof, or the sidewalks or streets in front of or adjoining the Demised Premises, or the rent, income, or other payments received from subtenants by Tenant or anyone claiming by, through, or under

Landlord a sum equal to one-twelfth ($\frac{1}{12}$) of the next annual payment of the taxes falling due, plus one-twelfth ($\frac{1}{12}$) of the total annual insurance premiums required to be paid by Tenant under said Article 9. In the event that the amount on deposit with Landlord shall be insufficient to pay any installment of taxes or any insurance premium when the same shall become due and payable, then Tenant shall forthwith deposit with Landlord the deficiency. In the event that the amount of the taxes against the Demised Premises or insurance premiums for insurance required to be furnished under Article 9 hereof have not been fixed at the time when any such monthly deposit is herein required to be made, Tenant shall make such deposit based upon the amount of the taxes payable with respect to the Demised Premises during the preceding year and upon the amount of the insurance premiums last payable. If at any time the amounts held by Landlord under this Section, plus all amounts payable by Tenant hereunder during the next twelve (12) months, shall be more than sufficient to make timely payments of the taxes and insurance premiums payable during that period, then the excess will be credited toward payment of the next deposits to be made hereunder.

Notwithstanding the foregoing provisions of this Section 2.04, if the provisions of the Long-Term Mortgage require deposits for taxes or insurance premiums to be made with the holder of such mortgage instead of with Landlord, Tenant shall make such deposits with Landlord at least twenty (20) days before they are required to be made with the holder of such mortgage, and Landlord will pay the same over to such holder when due.

Section 2.05. So long as Tenant shall continue to make due and prompt payment of net rent under Section 2.01 and deposits under Section 2.04, Landlord shall promptly pay the taxes and insurance premiums covered by such deposits and payments on the Long-Term Mortgage as and when the same severally become due and payable and shall promptly forward to Tenant receipted bills or other satisfactory evidence showing such payment, and Tenant shall not be required to furnish the proof of payment of such taxes provided for in Section 3.01 hereof or proof of payment of insurance premiums. If Tenant shall have paid the net rent and made the deposits herein provided for, and if Landlord shall have failed to pay any installment of taxes prior to the time when any interest or penalty would accrue thereon, or any insurance premium prior to the time when the same is due and payable, or any payment on the Long-Term Mortgage at least three (3) days prior to the expiration of the applicable grace period, Tenant may, at its option, on notice to Landlord, pay any such taxes, insurance premiums,

the adjustment made pursuant to Section 2.01(d)(ii), plus (ii) the amount then payable under Section 2.01 (c).

(f) The provisions of Section 2.01 (c), (d), and (e) are subject to further adjustment under the circumstances described in Section 11.04 in the manner therein provided.

(g) Whenever the rent shall be adjusted under any of the foregoing Subparagraphs (c), (d), (e), or (f), the parties will enter into a further supplement to this lease exactly fixing the amount of the monthly net rent effective on the first day of the month in which such computation is to be made.

Section 2.02. It is the purpose and intent of Landlord and Tenant that the net rent shall be net to Landlord, so that this lease shall yield, net, to Landlord, the net rent specified in Section 2.01 hereof in each month during the term of this lease, and that all costs, expenses, and charges of every kind and nature relating to the Demised Premises (except the taxes of Landlord referred to in Section 3.04 of Article 3 hereof, and any payments on account of interest or principal under any mortgage or deed of trust which shall be a lien on the fee of the Demised Premises) which may arise or become due during the initial term or any renewal term of this lease shall be paid by Tenant, and that Landlord shall be indemnified and saved harmless by Tenant from and against the same.

Section 2.03. The net rent shall be paid to Landlord without notice or demand and without abatement, deduction, or setoff, except as otherwise expressly provided in this lease.

Section 2.04. On the first day of the month on which Tenant shall first become obligated under Section 3.01 hereof to pay real estate taxes and other charges and under Section 9.01 hereof to pay insurance premiums, Tenant shall deposit with Landlord a sum equal to the aggregate of one-twelfth ($1/12$) of the next annual payment of real estate taxes and other charges falling due, which are payable as additional rent under Article 3 hereof (hereafter in this Section 2.04 collectively referred to as a "tax" or "taxes"), multiplied, as to each such tax, by the number of months (including any fraction of a month as a whole month) intervening between and including the month in which the previous installment of such tax became due and payable and the first day of the month following the month in which such deposit is to be made, together with the accrued insurance premiums payable by Tenant under Article 9 hereof, computed from the last day on which each such premium was paid to the said first day of the month following the month in which such deposit is to be made. Thereafter, on the first day of each and every month during the term, Tenant shall deposit with

Premises shall be rented to subtenants who have become obligated to commence paying subrent thereon (the initial payments made on the execution of their subleases to be treated as paid on the days on which they are applied to subrent under the terms of such subleases); or

   (iii) April 1, 1968;

net rent shall be computed at the monthly rate of Thirty-six Thousand Nine Hundred Seventeen Dollars ($36,917), subject to adjustment as provided in the following sentence and in Subparagraph (d) hereof. In the event, however, that Landlord's Unrecovered Costs, as defined and determined under the provisions of the First Supplement hereto, shall be less than Two Million Seven Hundred Thousand Dollars ($2,700,000), the monthly net rent so computed shall be reduced by three-quarters of one percent (.75%) of the difference or by Twenty Thousand Two Hundred Fifty Dollars ($20,250), whichever is less.

  (d) (i) Commencing on the date on which the Long-Term Mortgage shall be placed, if that be the first day of a month, otherwise on the first day of the following month and on the first day of each month thereafter and continuing until the first day of the first month which shall be a full thirty (30) years after the placing of the Long-Term Mortgage, net rent shall be computed at the monthly rate of One Hundred Seventy-one Thousand Nine Hundred Seventeen Dollars ($171,917), less any adjustment theretofore made or thereafter to be made pursuant to the last sentence of the foregoing Subparagraph (c).

  (ii) If, however, the aggregate annual payments of principal and interest payable under the terms of the Long-Term Mortgage shall, at any time, be greater or less than One Million Six Hundred Twenty Thousand Dollars ($1,620,000), the monthly net rent so computed shall then be increased or decreased, as the case may be, by one-twelfth ($1/12$) of the difference.

  (iii) If the Long-Term Mortgage shall be placed on a date other than the first day of a month, on such date Tenant shall pay as rent an amount equal to interest on the Long-Term Mortgage computed from such date until the first day of the following month, it being the intention of this Subparagraph (d) that Tenant shall pay as net rent each month, in addition to the amount computed as provided in Subparagraph (c) hereof, a proportionate amount of the next payment of principal and/or interest next becoming due on the Long-Term Mortgage.

  (e) Beginning on the first day of the first month which shall be a full thirty (30) years after the placing of the Long-Term Mortgage, the monthly net rent shall be (i) Sixty-seven Thousand Five Hundred Dollars ($67,500) plus or minus, as the case may be, 50 percent (50%) of

hereof with the same force and effect as though herein at length set forth;

TO HAVE AND TO HOLD the Demised Premises for the term of thirty-five (35) years to commence on the fifteenth day of............, ... and to end on the fourteenth day of ...., ..., both dates inclusive (unless such term shall be renewed or sooner terminated as hereinafter provided), upon the following agreements, terms, covenants, and conditions.

ARTICLE 2
Rent and Deposits for Taxes and Insurance

Section 2.01. Tenant covenants and agrees to pay to Landlord, in such coin or currency of the United States of America as at the time of payment shall be legal tender for the payment of public and private debts, at Landlord's address specified in or furnished pursuant to Article 26 hereof, during the term, a net rental computed as hereinafter provided. Such net rental (hereinafter called the "net rent") shall be in addition to all other payments to be made by Tenant as hereinafter provided and shall be paid monthly in advance on the first day of each calendar month during the term of this lease. The net rent shall be computed in the following manner:

(a) From the date hereof until net rent shall become payable under the following Subparagraph (b), there shall be no net rent due or payable.

(b) Whenever subtenants shall be obligated under the terms of their subleases to pay subrents, which, computed on a monthly basis, should be in an amount at least equal to the net rent as computed in this Subparagraph (b) (the initial payments made on the execution of their subleases to be treated as paid on the days on which they are applied to subrent under the terms of such subleases) and continuing until net rent shall become payable under the following Subparagraph (c), net rent shall be paid each month in the amount by which a fraction of the monthly rent computed at the rate provided in the following Subparagraph (c) for such month exceeds Thirteen Thousand Dollars ($13,000). The numerator of such fraction shall be the number of square feet of space rented to subtenants who have, on the first day of such month, become obligated to commence paying rent thereon, and denominator of such fraction shall be 1,200,000.

(c) From and after the earliest of:

(i) a date twenty-four (24) months after construction of the Project commences;

(ii) the date when 700,000 square feet of space in the Demised

THIS INDENTURE OF LEASE made as of the .... day of
............, 19..., between ....Co., a general
partnership organized and existing under the laws of the State of
.... (whose partners are A and B), having its principal office in the City and County of ....,
...................., party of the first part, hereinafter referred to as
"Landlord", and ...., Ltd., a limited partnership, organized and existing under the laws of the State of ....
and having its principal office at ....
...................., party of the second part, hereinafter referred to
as "Tenant":

WHEREAS, by deed bearing even date herewith Partner A, for and on behalf of Landlord, acquired title to the premises hereinafter described on which Landlord desires to erect and construct a retail shopping center complex, hereinafter called "the Project", containing approximately 1,200,000 square feet of rentable space and providing parking space in the ratio of 2½ square feet thereof to each square foot of such rentable space, which shall thereafter be operated by Tenant; and

WHEREAS, the parties hereto are simultaneously herewith entering into a First Supplement hereto providing for the erection and construction of the Project by Tenant acting for and on behalf of Landlord and the means by which the Project shall be paid for and financed, such supplement and any other agreements supplemental hereto or in modification or amendment hereof being hereinafter included in the term "this lease" as used herein.

Now, THEREFORE, this Indenture,

WITNESSETH:

That in consideration of the premises and of the mutual covenants and agreements herein and in said supplemental agreement contained:

ARTICLE 1
Demised Premises—Term of Lease

Section 1.01. Landlord hereby demises and leases to Tenant, and Tenant hereby hires and takes from Landlord, the premises described in Schedule A hereto annexed and made part hereof with the same force and effect as though herein at length set forth, which premises are hereinafter called "the Demised Premises";

SUBJECT to the estates, interests, liens, charges, encumbrances, and matters set forth in Schedule B hereto annexed and made part

INDEX

ARTICLE		PAGE
1	Demised Premises—Term of Lease	App. B-114
2	Rent and Deposits for Taxes and Insurance	App. B-115
3	Taxes and Other Charges	App. B-119
4	Assignments, Leasehold Mortgages, and Subleases; Operation Statements	App. B-122
5	Alterations	App. B-130
6	Repairs	App. B-132
7	Mechanics' and Other Liens	App. B-132
8	Requirements of Law	App. B-133
9	Insurance	App. B-134
10	Destruction—Fire or Other Causes	App. B-137
11	Condemnation	App. B-141
12	Subordination	App. B-145
13	Landlord Not Liable for Injury or Damage	App. B-148
14	No Rent Abatement	App. B-148
15	Access to Premises	App. B-148
16	Vaults	App. B-149
17	No Unlawful Occupancy	App. B-149
18	Indemnity	App. B-149
19	Default	App. B-150
20	No Representations by Landlord	App. B-156
21	End of Term	App. B-156
22	Quiet Enjoyment	App. B-157
23	Renewal Privileges	App. B-157
24	Arbitration	App. B-158
25	Estoppel Certificate	App. B-160
26	Notices	App. B-160
27	Rights of Leasehold Mortgagee	App. B-161
28	Shoring	App. B-163
29	Definitions	App. B-163
30	Land to Be Conveyed to the City	App. B-166
31	Lease of Adjacent Land	App. B-166
32	Option Agreement on Portion of Demised Premises	App. B-167
33	Miscellaneous	App. B-169
	Signatures	App. B-172
	Acknowledgements	App. B-172
	SCHEDULE A	App. B-173
	SCHEDULE B	App. B-173

the parties hereto immediately upon such substitute lessor succeeding to the interest of the Landlord under said Sublease provided, however, that the Tenant shall be under no obligation to pay rent to such substitute lessor until Tenant receives written notice from such substitute lessor that it has succeeded to the interest of the Landlord under the said Sublease.

5. Tenant hereby waives the provisions of any statute or rule of law now or hereafter in effect which may give or purport to give it any right or election to terminate or otherwise adversely affect its said Sublease and the obligations of Tenant thereunder by reason of the termination of said Ground Lease or any foreclosure proceeding.

6. This agreement may not be altered, modified, or amended except in writing signed by all the parties hereto.

7. This agreement shall be binding upon the parties, their respective heirs, successors and assigns.

IN WITNESS WHEREOF, the parties hereto have set their hands and seals the day and year first above written.

....
....
                              ....Insurance Company
....

COMMENT: See discussion at ¶ 6.02[2][6].

Form 6.2

GROUND LEASE ON UNSUBORDINATED FEE

LEASE

Landlord: .... Company

Tenant: ...., Ltd.

Demised Premises: ....
....
.... County,
.... State.

Dated: As of ...., ...

WHEREAS, Landlord entered into a Sublease with Tenant dated ...., by which Landlord leased to Tenant space located in the aforesaid premises, and

WHEREAS, Mortgagee as a condition to making a mortgage loan on said premises has requested the execution of this Agreement.

NOW, THEREFORE, in consideration of the mutual covenants and agreements herein contained and to induce Mortgagee to make said mortgage loan upon said premises and in consideration of the sum of One Dollar ($1.00) by each of and the parties hereto paid to the other, receipt thereof is hereby acknowledged, the parties do hereby covenant and agree as follows:

1. Ground Lessor agrees that so long as tenant is not in default in the payment of rent or additional rent, or in the performance of any of the terms, covenants, and conditions of the Sublease on the Tenant's part to be performed. Tenant's possession of the premises and its rights and privileges under the Sublease, or any renewal thereof, shall not be diminished or interfered with by Ground Lessor.

2. So long as Tenant is not in default beyond any period given to cure such default in the performance of any of the terms, covenants, or conditions of said Sublease on the Tenant's part to be performed, Mortgagee will not join Tenant as a party defendant in any action or proceeding for the purpose of terminating Tenant's interest and estate under said Sublease in the event of default under the mortgage or otherwise.

3. Tenant agrees that in the event said Ground Lease is terminated for any reason other than the expiration of the term or any extension of the term thereof, or in the event any proceedings are brought for the foreclosure of said mortgage, it does hereby attorn to the Ground Lessor, its successors and assigns (successors and assigns being herein defined to include Mortgagee and/or Purchaser at any foreclosure sale of the premises), said Ground Lessor, its successors and assigns being deemed to have assumed and agreed to be bound, as substitute lessor, by the terms and conditions of said Sublease until the resale or other disposition of the interest of the Ground Lessor, its successors and assigns, in said premises, except that such assumption shall not be deemed of itself an acknowledgment by the Ground Lessor, its successors and assigns, of the validity of any then existing claims of Tenant against the prior Landlord; all rights and obligations under said Sublease to continue as though said Ground Lease had not terminated or such foreclosure proceedings had not been brought, except as aforesaid.

4. Tenant's attornment by these presents is effective and self-operative without the execution of any other instruments on the part of

remedies set forth in the Commitment, including the provision for liquidated damages, shall not constitute the only remedies available to the Permanent Lender in the case of any breach of this agreement by the Temporary Lender or the Borrower.

Tenth: Construction of Agreement. This agreement shall be construed in accordance with the laws of the State of ....

IN WITNESS WHEREOF, the parties have duly executed this agreement the day and year first above written.

By: ....
Vice-President

By: ....
.... Life Insurance Company

By: ....
Vice-President

COMMENT: See discussion of Buy-Sell Agreement at ¶¶ 3.04[14], 4.05.

Form 6.1

ATTORNMENT AND NONDISTURBANCE AGREEMENT BETWEEN GROUND LESSOR, TENANT AND MORTGAGEE

THIS AGREEMENT made and entered into the .... day of ...., 19...., by and between .... (hereinafter called Tenant), ... (hereinafter called Ground Lessor) and .... Insurance Company, a .... corporation (hereinafter called Mortgagee),

WITNESSETH:

WHEREAS, the Ground Lessor is owner of the fee simple title to the premises situated at ...., known as .... and more particularly described in the Ground Lease dated ...., between Ground Lessor and ...., Ground Lessee (hereinafter called Landlord), for a term of .... (....) years, which Lease is recorded in .... (hereinafter called Ground Lease) and

Loan Note nor will it assign, transfer, or sell the Building Loan Note and the Building Loan Mortgage to anyone else, unless it shall have received written notice from the Permanent Lender that the Commitment has been cancelled by the Permanent Lender in accordance with the provisions thereof relating to such cancellation and termination. The provisions of the preceding sentence are subject to any requirement of law that the disposition of the assets of the Temporary Lender shall at all times be and remain within its control. The Borrower hereby confirms and consents to such agreement on the part of the Temporary Lender and warrants that it will not accept a first mortgage loan upon the aforesaid real property from any other lender during the term of the Commitment or any extension thereof by the Permanent Lender.

Fifth: Notices. All notices, demands, and requests hereunder shall be in writing and shall be deemed to have been properly given if sent by United States registered or certified mail, postage prepaid, addressed to the parties at the respective addresses set forth at the beginning of this agreement, or such other address as any of the parties may from time to time designate by written notice given as herein required. Notices, demands, and requests given in the manner aforesaid shall be deemed sufficiently served or given for all purposes hereunder at the time such notice, demand, or request shall be deposited in any post office or branch post office regularly maintained by the United States Government.

Sixth: Definitions. As used herein, the term "note" shall mean a note or a bond, and the term "mortgage" shall mean a mortgage or a deed of trust, as the Permanent Lender shall require.

Seventh: No Oral Modification. This agreement may not be changed, terminated or modified orally or in any other manner than by an agreement in writing signed by the parties hereto.

Eighth: Binding Effect. The covenants, agreements, rights, and options contained in this agreement shall be binding upon and inure to the benefit of the respective heirs, executors, successors, and assigns of the parties hereto and all persons claiming by, through, or under any of them.

Ninth: Specific Performance. Each party hereto shall be entitled to specific performance of the covenants, agreements, rights, and options contained in this agreement. It is the expressed intent of all parties hereto that the remedies of the Permanent Lender under the Commitment and the right of the Permanent Lender to resort to specific performance as herein provided shall be cumulative and that the

all of the terms and conditions of the Commitment and of this agreement, the Permanent Lender agrees to purchase from the Temporary Lender, the Building Loan Note and the Building Loan Mortgage. The Permanent Lender agrees to pay to the Temporary Lender for the Building Loan Note and the Building Loan Mortgage the aggregate of the Temporary Lender's principal advances under the Building Loan Agreement, in no event, however, to exceed the sum of .... Dollars ($............), or, if the requirement of Condition No. ...... of the Commitment shall not have been fulfilled, ... Dollars ($............), and the Temporary Lender will assign the Building Loan Note and the Building Loan Mortgage to the Permanent Lender by an assignment in form and substance satisfactory to the Permanent Lender. The Borrower and the Temporary Lender agree to furnish the Permanent Lender with such certificates of estoppel or no-defense as the Permanent Lender may reasonably require at the time of assignment. All fees and expenses connected with the sale and assignment shall be paid by the Borrower.

Second: Closing. The closing of the purchase and sale of the Building Loan Note and the Building Loan Mortgage (the "Closing") shall take place at the office of ...., at No. ...., or at such other place as may be designated by the Permanent Lender.

Third: Modification and Extension Agreement. On the Closing, the Borrower shall execute and deliver such modification and extension, if any, of the Building Loan Note and the Building Loan Mortgage as may be required to conform the terms thereof to the terms of the Commitment, and such other documents as are provided to be executed and delivered by the Borrower in accordance with the provisions of the Commitment, all in form and substance satisfactory to the Permanent Lender, and shall otherwise perform and observe all of the requirements of the Commitment on the part of the Borrower to be performed and observed. Prior to the Closing, the Building Loan Note and the Building Loan Mortgage may be modified or amended only with the prior written consent of the Permanent Lender.

Fourth: Restriction on Sale of Building Loan Note and Building Loan Mortgage. The Temporary Lender, in consideration, among other things, of this agreement on the part of the Permanent Lender to purchase the Building Loan Note and the Building Loan Mortgage at the price and upon the terms set forth herein, agrees that it will not accept payment of the principal indebtedness evidenced by the Building

WITNESSETH:

WHEREAS,

1. Heretofore and by agreement in writing dated ....,
19...., (the "Commitment"), made between the Permanent Lender and the Borrower, the Permanent Lender, subject to the terms and conditions set forth in the Commitment, agreed to make a loan to the Borrower in the sum of .... Dollars ($............), or in the lesser sum of .... Dollars ($............) if the requirements of Condition No. ...... of the commitment are not met, to be secured by a first mortgage upon certain described real property located at ....

2. The Commitment requires that the Borrower shall procure from the Lender furnishing the interim or construction financing an agreement, in form and substance satisfactory to the Permanent Lender, pursuant to which such Interim Lender shall agree to sell, assign, and transfer to the Permanent Lender, but subject nevertheless to compliance by the Borrower with all of the terms, provisions, covenants, and conditions of the commitment, any building loan note and mortgage executed and delivered by the Borrower to such Interim Lender.

3. The Temporary Lender and the Borrower have entered into an agreement (the "Building Loan Agreement") to provide the Borrower with funds for the construction of a .... upon the land described in the Commitment, and pursuant to the Building Loan Agreement the Borrower has executed and delivered its note or notes (collectively, the "Building Loan Note") in the sum of .... Dollars ($............), bearing interest at the rate of .... percent (....%) per annum, said Building Loan Note being secured by a first mortgage (the "Building Loan Mortgage") upon the aforesaid real property.

4. The Permanent Lender has approved the Building Loan Note and the Building Loan Mortgage, copies of which are annexed hereto as Exhibits A and B and made a part hereof.

5. This agreement is being executed and delivered by the parties in compliance with the aforesaid requirement contained in the Commitment.

NOW, THEREFORE, in consideration of the issuance of the Commitment by the Permanent Lender to the Borrower, and for other good and valuable consideration, the receipt whereof is hereby acknowledged, the parties hereto agree as follows:

First: Purchase and Sale. The Temporary Lender agrees to sell to the Permanent Lender, and subject to compliance by the Borrower with

(a) Allocation of miscellaneous funds from the Miscellaneous Code to some specific Construction Code contained in the Cost Breakdown by virtue of a change-order (AIA Form G701), which results in a cost increase within such specific Construction Code;

(b) Allocation of miscellaneous funds from the Miscellaneous Code to some specific "soft-cost" (nonconstruction) code (such as "Interest") by virtue of written approval of such allocation by Lender after written request for such allocation by Borrower.

PROVIDED, HOWEVER, that nothing by reason of any adjustment in the Categories of Nonconstruction Code Breakdown which may be made between Borrower and Lender from time to time shall constitute a waiver of Lender's right to insist that the monies thereafter be disbursed solely for the purposes intended hereby and *IN NO EVENT SHALL THE LENDER BE CALLED UPON TO ADVANCE ANY FURTHER MONIES UNLESS AND UNTIL THE BORROWER HAS TIMELY MET ALL CONDITIONS PRECEDENT TO COMMENCEMENT OF RENOVATION, AND SAID RENOVATION BASED UPON PERMITS, WHERE APPLICABLE, HAS BEEN COMMENCED AND IS IN PROGRESS.*

EXHIBIT B

This Exhibit, if an owner-builder is involved, lists a trade payments breakdown. Where a separate General Contractor is employed, a copy of the Construction Contract is attached.

COMMENTS: See discussion of Building Loan Agreement at ¶¶ 4.02[9], 4.04.

Form 4.2

BUY-SELL AGREEMENT

AGREEMENT made as of the .... day of ...., 19...., between and among .... a .... having its principal place of business at No. .... (the "Temporary Lender"), ... (the "Borrower"), and .... Life Insurance Company, a corporation having its principal place of business at ...., (the "Permanent Lender"),

IN WITNESS WHEREOF, this Building Loan Agreement executed as of the day and year aforesaid by Borrower and Lender.

WITNESS

.... By: ....
                                                                                                       General Partner

WITNESS

.... By: ....
                                                                                                        General Partner

EXHIBIT A

Nonconstruction Cost Breakdown

Item	*Amount*	*Initial Draw*	*Balance*
Land Acquisition Costs			
Interest			
Miscellaneous			
WSSC Permits			
Totals	_____	_____	_____

The balance to be drawn on account of the above items may only be taken down when Borrower is current and in good standing in all respects under the Promissory Note, Mortgage, this Loan Agreement, and any collateral and/or supporting documents, upon requisition in form satisfactory to Lender, at the following time or times, to wit:

1. Interest during construction may only be taken down from month to month, as interest expense is actually incurred and paid by Borrower to Lender, it being the case that the obligations of Borrower to pay interest is not conditioned upon the disbursement of the funds allocated for subject purpose. At any time, Lender can, without cause or accounting to Borrower, discontinue interest disbursements and/or reallocate interest to another construction or nonconstruction code and require Borrower to pay for interest with funds from nonloan sources.
2. Borrower's Architect's Fees shall be disbursed during construction in proportion to the work completed from time to time.
3. Reduction or use of the Miscellaneous Code may be accomplished by:

and use of Lender and in no event shall Lender be construed to be Borrower's agent, and in no event is Lender assuming Borrower's responsibility for proper payments to Contractor and others. It is specifically further intended that no party shall be a third party beneficiary hereunder except and unless it is specifically provided herein that any provision shall operate or inure to the use and benefit of a party, i.e., no subcontractor, or material supplier shall have any rights hereunder against Lender, or be entitled to the protection of any of the covenants herein contained, although such parties may have recourse to Borrower and/or Contractor as the case may be.

ARTICLE 26

This Building Loan Agreement and every undertaking made pursuant hereto is executed in behalf of .... by one or more officers or agents of the Bank in his or their capacity as such and not individually, and the obligations thereof shall be understood and expressly stated not to be binding upon any of the shareholders, officers, or agents of the Bank in his or their capacity as such and not individually, and the obligations thereof shall be understood and expressly stated not to be binding upon any of the shareholders, officers, or agents of the Bank, personally, but binding only upon the Assets of ....

ARTICLE 27

In the event that Lender is desirous of giving any notice to Borrower, the same may be given to any officer, director, partner, or agent of Borrower in person, or may be sent by registered or certified mail to Borrower at ...., ..., and such notice shall be deemed given when so personally delivered, subject to the proviso that where anything may be set forth and contained in said Application which is not set forth in the Note, Deed of Trust, and this Building Loan Agreement, or which is more expansive than any provisions of the latter three (3) documents, the provisions of the Application will be in effect, but wherever there may be any conflict between provisions of the Application and the Note, Deed of Trust, and Building Loan Agreement, or any Collateral Loan Document, the documents other than the Application shall be governing.

ARTICLE 28

This Building Loan Agreement shall be binding upon and inure to the use and benefit of Borrower and Lender and their respective heirs, legal representatives, successors, and assigns.

the Improvements, employing Borrower's Contractor or such other Contractor as Lender may deem appropriate and in its own best interest to complete the Improvements, and Borrower hereby gives Lender full power and authority to make such entry and to enter into such contract arrangements as may be necessary to complete the Improvements, and in this event, Lender shall be entitled to have any of the remaining undisbursed funds, whether cash deposited by Borrower or undisbursed loan proceeds (Construction and Nonconstruction) disbursed to it or under its direction in the payment of bills theretofore or thereafter contracted in connection with the construction, it is hereby expressly agreed between the parties hereto that all work remaining to be done and material still to be furnished shall be considered as work necessary for the conservation and preservation of the Project, and all sums advanced for such purposes over and above the total of the funds placed in escrow and the balance of loan proceeds, including reasonable attorneys' fees incurred by Lender incident to such default and completion of such construction or incident to the enforcement of any provision hereof, shall be an indebtedness of Borrower to Lender even though they may, when added to the monies advanced and disbursed under this Agreement, exceed the amount of the Note and Deed of Trust and shall be secured by the lien of the Deed of Trust as though same was part of the debt originally described and secured thereby, all of which are due and payable to Lender immediately, although the amount advanced in excess of the original principal sum of this loan shall not exceed 125 percent (125%) of the principal amount of the Note, and all such advances shall bear interest at the rate specified in the Note.

ARTICLE 24

In the event that Borrower shall default in any manner under the terms, provisions, and conditions of the Note, Deed of Trust, or this Building Loan Agreement, Lender shall have all the rights, privileges, options, and remedies reserved to it under said Note, Deed of Trust, and this Building Loan Agreement, and in addition, shall be entitled to cancel this Agreement by notice to Borrower, and/or by appropriate action to enforce such performance and correction of such defaults, and/or declare the amount of principal and interest secured by the Note, Deed of Trust, and this Building Loan Agreement due and payable and in default, and proceed to collect the same by foreclosure or other remedy.

ARTICLE 25

All of the terms, provisions, conditions, and requirements made and set forth herein by Lender are for the sole and exclusive protection

critical times during construction to determine that the work is progressing in a timely manner and in compliance with the Plans and Specifications and to certify with each requisition of loan proceeds that all construction to date of requisition has been completed to the extent indicated in Contractor's Requisition and if such be the case, indicating any variances where the amount approved may be less than that requisitioned by the Contractor, and that the work to the extent so indicated is in accordance with the Plans and Specifications and to furnish Lender with full and complete reports on construction, for all of which Architect shall look solely to Borrower for payment of any fees, and not to Lender or Project.

ARTICLE 23

In addition to any other right hereinbefore reserved unto Lender for default of Borrower, without benefit of notice or grace period, if Borrower's Contractor shall fail to perform according to the terms of the Building Loan Agreement or permits conditions to arise or exist so that performance will be rendered difficult or hazardous for Lender, or if Borrower shall fail, neglect or refuse to perform either or any of Borrower's promises or agreements hereunder, or breach any promises, covenants, warrants, or agreements made hereby or made under the Note hereinabove mentioned or the Deed of Trust securing the same, or under any other collateral loan documents, or if it becomes apparent in the sole judgment of Lender that Borrower's Contractor will not complete said buildings and Improvements within the time specified herein, or if construction shall cease before completion and remain abandoned for a period of ten (10) days, or if Borrower or any endorser and guarantor of the Note should become insolvent or make an assignment for the benefit of creditors, or if an involuntary petition in bankruptcy is filed against or a voluntary petition in bankruptcy is filed by the Borrower or any endorser or guarantor of the Note, or if a conservator or trustee is appointed for the assets of Borrower or any endorser or guarantor of the Note, then in any of such events, Borrower shall be considered in default hereunder, and Lender may, at its option, without benefit of any notice or grace period, withhold further disbursements hereunder, and in addition to all other remedies provided by the Mortgage Loan Documents and by law, either:

A. Declare all sums evidenced by the Note hereinabove mentioned and secured by said Deed of Trust and all sums hereunder to be immediately due and payable and unless the same are paid on demand, foreclose said Deed of Trust; or

B. Enter into and upon the Project and complete construction of

day of a month, and shall be furnished to Borrower and Borrower's Request for Disbursement and Contractor's Requisition furnished to Lender on or about the first day of the following month, and in any event the same shall be furnished to Lender in no less than five (5) business days prior to the date on which any advance is desired, and an executed copy of the same shall be simultaneously furnished to Borrower's Architect. Such documents shall further be accompanied by the following:

(i) Certificate of Borrower's Architect in form acceptable to Lender;

(ii) Contractor's receipt and partial Release of Lien for all funds previously disbursed on account of construction of the Improvements and evidence from Borrower or Contractor, or both, of the payment of bills for work, labor, material, supplies, and equipment for all sums advanced through the last prior request for disbursement and Contractor's Requisition. Final payment shall be not less than .... percent (....%) of the original Construction Fund.

K. All payments may be made by Lender at its discretion to Borrower, or Contractor, or to Borrower and Contractor jointly, or to the Borrower, Contractor and its Subcontractors and Material Suppliers where circumstances so warrant in the sole judgment of the Lender.

ARTICLE 20

Where any disbursing agent is utilized, whether Title Company or other party, such party shall procure and deliver an Insured Closing Letter to Lender in form and content required by Lender and such other Instrument as Lender may require whereby the disbursing agent agrees to receive and handle the funds in compliance with the provisions of this Building Loan Agreement and acknowledges that it will not commingle any funds received with its own funds, and that the same will be disbursed in account or accounts used as a fiduciary for escrow or loan disbursement purposes.

ARTICLE 21

In the event Borrower fails to construct and complete said Improvements in accordance with the terms and provisions of this Building Loan Agreement, Borrower hereby assigns to Lender the right to possess and use the Plans and Specifications for the purpose of completing said Improvements.

ARTICLE 22

Borrower shall cause its Architect, at Borrower's expense, to make regular inspections of the site as construction progresses and at all

tractor to prepare and submit to Lender a written schedule, in Affidavit form where required by Lender, setting forth the name and address of each party employed as a Subcontractor and/or Material Supplier in connection with construction of the Improvements, the amount of such Subcontract or Material Purchase Order, and the status of performance and payment under each Subcontract and Material Purchase Order, and, where requested by Lender, Borrower shall cause Contractor to furnish to Lender and Contractor shall furnish to Lender, signed copies of each and every Subcontract and/or Material Purchase Order. And, Lender is hereby given the right by Borrower and Contractor to make inquiry of all Subcontractors and Material Suppliers to verify and determine the status of all matters pertaining to Subcontracts and Material Purchase Orders.

I. As a condition to final advance of the Construction Fund, which will include final advance to Contractor under the Construction Contract, Lender shall be furnished by Contractor with Final Contractor's Affidavit as required under the Mechanic's Lien Law of the .... of .... and Contractor's final release of Lien. In addition to Lender being furnished with Certificates of Substantial Completion by Borrower's Architect, Lender's independent Architect or Construction Inspector and with Certificate or Certificates of Occupancy issued by the appropriate governmental agency for all of the Improvements, the form and content of all such Certificates and/or Certifications to be as specified by Lender. Lender shall be entitled to such evidence and proof as it deems appropriate from Borrower and Contractor to establish that upon final disbursement, the entire cost of completing the Improvements will have been fully paid.

J. Advances of the Construction Fund shall be made monthly during progress of construction in a sum not to exceed .... percent (....%) of the value of all labor and materials incorporated in the construction since the date of the last previous advance of funds therefor, and in addition thereto, at the option of Lender, Lender may disburse and advance monthly a sum not to exceed .... percent (....%) of the value of materials acceptably stored at the job site, but in no event will Lender disburse any monies for such account where the materials acceptably stored on the site cannot be reasonably utilized in construction in ordinary course within several weeks next following. The amount requested by Contractor shall be set forth in a Contractor's Requisition and shall relate to the Cost Breakdown previously approved by Lender, which Contractor's Requisition will be accompanied by Borrower's Request for Disbursement. Generally, Contractor's Requisition shall include work through the twenty-fifth (25th)

Title Binder or policy to Lender insuring its examination of the title current will certify to Lender in writing that there have been no instruments filed of record to the date of each advance which in any way disturbs the priority of the first mortgage lien of Lender, and that there have not been filed any liens against the Project, and that upon making of such advance by Lender the amount so advanced, and all prior advances made under the Mortgage, are insured as being secured by Lender's first mortgage lien, to be confirmed by Endorsement to the Title Binder or Policy to be forthwith issued after receipt of advice of the making of each such advance by Lender, or Lender shall furnish the funds to be advanced to Title Company, with instructions for it to examine title and disburse proceeds, in each instance, when it is assured that the advance can be made with the foregoing assurance of full coverage therefor and for prior advances, as secured by the first mortgage lien of Lender's Deed of Trust, with appropriate Title Endorsements to be issued and delivered to Lender. Borrower, in order that Title Company can issue such written Certification and Endorsement as is required from time to time agrees to fully observe and comply with any regulations and requirements which the Title Company may make with respect to the title, disbursement of advances, and proof of payment as to construction bills, partial releases of lien, waivers, inspections and surveys.

E. Prior to making payment under each request for disbursement and accompanying Contractor's Requisition, Borrower shall furnish Lender with Construction surveys as required by Lender, reflecting that all Construction by Borrower is within the boundary lines of the Land and not in violation of any building setback lines or restrictions, and as a condition to the final advance shall furnish Lender with a final Survey reflecting all Improvements in place, including all walkways and paved parking areas, all existing easements, and the location of all utility lines, both underground and overhead, all surveys to be duly certified to and prepared by a licensed and registered Survey or authorized to do business in the .... of ....

F. Notwithstanding provision for inspection and approval of construction by Borrower's Architect, and for his certifications, in no event will the amount to be paid out of the Construction Fund be in excess of the amount approved by Lender's independent inspecting Architect or Construction Inspector.

G. If Lender utilizes Title Company as a Disbursing Agent, all costs and fees of Title Company incurred therefor shall be paid by Borrower.

H. Prior to payment under each request for disbursement and accompanying Contractor's Requisition, Borrower shall cause its Con-

it will have been determined whether Borrower will have to deposit cash funds or make other arrangements satisfactory to Lender in its sole discretion to complete the Nonconstruction or Construction Funds in accordance with Lender's determination provided hereinbefore.

ARTICLE 19

When all of the foregoing prerequisites entitling Borrower to the advance of Construction Funds have been met, and Borrower continues to be in good standing and not in default hereunder, the Construction Fund shall be advanced in payment for construction of the Improvements in the time and manner hereinafter provided. Said Construction Fund may be comprised of loan proceeds and funds of or from Borrower.

A. The Contractor's Requisition and Borrower's request for disbursement shall be on forms designated by Borrower and/or prepared and furnished by Borrower, containing such certifications required of, and signed by, Contractor and/or Borrower, respectively, under oath as Lender may require, and may be accompanied by all such other documents which may be called for herein to substantiate entitlement of Borrower and/or its Contractor, as the case may be, to the funds requisitioned.

B. Prior to payment under each request for disbursement and accompanying Contractor's Requistion, Borrower and/or Contractor shall furnish to Lender from time to time as and when required by Lender, evidence satisfactory to Lender that Borrower and Contractor have obtained or can obtain all necessary materials as and when required for completion of construction in accordance with the Plans and Specifications, and this shall be a condition precedent to making any disbursement from the Construction Fund.

C. Prior to payment under each request for disbursement and accompanying Contractor's Requisition, should it appear that the proceeds of the Construction Fund remaining undisbursed will be insufficient to complete all of the Improvements in accordance with the Plans and Specifications and to pay for all labor, material, and costs in the premises, Borrower shall upon demand of Lender deposit with Lender additional monies in a noninterest bearing account which shall, when added to the undisbursed proceeds of the Construction Fund, be sufficient to complete and pay for the Improvements, costs and expenses in connection therewith, and the amount so deposited by Borrower shall be disbursed to pay for the Improvements before any additional advance will be paid out from the Construction Fund.

D. Prior to payment under each request for disbursement and accompanying Contractor's Requisition, the Title Company issuing the

ARTICLE 16

Anything in said Note, Deed of Trust, or this Agreement to the contrary notwithstanding, it is understood and agreed by the parties that if by reason of acceleration, interest paid hereunder shall exceed the maximum amount permitted by law as to the maker, such excess which exceeds the maximum permitted by law as to the make shall be credited by Lender on interest accrued or principal, or both, at the time of acceleration so that the maker of such interest shall not exceed the maximum amount permitted by law, and being expressly understood, however, that any such credit will not cure any default. Anything in said Note, Deed of Trust, or this Agreement to the contrary notwithstanding, it is understood and agreed by Lender and endorsers or guarantors of the Note that if by reason of acceleration, the interest hereunder shall exceed the maximum amount permitted by law as to the endorsers or guarantors shall be credited by Lender on interest accrued or principal or both, at the time of acceleration, so that as to endorsers or guarantors, such interest shall not exceed the maximum amount permitted by law, provided that this sentence shall only apply for the purpose of computing the amount of the liability of the endorsers or guarantors.

ARTICLE 17

Nothing herein shall be construed to waive or diminish any right or security of Lender under the Note and Deed of Trust hereinabove described. It is the purpose and intent hereof to provide safeguards, protection, and rights to Lender in addition to those provided in said Note and Deed of Trust and to better secure said Lender for and on account of said construction loan.

ARTICLE 18

The initial advance of Nonconstruction Funds and the remaining balance of Nonconstruction Funds are as set forth in attached Exhibit B. These funds are to be disbursed when Borrower is current and in good standing hereunder for the purposes of making payment of the specified item or expense as the same may be incurred from time to time, and upon any default, any amount remaining undisbursed allocated as Nonconstruction Funds may be applied and disbursed to pay for construction of the Improvements or may be used and applied in such other manner as the Note, Deed of Trust, and Building Loan Agreement may permit.

After initial advance of the Nonconstruction Funds, no further advances of any Nonconstruction Funds or Construction Funds shall be made until such time as all conditions have been met which would entitle Borrower to disbursement of Construction Funds, at which time

ARTICLE 14

Borrower shall permit a representative of Lender, Architect, or of Title Company (which term as used herein and hereafter refers to issuer of the Commitment or Policy) to enter and inspect the mortgaged premises at all reasonable times.

ARTICLE 15

Borrower shall not assign this Building Loan Agreement nor any part of any advance to be made hereunder, nor convey, nor further encumber said premises, nor change Title Company, Architect, or Contractor without Lender's written consent. The interest of Lender in the Building Loan Agreement, and in the Note, Deed of Trust and other Collateral Loan Documents, may be assigned by Lender and nothing thereby shall relieve Borrower or any Guarantor of the obligation or obligations of Borrower from liability, and the successor of Lender shall succeed to and be possessed of all of the rights of Lender to the same force and effect as though such party was the original Lender.

Borrower shall not make any conveyance of the mortgaged premises without the written consent of Lender and without assumption of the obligation created hereunder by the grantee of Borrower, and if any conveyance is made without such written consent and/or without such assumption, then and in that event and at option of Lender, and without notice to Borrower, all sums of money due on the Note and secured by the Deed of Trust and hereunder shall immediately and concurrently with such conveyance become due and payable and in default whether or not the same are so due and payable and in default by the specific terms hereof, in which event Lender shall have no further obligation to make any disbursements hereunder.

If Borrower is a corporation, then the sale or transfer of stock in Borrower of interests aggregating twenty percent (20%) or more of the present outstanding capital stock of Borrower shall be classified as a transfer made in the same manner as though Borrower had conveyed its interest in the mortgaged premises without Lender's consent, which consent shall not be unreasonably withheld where Borrower desires to sell stock to raise additional equity capital for the project, except that this covenant shall not be applicable where any transfer of stock is between parties already stockholders of Borrower or transfers of stock by reason of the death of any individual stockholder. If Borrower is a partnership, any sale or transfer of a partnership interest shall also be treated in the same manner as though it was a conveyance by Borrower of the encumbered premises, except where the sale or transfer of any partnership interest is between persons already partners of Borrower or the transfer is by reason of the death of any individual partner.

all policies of such insurance shall be written to cover the Improvements and onsite materials against such hazards, including Other Perils, in such amounts, and in such form, as Lender may from time to time require, and written in companies with a policyholder's rating of "A" or "A+" in Best's latest rating guide. All such policies shall be in amounts which do not exceed three percent (3%) of the issuing company's policyholder's surplus and shall be delivered to Lender with premiums fully paid by Borrower.

ARTICLE 9

Borrower specifically agrees to have any mechanics' liens which may be filed against said job or premises, released or bonded within ten (10) days of the date of filing of the same, time being of the essence.

ARTICLE 10

Borrower hereby agrees that any taxes or assessments on the above-described Project which may become due or be payable during the existence of the Deed of Trust will be promptly paid and discharged.

ARTICLE 11

Lender shall be entitled to deduct from the initial advance the cost of preparation of papers, Lender's attorney's appraisal and inspections, and insurance and other incidental charges. Lender is also entitled to deduct from all advances any accrued interest not otherwise paid.

ARTICLE 12

If Borrower, during the progress of the work, neglects to employ a watchman for the protection of the Project, Lender may employ a watchman or watchmen for this purpose, and any amount thus expended shall be deemed to be secured by the Note and Deed of Trust and may be charged, at the option of Lender, to any advance thereafter becoming due.

ARTICLE 13

Borrower will furnish to Lender, whenever requested to do so, satisfactory evidence, showing that all monies theretofore advanced or paid by Lender on account of the Loan, have actually been paid or applied for the construction of the Project by Borrower, and until such evidence is produced, at the option of Lender, no other or further advances or payments need be made by it hereunder.

ARTICLE 6

When all conditions authorizing and permitting construction of the Improvements have been secured, being within the time required therefor, Borrower agrees that it shall construct or cause to be constructed the Improvement in a first-class and good and workmanlike manner in accordance with the approved Plans and Specifications, and in compliance with all restrictions, conditions, ordinances, codes, regulations and laws of all Governmental Agencies having jurisdiction over or an interest in the same, such construction to be entirely on the Land and to be accomplished so that the same will not encroach upon or overhang any easement or right of way or land of others, and that the Improvements when erected shall be wholly within any building setback or restriction lines, and that Borrower shall cause construction of said Improvements to be carried on continuously, diligently, and with dispatch to the end that all said Improvements shall be substantially completed and Certificate or Certificates of Occupancy duly issued therefor on or before ...., 19...., and Borrower shall fully pay for all said Improvements, including all building or buildings, appurtenances and the fixtures, equipment, landscaping, walls, driveways, approaches, and walks which may be called for in said Plans and Specifications, without the foregoing enumeration being in limitation thereof, and all materials contracted or purchased for delivery to the Project, and all labor contracted or hired for or in connection therewith shall be used and employed solely in connection with construction of said Improvements and only in compliance with the said Plans and Specifications.

ARTICLE 7

No extra work nor materials nor change in Plans and Specifications shall be ordered or authorized by Borrower without the written consent of Lender. If Lender shall consent to any such extra work or materials or change in Plans and Specifications, Borrower shall immediately deposit with Lender the amount of the cost thereof. Such additional deposit shall be disbursed upon the completion of such extras or changes, subject to applicable .... percent (....%) holdback to be disbursed at time of final payment after completion of the Improvements.

ARTICLE 8

The interest of Lender shall at all times be protected by adequate Builder's Risk Insurance, completed value on a nonreporting form, and

loan proceeds allocated to pay for cost of Construction, will aggregate the amount or value of the work under Contract price under Construction Contract, together with deposit of such other funds, if any may be required by Lender, to guarantee payment of other obligations which may be incurred during Construction, such as interest, taxes, and the like.

T. Such other certifications and documents as Lender may reasonably require pertaining to initial disbursement of funds to pay for construction.

In no event shall Lender be required to disburse any funds unto Borrower, or for account of Borrower, when there exists any default under any of the terms, provisions, and conditions of the Note, Deed of Trust or herein, whether or not any grace or acceleration period, if any, has expired.

Assuming that the initial disbursement has been made hereunder of funds for other than cost of Construction (the requirements of Items A through R above having been duly met), if Borrower on or before ...., 19...., has not complied with the conditions necessary to authorize disbursement of funds hereunder for payment of construction (the requirements of Items S through T above having been duly met) and has not caused construction to be actually commenced, then Lender at its option shall have, and is hereby given, the right at any time on or after ...., 19.... to accelerate and declare entirely due and payable the indebtedness due on the Note, Deed of Trust and hereunder, in the same manner as though the loan had been fully disbursed and said date was the final maturity date for payment hereunder, and said Lender may enforce the Note, Deed of Trust, and this Building Loan Agreement against the Borrower and/or the security, or both, in addition to having the right to proceed under the Guaranty.

ARTICLE 5

Hereunder, the loan proceeds are designated into "Nonconstruction Funds" and "Construction Funds," the same being respectively established as .... Dollars ($............) and .... Dollars ($............), to be disbursed as hereinbefore and hereafter provided. Whenever it may be proper so to do Borrower and Lender have agreed thereto in writing, the amounts allocated to the Nonconstruction Funds and Construction Funds may be adjusted, but it is intended that in no event shall the Construction Funds hereunder, together with any cash contributions thereto by Borrower, be less from time to time than the amount remaining or unpaid on the Contract Price under Construction Contract.

P. All building permits from applicable government authorities having jurisdiction necessary to authorize and permit construction of the improvements to be commenced.

Q. Satisfactory Soils Report.

R. Written joinder herein, by signature hereon or separate instrument, of Architect and Contractor consenting to the terms and conditions relating to them hereinafter specified, and which in any event acknowledge the following: As to Architect—that he has and claims no lien against the Project for all of his designing architectural services and will claim no lien against the same for his supervisory services to be furnished, that he will perform supervisory services during construction including inspection of Project from time to time and approving and disapproving Contractor's Requisitions for Payment, upon reasonable notice and at no expense to Lender, and that for payment of any fees for supervisory services he will look solely to Borrower, and that he will continue to render his supervisory services to Lender regardless of default in payment therefor by Borrower, and that Lender may use the Plans and Specifications for the Project for any appropriate purpose connected therewith without any further charge by the Architect; and, as to the Contractor—that all rights, claims, and liens are subordinated to the lien, operation and effect of the Deed of Trust and all advances thereunder, that requisitions will be submitted on a form satisfactory to Lender, accompanied by such certifications and other evidence of payment of obligations as Lender may require, that it will not undertake to perform any extra work, furnish additional materials, or change construction from the approved Plans and Specifications without consent of Lender having been first obtained, and that it will, upon demand of Lender after default of Borrower hereunder and/or under Construction Contract, complete the work called for under the Construction Contract for the then remaining undisbursed portion of the construction fund allocated herein to pay for cost of construction (including loan funds and any funds deposited with Lender by Borrower for the purpose of completing construction fund), all without rendering in latter instance the Lender personally liable unto the Contractor under Construction Contract.

After the foregoing requirements have been met and certain initial disbursements provided for hereinafter may have been made to Borrower, being disbursements for other than payment of cost of construction, no further disbursements will be made hereunder unless and until Borrower has furnished Lender, at Borrower's expense and within the time hereinafter required, the following:

S. Deposit with Lender of cash funds, if any may be required, which when added to the then remaining undisbursed balance of the

of supervisory fees, if any, and who will not look to Lender or Project therefor.

I. Evidence satisfactory to Lender that the subject loan is duly authorized by the ...., that the execution of the Loan Documents is not in violation of the .... or any other contractual obligations of the Borrower, which may include a signed copy of the ....
....

J. Guaranty, in original and at least one copy form, executed by .... and .... individually and unconditionally, jointly and severally, in form and content satisfactory to Lender, guaranteeing payment of the indebtedness of Borrower evidenced by the Note, Deed of Trust, and hereunder.

K. Evidence satisfactory to Lender that Borrower has paid for all costs incident to this mortgage loan, including, without limiting the generality of the foregoing, title insurance premium, survey, recording fees, State and Documentary Stamps, and Lender's attorneys' fees. (Where any of the foregoing costs are included within the initial disbursement to be made hereunder and are not required to be paid as a condition to recording of the Deed of Trust, the foregoing shall not be construed as requiring prepayment of such costs, and they may be paid simultaneously with initial disbursement hereunder.)

L. Such other certifications and documents to be executed by Borrower as Lender may reasonably require pertaining to the closing, initial disbursement and all subsequent disbursement of loan proceeds.

M. A permanent commitment from .... in the amount of .... Dollars ($............), said commitment to be assigned to Lender for the duration of construction and an executed Buy-Sell Agreement between Lender and .... whereby .... will purchase Lender's loan for .... Dollars ($............). Lender shall receive written receipt from ...., approving the loan documents, the plans and specifications, and the perimeter survey. Borrower agrees to execute any modifications of loan documents required by ....

N. A fully executed copy of the Construction Contract with Lender reserving the right to review, approve, and require changes in said Construction Contract.

O. A payment and performance bond in the amount of the contract price stated in the Construction Contract between Borrower and ...., with a surety company satisfactory to Lender with the contents of said payment and performance bond satisfactory to Lender's counsel.

A. Original Title Insurance Policy of ...., insuring the Deed of Trust to be a first lien upon the Project, the form of which Policy shall be satisfactory to Lender, subject only to such exceptions as Lender may approve, such Policy to be for the full amount of the loan although it may contain a pending disbursements clause in form satisfactory to the Lender, it being the case that such Policy will be endorsed from time to time to cover the loan amount disbursed on account of the Note and Deed of Trust.

B. A current Perimeter Survey of the Land, reflecting no encroachments and showing all existing easements, surrounding and abutting rights-of-way, in form and content satisfactory to Lender.

C. Evidence satisfactory to Lender as to the present zoning of the Land establishing that the Improvements may be constructed upon the Land without violating said zoning, and if applicable, further evidence to the effect that the construction meets requirements of any other Governmental Agency having jurisdiction including, but not withstanding, the Environmental Protection Agency.

D. Evidence satisfactory to Lender that the power, water and sewer services are available for the Project, during construction and upon completion so as to furnish applicable services and meet requirements of all Governmental Agencies having jurisdiction; and evidence of payment by Borrower of water and sewer taps.

E. A set of the Plans and Specifications prepared by Architect (being the Plans and Specifications which are identified in the Construction Contract, if applicable) and approved by Lender and ....

F. Original Assignment of Leases approved by Lender in form and content.

G. Original Builder's Risk Insurance Policy complying with provisions of the Deed of Trust and Application, containing a loss payable clause in favor of Lender, written in a company or companies acceptable to Lender, covering Project for its full insurable value, and evidence of the existence of such Workmen's Compensation, Public Liability and Property Damage Insurance coverage as the Borrower and/or its Contractor (if applicable) may be required to carry in accordance with the Application and Construction Contract (if applicable).

H. Evidence satisfactory to Lender that Architect's fees for design have been paid, waived, or otherwise taken care of so that Architect will claim no lien therefor, Lender may use the Plans and Specifications to complete the Improvements upon Borrower's default without further payment therefor to Architect, and that arrangements satisfactory to Lender have been made for supervision of construction of the Improvements by said Architect, who will look solely to Borrower for payment

signed by Borrower if an Owner-Builder and by Borrower and Contractor if separate Contractor and Construction Contract are applicable. Aggregate of Cost Breakdown equals Construction Fund if Borrower is Owner-Builder, which is set forth in Exhibit B.

H. *Contractor.* ....

I. *Construction Contract.* Agreement dated between Borrower as Owner and Contractor as Contractor whereby Contractor has agreed to construct the Improvements for a Contract Sum not to exceed .... Dollars ($............) in accordance with the approved plans and Specifications.

ARTICLE 2

Lender shall make to Borrower and Borrower shall accept from Lender a loan in the principal sum of .... Dollars ($............) evidenced and secured by the Note and Deed of Trust, and the proceeds of which loan will be disbursed as provided in this Building Loan Agreement. Borrower agrees to pay to Lender the principal and interest, as the case may be, in the amount, at the time and in the manner provided for in the Note, at the interest rate set forth therein, the interest to be based upon the outstanding principal balance due from time to time on said Note.

ARTICLE 3

Borrower warrants and assures Lender that the Deed of Trust shall at all times be and constitute a first mortgage lien upon the Project, superior and prior in lien and dignity to any and all other liens, rights, and claims of all parties whomsoever, except for the lien of current real estate taxes and such taxes for subsequent years. Said Deed of Trust shall be superior in lien and dignity to the liens, rights, and claims of all parties whomsoever for all work, labor, materials, supplies, equipment, rental of equipment and the like to be furnished in connection with construction of Improvements upon the Land. Borrower warrants that at time of execution and delivery of the Note and Deed of Trust no work has been commenced upon the Land by, through or under Borrower or any other party, and there will have been no commencement of such work or storage of materials thereon at the time of recording said Deed of Trust.

ARTICLE 4

Prior to the initial advance of any loan funds hereunder, Borrower shall furnish Lender, at Borrower's expense, assuming that the Deed of Trust has been recorded, the following:

called "Borrower," and ....
.... with power to protect, exercise and enforce all the rights and perform all the obligations of the Lender herein, hereinafter called "Lender."

WITNESSETH:

THAT for and in consideration of Ten Dollars ($10.00) and other good and valuable considerations this day paid by Borrower and Lender each to the other, receipt of which considerations is hereby acknowledged, and to induce Lender to disburse the proceeds of its First Mortgage Loan hereinafter described, the said Borrower and Lender do hereby represent, warrant, covenant, and agree each with the other as follows:

ARTICLE 1

Borrower and Lender agree that certain terms of reference used herein for convenience mean and refer to the following, to wit:

A. *Note.* A certain Promissory Note of even date, in the principal sum of .... Dollars ($............), executed by Borrower and delivered to Lender, being the Note which is secured by Deed of Trust, the terms of which Note are incorporated herein by reference.

B. *Deed of Trust.* The Mortgage of Real Property of even date executed and delivered by Borrower, securing the Note, the terms of which Deed of Trust are incorporated herein by reference, and encumbering the Land situate in ...., ..., described in Exhibit A annexed hereto and marked "Legal Description."

C. *Land.* The real property last hereinabove described encumbered by Deed of Trust.

D. *Improvements.* ....
....
....
....

E. *Application.* Application of Borrower to Lender dated ...., as accepted by Lender, and any further modifications, qualifications, and amendments thereto agreed on between said parties, the provisions of all of which are incorporated herein by reference.

F. *Architect.* ....

G. *Cost Breakdown.* The Schedule allocating the work and amounts therefor into various trades and items satisfactory to Lender,

2. Tenant agrees that in the event any proceedings are brought for the foreclosure of any such ...., it will attorn to the purchaser of such foreclosure sale and recognize such purchaser as the landlord under said lease. Said purchaser, by virtue of such foreclosure to be deemed to have assumed and agreed to be bound as substitute Landlord, by the terms and conditions of said lease until the resale or other disposition of its interest by such purchaser, except that such assumption shall not be deemed of itself an acknowledgment of such purchaser of the validity of any then existing claims of Tenant against the prior Landlord. All rights and obligations herein and hereunder to continue as though such foreclosure proceedings had not been brought, except as aforesaid. Tenant agrees to execute and deliver to any such purchaser such further assurance and other documents, including a new lease upon the same terms and conditions as the said lease, confirming the foregoing as such purchaser may reasonably request. Tenant waives the provisions of any statute or rule of law now or hereafter in effect which may give or purport to give it any right or election to terminate or otherwise adversely affect the said lease and the obligations of Tenant thereunder by reason of any such foreclosure proceeding.

The provisions of this Agreement are binding upon and shall inure to the benefit of the heirs, successors, and assigns of the parties hereto.

IN WITNESS WHEREOF the parties hereto have executed these presents the day and year first above written.

Life Insurance Company
By: ....

By: ....

The terms of the above Agreement are hereby consented and agreed to.

Owner and Landlord
By: ....

COMMENT: See discussion at ¶ 3.06[6].

Form 4.1

BUILDING LOAN AGREEMENT

THIS BUILDING LOAN AGREEMENT, made and entered into .... original and one copy this .... day of ...., 19...., by and between ...., a ...,

Form 3.14

ATTORNMENT AND NONDISTURBANCE AGREEMENT BETWEEN MORTGAGEE AND OCCUPANCY SUBTENANTS

THIS AGREEMENT dated the .... day of ...., 19 ...., between .... Life Insurance Company, a corporation duly organized and existing under the laws of the State of ...., having its principal place of business at ...., (hereinafter referred to as Life), and .... (hereinafter referred to as Tenant).

WITNESSETH:

WHEREAS, Tenant has entered into a lease dated the .... day of ...., 19 ..... (hereinafter referred to as said lease) leasing certain premises in ...., said premises more particularly described in said lease, and

WHEREAS, Life is the holder of a certain Note in the sum of .... secured by a .... upon premises of which the leased premises are a portion, the lien of said .... being prior to the Tenant's leasehold estate, and

WHEREAS, Tenant desires to be assured of the continued use and occupancy of the premises under the terms of said lease, and

WHEREAS, Life agrees to such continued use and occupancy by Tenant provided that by these presents Tenant agrees to recognize and attorn to Life or purchaser in the event of foreclosure or otherwise.

NOW, THEREFORE, in consideration of the premises and the sum of One Dollar ($1.00) by each party in hand paid to the other, receipt of which is hereby acknowledged, it is hereby mutually covenanted and agreed as follows:

1. In the event it should become necessary to foreclose the said .... or ...., and Life should otherwise come into possession of the premises, Life will not join Tenant under said lease in summary or foreclosure proceedings and will not disturb the use and occupancy of Tenant under said lease so long as Tenant is not in default under any of the terms, covenants, or conditions of said lease and has not prepaid the rent except monthly in advance as provided by the terms of said lease.

Dated: ...., 19....

Attached to and forming part of Policy No. ....

....
(Signature for Company)

COMMENT: See discussion at ¶¶ 3.04[12][b], 3.08[4][d], and Article 4.5 in Form 3.4.

Form 3.13

CERTIFIED INVENTORY

RE: Loan No. ....
     Legal No. ....
     Property ....

The undersigned, the borrower (mortgagor) under the above-captioned loan, hereby certifies that the annexed schedule is a true, accurate, and complete inventory showing the make, model, serial number, and location of all personal property used in the management, maintenance, and operation of the Real Property above referred to (other than trade fixtures or personal property of space tenants); and the undersigned further certifies that the items specified in said inventory constitute all of the fixtures and personal property required for the proper management, maintenance, and operation of the Real Property above referred to; and the undersigned further certifies that all of said items are owned by the undersigned free and clear of conditional sale contracts and other title retention agreements (except hereinafter specified). The within certification is being made and given by the undersigned in order to induce .... Insurance Company to make the loan above referred to with the knowledge of the undersigned that said .... Insurance Company is relying upon the within certification in making said loan.

....

Dated: ...., 19....

COMMENT: See discussion at ¶¶ 3.04[12], 3.09[2].

owner of obligations secured by first trust or loan deed, hereafter designated as the mortgagee, as interest may appear, and this insurance, as to the interest of the mortgagee only therein, shall not be invalidated by any act or neglect of the mortgagor or owner of the within described property, nor by any foreclosure or other proceedings or notice of sale relating to the property, nor by any change in the title or ownership of the property, nor by the occupation of the premises for purposes more hazardous than are permitted by this policy; provided, that in case the mortgagor or owner shall neglect to pay any premium due under this policy the mortgagee shall, on demand, pay the same.

Provided, also, that the mortgagee shall notify this Company of any change of ownership or occupancy or increase of hazard which shall come to the knowledge of the mortgagee, and unless permitted by this policy, it shall be noted thereon and the mortgagee shall, on demand, pay the premium for such increased hazard for the term of the use thereof, otherwise this policy shall be null and void.

This Company reserves the right to cancel this policy at any time as provided by its terms, but in such case, this policy shall continue in force for the benefit only of the mortgagee for ten (10) days after notice to the mortgagee of such cancellation and shall then cease, and this Company shall have the right, on like notice, to cancel this agreement.

Whenever this Company shall pay the mortgagee any sum for loss or damage under this policy and shall claim that, as to the mortgagor or owner, no liability therefore existed, this Company shall, to the extent of such payment, be thereupon legally subrogated to all the rights of the party to whom such payment shall be made, under all securities held as collateral to the mortgage debt, or may, at its option, pay to the mortgagee the whole principal due or to grow due on the mortgage with interest, and shall thereupon receive a full assignment and transfer of the mortgage and of all such other securities; but no subrogation shall impair the right of the mortgagee to recover the full amount of its claim.

ORDER OF PRECEDENCE

Loss or damage, if any, under this policy shall be payable to .... Insurance Company as interest may appear under all present or future mortgages or as present or future owner of obligations secured by trust or loan deeds, in order of precedence of such mortgages, trust or loan deeds, in accordance with the terms of the standard mortgage clause attached, it being understood that no notice of increase or decrease in any mortgagee's interest is required.

Form 3.11

MORTGAGOR'S ESTOPPEL AFFIDAVIT

KNOW ALL MEN BY THESE PRESENTS THAT:

The undersigned, a general partner in The .... Company, the owner of the premises located in the City of ...., described in that certain Deed of Trust dated ...., 19...., securing a loan in the face amount of .... Dollars ($. ....) and recorded in Clerk's Office ...., which Deed of Trust and Note secured thereby are being assigned by............... Bank of .... to .... Insurance Company, hereby certifies that the amount due upon said Note is ...., Dollars principal together with interest thereon at the rate of .... percent (....%) per annum from the date on which the said .... Insurance Company purchases said Note; that said Deed of Trust is a valid first lien on the property described therein for the full amount of principal and interest now owing thereon; that there are no defenses or offsets to said Deed of Trust or Note; and that all other provisions of the said Note and Deed of Trust are in full force and effect.

This .... day of ...., 19.....

By ....

Subscribed and sworn to
before me this .... day
of ...., 19.....
....

COMMENT: See discussion at ¶¶ 3.90[2], 4.03[1]

Form 3.12

STANDARD MORTGAGE CLAUSE

(For Use in Connection With First Mortgage Interest on Real Estate)

Loss or damage, if any, under this Policy, shall be payable to .... Insurance Company as first mortgagee or

This Attorney's Certification is to be issued on the letterhead of the Attorney executing same.

COMMENT: See discussion at ¶ 3.09[2].

Form 3.10

ARCHITECT'S CERTIFICATE

Address of Premises: ....

The undersigned ....,
Architect for ....,
hereby certifies that the construction of the building(s), including grading, landscaping, and all other on- and off-site improvements, on and with respect to premises described in Mortgage Loan Commitment dated .... issued by .... Insurance Company to .... has been substantially completed in a first-class workmanlike manner in accordance with plans and specifications approved by .... Insurance Company and with all applicable requirements of law (including all zoning and building code requirements), and that said building(s) and improvements and the use thereof comply with all applicable rules and regulations of governmental authorities having jurisdiction of said premises so as to entitle the owner of said premises to full use and occupancy of said premises for the purpose for which it was improved and to the issuance of such certificates authorizing occupancy of said building(s) as said government authorities issue upon completion of improvements, and readiness thereof for use and occupancy. The undersigned further certifies that he is familiar with the terms of said Mortgage Loan Commitment and that he made such periodic inspections of said premises during the course of such construction as he deemed necessary as the basis for the certifications set forth herein.

....

COMMENT: See discussion at ¶¶ 3.04[9], 3.04[11], 3.09[2].

COMMENT: See discussion of disbursement letter at ¶ 3.09[2]. Since the permanent lender requires that interest commence with the wiring of the funds, it is probable that until the construction loan is paid off the borrower will, in effect, have to pay interest on both loans. Depending upon the relationship that the borrower has with the construction lender, a construction lender will sometimes waive the double interest for a day or two.

Form 3.9

ATTORNEY'S CERTIFICATION

Re: Legal No.
 Property

The undersigned hereby certifies as follows:

(1) That all of the improvements and their use re the above-captioned Real Property comply fully with all applicable zoning and building laws, ordinances and regulations, and all other applicable federal, state, and municipal laws and requirements; and

(2) That the loan is in all respects legal and does not violate any laws or other requirements of any governmental authority having jurisdiction; and the loan instruments are in all respects valid, existing, and enforceable instruments against the makers thereof; and

(3) That all streets necessary for access to the Real Property above referred to are completed, dedicated, and accepted for maintenance and public use by the appropriate governmental authorities; and

(4) That at the time the funds disbursed in connection with the above captioned loan were disbursed:

 (a) The Real Property had not been taken, in whole or in part, in condemnation or in any other similar proceedings, and no such proceedings were pending; and

 (b) That the borrower and all tenants whose leases have been assigned as security, if there be any, and the leases of all such tenants were not the subject matter of any bankruptcy, reorganization or insolvency proceeding or any other debtor-creditor proceedings; and

(5) That .... Insurance Company has a good, valid, and enforceable first security lien in and to all fixtures and personal property.

....

filed. Your closing attorney is requested to confirm this for my file.

7. *Compliance With Commitment Conditions 10, 12 & 15.* That your closing attorney certify to us that at the time of the disbursement of our funds, no part of the property had been taken in condemnation or similar proceeding and that no such proceeding is pending; that neither the borrower corporation nor Tenant are the subject of any reorganization or any bankruptcy or insolvency proceeding.

8. *Tax and Insurance Deposits.* That at the closing, collect whatever is considered necessary by ...., our servicing agent, in the way of pro rata deposits to properly implement numbered Paragraph 9 of the Deed of Trust so as to assure that adequate funds will be on hand on the next ensuing tax and insurance premium payment dates. The amount collected should be remitted to our servicing agent with advice to us.

9. *Hazard Insurance.* That you or our servicing agent have in possession for submission to me immediately following the closing, the hazard insurance policy reflected by Insurance Binder issued by .... Insurance Company under date of ......,19..., with standard mortgage clause in our form attached, which policy must be written with an eighty percent (80%) coinsurance clause and contain a provision waiving subrogation.

10. *Security Deposit Refund.* That you refund to those entitled thereto the .... Dollars ($. ......) security deposit against appropriate receipt. Our records indicate that the deposit was made by borrower's check No. ...., dated ...., 19....

11. *Fees and Expenses.* The borrower is responsible for all fees, charges, and expenses connected with this transaction and closing. Please, therefore, make whatever arrangements you consider necessary to assure payment of all such items prior to the disbursement of our funds.

As soon as you have tentatively scheduled the closing date, please request our funds by a telephone call to me. Such request should not be made until you are assured that all our requirements, as well as such additional ones as you or your closing attorney may have, have been met or will be met prior to bank closing on the date fixed.

Your report on the closing should be sent to me as soon as it has taken place, together with all documentation relating to the loan, except for the final title policy and instruments handed in for filing or registration, which should follow in due course.

Please acknowledge receipt of this letter by signing and returning the enclosed carbon copy.

Very truly yours,

....

Encs.   Associate Counsel

certified or reproduction copy of the aforesaid Assignment. Several copies of our Notice form are enclosed.

5. *Title Insurance.* That Title Insurance Company of . . . . is ready, willing, and able to issue its loan policy in ALTA revised 1976 form insuring this Company by name, and as the sole insured, as of a time subsequent to the disbursement of our funds as the holder of a valid, subsisting, and enforceable first lien on the fee simple title to the real property described in the aforesaid Deed of Trust, as amended, in the amount of . . . . Dollars ($. . . . . . .), subject only to taxes not yet due and payable.

Items 2, 3, and 4 of title report dated . . . . ,19. . ., are to be omitted from the final title policy. The property description in said report refers to an engineer's survey dated . . . . ,19. . . . The survey in question is actually dated . . . . ,19. . . .

If the Lease is reflected in the title policy, it must be accompanied by a statement that it has been assigned to us.

6. *UCC Lien Requirements.* The following are applicable to the requirements for a first UCC lien as called for by the last paragraph on page 1 of the Commitment.

(a) *Certified Inventory.* That the inventory contemplated by Commitment Condition 3, certified by the borrower and its President, be submitted to our real estate office for transmittal to me, with his recommendations. Our funds will not be wired until said inventory has been approved.

(b) *Security Agreement.* That your closing attorney draft and submit for my approval a security agreement covering all of the fixtures and personal property used in the management, maintenance, and operation of the Project, including all items listed on the aforesaid Certified Inventory, as well as substitutions for, or replacements of, such items. A copy of the Inventory should be attached to the security agreement as an exhibit.

(c) *UCC Financing Statement.* That your closing attorney draft and submit to me for approval, execution by this Company, and return to him for appropriate filing in the office required under . . . . [state] law, at the time of closing, a UCC Financing Statement.

(d) *Opinion re First Lien.* That immediately following the closing, your attorney furnish the Company with his unqualified Opinion that it has a valid, subsisting, and enforceable first lien on all of the fixtures and personal property covered by the chattel trust instrument, free of conditional sales contracts or other title retention arrangements.

(e) *Refiling Requirement.* It is our understanding that in order to continue the chattel lien beyond five (5) years, a Continuation Statement must be filed within the six (6)-month period immediately preceding the expiration of five (5) years from the date the Financing Statement is

.... has no further obligations to it under or by virtue of the Buy and Sell Agreement dated ....,19....

Item (b) above assumes that any interest owing to the Bank to the date of the takeout closing will be collected from the borrower at said closing and paid over to the Bank.

We understand that no one other than the Bank has any right, title, or interest in the loan. If such is not the case, please let me know at once.

3. *Mortgagor's Estoppel Certificate.* That the borrower causes to be executed, subscribed and sworn to an appropriate estoppel certificate. The enclosed sample Mortgagor's Estoppel Affidavit contains our requirements and should be used as a guide. It should be executed by the borrower corporation.

4. *Lease Requirements.* The following requirements are applicable to the lease with the Borrower and ....(hereinafter referred to as "Tenant") dated ....,19...:

(a) *Landlord's Duplicate Original.* That Landlord's Duplicate Original of the aforesaid Lease be in your hands prior to the closing and mailed to me thereafter for retention by us. This Lease must, at the time of closing, provide for annual rental of .... Dollars ($.......) payable in equal monthly installments of .... Dollars ($.......) as required by Commitment Condition No. 25.

(b) *Opinion re Survival of Lease.* That your closing attorney, ..., certify to us that the aforesaid Lease would not be cut off in the event of foreclosure of, or sale under power contained in, the Deed of Trust. If he cannot render such an opinion without an attornment agreement or a subordination of the Deed of Trust to the Lease, appropriate documentation should be drafted and submitted to me for approval and, if necessary, execution by the Company.

(c) *Assignment of Lease.* That all of lessor's right, title, and interest in said Lease be assigned to this Company on this Company's form of Assignment of Lessor's Interest in Lease, several blank copies of which are enclosed, and that said Assignment be filed for registration.

(d) *Tenant's Acceptance Letter.* That you obtain prior to the closing an acceptance letter from said Tenant on our form of acceptance letter, several copies of which are enclosed. This should be sent to me directly following the closing.

(e) *Notice of Lease Assignment.* That you serve on Tenant, either personally against signed acknowledgment of receipt or by registered mail return receipt requested, as soon as the closing has taken place, Notice of Lease Assignment on our form, together with a

Form 3.8

CLOSING DISBURSEMENT LETTER TO TITLE COMPANY

At the opening of business on a date to be fixed by telephone agreement as soon as we are assured that all the conditions of our Commitment have been met, this Company will wire the sum of . . . . Dollars ($. . . . . . .) to . . . . Bank in . . . . , your city, for the account of . . . . Bank & Trust Company, your city, for credit to . . . . Title Company, Inc.'s Escrow Account No. . . . . The amount represents the takeout loan proceeds of . . . . Dollars ($. . . . . . .) plus refund of the . . . . Dollars ($. . . . . . .) security deposit.

You are authorized and requested to disburse the . . . . Dollars ($. . . . . . .), but only on the following conditions:

1. *Assignment of Loan.* That all of . . . . Bank's (hereinafter referred to as "Bank") right, title and interest in and to the Note for . . . . , Dollars ($. . . . . . .) dated . . . . , 19. . . , the Deed of Trust dated the same date and registered in . . . . , on . . . . , 19. . . , as amended by Deed of Correction registered on . . . . , 19. . . , in . . . . Page. . . . , securing said Note and in the property described in said trust deed, as amended, are duly, validly, effectively, and enforceably assigned to this Company.

It is my understanding that the foregoing is to be accomplished by a "without recourse" endorsement and delivery of the Note and the execution and registration of an assignment of the Deed of Trust. The sample form of Assignment enclosed should be used as a guide in drafting the instrument, provided it is valid and enforceable according to its tenor under . . . . [state] law. Both the Deed of Trust and the Correction Deed are to be recited in the first paragraph and the amount, interest rate, and "interest from" date to be shown in the second paragraph are . . . . Dollars ($. . . . . . .) and . . . percent (%) and the closing date, respectively.

The Assignment and its registration must, of course, be reflected in Schedule A of the title policy.

The endorsed Note should be mailed to me by certified mail immediately following the closing.

2. *Assignor's Written Acknowledgment.* That Bank acknowledges in writing (a) that it has advanced the full . . . . Dollars ($. . . .) to the borrower, (b) that it has received payment in full for the loan being assigned to us, including the full amount of the principal thereof as well as interest to the date of the closing of our takeout, and (c) that

Form 3.7

TENANT'S ACCEPTANCE LETTER

.....................Insurance Company
....
....

                        Re:

Dear...................:

    The undersigned, as tenant under that certain Lease dated ...., made with ...., as Landlord, does hereby certify:

(1) That its leased premises at the above location have been completed in accordance with the terms of the Lease, that it has accepted possession of said premises, and that it now occupies the same;

(2) That it began paying rent on ...., 19...., and that, save only as may be required by the terms of the Lease, no rental has been paid in advance;

(3) That there exist no defenses or offsets to enforcement of the Lease by the Landlord, and that there are, as of the date hereof, no defaults or breaches on the part of the Landlord under the Lease known to the undersigned;

(4) That the Lease is now in full force and effect and has not been amended, modified, or assigned, except by agreements dated . ... (if none, so state).

    It is understood that you require this statement from the undersigned as a condition to the making of a loan to the owners of ...., secured by a first mortgage thereon and also by an assignment of the Lease as collateral security.

Dated: ...., 19....

                                   ....
                                                Tenant

COMMENT: See discussion at ¶¶ 3.08[4][i], 3.09[2].

Form 3.6

NOTICE OF LEASE ASSIGNMENT

Dear ....: Premises:
                                              Lease between ...., Lessor
                                              and..................., Lessee

This is to notify you that in accordance with the terms of the Assignment of Lessor's Interest in Lease, a copy of which Assignment is annexed to this letter and furnished to you so that you may be fully informed of its terms, there was duly assigned to the undersigned .... Insurance Company, a .... corporation having its principal office at ...., the entire interest of the Lessor in the above-mentioned Lease.

You are further notified that all rental payments under your Lease shall continue to be paid as heretofore in accordance with the terms of your Lease unless you are otherwise notified in writing by .... Insurance Company.

Your attention is also particularly called to the following matters:

1. Under the provisions of the Assignment, it is expressly provided that unless the written consent of .... Insurance Company is first obtained, no cancellation, surrender, or modification may be made of the Lease, and no rentals shall be paid other than as now provided in the Lease or in such modification of the Lease as may receive the written approval of .... Insurance Comapny.
2. The interest of the Lessor in the Lease has been assigned to .... Insurance Company solely as security for the purposes specified in the Assignment and .... Insurance Company assumes no duty, liability, or obligation under the Lease or any extension or renewal of the Lease either by virtue of the Assignment or by any subsequent receipt or collection of rents under the Assignment.

                    Very truly yours,

                    .... Insurance Company

Enclosure   By...................................

COMMENT: See discussion at ¶¶ 3.08[4][i], 3.09[2].

13. Mortgagee may take security in addition to the security already given Mortgagee for the payment of the principal and interest provided to be paid in or by the Obligation or by the Mortgage or release such other security, and may release any party primarily or secondarily liable on the Obligation, may grant or make extensions, renewals, modifications, or indulgences with respect to such Obligation or Mortgage and replacements thereof, which replacement of said Obligation or Mortgage may be on the same or on terms different from the present terms of said Obligation or Mortgage, and may apply any other security thereof held by it to the satisfaction of such Obligation, without prejudice to any of its rights hereunder.

14. Owner shall give Mortgagee notice immediately upon entering into a lease of any part of the above-described real estate, which lease is not hereinabove listed, and upon notice from Mortgagee to Owner to that effect, said lease shall be deemed included in this assignment as though originally listed herein.

15. Failure of the Mortgagee to avail itself of any of the terms, covenants, and conditions of this assignment for any period of time, or at any time or times, shall not constitute a waiver thereof. The rights and remedies of Mortgagee under this instrument are cumulative and are not in lieu of but are in addition to any other rights and remedies which Mortgagee shall have under said Obligation and Mortgage. The rights and remedies of Mortgagee hereunder may be exercised from time to time and as often as such exercise is deemed expedient.

16. No change, amendment, modification, abridgment, cancellation, or discharge hereof or of any part hereof, shall be valid unless consented to in writing by Mortgagee.

17. All covenants and agreements herein shall apply to, inure to the benefit of, and bind the respective heirs, executors, administrators, successors, and assigns of Owner and Mortgagee.

IN WITNESS WHEREOF this assignment has been duly executed and sealed by Owner.

....

By ....

........................(L.S.)

COMMENT: See discussion of assignment at ¶¶ 3.05, 3.08[4][i].

shall not transfer or convey title to said premises to any lessee without requiring such lessee, in writing, to assume and agree to pay the Obligation in accordance with the terms, covenants, and conditions of the Obligation and the Mortgage, and the payment to Mortgagee by such lessee of so much of the purchase price as shall be deemed necessary by Mortgagee in reduction of the outstanding principal of the Obligation, in the inverse order of maturity, which payment, if made during the period that said Obligation permits prepayment, shall include applicable prepayment charges as set forth in said Obligation. In the event said Lease permits cancellation thereof on payment of consideration and said privilege of cancellation is exercised, the payments made or to be made by reason thereof are hereby assigned to Mortgagee to be applied, at the election of the Mortgagee, to reduce the amount of the principal of said Obligation in the inverse order of maturity or to be held in trust by the Mortgagee as further security without interest for the payment of the principal and interest provided to be paid by the Obligation.

10. Owner will not alter, modify, or change the terms of any guaranties of the Lease or cancel or terminate such guaranties, nor consent to any assignment of the Lease or any subletting thereunder, nor request, consent, or agree to or accept a subordination of the Lease to any mortgage or other encumbrance now or hereafter affecting the premises without the prior written consent of Mortgagee. Owner will not consent to or permit a material alteration of or addition to the premises by the lessee without prior written consent of Mortgagee unless the right to alter or enlarge is expressly reserved by lessee in its Lease.

11. Owner will not execute any other assignment of the Lease or of any interest therein or of any of the rents payable thereunder. Owner will perform all of its covenants and agreements as lessor under the Lease and will not suffer or permit to occur any release of liability of lessee or the accrual of any right in lessee to withhold payment of rents. Owner will give prompt notice to Mortgagee of any notice of Owner's default received from the lessee or from any other person and will furnish Mortgagee with complete copies of said notice. If requested by Mortgagee, Owner will enforce the Lease and all remedies available to Owner against the lessee in case of default by lessee under said Lease.

12. Notwithstanding any variation of the terms of the Obligation and/or the Mortgage, including increase or decrease in the principal amount thereof or in the rate of interest payable thereunder or any extension of time for payment thereunder or any release of part or parts of the lands subject to the Mortgage, the Lease and the benefits hereby assigned shall continue as additional security in accordance with the terms of this assignment.

equity of redemption in said premises. Prior to actual entry and taking possession of the premises by Mortgagee, this assignment shall not operate to place responsibility for the control, care, management, or repair of said premises upon Mortgagee or for the carrying out of any of the terms and provisions of said Lease. Should Mortgagee incur any liability by reason of actual entry and taking possession or for any other reason or occurrence or sustain loss or damage under said Lease or under or by reason of this assignment or in the defense of any such claims or demands, Owner shall immediately upon demand reimburse Mortgagee for the amount thereof including interest at 6 percent (6%), costs and expenses and reasonable attorneys' fees, and Mortgagee may retain possession and collect the rents, income, and profits and, from time to time, apply them in or toward satisfaction of, or reimbursement for, said loss or damage.

7. Owner represents that Owner now is the absolute owner of said Lease, with full right and title to assign the same and the rents, income, and profits due or to become due thereunder; that said Lease is valid, in full force and effect, and has not been modified or amended except as stated herein; that there is no outstanding assignment or pledge thereof or of the rents, income, and profits due or to become due thereunder; that there are no existing defaults under the provisions thereof on the part of either party; that the lessee has no defense, setoff or counterclaim against Owner; that the lessee is in possession and paying rent and other charges under the Lease and as provided therein; and that no rents, income or profits payable thereunder have been or will hereafter be anticipated, discounted, released, waived, compromised, or otherwise discharged except as may be expressly permitted by said Lease. Owner covenants not to cancel, abridge, surrender, or terminate said Lease or change, alter, or modify the same, either to reduce the amount of said rents, income, and profits payable thereunder, or otherwise change, alter, abridge or modify said Lease, or make any subsequent assignment of said Lease, or consent to subordination of the interest of the lessee in said Lease without the prior written consent of Mortgagee. Any attempt at cancellation, surrender, termination, change, alteration, modification, assignment, or subordination of the Lease without the written consent of Mortgagee shall be null and void.

8. Owner agrees to execute and deliver to Mortgagee and hereby irrevocably appoints Mortgagee and its successors and assigns as its agent and attorney in fact to execute and deliver during the term of this assignment such further instruments as Mortgagee may deem necessary to make this assignment and any further assignment effective.

9. Said Lease shall remain in full force and effect irrespective of any merger of the interest of the lessor and lessee thereunder. Owner

4. Owner irrevocably consents that the lessee under said Lease, upon demand and notice from Mortgagee of Owner's default under said Obligation, under said Mortgage, or under this assignment shall pay said rents, income, and profits under said Lease to said Mortgagee without liability to said lessee for the determination of the actual existence of any default claimed by said Mortgagee. Owner hereby irrevocably authorizes and directs lessee, upon receipt of any notice of Mortgagee stating that a default exists and that payments are due under or in the performance of any of the terms, covenants, or conditions of said Obligation or of said Mortgage or of this assignment, to pay to Mortgagee the rents, income, and profits due and to become due under the Lease. Owner agrees that lessee shall have the right to rely upon any such notices of Mortgagee that lessee shall pay such rents, income, and profits to Mortgagee, without any obligation or without any right to inquire as to whether such default actually exists and notwithstanding any claim of Owner to the contrary. Owner shall have no claim against lessee for any rents paid by lessee to Mortgagee. Upon the curing of all defaults in the payments due under or in the performance of any of the terms, covenants, or conditions of the said Obligation or the said Mortgage, Mortgagee shall give written notice thereof to lessee, and thereafter, until further notice from Mortgagee, lessee shall pay the rents, income, and profits to Owner.

5. Mortgagee shall have the right to assign Owner's right, title, and interest in said Lease to any subsequent holder of said Mortgage and to any person acquiring title to the mortgaged premises through foreclosure or otherwise. After Owner shall have been barred and foreclosed of all right, title, interest, and equity of redemption in said premises, no assignee of Owner's interest in said Lease shall be liable to account to Owner for the rents, income, and profits thereafter accruing.

6. Owner agrees to indemnify and hold Mortgagee harmless of and from any and all liability, loss, or damage which Mortgagee may incur under said Lease or by reason of this assignment, and of and from any and all claims and demands whatsoever, which may be asserted against Mortgagee by reason of any alleged obligation or undertaking to be performed or discharged by Mortgagee under said Lease or this assignment. Nothing herein contained shall be construed to bind Mortgagee to the performance of any of the terms and provisions contained in said Lease, or otherwise to impose any obligation on Mortgagee including, without limitation, any liability under the covenant of quiet enjoyment contained in said Lease in the event that the lessee shall have been joined as party defendant in any action to foreclose said Mortgage and shall have been barred and foreclosed thereby of all right, title, interest, and

and not Owner shall be and be deemed to be the creditor of (each) lessee in respect of assignments for the benefit of creditors and bankruptcy, reorganization, insolvency, dissolution, or receivership proceedings affecting such lessee, (without obligation on the part of Mortgagee, however, to file or make timely filings of claims in such proceedings or otherwise to pursue creditor's rights therein) with an option to Mortgagee to apply any money received by Mortgagee as such creditor in reduction of the aforesaid principal or interest or any other indebtedness secured or to be paid by said Mortgagee.

2. Owner agrees that in the event of default in the performance of any of the terms, covenants, and conditions of said Obligation or of said Mortgage or of this assignment and until such default shall have been fully cured, the license reserved herein by Owner shall cease and terminate, and Mortgagee is hereby authorized at its option to enter and take possession of the leased premises, or any part thereof, and to perform all acts necessary for the operation and maintenance of said premises in the same manner and to the same extent that Owner might reasonably so act. In furtherance thereof and not by way of limitation, Mortgagee is empowered, but shall be under obligation to collect the rents, income, and profits under said Lease, to enforce payment thereof and the performance of any and all other terms and provisions of said Lease, to exercise all the rights and privileges of Owner thereunder including the right to fix or modify rents, to demand and sue for possession of the premises covered by said Lease, to relet the premises or any part thereof, and to collect the rents, income, and profits under such new lease. Mortgagee shall, from time to time, apply the net amount of income after payment of all proper costs and charges, including loss or damage referred to hereinafter in Paragraph 6 and including reasonable attorneys' fees, to the sums then due to said Mortgagee under said Obligation and Mortgage. The manner of the application of such net income, the reasonableness of the costs and charges to which such net income is applied, and the item or items which shall be credited thereby shall be within the sole and uncontrolled discretion of said Mortgagee. Such entry and taking possession of the leased premises or any part thereof may be made by actual entry and possession or by written notice served personally upon or sent by registered or certified mail to the last owner of the mortgaged premises appearing on the records of Mortgagee as Mortgagee may elect, and no further authorization shall be required. Mortgagee shall only be accountable for money actually received by it pursuant to this assignment.

3. Upon payment to Mortgage of the full amount of the indebtedness secured by the Mortgage as evidenced by a recorded satisfaction or release of the Mortgage, this assignment shall be void and of no effect.

Form 3.5

ASSIGNMENT OF LESSOR'S INTEREST IN LEASE

BY THIS ASSIGNMENT dated ...., 19...., ...
....
hereinafter referred to as "Owner," for the consideration of One Dollar ($1.00), with intent to be legally bound hereby, and as an inducement for the making of the loan evidenced and secured as hereinafter described, hereby assigns unto ...., a corporation organized under the laws of the State of .... and having its principal place of business at ...., hereinafter referred to as "Mortgagee," all the right, title, and interest of Owner in, under, or by virtue of the following described lease or leases, and all extensions, renewals, modifications or replacements thereof, and any and all guaranties of the lessee's obligations under any provisions thereof and under any and all extensions and renewals thereof (any such lease or leases being hereinafter referred to collectively as the "Lease"), to wit:

....
(Name of Lessee)   (Date of Lease)   (Date of Modification, if any)

TO HAVE AND TO HOLD said Owner's right, title, and interest unto Mortgagee, its successors and assigns as security for the payment of the principal and interest provided to be paid in or by Owner's bond, note, or obligation (herein called "Obligation") dated ...., 19...., and for the performance of the agreements of Owner contained in the mortgage, deed of trust, or other security instrument (herein called "Mortgage") made by Owner to, or to a trustee for, Mortgage dated ...., 19...., and recorded or to be recorded at or prior to the recording of this assignment, covering the following described real estate: ....
....
reserving, however, a license to collect, except as hereinafter provided, the rents, income, and profits accruing by virtue of said Lease as they respectively become due, but not in advance, and to enforce the agreements of said Lease, so long as there is no default by Owner in any of the terms, covenants, or provisions of said Obligation or of said Mortgage, or of this assignment.

Owner covenants as follows:
1. Notwithstanding said license the Owner agrees that Mortgagee

loan secured by this Deed of Trust was made and transacted solely for the purpose of carrying on or acquiring a business or commercial investment within the meaning of said Article ......, Section ......, Annotated Code of ....

10.13. *Saving Clause.* If any clauses or provisions herein contained operate or would prospectively operate to invalidate this Deed of Trust in whole or in part, then, such clauses and provisions only shall be held for naught, as though not herein contained, and the remainder of this Deed of Trust shall remain operative and in full force and effect.

10.14. *Headings.* The Article headings and the Section and Subsection entitlements hereof are inserted for convenience of reference only and shall in no way alter or modify the text of such Articles, Sections, and Subsections.

10.15. *Deed to Secure Future Advances.* Grantor covenants and agrees to perform each and every of the covenants and agreements on the part of Grantor contained in the Loan Agreement and Commitment, the terms of which are by reference hereto made a part hereof, the performance of such covenants and agreements on the part of the Grantor being secured by the lien hereof as fully and to the same extent as the Note secured hereby. The lien hereof also secures the payment by Grantor to Beneficiary of all sums of the Loan Agreement, together with interest and any other sums payable by Grantor to Beneficiary under the terms of the Loan Agreement. The Note secured from the date of advances and such advances secured hereby shall not exceed the principal amount of the Note plus interest accrued thereon and other sums payable by Grantor to Beneficiary under the Construction Loan Agreement and this Deed. Failure of the Grantor to comply with and perform the obligations of Grantor under the Loan Agreement or Commitment or a default by Grantor under the terms of the Loan Agreement shall constitute an Event of Default hereunder and shall render all amounts due under the Loan Agreement, this Deed and the Note secured hereby immediately due and payable at the option of the Beneficiary. This Deed of Trust and all of the instruments evidencing the debt hereby secured shall likewise secure any extension or renewal of the Note or Notes hereby secured or which may be executed and delivered in substitution therefor. The lien and priority hereof shall in no manner be affected by such renewal, extension, or substitution.

COMMENT: See ¶ 4.03[2][b] for discussion of future advance clause.

provisions of this Subsection or by reason of the Security Documents, and any funds expended by Beneficiary to which it shall be entitled to be indemnified, together with interest thereon at a rate of not less than 12 percent (12%) per annum from the date of such expenditures, shall constitute additions to the Indebtedness and shall be secured by the Security Documents and shall be paid by Grantor to Beneficiary upon demand.

10.5. *Covenants Running With the Land.* All covenants contained in the Security Documents shall run with the Mortgaged Property.

10.6. *Successors and Assigns.* All of the terms of the Security Documents shall apply to and be binding upon and inure to the benefit of the successors and assigns of Grantor and Beneficiary respectively, and all persons claiming under or through them.

10.7. *Severability.* In case any one or more of the Obligations shall be invalid, illegal, or unenforceable in any respect, the validity of the remaining Obligations shall be in no way affected, prejudiced, or disturbed thereby.

10.8. *Modification.* The Security Documents and the terms of each and all of them may not be changed, waived, discharged or terminated orally, but only by an instrument or instruments in writing, signed by the party against which enforcement of the change, waiver, discharge or termination is asserted.

10.9. *Counterparts.* This Deed may be executed in any number of counterparts, each of which shall be an original, but all of which together will constitute one instrument.

10.10. *Applicable Law.* The Security Documents and Note shall be governed and construed according to the laws of the State of ....

10.11. *No Release in Default.* No partial release of the premises herein described shall be sought or requested to be executed at any time when there shall be any default or delinquency by the Grantor in any material term, provision, covenant or condition hereof or of the Note secured hereby.

10.12. *Nature of Loan.* The Grantor hereby represents and warrants that it is a business or commercial organization within the meaning of Article ...., Section ...., Annotated Code of .... and further represents and warrants that the

represented the sufficiency, legality, effectiveness, or legal effect of the same, or of any term, provision, or condition thereof, and such acceptance or approval thereof shall not be or constitute any warranty or representation with respect thereto by Beneficiary.

10.3. *Notice.* All notices, demands, requests and other communications required under the Security Documents and the Note shall be in writing and shall be deemed to have been properly given if sent by United States first-class mail, postage prepaid, addressed to the party for whom it is intended at its address set forth in the Definitions hereof. Any party may designate a change of address by written notice to the others, given at least ten (10) days before such change of address is to become effctive.

10.4. *Beneficiary's Right to Perform the Obligations.* If Grantor shall fail to make any payment or perform any act required by the Note or the Security Documents, then, at any time thereafter, with notice as herein provided to or demand upon Grantor and without waiving or releasing any obligation or default, Beneficiary may make such payment or perform such act for the account of, and at the expenses of, Grantor and shall have the right to enter the Land and/or Buildings for such purposes and to take all such action thereon and with respect to the Mortgaged Property as may be necessary or appropriate for such purpose. All sums so paid by Beneficiary and all costs and expenses, including, without limitation, reasonable attorneys' fees and expenses so incurred, together with interest thereon at a rate of not less than 12 percent (12%) per annum from the date of payment or incurring, shall constitute additional indebtedness secured by the Security Documents and shall be paid by Grantor to Beneficiary on demand. If Beneficiary shall elect to pay any Imposition, Beneficiary may do so ten (10) days after written notice of such election by Beneficiary is given to Grantor and in reliance on any bill, statement, or assessment procured from the appropriate public or nonpublic office, without inquiring into the accuracy thereof or into the validity of such Imposition. Similarly, in making any payments to protect the security intended to be created by the Security Documents, Beneficiary shall not be bound to inquire into the validity of any apparent or threatened adverse title, lien, encumbrance, claim or charge before making an advance for the purpose of preventing or removing the same; provided that such payment shall not be made until ten (10) days after written notice of the intent to make such payment is given to grantor. Grantor shall indemnify Beneficiary for all losses and expenses, including reasonable attorneys' fees, incurred by reason of any acts performed by Beneficiary pursuant to the

ARTICLE 9
Assignment of Leases and Rents

COMMENT: See discussion of assignment at ¶¶ 3.05, 3.08[4][i].

In order to further secure the payment of the Indebtedness and the observance, performance, and discharge of the Obligations, Grantor hereby sells, assigns, transfers and sets over to Beneficiary all of Grantor's right, title and interest in, to, and under the Leases, and in and to the Rents.

9.1. *Performance Under Leases.* Grantor will, at its cost and expense, perform and discharge, or cause to be performed and discharged, all of the obligations and undertakings of Grantor or its agents under the Leases, and will use its best efforts to enforce or secure, or cause to be enforced or secured, the performance of each and every obligation and undertaking of the respective tenants under the Leases, and will appear in and defend at its cost and expense, any action or proceeding arising under or in any manner connected with the Leases or the obligations and undertaking of any tenant thereunder.

9.2. *No Third-Party Assignments.* Grantor shall not assign or otherwise encumber future rental payments under the Leases.

ARTICLE 10
Miscellaneous

COMMENT: See discussion at ¶ 3.08[4][j].

10.1. *Loan Expenses.* Grantor shall pay all costs and expenses in connection with the preparation, execution, delivery, and performance of the Security Documents, including (but not limited to) fees and disbursements of its and Beneficiary's counsel, broker's fees, recording costs and expenses, stamp and other taxes, surveys, appraisals and policies of title insurance, physical damage insurance and liability insurance.

10.2. *No Representation by Beneficiary.* By accepting or approving anything required to be observed, performed or fulfilled, or to be given to Beneficiary pursuant to the Security Documents, including (but not limited to) any officer's certificate, balance sheets, statement of profit and loss or other financial statement, survey, appraisal or insurance policy, Beneficiary shall not be deemed to have warranted or

affecting all or any part of the Mortgaged Property or any easement therein or appurtenance thereof, including severance and consequential damage and change in grade of streets, and will deliver to Beneficiary copies of any and all papers served in connection with any such proceedings. Grantor hereby assigns, transfers, and sets over to Beneficiary all rights of Grantor to any award or payment in respect of (a) any taking of all or a portion of the Mortgaged Property as a result of, or by agreement in anticipation of, the exercise of the right of condemnation or eminent domain; (b) any such taking of any appurtenances to the Mortgaged Property or of vaults, areas or projections outside the boundaries of the Mortgaged Property, or rights in, under, or above the alleys, streets, or avenues adjoining the Mortgaged Property, or rights and benefits of light, air, view or access to said alleys, streets, or avenues, or for the taking of space or rights therein below the level of or about the Mortgaged Property; and (c) any damage to the Mortgaged Property or any part thereof due to governmental action, but not resulting in a taking of any portion of the Mortgaged Property, such as, without limitation, the changing of the grade of any street adjacent to the Mortgaged Property. Grantor hereby agrees to file and prosecute its claim or claims for any such award or payment in good faith and with due diligence and cause the same to be collected and paid over to Beneficiary and hereby irrevocably authorizes and empowers Beneficiary, in the name of Grantor or otherwise, to collect and receive any such award of payment and, in the event Grantor fails to act, or in the event that an Event of Default has occurred and is continuing, to file and prosecute such claim or claims.

8.1. *Application of Proceeds.* All proceeds received by Beneficiary with respect to taking of all or any part of the Mortgaged Property or with respect to damage to all or any part of the Mortgaged Property from governmental action not resulting in a taking of the Mortgaged Property, shall be applied as follows, in the order of priority indicated: (a) to reimburse Beneficiary for all costs and expenses, including reasonable attorneys' fees incurred in connection with collecting the said proceeds; (b) to the payment of accrued and unpaid interest on the Note; (c) to the prepayment of the unpaid principal of the Note, without premium; and (d) to the payment of the balance of the Indebtedness, and the balance, if any, will be paid to Grantor, provided that Beneficiary shall have the option to specify the manner in which such proceeds shall be disbursed by Grantor, and such release of such proceeds to Grantor shall not affect the lien hereof or reduce the amount of the Indebtedness.

proceeds and avails of such sale, or in an amount equal to the commission allowed trustees for making sales of property under decrees of the court having jurisdiction, whichever is greater; and

(b) Second, to pay whatever may then remain unpaid on account of Indebtedness and the interest thereon to the day of payment, whether the same shall be due or not, it being agreed that said Notes shall, upon such sale being made before the maturity of said Notes, be and become immediately due and payable at the election of the Beneficiary and to pay all of the indebtedness and any other sums secured hereby; and

(c) Third, to pay the remainder of said proceeds, if any, less the expense, if any, of obtaining possession, to said Grantor or other party lawfully entitled to receive the same, upon the delivery and surrender of possession of the premises aforedescribed sold and conveyed and delivery of all records, books, bank accounts, leases, agreements, security deposits of the lessees and all material relating to the operation of said premises to the said purchaser or purchasers.

Beneficiary shall account to Grantor for any surplus, and Grantor shall be liable to Beneficiary for any deficiency.

7.11. *Tender of Payment of Default.* Upon any default by Grantor and following the acceleration of maturity as herein provided, a tender of payment of the amount necessary to satisfy the entire indebtedness secured hereby made at any time prior to foreclosure sale (including sale under power of sale) by the Grantor, their successors or assigns or by anyone on behalf of the Grantor, their heirs, successors or assigns, shall constitute an evasion of the prepayment terms hereunder and shall be deemed to be a voluntary prepayment thereunder, and any such payment to the extent permitted by law will, therefore, include the premium required under the prepayment privilege, if any, contained in the Note secured hereby, or if at that time there be no prepayment privilege, then such payment will, to the extent permitted by law, include a premium of 5 percent (5%) of the then principal balance.

ARTICLE 8
Condemnation

COMMENT: See discussion at ¶ 3.08[4][h].

Grantor shall give Beneficiary immediate notice of the actual or threatened commencement of any proceedings under eminent domain

7.6. *Release of Collateral.* Beneficiary may release, regardless of consideration, any part of the security held for the Indebtedness or Obligations without, as to the remainder of the Security, in any way impairing or affecting the liens of the Security Documents or their priority over any subordinate lien.

7.7. *Other Collateral.* For payment of the Indebtedness, Beneficiary may resort to any other security therefor held by Beneficiary in such order and manner as Beneficiary may elect.

7.8. *Waiver of Redemption, Notice, Marshalling, Etc.* Grantor hereby waives and releases: (a) all benefit that might accrue to Grantor by virtue of any present or future law exempting the Mortgaged Property, or any part of the proceeds arising from any sale thereof, from attachment, levy or sale on execution, or providing for any appraisement, valuation, stay of execution, exemption from civil process, redemption or extension of time for payment, and (b) unless specifically required herein, all notices of Grantor's default or of Beneficiary's election to exercise, or Beneficiary's actual exercise, of any option or remedy under the Note or the Security Documents, and (c) any right to have the Mortgaged Property marshalled.

7.9. *Discontinuance of Proceedings.* In case Beneficiary shall have proceeded to enforce any right under the Note or the Security Documents and such proceedings shall have been discontinued or abandoned for any reason, then in every such case Grantor and Beneficiary shall be restored to their former positions and the rights, remedies, and powers of Beneficiary shall continue as no such proceedings had been taken.

7.10. *Application of Proceeds.* The proceeds of any sale of all or any portion of the Mortgaged Property and the earnings of any holding, leasing, operation or other use of the Mortgaged Property shall be applied by Beneficiary in the following order:

(a) First, to pay all proper costs, charges, attorneys' fees and expenses, including the fees and costs herein provided for, and to pay or repay to the Trustee or Beneficiary all monies advanced by them or either of them for taxes, insurance and assessments, or otherwise, with interest thereon as provided herein, and to pay all taxes, general and special, due upon said premises at the time of sale, and to pay any other liens prior to the lien of this Deed of Trust unless said sale is made subject to such tax or other lien, and to pay a commission to the person or persons making the sale in the amount of 2 percent (2%) of the

7.3. *Remedies Cumulative and Concurrent.* The rights and remedies of Beneficiary as provided in the Note and in the Security Documents shall be cumulative and concurrent and may be pursued separately, successively, or together against Grantor or against other obligors or against the Mortgaged Property, or any one or more of them, at the sole discretion of Beneficiary and may be executed as often as occasion therefor shall arise. The failure to exercise any such right or remedy shall in no event be construed as a waiver or release thereof.

7.4. *Strict Performance.* Any failure by Beneficiary to insist upon strict performance by Grantor of any of the terms and provisions of the Security Documents or of the Note shall not be deemed to be a waiver of any of the terms or provisions of the Security Documents or the Note, and Beneficiary shall have the right thereafter to insist upon strict performance by Grantor of any and all of them. Failure of the beneficiary to exercise the option for acceleration of maturity and/or foreclosure following any default as aforesaid or to exercise any other option granted to the Beneficiary hereunder in any one or more instances, or the acceptance by Beneficiary of partial payments hereunder shall not constitute a waiver of any such default, but such option shall remain continuously in force. Acceleration of maturity, once claimed hereunder by Beneficiary, may, at the option of Beneficiary, be rescinded by written acknowledgment to that effect by the Beneficiary, but the tender and acceptance of partial payment alone shall not in any way affect or rescind such acceleration of maturity.

7.5. *No Conditions Precedent to Exercise of Remedies.* Neither Grantor nor any other person now or hereafter obligated for payment of all or any part of the Indebtedness shall be relieved of such obligation by reason of the failure of Beneficiary to comply with any request of Grantor or of any other person so obligated to take action to foreclose on this Deed or otherwise enforce any provisions of the Security Documents or the Note, or by reason of the release, regardless of consideration, of all or any part of the security held for the Indebtedness, or by reason of any agreement of stipulation between any subsequent owner of the Mortgaged Property and Beneficiary extending the time of payment or modifying the terms of the Security Documents or Note without first having obtained the consent of Grantor or such other person; and in the latter event, Grantor and all other such persons shall continue to be liable to make payment according to the terms of such extension or modification agreement, unless expressly released and discharged in writing by Beneficiary.

public advertisement to be made as they deem advisable, and any such sale may be adjourned by the Trustees by announcement at the time and place to which the same shall be so adjourned. Upon the completion of any sale, the Trustees shall execute and deliver to the purchaser or purchasers a good and sufficient deed of conveyance or assignment and transfer, lawfully conveying, assigning, and transferring the property sold. The receipt of the Trustees after payment to them of such purchase money, shall be full and sufficient discharge of any purchaser or purchasers of the premises, sold as aforesaid for the purchase money; and no such purchaser, or his representatives, grantees, or assigns, after paying such purchase money and receiving such receipt, shall be bound to see to the application of such purchase money.

7.1.5. *Commissions and Release Fees.* Upon foreclosure, Trustee shall be entitled to retain as compensation a commission equal to 2 percent (2%) of the proceeds of sale on foreclosure. Trustee shall be entitled to receive not more than $7.50 for each Deed of Release executed.

7.1.6. *Commissions Upon Advertisement.* Immediately upon the first insertion of an advertisement of any sale of the premises, or any part thereof under this Deed of Trust, there shall be and become due and owing by Grantor a commission on the total amount of the indebtedness hereby secured equal to one-half (½) the percentage allowed on commissions to trustees making sales under orders or decrees of any court having jurisdiction, and the Beneficiary shall not be required to receive the principal and interest only of the said indebtedness hereby secured in satisfaction thereof, but said sale may be proceeded with unless, prior to the day appointed therefor, tender is made of said principal, interest, commissions and all expenses and costs incident to such sale.

7.1.7. *Other.* The Beneficiary may exercise any other remedy specifically granted under the Security Documents or now or hereafter existing in equity, at law, by virtue of statute or otherwise.

7.2. *Separate Sales.* Any real estate or any interest or estate therein sold pursuant to any writ of execution issued on a judgment by virtue of the Note or this Deed or the other Security Documents, or pursuant to any other judicial proceedings under this Deed or the other Security Documents, may be sold in one parcel, as an entirety, or in such parcels and in such manner or order as Beneficiary, in its sole discretion, may elect.

time may make all necessary or proper repairs, renewals, replacements and useful or required alterations, additions, betterments, and improvements to and upon the premises as to it may seem judicious and pay all proper costs and expenses of so taking, holding, and managing the same, including reasonable compensation to its agents, servants, attorneys and counsel, and any taxes, assessments and other charges prior to the lien of this Deed of Trust which, the Beneficiary may deem it wise to pay, and in such case the Beneficiary shall have the right to manage the premises and to carry on the business and exercise all rights and powers of Grantor, either in the name of Grantor or otherwise, as the Beneficiary shall deem advisable; and Beneficiary shall be entitled to collect and receive all earnings, revenues, rents, issues, profits and other income thereof and therefrom. After deducting the expenses of operating the premises and of conducting the business thereof, and of all repairs, maintenance, renewals, replacements, alterations, additions, betterments, improvements, and all payments which it may be required or may elect to make for taxes, assessments, or other proper charges on the premises, or any part thereof, as well as just and reasonable compensation for all agents, clerks and other employees and for all attorneys and counsel engaged and employed, the monies arising as aforesaid shall be applied to the indebtedness secured hereby. Whenever all that is due upon the principal of and interest on the Notes and under any of the terms of this Deed of Trust shall have been paid and all defaults made good, the Beneficiary shall surrender possession to Grantor. The same right to entry, however, shall exist if any subsequent Event of Default shall happen.

7.1.4. *Foreclosure and Private Sale.* Sell the Mortgaged Property, in whole or in part, and in the case of default of any purchaser or purchasers shall resell all the premises as an entirety, or in such parcels as the Beneficiary shall in writing request, or, in the absence of such request, as the Trustees may determine at public auction at some convenient place in the jurisdiction where the premises are situate, or in such other place or places as may be permitted by law, at such time, in such manner, and upon such terms as the Trustees may fix and briefly specify in the notice of sale, which notice of sale shall state the time when and the place where the same is to be made, shall contain a brief general description of the premises to be sold and shall be sufficiently given if published in at least one newspaper printed in the English language and customarily published in the place or places where such sale is to take place in such manner and at such time or times as may be required by law, and the Beneficiary or the Trustees shall cause further

6.8. *Taxation of Mortgage*. In the event of the passage, after the date of this Deed of Trust, of any law of ...., deducting from the value of land for the purposes of taxation of any lien thereon, or changing in any way the laws for the taxation of mortgages or deeds of trust or debts secured by mortgage or deed of trust for state or local purposes, or the manner of the collection of any such taxes so as to affect this Deed of Trust, or upon the rendition by any court of competent jurisdiction of a decision that any undertaking by Grantor as in this paragraph provided is legally inoperative, or if the United States Government or any state, county, municipal or other governmental subdivision shall require internal revenue or other documentary stamps hereon or on the Notes secured by this Deed of Trust, or either of them;

6.9. *Foreclosure of Other Liens*. If the holder of a junior, subordinated or senior mortgage, Deed of Trust or other lien on the Mortgaged Property (without hereby implying Beneficiary's consent to any such junior, subordinated or senior mortgage, Deed of Trust or other lien) institutes foreclosure or other proceedings for the enforcement of its remedies thereunder.

ARTICLE 7
Default and Foreclosure

COMMENT: See discussion at ¶ 3.08[4][g].

7.1. *Remedies*. If an Event of Default shall occur, Beneficiary may, at its option, exercise any or all of the following remedies:

7.1.1. *Acceleration*. Declare the unpaid portion of the Indebtedness to be immediately due and payable, without further notice or demand (each of which hereby is expressly waived by Grantor), whereupon the same shall become immediately due and payable;

7.1.2. *Entry on Mortgaged Property*. Enter upon the Mortgaged Property and take possession thereof and of all books, records and accounts relating thereto;

7.1.3. *Operation of Mortgaged Property*. Enter and take possession of the premises and may exclude Grantor, its agents and servants, wholly therefrom, having and holding the same, may use, operate, manage and control the premises or any part thereof, and upon every such entry the Beneficiary, at the expense of the premises, from time to

due observance or performance of any of the Obligations other than payment of money and such default shall not be curable, or if curable shall continue for a period of thirty (30) days grace after written notice thereof from the Beneficiary to Grantor (unless such default, if curable, requires work to be performed, acts to be done or conditions to be remedied, which by their nature cannot be performed, done or remedied, as the case may be, within such thirty (30) days period and Grantor shall diligently and continuously process the same to completion);

6.3. *False Representation.* If any representation or warranty made by Grantor or others in, under, or pursuant to the Note or the Security Documents shall prove to have been false or misleading in any material respect as of the date on which such representation or warranty was made;

6.4. *Judgment.* If a final judgment for the payment of money in excess of Twenty-five Thousand Dollars ($25,000) shall be rendered against Grantor and the same shall remain undischarged for a period of thirty (30) consecutive days, during which period execution shall not be effectively stayed;

6.5. *Voluntary Bankruptcy, Etc.* If Grantor shall (a) voluntarily be adjudicated a bankrupt or insolvent, (b) seek or consent to the appointment of a receiver or trustee for itself or for all or any part of its property, (c) file a petition seeking relief under the bankruptcy or similar laws of the United States or any state or any other competent jurisdiction, (d) make a general assignment for the benefit of creditors, or (e) admit in writing its inability to pay its debts as they mature;

6.6. *Involuntary Bankruptcy, Etc.* If a court of competent jurisdiction shall enter an order, judgment, or decree appointing, without the consent of Grantor, a receiver or trustee for it or for all or any part of its property or approving a petition filed against it seeking relief under the bankruptcy or other similar laws of the United States or any state or other competent jurisdiction, and such order, judgment or decree shall remain in force undischarged or unstayed for a period of thirty (30) days;

COMMENT: See discussion at ¶ 4.02[12] concerning bankruptcy of the borrower.

6.7. *Dissolution.* If Grantor or any Guarantor shall dissolve or liquidate and such dissolution or liquidation is not in connection with a merger or consolidation under Article 4.1;

ciary, unless actually replaced by an article of equal suitability and value, owned by Grantor, free and clear of any lien or security interest except such as may be approved in writing by Beneficiary.

5.4. *Other Liens.* Grantor will not, without the prior written consent of Beneficiary, create or permit to be created or to remain, any mortgage, pledge, lien, lease, encumbrance or charge on, security interest in, or conditional sale or other title retention agreement, whether prior or subordinate to the liens of the Security Documents, with respect to the Mortgaged Property or any part thereof or income therefrom, other than the Security Documents and the Permitted Encumbrances.

5.5. *Mechanic's Lien.* Grantor will not permit any mechanic's lien to be filed against the Mortgaged Property or any part thereof and remain unsatisfied or not bonded so as to remove same for a period of thirty (30) days after filing thereof.

5.6. *No Dividend by Grantor.* Grantor covenants and agrees that he shall not, prior to the full payment and discharge of the Indebtedness, declare or pay any dividend of any kind.

5.7. *No Transfer of Ownership.* Grantor covenants and agrees that he shall not, prior to the full payment and discharge of the Indebtedness, convey or transfer ownership, in whole or in part, of the Mortgaged Property except as hereinafter provided, and any such transfer or conveyance shall constitute an event of default as hereinafter described in Article 6.

ARTICLE 6
Events of Default

COMMENT: See discussion at ¶ 3.08[4][f].

The term "Event(s) of Default," as used in the Security Documents and in the Note, shall mean the occurrence or happening, from time to time, of any one or more of the following:

6.1. *Payment of Indebtedness.* If Grantor shall default in the due and punctual payment of all or any portion of any installment of the Indebtedness as and when the same shall become due and payable, whether at the due date thereof or at a date fixed for prepayment or by acceleration or otherwise;

6.2. *Performance of Obligations.* If Grantor shall default in the

amount of such estimated cost shall thereupon become due and payable by Grantor to be applied upon the indebtedness secured hereby unless within such period Grantor, at its own cost and expense, shall have completed or shall have commenced, and thereafter with diligence, completes such repairs and replacements. In such event, Grantor shall also reimburse Beneficiary the cost of such survey, the same being secured hereby. If the survey determines such maintenance to be adequate, then the cost therefor shall be at the expense of the Beneficiary.

4.17. *Further Assurances.* Grantor shall, upon five (5) days written notice from Beneficiary, execute and deliver such additional financing statements, deeds of Trust, Supplemental Deeds of Trust, or other security agreements which may from time to time be reasonably required to protect and preserve the security of the Mortgaged Property.

ARTICLE 5
Negative Covenants

COMMENT: See discussion at ¶ 3.08[4][e].

5.1. *Use Violations, Etc.* Grantor will not use the Mortgaged Property or any part thereof or allow the same to be used or occupied for any purpose other than as .... and directly related purposes or for any unlawful purpose or in violation of any certificate of occupancy or other permit or certificate, or any law, ordinance or regulation, or any restrictions or reservations covering or affecting the use or occupancy thereof, or suffer any act to be done or any conditions to exist on the Mortgaged Property or any part thereof or any article to be brought thereon, which may be dangerous unless safeguarded as required by law, or which may, in law, constitute a nuisance, public or private, or which may make void or voidable any insurance then in force with respect thereto.

5.2. *Alterations, Etc.* Grantor will not commit or knowingly permit any waste of the Mortgaged Property or any part thereof or make or permit to be made any alterations or additions to the Mortgaged Property which would have the effect of materially diminishing the value thereof.

5.3. *Replacement of Fixtures and Personalty.* Grantor will not permit any of the Fixtures or Personalty to be removed at any time from the Land and/or Buildings without the prior written consent of Benefi-

COMMENT: See discussion of escrows at ¶ 3.04[6].

4.14. *Payment of Indebtedness.* Grantor covenants that it will duly pay and discharge the Indebtedness in accordance with the terms and conditions of the Security Documents.

4.15. *Maintenance of Books and Records.* The Grantor and all subsequent owners of the Mortgaged Property shall keep and maintain full and correct books and records showing in detail the earnings and expenses of said premises and shall permit the Beneficiary or its representatives to examine such books and records and all supporting vouchers and data at any time and from time to time on request, at its offices, hereinbefore identified, or at such other location as may be mutually agreed upon; within ten (10) days after demand therefor and, in any event, within ninety (90) days following the expiration of Grantor's first fiscal year and following the expiration of each fiscal year thereafter during the terms of this Deed of Trust, will furnish to the Beneficiary a statement showing in detail all such earnings and expenses since the last such statement, verified by the affidavit of the Grantor or then owner, or if the same be a corporation, by an affidavit of its principal executive officer, and in the event that the owner shall refuse or fail to furnish any statement as aforedescribed, or in the event such statement shall be inaccurate or false, or in the event of the failure of the Grantor or any subsequent owner to permit the Beneficiary or its representative to inspect the said premises or the said books and records on request, the Beneficiary may consider such acts of the Grantor as a default hereunder and may proceed in accordance with the rights and remedies afforded it under the provisions of this instrument.

COMMENT: See discussion at ¶ 3.04[3][a] of the "audit" provision in connection with the lender's requirement that the borrower pay "additional compensation" over and above the regular amount of interest.

4.16. *Survey of Independent Realtor.* The Beneficiary shall have the right, at any time and from time to time, to engage an independent Realtor to survey the adequacy of the maintenance of the Mortgaged Property. If found inadequate, such realtor shall determine the estimated cost of such repairs and replacements necessary to protect and preserve the rentability and useability of the said premises, and the Grantor does hereby acknowledge that the security of this Deed of Trust is thereby impaired to the extent of the estimated cost of such repairs and replacements. In such event, at the option of the Beneficiary and within sixty (60) days after written demand therefor, a sum equal to the

interest thereunder will be in danger of being sold, forfeited, terminated, cancelled or lost, (iii) Grantor shall have furnished such security as may be required in the proceedings or as may be reasonably requested by Beneficiary.

4.11. *Grantor's Assent.* Upon the occurrence of any of the Events of Default, then upon any and every such default so made:

(a) The Grantor, in accordance with the applicable rules of .... Rules of Procedure or any Public General Law or Public Local Law of the State of .... relating to Deeds of Trust or mortgages, including any supplements, amendments, or additions thereto, does hereby assent to the passage and entry of decree by the Circuit Court of the city or county in which the Mortgaged Property herein described is located; or

(b) The Trustee or substitute Trustee or Trustees shall have the power and duty to sell, and in the event of default by any purchaser, to resell the Mortgaged Property.

4.12. *Performance of the Commitment.* Grantor shall timely comply with, abide by, and perform all of the terms and conditions of the Commitment, dated ...., 19.....

4.13. *Tax and Insurance Escrow.* Supplementing the provisions of Articles 4.3 and 4.5 hereof, if the Note shall be payable in monthly or other periodic payments of principal and/or interest, and if required by Beneficiary, the Grantor shall pay to Beneficiary on the payment date of installments of principal and interest together with and in addition to such installment of principal and interest, until the Note is fully paid, an installment of the Impositions and insurance premiums for such insurance as is required hereunder, next due on the Mortgaged Property in an amount sufficient, as estimated by Beneficiary, to accumulate the sums required to pay such Impositions and insurance thirty (30) days prior to the due date thereof. Amounts held hereunder shall not be, nor be deemed to be, trust funds, but may be commingled with the general funds of Beneficiary, and no interest shall be payable in respect thereof. Upon demand of the Beneficiary, the Grantor agrees to deliver to the Beneficiary such additional monies as are necessary to make up any deficiencies in the amounts necessary to enable the Beneficiary to pay such Impositions and insurance premiums. In the event of a default by the grantor in the performance of any of the terms, covenants or conditions in the Note or Security Documents, the Beneficiary may apply to the reduction of the sums secured hereby, in such manner as the Beneficiary shall determine, any amount under this Article 4.13 remaining to the Beneficiary's credit.

if any, shall be sufficient for the purpose, commence and diligently continue to restore, repair, replace, rebuild or alter the Mortgaged Property as nearly as possible to its value, condition, and character immediately prior to such damage or destruction.

COMMENT: See discussion of insurance clause at ¶¶ 3.08[4][d], ¶ 3.04[12].

4.7. *Performance of Other Agreements.* Grantor will not violate any of the terms, provisions, covenants, agreements or restrictions and will timely comply with, abide by, and perform all of the terms, agreements, obligations, covenants, restrictions and warranties expressed as binding upon it under any lease, easement, or other agreement to which it is or is not a party with respect to or affecting the Mortgaged Property or any part thereof.

4.8. *Inspection.* Grantor will permit Beneficiary at all reasonable times to inspect Mortgaged Property.

4.9. *Hold Harmless.* Grantor shall save the Beneficiary and the Trustee harmless from all costs and expenses, including reasonable attorneys' fees and costs of a title search, continuation of abstract and preparation of survey, incurred by reason of any action, suit, proceeding hearing, motion or application before any Court or administrative body in and to which the Beneficiary or the Trustee may be or become a party by reason of this Trust, including but not limited to condemnation, bankruptcy, and administration proceedings, as well as any other of the foregoing wherein proof of claim is by law required to be filed or in which it becomes necessary to defend or uphold the terms of this Trust, and all money paid or expended by Beneficiary or Trustee in that regard, together with interest thereon from day of such payment at the rate set forth in said Notes, shall be so much additional indebtedness secured hereby and, except as otherwise provided herein, shall be immediately and without notice due and payable by Grantor.

4.10. *Contest of Tax Assessments, Etc.* After prior written notice to Beneficiary, in the case of any material item Grantor at its own expense may contest by appropriate legal proceedings, promptly initiated and conducted in good faith and with due diligence, the amount or validity or application, in whole or in part, of (a) any of the legal requirements referred to in Article 4.2, or (b) any Imposition, provided that (i) in the case of any unpaid Imposition, such proceedings shall suspend the collection thereof from Grantor and from the Mortgaged Property, (ii) neither the Mortgaged Property nor any part thereof or

ciary to collect, adjust, and compromise any losses under any of the insurance aforesaid and after deducting costs of collection to apply the proceeds at its option as follows: (a) as a credit in the inverse order of maturity, upon the indebtedness secured hereby, or (b) to restoring the improvements, in which event Beneficiary shall not be obligated to see to the proper application thereof nor shall the amount so released or used be deemed a payment on any indebtedness secured hereby, or (c) to deliver same to the owner of said premises. In the event of foreclosure of the Deed of Trust or other transfer of title to the premises in extinguishment of the indebtedness secured hereby, all right, title, and interest of the Grantor, in and to any insurance policies then in force, shall pass to the purchaser or grantee. In the event of damage to the Mortgaged Property prior to disbursement of the full principal sum secured hereby, no further disbursement shall be required until such damage is repaired or satisfactory arrangements made therefore. Beneficiary may, but shall not be obligated to, make premium payments to prevent such cancellation, and such payments shall be accepted by the insurer. In addition, Grantor shall furnish to Beneficiary duplicate executed copies of each such policy at the time of execution hereof, and copies of each renewal policy not less than thirty (30) days prior to the expiration of the original policy or the preceding renewal policy (as the case may be), together with receipts or other evidence that the premiums thereon have been paid; and furnish to Beneficiary on or before 120 days after the close of each fiscal year of Grantor a statement certified by a duly authorized officer of Grantor of the amounts of insurance maintained in compliance with this subsection, of the risks covered by such insurance and of the insurance company or companies which carry such insurance. In addition, grantor shall carry and maintain such liability and indemnity insurance as may be required from time to time by the Beneficiary. Certificates of such insurance, premiums prepaid, shall be deposited with the Beneficiary and shall contain provision for ten (10) days prior notice to the Beneficiary prior to any cancellation thereof.

4.6. *Restoration Following Casualty.* In the event of the happening of any casualty, of any kind or nature, ordinary or extraordinary, foreseen or unforeseen (including any casualty for which insurance was not obtained or obtainable), resulting in damage to or destruction of the Mortgaged Property or any part thereof, Grantor will give notice thereof to Beneficiary and if Beneficiary elects to apply the insurance proceeds to the restoration, as provided in Article 4.5, repair or replacement of the Mortgaged Property, grantor will promptly, at Grantor's sole cost and expense, whether or not the insurance proceeds,

4.3. *Payment of Imposition.* Grantor will duly pay and discharge, or cause to be paid and discharged, the Imposition, such Impositions or installments thereof, to be paid not later than the due date thereof, or the day any fine, penalty, interest, or cost may be added thereto or imposed by law for the nonpayment thereof (if such day is used to determine the due date of the respective item); provided, however, that if, by law, any Imposition may, at the option of the taxpayer or other person obligated to pay it, be paid in installments (whether or not interest shall accrue on the unpaid balance of such Imposition), Grantor may exercise the option to pay the same in such installments.

4.4. *Repair.* Grantor will keep the Mortgaged Property in good order and condition and make all necessary or appropriate repairs, replacements and renewals thereof, and additions and betterments and improvements thereto, interior and exterior, structural and nonstructural, ordinary and extraordinary, foreseen and unforeseen, and use its best efforts to prevent any act or thing which might impair the value or usefulness of the Mortgaged Property or any part thereof.

4.5. *Insurance.* Grantor shall keep the improvements now existing or hereafter erected on the premises insured as may be required from time to time by the Beneficiary against loss or damage by an abatement of rental income resulting from fire, and such other hazards, casualties, and contingencies (including but not limited to war risk insurance, if available) in such amounts and for such periods as reasonably may be required by the Beneficiary and will promptly pay when due any premiums on such insurance. All such insurance shall be carried by companies approved by the Beneficiary and the policies and renewals thereof shall be deposited with and held by the Beneficiary and have attached thereto standard noncontribution mortgagee clause (in favor of and entitling Beneficiary to collect any and all proceeds payable under such insurance), as well as standard waiver of subrogation endorsement, all to be in a form acceptable to the Beneficiary. Grantor shall not carry separate insurance, concurrent in kind or form or contributing, in the event of loss, with any insurance required hereunder. In the event of a change in ownership of the premises (in its entirety), immediate notice thereof by mail shall be delivered to all insurers, and in the event of loss, Grantor will give immediate notice to the Beneficiary. If any such insurance policy be subject to cancellation or be endorsed or sought to be endorsed to effect a change in coverage for any reason whatsoever, such insurer will promptly notify Beneficiary and such cancellation or change shall not be effective as to Beneficiary for thirty (30) days after receipt by Beneficiary of such notice. Grantor hereby authorizes Benefi-

3.4. *Mortgaged Property and Other Property.* Grantor has good and marketable title in fee simple to the Land and Buildings and good and marketable title to the Fixtures and Personalty, free and clear of any liens, charges, encumbrances, security interests, and adverse claims whatsoever, except the Permitted Encumbrances.

3.5. *Taxes.* Grantor has filed all federal, state, county and municipal income tax returns required to have been filed by it and has paid all taxes which have become due pursuant to such returns or pursuant to any assessments received by it, and Grantor does not know of any basis for additional assessment in respect to such taxes.

3.6. *Litigation.* There is not now pending against or affecting Grantor, nor, to the knowledge of Grantor, is there threatened, any action, suit or proceeding at law or in equity or by or before any administrative agency, which, if adversely determined, would materially impair or affect its financial condition or operation.

ARTICLE 4
Affirmative Covenants

COMMENT: See discussion at ¶ 3.08[4][d].

Until the entire Indebtedness shall have been paid in full, Grantor hereby covenants and agrees as follows:

4.1. *Corporate Existence.* Grantor will preserve and keep in full force and effect its corporate existence, rights, franchises and trade names.

4.2. *Compliance with Laws.* Grantor will promptly and faithfully comply with, conform to, and obey all present and future laws, ordinances, rules, regulations and requirements of every duly constituted governmental authority or agency and of every Board of Fire Underwriters having jurisdiction, or similar body exercising similar functions, which may be applicable to it or to the Mortgaged Property, or any part thereof, or to the use or manner of use, occupance, possession, operation, maintenance, alteration, repair or reconstruction of the Mortgaged Property, or any part thereof, whether or not such law, ordinance, rule, order, regulation or requirement shall necessitate structural changes or improvements or interfere with the use or enjoyment of the Mortgaged Property.

ARTICLE 3
Representations and Warranties

COMMENT: See discussion at ¶ 3.08[4][c].

Grantor hereby represents and warrants to Beneficiary that:

3.1. *Organization, Corporate Power, Etc.* Grantor (a) is a corporation duly organized, validly existing and in good standing under the laws of the State indicated in the preamble hereof; (b) has the corporate power and authority to own its properties and to carry on its business as now being conducted; (c) is qualified to do business in every jurisdiction in which the nature of its business or its properties makes such qualification necessary, and (d) is in compliance with all laws, regulations, ordinances and orders of public authorities applicable to it.

3.2. *Validity of Loan Instruments.* (a) The execution, delivery and performance by Grantor of the Note and the Security Documents, and the borrowing evidenced by the Note (i) are within the corporate powers of Grantor, (ii) have been duly authorized by all requisite corporate action, (iii) have received all necessary governmental approval, and (iv) will not violate any provision of law, any order of any court or other agency of government, the articles of incorporation by bylaws of Grantor or any indenture, agreement, or other instrument to which Grantor is a party or by which it or any of its property is bound or be in conflict with, result in a breach of or constitute (with due notice and/or lapse of time) a default under any such indenture, agreement or other instrument, or result in the creation or imposition of any lien, charge, or encumbrance of any nature whatsoever upon any of its property or assets, except as contemplated by the provisions of the Security Documents; and (b) the Note and the Security Documents, when executed and delivered by Grantor, will constitute the legal, valid, and binding obligations of Grantor and other obligors named therein, if any, in accordance with their respective terms.

3.3. *Other Information.* All other information, reports, papers, and data given to Beneficiary with respect to Grantor or to others obligated under the terms of the Security Documents are accurate and correct in all material respects and complete insofar as completeness may be necessary to give Beneficiary a true and accurate knowledge of the subject matter.

described shall not exclude any item of personal property not specifically mentioned.

(r) *Rents*—All of the rents, revenues, income, profits and other benefits arising from the use and enjoyment of all or any portion of the Mortgaged Property.

(s) *Security Agreement*—The Security Agreement contained in this Deed of Trust, wherein and whereby Grantor grants a security interest in the Personalty and the Fixtures to Beneficiary.

(t) *Security Documents*—This Deed, the Security Agreement, and the Construction Loan Agreement, now or hereafter securing the payment of the Indebtedness or the observance or performance of the Obligations.

(u) *Trustee or Trustees*— ....

(v) *Grantors*— ....

ARTICLE 2
Grant

COMMENT: See discussion at ¶ 3.08[4][b].

Now, therefore, the Grantor, in consideration of the premises and the sum of Ten Dollars ($10.00), the receipt of which is hereby acknowledged by Grantor, and in order to secure payment of the Indebtedness and the performance and discharge of the Obligations, does by these presents grant, bargain, sell, assign, convey and warrant unto the Trustees, their successors and assigns forever, in fee simple, the Mortgaged Property, subject, however, to the Permitted Encumbrances, to have and to hold the Mortgaged Property unto the Trustees, their successors and assigns forever.

2.1. *Possession.* Until an Event of Default, Beneficiary shall permit Grantor to possess and enjoy the Mortgaged Property and to receive the rents, issues and profits thereof.

2.2. *Condition of Grant.* The condition of these presents is such that if Grantor shall pay or cause to be paid the Indebtedness as and when the same shall become due and payable and shall observe, perform and discharge the Obligations, then Beneficiary shall release and reconvey unto and at the cost of Grantor the Mortgaged Property.

(l) *Maturity Day*—The Maturity Day as stated in the Note.

(m) *Mortgaged Property*—The Land and the Buildings and the Fixtures and the Personalty, together with:

    (i) All rights, privileges, tenements, hereditaments, rights-of-way, easements, appendages and appurtenances of the Land and/or the Buildings belonging or in anywise appertaining thereto, or which hereafter shall in any way belong, relate, or be appurtenant thereto, *whether now owned or hereafter acquired by Grantor;* all right, title, and interest of Grantor in and to any streets, ways, alleys, strips or gores of land adjoining the Land or any part thereof; and

    (ii) All of Grantor's right, title and interest in and to any award or awards heretofore made or hereafter to be made by any Municipal, State or Federal authorities or Boards to the present, and all subsequent owners of the Land and/or the Buildings and/or the Fixtures and/or the Personalty, including any award or awards or settlements hereafter made resulting from condemnation proceedings or the taking of the Land and/or the Buidings and/or the fixtures and/or the Personalty or any part thereof under the power of eminent domain or for any change or changes of grade of streets affecting the Land and/or the Buildings and/or the Fixtures and/or the Personalty; and

    (iii) All the estate, right, title, interest, claim or demand whatsoever of Grantor, either at law or in equity, in and to the Land and the Buildings and the Fixtures and the Personalty.

(n) *Note*—The Deed of Trust Note, dated as of even date with this Deed, made by Grantor to the order of Beneficiary in the amount secured by this Deed.

(o) *Obligations*—Any and all of the covenants, promises, and other obligations (other than the Indebtedness) made or owing by Grantor or others to or due to Beneficiary under and/or as set forth in the Note and/or the Security Documents and/or otherwise.

(p) *Permitted Encumbrances*—Easements, restrictions, zoning laws and ordinances, minor encroachments and other irregularities in title and other similar encumbrances that do not individually, or in the aggregate, materially detract from the value of the Mortgaged Property or impair the use thereof for the purposes intended, or subject such use to the risk of being impaired.

(q) *Personalty*—All of the right, title and interest of Grantor in and to all furniture, furnishings, equipment, machinery, and all other personal property (other than Fixtures) nor or hereafter located in, upon or about the Land and the Buildings, and as more specifically described in Schedule B attached hereto and made a part hereof. The enumeration of any specific article of personal property herein

(a) *Beneficiary*—..

(b) *Buildings*—Any and all buildings, improvements, alterations, or appurtenances now standing or at any time hereafter constructed or placed upon the Land or any part thereof.

(c) *Construction Lender*—..................................

(d) *Construction Loan Agreement or Loan Agreement*—The Construction Loan Agreement dated ...., 19..., between Grantor and Construction Lender.

(e) *Event(s) of Default*—The happenings and occurrences described in Article 6 of this Deed.

(f) *Fixtures*—All fixtures located upon or within the Buildings or now or hereafter attached to, or installed in, or used in connection with any of the Building and Improvements, including, but not limited to, any and all partitions, dynamos, screens, awnings, motors, engines, boilers, furnaces, pipes, plumbing, elevators, cleaning, call and sprinkler systems, fire extinguishing apparatus, and equipment, water tanks, heating, ventilating, air-conditioning and air-cooling equipment (including all furnaces, heaters, boilers, plants, units, systems, condensers, compressors, motors, ducts and apparatus), built-in refrigerated rooms and gas and electric machinery, appurtenances and equipment. Fixtures as herein defined are also, without limiting the generality hereof, more particularly described in Financing Statement between Grantor and Beneficiary executed simultaneously herewith.

(g) *Grantor*—...

(h) *Impositions*—All (i) real estate and personal property taxes and other taxes and assessments, including, but not limited to .... (ii) other taxes, assessments, fees and governmental or nongovernmental charges levied, imposed or assessed upon or against Grantor or any of its properties.

(i) *Indebtedness*—The principal of and/or interest on, and all other amounts, payments and premiums due under the Note, and all other indebtedness of Grantor to Beneficiary under and/or secured by the Security Documents and/or otherwise.

(j) *Land*—The real estate, easements, and rights described in Schedule A attached hereto.

(k) *Leases*—Any and all leases, subleases, licenses, concessions, or grants of other possessory interests now or hereafter in force, oral or written, covering or affecting the Mortgaged Property, or any part thereof.

signed contained in every instrument now evidencing or securing said indebtedness. No extension of the time for the payment of this note or any installment hereof made by agreement with any person now or hereafter liable for the payment of this note shall operate to release, discharge, modify, change or affect the original liability under this note, either in whole or in part, of any of the undersigned not a party to such agreement. This note is secured by a deed of trust of even date herewith which is a lien on real estate in .... County, ..., and shall be construed by the laws of the State of ....

Notwithstanding any provision herein or in any instrument now or hereafter securing said indebtedness, the total liability for payments in the nature of interest shall not exceed the limits now imposed by the usury laws of the State of ....

Form 3.4

MORTGAGE DEED OF TRUST—ANNOTATED

THIS DEED OF TRUST, made this .... day of ...., 19...., by and between ...., hereinafter referred to as "Grantor" and .... and ...., hereinafter referred to as "Trustee";

WHEREAS, Grantor proposes to erect substantial improvements on the Land and, in order to finance the construction thereof, will borrow the amount of the Note from ...., hereinafter referred to as "Beneficiary" pursuant to a Building Loan Agreement between them, of even date hereof and Grantor has executed and delivered to the Beneficiary its Note, or so much thereof as may be advanced in accordance with the terms of said Building Loan Agreement.

ARTICLE 1
Definitions

COMMENT: See discussion at ¶ 3.08[4][a].

Grantor, Trustee, and Beneficiary agree that, unless the context is otherwise specified or required, the following terms shall have the meanings herein specified, such definitions to be applicable equally to the singular and the plural forms of such terms:

Form 3.3

NOTE

$....................   Date...........

............, State ....

For Value Received, the undersigned (and if more than one, each of the undersigned, jointly and severally) hereby promises to pay to Life Insurance Company, or order, the principal sum of .... Dollars ($............) together with interested to be computed from ...., upon the unpaid principal, at the rate of .... percent (....%) per annum until fully paid. The principal and interest shall be paid in lawful money of the United States at the principal office of .... Insurance Company, in New York City, New York, or at such other place as the legal holder of this note may from time to time designate in writing, by monthly installments in the amount of .... Dollars ($............) each, due and payable on the first day of each and every month, commencing on the first day of ...., 19....; except that monthly installment payments shall not extend beyond the first day of ...., 19...., on which date any principal and interest remaining unpaid shall be due and paid in full.

While any default exists in the making of any of said payments or in the performance or observance of any of the covenants or agreements of this note or of any instrument now or hereafter evidencing or securing the indebtedness evidenced hereby, the undersigned further jointly and severally promise to pay, on each date aforesaid, additional interest, on the principal balance of this note then outstanding at the rate representing the difference between the aforesaid rate and ...... percent (....%) per annum, provided that any additional interest which has accrued shall be paid at the time of, and as a condition precedent to, the curing of any default. Upon any such default, the holder of this note may apply payments received on any amounts due hereunder or under the terms of any instrument now or hereafter evidencing or securing said indebtedness as said holder may determine and, if the holder of this note so elects, notice of election being expressly waived, the principal remaining unpaid with accrued interest shall at once become due and payable.

The undersigned jointly and severally waive presentment, protest and demand, notice of protest, demand and dishonor and nonpayment of this note and agree to pay all costs of collection when incurred, including reasonable attorneys' fees, and to perform and comply with each of the covenants, conditions, provisions, and agreements of any of the under-

Fm. 3.2 REAL ESTATE FINANCING App. B-42

closing) that, until loan repayment, information as to the loan, the property, and the credit of the borrower, any tenant, any guarantor of the loan, or any lease and any future owner may be made available to such participant and to any future potential purchaser of the loan or any part thereof. Upon our being advised of any such participation, either by endorsement hereon by each participant of its acceptance of this application for the loan share specified, or by mailing to applicant prior to loan closing of an executed counterpart of a partial transfer of this application by .... to such participant, with acceptance thereof by the latter, (a) we shall look solely to each participant for its loan portion; (b) we shall, on request, deliver a separate note to each participant and cooperate in closing the loan on any loan portion taken by .... at its .... office; (c) any payments of fees and charges payable hereunder shall be payable to the participant(s) entitled thereto in accordance with their separate agreement; and (d) .... (and any other participant Trust's) obligations under this agreement shall not be personally binding upon, nor shall resort be had to the private property of, any of the trustees or shareholders, officers, employees or agents of such Trust, but the Trust property of such Trust only shall be bound, and each other agreement of such Trust relating to the loan may contain a similar provision.

Submitted by: ....
                            (If Organization, its name, if not, Signature of Applicant)

Address: ....
                            (Signature for Organization—State title below line)

      ....   Date: ....

Applicant's Mailing Address: ....

ACCEPTED AND AGREED TO:

Date:..............   By: ....

ments, and insurance, a call option in mortgagee if, without its consent, all or part of the property is transferred or further encumbered or a material change in identity or control of mortgagor occurs (other than through death), and a requirement for furnishing financial statements, certified to .... satisfaction, of borrower, tenants, any future owner, and any guarantor of the loan or of any lease assigned to ...., and of the property operations.

COMMENT: See discussion at ¶¶ 3.04[6], 3.04[8].

6. Neither the endorsement of any check or draft nor the deposit of any payment delivered pursuant to this application shall be construed as an approval of this application by .... No waiver, assignment, extension or modification shall be effective against ... ., except as specified in a writing signed by it.

COMMENT: See discussion at ¶ 3.04[10].

7. We represent that we have no other commitment on the property and agree that, when accepted by ...., this application will constitute an agreement by us to close the loan on the terms set forth in the accepted application. We represent and agree that the loan funds are required for business or commercial purposes, are not intended to be used and will not be used for family, household, agricultural, or personal purposes, and that truth in lending and similar laws, federal and state, and interest equalization and similar tax laws, do not apply to the loan. We agree that, if more than one advance is provided for, the terms, including the expiration date, shall apply to each advance.

8. We hereby agree that the loan shall be without cost to ...., and we assume liability for and shall pay all costs and expenses required to satisfy the conditions hereof and the making of the loan, including, without limitation, all reasonable expenses for examination and evidence of title, taxes of any nature, survey costs, and recording and attorneys' fees, whether or not the loan closes.

COMMENT: See discussion at ¶ 3.04[15].

9. We recognize that other lenders, including ...., a real estate, may participate in the loan at its inception or thereafter, whereupon each representation and agreement herein shall also run to, and each reference herein to .... shall also refer to such participant, and we consent (the consent to survive loan

of, and no material adverse change in the financial condition of, any borrower, tenant under a lease to be assigned to or guarantor of the loan or any such lease, has occurred or is contemplated, and that no judicial or administrative actions or proceedings are pending affecting any of them or the property, which if adversely determined would materially adversely affect the loan.

COMMENT: See discussion at ¶ 3.04[17].

(c) Evidence that the improvements are undamaged, may be legally occupied free of violation (or claimed violation) of environmental, flood plain, building and zoning laws or other applicable legal and insurance underwriter's requirements, and if not now completed have since been completed and paid for and are ready for occupancy, all to the satisfaction of .... in accordance with plans and specifications approved by ....

COMMENT: See discussion at ¶ 3.04[9].

(d) Fire, extended coverage, and other usual insurance, with standard mortgagee clause, in companies, amounts, and with coinsurance satisfactory to ....

COMMENT: See discussion at ¶ 3.04[12].

(e) As to any leasehold to be mortgaged (which lease must be in all respects satisfactory to ...., in force and free from default), an estoppel certificate from the lessor thereunder. And

(f) An opinion of title (supported by an abstract) or title insurance, as required by ...., from counsel or one or more title companies satisfactory to ...., showing title in the mortgagor satisfactory to ...., the aforementioned note, mortgage, and any desired security agreement, a current survey by a licensed engineer or surveyor satisfactory to .... evidence of compliance with the provisions of this application, an opinion of borrower's counsel (if requested), and other instruments deemed necessary by .... or its counsel for the proper closing of the loan.

COMMENT: See discussion at ¶ 3.04[15].

5. The mortgage may include, without limitation, provision for non-interest-bearing monthly escrow deposits for estimated taxes, assess-

.... (which date of approval will usually precede the date of acceptance hereof). The billing or acceptance of any quarterly installment, whether before or after, or for a period extending beyond, the expiration date and regardless of the stage of completion of any required construction or of the stage of compliance with any other term hereof, shall not waive any term hereof or extend the expiration or any other date herein or be deemed an approval of any matter unless so stated in writing by .... That part of any quarterly installment collected and allocable to a period after the expiration date or after disbursement of the entire loan shall be refunded.

COMMENT: See discussion at ¶ 3.06.

3. We shall furnish promptly such additional information as shall be requested by .... or its counsel, and we shall extend to .... the privilege of erecting its customary sign on the property during construction and of participating in ground-breaking and opening ceremonies.

4. At or prior to closing we shall furnish in form, substance, and enforceability satisfactory to .... and its counsel:

(a) Leases in force, free from default, with term commenced to tenants in possession and on terms satisfactory to ...., accompanied by estoppel certificates, and assigned as additional security by instrument to be recorded (and notice of such assignment to be given to the tenants). The tenants and terms below (except those, if any, preceded by an asterisk, which denotes they are satisfactory but not required) must be included, and no tenant shall have paid rent more than thirty (30) days in advance or be entitled to any set-off. The acceptance of this application after receipt by .... of a copy of any lease is not to be considered as approval of such lease unless so stated by ....

COMMENT: See discussion at ¶¶ 3.05, ¶ 3.08[4][i].

Tenant	*Space*	*Term*	*Annual Rental*	*Percentage Rent*
......	......	......	....	....
......	......	......	....	....
......	......	......	....	....

(b) Evidence that borrower owns the property, that since the date of this application no material change in the identity of or control

(a) If the loan is not closed by ...., 19...., or earlier if all conditions for the loan are fulfilled to satisfaction (but .... shall not be required to disburse the loan prior to ...., 19....); or

(b) If the lender furnishing interim mortgage financing, if any, and the borrower shall not enter into an agreement in standard form for the sale and purchase of the interim loan within thirty (30) days after the date of acceptance of this application or of the making of a commitment for such interim loan, whichever is later; or

COMMENT: See discussion at ¶ 3.04[14].

(c) If this is an application for a construction loan, and borrower fails to enter into a Building and Loan Agreement in standard form incorporating the pertinent provisions of this application by ...., 19....; or

(d) If, as to required improvements not now completed, architectural, structural, mechanical and electrical plans and specifications and a soils report are not furnished to .... within .... days after its acceptance of this application, or if such plans and specifications or report or any materials, workmanship or design are unsatisfactory to .... and not promptly corrected to .... satisfaction (approval not to be unreasonably withheld, and not to impose any responsibility on .... as to adequacy or legality); or

(e) If any loan held by .... on the property (including any prior advance hereunder) or on any other property of applicant or borrower or of an entity in which either has a material interest, directly or indirectly, is in default.

2. We hereby pay, or shall pay on demand

   (a) An (appraisal) (service) charge of ....Dollars ($.....), not returnable.

   (b) In consideration for .... processing this application and for arranging for funds to be available for disbursement hereunder, (i) a cash deposit of ....Dollars ($.....) to be held without interest and returned only upon closing the entire loan (or any advance) or if .... fails to approve the application within a reasonable time, and (ii) a nonreturnable commitment fee of ....Dollars ($.....), plus .... percent (....%) per annum, on .... payable quarterly in advance from the date the loan is approved by with a charge of .... percent (....%) during the .... loan year declining .... percent (....%) per annum each loan year thereafter to not less than one percent (1%) (prepayments to be on interest dates after thirty (30) days notice for part and sixty (60) days for full prepayment, with loan years to be calculated from the first interest date). The loan is to be evidenced by one or more bonds or notes (the "note") of ......

....
(borrower)
and secured by a mortgage or trust deed (the "mortgage"), all as required by ......, creating a first lien on the unencumbered marketable fee simple absolute title to the following property (such lien, however, to be on an unencumbered marketable leasehold estate as to any leasehold mentioned below, with the fee simple title to the leasehold area to be absolute and subject to no encumbrances prior to said leasehold; and such lien to be on the absolute and unencumbered title to the equipment and personal property mentioned below, and to be supplemented by a security agreement, if desired by ......; and all the foregoing property to be owned absolutely by borrower for his own account and not as agent or trustee for another except as expressly stated, with the real estate to be an independent tax lot, taxed separately from other property):

Land Description: ....
(show location-address-size—if part leasehold, specify part)
....

City: ....County: ....State: ....

Description of Improvements:..................................

    COMMENT: For discussion of prepayment clause, see ¶ 3.04[5].

Equipment: All property reasonably necessary or appropriate for proper operation of premises. There must be included (without limitation)..
....

If all or part Leasehold, Term: ....
                                         From   To

    Annual Net Rental: $............
    Options to Renew or Purchase: ....

Purpose of Loan: ....

1. We hereby agree that .... obligation hereunder shall terminate at the option of:

lien on the fee and lessor's interest in such ground lease and shall be assigned to this Company as additional security. The ground lessee must join the fee owner in the execution of the Deed of Trust for the purpose of obligating itself to comply with mortgage covenants.

26. The fee holder listed in the commitment is to join in the execution of the Deed of Trust and in the execution of the Note if such execution of the Note is necessary under .... state law to subject his fee interest, including the rents, issues, and profits arising therefrom, to the lien of this Company's mortgage, and to assure this Company of a valid and enforceable first lien on such fee title and the rents, issues, and profits arising therefrom. In the event such execution of the Note by the fee owner is required, the loan documents shall contain a provision that the Company will not seek a judgment against the fee owner for any personal liability.

27. Simultaneously with the acceptance of this commitment, as consideration for our making the commitment and holding the funds available for you, you will pay us the sum of $8,000, which shall be retained by us irrespective of whether or not the loan contemplated hereby closes. We have received your check in the amount of $16,000, which, upon your acceptance of this commitment, we will credit $8,000 in payment of the above sum and $8,000 as partial payment of the Security Deposit required in Condition No. 19 of this commitment. If the commitment is not accepted within fifteen (15) days, we will credit $16,000 to the application fee.

COMMENT: See discussion at ¶ 3.06.

Form 3.2

PERMANENT MORTGAGE LOAN APPLICATION-COMMITMENT—ANNOTATED

We hereby apply to .... for a mortgage loan of ....Dollars ($.....) for .... years .... months (from the first or only advance) (from the earlier of the final advance or the expiration date referred to in 1 (a) below) with interest at ....percent (....%) per annum.

COMMENT: See discussion at ¶ 3.04[1].

We are to have the right after .... loan years to prepay up to ....Dollars ($.....) in any one loan year (noncumulative) without charge and to prepay additional amounts after .... loan years

$10,070, and (b) the balance is to be advanced if and when said leasing requirement has been met, but not later than ...., 19...., and the monthly payments shall be increased at the time of such advance to an amount sufficient to completely amortize the loan by the maturity date.

The mortgagor shall also certify to this Company in writing at the time of closing that in leasing space in the Real Property it has complied with all applicable federal, state and municipal laws, orders, rules and regulations regulating or controlling the rents which the mortgagor is permitted to charge.

COMMENT: See discussion at ¶ 3.04[2].

22. Option to Accelerate Loan. During the fifteenth (15th) loan year, the company, upon six (6) months notice, will have the option to require an increase of monthly payments to amortize the loan in twenty-five (25) years from the date of closing rather than thirty (30) years. In the event this option is exercised, the mortgagor shall have the right to prepay the loan in full without prepayment charge within six (6) months after notice of the exercise of the option is given by this Company.

COMMENT: See discussion at ¶ 3.04[4].

23. Buy and Sell Agreement. Prior to ...., 19...., you shall have obtained a construction loan from an interim lender satisfactory to us, evidenced by loan documents incorporating the terms of the permanent loan to be made by this Company, which documents shall be first approved by us, and on or before such date, you and such interim lender shall have also entered into a written agreement with, and in form and substance satisfactory to this Company assuring us of the right to purchase such loan documents.

For your guidance, a sample form of a Buy and Sell Agreement is enclosed.

COMMENT: See discussion at ¶ 3.04[14].

24. Receipt of monthly construction progress reports satisfactory to this Company should be prepared by a licensed engineer. All fees and expenses incurred for the preparation of these reports are to be paid by the mortgagor.

25. The terms, provisions, and conditions of the ground lease shall comply with this Company's substantive requirements as well as such requirements as to form and substance as and shall be necessary to secure the approval of our local counsel and the Office of the General Counsel. Any such ground lease shall be subordinate to this Company's

in writing signed by the parties hereto. See page(s) .... for supplementary conditions which are incorporated herein and made a part hereof.

INSURANCE COMPANY

By: ....

TO INSURANCE COMPANY

The undersigned hereby unconditionally confirms the foregoing commitment in accordance with the terms and conditions therein contained and agrees to be bound thereby, and in accordance therewith agrees that the mortgage loan that you have agreed to make or purchase will be accepted or sold by the undersigned on the terms and conditions set forth herein.

Date: ....

....

ADDENDUM

MORTGAGOR: ...., a general partnership; ground lessee; and .... fee owners, who are to subject entire site to the lien of the mortgage.

SUPPLEMENTARY CONDITIONS

21. Leasing Requirements. The annual rental from not more than 79.5 percent of the rooms in the buildings of the Real Property on an unfurnished basis shall not be less than $273,546, and the space rented shall be rented on a basis so that if the buildings were 100 percent rented, the annual rental would be at least $343,800. Such rooms shall be occupied by tenants on a current rent-paying basis under written leases or rental agreements having terms of not less than one year. The mortgagor shall deliver to us a rent-roll certified to be correct and indicating the apartments of which said rooms comprise the total rooms relied upon to satisfy this condition. No rental concessions to tenants shall have been made, and said certificate should so state.

If by ....,19....,[*closing date*] said annual rental has not been achieved on the foregoing basis, the loan is to be closed as a two-payment loan, i.e., (1) the amount of $1,280,000 is to be paid out not later than ...., 19...., without said leasing requirement, in which event the monthly installments of interest and principal shall be

conditions of this commitment, unless we have waived such default in writing, our obligations hereunder shall cease as of said expiration date or as of such earlier date, but your obligation for the payment of damages by reason of such default shall survive until fully paid and satisfied. Your acceptance of any other loan commitment with respect to the Real Property, except for said interim financing, shall be deemed a default hereunder.

COMMENT: See discussion at ¶ 3.06.

19. Security Deposit. Concurrently with your acceptance hereof, and so long as this commitment shall remain in effect, you shall maintain on deposit with us as security for the performance of your obligations hereunder $32,000 in cash,* which we shall hold but not in trust and without interest. If for any reason the transaction contemplated hereby is not consummated and the Loan is not acquired by us within the time herein set forth for such consummation and acquisition by us, we shall have the right, in our absolute discretion, and without the requirement of any notice to you, to apply said amount in payment of the liquidated damages provided for in the preceding paragraph. It is further understood that if the Loan herein contemplated shall not have been acquired by us as herein provided, we shall return the aforesaid deposit to you.

COMMENT: See discussion at ¶ 3.06.

20. Expiration Date—Date of Closing.** Our obligation under this commitment to make or purchase this mortgage loan and your obligation to accept or sell may be extended by us beyond the last mentioned date in writing, from time to time, in our sole discretion, if the conditions of this commitment have not been met by said date.

Your confirmation of this commitment must be indicatd by your signing and returning to us the enclosed counterpart within fifteen (15) days from the date hereof. Until receipt thereof by us, we will have no obligation hereunder. This commitment supersedes any and all previous commitments with respect to this transaction and may be modified only

---

*See Condition No. 27. The balance of $24,000 may be in the form of an Irrevocable Letter of Credit satisfactory to us.

**The acquisition of the loan by us shall take place on ...., 19...., provided all of the conditions of this commitment have been met, but we shall have the option to acquire the loan at such earlier date as we may determine.

void. It is understood, however, that consent will not be withheld to assignment of the commitment to a bank or other financial institution for the purpose of obtaining interim financing. This commitment cannot be changed, discharged, or terminated orally, but only by an instrument in writing signed by the party against whom enforcement of any change, discharge, or termination is sought.

COMMENT: See discussion at ¶ 3.04[10].

17. Expenses. Your confirmation of this commitment shall constitute your unconditional agreement to pay all fees, expenses, and charges in respect to the Loan, or its making or transfer to us or in any way connected therewith including, without limiting the generality thereof, the fees and expenses of local counsel should local counsel be employed by us in connection with this transaction, title insurance and survey costs, recording and filing fees, mortgage taxes, documentary stamps, and any other taxes, fees, and expenses payable in connection with this transaction. We shall not be required to pay any premium or other charge or any brokerage fee or commission or similar compensation in connection with this transaction, and by your confirmation of this commitment you agree to defend, indemnify, and hold us harmless against and from any and all claims for any fees, charges, commissions, taxes, and compensation in connection with the Loan or its making or transfer to us or in any way connected therewith. Your obligation for such expense, fees, charges, compensation, and taxes shall be in addition to your obligation to pay the amount of liquidated damages, if any, hereinafter referred to.

COMMENT: See discussion at ¶ 3.04[15].

18. Liquidated Damages. In consideration of our making this commitment and holding ourselves willing and ready to acquire the Loan within the time hereinafter stated, and in further consideration of the substantial services that we as prospective mortgagee have rendered and will be required to render and incur in preparation for the closing, and in view of the difficulty of ascertaining the amount of damages that would be sustained by us should this Loan not be acquired by us, your acceptance of this commitment shall constitute your unconditional obligation to pay .... Insurance Company, as liquidated damages, the sum of $32,000 on our demand, if the Loan has not been acquired by us on or before the expiration date of the commitment as herein set forth in full compliance with the conditions of this commitment. If the Loan has not been acquired by us by the said expiration date or if you have defaulted prior to said date in any of the terms or

delivered to us, insuring us as a holder of the indebtedness secured by the first mortgage or deed of trust provided for herein, subject only to such exceptions as shall be approved by our Office of the General Counsel. The title policy shall show no delinquent taxes and assessments affecting the Real Property or any part thereof on the date of closing.

COMMENT: See discussion at ¶ 3.04[15].

12. Compliance With Law. Evidence satisfactory to us shall be furnished, certifying that all improvements and their use comply fully with all applicable zoning and building laws, ordinances and regulations, and all other applicable federal, state and municipal laws and requirements. The Loan and our making or purchase thereof shall be in all respects legal and shall not violate any applicable law or other requirement of any governmental authority.

COMMENT: See discussion at ¶ 3.04[9].

13. Survey. Within a reasonable time prior to date of closing, a survey of a licensed surveyor satisfactory to us and the title company, prepared after completion of improvements and dated not more than thirty (30) days prior to closing, shall be furnished us. The survey shall show dimensions and total square foot area of the Real Property; interior lot lines, if any; dimensions and location of improvements; parking areas; easements, if any; location of adjoining streets; and the distance to and names of nearest intersecting streets; and such other details as to the Real Property as may be requested by us.

COMMENT: See discussion at ¶ 3.04[15].

14. Estoppel. If we are to acquire the Loan by assignment, we must be furnished with estoppel affidavit of the mortgagor or interim mortgagee stating the amount then unpaid on the evidence of indebtedness and that no defenses or setoffs exist with respect thereto. A certificate as to disbursement of the full amount of our Loan and such other documents and certificates as we shall require shall also be furnished.

15. Street Dedication. All streets necesssary for access to the Real Property must be completed, dedicated, and accepted for maintenance and public use by the appropriate governmental authorities and satisfactory evidence thereof submitted to us.

16. Assignability. Neither this commitment nor the Loan proceeds shall be assignable without our prior written consent, and without such consent there shall be no right to designate a payee of such Loan proceeds. Any attempt at assignment without such consent shall be

and we shall be furnished with evidence satisfactory to us that all the aforesaid are paid for or that adequate provision is made therefor. Any work or materials not directly noted in the plans and specifications but necessary for the proper carrying out of the intention thereof are to be implied and are to be provided for as if specifically described. Incorporation into the improvements of any work or materials or equipment that do not conform to such standards at any time during the course of the work shall be deemed an immediate default hereunder.

7. Architect's Certificate. Prior to date of closing, a final certificate of completion by the mortgagor's architect .... shall be delivered to us, certifying that the buildings and improvements have been completed in accordance with the final plans and specifications approved by us and in accordance with applicable law, on a form of architect's certificate furnished by us.

8. Audit. The mortgage documents shall contain a covenant requiring the mortgagor, without expense to us, to furnish an annual audit of the operation of the Real Property, showing in reasonable detail total rents received and total expenses together with annual balance sheets and profit and loss statements, prepared and certified by a certified public accountant, within 120 days after the close of each fiscal year, and such interim balance sheets and profit and loss statements as may be required by us.

9. Waiver of Redemption. If the statutes of the state in which the Real Property is located provide a right of redemption but permit the mortgagor to waive that right, such provision shall be incorporated in the mortgage documents.

10. No Material Change. Except as may be otherwise provided herein, the Loan, the income and expenses of the Real Property, the occupancy leases, and all other features of the transaction shall be as represented in the mortgage loan application without material change.

Prior to date of closing, no part of the Real Property shall have been damaged and not repaired to our satisfaction, nor taken in condemnation or other similar proceeding, nor shall any such proceeding be pending. Neither the mortgagor nor any tenant under any lease to be assigned as security nor any guarantor of the Loan or any such lease shall be the subject of any bankruptcy, reorganization, or insolvency proceeding. No default shall have occurred and be continuing in the performance of any obligation in the instruments evidencing or securing the Loan or incidental thereto.

COMMENT: See discussion at ¶ 3.04[17].

11. Title Insurance. Title insurance, in form and issued by title company(ies) satisfactory to us in the amount of the Loan shall be

maintenance, and operation of the Real Property (other than trade fixtures or personal property of space tenants) shall be delivered to our mortgage loan manager and shall have attached thereto a certification by the mortgagor that said inventory is a true and complete schedule of the fixtures and personal property used in the management, maintenance, and operation of the Real Property, and that the items specified in said inventory constitute all of the fixtures and personal property required for the proper management, maintenance, and operation of the Real Property, and that all of said items are owned by mortgagor free and clear of conditional sales contracts and other title retention arrangements, except as specified in the certification.

If any of said items are not thus free and clear, please specify in the certification which items are not free and clear, the names of persons having an interest in the personal property, the nature of their interest, if the interest is evidenced by a written instrument, the date and place of recording of the instrument and the amount of the indebtedness for which the interest in the personal property was given or retained as security.

4. Commencement and Completion of Construction. Final plans and specifications for the improvements contemplated by this commitment must be approved by us prior to commencement of construction. Construction shall commence on or before ...., thereafter be diligently prosecuted, and shall be completed on or before .19...... Failure so to do, unless time for commencement and/or completion is extended by us in writing, shall be deemed a default hereunder. A report from our appraiser, confirming compliance with the condition of completion in accordance with the plans and specifications as appraised must be furnished us prior to date of closing.

COMMENT: See discussion at ¶ 3.04[11].

5. Changes in Final Plans and Specifications. No change of any substance shall be made in the final plans and specifications approved by us pursuant to General Condition 4 without prior written approval by us. The making of such change without our prior written approval and its incorporation into the structure shall be deemed a default hereunder. Two copies of final plans and specifications and any changes thereto shall be furnished us.

6. Standards of Construction. The buildings and all other improvements contemplated by this commitment, including grading, landscaping, and all other on- and off-site improvements, shall be made and completed of first-class materials and in a good, substantial and workmanlike manner in accordance with the plans and specifications approved by us and shall be fully equipped with first-class equipment, the Real Property shall be satisfactory to us, including the term, the tenants, and the rent payable. Within a reasonable time prior to date of closing, you shall meet our requirements as to which leases, if any, shall be made superior and which shall be made subordinate to the mortgage.

COMMENT: See discussion at ¶¶ 3.08[4][i] and 3.05. This clause is inapplicable to apartment building loans.

A complete list of each and every lease and any security deposits made thereunder of any part of the Real Property shall be delivered to our mortgage loan manager. Said list shall show unit number, type, name of tenant, monthly rental, date to which paid, term of lease, date of occupancy, date of expiration and any and every special provision, concession, or inducement granted to tenant.

GENERAL CONDITIONS

1. Approval of General Counsel. The form and substance of each and every document evidencing the Loan and the security therefor or incident thereto, and any proceedings incident thereto, and the title and evidence thereof must be satisfactory to our Office of the General Counsel.

COMMENT: See discussion at ¶ 3.04[13].

2. Hazard Insurance. Policies, in form and issued by companies satisfactory to us, of fire and extended coverage and such other hazard insurance (including war damage insurance, if available from the U.S. Government or any agency thereof) as we may require, are to be delivered to us (and maintained during the term of the Loan) with acceptable mortgagee clauses in our favor and, where required by us, waiver of subrogation clauses attached, in the amount (if written at 80 percent co-insurance) of at least $1,600,000, together with evidence of payment of premiums thereon. Should we require or be furnished with a higher co-insurance percentage, a proportionately higher amount of insurance will be required. A higher co-insurance percentage will be required in any event to conform to requirements of occupancy leases. We will also require insurance in an amount sufficient to cover fixtures and articles of personal property to the extent the latter are required as security for the mortgage. An insurance schedule for our approval must be submitted at least fifteen (15) days prior to closing.

COMMENT: See discussion at ¶ 3.04[12].

3. Certified Inventory. An inventory showing make, model, serial number, and location of all personal property used in the management,

COMMENT: See discussion at ¶ 3.04[5].

THE SECURITY

The evidence of indebtedness shall be secured by a mortgage or deed of trust which shall be a first lien on the marketable fee simple absolute title to the real property, the appurtenances thereto, and the improvements to the property described herein and in the mortgage loan application (herein collectively called the "Real Property") and such other security as is hereinafter described, subject only to such encumbrances as shall be acceptable to us and free of the possibility of any prior mechanics' or materialmen's liens or special assessments for work completed or under construction on the date of closing.

The Real Property
   Location: ....
   Plot Size: 204,730 sq. ft. (4.7 acres ±)
   General Description of Improvements: 13-2 sty. frame and masonry air conditioned apt. bldgs., recreation bldg. with sauna and laundry, swimming pool, shuffleboard, handball court and putting green, on-site parking for 180 cars including 120 covered spaces net rentable area 114,420 sq. ft. 120 apts.—450 rms.—150 full baths—60 half baths.
   Layout:
      30—3½ rm., 1 bedrm., 1 bath
      60—3½ rm., 1 bedrm., 1½ bath
      30—4½ rm., 2 bedrm., 2 bath

Fixtures and Personal Property. A chattel mortgage constituting a first lien, free of conditional sales contracts and other title retention arrangements (except as approved by us in writing) is required on all fixtures and personal property used in the management, maintenance, and operation of the Real Property (other than trade fixtures or personal property of space tenants).

Occupancy Leases. Each lease of any part of the real Property shall be executed in form satisfactory to our Office of the General Counsel and assigned to us as additional security for the Loan. The assignment shall be recorded and notice thereof served on the tenants. As to each lease to be assigned, the lease shall be in full force and effect, there shall be no rental offsets or claims or defenses to enforcement of the lease, the tenant shall have accepted its premises, confirmed commencement of the lease term, and shall have acknowledged that it is in occupancy and paying rent on a current basis. Evidence to that effect satisfactory to us shall be furnished us. The substance of all leases affecting any part of

Form 3.1

PERMANENT MORTGAGE LOAN COMMITMENT—ANNOTATED

............, 19....

.... Insurance Company will make the first mortgage loan, identified below and herein referred to as the "Loan," based on the representations made in the mortgage loan application, subject, however, to compliance with each of the terms and conditions set forth herein prior to date of closing of the Loan.

THE LOAN

Mortgagor: ....

Loan Amt.: $1,600,000   Int. Rate: 8¾ percent (8¾%)per annum- Term: thirty (30) years zero (0) months

COMMENT: See discussion at ¶ 3.04[1].

REPAYABLE: MONTHLY INSTALLMENTS OF $12,587.21 INCLUDING INTEREST, THE BALANCE OF PRINCIPAL, IF ANY, TO BE PAID ON MATURITY OF THE LOAN.

REQUIRED DEPOSITS: MONTHLY DEPOSITS OF 1/12TH OF THE ANNUAL TAXES AND HAZARD INSURANCE PREMIUMS AS ESTIMATED BY US TO ACCUMULATE FOR SUCH CHARGES WHEN DUE. NO INTEREST SHALL BE PAYABLE ON SUCH DEPOSITS. INSTALLMENTS AND DEPOSITS SHALL BE DUE AND PAYABLE ON THE TENTH DAY OF EACH MONTH.

COMMENT: See discussion at ¶ 3.04[6].

Prepayment Privilege: No privilege is reserved to prepay principal during the first fifteen (15) loan years. Beginning with the sixteenth loan year, and upon sixty (60) days written notice, privilege is reserved to pay the loan in full on any interest date, upon payment of a prepayment charge of 5 percent (5%) if the loan is paid in full during the sixteenth loan year, such prepayment charge to decline one-quarter of one percent (¼ of 1%) per year beginning with the seventeenth loan year. The prepayment charges are to be computed on the unpaid principal balance at the time of such prepayment. It is understood and agreed that the sixteenth loan year stated herein commences on the expiration of fifteen (15) years from the date of the first required amortization payment.

(3) To pay Limited Partners any remaining balances credited to their drawing or capital accounts;

(4) To pay General Partners any remaining balances credited to their drawing or capital accounts.

ARTICLE 7
MISCELLANEOUS

Section 7.1. *Arbitration.* Any dispute arising out of or in connection with this Agreement shall be decided by arbitration in accordance with the ten prevailing commercial arbitration rules of the American Arbitration Association, and judgment thereon may be entered in any court having jurisdiction thereof.

Section 7.2. *Binding Effect.* This Agreement shall be binding upon, and inure to, the benefit of the heirs, executors, administrators, personal representatives and assigns of the respective Partners.

Section 7.3. *Applicable Law.* This Agreement shall be construed in accordance with the laws of the State of ....

Section 7.4. *Amendment.* This Agreement may be amended with the written consent of the General Partners and Limited Partners owning at least 50 percent (50%) of Partnership capital.

Section 7.5. *Notices.* Any notice required or desired to be given to any Partner or the Partnership shall be in writing and shall be sufficient if sent by registered or certified mail to the last known address of the Partner, or in the latter case, the principal office of the Partnership.

IN WITNESS WHEREOF, the Partners have executed this Agreement on ...., 19.....

General Partners:

....

....

Limited Partners:

....

....

goodwill in the partnership agreement. Such payments would be regarded as "income payments" under I.R.C. § 736(a), but the estate of the deceased partner would pay no income tax on the payments, since it would receive a stepped-up (to fair market value) basis in the partnership interest under I.R.C. § 1014. In the case of a retiring partner who stands on a less equitable footing, there would be taxable gain, but it would be capital gain if the partnership doesn't own collapsible assets.

Finally, it is quite appropriate and feasible to fund a buy-sell agreement with life insurance policies on the lives of all general partners which are owned and paid for by the partnership. In this way, the continuing partners could be relieved from the potential ordeal of foregoing the use of precious working capital to fund their obligation to a retiring partner or to the estate of a deceased partner imposed by the buy-sell agreement.

ARTICLE 6
Dissolution and Termination of the Partnership

Section 6.1. *Causes of Dissolution.* The Partnership shall not be dissolved prior to the expiration of the Partnership term except in the event (1) any General Partner retires, dies, is expelled, becomes incompetent and/or bankrupt and the business is not continued by the remaining General Partners in accordance with Section 5.2(1); or (2) all of the Partners, both General and Limited, unanimously agree to dissolve.

COMMENT: Observe that U.P.A. §§ 31(2) and 32 permit other causes of dissolution; however, any partner dissolving the partnership in contravention of the Agreement would probably subject himself to damages. (See U.P.A. § 38(2).)

Section 6.2. *Winding up the Partnership.* In winding up the affairs of the Partnership after dissolution, the Partners shall continue to share profits and losses in the same manner as before dissolution, and the liquidation proceeds shall be applied in the following priority:

(1) To pay all amounts owed to creditors of the Partnership other than Partners;
(2) To pay Partners for unpaid salaries and loans made to the Partnership;

retiring partner's interest to an outsider, and to lessen the economic burden on the deceased partner's family by automatically converting his interest into a certain cash sum. The sale of an interest to a stranger, whether it be the widow or child of the deceased partner or transferee of a retiring partner, might disrupt the personal interrelationship between the managing partners. Yet Section 5.2 hereof addresses this concern simply by making the assignee an "additional" limited partner without the right to partake in management decisions. In the case of a deceased general partner, it is ordinarily preferable for the family to liquidate the partnership interest, since the liquidation proceeds can be used to pay the debts of the estate and/or perhaps can be invested in a more appropriate income-producing medium. Also, while the valuation set forth in a "right of first refusal agreement" (Section 5.1(2)) is not binding on the Revenue Service for federal estate tax purposes, the valuation fixed in a "buy-sell" agreement is, under most circumstances, whether or not the partnership is obligated to purchase the interest.

Obviously, the continuing partners would prefer a low valuation figure, whereas the retiring partner or representative of the deceased partner would favor a high valuation. Accordingly, in a time of rising prices and liberal depreciation rules, the former group would seek a valuation of partnership assets based on book value, and the latter group would press for use of a fair market valuation. However, since every general partner must view himself in the dual role of either a prospective *remaining* partner, or a prospective retiree or decedent, a rational compromise might be to adjust the book value by some agreed-upon percentage (e.g., 50 percent) of the increase or decrease in fair market value over book value. Perhaps the most frequent mode of valuation is simply to use book value because it is simple and avoids the guesswork and conflicts associated with appraisal. Yet use of book value may be onerous to either side when it varies significantly from fair market value. In any event, this is something that must be discussed candidly and planned early, rather than relegated to a post-hoc determination.

From a tax perspective, an entity-retirement is preferable to a cross-purchase arrangement where the partners agree that some goodwill exists since the partnership would be entitled to deduct any payments for goodwill if no reference is made to

allocate value to goodwill by amending the partnership agreement retroactively, afortiori, any ad hoc determination on whether to arrange a liquidation versus a sale and/or whether to recognize goodwill should be recognized. (See David Foxman, 41 T.C. 535 (1964); Crenshaw v. United States, 116 F.2d 737 (5th Cir. 1971); and Comm'r v. Jackson Inv. Co., 346 F.2d 187 (9th Cir. 1965).)

Section 5.2. *Death of a General Partner*

(1) The retirement, expulsion, death, incompetency and/or bankruptcy of a General Partner shall dissolve the Partnership unless the business is continued by the remaining General Partners with the written consent of a majority of the then-remaining Partners, both General and Limited [with the written consent of Limited Partners owning collectively at least 50 percent (50%) of Partnership capital]. If the remaining General Partners continue the business of the Partnership, the personal representative or assignee of the retiring, expelled, deceased, incompetent, or bankrupt General Partner shall become an additional Limited Partner with the same right to share profits and losses and with the same balance in his capital and/or drawing account as had been owned by the retiring, expelled, deceased, incompetent, or bankrupt General Partner.

(2) OPTIONAL—*Buy-Sell Agreement on Death of a General Partner.* On the death or retirement of any General Partner, the Partnership will be required to acquire the interest of the deceased or retiring Partner. The value of the interest so acquired shall equal in amount the sum of the deceased (or retiring) Partner's capital account and his proportionate share of Partnership net income or loss accrued to the date of this death or retirement, unless included in his drawing account. Within sixty (60) days after the death or withdrawal of the Partner, he or his personal representative shall receive from or pay to the Partnership any positive or negative balance in his drawing account, as the case may be. In valuing his interest, all Partnership assets shall be valued at book value except that the parties shall determine separately the fair market value of the Partnership's unrealized receivables (as defined in I.R.C. § 751(a)), if any; inventory items (as defined in I.R.C. § 751(d)(2)), if any; and real property, if any. Fifty percent (50%) of the difference between the fair market and book value of these items, if any, shall increase or decrease the deceased or retiring Partner's capital account, as the case may be.

COMMENT: The purpose of the buy-sell agreement is primarily twofold: to obviate the need for a sale of the deceased or

By doing so, they can thereafter increase *their* basis in the assets (for purposes of maximizing their share of depreciation and/or minimizing their share of ordinary gain from a future sale of such assets) if the partnership elects an adjustment to basis of partnership property under I.R.C. § 754. (See I.R.C. § 743(b) and regulations thereunder.) The selling partner will want to minimize the amount allocable to collapsible assets, since his gain attributable to the sale of such property will be ordinary income under I.R.C. § 741. Since the interests of the selling partner and remaining purchasing partners are antithetical, any arm's-length allocation will generally be respected by the Revenue Service. (Reg. § 1.751-1(c)(3).)

Likewise, the partnership may own a substantial amount of goodwill or "going concern" value as reflected by the fact that the success of the venture is dependent upon the personal efforts of the partners and/or the prospective purchaser is willing to pay a price that exceeds the selling partner's prorated market value share of the partnership's net assets. If the partnership wishes to exercise its prerogative to acquire the interest of the retiring partner, the general partners may wish to effect the acquisition by means of a liquidating distribution under I.R.C. § 736 (an "entity-retirement" arrangement) rather than by means of a group purchase by the remaining partners (a "cross-purchase" agreement). The advantage of the former is that additional payments for goodwill are treated as ordinary income payments under I.R.C. § 736(a), which reduce the taxable income of the remaining partners if no value is assigned to goodwill in the partnership agreement. (I.R.C. § 736 (b)(2)(B).) If, on the other hand, the interest of the retiring partner is formally purchased by the remaining partners, the amount allocable to goodwill would produce only capital gain for the retiring partner, and the continuing partnership would be forced to capitalize the payment for goodwill. The purpose of the language in Section 5.1 is to accord the general partners maximum flexibility in resolving this potential tax conflict by negotiations between the parties at the time of acquisition, if this becomes necessary. Again, since the tax interests of the parties are antithetical, the regulations regard as correct any valuation of goodwill arrived at by the parties in an arm's-length agreement. (Reg. § 1.736-1(b)(1).) Since form reigns supreme over substance in this area, so that the parties can even change their minds on whether or not to

thereof shall be entitled to purchase the interest or portion thereof on a prorated basis determined by a majority of the General Partners. In the event the entire interest is not acquired in the foregoing manner, the retiring Limited Partner may sell his interest or the remaining portion thereof to the proposed transferee on the terms contained in the notice of sale.

If the interest of the retiring Partner is acquired by the Partnership or collectively purchased by the remaining Partners, the General Partners at the time of acquisition shall at their option separately determine the amounts of the liquidating distribution or, in the latter case, the amounts of the purchase price allocable to the value of the retiring Partner's interest in the Partnership's unrealized receivables (as defined in I.R.C. § 751(a)), if any, inventory items (as defined in I.R.C. § 751(d)(2)), and goodwill, if any.

COMMENT: While the sale of a limited partner's interest to a stranger is of less concern than a change in the composition of the managerial group, it may be appropriate to restrict transferability by means of a "right of first refusal" agreement to help keep a cohesive group of investors intact so that it can more effectively interact with the managing partners. Moreover, there may be a legal reason for constricting the class of persons to whom an interest can be assigned; for example, the partnership may want to exercise its right of first refusal to prevent a sale to a nonresident assignee that might threaten the partnership's intrastate exemption from federal or local securities laws. The basic purpose of a right of first refusal is to strike a reasonable balance between respecting the proprietary rights of a selling partner and protecting the remaining partners against intrusions by outsiders. By contrast, the more onerous type of restriction on alienability imposed by Section 5.1(1) may render the partnership interest so unmarketable as to discourage participation by an attractive would-be investor. In addition, this right of first refusal is regarded under Reg. § 301.7701-2(e)(2) as merely a "modified" form of "free transferability of interest" and, as such, is accorded less weight than full transferability in determining whether the organization sufficiently resembles a corporation to be taxed as one.

If the partnership owns untaxed accounts receivables and/or appreciated dealer realty and is accordingly regarded as "collapsible" under I.R.C. § 751, the general partners may want the right to allocate a maximum amount of the selling price to the selling partner's interest in such collapsible assets.

ARTICLE 5
Death or Retirement of Partner

Section 5.1. *Sale of a Partnership Interest.*

(1) *Sale of General Partner's Interest.* A General Partner may not sell or transfer his interest in Partnership capital and/or profits without the written consent of a majority of the then-remaining Partners, both General and Limited [without the written consent of Limited Partners owning collectively at least 50 percent (50%) of Partnership capital], which consent shall not, depending on the circumstances, unreasonably be withheld. Such sale or other disposition may, at the option of the remaining Partners, cause a dissolution of the Partnership in accordance with Section 5.2(1) of this Agreement.

> **COMMENT: Very often the success of the venture will depend upon how well the managing partners interrelate; in addition, the limited partners have in effect bargained for the personal and often unique services of the general partners. Indeed, but for the participation of certain decision-makers, some of these investors may well have decided to invest elsewhere. Accordingly, the remaining general partners, and to a greater degree the limited partners, should be able to restrict the alienability of a general partner's interest. Observe also that under Section 5.2 any transferee or successor in interest of a deceased or retiring general partner becomes a limited, and not general, partner.**

(2) OPTIONAL—*Sale of Limited Partner's Interest—Right of First Refusal.* If any Limited Partner intends to sell or transfer his Partnership interest, said Partner must at least sixty (60) days prior to disposition of his interest, notify the remaining Partners of his intent and identify in writing the proposed transferee and terms of sale. Within forty (40) days after the receipt of such notice, the Partnership may elect to acquire said interest at the price and on the terms proposed to the prospective transferee by means of a liquidating distribution, or if the majority of the remaining Limited Partners agree, by causing all the remaining Partners to purchase said interest on a prorated basis in accordance with the ratio of each Partner's capital interest to the total amount of Partnership capital owned by all the Partners. In the event the interest of the retiring Partner is not acquired by the Partnership or by the remaining Partners collectively, the interest shall next be offered to the remaining Partners as individuals at the price and terms proposed to the prospective transferee. Within twenty (20) days after receipt of the offer, each Partner desiring to purchase the interest or a portion

discretion, be reasonably necessary to perform their duties. Each General Partner may engage in transactions connected with the business of the Partnership and may hold interests in other business ventures of every kind for his own account whether or not such business ventures are in direct or indirect competition with the business of the Partnership and whether or not the Partnership also has an interest therein.

> **COMMENT: The authorities indicate that the fiduciary requirement imposed on partners by both the common law and U.P.A. § 21 is satisfied so long as the competing or dealing partner fully discloses his activities and deals with the partnership on an arm's-length basis. Cf. I.R.C. § 707(a), which provides that absent special circumstances a partner-partnership transaction shall be considered as occurring for tax purposes between the partnership and one who is not a partner.**

Section 4.4. *Partnership Books.* The Partnership books shall fully and accurately reflect the transactions of the Partnership and such books, together with a certified copy of the Certificate of Limited Partnership and any amendments thereto, shall at all times be maintained at the principal place of business of the Partnership and shall be open to the reasonable inspection of the General Partners, original and substituted Limited Partners, and/or their duly authorized representatives.

> **COMMENT: Under U.L.P.A. § 19(3), an assignee who does not become a "substituted" limited partner (because one of the remaining partners objects and the certificate does not empower the assignor to so designate his transferee) has no automatic right to require an account of partnership transactions or to inspect the partnership books.**

Section 4.5. *Accounting Method and Annual Reports.* The Partnership shall maintain its accounting records and report its income for tax purposes on the accrual basis. In addition, the General Partners shall have the books and records of the Partnership examined each year by an independent Certified Public Accountant who shall prepare, on an annual basis, financial statements based on such examination and shall distribute copies thereof to all Partners.

> **COMMENT: Since limited partners cannot partake in management decisions, they should be as well informed as possible about the yearly operations and profitability of the enterprise.**

percent of $120,000) would be the partners' distributive share, and the remaining $4,000 payable to the partners would be guaranteed payments. (See Reg. § 1.707-(c), Examples (1)-(4).) The distinction between a guaranteed payment and adjusting the distributive shares of partnership income is important for tax planning when a partner with an already large profit share wants to minimize his percentage share to avoid a disallowance of a loss (under I.R.C. § 707(b)(1)) or conversion of gain into ordinary income (under I.R.C. § 707(b)(2)), in the event he sells property to the partnership. A pitfall associated with guaranteed-payment treatment is that the entire payment is treated as ordinary income to the payee, even when the payment is funded entirely from capital gains proceeds.

ARTICLE 4
Administrative Provisions

Section 4.1. *Management of the Partnership*. The business of the Partnership shall be managed and controlled solely by the General Partner(s).

COMMENT: This provision simply acknowledges what is required by U.L.P.A. § 7. But observe that the limited partners may nevertheless be consulted and their advice solicited prior to decisions by the general partners. In addition, the authorities suggest that the limited partners can perform ministerial functions and in extraordinary situations even directly perform managerial chores without subjecting themselves to external liability. See text discussion in note 29 at ¶1.05[1].

Section 4.2. *Authority of General Partners*. The General Partners are authorized on behalf of the Partnership to do and perform whatever in their sole discretion is reasonably necessary to effectuate the purposes of the Partnership. By way of the foregoing, the General Partners, except as provided in U.L.P.A. § 9, have all the rights and powers and are subject to all the restrictions and liabilities of a partner in a partnership without limited partners.

COMMENT: This all-inclusive approach is preferable to a detailed enumeration of the general partners' rights and responsibilities, since in the latter case any inadvertent omission may cause negative inferences to be drawn.

Section 4.3. *Outside Activities*. The General Partners shall devote whatever time and attention to Partnership business as may, in their sole

allocate a disproportionate share of capital gains or depreciation losses to a high-bracket partner, general or limited, provided, however, that the allocation is not forgotten by the affected partner in any subsequent business reckoning with his fellow partners.

In addition, under I.R.C. § 704(c), any precontribution appreciation or depreciation in property contributed to the partnership can be taken into account in allocating partnership depreciation and/or gain and loss.

Section 3.2. *Salaries and Other Compensation.*

(a) No interest shall be payable in respect to the Partners' Capital Accounts.

(b) No salary shall be paid to the General Partners for services rendered.

[*ALTERNATIVE PROVISION—Section 3.2A. Salaries*]

Section 3.2A. *Salaries.* The General Partners shall each receive a salary equal to 5 percent (5%) of annual net Partnership profits, computed without regard to the salary deduction, but not less than $10,000 per annum, and any such salaries earned or paid shall, like any other expense, be deductible from Partnership income in determining the profits or losses for distribution to the Partners under Section 3.1.

COMMENT: The purpose of Section 3.2(b) is to reinforce the tax posture of the partnership with respect to Section 3.1A. If the general partners insist upon a minimum guaranteed level of compensation, the salaries paid will be regarded as a guaranteed payment under I.R.C. § 707(c) to the extent such payments are determined without regard to partnership income. Such payments are deductible under I.R.C. § 162(a) as ordinary and necessary business expenses, if not capital in nature. To the extent the payment is geared to partnership income, it is merely regarded as an extra distributive share of ordinary partnership income to the recipient partner, which reduces the income share that would otherwise be paid to the remaining partners. So, for example, if under Section 3.2A each of the general partners received at the end of the fiscal year $15,000 (5 percent of net partnership profits totaling $300,000), no part of the $15,000 would be a guaranteed payment. However, if the partnership had a net income of $120,000, $6,000 (5

(4) *Receipt of Interest in Profits.* Of all the alternatives this is ordinarily preferable in the case of appreciating income-producing property, since a right to future profits is not presently taxable under Reg. § 1.721-1(b)(1) and, under ALTERNATIVE PROVISION—Section 3.2 herein, the partner will be receiving a disproportionate amount of preferred capital or § 1231 gain when the investment property is sold prior to or at liquidation. However, see Sol Diamond, 56 T.C. 530 (1971), aff'd 492 F.2d 287 (7th Cir. 1974), where the Tax Court disregarded the language in Reg. § 1.721-1(b)(1) and held that the taxpayer's receipt of a right to *future* profits was immediately taxable as ordinary compensation income. However, most commentators feel that the *Diamond* decision is distinguishable from the ordinary profit-sharing arrangement since the value of the taxpayer's profit share was measurable (he sold it for $40,000 three weeks after receiving it), and he received it for *past* services rendered.

Moreover, this type of allocation should withstand an attempt by the IRS to characterize the extra capital gain as disguised *ordinary* compensation income in that the "character" of any item included in a partner's distributive share is, under I.R.C. § 702(b), fixed by reference to the business of the partnership and not that of the partner. (See Reg. § 1.702-1(b).) For example, the Service itself has applied this theory in holding that a partner's distributive share of partnership loss resulting from the forced sale of depreciable property was an I.R.C. § 1231 loss rather than an ordinary loss, notwithstanding the partner's past and present status as a real estate dealer. (Rev. Rul. 67-188, 1967-1 C.B. 216.) Moreover, the taxpayer's case for capital gain treatment would be further strengthened under ALTERNATIVE PROVISION—Section 3.2 herein if the partner also owns some partnership capital.

In addition, I.R.C. § 704(b), as amended by the 1976 Tax Reform Act, engenders the partners with flexibility in allocating special income and deduction items among themselves—a valuable tax-planning device that is not available to their corporate counterparts and that represents an important advantage of partnership over corporate taxation. However, any special allocation under I.R.C. § 704(b) will be recognized only if it has "substantial economic effect," in that the capital accounts of the partners are affected independently of tax consequences. (Reg. § 1.704-1. See also discussion in text at 1.05[3][b].) So, for example, the partnership agreement could

(1) *Present Transfer of Vested Interest in Partnership Capital.* The receipt of an unrestricted interest in partnership capital at a below-arm's-length price is immediately taxable, and to make matters worse, such a bargain-purchase of capital is regarded as disguised compenstion income and is accordingly taxable at the ordinary income rate. (Reg. § 1.721-1(b)(1).) Of course, any time the partner is charged with ordinary compensation income, whether in the form of an extra share of capital or simply as a salary, the partnership is entitled to an offsetting ordinary and necessary expense deduction. (I.R.C. § 707(c).) This extra share of capital could be in the form of overcrediting the general partners' capital accounts in exchange for their contribution to the partnership of either an option to purchase property (see Section 2.1A hereof) or the property itself (see Section 2.1B hereof). However, while the general partners presumably have some leeway to ascribe an inflated market value to contributed property (see language in first parenthetical of Reg. § 1.721-1(b)(1)), any egregious overvaluation on their part will subject themselves to a challenge by the IRS that the extra capital received is nothing more than disguised compensation income.

(2) *Transfer of Restricted Interest in Capital.* If, for business reasons, the limited partners want to restrict the capital interests of the general partners (e.g., make the interest nonassignable and forfeitable until the general partners demonstrate managerial competence), and the partnership owns property that is appreciating in value at a fast rate, the general partners should consider electing recognition of gain on the *present* value of the interest under I.R.C. § 83(b) so that any subsequent appreciation in value prior to the lapse of the restrictions will be taxed as capital gain and not as ordinary income (under Reg. § 1.721-1(b)(1)) when the interest in partnership capital is sold or liquidated.

(3) *Receipt of Promise of Future Transfer of Capital.* Of all the alternatives, this is perhaps the most onerous for the general partner since, under Reg. § 1.721-1(b), he would not recognize any income until he receives his capital interest, at which time the entire appreciated value would be treated as ordinary compensation income, and he would be denied the right to use a Section 83(b) election. (Cf. United States v. Frazell, 335 F.2d 487 (5th Cir. 1964).)

[*OPTIONAL PROVISION—Section 2.8. Indemnification of General Partners*]

Section 2.8. *Indemnification of General Partners.* Each General Partner shall be entitled to prompt indemnity from the Partnership for any payment or liability reasonably made or incurred in connection with any act performed by said General Partner within the scope of his authority, except for acts of malfeasance, or gross negligence or misrepresentation, provided that any indemnity shall be paid only out of and to the extent of Partnership assets.

COMMENT: Such an indemnity agreement will not cause the organization to be characterized as possessing "limited liability" and thereby more closely resembling a corporation for tax purposes, since under local law the general partners remain liable to such outside creditors, notwithstanding such agreement. [Reg. § 301.7701-2(d)(1).]

ARTICLE 3

ALLOCATION OF PROFITS AND LOSSES AND SALARIES

Section 3.1. *Profits and Losses.* All Partnership profits and losses shall be distributed in the following proportions:

The General Partners shall receive 10 percent (10%) of all profits and losses. The balance of 90 percent (90%) shall be allocated among all the Partners in proportion to their ownership of Partnership capital.

[*ALTERNATIVE PROVISION—Section 3.1A. Profits and Losses*]

Section 3.1A. *Profits and Losses.* All Partnership profits and losses shall be distributed in the following proportions:

The General Partners shall receive 20 percent (20%) of all capital and I.R.C. § 1231 gains and losses. The balance of 80 percent (80%), and the entire amount of gains and loss, exclusive of capital and I.R.C. § 1231 gains and losses, shall be allocated among all the Partners in proportion to their ownership of Partnership capital.

COMMENT: A common method of compensating the general partner for his promotional and managerial services is to have him receive an interest in partnership capital or profits disproportionate to the interests received by outsiders for the same amount of consideration paid. If the partnership owns rental income-producing realty that is likely to appreciate in value, it should consider the following alternatives:

the general partners with maximum flexibility in characterizing the advance as a loan or contribution depending upon the tax circumstances. For example, a partner with bargaining clout in a not-so-solvent partnership may insist that the advance be regarded as a loan. He would then become eligible for ordinary (and not capital) loss treatment under I.R.C. § 166(a)(1) if the debt is not paid and is proximately related to the taxpayer's trade or business. Otherwise, the additional capital contribution would increase the partner's tax basis and capital loss when the interest is sold (I.R.C. § 741(a)) or liquidated (I.R.C. §§ 731(a)(2), 736 (b)(1)). Whether the advance is denominated as a loan or capital contribution, the partnership income would be reduced by any amounts paid to the payor-partner, since in the former case the partnership would be entitled to an interest deduction, and in the latter case the amounts paid for use of the contributing partner's capital would either reduce the other partners' distributive share of income, or if the payments are fixed, generate an ordinary and necessary business expense deduction. (See Reg. § 1.707-1(c).) (Observe that U.P.A. § 18(c) requires that interest be paid on such advances.)

On the other hand, the payor-partner might prefer to have the advances be regarded as additional capital contributions so that he can increase his potential loss write-off under I.R.C. § 704(d), especially if he is a limited partner and the partnership uses recourse financing. Or perhaps he may demand that the partnership agreement be amended to allocate all partnership losses to him until all of his additional capital contributions have been wiped out. In this way, he will secure the earliest possible deduction if his additional contributions are exhausted because of future operating losses. In the event the partnership revives, subsequent profits of the partnership could be utilized to restore the contributing partner's capital account to its original amount. Since the special reallocation *could* affect the partners' dollar amounts in their capital accounts and has a business purpose, it would be recognized under I.R.C. § 704(b)(2), as amended. Specifically, if the failing partnership did not recover, the contributing partner could wind up with an economic loss at dissolution. Cf. Jean V. Kresser, 54 T.C. 1621 (1970), a similar type of special allocation failed because the reallocation of profits and losses, which the taxpayer failed to prove, was exclusively tax-motivated and could not in the long run change the partners' dollar amounts of capital.

ner in a highly leveraged partnership (where contributions are minimal relative to the total partnership undertaking) may be forced to forgo sharing fully in the *tax* losses of the partnership. For example, suppose limited partner X's distributive share of losses for 1980 is $12,000 (generated by a fast depreciation write-off and low amortization), but his capital contribution and resultant capital account is only $10,000. While in a real estate investment partnership using nonrecourse financing (see Comment at Section 2.8 hereof) X's adjusted basis for purposes of the loss limitation imposed by I.R.C. § 704(d) is bound to be far in excess of $12,000, the IRS will nonetheless most probably argue sham if X takes a $12,000 tax loss and his capital account or drawing account is only debited by $10,000. Accordingly, in a successful venture the partner-taxpayer may be forced to suffer such a temporary deficit in his capital account (technically a liability to the partnership) for the purpose of maximizing his tax-shelter trade-off of ordinary income (to the extent of the depreciation offset against his outside income) for capital gain. For these reasons, Alternative Provision—Section 2.6A is preferable.

Section 2.7. *Loans to the Partnership.* The Partnership shall obtain only nonrecourse financing; accordingly, neither the General Partners nor Limited Partners will be subjected to personal liability with respect to such financing, and the lenders, with respect to any construction, permanent and/or other loan to the Partnership, shall have recourse only against Partnership assets for repayment.

In the event an advance is made to the Partnership by a Partner, such advance shall be deemed in the sole discretion of the General Partners to be either a loan or a capital contribution to the Partnership.

COMMENT: The purpose of the language in the first paragraph is to secure for the limited partners in a leveraged real estate investment partnership (where capital contributions are minimal relative to the total partnership undertaking) an increase in their tax bases equal to their pro rata share of mortgage liabilities. (I.R.C. §§ 704(d), § 752; Reg. § 1.752-1(e).) Maximizing the adjusted basis of the limited partner's partnership interest is of vital importance in any tax-shelter enterprise, since in the early years depreciation losses and tax-free distributions decrease the partner's basis, which is itself the ceiling amount for future deductible losses and tax-free distributions under I.R.C. §§ 704(d) and 731(a)(1), respectively.

The language in the second paragraph is intended to invest

COMMENT: It is advisable to both define with particularity the term "capital account" and maintain relatively fixed and stable capital accounts for each partner, since numerous important tax consequences depend on the amount of a partner's interest in partnership capital. See, for example I.R.C. §§ 707(b) (disallowing losses and rendering gain ordinary on sales between a partner and a related partnership), 704(c)(3) (permitting a special allocation of income and deduction items only if the partner's interests in capital and profits correspond to their undivided interests in contributed property), and 708 (b)(1)(B) (providing for termination if during any twelve-month period there is a sale or exchange of 50 percent or more of the total interest in partnership capital or profits). Moreover, neither law (e.g., IRC and UPA) nor standard accounting usage decides whether withdrawals of cash or retention of earnings are to be regarded as capital adjustments or debt transactions absent agreement by the partners.

Section 2.6. *Liability of Limited Partner.* No Limited Partner shall be personally liable for any debts of the Partnership (or for any loss beyond the amount of his capital interest as a Limited Partner.)

[*ALTERNATIVE PROVISION—Section 2.6A. Liability of Limited Partner*]

Section 2.6A. *Liability of Limited Partner.* No Limited Partner shall be personally liable *to outsiders* for any liability or net loss of the Partnership beyond the amount of his capital interest as a Limited Partner.

COMMENT: This first customary phrase in Section 2.6 is designed merely to quiet the trepidations of the unknowledgeable investor, since it states what is obvious at local law (U.L.P.A. § 1) but, of course, presupposes that the Limited Partners will not partake of management control (U.L.P.A. § 7). However, the second and parenthetical phrase poses, in the authors' judgment, a real, albeit subtle, tax pitfall for the unwary. Section 18(a) of the Uniform Partnership Act and U.L.P.A. §§ 7 and 17(1) when read in pari materia provide that the limited partner, unlike the general partner, may not be forced to absorb losses "beyond the amount of his capital interest" (capital account), but limited partners can tolerate a temporary deficit in their capital or drawing accounts. (See 68 C.J.S. "Partnership" § 478(b)(1).) Otherwise, a limited part-

Partnership. In addition, the General Partners reserve the right to sell additional limited partnership interests in exchange for cash contributions aggregating not more than .... Dollars ($.....) (in excess of the sum of $80,000 contributed by the original Limited Partners) in the event that this becomes necessary in the judgment of the General Partners. The allocation of profits and losses among the Partners shall accordingly be adjusted pursuant to Section ....

> **COMMENT:** Often, the syndicate will need to raise additional venture capital since in most cases the amount of the construction financing and total construction costs and/or carrying charges can only be estimated at the inception of the venture. Characterizing "gap" contributions as loans may induce such contributions since loans have priority over capital contributions in distributions following dissolution (U.P.A. § 40(b) and Section 5.2 hereof); however, interest can be paid on such advances whether they be denominated as loans or capital contributions. (U.P.A. § 18(c).)
>
> It is advisable that a ceiling amount for additional contributions be specified; otherwise, the prudent investor fearing an open-ended dilution of his equity may be deterred from investing in a particular project.

Section 2.4. *Capital Accounts and Distribution of Profits.* An individual capital account shall be established for each Partner equal to his original capital contribution, credited by (1) his additional contributions to capital and (2) his share of Partnership profits if transferred from his drawing account, and debited by (1) distributions to him that reduce his interest in Partnership capital and (2) his share of Partnership losses if transferred from his drawing account.

Section 2.5. *Drawing Accounts.* An individual Drawing Account shall be maintained for each Partner, which shall be credited by his share of Partnership profits, and debited by (1) his share of Partnership losses, and (2) all his withdrawals during the year, which shall be limited to such amounts as the General Partners determine from time to time. A credit balance in the Partner's Drawing Account shall constitute a liability of the Partnership to the Partner involved, and shall not increase such Partner's interest in Partnership capital unless the General Partners determine otherwise. A debit balance in the Partner's Drawing Account shall constitute a liability of the Partner involved to the Partnership and shall not decrease such Partner's interest in Partnership capital unless the General Partners determine otherwise.

($.....), if the leasing requirement (referred to in paragraph (iv) above) pursuant to condition No. .... of the Permanent Mortgage Loan Commitment is not met.

(e) *OPTIONAL:* It is understood and agreed that if ACE INSURANCE CO. does not purchase from CONSTRUCTION LOAN BANK the note secured by the first mortgage (deed of trust) by ...., 19...., [*closing date*], then the General Partners will, within a reasonable time, obtain for and on behalf of the Partnership a long-term loan (or loans) sufficient in amount to pay and satisfy the indebtedness to CONSTRUCTION LOAN BANK, evidenced by the aforesaid note in favor thereof, and on such terms and conditions as in the discretion of the General Partners may be in the best interests of the Partnership, and shall give written notice of the terms of such substitute loan(s) to the Limited Partners, who will have sixty (60) days to accept or reject the terms of the substitute loan(s). If for any reason such terms are not acceptable to at least a majority of the Limited Partners, then within thirty (30) days after written notice of such rejection, the General Partners shall redeem the interests of the Limited Partners by returning their initial capital contributions.

Section 2.2. *Limited Partners and Their Contributions.* The original Limited Partners and their initial capital contributions to the Partnership shall be as follows:

Limited Partner	*Initial Capital Contribution*
ALVIN ADAMS	$20,000
BEN BRUCE	20,000
CHARLES CAROL	20,000
DAN DAILY	20,000

Section 2.3. *Additional Capital Contributions.* In the event the General Partners at any time deem additional capital contributions reasonably necessary to fund increased construction costs and/or financing costs, and/or to otherwise conduct the business of the Partnership, the Limited Partners shall make such subsequent capital contributions as are needed in proportion to their capital interests (as defined in Section ....) within thirty (30) days after written request by the General Partners, but in no event shall the Limited Partners be required to make additional contributions aggregating more than .... Dollars ($.....). If any Limited Partner fails to make such additional contribution(s), the other Partners, both General and Limited, shall be afforded the opportunity to advance the needed amount(s), which may, in the discretion of the General Partners, be regarded as loans to the

nership, the capital accounts of the General Partner(s) will be credited with a sum ($10,000) equal to the excess of the fair market value of the property (as determined by the General Partner(s)) over the amount of liabilities to which the property is subjected.

(d) *OPTIONAL:* The General Partner(s) covenant and agree as follows:

    (i) The General Partner(s) will complete or cause to be completed on the property by ...., 19...., [*closing date*] the improvements contemplated by and in accordance with the plans and specifications (described in Exhibit A to the Note Purchase Agreement) prepared by Mr. Alan Architect, which require approval by CONSTRUCTION LOAN BANK, pursuant to condition No. .... of the Construction Loan Agreement and ACE INSURANCE CO., pursuant to condition No. .... of the Permanent Mortgage Loan Commitment Letter.

    (ii) By ...., 19...., [*closing date*] the property will be free and clear of all liens and encumbrances other than those set forth in Schedule B of that certain title Policy No. .... issued by ...., dated ...., 19...., as required by condition No. .... of the Permanent Mortgage Loan Commitment.

    (iii) The General Partner(s) will not permit the aggregate amount of the principal balance of outstanding indebtedness under the aforesaid notes to exceed at any time their present amounts.

    (iv) By ...., 19......., [*closing date*] the General Partner(s) will use their best efforts to create an aggregate annual gross rental (rent-roll) payable under valid and enforceable apartment leases covering apartments on the property with an original term of not less than one year, free of concessions, allowances, or offsets, to be equal to $ .... from not more than ...... percent (...%) of the number of total apartment units.

    (v) The General Partner(s) will perform or cause to be performed all the *other* conditions and requirements of the Note Purchase Agreement necessary or appropriate to require ACE INSURANCE CO. to purchase from CONSTRUCTION LOAN BANK on or before ...., 19...., [*closing date*] the aforesaid note secured by the first mortgage [deed of trust] covering the property in the platform amount of .... Dollars ($.....), or if need be, in the lesser amount of .... Dollars

to a first mortgage [deed of trust] in favor of CONSTRUCTION LOAN BANK, dated ...., 19...., securing an "interest only" note ...., Dollars ($ ....), and subject to a subordinated or second purchase-money mortgage [deed of trust] in favor of SAM SELLER, dated ...., 19...., securing an "interest-only" purchase-money note in the principal amount of .... Dollars ($. ...). The former note was issued by SMITH & JONES, a partnership composed of the General Partners [by the ACME CORP., as principal and not as the agent of the partnership—a corporation comprised of SMITH and JONES, as shareholders] pursuant to a Construction Loan Agreement between the SMITH & JONES partnership [the ACME CORP.] and the CONSTRUCTION LOAN BANK. Simultaneously with the conveyance to the Partnership of the property, the following shall also occur:

    (a) The General Partner(s) will cause to be assigned to the Partnership all of the rights and benefits of, in, to and/or under the following:
- (i) The Construction Loan Agreement with CONSTRUCTION LOAN BANK;
- (ii) The Permanent Mortgage Loan Commitment with ACE INSURANCE CO.;
- (iii) That certain Note Purchase ("Buy-Sell") Agreement dated ...., 19...., between the SMITH & JONES partnership [the ACME CORP.] as borrower, the CONSTRUCTION LOAN BANK as construction lender, and ACE INSURANCE CO., as permanent lender, whereunder the parties agree that ACE INSURANCE CO. will purchase the aforesaid first mortgage [deed of trust] note from CONSTRUCTION LOAN BANK on or before ...., 19....., [*closing date*] if the conditions in the Construction Loan Agreement and Permanent Mortgage Loan Commitment are met, which Agreements are incorporated by reference in the Note Purchase Agreement, respectively, as exhibits A and B thereof;
- (iv) The Construction Contract Agreement for construction work, dated ...., 19...., with the SMITH & JONES partnership [the CONTRACTOR].

    (b) The Partnership will assume and agree to observe and perform all of the obligations and covenants of, in, to and/or under the aforesaid Agreements, except that the General Partners in their capacity as agents of the Partnership will not assume the indebtedness evidenced by the aforesaid mortgage [deed of trust] notes.

    (c) Upon the assignment of the aforesaid Agreements to the Part-

is unlikely, the remaining general partners *must* continue the business of the partnership in the event one of their colleagues dies, becomes insane, or retires prior to the expiration of the stated period. (See Reg. §§ 7701-2(b)(3), 7701-3(b), Examples (1),(2).) Finally, a partnership with a fixed term, unlike one of indefinite duration, cannot, absent an agreement to the contrary, be dissolved at the will of any partner. (U.P.A. § 31(1)(b).) And if a dissolution in contravention of the partnership agreement occurs, the UPA grants to the innocent partners the right to damages for breach of contract and the right to continue the business. (U.P.A. §§ 38(2), 31(2).)

ARTICLE 2
Capital Contributions and Loans

Section 2.1. *General Partners and Their Contributions.* The General Partners and their initial capital contributions to the Partnership shall be as follows:

General Partners	Initial Capital Contribution
JOHN SMITH & TOM JONES (or, the ACME CORP.)	$10,000

[*ALTERNATIVE PROVISION—Section 2.1A*]

Section 2.1A. It is acknowledged that the General Partner(s) JOHN SMITH and TOM JONES [the ACME CORP.] have [has] acquired an option to purchase the real property described in Exhibit A, attached hereto. Upon the execution of this Agreement by the General Partners and by the original Limited Partners, the General Partners will convey said option for and in exchange of a total capital account of $10,000. Said sum represents the value of the option over and above the cost ($1,000) of said option. The cost of said option is to be reimbursed to the General Partners out of Partnership assets as soon as practical after the original Limited Partners have made their capital contributions.

[*ALTERNATIVE PROVISION—Section 2.1B*]

Section 2.1B. It is acknowledged that the General Partner(s) JOHN SMITH and TOM JONES [the ACME CORP.] have [has] acquired real property described in Exhibit A, attached hereto, subject

phraseology suggests that the character of an item is fixed for tax purposes at the partner level, the latter phraseology infers that such characterization is determined at the partnership level, without regard to the trade or business of each partner. Unfortunately, neither the legislative history nor the regulations at Reg. § 1.702-1(b) expressly resolve this ambiguity; however, the examples in the regulations and in Rev. Rul. 67-188, 1967-1 C.B. 216 both suggest that the character is fixed at the partnership level.

Section 1.3(2). *General Purpose.* The Partnership may also acquire, own, hold, improve, develop, operate, and manage real property other than the property referred to in Paragraph 1.3(1) above, and with respect to all Partnership property do all things reasonably incidental thereto, including (by way of illustration) mortgaging, refinancing, selling, leasing and subleasing or otherwise disposing of said property and the improvements at any time.

Section 1.4. *Term of the Partnership.* The term of the Partnership commenced on January 1, 1976, the date the original Agreement and Certificate of Limited Partnership was filed with the appropriate authority of the State of ...., as required by the .... Uniform Limited Partnership Act, and shall expire on December 31, 1985, unless sooner terminated in accordance with Section .... or any other provision of this agreement.

COMMENT: For certain reasons, a limited partnership, unlike a general partnership, is often one of limited duration. First, the former is more suited for ownership of fixed-term investment property such as an apartment building that the partners plan to sell once accelerated depreciation is exhausted. By contrast, the latter form of ownership is more conducive as the organizational framework for conducting an ongoing active trade or business. Moreover, since the limited partners must forgo the right to participate in management control, they are more likely to insist upon a return of their venture capital on or before a certain date. In addition, the mere fact that the partnership is to continue for a stated period (i.e., ten years in this case) or until the completion of a stated undertaking does not ordinarily mean that the organization is more likely to resemble and be taxed like a corporation. The corporate attribute "continuity of life" would exist only if no member has the power to dissolve the partnership *and,* which

intending to extend credit to the partnership. Accordingly, there must be substantial compliance with the informational and recordation requirements of U.L.P.A. § 2 in order to create limited liability for the limited partners.

Another preliminary consideration is whether the partnership agreement, as drafted, can pass muster under the Section 7701 regulations. In addition, if the promoter-general partners incorporate (ACME CORP.) to avoid unlimited liability, the corporate general partner must comply with the net asset tests of Rev. Proc. 72-13. Otherwise, the limited partnership may be treated like a corporation for tax purposes. See discussion at ¶1.05 [4][a].

Section 1.2. *Name and Place of Business.* The Partnership shall be conducted under the name of LAND DEVELOPMENT COMPANY and its principal place of business in the State of ...., unless changed by action of the General Partners upon notice to the Limited Partners, shall be located at ...., or at such other or additional place or places as may be designated by the General Partners.

Section 1.3(1). *Specific Purpose.* The primary and specific purpose of the Partnership is to acquire that certain parcel of unimproved land, situated in the City of ...., ... County, State of ...., more particularly described in Exhibit "A" attached hereto; to construct apartment buildings thereon; and to operate, maintain, and manage said apartment buildings *as an investor for residential rental purposes.*

COMMENT: While a self-serving declaration as to the purpose of the partnership is not determinative of federal tax consequences, it nonetheless may be somewhat persuasive in the event a close question arises at audit as to whether the partnership should, as a dealer, be charged with ordinary gain, or, as an investor, with capital gain on the sale of partnership property. Section 702(b) of the Internal Revenue Code provides that "the character of any item of income, gain, loss, deduction, or credit included in a partner's distributive share...shall be determined as if such item were realized *directly from the source* from which realized by the partnership, or *incurred in the same manner as incurred by the partnership.*" (Emphasis added.) Whereas the penultimate

6.3	Ground Lease Option and Development Agreement: Involving Ground Lease on Unsubordinated Fee	App. B-175
6.4	Land Purchase-Leaseback Transaction Sales Contract	App. B-177
8.1	Three-Cornered Exchange Agreement	App. B-185
9.1	Bond and Agreement Procedures for Residential Development	App. B-197
9.2	Set-Aside Letter	App. B-206
9.3	Master Development Loan Agreement	App. B-207
10.1	Master Deed for Condominium	App. B-223
10.2	Construction Loan Commitment Letter for Condominium Financing	App. B-232
11.1	Loan Participation Agreement	App. B-242
11.2	Separate Noteholder's Agreement	App. B-246
11.3	Master Mortgage Warehouse Security Agreement and Financing Statement	App. B-248
11.4	Joint Venture Agreement	App. B-261

Form 1.1

LIMITED PARTNERSHIP AGREEMENT—ANNOTATED

This is a limited partnership agreement executed this ...... day of ...., 19 ...., by and among JOHN SMITH, TOM JONES [the ACME CORP. comprised of SMITH AND JONES] as general partner(s), and ALVIN ADAMS, BEN BRUCE, CHARLES CAROL, AND DAN DAILY as limited partners.

ARTICLE 1
General

Section 1.1. *Formation.* The parties hereto hereby form a limited partnership (hereinafter called the "Partnership") pursuant to the provisions of the Uniform Limited Partnership Act of the State of .... The partners shall sign and file for record a certificate of limited partnership as required by the aforesaid Act.

COMMENT: The major purpose of U.L.P.A. § 2, which requires recordation of a limited partnership certificate, is to give notice of any limited liability of a partner to persons

Appendix B
SAMPLE FORMS AND AGREEMENTS

Form		Page
1.1	Limited Partnership Agreement—Annotated	App. B -2
3.1	Permanent Mortgage Loan Commitment—Annotated	App. B-26
3.2	Permanent Mortgage Loan Application-Commitment—Annotated	App. B-36
3.3	Note	App. B-43
3.4	Mortgage Deed of Trust—Annotated	App. B-44
3.5	Assignment of Lessor's Interest in Lease	App. B-69
3.6	Notice of Lease Assignment	App. B-75
3.7	Tenant's Acceptance Letter	App. B-76
3.8	Closing Disbursement Letter to Title Company	App. B-77
3.9	Attorney's Certification	App. B-81
3.10	Architect's Certificate	App. B-82
3.11	Mortgagor's Estoppel Affidavit	App. B-83
3.12	Standard Mortgage Clause	App. B-83
3.13	Certified Inventory	App. B-85
3.14	Attornment and Nondisturbance Agreement Between Mortgagee and Occupancy Subtenants	App. B-86
4.1	Building Loan Agreement	App. B-87
4.2	Buy-Sell Agreement	App. B-106
6.1	Attornment and Nondisturbance Agreement Between Ground Lessor, Tenant and Mortgagee	App. B-110
6.2	Ground Lease on Unsubordinated Fee	App. B-112

Table 3

TABLE 3. Analysis of State Usury Statutes
(continued)

State	Maximum Contract Rate				Home Mortgage Exceptions	
	Individual	Unincorporated Business	Corporation	FHA & VA	Conventional	
South Carolina *Code Ann.* § 34-31-30	UCCC—12% § 37-3-201	8% 1% over the Federal Reserve discount rate—commercial agricultural loans up to $50,000 (until 6/30/81)	N/L—corporations with $40,000 capital § 34-31-80	X	Until 6/30/81, first mortgage loans: N/L—over $100,000 N/L—under $100,000 if a fixed rate with no prepayment penalty	
South Dakota *Comp. Laws Ann.* § 54-3-7	12% (reverts to 10% 7/1/81) N/L—regulated lenders		N/L § 54-3-7.1	X § 51-18-28	N/L—real estate loans by regulated lenders	
Tennessee *Code Ann.* §§ 47-14-102, 47-14-103	5 percentage points above Federal Reserve discount rate (18% maximum)			X §§ 35-327 & 35-328	Residential loan rate set at 2 percentage points above the FNMA monthly auction rate (must be 15 years or longer; rate may not exceed 18%) § 47-14-202	
Texas *Const. Art. 16, § 11* *Rev. Civ. Stat. Ann.* *Art. 5069-1.04*	10% 18%—over $250,000 (except loans secured by residences, agricultural or ranch land). *Art. 5069-1.07(b)*		18%—$5,000 or more *Art. 1302-2.09*	X *Art. 5069-1.09*	For loans secured by 1- to 4-family residential property, the lesser of (a) 12% or (b) 2% over the long-term (10-yr.) U.S. Gov't bond yields (until 9/1/81) *Art. 5069-1.07(d)*	
Utah *Code Ann.* § 70B-3-201	UCCC—18%	N/L § 70B-3-605	N/L § 70B-3-605	FHA only § 33-3-1		
Vermont *Stat. Ann. Tit. 9, § 41*	12%	N/L Tit. 9, §46(2)	N/L Tit. 9, § 46(1)	X Tit. 9, § 46(4)		
Virginia *Code* § 6.1-330.11	8%	N/L—$5,000 or more § 6.1-330.44	N/L § 6.1-330.43	X § 6.1-330.38	N L—first mortgage loans § 6.1-330.37	
Washington *Rev. Code* § 19.52.020	12%	12% N/L—over $50,000 § 19.52.080	12% N/L—over $50,000 § 19.52.080	MSBs only § 32.20.040		
West Virginia *Code* § 47-6-5	8% N/L—business loans to individuals over $20,000	N/L	N/L § 47-6-10	X §§ 31A-4-27 & 31A-4-29	Commissioner sets rates for mortgage loans at up to 1½ percentage points over the average yield on long-term (20-yr.) U.S. Gov't bonds § 47-6-5b	
Wisconsin *Stat. Ann.* § 138.05	N/L (until 11/1/81)	N/L (until 11/1/81)	N/L	X § 219.03	N/L—first lien residential mortgages and conventional mortgage loans exceeding $25,000 (until 11/1/81)	
Wyoming *Stat. Ann.* § 40-14-310	UCCC—10%	N/L § 40-14-358	N/L § 40-14-358		18%—realty loans § 40-14-305	

Copyright © June 1980 by American Bankers Association. All rights reserved.

State	Maximum Contract Rate				Home Mortgage Exceptions	
	Individual	Unincorporated Business	Corporation	FHA & VA	Conventional	
New York Banking Law § 14-a Gen. Oblig. Law § 5-501	10½%—may rise ¼% every 3 months until it reaches ceiling of 2 percentage points over monthly index of U.S. Gov't (10-yr.) bond yields (until 12/15/80) N/L—$250,000 or more except loan secured by 1- to 2-family residential property 5% over 90-day discount rate set by N.Y. Federal Reserve Bank—$25,000 or more Banking Law § 108(9) Interest at 25% or more is criminal usury. Penal Law § 190.40		N/L Gen. Oblig. Law § 5-521	X Gen. Oblig. Law § 5-501(5)	X	
North Carolina Gen. Stat. § 24-1.1	12%—$25,000 or less N/L—over $25,000		N/L § 24-9	X § 53-45	N/L—first mortgage on residential real property if lender is bank, S&L, credit union, or federally insured mortgagee 10%—to $10,000 N/L—$10,000 or more } other lenders § 24-1.1A	
North Dakota Cent. Code § 47-14-09	Greater of 7%, or 5½ percentage points over rate paid on 30-month CDs (current rate is 10%) N/L—loans to partnerships N/L—over $35,000		N/L	X § 6-03-50	12%—loans by S&Ls § 7-02-04	
Ohio Rev. Code Ann. § 1343.01	8% N/L—over $100,000 Interest at more than 25% is criminal usury.	8% N/L—over $100,000 § 2905.21	N/L § 1701.68	X	Residential mortgages—3 percentage points over the 4th Federal Reserve District 90-day discount rate	
Oklahoma Stat. Ann. Tit. 14A, § 3-201	UCCC—10%	45%	N/L	X	18%—realty loans Tit. 14A, § 3-105 45%—all loans other than consumer loans and consumer-related loans	
		Tit. 14A, § 3-605	Tit. 18, § 1.26	Tit. 6, §§ 2041 & 2043	Tit. 14A, §3-605	
Oregon Rev. Stat. § 82.010	10%[3] N/L—over $50,000	12% N/L—over $50,000		X § 82.115	12%—real estate loans N/L—all loans over $50,000	
Pennsylvania Stat. Ann. Tit. 41, §§ 201, 301	6%[4] N/L—over $50,000	6%[4] N/L—over $10,000	N/L	X Tit. 41, § 302	Mortgage rate set monthly at 2½ percentage points over index of long-term U.S. Gov't bond yields[4] N/L—all loans over $50,000 N/L—loans secured by real estate lien other than 1- to 2-family residential mortgage	
Rhode Island Gen. Laws Ann. § 6-26-2	21%	21%	21%			

[3] In addition to the rates shown, banks may charge an 8% add-on or 15% on loans up to $50,000. § 708.480(1)(a).
[4] All direct loans may bear a rate of 5% above the Federal Reserve discount rate.

Table 3

TABLE 3. Analysis of State Usury Statutes
(continued)

State	Maximum Contract Rate				Home Mortgage Exceptions	
	Individual	Unincorporated Business	Corporation	FHA & VA	Conventional	
Missouri *Ann. Stat. § 408.030*	Director of Division of Finance sets rate quarterly at 3% over monthly index of long-term U.S. Gov't (10-yr.) bond yields rounded to nearest 1/10%	N/L—over $5,000 (except agricultural or residential real estate loans) §§ *408.035(2) & 408.015(6)*	N/L § *408.035(1)*			
Montana *Code Ann. § 31-1-107*	Up to $150,000—greater of 10%, or 4 percentage points over the 9th Federal Reserve District 90-day discount rate Over $150,000 to $300,000—greater of 10%, or 5 points over the discount rate N/L—over $300,000			FHA only § *32-1-434*		
Nebraska *Rev. Stat. §45-101.03*	16%—over $100,000	N/L—over $25,000 N/L—loans to partnerships § *45-101.04*	N/L § *45-101.04*	X § *45-101.04(5)*		
Nevada *Rev. Stat. § 99.050*		18%		X § *662-095*		
New Hampshire *Rev. Stat. § 336:1*	N/L	N/L	N/L			
New Jersey *Stat. Ann. § 31:1-1*	Comm'r may set a rate not to exceed 8% over long-term U.S. Gov't bond index (maximum nonresidential loans—8%)[2] N/L—$50,000 or more except 1- to 6-family first mortgage loans		N/L § *31:1-6*	X	For 1- to 6-family first lien residential mortgage, Comm'r may set rate up to 8% over long-term U.S. Gov't bond index	
New Mexico *Stat. Ann. § 56-8-11*	Greater of 10% (secured), 12% (unsecured), or 3% over the Federal Reserve discount rate	N/L—$500,000 or more § *56-8-9(C)*	N/L § *56-8-9(B)*	X § *58-8-2*	For 1- to 4-family residential, mobile home & condominium loans, 1% above the FNMA auction rate, computed quarterly § *58-7-4*	

[2] Six percent, absent action by Commissioner fixing rate.

Table 3

State	Maximum Contract Rate				Home Mortgage Exceptions
	Individual	Unincorporated Business	Corporation	FHA & VA	Conventional
Indiana Code Ann. § 24-4.5-3-201	UCCC—18%	N/L § 24-4.5-3-605	N/L § 24-4.5-3-605	FHA—banks only. § 28-1-11-3(b) FHA & VA—S&Ls only. § 28-1-21-23(g)	15%—realty loans § 24-4.5-3-105
Iowa Code Ann. § 535.2	15% N/L—personal, family or household loans exceeding $35,000 (until 7/1/83)	N/L	N/L § 535.2(2)		N/L—real estate acquisition loans (until 7/1/83)
Kansas Stat. Ann. § 16a-2-401	UCCC—18%	10% § 16-207	N/L § 17-7105		Mortgage rate set monthly at 1½% above average weighted yield of FHLMC weekly purchase program. § 16-207
Kentucky Rev. Stat. § 360.010	Lesser of 19%, or 4% over the Federal Reserve discount rate N/L—over $15,000	Lesser of 19%, or 4% over the Federal Reserve discount rate N/L—over $15,000 N/L—to a limited partnership or business trust § 360.025	N/L § 386.030	X	
Louisiana Civ. Code Ann. Art. 2924	8%	8% § 360.027	N/L R.S. §12:703	X R.S. § 9:3504	12%—realty loans R.S. § 9:3503
Maine Rev. Stat. Ann., Tit. 9-A, § 2-401	UCCC—12¾%	N/L no provision	N/L no provision		N/L—first mortgage loans by a supervised financial institution Tit. 9-B, § 432 & Tit. 9-A, §1.202
Maryland Com. Law § 12-103	18%	N/L—over $5,000 § 12-103(e)	N/L—over $5,000 § 12-103(e)	X § 12-103(d)	N/L—residential realty loans § 12-103(b)
Massachusetts Ann. Laws, Ch. 107, § 3	N/L	N/L	N/L		
Michigan Stat. Ann. § 19.15(1)	7% N/L—business loans. § 19.15(71) Interest at more than 25% is criminal usury. § 19.15(51)		§ 19.200(275)	X § 19.15(1)(c)	N/L—loans on one family dwellings by regulated lenders (until 12/31/81) 11%—mortgage loans and land contracts by non-regulated lenders N/L—loans of $100,000 or more, secured by real estate other than a 1-family home (until 12/31/81) § 19.15(1)(c)
Minnesota Stat. Ann. § 334.01	8% N/L—over $100,000	4½ percentage points over Federal Reserve discount rate § 334.011	N/L § 334.021	X § 47-21	Commissioner sets rate at monthly index of FNMA auction rate of previous month, rounded to next higher ¼% (until 11/30/82) § 47.20
Mississippi Code Ann. § 75-17-1	Greater of 10%, or 5% over the Federal Reserve discount rate (until 6/30/82)	Greater of 15%, or 5% over the Federal Reserve discount rate—over $2,500 (until 6/30/82)	Greater of 15%, or 5% over the Federal Reserve discount rate (until 6/30/82)	X § 43-33-307	Greater of 10%, or 5% over the long-term (20-yr.) U.S. Gov't bond index (until 6/30/82)

TABLE 3. Analysis of State Usury Statutes
(continued)

State	Maximum Contract Rate				Home Mortgage Exceptions	
	Individual	Unincorporated Business	Corporation	FHA & VA	Conventional	
Arkansas *Const., Art. 19, § 13* *Stat. Ann. § 68-602*	10%	10%	10%			
California *Const., Art. XV, § 1*	Non-regulated lenders—greater of 10%, or 5% over Federal Reserve discount rate Regulated lenders—N/L			X *12 U.S.C. § 1709-1a*		
Colorado *Rev. Stat. § 53-201*	UCCC—12% *§ 5-3-605*	45% *§ 5-3-605*	45% *§ 5-3-605*		13%—realty loans (until 7/1/81)	
Connecticut *Gen. Stat. § 37-4*	12%		18%—over $10,000 *§ 37-9*		N/L—any loan by bank or S&L N/L—realty loans over $5,000 *§ 37-9*	
Delaware *Code Ann.,* *Tit. 6, § 2301*	5 percentage points over the Federal Reserve discount rate N/L—over $100,000		N/L *Tit. 6, § 2306*	X	Residential mortgage loans—5 percentage points over the Federal Reserve discount rate	
District of Columbia *Code Ann.* *§§ 28-3301, 28-3309*	15%	N/L—over $5,000	N/L	X *Reg. 70-38 & 28-3307*	15% *D.C. Law 3-38*	
Florida *Stat. Ann. § 687.02*		18% N/L—over $500,000 Interest at more than 25% is criminal usury. *§ 687.071*		X *§ 687.03(2)(a)*	N/L—loans by S&Ls. *§ 665.395* N/L—loans by other lenders. *§ 687.12*	
Georgia *Code Ann. § 57-101*	10½%	10½% N/L—over $3,000 *§ 57-118*		X *§ 57-101.1(b)*	Residential loan rate set at 2½ percentage points over the monthly index of long-term U.S. Gov't (20-yr.) bond yields N/L—any loan over $100,000 *§§ 57-101.1; § 57-119*	
Hawaii *Rev. Stat.* *§§ 478-3, 478-8*	12% N/L—over $750,000	12% N/L—over $750,000	12% N/L—over $750,000	X *§§ 402-11 & 478-8*	N/L—first lien residential mortgages and mortgage loans secured by "alternative mortgage instruments" *§ 478-8*	
Idaho *Code § 28-22-105*	UCCC—18% *§ 28-33-201*	13% N/L—over $25,000 if not secured by a residential mortgage and not subject to UCCC			13%—residential realty loans *§ 28-33-105*	
Illinois *Ann. Stat., Ch. 74,* *§ 4(1)*	9%	N/L	N/L	X	N/L—until 12/31/81 *Ch. 74, § 4(2)*	

TABLE 3. Analysis of State Usury Statutes

This chart is intended to present an overview of the law in each state and the District of Columbia placing an interest rate ceiling on mortgage loans. The format displays the maximum contract rate for individuals, unincorporated businesses, and corporations, respectively. EXCEPT AS NOTED UNDER THE FHA/VA OR CONVENTIONAL MORTGAGE COLUMNS, THE INDIVIDUAL CONTRACT RATE IS APPLICABLE TO HOME MORTGAGE LOANS.

Significant factors, not taken into account in this analysis, are certain federal laws providing exemptions from state interest ceilings. For example, P.L. 96-153 exempts mortgages insured under Title I or II of the National Housing Act from state usury provisions. P.L. 96-128 similarly exempts VA loans from state usury laws. P.L. 96-221 permanently preempts state usury ceilings for first lien home mortgage and mobile home loans unless a state reimposes a usury limit and explicitly overrides the federal preemption by April 1, 1983. Federally insured lenders may also make business and agricultural loans of $25,000 or more at a rate not exceeding 5% over the Federal Reserve discount rate until April 1, 1983 (or earlier if the state overrides the federal provision). In addition, federally insured institutions may permanently charge 1% over the Federal Reserve discount rate, thus obtaining parity with national banks. The chart makes no attempt to detail the specific loan rates for the wide variety of personal loans such as bank instalment loans, loans by licensed lenders, and the like.

The figures given are annual interest rates, with the entry "N/L" as an abbreviation for "No Limit." "UCCC" refers to the Uniform Consumer Credit Code. Individual contract rates in those states which have adopted the UCCC or a variant are those which are applicable only to consumer loans by non-supervised, non-regulated lenders. Citations listed under the name of each state are supplemented by a notation under a particular entry where appropriate.

—*Office of the State Legislative Counsel
American Bankers Association*

THIS CHART IS INTENDED TO PROVIDE AN OVERVIEW
AND NOT A DEFINITIVE ANALYSIS OF THE LAW IN EACH STATE.

State	Maximum Contract Rate			Home Mortgage Exceptions	
	Individual	Unincorporated Business	Corporation	FHA & VA	Conventional
Alabama Code § 8-8-1	8%[1]	N/L—$5,000 or more (until 12/1/81) § 8-8-5	15%—$10,000 to $100,000 N/L—$100,000 or more § 8-8-3	X § 8-8-6	18%—real estate loans § 5-19-3(f)
Alaska Stat. § 45.010(b)	5 percentage points over the discount rate charged by the 12th Federal Reserve District N/L—over $100,000				
Arizona Rev. Stat. § 44-1201	N/L	N/L	N/L	X § 44-1206	N/L

[1] But see Fletcher v. Tuscaloosa Federal Savings & Loan Ass'n, 294 Ala. 173, 314 So. 2d 51 (1975).

Table 2

TABLE 2. Mortgage Debt Outstanding
($ millions; end of period)
(continued)

Type of Holder, and Type of Property	1977	1978	1979	1978 Q4	1979 Q1	1979 Q2	1979 Q3	1979 Q4
51 Federal Home Loan Mortgage Corporation	6,610	11,892	15,180	11,892	12,467	13,708	14,421	15,180
52 1- to 4-family	5,621	9,657	12,149	9,657	10,088	11,096	11,568	12,149
53 Multi-family	989	2,235	3,031	2,235	2,379	2,612	2,853	3,031
54 Farmers Home Administration	18,783	22,394	27,697	22,394	24,129	25,551	26,870	27,697
55 1- to 4-family	11,397	13,400	14,884	13,400	13,883	14,329	14,972	14,884
56 Multi-family	759	1,116	2,163	1,116	1,465	1,764	1,763	2,163
57 Commercial	2,945	3,560	4,328	3,560	3,660	3,833	4,054	4,328
58 Farm	3,682	4,318	6,322	4,318	5,121	5,625	6,081	6,322
59 Individual and others[3]	138,199	154,173	177,534'	154,173	158,999	165,687	171,886	177,534'
60 1- to 4-family	72,115	82,567	96,047'	82,567	85,354	89,345	92,565	96,047'
61 Multi-family	20,538	21,393	23,439	21,393	21,637	22,094	22,920	23,439
62 Commercial	21,820	22,837	24,979'	22,837	23,230	23,770	24,442	24,979'
63 Farm	23,726	27,376	33,069'	27,376	28,778	30,478	31,959	33,069'

[3] Other holders include mortgage companies, real estate investment trusts, state and local credit agencies, state and local retirement funds, noninsured pension funds, credit unions, and U.S. agencies for which amounts are small or separate data are not readily available.

NOTE: Based on data from various institutional and governmental sources, with some quarters estimated in part by the Federal Reserve in conjunction with the Federal Home Loan Bank Board and the Department of Commerce. Separation of nonfarm mortgage debt by type of property, if not reported directly, and interpolations and extrapolations when required, are estimated mainly by the Federal Reserve. "Multifamily debt" refers to loans on structures of five or more units.

SOURCE: 66 **F.R.B.** No. 5, at A51 (May 1970).

App. A-13 APP A—ANCILLARY DATA Table 2

					1979			
Type of Holder, and Type of Property	1977	1978	1979	1978 Q4	Q1	Q2	Q3	Q4
26 Federal and related agencies	70,006	81,853	97,293	81,853	86,689	90,095	93,143	97,293
27 Government National Mortgage Association								
28 1- to 4-family	3,660	3,509	3,852	3,509	3,448	3,425	3,382	3,852
Multi-family	1,548	877	763	877	821	800	780	763
29	2,112	2,632	3,089	2,632	2,627	2,625	2,602	3,089
30 Farmers Home Administration	1,353	926	1,274	926	956	1,200	1,383	1,274
31 1- to 4-family	626	288	417	288	302	363	163	417
32 Multi-family	275	320	71	320	180	75	299	71
33 Commercial	149	101	174	101	283	278	262	174
34 Farm	303	217	612	217	191	484	659	612
35 Federal Housing and Veterans Administration	5,212	5,419	5,764	5,419	5,522	5,597	5,672	5,764
36 1- to 4-family	1,627	1,641	1,863	1,641	1,693	1,744	1,795	1,863
37 Multi-family	3,585	3,778	3,901	3,773	3,829	3,853	3,877	3,901
38 Federal National Mortgage Association	34,369	43,311	51,091	43,311	46,410	48,206	49,173	51,091
39 1- to 4-family	28,504	37,579	45,488	37,579	40,702	42,543	43,534	45,488
40 Multi-family	5,865	5,732	5,603	5,732	5,708	5,663	5,639	5,603
41 Federal Land Banks	22,136	25,624	31,277	25,624	26,893	28,459	29,804	31,277
42 1- to 4-family	670	927	1,552	927	1,042	1,198	1,374	1,552
43 Farm	21,466	24,697	29,725	24,697	25,851	27,261	28,430	29,725
44 Federal Home Loan Mortgage Corporation	3,276	3,064	4,035	3,064	3,460	3,208	3,729	4,035
45 1- to 4-family	2,738	2,407	3,059	2,407	2,685	2,489	2,850	3,059
46 Multi-family	538	657	976	657	775	719	879	976
47 Mortgage pools or trusts[2]	70,289	88,633	119,278	88,633	94,551	102,259	110,648	119,278
48 Government National Mortgage Association								
49 1- to 4-family	44,896	54,347	76,401	54,347	57,955	63,000	69,357	76,401
Multi-family	43,555	52,732	74,546	52,732	56,269	61,246	67,535	74,546
50	1,341	1,615	1,855	1,615	1,686	1,754	1,822	1,855

[2] Outstanding principal balances of mortgages backing securities insured or guaranteed by the agency indicated.

Table 2   REAL ESTATE FINANCING   App. A-12

TABLE 2. Mortgage Debt Outstanding
($ millions; end of period)

	Type of Holder, and Type of Property	1977	1978	1979	1978 Q4	1979 Q1	1979 Q2	1979 Q3	1979 Q4
1	All holders	1,023,505	1,172,754	1,334,373'	1,172,754	1,206,213	1,252,426	1,295,644	1,334,373'
2	1- to 4-family	656,566	761,843	872,191'	761,843	784,546	816,940	846,115	872,191'
3	Multi-family	111,841	121,972	130,758'	121,972	123,965	125,916	128,256	130,758'
4	Commercial	189,274	212,746	239,093'	212,746	217,495	224,499	233,120	239,093'
5	Farm	65,824	76,193	92,331'	76,193	80,207	85,071	89,153	92,331'
6	Major financial institutions	745,011	848,095	940,268'	848,095	865,974	894,385	919,967	940,268
7	Commercial banks[1]	178,979	213,963	246,763	213,963	220,063	229,564	239,363	246,763
8	1- to 4-family	105,115	126,966	146,077	126,966	130,585	136,223	142,038	146,077
9	Multi-family	9,215	10,912	12,585	10,912	11,223	11,708	12,208	12,585
10	Commercial	56,898	67,056	77,737	67,056	68,968	71,945	75,016	77,737
11	Farm	7,751	9,029	10,364	9,029	9,287	9,688	10,101	10,364
12	Mutual savings banks	88,104	95,157	98,924	95,157	96,136	97,155	97,929	98,924
13	1- to 4-family	57,637	62,252	64,717	62,252	62,892	63,559	64,065	64,717
14	Multi-family	15,304	16,529	17,183	16,529	16,699	16,876	17,010	17,183
15	Commercial	15,110	16,319	16,965	16,319	16,488	16,662	16,795	16,965
16	Farm	53	57	59	57	57	58	59	59
17	Savings and loan associations	381,163	432,808	475,797	432,808	441,358	456,543	468,307	475,797
18	1- to 4-family	310,686	356,114	394,436	356,114	363,723	377,516	387,992	394,436
19	Multi-family	32,513	36,053	37,588	36,053	36,677	37,071	37,277	37,588
20	Commercial	37,964	40,641	43,773	40,641	40,958	41,956	43,038	43,773
21	Life insurance companies	96,765	106,167	118,784'	106,167	108,417	111,123	114,368	118,784'
22	1- to 4-family	14,727	14,436	16,193'	14,436	14,507	14,489	14,884	16,193'
23	Multi-family	18,807	19,000	19,274'	19,000	19,080	19,102	19,107	19,274'
24	Commercial	54,388	62,232	71,137'	62,232	63,908	66,055	68,513	71,137'
25	Farm	8,843	10,499	12,180'	10,499	10,922	11,477	11,864	12,180'

[1] Includes loans held by nondeposit trust companies but not bank trust departments.

APP. A—ANCILLARY DATA

Table 1

State	Maximum Ratio of Loan Value	Maximum Term	Loan Limit: Aggregate—One Borrower	FHA- or VA-Insured or Guaranteed Loans Exempt From Loan Restrictions
Washington			One borrower: Shall not exceed 15% of capital and surplus	Yes
West Virginia				Yes
Wisconsin			Aggregate: 50% capital, surplus and deposits, but loans exceeding this limit may be authorized by directors of bank under certain conditions	Yes
Wyoming	• 50% • 75% • 75% • 90%	• 5 years • 10 years, 40% amortized • 20 years, fully amortized • 30 years, fully amortized	Aggregate: 10% capital and surplus or 70% deposits, whichever is greater, but uninsured loan may not exceed 20% of capital, surplus and deposits	Yes

SOURCE: State Bank Supervisors, *Profile of State Chartered Banking* (1980), December 31, 1979

Table 1 REAL ESTATE FINANCING App. A-10

TABLE 1. State Statutory Limitations on Commercial Bank Real Estate Loans, December 31, 1979
(continued)

State	Maximum Ratio of Loan Value	Maximum Term	Loan Limit: Aggregate—One Borrower	FHA- or VA-Insured or Guaranteed Loans Exempt From Loan Restrictions
South Dakota	Statutes are silent			Yes
Tennessee			25% of capital, surplus and undivided profits	Yes
Texas	• 60% • 70% • 90%, 1- to 4-family dwelling	• 15 years, 40% amortized • 30 years, fully amortized	Aggregate: General loan limit applies	Yes
Utah			One borrower: 15% of capital and surplus	Yes
Vermont	• 60%, timber lands, mines, and quarries • 60%, industrial plants • 75% • 90%; 95% if in state, 1- or 2-family dwelling • 60%	• 10 years • 20 years • 40 years, fully amortized payments made at least annually • 40 years, fully amortized payments made at least every 6 months • 1 year		Yes
Virginia	• 50% • 90%	• 30 years, 3½% amortized per year	Aggregate: 100% capital and surplus or 70% time and saving deposits, whichever is greater	Yes

State	Maximum Ratio of Loan Value	Maximum Term	Loan Limit: Aggregate—One Borrower	FHA- or VA-Insured or Guaranteed Loans Exempt From Loan Restrictions
Pennsylvania *(continued)*	• 75%, unimproved real estate, provided utilities, streets, etc., necessary for development have been completed	• 5 years		
Puerto Rico				Yes
Rhode Island (applicable only to savings departments)	• 50%, unimproved real estate • 75%, improved real estate • 80%, improved real estate • 90%, improved real estate in a residential neighborhood and designed for not more than 4 families	• 30 years, fully amortized • 30 years, fully amortized • 30 years, fully amortized	Aggregate: 80% savings deposits or up to 90% savings deposits with excess over 80% insured by U.S. Government or a private insurer	No
South Carolina	• 90%, first lien improved real estate • 66⅔%, first lien improved real estate • 75%, first lien improved real estate • 75%, first lien improved real estate • 90%, first lien improved real estate	• 1 year • 5 years • 10 years, 40% amortized • 15 years, 60% amortized • 30 years, fully amortized	Aggregate: 50% capital plus, 50% deposits One borrower: Total of all loans cannot exceed 15% of capital stock, capital notes and debentures, and surplus of the bank with the approval of two-thirds of the directors; however, loans to directors and officers of the bank are limited to 10% of these accounts	Yes

Table 1 REAL ESTATE FINANCING App. A-8

TABLE 1. State Statutory Limitations on Commercial Bank Real Estate Loans, December 31, 1979
(continued)

State	Maximum Ratio of Loan Value	Maximum Term	Loan Limit: Aggregate—One Borrower	FHA- or VA-Insured or Guaranteed Loans Exempt From Loan Restrictions
Oregon	• 80% • 90% • 90% • 95%	• 5 years • 10 years, 40% amortized • 30 years and 62 days, fully amortized, excess over 90% must be insured • 30 years	Aggregate: 25% capital and surplus, plus 10% demand deposit, plus 75% time deposits One borrower: 25% capital and surplus, plus debentures over 5 years	Yes
Pennsylvania	• 66⅔%, improved real estate • 80%, improved real estate • 90%, not over $40,000; one-family dwelling • 95%, provided principal in excess of 75% is made in reliance upon a private company mortgage insurance or a guarantee acceptable to the department • 66⅔%, unimproved real estate	• 10 years, unamortized • 30 years, fully amortized • 30 years, fully amortized • 30 years, fully amortized • 3 years	Aggregate: 100% capital, capital securities, and surplus or 70% of total time and savings deposits, whichever is greater One borrower: 10% capital surplus, undivided profits, and capital securities	Yes

APP. A—ANCILLARY DATA

Table 1

State	Maximum Ratio of Loan Value	Maximum Term	Loan Limit: Aggregate—One Borrower	FHA- or VA-Insured or Guaranteed Loans Exempt From Loan Restrictions
New Mexico	• 66⅔% unimproved • 75% partially or being improved • 90% improved by building	• 30 years, fully amortized • 30 years, fully amortized • 30 years, fully amortized	Aggregate: 100% time and savings deposits	Yes
New York	• 66⅔% unimproved real estate • 75% improved real estate • 80% improved or 2-family dwelling • 95% appraised value, 1- or 2-family dwelling	• 40 years	One borrower: 10% of capital funds of the bank	Yes
North Carolina				Yes
North Dakota	• 90%	• 30 years, fully amortized	Aggregate: 100% capital and surplus or 66⅔% time and savings deposits, whichever is greater	Yes
Ohio	• 66⅔% unimproved real estate • 75% improved real estate • 90% improved real estate	• 10 years • 10 years • 30 years, equal and full amortization	Aggregate: 10% of paid in capital, surplus, and capital securities	Yes
Oklahoma	• 80% • 85% • 80%	• 5 years • 10 years, 40% amortized • 25 years, fully amortized	Aggregate: 100% capital and surplus or 70% time and savings deposits, whichever is greater	Yes

TABLE 1. State Statutory Limitations on Commercial Bank Real Estate Loans, December 31, 1979
(continued)

State	Maximum Ratio of Loan Value	Maximum Term	Loan Limit: Aggregate—One Borrower	FHA- or VA-Insured or Guaranteed Loans Exempt From Loan Restrictions
Nebraska	• 75% first lien and first mortgage • 80%, improved real estate, not a first mortgage • 90%, improved real estate, first mortgage • 90%, improved real estate, first mortgage • 95%, improved real estate, first mortgage	• 5 years • 10 years, fully amortized • 10 years, 60% balloon payment • 25 years, fully amortized • 30 years, fully amortized, excess over 70% must be insured by a private company	Aggregate: 100% capital, surplus and undivided profits, or 70% time and savings deposits, or 20% total deposits, whichever is greatest	Yes
Nevada	• 80%	• 30 years	One borrower: 25% of unimpaired capital and surplus	Yes
New Hampshire	• 70%		Aggregate: limitation included 15% of capital and surplus	Yes
New Jersey	• 90%	• 40 years	Aggregate: 80% of time deposits One borrower: 10% of capital funds including capital stock, surplus, undivided profit, capital note. Contingency reserves and any nonallocated valuation reserves less tax liability that would occur if transferred from the reserve to individual profits	Yes

APP. A—ANCILLARY DATA — Table 1

State	Maximum Ratio of Loan Value	Maximum Term	Loan Limit: Aggregate—One Borrower	FHA- or VA-Insured or Guaranteed Loans Exempt From Loan Restrictions
Massachusetts (continued)	• 80%, improved real estate	• 25 years, fully amortized and at least 40% amortized within 10 years		
Michigan	• 80%	• 30 years	Aggregate: 70% time savings deposits	Yes
Minnesota	• 50%		First mortgages on improved property in this state, or adjoining state within 20 miles of the principal bank office in excess of 50% of current appraisal included in lending limit of 20% of capital and surplus, but not to exceed 25% of capital and surplus	Yes
Mississippi	Statutes are silent		One borrower: Shall not exceed 15% of aggregate paid-in capital and surplus of bank	Yes
Missouri			Aggregate: Real estate loans are treated like any other loan and are subject to usual legal loan limit	Yes
Montana			Aggregate: 100% capital and surplus or 60% time and savings deposits, whichever is greater	Yes

Table 1 REAL ESTATE FINANCING App. A-4

TABLE 1. State Statutory Limitations on Commercial Bank Real Estate Loans, December 31, 1979
(continued)

State	Maximum Ratio of Loan Value	Maximum Term	Loan Limit: Aggregate—One Borrower	FHA- or VA-Insured or Guaranteed Loans Exempt From Loan Restrictions
Iowa	• 75% • 90% (mortgage insurance equal to 20% of loan)	• 20 years, equal and full amortization • 30 years, fully amortized	One borrower: Bank loan limit prevails as to total indebtedness per borrower	Yes
Kansas	No specific restrictions			
Kentucky	General loan limits apply			Yes
Louisiana	No restrictions			No
Maine	No restrictions			Yes
Maryland	Subject only to bank's legal lending limit, limit of 10% of capital and surplus			No
Massachusetts	• 50%, improved farm land • 50%, improved real estate • 60%, improved real estate	• 3 years; 5 years if at least 2% per year of principal is repaid • 5 years • 3 years; 5 years if at least 2% per year of principal is repaid	Aggregate: 15% of total deposits	Yes

Table 1

State	Maximum Ratio of Loan Value	Maximum Term	Loan Limit: Aggregate—One Borrower	FHA- or VA-Insured or Guaranteed Loans Exempt From Loan Restrictions
Delaware				Yes
Florida[1]				No
Georgia	• 75% loan-to-value • 90% loan-to-value • 100% loan-to-value, construction loan	• 5 years, unamortized • 30 years, fully amortized • 24 months residential, 60 months commercial or industrial	Aggregate with all other loans limited to 20% of statutory capital base	Yes
Hawaii	• 80%		Aggregate: 75% of savings deposit plus 25% of bank capital, surplus, and commercial deposits on obligations served by real estate	No
Idaho	• 50% • 66⅔% • 80%	• 5 years • 10 years, 40% amortized • 30 years, fully amortized	Aggregate: 100% capital and surplus or 70% time and savings deposit, whichever is greater One borrower: 20% of aggregate paid-in capital and surplus of bank	Yes
Illinois			Aggregate: 15% capital and surplus unless qualified for excess, in which case limitations; 50% of capital and surplus including all obligations of borrower	Yes
Indiana	• 50% • 66⅔% • 90%	• 5 years • 10 years, 40% amortized • 30 years, fully amortized	Aggregate: 100% total sound capital, 40% total deposits, or 75% time deposits, whichever is greatest	Yes

[1] By statute, state banks may make real estate loans under the same restrictions as national banks.

Table 1   REAL ESTATE FINANCING   App. A-2

TABLE 1. State Statutory Limitations on Commercial Bank Real Estate Loans, December 31, 1979

State	Maximum Ratio of Loan Value	Maximum Term	Loan Limit: Aggregate—One Borrower	FHA- or VA-Insured or Guaranteed Loans Exempt From Loan Restrictions
Alabama				Yes
Alaska	• 80% • 90%	• 25 years • 30 years		Yes
Arizona			One borrower: 15%	Yes
Arkansas				Yes
California	• 60% • 90% • 85%, construction loan	• 10 years • 30 years, equal monthly installments • 60 months	Aggregate: 70% of savings and time deposits One borrower: 20% capital stock, surplus, capital notes and debentures	Yes
Colorado	• 50% • 90% • 75%	• 5 years • 30 years, 35 years if for construction of one or more buildings; fully amortized • 7 years, fully amortized	Aggregate: 100% capital and surplus, or 70% time and savings deposits, or 25% interest-bearing securities, whichever is greatest	
Connecticut	• 50% • Construction loan, no limit • 90%, not over $25,000	• 24 months or 36 months with approval of Bank Commissioner • 40 years, fully amortized in equal at least semiannual payments	Aggregate: 25% of capital and surplus or 25% of commercial deposits, whichever is greater	Yes

Appendix A
ANCILLARY DATA

Page

Table 1 State Statutory Limitations on
Commercial Bank Real Estate Loans................. App. A- 2

Table 2 Mortgage Debt Outstanding .... App. A-12

Table 3 Analysis of State Usury Statutes .... App. A-15

The value of the property exceeding the $75,000 mortgage is treated as a gift to Y.

In the case of charitable donees, the transaction can also be treated as part sale and part gift,[253] but the taxpayer is required to allocate his basis between the gift portion and the sale portion; the portion allocated to the sale is the amount of basis that bears the same ratio to the fair market value as the mortgage bears to the fair market value.[254] The donor then realizes gain equal to the difference between the mortgage and the basis allocated to the sale portion.[255]

The subject of abandonment is discussed at length in ¶12.3[3], which deals with transfers to the mortgage.

---

[253] See Rev. Rul. 75-194, 1975-1 C.B. 1975-1 C.B. 80. Reg. §§ 1.1011-2, 1.170A-4.
[254] Reg. § 1.1011-2(b).
[255] Reg. §§ 1.1011-2(a)(3), 1.1011-2(c), *Example 7*.

For example, when the owner of mortgaged property transfers it to a controlled corporation, he will recognize gain in the amount of the excess of the debt over the owner's basis in the property.[250]

> *Example 1.* X owns depreciable income-producing real property with a fair market value of $100,000 and a basis of $50,000. He contributes property to X, Inc., a wholly owned corporation in exchange for X, Inc. stock worth $100,000. Under general rules, X realizes a gain of $50,000, but need not recognize such gain under rules set forth in I.R.C. § 351.

> *Example 2.* Assume the same facts as are in Example 1, with the following modification. The property is subject to a mortgage in the amount of $75,000. X will realize gain of $50,000 but will recognize $25,000, the amount equal to the excess of liabilities over basis in the contributed property.

It should be noted that because X owns more than 80 percent of X, Inc., the gain will be taxed as ordinary income, not capital gain, even if the property constitutes a capital asset in X's hands.[251]

[3] Gifts, Abandonment

When the owner of mortgaged property makes a gift of it, it has been held in the case of a noncharitable donee that the transaction is to be treated as a sale to the extent that the value of the property exceeds the mortgage.[252]

> *Example.* X owns property worth $100,000, with a basis of $50,000, subject to a mortgage of $75,000. If X gives the property to Y, X will realize gain in the amount of $25,000, computed as follows.

Amount realized (the mortgage)	$75,000
Less basis	50,000
Taxable gain	$25,000

---

[251] I.R.C. § 1239 (exchange of depreciable property with corporation of which transferor owns 80 percent of or more of the value of stock is taxed as ordinary gain).

[252] See Joseph W. Johnson, 59 T.C. 791 (1973), *aff'd* 495 F.2d 1079 (6th Cir. 1974), *cert. denied* 419 U.S. 1040 (1974). See discussion of *Crane* doctrine at §12.01[3].

Example. X purchases property worth $100,000 by paying $10,000 in cash and financing $90,000 with a mortgage loan. After two years, X has paid $5,000 of the mortgage and taken $20,000 of depreciation. X sells the property for $95,000 with the buyer paying $10,000 and assuming or taking subject to the $85,000 mortgage loan balance. X realizes a gain of $15,000, computed as follows.

Original basis		$100,000
Less depreciation	$20,000	
Adjusted basis at sale		$ 80,000
Amount Realized		
Cash	$10,000	
Mortgage Amount	$85,000	
		95,000
Gain ($95,000 − $80,000)		$ 15,000

The result would be the same if X purchased the property for cash and later obtained a mortgage in the amount of $85,000 on the property. The amount realized includes any mortgage on the property transferred whether connected with its acquisition or placed afterward.[248]

[2] Transfers to Other Entities

If the owner of property transfers the property to a controlled entity, such as a corporation controlled by him or a partnership in which he is a principal partner, the transfer can result in taxable gain despite the usual rule that such transfers are not taxable.[249] This will occur when the liabilities on the property exceed the owner's basis in the property.

C.B. 214; Gavin S. Millar, 67 T.C. 656 (1977), *aff'd* Millar v. Comm'r, 577 F.2d 212 (3d Cir., 1978). It appears likely that other courts will follow this rule.

[248] See Mendham Corp., 9 T.C. 320 (1947); Lutz v. Schramm, 1 T.C. 682 (1943).

[249] See I.R.C. § 351 (transfer to 80 percent-owned corporation generally tax-free); I.R.C. § 721 (tax-free transfers to partnership in exchange for partnership interest).

[250] I.R.C. § 357(c). A similar effect can occur in cases of dispositions to a partnership, but the recognition of gain will not be automatic as in the case of a corporation. This will occur when the other partner's share of the liabilities exceed the contributing partner's basis in his partnership interest. For an example of the recognition of gain under these circumstances, see Reg. §§ 1.752-1(c), 1.752-1(d); I.R.C. § 731. For a detailed analysis of the effect of mortgage liabilities in connection with transfers to partnerships, see 1 Mckee, Nelson & Whitmire, *Federal Taxation of Partnerships and Partners* ¶ 6.03[3] (1977).

gee treat his debt when the first mortgage is foreclosed and his security interest is eliminated? The rule holds that a second mortgagee cannot take a bad-debt deduction until the worthlessness of the debt is established.[243] It has been held that a combination of foreclosure on a first mortgage and insolvency of the debtor was sufficient to justify a bad-debt deduction.[244] Of course, if the second mortgagee can establish worthlessness or partial worthlessness, earlier, the second mortgagee would be entitled to a deduction at such time.

¶ 12.04 DISPOSITION OF MORTGAGED PROPERTY

The tax benefits of mortgaging out and including debt in basis are balanced by including the amount of debt encumbering the property as part of the amount realized when the property is disposed of. There are numerous ways in which property may be transferred, including sale, taxable or nontaxable exchange, transfers to other entities, i.e., partnerships or corporations, gifts or abandonment. The consequences of these transactions vary, but the effect of a mortgage on the property is similar in virtually every instance: it will either increase gain or reduce loss, whether the gain or loss is recognized at the time of the dispostiion or deferred in a nontaxable disposition.

[1] Sales and Taxable Exchanges

Included in this discussion are all sales and taxable exchanges,[245] including transfers to a corporation which is not controlled by the transferor. The taxpayer will treat the cash and the fair market value of other property received *plus* the face amount of mortgage on the property as the "amount realized" for the purpose of determining gain or loss from the disposition, irrespective of personal liability on the debt.[246] The result is not changed if the seller is personally liable on the debt, and the buyer merely takes subject to the mortgage.[247]

---

[244] Walter F. Burrows, 38 B.T.A 236 (1938), *nonacq.* 1938-2 C.B. 38.

[245] The effect of mortgages in tax-free exchanges is discussed at ¶ 8.02[3].

[246] See, e.g., Crane v. Comm'r, 331 U.S. 1 (1947); Mendham Corp., 9 T.C. 320 (1947); Lutz v. Schramm Co., 1 T.C. 682 (1943).

[247] There is some lingering doubt in cases of nonrecourse debt whether the amount realized includes the excess of the face amount of debt over the fair market value of the property transferred. See McGuire, "Tax Shelter Partnership Liabilities in Excess of Basis," 36th Annual N.Y.U. Tax Inst. on Fed. Tax. 1443, 1446-1453 (1978) (citing opinions of several commentators). Crane v. Comm'r, note 246 *supra*, at 14 n.37. See discussion at note 134 *supra*. The IRS has taken the position that fair market value is irrelevant for this purpose and has succeeded with this contention in the courts. See Rev. Rul. 76-111, 1976-1

When the mortgagee is directly engaged in the real estate sales business, the gain would be taxable as ordinary income would if the property will be held for sale in the ordinary course of the taxpayer's business.[237] By contrast, if the mortgagee is a non-dealer and uses the property in its regular trade or business as depreciable income-producing property, or holds it for more than one year, the rules of I.R.C. § 1231 will apply. Gains would be taxable as capital gains and losses generally as ordinary losses.[238]

The nature of the gain or loss of mortgagees in the business of lending money and dealing in mortgages depends upon what is done with the property.[239] As noted above, if it becomes depreciable property held as an income-producing asset or becomes used as business property and held for more than one year, it appears that the rules of I.R.C. § 1231 would again apply. On the other hand, if the mortgagee generally sells such property and engages in "dealer-type" activities,[240] gains and losses from such sales would be taxable as ordinary income.[241]

[6] Loss of a Second Mortgagee

A second mortgagee is in essentially the same tax position as a first mortgagee, that is, the second mortgagee is a creditor who may collect on his debt through the same means employed by a first mortgagee.[242] Consequently, any loss incurred by a second mortgagee, including its timing, amount, and nature is subject to the same rules under I.R.C. § 166 as a first mortgagee.

However, the second mortgagee is in a unique position, as creditor, because of his subordinated debt position. How should such a mortga-

---

[237] I.R.C. § 1231(b)(1)(B). Cf. Rev. Rul. 74-159, 1974-1 C.B. 232 (dealing with banks and finance companies selling foreclosed properties).

[238] I.R.C. § 1231(b)(1); Rev. Rul. 68-661, 1968-2 C.B. 607.

[239] See S. Rep. No. 1881, 87th Cong., 2d Sess. 47-48 (1962); Rev. Rul. 74-159, 1974-1 C.B. 232; Parkersburg State Bank v. United States, (unreported officially). Civ. No. 71-C-2028-C (N.D. Iowa, May 25, 1973), 74-1 U.S.T.C. ¶ 9124.

[240] For the distinction between a "dealer" in real property and an investor, see ¶ 9.05[1]. Generally, frequent sales activity, advertising, use of brokers, etc., indicates "dealer" status, i.e., the seller is holding property primarily for sale in the ordinary course of business.

[241] I.R.C. § 1221(1); Parkersburg State Bank v. United States, cited in note 235 *supra*; Girard Corn Exch. Bank, 22 T.C. 1343 (1954), *acq.'d* 1955-1 C.B. 4; Rev. Rul. 74-159, 1974-1 C.B. 232.

[242] See discussion at ¶¶ 7.04, 7.05, 7.06

[243] See Theatre Inv. Co. v. Comm'r, 119 F.2d 477 (9th Cir. 1941); Arthur Berenson, 39 B.T.A. 77 (1939), *aff'd per curiam* 113 F.2d 113 (2d Cir. 1940).

If title is transferred and the reacquisition is by foreclosure, there is no available authority. Based on the scant evidence of congressional intent and in the absence of any clear authority to the contrary, it seems that the results should be determined by looking to the nature of the original sale for the nature of the gain. This approach is also most consistent with the statutory limitations on the amount of gain recognized: The limitations are based upon the total gain from the original sale and the amount of income reported from the sale.

The regulations, albeit vague, seem to rely upon pre-Section 1038 rules for mortgagee acquisitions at foreclosure. How these rules apply to a foreclosure where the seller is the mortgagee is unclear.[231] If the usual two-transaction rule is applied, the taxpayer might realize ordinary loss or gain on the collection portion and capital gain or loss on the exchange portion. Conceivably, an allocation might be required. It seems, however, that the simpler approach of looking to the nature of the original sale is warranted under the present law.

The problem of characterization of the gain is not likely to occur often, for the simple reason that deferred payment sales under which gain on the sale is deferred are limited to the situations where the seller's note has no value. In most cases where gain results from a reacquisition, the installment method has been used, and the nature of the gain will be determined by reference to the original transaction.

[5] Mortgagee's Disposition of Property Acquired From Mortgagor

The mortgagee's basis in property obtained from the mortgagor is its fair market value whether obtained by a voluntary conveyance[232] or a foreclosure.[233] In cases of foreclosure, the bid price is presumed to be the fair market value unless a different value is established by clear and convincing evidence.[234] When the property is disposed of by the mortgagee, gain or loss will be realized measured by the difference between the amount realized and the basis.[235]

The nature of the gain will depend upon the business of the mortgagee. If the mortgagee is not in the lending, mortgage finance, or real estate business, the property would probably constitute a capital asset; gain or loss would be taxable as capital gain or loss.[236]

---

[231] See Handler, note 85 *supra*, at 221.
[232] Kohn v. Comm'r, 197 F.2d 480 (2d Cir. 1952).
[233] Reg. § 1.166-6(c).
[234] Reg. § 1.166-6(b)(2); Community Bank, 62 T.C. 503 (1974).
[235] I.R.C. § 1001.
[236] I.R.C. § 1221. See, e.g., Kanawha Valley Bank, 4 T.C. 252 (1944), *acq.* 1946-1 C.B. 3.

ment has the effect of increasing the seller's basis in the reacquired property.[223]

The theory of I.R.C. § 1038 that the reacquisition constitutes a "nullification" of the original sale, which leaves the seller in essentially the same position. Accordingly, the seller's holding period of the property includes the period of ownership before the sale, but not the period between the sale and the reacquisition.[224] The holding period prior to the sale must be determined in accordance with the usual rules governing holding period.[225]

The last major consideration with respect to I.R.C. § 1038 reacquisitions is the nature of the gain. Here the answers are very uncertain. The regulations are unclear; there is no case law and the commentators have provided diverse opinions.

The simplest approach, and the one apparently intended by Congress, would be to treat the gain as if derived from the original transaction.[226] The regulations, however, appear to follow the rules in effect before I.R.C. § 1038 concerning the nature of gain. In respect to installment sales, the regulations do provide that gain on the reacquisition is treated as gain derived from the original sale.[227] However, in cases of other deferred payment sales the regulations provide that the nature of the gain depends upon whether title passed to the buyer and, if so, whether the conveyance back to the seller was voluntary.[228]

The regulations contain only two cryptic illustrations: (1) If the title was transferred in the original sale and the conveyance back to the seller was voluntary, the gain is taxed as ordinary income; (2) if the debt constitutes a security under I.R.C. § 165(g), the gain is capital gain.[229]

Apart from the examples in the regulations, the following rules, derived from pre-Section 1038 law would seem to apply. If title is *not* transferred to the seller (as in the case of a conditional sale), any gain is likely to be taxed as ordinary income in the nature of liquidated damages or consideration for an option.[230]

---

[223] See text accompanying note 216 *supra*.

[224] See Reg. § 1.1038-1(g)(3).

[225] These rules are set forth in I.R.C. § 1223.

[226] See S. Rep. No. 1361, 88th Cong., 2d Sess. 9 (1964) ("...thus, for example, the gain by dealers in real estate as determined under [I.R.C. § 1038] will be ordinary income...").

[227] Reg. §§ 1.1038-1(d), 1.453-9.

[228] Reg. § 1.1038-1(d).

[229] Reg. § 1.1038-1(d). Cf. Reg. §§ 1.453-6(b), 1.453-6(c) (effective for years beginning before September 3, 1964, the regulation spells out consequences of repossessions in cases of deferred sales).

[230] See, e.g., Ralph A. Boatman, 32 T.C. 1188 (1959).

B. *Application of Limitation*

Sales Price		$100
Less:		
Adjusted basis	$80	
Gain previously reported	6	
Payments on reacquisition	5	
Limitation on gain		$ 9

X reports $9 as the recognized gain on reacquisition.

The basis of the property received on the reacquistion is equal to the sum of (1) the basis of the obligation at the time of the reacquisition, (2) the amount of gain recognized on the reacquisition, and (3) payments made by the seller in connection with the reacquisition.[219]

In the above example the basis of the reacquired property is $70, computed as follows:

Basis in the debt under I.R.C. § 453 (excess of face value over the amount that would be returned as income if note were paid in full):

$$70(\text{face value of note}) - \left(70 \times \frac{20(\text{gross profit})}{100(\text{contract price})}\right) = \$56$$

Gain reported from reacquisiton	9
Plus money paid on reacquisition	5
Seller's basis in the reacquired property	$70

There are special rules regarding treatment of (1) debt that arises from the original sale and (2) debt that has been subject to a deduction by the seller as partially worthless. First, a bad-debt deduction is never allowable as a result of the reacquisition.[220] Second, if any of the debt has been previously deducted as partially worthless, the amount deducted will be treated as recovered by the seller in the reacquisition, and the seller will generally be required to include that amount in gross income.[221] Third, the basis of the debt to the seller will be increased by the amount deemed recovered.[222] Because the seller's basis in the reacquired property is determined by his basis in the debt, this adjust-

---

[219] I.R.C. § 1038(c); Reg. § 1.1038-1(g)(1).

[220] I.R.C. § 1038(a).

[221] Reg. § 1.1038-1(f)(2). The seller will not recognize income to the extent that the deduction provided no tax benefit. I.R.C. § 111.

[222] I.R.C. § 1038(d)(2); the seller may increase his basis in the debt only by the amount included in income as a result of the deemed recovery. Reg. § 1.1038-1(f)(3); see I.R.C. § 111.

Money received prior to reacquisition	$30
Less amount of gain reported under installment method	
$\dfrac{80 \text{ (gross profit)}}{100 \text{ (contract price)}} \times 30 \text{ (prior payments)}$	24
Gain recognized on the reacquisition	$ 6

However, under I.R.C. § 1038(b) the gain that must be recognized cannot exceed the net gain on the original sale (sale price less seller's adjusted basis in the property) less the amount of gain reported prior to the reacquisition and less the seller's reacquisition costs.[216] The sale price of the property is reduced by sale expenses properly deductible in determining gain or loss on such sale, such as commissions, legal fees, advertising expenses, appraisal fees, recording fees, and the like.[217] Because of this limitation, unless the seller deferred recognition of gain, through an installment sale election, for example, there should be no gain on the reacquisition. All the gain would have been reported prior to the reacquisition.

The reacquisition costs include: (1) acquisition-related expenses such as attorneys' fees, court costs, recording fees; (2) payments to the purchaser; and (3) the assumption by the seller of indebtedness secured by the property, or taking by the seller of the property, subject to the extent of such indebtedness.[218]

Assume in the first example that the basis for the property was $80 and that X paid $5 at the time of the reacquisition. X will recognize a gain in the amount of $9, computed in two steps, as follows.

A. *Gain Before Limitation*

Money received before acquisition	$ 30
Less gain reported under installment method	
$\dfrac{20 \text{ (gross profit)}}{100 \text{ (contract price)}} \times 30$	6
Gain realized on the reacquisition	$ 24

---

[216] I.R.C. § 1038(b)(2).

[217] I.R.C. § 1038(b)(2); Reg. § 1.1038-1(c)(3). If such expenses were properly deducted as a business expense, e.g., when incurred by a dealer in real estate, they do not reduce the selling price for this purpose. See Reg. § 1.1038-1(c)(3).

[218] See Reg. § 1.1038-1(c)(4). For example, if the buyer had obtained a first mortgage loan from a bank at the time of the original sale and gave the seller a second mortgage, the seller would be deemed to make a payment equal to the first mortgage if the property is subject to the first mortgage at the time of its reacquisition by the seller.

indebtedness encumbering the property, which arose after the date of the original sale.[207]

It also does not matter how the seller reacquires the property. Any method will suffice: foreclosure, voluntary conveyance, or abandonment by the buyer.[208] The seller also may reacquire the property from a subsequent purchaser or from anyone holding the property subject to the original indebtedness.[209]

Once the requirements of I.R.C. § 1038 are met, its application is mandatory: No loss will be recognized and recognition of gain is limited to the excess of (1) the amount of money and (2) the value of property received prior to the reacquisition over the gain reported as income in respect to the payments prior to the reacquisition.[210]

The payments received prior to reacquisition do not include the value arising from the sale of the buyer's obligations to the seller.[211] payments received by the seller include: (1) indirect as well as direct payments by the buyer, such as payments made on indebtedness to which the property was subject at the time of the sale and on which the seller is personally liable,[212] and (2) payments that are with respect to the original sale made by the buyer at the time of the reacquisition.[213] Interest of any kind, however, is not included as payments received or as gain that has been reported for purposes of computing the gain on reacquisition.[214] The gain to be reported as income for periods prior to the reacquisition includes gain reportable in the year of acquisition, in respect of payments made prior to the reacquisition.[215]

The application of these rules can be demonstrated as follows.

Example. X sells real property with a basis of $20 to Y for $100. Y pays $10 and executes an installment note for $90, payable ratably over nine years. X elects to report the income on the installment method. After Y makes two annual payments, and defaults, X reacquires the property in complete satisfaction of the note. X recognizes gain in the amount of $6, computed as follows:

---

[207] *Id.*
[208] Reg. § 1.1038-1(a)(3)(ii).
[209] Reg. § 1.1038-1(a)(4).
[210] I.R.C. § 1038(b); Reg. § 1.1038-1(b)(1).
[211] *Id.*
[212] Reg. § 1.1038-1(b)(2)(i).
[213] Reg. § 1.1038-1(b)(2)(ii).
[214] Reg. § 1.1038-1(b)(2)(iii).
[215] Reg. § 1.1038-1(b)(1)(ii).

If X were a corporation not in the business of lending, its exchange gain would be capital gain and its bad-debt loss would be deductible as an ordinary bad-debt deduction.

Reacquisitions by the Mortgagee: I.R.C. § 1038. Part of the financing package for the acquisition of real property often includes a "purchase-money mortgage" under which the seller agrees, in effect, to lend part of the purchase price to the buyer by accepting payment of part of the purchase price over a period of time.[201]

Section 1038 of the Internal Revenue Code provides generally that if a sale of real property gives rise to an indebtedness to the seller secured by the transferred property, and the seller reacquires the property in partial or complete satisfaction of the indebtedness, then no loss is recognized and gain will be recognized only under certain limited circumstances.[202]

The section is applicable to a "sale" of real property giving rise to secured indebtedness, including transactions such as conditional or "installment land" sales where title does not pass immediately to the purchaser.[203] An indebtedness will be secured for purposes of the section if the seller has the right to obtain title or possession of the property, or both, on a default by the buyer, whether or not the buyer is personally liable for the debt.[204]

For I.R.C. § 1038 to apply, the seller must reacquire the property in complete or partial satisfaction of the debt resulting from the sale.[205] Thus, if the seller pays consideration to the purchaser other than the discharge of the purchaser's indebtedness on the reacquistion, I.R.C. § 1038 generally will not apply unless (1) the additional consideration was provided for in the original contract of sale or (2) the seller was in default or default was imminent at the time of the reacquisition.[206] Additional consideration includes (1) any property or money transferred to the buyer or (2) taking property subject to, or by assuming, post-sale

---

[201] See discussion at ¶¶ 8.04, 9.01[1].

[202] I.R.C. §§ 1038(a), 1038(b).

[203] Reg. § 1.1038-1(a)(2). The regulations also provide that I.R.C. § 1038 will not apply to sales of cooperative housing stock described in I.R.C. § 121(d)(3) or § 1034(f), to an exchange of property or to a disposition treated as a sale under I.R.C. §§ 121(d)(4), 1034(i)(relating to the sale or exchange of a residence). See discussion of installment land contracts at ¶ 8.03.

[204] Reg. § 1.1038-1(a)(2)(ii).

[205] The regulations state that "the reacquisition must be in furtherance of the seller's security rights in the property with respect to indebtedness to him that arose at the time of the sale." Reg. § 1.1038-1(a)(3).

[206] *Id.*

right has not been released or abandoned.[200]

The rules are illustrated in the following examples.

Example 1. Individual X, in the trade or business of lending, lends Y $250,000 and secures the loan with a mortgage. During the next two years, Y pays $20,000 of the principal of the loan but then defaults. X pays property tax assessments on the property in the amount of $5,000, forecloses on the property, and successfully bids in at $200,000. The foreclosure expenses are $5,000, and the fair market value of the property is $190,000.

Transaction 1: Debt Collection

Initial basis		$250,000
Less principal payments	$20,000	
Plus property tax payments (treated as additional loan)	5,000	
Basis in debt		$235,000
Less amount realized on sale (bid price less expenses $200,000 − $5,000)		195,000
Bad-debt loss		($ 40,000)

Transaction 2: The Exchange

Fair market value of property	$190,000
Less bid price applied to purchase	200,000
Loss on Exchange	($ 10,000)

The bad-debt deduction and the exchange loss will be ordinary.

Example 2. Assume the same facts as in Example 1, except that X successfully bids in at $150,000.

Transaction 1: Debt Collection

Basis in debt	$235,000
Less amount realized on sale ($150,000 − $5,000)	145,000
Bad-debt Loss	($ 90,000)

Transaction 2: The Exchange

Fair market value of property	$190,000
Less bid price applied to exchange	150,000
Gain on exchange	$ 40,000

---

[200] Securities Mortgage Co., 58 T.C. 667 (1972).

property.[194] Decided cases and Treasury regulations provide, however, that the bid price is presumed to be the fair market value of the property; this presumption can be rebutted by either the government or the taxpayer showing clear and convincing proof to the contrary.[195] The gain or loss from this second transaction is determined by subtracting the bid price from the amount realized.[196] Consequently, in any case where the mortgagee can demonstrate by clear and convincing proof that the value of the real property is less than the bid price, he will be entitled to an additional loss measured by such difference. Conversely, if the Internal Revenue Service can show that the value of the property is more than the bid price, the mortgagee should be taxable on the difference as gain on the exchange. Consistent with the theory of the exchange transaction, the basis of the property acquired by the mortgagee is equal to its fair market value on the date of acquisition.[197]

The nature of the gain or loss on the second transaction has been generally held to be capital.[198] The Internal Revenue Service has indicated, however, that the nature of gain or loss on the exchange of the note is to be determined by the usual rules, with the result that when a mortgagee acquires the mortgage debt in the ordinary course of a lending business, or the business of dealing in real estate and mortgages, the mortgagee would be entitled to ordinary loss deductions or would be taxable on the gain at ordinary rates.[199]

Under these rules, it is possible for a corporation that is not in a lending trade or business to bid low at foreclosure and obtain a large ordinary bad-debt deduction. The loss will be offset by a *capital gain* if the value of the property exceeds the bid price because the note would be a capital asset of the corporation.

The tax results of the second transaction must be reported in the year the transaction is finalized. Where the mortgagor has a right of redemption, it has been held that the transaction is final even if that

---

[194] *Id.* Cf. Community Bank, 62 T.C. 503 (1974) (court held that presumption applies that bid price equals fair market value).

[195] See Community Bank, 62 T.C. at 503; Securities Mortgage Co., 58 T.C. 667 (1972). Reg. § 1.166-6(b)(2).

[196] Reg. § 1.166-6(b)(1).

[197] Reg. § 1.166-6(c); see Philadelphia Park Amusement Co. v. United States, 126 F. Supp. 184 (Ct. Cl. 1954) (basis of property received in taxable exchange is its fair market value).

[198] See Larson v. Cuesta, 120 F.2d 482 (5th Cir. 1941); Hadley Falls Trust Co. v. United States, 110 F.2d 887 (1st Cir. 1940); Clarkson Coal Co., 46 B.T.A. 688 (1942).

[199] See Rev. Rul. 72-238, 1972-1 C.B. 65 (holding that bank mortgagee realizes ordinary gain on the second step of the transction); Robinson, note 78 *supra* ¶ 10.06; Handler, note 85 *supra,* at 209-210.

The consequences of the first transaction are similar to those resulting from a foreclosure sale to a third party. The bid price, although often unrelated to the value of the property, is treated as the gross proceeds from the sale,[186] and the mortgagee is generally entitled to a bad-debt deduction if the basis in the debt exceeds the bid price.[187] The nature of the loss is subject to the same considerations as in a foreclosure sale to third parties, i.e., whether the debt constitutes a business debt.[188] If the bid price exceeds basis, the mortgagee will realize gain that will be taxable as ordinary income from the collection of a note.[189]

If the bid price is high enough to cover unpaid and unreported interest on the debt, the mortgagee will be required to include such interest in income.[190] The mortgagee is deemed to have received payment for the interest even though the value of the property is less than the principal of the debt: the bid price is deemed conclusive for this purpose.[191] The time for reporting the results of this first transaction are the same as in a foreclosure sale to a third party.[192]

The second transaction consists of an exchange of the mortgage obligation for the mortgaged property.[193] The amount realized on the exchange by the mortgagee is equal to the fair market value of the

---

would be determined under those same rules. The Supreme Court, however, precluded this result by holding that the *bid price* is conclusive evidence of the fair market value and is the touchstone for measuring the *foreclosure* loss. See Helvering v. Midland Life Ins. Co., 300 U.S. 216 (1937). Because the bid price is often artificial, the Treasury Regulations and subsequent cases have skirted the Midland holding by creating the fiction of a second exchange transaction in which the value of the property is determinative and by interpreting the Midland decision to hold that the bid price conclusively equals value only in regard to the first transaction—the debt collection process.

[186] Reg. § 1.166-6(a); See Helvering v. Midland Mut. Life Ins. Co., 300 U.S. at 216.

[187] *Id.* Community Bank, 62 T.C. 503 (1974), *acq.* 1975-1 C.B. 1.

[188] See discussion at ¶ 12.03[2][b][iii].

[189] See cases cited in note 155 *supra*; Humphrey v. Comm'r, 162 F.2d 853 (5th Cir. 1947).

[190] See Helvering v. Midland Mut. Life Ins. Co., 300 U.S. at 216; cf. Nichols v. Comm'r, 141 F.2d 870 (6th Cir. 1914) (distinguishing *Midland* but recognizing its authority); Manufacturer's Life Ins. Co., 4 T.C. 811 (1945), *acq.* 1947-1 C.B. 13 (distinguishing *Midland* where no bid was made).

[191] *Id.*

[192] See discussion at ¶ 12.03[4][b][i].

[193] See Reg. §§ 1.166-6(b), 1.166 6(c); Helvering v. New President Corp., 122 F.2d 92, 97 (8th Cir. 1941); Korth v. Zion's Sav. Bank & Trust Co., 148 F.2d 170 (10th Cir. 1945); Securities Mortgage Co., 58 T.C. 667 (1972).

(4) A deficiency judgment is obtained in the year of foreclosure and is uncollectible.[182]

If local law permits a deficiency judgment and such judgment appears to be collectible, the mortgagee does not report the loss until such judgment is collected or proven worthless.[183] If part of the deficiency judgment is worthless and it stems from a business debt, the mortgagee could take a deduction in the year of worthlessness for the worthless portion. On the other hand, when the foreclosure results in gain, it is reportable in the year of foreclosure. Additional gain is reported if further collections are made pursuant to a deficiency judgment.

The time for reporting gain or loss by the mortgagee is not affected by any right of redemption by the mortgagor: such rights are exercisable only against the purchaser and have no bearing on the finality of the transaction for the mortgagee.[184]

[ii] Foreclosure Sale to Mortgagee. If the foreclosure sale does not produce bids equal to the debt, the mortgagee will often bid as high as the outstanding debt and thereby obtain possession of the property. The consequences to the mortgagee depend generally upon whether the mortgagee was the seller of the mortgaged property. If the mortgagee was not the seller, the transaction is governed by general principles derived from case law and pertinent regulations. If the mortgagee was the seller of the property, special statutory rules under I.R.C. § 1038 apply.

Not Involving I.R.C. § 1038. When a mortgagee buys in at the foreclosure sale, he is treated constructively for tax purposes as if he had engaged in two transactions. In the first transaction, the mortgagee acts as a creditor collecting the debt and receiving the bid price as the proceeds from the sale. In the second transaction, the mortgagee engages in an exchange of his note for the property acquired at the foreclosure sale.[185]

---

[182] See Doris D. Havemeyer, 45 B.T.A. 329 (1941), *acq.* 1942-1 C.B. 8.

[183] See Reg. § 1.166-6(a); Vancoh Realty Co., 33 B.T.A. 918 (1936), *nonacq. on other grounds* XV-2 C.B. 49.

[184] William C. Heinemann & Co., 40 B.T.A. 1090 (1939).

[185] See Reg. §§ 1.166-6(a), 1.166-6(b); Nichols v. Comm'r, 141 F.2d 870, 876 (6th Cir. 1944); Hadley Falls Trust Co. v. United States, 110 F.2d 887 (1st Cir. 1940); Community Bank, 62 T.C. 503 (1974); Rev. Rul. 72-238, 1972-1 C.B. 65. It is arguable that the transaction should be treated the same as a voluntary conveyance. There would be one transaction and the mortgagee would be entitled to a loss or gain measured by the difference between the value of the property and the basis in the debt. The nature and timing of any gain or loss

foreclosure and the amount of unpaid interest on the debt included in income.

Step 3: Add any deficiency collected to the amount of proceeds from the sale.

> *Example.* In 1978, X lends Y $100,000. The loan is secured by real property purchased by Y. During the next two years, Y makes payments of $10,000 on the principal of the debt. Interest in the amount of $18,000 falls due, which is unpaid but reported as income by X, an accrual-basis taxpayer. In 1980, X pays certain local tax assessments against the property, in the amount of $5,000, and in 1981 causes the property to be sold in a foreclosure sale. The expenses of foreclosure are $1,000, and the sales proceeds are $80,000. X realizes a loss of $34,000, computed as follows.

Step 1: Net Proceeds
Gross proceeds less expenses
($80,000 − $1,000) $ 79,000
   Less:

Step 2: Basis of Debt at Foreclosure
Initial basis (amount advanced) $100,000
   Less principal payments $10,000
   Plus unpaid, accrued interest   18,000
   Plus additional advances   5,000
Basis at foreclosure   113,000

Loss realized (excess of 2 over 1)   ($ 34,000)

If X subsequently collects $10,000 from Y in a deficiency action, the loss would be $24,000.

The mortgagee must report the loss in the year the debt, including any deficiency, becomes worthless.[180] Accordingly, the loss will be reportable in the year of foreclosure under any of the following circumstances:

(1) There is no deficiency;
(2) No deficiency can be obtained because of local law or because the debt is nonrecourse;
(3) It is apparent that the right to collect the deficiency is worthless[181]; or,

---

[180] Reg. § 1.166-2(a). See discussion of deficiency judgment at ¶3.08[4][g].
[181] See Reg. § 1.166-2(b); Doris D. Havemeyer, 45 B.T.A. 329 (1941), *acq'd.* 1942-1 C.B. 8.

constitutes a security under I.R.C. § 165(g) (generally, corporate debt in registered form or with interest coupons) and a capital asset, the loss would be treated as derived from the sale or exchange of a capital asset.[176]

It is also possible for the mortgagee to recognize gain from the foreclosure if the debt was acquired at a discount, or if the mortgagee has already taken a deduction for the partial worthlessness of the debt. In either case, the basis for the debt could be lower than the face amount of the debt, creating the possibility that net proceeds will exceed that basis and will produce taxable gain.

The gain will be taxable as ordinary income if it is attributable to a discount purchase, under the rule that collections by a purchaser of a note in excess of the purchase price do not constitute capital gains.[177] The excess of proceeds over basis will also be taxable as ordinary income if attributable to a partial write-off of the debt, to the extent the deduction for partial worthlessness provides the creditor with a tax benefit.[178]

If the net proceeds of the sale exceed the face amount of the note, the excess will be taxable to the mortgagee as ordinary interest income to the extent of any unpaid interest, unless it has been previously reported as income.[179]

The rules for computing gain or loss of the mortgagee can be summarized as follows.

Step 1: Determine the net proceeds (gross proceeds less expenses of foreclosure) and subtract the basis computed in Step 2.

Step 2: Determine the mortgagee's basis in the debt at the time of foreclosure. The initial basis is reduced by any principal payments made by the mortgagor and increased by additional advances made before the

---

[176] I.R.C. §§ 166(e), 165(g)(2). A bank is entitled to a bad-debt loss in this instance under a special rule set forth in I.R.C. § 582.

[177] See, e.g., Galvin v. Hudson, 20 T.C. 734 (1953), *aff'd per curiam* 216 F.2d 748 (6th Cir. 1954); Hale v. Helvering, 85 F.2d 819 (D.C. Cir. 1936); Rev. Rul. 68-523, 1968-2 C.B. 82.

[178] See First Nat'l Bank of Lawrence County, 16 T.C. 147 (1951); Merchants Nat'l Bank of Commerce v. Comm'r, 199 F.2d 657 (5th Cir. 1952). To the extent that no tax benefit was provided the mortgagee by the write-off of the mortgage, he would be entitled to a recovery exclusion under I.R.C. § 111, and no income would be recognized.

[179] Herbert's Estate v. Comm'r, 139 F.2d 756 (3d Cir. 1943), *cert. denied* 322 U.S. 752. Cf. Helvering v. Midland Mut. Life Ins. Co., 300 U.S. 216 (1937) (involving foreclosure sale to mortgagee where bid price included interest). An accrual-basis taxpayer would generally have reported the unpaid interest as income. See Reg. § 1.451-1.

settled.[167] If the mortgagor wishes to expedite the finality of the sale, he can execute a quitclaim deed which will effectively release any redemption rights.[168]

[b] Consequences to Mortgagee

The tax implications of the foreclosure sale for the mortgagee depend upon whether the sale is to a third party or whether the mortgagee acquires the property by bidding in at the foreclosure sale. We will first analyze the simpler case, a sale to a third party.

[i] Foreclosure Sale to Third Party. In the vast majority of foreclosure sales, the mortgagee will realize a gain or loss computed by subtracting the sum of (1) net proceeds obtained from the sale and (2) any deficiency judgments collected from the debtor, from the mortgagee's basis in the debt.[169] For this purpose, the net proceeds equal gross proceeds of sale less expenses of foreclosure.[170] It should also be noted that payments to preserve the value of the security *prior to* foreclosure are treated as additional loans which increase the mortgagee's basis in the debt.[171]

Any loss will usually be treated as a bad-debt loss deductible as either an ordinary loss or a short-term capital loss pursuant to the rules of I.R.C. § 166.[172] Thus, if the mortgagee is a corporation or if the debt is directly connected with the individual taxpayer's business, either at the time incurred or at the time it became worthless, it will produce a loss deductible against ordinary income.[173] If the mortgagee has reported unpaid interest as income, the deduction will be increased by such interest, to the extent the proceeds are insufficient to pay the unpaid interest.[174]

There are two exceptions to the treatment of the loss realized by the mortgagee as a bad-debt loss: (1) If the mortgage debt constitutes an installment obligation within the meaning of I.R.C. § 453, the loss or gain will be taxed as if realized from the original sale.[175] (2) If the debt

---

[167] See Morton v. Comm'r, 104 F.2d 534 (4th cir. 1939).

[168] See Sherwin A. Hill, 40 B.T.A. 376 (1939), *rev'd on other grounds* 119 F.2d 421 (6th Cir. 1941).

[169] For a discussion of the determination of the mortgagee's basis, see ¶12.03[2][6][11].

[170] Reg. § 1.166-6(a).

[171] See Estate of Lucy S. Schieffelin, 44 B.T.A. 137 (1941).

[172] For a full discussion of those rules, see ¶12.03[2][b][iii].

[173] Reg. § 1.166-5(b).

[174] See Reg. §§ 1.166-6(a)(2), 1.166-1(e).

[175] I.R.C. § 453(d)(1).

debt, the amount of gain will be reduced by subsequent payment of any deficiency judgment.

Assume in our example that X had taken $50,000 of depreciation and the outstanding balance of the debt is $80,000. The net proceeds on the foreclosure sale are $75,000. At the time of the foreclosure sale X should[162] realize a $10,000 gain, computed as follows:

Amount realized (mortgage debt unpaid)	80,000
Mortgagor's adjusted basis	$70,000
(initial basis less depreciation)	
Gain	$10,000

If X is personally liable on the debt and the $10,000 deficiency were collected later, the gain would be reduced to $0.

If the sale proceeds exceed the principal amount of the debt, the mortgagor may deduct any interest included in the foreclosure price,[163] unless the interest was previously deducted by the mortgagor.

Since the foreclosure sale is treated as a sale, the nature of the gain or loss is governed by the usual rules concerning capital versus ordinary income.[164] The nature of the mortgagor's deduction, if a deficiency judgment is collected by the mortagee, is governed by the treatment of the original foreclosure sale transaction.[165]

The mortgagor must report the gain or loss in the year the sale is final. If the mortgagor has a right of redemption under state law, the sale is not final until such right expires or becomes worthless.[166] Where there is no right of redemption, the transaction is reported in the year of foreclosure. The gain or loss will also not be reportable until the foreclosure decree becomes final and any appeal by the mortgagor is

---

[162] See note 157 *supra*.

[163] Margaret E.J. Malmstedt, 35 T.C.M. 199 (1976); Harold M. Blossom, 38 B.T.A. 1136 (1938), *acq.* 1939-1 C.B. 4.

[164] Neils Schultz, 44 B.T.A. 146 (1941), *acq.* 1941-1 C.B. 9; Charles H. Black, Sr., 45 B.T.A. 204 (1941), *acq.* 1941-2 C.B. 2 (foreclosure loss by dealer in real estate held ordinary loss); McCarty v. Cripe, 201 F.2d 679 (7th Cir. 1953) (foreclosure loss on farm property used in trade or business allowed as ordinary loss under I.R.C. § 1231); Gilford v. Comm'r, 201 F.2d 735 (2d Cir. 1953) (foreclosure loss on improved property allowed as ordinary loss under § 1231).

[165] Harry H. Diamond, 43 B.T.A. 809 (1941); Charles H. Black, Sr., 45 B.T.A. 204 (1941), *acq.* 1941-2 C.B. 2.

[166] See, e.g., Derby Realty, 35 B.T.A. 335 (1937), *acq.* 1938-1 C.B. 9; J.C. Hawkins, 34 B.T.A. 918 (1936), *acq.* 1937-2 C.B. 13, *aff'd* 91 F.2d 354 (5th Cir. 1937); Securities Mortgage Co., 58 T.C. 667 (1972).

instance, the amount realized is the outstanding mortgage indebtedness that encumbers the transferred property.[160]

> *Example.* X acquires an office building for $120,000, financing $100,000 of the purchase with a mortgage loan from a bank. Two years later, after X has paid $20,000 on the loan and taken $20,000 in depreciation deductions, the bank forecloses on the building and the foreclosure sale yields net proceeds of $80,000. The mortgagor realizes a loss in the amount of $20,000, computed as follows.

Mortgagor's basis		$120,000
Less depreciation	$20,000	
Mortgagor's adjusted basis		$100,000
Amount realized (mortgage debt unpaid)		80,000
Loss		($ 20,000)

If the mortgagor is personally liable for the debt and a deficiency results from the sale, the tax consequences are the same as in the example until the mortgagor pays the deficiency. At that time, he is entitled to increase the amount of loss by the amount of the deficiency payment.[161]

> Assume that the proceeds from the foreclosure sale above were only $60,000. As a result of the foreclosure, X would still have a loss of $20,000. If X subsequently pays the deficiency, his loss would be increased to $40,000.

As indicated above, a taxpayer will realize gain from the foreclosure if the debt exceeds his basis. Where there is personal liability on the

---

Merrit, Sr., 400 F.2d 417 (5th Cir. 1968) (involving IRS seizure of stock). But see McCarty v. Cripe, 201 F.2d 679 (7th Cir. 1953); R.H. McNeil, 251 F.2d 863 (4th Cir. 1955), both of which indicate an opposite conclusion.

[160] See Crane v. Comm'r, 331 U.S. 1 (1947); Gavin S. Millar, 67 T.C. 656 (1977), *aff'd* 577 F.2d 212 (3d Cir. 1978). Surprisingly, the tax consequences of such a common event are not clear. It has been contended that the amount realized is limited to the net proceeds from the sale (gross proceeds less expenses of foreclosure). Compare Robinson, *Federal Income Taxation of Real Estate* ¶9.03[1](1979) with Anderson, note 77 *supra*, at 163. Handler, note 85 *supra*, at 227-230. There is also a persisting, but probably incorrect, contention that the amount realized is limited to fair market value where there is no personal liability, based upon the infamous footnote 37 in the *Crane* opinion. See the discussion at note 134 *supra*.

[161] See Harry H. Diamond, 43 B.T.A. 809 (1941); Charles H. Black, Sr., 45 B.T.A. 204 (1941), *acq.* 1941-2 C.B. 2.

debt is a business debt, the mortgagee might deduct the worthless portion before the conveyance, although the value of the property ultimately received will determine the amount of the loss. Finally, the mortgagee should be wary of agreements worded in such a manner that a court could hold that the settlement was in exchange of valuable consideration other than the property conveyed by the mortgagee. Such consideration would preclude a bad-debt deduction.

[4] Foreclosure Sales

When agreement is impossible, the usual remedy is foreclosure and sale by a court order pursuant to the mortgage, or a sale by a mortgagee or trustee under a deed of trust power of sale contained in the mortgage or deed of trust. The sale might be made to a third party, or the mortgagee might "bid in" for the property. The proceeds of the sale are paid first to the lienholders in order of their priority and then to the mortgagor. If the sale does not yield enough to pay the entire debt, and the mortgagor is personally liable for the debt, in most jurisdicitions the mortgagee is entitled to bring an action to recover the deficiency from the debtor. In addition, in some jurisdictions the debtor has a right for a prescribed period of time to redeem, i.e., purchase, the property from the purchaser at the foreclosure sale.[157]

[a] Consequences to the Mortgagor

A transfer via a foreclosure sale is taxable to the mortgagor as a sale or exchange of the property, whether or not the mortgagor is personally liable for the debt.[158] The amount and nature of the gain or loss are measured according to standard rules governing sales or exchanges: there will be a gain if the amount realized (net foreclosure proceeds) exceeds the mortgagor's adjusted basis in the property and there will be a loss if that basis exceeds the amount realized.[159] In either

---

[157] See discussion at ¶3.08[4][g].

[158] Helvering v. Hammel, 311 U.S. 504 (1941); Electro-Chemical Engraving Co. v. Comm'r, 311 U.S. 513 (1941); Comm'r v. Abramson, 124 F.2d 416 (2d Cir. 1942); Ann S. Russo, 68 T.C. 135 (1977); Gavin S. Millar, 67 T.C. 656 (1977), aff'd 577 F.2d 212 (3d Cir., 1978).

[159] I.R.C. § 1001. Gain is likely to result if the taxpayer has reduced his basis in the property by taking substantial depreciation deductions in a highly leveraged investment, i.e., a tax shelter. See ¶1.05[2]. There is a possibility that no loss will be recognized on the foreclosure sale of the property to a "related party" under I.R.C. § 267. The case law indicates generally that I.R.C. § 267(a)(1) does apply to preclude recognition of loss in such a transaction. See Thomas Zacek, 8 T.C. 1056 (1947); E.E. Hassen, 63 T.C. 175 (1974); J.H.

extent of such non-payment unless such interest has been previously reported as income by the taxpayer.[154] If the value of the property exceeds basis but does not exceed the principal of the debt, gain would be taxable as ordinary income from the collection of a debt,[155] unless an arm's-length agreement between the creditor and the debtor allocates a portion of the payment to unpaid interest.[156] If the agreement allocates a portion of the payment to interest, that portion will be reportable as ordinary income unless the interest has been previously reported by the taxpayer. Because all rights are settled as of the time of the conveyance, the mortgagee will recognize gain or loss in the year the conveyance occurs regardless of the accounting method used.

[c] Planning the Voluntary Conveyance

The key consideration with respect to any of the voluntary conveyance is the fair market value of the property. For the mortgagor, if the property is worthless and the worthlessness can be established, the mortgagor might be able to structure the conveyance as an abandonment of worthless property which results in an ordinary, as opposed to a capital, loss. To do so, the mortgagor should clearly state an intention to abandon and should carefully document the claim of worthlessness. If it appears that gain might result, the mortgagor should be careful to show the existence of any exchange of the property for cancellation of the debt in order to secure capital gains treatment.

For the mortgagee, the value of the property is the measure of his recovery on the debt and, hence, the gain or loss on the transfer. A loss will usually result, and the loss will be deductible generally under the bad-debt provisions. Therefore, the mortgagee should carefully document the position that the portion of the debt not satisfied was indeed worthless. This might be done in the case of nonrecourse debt by evidence of the value of the property. Where the mortgagor is personally liable, evidence of worthlessness would be derived from the debtor's financial condition and unsuccessful attempts to collect the debt. If the

---

[154] The interest would have been previously reported by an accrual-basis taxpayer. See note 150 *supra*.

[155] See, e.g., Hale v. Helvering, 85 F.2d 819 (D.C. Cir. 1936); Weiner v. Comm'r, 316 F.2d 451 (3d Cir. 1963); E.D. Rivers, Jr., 49 T.C. 663 (1968); Clement O. Dennis, 57 T.C. 352 (1971), *aff'd* 473 F.2d 274 (5th Cir. 1973); Rev. Rul. 68-523, 1968-2 C.B. 82. If the debt qualifies under I.R.C. § 1232, and if the conveyance constitutes retirement of the debt within the meaning of that section, the conveyance will constitute a sale or exchange giving rise to capital, gain treatment subject to the special rules governing original issue discount. See ¶ 12.02[1][b].

[156] See discussion at ¶12.02[1][a].

transaction is treated as a sale or exchange, and if a capital asset is transferred, capital gain or loss would result from the voluntary conveyance, reportable in the year the conveyance occurs.[148]

[b] Consequences to Mortgagee

When the mortgagee accepts the mortgaged property in full satisfaction of the debt, it will realize a loss equal to the excess of the basis in the debt over the fair market value of the property transferred, or a gain equal to the excess of the value of the property over the basis in the debt.[149] The loss will be increased, or the gain reduced, by any interest which remains unpaid after the transfer and which the mortgagee has previously reported as income.[150] The mortgagee's basis in the transferred property will be the fair market value of the property.[151]

If the transaction generates a loss, the mortgagee is generally entitled to a bad-debt deduction,[152] the nature and timing of which are subject to the rules discussed at ¶¶ 12.03[2][b][i] and [ii]. The exceptions to the rule that the transaction is treated as a bad-debt loss, discussed in ¶ 12.03[2][b][ii], apply as well.

As noted above, gain will be realized to the extent that the value of the property exceeds the mortgagee's basis in the debt. If there is unpaid interest and the value of the property exceeds the principal balance on the note, such excess will be taxable as payment of that interest[153] to the

---

absence of personal liability). Cf. Fred H. Lenway & Co., 69 T.C. 620 (1978) (court questions validity of doctrine in light of *Crane,* dissenting opinion would overrule the doctrine); Ann S. Russo, 68 T.C. 135 (1977) (indicating consideration unnecessary for existence of sale involving nonrecourse debt); Eugene L. Freeland, 74 T.C. 970 (1980) (court held that voluntary conveyance to mortgagee constitutes a sale or exchange).

[148] I.R.C. § 1221.

[149] See, e.g., Bingham v. Comm'r, 105 F.2d 971 (2d Cir. 1939); Comm'r v. Spreckles, 120 F.2d 517 (9th Cir. 1941); Rev. Rul. 68-523 1968-2 C.B. 82.

[150] A taxpayer reporting income on the accrual method would report unpaid interest as income when the interest falls due. Reg. § 1.461-1. Only such unpaid income items result in a bad-debt deduction. See Reg. §§ 1.166-1(d), 1.166-1(e).

[151] See, e.g., Kohn v. Comm'r, 197 F.2d 480 (2d Cir. 1952); W.D. Haden Co. v. Comm'r, 165 F.2d 588 (5th Cir. 1948).

[152] See Bingham v. Comm'r, 105 F.2d at 971; Comm'r v. Spreckles, 120 F.2d at 517; Comm'r v. National Bank of Commerce of San Antonio, 112 F.2d 946 (5th Cir. 1940).

[153] See Manufacturers Life Ins. Co., 43 B.T.A. 867 (1941). There will not be a payment of interest simply because such unpaid interest is deemed satisfied unless the value of the property exceeds the principal of the note. See Helvering v. Missouri State Life Ins. Co., 78 F.2d 778, 780 (8th Cir. 1934); Manhattan Mut. Life Ins. Co., 37 B.T.A. 1041, 1043 (1938), *acq.* 1938-2 C.B. 20.

If an abandonment loss is justified, it will be deductible in the year of worthlessness and abandonment of the property.[142] Presumably, the amount of the deduction would equal the excess of the debtor's basis in the property over the amount of the outstanding indebtedness.[143] It is possible, if the debt exceeds the debtor's basis in the property, that a gain *taxable* as *ordinary income* will result from an attempted abandonment.[144] The gain would be ordinary income even if the property is a capital asset, since there is no sale or exchange. If there is a possibility of gain, the debtor can of course, easily avoid abandonment treatment by awaiting foreclosure or by arranging for a voluntary conveyance in exchange for cancellation of the debt.

Where the mortgagor is not personally liable for the debt, there is substantial, yet dated, authority for the proposition that a voluntary conveyance to the mortgagee will not be treated as a sale or exchange.[145] These cases hold that a release of liability on nonrecourse debt is not consideration and, hence, there is no "exchange." Rather, the loss realized is held to be in the nature of an abandonment loss giving rise to an ordinary deduction; similarly, any gain would be taxable as ordinary income.[146] The continuing viability of this doctrine is questionable, however, in light of *Crane* and other more recent authorities, and it appears likely that the gain or loss from such a transaction would be treated as gain or loss from the sale or exchange of the asset.[147] If the

---

[142] See, e.g., Comm'r v. Hoffman, 117 F.2d 987 (2d Cir. 1941); A.J. Indus. v. United States, 388 F.2d 701 (Ct. Cl. 1967).

[143] It appears that this result would be dictated by Crane v. Comm'r, 331 U.S. 1 (1947), which treats the outstanding indebtedness as an amount realized on *any* disposition, even an abandonment. Cf. Parker v. Delaney, 186 F.2d 455 (1st Cir. 1950) (dictum). Admittedly, it is hard to rationalize reducing the loss deduction by treating the debt balance as an "amount realized" when the premise of the abandonment producing an ordinary deduction versus capital loss is that the debtor has received no consideration. It seems unlikely, however, that a court would allow a deduction for the entire basis.

[144] Cf. Parker v. Delaney, 186 F.2d at 455 (dictum); see Handler, note 84 *supra,* at 244.

[145] See, e.g., Stokes v. Comm'r, 124 F.2d 335 (3d Cir. 1941); Comm'r v. Hoffman, 117 F.2d 987 (2d Cir. 1941); Polin v. Comm'r, 114 F.2d 174 (3d Cir. 1940); Bert Burnquist, 44 B.T.A. 484 (1941). Cf. Comm'r v. Crane, 153 F.2d 504, 506 (2d Cir. 1945), *aff'd on other issues* 331 U.S. 1 (1946) (dictum citing the above as authority); Blaine S. Fox, 61 T.C. 704, 715 (1974) (citing above authorities).

[146] *Id.*

[147] See Rev. Rul. 76-111, 1976-1 C.B. 214 (conveyance to mortgagee in exchange for cancellation of nonrecourse indebtedness held to be sale or exchange); Gavin S. Millar, 67 T.C. 656 (1977), aff'd 577 F.2d 212 (3d Cir., 1978) (involuntary conveyance to mortgagee treated as sale or exchange despite

results from the voluntary transfer. Where the mortgagor is personally liable for the debt, conveyance to the mortgagee is likely to be treated as a sale or exchange,[137] and if the asset transferred is a capital asset, or real property used in a trade business (Section 1231 asset), the gain or loss will be capital in nature and will be reportable in the year of the sale or exchange.[138]

Under very limited circumstances, a personally liable debtor might be entitled to treat the transaction as abandonment of a worthless asset, which gives rise to an ordinary loss deduction because there is no "sale or exchange."[139] To support such a deduction, the debtor would be required to establish the worthlessness of the property, the absence of consideration for the act of abandonment, and the year that worthlessness occurs.[140] This is an almost insurmountable hurdle if the mortgagee forecloses on the property after the abandonment, and the debt is canceled. The courts have tended to treat the two transactions—the abandonment and subsequent foreclosure—as one transaction; the release of liability in connection with the foreclosure is treated as consideration for the transfer of the property. Accordingly, no abandonment deduction would be allowable.[141]

---

[137] Kaufman v. Comm'r, 119 F.2d 901 (9th Cir. 1941); Rogers v. Comm'r, 103 F.2d 790 (9th Cir. 1939); Pender v. Comm'r, 110 F.2d 477 (4th Cir. 1940), *cert. denied* 310 U.S. 650. The debtor is treated as having exchanged the property in consideration of a release from liability. It is noteworthy that this rule applies even if the value of the property is less than the amount of debt canceled. Logically, there are two possibilities in such event: (1) a sale or exchange to the extent that the debt equals the value, and (2) a cancellation of the debt in excess of the value of the property. However, authority up to now has generally provided little support for separating the tax consequences. See Peninsula Properties Co., 47 B.T.A. 84 (1942); Unique Art Mfg. Co., 8 T.C. 1341 (1947); Rev. Rul. 76-111, 1976-1 C.B. 214. But see Reg. § 1.1017-1(b)(5), and Harry L. Bialock, 35 T.C. 649 (1961), *acq.* 1961-2 C.B. 4, which suggests that a bifurcated approach is appropriate under certain circumstances.

[138] I.R.C. §§ 1221, 1231(b)(1). See Comm'r v. Union Pac. R. Co., 86 F.2d 637 (2d Cir. 1936).

[139] I.R.C. § 165(a). See Rhodes v. Comm'r, 100 F.2d 966, 970; Bickerstaff v. Comm'r, 128 F.2d 366 (5th Cir. 1942). Cf. Reg. §§ 1.167(a)-8, 1.165-2 (mentioning abandonment of property). I.R.C. §§ 165(c)(1), 165(c)(2) would entitle the debtor to a deduction for such a loss only if it arose in his trade or business or in a transaction entered into for profit.

[140] See Comm'r v. Abramson, 124 F.2d 416 (2d Cir. 1942). Cf. A.J. Indus. v. United States, 388 F.2d 701 (Ct. Cl. 1967).

[141] See Comm'r v. Green, 126 F.2d 70 (3d Cir. 1942); Stamler v. Comm'r 145 F.2d 37 (3d Cir. 1944); Richter v. Comm'r, 124 F.2d 412 (2d Cir. 1942), all indicating that the abandonment and subsequent foreclosure will be treated as one transaction.

amount realized on the disposition of the property.[135] Although the case decisions are in conflict, it appears that an insolvent mortgagor will be treated as realizing gain only to the extent that the cancellation of indebtedness renders him solvent.[136]

> *Example.* Assume X owns real property that he purchased from Y for $100,000 by paying $10,000 cash and borrowing $90,000 on a nonrecourse basis. The debt was secured by a mortgage on the property. At the end of the fifth year, X's adjusted basis in the property has been reduced to $70,000, and the outstanding balance of the debt is $80,000. X voluntarily conveys the property to Y who cancels X's indebtedness, and X is solvent before and after the conveyance.
>
> *Result:* X has a gain from the disposition of the property in the amount of $10,000. The result would not be affected if the value of the property were less than $80,000.

The nature of the gain to the mortgagor and the appropriate time for reporting the gain or loss depend upon what kind of "disposition"

Tax L. Rev. 159 (1966); Stone, note 80 *supra,* at 559; Handler, note 85 *supra,* at 235. Indeed, one often-cited Tax Court opinion has so held. See Leland S. Collins, 22 T.C.M. 1467 (1963). However, the Service has reached the opposite conclusion, and in Rev. Rul. 76-111, 1976-1 C.B. 214, held that the value of the property transferred is not relevant to the determination of gain or loss on the disposition. Moreover, at least two courts have reached the same conclusion; see Gavin S. Millar, 67 T.C. 656 (1977), *aff'd* Millar v. Comm'r, 577 F.2d 212 (3d Cir., filed June 12, 1978). Cf. Lutz v. Schramm, 1 T.C. 682 (1943) (a pre-*Crane* case, holding value of property irrelevant). It seems likely that other courts would adopt this position.

[135] See Parker v. Delaney, 186 F.2d at 455; Lutz v. Schramm, 1 T.C. at 682.

[136] Turney's Estate v. Comm'r, 126 F.2d 712 (5th Cir. 1942); Lakeland Grocery Co., 36 B.T.A. 289 (1937); Dallas Transfer & Terminal Warehouse Co. v. Comm'r, 70 F.2d 95 (5th Cir. 1934); Main Properties, Inc., 4 T.C. 384 (1944), *acq.* 1945 C.B. 5. Contra, Estate of Delman, 73 T.C. 15 (1979). This exception applies even if there is personal liability and stems from the insolvency exception to the rule that cancellation of indebtedness causes the debtor to realize income. See the cases cited and the discussion at note 81 *supra.* This exception seems misplaced because the transaction is treated as an exchange of the property for the release of liability, even when the debt exceeds the value of the property transferred. See, e.g., Peninsula Properties Co., 47 B.T.A. 84 (1942); Rev. Rul. 76-111, 1976-1 C.B. 214. Courts have generally refused to treat any portion of the transaction as a debt cancellation. See, e.g., Unique Art Mfg. Co., 8 T.C. 1341 (1947). But see Harry L. Bialock, 35 T.C. 649 (1961), *acq.* 1961-2 C.B. 4. Since the transaction is viewed as a "sale," and insolvent taxpayers are required to report gain on sales, the exception derived from cancellation of indebtedness doctrines should be irrelevant.

[c] Tax Planning

When the mortgagee and the mortgagor agree to a debt restructuring, the parties would be advised to limit the adjustments to avoid forcing the mortgagor to realize taxable gain, i.e., avoid a debt cancellation, which would only increase the mortgagor's financial problems. In any event, the mortgagee will need to carefully document its efforts to collect on the debt and to pin down the debtor's financial condition in order to justify a deduction for worthlessness of the debt should it become necesary to accept less than the full amount owed by the mortgagor.

[3] Voluntary Conveyance to Mortgagee, Deed in Lieu of Foreclosure, Abandonment

If the mortgagee and mortgagor cannot agree to restructure the debt or otherwise work out their difficulties, they may agree to a deed in lieu of foreclosure: the mortgagor would surrender the property to the mortgagee in full satisfaction of the outstanding indebtedness. Assuming the mortgagee is willing to hold the property, this simple procedure avoids the expense of a foreclosure sale.[132] Or the mortgagor may attempt simply to abandon the property, usually resulting in an indirect transfer to the mortgagee.

[a] Consequences to Mortgagor

On a voluntary conveyance of mortgaged property to the mortgagee, the mortgagor will realize gain or loss equal to the difference between the outstanding balance of the indebtednesss and the mortgagor's basis in the property transferred, irrespective of whether the mortgagor is personally liable on the note[133] and irrespective of the value of the property.[134] The amount of the liability is treated as an

---

[132] See discussion at ¶3.08[4][g].

[133] See Parker v. Delaney, 186 F.2d 455 (1st Cir. 1950); Lutz v. Schramm, 1 T.C. 682 (1943); Kaufman v. Comm'r, 119 F.2d 901 (9th Cir. 1941); Rev. Rul. 76-111, 1976-1 C.B. 214. Cf. Crane v. Comm'r, 331 U.S. 1 (1947). See discussion at ¶ 12.01[3].

[134] In Crane v. Comm'r, 331 U.S. at 14, n.37, it was indicated that mortgage debt on the transferred property might not be treated as an amount realized on a disposition where the debt exceeds the value of the property and the debtor is not personally liable. This famous "footnote 37" issue has led some to postulate that gain would be realized under such circumstances only to the extent of the value of the property. See, e.g., Adams, "Exploring the Outer Boundaries of the Crane Doctrine; An Imaginary Supreme Court Opinion," 21

entered into for profit, the mortgagee might be entitled to a deduction, irrespective of the origin of the debt.[131]

The following examples illustrate the foregoing concepts with respect to the settlement of a debt at a discount.

> *Example 1.* X, an individual in the business of lending money lends money to Y to enable him to purchase real estate. The purchase price is $10,000, and the loan is for $9,000. Y pays $2,000 of the principal over the next five years. At that time, it becomes apparent that the borrower is in financial straits and that the property is worth substantially less than the outstanding balance of the loan. Accordingly, X allows the borrower to pay off the entire loan for $5,000. X would be entitled to a bad-debt deduction (against ordinary income) in the amount of $2,000 if it can show that the $2,000 debt was worthless. The basis in the debt was originally $9,000 but was reduced by $7,000 of principal payments. The lender received only $5,000 in payment. X might have been entitled to a partial write-off if it could have established partial worthlessness before the debt was paid at a discount.
>
> *Example 2.* X, an individual, sells to Y real estate he owns as an investment for a sales price of $10,000, payable $1,000 cash and with a nine-year purchase-money $9,000 loan. X elects to report the gain on the installment method. X's basis in the property is $5,000. After three years (and $3,000 in payments), it becomes apparent that the borrower is in desperate financial trouble, and the value of the security is questionable. X accepts an offer by Y to settle the entire balance of the debt ($6,000) for $2,000. X's basis in the debt is equal to the excess of the face value $6,000 over the amount that would be returned as income if the note were paid in full ($6,000 × $5,000/$10,000 = $3,000), or $3,000. X is entitled to a capital loss of $1,000 since the loss is treated as a loss on the sale or exchange of the real estate that X held as an investment and not a bad-debt loss deduction.

---

[131] I.R.C. §§ 162, 165. An ordinary loss deduction was allowed under these circumstances in West Coast Sec. Co., 14 T.C. 947 (1950), *acq.* 1950-2 C.B. 4, and First Nat'l Bank of Durant, 6 B.T.A. 545 (1927); cf. Thomas v. Comm'r, 100 F.2d at 408 (dictum that such a transaction generates Section 165 loss not bad-debt deduction if from a transaction entered into for profit). The deduction will not be applicable if the creditor receives other bargained for consideration. See N. Lucille Harrison, 59 T.C. 578 (1973) (disallowing loss deduction where other consideration received, distinguishing West Coast Securities). Cf. Blanche F. Davies, 54 T.C. at 170 (holding no bad-debt deduction allowed on compromise where other consideration received).

debt is acquired or at the time it becomes worthless.[125] Thus, debt obtained from a trade or business may be deducted although the taxpayer is no longer in a trade or business when the debt becomes worthless.[126] If a lender is in the business of making real estate loans or dealing in the sale of real estate as a business, the worthless mortgage debts arising from that business qualify as business bad debts.[127] Worthless debt in connection with a casual sale of real estate held for investment would not qualify for deduction against ordinary income.

There are several exceptions to the general rule that the lender is entitled to an ordinary bad-debt deduction. When the worthless obligation is an installment obligation, the loss is treated as derived from the original sale transaction and will have the same character as the gain or loss on the sale of the asset originally sold to the mortgagor.[128] Similarly, if the taxpayer reports the sale under the deferred-payment method and does not recover his basis, the loss is treated as derived from the sale or exchange of the asset originally sold. Finally, if the note of the mortgagor constitutes a security within the meaning of I.R.C. § 165(g) (generally, a corporate obligation in registered form or with interest coupons), the worthlessness loss will be treated as a loss from the sale or exchange of a capital asset and not as a bad-debt loss.[129]

A bad-debt loss deduction will also be unavailable if the mortgagee accepts less than the face value of the debt for reasons other than worthlessness. If the debt is a nonbusiness debt, it appears that no deduction would be available under such circumstances.[130] However, if the discount is offered in order to further the mortgagee's trade or business, e.g., to obtain working capital, or is offered in a transaction

---

[125] I.R.C. § 166(d)(2). Reg. § 1.166-5(b). See J.T. Dorminey, 26 T.C. 940 (1956).

[126] See Reg. § 1.166-5(d), *Example 1*.

[127] See Estate of Theodore Gutman, 18 T.C. 112 (1952), *acq.* 1952-2 C.B. 2. Cf. Rev. Rul. 72-238, (notes held by bank in connection with lending business are not capital assets). The making of loans as part of general investment activity will not give rise to business debts. See Higgins v. United States, 312 U.S. 212 (1941); Whipple v. Comm'r, 373 U.S. 193 (1963). Cf. Generes v. United States, 405 U.S. 93 (1972) (dealing with shareholder's loans to corporation).

[128] I.R.C. § 453(d)(1).

[129] I.R.C. §§ 166(e), 165(g). There are special rules for banks and savings and loan associations that permit them to deduct the loss as a bad-debt loss. I.R.C. § 582(a).

[130] See Blanche F. Davies, 54 T.C. 170 (1970); Leon S. Black, 52 T.C. 147 (1969). Cf. W.F. Taylor, 38 B.T.A. 551 (1938) (dictum stating that voluntary compromise of valuable debt not deductible as bad-debt loss); Thomas v. Comm'r, 100 F.2d 408 (2d Cir. 1938) (disallowing bad-debt loss for voluntary settlement of valuable nonbusiness debt).

basis is equal to the excess of the face value of the obligation, over the amount of income that would be reported if the note were to be paid in full.[117] If the taxpayer uses a deferred payment sale—reporting no income until payments exceed the basis of the property sold[118]—it appears that the mortgagee's basis in the note will be the same as his basis in the transferred property.[119]

The initial basis is increased by (1) additional amounts loaned to the mortgagor and (2) payments made by the mortgagee in order to preserve the value of his security, e.g., payment of unpaid tax assessments.[120] The basis is reduced by (1) principal payments made by the mortgagor and (2) any prior deductions for partial worthlessness of the debt.[121]

[iii] Nature of the Loss: Business vs. Nonbusiness Debt. The nature of the loss depends upon the taxpayer and the source of the debt. A corporate taxpayer reports the bad-debt loss as a deduction against ordinary income.[122] If an individual is the creditor, the worthlessness of the debt will be taxed as a short-term capital loss,[123] unless it can be shown that the debt was a business bad debt.[124]

A debt qualifies as a business debt if the debt bears a direct relationship to the trade or business of the lender, either at the time the

---

[117] Reg. § 1.453-9(b)(2). See discussion of installment method at ¶9.04.

[118] See Reg. § 1.453-6(a)(2). This method is available only in the rare and extraordinary circumstance that the purchaser's obligations have no ascertainable value. Burnet v. Logan, 283 U.S. 404 (1931); Wingate E. Underhill, 45 T.C. 489 (1966).

[119] See Handler, note 85 *supra,* at 196; Philadelphia Park Amusement Co. v. United States, 126 F. Supp. at 184 (dictum).

[120] See Estate of Lucy S. Schieffelin, 44 B.T.A. 137, 140 (1941), *acq.* 1941-1 C.B. 9. The payments by the mortgagor are treated as additional advances to the mortgagee. Presumably, the advances to the mortgagee are the equivalent of taking a mortgage out on the property and do not serve to increase the *mortgagor's* basis in his property. The amount realized by the mortgagor on eventual disposition, however, would be increased by the additional mortgage debt, assuming that the new loans are secured by the same mortgage instrument.

[121] Motor Prods. Corp., 47 B.T.A. 983, 1001 (1942), *aff'd per curiam* 142 F.2d 449 (6th Cir. 1944); Bank of Newberry, 1 T.C. 374 (1942), *acq.* 1943 C.B. 2; Ludlow Value Mfg. Co. v. Durey, 62 F.2d 508 (2d Cir. 1933). A deduction for partial worthlessness is available only for business bad debts. I.R.C. § 166(d); Reg. § 1.166-5(a)(2).

[122] I.R.C. §§ 166(a)(1).

[123] I.R.C. § 166(d)(1)(b). A short-term capital loss will first be applied to reduce capital gains. To the extent such losses exceed capital gains, the losses can offset ordinary income up to $3,000 per year. Unused losses can be carried over future tax years. I.R.C. §§ 1211, 1212.

[124] I.R.C. § 166(d)(1)(A).

lender receives property in settlement of the debt, however, his deduction is limited to the difference between the amount received and his basis in the debt.[110] If the creditor simply cancels a portion of the debt because the debt is partially worthless, he would be entitled to a deduction equal to his basis in the amount of debt canceled, assuming the lender is a corporation or the debt is a business debt.[111]

The lender's initial basis in the debt depends upon how the debt was obtained. If the lender advanced cash to the borrower, the basis in the loan is equal to the amount advanced,[112] and if the debt is purchased by the mortgagee his basis will equal the purchase price for the debt.[113] As a general rule, if the debt arose from a sale of the mortgaged property from the mortgagee to the mortgagor, the mortgagee's basis in the debt of the mortgagor will be equal to the face amount of the purchase-money indebtedness includible as "amount realized" from the sale, where the mortgagee does not defer the reporting of any gain from the sale.[114] For a cash-method mortgagee, the amount of the mortgagor's note included as the amount realized will be equal to the fair market value of the note.[115] It appears that an accrual-method taxpayer will be required to include the full face value of the note as income from the sale, irrespective of its fair market value.[116]

When the mortgagee defers reporting gain on the sale to the mortgagor, the rules are somewhat more complicated. If the installment method of reporting gain is used under I.R.C. §453, the mortgagee's

---

[110] See I.R.C. § 166(b). Cf. Comm'r v. Spreckels, 120 F.2d 517 (9th Cir. 1941); Rev. Rul. 74-621, 1974-2 C.B. 405; Rev. Rul. 68-523, 1968-2 C.B. 82; Bingham v. Comm'r, 105 F.2d 971 (2d Cir. 1939); Reg. § 1.166-6(a)(1). It is important to note that debts arising from unpaid rights to income such as rent, dividends, wages, or interest have a zero basis and, therefore, will not be allowed as a deduction unless included in income pursuant to the taxpayers accounting method no later than the year in which the bad-debt deduction is claimed. Reg. § 1.166-1(e).

[111] I.R.C. § 166(a)(2). Only this type of debt gives rise to a deduction for partial worthlessness. Of course, even if the worthless portion is not canceled, the mortgagee could deduct the worthless part of the debt under these circumstances.

[112] I.R.C. §§ 1011, 1012.

[113] I.R.C. §§ 1012. See Reg. § 1.166-1(d)(2)(i)(b).

[114] See generally Handler, note 85 *supra,* at 195-197 and I.R.C. § 1001(b).

[115] See Reg. § 1.453-6(a); Philadelphia Park Amusement Co. v. United States, 126 F. Supp. 184 (Ct. Cl. 1954); Comm'r v. Jones Co., 75-2 U.S.T.C. ¶ 9732, *rev'g* 60 T.C. 663 (1973).

[116] Reg. § 1.451-1. See Morris, *Real Estate Tax Planning* 64 (1977).There are some who would contend that even an accrual-basis taxpayer must include only the value of the note in income. See Arthur Andersen & Co., *Federal Taxes Affecting Real Estate* ¶ 7.02[4] (1978). Cf. George L. Castner Co., 30 T.C. 1061, 1068 (1955) (dictum).

individual taxpayer if the debt arose in connection with his trade or business.[99] The amount of the deduction is the adjusted basis of the taxpayer in the worthless debt.[100] An individual taxpayer will be entitled to a short-term capital loss and not an ordinary deduction unless the debt is created, acquired, or incurred in the taxpayer's trade or business.[101] These three elements—the timing, the amount, and the nature of the deduction—will be considered separately.

[i] Timing of the Deduction. The debt may be deducted only in the year of worthlessness, determined from all relevant facts and circumstances, including the value of any security for the debt and the financial condition of the borrower.[102] The regulations provide that legal action is not required if the taxpayer can establish that the note is otherwise uncollectible and that legal action would be pointless.[103] According to the regulations, bankruptcy is very strong evidence of worthlessness of the unsecured debts of the bankrupt.[104]

The burden of proving worthlessness is on the mortgagee and can be established by showing that a prudent person would have written off the debt.[105] Undoubtedly, the best evidence of worthlessness is a debt reduced to judgment that has been returned unsatisfied.[106] But situations short of fruitless litigation have been held to indicate worthlessness, such as reversals in the debtor's business[107] or a showing that the security for the debt is worthless.[108] It is advisable for the creditor to carefully document efforts to (1) collect the debt, (2) ascertain the financial condition of the debtor, and (3) value the mortgaged property in order to support the timing of the deduction.

[ii] Deduction Equals Mortgagee's Basis in the Debt. The second element relates to the amount of the deduction: the amount of the deduction is equal to the lender's adjusted basis in the debt.[109] Where the

---

[99] I.R.C. § 166(d)(1)(A).

[100] I.R.C. § 166(b).

[101] I.R.C. §§ 166(d)(1)(B), 166(d)(2).

[102] Reg. § 1.166-2(a).

[103] Reg. § 1.166-2(b).

[104] Reg. § 1.166-2(c)(1), 1.166-2(c)(2).

[105] Reading Co. v. Comm'r, 132 F.2d 306 (3d Cir. 1942), *cert. denied* 318 U.S. 778; Ott, 26 T.C.M. 540 (1967).

[106] See Weiss, 24 T.C.M. 432 (1965); Meurer Steel Barrel Co., 7 B.T.A. 64 (1927), *acq.* VII-1 C.B. 21.

[107] See, e.g., Washington Inst. of Technology, Inc., 10 T.C.M. 17 (1951).

[108] Portland Mfg. Corp., 56 T.C. 58 (1971), *acq.* 1972-2 C.B. 2, *aff'd on another issue* 75-1 U.S.T.C. ¶ 9449; E.C. Olson, 10 T.C. 458 (1947), *acq.* 1948-2 C.B. 3; A.W. Skaer, 10 B.T.A. 247 (1928).

[109] I.R.C. § 166(b).

debt, pursuant to rules and regulations set forth in I.R.C. § 1017. It is important to note that the canceled debt must be applied first to reduce the basis of the property subject to the lien of that debt or of the property that was purchased with the proceeds of the canceled debt.[94]

[ii] Restructuring of the Debt. As indicated above, the parties may agree to restructure the debt, short of actual cancellation of the debt. If the mortgagee agrees to extend the maturity of the loan, to reduce or to increase the interest rate, to defer the payment of either principal or interest, or to add unpaid interest to the principal, neither the mortgagor or the mortgagee will realize income.[95] If the interest owing is deferred, a cash-basis taxpayer cannot deduct the interest until it is paid. An accrual-basis taxpayer may deduct the interest as it accrues, regardless of when it is paid.[96] However, should the principal amount of the loan actually be reduced, the cancellation of indebtedness rules will govern.

[b] Consequences to Mortgagee

When a mortgagee permits settlement of the debt for less than the outstanding balance, or cancels a portion of the debt, the mortgagee will generally be entitled to a deduction for the worthlessness or partial worthlessness of the debt under I.R.C. § 166.[97] This is commonly known as the "bad debt" deduction. An understanding of the nature of this deduction is essential to a consideration of the tax consequences of losses realized by a mortgagee in connection with the mortgage indebtedness.

Generally, I.R.C. § 166 provides that a taxpayer is entitled to a deduction for any bona fide debt that becomes worthless during the taxable year or for that part of the debt that becomes worthless during the taxable year.[98] A worthless debt, however, is deductible only by an

---

[94] Reg. §§ 1.1017-1(a)(1), 1.1017-1(a)(2). This enables the taxpayer to do under the statute what was allowed under the cases cited at note 85 *supra,* except that trade or business requirement does not exist under a judicially created exception form non-corporate debts.

[95] Rev. Rul. 73-160, 1973-1 C.B. 365 (change of rate and maturity); Sam F. Sotar, 27 T.C.M. 194 (1968); Rev. Rul. 68-419, 1968-2 C.B. 196; Rev. Rul. 55-429, 1955-2 C.B. 252.

[96] See Rev. Rul. 70-697, 1970-2 C.B. 38, Reg. § 1.461-1(a)(2); Rev. Rul. 70-56, 1970-2 C.B. 37.

[97] I.R.C. § 166; Reg. § 1.166-1(a). A bona fide debt is one that arose from a valid and enforceable obligation to pay a fixed or determinable amount of money. Reg. § 1.166-1(c).

[98] I.R.C. §§ 166(a)(1), 166(a)(2).

requires the debtor to reduce his basis in the mortgaged property.[85] It is questionable whether this exception, which relies upon the absence of personal liability, has any vitality in light of the development of the *Crane* doctrine, which ignores personal liability and allows a taxpayer to include nonrecourse debt in basis while requiring the taxpayer to include the amount of such debt as part of the amount realized on a dispostiion.[86]

Even if income is realized from a discharge of indebtedness, a debtor may choose to defer recognition of the gain by making an election to reduce the basis of property owned by the debtor by the amount of the canceled debt.[87] This alternative is available to all corporate debtors and to noncorporate debtors if the debt arose in connection with the debtor's trade or business.[88] The deferral election is available for nonrecourse as well as recourse liabilities.[89]

Whether the debt is incurred or assumed in connection with a trade or business is answered by looking at all facts and circumstances surrounding the debt.[90] The regulations indicate that if the proceeds of the debt are used to purchase, improve, or repair property used in a trade or business, the election will be available.[91] The mere fact that the debt is secured by trade or business property, however, will not be sufficient.[92]

In order to obtain the deferral, the taxpayer must file a proper election[93] to reduce the basis of his assets by the amount of canceled

---

[85] Fulton Gold Corp., 31 B.T.A. 519 (1934); Hotel Astoria, Inc., 42 B.T.A. 759. The exact nature of the exception is unclear, leading some commentators to treat it merely as part of the second exception. See Robinson, *Federal Income Taxation of Real Estate* ¶9.02[2] (1979), and others who treat it as a separate exception, see Handler, "Tax Consequences of Mortgage Foreclosures and Transfers of Real Property to the Mortgagee," 31 Tax. L. Rev. 193, 235-236 (1976) (hereinafter cited as Handler). The primary difference between this and the second exception appears to be that this exception does not depend upon the value of the property and will not apply if the mortgagor has personal liability. See discussion of nonrecourse financing at ¶1.05[4][b].

[86] See Handler, note 85 *supra,* at 236, n.176. See the discussion of the *Crane* doctrine at ¶¶ 12.01[3][a], 12.01[3][b].

[87] I.R.C. §§ 108(a), 1017.

[88] I.R.C. § 108; Reg. § 1.108(a)-1(a)(2). For an additional discussion of a debt incurred in a taxpayer's trade or business see ¶ 12.03[2][b][iii] and notes 110, 111 *infra.*

[89] See Reg. § 1.108(a)-1(a)(1); Rev. Rul. 67-200, 1967-1 C.B. 15.

[90] Reg. § 1.108(a)-1(a)(2).

[91] *Id.*

[92] *Id.*

[93] Reg. § 1.108(a)-2 provides that the taxpayer must file the election on Form 982 for the taxable year in which the indebtedness is canceled.

lation.[80] This rule applies whether a portion of the debt is simply canceled or whether the debtor repays the entire debt for less than the amount due and retains the property securing the debt. Courts applying this general rule have spawned a number of exceptions that might apply in the case of mortgaged real estate.

The most far-reaching exception is the fact that the general rule does not apply to insolvent taxpayers.[81] If the cancellation renders the taxpayer solvent, the taxpayer will realize income only to the extent of the newfound solvency.[82] A debtor is insolvent for this purpose if the current fair market value of his assets is less than his liabilities, including goodwill and other intangibles.[83]

A second exception pertains to purchase-money indebtedness. If the debt reduction is the product of direct negotiations to reduce the purchase price and the value of the property does not exceed the uncanceled portion of the debt, it has been held that debt reduction constitutes a price reduction that does not produce taxable income.[84]

A third exception has been applied in cases involving nonrecourse refinancing. When the debt is settled at a discount by cash or by a transfer of property other than the property securing the debt, it has been held that no gain is realized; instead, the transaction merely

---

[80] I.R.C. § 61(a)(12); Reg. § 1.61-12. The doctrine manifested in the Code and regulations stems from the seminal case of United States v. Kirby Lumber, 284 U.S. 1 (1931). For a thorough analysis of the genesis of the doctrine and the numerous exceptions discussed in the text, see Stone, "Cancellation of Indebtedness," 34th Annual N.Y.U. Inst., Pt. I, at 555 (1976); see also Suwalsky & Chirelstein "Cancellation of Indebtedness," BNA Tax Management Portfolio 58-3rd (1976); Eustice, "Cancellation of Indebtedness and the Federal Income Tax: A Problem of Creeping Confusion," 14 Tax. L. Rev. 225 (1959). For a discussion of the satisfaction of debt by the transfer of property worth less than the debt, see discussion at ¶12.03[3].

[81] See Dallas Transfer & Terminal Warehouse Co. v. Comm'r, 70 F.2d 95, 96 (5th cir. 1934); Lakeland Grocery Co., 36 B.T.A. 289 (1937); Main Properties Inc., 4 T.C. 364 (1944), acq. 1958-2 C.B. 29.

[82] Lakeland Grocery Co., 36 B.T.A. at 289; Capital Coal Corp. v. Comm'r, 250 F.2d 361 (2d Cir. 1957), cert. denied 356 U.S. 936 (1958).

[83] J.A. Maurer, Inc., 30 T.C. 1273 (1958); Conestoga Tranp. Co., 17 T.C. 506 (1951).

[84] See Helvering v. A.L. Killian Co., 128 F.2d 433 (8th Cir. 1942); Hirsch v. Comm'r, 115 F.2d 656 (7th Cir. 1940); Comm'r v. Sherman, 135 F.2d 68 (6th Cir. 1943); Fifth Avenue-14th St. Corp. v. Comm'r, 147 F.2d 453 (2d Cir. 1945). Where the property value exceeded the remaining debt after deduction, the exception has been held inapplicable. See L.D. Coddon & Bros., Inc., 37 B.T.A. 393 (1968); John E. Montgomery, 65 T.C. 511 (1975); Comm'r v. Coastwise Transp. Co., 71 F.2d 104 (1st Cir. 1934).

¶ 12.03 TAX CONSEQUENCES OF MORTGAGOR'S DEFAULT

[1] Overview

The most complicated issues with respect to mortgage financing arise when a mortgagor defaults in payments under the mortgage. The parties are confronted with numerous alternatives, including conveyance to the mortgagee by strict foreclosure, foreclosure and sale to a third party or to the mortgagee, or voluntary conveyance to the mortgagee, e.g., a deed in lieu of foreclosure.[79] In lieu of such draconian measures, the parties may agree to a compromise of the debt. This may range in form from partial cancellation or settlement of the debt at a discount to a mere extension of maturity or a waiver of payments of principal and/or interest.

The tax consequences to the parties, even when relatively well settled, appear to depend upon otherwise insignificant differences in form, and thus provide fertile ground for effective planning. Other issues are not finally resolved, for example, the nature of a mortgagor's loss when he abandons mortgaged property to the mortgagee. Careful planning can help avoid the areas that provide a potential for adverse resolution and can minimize the potential for difficulty with the IRS.

This section of the chapter will cover the tax consequences to the parties in the multiplicity of possible situations arising from default, beginning with the effects of a compromise of the indebtedness and proceeding to the more drastic measure of foreclosure. At each juncture, planning hints will be provided to pragmatize the legal discussion.

[2] Compromise of Mortgage Indebtedness

The debt secured by the mortgage may be compromised in essentially two ways: (1) a partial cancellation of the debt, e.g., via settlement at a discount, and (2) a restructuring of the debt. The alternatives produce very different tax results.

[a] Consequences to Mortgagor

[i] Debt Cancellation, Settlement at Discount. If debt owed by a taxpayer is canceled, in part or entirely, the general rule is that the debtor will realize ordinary taxable income to the extent of the cancel-

---

The income on foreclosure would thus be reduced by the amount of the assigned rents without producing any income to the mortgagor, an anomalous result after *Crane*.

[79] See discussion at ¶ 3.08[4][g].

Payments made after foreclosure of expenses accruing after foreclosure are subject to the general rules governing deductibility of expenses.[73]

[4] Assignment of Rents to Mortgagee

During the course of the mortgage loan, the mortgagor may assign rents to the mortgagee pursuant to security-related provisions in the mortgage agreement or pursuant to an agreement with the mortgagee executed to avert foreclosure.[74] The rents paid to the mortgagee are usually applied to the principal and interest owing on the debt.

The payments received by the mortgagee are not taxable as income to the mortgagee,[75] unless, of course, the payments are applied to interest on the debt.[76] Rather, the mortgagor remains taxable on the rents as the continuing owner of the property.[77] Although there is some authority to the contrary, it is likely that this result will apply even if the mortgagor is not personally liable on the indebtedness.[78]

---

[73] Cf. Gordon I. Hyde, 64 T.C. 300 (1975) (no deduction allowed because expenses accrued before acquisition).

[74] See discussion at ¶ 308[4][i].

[75] E.J. Murray, 21 T.C. 1049 (1954), *aff'd* 232 F.2d 742 (9th Cir. 1956); Comm'r v. Penn Athletic Club Bldg., 176 F.2d 939 (3d Cir. 1949); Hadley Falls Trust Co. v. United States, 22 F. Supp. 346, 353 (D. Mass. 1938) *rev'd on another point* 110 F.2d 887 (1st Cir. 1940).

[76] I.R.C. § 61(a)(4).

[77] See Murray v. Comm'r, 232 F.2d 742 (9th Cir. 1956) (owner taxable on rents collected by mortgagee and credited against debt after redemption by owner); William A. Clementson, 27 T.C.M. 559 (1968) (involving assignment of rents to creditors); Helvering v. Horst, 311 U.S. 112, 115 (1940) (holding that assignment of right to income from property does not relieve owner of taxability of the income).

[78] See Ethel S. Ane, 22 T.C. 756, 761 (1954) (lease provided for direct payments to mortgagee, lessor not personally liable on debt, held: lessor taxable on assigned rent); Anna L. Hilpert, 4 T.C. 473, 477 (1944) (holding mortgagor taxable on assigned rents credited against nonrecourse mortgage liability), *rev'd* 151 F.2d 929 (5th Cir. 1945). Other commentators have indicated that where the debtor is not personally liable there is no income when rents are applied to the debt, citing the reversal of the Tax Court in the *Hilpert* case. See e.g., Anderson, *Tax Planning of Real Estate* 148 (7th ed. 1977). The *Hilpert* case, which involved a complicated set of facts was decided before Crane v. Comm'r, 331 U.S. 1 (1947), discussed at ¶ 12.01[3][a], which held that the amount realized on disposition of mortgaged property includes the amount of mortgage, indebtedness even if there is no personal liability. See Parker v. Delaney, 186 F.2d 455 (1st Cir. 1950). First, the conclusion in *Hilpert* is inconsistent with the basic rule that income from property is taxed to the owner of the property. See, e.g., Helvering v. Horst, 311 U.S. 112 (1940). Second, the amount realized on a subsequent foreclosure by the mortgagee would include only the remaining debt.

only to the extent that the investment-type income is not derived from a trade or business.[65] Investment expenses are defined as deductions directly connected with production of the investment income.[66]

Real property subject to net leases will not be considered property held for investment if (1) the business expenses (exclusive of taxes, interest, depreciation, and bad debts) exceed 15 percent of gross rent from the property, or (2) the lessor is not guaranteed a specified return on the property and is not guaranteed against loss in whole or in part.[67] The owner, however, may elect out of the 15 percent restriction if the property has been in use for over five years.[68] If property is subject to two or more leases, the owner can elect to aggregate the leases for purposes of the 15 percent test. If the real property is treated as an investment, interest deductions on the mortgage will be subject to the limitations contained in the statute. Investment interest that is disallowed may be carried forward to succeeding taxable years as interest paid or accrued in that year.[69]

[3] Mortgagee's Expenses

The mortgagee might incur expenses in connection with the mortgaged property in order to preserve the value of his security interest. These expenses might include repairs, insurance and unpaid tax assessments on the property, or loan payments on senior mortgages. Such payments are treated as additional loans to the mortgagor and, therefore, are not deductible by the mortgagee.[70] Instead, the payments increase the mortgagee's basis in his debt and will, in turn, increase any bad-debt deduction if the mortgage debt later becomes partially or entirely worthless.[71]

If the mortgagee acquires the property through foreclosure, payments made after the foreclosure increase the mortgagee's basis in the property acquired if the payments accrued prior to the foreclosure.[72]

---

[65] I.R.C. § 163(d)(3)(B).

[66] I.R.C. § 163(d)(3)(C). The expenses must be deductible under I.R.C. §§ 162 (business expenses), 164(a)(1) or 164(a)(2) (taxes), 166 (bad-debt deduction), 167 (depreciation), 171 (bond premium), 212 (expenses of producing income), 611 (depletion).

[67] I.R.C. §§ 163(d)(4)(A)(i), 163(d)(4)(A)(ii).

[68] I.R.C. § 163(d)(6)(B).

[69] I.R.C. § 163(d)(2).

[70] Estate of Lucy S. Schieffelin, 94 B.T.A. 137, 140 (1941), *acq.* 1441-1 C.B. 9.

[71] I.R.C. § 166.

[72] Estate of Lucy S. Schieffelin, 44 B.T.A. 137, 140 (1941), *acq.* 1941-1 C.B. 9; Hadley Falls Trust Co. v. United States, 110 F.2d 887 (1st Cir. 1940); Missouri State Life Ins. Co. v. Comm'r, 78 F.2d 778, 781 (8th Cir. 1934).

determined generally by the agreement of the parties; in the absence of agreement the rules discussed in ¶ 12.02[1] apply.[56]

This rule does not apply to prepayment of interest that relates to a taxable year later than the year of payment; the taxpayer is required to deduct such prepaid interest as it accrues, irrespective of the usual accounting method employed.[57]

The mortgagor will also be entitled to an interest deduction for prepayment penalties, late payment charges, and the like.[58] The payments are viewed simply as additional charges for using borrowed money.[59] The prepayment penalty is deductible even if the loan is repaid to obtain new financing: the mortgagor is not required to treat the penalty as a cost of the new loan and amortize it over the life of that loan.[60] As a corollary of this rule, the penalties are includable as interest in the income of the mortgagee.

[b] Investment Interest Limitations

Interest deductions by a noncorporate mortgagor are subject to a statutory limitation on the amount of "investment interest" that may be deducted.[61] "Investment interest" is defined as interest on indebtedness "incurred or continued to purchase or to carry property held for investment"[62]; it does not include interest on a construction loan for property to be used in a trade or business.[63] Basically, the amount of deductible investment interest is limited to the sum of (1) $10,000 ($5,000 in the case of a married individual filing a separate return), (2) the excess of investment income over investment expenses, and (3) the excess of out-of-pocket business expenses incurred in connection with a net lease (a lease under which the lessee is responsible for almost all of the expenses associated with owning and operating the property) over rental income from such lease.[64] Investment income is comprised of gross income from dividends, interest, rent, royalties, net short-term capital gain attributable to investment sales, and recapture income, but

---

[56] See Huntington-Redondo Co., 36 B.T.A. 116 (1937), *acq.* 1937-2 C.B. 14. See also notes 38-41 *supra* and accompanying text.

[57] I.R.C. § 461(g). See the discussion in the text accompanying note 8 *supra*.

[58] Rev. Rul. 57-198, 1957-1 C.B. 94.

[59] See General Am. Life Ins. Co., 25 T.C. 1265 (1956), *acq.* 1956-2 C.B. 5.

[60] 12701 Shaker Blvd. Co., 36 T.C. 27 (1961), *aff'd* 312 F.2d 749 (6th Cir. 1963).

[61] I.R.C. § 163(d). Also see discussion at ¶ 1.05[2][d].

[62] I.R.C. § 163(d)(3)(D).

[63] I.R.C. § 163(d)(4)(D).

[64] I.R.C. § 163(d)(1).

capital gain.[47] However, when the bond is retired a portion of the "original issue discount" must be included in ordinary income.[48] For this purpose, "original issue discount" means the excess of the redemption price at maturity over the issue price.[49] The noteholder is also generally required to include in gross income as interest each year a ratable portion of original issue discount.[50] To the extent that an amount of the discount is included in income, the noteholder's basis in the note is increased.[51]

[2] Mortgagor's Tax Treatment of Mortgage Payments

[a] Interest vs. Principal

The mortgagor is entitled to a deduction for the interest on the mortgage debt[52] that accrues when the mortgagor has equitable or legal title to the property, whether or not he is personally liable on the debt.[53] If the interest falls due before the mortgagor owns the property, it must be capitalized as a cost of the property when it is paid.[54] If the mortgagee is a cash-basis taxpayer, he deducts the interest in the year it is paid; an accrual-basis taxpayer deducts it in the year it accrues ratably over the loan.[55] The amount of each payment that constitutes interest is

---

[47] I.R.C. § 1232(a).

[48] I.R.C. § 1232(a)(2)(A). This rule applies only to corporate bonds issued after May 27, 1969. The amount includable is calculated by making an allowance for any original issue discount includable in income before retirement. See note 39 *supra* and accompanying text.

[49] I.R.C. § 1232(b).

[50] I.R.C. § 1232(a)(3)(A). The ratable portion is equal to the total original issue discount divided by the number of complete months from the issue date to the maturing date. A subsequent holder of the note is entitled to credit for amounts previously includable and for the excess, if any, of his purchase price over the issue price plus previously includable discount income. I.R.C. § 1232(a)(3)(B).

[51] I.R.C. § 1232(a)(3)(E).

[52] I.R.C. § 163, but see I.R.C. § 189 for special rules governing interest attributable to the construction period of real property. See discussion at ¶1.05[2][d].

[53] New McDermott, Inc., 44 B.T.A. 1035 (1941), *nonacq.* 1954-1 C.B. 8; Reg. § 1.163-1(b). The ownership of legal or equitable title in the property is sufficient to justify the deduction. If a mortgagor transfers property but remains liable on the debt, he can probably deduct any interest payments. See Walther v. Comm'r, 316 F.2d 708 (7th Cir. 1963); contra, J. Simpson Dean, 35 T.C. 1083 (1961).

[54] See Rodney, Inc. v. Comm'r, 145 F.2d 692 (2d Cir. 1944).

[55] I.R.C. § 163(a); see Higginbotham-Bailey-Logan Co., 8 B.T.A. 566 (1927). Cf. James Bros. Coal Co., 41 T.C. 917 (1964).

an agreement, the taxpayer will be confronted with an allocation by the IRS, which if presented to a court would be presumptively correct.[41] The parties would be well advised to make some allocation arrangement to avoid conflict with the IRS.

[b] Mortgages Purchased at Discount

It is not unusual for a mortgage to be purchased or issued at a discount. The consequences to a lender who issues a loan at a discount have already been discussed.[42] But what about an acquired mortgage? How is the gain to be reported? The answer is not simple.

To begin with, the gain on the collection of a note is, in most instances, taxable as ordinary income, not capital gain, because there is no sale or exchange.[43] But if the note is repaid in installments, must the noteholder apportion each payment between discount gain and return of basis in the note? The answer appears to be that if it is likely that the entire loan will be repaid, the noteholder must first subtract the interest portion of the payment and then allocate the payment pro rata between discount gain and return of basis.[44] Thus, for example, where it appears likely that the loan will be repaid because it is secured by property with a value exceeding the amount owing, the noteholder must apportion each loan payment.[45]

> *Example.* Assume X acquires a note, secured by property worth $100, at a discount. The note has a face amount of $100, and X purchases it for $80. The note is to be paid with 5 percent interest on the outstanding balance over a five-year period. If X receives a payment of $15 at the end of the first year, it will be allocated $5 to interest, $8 to return of basis (80/100 × 10) and $2 to discount gain taxable as ordinary income.[46]

A different and complex set of rules applies if the note is a capital asset in the hands of the holder and if it is issued by a corporation. Collection of the corporate note through "retirement" of the security is treated as a sale or exchange under the Code, gain is generally taxed as

---

[41] Weldon D. Smith, 17 T.C. 135, 144 (1951), *rev'd on other grounds* 203 F.2d 310 (2d Cir. 1953), *cert. denied* 346 U.S. 816.

[42] See ¶ 12.01[2][b].

[43] I.R.C. § 1221; see, e.g., Merchant's Nat'l Bank of Mobile, 199 F.2d 657 (5th Cir. 1952); A.B. Culbertson, 14 T.C. 1421 (1950), *acq.* 1950-2 C.B. 1.

[44] See, e.g., Liftin v. Comm'r, 317 F.2d 234 (4th Cir. 1963), *aff'd* 36 T.C. 909, (1961); W.H. Potter, 44 T.C. 159 (1966).

[45] See Edna Morris, 59 T.C. 21 (1972), *acq.* 1973-2 C.B. 3.

[46] This example is based on Shapfa Realty Corp., 8 B.T.A. 283 (1927).

¶ 12.02 TAX CONSEQUENCES DURING THE MORTGAGOR-MORTGAGEE RELATIONSHIP

[1] Mortgagee's Tax Treatment of Mortgage Payments

[a] Distinction Between Interest and Principal

The part of the payments received by the mortgagee that constitutes interest on the loan is ordinary income to the mortgagee.[34] That portion that is a repayment of principal loaned by the mortgagee is a non-taxable return of capital to the mortgagee.[35] Generally, the agreement of the parties governs the allocation between interest and principal as to each payment received,[36] as long as the agreement is contemporaneous with the payment or is made during the same taxable year as the payment.[37] Questions of allocation often arise, however, when the lender receives a lump-sum payment on the loan, and the loan agreement does not specify any allocation.

The general rule for voluntary partial payments of debt with interest outstanding is that the payment is applied first to interest.[38] If a full settlement of the debt is made, however, payments are first deemed made for principal.[39] In the absence of an agreement, the decision might also rest on state law governing the allocation.[40] Also, in the absence of

---

[34] I.R.C. § 61(a)(4).

[35] See Charles M. Howell, 21 B.T.A. 757, 781 (1930), *acq.* X-1 C.B. 30. This is not true if the debt was purchased at a discount (see the discussion in the text at notes 47-51 *infra*), or if the mortgagee has written off part of the debt as worthless. To the extent the "worthless debt" is recovered, it will be included in income except to the extent that the bad-debt deduction provided the lender with no tax benefit. See I.R.C. § 111.

[36] See, e.g., Robert H. Gries, 9 T.C.M. 419; (1950),Huntington Redondo Co., 36 B.T.A. 116 (1937), *acq.* 1937-2 C.B. 14; Rev. Rul. 63-57, 1963-1 C.B. 103. A court might infer an agreement, e.g., from records of the parties. Cf. George S. Groves, 38 B.T.A. 727, 737 (1938) (court found no such agreement).

[37] See Huntington Redondo Co., 36 B.T.A. 116 (1937), *acq.* 1937-2 C.B. 114; cf. Central Cuba Sugar Co., 198 F.2d 214, 217 (2d Cir. 1952), *cert. denied* 344 U.S. 874 (holding agreement in later year not binding).

[38] See Estate of Paul M. Bower, 2 T.C. 1, 5 (1943), *acq.* 1943 C.B. 3; Theodore R. Plunkett, 41 B.T.A. 700, 709 (1940), *acq.* 1940-1 C.B. 3, *aff'd on other grounds* 118 F.2d 644 (1st Cir. 1941). Rev. Rul. 70-647, 1970-2 C.B. 38.

[39] See William Justin Petit, 8 T.C. 228, 236 (1947); cf. Manufacturer's Life Ins. Co., 43 B.T.A. 867 (1941), *acq.* 1941-1 C.B. 47; and Manhattan Mut. Life Ins. Co., 37 B.T.A. 1041 (1938) (mortgagee recognizes interest income on voluntary conveyance only to the extent value of transferred property exceeds debt principal owing); George R. Newhouse, 59 T.C. 783 (1973) (in case of insolvent mortgagor foreclosure payments deemed applied to *principal* first).

[40] See Estate of Buckley, 37 T.C. 664 (1962) (court looked to New York law and applied payment to interest first).

from mortgage refinancing in excess of current indebtedness once construction has been completed and/or the real estate has appreciated in value. The net refinancing proceeds may be distributed tax-free since the placement of a mortgage even in excess of the tax basis of the property merely represents a borrowing of money and does not itself constitute a taxable event.[30] However, if a corporation owns the property, such distribution is taxable to shareholders as a dividend to the extent of the corporation's earnings and profits.[31]

Example. X acquires property worth $100,000 by paying $50,000 in cash and assuming a $50,000 mortgage on the property. During the next ten years, X takes depreciation deductions in the amount of $25,000 and pays off $40,000 of the loan. In the fifth year the property is worth $150,000. He obtains a loan of $100,000 secured by the property. X will realize no gain and his basis in the property is $75,000.

Original basis	
($50,000 payment + $50,000 loan)	$100,000
Less: depreciation	25,000
Basis at time of loan	$ 75,000
Amount of loan proceeds	100,000
Economic gain not realized for tax purposes	$ 25,000

Suppose that the owner obtains a release of personal liability for the debt at some time after he mortgages the property. Will that release cause the owner to realize income? Despite the usual rule that cancellation of such debt constitutes taxable exchange,[32] it has been held that the mere release of *personal* liability will not cause the property owner to realize gain.[33]

---

[30] E.g., Woodsam Associates, 198 F.2d 357 (2d Cir. 1952).

[31] I.R.C. §§ 301, 316. Even if at the time of distribution the corporation has no earnings and profits, but a mortgage loan exceeds in amount the adjusted basis of the secured property, such excess will itself be treated temporarily as earnings and profits and constitute a taxble dividend if the loan is insured or guaranteed by FHA or other U.S. agencies. See I.R.C. § 312(i). To make matters worse, the corporation may be treated as collapsible. See *Raymond Burge,* 28 T.C. 46 (1957), *aff'd* 253 F.2d 765 (4th Cir. 1958); Rev. Rul. 57-357, 1957-2 C.B. 9.

[32] See the discussion in ¶ 12.03[2].

[33] See Woodsam Associates, 198 F.2d 357 (2d Cir. 1952).

example, the Tax Court reaffirmed the *Crane* rule in both *Manual Mayerson*[26] and *David F. Bolger*,[27] where the respective taxpayers had a nominal and zero cash investment in the properties besides being exculpated from personal liability on their mortgages. This was based on the assumption that a capital investment equal to the mortgages would eventually occur. The Service later acquiesced in the *Mayerson* decision because the property had been acquired at its fair market in an arm's-length transaction, but warned that it would not recognize transactions designed to artificially inflate the depreciation deduction.[28]

However, in *Franklin Estate v. Comm'r*,[29] the Ninth Circuit disallowed depreciation and interest deductions to a nonrecourse purchaser of some motel property leased back to the seller, notwithstanding a $75,000 payment by the purchaser. This was decided because the unpaid balance of the purchase price (and purchase-money indebtedness) exceeded the fair market value of the property during the ten-year preballoon payment period. Unlike *Mayerson* and *Bolger*, the taxpayer had failed to prove that the $1,244,000 purchase price had *any* relationship to the actual value of the property that would yield an equity in the property the purchaser could not prudently abandon. Consequently, this failure to show a net investment or equity in the property prompted the court to treat the transaction as merely a ten-year option to purchase the property, rather than as a genuine purchase funded by real indebtedness.

Therefore, the careful use of nonrecourse financing under the *Crane* doctrine still appears to be a valuable tax planning tool, but beware that even without further legislative restrictions on the doctrine, the Service will undoubtedly continue its attempt in the courts to curtail the benefits wrought by *Crane*.

[4] Mortgaging Out

Another tax-shelter device available to individuals and partners is the so-called mortgaging out, or windfall financing device, which results

---

[26] 47 T.C. 340 (1966), *acq.* 1969-1 C.B. 21. Cf. Franklin Estate v. Comm'r, *aff'g* 64 T.C. 752 (1975), 544 F.2d 1045 (9th Cir. 1976).

[27] 59 T.C. 760 (1973).

[28] Rev. Rul. 69-77, 1969-1 C.B. 59.

[29] 64 T.C. 752 (1975), 544 F.2d 1045 (9th Cir. 1976). The *Crane* doctrine has also been attacked in those cases where the indebtedness is unrealistic because of its contingent nature. See Columbus & Greenville R.R., 42 T.C. 834, 848 (1964), *aff'd* 358 F.2d 924 (5th Cir. 1966), *cert. denied* 385 U.S. 827; Albany Car Wheel Co., 40 T.C. 831 (1963), *aff'd per curiam* 333 F.2d 153 (2d Cir. 1964); Leonard Marcus, 30 T.C.M. 1263 (1971); Marvin M. May, 31 T.C.M. 279 (1972).

mortgage. For example, where real estate having a value of $100,000 is acquired by a taxpayer who pays $20,000 and assumes an $80,000 mortgage for which he is personally liable, or by a taxpayer who pays $20,000 but only takes subject to the mortgage so that he is not personally liable, the tax basis for the purchaser in both instances is $100,000 for purposes of computing depreciation and gain or loss on the sale or exchange of the realty. The assumption underlying the doctrine is that the taxpayer will later have to invest an additional amount equal to the indebtedness in order to retain the property, and hence, at the start he is given credit in his basis for such assumed later investment. This approach also permits depreciation at a rate consistent with the market value of the property when acquired and affords competitive equality with other taxpayers owning unencumbered property. Otherwise, in our example, the taxpayer would be allowed a depreciation deduction in year one based on his equity in the property of about $20,000, rather than based on its $100,000 intrinsic value. Moreover, he would be entitled to more depreciation toward the end as the debt is paid, even though the value of the property is declining. Finally, equating personal liability with no personal liability under the *Crane* doctrine seems responsive to the reality that personal liability is somewhat meaningless because of corporate ownership, use of straw men, and the fact that according to one study dealing with foreclosure, only 7 percent of the dollar amount of deficiency judgments is ever realized.[23]

As a corollary to the rule that basis includes mortgage indebtedness, payments of principal to the lender do not increase the mortgagor's basis in the property,[24] and the mortgage indebtedness in basis must be balanced by a similar inclusion of the indebtedness in amount realized[25] upon a sale or other disposition of the property.

For a discussion of the impact of the *Crane* doctrine on tax sheltering of the real estate investor's income, see ¶ 1.05[2]. Also, see ¶ 1.05[4][b] for a discussion of how the *Crane* doctrine relates to the basis problem caused by recourse financing in limited partnerships.

[b] Effects in Nonrecourse Financing

Notwithstanding unsuccessful attacks by the Commissioner on applying the *Crane* doctrine to the use of nonrecourse financing, recent case law suggests that the doctrine has its obvious threshold limits. For

---

[23] Prather, "A Realistic Approach to Foreclosure," 14 Bus. Law. 132 (1958).

[24] E.g., Blackstone Theatre Co., 12 T.C. 801 (1949), *acq.* 1949-2 C.B. 1.

[25] I.R.C. § 1001(b); see Parker v. Delaney, 186 F.2d 455 (1st Cir. 1950).

[b] Fees, Points, and Discount to the Mortgagee

Fees paid to the mortgagee for the performance of services in connection with issuing the loan are includable in gross income.[16] The same is true for points and discount income arising from the transaction.[17] The manner in which the income is reported depends upon the mortgagee's accounting method. If points are paid from sources other than the loan itself, a cash-basis taxpayer includes the amounts in income when received, and an accrual-basis taxpayer includes them when received or when the right to the payments becomes fixed, whichever is earlier.[18]

When the points are held back from the amount disbursed to the borrower, i.e., the loan is discounted, the result depends upon whether the points constitute interest or charges for services. If for services, a cash-basis lender includes the amounts in income when they are paid or when the loan is disposed of, and an accrual-basis taxpayer includes the amounts in income in the year the loan is made.[19]

If the points are interest, a cash-basis taxpayer includes the points in income as the note is paid, and an accrual-basis taxpayer includes the amounts in income ratably over the life of the loan as each note becomes due, or as actually received, if earlier.[20]

[3] The *Crane* Doctrine

[a] Determination of Cost Tax Basis

The so-called *Crane* doctrine, first enunciated in *Crane v. Comm'r*,[21] provides that when property is acquired for cash and a mortgage, the cost tax basis[22] of the property includes the mortgage indebtedness, whether or not the purchaser is personally liable under the

---

[16] I.R.C. § 61(a). Cf. Metropolitan Mortgage Fund, 62 T.C. 110 (1975) (charges are includable in income in the year during which the loan was extended).

[17] See Rev. Rul. 70-540, 1970-2 C.B. 101; Rev. Rul. 74-607, 1974-2 C.B. 149.

[18] Rev. Rul. 70-540, 1970-2 C.B. 101.

[19] Rev. Rul. 70-540, 1970-2 C.B. 101; Metropolitan Mortgage Fund, 62 T.C. 110 (1975).

[20] Rev. Rul. 70-540, 1970-2 C.B. 101. Cf. Rev. Rul. 72-100, 1972-2 C.B. 38. When a construction lender receives these payments from the permanent financing, the cash-basis lender includes them in income at that time, and the accrual-basis taxpayer reports the income ratably over the life of the loan. See Rev. Rul. 72-100, 1972-2 C.B. 38; Rev. Rul. 74-607, 1974-2 C.B. 149.

[21] 331 U.S. 1 (1947).

[22] I.R.C. §§ 1001, 1011, 1012.

deducted currently.[9] Thus, for example, if a taxpayer prepays the first five years of interest, he may deduct the amount paid ratably over the five-year term, whatever his accounting method. This was the rule for accrual-basis taxpayers before the Tax Reform Act of 1976, and it continues to apply.

It is also possible that the bank will simply withhold part of the loan as an advance payment of interest. This difference between the face amount of the loan and the amount received is known as "discount." An example of a loan discount is a loan with a face amount of $100,000 whose borrower is entitled to receive only $95,000; the discount is $5,000. The discount is treated as an interest charge for the entire loan period and is not deductible at the time the loan is obtained.[10] Instead, an accrual-basis taxpayer must amortize the loan discount on a straight-line basis over the life of the loan.[11] A cash-basis taxpayer may deduct the discount only when the principal payments are made on the loan,[12] and for this purpose must allocate a pro rata portion of the deduction (with respect to the discount) to the period in which an installment payment of loan is made.[13]

[2] The Cost of Lending

[a] Fees and Payments by the Mortgagee

The mortgagee, like the mortgagor, often incurs expenses in connection with the mortgage loan. If the mortgagee is in the business of making loans, most general expenses of the business are deductible under I.R.C. § 162. However, certain specific fees paid by the mortgagee, such as brokers' fees and finders' fees paid to a third party as compensation for introducing the borrower to the lender, must be capitalized and amortized by the mortgagee over the life of the loan.[14] If the lender does not hold the mortgage to produce income or is not in the business of lending or dealing in real estate and/or mortgages, the specific costs which must be capitalized cannot be deducted.[15]

---

[9] See I.R.C. § 461(g)(2).

[10] See, e.g., James Bros. Coal Co., 41 T.C. 917, 921-922 (1964) (accrual-basis taxpayer); Alan A. Rubnitz, 67 T.C. 621 (1977) (cash-basis taxpayer); Donald L. Wilkerson, 70 T.C. 240 (1978) (cash-basis taxpayer).

[11] See James Bros. Coal Co., 41 T.C. 917 (1964); Rev. Rul. 74-395, 1974-2 C.B. 45; Higginbotham-Bailey-Logan Co., 8 B.T.A. 566, 577 (1927). Cf. Rev. Rul. 72-100, 1972-2 C.B. 122.

[12] See, e.g., Donald L. Wilkerson, 70 T.C. 240 (1978); Parks v. United States, 434 F. Supp. 206 (N.D. Tex. 1977).

[13] John R. Hopkins, 15 T.C. 160 (1950).

[14] See Rev. Rul. 57-400, 1957-2 C.B. 520.

[15] I.R.C. § 263.

Another type of fee commonly paid by a borrower is a commitment fee. The fee compensates the prospective lender for agreeing to keep funds available for a set period of time for a loan to be made during that period. As a general rule, a commitment fee is treated as an ordinary and necessary business expense, deductible if incurred in carrying on a trade or business or for the production of income.[4]

[b] Points and Discount

A mortgagor will often pay to the lender "points," that is, percentage points of the loan. The points may be a charge for the use or forbearance of money, i.e., interest,[5] or they may be in part or entirely a charge for services rendered by the mortgagee.[6] If points are charged for services, the points are part of the cost of the loan and are subject to the same rules as other capital costs incurred to obtain a loan. To determine what portion of the points is for services, a court will examine the facts surrounding the payment, including the value of any services, comparable charges by other banks, the relationship of the stated interest to the state of the money market, etc.[7]

Points that constitute interest, on the other hand, are subject to specific statutory rules. Under I.R.C. § 461(g), the taxpayer on a cash basis must amortize all prepayments of interest over the period to which the interest relates,[8] except that points paid on a home mortgage can be

---

[4] See Rev. Rul. 56-136, 1956-1 C.B. 92. Cf. Rev. Rul. 74-395, 1974-2 C.B. 4546 (holding FNMA commitment fee to be *prepaid interest* and not a deductible business expense when the fee was held to be for the use of money in connection with an existing loan). See discussion of commitment fees at ¶ 3.06.

[5] See Rev. Rul. 69-188, 1969-1 C.B. 54; L-R Heat Treatment Co., 28 T.C. 894, 896-897 (1957); Alan A. Rubnitz, 67 T.C. 621 (1977).

[6] See Rev. Rul. 69-188, 1969-1 C.B. 54 requiring taxpayer to establish that points were not for services.

[7] See Donald L. Wilkerson, 70 T.C. 240 (1978) (FHA point finance fee held part interest and part services).

[8] Prior to the Tax Reform Act of 1976 (1976 TRA), there was a great deal of controversy concerning the deductibility of prepaid interest by cash-basis taxpayers. The IRS successfully contended that the rule normally applicable to accrual-basis taxpayers must apply, i.e., deduction of the payment over the period to which the interest related. However, the Service did permit prepayment by cash-basis taxpayers for not more than twelve months beyond the close of the current year, if the prepayment did not result in a material distortion of income. See Rev. Rul. 68-643, 1968-2 C.B. 76; Andrew A. Sandor, 62 T.C. 469 (1974) *aff'd* 536 F.2d 874 (9th Cir. 1974); S. Rex Lewis, 65 T.C. 625, 629-630 (1975) 1976 TRA added Section 461(g), which ended the controversy. The usual rule for cash-basis taxpayers is that interest is deductible when "paid." I.R.C. § 163. See the discussion of interest at ¶¶ 12.02[1][a], [2][a].

¶ 12.01[1][a]   REAL ESTATE FINANCING   12-2

        [b] Consequences to Mortgagee 12-28
        [c] Planning the Voluntary Conveyance 12-29
    [4] Foreclosure Sales 12-30
        [a] Consequences to Mortgagor 12-30
        [b] Consequences to Mortgagee 12-33
            [i] Foreclosure Sale to Third Party 12-33
            [ii] Foreclosure Sale to Mortgagee 12-36
    [5] Mortgagee's Disposition of Property Acquired
        From Mortgagor 12-45
    [6] Loss of a Second Mortgage 12-46

¶ 12.04   Disposition of Mortgaged Property...................... 12-47
    [1] Sales and Taxable Exchanges 12-47
    [2] Transfers to Other Entities 12-48
    [3] Gifts, Abandonment 12-49

¶ 12.01 TAX CONSEQUENCES OF A MORTGAGE ON REAL PROPERTY

[1] The Cost of Obtaining a Mortgage Loan

[a] Fees

In a typical mortgage loan transaction, the mortgagor will incur various expenses in connection with obtaining the loan. These include, for example, attorneys' fees, appraisal fees, financing fees charged by the lender for services in connection with the loan, recording fees, title and survey fees, and brokers' commissions. These fees are treated as capital expenditures that are not deductible by the mortgagor when paid or incurred. If the costs are incurred in the carrying on of a trade or business or for the production of income, they may be amortized on a straight-line basis by the mortgagor over the life of the loan to which they relate.[1] The same rule applies for the costs of renewing or extending an existing loan: they must be amortized over the life of the new loan.[2] If the property is disposed of or the loan prepaid, the owner is entitled to a deduction for the entire amount of unamortized deductions, even if the loan is prepaid solely to obtain a new loan from the same lender.[3]

---

[1] See, e.g., Anover Realty Corp., 33 T.C. 671 (1960); Julia Stow Lovejoy, 18 B.T.A. 1179 (1930). Cf. Lyndell E. Lay, 69 T.C. 421 (1977); I.R.C. §§ 162, 212.

[2] See Julia Stow Lovejoy, 18 B.T.A. 1179 (1930).

[3] See S & L Bldg. Corp., 19 B.T.A. 788 (1930), *acq.* X-1 C.B. 60 (1931); 12701 Shaker Blvd. Co., 36 T.C. 255 (1961) (loan prepaid with loan from different mortgagee); Metropolitan Properties Corp., 24 B.T.A. 220 (1931), *acq.* X-1 C.B. 5 (1932); Buddy Schoellkopf Prods., Inc., 65 T.C. 640 (1975) (new loan with same lender).

Chapter 12

TAX ASPECTS OF MORTGAGE FINANCING

		Page
¶ 12.01	Tax Consequences of a Mortgage on Real Property	12- 2
	[1] The Cost of Obtaining a Mortgage Loan	12- 2
	[a] Fees	12- 2
	[b] Points and Discount	12- 3
	[2] The Cost of Lending	12- 4
	[a] Fees and Payments by the Mortgagee	12- 4
	[b] Fees, Points, and Discount to the Mortgagee	12- 5
	[3] The Crane Doctrine	12- 5
	[a] Determination of Cost Tax Basis	12- 5
	[b] Effects in Nonrecourse Financing	12- 6
	[4] Mortgaging Out	12- 7
¶ 12.02	Tax Consequences During the Mortgagor-Mortgagee Relationship	12- 9
	[1] Mortgagee's Tax Treatment of Mortgage Payments	12- 9
	[a] Distinction Between Interest and Principal	12- 9
	[b] Mortgages Purchased at Discount	12-10
	[2] Mortgagor's Tax Treatment of Mortgage Payments	12-11
	[a] Interest vs. Principal	12-11
	[b] Investment Interest Limitations	12-12
	[3] Mortgagee's Expenses	12-13
	[4] Assignment of Rents to Mortgagee	12-14
¶ 12.03	Tax Consequences of Mortgagor's Default	12-15
	[1] Overview	12-15
	[2] Compromise of Mortgage Indebtedness	12-15
	[a] Consequences to Mortgagor	12-15
	[i] Debt Cancellation, Settlement at Discount	12-15
	[ii] Restructuring of the Debt	12-18
	[b] Consequences to Mortgagee	12-18
	[i] Timing of the Deduction	12-19
	[ii] Deduction Equals Mortgagee's Basis in the Debt	12-19
	[iii] Nature of the Loss: Business vs. Nonbusiness Debt	12-21
	[c] Tax Planning	12-24
	[3] Voluntary Conveyance to Mortgagee, Deed in Lieu of Foreclosure, Abandonment	12-24
	[a] Consequences to Mortgagor	12-24

this will not occur in the immediate future. First, most economists predict that the 1980s will see a continued period of inflation. Second, certain life insurance companies have set up separate equity departments with substantial capital to invest. Third, these insurance companies have spent millions of dollars on computer processing data banks that can gather information on sales, values, and rents nationwide. Additionally, several of these companies, in anticipation of decreased loan involvement, are terminating their mortgage loan correspondent relationships with mortgage bankers. These life insurance companies are also purchasing vacant land in large metropolitan areas as long-term investments, which they will develop on their own or joint venture with a developer. Moreover, the prevailing reluctance of lenders to fund equity capital before completion of the development has also been overcome by several life insurance companies with an agreement to seed at inception the joint venture with equity capital.

In conclusion, the authors are of the opinion that notwithstanding the problems discussed at ¶ 11.02[3] and summarized at ¶ 11.02[6], joint ventures between developers and institutional investors, both foreign and domestic, are not only destined to endure, but will become the norm rather than the exception during the 1980s.

right purchase obviates the need to grapple with the complexities and pitfalls inherent in any joint venture agreement. The problems and conflicts of dealing with the developer as a partner can be avoided and yet allow the institution to maintain a passive position by retaining the services of an outside managing agent pursuant to a carefully drafted management contract.

On the other hand, joint venturing is unfavorable to developers who feel that (1) they are essentially selling a participation in a future income stream to the lender at cost and are thereby losing the incremental value in the property upon its completion, and (2) they can receive more cash dollars, in most cases, by completing the project on their own and then selling the project to a syndicate of investors for its completion value. Indeed, the only real advantage for the developer has been its ability to immediately obtain permanent financing, along with equity financing, at favorable rates from the institutional co-venturer. However, during the last business recession, developers discovered that along with equity financing, permanent loan funds were available, but on loan terms that were not very attractive. Moreover, most had to wait for their equity financing until after the improvements were completed.

[7] Renewed Interest in Institutional Joint Ventures

Some new, innovative investing techniques have been introduced. For example, some lenders taking a combined loan and equity position are obtaining the option to convert a part or all of their loan to a full equity share. One obvious problem at the time of making the loan-equity commitment is: What is the debt-equity conversion price ratio? Normally this will be carefully negotiated, but will probably be higher than the present value of the project at inception, but lower than the market rate at the time of the conversion. Another not so obvious problem is whether such an option to convert is unenforceable as a clog on the mortgagor's common law right to an equity of redemption. It is the author's belief that such a conversion right does not fall within the parameters of clogging the equities of redemption in that the mortgagor is not being divested of his estate but is merely satisfying indebtedness via the granting of a joint venture interest. In addition, some lenders are insisting on a conversion option back from equity to debt, either by making the loan themselves or by using another lender.

Faced with the prospect of continued double-digit inflation, some large permanent lenders now appear to be leaning heavily toward positions in equities as opposed to loans. The possibility exists, though, that once the market calms down and increased funds become available for loan commitments, this appetite for equities will disappear just as it has in the past; however, for several reasons, there is a good chance that

partnership, which is the ceiling amount of his tax-loss allowance as a partner.[108] In addition, if the institutional investor should demand a preferred and disproportionate share of net cash flow equal to some percentage of its equity investment, the developer-partner may be charged with a distributive share of taxable income that exceeds its share of cash flow. The reason being that, absent an agreement to the contrary, each partner's share of taxable income is based on its respective interest in the partnership, as determined by all facts and circumstances, including its share of partnership profits and losses and rights to distribution of capital upon liquidation, as well as its right to cash flow. Accordingly, counsel for the developer should insist upon an allocation of taxable income in the partnership-joint venture agreement that is consonant with each co-venturer's rights to the net cash flow of the partnership.[109]

[6] Summary of Problems Inherent in Joint Venturing

Lenders and developers have been sitting on opposite sides of the fence for so long that any joint effort between them is bound to encounter difficulties. Specifically, the co-venturing developer, especially if he has been a partner in partnerships with private and non-institutional investors, will want to take the position that "whatever is good for the goose should be good for the gander." By contrast, the institutional co-venturer will approach the transaction with a firm belief in the "golden rule"—"he who has the gold rules." No matter how sophisticated the institutional investor, it will view the transaction from the perspective of a secured creditor and will frequently employ the business judgments and guidelines it has developed over the years for itself as a lender. For example, most institutional investors still refuse to enter into a joint venture and disburse their share of equity funds prior to the completion of construction. The institutional investor does not want to expose itself to the open-end liability and risks arising during the construction period, and feels that it must insulate its public image from any adverse publicity that might arise from an adverse environmental impact statement or some breach of a federal, state, or municipal law or regulation.

In addition, institutional investors seeking equity positions have been discovering that direct purchases of existing projects can be easier and more advantageous than the joint venture arrangement. An out-

---

[108] See I.R.C. §§ 704(d), 752(a) and discussion at ¶¶ 1.05[4][b], 12.01[3].
[109] See I.R.C. § 704(b)(1) and discussion at ¶ 1.05[3][b].

[e] Dissolution

Subject to the UPA and ULPA provisions governing dissolution and termination of partnerships,[105] the institutional investor will require that if the developer should die, the estate of the decedent will remain liable for capital contributions, but will receive its share of profits as a passive investor without the right to share in the control of joint venture business. In addition, the institution will have the option to purchase the decedent's interest at some prearranged formula price based on the then-appraised value of the real estate and other assets owned by the partnership venture. Similarly, if the developer should become bankrupt, the agreement will customarily deactivate the interest of the developer to avoid control by the bankruptcy trustee and will allow the institution to buy out the developer's interest.[106] Where the developer was managing the property and subsequently had filed for a Chapter 11 or 12 reorganization, it is doubtful that the foregoing provision would be recognized by a bankruptcy court; in such reorganizations the insolvent debtor normally retains control over his property and assets.

[f] Tax Considerations

The following tax considerations are of importance to the participant in a joint venture: (1) insuring taxation of the joint venture as a partnership rather than a corporation, (2) taxation of a service partner who receives a disproportionate share of capital or profits, (3) tax consequences of selling a partnership interest, (4) effect of debt on the basis held by a partner in his partnership interest, and (5) special allocations of depreciation and other deductions for tax purposes.[107] A specific tax concern of the developer-co-venturer is that in the event the institutional co-venturer supplies a significant portion of the investment funds, such investment, if possible, should be structured as a loan to the joint venture-partnership and not as a capital contribution. In this way, the developer can obtain the benefit of an increase in its tax basis in the

---

[105] Under U.P.A. § 31, dissolution is caused by the death or bankruptcy of any partner or by the express will of any partner in contravention of the partnership agreement. In the case of a limited partnership, the death of a limited partner will not dissolve the partnership, but the retirement, death, or insanity of a general partner does, unless the partnership is continued by the remaining general partners under a right to do so in the certificate or with the consent of all the partners. U.L.P.A. §§ 20, 21.

[106] See Sections 7.01, 7.02 of Form 1.4 in Appendix B.

[107] See discussion at ¶¶ 1.05[3][b], 1.05[4][a], 1.05[4][b]. For a general tax discussion of partnerships geared to a limited partnership, see author's comments in Form 1.1, a sample limited partnership agreement, in Appendix B.

are to its co-venturer, so that in the event the venture fails it will not be precluded from exercising its rights as mortgagee as defined in the mortgage instrument.

[d] Buy-Sell Agreement and Transfer of Venture Interest

Many agreements provide that in the event of an irreconcilable dispute among the co-venturers, either may purchase the capital and profit share of the other. Generally, one co-venturer stipulates a price and the other party has the option of either buying or selling at a pro rated percentage of the stipulated price.[101] Some even provide for a mutual buy-sell privilege if for some other reason the parties wish to terminate the venture, but in most cases, the agreement stipulates how frequently the privilege can be exercised by the parties.[102] While such privilege is mutual by its terms, it can, in effect, be one-sided in favor of the institutional lender since few developers would have the same ready access to buy-out funds.[101a] Under such provision, the developer should be given a substantial period of time within which to raise the necessary capital. Frequently, the success of a venture organized as a general partnership depends on how well the co-venturers interrelate in exercising their management and control responsibilities. In some cases, the institutional investor has, in effect, bargained for the personal and often unique management skill of the developer; in fact, if it were not for the developer's participation, the institution might well have decided to invest elsewhere. Accordingly, most joint venture agreements provide that if either party receives an offer to purchase its interest from a third party, the offeree must give its co-venturer a right of first refusal at the same price and on the same terms.[103] In addition, subject to the foregoing exception, the typical agreement also provides that a co-venturer may neither sell, assign, nor pledge its interest, except to an affiliated entity.[104] However, frequently, the developer wants to be able to make a profit on the transfer of its interest to a third party. If this be the case, the parties, by way of compromise, might permit the developer to transfer some portion of its interest after a stipulated period of time. Another compromise would be to permit the developer to pledge or assign its distributive share of cash flow, but not its share of partnership assets.

---

[101] See Section 4.03 of Form 11.4 in Appendix B.

[101a] One author has suggested the possibility that this buy-out may be overreaching by the lender, tempting a court to circumvent or void such a provision. See Kane, "The Mortgagee's Option to Purchase Mortgaged Property," in *Financing Real Estate During the Inflationary 80s,* at 123-139 (1981).

[102] See Section 6.04 of Form 11.4 in Appendix B.

[103] See Section 6.03 of Form 11.4 in Appendix B.

[104] See Sections 6.01, 6.02 of Form 11.4 in Appendix B.

majority consent (where there are two or more co-venturers) with respect to such matters as selling or mortgaging joint venture assets, making substantial capital improvements, borrowing funds, settling insurance or condemnation claims, or taking any legal action on behalf of the venture except to collect rentals and other accounts payable to the venture.[94]

Finally, if the institutional investor is a REIT, any substantial delegation of control to the developer or other nontrustee manager may raise questions about whether the "centralization of management" test has been violated[95] and whether the rental income from the property being managed meets the "passive income requirement" of I.R.C. § 856(d)(1).[96]

[c] **Default Remedies**

In the event any of the co-venturers fails to make its capital contributions, pay its share of joint venture expenses, or comply with any other obligation required of it under the joint venture agreement, the nondefaulting party could bring an action directly against the defaulting party for damages, or, where appropriate, for specific performance or restitution.[97] Also, if some duty to the partnership venture has been breached, the nondefaulting party can bring an action for accounting even prior to dissolution, if such relief is just and reasonable.[98]

Under most joint venture agreements, if the default consists of a failure to make a required capital contribution or other payment of money, the nondefaulting venturer can make the payment on behalf of the defaulting party and thereby purchase a portion of the latter's interest equal to whatever percentage the unpaid payment represents in relationship to the total net value of the venture.[99] Alternatively, the nondefaulting venturer would have the right to purchase the entire interest of the defaulting party for a price equal to the net balance of the latter's capital account.[100]

Finally, if the institutional co-venturer is supplying the permanent loan financing, it should carefully define and limit in the joint venture agreement and mortgage documents what its fiduciary responsibilities

---

[94] See Section 4.02 of Form 11.4 in Appendix B.
[95] I.R.C. § 856(a)(1); Reg. §§ 1.856-1(b)(1), 1.856-1(d)(1), 301.7701-2(c); Rev. Rul. 72-254, 1972-1 C.B. 207.
[96] See Rev. Rul. 75-52, 1975-1 C.B. 198.
[97] See Crane & Bromberg, note 59 *supra*, at § 69.
[98] *Id.* § 70; U.P.A. § 22(d).
[99] See Section 8.02(3) of Form 11.4 in Appendix B.
[100] See Section 8.02(4) of Form 11.4 in Appendix B.

entity is a general partnership, the institutional investor will want to exercise some measure of control over the affairs of the venture both during construction and afterward, when the project is being leased and managed by the developer or some outside managing agent. Even if the institutional investor does not make any capital contribution until the construction is completed, it will nevertheless in most cases require at least some measure of control over such matters as approval of the plans and specifications and inspection of construction.[91]

Inasmuch as the typical institutional investor (despite the recent spate of foreclosures) lacks both the experience and personnel to manage the daily operation of the property, it will delegate this function to the developer or some third-party agent. However, it will usually reserve the right to dismiss such party as manager and perhaps furnish the developer with a choice from among three or four potential substitutes selected by the institution. Some developers have been successful in fettering the institution's right to discharge the manager without just cause and in demanding equal rights with respect to the hiring and firing of any outside manager. The institutional investor will also frequently require a strict accounting of the manager's day-to-day control over receipts and expenditures by means of a quarterly or year-end accounting and audit procedure, not only to safeguard the fiscal integrity of the project, but also to prevent self-dealing by the developer or third-party manager that does not benefit the project.[92] In regard to the latter, the agreement may also provide either that any contract with a related party be approved by all co-venturers or that the contract price for goods and services be reasonable for the area in which the property is situated.[93] Also, where disbursements do not require the signature of the institutional investor's representative, the developer may be prohibited from either spending or withdrawing, as reserves, more joint venture funds than are "reasonably" or "customarily" necessary to meet operating expenses over the next few months or to cover contingencies that are likely to arise in the foreseeable future.

While the institutional investor does not want to impede unduly or to interfere with the manager in his day-to-day operations, the institution must reserve unto itself sufficient control over major management or policy decisions as protection from loss of its capital investment, from adverse publicity, or from being subjected to personal liability if the joint venture is organized as a general, not limited, partnership. Accordingly, the institution will require either unanimous consent or

---

[91] See Section 2.01 of Form 11.4 in Appendix B.
[92] See Sections 3.04, 3.05 of Form 11.4 in Appendix B.
[93] See Section 4.02 of Form 11.4 in Appendix B.

While it is understandable why the institutional investor refuses to assume a "carte blanche" responsibility for the cost overruns of the developer, this limitation is onerous in that it indirectly saddles the developer with the burden of insuring completion of the project as per the original estimated costs, even though cost overruns that are beyond the developer's control may occur.[90]

A compromise solution to this cost-overrun problem would be for the parties to split the expenses caused by the cost overrun, and, if necessary, allow the institutional investor, at its option, to terminate the venture agreement if total cost overruns exceed a stipulated percentage of the original estimate for total cost. Alternatively, the agreement could require the institutional investor to fund its share of the cost overrun up to a stated maximum amount on the condition that it receive, in exchange, a preferred position on the venture's cash flow until it is reimbursed for the extra outlay of funds. An alternative solution would be to reallocate partnership capital from the developer's capital account to that of the institutional investor on the basis of a pre-arranged formula, in the event the latter partner makes additional capital contributions to cover such cost overruns. However, to avoid a total "squeeze out" of the developer, it should be entitled to retain a guaranteed minimum percentage of the partnership's net assets and should be accorded the opportunity to repurchase any partnership interest or capital so reallocated by paying to the institutional investor an amount that would enable the institution to recoup its extra outlay of capital and receive a fair rate of interest to be agreed upon by the parties.

Furthermore, cost overruns may result in deleterious consequences for the developer, even where the institution has agreed to furnish all the equity capital. For example, the institution will probably insist that it recoup all its capital contributions before there is any allocation of cash flow to the developer. Consequently, the developer could wind up with nothing for a number of years after the project becomes income-producing.

[b] Allocation of Control

A harried and perplexed vice-president of an institutional investor once defined a joint venture as an arrangement in which, at its inception, the institutional investor contributes cash and the developer its experience, and, at its conclusion, the developer has the cash and the institutional investor the experience. Accordingly, if the ownership

---

[90] See discussion at ¶ 4.04[5].

will be tailored to the particular joint venture transaction, the developer must bear in mind that the institutional investor will probably approach the transaction from the perspective of a preferred creditor rather than as a co-entrepreneur. For example, in most cases, the institution will not contribute any venture capital until the project is completed, free of liens and in accordance with the plans and specifications, and will reserve the option to terminate the agreement if the project is not completed by some certain date.[89]

[a] Allocation of Capital Contributions

An important threshold consideration for both parties is how much equity capital each will contribute to the venture. In some cases, the developer will contribute its skill and expertise but will make no capital contributions, while in other cases the developer will be required to match the capital contributions of its institutional co-venturer, either in hard cash or at least in "soft" equity. The audited costs upon which the capital contributions of the parties are based should be carefully defined. They are frequently determined by the relative bargaining clout of each party. For example, in Section 3.02 of the sample agreement, Form 11.3, there is no inherent reason why the capital contribution of the institutional investor should not include reimbursement of the developer for its share of the leasing commissions, promotion and advertising expenses, and mortgage brokerage fees other than the fact that the institution has successfully demanded that such items be excluded from the list of audited costs.

Ordinarily, the institution will impose a ceiling limit on its capital contributions, and in many instances, any cost overrun that increases this ceiling must be borne by the developer. To make matters worse for the developer, the agreement may also provide that the developer's funding of such cost overruns will not be deemed additional capital contributions of the venture nor will the developer be entitled to recoupment for such payments from the net cash flow of the venture.

---

[89] One disadvantage of this approach whereby the joint venture does not acquire the property until after construction is completed and the necessary certificate of occupancy issued is that the joint venture partnership may be denied "first user" status and accordingly be deprived of its right to use accelerated depreciation for tax purposes. I.R.C. § 1250. While such fast write-off is not indispensible to a quasi-exempt institution like a life insurance company, such inability to use accelerated depreciation could be extremely detrimental for an individual developer in a high tax bracket. See Section 2.01 of the sample joint venture agreement, Form 11.4, in Appendix B, and discussion at ¶ 11.02[3][a].

estate investment trusts),[84] since its subsidiary could be taxed at the maximum 46 percent corporate rate. While the filing of consolidated returns cannot be employed by insurance companies and REITs to eliminate this tax disadvantage,[85] the problem can be ameliorated to some degree by carefully manipulating the capital structure of the subsidiary. Since interest paid by the subsidiary on its indebtedness to its parent corporation is deductible, the taxable income of the subsidiary can be reduced by increasing its debt-to-equity ratio, provided that the loans from the parent have all the characteristics of genuine indebtedness and the subsidiary is not too undercapitalized.[86]

From a nontax standpoint, several advantages may be obtained for the parent corporation or trust. First, where the subsidiary and not the parent is a co-venturer in a general partnership venture, the assets of the parent are protected against suits brought by co-partners or outside creditors of the partnership, unless the court decides to "pierce the corporate veil" and hold the parent liable for the actions of its subsidiary.[87] Moreover, since the parent and not the subsidiary would make the permanent mortgage loan to the venture, the mortgage would not be subordinated to the claims of other partnership creditors and, in the case of a limited partnership, the parent as a nonpartner could unquestionably take and hold the partnership real estate as mortgage collateral.[88] Still another advantage is that by using an intermediary to engage in the joint venture, the parent can to some degree shield itself from any adverse publicity concerning the venture and can retain at least a modicum of anonymity.

[5] Analysis of Joint Venture Agreement

While the institutional investor's standard form of joint venture agreement will be subject to negotiation and, like any legal document,

---

[84] REITs can avoid payment of any corporate tax on their distributions provided they pay out at least 95 percent of their taxable earnings to their trust beneficiaries. See I.R.C. § 857.

[85] I.R.C. § 1504(b).

[86] E.g., Isidor Dobkin v. Comm'r. 15 T.C. 31, *aff'd* 192 F.2d 392 (2d Cir. 1951); see I.R.C. § 385.

[87] Courts are more likely to find the broader business entity liable when the business affairs of the corporations are intertwined and the separate corporate formalities are not followed: Compare Sisco-Hamilton Co. v. Lennon, 240 F.2d 68 (7th Cir. 1957), with Berkey v. Third Ave. Ry., 244 N.Y. 84, 155 N.E.58 (1926); or, where the subsidiary and parent are operating portions of a single enterprise and the subsidiary is severely undercapitalized. See Erickson v. Minnesota & O. Power Co., 134 Minn. 209, 158 N.W. 979 (1916).

[88] See discussion at ¶ 11.02[3][b].

organized to assume control of the venture as corporate general partner without exposing the assets of the parent company to personal liability, the subsidiary would have to own substantial assets; otherwise, the venture might be treated by the Revenue Service as an "association," taxable as a corporation.[76] Another problem with the limited partnership format is that a literal construction of Section 13 of the Uniform Limited Partnership Act (ULPA) seems to prohibit the institution, as a limited partner, from making a mortgage loan to the venture since, under this section, "no limited partner shall...receive or hold as collateral security any partnership property...." Fortunately, however, the case law[77] and Official Comment of the Commissioners on Uniform State Laws[78] suggest that the limited partner may lend money to the venture partnership as a secured creditor if the partnership is solvent at the time the loan is made.

By contrast, if the joint venture is organized as a general partnership, the institutional investor would be personally liable for the debts of the partnership,[79] but it could, without qualification, hold a mortgage on partnership property (subject, of course, to the prior claim of outside creditors)[80] and could exercise control over the affairs of the venture, while avoiding double taxation and the other tax problems posed by corporate ownership.[81]

[b] Indirect Subsidiary Investment in Joint Ventures

Some institutional investors, including life insurance companies, prefer to participate in joint ventures by using as their intermediary either a single corporate subsidiary for all transactions or separate subsidiaries for each joint venture transaction. From a tax perspective, subsidiary investment is disadvantageous if the institutional investor is quasi-exempt from full corporate taxation (e.g., life insurance companies,[82] mutual savings banks, savings and loan associations,[83] and real

---

[76] Rev. Proc. 72-13, 1972-1 C.B. 735. See discussion at ¶ 1.05[4][a].

[77] E.g., Hughes v. Dash, 309 F.2d 1 (5th Cir. 1962). See discussion in article by Roegge, note 40 *supra*, at 603-607.

[78] U.L.P.A. § 1, Comment Fifth, 6 Uniform Laws Annot. 562 (Master ed. 1960).

[79] U.P.A. § 15.

[80] See note 62 *supra*.

[81] See discussion at ¶ 1.05[3].

[82] I.R.C. §§ 801-820.

[83] Under I.R.C. § 591, savings institutions are allowed a deduction for dividends paid on deposits.

Kessing v. National Mortgage Corp.[71] In that case, the defendant gave the plaintiffs a $250,000 mortgage loan, at the maximum rate of interest, on the condition that it be able to purchase, for $25, a share in the venture, as limited partner, entitling it to receive a 25 percent share in both partnership capital and profits. The court found that, with the extra profit share, the defendant's expected or "hoped for" yield on its loan investment increased to between 16 and 20 percent interest, which rendered the loan transaction usurious.

Fortunately, however, if additional consideration is paid for the loan, the courts in most jurisdictions (including New York)[72] would either spread the consideration over the term of the loan or would regard the income from the additional consideration as the interest to be added to the fixed interest.[73] For example, in a jurisdiction with a maximum interest ceiling of 8 percent, a $100,000 five-year interest-only loan with a 6 percent face rate would not be rendered usurious if the lenders should receive a $10,000 bonus for making the loan in the form of a joint venture interest.

[4] Selecting the Ownership Entity

[a] General vs. Limited Partnership

While corporate ownership poses the advantage of limited liability for the co-venturers as stockholders, the problem of double taxation and other tax considerations make its use as the ownership entity for the joint venture impractical in most cases.[74] Therefore, selecting the ownership vehicle usually narrows to a choice between the general and the limited partnership formats. While this topic is fully covered at ¶ 1.04, the following considerations are especially germane in deciding how to structure the joint venture arrangement.

From the perspective of the institutional investor, the limited partnership is generally not a feasible choice because while the institution, as a limited partner, would not be personally liable for the debts of the partnership venture, it would be precluded from participating with the developer-general partner in the control and management of venture affairs.[75] While a subsidiary of the institutional investor could be

---

[71] 278 N.C. 523, 180 S.E.2d 823 (1971).

[72] E.g., Reisman v. William Hartman & Son, Inc., 51 Misc. 2d 293, 273 N.Y.S.2d 295 (1966).

[73] See Hershman, note 70 *supra*, at 317.

[74] See complete discussion of the advantages and disadvantages of corporate ownership at ¶ 1.05.

[75] U.L.P.A. § 7. For a discussion of what constitutes partaking in control under the U.L.P.A., see discussion at ¶ 1.05[1].

binding, the institutional lender would lose its certitude about obtaining the joint venture interest because there can generally be no specific performance of a partnership (joint venture) agreement even though the subject matter of the partnership agreement involves real property.[67] One possible compromise would be for the mortgage commitment to provide that the loan shall be callable if a joint venture agreement is not consummated within a stated period of time after the long-term mortgage loan is made.[68]

[c] Usury Considerations

A commonly cited advantage in using the joint venture device, as opposed to the contingent-interest kicker,[69] is that the usury laws do not apply to an institutional investor's purchase of a joint venture interest as a concomitant to making a permanent mortgage loan, if the institution pays a fair market value amount for its interest. However, if the joint venture interest is a condition precedent to making the mortgage loan and it is worth more than the institution paid for it, this additional value, when added to the interest payable on the loan, could arguably render the lender's return usurious on the rationale that anything of value obtained by the lender in connection with making the loan, either directly or through a subsidiary, may be considered interest.[70]

Because of the recent vintage of the joint venture device and the frequent use of circumvention devices (such as the exemption for loans made to corporate borrowers) to enable the lender to charge a market rate of interest in excess of the statutory maximum, little case law is squarely on point. Indeed, only one case appears relevant, namely squarely on point. Indeed, only one case appears relevant, namely

---

[67] E.g., Rabinowitz v. Borish, 43 F. Supp. 413 (D.N.J. 1942); Maxa v. Jones, 148 Md. 459, 129 A. 652 (1925).

[68] See Roegge, Note 37 *supra*, at 571.

[69] See discussion at ¶ 5.05[8].

[70] See generally Hershman, "Usury and 'New Look' in Real Estate Financing," 4 Real Prop. Prob. & Tr. J. 315-326 (1969). For example, in Mission Hill Dev. Corp. v. Western Small Business Inv. Co., 260 Cal. App. 2d 923, 67 Cal. Rptr. 505 (1968), defendants gave plaintiffs a $500,000 loan in exchange for two five-year notes at 9½ percent per annum and an option to purchase 62 acres of land owned by plaintiff for one-half its market value. The appellate court affirmed the lower court's finding that the options were "a device to hide an agreement to pay an additional 10 percent interest per year over and above the 9½ percent called for under the terms of the note" by applying a substance-over-form approach to the facts. But see Bokser v. Lewis, 383, Pa. 507, 119 A.2d 67, *cert. denied* 351 U.S. 965 (1956), wherein the Pennsylvania Supreme Court held that an agreement to make a $10,000 one-year loan at the maximum rate of interest and sell to the lender stock at a per-share price equal to $25 less than book value did not taint the loan with usury.

to change them fast enough to effectively negotiate two positions.[61]

Another related concern of the lender is that when it makes the permanent loan, other creditors of the joint venture, upon either a foreclosure or bankruptcy, could argue that the permanent loan was in reality an additional capital contribution to the venture rather than a loan made by a secured creditor, if the loan commitment letter and joint venture agreement are not carefully drafted to indicate otherwise. Moreover, if the co-venturing institution is a general partner, its claims against the partnership are subordinate to those of outside creditors, whether the institution is claiming as a lender[62] or as a partner seeking to recoup its capital contributions.[63] Moreover, under Section 101(2) of the Bankruptcy Reform Act of 1978, the co-venturing lender would be considered an "insider" and, as such, could not participate as a creditor in the approval of any Chapter 11 reorganization plan.[64] Accordingly, a cautious lender will insist that the venture not incur any additional indebtedness, whether secured or unsecured.

However, if the institutional investor refuses to supply the permanent financing in order to avoid these problems, the developer might object on the ground that the prospect of such financing at favorable rates was what induced it to agree to the joint venture arrangement. A possible compromise solution might be for the institutional co-venturer to merely issue a standby loan commitment[65] for little if any front-end fee[66]. This would enable the venture to obtain its construction financing and shop around for better permanent financing elsewhere before asking the institution to supply the long-term mortgage loan.

If, however, the institutional co-venturer does issue its commitment to make the long-term mortgage loan and a construction lender relies upon such commitment in agreeing to furnish the construction financing, a problem may arise if the co-venturer's takeout commitment is conditioned upon a satisfactory joint venture agreement between it and the developer. Most construction lenders will object to any such condition and prefer that the permanent loan commitment omit all reference to the joint venture. However, if the two commitments are not mutually

---

[61] See Hartman, Note 51 *supra*, at 63.

[62] Observe that under Section 40(b) of the UPA the claims of outside creditors are accorded preferential treatment over the claims owning to partners as creditors of the partnership. See also *In re* Rice, 164 F.509 (E.D. Pa. 1908); *In re* Effinger, 184 F. 728 (D. Md. 1911).

[63] E.g., Wallerstein v. Erwin, 112 F. 124 (3d Cir. 1901).

[64] See 11 U.S.C. §§ 101(2), 1126(c).

[65] See ¶ 3.07.

[66] Since the institution itself is one of the venturers, it would, in any event, be paying half of the standby front-end fees.

venture without risk" syndrome. Exasperated developers' attorneys are prone to point out that the joint venture agreement, as prepared by counsel for the lender, is often so replete with proscriptions and restrictions on the conduct of the developer that it reads more like a trust indenture than a true partnership agreement. The probable explanation for this phenomenon is that the institutional investor and its counsel frequently view the transaction from the traditional preferred-security vantage point of a mortgagee. In addition, the institutional investor, especially a life insurance company, is bound to be extremely sensitive about protecting and enhancing its public image. For example, a company like Prudential Life Insurance Co., long identified with "a piece of the rock," might be disinclined to venture and commit itself to a piece of land if environmental problems and adverse publicity could tarnish its image in the minds of surrounding neighbors, who may be customers. Also, lenders have concerned themselves with deciding whether union contractors should be required for the construction of the project, and fears have been raised among lenders that during the construction period some of their construction funds might be used without their knowledge and consent to "influence" building inspectors and other local public officials. In fact, this latter concern explains in part why most institutional lenders refuse as a matter of policy to co-venture with a developer until the improvements have been substantially or fully completed.

From the developer's perspective, the problem of sharing control over policy and management decisions arises once a decision is made to utilize the general partnership format. For example, while most developers take professional pride in their ability to think and make decisions extemporaneously, institutional investors are by their very natures extremely cautious and prefer the time-consuming committee approach to making decisions.

[b] Problems for Institution Acting as Both Co-Venturer and Permanent Lender

Another practical dilemma for the lender desirous of participating in a joint venture has been whether or not to make the permanent loan to the venture. In most cases, the institution or a subsidiary corporation will commit itself simultaneously to both and use the same loan officers and attorneys to negotiate, underwrite, and close both the loan and ownership aspects of the venture. However, what is good for the joint ventures, may not be good for the permanent lender and vice versa, and it is difficult for the same personnel to wear two hats at the same time or

differs from the partnership form in that it has sometimes been said that corporations should not be permitted to be partners at local law, whereas corporations may always enter joint ventures.[57] The rationale for the distinction holds that since a joint venture is limited in time and scope, it entails less delegation of managerial authority and therefore impinges less upon the statutory mandate that a corporation be managed by its board of directors. Finally, one co-venturer can sue the others at law with respect to joint venture transactions,[58] and the venturers can bind one another only with respect to the usual narrow joint venture purpose.[59]

In most other respects, joint ventures are either analogized to or simply treated as partnerships and are accordingly governed by local law rules applicable to partnerships. In addition, the term "joint venture" is included with the ambit of the tax definition of a partnership.[60] However, regardless of whether such pooling of risk capital is treated as a partnership or tenancy in common, in common parlance all such associations between lender and developer are referred to as joint ventures.

[3] Concerns of Co-Venturers

[a] Psychological Barriers

Perhaps the greatest psychological hurdle faced by the parties in dealing with one another is the institutional lender's "wanting to

---

[57] U.P.A. § 6 defines a partnership as "the association of two or more persons to carry on as co-owners a business for profit." While U.P.A. § 2 defines "person" to include corporations and other associations, there is authority that the UPA does not confer a capacity to make a contract of partnership with an individual or person who, by the law governing capacity, is incompetent to make such a contract. 68 *C.J.S.* "Partnership" § 5a. In New York the Attorney General has held that the term "person" in its version of the UPA does not give a corporation the right to enter into a partnership. 1935 N.Y. Op. Att'y Gen. 230. However, such authority is based on Bus. Corp. Law § 2.02(a)(15) (McKinney 1963). In the majority of other states such authority likewise exists. E.g., Memphis Natural Gas Co., v. Pope, 178 Tenn. 580 161 S.W.2d 211, (1941), *aff'd* Memphis Natural Gas Co. v. Beeler, 315 U.S. 649 (1941). See 68 *C.J.S.* "Partnership" § 5.

[58] E.g., Miller v. Walser, 42 Nev. 497, 181 P. 437 (1919); Galloway v. Korzekwa, 346 F. Supp. 1086 (D. Miss. 1972). Ordinarily, partners must sue in equity for an accounting, whereas a joint venturer can sue both at equity and at law for breach of contract. But some courts have held that the co-venturers cannot sue each other at law during the existence of the venture unless no business has been transacted. E.g., Janofsky v. Wernick, 362 F. Supp. 1005 (D.N.Y. 1973).

[59] Crane & Bromberg, *Law of Partnership* § 35 at 194 (1968).

[60] I.R.C. § 7701(a)(2).

destined to endure,[51] and they are being heralded as the wave of the future.

[2] Legal Definition

Ordinarily, the institutional lender and the developer will own and operate the realty by using the general or limited partnership format, and many joint venture agreements will expressly refer to the particular jurisdiction's version of the Uniform Partnership Act (UPA) or Uniform Limited Partnership Act (ULPA) as its interpretational reference point. Indeed, somewhat dated legal authorities view the joint venture as but a form of partnership,[52] namely, one created for a single undertaking or purpose that normally does not require the full attention of the participants and is of short duration. Others opine that a joint venture is a legal entity, separate and distinct from a partnership.[53] Nonetheless, the prevailing view holds that some differences in legal consequences can exist, but for the most part these differences can be explained by the fact that any entity treated by a court as a nonpartnership joint venture would not be subject to the Uniform Partnership Act. For example, the joint venture, like the tenancy in common, does not provide any automatic or simple mechanism for holding title to real property.[54] If title and control are not held by a trustee, nominee, or other agent, then all of the co-owners must authorize and execute any mortgage refinancing, leasing, or conveyance instrument, and complications are apt to ensue upon the death, insolvency, or incompetency of an individual member.[55] In addition, any co-venturer has the right at equity to bring at any time an action for partition and/or demand an accounting, absent an agreement to the contrary.[56] Moreover, the joint venture

---

[51] E.g., Hartman, "Economics Makes Strange Bedfellows: The Institutional Joint Venture," Real Est. Rev. 62-66 (1972).

[52] E.g., Mechem, "The Law of Joint Adventures," 15 Minn. L. Rev. 644, 666 (1931).

[53] E.g., Comment, "Joint Venture or Partnership," 18 Fordham L. Rev. 114 (1949). See generally Note, "A Partnership and A Joint Adventure Distinguished," 33 Harv. L. Rev. 852-854 (1920).

[54] Any nonpartnership joint venture not subject to the UPA cannot take advantage of U.P.A. § 8 (3), which permits the partnership, itself, to hold title to real estate.

[55] 48 *C.J.S.* "Joint Adventures" § 7. The venture might not be "dissolved" on the death or withdrawal of a venturer as would a partnership under U.P.A. § 31.

[56] *Id.* § 12. A partner's right to an accounting is circumscribed to some degree by U.P.A. §§ 21, 22; in addition, U.P.A. § 38(1) gives each partner on dissolution, the right to have any surplus distributed in cash, which obviously precludes partition unless all partners agree to it.

tive type of joint venture called "split financing."[45] For example, an insurance company would purchase real estate from the developer and lease it back (a traditional sale-leaseback). The company would then make a leasehold mortgage to the developer, secured by the developer's leasehold estate, and receive contingent interest on the leasehold loan together with a leasehold or gound rental consisting of both a base fixed rental plus a contingent rent geared to the developer's income from the property.

However, use of the contingent-interest kicker poses serious usury problems,[46] and, while its use has continued, both it and the sale-leaseback merely whetted the lenders' appetites for what they were really seeking as the main course, namely, a "true" equity participation whereby they could participate as full partners in the profits from the property being financed with their loan funds. Indeed, what better marriage could be arranged than one between the developer with experience but without capital and the lender with capital to invest but without experience in constructing and managing income-producing real estate? Doubtless, the typical institutional lender supplying between 75 to 90 percent of the venture capital[47] has felt at one time or another a regret at being limited to a fixed mortgage return, while the leverage-minded developer with as little as a 10 or 15 percent cash investment reaps all of the investment rewards. True, the developer assumes the risk of loss, as well, but after the 1973-1974 real estate crunch involving many nonrecourse loans and bankruptcy decisions against lenders, lenders have become less certain about who it is that really bears the loss when the project goes "bellyup." Consequently, lenders slowly began to acquire true equity interest in office buildings, shopping centers, apartment projects, and other commercial real estate. The pace soon quickened, and by the end of 1978 real estate directly owned by life insurance companies (exclusive of home and branch offices) amounted to $11.8 billion, and the amount of their total real estate holdings more than doubled between 1968 and 1978.[48] However, serious problems have emerged with the joint venture device,[49] some of which cannot be resolved even by means of careful draftsmanship in the joint venture agreement[50]; however most commentators feel that joint ventures are

---

[45] See discussion at ¶ 8.09.
[46] See discussion at ¶ 5.05[8].
[47] See discussion at ¶¶ 2.02[1][d], 2.02[2][d], 2.02[3][d], 2.02[4][c].
[48] American Council of Life Insurance, *1979 Life Insurance Fact Book* 84(1978).
[49] See discussion at ¶ 11.02[3].
[50] See discussion at ¶ 11.02[5].

Life insurance companies are not only the chief source of permanent financing for income-producing real estate.[39] They have also emerged as the largest group of institutional lenders involved in real estate joint ventures since the middle 1960s, when this type of equity participation between lenders and developers first became popular. Traditionally, these conservative companies have rarely ventured beyond their fixed-interest mortgage realm. However, when their regulatory statutes were amended to permit them to invest in income-producing real estate,[40] many life insurance companies for the first time began to engage in sale-leaseback transactions,[41] chiefly as a device to combat inflation. Ordinarily, the leaseback is a net long-term lease that provides for renewals at moderately higher rentals, based on the then-reappraised value of the real estate.[42] Moreover, while the seller-lessee usually reserves the right to repurchase the property at the end of the lease term, the institutional investor, as owner-lessor, will ordinarily be able to take some advantage of the appreciation in land value caused by inflation. If the repurchase-option price is set too low, the transaction might be viewed by the Internal Revenue Service as a disguised loan, in which event the deduction for ground rent would be denied.[43] However, despite these built-in safeguards, the sale-leaseback has generally proven to be a rather limited anti-inflation device for insurance companies and other institutional investors. Consequently, in the early and middle 1960s (especially since the 1966 credit crunch) institutional lenders began resorting to another type of inflation hedge called the contingent-interest "kicker,"[44] whereby lenders demand from their borrowers "additional compensation" (in addition to the regular face amount of interest) equal to some percentage of the amount by which the gross or net income from the property exceeds a specified base rental income amount. Both these techniques were sometimes combined into a primi-

---

[39] See discussion at ¶¶ 2.01[2], 2.02[1][c].

[40] In 1946 the New York Insurance Law was amended by adding Paragraph (h) to Section 81(7). 1946 N.Y. Laws, Ch. 509, § 1 (169th Sess., April 5, 1946). As amended, N.Y. Ins. Law § 81(7)(h) (McKinney Supp. 1979). Almost simultaneously, other states including New Jersey and Massachusetts enacted similar legislation, and today, ownership by life insurance companies of real estate for investment purposes is permitted, in some form or another, in every state. For both an excellent historical discussion of this point and a general discussion of joint ventures, see Roegge, Talbort & Zinman, "Real Estate Equity Investments and the Institutional Lender: Nothing Ventured, Nothing Gained," 39 Fordham L. Rev. 579-648 (1971) (hereinafter cited as Roegge).

[41] See discussion at ¶¶ 2.02[1], 6.04.

[42] See discussion at ¶ 6.04.

[43] See discussion at ¶ 6.04[3][b].

[44] See discussion at ¶ 3.04[3][a].

However, certain legal considerations arise that still may warrant the close attention of lender's counsel. For example, where two separate notes are secured by the same mortgage, the holders of both notes would have to agree to a foreclosure unless the mortgage expressly provides that a default in either note constitutes a default under both.[35] In addition, the noteholders' agreement should address some of the same questions dealt with in the loan participation agreement; when a default should prompt foreclosure and whether any of the noteholders can bypass the foreclosure remedy and bring a separate suit on the note, assuming of course that the maker is personally liable and the property is not located in a "single action" jurisdiction like California.[36] In order to properly bind the successors and assigns of any of the noteholders, both the promissory note and underlying mortgage or deed of trust should incorporate by reference the noteholders' agreement.

¶ 11.02 JOINT VENTURES BETWEEN INSTITUTIONAL LENDERS AND DEVELOPERS

[1] Historical Development as Hedge Against Inflation for Institutional Lenders

As a concomitant to making a permanent mortgage loan, life insurance companies and other institutional lenders will sometimes engage in a "joint venture" with the borrower-developer by purchasing an equity interest in a partnership organized by the developer to own and operate the secured property. In most instances, this shift from a fixed return mortgage loan to a fluctuating equity investment occurs during a period of inflation. Mortgage money is tight, interest rates are high, and the bargaining position of lenders, whose mortgages are being repaid in declining-value dollars, is relatively strong. At such times, these lenders or their subsidiaries will acquire a joint-venture position in the mortgaged income-producing property as a hedge against capital erosion due to inflation. Sometimes the lender will also acquire a joint-venture interest in lieu of a contingent interest "kicker"[37] (so that it will not run afoul of local usury restrictions),[38] or perhaps as an alternative to what would otherwise be a less attractive investment in stocks or bonds when the prices of either or both are falling.

---

[35] Osborne, *Mortgage* § 319 (2d ed. 1970).

[36] See ¶ 3.08[4][g]. See Section 7 of Form 11.2 in Appendix B.

[37] Additional interest geared to the mortgagor's gross or net income from the mortgage property. See discussion at ¶ 3.04[3][a].

[38] See discussion at ¶ 11.02 [3][c].

the certificate maturity dates should correspond to the underlying loan's maturity; otherwise, the lead may be confronted with an obligation to repurchase, which may cause the very problem of overlending that prompted the lead's use of the loan participation device.

Since the participants are not creditors of the borrower and must stand or fall together in the event of a serious default by the borrower, the agreement should spell out with precision the events of default, the parties who may declare them, what termination provisions obtain if the lead decides to abandon the loan or if the major participants want to liquidate their position, and what discretion the lead has as to whether and when to exercise its foreclosure and other remedies as mortgagee.[33] The attorneys for the participants may want the latter decision to be based on majority rule; otherwise, the lead might be tempted, at the expense of the participants' best interests, to "carry" its defaulting borrower-customer for an imprudent period of time. However, based on experience, the authors are of the opinion that in the event of a major default the language in the agreement is frequently of little avail in resolving differences in opinion among the participants on how to proceed, and that in most cases time demands will pressure them towards an agreed-upon course of action. The agreement should deal with what discretion, if any, the lead should have to modify the loan agreement, substitute participants, waive defaults, release or substitute the mortgage collateral, grant extensions, etc. Finally, the participants should reserve the right to approve the form of the note, deed of trust, and all of the collateral loan documents.[34]

[8] Separate Notes Secured by One Mortgage

As noted at ¶¶ 11.01[6][a], 11.01[6][b], and 11.01[6][c], several legal problems may arise when the lead alone holds the note and mortgage and sells beneficial interest in the loan to other lenders. Accordingly, where administratively feasible and when the loan participants can avoid any "doing business" problems in the state where the loan is being made, it would be safer for each lender to receive a separate note, which could then be held and serviced by a representative lender acting for the group pursuant to an agency or noteholders' agreement. Each lender would become a creditor of the borrower, and would not be merely obtaining an equitable interest in the note and mortgage collateral.

---

[33] See Section 5 of Form 11.1 in Appendix B.
[34] See Section 10 of Form 11.1 in Appendix B.

[d] Lead Lender's Compliance With Securities Laws

A serious legal problem for the lead lender results from several recent cases involving loan participations. Federal courts have evinced an increasing willingness to view the loan participation certificate as a "security" within the ambit of the Securities Exchange Act of 1934. Moreover, even if the certificate were exempt from the Act's registration requirements, the lead would have an obligation under the antifraud provisions of the Act (especially Rule 10b-5) to make a full and truthful disclosure of all material facts relevant to the participation, such as the credit standing of the borrower; otherwise, it could become liable for any losses sustained by the participants.[30]

[7] The Loan Participation Agreement

Since the lead is the only publicly secured party, and neither the loan documents nor borrower-lead contract mentions the participants (either as co-lenders or secured parties), the participants should require language in the agreement that the participants will become the owners of undivided fractional interest in all notes and underlying mortgage collateral to be held by the lead (except for its share) in trust for the participants. This should be done in order to more firmly establish a trust relationship among the parties. It should also state that the participants will be treated as beneficiaries (and secured creditors of the lead) by the lead's trustee in bankruptcy. Provision should also be made that the lead, as custodian of all evidence of indebtedness and mortgage collateral, shall take proper care of both, and be exclusively liable to the borrower for any dereliction in its responsibilities as payee and mortgagee. However, most lead lenders will insist that any liability on their part to the participants be confined to losses arising from their gross, but not ordinary, negligence. The agreement should also specify how payments, expenses, and setoffs shall be shared; the usual agreement provides that the lead and the participants will share these items on a pro rata basis.[31] It should also spell out what happens if any of the participants are unable or unwilling to make the agreed-upon advances.[32] As a protective measure, the lead lender should consider reserving its right to reduce or cancel the commitment to the borrower and other participants if advances are not made by any of the important participants. Obviously,

---

[30] See Lehigh Valley Trust Co. v. Central Nat'l Bank, 409 F.2d 989 (5th Cir. 1969); NBI Mort. Inv. Corp. v. Chemical Bank, 75 Civ. Action No. 3411 (S.D.N.Y. 1976).

[31] See Section 3, 4, and 8, respectively, of Form 11.1 in Appendix B.

[32] See Section 1 of Form 11.1 in Appendix B.

property subject to the outstanding interests of the beneficiaries.[23] Accordingly, if the lead lender should become bankrupt while the promissory note is the property of the bankrupt lead's estate, the participants, as both beneficiaries and secured creditors of the lead, would be entitled to their proportional shares of the payments (but not setoffs)[24] received by the lead's trustee or receiver. To protect themselves, the participants should demand that the participation funds and payments held by the lead be segregated from its other monies;[25] otherwise, if the participation funds held in trust for the participants cannot be identified as such, the participants would be relegated to the status of general creditors of the lead's estate.[26]

[c] Piggyback Protection From Usury Laws Unlikely for Loan Participants

Suppose a nonexempt lender directly participates in making an otherwise usurious loan with an exempt lead lender or, alternatively, suppose the nonexempt lender originates the loan and participates with an exempt lender solely for the purpose of circumventing the usury law. Although no decisional authority is squarely on point, it is reasonable to assume that a court would hold, on a substance-over-form rationale, that the interest portion of the illegal loan attributable to the nonexempt lender is usurious.[27] In *Sondeno v. Union Commerce Bank*,[28] the California Court of Appeals held that the defendant foreign lender was exempt, on its own accord, from the usury law as a bank conducting business under California banking law. However, the court, in dictum, stated that, had the foreign lender not been exempt, its participation with an exempt local lead lender would not have removed the taint of usury, although the domestic lender would obviously remain exempt with respect to its portion of the loan.[29]

---

[23] 4A *Collier on Bankruptcy* § 70.25[1] (14th ed. 1976).

[24] FDIC Receiver v. Mademoiselle of Cal. 379 F.2d 660 (9th Cir. 1967).

[25] See Section 6 of Form 11.1 in Appendix B.

[26] 4A *Collier on Bankruptcy* § 70.25[2]; the prevailing view in trusts is that "a beneficiary who cannot find the trust property has no lien or charge spread over the entire estate of the faithless trustee." Gulf Petroleum, S.A. v. Collazo, 316 F.2d 257 (1st Cir. 1963).

[27] See Comment, "Comprehensive View of California Usury Law" 6 S. U.L. Rev. 166, 182 (1974).

[28] 71 Cal. App. 3d 391, 139 Cal. Rptr. 229 (1977).

[29] *Id.* at 394.

corded claims.[19] Therefore, participating lenders traditionally have relied for their protection on both the terms of the participation agreement and their confidence in the lead lender's willingness to faithfully perform its fiduciary duties as the trustee of their interests.

The lead lender itself may also encounter problems in its capacity as fiduciary. For example, if the lead lender has made other loans on its own account to the same borrower and discovers that the borrower is in financial difficulty, it may be compelled to forgo its remedy of acceleration with respect to such other loans if such accelerations would jeopardize the ability of the borrower to meet his obligations under the participation loan. Otherwise, it might breach its fiduciary responsibility to the other loan participants.[20]

[b] Bankruptcy of the Borrower or Lead Lender

Not only do the loan participants lack standing to assert their claims directly against the mortgage collateral, but they must also rely upon the lead lender for protection if the borrower should go bankrupt since the lead is the only party qualified to file a proof of claim against the bankrupt's estate for the remaining balance due on the participation loan.[21] In addition, it has been held that a participant cannot "set off" its share of the loan participation against the funds of the bankrupt borrower on deposit with it (thereby reducing its claim against the lead lender). This is based on the rationale that since the participant bank was not a party to the loan agreement and did not retain any indicia of control over the borrowing relationship, it was not a creditor of the bankrupt borrower and therefore could only look to the lead lender for satisfaction of its claim.[22]

The rule is well settled that where the bankrupt was in possession of property impressed with a trust, the trustee in bankruptcy holds such

---

[19] For example, if the lead lender shoud record its release of the mortgage after receiving payment from the borrower, the borrower could sell the real estate to a bona fide purchaser free of the mortgage and thereby extinguish the security for the loan participation.

[20] For an analogous situation involving a bank acting as a corporate trustee on behalf of bondholders, see Dabney v. Chase Nat'l Bank of City of New York, 196 F.2d 668, (2d Cir. 1952).

[21] However, as a logical corollary, no trustee in bankruptcy should be able to contest the amount of the lead's secured claim on the rationale that a portion thereof actually belongs to the participants.

[22] *In re* Yale Express Sys. Inc., 245 F. Supp. 790 (S.D.N.Y. 1965). The holding in *Yale* was approved but distinguished by the court in *In re* Erie Forge & Steel Corp., 456 F.2d 801, 806 (3d Cir. 1972).

the one mortgage are issued to each lender, or where the participant is identified in the financing statement and other security documents executed by the borrower.[16] Accordingly, where one promissory note is payable to and held by the lead lender it alone is designated as the mortgagee of record, and since Article 9 of the Uniform Commercial Code does not apply to the transaction,[17] according to the public records, the lead lender becomes the only party with a security interest in property. Moreover, this absence of a debtor-creditor relationship between the borrower and participating lenders is not altered by mention of the latter in the lead-borrower loan agreement, unless they are specifically named as third-party beneficiaries. Consequently, unless the participants enter into separate side agreements with the borrower, they cannot assert separate creditor claims against the borrower. They can only look to their lead lender and the loan participation agreement for satisfaction of claims arising out of the mortgage transaction. So, for example, if the borrower should default and the lead lender refuses to foreclose (pursuant to its discretionary authority under the participation agreement), perhaps because the borrower is a good customer, the participants' only recourse would be to bring an equitable action against the lead (by way of specific performance or otherwise) if its refusal constitutes an egregious abuse of its discretionary authority to act as trustee for the benefit of the other lenders. However, if such refusal contravenes the terms of the participation agreement, the participants would be able to sue the lead for breach of contract, thus obviating their need to seek equitable relief. Otherwise, the participating lenders may be forced to buy out the lead's share of the loan (if allowed under the participation agreement), at best a last-resort solution since the participants would be placed in the precarious position of possibly "throwing good money after bad."[18]

Moreover, because the lead is the sole mortgagee of record, the participants are in the same vulnerable position as would be any unsecured creditors with respect to the claims of bona fide third parties who take the mortgaged property without notice of their prior unre-

---

[16] *In re* Fried Furniture Corp., 293 F. Supp. 92 (E.D.N.Y. 1968); Heights v. Citizens Nat'l Bank, 463 Pa. 48, 342 A.2d 738 (1975).

[17] Generally, sales of participatory interests in collateral other than chattel paper, contract rights, and accounts are not covered by Article 9. U.C.C. § 9-102. Moreover, Article 9 *expressly does not apply* to the creation or transfer of an interest in or lien on real estate. U.C.C. § 9-104(j). See Armstrong, "The Developing Law of Participation Agreements," 23 Bus. Law. 689, 691 (1968).

[18] See Section 5 of Form 11.1 in Appendix B.

certain that there is both adequate hazard insurance and title policy supporting the loan.
5. The lender should insist on standardizing its settlement procedures and should make the settlement agent aware of its responsibility to both the lender and the originator.

At closing, perhaps the greatest risk incurred by lenders engaged in warehouse financing is that they tend to conduct such transactions in a very casual and informal manner. Often, none of the above safeguards are required. Traditionally, commercial bankers have long-standing and profitable relationships with mortgage bankers and are embarrassed to ask for these cumbersome protections. Moreover, these foregoing safeguards are frequently both costly and time consuming for the mortgage company. However, where a commercial bank is effecting a warehouse credit line with other commercial banks, it is both prudent and seemly to ask for the foregoing safeguards.[14]

[5] Permanent Loan Participations

In contrast to construction loan participations, long-term loan participations are not actively pursued by permanent lenders. As the largest suppliers of permanent financing, life insurance companies are generally able to avoid "doing business" problems. Unlike commercial banks, because of their business volume many are licensed to do business in every state. Moreover, the large companies, with billions of dollars of assets, seldom need to rely on other lenders for funding assistance, and local statutory lending limits are generally quite liberal.[15] However, life insurance companies will from time to time engage in loan participations as a risk-spreading device where the loan amount is unusually large or where the risk factor is high, such as in the case of a multimillion-dollar urban renewa loan.

[6] Legal Pitfalls

[a] No "Privity" Between Participant and Borrower

As noted earlier, the participating lenders have no direct legal relationship with the borrower except where separate notes secured by

---

[14] An example of a mortgage warehousing security agreement is found as Form 11.3, Appendix B.

[15] For example, in New York, life insurance companies are permitted to lend up to the greater of $30,000 or 2 percent of their admitted assets on a single parcel of property. N.Y. Ins. Law § 81.6(a) (McKinney Supp. 1979).

commercial banks to close and record mortgage loans in their own names, pledging the secured mortgage notes as collateral with the banks. Thereafter the banks hold onto or "warehouse" the mortgage loans until they are reassigned and sold to some permanent lender. From the time it advances the loan funds until the time at which the loans are purchased by the permanent lender, any lender engaging in warehouse financing should secure its position by obtaining as collateral the various notes and mortgages executed in favor of the mortgage banker-originator. There are essentially two ways to obtain such security interest: the first is to file a Uniform Commercial Code Financing Statement covering the collateralized notes and mortgages[12] and to provide in the security agreement and the ancillary loan documents that upon repayment by the originator, both the lien and collateral will be released; the second is to arrange to have the actual notes and mortgages endorsed and delivered by the originator over to the lender as collateral, which would then be returned prior to the permanent funding.

A lender engaged in warehouse financing should consider the following:

1. The lender's security interest should blanket the mortgage banker-originator's contractual right as correspondent[13] to any servicing fees, and it should also cover any after-acquired notes and mortgages.
2. All documents being retained by the originator should state that they are being held in trust and on behalf of the lender.
3. If possible, the particular permanent investor's commitment should be identified before the lender advances any funds. If such identification is impossible, the warehouse agreement should state that the identification process will take place within a certain period of time after the initial funding. Moreover, the lender should make certain that it is dealing with a satisfactory permanent investor of substantial means, that the permanent investor's commitment be assigned to the lender, that such assignment be acknowledged by the permanent investor, and that the permanent investor agree to disburse the proceeds directly to the lender upon funding.
4. As a standard requirement for closing, the lender should make

---

[12] See U.C.C. § 9-403. However, in the case of warehousing, perfecting the security interests of the warehouser-lender can, as a practical matter, be extremely difficult because in many cases the collateral pool changes continuously as underlying notes and obligations become substituted for one another.

[13] See discussion at ¶ 2.03[2].

chise taxes, filing reports with state authorities (often including a list of resident shareholders), and subjecting itself to the jurisdiction of the courts within the state.[6] If these requirements are not met, a few states, such as Ohio[7] and Indiana,[8] impose criminal sanctions against the officers of the offending corporation. In others, if the borrower should default and the mortgage be foreclosed, the defendant-mortgagor could argue that since the lender was illegally engaged in business within the state its mortgage is unenforceable or even void at its inception.[9] While many state statutes carve out an exception from the "doing business" prohibition for the foreign lender who consummates the loan transaction and has the mortgage and other loan documentation executed outside the state,[10] some states, such as Connecticut,[11] require loans in their states to be purchased from a local lender in order for the foreign lender to avoid any "doing business" problems. Consequently, as a means of engaging in interstate lending without running afoul of the "doing business" problem, commercial banks and other lenders frequently participate in loans originated by local correspondents. However, since a bank or other foreign lender may inadvertently be doing business in the state by virtue of its other nonloan activities and because there is considerable variation in the banking and "doing business" statutes of the various states, a confirmation from the lead bank and/or its local counsel that the intended purchase of the participation interest does not constitute "doing business" should always be required by the foreign lender participating in the loan transaction.

[4] "Warehousing" Mortgage Loans

The practice known as "warehousing" is closely related to loan participation. Mortgage bankers use their revolving lines of credit with

---

[6] E.g., Cal. Corp. Code §§ 2100-2116 (West 1977).

[7] Ohio Rev. Code Ann. § 1703.99 (Page 1979).

[8] Ind. Code Ann. § 23-1-11-14 (Burns 1972).

[9] E.g., John Hancock Mut. Life Ins. Co. v. Girard, 64 P.2d 254 (1936). In a few states, such as Arkansas, the mortgage would be void. Ark. Stat. § 64-1202 (Bobbs-Merrill 1947). However, if the mortgage is initially voidable (and not void), in most states it could be rendered enforceable if the lender pays the appropriate penalties and any delinquent taxes and thereby obtains the necessary certificate of authority or other approval to do business in the state. E.g., N.J. Stat. Ann. § 14A:13-11(1) (West 1969).

[10] E.g., Cal. Corp. Code § 191(d) (West 1977). In Illinois, a foreign bank may make loans on property by executing the note and mortgage in Illinois without being classified as "transacting business," and such mortgage may be enforced by Illinois courts. Ill. Ann. Stat. Ch. 32, § 212 (Smith-Hurd 1979). See also Industrial Acceptance Corp. v. Haering, 253 Ill. App. 97 (1929).

[11] E.g., Conn. Gen. Stat. § 36-5A (West 1979).

met because of its lending limits,[5] credit policies, or lack of loanable funds. For example, within recent years, smaller rural banks have been able to meet the credit demands of their customers by developing correspondent relationships with large city-based banks. These city-based banks have billions of dollars to invest, and can share with the local lead banks in attractive loans that might not otherwise be offered to them in their own geographical areas. Indeed, as construction costs have risen, even the larger city banks, with sizeable lending limits per loan, are sometimes forced to act as lead lenders themselves and to originate loan participations in order to finance the construction of office buildings which, in some cases, cost upward of $15 million. In addition to this urban to rural shift in loanable funds, a national symbiotic network of corresponding banks has employed the loan participation device to reallocate credit from those regions of the country experiencing a capital surfeit (like New England) to those areas (like the South and West) in need of extra loan funds. Sometimes the lead bank's motivations for organizing a loan participation are to have some local correspondent bank administer a distant construction loan and to take advantage of its knowledge of local conditions and the peculiarities of local law. In addition, the participating bank may be willing to increase its correspondent balances with the lead lender in exchange for a share of an attractive loan. Conversely, a local participating bank that buys a loan share within its banking area may be able to use the transaction as the basis for making contacts that may generate additional business for the local bank. For example, if the project under construction is rental property, the local bank may be able to obtain the management account once the project is complete, and may perhaps solicit the developer's local banking business.

In addition, commercial banks, like other corporate lenders, cannot transact business in a foreign state without qualifying to do business in that state. However, qualification can be both expensive and troublesome, and the penalties for noncompliance can be extremely severe. For example, in most states such as California, if a foreign participating lender is engaged in a loan transaction that constitutes doing business within the state, it must qualify for doing business by filing certain documentation (e.g., application to qualify, copies of certificate, and articles of incorporation), paying filing fees, paying income and fran-

---

[5] For example, a national bank can lend to any one borrower no more than an amount equal to 10 percent of the bank's paid-in capital stock and unimpaired surplus. 12 U.S.C. § 84. Moreover, the Office of the Comptroller and its bank examiners discourage national banks from making direct loans outside their immediate marketing areas because of the added difficulties involved in connection with collecting such loans.

[2] Participant Lenders in Construction Financing

Most loan participations involve large construction loans shared by commercial banks that frequently maintain correspondent relationships with one another. Many commercial banks provide loan participations for their correspondents as a correspondent service. Generally, the lead bank assumes full responsibility for serving the loan during the construction period (e.g., collecting interest payments, supervising disbursements under its building loan agreement), and, in exchange, receives more than its pro rata share of loan fees or interest payments.

Some REITs have also developed correspondent relationships with commercial banks with whom they regularly participate in construction financing. Frequently, savings and loans, attracted by the high yields offered by construction loans, will seek participations with commercial banks, especially when they lack the expertise to oversee construction and administer the loans themselves. Also, by participating as the senior lienholder with a private lender, federally chartered and state chartered Federal Savings and Loan Insurance Corporation-insured savings and loans are permitted by the Federal Home Loan Bank Board to offer home builders and other developers loans with higher loan-to-value ratios than would otherwise be permitted under their regulatory scheme or by their underwriting policies.[3] Also, since 1969 the Federal National Mortgage Association (Fannie Mae) has participated with qualified institutional lenders on loans originated by the latter to fund the construction of low- and moderate-income multi-family housing projects. Pension funds, with their huge investment reserves, contribute indirectly to construction loan participations through their equity investments in REITs. While strictly regulated life insurance companies are allowed by local law to engage in loan participations,[4] they generally do so on a very limited basis. Their construction lending activities are almost always confined to projects in which they have an equity interest or in respect to which they supply the permanent financing.

[3] Business and Legal Reasons for Loan Participations

By use of the participation device, a commercial bank or some other financial institution, acting as the lead lender, can satisfy the credit demands of its valuable depositors which otherwise might not be

---

[3] See discussion of "piggyback" mortgages at ¶ 8.07.
[4] E.g., N.Y. Ins. Law § 81.6(a) (McKinney, Supp. 1979).

[d] Buy-Sell Agreement and Transfer
of Venture Interest 11-28
[e] Dissolution.. 11-29
[f] Tax Considerations............................... 11-29
[6] Summary of Problems Inherent in
Joint Venturing...................................... 11-30
[7] Renewed Interest in Institutional
Joint Ventures...................................... 11-31

¶ 11.01 LOAN PARTICIPATIONS

Occasionally, an institutional lender participates with other lenders in making a single mortgage loan to the same borrower. Also, as discussed at ¶ 11.02, life insurance companies and other institutional lenders sometimes join with developers, as equity participants, in the ownership and development of real estate.

[1] Definition

A loan participation is a shared loan arrangement among two or more institutional lenders whereby one of them, called the "lead," parcels out portions of the loan into shares it then sells, generally without recourse, to the other "participant" lenders who receive, among themselves, undivided fractional interests in both the loan and the underlying collateral. In most cases, the participants have no direct legal relationship with the borrower. The promissory note is payable exclusively to the lead lender, which holds it and the mortgage collateral (except for its own share) in trust for its participants and is empowered by them to collect and distribute the principal and interest payments. The only evidence the participant has of its advance of funds is the certificate issued by the lead lender, and the rights and obligations of the lead and participants to one another are spelled out in the participation agreement to which the borrower is not a party.[1]

Alternatively, where feasible, separate notes may be issued to each lender, in which event each would become a separate creditor of the borrower and receive, as collateral, a joint interest in the underlying mortgage.[2]

---

[1] See ¶ 11.01[7] and the sample loan participation agreement, Form 11.1 in Appendix B.

[2] See ¶ 11.01[8] and the sample separate noteholder's agreement, Form 11.2 in Appendix B.

Chapter 11

LOAN PARTICIPATIONS AND JOINT VENTURES BY INSTITUTIONAL LENDERS

Page

¶ 11.01 Loan Participations 11- 2
    [1] Definition 11- 2
    [2] Participant Lenders in Construction Financing 11- 3
    [3] Business and Legal Reasons for Loan
        Participations 11- 3
    [4] "Warehousing" Mortgage Loans 11- 5
    [5] Permanent Loan Participations...................... 11- 7
    [6] Legal Pitfalls...................................... 11- 7
        [a] No "Privity" Between Participant
            and Borrower 11- 7
        [b] Bankruptcy of the Borrower or Lead
            Lender 11- 9
        [c] Piggyback Protection From Usury Laws
            Unlikely for Loan Participants 11-10
        [d] Lead Lender's Compliance With
            Securities Laws 11-11
    [7] The Loan Participation Agreement 11-11
    [8] Separate Notes Secured by One Mortgage.............. 11-12

¶ 11.02 Joint Ventures Between Institutional Lenders
      and Developers 11-13
    [1] Historical Development as Hedge Against
        Inflation for Institutional Lenders 11-13
    [2] Legal Definition 11-16
    [3] Concerns of Co-Venturers 11-17
        [a] Psychological Barriers 11-17
        [b] Problems for Institution Acting as
            Both Co-Venturer and Permanent Lender 11-18
        [c] Usury Considerations........................... 11-20
    [4] Selecting the Ownership Entity 11-21
        [a] General vs. Limited Partnership 11-21
        [b] Indirect Subsidiary Investment in Joint
            Ventures 11-22
    [5] Analysis of Joint Venture Agreement.................. 11-23
        [a] Allocation of Capital Contributions 11-24
        [b] Allocation of Control 11-25
        [c] Default Remedies 11-27

Baltimore, and, to a lesser extent, Washington, D.C.. To the would-be purchaser, cooperative ownership is not as flexible and economically rewarding as condominium ownership. The purchaser is normally locked into the existing financing arrangements of the blanket mortgage and unless the blanket mortgage can be refinanced, the seller must take back substantial deferred financing that represents the increase in the purchaser's appreciated equity. Commercial banks will give commercial loans if secured by a stock pledge of a cooperative owner; nevertheless, outside New York, most of these commercial loans are of short duration—not more than three to seven years—which means that a would-be purchaser must, on a resale, come up with a large down payment.[68]

---

[68] For comparisons between a condominium and a cooperative, see generally Clurman, *Condominiums and Cooperatives* (1970), *Cooperatives and Condominiums* (J. McCord, Ed., 1969), and *HUD Condominium-Cooperative Study* (1975).

mortgage covering the entire project. Consequently, the cooperator's stock interest may be less marketable than a condominium unit since a prospective purchaser may not be able to refinance the purchase price with his own individual mortgage.

For example, suppose X owns a cooperative apartment for twenty years and the blanket mortgage indebtedness is paid down to 50 percent of its original principal amount. Also during the twenty-year period, the value of the apartment has perhaps doubled. If X then wants to sell, his purchaser has no way to finance the increased value in the property through a mortgage and must pay cash for this increase in value of the equity, along with assuming X's share of the blanket mortgage liability. In some states, such as New York,[67] special legislation exists to authorize "home mortgage" financing of the cooperative apartment, but elsewhere this problem remains. This disadvantage could perhaps be surmounted if the cooperative corporation were willing to write the lease and issue stock in mortgageable form, and local lenders could be persuaded to accept a lien on the stock rather than on the fee as security for their permanent mortgage loans to the purchasers. In some instances, lenders have been known to finance the purchaser's acquisition costs based merely upon the high credit rating of the purchaser rather than on mortgage financing. In any event, before this option is selected, inquiry should be made of local permanent lenders to determine whether such mortgage financing is both legal and practical. It should be pointed out to them that as a matter of circumstances and form, the security for their mortgage would essentially be the same, whether the lien is on the stock (cooperative) or on the fee (condominium), and that "ownership" of a cooperative is as tangible a concept as a matter of law as "ownership" of a condominium.

The primary sources of the cooperative apartment blanket mortgages are savings associations and insurance companies. Conservative permanent lenders will often issue a commitment based upon 75 percent of loan-to-value ratio as an apartment rental project. They assume that if the cooperative is a failure and must be converted to a rental project, the project can still carry the mortgage loan. However, other lenders, when the supply of mortgage funds is readily available, will often lend up to 65 percent of the contemplated sellout price. The cooperative concept is very rare outside such cities as New York, San Francisco,

---

[67] See N.Y. Banking Law §§ 103-5, 235-8-a, 380-2-a (McKinney Supp. 1979). See also 12 C.F.R. §§ 541.10-4, 545.6-1(b) where the federal savings and loan associations are permitted to make loans secured by individual units in cooperative housing projects on similar terms as loans on single-family dwellings.

common elements by means of a long-term management contract with the cooperative corporation[65]; and (4) the unit stockholders would have limited liability with respect to both tort and contract actions arising from their ownership and management of the common areas.[66] From a tax perspective, the tax deductions available to condominium unit owners are also available to cooperative stockholders under I.R.C. § 216 so long as at least 80 percent of the corporation's gross income is derived from tenant-shareholders, not outside income such as from commercial rentals.

From a construction lender's perspective, cooperative financing is essentially the same as condominium financing. However, the permanent financing aspects are quite dissimilar and pose serious problems for both the developer and the tenant-shareholders. Since the cooperative corporation itself holds title to the land and structures, it alone may arrange for mortgages on the property and it alone is solely liable for property tax assessments. Consequently, each shareholder must accept whatever financing terms are arranged by the corporation, and should one shareholder default in his share of the blanket mortgage or tax payment, to prevent foreclosure the others must assume this obligation. Of course, any defaulting cooperator's stock and leasehold interest are forfeitable, and his equity interest can be sold to reimburse the other cooperators, but any mass default could bring down the entire project.

Another disadvantage is that unlike the condominium unit, the stock and proprietary lease acquired by the cooperator do not constitute real property and in some jurisdictions may not qualify for traditional home mortgage loans under the local regulatory statutes governing the lending practices of savings and loans and banks. In addition, local lenders may be wary about making any type of permanent mortgage loan when the security for the loan is only a lien on stock and not real estate, and where the mortgage would be subordinate to the first

---

corporation, has been held to be an interest in personalty for purposes of determining the perfection and priority of creditors' liens. See State Tax Commission v. Shor, 43 N.Y.2d 151, (1977). Accordingly, foreclosure of a cooperative loan pursuant to the Uniform Commercial Code obviates the difficulties and expense of judicial foreclosure of a mortgage loan secured by real property.

[65] As noted at note 48 *supra,* most condominium statutes limit in some fashion the developer's long-term control over common areas. In the case of a cooperative, such self-dealing by the developer is not voidable by the subscribers if the terms are disclosed at the time of purchase. See Northridge Coop. Section No. 1 v. 32nd Ave. Constr. Corp., 2 N.Y.2d 514, 141 N.E.2d 802, 16 N.Y.S.2d 404 (1957).

[66] In some jurisdictions, condominium unit owners are exculpated from such liability by statute. E.g., Va. Code § 55-79.80:1 (Cum. Supp. 1975).

would be buying seasoned loans; (2) the interest rates on residential loans sometimes exceed rates charged to their commercial borrowers; (3) purchasing in bulk would decrease its expenses and enable the insurance company to fund large amounts in a single funding; (4) the loans are recourse as opposed to the typical nonrecourse commercial loan.

Certain large insurance companies, such as New York Life and Aetna, have already begun to buy seasoned subdivision end loans, and perhaps in the not-too-distant future, life insurance companies will start to fund condominium end loans by means of a similar bulk-type arrangement.

¶ 10.03 COOPERATIVE FINANCING

In the case of cooperative ownership, fee title to the entire project (including the land, structure, and common areas) is held by a corporation, with every shareholder-occupant merely receiving a proprietary lease covering a particular residential unit and granting use of the common areas. The chief advantages of cooperative ownership over condominium ownership are: (1) the individual cooperative units can be sold at a lower price where favorable underlying or blanket mortgage financing can be retained by the cooperative housing corporation[64]; (2) a majority of the board of directors of a cooperative can arbitrarily reject a prospective purchaser or sublessee (except on the grounds of race, creed, color, national origin, sex, marital status or disability) whereas a condominium's board of managers' control over purchases is ordinarily limited to a mere right of first refusal; (3) since stock in a cooperative housing corporation is in the nature of personalty and not realty, a permanent lender holding a security interest in such stock can avoid the expense and delay of judicial foreclosure to dispossess a defaulting stockholder[64a]; (4) the developer can retain management control over the

---

[64] The economics of ownership of a cooperative frequently compel its use instead of a condominium. For example, a building due to be converted may be subject to an existing mortgage with a low interest rate—perhaps a 7 percent loan with ten or fifteen years to maturity. Assuming this mortgage does not contain a due on sale provision, in states where such provisions are enforceable, it is desirable to retain the favorable financing and the cost of acquiring a unit in the building would be less than if it were a condominium. See discussion at ¶ 3.04[8]. In addition, most mortgages contain provisions which prohibit a conveyance to fractionalized interests such as condominium units, and refinancing will add substantially to the carrying charges of individual purchasers.

[64a] In New York, an interest in a cooperative apartment, which is a stock certificate in the corporation and a proprietary leasehold granted by the

sponsor may be able to obtain bridge financing from some other lender. Ordinarily, short-term (two- or three-year) interest-only bridge financing with 60 to 80 percent loan-to-value ratio can be had from savings and loans (frequently as part of a loan package including the permanent takeouts) or from a commercial bank. The personal guaranty of the sponsor is normally required. Financing of this nature enables the sponsor to sell the condominium units before amortization payments become due on the new bridge loan. Part of the gap financing proceeds would be used to pay off the existing mortgage indebtedness, and the balance would be funded like an ordinary construction loan; disbursements would be made as the construction progressed toward completion.

If the existing mortgage carries a low rate of interest or contains a steep prepayment penalty, the resourceful sponsor or developer may find it economically attractive to obtain a "wraparound bridge loan."[63] This would enable the developer to retain the existing loan indebtedness during the conversion period, while permitting the wraparound mortgagee to fund only the amount of the conversion costs and earn a higher-than-first-mortgage yield on its disbursements. Alternatively, the conversion costs could be funded by means of an ordinary second mortgage or from cash based on an unsecured line of credit with a bank. Under such an arrangement, the existing mortgage and second mortgage loans would be paid off with unit sales proceeds when enough units have been sold "on contract" to persuade the permanent lender to refinance the purchase contracts by means of "end-loan financing."

On large-scale multimillion dollar conversions, problems may be encountered in procuring a takeout of permanent loans for the individual units to be purchased, or what is commonly called "end-loan financing." Few savings and loan associations have the funding capability to engage in such financing. While some of the financing for these large projects has been accomplished by a consortium of savings and loans, another obvious source of financing would be the insurance companies, which traditionally have declined to engage in such financing for the same reason that they do not make single-family residential loans—namely, to avoid the large overhead costs associated with making such small-sized loans. However, it is possible that a mortgage banker, or even a construction lender, could process and close the individual end loans, retain a certain percentage (e.g., 10 percent) for its portfolio, sell the remainder (e.g., 90 percent) in bulk to a life insurance company, and even service the entire portfolio.

The advantages to a life insurance company would be several: (1) it

---

[63] See discussion of wraparound financing at ¶ 7.04[3].

Moreover, lenders often prefer to finance large projects in phases; they can reduce their underwriting risks by making Phase II financing contingent upon a successful Phase I.

[5] Condominium Conversion of Rental Units

Over the past decade or so, rents have failed to keep pace with escalating fuel, labor, utility, and other operating expenses, which has prompted owners of existing rental properties to convert these units into condominiums and has prompted lenders to become more cautious about underwriting new apartment building loans, notwithstanding the current shortage in existing stocks of multifamily dwellings. Accordingly, once the existing rental projects become overdepreciated and the tax-shelter benefits decline, conversion of these rental units into condominiums has become a popular way for investors to increase their rates of equity return. Indeed, in some cities, such as Chicago, New York, and Houston, there has been a frenzy of conversion activity, and in approximately fifteen communities including the District of Columbia the local authorities became so worried that they recently enacted a police-power-based condominium moratorium statute.[62] In these locations, condominium conversions have become so successful that apartment building owners can sell projects at prices greatly in excess of values based on capitalized earnings to would-be converters. Notwithstanding this trend toward conversions, many lenders worry about the viability of proposed conversions in situations where the property is located in neighborhoods that are primarily renter-oriented or where the project is obsolescent and must compete with new projects that offer such amenities as swimming pools, balconies, recreation rooms, etc.

When an existing apartment building is converted to condominium ownership and there is existing financing, the developer or sponsor normally will obtain a "bridge" or "gap" loan to pay off the existing loan (including prepayment penalties, if any) and to defray the costs of conversion (including marketing, renovation, and interest costs during conversion). If the financing is procured from the existing lender, the existing note could be amended to provide for proration of the indebtedness among the units. The mortgage could also be modified to provide for partial releases and a proration of the lien among the units. It could also be amended to include a new legal description.

If the existing mortgagee refuses to refinance the existing loan, the

---

[62] The lifting of the condominium moratorium in the District of Columbia requires a ninety-day notice to be provided to all tenants prior to eviction. This ninety-day notice provision has recently been increased to six months.

permanent lenders are willing to subordinate their mortgages if, at local law, they are not required to invest in unencumbered first mortgages and if the mortgages on the other units are subordinated. This insures that the common-expense charges will be collected.

Finally, of major concern to the lender is that the value of the condominium unit can be impaired if the common areas are not properly maintained and are allowed to deteriorate. Notwithstanding its lien on the mortgagor-unit owner's undivided ownership interest in the common elements, the lender has no direct legal control over the use of the common areas. Some lenders insist upon a provision in the mortgage stating that if waste occurs in the common areas, such waste constitutes a default under the unit owner's mortgage and allows the lender to call the loan. This is inherently unfair because the unit owner, aside from having one vote in the condominium association, does not really have the ability to control or cure waste arising outside his unit. More importantly, the permanent lender does not really receive protection from such a clause. By the time waste is discovered by the permanent lender, the damage may be too late to remedy and, after foreclosure, it may be difficult to resell the unit. A more protective and equitable solution would be to assure the permanent lender that there are adequate reserves for maintenance and replacements and possibly even assure the lender that the condominium association must correct such deficiencies in the common elements at the request of a stipulated percentage of the permanent lenders.

[4] Phasing

As noted earlier, the construction lender may attempt to motivate the developer to pay full attention to completing the sale of all units by holding up his profits with high release prices up to 100 percent of the net sales proceeds. In response, many developers elect to "phase" by constructing the condominium project in stages. Although phased development might increase the overall costs of the project and might increase the required legal documentation,[61] such phasing might be necessary to save the developer from a ruinous cash squeeze caused by high release prices, and, in some cases, the added expense and legal complexities might be more than offset by the developer's ability to charge higher per-unit prices in Phase II if all goes well with Phase I.

---

[61] Maryland and Virginia allow for expanding and, in the case of Virginia, contracting condominium regimes. See Va. Code §§ 55-79.63, 55-79.64 (Michie Cum. Supp. 1979), and Md. Real Prop. Code Ann. § 11-117 (Michie Cum. Supp. 1979).

☐ What insurance coverage is required?
☐ Is there provision for construction of additional living units?
☐ Are unit air-lot surveys recorded?
☐ Are there any unusual provisions?
☐ Is the declaration silent on typical matters?
☐ Are powers and duties of officers defined?

SOURCE: Mortgage Guaranty Insurance Corp.

[d] Permanent Loan Documentation

At the present time, there is a lack of standardization of condominium documents, and consequently lenders, other than the original lender, may be unwilling to make "spot" loans on future unit resales because of the time and expense involved in carefully reviewing de novo the condominium documentation. To ameliorate this problem, the original lender could insist upon the use of documents that conform to the requirements of either "Freddie Mac," "Fannie Mae," the Veterans Administration, or some other agency active in the secondary mortgage market. Use of these standards would facilitate sale of the loans in the secondary market and would enhance the chance for new mortgage financing on resale.

The mortgage or deed of trust instrument should provide that any breach by the mortgagor of its obligations under the condominium documents constitutes a default under the mortgage. The condominium documents should require notice of default to the lender and should afford the lender a reasonable opportunity to cure such default by the mortgagor-unit owner. Ordinarily, permanent lenders will also require that the condominium documents not be amended without their prior written consent. Some lenders will also seek language in the documents giving them the right to inspect the books and records of the unit owners association, to inspect the common areas, to receive notice of meetings and specified acts of the association, to require that insurance proceeds be utilized to repair or restore damage to units or the common areas, to require that the unit owners association maintain adequate reserves for maintenance and capital improvements, and to require that the mortgagee or purchaser at a foreclosure sale be exempt from first refusal rights in the association, and other resale restrictions if such mortgagee or purchaser steps into the shoes of the mortgagor at foreclosure. In addition, most lenders will require that the condominium documents include specific language subordinating common-area expense charges and liens to the permanent first mortgage. In those jurisdictions permitting common-expense liens to take lien priority over mortgages, some

- ☐ Is monthly maintenance charge reasonable?
- ☐ When does developer control expire?
- ☐ Can common areas or facilities be enlarged later?
- ☐ Are there TV and parking restrictions?

OWNERS ASSOCIATION

- ☐ Is association empowered to collect monthly maintenance fees?
- ☐ What is penalty for nonpayment? How enforced?
- ☐ Is association required to notify lender of default in common-area charge payments?
- ☐ Is association solvent?
- ☐ Is association balance sheet and operating statement data available?
- ☐ Is provision being made for reserve funds for major maintenance items?
- ☐ Does association provide professional management? Review management contracts?
- ☐ When does builder turn over control to owners?
- ☐ Is insurance adequate?
- ☐ Does association approve new owners?
- ☐ Is time allowed for owner approval reasonable?
- ☐ Must association advise lenders of maintenance payment default?

CONDOMINIUM DECLARATION

- ☐ Is declaration recorded?
- ☐ What are occupancy restrictions? Children? Pets? Renters? Family members? Guests?
- ☐ Can units be rented on long-term basis?
- ☐ Is a rental pool permitted?
- ☐ Are resales restricted?
- ☐ What are unit owners' voting rights?
- ☐ Provisions for amendments?
- ☐ When does builder's control terminate?
- ☐ What percentage of units must be sold before the condominium declaration is filed?
- ☐ Any restrictions on owners' mortgage financing?
- ☐ What are rights of mortgagee-in-possession?
- ☐ How are insurance proceeds applied?
- ☐ Is there an obligation to repair and rebuild?

[c] Permanent Lender Checklist for Review of Condominium Project

The following checklist has been used by the Mortgage Guaranty Insurance Corporation to help decide whether to become the permanent lender on a particular condominium project.

PHYSICAL CHARACTERISTICS OF PROJECT AND NEIGHBORHOOD

☐ Parking ratio? Adequate?
☐ Is parking owned? Rented? Assigned? Uncontrolled?
☐ Are balconies of adequate size? One or more for each unit?
☐ Do balconies permit owners to clean own windows?
☐ Any design elements that increase maintenance cost?
☐ Is maintenance of common areas good?
☐ Is exterior design acceptable to market?
☐ Are floor plans acceptable to market?
☐ Is there proper mix of one-, two-, and three-bedroom units?
☐ Are streets public or private?
☐ Who provides police and fire protection?
☐ How is trash pickup handled? At whose expense?
☐ Are utilities public or private?
☐ Is unit price and quality comparable to neighborhood?
☐ What is density of dwelling units per acre?
☐ Is project large enough for efficient management?
☐ Is ethnic mix appropriate?

COMMON AREAS

☐ Are common areas defined?
☐ Are limited common areas defined? Who maintains?
☐ Are there restrictions on use of common and limited common areas?
☐ Are common facilities rented or owned?
☐ Are common areas encumbered?
☐ Is common-area ownership equal or proportioned?
☐ Are recreational facilities adequate? Superadequate?
☐ Are there any club membership privileges or requirements?
☐ What does common-area maintenance charge include? Taxes? Insurance? Common-area maintenance? Central heat and/or air conditioning? Window cleaning?

insurance standards be set forth in the condominium documentation to prevent an economy-minded—but inefficient—board of managers from scaling down coverage to inadequate levels after control passes from the developer. In the absence of statutory limitation of liability,[53] this management control of the common elements may result in contractual liability for the unit owners as principals on all authorized contracts of the unincorporated association,[54] while liability for unauthorized contracts may be based on apparent authority.[55] Incorporation of the association, if permitted under local law, might not alleviate this potential liability; the corporation could be construed as the agent of the owners of the common areas, enabling liability to be predicated upon the unit owners' status as undisclosed or partially disclosed principals.[56] There is also a risk of unlimited tort liability, absent statutory limitation,[57] for injuries to nonresidents caused by defective construction or maintenance of the common areas, which each unit owner would have a duty of care to keep safe.[58] Vicarious liability also could arise for the torts of employees of the association committed within the scope of employment.[59] The permanent lender should also require a separate title insurance policy for each unit, especially since condominium titles involve questions of air space as well as ground lines. In addition, it should require an affirmative endorsement insuring the validity of the creation of the condominium under the applicable state statute.

Miscellaneous. Some miscellaneous matters of concern to the permanent lender are: (1) refusal by the developer to relinquish control over the common areas or management association for an excessive period of time after the project has been completed; (2) unfair long-term developer control of management contracts, utilities, or recreational leases[60]; (3) potential reduction in the value of the units caused by the developer adding additional units without being required under the condominium documents to enlarge the common areas; and (4) provisions in the condominium documents giving the unit owners association a lengthy right of first refusal to purchase units offered for resale.

---

[53] For an example of a statute limiting contractual liability, see Fla. Stat. Ann. § 718.119(1) (West Supp. 1978).

[54] See Rohan & Reskin, note 12 *supra,* § 6.03(2).

[55] See *id.* See also *Restatement (Second) of Agency* § 159 (1957).

[56] See *Restatement (Second) of Agency* §§ 144, 186 (1957).

[57] For an example of a statute limiting the unit owner's tort liability, see Fla. Stat. Ann. § 718.119(2) (West Supp. 1978).

[58] See Prosser, *Torts* §§ 57-63 (4th ed. 1971).

[59] *Id.* § 70.

[60] See note 48 *supra.*

rable buildings. Accordingly, a prudent permanent lender should carefully review the projected assessments; if they are underestimated, the marketability and resale value of the units could be seriously affected. To reduce the impact of these assessments, several methods have been devised to generate income from outside sources. This can be used to fund expenses for management and maintenance of the portions of the common areas devoted to residential use. For example, outsiders may be charged for the privilege of using condominium services or facilities, or concession income can be obtained from suppliers of services to condominium residents. Perhaps more popular is the leasing of space in the common areas to commercial tenants, providing a flow of rental income that can help to decrease or even offset completely the financial burden of maintaining the residential common areas.[50] Moreover, by leasing space to commercial tenants such as grocers, barbers, and pharmacists, the unit owners in such "multi-use" condominiums benefit from the proximity of desired services. Use of rent from commercial common areas to reduce assessments involves an inherent tax problem, however, that can undercut the desirability of "assessment-free" condominium ownership: The net income from outside sources used to defray maintenance assessments may constitute taxable income both to the unit owners' association and to the individual unit owners.[51]

Insurance. Another area of concern for the permanent lender is whether the unit owner's association is carrying sufficient hazard insurance on the structural improvements. If it is not, the association may have insufficient insurance proceeds to repair or restore in the event of a casualty loss even though it may be obligated to do so under the condominium documentation. Moreover, if the applicable state statute, condominium bylaws, or master deed requires that the insurance proceeds be used for restoration purposes, the lender would be precluded from requiring that the proceeds be used to scale down the mortgage indebtedness (as may be the case in a conventional rental project[52]), notwithstanding language to that effect in the loan documents. In addition, the permanent lender should insist that minimum liability

---

concern, which also manages other properties, often can purchase utility services at cheaper bulk rates. Moreover, experience has shown that occupants and commercial tenants meet their obligations more punctually when dealing with professionals. See Ferrer & Stecher, note 7 *supra,* § 472.

[50] *Id.* § 431, at 300, n.2.

[51] For a discussion of the double taxation problem and possible solutions, see Madison, "Multi-Use Condominiums to Avoid Double Taxation of Outside Income," 16 Wm. & Mary L. Rev. 37 (1974).

[52] See discussion at ¶ 3.08[4][d].

and loans are authorized to make 80 percent loans (without dollar limit), 90 percent first mortgage loans up to $75,000, and 95 percent loans up to $60,000.[46]

[b] Permanent Lender's Considerations

Physical Characteristics. Since the permanent lender will be involved in the project on a long-term basis, it will be concerned with the permanent physical characteristics of the structure and site that affect the habitability and marketability of the units. For example, it will scrutinize the mix of unit prices and sizes, parking ratios, density of dwelling units per acre, and a host of other factors summarized in the checklist at ¶ 10.02[3][c].

Common Area Assessments. Greatly detracting from the condominium's desirability are the often excessive and unanticipated assessments that the unit owners must pay to maintain and manage the common areas. In a highly competitive market, developers have been known to lure buyers by understating estimated assessments.[47] Even once the true costs are established, they can escalate because of inflation, self-dealing by manager-developers before the unit owners association assumes management duties,[48] or inefficient owner management once the association is in control.[49] Consequently, the owners may pay monthly assessments that, when added to property tax and mortgage payments, equal or exceed monthly rentals paid by neighbors in compa-

---

[46] See discussion at ¶ 2.02[3][d].

[47] See N.Y. Times, June 2, 1974, Sec. 1, at 1, col. 7. Assessments to cover "hidden" costs often will increase by as much as 35 percent, and in some cases 50 to 60 percent, over the original estimates. Sheldon, *Know the Ins and Outs of Condominium Buying* 40 (1973).

[48] Condominium statutes may permit the developer to control the common areas for a limited time or until most of the units are sold. E.g., Va. Code Ann. § 55-79.74 (Cum. Supp. 1974). Occasionally, a developer will manage the common areas himself during this period or will secure a long-term management contract with an insider and, in either case, charge an excessive rate of compensation. The statute might require unit-owner ratification of such long-term contracts initiated by the developer, however. E.g., *id.* § 55-79.74(b) (Cum. Supp. 1974).

[49] The unit owners association can engage the services of a professional manager and avoid the costs and inefficiency of owner management; a nonprofessional board often does not devote the time necessary for proper careful management, and it may not have the requisite experience to handle efficiently matters such as local assessments, taxes, insurance, zoning ordinances, and hiring and supervising of personnel. In addition, a professional management

(4) It obtains an endorsement to the title policy insuring that the condominium regime is validly created pursuant to the applicable state law.

These protections also benefit the permanent lenders on whom the construction lender will rely for repayment of its loan.

Securing Hidden Income. Many condominium projects are structured to enable the developer to lease ground floor space to commercial tenants or include a recreational amenities package on a long-term lease between the developer and the condominium association. The foregoing constitutes an income stream to the developer, which should be secured as additional collateral for the construction loan.

[3] Permanent Financing

Since each condominium unit is a separate parcel of real estate, an advantage of condominium ownership over stock ownership in a cooperative housing corporation is that the permanent lender will receive as security for its loan, a mortgage on real estate rather than merely a lien on stock and a pledge of the stockholder's proprietary lease in the cooperative housing corporation. In contrast to blanket mortgage financing of a cooperative, individual unit financing of either a condominium or cooperative enables the lender to deal on a personal basis with, and assess the credit standing of, each individual unit owner.

[a] Sources of Permanent Mortgage Funds

The three major sources of permanent loan funds for purchasers of condominium units are savings and loan associations, commercial banks, and mortgage bankers. While most commercial banks shy away from unit permanent financing, savings and loans welcome such loans and will frequently provide the interim financing to the developer to satisfy their portfolio requirements and attract the permanent financing. Indeed, when faced with competition, savings and loans frequently charge lower rates on the construction financing in exchange for the opportunity to furnish all the eligible unit owners with permanent financing. Savings and loans and banks usually offer conventional permanent financing at a 75 to 80 percent loan-to-value ratio. However, since the marketability of the units is so heavily influenced by the ability of the purchasers to leverage their acquisition costs, savings and loans—at the behest of the developer—will sometimes make maximum loan-to-value ratio loans. For example, at present, federally chartered savings

The lender should also require that the sales contract not be recorded and should have the contract stipulate that any execution thereof will not create any lien or lien rights in favor of a purchaser, with the purchaser expressly waiving or relinquishing any such lien rights it might have at law or equity. In addition, some lenders will require language that the contract is expressly subordinate to the construction loan, including any modifications, renewals, increases, or advances made thereunder. Finally, to avoid any potential conflict or problems between the construction lender and the prospective purchasers upon foreclosure of the project during construction, most lenders will insist that the following language be included in the sales contract:

> If Construction Lender by foreclosure or deed in lieu of foreclosure succeeds to ownership of the premises, including the residential apartments, Construction Lender shall have the right at its option to cancel said contract. In the event Construction Lender elects to cancel the contract, Construction Lender is obligated to return only those down payments actually received in hand by Construction Lender from Seller or Seller's agent.
>
> Construction Lender shall be in no way obligated to Purchaser for any down payments it has not received from Seller nor shall any liability be construed from Construction Lender's failure to receive any deposits from Seller, and Purchaser hereby relinquishes any right to place a judgment lien on the premises.

Declaration or Master Deed. Since the construction lender subordinates its mortgage to the condominium regime by recording (or by recording and joining in) the master deed, any subsequent foreclosure of the subordinated mortgage will merely allow the lender to receive title to the property subject to the recorded master deed or declaration.[45] Accordingly, the lender should make certain that:

(1) The condominium lien for assessments be subordinate to the construction loan, and in the event of foreclosure the lender be not liable for the payment of back assessments;
(2) The lender not be fettered by the usual restrictions on the right to sell and lease the units in the event of foreclosure;
(3) The lender be notified of all meetings of boards of directors of the condominium association and that there be a stipulation that no condominium documents be amended without its prior written consent;

---

[45] But see note 41 *supra.*

ness) and the developer (as a partial return of his equity and sales profits). In some instances, as a safety hedge, especially when the project is speculative or the sales pace is slow, the lender will demand that the entire net proceeds from sales be used to scale down the mortgage indebtedness. Sometimes, however, the lender will permit the developer to keep a portion of the proceeds after the sales program is well under way, especially where the developer has been required to put up a substantial amount of "front money." Such allocation is a matter of negotiation between the parties; however, at a minimum, the developer should insist that it be allowed to immediately recoup its closing costs as seller out of the sales proceeds. While construction lenders are naturally concerned about the developer becoming apathetic about the project after receiving its front money and profits, the recent real estate malaise demonstrated how high release prices—85 to 90 percent release price per unit—can render developers insolvent by depriving them of sufficient cash inflow to pay their overhead expenses and maintain their daily operations.

[d] Construction Lender's Review of Condominium Documents

The construction lender will carefully review the condominium master deed, bylaws, sales contract, and public offering statement or property report (if required by local or federal law) since, once the documents are recorded or filed,[43] the lender may be forced to step into the shoes of the developer in the event of a foreclosure and will become the owner of the condominium property subject to a legal structure based on the several documents. In addition, the requirements of the permanent lender will greatly concern the construction lender because its loan will be repaid with permanent mortgage funds. Accordingly, the prudent construction lender will also review the documentation from the perspective of the permanent lender and will incorporate the latter's requirements in the construction loan commitment letter.[44]

Sales Contract. The construction lender will be bound by the language contained in the contract if it forecloses and, as the new owner, seeks to enforce it against purchasers. Accordingly, the lender should insist on reviewing the content of the agreement and should prohibit changes without its consent because unfulfilled sales agreement obligations may involve special promises to a particular purchaser that the lender is not staffed to meet.

---

[43] See note 41 *supra.* See sample master deed, reproduced as Form 10.1 in Appendix B.

[44] A sample commitment letter, Form 10.2, is reproduced in Appendix B.

bound to be the subject of careful negotiations between the parties. The construction lender will consider a number of underwriting factors in determining whether to impose such a requirement, and, if so, how restrictive it will be. For example, the lender will scrutinize the developer's financial position, his backing, and whether any guarantees are involved. In regard to the latter, if local law requires the lender to first foreclose against the real estate, obtain a deficiency judgment, and prove that the developer is insolvent before proceeding against the guarantors, the lender will also be more likely to impose a presales requirement than if at local law it could proceed directly against the guarantors. The lender will obviously look at the developer's record of success in the local market and the timing and amount of the developer's equity contributions. The lender will also be more likely to impose a presales requirement where the condominium design is specialized, as in the case of many commercial and multi-use condominiums, since the number of potential tenants would be significantly reduced in the event the lender is forced to foreclose and operate the project as a rental property. In the event a presales condition is imposed, the construction lender may also insist that the condominium documents not be recorded until and unless the condition is met; in the event that if the project is not selling successfully, the construction lender would have the right to foreclose and operate the property as a rental project.

Release Requirement. The statutes of most jurisdictions prohibit a condominium unit from being conveyed subject to a blanket construction mortgage.[42] From a unit purchaser's point of view, a blanket mortgage is most undesirable unless subject to an adequate release provision that may be exercised even following a default by the blanket mortgagor. Individual units are released from the lien of the mortgage upon the payment on account of the loan at a specified release price. The release must cover both the unit and its associated interest in common elements. In jurisdictions with a substantial mortgage tax, it may be desirable, prior to commencement of construction, to create individual mortgages on separate units. These units could then be sold subject to the mortgage. This can become quite complex, with the problem of creating an adequate description of individual units prior to construction.

When the condominium units are sold and released, the question arises as to how the sales proceeds will be allocated as between the construction lender (as a partial repayment of the mortgage indebted-

---

[42] E.g., Va. Code Ann. § 55-79.46 (Supp. 1974).

[c] Presale and Release Requirements

Presale Requirement. The construction loan mortgage or deed of trust will generally cover the land and the improvements to be constructed. Although the mortgage is recorded prior to commencement of construction to accord the construction lender lien priority over any intervening mechanics' or other liens,[40] the master deed (establishing the condominium regime) is generally recorded some time after construction commences, upon the satisfaction of a variety of conditions imposed by the lender. Otherwise, if these conditions are not met by the developer after the condominium declaration or master deed is recorded, the subsequent foreclosure by the lender could not extinguish the condominium regime and the lender would be precluded from operating the project as a rental building.[41] Invariably, the condominium documents (e.g., master deed, bylaws, sales contract, and public offering statement or property report, if required by local or federal law) must first be approved by the construction lender and perhaps by the permanent lender as well. The construction lender will also require the developer to furnish proof that the proposed construction and underlying documentation has been approved by the appropriate state and local regulatory authorities. Prior to the filing of the condominium documents, the lender may also require completion of construction to a specified stage, in conformity with approved plans and specifications. The lender will also demand title insurance to insure the validity of the formation of the condominium regime under state law, a current three-dimensional survey indicating there are no encroachments, and evidence that adequate hazard and liability insurance is being carried.

Finally, as noted earlier, many lenders will only underwrite and fund the loan based on the full sellout value if a preestablished presales requirement is met by the developer. Sometimes a construction lender will even refuse to authorize the first construction draw or progress payment until and unless the stipulated presales condition is achieved by the developer. Accordingly, the imposition of a presales condition is

---

[40] See discussion at ¶ 4.02[6][a].

[41] However, courts in some jurisdictions take the common-law position that if the construction mortgage is recorded before the master deed is filed, a subsequent foreclosure by the construction lender would wipe out the condominium regime unless the prior mortgage is subordinated to the condominium declaration or master deed. However, in many of these states the construction mortgagee, by joining in the recordation of the master deed, will automatically subordinate the construction mortgage to the condominium regime. E.g., Fla. State Ann. § 718.104(3) (West Supp. 1978). See Dwyer, "Protecting the Rights of Purchasers of Condominium Units," 3 Fordham Urb. L.J. 479 (1975).

Also, a few states have laws that regulate and limit the ability of a developer to use down payments received from prospective purchasers.[35] In Florida, a developer can use down payments for construction of the project provided the contract clearly so states. In the event the contract does not, the developer is liable for a fraudulent misuse of the deposit.[36] If a lender has knowledge of the developer's misuse of the deposits in the construction of condominium contrary to statutory regulation, the aggrieved contract purchasers arguably might have a cause of action for the return of the deposit. This cause is based on a theory of unjust enrichment against the construction lender if the latter should foreclose upon the construction loan. However, where local law does not mandate that these funds be escrowed and the purchase contract is either executed after the construction mortgage has been recorded or subordinated by agreement of the purchaser to the lien of the construction mortgage, the construction lender would be under no obligation to enforce the purchase contract or to return the earnest money of the purchaser.[37] Nevertheless, if the developer uses these funds to help finance his other ventures, one commentator has suggested that the lender may later be forced to credit the purchasers with the amounts of such diverted funds under a third-party beneficiary theory—if the developer's default is attributable in part to the lender's negligence in not overseeing the developer's use of the construction loan funds.[38]

If the developer is inexperienced, a construction lender should closely monitor and review the developer's compliance with the various state and federal regulatory constraints. On the other hand, if the developer is wise to the ways of condominium development and regulation and has worked well with the lender in the past, such high degree of control should not be necessary.[39]

---

[35] For example, the State of Maryland requires that all deposits for condominium units not completed at the time of sale be segregated in a separate escrow account by the seller, or that a corporate surety bond be furnished. Md. Real Prop. Code Ann. § 10-301 (Cum. Supp. 1976). Virginia also requires that such funds be held in escrow, but adds that "such escrow funds shall not be subject to attachment by the creditor of either the purchaser or the developer." Va. Code Ann. § 55-79.95 (Cum. Supp. 1974).

[36] Fla. Stat. Ann. §§ 18.201 to 18.202 (West Cum. Supp. 1978).

[37] See State Sav. & Loan Ass'n v. Kauaian Dev. Co., 50 Hawaii 540, 445 P.2d 109, 121, 122 (1968).

[38] Osborne, Nelson & Whitman, *Real Estate Finance Law* § 13.3 (1979).

[39] Generally, see "Symposium on the Law of Condominiums," 48 St. John's L. Rev. xi, xv (1974).

the Act applies, no purchase price payments, deposits, or purchase commitments may be accepted, nor may sales literature be disseminated or indications of interest be solicited prior to the filing of a registration statement.[33] In addition, the Interstate Land Sales Full Disclosure Act (ILSFDA) has consistently been applied by HUD's Office of Interstate Land Sales Regulation (OILSR) to the sale of condominium units. As the name implies, the primary purpose of the statute is to require the seller of subdivided property to make a full, complete, and accurate disclosure to the purchaser of all relevant information (in a document known as the "Property Report") prior to consummation of the sale, if the transaction is effectuated through use of the mails or other means of interstate commerce.[34]

---

rated in Release No. 33-5347, entitled "Guidelines as to the Applicability of the Federal Securities Laws to Offer and Sales of Condominiums or Units in a Real Estate Development." The release exempted condominiums that are sold as primary residences, but extended coverage under the Securities and Exchange Act to condominiums not sold as a primary residence but as a resort or vacation home. Essentially, an offering of a condominium unit would be considered an offering of a security if the unit is sold under: (1) a rental arrangement with emphasis on economic benefit to be realized from the efforts of the developer-promoter; (2) the offer of a participation in a rental pool; and (3) the offering of a rental or similar arrangement whereby the purchaser must hold his unit available for rental for any part of the year, use an exclusive rental agent, or is otherwise materially restricted in the occupancy or rental of his unit. Securities Act Release 33-5347, 17 C.F.R. § 231.5347 (Jan. 4, 1973). By contrast, while the stock interest in a cooperative housing corporation is subject to local regulation, the U.S. Supreme Court in United Housing Foundation, Inc. v. Foreman, 421 U.S. 837 (1975), ruled that such stock sales in a nonprofit housing cooperative were not "securities" for purposes of the federal securities acts. See also Frome, "Cooperatives and Condominiums as Securities," 4 Real Est. Rev. 35(1975).

[33] Securities Act. Release 33-5382 (April 9, 1973).

[34] 15 U.S.C. §§ 1701 et seq. (1970). For a more detailed discussion of ILSFDA, see ¶ 9.03. According to OILSR, condominium units are the equivalent of lots in a subdivision and distinguishable from houses (which fall beyond the intended scope of the statute) on the rationale that the right to condominium space is a form of ownership rather than a structural description. See 38 Fed. Reg. 23,866 (1973); Rohan & Reskin, note 12 *supra,* § 18A.02. Accordingly, to exempt the condominium unit sale from ILSFDA, the unit must either be completed before it is sold or sold under a contract obliging the developer to complete construction of the unit within two years after the sales contract is executed. *Id.* See generally Kerr, *What the Home Builder and Developer Should Know About the Interstate Land Sales Full Disclosure Act* (1975), and Ingersoll, *Interstate Land Sales 1973: How to deal With HUD's New Regulations* (2d ed. 1973).

right to turn down prospective purchasers because of lack of income, etc., the lender should nevertheless commit itself as to the exact amount of loan funds to be committed to a permanent borrower on a particular project and should also indicate how long the commitment will be binding. The construction lender should insist that the commitment letter be written for its benefit as well as for the developer, or at least be assignable to the construction lender in the event of a default by the developer. The commitment should further specify what eligibility requirements, if any, must be met by any prospective purchaser-mortgagor.

[b] State and Federal Regulation

A few states, including Virginia and Florida,[28] have laws of the full disclosure variety that regulate the offering and sale of condominium units to purchasers. For example, under the Virginia statute the developer must file a registration statement with the Virginia Real Estate Commission before a condominium project may be marketed to the general public. Also, prospective purchasers must be given a current public offering statement containing all relevant data, and the sale is subject to cancellation by the purchaser within ten days from the date of the sale or delivery of the statement, whichever is later.[29] It is well settled that the mere offering of condominium units to public purchasers will be deemed to be the sale of real estate and not the sale of a security; hence, no registration is required with the Securities Exchange Commission or, at the local level, with state agencies administering compliance with local "blue sky" laws.[30] However, it is now clear that, unless the transaction is exempt,[31] Securities and Exchange Commission registration and compliance with local security regulation laws will be required where the condominium documents and sales literature refer to a rental agency or pool that permits the unit owner to rent his unoccupied premises to third parties. This is so because the SEC has opined that the holding out of the rental feature to a potential buyer transforms the transaction into a sale of an "investment contract" or "security" within the meaning of the Securities and Exchange Act of 1934.[32] Moreover, if

---

[28] E.g., Fla. Stat. Ann. §§ 718.504, 718.505 (West 1978).

[29] Va. Code Ann. §§ 55-79.88(a), 55-79.88(c) (Cum. Supp. 1974).

[30] Rohan & Reskin, note 12 *supra,* § 3.05 (1977).

[31] For a discussion of the private offering, intrastate, and other exemptions from the SEC registration requirement, see ¶ 1.05[1] at note 36.

[32] In 1972, a real estate advisory committee was established by the SEC to assist the Commission in real estate securities. Most of the recommendations in the committee's report (popularly known as the Dickey Report) were incorpo-

project.[24] While there are some closing costs and certain minimal advertising and marketing expenses associated with a rental project, a condominium project ordinarily entails additional costs that may include construction and furnishing of display models, substantial advertising and marketing costs relating to the sale of the condominium units, closing costs relating to the sale of the units, additional legal fees incurred in connection with the drafting of the complex condominium documents, and certain additional architectural and surveying expenses in connection with subdividing the land for condominium use.

In the past, many lenders applied a conservative underwriting approach, under which the construction loan-to-value ratio would be predicated on a rental and not to a condominium sellout value. By contrast, if the developer could show a sufficient rate of return, other lenders would underwrite the loan as a true condominium loan based on the loan sellout value.[25] In light of the high number of unsold condominium units on the market a short time ago—in various stages of foreclosure—most lenders have now become extremely cautious in their underwriting of these loans[26] and frequently refuse to base their loan amounts on the condominium's full projected sales value. However, in the past, certain experienced developers were able to convince lenders to fund, based on a full sellout value, on the condition that the difference between rental value and sellout value would not be disbursed by the lender until a presale requirement as to the number of units sold was met by the developer. Whether or not this approach will continue remains to be seen.

Another area of concern to the construction lender is the confusion involving permanent takeouts. In a conventional rental project, the construction lender concerns itself primarily with whether the developer has obtained a permanent loan commitment assuring repayment of the construction loan.[27] However, in response to permanent lenders' underwriting requirements as to prospective purchasers of condominium units, in the case of a condominium loan many construction lenders do not emphasize this takeout requirement. Condominium takeouts differ from normal rental takeouts in number, and in the fact that the respective mortgagors are unknown and ordinarily free to arrange permanent financing with a mortgagee of their choice; thus, a prudent construction lender should examine the standard form of takeout employed by savings and loans associations and other local permanent lenders. While in its commitment a permanent lender should have the

---

[24] See discussion at ¶ 4.02[3].
[25] See Romney, *Condominium Development Guide* 7-17 (1974).
[26] See generally Williams, *The Great Condominium Ripoff* (1974).
[27] See discussion at ¶ 4.01[1].

revisions of some state statutes to require stringent disclosure of material items[21] to purchasers and to permit the sophisticated options of time-sharing as well as expanding and contracting the condominium, the overall financing of condominiums is still a complex area. Incidentally, in the area of specific performance, at least one state court has recognized a possible distinction between a condominium and a house.[22]

Finally, financing the interim construction of a condominium project differs from that of financing a subdivision in that the subdivision builder can stop construction if sales are not progressing; the condominium project must be completed once construction starts. Accordingly, the construction lender's major risk in providing financing is that the units may not sell.

[2] Construction Financing

A real estate improvement is not a condominium until a declaration or master deed is recorded.[23] In this respect, condominium property is no different in terms of construction than a rental project. However, there are other risks and pitfalls peculiar to a condominium regime that will change the construction lender's standard requirements and conditions for making the construction loan, as well as change the scope of its review of the construction loan documentation. These areas of concern deal with (1) underwriting, (2) compliance with state laws, (3) presale and release requirements, and (4) review of condominium documents.

[a] Underwriting Analysis

In the case of a rental project, lenders normally lend 100 percent of the construction costs, based upon an appraisal of the completed rental

---

[21] Virginia's innovative condominium statute is a good example. Va. Code Ann. §§ 55-79.39 – 55-79.103 (Cum. Supp. 1974). The Virginia Condominium Act requires registration and public disclosure by way of an offering statement. Va. Code Ann. §§ 55-79.89 – 55-79.90 (Cum. Supp. 1974).

[22] In Centex Homes Corp. v. Boag, 128 N.J. Super. 385, 320 A.2d 194 (1974), the New Jersey Superior Court, Chancery Division, held that a condominium developer was not entitled to specific performance to force a purchaser to take title to his unit. The court stated that it would no longer specifically enforce real estate contracts absent a showing that the real property in question is unique and that monetary damages would be inadequate. The court held that condominium units had no unique quality, but were but one of hundreds of virtually identical units. It would appear logical that the court's reasoning could also be extended to the typical tract house development of suburban living.

[23] A sample master deed, Form 10.1, is reproduced in Appendix B.

agement and maintenance of the common areas,[18] and a large project often can be practicably cared for only by collective action of the unit owners.

¶ 10.02 CONDOMINIUM FINANCING

[1] Subdivision and Condominium Financing Distinguished

In the mid-1960s, when the infatuation with condominiums began, many real estate lenders scoffed at the idea that condominium financing was specialized or different from typical single-family-home subdivision financing. However, through experience, they discovered some significant differences in these two types of financing. First of all, it was found that market absorption data for single-family homes were not indicative of condominium absorption. Thus, lenders did not have the necessary underwriting data to analyze proposed condominium loans. However, as statistics developed on existing condominium projects in those areas where condominium development had become commonplace, lenders were given the resources necessary to adequately underwrite and review condominium loans. A second factor that distinguishes the condominium project from the typical subdivision project is the legal complexity of condominium ownership.[19] Since condominiums are creatures of state statutes, careful attention must be given to complying with the applicable enabling legislation. The lender, the developer, and the attorney must work with master deeds, bylaws governing the condominium association, articles of incorporation, possible recreation leases, common elements, limited common elements, phase development, expandable condominiums, and contracting condominiums. To the extent that documentation is becoming standardized by way of the Federal National Mortgage Association (FNMA, or "Fannie Mae") and the Federal Home Loan Mortgage Corporation (FHMLC, or "Freddie Mac"),[20] some of this complexity will be eased. However, with the advent of consumerism in condominium legislation and the recent

---

[18] See, e.g., Md. Real Prop. Code Ann. § 11-109 (Cum. Supp. 1974); N.Y. Real Prop. Law § 339-v(1)(a) (McKinney Cum. Supp. 1978). See generally Rohan & Reskin, note 12 *supra,* § 6.02(3).

[19] While the law of condominiums is but a peculiar type of subdivision law, nevertheless, very few states have attempted to coordinate condominium subdivision with that of typical subdivision of land. For example, in Ohio, the Attorney General ruled that property is not able to qualify under the Ohio Condominium Statute where it consisted of clusters of land lots and where the common areas consisted merely of roads and other types of commonly used property. See Att'y Gen. Op. No. 71-031 (1971).

[20] See discussion at ¶ 10.02[3][d].

forth in the declaration.[13] The percentage ordinarily is a ratio of the value of the apartment unit to the value of the entire condominium property,[14] and the unit owner's voting power and share of the common areas' profits and expenses generally are based upon this percentage.[15] Each unit owner owns his share of the common areas as a tenant in common,[16] but since occupancy would be untenable without free access to all of the general common areas, partition of these areas is prohibited.[17] An association of unit owners generally is responsible for man-

---

distinct categories: general common areas and limited common areas. The general common areas are available for use by all unit owners and include such elements as the underlying land, yards, gardens, garbage incinerators and other utility equipment, swimming pools, golf courses and other recreational facilities, and the building's foundation, lobby, basement, and other structural components—generally, all structures and facilities existing for common use. See FHA Model Condominium Act § 2(f). The limited common areas are available only for use by more than one but less than all unit owners and may include such elements as elevators, stairways, and balconies. Stores, offices, and other commercial or recreational facilities leased to outsiders also may be included in the common areas.

[13] FHA Model Condominium Act § 6(a).

[14] *Id.*

[15] *Id.* § 10. The FHA Model Condominium Act defines "common profits" as "the balance of all income, rents, profits and revenues from the common areas and facilities remaining after the deduction of the common expenses." *Id.* § 2(h). "Common expenses" are the "expenses of administration, maintenance, repair or replacement of the common areas and facilities." *Id.* § 2(g). Such expenditures are funded by assessments by the association against the unit owners or by other income derived from the common areas, such as rental income from commercial tenants; they may include outlays for salaries, utilities for the common areas, services, professional fees, insurance, equipment, and supplies.

If the condominium consists essentially of only one type of unit, with only minimal differences among the unit owners' interests in the common elements, it may be more feasible to allocate one vote and an equal share of the common areas profits and expenses to each unit. Most statutes permit this variation by providing that profits and expenses are to be allocated as determined in the declaration or bylaws. See, e.g., Fla. Stat. Ann. § 711.14 (West Cum. Supp. 1972); Ohio Rev. Code Ann. § 5311.08 (Page Supp. 1978). See generally Rohan & Reskin, note 12 *supra*, § 6.02(1).

[16] Rohan & Reskin, note 12 *supra*, § 5.02.

[17] See, e.g., Md. Real Prop. Code Ann. § 11-107(a) (Supp. 1974); N.Y. Real Prop. Law § 339-i(3) (McKinney 1968); Va. Code Ann. § 55-79.55(g) (Cum. Supp. 1974).

The FHA Model Condominium Act provides: "The common areas and facilities shall remain undivided and no apartment owner or any other person shall bring any action for partition or division of any part thereof.... Any convenant to the contrary shall be null and void." FHA Model Condominium Act § 6(c).

enabling statutes follow the FHA model statute, although some variations exist in most of the statutes.[7]

The typical statutory scheme establishes a legal structure based on several organizational documents. A declaration or master deed, recordation of which establishes the condominium as a legal entity, usually contains such project identification information as a description and allocation of the common areas and facilities, the floor plans, and the legal descriptions of the land, buildings, and individual units.[8] Bylaws are required to control the internal management of the condominium,[9] to provide rules for the management of the common areas, and to establish the means for collecting a pro rata share of the common expenses from the unit owners.[10] The third organizational instrument is the deed, by which the interest in each unit, along with an appurtenant interest in the common areas, is conveyed to each unit owner.[11]

Each unit owner is entitled to an undivided interest in the common areas,[12] inseparable from his apartment ownership, in a percentage set

---

[7] For the verbatim text and comparative analysis of the FHA Model Condominium Act and the state statutes, see 1 & 2 Ferrer & Stecher, *Law of Condominium* (1967) (hereinafter cited as Ferrer & Stecher).

[8] Section 11 of the FHA Model Condominium Act requires the declaration to describe the common areas and facilities and to provide for the "value of the property and of each apartment, and the percentage of undivided interest in the common areas and facilities appertaining to each apartment and its owner for all purposes, including voting." See note 23 *infra*.

[9] The bylaws ordinarily should provide for the election of officers and members of an executive committee who will manage the daily affairs of the condominium on behalf of all unit owners. 1 Ferrer & Stecher, note 7 *supra*, § 7.

[10] The FHA Model Condominium Act suggests that the bylaws address the following subjects:

(f) Maintenance, repair and replacement of the common areas and facilities and payments therefore, including the method of approving payment vouchers.
(g) Manner of collecting from the apartment owners their share of the common expenses.
(h) Designation and removal of personnel necessary for the maintenance, repair and replacement of the common areas and facilities.
(i) Method of adopting and of amending administrative rules and regulations governing the details of the operation and use of the common areas and facilities.

FHA Model Condominium Act § 19.

[11] The FHA Model Condominium Act requires the deed to specify the percentage of undivided interest in the common areas to which the unit owner is entitled. *Id.* § 12.

[12] For a comprehensive examination of the operational and legal aspects of the common areas, see 1 Rohan & Reskin, *Condominium Law and Practice* § 6 (1977) (hereinafter cited as Rohan & Reskin); 1 Ferrer & Stecher, note 7 *supra*, §§ 431-440, 451-476, 491-497. The common areas may be divided into two

satisfaction and tax benefits[3] of home ownership. This is particularly true in urban areas where the scarcity of economically desirable land necessitates more intensive land use and places individual ownership of a detached home beyond the economic reach of many families. Confronted with suspicious consumers accustomed to detached houses situated on plots of land, condominium developers creatively packaged this new legal concept by offering such amenities as swimming pools, golf courses, and marinas. Next came the introduction of retirement condominiums, resort condominiums, rental condominiums, and multi-use condominiums. Then, when the real estate bubble burst, a new marketing device called "time sharing" came into being, whereby several families or friends, or even groups of strangers, get together and purchase the right to use a condominium at a given period of time over a given period of years or purchase a fee simple right to the use of a condominium for a certain period of time.[4] In times of stress, ingenuity flourishes.

An examination of the statutory framework governing condominium ownership is necessary to understand the specific financing issues to be considered. Condominium development is encouraged by Section 234 of the National Housing Act of 1961,[5] which authorizes the Federal Housing Administration (FHA) to insure both permanent and construction mortgages on condominium projects in states that allow condominium ownership. To establish guidelines for state legislation that would satisfy the requirements of Section 234 and yet allow necessary modification by local law, the FHA drafted a model statute.[6] Most state

---

[3] The condominium unit owner, as a homeowner, is entitled to several tax benefits not available to a taxpayer who merely rents his residence. These include: deduction for payment of local property taxes, I.R.C. § 164(a)(1); deduction for mortgage interest paid, I.R.C. § 163(a); depreciation deduction if the residence is converted to rental property, I.R.C. § 167; deduction for casualty losses not reimbursed by insurance, I.R.C. § 165; postponement of recognition of gain on the sale of the unit if it is the seller's principal residence, I.R.C. § 1034; exclusion of realized gain from the taxable income of elderly taxpayers upon the sale of the unit, I.R.C. § 121. See Rev. Rul. 64-31, 1964-1 C.B. 300.

[4] There are several legal methods of structuring the time-sharing concept. For example, one method is when a group of buyers purchase as tenants in common, whereupon they execute an occupancy agreement delineating each buyer's right to a stated time. There is also the interval approach, where each buyer receives an estate for years with a vested remainder at the end of an estate for years as tenants in common.

[5] 12 U.S.C. § 1715 (1970).

[6] FHA Model Condominium Act (1962).

Chapter 10

CONDOMINIUM AND COOPERATIVE FINANCING

		Page
¶ 10.01	Legal Structure of Condominium Ownership	10- 1
¶ 10.02	Condominium Financing	10- 5
	[1] Subdivision and Condominium Financing Distinguished	10- 5
	[2] Construction Financing	10- 6
	[a] Underwriting Analysis	10- 6
	[b] State and Federal Regulation	10- 8
	[c] Presale and Release Requirements	10-11
	[d] Construction Lender's Review of Condominium Documents	10-13
	[3] Permanent Financing	10-15
	[a] Sources of Permanent Mortgage Funds	10-15
	[b] Permanent Lender's Considerations	10-16
	[c] Permanent Lender Checklist for Review of Condominium Project	10-19
	[d] Permanent Loan Documentation	10-21
	[4] Phasing	10-22
	[5] Condominium Conversion of Rental Units	10-23
¶ 10.03	Cooperative Financing	10-25

¶ 10.01 LEGAL STRUCTURE OF CONDOMINIUM OWNERSHIP

Condominiums[1] have become an increasingly popular method[2] of combining the convenience of apartment rental with the psychological

---

[1] "Condominium" is a Latin word meaning joint ownership or control. *Webster's Third New International Dictionary* 473 (1969). When applied to housing, the term connotes individual ownership of one or more units of airspace in a multi-unit structure, together with a proportionate undivided interest in the land and other common areas and facilities that serve the structure. These common areas and facilities, which are owned in common with other unit owners, include areas such as hallways, parking facilities, heating plants, recreational areas, and commercial facilities.

[2] Based on figures compiled by the Department of Commerce in 1978, new starts for condominiums (156,000) represented 7.7 percent of all new construction starts compared to 5.9 percent in 1977. See Bureau of Census, *Construction Report Series C-20* (March 1979).

(2) How long the property is held prior to sale and what is the scope and nature of the taxpayer's efforts to sell the property;
(3) To what extent the taxpayer has subdivided, developed, and advertised the property and whether he has employed a business office and sales representatives under his control to promote the sales; and
(4) How frequent and continuous are the sales.[116]

The fact that a taxpayer has a history of being a "dealer" is relevant, but does not preclude the taxpayer from qualifying for capital gain treatment if the particular property involved was held primarily for "investment" purposes.[117]

[2] Statutory Relief for the Investor-Subdivider

In enacting I.R.C. § 1237, Congress recognized the plight of the investor who might be required to subdivide the property to dispose of it at a reasonable price and yet who because of his subdivision activities would probably be denied capital gain treatment.[118] Section 1237 provides that if certain requirements are met, the taxpayer (other than a corporation) will not be characterized as a dealer merely because he subdivides real estate for purposes of its sale. However, this statutory relief will not lie if the subdivider-taxpayer was previously a "dealer" with respect to the particular property being sold or is a "dealer" with respect to any other real property in the year of sale.[119] In addition, the taxpayer may not make any improvements on the property being sold that substantially enhance the value of such property.[120] Unless the property is acquired by inheritance or devise, the taxpayer must hold the property for at least five years prior to its sale.[121] However, even if the taxpayer's land qualifies in all respects under Section 1237, gain will be treated as ordinary income to the extent of 5 percent of the selling price in and after the taxable year in which the sixth lot or parcel is sold from the tract.[122]

---

[116] E.g., Howell v. Comm'r, 57 T.C. 546 (1972), *acq.* 1974-2 C.B. 3; Estate of Freeland v. Comm'r, 393 F.2d 573 (9th Cir. 1968), *cert. denied* 393 U.S. 845 (1968) *rehearing denied* 393 U.S. 956 (1968).
[117] E.g., Scheuber v. Comm'r, 371 F.2d 996 (7th Cir. 1967).
[118] S. Rep. No. 1622, 83d Cong., 2d Sess. 115 (1954).
[119] I.R.C. § 1237(a)(1).
[120] I.R.C. § 1237(a)(2).
[121] I.R.C. § 1237(a)(3).
[122] I.R.C. § 1237(b)(1). For a more in-depth discussion of I.R.C. § 1237, see Robinson, *Federal Income Taxation of Real Estate* ¶ 12.05[3] (1973). Also, see Sills, "The 'Dealer-Investor' Problem: Observations, Analysis, and Suggestions for Future Development," 2 J. of Real Est. Tax. 51-67 (1974).

that the Internal Revenue Service will consent to a revocation of such election (made prior to promulgation of final regulations) if the request is made within a reasonable time after the final regulations are issued. Accordingly, after the regulations are published, taxpayers will have the flexibility to change their method for reporting gain on such contingent sales if the need should arise.

Under the typical purchase-money mortgage arrangement, the deferred-payment method would not be available, under prior or present law, even with respect to a sale by a cash-basis taxpayer, since secured notes of this type are in most cases readily salable.[113] Moreover, if the seller-mortgagee does not report the full face value of the note in the year of sale and it is subsequently determined that the note when received was the cash equivalent of some portion of its face value, the seller will be charged with ordinary income when the balance of the note's face value is collected, even though the sale of the underlying property qualifies for capital gain treatment.[114] Accordingly, the only way the seller-mortgagee can obtain deferral in the recognition of his taxable gain on the sale would be for the taxpayer not to "elect out" of the installment method for reporting his gain.

¶ 9.05 CAPITAL GAIN TREATMENT FOR THE INVESTOR-SUBDIVIDER UNDER I.R.C. § 1237

[1] Tax Status as Dealer vs. Investor

Gain or loss on the sale or exchange of real estate held by the taxpayer as inventory or primarily for sale to customers in the ordinary course of his trade or business will be taxed as ordinary "dealer" income or loss rather than as capital gain or loss.[115] The determination of whether the sale has been made in the ordinary course of trade or business depends upon all the surrounding facts and circumstances in each particular case. However, the following factors are frequently cited by the Service and the courts in deciding whether "investment" property or "dealer" property is being sold:

(1) Whether the taxpayer acquired the property with the intention of holding it for investment purposes or with the purpose of selling it to customers in the ordinary course of his trade or business, and what the taxpayer's intentions were in this regard at the time of sale or exchange;

---

[113] E.g., Ruth Iron Co. v. Comm'r, 26 F.2d 30 (8th Cir. 1928).
[114] Culbertson v. Comm'r, 14 T.C. 1421 (1950).
[115] I.R.C. §§ 1221(1), 1231(b)(1). See Malat v. Riddell, 383 U.S. 569 (1966).

recovery in transactions where the gross profit or the total contract price (or both) cannot be readily ascertained."[112] Under the new law, if there is a stated maximum selling price, income from the sale will be reported on a pro rata basis with respect to each installment payment by using the maximum selling price to determine the total contract price and gross profit ratio. The maximum selling price will be determined based on the "four corners" of the contract of sale as the largest price which could be paid to the seller, assuming all contingencies, formulas, and so forth, operate in the seller's favor; however, incidental or remote contingencies will not be taken into account in making any such determination. If it is subsequently determined that a contingency will not be satisfied, causing the maximum selling price to be reduced, the seller's income from the sale will be recomputed, and the taxpayer would then report reduced income with respect to each installment payment received in the taxable year of adjustment as well as subsequent taxable years. If the seller has already reported more income than the total recomputed income, the excess will be deductible as a loss in the year of adjustment.

Example. Seller owns a shopping center with an adjusted basis in the Seller's hands of $300,000 and agrees to sell the property to Buyer based on their understanding that Buyer will pay each year to Seller over the next six years $50,000 plus 10 percent of his gross rental income, but in no event shall seller receive more than $100,000 in any of the six years.

The maximum selling price is $600,000, and the ratio of gross profit ($300,000) to contract price ($600,000) is 50 percent, so one-half of each payment is regarded as taxable income.

If the selling price is so indefinite that no maximum selling price can be calculated, but the price is payable over a definite period of time, the taxpayer will be allowed to recoup his tax basis ratably over the payment period. In a case where both the selling price and payment period are indefinite the regulations will permit a ratable basis recovery over some reasonable period of time.

Example. In the previous example, if there were no maximum payment amount, each year Seller would be allowed to recover his $300,000 basis ratably over the six-year payment period, and accordingly, $50,000 of each payment in each of the six years would be treated as a non-taxable return of his capital.

Until final regulations are promulgated with respect to contingent sales, the taxpayer may not be in a position to decide whether to elect not to utilize installment reporting. However, it is anticipated

---

[112] Section 2 of the Act adding new I.R.C. § 453(i)(2), effective for dispositions after October 19, 1980.

receivables from lot sales. The position of the Service under prior law was that "the obligations of the purchaser received by the vendor are to be considered as an amount realized to the extent of their fair market value...[and] only in rare and extraordinary cases does property have no fair market value."[109] However, in *Ennis v. Comm'r,* the Tax Court held that such installment land contractual obligations were not cash equivalent and "amount realized" to a cash-basis vendor where the contract of sale "merely requires future payments and no notes, mortgages, or other evidence of indebtedness such as commonly change hands in commerce, which could be recognized as the equivalent of cash...."[110] In a subsequent decision involving the same contract, the Service argued that land contracts such as the one in the case were freely bought and sold in Michigan and accordingly have ascertainable fair market values. Again, the Tax Court held that the particular contract involved was not cash equivalent because the contract was not readily salable at a reasonable discount and hence had no ascertainable market value.[111] Despite these decisions, the Service steadfastly maintained its position; hence, it would appear that under prior law the deferred-payment method could be safely used only where the contract has no ascertainable market value because the credit standing of the purchaser-debtor was poor, the condition or value of the underlying property was speculative, the total consideration to be received by the seller was subject to contingencies (e.g., geared to future cash flow), or the contract was nonassignable.

However, under the Installment Sales Revision Act of 1980, installment reporting is now applicable to sales with a contingent selling price; for example, where the amount to be paid for some real estate depends upon future earnings. Now that Congress has expanded the use of installment reporting, it intends to limit use of the deferred-payment method to those "rare and extraordinary cases" involving contingent sales—when the fair market value of the purchaser's obligation cannot reasonably be ascertained. The new law expressly authorizes the Treasury Department to promulgate regulations "providing for ratable basis

---

[109] Reg. § 1-453-6(a).

[110] 17 T.C. 465, 470 (1951).

[111] Estate of Ennis v. Comm'r, 23 T.C. 799, 802 (1955), *nonacq.* 1956-1 C.B. 6. But see Warren Jones Co. v. Comm'r, wherein the Ninth Circuit reversed the Tax Court in holding a cash-basis vendor taxable upon receipt of an installment contractual obligation even though the contract was salable at a 42 percent discount from the face value. The Ninth Circuit concluded that the contract had an ascertainable fair market value notwithstanding that it may not have been cash equivalent. 524 F.2d 788 (1975), *rev'g* 60 T.C. 663 (1973).

kind exchange will not be treated as a "payment" for purposes of installment-method reporting. Thus, in reporting gain on the exchange under the installment method, where an installment obligation is received in addition to the like-kind property, the gross profit will be the amount of gain recognized on the exchange if the installment obligation were satisfied in full at its face amount. Also, the total contract price will not include the value of the like-kind property, but instead will consist solely of the sum of the money and the fair market value of other property received, plus the face amount of the installment obligation.[107]

[7] Using the Deferred-Payment Method to Report Gain

In some limited situations it may be possible for a *cash-basis* taxpayer to avoid reporting gain where the entire selling price is not received in the year of sale and where the statutory requirements for utilizing the installment method of reporting have not been met. Under prior case law, installment reporting was generally not allowed unless the selling price was fixed and determinable. Under the deferred-payment method (also known as the cost-recovery method), if all that the cash-basis seller received was a mere contractual obligation of the purchaser to pay the purchase price, and the contract itself was neither readily negotiable nor readily capable of being valued, the seller need not have reported any gain on the sale until he recovered his cost basis in the property. Such obligation would not be equivalent to the receipt of cash.[108]

The obvious advantage of the deferred-payment method over the installment method for reporting income is that the seller will have the full use of the cash proceeds of the sale without diminution by any tax payment until the installment payments equal his cost basis in the property. However, unlike the installment method, the gain will not be spread over the life of the contract, but will instead be bunched in the final years of the installment period.

Under the typical installment land contract, the seller retains legal title as security until the purchaser has either fully paid the purchase price or made sufficient installment payments to warrant transfer of title. Unless unusual conditions are stipulated in the land contract, such contracts are normally salable at a steep discount. Indeed, to assemble additional working capital, land developers frequently will factor their

---

[107] Section 2 of the Act adding new I.R.C. § 453(f)(6), effective for dispositions after October 19, 1980.
[108] Burnet v. Logan, 283 U.S. 404 (1931). See Johnston v. Comm'r, 14 T.C. 560 (1950); Reg. § 1.453-(6)(a)(2).

payer and/or the taxpayer's spouse. The general purpose of the new law is to deter transactions designed to give the related purchaser the benefit of depreciation deduction based upon a stepped-up cost basis prior to the time the seller is required to include in income the gain on the installment sale. For transactions to which the special rule applies, the deferred payments will be deemed to be received in the tax year in which the sale occurs.[102] The new law also changes the definition of related persons for purposes of I.R.C. § 1239(a), which, to conform to the new installment-sale rule, precludes capital gain treatment for gain on the sale of depreciable property between related parties.[103]

However, in the case of transfers that are treated as tax-free transfers to a controlled corporation or partnership,[104] the present law will continue to apply and will not be affected by this provision. Also, new I.R.C. § 453(g)(2) offers an "escape-hatch" by providing that the new rule will not apply if it is established to the satisfaction of the Commissioner that the sale did not have as one of its principal purposes the avoidance of federal income taxes. Thus, the special rules will not apply if, at the time of the installment sale, the husband and wife are legally separated under a decree of divorce or separate maintenance, or if the sale occurs pursuant to a settlement in a proceeding that culminates in a decree of divorce or separate maintenance.

[6] Liberalization of Rules for Like-Kind Exchanges Coupled With Installment Sales

Under present law, the transfer of property for cash payments and like-kind property may qualify for both installment-method reporting and non-recognition treatment with respect to gain attributable to the like-kind exchange.[105] In such case, the gain to be recognized under the installment method is the total gain realized on the transaction, less the gain eligible for non-recognition under the like-kind ("tax-free exchange") provisions. However, under prior law, the value of the like-kind property received by the seller is considered in determining the amount of the selling price, the contract price, and the payments received for purposes of the installment sale rules.[106] Under the new law, property permitted to be received without recognition of gain in a like-

---

[102] Section 2 of the Act adding new I.R.C. § 453(g) effective for dispositions after October 19, 1980.

[103] Section 5 of the Act amending I.R.C. §§ 1239(b), 1239(c).

[104] See I.R.C. §§ 351, 362, 721, and 723.

[105] See I.R.C. § 1031; Rev. Rul. 65-155, 1965-1 C.B. 356. See discussion at ¶ 8.02.

[106] Rev. Rul. 65-155, 1965-1 C.B. 356; Clinton H. Mitchell, 42 T.C. 953, 965 (1964); Albert W. Turner, T.C. Memo. 1977-437.

[5] Sales to Related Parties Restricted

To eliminate past tax abuse in use of the installment method by related parties, the new law imposes stringent rules with respect to installment sales to related parties who subsequently dispose of the property and also with respect to sales of depreciable property (including real estate) between closely related parties.

[a] Restrictions on Intra-Family Transfers of Appreciated Property

Under prior law, a taxpayer was allowed to make an installment sale of appreciated property to a spouse, child, or some other related party who could then "cash out" by immediately reselling the property. The seller would thus achieve deferral of recognition of gain while cash proceeds were received within the related party group. In addition, the related-party purchaser would receive a cost basis in the party (including the portion of the purchase price payable in the future) and thus recognize gain or loss only on the post-resale appreciation or depreciation in the value of the property. In the leading case, *Rushing* v. *Comm'r*, the test was held to be that in order to obtain the deferral benefits, the "seller may not directly or indirectly have control over the proceeds or possess the economic benefit therefrom."[100] Effective for installment sales (first dispositions) after May 14, 1980, a resale by the related buyer will generate gain recognition for the original seller (on the basis of the gross profit ratio) to the extent that the amount realized on the resale exceeds the payments received on the installment sale.[101]

[b] New Accrual Rules for Sales of Depreciable Property Between Related Parties

Under the new law, the accrual method of accounting is, in effect, required for deferred-payment sales of depreciable property, including real estate, between the following related parties: (1) the taxpayer and its spouse; (2) the taxpayer and a partnership or corporation that is 80 percent owned by the taxpayer and/or its spouse; and (3) between partnerships and corporations that are 80 percent owned by the tax-

---

[100] 52 T.C. 888 (1969) *aff'd* 441 F.2d 593 (5th Cir. 1971).
[101] Section 2 of the Act adding new I.R.C. §§ 453(e), 453(f).

perhaps incur some gift-tax but no income-tax liability, since the taxpayer would not be benefitted in any material way.[94] However, this argument overlooks the fact that the installment buyer, as donee, would directly benefit by obtaining a cost basis through the installment sale (which reflects future payments that will never be made) rather than a carryover basis (equal to the donor's basis), as would have been required in the case of a direct gift.[95] Effective for installment obligations becoming unenforceable after October 19, 1980, the new rule is that such cancellation will be treated as a disposition of the obligation and that the seller will recognize gain or loss to the extent of the difference between its basis and its fair market value at the time of disposition.[96] In addition, under the new law the same tax treatment will apply when an installment seller dies holding an installment obligation. Any previously unreported gain from an installment sale will be recognized by a deceased seller's estate if the obligation is transferred or transmitted by bequest, devise, or inheritance to the obligor, or is cancelled by the executor.[97]

[c] Distribution of Installment Obligation Pursuant to Section 337 Liquidation Allowed Under New Law

A recurring problem for stockholders in a corporation holding real estate has been that while a shareholder was allowed to utilize the installment method to report gain on the sale of stock to an unrelated buyer in the event of a one-year liquidation under I.R.C. § 337 (which eliminates tax on the corporate level), the liquidating distribution of an installment obligation would, under prior law,[98] precipitate recognition of the gain for the distributee-shareholder. This created a problem where the corporation desired to sell its real estate, but the purchaser refused to accept stock in the corporation. Effective for distributions of installment obligations after March 31, 1980, the new rule provides that any installment obligation received by a distributee-shareholder during a Section 337 liquidation will not, subject to a few exceptions, be treated as a payment received by the shareholder in exchange for stock. Instead, the shareholder will be allowed to report installment gain as payments are received on the installment obligation.[99]

---

[94] This cancellation technique is based on the dubious holding in Miller v. Usry, 160 F. Supp. 368 (W.D. La. 1958).

[95] I.R.C. § 1015.

[96] Section 2 of the Act adding new I.R.C. § 453B(f).

[97] Section 3 adding new I.R.C. § 691(a)(5) effective for decedents dying after October 19, 1980.

[98] See prior I.R.C. § 453(d).

[99] Section 2 of the Act adding new I.R.C. § 453(h).

or the seller disposes of the obligation instead of holding it until it is collected, gain or loss will be recognized in the taxable year of such satisfaction or disposition equal to the difference between the seller's basis in the obligation and (1) the amount realized, in the case of satisfaction at other than face value or in the case of a sale or exchange, or (2) the fair market value of the obligation at the time of disposition, if such disposition is otherwise than by sale or exchange.[90] The basis of an installment obligation is the excess of the face value of the obligation over an amount equal to the income that would be reported were the obligation to be satisfied in full.[91] The Code also provides that any gain or loss so resulting will be considered as resulting from the sale or exchange of the property in respect to which the seller had received the installment obligation.[92] The impact of this rule is generally to tax in the year of sale or other disposition the profit from the installment sale that would otherwise be deferred over the installment period.

Example. Returning to the facts in the previous example, if the purchaser were to make its first $5,000 installment payment in 1982 (instead of 1981), and prior to such payment the seller sold the notes (totaling $50,000 in face value) in 1982 for $45,000, the seller would in that year recognize gain in the amount of $10,000. Such amount equals the difference between the amount realized on the sale of the notes ($45,000) and the seller's basis in the installment obligations (35,000), which basis equals the excess of the $50,000 face value of the notes over the $15,000 amount of income the seller would have reported over the installment period had the notes been satisfied in full ($18,000 gross profit ÷ $60,000 contract price, or 30 percent of the $50,000 face value of the notes equals $15,000).[93]

[b] Cancellation of Installment Obligation, by Gift or Bequest, Is a Disposition

Under prior law, it had been argued that the installment obligation disposition rules could be avoided by making gift cancellations of the obligation or the installments as they became due. Specifically, it was held that by making an installment sale and then cancelling the obligation, or by making a number of installment payments, the seller should

---

[90] See prior I.R.C. § 453(d)(1); Reg. § 1.453-9(b)(1).
[91] See prior I.R.C. § 453(d)(2); Reg. § 1.453-9(b)(2).
[92] See prior I.R.C. § 453(d)(1); Reg. § 1.453-9(a).
[93] For a more in-depth discussion, see Robinson, *Federal Income Taxation of Real Estate* ¶ 12.03 (1973).

Example. Seller transfers title to Blackacre worth $100,000, which is encumbered with a $40,000 mortgage and which has an adjusted basis in the seller's hands of $80,000 to the purchaser on January 1, 1981 in exchange for $10,000 in cash at the closing and a $50,000 purchase-money mortgage from the purchaser. The mortgage is payable in annual installments of $5,000, bears an annual interest rate of 6 percent, and provides that the first installment will become due and payable on June 1, 1981. Commissions and selling expenses amount to $2,000. The results are as follows:

Gross profit on sale:		
Selling price		$100,000
Less:		
Adjusted basis	$80,000	
Selling expenses	2,000	82,000
		$18,000
Contràct price:		
Selling price		$100,000
Less existing mortgage		40,000
		$60,000
Payments received in year of sale:		
Cash at closing		$10,000
Installment received 6/1/79		5,000
		$15,000

Gain reportable in year of sale:

$$\frac{\$18,000 \text{ (gross profit)} \times \$15,000 \text{ (payments in year of sale)}}{\$60,000 \text{ (contract price)}} = \$4,500$$

Accordingly, $4,500 is reported as taxable gain in the year of sale (1981) and 18/60, or 30 percent, of each of the $5,000 installments received in 1982 through 1991 ($1,500) will be reported as gain, and the balance ($3,500) will be treated as a nontaxable return of the seller's basis in the property. Over the remaining nine-year installment period, the sum of the gain to be reported (9 × $1,500 = 13,500) plus the gain reported in 1981 ($4,500) will equal the total gross profit or gain to be realized on the sale ($18,000).

[4] Sale or Other Disposition of Installment Obligations Under the New Law

[a] General Rule

If the installment obligation is satisfied at other than its face value,

We disagree. It has been long settled that *secured notes stand on the same plane as unsecured notes for purposes of the installment sale limitation on year-of-sale payments.* Both are mere promises to pay. The maker of either instrument permanently surrenders nothing of value except his promise. *The giving of security is not payment and does not transform the promise to pay into a completed payment.* It merely makes the promise more certain of fulfillment.

The value or cash-equivalency of the security cannot adequately serve as criterion in the present context. It would be impractical for the taxpayer and the I.R.S. to evaluate a security and determine whether its 'quality' was such as to create some indeterminate and indeterminable level of risk that the note payee would or would not get paid. Moreover, consideration of the 'quality' of security would unfairly penalize those most careful and successful in protecting themselves against buyer default, who would thereby disqualify themselves from the tax advantages of installment reporting. Hence, the government's certainty of collection' theory must be rejected.[85]

However, as a note of caution to tax planners, remember that third-party notes and other marketable obligations (prior to default by the purchaser) are deemed (under both prior and present law) to be payments to the seller.[86]

[3] Illustration of How To Report Gain Under Installment Method

If a timely election not to use installment reporting is not filed, and at least one payment is to be received in a taxable year subsequent to the year of sale, the seller of real estate may utilize the installment method by reporting as gain, each year, that portion of each installment payment that corresponds to the ratio of "gross profit"[87] on the sale (total gain to be realized on the sale) to the total "contract price."[88] The remainder of the payment is treated as a nontaxable return of basis or capital.[89]

---

[85] *Id.* at 85,051 (footnotes omitted and emphasis added).

[86] See note 66 *supra*.

[87] Reg. § 1.453-1(b). Gross profit means the selling price less the seller's adjusted basis in the realty, and, in the case of a sale of real estate by a person other than a dealer, is reduced by commissions and other selling expenses. *Id.*

[88] The contract price is the selling price; however, it does not include the amount of any existing mortgage, except to the extent that the mortgage assumed, or taken subject to, exceeds the seller's basis in the property. Reg. § 1.453-4(c).

[89] Reg. § 1.453-1(b)(1).

(3) The escrow should be irrevocable and neither party should be able to accelerate the time of payments;
(4) The purchaser should be entitled to the income earned on the escrow deposits; and,
(5) Future escrow payments should be made subject to a "substantial restriction" (in addition to the payment schedule) with respect to the seller's right to receive payment. This insures that some risk that the future payments might not be made to the seller must exist. (This item is of singular importance.) An example of the latter, posed in Revenue Ruling 77-294, is a condition in the escrow agreement that the seller would forfeit all rights to the amounts held in escrow if the seller should violate its covenant not to compete at any time during the escrow period.

A very important development under the new law, effective for dispositions after October 19, 1980, is new I.R.C. § 453(f)(3), which provides that, except for demand obligations and certain readily traded securities, "the term 'payment' does not include the receipt of evidence of indebtedness of the person acquiring the property *whether or not payment of such indebtedness is guaranteed by another person.*" (Emphasis added.) Also, the Senate Finance Committee report makes it clear that the rule applies in order to prevent the purchase-money obligation of the purchaser being counted as a "payment" under the installment method, regardless of who the guarantor is, even if it is a bank issuing a standby letter of credit. The Tenth Circuit, in *Sprague* v. *United States*,[84] reached the same result under prior law. The rationale underlying this new rule is more important than the letter of the rule itself. It would seem to follow that the real issue is not whether the seller is relying on the general credit of the purchaser. If so, almost any kind of security will pass muster under the doctrine of constructive receipt. Payments taken into account as being received in a taxable year would not include the purchaser's obligation of future payment, whether dischargeable in money or other property, unless the obligation (e.g., demand obligations) expressly falls beyond the scope of I.R.C. § 453(f)(3). Indeed, the Tenth Circuit, in *Sprague* v. *United States,* adopted this line of reasoning:

> The Government says the nature of the security makes the notes certain of collection. Because [the seller] Pelham was virtually guaranteed collection of cash equalling the value of the security, says the Government, the security is the equivalent of cash and Pelham should be treated as if it had collected that cash at the time of sale.

---

[84] See note 82 *supra.*

seller agreed to cancel the deed of trust in consideration of the purchaser depositing the balance of the purchase price with an escrow agent. As noted earlier,[81] arrangements of this sort are commonplace. Frequently, the seller of undeveloped land will refuse to subordinate its lien position (e.g., take a second mortgage) to that of an institutional lender willing to make a first-mortgage land development loan to the purchaser-developer, and the escrow solution may be the only way to enable the purchaser to go forward with the financing of the necessary improvements on the land.

In a recent Court of Appeals decision, *Sprague* v. *United States* (decided on August 14, 1980),[82] involving the partnership sale of stock on the installment basis, where the seller assigned the buyer's notes for the balance of the price as substituted collateral to its creditor-banks to secure the release of the stock, the Tenth Circuit held (for purposes of the 30 percent limitation rule) that the partnership had not constructively received the value of non-cashable letters of credit issued to the banks to secure the buyer's notes because the notes were mere promises to pay, and the security did not constitute payment of the notes. By way of dictum, the court suggested that the status of a cash-equivalent escrow still remains in doubt: "As reflected in the foregoing [cash escrow] cases, the essence of that determination is the effective relief of a purchaser, at the time of sale, from his obligation to pay, and the substitution of an intermediary as obligor. The purchaser sheds his obligation by irrevocably placing in escrow sufficient cash or its equivalent to pay the full amount of his debt to the seller. At that point, the transaction is essentially complete for the purchaser, who has no further interest in it. The escrow agent becomes a substitute obligor if, at the time of sale, the seller is able to look to the escrowed funds for unconditional periodic payment of the purchase price."[83] Accordingly, pending more conclusive judicial review of the Service position, the prudent course of action would be for the real estate seller to avoid any cash or cash-equivalent escrow arrangement. If that is not possible, the following precautionary measures should be taken to help preclude treatment of the escrowed assets as payments in the year of escrow (generally, the year of sale) under I.R.C. § 453:

    (1) If possible, the escrow should be effected subsequent to the year of sale;

    (2) The escrow should be a true installment obligation;

---

[81] See discussion at ¶¶ 9.01[1][d], 9.01[2].

[82] 627 F.2d 1044, 1980-2 U.S.T.C. ¶ 9621 at 85,049 (10th Cir. 1980) *rev'g* 42 A.F.T.R.2d 78-5877, 1978-2 U.S.T.C. ¶ 9650 (W.D. Okla. 1978).

[83] See dictum at 1980-2 U.S.T.C. ¶ 9621 at 85,053.

Obviously, the repeal of the 30 percent limitation under the new law obviates the use of such a circumvention device. However, use of escrow arrangements is commonplace in real estate financing, especially with respect to subdivision financing.[77] Consequently, the question remains as to whether such escrows will be treated as "payments" (at the date of escrow), under both the new law and the doctrine of constructive receipt, when they are merely being utilized to achieve a business, rather than tax avoidance, purpose. In a typical escrow situation, the seller has no enforceable right to receive the cash or certificates of deposit that have been placed in escrow prior to the agreed-upon release date except when there is a default in payment by the purchaser. If at each stage the escrow deposits are irrevocable, and no contingency will accelerate the time of the payment of the installment obligations, and if the purchaser continues to remain liable for the payment of the remaining installments and recognizes tax liability for the interest earned on the escrow deposits, it would appear that sufficient limitations on the purchaser's right to receive the escrow payments or deposits exist. This would forestall operation of the doctrine of constructive receipt. However, in Revenue Ruling 73-451,[78] the Service ruled that under the foregoing circumstances a sale of real property did not qualify for installment reporting where the entire purchase price was placed into escrow—and a deed delivered to the purchaser—at the time of the sale because the buyer's obligations had been met in full and "the taxpayer (seller) was not relying on the installment obligation of the buyer, but upon the escrow deposit to make the payments in connection with the sale...."

Moreover, in a reversal of its earlier position,[79] the Service ruled in 1977 that the substitution of a cash escrow as security (in lieu of a deed of trust) constituted a payment of the remaining unpaid balance due on the installment obligation.[80] Revenue Ruling 77-294 involved a seller of land who received 10 percent of the purchase price as a down payment and six equal interest-bearing notes that were secured by a deed of trust due on an annual basis. Later in the same year of sale, when the purchaser sought to subdivide the property and sell individual lots, the

---

total sales price in cash and insisted instead that the funds be deposited in escrow as security for the installment obligation of the purchaser. In *Oden,* certificates of deposit with principal amounts and maturity dates corresponding to the purchaser's installment obligations were placed in escrow as security, and it was concluded that the sellers looked to the certificates for payment (and not merely as security) rather than the obligations of the purchasers to make the installment payments.

[77] See discussion at ¶ 9.01[1].
[78] 1973-2 C.B. 158.
[79] Rev. Rul. 68-246, 1968-1 C.B. 198.
[80] Rev. Rul. 77-294, 1977-2 C.B. 173.

percent of the "total contract price" is received, under the present rules there is still a deferral of recognition of 10 percent of the gain. However, as a note of caution to tax planners, under present as well as prior law—where the purchaser purchases the real estate subject to a preexisting mortgage (or assumes the mortgage)—any amount by which the mortgage amount exceeds the seller's basis in the property is part of the "total contract price" (as defined in ¶ 9.04[3]) and such excess will be deemed to be cash received by the seller in the year of sale.[75] Also, the new law does not help resolve the issue of whether or not a mortgage that the seller, rather than the purchaser, is required to pay is properly treated as being within the ambit of the foregoing rule.

[c] Use of Escrow Arrangements and Third-Party Guarantees Under the New Law

As noted earlier, one way to bypass the 30 percent requirement under prior law was to escrow all of the purchaser's initial payments in excess of the 30 percent amount on the condition that the seller must render further performance before it was entitled to receive the escrow funds. However, if, prior to the escrow, the seller had the unconditional right to receive the payments, the amounts placed in escrow during the year of sale were deemed to have been received by the seller at the time of the escrow under the doctrine of "constructive receipt."[76]

---

[75] Reg. § 1.453-4(c). In two letter rulings, conveyances of land were expressly made subject to the unpaid balances owing on the prior indebtedness against the property. In both instances, all payments of the purchaser were to be made directly to the seller, who was obligated to continue to make payments on the underlying mortgage indebtedness. The Service concluded that even though the purchaser itself would not make direct payments to the mortgagee, the property was sold "subject to the mortgage"; accordingly, the mortgage comprised part of the payments by the purchaser in the year of sale (to the extent the mortgage exceeded the seller's basis) and part of the selling price of the property for purposes of the 30 percent limitation on the use of installment reporting. IRS Ltr. Ruls. 7814010 (Dec. 23, 1977), and 7814011 (Dec. 29, 1977), CCH IRS Letter Rulings Reports. Cf. Stonecrest Corp., 24 T.C. 659 (1955), and United Pac. Corp., 39 T.C. 721 (1963), with F.J. Voight, 68 T.C. 99 (1977).

[76] See Reg. § 1.451-2, which defines and discusses the doctrine of constructive receipt. See Williams v. United States, 219 F.2d 523 (5th Cir. 1955), wherein title to timber land immediately passed to the purchaser, and prior to escrow, the purchaser had been willing to immediately pay the full purchase price. Cf. Pozzi v. Comm'r, 49 T.C. 119 (1967) and Oden v. Comm'r, 56 T.C. 569 (1971), appeal to Fifth Circuit dsm'd (1971), wherein the Tax Court seemed to rely on substance over form principles in holding that installment reporting should not be allowed because the parties in both cases had not intended a bona fide installment sale. In *Pozzi,* the seller rejected the purchaser's offer to pay the

Perhaps the most significant change under the new law for sellers of real property is that this 30 percent limitation has been eliminated.[74] Consequently, under present law, effective for dispositions even prior to October 19, 1980 (if they occur in taxable years ending after such date), regardless of how much is received in the year of sale, the tax becomes due proportionately as payments are received. For example, if 90

---

780. However, the Service might have argued that the controlling stockholder in effect first contributed the property to the corporation, in which event the corporation would receive a "substituted" (carryover) basis in the property (under I.R.C. § 362(a)) or, in the latter alternative, the original seller would receive a "substituted" basis in its stock (under I.R.C. § 358(a)) so that in either case the seller would be taxed on the entire gain without benefit of installment treatment. See Russell Inc., 36 T.C. 965 (1961). Accordingly, if a newly formed corporation was involved, the transaction must have been so structured that it would not have been regarded as a tax-free exchange under I.R.C. § 351. In addition, the intermediary corporation that purchased the property on the installment basis should have issued its notes and become liable to the original seller for payment and given security to the seller for its installment obligation; otherwise, it might have been treated as a mere agent or conduit of the seller, in which event the transaction would be attacked by the Service as a cash sale by the original seller. Compare Rogers v. Comm'r, 1 T.C. 629 (1943) wherein these formalities were respected and the Tax Court held there was substance in the sale to the intermediary corporation because it served a real business purpose in relieving the purchasers of personal liability for the balance due on the installment obligations of the corporation whose stock it had acquired from the seller, with McInerney v. Comm'r, 82 F.2d 665 (5th Cir. 1936), wherein the intermediary corporation had given neither notes nor security to the seller, had no assets and business, and whose only function was to complete the particular sale and transfer. Id. at 667. A variation on this theme would have been for the seller to utilize as the intermediary a family member or other controlled individual who, after purchasing the property on the installment basis, would have made an all-cash sale to the third-party purchaser. However, this approach yielded mixed results for the taxpayer wishing to bypass the 30 percent limitation. Compare Nye v. Comm'r, 407 F. Supp. 1345 (D.N.C. 1975), wherein a prearranged sale of stock by wife to husband was so structured as to enable the latter to use the cash proceeds to meet his loan obligations, and the transaction qualified, with Wrenn v. Comm'r, 67 T.C., 576 (1976), where the wife-installment purchaser was deemed to be a mere "straw" acting as a conduit for the husband-seller, since there was no purpose for the transaction other than tax avoidance.

[73] A final technique for satisfying the 30 percent test while providing the seller with sufficient cash in the year of sale would have been for the seller to immediately sell or otherwise dispose of the purchaser's notes for additional cash in the year of the sale. This approach should not have disqualified the transaction for installment reporting inasmuch as the Treasury regulations acknowledge that the disposition of the purchaser's notes to a third party shall not be deemed a "payment" for purposes of I.R.C. § 453. See Reg. § 1.453-4(c).

[74] Section 2 of the Act repealing I.R.C. § 453(b)(2)(B) and adding new I.R.C. § 453 (b)(1).

arrangements to postpone the seller's receipt of any down payment;[68] (2) refinancing of the property prior to sale;[69] (3) a loan from the buyer to the seller in lieu of a down payment;[70] (4) fragmenting the sale if multiple assets were being sold to the same purchaser;[71] (5) sale to an affiliated entity;[72] and finally, (6) sale of the purchaser's notes to a third party for cash.[73]

---

[68] E.g., Minnie Ebner, 26 T.C. 962 (1956), *acq.* 1956-2 C.B. 5. See discussion of escrow devices under present law at ¶ 9.04[2][c].

[69] As noted earlier, payments in the year of sale include only cash paid and the value of other property given by the purchaser to the seller. Accordingly, another circumvention device was for the seller to merely refinance an existing mortgage or to place a mortgage in the property prior to its sale to the purchaser. By doing so, the seller might have been able to "cash out" more than 30 percent of the value of the real estate without disqualifying itself for subsequent installment sale treatment, provided that the financing transaction was not linked to the sale negotiations with the purchaser.

[70] Another possibility would have been for the purchaser to reduce the amount of the down payment in the year of sale to less than 30 percent of the selling price and then make a loan to the seller to meet his immediate cash requirements. If the amount purporting to be a loan was evidenced by the personal, unqualified obligation on the part of the seller to repay the sums advanced and was not payable out of the proceeds of the installment sale, the cash advance to the seller would not have been regarded as part of the payment in the year of sale even though the seller received the advance in the same year. Rev. Rul. 55-234, 1953-2 C.B. 29. Cf. James Hammond, 1 T.C. 198 (1942). See also Minnie Ebner, note 68 *supra.*

[71] If multiple assets were being sold to the same purchaser (e.g., sale of an apartment building plus sale of personal property such as refrigerators and air conditioners) and the sales documentation reflected separate sales of each asset, it may have been possible for the seller to receive all cash for some assets while taking less than 30 percent for others and thereby obtain in cash more than 30 percent of the aggregate selling price without disqualifying the transaction for installment reporting. In *Monaghan v. Comm'r,* the taxpayer who owned a retail store sold his inventory for cash while separately selling the remainder of the business assets under an installment sales contract. The Tax Court held that the cash received for the inventory did not have to be combined with the cash received from the other sale for purposes of the 30 percent test. Consequently, the latter sale qualified for installment reporting even though the total cash received by the seller in the year of sale exceeded more than 30 percent of the total selling price. 40 T.C. 680 (1963), *acq.* 1964-2 B.C. 6. See also Spivey v. Comm'r, 40 T.C. 1051 (1963), *acq.* 1965-2 B.C. 6.

[72] Still another possibility for bypassing the 30 percent requirement would have been for the seller to make an installment sale to a controlled intermediary such as an already existing or newly formed corporation, which would in turn make an all-cash sale to the original purchaser. Alternatively, the stock of the intermediary corporation could have been sold for cash to the original purchaser after the property was sold (on the installment basis) by the original seller to the corporation. See Estate of Henry Rogers v. Comm'r, 1 T.C. 629, 632-633, (1943) *aff'd on other grounds* 143 F.2d 695 (2d Cir. 1944), *cert. denied* 323 U.S.

Under prior law (I.R.C. § 453(b)(2)(B) and present law (I.R.C. § 453(f)(3)), the term "payment" excludes the purchaser's evidence of indebtedness; otherwise, the installment obligation would, under prior law, always have disqualified the transaction from installment reporting and under present law would have precluded the seller from receiving deferral treatment with respect to such purchase-money indebtedness. It would thus have defeated the purpose of the statute. Under present law, the term "payment" does not include such evidence of indebtedness even if such indebtedness is guaranteed by a third party, except for demand obligations and certain readily traded securities.[65] It was frequently difficult to determine whether the payments in the year of sale exceeded 30 percent of the "selling price" of the property being sold,[66] and yet the very utilization of installment reporting depended on a strict showing by the taxpayer that this requirement had been met.[67] Accordingly, sellers were forced to utilize a variety of circumvention devices to avoid the 30 percent limitation. These included the use of: (1) escrow

---

[65] Section 2 of the Act adding new I.R.C. § 453(f)(3).

[66] Payments in the year of sale include not only all cash payments made to the seller (e.g., deposits, option payments, or installment payments applied to the purchase price), but also property other than cash received by the seller, such as the market value of third-party notes and obligations payable to the purchaser. However, payments in the year of sale did not include any indirect payments to third parties for the seller's benefit, such as payments by the purchaser of the seller's liabilities, where such payments were not incurred for the purpose of avoiding the 30 percent limitation rule. Rev. Rul. 73-555, 1973-2 C.B. 159, revoking Rev. Rul. 60-52, 1960-1 C.B. 186; also see United States v. Marshall, 357 F.2d 294 (9th Cir. 1966), wherein it was held that the purchaser's assumption of the seller's current trade liabilities was not "payments" in the year of sale. Nonetheless, attorney's fees, brokerage commissions, and other payments directly related to the sale were treated as payments in the year of sale, if such an arrangement was made to avoid the 30 percent limitation rule. E.g., Wagegro Corp. v. Comm'r, 38 B.T.A. 1225 (1938); Ronald w. Sholund, 50 T.C. 503 (1968) (if such liabilities were specified in the contract to be paid out of the purchase price, and were in fact paid in such tax year). But if such liabilities are not expressly assumed by the purchaser under the terms of the sales contract or escrow and the payments are made by the purchaser after the taxable year of sale of the property, they will not be regarded as "payments" made by the purchaser in the year of sale. E.g., Katherine Watson v. Comm'r, 20 B.T.A. 270 (1930), acq. X-1 C.B. 68.

[67] E.g., Westrom v. Comm'r, 25 T.C.M. 1019 (1966); cf. Lewis Ludlow, 36 T.C. 102 (1961), acq. 1961-2 C.B. 5, wherein the amount received in the year of sale inadvertently exceeded 30 percent of the selling price, but the excess over the intended amount was immediately returned to the purchaser in the year of sale. The Tax Court held that the transaction qualified for installment reporting since the parties had intended to meet the 30 percent requirement, and the refund was made in the year of sale.

property could not utilize the installment method if the total purchase price were payable in a lump sum in a taxable year subsequent to the year of sale. The rationale for this view was simplistic; namely, that the "installment" concept precluded any single payment sale not payable in installments in two or more taxable years. Effective for dispositions after October 19, 1980, and even for those prior to such date that occur in tax years ending after October 19, 1980, gain from the sale of real estate where at least one payment is to be received in a taxable year subsequent to the year of sale will qualify for the installment method, even if no down payment is received by the seller in the year of sale.[61] This liberalization obviously makes qualification much easier for sellers, and even enables a seller receiving a lump-sum payment to shift his recognition of gain to a tax year subsequent to the year of sale by simply requiring in the contract of sale that the payment be made in such subsequent year.

[ii] 30 Percent Limitation on Payments in Year of Sale Eliminated. Under prior law, if a payment was received in the year of sale it could not exceed 30 percent of the gross "selling price" of the property. The total "selling price" of the property includes not only the amount of cash and value of other property received by the seller over the duration of the contract, but also includes the total amount of all mortgages on the property, whether or not the mortgages are assumed by the purchaser.[62] In computing the selling price, the obligations of the purchaser are included at their face amount regardless of their actual market value. Commissions and other selling expenses paid or incurred by the seller reduce neither the amount of the selling price nor the amount of the payments received by the seller in the year of sale.[63] The amount of the selling price must still be reduced by any "imputed interest" under I.R.C. § 483, which may be a tax pitfall for any seller who charges less than 6 percent simple annual interest under the terms of the installment sale contract or purchase-money mortgage.[64]

---

[61] Section 2 of the Act adding new I.R.C. § 453(b)(1).

[62] Reg. § 1.453-4(c).

[63] *Id.*

[64] Note that under the Act the imputed interest rules still apply. I.R.C. § 483 treatment applies only to payments that are due more than six months after the date of sale, under a contract that provides for a selling price of more than $3,000 and that one or more payments are due more than one year from the date of sale. If interest is stipulated in the contract, there will be unstated interest only if the rate is less than: (1) 4 percent per annum simple interest for payments on account of a sale or an exchange of property entered into before July 24, 1975, or (2) 6 percent per annum simple interest for payments on account of a sale or an exchange of property entered into after July 24, 1975. Reg. § 1.483-1.

any disposition of an installment obligation—even by way of gift or cancellation—will generate taxable gain for the holder.

[2] Requirements For Using Installment Method Under New Law

[a] Timely Election Need No Longer Be Filed

Under prior law, a taxpayer who elected to report his gain was required to show a computation of the gross profit from the sale on his income tax return (or on a statement attached thereto) for the year of the sale.[57] Effective for dispositions after October 19, 1980, installment reporting automatically applies to a qualified sale unless the taxpayer affirmatively elects for it not to apply.[58] Unless future Treasury regulations provide otherwise, the choice against installment method reporting must be made on or before the due date for filing the income tax return for the taxable year in which the sale occurs. This due date includes extensions of time for filing. It is anticipated that reporting the entire gain in gross income for the taxable year in which the sale occurs will operate as an election, and that such election will be irrevocable without the consent of the Internal Revenue Service. The tax planner might consider recommending such election to report the entire gain from an installment sale under special circumstances; for example, where gain in the year of sale could be utilized to offset expiring loss carryovers of the taxpayer, or where installment-method gain might be taxed in subsequent higher-tax bracket years of the taxpayer.

[b] Limitations on Payments by Purchaser in Year of Sale Eliminated

[i] Two Payment Rule Eliminated. Under prior law, the Internal Revenue Service[59] and the courts[60] took the position that a seller of real

---

[57] Reg. § 1.453-8(b). Under prior law, the Service had ruled that it would accept a delinquently filed election if made on either a late original return for the year of sale or on an amended return for the year of sale, provided, however, that the statute of limitations had not run with respect to the year of sale and that no prior inconsistent election had been filed. Rev. Rul. 65-297, 1965-2 C.B. 152. Once made, the seller could not revoke the election even by filing an amended return for the year of sale. Rev. Rul. 56-396, 1956-2 C.B. 298.

[58] Section 2 of the Act repealing I.R.C. § 453(b)(1) and adding new I.R.C. § 453(d).

[59] See Rev. Rul. 69-462, 1969-2 C.B. 107, as amplified by Rev. Rul. 71-595, 1971-2 C.B. 223.

[60] E.g., Baltimore Baseball Co. v. United States, 481 F.2d 1283 (Ct. Cl. 1973); 10-42 Corp., 55 T.C. 593 (1971).

bracket and tax liability by spreading the capital gain over the installment period.[54]

(4) Under prior tax law, the seller could reduce the amount of his "preference" income (e.g., the 50 percent untaxed portion of long-term capital gain prior to 1979) subject to the 15 percent minimum tax by offsetting his preference income by the amount of the annual exemption each year during the installment period. Under the new alternative maximum tax for noncorporate taxpayers imposed by the Revenue Act of 1978, the seller may (as of January 1, 1979) be able to reduce his tax rate applicable to the excluded portion (60 percent) of his capital gains from 25 percent to 20 percent or from 20 percent to 10 percent by spreading the amount of the gain over the installment period.[55]

[1] Overview of Changes

In enacting the Installment Sales Revision Act of 1980,[56] Congress effectuated the first major overhaul of the installment sales rules. While the Act provides some new restrictions to eliminate certain tax abuses, the new law simplifies the provisions under I.R.C. § 453 and makes qualification for tax-deferral treatment by the seller much easier and less cumbersome. Among the more significant changes affecting installment sellers of real estate are those that (1) eliminate the 30 percent limitation on payments by the purchaser in the year of sale; (2) do away with the requirement that the purchase price be payable in two or more tax-year installments; (3) qualify sales involving a contingent selling price for installment reporting; and (4) render installment reporting automatic, so that the taxpayer need no longer elect to use this method for reporting gain in order to take advantage of the tax-deferment benefits. However, the Act also provides stringent new rules with respect to sales between related parties and makes it clear that, as a general rule,

---

[54] Revenue Act of 1978 § 402, amending I.R.C. § 1202; Revenue Act of 1978 § 401, repealing I.R.C. §§ 1201(b), 1201(c).

[55] Revenue Act of 1978 § 421(a), adding I.R.C. § 55. See discussion at ¶ 1.05[2][d].

[56] Pub. L. 96-471 (hereinafter cited as "the Act"), enacted October 19, 1980; for its legislative history see H.R. Rep. No. 96-1042 (May 21, 1980); and S. Rep. No. 96-1000 (Sept. 26, 1980). In general, the provisions of the Act are effective for dispositions of property made after October 19, 1980. However, two of the most important liberalizing rules—those eliminating the 30 percent limitation and the two-payment requirement—will apply to transactions occurring in taxable years ending after the date of enactment even if the actual disposition took place before the date, and the related party installment sale rules apply to installment sales (first dispositions) after May 14, 1980.

¶ 9.04 SELLER'S USE OF INSTALLMENT METHOD FOR REPORTING INCOME (I.R.C. § 453) UNDER INSTALLMENT SALES REVISION ACT OF 1980

If a purchaser is able to negotiate an installment purchase contract or purchase-money mortgage with the seller, the seller is entitled to use the installment method for reporting his taxable income (but not loss) from the sale. As explained in the following discussion, this option may be a strong inducement for the seller to enter into such an agreement.

When real property is sold at a gain, the seller must report the entire gain in the year of sale even though payment by the purchaser is deferred over a period of time and the seller receives little if any down payment in the year of sale to fund the payment of the tax liability. However, under the installment sale provisions of I.R.C. § 453, the seller may elect to spread his tax liability over the period of time during which he receives his installment payments. Under this method, a pro rata portion of the total gain to be realized is taxed on the receipt of each payment due under the sales contract or purchase-money mortgage, in which event the following advantages may accrue to the seller:

(1) If the entire gain were taxable in the year of sale, the seller would obviously have less after-tax proceeds from the down payment available for reinvestment purposes. Moreover, absent such election, the seller would be compelled to immediately report the entire gain, notwithstanding that its ultimate receipt would depend upon the solvency and reliability of the purchaser to make the promised payments.

(2) If the gain is taxed at the progressive "ordinary" income tax rates either because the seller is a "dealer" for tax purposes[51] or because the income-producing real estate being sold is subject to depreciation recapture,[52] the spreading of the gain over the installment period may result in a lower tax bracket and lower tax liability for the seller.

(3) Under prior law, if the real estate being sold was either a capital asset or an asset used in the seller's "trade or business,"[53] spreading the capital gain could reduce the individual seller's tax rate on the gain. The maximum alternative rate for noncorporate taxpayers was eliminated on December 31, 1978 under the Revenue Act of 1978. Long-term capital gains are now taxed at the progressive ordinary income rates (except for the excluded portion which is now 60 percent instead of 50 percent); accordingly, under the new law the seller may be able to reduce his tax

---

[51] See discussion at ¶ 9.05[1].
[52] I.R.C. § 1250. See discussion at ¶ 1.05[2][d].
[53] See I.R.C. § 1221 (capital asset) and § 1231 (trade or business property).

receives by assignment the developer's installment sales contracts (usually as a security for the loans); or (3) where, as a result of its lending arrangement, the lender comes within the statutory definition of "developer" or "agent" due to its influence or control over operations of the subdivision.

It is not uncommon for a lender to find itself the owner of a subdivision as a result of a developer's default on a loan, either as a result of foreclosure proceedings or by means of a stock transfer provided for in the loan agreement. Assuming that the lender does not wish to become a member of the land sales industry but only wishes to recoup its losses by sale of the entire unsold portion of the subdivision to another developer, it should obtain an order exempting such a sale of the subdivision from ILSFDA.[48] A sale by the lender, absent such an exemption order, is a violation of ILSFDA. The Statement of Record and the Property Report filed by the developer who defaulted on the loan are no longer valid. If the lender sells the subdivision to a new developer, the sale can be rescinded pursuant to Section 1404(b) of ILSFDA.[49]

Where installment contracts are assigned to the lender as security for a loan or where the lender purchases the installment contracts, it is possible that a lot purchaser has a cause of action against the lender. As of this writing, there has not been any litigation concerning this possibility. However, it is probable that in a situation where the lender was the assignee of lot purchasers' installment agreements as well as the construction lender, a holder-in-due-course defense could not be successfully asserted.

A number of suits have been filed against lenders by purchasers seeking to hold them liable under Section 1410 of ILSFDA for damages resulting from misrepresentations made at the time of sale. To date, the courts have been unanimous in dismissing the actions because the purchasers have been unable to show that the lenders were "developers" or "agents" under Sections 1402(4) and 1402(5) of ILSFDA.[50] Only persons falling into these two categories or acting on their behalf are liable under Section 1410 of the Act. However, the courts have not precluded the possibility that a lender would be liable under certain circumstances.

---

[48] An exemption order for such a transaction is provided for in 24 C.F.R. § 1710.14. This section of the regulations provides for an exemption from ILSFDA where a single transaction is involved and enforcement of the Act is not necessary for the protection of the public.

[49] 15 U.S.C. § 1703(b).

[50] 15 U.S.C. §§ 1901(4), 1901(5).

(4) Nature of the offering:
  (a) Sale of lots by a government unit or agency.[43]
  (b) Sale of lots pursuant to foreclosure or other court order.[44]
  (c) Sale of lots absent a common promotional plan to offer fifty or more lots for sale.[45]

In addition to the foregoing self-operating exemptions, a developer may be able to procure an exemption by giving notice to and receiving an action letter from OISLR in the event the sale or leasing involves a site in respect to which his promotional efforts are confined to the local community,[46] or where the lots are sold free and clear of any liens, encumbrances, and/or adverse claims at the time the contract is executed and certain on-site inspection, deposits, and delivery of deed requirements are met.[47]

[4] Concerns of the Lender

[a] Protection of Security Interest

The importance of the Interstate Land Sales Full Disclosure Act to the lender lies principally in the lender's concern for the security of its loan, which, with subdivision financing, frequently consists of a reliance on the developer's receipt of installment sales contracts or promissory notes. Should the developer fail to meet the requirements of the Act, the lender's security may be jeopardized, since land sales may be suspended by administrative action, and the developer, at the least, is vulnerable to a possible action for rescission and restitution of monies paid in each sales transaction. Thus, before granting a loan to a developer, the lender should seek a reliable opinion regarding the developer's status under ILSFDA.

[b] Direct Liability Under the Act

A secondary consideration is that under certain circumstances, the lender may actually become directly liable under the Act. The circumstances that would give rise to such liability are: (1) where the lender, as a result of the developer's default on a loan, forecloses on the subdivision and becomes the developer in fact; (2) where a lender purchases or

---

[43] 24 C.F.R. § 1710.10(g).
[44] 24 C.F.R. § 1710.10(d).
[45] 24 C.F.R. § 1710.10(a).
[46] 24 C.F.R. § 1710.14.
[47] 24 C.F.R. § 1710.11.

minimum standards for subdivision lot development have been specified.[31]
- (b) Sale of subdivision lots, all of which contain five or more acres.[32]
- (c) Sale of improved land containing residential, commercial, or industrial improvements, or land in respect to which the seller is obligated to construct such improvements within a two-year period.[33]
- (d) Sale of land restricted to commercial or industrial development by zoning regulations or by recorded declarations of covenants.[34]
- (e) Leases of lots for a lease term of less than five years where the lessee is not required to renew the lease.[35]

(2) Nature of the purchaser:
- (a) Sales of lots to a builder or other purchaser who acquires lots in order to engage in the construction business.[36]
- (b) Sales of lots to a purchaser who plans to sell the lots in the normal course of his business.[37]
- (c) Sale of lot where a purchaser has leased and maintained his primary residence on the lot (e.g., a lot in a mobile home subdivision) for at least one year.[38]
- (d) Sales of lots to a governmental unit or agency.[39]

(3) Number of the lots involved:
- (a) Sales of subdivision lots where fewer than fifty lots are sold and no more than one-forth of the total lots are platted of record.[40]
- (b) Sales of lots in scattered sites where fewer than fifty lots are sold.[41]
- (c) Sales of no more than twelve lots each year and such limit has not been exceeded during the preceding five years.[42]

---

[31] 24 C.F.R. § 1710.12.
[32] 24 C.F.R. § 1710.10(b).
[33] 24 C.F.R. § 1710.10(c).
[34] 24 C.F.R. § 1710.10(j).
[35] 24 C.F.R. § 1713(c)(2).
[36] 24 C.F.R. § 1710.10(i).
[37] 24 C.F.R. § 1710.13(c)(4).
[38] 24 C.F.R. § 1710.13(c)(9).
[39] 24 C.F.R. § 1710.13(c)(8).
[40] 24 C.F.R. § 1710.13(c)(3).
[41] 24 C.F.R. § 1710.13(c)(7).
[42] 24 C.F.R. § 1710.13(c)(6).

[2] Compliance Procedures

Land developers subject to the Act must file with the Office of Interstate Land Sales Registration (OILSR), Department of Housing and Urban Development (HUD), a "Statement of Record" that substantiates and sets forth information in detail.[28] A summary of this information, called the "Property Report," must be furnished to the purchaser or lessee in advance or at the time of his signing any contract or agreement for the purchasing or leasing of a lot, and the report must be both accurate and complete in its informational content.[29] The Property Report is presented in a question-and-answer format, which includes such pertinent information as: the name and location of the developer and the subdivision; distances by road to nearby communities; mortgages and liens on the property, if any; taxes and special assessments to be paid by the purchaser; escrow and title arrangements with any accompanying restrictions; easements or covenants and their impact on the purchaser; availability of utilities and facilities; etc.[30]

[3] Exemptions

On April 10, 1979 OISLR issued new regulations in the *Federal Register* that revised the Property Report informational requirements, clarified its policies concerning exemptions in accordance with old and new provisions of the Act, and created new rules for additional "regulatory exemptions." In addition, most of the exemptions have been rendered "self-operating," inasmuch as qualification for exempt status no longer requires a prior determination by OISLR.

Most briefly, the following is a list of the major self-operating old and new exemptions based on the nature of the real estate sold or leased, the nature of the purchaser, the number of the lots involved, and the nature of the offering:

(1) Nature of the property sold or leased:
   (a) Sale of single-family lots situated in a city or country where

---

[28] The regulations (24 C.F.R. §§ 1700-1702, 530 (1979)) deal with the nature and presentation of the facts to be disclosed, and if in the judgment of OILSR the document meets these requirements, it will take effect thirty days after it is filed, unless the developer is notified of an earlier date. 24 C.F.R. § 1710.21 (1979). If the filing is inadequate, OILSR will notify the developer that the Statement of Record's effective date has been suspended until the necessary amendments are made. Once the amendments are received, the Statement will become effective in thirty days, unless they are found to be lacking.

[29] See note 24 *supra*.

[30] 15 U.S.C. § 1707.

authorize criminal,[25] injunctive,[26] and administrative proceedings[27] (including suspension of lot sales by administrative action) against not only the land developer but also the sales agency for violations under the Act.

---

violated, a purchaser may also sue for damages. This provision covers failure to deliver the Property Report, as mentioned above, and also the prohibition against fraudulent and deceptive sales practices. To date the case law indicates that the purchaser's statutory remedy is more direct than at common law. In Hoffman v. Charnita, 58 F.R.D. 86 (M.D. Pa. 1973), the court held that for a purchaser to recover damages he need only prove the existence of a material misrepresentation in the Property Report. *Id.* at 88. See also Tober v. Charnita, 58 F.R.D. 74 (M.D. Pa. 1973). By contrast, in a common-law action based on the fraudulent representations of the vendor, a purchaser would have to prove the following: (1) that the representation was made as a statement of fact, (2) that it was false and known to be so by the vendor, (3) that the vendor made the representation for the purpose of causing the purchaser to rely upon it, and (4) that the purchaser did so rely to his injury. Prosser, *Law of Torts* §§ 105-110 (4th ed.). 15 U.S.C. § 1709(e) limits the amount recoverable to "the purchase price of the lot, the reasonable cost of improvements and reasonable court costs."

[25] 15 U.S.C. § 1717 of the Act provides: Any person who willfully violates any of the provisions of this title or the rules and regulations prescribed pursuant thereto, or any person who willfully, in a statement of record filed under, or in a property report issued pursuant to, this title, makes any untrue statement of a material fact or omits to state any material fact required to be stated therein, shall upon conviction be fined not more than $5,000 or imprisoned not more than five years or both."

[26] The power to enjoin practices that violate the provisions of ILSFDA is given to the Secretary of HUD under 15 U.S.C. § 1714(a). This provision enables the Secretary to prevent a developer from conducting his business until he has complied with ILSFDA. One case, Lynn v. Beard Land Co., No. TY-74-273-CA (E.D. Tex., Tyler Div., filed Oct. 30, 1974), held that this provision can also be used by the government to compel a developer to refund money to purchasers who have the right to rescind under the Act and wish to exercise that right. The court in this case found that it had the authority under 15 U.S.C. §§ 1714(a) and 1719 to grant mandatory relief requiring the defendants to make refunds to purchasers who elect to rescind their contract pursuant to 15 U.S.C. § 1703(b).

[27] In administering this statute, OILSR has the authority under 15 U.S.C. § 1706(d) to suspend the effectiveness of any Statement of Record which "includes any untrue statement of material fact or omits to state any material fact required to be stated therein or necessary to make the statement therein not misleading." A filing may also be suspended whenever changed circumstances render it no longer accurate. 15 U.S.C. § 1706(c). A suspension remains in effect until the necessary amendment is filed and made effective by OILSR. A developer may request a hearing on any suspension pursuant to 24 C.F.R. § 1720.160 (1979). Thus, a developer may find himself unable to conduct his business where a material fact changes (even one not within his control) that affects his subdivision.

of all relevant information about the property prior to consummation of the sale or lease. The Act was the product of a number of congressional hearings on the land sales industry that began in 1963. The hearings dealt with the problem of fraudulent land sales, especially as they affected retired individuals. Specifically, Congress was concerned with the sale of raw, undeveloped acreage that had little or no potential for suitability as a homesite. The Act is aimed at the high-pressure tactics of some land developers and salespeople who, to "close the sale," make promises and representations to prospective purchasers that may not or cannot be performed. The approach of the statute is to require full disclosure,[22] to prohibit fraudulent and deceptive sales practices,[23] to furnish consumers with broad civil remedies (including rescission and damages[24]), and to

---

intended. An exception to this occurs in the case of a subdivision in which the promotion of the common facilities is the main inducement to purchase, as in the case of a recreational development. In such a case, completion is viewed by OILSR to include those facilities. See "Condominiums and Other Construction Contracts—Guidelines," 39 Fed. Reg. 7824 (Feb. 2, 1974).

[22] ILSFDA was patterned after the disclosure approach of the Securities and Exchange Acts of 1933 and 1934. This fact has had an important bearing on what judicial interpretation of ILSFDA there has been to date. E.g., McCown v. Heidler, 527 F.2d 204 (1975).

[23] 15 U.S.C. § 1703(a)(2).

[24] The statutory remedies of rescission and damages are stronger than those available at common law to a vendee under an installment land contract. 15 U.S.C. § 1703(b) provides the purchaser with an unqualified right to void his contract unless he received a valid Property Report at the time of or prior to signing his contract or agreement for the purchase or lease of a lot. In Rockefeller v. High Sky, Inc., 394 F. Supp. 303 (E.D. Pa. 1975), the court found that this right existed even where the developer alleged substantial compliance and furnished all the information that a Property Report would have provided. The purchaser need only have proved he signed the contract prior to receipt of the Property Report. The only affirmative statutory defense available to the developer is the statute of limitation embodied in 15 U.S.C. § 1711, which runs two years from the signing of the contract. See Jacobsen v. Woodmoor Corp., 400 F. Supp. 1 (W.D. Mo. 1975); Hall v. Bryce's Mountain Resort, Inc., 379 F. Supp. 165 (W.D. Va. 1974). A second ground for rescission is provided by this section where the Property Report is delivered less than forty-eight hours prior to the signing of the contract. In such a case, the purchaser may revoke the contract within three business days of its execution. The exercise of this right provides the purchaser with a defense for his failure to perform as well as giving him the right of restitution in the event that he fulfills the contract. In addition, under 15 U.S.C. § 1709(b) the purchaser may forgo his right to rescind and sue for damages.

15 U.S.C. § 1709 authorizes a civil suit for damages when any part of the Statement or Record (once it becomes effective) or the Property Report at the time of sale contains an untrue statement of a material fact or omits stating a material fact required to be stated therein. In addition, when 15 U.S.C. § 1703 is

antee may not exceed 80 percent of the estimated value of the land before development, plus 90 percent of the estimated development costs. Loans to date have ranged from between $120,000 to $16 million, and the approval criteria for Title X financing, administered by HUD's New Communities Administration, have been less onerous than under Title VII of the Housing and Urban Development Act of 1970. The interest rate on Title X loans is based on the FHA ceiling in effect at the time the loan is closed. While FHA fees and mortgagee service fees (discounts) may increase the effective rate somewhat, Title X financing is bound to be cheaper than conventional financing since conventional loans are regarded as high risk because they are funded before the project establishes a marketing record and, absent mortgage insurance, carry interest rates, including fees, as high as six points above prime. In addition, conventional loans of this type normally have a loan-to-value ratio of no more than 50 percent, require repayment within five years, and frequently require the developer to personally guarantee the loan. By contrast, Title X financing allows the developer to obtain a high loan-to-value ratio, to repay the loan over a ten-year period, and to obtain a nonrecourse loan. Finally, with the recent curtailment in the activities of construction and development REITs, Title X financing promises to be an important source of site acquisition and development financing, since the other private institutional lenders and state agencies tend to shy away from these high-risk-type loans.[18]

¶ 9.03 EFFECT OF INTERSTATE LAND SALES FULL DISCLOSURE ACT ON SUBDIVISION FINANCING

[1] Purpose of the Act

As the name implies, the basic purpose of the Interstate Land Sales Full Disclosure Act (ILSFDA)[19] is to require the seller or lessor of subdivided property (where more than fifty lots are being offered for sale[20] and where a building is not erected or being erected on the lot[21]) to make a full, complete, and accurate disclosure to the purchaser or lessee

---

[18] For a good general discussion of Title X and Title VII financing, see Hopfl, "Financing Land Development Under Title X," 5 Real Est. Rev. 118 (1975).

[19] 15 U.S.C. § 1701 (1974); Pub. L. 90-448, § 1401, 82 Stat. 590 (1968) (hereinafter the Act will be cited by U.S. Code sections).

[20] 15 U.S.C. § 1702(a)(1).

[21] 15 U.S.C. § 1702(a)(3). Under this exemption, a unit must be completed before it is sold or it must be sold under a contract obligating the seller to erect the unit within two years of the contract date. OILSR considers completion to occur when the purchaser is able to occupy the unit for the purpose it was

advances will be made to fund the construction of the land improvements, such as storm sewers, sanitary sewers, gravel and paving of streets, clearing and grading, curbs and gutter, water filtration, etc. Prior to making land improvement disbursements, the lender normally wants to review the development contract and receive copies of all necessary grading and clearance permits. The method of disbursement is similar to that of a construction loan. Prior to each disbursement, the lender requires a rundown of title and receipt of partial waivers on work or materials furnished to date.

As a final precautionary note, the developer-subdivider should familiarize itself carefully with the local subdivision ordinances and study the adjacent land prior to purchasing its first tract of land.[16] Preferably, the developer should start by selling only one or two lots to its custom-home builder customer. Also, it is the quality and not the quantity of the improvements that can build its track record with both the county planning boards and prospective institutional lenders. In addition, a subdivider should be thoroughly familiar with the needs of the local builders in the area. They can often provide valuable advice to the subdivider in his quest for raw acreage that will be suitable for subdivision development.

¶ 9.02 TITLE X FINANCING

Title X financing[17] is a federally sponsored mortgage insurance program designed to support the private development of building sites for residential and related uses. The legislative aim of Title X is not limited to the financing of planned unit developments, but also is designed to encourage development of conventional new subdivisions and extensions of existing neighborhoods. To be eligible, the developer must convince the local FHA authority that the local market is capable of absorbing the number of lots proposed for any one development phase, that sufficient public services (e.g., schools and fire and police protection) and utilities (e.g., water and sewer) will be available to service the project, and that certain environmental impact requirements will be met.

The program does not impose any absolute dollar ceiling on the mortgage guarantee; however, the maximum amount of the loan guar-

---

[16] For an excellent analysis on how to assemble land, see Halstead, Jr., "How the Land Assembler Chooses His Targets," 3 Real Est. Rev. 54 (1973).

[17] Title X of the Housing and Urban Development Act of 1965, as amended by the Housing and Community Development Act of 1974; 12 U.S.C. 1749 (aa) (1978).

(5) A lender should not waive any right it has to review and approve any revisions of the plans, profiles, and specifications regarding set-aside improvements and of equal importance, any extension of time to complete the set-aside improvements should not exceed the term of the loan. To avoid any open-ended liability, the lender should also require that its obligations under the set-aside letter to the subdivision authority terminate on a specific date.

In issuing set-aside letters, a lender should make certain that its servicing department does in fact hold back the actual set-aside amount from the committed loan funds. The lender should also make certain that the loan documents specifically refer to any set-aside amount paid to the subdivision authority as a loan advance that the borrower is required to pay interest on and, in fact, repay as part of the outstanding total indebtedness loan to borrower.[13]

As noted earlier, a lender should familiarize itself with the subdivision procedures and requirements. For example, the subdivision authority will be influenced by the previous track record of the borrower in completing subdivision improvements on previous projects.

[4] Loan Documentation

With the exception of a buy-sell agreement and a building or construction loan agreement, the documentation for a land development loan is similar in all respects to that of a construction loan.[14] As noted in ¶ 9.01[2], a subdivision loan will be repaid from the lot sales proceeds and not from the proceeds of a permanent takeout commitment. Where the land is to be improved, a lender normally requires a development loan agreement that performs a function similar to that of a construction loan agreement. A land development loan is normally divided into two stages. In the first stage, the land disbursement stage, the lender normally will disburse an initial amount of the loan necessary to have the developer acquire the property. The lender normally requires that certain conditions be accomplished prior to the first advance, such as receipt of a title insurance policy insuring priority of its mortgage lien, receipt of a copy of the recorded subdivision plat, and evidence that the construction and use of the proposed improvements conform to present zoning regulations.[15] After the initial loan advance, the subsequent

---

[13] See Article I(3) of Form 9.3, a sample master development loan agreement, in Appendix B.

[14] See discussion at ¶¶ 4.02, 4.03, and 4.04.

[15] See Article I of Form 9.3 in Appendix B.

jurisdiction. As for noncorporate bonds, these may be acceptable provided they are secured by either cash escrows or irrevocable letters of credit or set-aside letters furnished by the lender on the development.

One problem that developers and lenders often discover in the bonding area is that surety companies in many jurisdictions throughout the country have stopped writing subdivision bonds because of the high risk involved. Where developers do not have sufficient financial strength to persuade a bank to give a letter of credit to the subdivision board, the subdivision lender on the proposed project will frequently rely upon so-called set-aside letters.[12] By issuing a set-aside letter, the subdivision lender is essentially agreeing to set aside funds from the loan amount. These funds can only be disbursed to the developer after the subdivision authority has approved the completion of those improvements and facilities required as a condition precedent to subdivisional approval. Lender's counsel should carefully review set-aside letters. From a lender's standpoint, the sample set-aside letter (see Form 9.2) lacks the following protective provisions that should be demanded by lender's counsel:

(1) The subdivision authority is under no time constraint with respect to approving or disapproving a request for reduction of the set-aside amount. Lender's counsel should insist that the subdivision authority approve or disapprove in writing the submitted request for reduction within a reasonable time (e.g., sixty days) after the borrower has submitted a request for reduction of the set-aside work already completed to the date of the request.

(2) In the event of the borrower's default or failure to complete the set-aside improvements and facilities, the lender, at its option, should have the right to commence construction to complete the improvements within a reasonable period of time.

(3) The lender should also insist that if the subject property or the borrower is the subject of a bankruptcy proceeding or reorganization, the subdivision authority will agree to allow the lender to recommence construction of the improvements as soon as the lender or its nominee receives title to the property.

(4) Where the subdivision authority does receive the set-aside amount, it should agree that any excess funds be returned to the lender after the set-aside improvements have been completed.

---

[12] A standard form for a set-aside letter is reproduced in Appendix B, Form 9.2.

acreage, evidence of public liability and workmen's compensation insurance, satisfactory soils report, evidence of proper zoning, and, where required, subdivision approval.[9]

With the explosion in suburban growth rates, many jurisdictions have imposed master plans (sometimes rational, other times not) to control and avoid suburban sprawl.[10] By enacting these master plans, suburban localities have sought to enhance the quality of suburban growth and to minimize the impact that it has on existing suburban facilities. To implement the master plans, many suburban jurisdictions have created subdivision approval committees. These committees draw on various personnel from public works, roads, school district, public utilities, community development, and parks and recreation departments, and the developer may have to obtain approvals from all the various governmental agencies involved. As a condition of subdivision approval, many jurisdictions require the developer to enhance the public domain by dedicating park land, improving streets, or building streets and roads, underground water and sewer systems and schools, or even perhaps by contributing to a school fund. To enforce the developer's compliance, some jurisdictions have enacted binding agreements that are bonded. Counsel for the lender and the developer should carefully familiarize themselves with these agreements.[11]

Essentially, an agreement of this nature is supported by a bond on all projects and the agreement obligates the developer to construct required improvements in accordance with approved subdivision or site plans. The amount of the bond required is predicated on the estimated cost of the improvements covered by the agreement, which may be determined by the jurisdiction staff's review of the plans submitted by the developer. The actual amount of the bond may typically be equivalent to approximately 115 percent of the estimated cost of improvements, the additional 15 percent serving as a hedge for engineering costs, contingencies, and inflationary factors that may come into play should the improvements not be completed by the developer in a timely manner. The jurisdiction may not accept a personal guarantee from a developer, but may accept corporate bonds from an established surety company with an attorney-in-fact recorded in the land records of the

---

[9] All of these requirements, except for subdivision approval, have been discussed at ¶ 3.04.

[10] See Vilander, "Outer City: Suburbia Seeks New Solutions," 1 Real Est. Rev. 9 (1972).

[11] For example, Fairfax County, Virginia, as one of the most developed and affluent counties in the country, has a very sophisticated "bond and agreement procedure" for all residential development in the county, a copy of which is found in Appendix B, Form 9.1.

contemplated, it is imperative that the tract of land be improved and be legally subdivided. If the land is not legally subdivided, a problem could arise in the event of default and foreclosure as to which lender had the first lien position, since on the local tax rolls the property would be treated for foreclosure purposes as undivided and still consisting of one large tract of land.[7]

[2] Financing by Institutional Lender

Some of the greatest lending losses incurred by mortgage REITs resulted from the making of risky land acquisition and development loans. These loans resulted in part from poor underwriting coupled with an overall failure or inability to understand the economics of investing in raw land. For example, some loans were even made without prior site inspections. Nevertheless, important lessons have been learned as to how to underwrite a safe land development loan. One primary rule has become obvious, namely, that the subject property should be in an area that has already experienced residential growth in the direction of the subject property. However, success in the subdivision area may also create an undesirable lending situation. The lender should be aware in its underwriting as to how many other subdivision projects are or will be taking place in the immediate vicinity of the subject property. The lender should also be concerned with how long it will take to improve the property.

Since the only source for repayment of the lender's loan is the revenues from the sale of the finished lots, some lenders require bona fide contracts of sale executed with builders as purchasers, which contracts are conditionally assigned to the bank in the event of foreclosure.[8] However, since these contracts are only as good as the financial solvency of the builder-purchaser and no income stream can be generated from the real estate until the lots are sold (other than from such land activities as planting Christmas trees or allowing campsites), many lenders will require substantial assets and liquidity in the borrowing entity as a condition of making the loan.

[3] Approvals and Requirements for Closing Land Development Loan

As a condition of closing the land development loan, the lender will require a satisfactory title insurance policy, a survey showing exact

---

[7] For a more general discussion of purchase-money financing, see ¶¶ 7.04[1], 8.04.

[8] See note 6 *supra*.

exceed a specified sum. Further restrictions may include the requirement of periodic repayments of interest and principal, limitations on interest rates, notice to seller of developer's defaults and reasonable time for seller to cure such defaults, and a requirement that any default on the first deed of trust shall cause an automatic default under the subordinated purchase-money trust.

If the permissible terms of the development lien instrument are sufficiently restrictive, the subordination provision can be made self-operative in the purchase-money lien instrument, or it can at least be reduced to a mere mechanical procedure without unreasonably diminishing the seller's security. The seller must be assured that he is subordinating his position only to that of the development lender and not to liens that may subsequently attain lien priority over the development lender's lien. For example, certain liens (e.g., local property tax) may by statute be accorded automatic lien priority over recorded liens created by contract. Also, if a purchase-money lien is subordinated to a development loan lien, will the purchase-money lien also be automatically subordinate to mechanics' liens, materialmen's liens, governmental improvement assessments, and the like? In those jurisdictions where such is the case, the seller may have subordinated to substantially more than he had anticipated. Where the subordination results in the conversion of a purchase-money deed of trust or mortgage to a second deed of trust or mortgage with no preferential status, additional unanticipated subordination occurs. While contractual liens cannot preclude after-arising statutory liens from gaining priority, the subordination can restrict the amount of the development loan (principal, interest, costs, attorney's fees, etc.) to which it is subordinate and thereby permit the seller to make a more realistic evaluation of his downside risk in determining whether or not his security is being diminished beyond a reasonable level.

One area of compromise that a developer can suggest to the institutional lender and the purchase-money noteholder is to give the institutional lender, at the initial closing, a first lien position as to a certain portion of the land to be immediately developed and a second lien position behind the purchase-money noteholder's first lien position as to the balance of the land to be subsequently developed. This "rollover" method of subdivision financing is also economical to the developer. Costlier funding from the higher interest rate development loan can be delayed until such time as the developer is actually ready to develop and improve the lots. At such time, the institutional lender can make an additional land acquisition advance, and the purchase-money noteholder could then release a portion of the land to the first lien position of the institutional lender. If this type of rollover financing is

In jurisdictions that provide that in the absence of designation the noteholder may apply prepayments to the last installment under the note, from the developer's standpoint it is important that any prepayments of the deed of trust or mortgage will apply to the next installment or installments due under the mortgage or deed of trust note.

[d] Subordination of Purchase-Money Financing

Since the demise of the mortgage REIT as a primary lending source, commercial banks are now the major lenders that make land development loans, and most banks will require a first lien position. However, the seller is generally reluctant to give up its lien priority position unless it is given reasonable assurances that the proceeds of the senior development loan will be utilized to improve the real estate that the seller holds as security. This insures that the value of the property will be increased by at least the unpaid amount of the development deed of trust or mortgage indebtedness.

The seller that subordinates its purchase-money indebtedness should be concerned about the reputation of the financial institution making the development loan, the amount of the loan, the method by which it is disbursed, and the restrictions that the institutional lender will place on the use of the loan draws by the developer. Conversely, the developer wants loan terms as liberal as possible and does not want to give the seller a veto power over the loan commitment after he has completed the purchase of the real estate. A provision stating that the seller must not be unreasonable in withholding its consent to the development loan commitment is not an acceptable compromise. The terms of the development loan are sufficiently complex to permit honest differences of opinion as to the diminution of the seller's security where it is required to subordinate its lien position. Moreover, the developer cannot afford the time delay or expense of litigation that may ensue if such consent is predicated upon the "reasonableness" of the seller.

Consequently, to resolve this problem the subordination provision in the purchase-money deed of trust must be virtually self-operative and yet sufficiently restrictive to protect the seller's security interest in the property. The subordination provisions normally provide that the purchase-money deed of trust or mortgage will be subordinated to: (1) a bona fide development loan, (2) the proceeds of which are to be used exclusively for the improvements to be placed on the real estate, and (3) not in excess of X percent of the cost of said improvements, (4) which loan shall be made by a bank, savings and loan association, insurance company, or other satisfactory institutional lender, and (5) the outstanding principal and accrued interest thereon and all other costs in connection therewith for which the property stands as security shall in no event

(2) Which does not preclude access of utilities to the unreleased land;

(3) Which does not diminish the economic value of the unreleased land to a point where its value in excess of the balance due on the seller's note will not provide adequate security for the repayment of the balance due at all stages of development. As a matter of standard practice, the release provisions should also stipulate that the preparation of releases by the seller's attorney will be paid for by the buyer.[5]

In jurisdictions that require the recordation of a subdivision plat (which has the effect of dedicating to the governmental body streets, alleys, utilities, and drainage easements), it may become necessary for the developer to obtain the release of certain areas and easements in addition to obtaining a provision for the orderly release of acreage or lots. If possible, these former releases should be obtained without prepayment of any of the deferred purchase price called for in the release provision. In jurisdictions that require the developer to post a subdivision or completion bond with corporate surety to guarantee the completion of all those improvements, the seller should be willing to release from the deed of trust or mortgage so much of the land as is contained in such streets, alleys, utilities, and drainage easements without requiring any prepayment. This is to the seller's benefit inasmuch as its security will be substantially enhanced as the result of the bond that guarantees the subdivision improvements will be completed once it is posted when the plat is recorded. Thereafter, in the event of default, the seller will receive back or be able to sell at foreclosure completely improved subdivision lots or lots whose completion is bonded, as opposed to the raw acreage originally sold. Such a provision may assume the following format:[6]

> The noteholder and trustees agree, at the grantor's (purchaser's) request, without the requirement of any additional payment, to join in any subdivision plat for purposes of releasing from the lien of the deed of trust all required streets, alleys, utility and drainage easements as may be required in the proper development of the property for single-family subdivision purposes, at such time as a subdivision plat and a subdivision bond in form and substance acceptable to the County of .... is recorded and filed.

---

[5] See Thau, "Turning Raw Land Into Pay Dirt," 2 Real Est. Rev. 73 (1972).

[6] See Nochimson, "How the Land Packager Makes His Deal," 4 Real Est. Rev. 64 (1974), for an excellent discussion on structuring releases and arranging purchase-money financing.

ing becomes a negotiable issue. Where a large down payment is made to the seller of the land, and completion bonds for the improvements are procured, nonrecourse purchase-money financing should be obtainable.

[c] Release Provisions

If the seller refuses to subordinate its purchase-money deed of trust or mortgage to the developer's site development, construction, and/or permanent loan, the developer may be able to resolve the problem by initially excluding a portion of the land from the lien instrument that it gives the seller in consideration for the cash paid at settlement and by obtaining appropriate provisions for the release of portions of the secured property for each installment or prepayment made thereafter. Absent such provision, the developer must pay off the purchase-money lien before he can finance and commence development of the real estate. If not, he could lose the leverage and working capital advantage that he initially obtained from the seller. On the other hand, the seller does not want its security diminished by a haphazard or checkerboard release of numerous small parcels that could result in its remaining security being landlocked, inaccessible, or cut off from required utilities, or could render the remaining property insufficient in value to properly secure the balance due on its note.

A provision providing for the release from the lien of the deed of trust or mortgage in terms of a specified amount per acre or per lot (if the real estate has been or will be subdivided and platted of record in accordance with all applicable governmental requirements) may be made sufficiently restrictive to both to accomplish the developer's objectives and also protect the interests of the seller. As in the case of the subordination provision, from the developer's standpoint, the release provision should be made virtually self-operative or reduced to a mere mechanical procedure in order to avoid the need for consent and approvals that might result in delays or litigation. To protect the seller, such a release provision should be restricted to the release of parcels of land or lots:

(1) Which parcels are contiguous[4] from front to rear or in such other direction so as not to consume road frontage or preclude ingress or egress;

---

[4] The use of the word "contiguous" does not in and of itself give the seller and purchaser protection. In Lawrence v. Shutt, 269 Cal. App. 2d 749, 75 Cal. Rptr. 533 (1969), a court held as unenforceable a release clause because of its uncertainty, which stated "any portion...released shall be contiguous to a portion thereof previously released."

which to cure to protect the purchaser from a technical default that would allow the seller to foreclose and acquire back his property at its enhanced market value. If, upon a default, the seller reacquires the mortgaged property, the Internal Revenue Code provides generally that no loss will be recognized, no bad-debt deduction will be allowed, and only limited amounts of gain may be recognized by the seller-taxpayer.[3]

[b] Exculpatory Clauses

Historically, developers of real estate have sought to minimize their financial exposure not only for purposes of insulating their other sound investments from the potential risk of one project failure (as well as avoiding bankruptcy because of one unsuccessful venture), but also in order to expand their lines of credit and broaden their borrowing base, of critical importance to developers. With respect to improved property, a purchaser should strenuously insist that the purchase-money financing be without recourse, since the seller can, in the event of default, acquire back the property and return to the position prior to the sale. This approach should also be attempted in the case of purchase-money financing of unimproved land, but because of the inherent risks to the seller involved with subdivision financing, the case for nonrecourse financing is less defensible. Where the seller of the land has not agreed to subordinate the purchase-money financing to the loan of an institutional lender, the purchase-money financing should be without recourse, for, if any default should arise, the seller of the land would be able to reacquire his property. However, where the seller has agreed to subordinate the purchase-money financing to a land development loan from an institutional lender, the seller may, in the event of the purchaser's default, lose its right to reacquire the land because of the institutional lender's prior lien position. This problem can be ameliorated somewhat by the purchase-money noteholder requiring, as a condition of subordination, that the institutional lender notify the purchase-money noteholder in the event of the purchaser's default and grant the purchase-money noteholder a reasonable opportunity to cure the default under the first mortgage trust. However, this is not a completely satisfactory solution. It is quite conceivable that the purchase-money noteholder would not have funds available to cure a default under the mortgage of the institutional lender, or would even have the wherewithal to step in and finish improvements that were not properly installed by the developer. Clearly, in such a situation, nonrecourse purchase-money financ-

---

[3] See discussion at ¶ 12.03[4][b].

actually is. For example, a developer may be able to acquire a choice piece of property, but by the time the property is improved, subdivided, and "comes on stream," the market may have changed for the worse. In the intervening time, there may have been other properties subdivided and improved in the vicinity, and, indeed, the economy may have entered into a recession, precluding builders from developing houses. There is not much that one can do with subdivided and improved lots other than to wait out the economic downswing. In arranging financing, the developer should make certain that the term of the loan is for a sufficient period of time—or at least can be extended for an additional fee—to enable him to ride out any slump in the market.

[1] Purchase-Money Financing

Because of the inherently risky nature of subdivision financing and the lack of any income stream prior to the sale of the subdivision lots, institutional lenders will generally only fund between a 50 to 75 percent loan-to-value ratio loan; accordingly, unless a developer is willing to commit a large amount of equity money to the project, purchase-money financing is essential.

Persuading the seller to take back purchase-money financing is not extremely difficult; in fact, an arrangement of this nature is the rule rather than the exception. Frequently, the seller of the property will be able to receive a higher purchase price for the land if purchase-money financing is provided. The interest rate is normally fixed and should not be greater than the prevailing interest rate on a conventional first mortgage or deed of trust. Indeed, interest on the purchase-money note is often below market rates. A current example would be a four-year deed of trust, interest only, at the rate of 9 percent during the first two years and 10 percent for the second two years.

[a] Prepayment and Default Provisions

To allow for refinancing and development financing, the purchase-money financing should be prepayable, at any time, without penalty, subject to a seller's reasonable requirement of requesting installment sales treatment under I.R.C. § 453.[2] The purchase-money mortgage or deed of trust should contain a notice of default provision regarding monetary and nonmonetary defaults as well as a reasonable time in

---

[2] See discussion at ¶ 9.04.

[b] Cancellation of Installment Obligation, by
    Gift or Bequest, Is a Disposition 9-34
[c] Distribution of Installment Obligation Pursuant
    to Section 337 Liquidation Allowed Under
    New Law 9-35
[5] Sales to Related Parties Restricted 9-36
    [a] Restrictions on Intra-Family Transfers of
        Appreciated Property............................ 9-36
    [b] New Accrual Rules for Sales of Depreciable
        Property Between Related Parties 9-36
[6] Liberalization of Rules for Like-Kind Exchanges
    Coupled With Installment Sales 9-37
[7] Using the Deferred-Payment Method to Report Gain 9-38

¶ 9.05 Capital Gain Treatment for the Investor-Subdivider
       Under I.R.C. § 1237 9-41
       [1] Tax Status as Dealer vs. Investor 9-41
       [2] Statutory Relief for the Investor-Subdivider 9-42

¶ 9.01 NATURE OF SUBDIVISION FINANCING

Subdivision financing generally involves the making of loans to a subdivider-developer to enable him to acquire raw land for the purpose of developing that land into finished lots, which are subsequently sold to home builders.[1] This area of financing poses great risks for the developer as well as the lender. For the subdivision lender there is the problem of a lack of a stable income stream to secure his mortgage indebtedness, the problem of obtaining a first lien position over existing purchase-money financing, and, in light of past failures, the uncertainties associated with underwriting a safe land development loan. For the developer who has purchased a tract of unimproved land, there is no appreciation or even liquidity in turning around and selling this property "as is." In order to cash out and make his profit after paying off the lender, he must convert this unimproved tract of land into finished and improved lots. However, reaching the finished-lot stage entails a myriad of governmental approvals and is not easily achieved. Even where the developer has successfully subdivided and improved the lots, there is another hurdle looming ahead, that of successfully selling the improved lots as quickly as possible. This may appear easier than it

---

[1] Some regional home builders, to avoid the subdivider's profit, have begun to bank land. Through the use of options and lines of credit from commercial banks, they attempt to tie up unimproved property for a period of time. If in the future the market is strong, they exercise the option, and request from a commercial bank a combination land development and construction loan.

Chapter 9

SUBDIVISION FINANCING

		Page
¶ 9.01	Nature of Subdivision Financing	9- 2
	[1] Purchase-Money Financing	9- 3
	[a] Prepayment and Default Provisions	9- 3
	[b] Exculpatory Clauses	9- 4
	[c] Release Provisions	9- 5
	[d] Subordination of Purchase-Money Financing	9- 7
	[2] Financing by Institutional Lender	9- 9
	[3] Approvals and Requirements for Closing Land Development Loan	9- 9
	[4] Loan Documentation	9-12
¶ 9.02	Title X Financing	9-13
¶ 9.03	Effect of Interstate Land Sales Full Disclosure Act on Subdivision Financing	9-14
	[1] Purpose of the Act	9-14
	[2] Compliance Procedures	9-17
	[3] Exemptions	9-17
	[4] Concerns of the Lender	9-19
	[a] Protection of Security Interest	9-19
	[b] Direct Liability Under the Act	9-19
¶ 9.04	Seller's Use of Installment Method for Reporting Income (I.R.C. § 453) Under Installment Sales Revision Act of 1980	9-21
	[1] Overview of Changes	9-22
	[2] Requirements for Using Installment Method Under New Law	9-23
	[a] Timely Election Need No Longer Be Filed	9-23
	[b] Limitations on Payments by Purchaser in Year of Sale Eliminated	9-23
	[i] Two Payment Rule Eliminated	9-23
	[ii] 30 Percent Limitation on Payments in Year of Sale Eliminated	9-24
	[c] Use of Escrow Arrangements and Third-Party Guarantees Under the New Law	9-28
	[3] Illustration of How to Report Gain Under Installment Method	9-32
	[4] Sale or Other Disposition of Installment Obligations Under the New Law	9-33
	[a] General Rule	9-33

reasonable overall constant payment and can shelter his rental income stream from taxation with deductions for depreciation, property taxes, and contract interest—an average constant and not a declining rate. The advantage to the investor is that it retains the benefit of a high-yield, inflation-hedged investment for a longer-than-normal "lock-in" period and can invest more money albeit at a higher risk, than would be possible for straight mortgage financing. Moreover, even though the term of the contract of sale is usually about ten years longer than would be made on a mortgage basis, the installment contract payments are geared to liquidate the installment over the normal mortgage period at somewhat below the current mortgage rate. Thus, for example, if the fixed contract payment is at the rate of 8½ percent of the purchase price, and the contract term is thirty-five years and seven months, the investor can write off his investment at a 7¼ percent yield in twenty-six years and seven months and continue to receive an additional nine years of contract payments, which, of course, would raise his average yield very substantially.[80]

---

[80] See Hershman, "Usury and 'New Look' in Real Estate Financing," 4 Real Prop., Prob. & T.J. 315, 321–323 (1969).

clear of all liens.[77] Such a sale of the property, free and clear of the prior fee mortgage, would extinguish the subordinate leasehold estate, leaving the leasehold mortgage with no security and no claim against the bankrupt fee owner's estate.[78] Other than having the fee mortgagee subordinate its lien to the leasehold estate, there is no protection available to a leasehold mortgage in this situation.

Although the borrower might obtain less financing proceeds under the fee mortgage method than under the previous sale-leaseback alternative, he would avoid a capital gains tax, would not forgo the benefit of future appreciation in the value of the land, and would retain a free hand in refinancing the entire project on a fee basis at a later date.

[3] Purchase and Installment Sale-Buyback

A final high-ratio technique (one step beyond the installment land contract) is the so-called sale-buyback, which can be used to achieve 100 percent financing for the developer. Under such an arrangement, the entire real estate, both land and projected improvements, is sold to an institutional lender or other investor such as an insurance company at a stated price—usually between 80 and 90 percent of economic value and equal to 100 percent of the developer's land and audited construction costs—and the developer simultaneously repurchases the real estate under a long-term installment contract. Since the developer is the "real" owner with equitable title and assumes both the benefits and burdens of ownership during the installment period, he can retain, by mutual agreement, the right to take the depreciation deductions.[79]

During the contract period, which is usually closed for a longer-than-normal period of about fifteen years, the investor not only recoups its capital outlay at a modest rate of interest but, in exchange for granting what amounts to a 100 percent mortgage loan, also receives an equity "kicker" in the form of a contingent payment geared to a percentage of the developer's net income (after subtracting the installment payments). The amortization period is usually ten years longer than it would be for a mortgage loan the developer can thus; maintain a

---

[77] Van Huffel v. Harkelrode, 284 U.S. 221 (1931). See discussion at ¶ 4.02[12][b].

[78] Exchange Nat'l Bank of Shreveport v. Head, 99 So. 272 (La. 1924).

[79] Depreciation is allowed to a purchaser, under an installment sale contract, who has equitable title despite the fact that he does not have legal title, but where he has the obligation to maintain the property and bear the risk of loss. E.g., J. I. Morgan, Inc., 30 T.C. 881, (1958), *rev'd on other issues* 272 F.2d 936 (9th Cir. 1959).

will sometimes make nonsubordinated fee mortgage loans at their prime rate with a loan-to-value ratio as high as 90 percent of the appraised value of the land.

> *Example.* In the previous hypothetical case, the developer should be able to get from an insurance company both a 90 percent fee mortgage (on $1 million land value) and a 75 percent leasehold mortgage (on $2 million building value) for a total financing amount of $2.4 million. The net result is that in comparison to a straight 75 percent fee mortgage, his equity requirement is reduced by $150,000 (from $750,000 to $600,000), or by 13 percent. One variation combining both of the techniques discussed above would be for the developer to then sell the land, subject to the fee mortgage, and lease the land back from the purchaser.

Underwriting such a high-ratio fee mortgage is justified because the security for the loan is not just the value of the land but also includes the ground rent receivable by the fee owner-mortgagor as ground lessor. Moreover, since the fee mortgage is unsubordinated, so that the underlying fee is not subject to the lien of the leasehold mortgage, foreclosure of the latter would not disturb the mortgagor's ownership of the fee. Conversely, if the fee mortgagee forecloses, it, or the purchaser at the foreclosure sale, would end up with ownership of the land, subject to the leasehold rent and leasehold mortgage—the ground lease would be recorded first and thereby have lien priority over the fee mortgage.

A regulated lender such as an insurance company would have to make a fee mortgage loan with such a high loan-to-value ratio under the leeway or "basket" clause of its state regulatory statute.[74] However, both loans would otherwise qualify since the fee mortgage covers "improved" real property, and the leasehold mortgage is not subject to any *prior* lien on the underlying fee.[75]

Even where regulatory requirements do not prohibit leasehold financing on a fee encumbered with a *prior* fee mortgage,[76] approval of such a loan is fraught with danger. For upon bankruptcy of the fee owner, the bankruptcy court has the right to sell the property, free and

---

[74] N.Y. Ins. Law § 81(17) (McKinney 1966); see discussion at ¶ 2.02[1][d].

[75] *Id.* § 81(6)(a), which, in the case of a leasehold mortgage, requires that the underlying real property not be subject to any prior lien.

[76] REITs are not prohibited from this type of financing; such a nonconforming loan can be made by an insurance company only under the leeway or basket clause of its state regulatory statute.

company or other permanent lender would yield a loan amount of $2.25 million. By contrast, if he sells the land and obtains a leasehold mortgage (with the same 75 percent loan-to-value ratio), he would end up with pretax proceeds of $2.5 million ($1 million land value plus 75 percent of $2 million building value). Note, however, that 100 percent financing of the land cost is only an optimum possibility that may not be realistic under certain facts and circumstances.[71]

Moreover, if the investor who purchases the land is willing to subordinate his fee interest to the lien of the leasehold mortgages in exchange for a higher ground rental or some other consideration, the developer could attain even greater leverage since the loan amount under such a "streamlined"[72] leasehold mortgage on a subordinated fee would include 75 percent of the appraised value of the land as well as the improvements. This high-ratio technique is referred to as the "subordinated land leaseback." Use of the "streamlined" leasehold mortgage in our example would yield a startling pretax total of $3.25 million for the developer—$1 million land value plus 75 percent of $3 million land-building value.[73]

[2] Fee Mortgage Plus Leasehold Mortgage

Where the land has substantially appreciated in value and a sale-leaseback would subject the developer to a heavy capital gains tax, he might consider leasing the land to a separate controlled entity, thereby splitting the ownership of the real estate into separate fee and leasehold interests and mortgaging each component separately. This combined financing feature will produce greater loan proceeds than single fee financing. While institutional lenders such as insurance companies are reluctant to make loans with abnormally high loan-to-value ratios, they

---

[71] The legal and tax aspects of a sale-leaseback of land only are discussed in greater detail at ¶ 6.04[1].

[72] See ¶ 6.02.

[73] Of course, this pre-supposes that the sublease or "occupancy" rentals will be sufficient in amount to enable the developer to pay the extra ground rent necessary to entice the purchaser of the fee to pay full value ($1 million), notwithstanding the condition that he subject the fee to the lien of the leasehold mortgage. Alternatively, the mortgagee might accept a "partial subordination" whereby the fee owner receives an unencumbered fee on the condition that he waive his right to the ground rent in the event of a default by the developer and the income from the property is insufficient to meet the debt service payments on the leasehold mortgage.

developer can obtain an extra tax deduction equal to the portion of the ground rent that represents the extra nondeductible amortization he would have paid on the larger fee mortgage had he purchased the underlying fee. Similarly, a sale-leaseback of land and *existing* improvements allows the owner to attain high-ratio financing. While such sale is a taxable event, the owner should be able to sell the real estate for 100 percent of its appraised value. By contrast, if the owner uses mortgage financing or refinancing to obtain additional working capital, he will not be taxed on the transaction, but the total loan amount will not normally exceed 75 percent of the appraised value of the property.[68]

Recently, developers have also used variations of the leasehold and leaseback financing theme to attain comparable or higher ratio financing. Generically, these techniques are referred to as component or "split financing" since they involve splitting the real estate owned by the developer into separate fee and leasehold interests and financing each component separately. Each type of component financing is geared to the particular financing, business, and tax needs of the developer, and may include one of the following.

[1] Sale-Leaseback Plus Leasehold Mortgage

A developer who owns the fee can sever the land from the improvements by selling the land for its market value to an institutional lender or other investor. The investor would then ground lease the land back to the developer and either the investor or another lender would make a leasehold mortgage loan to fund the construction costs of the improvements. The investor, as ground lessor, would get a specified ground rent plus a percentage rental or some other equity kicker as a hedge against inflation. In this manner, the developer might be able to obtain 100 percent financing for the land cost, whereas, had he obtained conventional mortgage financing, the loan-to-value ratio would be about 75 percent for both the land and the improvements.[69]

> *Example.* A developer wants to construct a shopping center costing $2 million on land he owns worth $1 million. Assuming the loan appraisal value of both the land and improvements is $3 million,[70] a regular 75 percent fee mortgage loan from an insurance

---

[68] Both leasehold and sale-leaseback financing are fully discussed in Chapter 6.

[69] See discussion at ¶ 2.02[1][d].

[70] Since lenders primarily use a capitalization-of-earnings ("income") approach to appraise the security property, the appraised value and cost figures may differ.

¶ 8.08 PARTICIPATION BY LENDER—THE "EQUITY KICKER"

In a climate of tight mortgage money, when the bargaining position of lenders is relatively strong, lenders will often insist upon some form of equity participation as a hedge against capital erosion due to inflation. In the colorful lexicon of the real estate industry, in a sound project the prospect of such an equity "kicker" will frequently induce an insurance company or some other institutional lender to engage in high-ratio financing. Such equity participations are discussed elsewhere and include the following:

(1) Percentage of borrower's annual gross income[63];
(2) Percentage of borrower's annual net income[64];
(3) Portion of any refinancing proceeds[65];
(4) Profit share as joint venturer.[66]

The major legal concern for the lender is whether such equity "kickers" are deemed to be additional interest and thus subject to the usury law in the particular jurisdiction where the loan is being made.[67] Frequently, the question is moot in that the regular, or market, interest rate charged by the lender exceeds the maximum rate allowed by local law. Accordingly, the borrower is forced to either use an exemption (for example, if the borrower is a corporation) or some circumvention device, in which event both the regular interest, as well as any additional interest, would be outside the ambit of the local statute. However, some institutional lenders are so cautious about usury violations that they will automatically use a wholly owned subsidiary to acquire certain equity interests, such as a joint venture share in the entrepreneurial profits.

¶ 8.09 COMPONENT OR SPLIT FINANCING

A developer can also achieve greater leverage by obtaining leasehold mortgage financing rather than fee mortgage financing. By leasing and not purchasing the fee, he can reduce his initial cost outlay and still obtain a leasehold mortgage to fund the construction costs of the improvements. Also, since land is not a depreciable asset for tax purposes, whereas the ground rent paid for the land is deductible, the

---

[63] See discussion at ¶ 3.04[3][a].
[64] *Id.*
[65] See discussion at ¶ 7.02.
[66] See discussion at ¶ 11.02.
[67] See discussion at ¶ 5.05[8].

is thereby able to offer a loan with a higher loan-to-value ratio than would otherwise be allowed by local law or by the underwriting policy of the lender.[61] For example, if the institutional lender lends out five-sixths of a 90 percent loan, it would end up with a safe 75 percent senior loan if the private lender is willing to fund the additional one-sixth of the total loan amount—the top 15 percent of the 90 percent mortgage.

[a] Lenders' Concerns

The principal advantage to the institutional lender is that it can safely participate in a transaction that requires high-ratio financing. In addition, the participation agreement will often permit the senior lender to purchase the junior portion of the loan after the loan has been amortized to a safe level (e.g., 75 percent), at which time the institutional lender will be able to add, at a modest expense, a seasoned loan to its investment portfolio.

For its part, the private lender will charge an interest premium for taking the junior lien position and will protect itself by requiring the borrower to pay for private mortgage insurance until the loan balance is amortized to a safe loan-to-value ratio.

[b] Borrowers' Considerations

The advantage to the borrower is that such high-ratio financing can obviate the need for secondary financing, which often requires a short amortization period and is generally more expensive because of higher interest rates and duplication of such mortgage closing costs as appraisal fees, title insurance, and recording fees.

[2] Collateralized Mortgage Loan

In contrast to loan participation, the "collateralized" mortgage loan enables banks and other institutional lenders to make the entire high-ratio loan; the excess portion of the loan is secured by collateral other than the secured real estate itself; for example, by time deposits of the borrower or by the guarantee of some responsible institution.[62]

---

agencies, FHA-approved mortgagees, and savings and loan service corporations). 12 C.F.R. §§ 545.6-4, 563.9-1, 563.9(g). However, it has been ruled that a joint loan without lien parity, such as one with a senior and junior position, is not a "participation" for purposes of the aforesaid restriction. Opinion of General Counsel, Federal Home Loan Bank Board, June 3, 1969.

[61] See discussion at ¶¶ 2.02[1][d], 2.02[2][d], 2.02[3][d], 2.02[4][c].

[62] See 12 C.F.R. § 7.2145, which authorizes national banks to make such loans.

the same bank. In attempting to arrange such a loan, the borrower may face the problem of convincing the lender to place the loan in the correct portfolio, since loans to municipalities may be subject to lower placement percentage limits than regular mortgage loans, of which the tax-exempt mortgage is but one, albeit exotic, variety.[58]

Recently, some economically unviable projects have been funded by means of tax-exempt financing, which has caused a spate of adverse publicity. Moreover, some state development authorities (e.g., Virginia) have recently been enacting inducement resolutions to obtain extra revenues with respect to proposed projects that have been rejected by the local industrial development authorities. At present, many commercial banks are insisting upon variable rates geared to a percentage of the current prime rate, which is discouraging borrowers from seeking this type of financing.

¶ 8.07 "PIGGYBACK" MORTGAGE LOANS

The "participation" loan, a single loan jointly made by two or more lenders using a single mortgage, along with the "collateralized" mortgage loan, are financing techniques, also referred to as "piggyback" mortgage loans, that are primarily used by home builders and increasingly by other developers, as well, to attain high-ratio financing.

[1] Loan Participation

For a variety of legal and business reasons, this well-established technique has been used by institutional lenders such as banks and savings and loan associations to parcel out portions of a single construction—or sometimes permanent—loan among themselves, either on the basis of lien parity or with senior and junior positions. For example, loan participation may be necessary where a loan amount requested by an important borrower exceeds the lender's lending limit for a single loan, or where participation with an out-of-state lender enables the lead lender to avoid local usury restrictions.[59]

A variation of this technique is the so-called "piggyback" mortgage whereby an institutional lender such as a bank or, since 1969, a savings and loan[60] participates as the senior lienholder with a private lender and

---

[58] The tax-exempt mortgage is also discussed at ¶ 3.04[3][b].
[59] The details of ordinary loan participation are discussed at ¶ 11.01.
[60] Both federally chartered and state-chartered FSLIC-insured savings and loans can engage in real estate loan participations only with "approved lenders" (insured banks and savings and loans, government secondary mortgage market

conventional non-tax-exempt construction loan that would be converted to a tax-exempt permanent loan after October 1982.

However, the $10 million ceiling can be circumvented by a developer who qualifies for and obtains an Urban Development Action Grant (UDAG) from the Department of Housing and Urban Development. When a UDAG is coupled with the $10 million exempt small issue, I.R.C. § 103 allows additional capital expenditures of $10 million. Thus, provided there has been no previous issuance of bonds in the same county or incorporated municipality, bonds may be issued for a project in the principal amount of $10 million, and capital expenditures may be made, in the three years prior to and the three years subsequent to the issuance, in the amount of $10 million. In this manner, projects requiring a total capital outlay of up to $20 million may be financed where significant UDAG funding and industrial development bond financing is combined.

The types of projects that may be financed vary from state to state. While some narrowly construe the phrase "industrial development facility" as applying only to manufacturing plants and other similar facilities, about a dozen or so other states, including New York and New Jersey, treat *retail facilities* as coming within the ambit of the phrase. Some expressly permit shopping center financing. However, to comply with state constitutional requirements, these enabling statutes either expressly or impliedly require that the bonds be issued for projects that fulfill some public purpose.[56]

To date, the major sources of tax-exempt financing have been banks, including savings and loans and mutual savings banks. One reason for bank activity in this lending area is that they are permitted to deduct interest relating to tax-exempt income, subject to certain limitations.[57] While such bond financing is customarily nonrecourse with respect to the municipal obligor, many banks have been able to secure a loan guarantee from the developer. If the mortgage lender is a commercial bank, the developer will frequently be able to obtain both the construction and permanent financing—"one-stop financing"—from

---

[56] E.g., N.J. Stat. Ann. §§ 34:1B-3(h); 34:1B-9 (West. Supp. 1978); N.Y. Gen. Mun. Law §§ 854(4), 858, 864 (McKinney 1974) (permits bond financing for commercial as well as industrial facilities). Where there is concern on the part of bond counsel as to whether a proposed facility comes within the definition of industrial facilities, as defined in a state enabling statute, some states have the equivalent of a declaratory judgment called a "validation" suit to determine the legality of bonds to be issued in the future. E.g., Va. Code Ann. § 15.1-214 (1973).

[57] See I.R.C. § 265(2).

to appraise the value of income-producing real estate for the purpose of complying with both internal and external constraints[53] on their loan to value ratios. But since the "income" approach involves capitalizing the projected earnings from the secured real estate, and the capitalization rate is theoretically related in part to the interest rate on the loan, the lower rate of interest enables the lender to use a lower capitalization rate and to fund the loan in a larger amount. Consequently, the loan amount for a tax-exempt mortgage is frequently larger than it is for an ordinary mortgage loan; however, the conservative appraisal policy of permanent lenders sometimes eliminates this added high-ratio advantage.[54]

By recent count, forty-eight states (all except California and Idaho) have enacted some form of tax-exempt bond legislation, and each has done so with reference to the requirements of I.R.C. § 103, including *inter alia* a confusing size limitation of $1 million and $10 million ceilings for small and large projects, respectively. One of the problems involved with industrial revenue financing is staging development within these capital expenditure limitations. Essentially, I.R.C. § 103 requires the user of the property not to exceed $10 million of capital expenditures within the county in which the revenue financing is to be provided. This limitation is measured by a duration of three years back from the date of issuance of the bond as well as three years forward. This $10 million ceiling includes the contemplated industrial revenue financing, all previous industrial revenue financing, all conventional financing, and all investments made for capital improvements.[55]

> *Example.* Suppose a developer made a $6 million capital expenditure to acquire property in a particular county during October 1979, and in June 1981 he wishes to build a $6 million facility to be financed by industrial revenue bonds. Under I.R.C. § 103, he can utilize only $4 million of industrial revenue financing and will be prohibited from making any additional capital expenditures within a three-year period after the date of issuance of the bonds. If he wants to utilize the full $6 million of additional industrial revenue financing, he can wait until after October 1982. However, another possibility would be for the developer to procure in June 1981 an "inducement" resolution from the local development authority, authorizing the purchasing and funding of tax-exempt bonds after October 1982. With this inducement resolution in hand, he could then commence construction of the facility with a

---

[53] See discussion at ¶ 3.04[1].
[54] See Williams, "Financing Shopping Centers With Tax-Free Funds," 5 Real Est. Rev. 67, 70 (1976).
[55] See I.R.C. § 103(b)(6)(D).

an individual or partnership and not a corporation; corporate losses cannot be passed through to the shareholder-investors.[51] Caution should also be observed about utilizing accelerated depreciation in light of the depreciation recapture rule and other restrictions imposed by the Tax Reform Act of 1976.[52]

Moreover, high-credit lease financing is feasible only if all the parties involved understand and accept the notion that the loan is a credit transaction akin to the issuance of a high-rated corporate bond. Since the lender looks to the unconditional promise to pay rent as the real security for the loan, the high-credit tenant, with its massive bargaining clout, must be willing to make concessions in the form of the lease agreement that it would otherwise refuse to make. In response, the developer, as landlord, must be able to induce such concessions by offering the tenant a low rental, as well as other benefits, in exchange for being able to obtain optimum leverage with respect to its acquisition and construction costs.

¶ 8.06 LOW-COST HIGH-RATIO FINANCING WITH TAX-EXEMPT MORTGAGES

The tax-exempt mortgage is essentially an industrial revenue bond structured as a tripartite mortgage loan that can significantly reduce a developer's interest costs on new construction. Generally, the mortgage loan is made to a municipality or municipal agency that places its bond with the lender and simultaneously engages in either a net lease (with an option to purchase) or installment sale of the mortgaged real estate with the developer. In practice, the developer is the real borrower on the loan; when the transaction is finalized, the mortgage lender has a first lien on the property and receives its debt service payments directly from the developer under the lease or sale contract that is assigned to the lender as additional collateral for the loan.

The purpose of the municipality's acting as a conduit is to qualify the mortgage interest income for tax-free treatment under I.R.C. § 103. Because the interest income is exempt from federal, and sometimes state, taxation, the lender is frequently willing to reduce the interest rate by 15 to 25 percent below the market rate for conventional loans. Moreover, permanent lenders traditionally use the "income approach"

---

[51] Losses can be passed through to stockholders of a Subchapter S corporation; however, such corporations cannot be used to own real property. See discussion at ¶ 1.06.

[52] See note 4 *supra,* and discussion at ¶ 1.05[2][d].

taking causes a rent reduction, the lender will insist that a portion of the award equal to such offset be applied to the mortgage indebtedness with only the balance of the award available for restoration of the premises. However, if the tenant remains obligated for the full rental, most lenders will permit the tenant to apply the entire award toward restoration of the untaken portion of the premises.

[d] Buy-Out by Tenant

In the event of an extreme circumstance, such as total destruction by an uninsured risk or total condemnation of the premises, some lenders will tolerate granting the tenant the right to cancel providing that the landlord has the option to sell the premises to the tenant at a price not less than the remaining mortgage indebtedness.

[e] Assignment of Lease to Lender

Since the lender will ordinarily require that any lease with a prime tenant be assigned to it as additional collateral for the loan,[49] it will *a fortiori* do so with respect to any bondable lease to protect itself if the landlord-borrower should become bankrupt, insolvent, or otherwise be in default under the terms of either the mortgage, lease assignment, or lease instrument. However, in the case of a bondable lease, the lender more often than not will also require that the rental payments be made directly to it, and not to the landlord, notwithstanding the attendant burden of accounting to the landlord for any rental receipts in excess of the debt service payments due on the loan.

[f] Subordination of Mortgage to Lease

Again, as is required of all leases with prime tenants, the bondable lease must have lien priority over the mortgage, especially in a jurisdiction where junior leases are automatically extinguished at foreclosure of the mortgage.[50]

[3] Planning Considerations

Because the major attraction of high-credit lease financing for investors is the depreciation tax shelter, the ownership entity should be

---

[49] See discussion at ¶ 3.08[4][i].
[50] See discussion at ¶ 3.05[6].

reason whatsoever, even if, for example, the landlord's title to the real estate fails, or the tenant is constructively evicted. Therefore, the lease must be noncancelable[45], and any default by the landlord cannot be used as the basis for a rental offset. The tenant's only recourse would be to bring an action for damages or to seek injunctive relief. In addition, the basic rent must be sufficient in amount to cover the debt service on the loan, and the initial lease term must be of sufficient duration to amortize the loan by maturity.[46] In regard to the latter, most high-credit tenants—such as AT&T—will seek a lease term of at least twenty years, with two or three five-year renewal options.

[b] Insurance Against Casualty Loss

In addition to the ordinary requirements[47] of the lender, the tenant must obligate himself to repair or restore the premises whether or not the insurance proceeds are sufficient in amount to fund such repair work or restoration. Since the rentals prime the mortgage, the lender will not permit any rent abatement or offset for the period during which the premises cannot be occupied; however, the tenant can protect itself against this contingency by procuring adequate occupancy insurance. Finally, all insurable risks must be covered, and the coverage amount must equal replacement cost.

[c] Condemnation

While presenting similar concerns to the lender,[48] the condemnation clause is often more difficult to negotiate. National chain-store tenants like J. C. Penney will frequently provide for an option to terminate in their standard form of lease even if the portion taken is insignificant or the taking is temporary, and will demand this right with respect to the parking areas as well. While lenders will not tolerate such an absolute right to cancel, most will accept a provision granting the tenant the option to terminate, in the event of a total taking, if the tenant agrees to pay the lender any difference between the condemnation award and the outstanding mortgage indebtedness. Otherwise, the lender will probably insist that the tenant remain liable for the full or reduced rental even if the entire premises are taken by eminent domain. Generally, if a partial

---

[45] *Id.*

[46] *Id.* Indeed, for this reason, many bondable leases are negotiated with the term, amount, and interest rate of a specific loan in mind.

[47] See discussion at ¶ 3.05[2].

[48] *Id.*

property is leased to a number of net or gross lease tenants.[41] However, in these inflationary times, lenders are wary of relying on gross leases, even where they contain escalation clauses providing for additional rentals to cover increases in real estate taxes or operating expenses. The major difficulty for the developer with the multiple-lease situation is that of confronting tenants with bargaining clout simultaneously and negotiating leases that are all bondable.

[1] Developer's Considerations

Normally, the trade-off for maximum financing is the fact that the developer must forgo any hedge against inflation and must accept a modest or zero cash flow since the rental is usually geared to the amount of the debt service payments. Moreover, the amount of the rental will be less than what the lessor could demand from a less solvent tenant. However, for very little, if any, equity investment, the developer and investors can take advantage of large depreciation deductions since their tax basis in the property will include the full leveraged amount of their acquisition costs, including the high-ratio mortgage indebtedness.[42]

[2] Lease Provisions Required by Lender

In addition to the other lease terms required of prime tenants by the lender[43], the lender, if a life insurance company, will insist that any "bondable" lease include the following terms.

[a] Rental Obligation and Term

The rental must be absolutely net so that the tenant pays all real estate taxes, all other taxes (except income), insurance premiums, repair and maintenance costs, and all other operational costs[44], excluding the debt service on the loan itself. Since the lender is relying primarily upon the value of the tenant's obligation to pay rent, it must be assured that under all circumstances the obligation will be met. Accordingly, the tenant must not be entitled to any rent abatement or offset for any

---

[41] For example, in New York, where more than one lease (but not more than six) is the security for the loan, the leases need not be net leases, but the aggregate rentals must provide for full amortization during the initial lease terms of not less than 90 percent of the loan obligation and must cover payment of those items required of a single net lease. See note 37 *supra*.

[42] See discussion note 21 *supra*.

[43] Discussed at ¶ 3.05.

[44] See note 37 *supra*.

amount (often on a nonrecourse basis) equal to 100 percent of either the appraised value of the property or the hard-cash costs[38] of the property to the developer, whichever is less. The rental stream and payment of the debt service is virtually assured if the credit of the tenant is sufficiently strong and the lease meets the requirements of the lender. Normally, the tenant is a corporation with a credit rating in the top three grades. Few individuals or partnerships have the requisite net worth, and in contrast to a corporation, a partnership may experience tax difficulties with the net lease arrangement[39] and, like the individual tenant, is subject to the vagaries of death or incompetency.[40] A long-term lease may also be bondable where the tenant is an undercapitalized subsidiary, if the parent corporation or parents (in the event of a joint venture) are willing to guarantee the lease. Occasionally, a lender will also accept as security a lease with a local governmental unit or agency where its rental commitment is supported by its ability to raise additional tax revenues should the need arise.

Normally, such financing presupposes a single high-credit tenant who leases the entire premises. However, subject to regulatory constraints on the lender, the borrower-lessor in some instances may be able to obtain high-ratio financing (often as high as 90 percent) where the

---

alia: (1) the lease is noncancelable, unless the lease provides for discharge of the debt or other satisfactory protection of the investment in the event of cancellation; (2) the loan is secured by an assignment of the lease or leases (up to a total of six); (3) the aggregate rentals from the lease are sufficient to pay all real estate taxes and assessments and all other taxes (except income), insurance premiums, repair and maintenance costs, and all other operational costs; (4) the landlord-borrower has at least a 10 percent equity in the leased real estate, unless a net lease of a single lessee is used and provides for 100 percent amortization; and (5) 100 percent of the loan amount is amortized over the initial term of the lease if the indebtedness is not secured by a mortgage on the leased real property; if so secured, only 90 percent need be so amortized.

[38] So-called "hard-cash" costs are essentially the costs of land acquisition and construction; whereas "soft-cash" costs refer to the opportunity costs incurred by the developer in expending his time and expertise on the project.

[39] For example, Reg. § 1.176-1(a) suggests that a partnership may be treated as but a tenancy in common for tax purposes if the co-owners of some leased realty do not provide services to the occupants. See discussion at ¶ 1.02. Similarly, if the partnership is deemed to be holding the real estate as a passive investment, it may be precluded from taking advantage of those Code sections (like I.R.C. § 163(d) dealing with excess investment interest) that confer exemptions or other preferential treatment to those taxpayers engaged in the active conduct of a trade or business.

[40] See Uniform Partnership Act §§ 31(4), 31(6); Uniform Limited Partnership Act § 20. Also, see discussion at ¶ 1.02[2].

ment, the developer, as landlord, assumes a totally passive position with respect to the real estate and receives a "net rental" for the duration of the lease term.[35] Also, the net lease must be "bondable,"[36] that is, a noncancelable lease[37] with a net rental sufficient in amount to cover the debt service on the loan and with a lease term long enough to fully amortize the loan by maturity. Since the security for the loan is primarily the rental obligation of the tenant and the value of the real estate only secondarily so, the lender will frequently underwrite a loan

---

unmarketable property; unlike apartment buildings, shopping centers, or office buildings, the building could only be used in a particular manner. To eliminate this risk, some institutional lenders acquire the right to take an assignment of the service contract with the power to substitute another laundry or computer company in the contract. Illustrative of this would be a hospital requiring a more efficient laundry service. The hospital would establish a subsidiary that will become the owner-mortgagor-occupant of a laundry building to be constructed. To induce a lender to become a mortgagee of the building, the hospital enters into a contract with the mortgagor equal to the duration of the mortgage, with payment by the hospital on the service contract equal to the monthly amortization payment to be made by the subsidiary on the mortgage. The service contract would give the mortgagee further protection by allowing the substitution of another laundry service as successor to the subsidiary in the long-term contract on the same terms in the event of a default on the mortgage. In actuality, the possibility of a default on the mortgage is slight in that the contract payment would be equal to the amortization payments on the mortgage. See Dwyer, "A Legal and Business Examination of the Contractually Supported Investment in Relation to the Corporate Guaranty," 23 Syracuse L. Rev. 33, 35 (1972).

[35] Leases that obligate the tenant to pay all or some operating expenses, including real estate taxes, maintenance, and repairs, are referred to as "net" leases, "net, net" leases, or even "net, net, net" leases, depending on how passive a position the landlord assumes with respect to the obligations arising out of the ownership and occupancy of the premises. This type of lease normally supports a mortgage loan for between 75 and 80 percent of the discounted present value of the future rentals under the lease.

[36] A net lease is deemed to be a "bondable" lease or a "financing" lease where the high credit rating of the tenant and its unconditional obligation to pay rent make the mortgage loan resemble a bond transaction. According to the panelists at a seminar on the subject held at the 1977 convention of the National Association of Corporate Real Estate Executives in New Orleans, the mortgage interest rate on such loans should be at least 25 basis points lower than the rate charged on loans secured merely by a net lease, and the loan amount will often equal 100 percent of the developer's costs.

[37] Life insurance companies are the major source of high-credit lease financing. This type of loan is usually made by the bond or private placement department and is, in most states, subject to local regulatory constraints. For example, in New York the Superintendent of Insurance has ruled by "circular letter," dated November 27, 1961, that such loans qualify for investment under N.Y. Insurance Law § 81(2)(a) as "corporate real estate obligations" if inter

income purchasers, who might not otherwise have the cash or qualify for mortgage financing, to buy and sometimes go into possession with a nominal down payment and low monthly payments.[30]

¶ 8.04 PURCHASE-MONEY MORTGAGE

A cautious attitude by institutional lenders toward high loan-to-value ratios has led to increased reliance by purchasers and sellers on the purchase money mortgage as a financing device. The purchase-money mortgage resembles the installment land contract in that a portion of the purchase price is deferred, and the seller can utilize the installment method of reporting his gain on the sale; however, in contrast to the latter, title immediately passes to the purchaser. The purchase money obligation is secured by a mortgage on all or part of the real estate,[31] with loan terms that are frequently more liberal than those offered by an outside lender when mortgage money is tight. Recently, the purchase-money mortgage has ceased to be merely a form of gap financing[32]—to be retired when the borrower obtains permanent financing—and is now frequently accepted by sellers as a secondary financing device to make their property more marketable to purchasers who, in today's market, might need the extra leverage to acquire the real estate.[33]

¶ 8.05 HIGH-CREDIT LEASE FINANCING

A key method of attaining optimum, if not total, leverage is for the developer to offer the mortgage lender, as security for its loan, not only the value of the real estate, but also the net worth of some high credit tenant who agrees to lease the entire premises.[34] Under such an arrange-

---

[30] For a discussion on the tax aspects of installment land contracts, see ¶ 9.04.

[31] In some states, the seller also retains a vendor's lien against the real estate as additional security for the payment of the promissory note, so that in the event of default the additional remedy of rescission is available to the seller.

[32] See discussion of gap financing at ¶ 7.04[2].

[33] For a more detailed discussion of the purchase-money mortgage, see ¶ 9.01[1].

[34] A similar financing arrangement whereby the lender relies not only on the value of the real estate but also on the contractual support of a third party as security for its loan is the so-called backup contract loan, used to finance certain types of real estate. For instance, a backup agreement would be utilized when a company requires the construction of a building with a limited use, such as a laundry facility or a building to house computers. Upon default, a mortgagee could, because of the particular nature of the building, acquire

latter case, between *A* and *B*) that clearly contemplates an exchange between them.[27]

¶ 8.03 INSTALLMENT LAND CONTRACT

Occasionally, a purchaser can leverage his acquisition cost by negotiating an installment, or conditional purchase contract with the seller. Under such an arrangement, the purchaser pays little, if any, down money upon closing the contract and thereafter pays the balance of the purchase price in periodic installments. The seller retains legal title as security until the purchaser has either fully paid the purchase price or has paid in enough money to warrant transforming the transaction into an executed sale, in which event the remaining indebtedness would be secured by a purchase money mortgage. The chief inducement for the seller is that in the event of a default, his contract remedies would be speedier and less cumbersome than those, like judicial foreclosure, which would be available to him as a mortgagee. And the seller would be able to spread his gain over the payout period by using the installment method for reporting his taxable income.[28] The purchaser can usually go into possession with a nominal or low down payment, postpone his closing costs until title closes, and sometimes acquire real estate when institutional financing is not readily available. However, since the seller frequently insists upon retaining legal title until the purchase-money obligation is paid, some contingency that may deprive the purchaser from obtaining title might occur during the payout period. For example, the seller might neglect to pay the local property taxes,[29] become bankrupt, or fail to pay some underlying mortgage that is prior in lien to any recorded contract of sale. In addition, any purchaser who plans to construct improvements or otherwise develop the land may be precluded from obtaining institutional financing to fund his development costs unless the seller is willing to transfer mortgageable title and accept a subordinated purchase money mortgage to secure the outstanding balance of the purchase price. Accordingly, installment land contracts are used primarily by sellers to sell completed projects and to market tracts of unimproved land, or by developers to sell en masse low-cost housing because it permits low-

---

[27] See Form 8.1, a sample three-cornered exchange agreement, in Appendix B.

[28] I.R.C. § 453.

[29] In most jurisdictions, a lien for unpaid property taxes is prior to any other lien or encumbrance, including a recorded contract of sale. E.g., Va. Code Ann. §§ 58-762, 58-1023.

(1) Do not let C be obligated to purchase Blackacre, by contract or escrow deposit, before he agrees to purchase and exchange Whiteacre. Otherwise, the Service could argue that a taxable sale of Blackacre took place, followed by a purchase of Whiteacre by C, acting as the agent of A (or, as in the latter example, B would be acting as the agent of A).[25]

(2) Have C purchase Whiteacre with his own money, and not with money belonging to A.[26]

(3) Do not have any cash other than boot (e.g., brokerage commissions) passing from A to C (or, in the latter case, from A to B), and establish a binding contract between A and C (or, in the

---

[25] E.g., James Alderson, 38 T.C. 215 (1962), *rev'd* 317 F.2d 790 (9th Cir. 1963). In that case, the Tax Court accepted this argument raised by the IRS. However, the Ninth Circuit reversed on the narrow grounds that from the outset, A had no intention to sell Blackacre for cash if it could be exchanged for other property of like kind; that the original escrow agreement, while originally contemplating a sale, had been amended to allow for an exchange if made within the stipulated time period; and that C had used its *own* funds to purchase Whiteacre prior to the exchange with A. 317 F.2d at 792, 793. Also, see John M. Rogers, 44 T.C. 126 (1965), *aff'd per curiam* 377 F.2d 534 (9th Cir. 1967), wherein A had first entered into an option agreement to sell Blackacre to C and then agreed to exchange Blackacre (subject to the option) for Whiteacre owned by B. However, before the deeds were delivered by A and B to one another (by escrow), C exercised his purchase option and paid cash to the escrow agent so that A had, in effect, purchased Whiteacre with money provided by C. Again, as in Carlton v. United States (discussed at note 24 *supra*) there is dictum to the effect that had C first purchased Whiteacre and exchanged it with A for Blackacre, the transaction would have qualified for tax-free treatment. 44 T.C. at 136.

However, if there is no prior absolute precondition that C purchase Blackacre, the transaction will qualify, notwithstanding a conditional obligation on C's part to do so if acceptable property for exchange is not found within an agreed period and even if C undertakes to exchange property with A which C does not own at the time the agreement with A is executed. Costal Terminals Inc. v. United States, 320 F.2d 333 (4th Cir. 1963); Antone Borchard, 1965-297 T.C. Memo. Also see Rev. Rul. 77-297, 1977-34 I.R.B. 12. This rule applies even if the exchange agreement reforms a contract for a cash sale between A and C. Leslie Q. Coupe, 52 T.C. 394 (1969), *acq.* 1970-2 C.B. XIX. To the same effect is where C's only obligation was to acquire a lot and construct a new building on it before exchanging it with A's property. J.H. Baird Publishing Co., 39 T.C. 608 (1962), *acq.* 1963-2 C.B. 4. Also see Rev. Rul. 75-291, 1975-2 C.B. 332.

[26] E.g., John M. Rogers, 44 T.C. 126 (1965), *aff'd per curiam* 377 F.2d 534 (9th Cir. 1967), discussed at note 25 *supra,* wherein the Tax Court held that A had constructively received cash from C (causing a sale of Blackacre) which A used to purchase Whiteacre even though the escrow agent was instructed to pay the proceeds directly to B. Also, see Carlton v. United States (discussed at note 24 *supra*). Cf. Leslie Q. Coupe, 52 T.C. 394 (1969), *acq.* 1970-2 C.B. XIX.

Under such an arrangement, A would have to find someone else (C) interested in buying Blackacre for cash. At A's behest, C would first buy B's property, Whiteacre, for cash, and then A and C would engage in a tax-free exchange so that A would receive Whiteacre and C would end up with Blackacre, as reflected by the following diagram:

DRAW FOLLOWING TWO DIAGRAMS

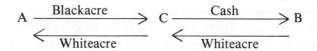

Or, in the alternative, A could exchange properties with B, who would then sell Blackacre to C for cash, as reflected by the following diagram:

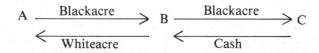

Such a tripartite exchange will qualify for nonrecognition treatment under I.R.C. § 1031 even when C's ownership of Whiteacre (or B's ownership of Blackacre) is transitory, or even if B deeds Whiteacre directly to A (or, as in the latter example, A deeds Blackacre directly to C), provided that the transactions are based on careful tax planning and the following caveats are observed by the parties[24]:

---

[24] The following case results herein and in notes 25 and 26 below are explained in terms of the *first* ABC hypothetical in ¶ 8.02[4]. E.g., W.D. Haden Co. v. Comm'r, 165 F.2d 588, 590 (5th Cir. 1948), wherein B (bypassing C) deeded Whiteacre directly to A and the Fifth Circuit disallowed A's loss, holding the transaction to be a tax-free exchange between A and B. Also, see Mercantile Trust Co. of Baltimore, 32 B.T.A. 82 (1935), *acq.* XIV-1 C.B. 13 (1935), wherein B deeded Whiteacre to C for cash and C exchanged with A Whiteacre for Blackacre. The Board of Tax Appeals held that since A's contract had been with C alone and C (not A) had acquired Whiteacre, C was not merely acting as A's agent; consequently, the transaction between A and C was a tax-free exchange. 32 B.T.A. at 85. Cf. Carlton v. United States, 385 F.2d 238 (5th Cir. 1967), wherein C assigned to A its contract to purchase Whiteacre and gave A the necessary cash to effectuate the purchase in A's name. The Fifth Circuit held the transaction to be a taxable sale of Blackacre to C by A followed by A's purchase of Whiteacre, but also held, by way of dictum, that had the parties followed their original plan (C acquiring title to Whiteacre and exchanging it for A's title in Blackacre), the transaction would have qualified for tax-free treatment. 385 F.2d at 241.

building X must give cash boot in the amount of $100,000 to the other party to the exchange. The following tax consequences would result to the original owner of X:

1. *Gain realized:*
   Amounts received in the exchange:

Market value of building Y	$900,000	
Outstanding mortgage on building X	500,000	$1,400,000
Less consideration paid in the exchange:		
Adjusted basis in building X	700,000	
Cash paid	100,000	
Outstanding mortgage on building Y	300,000	1,100,000
		$ 300,000

2. *Gain recognized (net boot received):*
   Amount of boot received:

Mortgage on property transferred		$500,000
Less boot given:		
Mortgage on property received	300,000	
Cash paid	100,000	400,000
		$100,000[23]

[4] Three-Cornered Exchange

Suppose A, the owner of some real estate (Blackacre), wants to acquire some like-kind real estate (Whiteacre) from its owner, B, in a tax-free exchange, but B insists upon receiving cash. While A may be able to sell Blackacre for cash, his net proceeds after payment of the gain tax may not cover the purchase price demanded by B, or, even if A could raise the necessary cash, he may feel that the tax cost of a sale and purchase is too high. For example, this could happen if Blackacre has a low tax basis relative to its market value because the improvements are overdepreciated, or because the value of the land has appreciated at a fast rate. Nonetheless, A may be able to effectuate the transaction by means of a "three-cornered" tax-free exchange.

---

[23] See Reg. § 1.1031(d)-2, *Example (2)(c)*.

amount of any gain recognized on the exchange.[20] Accordingly, in the foregoing example, the taxpayer's basis in building Y would be $700,000, since his $700,000 carryover basis would be decreased by the amount of the cash boot ($100,000) and increased by his taxable gain ($100,000).

Also, whenever an owner of real estate encumbered by a mortgage transfers it in an exchange, he is treated as being relieved of the remaining mortgage indebtedness whether or not the other party to the exchange assumes liability for such indebtedness.[21] Accordingly, the transferor constructively receives and the transferee constructively gives, cash boot equal to such remaining indebtedness. However, in many exchanges both properties are encumbered by a mortgage; in such cases a cash payment is frequently made by one of the parties to equalize the equities in the properties. When this happens, the taxpayer who both receives boot (by receiving cash or being relieved of the mortgage obligation) and gives boot (by paying cash or by accepting encumbered property)[22] will be deemed to have received boot only to the extent that the boot received exceeds the boot given.

> *Example.* Returning to our previous hypothetical case, suppose building X has a free and clear market value of $1 million but is subject to a $500,000 mortgage, and building Y has a free and clear value of $900,000 and is subject to a $300,000 mortgage. To equalize the equities and make the bargain fair, the owner of

---

[20] I.R.C. § 1031(d).

[21] *Id.* Under the so-called *Crane* doctrine (Crane v. Comm'r, 331 U.S. 1 (1947)), when property is acquired or constructed for cash and a mortgage, the cost tax basis of the property includes the mortgage indebtedness whether or not the purchaser or the developer is personally liable under the mortgage. The assumption underlying the doctrine is that the taxpayer will later have to invest an additional amount equal to the indebtedness in order to retain the property, and hence at the start is given credit in his basis for such assumed later investment. This approach also permits depreciation deductions at a rate consistent with the market value of the property when acquired and affords competitive equality with other taxpayers owning unencumbered property. Otherwise, the taxpayer would be allowed depreciation based only on his equity in the property, and his deductions would increase as the debt is paid, even though the value of the property is declining.

However, to prevent a tax windfall, the basis credit for the assumed investment must be balanced by a realization of the same amount when the property is sold or exchanged. Accordingly, when property is sold subject to a mortgage, the sale proceeds ("amount realized") include the amount of the outstanding indebtedness whether or not the seller was personally liable under the mortgage. See discussion at ¶ 12.01[3].

[22] *Id.* Reg. § 1.1031(d)-2.

property, or vice versa.[18] Moreover, the nature of the property is determined by reference to the status of the taxpayer seeking the tax benefits of the exchange. Accordingly, an owner of some business real estate (for example, an apartment that produces rental income) may exchange it for another apartment and still qualify for nonrecognition treatment even though the other party to the exchange is a dealer who buys and sells such real estate in the ordinary course of business.

[3] Effect of "Boot" and Mortgage on Computation of Gain or Loss

Whenever the equities in the properties to be exchanged are not identical, one party to the exchange will be required to make up the balance by giving cash or other non-"like-kind" property, in tax parlance called "boot." If boot is received in an otherwise tax-free exchange, it will not render the entire transaction taxable, but gain will be recognized to the extent of the boot received.[19]

> *Example.* A taxpayer who owns office building X worth $1 million, with a tax basis in his hands of $700,000, exchanges it for building Y worth $900,000 and, in addition, receives $100,000. Since the taxpayer receives boot in the amount of $100,000, his realized gain of $300,000 is recognized, or taxed, only to the extent of the boot received ($100,000), and the balance of the realized gain ($200,000) is not subject to immediate taxation.

In addition, the taxpayer's substituted basis in the new property is reduced by the amount of any boot received, but is increased by the

---

unproductive (non-income-producing) real estate can be held by a nondealer as "investment" property even though the holder will only realize a profit by reselling the property. However, any immediate resale would infer that the property was not held for an investment purpose. Regals Realty Co. v. Comm'r, 127 F.2d 931 (2d Cir. 1942).

Whether any particular property is "dealer" real estate depends primarily on the specific circumstances surrounding the exchange rather than the general tax status of the taxpayer. For example, one who holds real estate as an investor may be treated as a "dealer" with respect to a particular parcel that was acquired for immediate resale. Conversely, a change in purpose may cause a notorious "dealer" to hold property for investment purposes. E.g., Edwards Indus., Inc., 1974-120 T.C. Memo.; Climate Control, Inc., 1974-206 T.C. Memo. Cf. Heiner v. Tindle, 276 U.S. 582 (1928).

[18] Reg. § 1.1031(a)-1(a).

[19] I.R.C. § 1031(b). However, where cash or other boot forms a substantial part of the consideration to be received, the purported exchange may be treated as a sale, in which event the entire gain will be recognized. Bloomington Coca-Cola Bottling Co. v. Comm'r, 189 F.2d 14, 16 (7th Cir. 1951).

realty[8] and city realty can be exchanged for a farm or ranch,[9] even where the city real estate is rental and the farm or ranch is not.[10] Also, unimproved city lots held for resale were held to be like a building rented as stores,[11] hotel property like mineral rights in unimproved country land,[12] and a leasehold with thirty years or more to run could be exchanged for a fee interest.[13] Nevertheless, even though both land and buildings are termed "real estate," they are dissimilar by nature or character. Accordingly, a constructed office building cannot be exchanged for vacant land.[14] The Tax Court and the Internal Revenue Service have clashed over the issue of whether there can be a tax-free exchange of general partnership interests.[15] Both seem to agree, however, that an exchange of a general partner's interest for that of a limited partner is taxable even though the underlying assets of both partnerships are of "like kind."[16]

Likewise, the second requirement, that both properties in the exchange be "held for productive use in trade or business or for investment" has been broadly construed. While the nonrecognition rule expressly precludes the tax-free exchange of either "dealer" or residential real estate,[17] investment property can be exchanged for business

---

[8] Whether or not the real estate is improved is immaterial because this relates to its grade or quality and not to its kind or class. Reg. § 1.1031(a)-1(b).

[9] Reg. § 1.1031(a)-1(c)(2).

[10] E.R. Braley, 14 B.T.A. 1153 (1929), *acq.* VIII-2 C.B. 6 (1929).

[11] Burkhard Inv. Co. v. United States, 100 F.2d 642 (9th Cir. 1938).

[12] Comm'r v. Crichton, 122 F.2d 181 (5th Cir. 1941). In that case, the Fifth Circuit made the assertion that the distinction intended by the statute is the broad one between classes of properties, that is, between real and personal property and not between types of real estate. (122 F.2d at 182).

[13] Reg. § 1.1031(a)-1(c)(2). See Century Elec. Co. v. Comm'r, 192 F.2d 155 (8th Cir. 1951). Cf. Jordan Marsh Co. v. Comm'r, 269 F.2d 453 (2d Cir. 1959). Also see the discussion on loss disallowance and other tax pitfalls associated with the exchange of a fee for a thirty-year or more leaseback at ¶ 6.04[3][a].

[14] Rev. Rul. 67-255, 1967-2 C.B. 270.

[15] Compare Rollin E. Meyer Estate v. Comm'r, 58 T.C. 311 (1972), *aff'd* 503 F.2d 556 (9th Cir. 1974) *nonacq.* where Tax Court ruled that a general partner's interest in a general partnership can be exchanged for a general partner's interest in a limited partnership where both partnerships own the same kind of underlying assets—rental real estate, with Rev. Rul. 78-135, 1978-1 C.B. 256 where Service ruled that an exchange of equity interests is precluded by the parenthetical language in I.R.C. § 1031(a).

[16] *Id.*

[17] Neither "dealer" real estate (property held for sale to customers in the ordinary course of business) nor nonrental residential real estate fits within the ambit of the phrase "property held for productive use in trade or business or for investment." Also, in regard to the former, I.R.C. § 1031(a) expressly excludes "property held primarily for sale." Reg. § 1.1031(a)-1(b) makes it clear that

Example. Continuing the above example, assume that the investor has a remaining depreciable basis of $40,000 in building X, with a remaining useful life of twenty years and zero salvage value. The investor can write off $2,000 each year as a straight-line depreciation deduction. But if he acquires in the exchange some realty which includes a building having a fifteen-year useful life and zero salvage value and the same $40,000 depreciable basis carries over, the annual depreciation deduction jumps to $2,666 a year.

Obtain Higher Basis in More Leveraged Property. Since only *equities* and not market values count in valuating exchangeable properties, a third way to boost the owner's depreciation deductions would be for him to obtain new realty with a higher gross (albeit same or lower net) value since his substituted basis for depreciation of the new property would be stepped up by the extra amount of mortgage indebtedness attached to the new property.

Example. Returning to the original hypothetical case, assume that the original X realty is owned by the investor, free and clear of any mortgage indebtedness, and is worth $100,000. Instead of swapping it for another free and clear property worth $100,000, he might just as easily acquire some real estate worth twice as much ($200,000) that is subject to an existing $100,000 mortgage. While in both instances the respective equities or net values ($100,000) are the same, in the former case the investor would receive a new depreciable basis of $48,000 in building Y (80 percent of the $60,000 remaining aggregate basis in property X), assuming that the land to building ratio remains the same. By contrast, in the latter variation he would receive a step-up in his basis for depreciation from $40,000 (the remaining cost basis for building X) to $128,000 (80 percent of the sum of the $60,000 aggregate basis in X plus the new $100,000 indebtedness).[7]

[2] Requirements for Tax-Free Exchange

The first requirement under I.R.C. § 1031(a), that the properties in the exchange be of like kind, refers to their nature and character and not to their grade or quality, and in the case of real estate, has been interpreted broadly by the Internal Revenue Service and the courts. Accordingly, improved real estate may be exchanged for unimproved

---

[7] Reg. § 1-1031(d)-2, *Example (2).*

techniques that may be used to boost depreciation deductions in the event that a tax-free exchange is being contemplated.

[1] Techniques to Boost Depreciation Deduction

Tax-deferral exchanges are normally not arranged primarily for the purpose of increasing one's depreciation deductions. Accordingly, the following techniques pre-suppose that such exchanges are motivated by such nontax motives as the desire to acquire more attractive property or to diversify one's portfolio, the need to move to a better geographical location, or the need to eliminate management problems. These depreciation-boosting techniques can also be used in connection with any purchase of some new realty, whether or not preceded by a sale of the old real estate.

Improve Land-Building Ratio. As mentioned above, when a taxpayer exchanges either business or investment real estate for like-kind property, he receives a substituted basis in the new real estate equal to his adjusted basis in the old property; however, he is *not* bound by the land-building ratio applicable to the real estate being offered in exchange. Accordingly, if he can establish a more favorable allocation for the new real estate, one that reflects economic reality, he may obtain greater depreciation deductions than he would have been entitled to had he not engaged in the exchange.

> *Example.* Considering the facts of the previous example, but assuming that an appraisal establishes that 90 percent of the value of the new property Y is allocable to the building and 10 percent to the land, the investor would obtain a new $54,000 basis for depreciation equal to 90 percent of the $60,000 aggregate carryover basis ($20,000 land cost plus $40,000 remaining cost basis in building X); had the land-building ratio remained the same for property Y, he would have only a $48,000 basis for depreciation in building Y.[6]

Obtain New Realty With Shorter Useful Life. A second way to boost the depreciation allowance in connection with a tax-deferral exchange is for the investor to acquire new realty with improvements having a shorter useful life, assuming of course that the new property is possessed of other nontax advantages that outweigh the disadvantage of owning property with a shorter flow of future income.

---

[6] Rev. Rul. 68-36, 1968-1 C.B. 357.

basis of $60,000 ($20,000 land cost plus building cost depreciated down to $40,000) so that he can acquire apartment Y that is likewise worth $100,000 and that has a remaining useful life of twenty years and zero salvage value. If he sells the old apartment X for cash of $100,000, he will pay a capital gain tax of $8,000[5] ($40,000 gain − $24,000 capital gain deduction × 50%), and consequently, only $92,000 of net sale proceeds will be available to him for the purchase of the new property.

However, his tax basis in apartment Y will be its acquisition cost, $100,000, and assuming that an appraisal establishes that 80 percent of the value is allocable to the building and 20 percent to the land—the same ratio as for the old apartment—his basis for depreciation would be $80,000, and he would be entitled to a straight-line depreciation deduction each year of $4,000, worth $2,000 to him in tax savings.

If he opts instead for an exchange, he would be able to use the entire $100,000 value of apartment X to acquire apartment Y and would not now have to pay the $8,000 tax on the gain inherent in property X. However, the investor's new depreciable basis for the Y building would be 80 percent of the aggregate carryover basis of $60,000 ($48,000), and he would be entitled to straight-line depreciation of *only* $2,400 each year. Yet he would still be better off depreciation-wise than if he had not exchanged property X. While the building-land ratio (80%-20%) is the same for apartment Y as it is for X, it is *reapplied* to the *aggregate*—land plus building—carryover basis of $60,000; hence, the owner would end up with a new basis for depreciation of building Y of $48,000 instead of retaining the old overdepreciated basis of $40,000 in building X.

As illustrated by the example, any determination by an owner as to whether to sell or exchange his real estate for property of a like kind should take into account whether or not the immediate deferral of tax resulting from an exchange would outweigh the tax benefit to him of an increased depreciation allowance that might result from a sale-purchase. In that regard, the owner or his adviser should consider the following

---

[5] The Revenue Act of 1978 increased the capital gains deduction from 50 to 60 percent of net capital gains for individual taxpayers with respect to sales or exchanges on or after November 1, 1978. The new law also eliminated the alternative 25 percent tax on the first $50,000 of net long-term capital gains, effective January 1, 1979; it eliminated capital gains as an item of tax preference subject to the 15 percent minimum tax; and it now subjects capital gains to the new "alternative minimum tax." See discussion at ¶ 1.05[2][d].

property.[2] Accordingly, he is permitted to defer this inherent gain in the original property until he sells the replacement property he can therefore use the entire value of the former as consideration for the exchange. By contrast, if the owner were to first sell the original real estate, he would have available only the net sale proceeds, after payment of the gain tax (if any), for reinvestment in the "like-kind" property. The availability of this tax-deferral technique is especially important for the hard-pressed investor in a value-sliding or soft rental market; he must shift from sick to viable realty in order to survive, but cannot afford to pay the tax on the transaction.

However, if over-depreciated or other low-basis income-producing real estate is being offered for exchange, the taxpayer may wind up with a "substituted"[3] basis for depreciation in the new rental property that is small relative to its market value. Alternatively, if the owner's tax basis in the old property exceeds its market value, he would normally want to sell the real estate for cash and not engage in an exchange in order to recognize the tax loss, unless the greater depreciation allowance (substituted basis for exchange versus cost basis for purchase) would outweigh the value of the loss deduction.[4]

Example. An investor in a 50 percent tax bracket would like to dispose of building X worth $100,000 ($80,000 allocable to the building and $20,000 to land), in which he has an aggregate tax

---

[2] I.R.C. §§ 1031(a), 1031(d). In the event of a sale or other disposition of property, "realized" gain simply refers to the amount by which the value of what the taxpayer receives ("amount realized") exceeds his cost of other tax "basis" in what he gives up, "adjusted" to the date of the sale. Whatever portion of the realized gain that is taxable is referred to as "recognized gain." See I.R.C. §§ 1001, 1011, 1012.

[3] The Code applies the term "substituted basis" to those cases where the tax basis is continued or carried through from one taxpayer, or from one piece of property, to another.

[4] In some situations, when the taxpayer is in a very high tax bracket, the amount of the future depreciation allowance might be of more importance than either the deferment of gain recognition, especially if taxable at the capital gain rate, or even the recognition of a loss.

However, since the substitute property would be "used" real estate (in that the taxpayer would not be the original user), the taxpayer would not be able to use accelerated depreciation, except for used residential rental housing where the 125 percent declining-balance method is still available, if the remaining useful life at acquisition is twenty years or more. I.R.C. § 167(j)(5). Moreover, even when accelerated depreciation is available, the depreciation recapture rules for residential property (I.R.C. § 1250) and the mini-tax on accelerated depreciation as a "tax preference" item (I.R.C. § 56), have been made more restrictive under the Tax Reform Act of 1976. See discussion at ¶ 1.05[2][d].

¶ 8.01 INTRODUCTION

The real estate shake-out during the years 1974-1975 has had a prolonged effect on the underwriting attitude of institutional lenders toward real estate investments. Specifically, in today's market, lenders continue to be cautious about high loan-to-value ratios; gone are the days when developers, purchasers, and sellers could safely rely upon the availability of institutional financing at a reasonable cost to fund their construction or land transfer costs. The aim of this chapter is to discuss those high-ratio financing techniques used by developers and purchasers to leverage their acquisition costs, and the efforts by sellers to make their properties more marketable, especially when institutional financing becomes less available or more costly. These techniques run the gamut from the relatively well-known and long-established debt-financing technique known as purchase money financing to the recent and innovative use of such non-debtfinancing devices as the "equity kicker" and "sale-buyback of land." Some, like the "tax-free exchange," are tax-oriented; others, like high-credit lease financing, are not. All of these methods can theoretically be used to achieve 100 percent financing. This ideal is sometimes achieved by a developer or purchaser, while frequently, very close to 100 percent financing is obtained. However, the builder-developer or purchaser should keep in mind that one of the keys to success in real estate investing is maintaining the right balance between maximizing the rate of return on an equity investment and maintaining a "cushion" to act as a hedge against unexpected events. And, sometimes, in his quest for leverage the builder-developer may unwittingly jeopardize a successful operation by overfinancing the project. For its part, the lender will be seeking a return on its loan or equity investment commensurate with the risks that it takes and in light of the degree of projected inflation.

¶ 8.02 TAX-FREE EXCHANGE OF REAL ESTATE

Whenever an owner of real estate held for productive use in a trade or business—or for investment—contemplates its sale in order to finance the acquisition of similar property, he should consider the possibility of a tax-free exchange of so-called "like-kind" property.[1] While no potential gain is recognized on the exchange, the owner retains the same tax basis for the new real estate that he had in the old

---

[1] I.R.C. § 1031.

Chapter 8
SPECIAL TYPES OF HIGH-RATIO FINANCING

		Page
¶ 8.01	Introduction	8- 2
¶ 8.02	Tax-Free Exchange of Real Estate	8- 2
	[1] Techniques to Boost Depreciation Deduction	8- 5
	[2] Requirements for Tax-Free Exchange	8- 6
	[3] Effect of "Boot" and Mortgage on Computation of Gain or Loss	8- 8
	[4] Three-Cornered Exchange	8-10
¶ 8.03	Installment Land Contract	8-13
¶ 8.04	Purchase-Money Mortgage	8-14
¶ 8.05	High-Credit Lease Financing	8-14
	[1] Developer's Considerations	8-17
	[2] Lease Provisions Required by Lender	8-17
	[a] Rental Obligation and Term	8-17
	[b] Insurance Against Casualty Loss	8-18
	[c] Condemnation	8-18
	[d] Buy-Out by Tenant	8-19
	[e] Assignment of Lease to Lender	8-19
	[f] Subordination of Mortgage to Lease	8-19
	[3] Planning Considerations	8-19
¶ 8.06	Low-Cost High-Ratio Financing With Tax-Exempt Mortgages	8-20
¶ 8.07	"Piggyback" Mortgage Loans	8-23
	[1] Loan Participation	8-23
	[a] Lenders' Concerns	8-24
	[b] Borrowers' Considerations	8-24
	[2] Collateralized Mortgage Loan	8-24
¶ 8.08	Participation by Lender—The "Equity Kicker"	8-25
¶ 8.09	Component or Split Financing	8-25
	[1] Sale-Leaseback Plus Leasehold Mortgage	8-26
	[2] Fee Mortgage Plus Leasehold Mortgage	8-27
	[3] Purchase and Installment Sale-Buyback	8-29

to protect those junior mortgagees holding a mere equitable interest. The right to appoint the receiver can be a very valuable remedy. When a receiver is appointed by the senior mortgagee to collect the rents and profits, the senior mortgagee has a first right to the rents and profits collected, with the junior mortgagee entitled to any surplus remaining after the satisfaction of the senior mortgage. But where the junior mortgagee is able to move promptly and have a receiver appointed on its behalf, the junior mortgagee can bootstrap itself over the right of the senior mortgagee as to the profits and rents collected by the receiver prior to the assertion of the rights of a senior mortgagee. This functions on the theory that the mortgagee who moves first should be rewarded for his diligence; had it not been for his action, the rents accruing prior to the senior mortgagee's involvement would have been lost to the defaulting mortgagor.[35]

---

[35] See Sullivan v. Rosson, 223 N.Y. 217, 119 N.E. 405, 408 (1918); But see Bergin v. Robbins, 109 Conn. 329, 146 A. 724 (1929); See generally Osborne, Nelson & Whitman, *Real Estate Finance Law* § 4.46 (1979).

As the senior mortgagee owes no duty to the junior mortgagee to pay taxes or insurance, the junior mortgagee also owes no such duty to the senior mortgagee. However, where the junior mortgagee voluntarily pays taxes, some states allow the amount paid for taxes to constitute a preference over the first mortgagee's lien.[31]

In addition, some states recognize an equitable right in the junior mortgagee to insist upon a "marshaling of assets"[32], where the junior mortgage covers only a portion of the premises covered by the senior mortgage. For example, suppose a mortgagor owns Parcel 1 worth $10,000 and Parcel 2 worth $5,000 and gives the senior mortgagee a note secured by both parcels for $10,000. The mortgagor then gives the junior mortgagee a note secured only by Parcel 1 for $5,000. Assuming that both mortgages are recorded, and both mortgagees have actual notice of one another, what happens if the mortgagor defaults under both mortgages and the senior mortgagee decides to foreclose on Parcel 1 without foreclosing on Parcel 2? As against the mortgagor, the senior mortgagee is entitled to do so, but where there is a junior mortgagee involved, the senior mortgagee can be compelled at equity to enforce its mortgage to ensure that the junior mortgagee will be afforded as much protection as possible. Accordingly, in this simplified example, the assets of the mortgagor could be "marshaled" for the benefit of the junior mortgagee by forcing the senior mortgagee to first satisfy its indebtedness out of Parcel 2 before resorting to Parcel 1. Consequently, the junior mortgagee would not be totally ruined at foreclosure and, in the example, would be able to recover its full $5,000 indebtedness.[33]

Perhaps the most unusual preference afforded a junior mortgagee is the appointment of a receiver and the right to collect profits and rents. Courts have been far more liberal in approving the petition of a junior mortgagee than that of a senior mortgagee for appointment of a receiver.[34] This preference is historical in that, at common law, title was vested in the senior mortgagee, and all subsequent mortgagees had merely equitable interests or liens on the property. Since the appointment of a receiver was an equitable remedy, courts were far more willing

---

[31] E.g., Fischer v. Woodruf, 25 Wash. 149, 64 P. 923 (1901).

[32] Generally, "marshaling" is the ranking or ordering of several estates or parcels of land for the satisfaction of a judgment or mortgage to which all are liable. See 1 Black, *Judgments* § 440. When a senior mortgagee has a lien claim against two parcels and a junior mortgagee has but one source of security, a court at equity may require the senior mortgagee to satisfy his claim in a manner that affords maximum protection to the junior claimant.

[33] For a general discussion of marshaling of assets, see Osborne, *Mortgages* § 286 et seq.

[34] See discussion at ¶ 3.08[4][g].

accordance with the provisions of the senior mortgage; (5) that the junior mortgage continuously be subject to any and all leases upon the property.

With regard to condominium-construction financing, those construction lenders that permit secondary financing do so on two conditions. The first, a business condition, is that the second lienholder not be entitled to apply any sales proceeds to reduce its outstanding balance until the construction lender's lien has been completely repaid. The second—a legal requirement to prevent the construction lender from finding itself in a situation where it wants to release a condominium unit but the second mortgagee is not willing to release its lien because of a prior dispute with the developer—is that the second mortgagee execute and deliver in advance to the construction lender partial releases for the condominium units.

¶ 7.06 STATUTORY AND COMMON-LAW RIGHTS OF JUNIOR MORTGAGEE

At common law, holders of junior mortgages have slowly been given certain protections. For example, while the senior mortgagee is under no duty to foreclose its mortgage (in the event of a default thereunder) to mitigate damages and preserve any equity that would be available to the junior mortgagee,[26] the junior mortgagee not only can foreclose its own junior mortgage in the event of a default under both mortgages, but, if a foreclosure by the senior mortgagee should occur, the junior mortgagee can also protect itself by using the mortgagor's equitable right to redeem the property against the senior mortgagee.[27] Also, after a foreclosure by the senior mortgagee and extinction of the junior mortgagee's lien, the rights of the junior mortgagee to the property reattach if the mortgagor subsequently redeems the property.[28] However, this rule has been modified in certain states so that if after the redemption period the former mortgagor acquires the property by purchase, the junior mortgagee's lien does not attach to the property.[29] In a power of sale state, a junior mortgagee, unlike the senior mortgagee, can purchase at a sale under the first mortgage as an innocent purchaser and be protected as such.[30]

---

[26] See Osborne, *Mortgages* § 323 (1970).

[27] E.g., Seppala & Aho Constr. Co. v. Peterson, 367 N.E.2d 613 (Mass. 1977). See also discussion at ¶ 3.08[4][g].

[28] E.g., Martin v. Raleigh State Bank, 146 Miss. 1, 111 So. 448 (1927).

[29] E.g., Zandri v. Tendler, 123 Conn. 117, 193 A. 598 (1937).

[30] E.g., Mallory v. Agee, 226 Ala. 596, 147 So. 881 (1932). See discussion at ¶ 3.08[4][g].

senior mortgage. Even with such a cure provision granted by the first mortgagee, there are certain defaults such as bankruptcy or insolvency of the mortgagor that cannot be cured. In some cases, at the behest of the second mortgagee, the first mortgagee is willing to agree that in the event of bankruptcy or insolvency it will forbear action against the property provided the first mortgage is kept current and its lien is not impaired in any way during the bankruptcy proceedings. With the recent institution of automatic stay proceedings against foreclosing mortgagees, the first mortgagee is precluded from foreclosing upon the filing of a petition in bankruptcy. Accordingly, it would not behoove the second mortgagee to make payments on the first during a bankruptcy proceeding. Finally, a prudent lender, depending upon the financial reputation of the borrower, often requires that the payment of interest and principal, due under the first mortgage, be deposited with the second mortgagee three to five days prior to the due date under the first mortgage accompanied by the stipulation that the second mortgagee, upon receipt of payment, will make payments directly to the first mortgagee.

[2] Protection of Senior Lender

Permanent lenders sometimes require that some or all of the following terms and conditions be inserted in either a subordination agreement or the actual junior mortgage. Many of these effectively abrogate those previously discussed rights afforded the junior mortgagee. Briefly, these conditions are: (1) that the junior mortgage be and continue to be subject to and subordinate to the lien created by the senior mortgage; (2) that the junior mortgage be expressly subject to and subordinate to any and all advances in whatever amounts with interest thereon, and to any expenses, fees, and charges incurred that may even increase the indebtedness secured by the senior mortgage above the original principal amount, provided the same is advanced or incurred under any of the express provisions in the senior mortgage; (3) that the junior mortgagee agree that it shall not acquire by subrogation or otherwise any lien upon the estate, right or interest in the mortgaged premises, arising with respect to payment of real estate taxes, assessments, or other government charges, which is or may be prior in right to the senior mortgage, unless within a certain period of time, say sixty days following written notice from the junior mortgagee of such intention to pay such assessments the senior mortgagee shall fail or refuse to purchase or acquire by subrogation such prior lien, estate, right, or interest; (4) that the junior mortgagee agree to assign or release to the senior mortgagee all of its right, title, interest, and claims to insurance or condemnation proceeds for use by the senior mortgagee in

the validity of the secondary lien, and, where applicable, compliance with the usual closing requirements, such as receipt of estoppel certificates from tenants, survey, UCC financing statements, etc. However, it is also imperative for lender's counsel to review the existing first loan documentation and be certain that there are no onerous provisions, such as a due on encumbrance acceleration clause.[25]

[1] Protection of Junior Lender

The following second mortgage covenants should be added to ensure additional protection for the secondary lender:

(1) *Subject and subordinate to existing first mortgage only.* The second mortgagee should be certain that its contemplated second mortgage is only subordinate to the existing first mortgage. If the second mortgagee does not want its mortgage subordinate to renewals and extensions of the first mortgage, a negative covenant should be added to the second mortgage requiring that, without the prior written consent of the second mortgagee, the mortgagor is prohibited from renewing and/or extending the original first mortgage.

(2) *No change or modification of the first mortgage.* This requirement is self-explanatory. There should be no change in the terms and conditions of the existing first mortgage without prior consent of the second mortgagee. In the event of an increase in the first mortgage indebtedness, the second mortgagee should have the right to receive increased funds in order to reduce its outstanding indebtedness.

(3) *Notice of default and cross-default provision.* Any potential or actual default under the first mortgage should constitute a default under the second mortgage. In addition, the second mortgagee needs the right to be informed immediately of any default under the first mortgage. In some cases, it is not possible to receive said notice from the first mortgagee; however, the mortgagor should be obligated under the terms and conditions of the second mortgage to give the second mortgagee immediate notice of any existing default under the first mortgage. Where possible, the second mortgagee should also attempt to extract from the first mortgagee a right to cure any default under the first mortgage, usually within a stated period of time, with regard to a monetary default, and, in addition, be given a reasonable period of time to cure any nonmonetary default. Otherwise, as junior lienor, its security interest in the property could be threatened at foreclosure of the

---

[25] Discussed at ¶ 3.04[7].

payment, but are advanced in stages over a period of time. Most large title companies are willing to insure the priority of the subsequent disbursements based on a conventional subrogation principle of law, namely, to the extent that a wraparound mortgagee pays any installment of principal or interest or any other sums due under the first mortgage. The mortgagee in effect becomes entitled to the lien priority of the senior mortgagee. In giving this insurance, title companies usually insist upon conventional subrogation language in the mortgage and, in some cases, as set forth below, a separate subrogation agreement between the mortgagor and the wraparound mortgagee.

SUBROGATION AGREEMENT

WHEREAS, all or certain of the monies secured by the current mortgage of even date have not yet been advanced, but will be advanced by the wraparound mortgagee, as owner of the indebtedness and note secured by said mortgage, pursuant to the terms thereof, and to be applied from time to time to the payment of the remainder of the unpaid outstanding balance secured by the senior mortgage recorded as .... ;

NOW, THEREFORE, for valuable consideration and the amount of $10, receipt of which is hereby acknowledged, the Mortgagor does hereby authorize and empower the wraparound mortgagee to disburse the funds secured by said mortgage and to apply the same from time to time toward payment of part or all of the outstanding principal and interest secured by the senior mortgage recorded as......................, and it is expressly agreed by the parties hereto that upon each such disbursement the wraparound mortgagee secured by the current mortgage shall be and is hereby subrogated to all of the rights, title, interest and privilege which before such payment were vested in the senior mortgagee, holder of the senior mortgage, and that upon such payment the current mortgage shall be, to the extent of payment so made, a first and valid lien subrogated as aforesaid upon the secured premises.

In some cases, a wraparound lender will allow interest to be added to the principal indebtedness so that at the end of the term, the borrower will owe more than was actually disbursed. Accordingly, title companies have been willing to provide initial add-on coverage when the policy is issued.

¶ 7.05 DOCUMENTATION FOR SECONDARY FINANCING

The documentation for secondary financing is similar in most respects to that for first mortgage financing. The lender requires the execution of the note, deed of trust, or mortgage, a title policy insuring

liable for consequential damages or be required under the wraparound mortgage to actually advance funds to pay off the senior mortgage upon acceleration. This is normally unacceptable to most lenders. A compromise that has been accepted by most lenders and mortgagors is the use of an independent escrow or collection agent to minimize the chance of a breach in making any payment due under the senior mortgage. Separate provisions should be spelled out in the wraparound mortgage to the effect that the wraparound mortgagee shall reduce the constant payments of interest and amortization required under the wraparound note in the event the senior mortgagee applies any insurance or condemnation proceeds received by it in reduction of the indebtedness secured by the senior mortgage.

[b] Legal Problems

The three basic problem areas involved in using the wraparound mortgage are (1) usury, (2) recording statutes and state recording taxes, and (3) title insurance protection.

[i] Usury. As previously discussed, the yield to the wraparound lender will exceed the actual rate of interest stated in the promissory note because of the financial leverage gained by the inclusion of the outstanding principal balance of the senior mortgage in the wraparound lender's promissory note. Consequently, as noted earlier, the phenomenon has created uncertainty over the status of wraparound mortgages under the usury laws. Accordingly, a prudent wraparound mortgagee should require, where possible, a usury endorsement from the title company if its yield on the loan may exceed the local usury ceiling.[24]

[ii] State Recording and Disbursement Statutes. In states with substantial recording taxes, the question arises as to whether the tax is to be levied on the face amount of the wraparound promissory note or merely on those funds to be lent. In Virginia, for instance, the tax is levied on the face amount of the wraparound note. In some states, recording taxes exceed 5 percent of secured indebtedness; the difference in tax to be paid on a straight junior mortgage as opposed to a wraparound mortgage is thus substantial. This point should be carefully considered by the borrower, who is usually the one to pay all loan closing costs.

[iii] Title Insurance. A wraparound lender needs title insurance protection where the total funds are not to be advanced as a single

---

[24] See discussion at ¶ 5.05[7].

yield on the $500,000 loan to the wraparound mortgagee would be 14 percent, or 4 percent more than the face rate of 10 percent. Had the borrower procured an ordinary second mortgage, it probably would have to pay total interest of more than $150,000 per annum on both mortgages.[23a]

[a] Additional Covenants

The mortgage or deed of trust should identify itself as a wraparound instrument. Since under the wraparound mortgage the mortgagee is collecting not only its interest and principal payments but also the amortization payments under the senior mortgage, it must agree to pay to the holder of the senior mortgage all principal and interest due under the senior mortgage. In addition, the wraparound mortgagee should condition its agreement and liability to pay the senior mortgagee on its receiving from the mortgagor all payments due under the wraparound mortgage. Cautious wraparound mortgagees sometimes will also condition their liability to pay on the mortgagor's not being in default under the terms of either the senior or the wraparound mortgage. With the exception of the partial assumption to pay principal and interest due under the senior mortgage, which should be limited strictly to the benefit of the wraparound mortgagor so as to preclude the senior mortgagee from obtaining any third-party beneficiary rights against the wraparound mortgagee, the wraparound mortgagee should specifically not assume any of the additional covenants or obligations of the senior mortgage.

The wraparound mortgagor should insist that if the wraparound mortgagee fails to make payments to the senior mortgagee, it has the right to make such payments to the senior mortgagee and be allowed to receive a credit in the amount of such payment against the next payment due and payable under the wraparound mortgage. However, in a state that allows the mortgagee to accelerate upon failure to pay, this protection may not be sufficient if the wraparound mortgagee's failure to pay leads to an acceleration of the senior mortgage. Also, to protect the interest of the mortgagor, the wraparound mortgagee should be

---

[23a] Revenue Ruling 75-99, 1975-1 C.B. 197 seems to correctly preclude the transmutation of principal payments on the first mortgage into deductible interest payment on the wraparound mortgage by the borrower. Moreover, the use of a wraparound mortgage in excess of the seller's basis was included in the first year payments under the installment method of reporting. This inclusion was decided in part on the structuring of the wraparound documents with payments being made to an escrow agent instead of the wraparound mortgagee. See Goodman v. Comm'r, 74 T.C. No. 53 (1980).

[3] Wraparound Mortgage

Once an esoteric and curious device, the wraparound mortgage has become a standard and established means of obtaining secondary financing.[23] The wraparound mortgage is, by way of definition, a junior mortgage that secures a promissory note, the face amount of which is the total of the unpaid balance of the first note secured by the senior mortgage, and those funds advanced or to be advanced by the wraparound lender.

A wraparound mortgage is frequently utilized when prepayment of an existing first mortgage is impractical because the interest on the present financing is low or because the existing mortgage carries a steep prepayment penalty. Ordinarily, the wraparound lender will make a loan based on the current value of the property, but because the existing mortgage indebtedness is not discharged, it will advance to the borrower only the difference between the face amount of the wraparound loan and the principal amount of the existing indebtedness. The wraparound mortgagee need not assume the existing mortgage, but must merely agree to pay its debt service out of the payments received from the borrower on the wraparound mortgage. Because of the leverage provided by the low rate on the existing mortgage, the wraparound lender achieves a higher effective rate on the funds actually disbursed and is able to charge the borrower a rate below that which he would have to pay if the property were not so encumbered with a low rate mortgage. The loan-to-value ratio on a wraparound loan generally does not exceed 75 percent; yet the wraparound lender will ordinarily receive a higher-than-first-mortgage rate of return. The only difference is that the lien is a junior lien until the first mortgage is either repaid or prepaid.

> *Example.* Assume that an outstanding first mortgage on property worth $2 million secures a mortgage balance of $1 million at a simple annual interest rate of only 8 percent, and the wraparound lender plans to disburse additional funds of $500,000 at 10 percent per annum so that the total loan-to-value ratio would be 75 percent. The transaction would be structured as a wraparound promissory note so that the face amount of the note would be for $1.5 million at 10 percent interest. Since 10 percent interest on a $1.5 million note is $150,000, after paying and remitting to the senior mortgagee interest payments of $80,000, the wraparound mortgagee would retain $70,000 worth of interest payments. In effect, the actual

---

[23] See Gunning, "The Wraparound Mortgage, Friend or UFO?" 2 Real Est. Rev. 35 (1972).

mortgage loan. This is normal in a situation involving a permanent "platform loan" where the borrower does not meet a rent-roll requirement, and the first mortgagee funds only a floor amount, agreeing to fund the balance in the event the rent-roll requirement is met within a stated period of time.[21] In this case, the gap lender is often the construction lender. Where the gap lender has agreed prior to construction to make the gap loan, the document that ties together the construction loan, the gap loan, and the permanent loan is the buy-sell agreement.[22] In this agreement, a special provision is inserted providing that if the permanent lender's rent-roll holdback is not fulfilled at the time for the permanent closing, the construction lender agrees to disburse, at a concurrent closing date, funds equal to the amount withheld by the permanent lender pursuant to its commitment. These gap funds are normally evidenced by a promissory note secured by a junior mortgage subject and subordinate in all respects to the permanent loan documentation. The gap documents usually unequivocally state that, in the event the rent-roll requirement is not met during the rent-roll period, the permanent lender still retains the right on demand to purchase the gap note and discharge of record the second mortgage held by the construction lender. The borrower normally assigns to the construction lender all funds that would otherwise be payable to the borrower in the event the rent-roll requirement is met, with the construction lender agreeing to reassign to the borrower all funds that would be payable pursuant to the rent-roll requirement at such time as the gap loan note is paid in full. In addition, the permanent lender usually requires that the temporary lender and borrower agree that no funds will be disbursed under the gap documents, except at the closing of the permanent loan.

Normally, the permanent lender's rent-roll requirement involves a period that runs from between one to three years. However, the promissory note for the gap loan should be predicated on the possibility that the rent-roll requirement may not be met, and the terms should include a period of four to five years beyond the rent-roll requirement period, with a high enough interest rate to prompt the developer to refinance whenever it becomes feasible to do so. With regard to principal amortization, some gap lenders require none, while others require either partial amortization or amortization to the extent that there is net cash flow to be derived from the project.

Because of its prior position as construction lender, the gap lender usually has sufficient leverage with the permanent lender to receive adequate notice provisions and right-to-cure periods from the permanent lender.

---

[21] See discussion at ¶ 3.04[2].
[22] See discussion at ¶ 4.05.

partnership was concerned that the bank might utilize liability "for accounting" as a back-door method of acquiring personal liability. After the customary exculpatory language, the following paragraph that was acceptable to both the bank and the developer was added to the deed of trust and promissory note.

> Notwithstanding the foregoing limitation of liability, grantor shall be liable for a proper accounting of all income and rents collected to the end that all monies collected in any month should be first applied to debt service on the deeds of trust, taxes, insurance, operating expenses, reasonable repairs, and maintenance expenditures. The purpose of this indemnification is to prevent grantor from taking monies collected in a given month and creating a deficit or expense which would otherwise have been covered out of monies collected, without rendering grantor liable for any deficit where such monies collected are not sufficient to cover debt service and the enumerated operating expenses listed above. Nothing contained herein shall be deemed to make grantor liable for any distributions to grantor or as partners, made during the month in which monies collected were in excess of debt service, taxes, insurance, operating expenses, reasonable repairs and maintenance expenditures incurred during that month.

As consummated, the asset swap program also left the bank in a far more secure and profitable position. In its former position as a lead lender to the ailing REIT, the bank was collecting interest at ½ percent over prime. Moreover, if in fact the REIT subsequently went into bankruptcy this bank would be in the same position as many other creditors. By agreeing to the swap and transfer out, the bank was able to extricate itself from this ailing REIT and, more importantly, since the bank no longer had an outstanding loan with the REIT, it was not obligated to fund additional dollars based upon a ratio of outstanding indebtedness pursuant to the revolving credit agreement. The terms of the purchase-money financing were ten years at an interest rate of 4 percent for the first two years, then increasing by one percent for each year thereafter. While this was a rate far below the normal bank lending rate, it nevertheless was far above the rate the bank was receiving on the revolving credit agreement with the REIT. Of equal importance to the bank was the fact that it was receiving a purchase-money second trust on property with good potential, to be owned by a real estate partnership with professional expertise in managing office buildings.

[2] Gap Financing

Gap financing is subordinated temporary financing paid off when the first mortgagee disperses the full amount due under the first

[e] Example: Purchase-Money Financing in Today's Complex Real Estate Market

A variation of the purchase-money mortgage involves the asset swap programs of some troubled mortgage real estate investment trusts. Currently, some of the troubled REITs are indebted to major commercial banks for several billion dollars. While these line notes are technically secured by the assets of these REITs, they are actually unsecured and unprotected loans since the REIT assets often consist mainly *of mortgages in default*. Therefore, to continue the day-to-day existence of many of these troubled REITs, and to avoid bankruptcy that would profit no one, the banks have entered into revolving lines of credit with the REITs. The indebtedness is reduced in a systematic manner and, in some cases, if certain conditions are met, the commercial banks are obligated to fund additional loans to the ailing REITs. As an incentive or inducement for such revolving credit agreements, several of the REITs have instituted asset swap programs. Under these programs, the REITs bank lenders are allowed by written offers to bid on certain properties or mortgages owned by the REITs. The purchase price normally reduces the successful bank's outstanding loan to the REIT. In the case of a swap of real property as opposed to a mortgage, the bank successfully bidding in the project often wishes immediately to transfer the project to a real estate developer-entrepreneur because of banking prohibitions against its owning property outside the state; it may be quite willing to take back purchase-money financing in order to consummate the transaction.

In one example, an office building with a net value of $2 million in Washington, D.C., owned by a REIT, to avoid bankruptcy was transferred to a commercial bank in exchange for a reduction of approximately $1.5 million in the REIT's indebtedness. The bank, in turn, immediately transferred the property to a real estate partnership, and the deed from the REIT went directly to the real estate partnership to avoid a double transfer tax. The real estate partnership was required to pay the bank $250,000 for the building; however, the bank took back from the real estate partnership a purchase-money second mortgage that provided additional funds needed to complete improvements and to cover projected operating deficits for the next two years.

While the bank agreed to release the real estate partnership from any personal liability to repay the note, the bank was concerned with the possible diversion of income. In effect, the bank felt that the office building was sold to the real estate partnership on a "silver platter" and did not wish the real estate partnership to be in a position to milk the property by diverting income without any fear of personal liability in the event that the project went sour. At the same time, the real estate

mortgage.[18] But the fact remains that in a foreclosure of a purchase money-mortgage, courts have historically been very generous in permitting the mortgagor to set up claims of offset, recoupment, and/or counterclaims.

[ii] Concerns When Purchase-Money Mortgage Subordinated to Development Loan. In negotiating the terms of the subordination agreement with the purchaser, the seller should, where possible, condition the subordination agreement on some limitation of the loan-to-value ratio and debt service payable on the senior indebtedness, especially if the senior debt is a construction loan with a floating interest rate geared to the prime rate. Otherwise, the seller's margin of safety or "cushion" may be threatened because it holds the junior position. In addition, if the purchaser should refinance the senior indebtedness or resell the property, the seller-mortgagee should demand that it be entitled to recoup its capital from some agreed-upon share of the refinancing or sale proceeds in excess of the outstanding senior indebtedness. Ordinarily, the purchaser will demand that, upon any such allocation of proceeds, it be given credit for any capital improvements made by it prior to the sale. The seller-mortgagee should also require periodic operating information and audited income statements from the mortgagor so that it can anticipate prepayment or refinancing of the senior indebtedness, generally determined by the economic growth of the project.

[iii] Tax Considerations of Seller-Mortgagee

(1) *Installment method for reporting gain.* An important advantage in using either the purchase-money mortgage or installment land contract is that the seller can elect under I.R.C. § 453 to spread its gain from the sale of the property over the term of the payout period. Spreading the capital gain can possibly reduce the seller's tax rate; as of December 31, 1978 the maximum alternative rate for noncorporate taxpayers will end. Thereafter, long-term capital gains will be taxed at the progressive ordinary income rates.[19]

(2) *Repossession of property in event of default.* Under I.R.C. § 1038, the seller-mortgagee is taxable at foreclosure or repossession to the extent that any cash received prior to the take-over was not previously reported as gain on the installment sale.[20]

---

[18] Page v. Ford, 65 Ore. 450, 131 P. 1013 (1913).
[19] For a detailed discussion of this tax device, see ¶ 9.04.
[20] For a detailed discussion of this topic, see ¶ 12.03[4][b][ii].

that they are not so vague and uncertain as to render them unenforceable, he should be careful that they do not specify the terms of the development loan with too much particularity; if the terms are so stated, the entire purpose of the subordination provisions may be defeated. This might occur, for example, where the precise interest rate and the time for payment are specifically set forth in the subordination provisions, and the purchaser subsequently finds that he cannot obtain those precise terms from a development lender. Under these circumstances, the purchaser might find himself in the position of having to go back to the seller to renegotiate the terms of the subordination. For this reason, it is sound practice to have the subordination provisions set forth a range for each important term of the development loan that will be acceptable to the seller.[15]

[iii] Release of Purchase-Money Mortgage Lien. If the purchaser is a subdivider or other land developer who plans to develop the property in stages or sell portions of it in parcels prior to payment in full of the purchase-money obligation, it will need to obtain partial releases of lien from the seller as the development and sales progress. In that regard, the purchaser must consider the desirability of substituting other collateral for the parcels being released, whether or not to persuade the seller to execute the subdivision plat, as well as a host of other questions.[16]

[d] Considerations by Purchase-Money Mortgagee

[i] Right to Deficiency Judgment. Many legal commentators feel that deficiency judgments are an anathema to purchase-money financing, the theory being that the seller-mortgagee should, in the event of default, merely receive what was previously his—the property sold and nothing more. In some states such as California, recovery on a deficiency judgment is not possible with regard to purchase money financing.[17] Nevertheless, even in those states forbidding a deficiency judgment, counsel for purchaser should still, as a precautionary measure, insert nonrecourse language in both the mortgage and the note. Indeed, in one case a personal judgment was allowed on a purchase-money note even though a state statute prohibited any deficiency judgment on the

---

[15] See discussion at ¶ 9.01[1][d].

[16] For full coverage of additional considerations, see ¶ 9.01[1][c].

[17] E.g., Cal. Civ. Proc. Code § 580(b) (West 1976); Bargioni v. Hill, 59 Cal. 2d 121, 378 P.2d 593, 28 Cal. Rptr. 321 (1963); Mont. Rev. Codes Ann. § 93-6008 (1947); N.C. Gen. Stat. § 45-21.38 (1966). Ariz. Rev. Stat. § 33-729(A); see also, Uniform Land Transactions Act § 3-510(b) (1975).

gage will frequently come into existence as subordinated debt (e.g., second mortgage) because the existing financing on the property is insufficient, when added to the purchaser's cash investment, to cover the purchase price of the property. When new construction is involved, the purchase-money mortgage must often be subordinated to future indebtedness because the purchaser will need to obtain financing from some institutional lender in order to finance the cost of the improvements. Alternatively, the purchaser may want to simply refinance existing senior indebtedness. In either event, the purchaser must be mindful of the lien priority and other requirements that the future senior lender may demand; accordingly, when the seller negotiates conditions or restrictions in exchange for subordination of its purchase-money indebtedness, the purchaser must take care that the senior lender's requirements (discussed at ¶ 7.05) are taken into account. In its preliminary discussions with the prospective senior lender, the purchaser must also, of course, check to see if the former will tolerate keeping any junior liens (purchase money or otherwise) on the property once the improvements have been completed.[14] While sellers are obviously reluctant to subordinate their rights, most will do so if they are convinced that the sale depends on the purchaser's being assured of obtaining the financing necessary to develop the property. From the seller's point of view, subordinating his rights to the lien of the development loan not only helps him to make the sale, but also helps to increase the value of the property. This acts as security for his purchase-money obligation, since the property in its undeveloped state is less valuable than it will be when the contemplated development is completed. In addition, if he agrees to subordinate, the seller should be able to obtain a faster payout than if the purchase-money obligation is not subordinated. Where the purchase-money lien is subordinated to development financing, the purchaser's position with respect to obtaining the financing he needs is strengthened, since he is in a position to give the lender a primary lien on the property. The fact that the development lender is given a first lien on the property also means that the purchaser will not have to pay a premium to obtain the release of parcels from the lien of the purchase-money mortgage.

The purchaser will want the subordination provisions to be self-executing. He will want the purchase-money mortgage or deed of trust to provide that it will be automatically subordinated to the lien of any mortgage or deed of trust securing development financing, without any further action on the seller's part. While the purchaser may want to assure himself that the terms of the subordination are enforceable and

---

[14] See discussion at ¶ 3.04[7].

be paid off within ten years, but the buyer makes this type of deal on the assumption that rising values will enable him to pay the mortgage out of future appreciation in the value of the property.

[c] Considerations of Purchase-Money Mortgagor

[i] Concerns as Ordinary Mortgagor. In general, the legal and draftsmanship concerns of the purchase-money mortgagor parallel those of any ordinary mortgagor. For example, at common law the mortgagor has no right to prepay a mortgage unless the right is specifically spelled out in the mortgage or deed of trust note.[11] Accordingly, the purchaser-mortgagor should seek the right to prepay all or any portion of the unpaid note, from time to time, preferably without premium or penalty. Since the mortgagor is ordinarily required to pay property taxes as they become due, it should attempt to reserve for itself the right to contest in good faith the payment of any disputed taxes, and, if escrows are required, to receive the right to earn interest on any such funds.[12] Like any borrower, the mortgagor should attempt to procure nonrecourse financing by inclusion of an exculpatory provision in the purchase money mortgage note. This is particularly important if the borrower is a limited partnership; otherwise, the investor partners may not be able to receive tax losses in excess of their equity investments.[13] The mortgagor will also be concerned with the application of hazard insurance and condemnation proceeds under the terms of the mortgage instrument. Finally, within recent times, local governmental authorities have increasingly imposed moratoria on building activities and have, in many instances, refused to issue building permits because of inadequate sewer and water facilities, or in response to their concerns about the local environment and ecology. Thus, the purchaser-mortgagor should attempt to procure from the seller a provision in the purchase agreement and mortgage note suspending payments of principal in the event that proposed construction is prohibited because of any law or governmental rule, order, or directive, or in the event that building activities are substantially impeded because of any such governmental restrictions, or because of special and onerous requirements as to the use of building materials for the type of construction being contemplated.

[ii] Subordination of Purchase-Money Obligation to Development Loan. In the case of existing improvements, the purchase-money mort-

---

[11] See discussion at ¶ 3.04[5].
[12] See discussion at ¶ 3.04[6].
[13] See discussion at ¶ 1.05[4][b].

subject to an existing first mortgage for $1.2 million and has a net cash flow of $45,000 after expenses and debt service. After hard bargaining, the parties remain $100,000 apart, the owner asking $1.8 million, the buyer offering 1.7 million. At the buyer's price, he must put up $500,000 cash, on which the $45,000 cash flow would return 9 percent. Any more cash invested would mean that the property "won't show," that is, the return will be inadequate to permit syndication.

At this point, the use of a purchase-money second mortgage is proposed. If the seller would take a much smaller down payment, say $150,000 in cash, the purchaser would be willing to pay $1.85 million for the property, or $50,000 more than the original asking price. The gap of $500,000 between the lower down payment and the higher purchase price would be covered by a ten-year standing interest-only purchase-money second mortgage with interest at 6 percent.

As the following table indicates, the property now "shows"; the return is jacked up sharply.

SELLER'S ORIGINAL PROPOSAL

Purchase Price	$1,800,000	
Less: Existing Mortgage	1,200,000	
Cash required	$ 600,000	
Cash flow		$45,000
Return on $600,000 cash investment		7.5%

PURCHASE-MONEY (PM) MORTGAGE PROPOSAL

Purchase Price		$1,850,000	
Less: Existing mortgage	$1,200,000		
PM mortgage	500,000	1,700,000	
Cash required		$ 150,000	
Cash flow before PM mortgage interest			$45,000
Less: 6% on PM mortgage			30,000
Revised cash flow			$15,000
Return on $150,000 cash investment			10%

Note that the bargain 6 percent interest rate is justified because the seller is receiving an additional $50,000 in purchase price. If necessary, the seller can be offered an escalation, or step-up, interest rate. Alternatively, the no-amortization period can be reduced. All of these matters are subject to negotiation. Of course, the mortgage will have to

a few jurisdictions like California, a deficiency judgment may not be had against the purchase-money mortgagor.[10]

[b] Use to Facilitate Purchase Transaction

[i] High-Ratio, Low-Cost Financing for Purchasers. During the 1970-1971 real estate boom, the willingness on the part of institutional lenders to make land development loans at high loan-to-value ratios and at reasonable interest rates engendered the property markets with a high degree of liquidity. However, after the 1973-1974 crunch, today's cautious underwriting attitudes on the part of institutional lenders have popularized and changed the function of the purchase-money mortgage as a financing device. It has recently become more than a form of gap financing (retired when the developer obtains permanent financing), and now is frequently accepted by sellers as a secondary financing device to make their property more marketable to purchasers, who, in today's market, might need some extra leverage to acquire the real estate. The terms of purchase-money financing are usually quite liberal. The interest rates tend not to be as high as those traditionally demanded by second mortgage lenders and in many cases are as low as, if not lower than, conventional first-mortgage interest rates. The term may be for anywhere from two to seven years, with three to five being the customary range for commercial real estate transactions. The purchaser usually desires a longer term and, if the term is not satisfactory, will often request an option to extend for perhaps an additional one or two years. The note is usually prepayable at any time, and in most cases is interest only.

[ii] Closing With Less Cash at Higher Price. Another major use of the purchase money mortgage is to help consummate a purchase transaction that might not otherwise close because the seller wants more cash and the buyer needs more leverage to earn a decent return on its equity investment. In particular, it has often been used by developers when acquiring properties for syndication; a standing or low-interest purchase-money mortgage makes it possible to produce a cash flow from the property high enough so that, after the developer's share, enough remains to make the deal attractive for the other investors.

Example. A syndicator has been negotiating with the owner of an office building in a prime commercial area. The property is

---

[10] See Cal. Civ. Proc. Code § 580[b] (West 1976). See also discussion at ¶ 7.04[1][d][i].

¶ 7.04 SPECIAL TYPES OF SECONDARY FINANCING

[1] Purchase-Money Mortgage

[a] Legal Definition

A traditional purchase-money mortgage occurs when the seller agrees to defer a portion of the purchase price and the remaining purchase price indebtedness or "purchase-money obligation" is evidenced by the purchaser's promissory note and secured by a mortgage or deed of trust in favor of the seller that covers all or part of the real estate. The purchase-money mortgage resembles the installment land contract[4] in that a portion of the purchase price is deferred; however, in contrast to the latter, title immediately passes to the purchaser (possibly a precondition for development financing), and the seller's remedies are those of a mortgagee rather than a seller.[5] In all essential legal aspects, the purchase-money mortgage is like an ordinary mortgage, with the exception that in many jurisdictions a purchase-money mortgage (absent subordination by the mortgagee) is accorded lien priority over any other claim or lien attaching to the property through the vendee-mortgagor.[6] Accordingly, the purchase-money mortgage will prevail over a claim of dower, community property, or homestead, and over liens arising under judgments against the grantee-mortgagor.[7] It will also prevail over other previously executed mortgages that attach to the property; hence, the purchase-money mortgage is favored over "after-acquired property" clauses in prior mortgages designed to encumber the property once it becomes owned by the vendee-mortgagor.[8] However, a negligent purchase-money mortgagee who fails to promptly record his mortgage will not be protected under the recording statutes against a subsequent bona fide purchaser or mortgagee who takes without notice of the prior unrecorded claim unless the contest takes place in a so-called race-notice or race jurisdiction (as opposed to a pure "notice" jurisdiction) and the purchase-money mortgagee is fortunate enough to record first.[9] Also, in

---

[4] See discussion at ¶ 8.03.
[5] *Id.*
[6] See Osborne, *Mortgages* § 213 (1970).
[7] *Id.*
[8] E.g., Chase Nat'l Bank v. Sweeney, 261 N.Y. 710, 185 N.E. 803 (1933); County of Pinellas v. Clearwater Sav. & Loan Ass'n, 214 So.2d 525 (Fla. Dist. Ct. App. 1968). See discussion of these clauses at ¶ 3.08[4][a].
[9] See Tiffany, *Real Property* § 576 (3d ed. 1970).

and savings and loans do not engage in secondary financing. While commercial banks also follow this policy by not ordinarily engaging in secondary financing, some banks will make second mortgage loans to attractive customers on existing projects. They view such loans primarily as business loans only incidentally secured by the mortgaged real estate.

The secondary mortgage market is comprised mainly of the following types of lenders wishing to secure high yields on relatively short-term paper:

(1) Commercial financing companies, such as Walter E. Heller & Co. and AIC Financial Corporation;
(2) Industrial and financial corporations (or their wholly owned subsidiaries), such as General Electric Credit Corporation, C.I.T. Corporation, Aetna Business Credit, Inc. (a subsidiary of Aetna Life & Casualty Co.), and Westinghouse Credit Corp. (a subsidiary of Westinghouse Electric Corp.);
(3) Real Estate Investment Trusts, such as Property Capital Trust; and
(4) Other lenders including real estate financing companies, small business investment companies, foreign investors seeking dollar obligations without ownership responsibilities, and private individuals and syndicates.

As a rule of thumb, loan amounts vary between $100,000 to approximately $1.5 million; the loan period may range between one and ten years (without amortization if the term is short) and, at present, interest rates are generally four to five points over the prime rate.

For top-quality properties (e.g., shopping centers or office buildings with established long-term tenants), these lenders generally look for a net cash flow coverage of about 1.1 times the sum of debt service on the first mortgage and the proposed second mortgage. On lesser-quality properties such as apartments or motels, the coverage must be about 1.2 to 1.5 on total debt service. For example, if the property throws off a reliable net cash flow of $100,000 and the coverage is 1.5, no more than two-thirds, or $66,666, could go to service both the first and second mortgages. Another rule of thumb sometimes used for setting second mortgage loan-to-value ratio limits is the so-called five-times-the-bottom-line rule. For example, excess net income of $100,000, after payment of the first-mortgage debt service, might support a second mortgage loan of about $500,000.

real estate developer's demand for new first-mortgage permanent financing is unfortunately matched by a lack in supply of available mortgage funds.

(3) *Funds for first-mortgage refinancing are available but developer is unable to avail itself of said funds.* If the real estate developer desires additional financing on the first mortgage during the lock-in period, a refinancing or paying off of the first mortgage may be impossible under the terms of the mortgage note. Even where the real estate developer is past the lock-in period, the prepayment penalty is often onerous enough to preclude the paying off of the existing first-mortgage indebtedness.[1]

Some intrinsic reasons that preclude a developer from refinancing the first mortgage or procuring new first-mortgage financing are:

(1) *Cost of acquiring new first-mortgage financing greater than secondary financing.* This situation arises when the real estate developer has a very attractive existing first mortgage loan. In this case, it is cheaper to pay a higher rate of interest upon a small amount of new borrowed funds than to refinance the existing first mortgage.

(2) *Nature of the real estate transaction requires secondary financing.* Such a situation may arise, for example, in the event of a purchase-swap agreement with a real estate investment trust whereby a lead lender for the REIT cancels part or all of its indebtedness in exchange for a transfer to it of certain real estate owned by the REIT. The bank immediately thereafter tranfers the property to a real estate developer and takes back a purchase-money second. In such an instance, the bank has to be in a position to convert its unsecured line note into a secondary mortgage loan by way of a transfer of the priority to a third-party developer.[2]

¶ 7.03 LENDERS AND LOAN TERMS

Because of statutory lien priority requirements[3] and institutional conservatism, most permanent lenders such as life insurance companies

---

[1] See discussion at ¶ 3.04[5].
[2] See discussion at ¶ 7.04[1].
[3] See discussion of regulatory statutes in Chapter 2.

¶ 7.01 INTRODUCTION

Secondary financing, consisting of gap loan mortgages, purchase-money mortgages, wraparound mortgages, and other types of junior mortgages, plays a very important role in commercial real estate. As colorfully stated by one real estate broker, it is the grease that makes the project run smoothly; it is the cream that can make a real estate project more palatable for both the seller and the purchaser. Secondary financing can provide the extra funds needed to expand a real estate venture or can enable a willing construction lender to cover the developer's cost overrun when the permanent loan becomes funded. Actually, without this source of additional financing, many real estate projects or transactions involving a sale of real estate could never be made. However, it should not be assumed that secondary financing is the norm or that it is very readily available. Indeed, secondary financing, when procured or arranged, is considered an added extra, making for an unusual and creative financing transaction.

¶ 7.02 ADVANTAGES OVER REFINANCING A FIRST MORTGAGE

For a variety of reasons, an owner of real estate may turn to secondary financing instead of refinancing the first mortgage loan indebtedness by paying off the existing mortgage loan with a new and larger loan from the same mortgagee or from another mortgage lender. A real estate developer's use of secondary financing is based upon extrinsic factors beyond the control of the developer, as well as certain intrinsic reasons, some or all of which may be present to varying degrees at the same time. Extrinsic factors include:

(1) *Total unavailability of increased first financing because of the real estate involved.* In the case of financing certain specialized real estate projects, such as motels and hotels, which lenders essentially regard as business loans as opposed to real estate loans, mortgage lenders providing the first mortgage or trust financing require a very conservative loan-to-value ratio. They see an inherent risk in making such loans and probably will not be willing to increase the loan amount if the value of the property should appreciate. Only a limited number of permanent mortgage lenders are willing to make such permanent loans; the opportunity to obtain new financing is thus extremely limited.

(2) *Unavailability of first-mortgage financing because of market conditions.* Since real estate is a cyclical industry, frequently a

Chapter 7

SECONDARY FINANCING

		Page
¶ 7.01	Introduction	7- 2
¶ 7.02	Advantages Over Refinancing a First Mortgage	7- 2
¶ 7.03	Lenders and Loan Terms	7- 3
¶ 7.04	Special Types of Secondary Financing	7- 5

    [1] Purchase-Money Mortgage 7- 5
        [a] Legal Definition 7- 5
        [b] Use to Facilitate Purchase Transaction 7- 6
            [i] High-Ratio, Low-Cost Financing
                for Purchasers 7- 6
            [ii] Closing With Less Cash at
                Higher Price 7- 6
        [c] Considerations of Purchase-Money Mortgagor 7- 8
            [i] Concerns as Ordinary Mortgagor 7- 8
            [ii] Subordination of Purchase-Money
                Obligation to Development Loan 7- 8
            [iii] Release of Purchase-Money
                Mortgage Lien 7-10
        [d] Considerations by Purchase-Money Mortgagee 7-10
            [i] Right to Deficiency Judgment 7-10
            [ii] Concerns When Purchase-Money
                Mortgage Subordinated to
                Development Loan 7-11
            [iii] Tax Considerations of Seller-
                Mortgagee 7-11
        [e] Example: Purchase-Money Financing
            in Today's Complex Real Estate Market 7-12
    [2] Gap Financing 7-13
    [3] Wraparound Mortgage 7-15
        [a] Additional Covenants 7-16
        [b] Legal Problems 7-17
            [i] Usury 7-17
            [ii] State Recording and
                Disbursement Statutes 7-17
            [iii] Title Insurance 7-17

¶ 7.05	Documentation for Secondary Financing	7-18

    [1] Protection of Junior Lender 7-19
    [2] Protection of Senior Lender 7-20

¶ 7.06	Statutory and Common-Law Rights of Junior Mortgagee	7-21

alternatives (b) and (c) Realty would be "selling" the Section 1231 property worth $1 million for cash, and not exchanging it for the leaseback, the potential ordinary loss of $300,000 would be deductible in its entirety.[75] However, in alternative (d) the leaseback is worth $700,000, as reflected by realty's receipt of only $300,000 of boot and by the below fair market leaseback rental. Accordingly, the transaction would be regarded as a nontaxable exchange, and under I.R.C. § 1031(c) the entire loss, even the portion allocable to the boot received, would be disallowed or postponed if Realty should ever dispose of the leaseback.

[5] Component, or "Split," Financing

Recently, developers have also been employing variations of the leasehold and leaseback financing theme to attain high-ratio financing. Generically, these techniques are referred to as component, or "split," financing and include the sale-leaseback plus leasehold mortgage, the fee mortgage plus leasehold mortgage, and the purchase and installment sale-buyback.[76]

---

[75] Under I.R.C. § 1031(d), Realty would receive a carryover basis in the leaseback equal to its basis ($1.3 million) in the exchanged property, less cash received ($300,000), for a total new basis of $1 million. Accordingly, Realty could amortize the $1 million basis over the thirty-year leaseback term, and if the leaseback were sold for its market value of $700,000 in the first year, it would be entitled to a $300,000 loss deduction.

[76] These techniques are discussed fully at ¶ 8.09.

$28,000 to $944,000.[73] However, since the leaseback is worth more (by $100,000), the leaseback rentals and resultant deductions would decrease as an offset against future ordinary operating deductions. Moreover, since the leaseback is worth more, the amount of the leasehold mortgage would increase by $100,000, but the decrease in deductible rent would outmatch the resultant increase in deductible interest, and the interest would decline as the mortgage principal is repaid each year. Indeed, as the boot decreases and the leasehold mortgage increases, alternative (d) begins to look more and more, in substance, like straight debt financing—namely, alternative (a).

Conversely, if Realty is more concerned with the long-range tax picture, it could add more leaseback financing into the mix. For example, it could receive more cash boot, perhaps $400,000. Accordingly, the tax bite in the first year would be greater (28 percent of $400,000 versus 28 percent of $300,000), and the amount of after-tax working capital would decrease ($888,000 versus $916,000),[74] but the rental deductions would be higher because the leaseback is worth less. Finally, as the boot increases, Realty would be approaching straight leaseback financing—namely, alternative (c).

In conclusion, as the boot decreases, Realty would be trading a lesser capital gains tax for less in deductions against future operating income, and as the boot increases, the converse would be true. In either event, the amount of initial working capital would remain about the same. Of course, total reliance on general rules of thumb is almost always misplaced. Accordingly, any final decision on whether to use debt versus leaseback financing should be based on the mathematics of the particular situation, and should obviously take into account the nontax consideration—for example, the loss to the seller-lessee of any increase in land value when opting for the sale and leaseback.

Loss Disallowance Under I.R.C. § 1031. Finally, if Realty's book value in the property were $1.3 million instead of $300,000, the first-year tax results in alternatives (b), (c), and (d) would change. Since in

---

[73] If the boot received is only $200,000, the tax would be $56,000 (28 percent of $200,000) and net available working capital would be $144,000 plus the amount of the increased leasehold mortgage loan ($800,000) based on the more valuable leaseback, for a total of $944,000. On the other hand, if the boot remains the same at $300,000, the initial capital gain tax could be $84,000 (28 percent of $300,000), and the net working capital would be $216,000 plus the amount of the leasehold mortgage ($700,000), for a total of $916,000.

[74] If the boot received is $400,000, the tax would be $112,000 (28 percent of $400,000), and the after-tax amount of working capital would be $288,000 plus the amount of the reduced leasehold mortgage ($600,000), for a total of $888,000.

Short-term Results. Whereas debt financing (alternative (a)) is not a taxable event, the sale-and-leaseback alternatives are, unless I.R.C. § 1031 applies to postpone recognition of some of the potential gain ($700,000 in this instance) because Realty is transferring property with a basis of $300,000 and receiving $1 million plus a leaseback. However, I.R.C. § 1031 does not apply to alternatives (b) and (c) since a "sale," and not an exchange, took place. Under the "fair market value" test applied in both *Jordan Marsh* and *City Investing Co.* Realty could not be exchanging the property for the leasebacks since it would be receiving cash equal to the full $1 million value of the property. As a further indication that the leasebacks have no independent economic significance or value, the leaseback rentals in alternatives (b) and (c), unlike in (d), are not below fair market.[71] Also, in alternative (b), I.R.C. § 1031 could not apply even if the fee were exchanged for the leasehold since a leasehold of less than thirty years is not regarded as equivalent of "like kind" to a fee estate. Moreover, even if the nonrecognition provisions were applicable, it would not help Realty in either alternative (a) or (b) since it would have to recognize the potential gain ($700,000) to the extent of the cash or other boot received.[72] In this instance, the boot of $1 million would exceed the gain. However, chances are that Realty will sell the property anyway once the depreciation tax shelter diminishes, and the gain on the property, if it is held for at least nine months (and, after January 1, 1978, one year), in a trade or business will be taxable at capital gain rates under I.R.C. § 1231. In this instance, the tax would accordingly be $196,000 since the alternative 28 percent rate would apply.

Flexibility of Mixing Debt With Leaseback Financing. In most respects, alternative (d) is the optimum alternative; it best responds to both the short- and long-term needs of Realty Corporation. Specifically, if Realty is more concerned with its tax posture in the short run (that is, it needs some working capital but wants to minimize the initial tax bite), it could lessen the amount of the boot received to perhaps $200,000 instead of $300,000 and, as a result, receive a leaseback worth $800,000 instead of 700,000. Accordingly, I.R.C. § 1031 would still apply since the thirty-year leaseback has even more independent economic value and has, therefore, been "exchanged" for the fee. Consequently, the tax bite is less (28 percent of $200,000 versus 28 percent of $300,000) by $28,000, and the amount of available working capital is increased by

---

[71] In both instances, the rentals are calculated to enable Lender to recoup its purchase price and receive about a 5 percent extra rate of return each year.

[72] I.R.C. § 1031(b).

Question: How would the business and tax results of using debt financing (alternative (a)) compare in the short run, and long run, with use of:

(1) Sale-and-leaseback financing (alternatives (b) and (c)); and
(2) Combination of sale and leaseback with debt financing (alternative (d))?

The following chart of first year tax results will be useful in illustrating the subsequent analysis:

Alternative	Ownership	Realty's Cash Outflow	Depreciation	Interest	Rent	Total Deductions	Potential Capital Gain or Loss
15 yrs. (a)	Realty Corp.	$146,666 ↓	$ 3,333 K	$80,000 ↓	—	$ 83,333 ↓	-0-
15 yrs. (b)	Lender Ins. Co.	$116,666 K	—	—	$116,666 K	$116,666 K	28%[69] of $700,000 = $196,000
30 yrs. (c)	Lender Ins. Co.	$ 83,333 K	—	—	$ 83,333 K	$ 83,333 K	28% of $700,000 = $196,000
30 yrs. (d)	Lender Ins. Co.	$104,333 ↓	$10,000[70] K	$56,000↓	$ 25,000 K	$ 91,000 ↓	28% of $300,000 = $ 84,000

Key: K = constant
↓ decreasing

Long-Run Results. In the long run, alternative (b) clearly looks more attractive than the debt financing alternative (a). As expected, the cash outflow is greater with debt financing since the mortgage lender demands a higher rate of return than the owner-lessor during the same fifteen-year payout period. The lender, unlike the lessor, is not acquiring ownership of the land and benefiting from its appreciation in value. From a tax perspective, the sale and leaseback is clearly preferable since 100 percent of Realty's cash flow is deductible as rent; in alternative (a), the total deductions represent about 57 percent of Realty's cash flow. Moreover, with debt financing, the mortgage interest deduction will decline, as will the outstanding principal balance. So would depreciation if, as is generally the case, Realty had been using accelerated and not straight-line depreciation. By contrast, Realty's rent deduction in both leaseback alternatives (b) and (c) would remain constant over the respective leaseback periods.

---

[69] I.R.C. § 1201(a). The Revenue Act of 1978 reduced the alternative capital gains rate for corporations from 30 to 28 percent for taxable years after 1978. See discussion at ¶ 1.05[2][d].

[70] In effect, Realty paid $700,000 for the leaseback since it gave up property worth $1 million and received only $300,000. However, under I.R.C. § 1031(d), the basis in the leaseback is the basis of the property exchanged ($300,000) less cash received ($300,000) plus gain recognized ($300,000). Accordingly, Realty can amortize its carryover basis ($300,000) in the leasehold used in its trade or business over the thirty-year lease term, which produces a constant amortization deduction of $10,000 per annum.

(b) *Sale-leaseback.* Sell the realty to Lender Insurance Co. for $1 million with a fifteen-year leaseback at an annual rental of $116,666, with an option to renew based on 10 percent of the appraised value of the land.

(c) *Sale-leaseback.* Sell the realty to Lender for $1 million with a thirty-year leaseback at an annual rental of $83,333, with an option to repurchase based on 100 percent of the appraised value of the land. [*Note:* In both alternatives (b) and (c), Lender receives roughly a 5 percent rate of annual return over and above its recoupment of purchase price (disregarding any discount factor), somewhat less than what a mortgage lender or bondholder would demand.]

(d) *Combined sale-leaseback and debt financing.* Sell the realty to Lender for $300,000 with a thirty-year leaseback at an annual rental of $25,000. On the basis of the value of the leaseback, Realty can then borrow $700,000,[67] secured by a thirty-year mortgage repayable at $23,333 per annum, with annual interest of 8 percent on the outstanding principal balance. [*Note:* In a sale and leaseback the sales price can be manipulated, within reason,[68] to meet the working capital needs of the seller. For example, if Realty Corporation needed more initial capital, it could sell the property for more cash (e.g., $400,000) and, like any other borrower, pay out more annual rental (e.g., about $33,000) to enable Lender to recoup its capital and earn its 5 percent return.]

---

of the property's value, based on a capitalization of earnings reckoning. Moreover, some lenders, like life insurance companies, are limited by local law to a maximum loan-to-value ratio (e.g., 75 percent in New York). However, if the corporation obtained other debt financing by issuing preferred stock or by floating a bond issue, chances are that it might well obtain 100 percent financing if the corporation has a good credit rating because the lender would be looking to the net assets of the corporation, not just to the earnings potential of the property for security. In addition, for simplicity's sake, the mortgage in the example calls for a constant payment amortization, whereas the typical real estate mortgage involves a constant debt service payment so that the amortization or repayment of principal will increase over time.

[67] *Id.*

[68] *The sales price might be fixed well below market value in consideration of a reduced rental during the lease term.* If the sale resulted in an ordinary loss, taxpayer might enjoy an inflated deduction in the year of the sale, which would be partially offset by smaller rental deductions in future years. If the transaction were between related taxpayers (I.R.C. § 267) or affiliated organizations (I.R.C. § 482), the Commissioner could disallow any loss, or in the latter case, rewrite the transaction: An increase in sales price would lower the first year's loss; the lump sum increase would then be amortized over the lease term. If the original transaction were to produce a capital gain under either I.R.C. §§ 1221 or 1231, it is unlikely that the seller would deliberately accept an artificially low price; it is even more unlikely that the Commissioner would attempt to rewrite the transaction as indicated above.

character of the rent expenditure,[62] disallow loss recognition on the sale,[63] or charge the seller with ordinary income if gain is realized on the sale of depreciable property.[64]

[d] Treatment as Disguised Purchase

Finally, if the sale and leaseback involves a tax-exempt purchaser-lessor, the parties may be tempted to trade a high leaseback rental for a low repurchase price. This would enable the seller-lessee to obtain a higher rental deduction without disadvantaging the owner-lessor, either tax- or cash-wise. However, the Commissioner might argue that the transaction in substance amounted to nothing more than a disguised installment repurchase of the property and might accordingly disallow the rental payments as nondeductible installment payments.[65]

[4] Illustration of Leaseback Flexibility

The following hypothetical situation is illustrative of the foregoing tax rules and problems and the flexibility of the sale and leaseback as a financing tool in comparison to debt financing.

The Realty Corporation owns unencumbered land and buildings of equal value that together are worth $1 million, with an adjusted basis of $300,000 ($200,000 allocable to land and $100,000 to buildings). It desires to raise $1 million of additional working capital. Assume that the useful life of the buildings is thirty years, salvage value is zero, and the corporation is using straight-line depreciation. The corporation can pursue any of the following alternatives:

(a) *Debt financing.* Obtain a $1 million fifteen-year mortgage loan on the property, repayable $66,666 per annum with annual interest of 8 percent on the outstanding principal balance.[66]

---

[62] See I.L. Van Zandt v. Comm'r, 341 F.2d 440 (5th Cir. 1965), *cert. denied* 382 U.S. 814; Warren Brekke v. Comm'r, 40 T.C. 789 (1963), *vacated and remanded by 9th Circuit to Tax Court,* 25 T.C. Memo. 1063, 1966-208 T.C. Memo., *on other issues.*

[63] I.R.C. § 267 (sale to a family member or related party as defined in § 267(b); I.R.C. § 707(b)(1) (sale between a partnership and a controlling partner who owns more than a 50 percent partnership interest, or sale between two controlled partnerships).

[64] I.R.C. § 1239 (sale between husband and wife or between a corporation and a stockholder who owns 80 percent or more of stock); I.R.C. § 707(b)(2) (sale between a partnership and a controlling partner who owns more than 80 percent partnership interest, or sale between two controlled partnerships).

[65] See Starr v. Comm'r, 274 F.2d 294 (9th Cir. 1959).

[66] For comparison purposes, the $1 million loan amount used is somewhat unrealistic in that most permanent lenders would not lend more than 80 percent

(1) If possible, replace the repurchase option with a series of long renewal periods, or "water down" the option by making the repurchase optional with both the owner-lessor and the seller-lessee;
(2) Gear the option price to the fair market value of the property at the date of its exercise;
(3) Gear the initial sales price to the fair market value of the property at the date of sale;
(4) Avoid using a "net" leaseback, or placing the risk of casualty loss on the seller-lessee;
(5) Sell to an institutional lender only if it has other sale and leasebacks in its investment portfolio;
(6) Avoid any two-party arrangement between related taxpayers and, if possible, use an outside lender where other financing is involved.

[c] Reallocation of Leaseback Rental

If there is an option to renew at an unduly low rental, the Commissioner may urge that a portion of the rental paid during the original leaseback term be deferred as a prepaid expense to the renewal term. Otherwise, the lessee's taxable income arguably would be understated during the original term and overstated during the renewal period.[59] Or, if the rental for the original leaseback term is an escalating or de-escalating one, the Service may argue, on the same rationale, for even amortization of the entire rental payment over the entire leaseback period. In either event, a portion of the rental expenses would be disallowed as a current deduction and would instead be capitalized. Finally, if the sale and leaseback is between related parties, the Commissioner may attempt to denominate the lessee's payments as something other than a rent deduction,[60] reallocate any excessive rental paid as additional income to the lessee,[61] challenge the ordinary and necessary

---

[59] See Reg. § 1.461-1(a)(2). Main & McKinney Bldg. Co. v. Comm'r, 113 F.2d 81 (5th Cir. 1940), *cert. denied* 311 U.S. 688 (involving a straight lease transaction). Cf. Shelby Salesbook Co. v. United States, 104 F. Supp. 237 (N.D. Ohio 1952), and Alstores Realty Corp., 46 T.C. 363 (1966) (part of $1 million purchase price treated as prepaid rental income to taxpayer-purchaser where seller received $750,000 plus a two-and-a-half-year rent-free leaseback).

[60] For example, an excessive rental payment to a related individual may be treated as a nondeductible gift or personal expense. See Coe Laboratories, Inc., 34 T.C. 549 (1960). Or, an excessive rental paid to a shareholder-lessor by a corporate lessee may be treated as a constructive dividend. E.g., J.J. Kirk, Inc., 34 T.C. 130 (1960), *aff'd* 289 F.2d 935 (6th Cir. 1961).

[61] See I.R.C. § 482 and the regulations thereunder.

from the taxpayer to the bank. The United States Court of Appeals for the Eighth Circuit, in reversing the district court decision,[56] agreed with the Service and, after analogizing ownership for tax purposes to a "bundle of sticks," concluded that the taxpayer "totes an empty bundle..." because, inter alia, the option prices had not taken into account possible appreciation in building value or inflation, and the rental payments during the original term were exactly equal in amount to the mortgage payments.

The Supreme Court disagreed and held that this was a genuine multiparty transaction with economic substance not shaped solely by tax-avoidance features. Specifically, the Court cited the fact that the transaction was not simply a two-party arrangement between related taxpayers[57], but was rather a three-party transaction involving an independent investor and outside lenders. The Court also refused to characterize the transaction as nothing more than a mortgage agreement between the bank and the outside lenders, plus a loan from the taxpayer to the bank because (1) the taxpayer and not the bank was liable on the mortgage note; and (2) no legal obligation existed on the part of the bank to repay the $500,000 to the taxpayer since such would be the case only if and when the bank chose to exercise its options.[58]

While taxpayers may be encouraged by the Supreme Court's refusal (albeit without analysis) to draw any negative inferences from the fact that the purchase option and rental payments had been geared to the terms of the mortgage, it should also be noted that the Court was apparently influenced by the lower district court's finding that the rents were reasonable and that the option prices were negotiated at arm's length and represented fair estimates of market values. To a large extent, the Court was influenced by the fact that the sale-leaseback was compelled by a nontax motive, namely, the bank was unable because of certain regulatory constraints to carry its building plans into effect without resorting to some type of nonconventional financing arrangement.

[ii] **Tax Planning.** The following measures can be taken to help assure tax treatment as a sale:

---

[56] 536 F.2d 746 (8th Cir. 1976), *rev'd* 75-2 U.S.T.C. ¶ 9545 (E.D. Ark. 1975).

[57] On this point the Court distinguished this case from the *Lazarus* case cited in note 54 *supra*. 435 U.S. at 575.

[58] *Id.* at 576. However, the favorable option and lease renewal terms made it highly unlikely that the bank would abandon the building after it had in effect "paid off" the mortgage.

lessee would be entitled to deduct depreciation as the real owner of the property and would be entitled to deduct that portion of the so-called rental payments that constitute constructive "interest" on the constructive loan.[54]

[i] Frank Lyon Co. v. United States. While the precedential value of this case is limited by the uniqueness of its facts, the general approach taken by the Supreme Court offers guidance for the tax planner. In *Frank Lyon Co. v. United States*,[55] a state bank obtained commitments for both interim and permanent financing of an office building to be used as the bank's headquarters and principal banking facility. However, the bank was not itself able to take title to the improvements because of certain regulatory constraints, so it sold the building at the estimated cost of construction and leased the underlying fee to the taxpayer. It then leased back the building and subleased back the fee for twenty-five years with options to renew for an additional forty years. While the bank subordinated its fee interest to the lien of the leasehold mortgage, the taxpayer became obligated on the deed of trust note to both the construction lender and the permanent lender. These loan proceeds were used by the taxpayer, with $500,000 of its own equity funds, to pay the purchase price to the bank. Simultaneously, the bank obligated itself to pay, after construction was completed, a leaseback rental equal to the principal and interest payments on the permanent mortgage. It also acquired the option to repurchase the building at various times at prices equal to the unpaid balance of the long-term mortgage plus the taxpayer-lessor's initial investment ($500,000) compounded at a 6 percent annual rate of interest.

The Internal Revenue Service disallowed the taxpayer's deductions for depreciation and other expenses related to the building on the ground that the sale-leaseback was but a disguised loan of $500,000

---

as a matter of law inasmuch as there was evidence that the parties had intended a sale, that the repurchase price was "fair" and not unduly low, and that the lessee decided to exercise its purchase option because of the sudden availability of "wraparound" financing and not because he was under economic compulsion to do so.

[54] In Helvering v. F. & R. Lazarus & Co., 308 U.S. 252 (1939), the Supreme Court permitted depreciation to the taxpayer on the basis that the sale to, and leaseback from, a bank as trustee for some land-trust certificate holders was in substance a mortgage loan to the taxpayer. The Court sustained the findings of the Board of Tax Appeals to the effect that the "rent" was intended as a promise to pay an agreed-upon rate of interest on the loan, and the so-called depreciation fund was in reality a source for the amortization payoff. See Rev. Rul. 72-543, 1972-2 C.B. 87.

[55] 435 U.S. 561 (1978)

wants to avoid I.R.C. § 1031 so that a loss will be recognized, the amount of cash received should be close to the fair market of the transferred property, and the leaseback rental should likewise not be appreciably less than the fair market rental at the time the lease agreement is executed.[52]

[b] Treatment as Disguised Loan

The case law reflects another pitfall for the unwary. If the option to repurchase in the sale-and-leaseback agreement stipulates an unusually low price, or the agreement otherwise lacks the substantive appearance of a sale, a loss on the sale or leaseback rentals may be disallowed on the rationale that the transaction was, in substance, a loan in that the seller never intended to permanently divest himself of ownership.[53] However, offsetting the foregoing disadvantages is the fact that any gain on the purported "sale" would not be recognized. Moreover, the seller-

---

[52] See Leslie Co. v. Comm'r, 539 F.2d 943 (3d Cir. 1976), *aff'd* 64 T.C. 247, wherein the "fair market approach" was followed by the Tax Court and Third Circuit. Cf. Missouri Pac. R.R. v. United States, 497 F.2d 1386 (Ct. Cl. 1974) (sale-leaseback characterized as like-kind exchange despite the fact that seller received cash payment equal to fair market value of the property and the leaseback rental was at fair market value). See discussion of Frank Lyon Co. v. United States at ¶ 6.04[3][b][i].

[53] E.g., Sun Oil Co. v. Comm'r, 562 F.2d 258 (1977), *cert. denied* 436 U.S. 944 (1978), *rev'd and remanding Tax Court* 35 T.C.M. 173 (1976), where the Third Circuit held that a sale-leaseback between an oil company and an unrelated tax-exempt trust was in reality a mortgage and not a sale where the net leaseback rental was geared to amortization of the sale price and dropped sharply after a twenty-one-year primary lease term expired, notwithstanding likely appreciation in the value of the property, where the "rejectable" option to repurchase the property was in fact nonrejectable, and where the "fair appraisal value" option price was so formulated that the purchaser-lessor would be precluded from enjoying the appreciation in the value of the property. In another decision by the Third Circuit (decided prior to the *Lyon Co.* case), involving a sale-leaseback between unrelated parties, the court denied a loss to the seller-lessee where the leaseback rental was to be applied to the repurchase price and approximated the amounts received from the purchasor-lessor. Leeds & Lippincott Co. v. United States, 276 F.2d 927 (3d Cir. 1960). Accord, Frenzel v. Comm'r, 22 T.C. Memo. 1391, 1963-276 T.C. Memo. where the Tax Court disallowed rent deductions on leaseback where the taxpayers had an option to repurchase the property for 10 percent of its purchase price at the end of the leaseback period and where the renewal rents were very low. But cf. American Realty Trust v. United States, 498 F.2d 1194 (1974), where the Fourth Circuit sustained as not clearly erroneous a jury verdict that the sale-leaseback transaction was a bona fide sale and not a disguised secured loan. Even though the net leaseback rental was reduced by 50 percent of any reduction in the annual mortgage payments, and the seller-lessee was entitled to 50 percent of any refinancing proceeds, the court refused to hold that the transaction was a loan

court reasoned correctly that unlike *Century Electric*, the cash received by the taxpayer was the full equivalent of the value of the fee...."[48] Consequently, since the taxpayer had already received the full value of the property in cash, common sense dictated that the extra consideration received—the leaseback—had no independent economic value. This was reflected by the fact that the leaseback contract required a rental that was not below fair market. However, in Revenue Ruling 60-43,[49] the Revenue Service has indicated that it will not follow the decision in *Jordan Marsh*.

City Investing Co. v. Comm'r.[50] Finally, in *City Investing,* which involved a seller engaged in "liquidating" its properties, the Tax Court implicitly followed the "fair market value" approach of the Second Circuit in *Jordan Marsh* by holding that the taxpayer had sold his fee for a leaseback since the taxpayer had received in cash an amount that was not less than the fair market value of the transferred property. Reflective of this parity in market values was the fact that the leaseback rental was not less than the fair market rental of the property. However, the court disappointingly waffled on the sale versus exchange issue by stating that "it was not necessary...to decide whether the decision of the Court of Appeals for the Second Circuit in *Jordan Marsh* is inconsistent with the result in the earlier *Century Electric Co.* case" since the taxpayer in the instant case, unlike the cases cited, had transferred his property pursuant to an "adopted policy of liquidating its property holdings."[51] But again, the core issue presented by the sale versus "exchange" language in the statute is not whether, but how, the taxpayer will liquidate its property.

[ii] Tax Planning. Notwithstanding the nonacquiescence of the Revenue Service to the results in both *Jordan Marsh* and *City Investing Co.,* the rationale for these results ("fair market approach") is so compelling as to suggest that a taxpayer will be reasonably assured of obtaining nonrecognition treatment of gain, except to the extent boot is received, by arranging for a thirty-year or more leaseback and by limiting the amount of cash or other boot received to an amount significantly below the fair market value of the transferred property. Perhaps the ratio of cash to fair market value should not exceed $3/5$, the ratio present in the *Century Electric* case. Conversely, if the taxpayer

---

[48] *Id.* at 457.
[49] Rev. Rul. 60-43, 1960-1 C.B. 687.
[50] 38 T.C. 1 (1962), *nonacq'd* 1963-2 C.B. 6.
[51] *Id.* at 8.

the entire loss (or gain less boot) would go unrecognized, and in the case of a sale, the entire loss would be recognized regardless of whether boot was received by the seller. Unfortunately, neither the Code nor regulations define the term "exchange" with particularity, and one must therefore resort to the case authorities.

[i] Case Law Interpretations of "Exchange." *Century Electric Co. v. Comm'r.*[43] The first case to confront the issue involved a taxpayer who conveyed to a college a foundry building and land used in its manufacturing business. It had an adjusted basis of $531,000, and the owner received from the grantee both $150,000 and a ninety-five-year leaseback. The Eighth Circuit affirmed the Tax Court in disallowing the loss since the seller-lessee had received like property (the more-than-thirty-year leaseback) in "exchange" for the fee. The *tenuous* rationale for the decision was that since the taxpayer held the same property for the same use in the same business both before and after the transaction, the taxpayer's economic situation remained the same; therefore, no sale took place.[44] But under this standard, when would the economic situation of the taxpayer in a sale and leaseback ever change and produce a resultant sale? Ironically, the court ignored the real issue[45]— whether the leaseback was worth something. As a matter of common sense, a seller will expect to receive in value what he gives up. Accordingly, since the taxpayer gave up property worth as much as $250,000 (but not less than $205,780),[46] and yet received only $150,000 in cash with the leaseback, the leaseback must have been exchanged for the fee, inasmuch as the leaseback itself had independent economic significance.

Jordan Marsh Co. v. Comm'r.[47] The next case, decided by the Second Circuit eight years later, involved a department store concern that conveyed two parcels of land, with an adjusted basis of $4,770,000, and received as the quid pro quo a thirty-year leaseback and $2,300,000, which concededly represented the fair market value of the property. The Court reversed the Tax Court and held that the property was "sold" for cash and the taxpayer was accordingly entitled to a loss deduction. The

---

[43] 192 F.2d 155 (8th Cir. 1951), *cert. denied* 342 U.S. 954 (1952).

[44] 192 F. 2d at 160.

[45] *Id.* at 159, the court states that: "in the computation of gain or loss on a transfer of property held for productive use in a trade or business for property of a like kind to be held for the same use, the *market value of the properties of like kind involved in the transfer does not enter into the equation.*" (Emphasis added.)

[46] *Id.* at 157.

[47] 269 F.2d 453 (2d Cir. 1959).

recoups his capital at the end of the leaseback period. In the event of default, he (like the installment-contract vendor) can avail himself of the stronger contractual remedies (e.g., rescission, damages) and landlord remedies (e.g., action in ejectment) rather than the more cumbersome and expensive remedy of foreclosure.

[ii] Tax Considerations. While the seller-lessee is able to deduct rental payments in their entirety, the reciprocal disadvantage to the purchaser-lessor is that these payments are includable in full as ordinary rental income. By contrast, the portion of the debt service payments to a mortgage lender representing its return of capital (amortization) is not taxable. However, the tax impact to the purchaser is mitigated by his right for depreciation purposes to use a fresh tax basis equal to his purchase price. The foregoing tax disadvantage explains why the purchaser-lessor is usually a tax-exempt charitable organization such as a college or a quasi-exempt institution such as a life insurance company.

[3] Tax Pitfalls Inherent in Sale-Leaseback

[a] Loss Disallowed "Exchange"

Section 1031(a) of the Internal Revenue Code mandates nonrecognition of gain or loss if property held for productive use in a trade or business is *exchanged* solely for property of a like kind. In addition, if a taxpayer receives in exchange property not equivalent to the exchanged property, he must recognize his gain, but not loss, to the extent of the cash or fair market value of the tainted property ("boot") received. Since a leasehold of thirty years or more is regarded as like kind or equivalent to property held in fee, an individual or syndicate that holds property worth less than its depreciated cost (adjusted basis) would want to avoid an "exchange" of the property if a leaseback of thirty years or more is received by the seller.[42] Otherwise, an ordinary loss could not be recognized under I.R.C. § 1231.

But when is there an "exchange" versus a sale of a fee interest in property when the previous owner receives as consideration not only a long-term leaseback, but boot as well? For, in the case of an exchange,

---

[42] E.g., Capri, Inc. v. Comm'r, 65 T.C. 162, 181 (1975), wherein the loss on a sale of hotel assets was held deductible because even though the parties to the sale-leaseback transaction were related corporations and the Commissioner contended that the leaseback term would be automatically renewable, the term of the leaseback was less than thirty years, and there was no provision for renewal. See note 33 *supra*.

low the rental deductions and/or loss on the sale by treating the transaction as a "disguised" loan on the rationale that the so-called seller had never intended to permanently divest himself of ownership of the property.[39]

[ii] Tax Considerations. As previously mentioned, the individual or syndicate that uses a sale and leaseback is entitled to a rent deduction, which often will exceed the sum of the depreciation and mortgage interest it would have been entitled to had it retained title to the property and obtained a mortgage loan. This general rule is most applicable where a significant portion of the tax basis of the property is allocable to nondepreciable land and/or where the deductible depreciation remaining for the improvements has decelerated in amount. However, a sale of realty in a sale and leaseback, unlike a mortgage loan, is a taxable event, and it will generate taxable capital or Section 1231 gain unless the property is dealer realty, in which event the seller will be charged with ordinary income. However, if the seller-lessee receives a leasehold of thirty years or more *in exchange* for his fee title to the property, the transaction could qualify as a tax-free exchange under I.R.C. § 1031.[40] Accordingly, gain would be recognized and taxed only to the extent the seller-lessee receives cash or any other property (called "boot") in addition to the leaseback.[41] Moreover, if the property is sold for a loss, it may be deductible in full as an ordinary loss under I.R.C. § 1231 if the realty was used in the taxpayer's trade or business and held for more than nine months, or one year for tax years beginning in 1978. Finally, the amount of the lessee's rental deductions is determined by reference to the leaseback agreement itself. It normally is not subject to close scrutiny by the Commissioner, whereas the taxpayer must often, prove at audit the reasonableness of his estimates for useful life and salvage value in the event he retains ownership and claims depreciation deductions.

[b] Position of the Purchaser-Lessor

[i] Business Considerations. In contrast to a straight purchase, the purchaser in a sale and leaseback acquires investment property with a built-in tenant (the seller), and knows beforehand what the total of the prearranged rental and resultant rate of return will be. Moreover, the purchaser-lessor, unlike a mortgage lender, owns the property once he

---

[39] See discussion at ¶ 6.04[3][b].
[40] Reg. § 1.1031(a)-1(c)(2). See discussion at ¶ 8.02.
[41] I.R.C. § 1031(b).

Some accountants and commentators argue that rental payments constitute as inexorable an annual charge as the prorated amortization payments required in debt financing. They suggest that the balance sheet show the leasehold as a deferred expense asset (to be written off as the rentals are paid) and the rent obligation as a fixed liability.[35] In the case of debt financing, showing projected amortization payments as a fixed liability makes sense. The debtor has already received his consideration, the loan proceeds. In a sale and leaseback, however, the rental obligation of the seller-lessee is still contingent on performance of the lease agreement by the purchaser-lessor.[36] In addition, it is usually undesirable to create a deferred expense asset that has not in fact been paid for. Therefore, such an entry, while mechanically proper, would result in both a questionable asset and a questionable liability without serving any useful purpose. Indeed, such a "padding" of both sides of the balance sheet is likely to be more confusing than helpful to the lessee's creditors and investors. Accordingly, it would appear that this type of contingent liability should appear as merely a footnote on the balance sheet. This is not to say, of course, that the leasehold should not appear on the balance sheet as a fixed asset subject to amortization if the seller-lessee pays valuable consideration for the leaseback. For example, this would apply in a situation where owner sells Blackacre, worth $1 million, to an insurance company for $500,000 and receives the right to occupy the premises for less than the fair market rental.

Flexibility under usury law. Like the installment land contract device,[37] the sale and leaseback is, in form, a sale and not a loan to the purchaser. Accordingly, the usury restrictions on lending would not apply.[38]

Loss of Appreciation in Land Value. The most salient nontax disadvantage is an obvious one: The seller-lessee will lose possession of the premises, including improvements, upon the expiration of the leaseback term and will be deprived of the appreciation in land value to which he would have been entitled had he retained title to the land. The leaseback will frequently contain an option to repurchase, but the option price will generally be geared to the then fair market value of the property. Otherwise, the Commissioner could argue "sham" and disal-

---

[35] See Carey, "Corporate Financing through the Sale and Leaseback of Property: Business, Tax, and Policy Considerations," 62 Harv. L. Rev. 1, 12 (1948). See also Financial Accounting Standards Board Statement No. 13, at 29 (Nov. 1976), which suggests that certain "capital leasebacks be reflected as both an asset and a liability on the balance sheet."

[36] Cf. Levin v. Comm'r, 219 F.2d 588 (3rd Cir. 1955).

[37] See discussion at ¶ 5.05[5].

[38] See discussion at ¶ 5.05[4].

[a] Position of Seller-Lessee

As in the case of choosing between fee mortgage and leasehold mortgage financing, "rule of thumb" decision-making in the choice of sale-leaseback versus debt financing can be dangerous. Of necessity, any final decision must rest on a careful weighing of the following tax and nontax considerations:

[i] Business Considerations. *Greater Ability to Borrow.* For both purchase and mortgage loan appraisal purposes, the capitalized earnings of the property, and not the solvency or credit standing of the seller-lessee or mortgagor, determine the loan amount. Accordingly, the amount will generally be less in the latter case; loan-to-value ratios offered by mortgage lenders such as life insurance companies are regulated by local law.[33] By contrast, the seller in a sale-and-leaseback transaction should be able to sell the property for 100 percent of its appraised value. However, if the creditor-investor is relying upon the solvency of the borrower and not the earnings potential of the property (for example, where the realty only represents a fraction of the net assets and earnings of the borrower), the borrower should consider some other type of debt financing arrangement. For example, the borrower, if a corporation, would no doubt be able to procure more capital by issuing preferred stock or by issuing bonds than by a sale and leaseback. However, such a course of action might require the imposition of restrictions by a trust indenture agreement of preferred stock certificates, which might interfere with the borrower's ability to raise funds in the future.[34]

Effect on Balance Sheet of Borrower. In contrast to debt financing, the obligation of the seller-lessee does not reflect itself as indebtedness on the balance sheet, and a sale and leaseback results in replacing some fixed asset (the realty being sold) with a liquid asset (cash received). While the net assets of the seller-lessee remain the same, its borrowing ratios for the purpose of obtaining future credit would no doubt improve.

---

[33] See discussion of regulatory statutes at ¶ 2.02[1][d]. Typically, the maximum loan-to-value ratio on fee mortgages with a reasonably short amortization period (e.g., thirty-five years or less) is 75 percent. See N.Y. Ins. Law § 81(6)(a)(3) (McKinney 1966). However, these same regulatory statutes will often impose tight quantitative and qualitative constraints (other than loan-to-value restrictions) on the type of sale-and-leaseback transaction available to insurance companies.

[34] Maintenance of minimum working capital and debt-to-equity ratios are typical of the kinds of legal restrictions imposed by bond and preferred stock credits.

Fee simple title to the land only described in this Schedule A herein exclusive of a present possessory determinable interest in the reserved area, and the improvements located therein, which executory future interest shall ripen into a present possessory fee simple estate by operation of law (without the necessity of any future deed) upon termination or expiration of the leasehold estate reserved to the grantor in the deed to the insured as herein mentioned. Note, this policy specifically insures that the above referred to executory future interest (as created in the deed to the insured) does not violate the rule against perpetuities.

[2] Land and Improvements

A syndicate or other owner of land and *existing* improvements in need of additional working capital may find it more advantageous from a business or tax perspective to raise the capital by a sale-leaseback than by a mortgage loan or other type of debt financing.

The leaseback often is a net lease containing some provision for successive renewal periods or repurchase, and in all cases after the transaction, the same property is held by the previous owner for the same use in the same business. Accordingly, the economic position of the seller-lessee often remains the same in substance. As one court noted, "the only change wrought by the transaction was in the estate or interest of petitioner [seller] in the...property."[32] However, from a tax perspective, the seller-lessee (as previously noted) is entitled, in effect, to depreciate the land component under the guise of a "rental" payment. In addition, if the buildings are already fully depreciated, chances are that the seller-lessee's rental deduction allocable to the improvements will exceed the amount of depreciation and mortgage interest deductions he would have been entitled to had he retained ownership and obtained or refinanced a mortgage loan to fund his additional working capital needs.

By contrast, the purchaser-lessor, unlike a mortgage lender, will recoup its capital outlay in the form of ordinary rental income and will not receive a tax-free return of loan capital. However, this disadvantage is eliminated or ameliorated in the case of a tax-exempt or quasi-exempt purchaser such as an insurance company. Moreover, any appreciation in value of the land during the payout period will inure to the benefit of the purchaser-lessor who, unlike a mortgage lender, would own the land. The trade-off, however, is that the purchaser's rate of return over and above his capital outlay (purchase price) as reflected by the amount of leaseback rentals will probably be less than the rate of interest return obtainable by a mortgage lender.

---

[32] Century Elec. Co. v. Comm'r, 192 F.2d 155, 160 (8th Cir. 1951).

ments. On the other hand, as the new owner of the land, the institutional investor wants assurance that upon the expiration of the leaseback term, or sooner in the event of a lease default, it will be vested with clear title to the improvements as well as to the land.

[b] Drafting Approaches

There are two drafting approaches employed to resolve these antithetical objectives of the parties. The first is for the developer to convey title to the building as well as the land to the investor (although the purchase price will merely reflect the present value of the land), while reserving to the developer an estate for years in the improvements. The second method resurrects an old common-law future interest, executory interest. Under this method, the developer conveys the land by deed, together with a future interest in the buildings that becomes a possessory estate upon the expiration of the lease term, or sooner in the event of default and cancellation of the lease. Under traditional methods of conveyancing, there is no need for a subsequent deed, even if the institutional investor could procure it from the developer at the time of the termination of the lease. The advantage of this method is that it clearly reflects the intent of the parties to convey the land, but in the improvements, leaves both possessory and legal title with the developer.

[c] Title Problems

The rule against perpetuities is designed to prohibit remoteness in vesting of contingent future interests. Under most state statutes today, executory interests are held subject to the rule against perpetuities. An argument can and has been made in some jurisdictions[30] that the rule against perpetuities should not apply in commercial transactions. Moreover, the executory interest created in this manner is not an interest contingent upon a happening. In fact, the executory interest is subject to an event that is certain to happen, the expiration or termination of the ground lease within a stated time period. Consequently, an executory interest not subject to any condition precedent should not be in violation of the rule against perpetuities.[31] With regard to the title policy, the Schedule A language (in the American Land Title Association standard form of owner-mortgagee title policy) defining the estate should consist of the following type of language:

---

[30] E.g., Wong v. DeGrazia, 29 Cal. Rptr. 86, *aff'd in part and rem'd* 60 Cal. 2d 525, 386 P.2d 817, 35 Cal. Rptr. 241 (1963).

[31] 6 *American Law of Property* § 24.20 (A.J. Casner, ed., 1952).

established real estate lender, it would be better to use a sales contract to make it clear from the outset that an equity purchase rather than a disguised mortgage loan is being intended and contemplated by the parties.[27]

[1] Land But Not Improvements

A popular financing device used by developers has been to sever land from the improvements and then lease it back under a subordinated ground lease. By selling the land and leasing it back, the owner is able to receive one-hundred percent value for the land, whereas if the owner used conventional permanent financing, the loan-to-value ratio for land would be no more than eighty percent. Moreover, since land is a nondepreciable asset, by selling the land and leasing it back, the rent paid by the developer for the use of the land is a fully deductible tax item.

[a] Depreciation

If there are existing improvements with a large depreciation potential, or the construction of new improvements is contemplated, the developer, as seller-lessee of the land, will want to continue to take depreciation on the buildings or other improvements. While it is clear that the developer-lessee can depreciate his capital investment in the improvements where the estimated useful life of the improvements does not exceed the remaining term of the lease,[28] his right to depreciate deductions may cease if he relinquishes his economic interest in the improvements.[29] In addition, his first-user status for purposes of taking accelerated depreciation might be jeopardized if the developer-lessee were not to retain some measure of proprietary interest in the improve-

---

[27] See Form 6.4, a sample land purchase-leaseback transaction sales contract in Appendix B (used by several institutional investors in connection with a sale-leaseback of land, *but not* improvements).

[28] Reg. § 1-167(a)-4. Reg. § 1.162-11(b)(1) permits only straight-line amortization "in lieu of a deduction for depreciation" where the remaining term of the lease is shorter than the useful life of the improvement.

[29] In Rev. Rul. 61-217, 1961-2 C.B. 49, it was held that a lessee under a ninety-nine-year ground lease who erected, at his own cost, a commercial building thereon and then assigned the lease to another, could not continue taking depreciation deductions since he did not retain his capital investment or any economic interest in the improvements. However, such a lessee who merely subleased the improved realty for the remainder of the term was entitled to continue taking the deductions. Cf. Rev. Rul. 62-178, discussed in note 1 *supra*.

is of the opinion that the provisions of the lease are otherwise adequate to protect the interests of the leasehold mortgagee, the lease should expressly provide that title to all improvements shall be vested in the lessee throughout the period of the lease.

(9) There shall be no merger of the lease, nor of the leasehold estate created thereby, with the fee estate in the premises, by reason of the fact that the lease, or the leasehold estate created thereby, or any interest in either thereof, may be held directly or indirectly by or for the account of any person who shall own the fee estate in the premises or any portion therein, and no such merger shall occur unless and until all persons at the time having any interest in the fee estate and all persons having any interest in the lease or the leasehold estate, including the leasehold mortgagee, shall join in a written instrument effecting such merger.

¶ 6.04 SALE AND LEASEBACK FINANCING VS. DEBT FINANCING

Keeping in mind that land itself is not a depreciable asset, and its ownership thus does not provide any significant tax shelter, but that the rent paid for the use of land is deductible, the sale and leaseback can be seen as an appealing alternative to debt financing. If a developer uses leasehold mortgage financing, he not only can reduce his cash outlay, but can also take a rental deduction in lieu of making an extra nondeductible payment of fee mortgage principal. Similarly, the sale and leaseback of real property affords a developer the opportunity to increase his cash inflow and at the same time to depreciate land that he owns in the guise of rental payments.

As the term implies, a sale-leaseback typically involves the sale of realty (either land alone or land together with improvements) by a developer, syndicate, or other business concern to an institutional lender or other investor that simultaneously leases back the property to the seller on a long-term basis. Essentially, there are two major types of sale-leaseback financing. The first involves a sale-leaseback of land but not improvements; the second involves a sale-leaseback of both land and improvements. In connection with the latter, a comparison of sale-leaseback and debt financing will be presented along with a checklist of the advantages and disadvantages of both types of financing. Finally, some major tax pitfalls of sale-leaseback financing will be discussed together with tax planning suggestions.

A sale-leaseback is initiated by either a sales contract or a commitment from some institutional investor to engage in the transaction. If the investor committing itself to make the sale-leaseback is also an

steps to cure all defaults of the original lessee other than insolvency defaults and such other defaults, if any, as are not susceptible of being cured by the leasehold mortgagee;
(e) The leasehold mortgagee should be granted the right to cure any default on the part of the lessee, as well as the further right to enter upon the premises and to do all things necessary to that end.

(5) The leasehold mortgagee should be expressly authorized to exercise any renewal option granted to the lessee. If the lessee fails, within the time limit, to exercise any option of renewal, the leasehold mortgagee must be notified by registered mail in order that the latter, if it so chooses, may exercise the option, either on its own behalf or on behalf of the lessee.

(6) Appropriate permission should be granted to the lessee to include the interest of the leasehold mortgagee in all fire and other hazard insurance policies, pursuant to a standard mortgagee clause or endorsement and to deposit the originals or copies of all such policies with the leasehold mortgagee.

(7) Hazard insurance proceeds and any condemnation awards required by the lease to be applied to the restoration of the premises shall be held by the leasehold mortgagee, or by an institutional investor or bank or trust company satisfactory to the lessor, the lessee and the leasehold mortgagee, for application in accordance with the provisions of the lease (to the extent not inconsistent with the requirement of the lease and the provisions of the leasehold mortgage).

(Note: Rent insurance proceeds, if any, may be required to be applied first to payment of any unpaid obligations owing under the lease and thereafter to the payment of any unpaid obligations owing under the leasehold mortgage, with any remaining balance to go to the lessee.)

(8) The condemnation provisions of the lease must be approved by local counsel as providing adequate protection to the investment of the leasehold mortgagee. Unless local counsel in a particular jurisdiction should advise otherwise, the condemnation provision may state that the lessor shall receive all awards made with respect to the land (or portion thereof) taken, plus any consequential damage to any portion of the land not taken. The lessee shall also receive the balance of any such awards, with an additional provision to the effect that if the court shall not find such values, the parties receiving any portion of the total award shall hold the same in trust pending determination of the respective interests of the parties by agreement or arbitration. Unless local counsel

leasehold estate by foreclosure, assignment in lieu of foreclosure, or otherwise, and thereafter shall remain liable for such obligations only so long as the leasehold mortgagee remains the owner of the leasehold estate.

(3) If the leasehold mortgagee should become the owner of the leasehold estate, it may assign the lease without any requirement of the lessor's consent, and any purchase money mortgage delivered in connection with any such assignment shall be entitled to the benefit of all of the provisions of the lease with respect to a leasehold mortgage.

(4) The default provisions of the lease must be approved by this company and its special counsel as providing adequate protection to the leasehold mortgagee against the possibility of the loss of its investment through a termination of the lease by reason of the default of the lessee. In general, the lease should provide:

> (a) A copy of each notice of default, which the lessor may serve upon the lessee, shall also be served by registered mail upon the leasehold mortgagee;
> (b) In the event that the lessee shall fail to cure the default within the time proscribed by the lease, further notice to that effect shall likewise be given to the leasehold mortgagee by registered mail. The latter shall be allowed such additional time as may be required within which either to cure the default or to institute and complete foreclosure proceedings, or otherwise acquire title to the leasehold interest. Also, so long as the leasehold mortgagee shall be engaged either in curing the default or in proceeding to foreclose the mortgage, no such default shall operate, or permit the lessor, to terminate the lease;
> (c) Bankruptcy and other insolvency defaults should be applicable only with respect to the lessee, the then owner of the leasehold estate, and neither the bankruptcy nor the insolvency of the lessee shall operate, or permit the lessor, to terminate the lease so long as all rent and other payments required to be paid by the lessee continue to be paid in accordance with the terms of the lease;
> (d) If, for any reason, the lease should be terminated, the leasehold mortgagee shall be entitled to receive a new lease upon the same terms (except for any special requirements, such as a requirement for the construction of a new building, which has already been fulfilled by the lessee) and having the same relative priority as the original lease, provided the leasehold mortgagee agrees to take prompt

ninety days after the close of each lease year. It is understood that this percentage rental will be subordinate to the lien of the First Trust Holder.

Adjustment of Base Rent: The base rent is to be adjusted on the fifth anniversary of the execution of the lease and at the end of five-year increments thereafter, so that the base rent shall be equal to 8 percent of the fair market value of the land subject to the leasehold estate. Said fair market value is to be determined by an MAI appraiser satisfactory to Developer and Owner. All costs and expenses of such appraisals are to be borne by Owner.

However, many lenders will object to any change in the base ground rent until the leasehold mortgage has been fully amortized. In addition, if a percentage rental clause is contemplated, the lender will frequently tolerate an income base geared to the borrower's net income, but not one based on his gross income or cash inflow; the latter do not provide the borrower with any hedge against declining profits. The notion among lenders is that borrower-developers tend to be overanxious about closing a ground lease transaction and frequently are careless about protecting their future revenues against "tight" rental provisions. Lenders want to minimize the risk of a default that would force them to foreclose and take over the property. But if a leasehold mortgagee is required to step in at foreclosure, it must be able to live with any rental provisions acceded to by its predecessor-in-interest, the borrower.

[10] Outline of Minimum Ground Lease Requirements for Benefit of Leasehold Mortgagee

The ground lease should contain appropriate express provisions that cover the following matters:

(1) The lessee should be granted express authority, without any requirement of the consent or approval of the lessor,

    (a) To mortgage the leasehold interest;
    (b) To assign the lease and the leasehold estate created thereby, including, but not limited to, an assignment in lieu of foreclosure, to a leasehold mortgagee; and
    (c) To sublet the leased premises.

(2) The leasehold mortgagee shall not become personally liable for the obligations of the lease unless and until it becomes the owner of the

[8] Default Provisions

Most important, to protect its security interest, the mortgagee will require adequate notice, usually by registered mail, of any default under the ground lease, along with ample opportunity to cure the default under the ground lease. The leasehold mortgagee will also attempt to eliminate those events of default—like bankruptcy—that it cannot cure. Also, in the event the lease is prematurely terminated, it will demand the right to secure a new ground lease for the remainder of the term after foreclosure, on the same terms and conditions as the previous lease.[24] The advantage to the mortgagee of demanding a reasonable time (normally the time necessary to foreclose the leasehold mortgage) in which to obtain possession and cure the lessee's default over the latter requirement is that the agreement by the ground lessor to give the mortgagee a new lease is an executory contract that could be set aside by a trustee in bankruptcy.[25] The same pitfall exists with respect to the lessee's option to renew; therefore, most lenders require that the ground lessee exercise all of its renewal rights prior to the closing of the mortgage. This avoids any problems with executory contracts in the event the ground lessor should become bankrupt. Finally, note that the leasehold mortgagee wears two hats: that of a potential tenant with respect to the ground lessor, and that of a potential landlord with respect to an occupancy subtenant. It therefore must review both leases from opposite viewpoints.

[9] Changes in Ground Rent

Since the ground lease is apt to be long term,[26] the fee owner-ground lessor will often demand some type of rental adjustment clause, or "kicker," as a hedge against inflation. For example, a ground lease may contain the following types of provisions:

> *Percentage Rental:* Owner will receive 15 percent of net income in excess of a $110,000 "net income base" per annum. Net income is defined as gross rents received from the office building less operating expenses, repairs, debt service, ground rent, expenditure for improvements, real estate taxes, business and franchise taxes, and insurance premiums. This percentage rental will be due within

---

[24] See Article 27 of Form 6.2 in Appendix B.
[25] 11 U.S.C. § 365a (1978).
[26] Indeed, some jurisdictions like New York prohibit life insurance companies from investing in leasehold mortgages unless the unexpired term of the ground lease is no less than a certain number of years (twenty-one in New York). New York Ins. Law § 81(6)(a). See ¶ 2.02[1][d].

[6] Application of Hazard Insurance Proceeds

Ordinarily, the mortgagee would not only insist that it be a named insured under a standard mortgagee clause, with proceeds payable to it, but would also insist that it have the option to apply the insurance proceeds against the mortgage indebtedness rather than to fund the restoration of the premises—as would be a fee mortgagee in an analogous situation.[21] However, in this situation, the leasehold mortgagee must also contend with the fee owner, who generally has more bargaining power than the developer-mortgagor. The fee owner will waive its claim to the insurance proceeds only if the proceeds are made available for restoration of the premises. In response, the leasehold mortgagee will generally agree, provided that (1) there be no prohibition in the ground lease against the standard mortgagee clause naming it or an insurance trustee, like a bank or trust company; (2) there be no adjustment of losses without its consent; and (3) it retain control over the disbursement of proceeds. For example, it may require appropriate architects' certificates and mechanics' lien waivers or title insurance as conditions precedent to any disbursement, accompanied by some type of holdback prior to final disbursement.[22]

[7] Allocation of Condemnation Award

In the event of a total condemnation, the leasehold mortgagee will require that it receive the value of the leasehold improvements for the reduction of the outstanding mortgage indebtedness. Where the leasehold estate is not terminated by a partial taking, the mortgagee will generally consent to having the proceeds used to fund the restoration of the property, but will require protective provisions in the ground lease analogous to those discussed in connection with the distribution of hazard insurance proceeds. The lease should also expressly permit the leasehold mortgagee to participate in the condemnation proceedings, and the ground lease provisions should spell out what constitutes a total—as opposed to a partial—taking, and in the latter case how the ground rent will be reduced. In these respects, the language in the ground lease should be coordinated with the condemnation requirements of the prime subtenants.[23]

---

[21] See ¶¶ 3.04[12], ¶ 2.08 [4][d].

[22] See Articles 9.02, 9.03, 10.02 of Form 6.2 in Appendix B.

[23] See discussion at ¶ 3.05[2], and Articles 11.03, 11.04 of Form 6.2 in Appendix B.

leasehold mortgagee's liability shall cease after the leasehold mortgagee has assigned or transferred the lease to a third party.[18]

[3] Future Improvements

The ground lessee should not be obligated to make substantial future improvements beyond those to be financed by the leasehold mortgage. At a minimum, the lender will require that it be extricated from any such requirement if it should become the ground lessee.

[4] Antimerger Provision

If the ground lessee has an option to purchase the fee, there must be a provision prohibiting the merger of the leasehold and fee estates; otherwise, the security for the leasehold mortgage could be extinguished. Today, the doctrine of merger applies only if the parties clearly intend it. However, cautious lenders will still insist on language to the effect that if the two property interests merge, the leasehold mortgage will continue to encumber the "combined interest."

[5] Broad "Use" Clause and Mortgagee Consent to Change in Lease Terms

Since the mortgagee is not a party to the lease agreements, it will require that no terms or provisions of the ground lease, or occupancy subleases, be modified or deleted without its consent. As to the latter leases, the leasehold mortgagee (as would a fee mortgagee in an analogous situation) demands exclusive approval of all lease terms with prime tenants since the rental income stream from these subtenants will prime the mortgage.[19] The mortgagee will also require attornment agreements from the subtenants in the event of a termination of the ground lease for a noncurable default, as well as the creation of a new ground lease in favor of the mortgagee.[20]

In addition, the mortgagee will also require a broad "use" clause in the ground lease since, in the event the project falters and the mortgagee takes over, the mortgagee will want the flexibility to change the tenant mix and project design, and, if need be, to put the property to better use in whole or in part.

---

[18] See Articles 4.03 and 29 of Form 6.2 in Appendix B.
[19] See ¶ 3.05.
[20] See ¶ 6.03[8].

still place the leasehold mortgagee in an inferior position with respect to such matters as the sharing of hazard insurance and condemnation award proceeds.

[2] Right to Assign Leasehold Estate

The ground lessee must be able to freely assign its leasehold estate and, in the event the leasehold mortgagee takes over as lessee, its personal liability must be confined to the period during which it owns the leasehold estate. Absent such freedom of assignment, the leasehold mortgagee would not be able to realize its security by selling the ground lease after acquiring it at foreclosure unless it could obtain the consent of the ground lessor. In response, the ground lessor may suggest a compromise. Its consent would not be required for "any assignment to the mortgagee." However, such a provision would render the lease less marketable for the mortgagee; any purchaser who buys from the mortgagee would thereafter need the consent of the ground lessor in order to reassign the lease. Moreover, since the mortgagee often must provide purchase money financing to transfer the leasehold, it may require that such financing be allowed under the terms of the lease agreement.

In addition, a covenant against assignment may even prohibit the making of a mortgage and, a fortiori, the transfer to a trustee of property covered by a deed of trust in jurisdictions subscribing to the title theory approach to mortgage law.[15] Even in a lien theory state, the takeover of a leasehold estate by a mortgagee could arguably be construed as an assignment, notwithstanding an attempt to characterize it as an involuntary transfer by operation of law.[16]

Finally, the leasehold mortgagee should only be liable under the terms of the lease agreement, when and if it becomes the lessee. In some title states, such as Colorado and Maryland,[17] the mortgagee is, however, liable as soon as the deed of trust is recorded. Accordingly, a specific clause must be inserted in the lease agreement holding that the leasehold mortgagee is not personally liable until it actually acquires the leasehold interest. This same clause should also clearly specify that the

---

[15] E.g., Becker v. Werner, 98 Pa. 555 (1881).

[16] See Feldman v. Urban Commercial Inc., 64 N.J. Super. 364, 165 A.2d 854 (1960). But most cases hold to the contrary. E.g., Crouse v. Michell, 130 Mich. 347, 90 N.W.32 (1902).

[17] See Annot., 73 A.L.R.2d 1118 (1960). The theory is that when the mortgage is executed, the leasehold estate and its attendant liability are transferred constructively to the mortgagee.

since the lien of its leasehold mortgage would not cover the underlying fee. Consequently, in the event the ground lease is canceled or terminated as the result of a default by the ground lessee-mortgagor or some other contingency, the security for the mortgage loan would evaporate.[12] Accordingly, since the defeasible estate is created by the lease, the lender will require adequate protection for itself in the ground lease; special language in the leasehold mortgage would be of no avail in the event the ground lease is wiped out. Any attorney representing the developer-ground lessee should always negotiate lease provisions with the lender's requirements in mind in the event—no matter how unlikely—that the leasehold estate may be mortgaged at some time in the future. Otherwise, years later it may be impossible to renegotiate and obtain the necessary revisions demanded by the prospective lender.[13]

[1] Fee Owner Cannot Mortgage the Fee

The ground lease should include a negative covenant precluding the fee owner from mortgaging the fee. First, a mortgage on the underlying fee would prohibit most insurance companies from making a leasehold mortgage loan, if the fee mortgage were prior in lien to the leasehold estate.[14] Otherwise, the latter could be cut off by a foreclosure of the former, notwithstanding language in the lease or leasehold mortgage designed to protect the leasehold mortgagee. Some lenders will tolerate a fee mortgage that is inferior to the ground lease; if the ground lease is recorded before the fee mortgage, foreclosure of the latter could not threaten the leasehold estate. Alternatively, the lender might accept a "nondisturbance clause," pursuant to which the mortgagee, under a prior fee mortgage, agrees not to disturb the possession of the ground lessee in the event of foreclosure. However, this latter alternative would

---

[12] The trepidations of lenders making leasehold mortgages have been exacerbated by recent instances where trustees in bankruptcy have attempted to reject such mortgaged ground leases as being detrimental to the fee owner's bankrupt estate (e.g., Penn Central Railroad bankruptcy). In the event of the ground lessor's bankruptcy, there is the possibility that a court could direct that the property be sold free and clear of any mortgages that could wipe out the leasehold estate and the leasehold mortgage's security for its loan. Moreover, the mortgagee would have no claim or action against the ground lessor's estate in bankruptcy since the leasehold mortgagee would be neither a secured nor unsecured creditor of the ground lessor.

[13] See Article 12.01 of Form 6.2, a sample ground lease in Appendix B; also note that some of the following lender's requirements are cross-referenced to this document and are summarized in the outline of minimum groundlease requirements at ¶ 6.03[10].

[14] See note 4 *supra*. See also Form 6.3 in Appendix B.

ground rent, since the lender will be able to take into account the value of the subordinated land for appraisal purposes. Indeed, in some instances, the greater financing may be essential for the project to get off the ground.

(2) If the fee owner develops the land himself, he will have to put up the land as security in order to obtain mortgage financing.

(3) Most lenders will agree to exculpate the fee owner from personal liability with respect to the obligations contained in the mortgage.

[4] Protection for Fee Owner

In addition, and depending upon his bargaining position, the fee owner should attempt to procure the following protections: an agreement to subordinate that is specific and definite as to the type of lending institution, the amount, term, and interest rate of the loan, the constant, the loan-to-value ratio, etc.; assurance of notice from the mortgagee of any default of the lessee under the terms and conditions of the mortgage and a reasonable period in which to cure the same; and a deletion from the mortgage of such standard noncurable defaults as the bankruptcy of the mortgagor. Also included should be a provision that the mortgagee will not have the right to accelerate its loan upon the bankruptcy of the mortgagor-lessee—as long as the fee owner is willing to make the monthly mortgage payments, and a provision in the ground lease whereby any payments made by the fee owner to cure the mortgage are considered as additional rent. In addition, any default under the mortgage should constitute an automatic default under the ground lease. Moreover, in the case of a monetary default, provision should be made for quick termination of the ground lease. In the event of a default under, and termination of, the ground lease, the fee owner should be able to assume the role of the developer as mortgagor. Finally, in the event of a casualty, the mortgagee should permit the insurance proceeds to be used for the restoration of the improvements, rather than to be applied against the outstanding loan indebtedness. In that regard, the fee owner should be included as a named insured under the hazard policy and should require that adequate rental insurance be included in the policy.

¶ 6.03 LEASEHOLD MORTGAGE ON UNSUBORDINATED FEE: LENDER'S REQUIREMENTS

Straight leasehold financing on an unsubordinated fee affords the lender only the security of a leasehold estate and improvements thereon

leasehold estate, neither Lender nor its successor in interest will be able to receive the sublease rentals from the occupancy (prime) tenants to which the ground lessee would be entitled as sublessor. Lender would only be entitled to the lesser amount of ground rent from Developer as ground lessee.[9]

[b] Attornment by Subtenants

If Lender forecloses its lien on the fee and the inferior ground lease is extinguished, the occupancy subleases which attach to the ground lease will also be eliminated, and Lender will have lost the income from the occupancy tenants. Through attornment, Lender avoids this circumstance by having the prime tenants establish privity of contract with the ground lessor and its successors and assigns, including itself as mortgagee or purchaser at the foreclosure sale.[10] As a quid pro quo, the attorney for the tenant should demand assurance from the lender that it will accept the attornment and not disturb the tenant's use and occupancy of the premises. If not, Lender, its successor, or other purchaser at foreclosure could allow the lease to be canceled in order to obtain more favorable terms with a substitute tenant.[11]

[3] Advantage to Fee Owner

At this point, an obvious question is why the fee owner should go along with "streamlined" mortgage financing. He will be reluctant to subject his fee to the lien of the mortgage since he runs the risk of forfeiting his property in the event the developer-ground lessee defaults under the mortgage. The fee owner may also object to the lender's proscription against mortgaging of the fee.

The following are some arguments that the developer can use in negotiating with the fee owner:

(1) The developer can obtain greater financing to build more extensive improvements and be in a position to pay a higher

---

[9] Since Fee Owner assigned his interest under the ground lease to Lender as additional security, it would become operative when Developer defaulted under the mortgage. Hence, Lender would find itself in the anomolous situation of having both privity of estate and privity of contract with Developer, as ground lessee, even though Developer has defaulted under the mortgage.

[10] See Paragraph 2 of Form 6.1 in Appendix B.

[11] This rather archaic rule under which the sublease cannot survive extinguishment of the ground lease has been overruled by statute in some states (e.g., Ill. Rev. Stat. Ch. 30, § 39 (1967)) and has been rejected as too formalistic and inequitable by state courts in many, if not most, jurisdictions. 49 *Am. Jur. 2d* "Landlord and Tenant" § 512 (1970). Also, Form 6.1 in Appendix B.

these requirements and the relationships that they create are somewhat complex, the following is provided as an example:

Facts: Developer plans a $2 million shopping center complex on land he can purchase for $1 million or rent for $100,000 per year. To save the $1 million cash outlay, he negotiates a forty-year ground lease with Fee Owner and leases space to Prime Tenant and satellites, or secondary tenants. Lender Insurance Co. agrees to lend $2 million on the security of the leasehold and improvements thereon, providing all of the following conditions are met:

- Fee Owner agrees to subject his fee interest to the mortgage.
- The ground lease is subordinated to the mortgage.
- Fee Owner conditionally assigns his interest in the ground lease to Lender as additional security.
- The subtenants execute attornment agreements.

The configuration of the resultant agreements is illustrated by the following diagram.

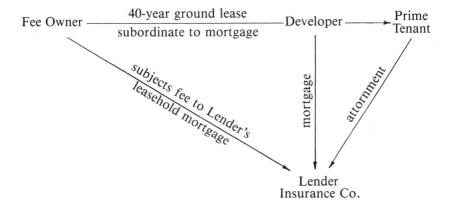

[a] Subordination of Ground Lease

Lender has Fee Owner execute the mortgage in order to acquire a mortgage lien on both the fee and Developer's leasehold estate, or, in effect, creates two mortgages. If the ground lease is made subordinate to the mortgage lien and Developer defaults, Lender, by foreclosing its mortgage lien on the fee, can eliminate the inferior ground lease and end up with a fee simple estate. However, if the ground lease were superior to the mortgage, it would survive the foreclosure, and Lender would have a fee simple estate subject to Developer's leasehold interest. Consequently, unless Lender also forecloses its lien on Developer's

subordinated land for appraisal purposes and thus make a larger loan based on a higher loan-to-value ratio. In fact, if the owner of the land has agreed to subject his fee interest to the mortgage, many lenders will simply use a straight mortgage on the fee to encumber the land and improvements and eliminate the leasehold mortgage entirely.

There are two methods available to accomplish subordination. The first method is to have the fee owner execute a separate subordination agreement. However, subordinating an ownership interest in land to the lien of a mortgage poses a conceptual problem for some lawyers who are accustomed to seeing only liens and other encumbrances subordinated to one another.[6] Consequently, most lenders prefer instead to have the fee owner join in the execution of the mortgage, and in those jurisdictions where a mortgage must be security to an indebtedness, the fee owner should join in the bond or note as well as in the mortgage.[7]

[2] Subordination of Ground Lease and Attornment

In addition, the lender will often require that the ground lease be subordinate to the lien of the mortgage by having the ground lease executed or recorded after the mortgage, or by having the ground lessee execute a subordination agreement. Also, the term of the ground lease must obviously be at least equal to the term of the mortgage, and it must provide expressly that the fee owner will join in the execution of the mortgage and subject its fee to the lender's lien. The lender will also frequently demand an assignment of the ground lessor's interest in the ground lease as additional security. Finally, the lender will probably require that the occupancy subtenants agree in the subleases or by separate instrument to "attornment," or recognition of the new fee owner (mortgagee or purchaser at foreclosure sale) as the new landlord in the event of foreclosure of the mortgage.[8] Since the rationale for

---

[6] Customarily, in a ground lease situation, the ground lessor agrees to subordinate his interest in the land to future construction and permanent loan financing and possibly refinancing of the permanent loan. Carefully drafted subordination agreements have normally been upheld by state courts.

However, the California Supreme Court, in a disturbing decision in Handy v. Gordon, 65 Cal. 2d 578, 422 P.2d 329, 55 Cal. Rptr. 769 (1967), while noting that the particular subordination agreement in question contained indefinite language, held it unenforceable on the grounds that it was unjust, unreasonable, and unfair to the defendant. In effect, the court applied a concept of fairness doctrine to the subordination clause. See Leon, "Subordination; A Handy Test of Fairness," 42 L.A. B. Bull. 264 (1967).

[7] However, most lenders will agree not to seek a judgment for any personal liability against the fee owner.

[8] See Form 6.1, in Appendix B.

tory statutes.[3] For example, a common statutory provision requires that mortgage loans be made only on leaseholds with unexpired terms of not less than twenty-one years.[4] In addition, the underlying fee interest in the realty "may not be subject to any prior lien and there may not be any condition or right of re-entry or forfeiture not insured against...."[5] Otherwise, if a mortgage on the fee has lien priority over the leasehold, a foreclosure of the fee mortgage could wipe out the leasehold estate, which is the security for the leasehold mortgage loan, and no provision in the leasehold mortgage could protect the leasehold mortgagee. Alternatively, if the underlying fee interest is forfeited under a "right of entry or condition broken," any leasehold interest attached to the fee would likewise be terminated. In response, the leasehold mortgage lender will require title insurance or some other assurance that the fee title is unencumbered or, as an alternative, that any fee mortgage be subordinated to the ground lease; it will thus survive foreclosure of the fee mortgage. The lender will also insist that any right of entry or possibility of reverter be waived, rendered inoperative by judicial action, or be insured against by a title company.

There are essentially three types of financing involving leasehold estates created by ground leases: leasehold mortgage financing on a subordinated fee, leasehold financing on an unsubordinated fee, and sale and leaseback financing.

¶ 6.02 LEASEHOLD MORTGAGE ON SUBORDINATED FEE: THE "STREAMLINED" MORTGAGE

A leasehold mortgage on a subordinated fee provides greater leverage for the developer and may provide certain advantages to the fee owner and mortgagee as well.

[1] Advantage to Developer

If the fee owner agrees to subject, or "subordinate," his fee interest to the lien of the leasehold mortgage arranged by the developer-lessee, the ability of the developer to procure mortgage financing is greatly enhanced. Since the security for the mortgage loan would not only be a defeasible leasehold estate subject to termination, but the fee interest as well, the lender would be able to take into account the value of the

---

[3] See ¶ 2.02[1][d].
[4] N.Y. Ins. Law § 81.6(a) (McKinney 1966).
[5] *Id.*

depreciation deductions since he would be entitled to recoup his capital investment in the improvements.[1]

For tax or business reasons the fee owner frequently will not wish to sell the land. For example, if the fee owner is a "dealer" for tax purposes or has a low tax basis in the property, he might obtain a higher, and possibly more secure, rate of return[2] by leasing as opposed to selling at a high tax cost and reinvesting the after-tax proceeds. Sometimes, owners of prime land, especially in urban areas, will refuse to sell because the anticipated rate of appreciation in land value is so high. In some instances, the landowner may simply not have the legal right to convey a fee interest.

[2] Regulatory Considerations

Since life insurance companies are the prime source of leasehold financing funds, the developer's attorney should be mindful of the lending constraints imposed on life insurance companies by local regula-

---

[1] Reg. § 1.162-11(b)(2). If the estimated useful life of the improvements is longer than the remaining term of the lease, the cost of the leasehold improvements can be amortized over the remaining lease term. However, the accelerated rates of depreciation are not available for "amortization". Improvements with a useful life shorter than the lease term may be depreciated by use of the accelerated methods. Reg. § 1.167(a)-4. Even though the lessee has vested legal title to the improvements in the lessor, the lessee will still be entitled to the depreciation or amortization deduction if it retains the beneficial enjoyment of the premises and bears the economic exhaustion of its capital investment in the property. See Comm'r v. F. & R. Lazarus & Co., 308 U.S. 252 (1939) (involving a sale-leaseback); see also Rev. Rul. 62-178, 1962-2 C.B. 91. If the lease term contains a renewal option, I.R.C. § 178 sets forth a complicated set of tests for determining the period over which the improvements can be depreciated or amortized. I.R.C. § 178 essentially provides that where the remaining initial lease term is less than 60 percent of the improvement's useful life at completion, the lease term will include renewal periods for purposes of depreciation or amortization. There is case law suggesting that a purchaser-ground lessor can also take a depreciation deduction in respect to improvements constructed by the ground lessee even though the remaining useful life of the improvements does not exceed the unexpired term of the lease and "duplicated" depreciation is also taken by the ground lessee on the same improvements. World Publishing Co. v. Comm'r, 299 F.2d 614 (8th Cir. 1962), *rev'd* 35 T.C. 7. But cf. M. Dematteo Constr. Co. v. United States, 433 F.2d 1263 (1st Cir. 1970), which followed Comm'r v. Moore, 207 F.2d 265 (9th Cir. 1953), *rev'd* 15 T.C. 906 (involving inherited property rather than property acquired by purchase).

[2] In some ground leases the fixed per annum rental amount is supplemented by an additional rental provision that, for example, may be geared to a percentage of the developer's sublease rental income or to any increase in the Consumer Price Index.

[3] Tax Pitfalls Inherent in Sale-Leaseback 6-24
    [a] Loss Disallowed "Exchange" 6-24
        [i] Case Law Interpretations of "Exchange" 6-25
        [ii] Tax Planning................................. 6-26
    [b] Treatment as Disguised Loan....................... 6-27
        [i] *Frank Lyon Co. v. United States* 6-28
        [ii] Tax Planning................................. 6-29
    [c] Reallocation of Leaseback Rental................... 6-30
    [d] Treatment as Disguised Purchase 6-31
[4] Illustration of Leaseback Flexibility 6-31
[5] Component, or "Split," Financing 6-36

¶ 6.01 LEASEHOLD VS. FEE MORTGAGE FINANCING

Leasehold mortgage financing arises when a developer decides to construct improvements on land that he leases rather than purchases from the fee owner. A number of factors enter into the decision to lease rather than purchase the fee.

[1] Tax and Business Considerations

In times of rising land costs and tight mortgage money, the developer who obtains leasehold financing can achieve greater leverage for himself or, as a syndicator, increase the rate of equity return to his investors. While the developer's cash outlay is less in leasehold financing, since he is not purchasing the fee, his cash earnings will often remain about the same. The ground rental will frequently be equal or close to the extra debt service he would pay had he obtained a larger fee mortgage to fund the cost of acquiring the land as well as the cost of constructing the improvements. The trade-off, of course, is that the developer, as a mere lessee, will forgo the benefit of realizing any appreciation in land value when the land is eventually sold.

Leasing may provide tax advantages for the developer. Since land is not a depreciable asset for income tax purposes, its ownership does not provide tax deductions. On the other hand, the ground rent paid for the land is deductible. Accordingly, part of the deductible ground rent really represents the extra nondeductible amortization the developer would have paid on the larger fee mortgage had he purchased the underlying fee. Moreover, the ground lessee-developer will still be entitled to the

Chapter 6

LEASEHOLD AND LEASEBACK FINANCING

		Page
¶ 6.01	Leasehold vs. Fee Mortgage Financing	6- 2
	[1] Tax and Business Considerations	6- 2
	[2] Regulatory Considerations	6- 3
¶ 6.02	Leasehold Mortgage on Subordinated Fee: The "Streamlined" Mortgage	6- 4
	[1] Advantage to Developer	6- 4
	[2] Subordination of Ground Lease and Attornment	6- 5
	[a] Subordination of Ground Lease	6- 6
	[b] Attornment by Subtenants	6- 7
	[3] Advantage to Fee Owner	6- 7
	[4] Protection for Fee Owner	6- 8
¶ 6.03	Leasehold Mortgage on Unsubordinated Fee: Lender's Requirements	6- 8
	[1] Fee Owner Cannot Mortgage the Fee	6- 9
	[2] Right to Assign Leasehold Estate	6-10
	[3] Future Improvements	6-11
	[4] Antimerger Provision	6-11
	[5] Broad "Use" Clause and Mortgagee Consent to Change in Lease Terms	6-11
	[6] Application of Hazard Insurance Proceeds	6-12
	[7] Allocation of Condemnation Award	6-12
	[8] Default Provisions	6-13
	[9] Changes in Ground Rent	6-13
	[10] Outline of Minimum Ground Lease Requirements for Benefit of Leasehold Mortgagee	6-14
¶ 6.04	Sale and Leaseback Financing vs. Debt Financing	6-17
	[1] Land But Not Improvements	6-18
	[a] Depreciation	6-18
	[b] Drafting Approaches	6-19
	[c] Title Problems	6-19
	[2] Land and Improvements	6-20
	[a] Position of Seller-Lessee	6-21
	[i] Business Considerations	6-21
	[ii] Tax Considerations	6-23
	[b] Position of the Purchaser-Lessor	6-23
	[i] Business Considerations	6-23
	[ii] Tax Considerations	6-24

receive 30 percent of the net profits from the property (based on the sale or appraised value of an office building to be erected on the lot), in addition to repayment of principal, was not usurious because the lender's profit return was subject to unusual "hazards" and the lender had not evinced an intent to evade the usury law.[182]

At the weak end of the risk scale the lender may assume the risk merely of not receiving the maximum interest permitted by law. In this situation which involves limited exposure for the lender, the court may strike a balance between the full amount of the legal interest that may not be realized and the interest in excess of the legal rate that may be received by the lender. In *Jameson v. Warren*,[183] a California court found an agreement usurious that provided for fixed interest close to the statutory limit. The contingent interest in *Jameson* was in the form of dividends from pledged stock. Although large dividends were anticipated, the agreement made the borrower liable for fixed interest close to the lawful limit. The court held that the agreement was intended to violate the usury laws.[184]

Bonus payment to the lender in the form of property at a price below its true value may readily be viewed as additional interest, especially if the property is not closely related to the loan transaction.[185]

---

[182] 250 Cal. App. 2d 341, 350, 58 Cal. Rptr. 297, 303 (1967).

[183] 91 Cal. App. 590, 596, 267 P. 372 (1928).

[184] See discussion of contingent interest "kickers" at ¶ 3.04[3][a].

[185] See Brown v. Cardoza, 67 Cal. App. 187, 191-192, 153 P.2d 767, 769 (1944); Mission Hill Dev. Corp. v. Western Small Business Inv. Co., 260 Cal. App. 2d 923, 927-928, 67 Cal. Rptr. 505, 507-508 (1968).

consent to the lender's assumption of the debt service on the existing mortgage. However, the course of action followed by the lender, who took over the debt service on the prior loan, effectively converted the transaction into a form of a wraparound mortgage. The decision therefore introduces considerable doubt as to the validity of wraparound mortgages under the usury statutes.[178]

[8] Contingent Compensation and Equity Participation by Lenders

Although many of the cases and treatises reflect separate rules of decision for lender compensation, subject to a contingency as opposed to compensation that involves the risk of nonrepayment, the concept of risk is the more basic and comprehensive.

The lender may assume a hierarchy of risks: risk of his capital; risk of its interest return; and risk of not receiving the maximum interest permitted by law.[179] In general, the greater the risk of nonrepayment, the further the transaction is removed from the effect of the usury statutes.

At one extreme is true equity participation in the enterprise by the lender as joint venturer, partner, or similar position as investor. Absent a fraudulent arrangement whereby the investor pays less than what its equity interest is worth, its equity participation will not be subject to a usury attack if it also makes a loan to the venture; the two transactions will be viewed as separate and distinct from one another. A fortiori, if the investor merely advances equity funds to the enterprise, usury could not apply since there would be no loan to which it could attach.[180]

In passing on financing arrangements in which the lender receives a share of the earnings or income from property in lieu of or in addition to fixed interest, the courts have raised the basic question of whether the substance of the transaction reveals an intent to evade the usury laws. Compensation to the lender in the form of a share of income, earnings, or profits will be categorized as interest unless there is substantial risk of nonpayment of capital or of the full legal interest, a risk that a prudent man would not incur in order to merely receive the legal interest.[181] For example, in *Thomassen v. Carr* a California court held that a transaction involving a borrower who received an eighteen-month interest-free loan to purchase a lot on the understanding that the lender would

---

[178] See also discussion at ¶ 7.04[3][b][i].

[179] See ¶ 5.02[3][b].

[180] *Id.*; Annot., 16 A.L.R.3d 475 (1967). Also see the more detailed discussion at ¶ 11.02[3][c].

[181] See cases collected in 16 A.L.R.3d 475.

amount of the new loan was actually that amount made available for the borrower's use. The court further found that the amount withheld by the lender to repay the original indebtedness had not been made available to the borrower's use because this money had not been applied to satisfy the original indebtedness.

However, it could be argued that if the senior mortgagee had, in effect, agreed to refinancing, it would have raised the interest rate on the existing indebtedness to equal the bargained-for rate on the new indebtedness and, where applicable under state law, would have consolidated the indebtedness. Actually, the borrower would have been paying the same amount of interest to the senior mortgagee on refinancing the total indebtedness as it would have paid on the total indebtedness secured by both the senior mortgagee's position and the wraparound mortgagee's position. The difference lies in the fact that in the wraparound situation there are by necessity two separate lenders, each receiving a different rate of return. While one lender may receive a rate of return exceeding the usury limit, the aggregate rate of return on the entire indebtedness nevertheless falls within the usury ceiling. In this regard, a wraparound is more like a refinancing of the senior mortgage than like a traditional second mortgage, except that the rate, terms, and amortization schedules differ from those of a senior mortgage. To the borrower in a wraparound transaction, the existing senior indebtedness, together with the funds to be advanced by the wraparound lender, are recast into one overriding indebtedness. Nevertheless, it remains to be seen whether a court would accept this approach.

By way of analogy, one tax ruling involved a real estate investment trust that made a wraparound loan in the amount of $400,000 at 8 percent, which, in effect, wrapped around an existing first trust indebtedness of $300,000 at 7 percent.[176] The borrower executed a note and a mortgage in the amount of $400,000 at 8 percent. The REIT advanced $100,000 to the borrower, who paid interest at the rate of 8 percent on the $400,000 note. The IRS in Revenue Ruling 75-99, in effect, followed the *Mindlin v. Davis* approach in holding that the indebtedness was less than the total amount of the wraparound loan. Accordingly, it held that only the interest on $100,000 was includable in the REIT's gross income for purposes of qualifying as a REIT under Internal Revenue Code Section 856,[177] which requires that a certain percentage of its gross income be derived from interest and other specified sources.

The agreed upon transaction in *Mindlin* was not wraparound mortgage. Unlike an ordinary wraparound loan, the borrower did not

---

[176] 1975-1 C.B. 197.
[177] I.R.C. §§ 856(c)(2), 856(c)(3).

interest, the hypothetical transaction should not be usurious. However, if the statute reads that a lender may not receive more than 15 percent interest, then on its face the transaction might be usurious. The answer, unfortunately, is beclouded by the fact that in many states there are decisions which have interpreted usury statutes in different ways; indeed, in some states there are conflicting state statutes. For example, the California Constitution provides that a lender is not to receive interest in excess of 10 percent.[172] However, the California statute[173] allows receipt of interest up to the 12 percent maximum rate.

The wraparound mortgage itself is not usurious on its face. Moreover, in the aggregate, the borrower never pays more than the lawful contract rate on the total outstanding balance for which he is liable. However, the economic reality lies in the fact that the compensation flowing from the borrower to the new lender includes a benefit in addition to the interest. The borrower cedes to the new lender the opportunity to use the outstanding principal on the first mortgage at a relatively low rate of interest. This acquisition of a business opportunity by the new lender may be viewed as the exaction of a collateral advantage from the borrower, a procedure that may lead to a finding of usury in a majority of jurisdictions.[174]

Alternatively, the issue may be addressed in terms of which party, lender or borrower, enjoys the actual use of the remaining principal of the first mortgage. Arguably, it is the borrower who enjoys the use of these wraparound funds by having them applied to eliminate his debt service on the first mortgage just as effectively as if he had received the money in cash and paid off the first mortgage himself. However, a contrary conclusion was reached in a Florida decision. *Mindlin v. Davis*[175] involved a refinancing transaction. Under the agreed terms, the lender was required to repay the existing indebtedness of the borrower, advancing the balance of the new loan in cash. The new lender, recognizing a good business opportunity, did not pay off the original low interest-rate loan immediately, but assumed the debt service. Although the borrower was relieved of required payments on his original loan, the court held that the transaction was usurious, finding the true

---

[172] Cal. Const. Art. 15, § 1 (West 1978).

[173] Cal. Civ. Code § 1916-2 (West 1972).

[174] See, e.g., *In re* Perry, 272 F. Supp. 73, 96 (S.D. Mo. 1967); Equitable Life Assurance Soc'y v. Kerpel, 38 Misc. 2d 856, 858, 38 N.Y.S.2d 1016, 1018 (1963); Klett v. Security Acceptance Co., 38 Cal. 2d 770, 780, 242 P.2d 873, 879 (1952). Contra, Commercial Credit Plan v. Chandler, 218 Ark. 966, 972, 239 S.W.2d 1009, 1012 (1951); Hatridge v. Home Accident & Life Ins. Co., 246 S.W.2d 666, 671 (Tex. 1951).

[175] 74 So. 2d 789, 793 (Fla. 1954).

found to be a loan, by which the supposed buyer merely obtains a security interest in the property.[168] In the case of sale and repurchase, there is almost no reported litigation.[169] By analogy to the sale-leaseback, it would seem that if the sale price is fully commensurate with the value of the property, the lender is well protected from usury claims. Provisions allowing the developer to reacquire the property during the term of the installment land contract may also be significant in some cases. But if the contract is long-term and early repurchase requires payment of all future installments, the developer will be strongly motivated not to exercise the option for early acquisition of the title. Such provisions would therefore evidence a bona fide sale to the investor.

[7] Wraparound Mortgage

A wraparound mortgage may be used advantageously only if the prospective borrower has an existing mortgage on the property, at a rate below the prevailing rate, a sufficient equity in the property to justify a second mortgage, and a need for additional financing. The distinctive feature of the wraparound mortgage is that the face amount of the new loan includes both the remaining balance on the existing first mortgage and an additional amount that is advanced to the borrower.[170] The borrower pays interest on the total amount of the wraparound mortgage at a stated rate that is at or below the lawful contract rate,[171] but is relieved of the burden of paying the installments on the prior first mortgage. The debt service on the first mortgage becomes the responsibility of the new lender, who may or may not assume the earlier mortgage.

The status of the wraparound mortgage under the usury statutes is by no means clear. Assume a wraparound mortgage is contemplated in a state with a usury ceiling of 15 percent interest. If the interest rate stated in the wraparound promissory note is 15 percent, but because of financial leverage the lender in effect would be receiving 17 percent, does this transaction violate the usury statute? In order to answer this question, it is necessary to look at the applicable state usury statute. If the statute provides that a borrower may not pay more than 15 percent

---

[168] See ¶ 5.05[4].

[169] The sale-repurchase arrangement was accepted as such by the court in Meridian Bowling Lanes, Inc. v. Brown, 90 Idaho 403, 415, 412 P.2d 586, 593 (1966).

[170] See general discussion of wraparound mortgages at ¶ 7.04[3].

[171] The stated interest rate is ordinarily below the prevailing rate, as an inducement for the borrower to use a wraparound mortgage.

¶ 5.05[6]

finance, the installment land contract is consequently of interest primarily as part of the sale repurchase method of financing, discussed in the following section.

[6] Sale and Repurchase of Realty

An imaginative arrangement for permanent financing is for the developer to sell the entire project to an investor for cash and then immediately repurchase the property on credit under a long-term installment land contract.[164] This method of sale and buy-back is similar to the sale-leaseback insofar as money flows from the investor to the developer pursuant to a sale, although the developer retains control and use of the property.[165] However, the tax and usury aspects of the sale-repurchase plan are quite distinct from those of the sale-leaseback.

The practical advantages of the sale-repurchase scheme of financing are realized because the Internal Revenue Service and the courts view the installment land contract from a different perspective. Under the tax laws and regulations, the substance of a sale on credit is recognized. The installment payments are not considered solely as a return of capital to the seller, and a portion of these payments is treated as interest, deductible to the buyer and taxable to the seller.[166]

In the usury area, it would seem logical that the sale-repurchase arrangement should attract the greatest judicial suspicion. The end result of the overall transaction is to leave the property in the hands of the original owner; in the interim, the developer receives money and pays it back to the investor at a substantial premium. In practice, however, the sale-repurchase arrangement ordinarily involves no significant risk of a usury problem because the judicial rule exempting installment sales from usury restrictions is so well established.[167]

A usury question will arise only if at the beginning of the transaction the sale of the property to the investor appears to be fraudulent. The danger is precisely the same one that is present in the sale-leaseback scheme: that what the parties have designated as a sale for cash will be

---

[164] See general discussion at ¶ 8.09[3].

[165] See discussion at ¶ 6.04.

[166] The total amount of imputed interest is essentially the time-price differential, that is, the difference between the price for sale on credit and the cash price. The amount of each installment that is deductible as interest is the total interest divided by the number of installments. The developer's interest deduction remains constant throughout the term of the installment land contract. The developer may further deduct depreciation because of his equitable interest in the improvements.

[167] See ¶ 5.02[2].

illusory sale.[159] But in some states, a transaction involving a sale that appears to be illusory will not be found usurious, absent a finding of an intent to to evade the usury laws.[160]

The more recent variation in the sale-leaseback arrangement has been in the original financing of a new development. The land on which the project is to be erected may be sold to an investor, with a leaseback to the developer. Unless the sale is found to be fraudulent, the rental payments cannot be usurious because they do not represent compensation for money loaned. The level of rent and the period of the lease can therefore be adjusted to provide a suitable return to the investor (even if it makes an accompanying mortgage loan) at no more than the lawful contract rate of interest, in order to fund the improvements. Moreover, the developer's burden of paying large ground rents is considerably lightened by the additional resulting tax deductions.[161]

[5] Installment Land Contract

Because of the well-established doctrine of time-price differential,[162] the owner of land may contract to sell it on credit, for any amount to which the buyer will agree. The buyer cannot successfully raise the defense of usury, even if the amount and number of installment payments are clearly unconscionable.

The installment land contract therefore provides a method by which an investor may receive large payments from a developer without running afoul of the usury statutes.[163] In the typical land development project, however, the developer owns or is in a position to acquire the land when he approaches the lender. In the area of commercial land

---

[159] See Gaither v. Clark, 67 Md. 18, 32 (1887); Banks v. Walters, 95 Ark. 501, 506, 130 S.W. 519, 521 (1910). See also Burr v. Capital Reserve Corp., 71 Cal. 2d 983, 996, 458 P.2d 185, 194, 80 Cal. Rptr. 345 (1969); cf. *In re* San Francisco Indus. Park, Inc., 307 F. Supp. 271, 276 (D. Cal. 1969) (involving bankruptcy proceedings against a bankrupt seller-lessee and instructive on difference between a sale-leaseback and mortgage transaction).

[160] See Plummer v. National Leasing Corp., 173 Neb. 557, 564, 114 N.W.2d 21, 25 (1962) (where court found that parties intended a genuine sale-leaseback notwithstanding disproportionate sales price).

[161] By contrast, if the land were not sold, no depreciation could be taken for the land. The developer also gains increased leverage by sale of the land at its fair market value. As in all sale-leaseback transactions, the developer stands to lose the appreciation of the property sold unless he can exercise an option to repurchase; however, the repurchase options most favorable to the developer will create the greatest risk of the transaction being deemed a loan rather than a sale. See ¶ 6.04[3][6].

[162] See ¶ 5.02[2].

[163] See general discussion of installment land contract at ¶ 8.03.

[4] Sale and Leaseback

The sale-leaseback is an established technique for gaining tax advantages in the refinancing of overdepreciated commercial real estate. As the nondeductible amortization of the mortgage becomes a significant portion of the debt service, and the peak years of accelerated depreciation have passed, the developer-manager can in effect refinance the project by selling it to an investor while retaining operational control through a leaseback arrangement.[154] Although the first applications of this financing device involved the sale-and-leaseback of both land and existing improvements, the method has also been used effectively by developers to obtain high-ratio financing by severing the building improvements from ownership of the underlying fee.

As a financing tool, the sale-leaseback has properly been acclaimed for the tax advantages it can create, without comparable regard for its utility as a usury circumvention device. Indeed, the sale-leaseback by its very nature is almost always free from usury restrictions. Since money flows from the investor to the developer pursuant to a sale rather than a loan, the usury laws, which by their terms apply only to interest on loans, cannot apply provided that the sale is real and not illusory.[155]

An important feature of the sale-leaseback is that the very same requirement—that the sale be a real one and not a sham—is necessary to obtain both tax and usury avoidance objectives. No dilemma is presented to the parties; they need only structure the transaction so that the facts and circumstances show a true conveyance and subsequent lease. Otherwise, the transaction may be viewed as merely a disguised loan for both usury and tax purposes.[156]

The strongest evidence of a sham conveyance is a provision that requires the seller-lessee to repurchase the property at a stated time or within a specified interval.[157] An option to repurchase, coupled with an unusually low option price or other circumstances that would compel a prudent developer to exercise the option, is also persuasive evidence of a disguised loan, whereby the supposed buyer actually receives only a security interest in the real estate.[158] Similarly, a sale price significantly lower than the value of the property is generally taken to indicate an

---

[154] See general discussion of sale-leaseback at ¶ 6.04.
[155] See ¶ 5.02[2].
[156] See discussion at ¶ 6.04[3][b].
[157] See Golden States Lanes v. Fox, 232 Cal. App. 2d 135, 42 Cal. Rptr. 568 (1965).
[158] See Kawauchi v. Tabata, 49 Haw. 160, 177, 413 P.2d 221, 231-232 (1966).

existence of the corporation,[145] the difference between the cash and market value of the distributed property and the distributee's adjusted basis in his stock will be accorded capital gain treatment unless the corporation is "collapsible." In this event, the gain will be ordinary income.[146] However, I.R.C. § 333 permits nonrecognition of gain at liquidation of a noncollapsible corporation to the extent that the corporation has no earnings and profits, and distributees have neither cash nor securities.[147] Finally, if the corporation distributes property in redemption of some of its stock or in partial liquidation, gain will be recognized equal to the excess of the value of the property over the distributee's adjusted basis in his relinquished stock.[148]

Generally, no gain or loss will be recognized to a corporation on the distribution of property in partial or complete liquidation.[149] However, when real estate subject to depreciation recapture[150] is distributed, ordinary income will be recognized by the corporation to the extent of the lesser of the gain or "additional depreciation" attributed to the property. The unrecognized gain inherent in an installment obligation must also be recognized by the corporation when distributed in liquidation.[151]

Alternatively, the corporation and its shareholders could sell the property as a "tax shelter" to outsiders and qualify for tax-free treatment, except for depreciation recapture, if (1) the corporation is not collapsible, (2) it adopts a plan of complete liquidation, (3) it distributes all of its assets (less those retained to meet liabilities) in complete liquidation within the twelve-month period beginning with the date of adopting the plan, and (4) the property sold is other than inventory or installment obligations.[152] If these requirements are met, gain or loss will only be recognized at the shareholder level. Such gain or loss will ordinarily be capital in nature and will be measured by the difference between the fair market value of the property received and the distributee-shareholder's adjusted basis in his stock.[153]

---

[145] I.R.C. § 331(a).
[146] See discussion at ¶ 1.05[3][a][ii].
[147] I.R.C. § 333(e)(1).
[148] I.R.C. §§ 317(b), 302(a), 346, 331(a)(2).
[149] I.R.C. § 336. However, if stock is redeemed, the corporation may recognize gain on its distribution of appreciated property. I.R.C. § 311(d).
[150] I.R.C. § 1250.
[151] I.R.C. § 453(d).
[152] I.R.C. § 337. See also I.R.C. § 1239, which imposes ordinary income treatment on any gain recognized on sale of depreciable property between related taxpayers.
[153] I.R.C. § 331(a).

that in jurisdictions, such as New Jersey, which follow the question-of-fact approach,[137] it would appear inconsistent for the borrower to argue for tax purposes that the financing corporation is but a trustee or agent acting on behalf of its individual or partnership shareholder, while for local usury law purposes the lender must take the position that the loan is in reality being made to the corporation.[138] However, as noted earlier, the decisional trend in these jurisdictions is not to pierce the corporate veil where an experienced real estate borrower is utilizing the corporate exemption to secure a loan for business purposes.[139] In any event, a cautious lender should certainly isolate itself as much as possible from knowledge about, or involvement with, any potential agency relationship between a corporate borrower and its shareholders.

Perhaps the safest course of action in a jurisdiction that rigorously follows the question-of-fact approach[140] would be the "in and out" approach. Here, the corporation would be made the beneficial owner of the property at the time of the loan[141] and sometime thereafter the property would be deeded back to the individual or partnership shareholders so that he or it could take advantage of the tax-shelter benefits associated with individual ownership. Under this approach, the validation of the loan would be insured by emphasizing the independence and viability of the corporate entity; however, the federal tax costs to the individual or partnership developer could be severe when the property is received from the corporation. First, taxable gain may be recognized to the distributee when the property is distributed to the individual or partnership shareholder. If the corporation effects a nonliquidating distribution of the property to a noncorporate distributee, that portion of the distributed cash or other property at fair market value,[142] which is out of the corporation's earnings and profits, is taxable as ordinary dividend income to the distributee-shareholder.[143] Otherwise, if the distribution is not a dividend[144] or if the distribution terminates the

---

[137] See discussion at ¶ 5.04[1].

[138] Interestingly, the Tax Court in the *Bolger* case states that "the existence of an agency relationship would have been self-defeating in that it would have seriously endangered, if not prevented, the achievement of those objectives which, in large part, gave rise to the use of the corporations, namely the avoidance of [usury] restrictions under state laws." 59 T.C. at 766. See also "Using a Dummy Corporate Borrower," note 133 *supra*, at 458.

[139] See ¶ 5.04[1].

[140] *Id.*

[141] For tax-free transfers into a "controlled" corporation, see I.R.C. § 351.

[142] I.R.C. § 301(b)(1)(A).

[143] I.R.C. §§ 301(c)(1), 316.

[144] I.R.C. § 301(c)(3)(A).

Claims decisions have sanctioned this trustee or agency theory approach where the applicable documentation (e.g., contracts, corporate resolutions) evidences a true agency relationship whereby the corporate agent exists independently of its principal and does not function solely because it is owned by the principal.[134] Accordingly, to fortify the agency relationship the corporation should: (1) receive more than a nominal fee for its services; (2) if possible, act as agent for unrelated third parties; (3) file an income tax return reporting its agency fees; (4) execute an agency agreement with the principals; (5) be limited under its articles of incorporation to agency activites precluding a finding by the Internal Revenue Service that it is engaging in business for itself; and (6) perform only those acts that are consistent with the agency relationship. In a Tax Court decision that is squarely on point, *David F. Bolger v. Comm'r,*[135] individual taxpayers organized ten corporations to acquire title to certain real estate, execute long-term net leases of the properties, and obtain financing to pay for the acquisition costs without running afoul of the local usury law restrictions on loans to individuals. Upon the consummation of the foregoing transactions, the corporations immediately conveyed the properties to the shareholders, subject to the corporations' obligations under the mortgages and leases with respect to which the shareholders did not assume personal liability. The Tax Court held that the corporations were separately taxable entities, primarily because the taxpayers had failed to prove the existence of a genuine agency relationship. For example, the court noted that "nominee" language existed in the pertinent documents only with respect to two of the ten corporations and that "neither party had sought separate treatment for particular transactions."[136]

Conceptually, the difficulty with the trustee or agency approach is

---

rations in a Nutshell: A Practitioner's Approach to Handling the Tax Problems," 1 J. Real Est. Tax. 391 (1974).

[134] See Caswal Corp. v. Comm'r, 19 T.C.M. 757, 763 (1960); K-C Land Co. v. Comm'r, 19 T.C.M. 183, 186 (1960); Compare Carver v. United States, 412 F.2d 233, 238-239 (Ct. Cl. 1969) (per curiam) (where corporate nominee acted on behalf of independent third party and not just for its sole stockholder) with Harrison Property Management Co. v. U.S., 475 F.2d 623, 626-627 (Ct. Cl. 1973) *cert. denied* 414 U.S. 1130 (1974) (where corporate agent was totally passive and dependent upon its owner-principals). See also Stillman v. Comm'r, 60 T.C. 897, 909 (1973), wherein the corporation had never executed an agency agreement, was not compensated for its services, and had never acted on behalf of unrelated third parties, which prompted the Tax Court to hold that the corporation was dominated by its individual stockholders and that a true agency relationship had not existed.

[135] 59 T.C. 760, 776 (1973).

[136] *Id.* at 766 n.3.

to the corporation.[126] However, the actual failure of this circumvention device has been in the tax area. The difficulty with this approach lies in the fact that the courts have almost invariably taxed and recognized the straw as a "viable corporate entity" whenever it is engaged in any business activity other than the holding of title.[127] Significantly, the mere act of borrowing and executing debt instruments has prompted courts to recognize the supposed straw as a separate taxable entity.[128]

Another more promising approach is predicated upon dicta in two benchmark Supreme Court decisions, *Moline Properties, Inc. v. Comm'r*,[129] and *National Carbide Corp. v. Comm'r*.[130] In both cases, the Court refused to ignore corporations as separate tax entities. In the former decision it noted that there was neither an agency contract nor an agency relationship between the corporation and its sole shareholder.[131] In the latter it stated, "What we have said does not foreclose a true corporate agent or trustee from handling the property and income of its owner-principal without being taxable therefor. . . . If the corporation is a true agent, its relations with its principal must not be dependent upon the fact that it is owned by the principal, if such is the case. Its business purpose must be the carrying on of the normal duties of an agent."[132] The approach suggested by this dictum is straightforward: The corporation holds legal title, as trustee, for the individual beneficial owners and/or merely acts as an agent for the beneficial owners rather than on its own behalf when it negotiates and consummates the desired mortgage loan. Accordingly, the corporation should be able to perform its ministerial functions as trustee and/or agent, such as managing the property and collecting rents, without being taxed on the income distributed to the beneficial owners.[133] Recent Tax Court and Court of

---

[126] See discussion at ¶ 5.04[1].

[127] E.g., Britt v. United States, 431 F.2d 227, 233, (5th Cir. 1970) (corporation, as partner, paid taxes and attorney's fees); Hagist Ranch Inc. v. Comm'r, 295 F.2d 351, 354 (7th Cir. 1961) (corporation executed leases and traded in properties); Tomlinson v. Miles, 316 F.2d 710, 713-714 (5th Cir. 1963) (corporation acquired and sold land); Taylor v. Comm'r, 445 F. 2d 455, 457, 1st Cir. 1971) (corporation performed minimal activities).

[128] See Paymer v. Comm'r, 150 F.2d 334, 336 (2d Cir. 1945); Strong v. Comm'r, 66 T.C. 12, 24-25, aff'd 77-1 U.S.T.C. ¶ 9240 (2d Cir. 1977); O'Neill v. Comm'r, 271 F.2d 44, 49 (9th Cir. 1959).

[129] 319 U.S. 436, 441 (1943).

[130] 336 U.S. 422, 429 (1949).

[131] 319 U.S. at 440.

[132] 336 U.S. at 437.

[133] See generally Comment, "Using a 'Dummy' Corporate Borrower Creates Usury and Tax Difficulties," 28 SW. L.J. 437, 454-457 (1974) (hereinafter cited as "Using a Dummy corporate Borrower"); Robinson, "Straw Corpo-

obligor to the effect that the instrument is valid and is not subject to offset or defense will estop the obligor from defending on grounds of usury.[121] But such an affidavit or certificate will prove ineffective if the purchaser of the mortgage has full knowledge of the details of the transaction.[122]

[3] Incorporation of the Borrower

Where the only usury exemption allowed is that for corporate borrowers, a developer may not have any alternative but incorporation, in order to fund his project. The challenging problem after incorporation is to preserve the tax-shelter benefits that primarily attract investors to commercial land enterprises. Depreciation and deductible items, the main ingredients of the tax shelter, will not pass through the syndicate and onto the tax returns of the individual investors if the corporation is a separate tax-paying entity.[123] In theory, then, the dilemma of having to choose between usury restrictions and a disadvantageous tax situation may be resolved through the mechanism of a corporation that is not separately taxable, at least with respect to the property under development. The Subchapter S corporation would be entirely suitable, but cannot be used with respect to rental property because of the passive income requirement.[124]

Two related approaches have been followed in the quest for a corporate form that is practical but not separately taxable. One approach is predicated on the notion that a "straw" or "dummy" corporation has no real tax existence apart from its owners and yet can evade usury restrictions by holding legal title to the property and consummating the loan.

Generally, when a corporation holds naked legal title solely for the benefit of its individual or partnership stockholders and serves no other business function, its existence as a separate tax entity will be ignored.[125] Theoretically, there is a potential risk that such a straw corporation would not succeed in avoiding the usury laws if the courts should find that the loan was actually made to the individual stockholders and not

---

[121] Annot., 110 A.L.R. 451, 457 (1937).

[122] DeKorwin v. First Nat'l Bank, 275 F.2d 755, 765 (7th Cir.), *cert. denied sub nom.* Jones v. Kaufman, 364 U.S. 824 (1960).

[123] See discussion at ¶ 1.05[2].

[124] I.R.C. § 1372(e)(5). See discussion at ¶ 1.06.

[125] See, e.g., United States v. Brager Bldg. & Land Corp., 124 F.2d 349, 350 (4th Cir. 1941); Shaw Constr. Co. v. Comm'r, 323 F.2d 316, 320-321 (9th Cir. 1963).

Estoppel. The majority view is that a borrower may be estopped from asserting usury as a defense against an innocent purchaser who has been induced to take the obligation by the borrower's conduct or representations.[116] The conduct or statements of the borrower must, of course, represent that the obligation is free of usury. Such representation can be indirectly made, as, for example, where the borrower merely indicates that the obligation is valid and enforceable.[117] In some states, the borrower's initiation of the usurious transaction will preclude the usury defense.[118]

Holder in Due Course. The law is not uniform; for example, in some jurisdictions the purchaser of a negotiable mortgage note is protected against usury claims by operation of the law governing negotiable instruments—if the purchaser qualifies as holder in due course, without notice of any matters such as commissions or fees on which the usury claim may be based.[119] In other states, this protection is not available to the purchaser of a mortgage who attempts to foreclose on the property.[120]

Affidavits and Estoppel Certificates. If there is any suspicion that the amount of discount at which a mortgage note has been sold is being exacted from the original borrower, the purchaser of the note, especially if he claims holder-in-due-course status, is well advised to obtain an affidavit from the holder, reciting that the holder is selling the note at discount for his own business purposes and that the discount is not being charged to the maker in any manner, either in whole or in part.

In a number of states, a similar affidavit or certificate from the

---

the lender was an investment company, which although an independent organization, had controlling interest in the borrowing entity. The court nevertheless found no usury in the arrangement whereby the borrower received the loan proceeds at par and the lender sold the note at discount to a completely independent buyer.

[116] Heubush v. Boone, 213 Va. 414, 192 S.E.2d 783, 789 (1972); Annot., 16 A.L.R.3d 510, 513 (1967).

[117] 213 Va. 414, 192 S.E. 2d 783, 791; Martin v. Ajax Constr. Co., 124 Cal. App. 2d 425, 432, 269 P.2d 132, 136 (1954).

[118] See Annot., 16 A.L.R.3d 510, 513 (1967). Contra, *id.* at 519.

[119] Obviously, the purchaser is not protected if the mortgage is usurious on its face. Furthermore, in the case of sale by a regular correspondent of a lender, the correspondent's knowledge may be and usually is imputed to the lender, on the basis of agency principles.

[120] The rationale for not allowing the purchaser to take advantage of the holder in due course doctrine is that the mortgage is but a chose in action which does not partake of the negotiable character of the note. See "Mortgage Investments and the Usury Problem," 10 Clev.-Mar. L. Rev. 343, 358-359 (1961).

While under the "rule of validation" the courts are apt to favor the lender in close cases, where the defense of usury is pleaded by the borrower, the lender's position would certainly be enhanced if the loan agreement is not a so-called adhesion contract that is nonnegotiable in its terms, but is one freely bargained for by a borrower who is relatively sophisticated and who has the aid of legal counsel.

[2] Sale of Mortgage Note at Discount; Estoppel; Holder in Due Course

Requirement of Bona Fide Sale. When the proceeds of a mortgage loan have been advanced to the borrower, the note is an asset of the lender, and he may sell it to a willing buyer at any agreed price. The bona fide sale of a mortgage note at discount is not controlled by usury statutes;[110] the sale is not a loan to which usury restrictions can apply.[111] Moreover, loan agreements are determined to be usurious or not as of the time at which they are made, not later.[112]

There can be no bona fide sale of a mortgage note at a discount unless there are three distinct parties in the overall transaction: the borrower, the lender who is also the seller of the note and who absorbs the discount, and the buyer. If the distinctions between the parties are blurred, usury problems may occur. For example, if the borrower directly absorbs the loss involved in sale at discount, the amount of the loss will be considered additional interest on the loan.[113] Similarly, if the mortgagee-seller is only a dummy, so that the loan is actually made by the supposed buyer to the borrower, the amount of the discount will again be categorized as interest, with the possible result that the overall transaction will be found to be usurious.[114] The doubtful cases are those in which there is some affiliation between the borrower and the lender-seller.[115]

---

[110] See generally Annot., 165 A.L.R. 626, 679 (1946).

[111] See ¶ 5.02[2].

[112] See, e.g., Sharp v. Mortgage Security Corp. of Am., 215 Cal. 287, 290-291, 9 P.2d 819, 820 (1932). In Conover v. Hobart, 24 N.J. Eq. 120 (1883), additional compensation paid by the vorrower to a third party, as inducement for the third party to purchase th mortgage, was found not to make the mortgage usurious, because the additional payment occurred after a valid mortgage loan had been made.

[113] An exception may be made if the discount absorbed by the borrower simply represents a permissible service that is due to the broker. See Webb v. Southern Trust Co., 227 Ky. 79, 83, 11 S.W.2d 988, 989 (1928).

[114] See, e.g., Janisse v. Winston Instrument Co., 154 Cal. App. 2d 580, 588, 317 P.2d 48, 54 (1957).

[115] For example, in Brown v. Crawford, 252 F. 248, 259, (D. Ore. 1918),

state connected with the transaction.[102] The rule is subject to the requirement that the parties have acted in good faith. There are a number of further qualifications. The contract must have a substantial relation to the state whose law governs, and foreign law will not be applied if it is in opposition to a strong public policy of the forum state.[103] However, if a majority of the contacts in the transaction are within a single state, the law of that state will be applied.[104]

For example, in *National Surety Corporation v. Inland Properties, Inc.*,[105] the apartment and shopping center loan was negotiated in New York, the note and mortgage were executed in New York, the note was payable in New York, the loan was closed and funded in New York, and the parties expressly stipulated that their rights and obligations under the note and mortgage would be governed by New York law. Notwithstanding the fact that the state in which the property was situated, Arkansas, had a strong public policy against usury, the court nonetheless held that New York rather than Arkansas law was controlling.

However, each state will seek to protect its residents[106] and its own lenders. As to national banks restricted by federal law,[107] it is not clear whether loans to out-of-state borrowers may be made at the higher rate as between the rate authorized by the bank's state and by the borrower's state.[108]

A rule that is particularly important—because it grants a measure of freedom to the parties—is that which allows the court to accept the choice of law indicated in the agreement as intended by the parties, if the choice is reasonable and made in good faith.[109]

---

was made), and Andrews v. Pond, 38 U.S. (13 Pet.) 65, 80 (1839) (place of performance). Cf. Fabs v. Martin, 224 F.2d 387, 401 (5th Cir. 1955); Lubbock Hotal Co. v. Guaranty Bank & Trust Co., 77 F.2d 152, 156 (5th Cir. 1935).

[102] *Restatement (Second) of Conflict of Laws* § 203 (1971).

[103] See, e.g., Trinidad Indus. Bank v. Romero, 81 N.M. 291, 294-295, 466 P.2d 568, 571-572 (1970) (rates of 12½ to 50 percent found to shock the conscience of the court).

[104] See, e.g., Aldens v. Packel, 524 F.2d 38, 53 (3d Cir. 1975), *cert. denied* 425 U.S. 943 (1976).

[105] 286 F. Supp. 173 (D. Ark. 1968), *aff'd* 416 F.2d 457 (1969) (per curiam).

[106] See, e.g., Rochester Capital Leasing v. K. & L. Litho Corp., 13 Cal. App. 3d 697, 703, 91 Cal. Rptr. 827, 830-831 (1970).

[107] 12 U.S.C. § 85 (Cum. Supp. 1974).

[108] Fisher v. First Nat'l Bank of Omaha, 548 F.2d 255, 257-258 (8th Cir. 1977), allowed the higher rate; Meador Brook Nat'l Bank v. Recile, 302 F. Supp. 62, 86 (E.D. La. 1969), is contra.

[109] See, e.g., Securities Inv. Co. v. Finance Acceptance Corp., 474 S.W.2d 261, 271 (Tex. 1971); Moody v. Bass, 357 F.2d 730, 732 (6th Cir. 1966) (per curiam). But cf. *Restatement (Second) of Conflicts of Laws*, § 203 Comment e, (1971).

¶ 5.05 CIRCUMVENTION DEVICES

The developer who is unable to obtain a mortgage loan at the lawful contract rate and who cannot avail itself of an exemption from the general usury statutes may have to consider a financing arrangement that avoids or circumvents the usury restrictions. This section considers a number of financing schemes that have been used, with greater or lesser success, to avoid usury problems.

In general terms, the usury restrictions may be avoided by structuring the financing arrangements so that the would-be borrower receives the money it needs as the proceeds from the sale of property to the lending institution or as an equity investment by the lender in the enterprise. Conversely, the lending institution would obtain repayment in the form of either rent or payments pursuant to an installment sale. Well-established legal doctrines governing estoppel and conflicts of laws may also apply to preclude the usury defense, or to place the transaction within the purview of a more favorable foreign statute. Finally, the borrower may try to use the corporate exemption by adopting the corporate form to a limited extent, hoping nevertheless to avoid unfavorable tax consequences.

Several of the financing arrangements discussed in this section provide advantages to the developer in areas unrelated to usury. The sale-leaseback, for example, may be selected to achieve larger tax deductions, or the sale-repurchase arrangement to achieve greater leverage.[100] However, almost all financial arrangements that give the lender a greater return than the lawful contract rate involve some usury-related hazards; accordingly, unless the project is clearly free of usury constraints because of a directly applicable exemption, it is important that the usury implications be recognized even in those arrangements selected primarily for reasons other than those dealing with usury evasion.

[1] Conflicts of Law

Sophisticated borrowers in states with stringent usury restrictions will sometimes "shop around" for a state where the usury law will satisfy the lender's requirements. The general rule for selecting the usury law to be applied when there is a conflict is the "rule of validation,"[101] which favors the lender by applying the law that will validate the transaction of any

---

[100] See discussion at ¶¶ 6.04, 8.09.

[101] The "rule of validation" originated in Miller v. Tiffany, 68 U.S. (1 Wall.) 298, 310 (1863). The rule combines the holdings in earlier leading decisions: Depau v. Humphreys, 10 Mart. 1, 17 (La. 1829) (place where contract

order to obtain a loan. After the borrower transferred his real estate to a newly formed corporation, he secured the loan, but subsequently defaulted. In refusing to vacate the foreclosure sale based on a usury defense, Justice Lehman of the Court of Appeals reasoned that "The [usury] law has not been evaded but has been followed meticulously in order to accomplish a result which all parties desired and which the law does not forbid."[98] As a result of these decisions, it seems apparent that in those jurisdictions recognizing a corporate exemption, a corporation may be formed solely for the purpose of borrowing money without running afoul of the usury law if the real estate loan is made for business purposes and if there has been no manifest overreaching by the lender.

[2] Exemptions Available to Limited Partnerships

An increasing number of states have expanded the corporate exemption or enacted a separate exception to permit partnerships and limited partnerships to borrow funds free of usury limitations. A specific partnership exemption eliminates the usury problem for most commercial real estate projects. A broad exception for business-purpose loans or for loans above a stated amount may directly provide the same relief to limited partnerships. They would additionally cover joint ventures and sole proprietorships, not always subsumed under the partnership exemptions.

In the absence of an exception for partnership borrowers or for business-purpose loans, special provisions allowing designated lending institutions to charge higher rates of interest may indicate that a funding source is available, without resort to circumvention techniques.

[3] FHA Mortgage Exemption

Although the presence of an FHA mortgage exemption is common to many usury statutes, the provisions do vary significantly from state to state. The exemption is generally available to locally chartered banks and frequently to savings and loan institutions and to insurance companies.[99] The FHA exemption is of primary importance in projects when land is being developed for resale.

---

[98] 254 N.Y. 319, 324, 172 N.E. 521, 522 (1930). On this issue see generally Hershman, "Usury and the Tight Mortgage Market—Revisited," 24 Bus. Law. 1121, 1132–1134 (1969).

[99] The exemption frequently is from investment regulations as well as from usury restrictions.

[1] Corporate Exemption

Historically, the corporate exemption has been the pioneer of the business-oriented exceptions to the general usury statutes. Not surprisingly, it has been seized upon as a circumvention device, and partly for this reason, has been the subject of continuous litigation.

The statutory variations from state to state dealing with nonprofit corporations are obviously of minimal significance to commercial land developers.[93] Provisions that merely prevent corporations from interposing the defense of usury have been construed broadly, as prohibiting even affirmative actions to avoid an obligation on grounds of usury.[94]

In situations where individual borrowers have been prompted by the lenders to incorporate in order to avoid the usury law, some courts like those in New Jersey and Florida have attempted to determine whether in fact the loan was made to the corporation or to the individual shareholder. In appropriate cases, the court may thus pierce the corporate veil where the lender has overreached his borrower.[95] But even in these so-called question-of-fact jurisdictions, the courts have been reluctant to permit the borrower to defend on the ground of usury where an experienced real estate borrower has utilized the corporate exemption to secure the loan for business purposes.[96] In other states like New York, the courts have generally applied a more formalistic approach in almost automatically recognizing the corporate exemption. For example, in the leading New York case of *Jenkins v. Moyse*,[97] an individual real estate borrower was told by the lender that he would have to incorporate in

---

[92] See Table 3 in Appendix A as a cross-referential guide.

[93] Some states retain the usury restrictions for nonprofit corporations while others do not. A middle ground is to allow a nonprofit corporation to waive the usury defense. Some statutes exempt loans to corporations only above a certain dollar amount. See also note 89 *supra*.

[94] See generally 63 A.L.R.2d 924, 927 (1959).

[95] See Gelber v. Kugelis Tavern, Inc., 10 N.J. 191, 89 A.2d 654 (1952); *In re* Greenberg 21 N.J. 213, 121 A.2d 520 (1956); Atlas Subsidiaries v. O.&O., Inc., 166 So. 2d 458 (Fla. 1964); See also Gangadean v. Flori Inv. Co., 11 Ariz. App. 512, 466 P.2d 63 (1970).

[96] See Monmouth Capital Corp. v. Holmdel Village Shops, Inc., 92 N.J. Super. 480, 224 A.2d 35 (1966); Tel Serv. Co. v. General Capital Corp., 227 So. 2d 667 (Fla. 1969) (where lender had required partnership to incorporate).

[97] 254 N.Y. 319, 172 N.E. 521 (1930). However, one commentator has noted a recent trend in lower New York court decisions to limit the availability of the corporate exemption to loans that are used for business purposes. See Comment, "Incorporation to Avoid Usury Laws," 68 Colum. L. Rev. 1390, 1392 (1968). See also Rabinowich v. Eliasberg, 159 Md. 655, 152 A. 437 (Md. 1930) (where court applied an estoppel theory to prevent the borrower from ignoring his own corporation).

(3) Type of lender or lending institution;
(4) Type of business entity of the borrower; and
(5) Form of the security (e.g., first versus second mortgage), and in some cases, the nature of the security.[90]

In addition, an exemption in some form is usually granted for FHA mortgage loans, and many states have codified the doctrine of time-price differential by statutorily exempting installment loans.[91]

Exemptions based on the amount or the purpose of the loan, whether business or personal, or on a combination of these two factors, ordinarily do not pose any serious problems of statutory construction, nor is their phraseology uncertain as to when they will apply. Similarly, exemptions for noncorporate business entities such as partnerships, limited partnerships, and joint ventures present few interpretational issues for the courts because the terms have well-established meanings. Logically, the same situation should prevail in regard to corporations; however, corporate exemption, as discussed below, is subject various limitations and to uncertainties in application.

Exceptions granted to particular lending institutions (frequently those that are separately regulated) may pose problems of statutory interpretation. Unfortunately, the variety of express exemptions adopted by the separate legislatures frequently requires that ambiguities as to meaning or legislative intent be resolved within the enacting state since out-of-state decisions generally are accorded relatively little weight or value because of statutory differences.

The extent of the various exemptions is also subject to variation. The statute may remove all usury restrictions from the exempted transaction or simply allow a higher lawful rate of interest; alternatively, the exemption may preclude the plea of usury as a defense or may permit the borrower to waive this protection.

The following sections address common exemptions that are significant to commercial real estate lending activities.[92]

---

[90] See Table 3 (Usury Statutes) in Appendix A. The nature of the security generally appears as a limitation to an established exemption. To curb abuse of the corporate exemption, several states have denied it to corporations whose assets are small holdings of one- or two-family dwellings.

[91] See, e.g., Grigg v. Wobinson Furniture Co., 78 Mich. App. 712, 732, 266 N.W.2d 898, 908 (1978), in which the court, in applying the Retail Installment Sales Act, expressly noted a legislative intent to continue observing the distinction between the interest charge on loans and the time-price differential charged on retail sales.

[92] See Table 3 in Appendix A as a cross-referential guide.

loan agreement, the courts have reached differing conclusions in cases where interest has become excessive because of acceleration.[84] The decisions most favorable to the lenders have allowed collection of the full interest amount, based on the original period of the loan, on the ground that the interest above the statutory maximum becomes payable only upon default, a contingency subject to the control of the borrower alone,[85] or that the contract must be tested for usury at the time the loan is made.[86] By contrast, the decisions most sympathetic to borrowers have found usury to exist where the rate of interest has or may be driven above the lawful limit by means of acceleration.[87] The reported cases also reveal two intermediate positions, similar in effect but conceptually distinct. Under the first approach, the courts will construe the agreement as requiring abatement of the excess interest if such a construction is possible;[88] the second approach is to view what might appear to be excess interest as really not interest but as a penalty that is not enforceable.[89] Under both of these middle positions, the lender avoids being cast in the role of usurer, but is unable to collect compensation beyond that permitted by the usury statutes.

¶ 5.04 STATUTORY EXEMPTIONS

Usury statutes invariably contain a number of express exemptions, most of which are based on one or more of the following factors:

(1) Amount or purpose of the loan;
(2) Form of the agreement, whether written or oral;

---

[84] See 66 A.L.R.3d 650 (1975).

[85] See, e.g., Mathis v. Holland Furnace Co. of Am., 109 Utah 449, 457, 166 P.2d 518, 522 (1946).

[86] See, e.g., Sharp v. Mortgage Security Corp., 215 Cal. 287, 290, 9 P.2d 819, 820 (1932).

[87] See, e.g., Home Credit Co. v. Brown, 148 So. 2d 257, 260 (Fla. 1962). In Texas, the presence of an acceleration clause in the agreement, under circumstances that would allow the lender to receive interest above the lawful limit, has been found to make the agreement usurious. See Shropshire v. Commerce Farm Credit Co., 120 Tex. 400, 418, 30 S.W.2d 282, 286, 39 S.W.2d 11, 14, *cert. denied* 284 U.S. 675 (1931). In Florida, the presence of an acceleration clause in the agreement, which could be used to collect excessive interest, coupled with actual acceleration of the obligation or foreclosure of the security, is sufficient for a finding of usury, even if the lender does not claim the excessive interest. See 66 A.L.R.3d 650, 668 (1975).

[88] See, e.g., Braniff Inv. Co. v. Robertson, 124 Tex. 524, 538, 81 S.W.2d 45, 52 (1935).

[89] See, e.g., Ruby v. Warrior, 71 Okla. 82, 86, 175 P. 355, 357 (1918); Tipton v. Ellsworth, 18 Idaho 207, 222, 109 P. 134 (1910).

tions,[78] because the failure to pay installments when due is not a contingency solely within the control of the borrower.[79]

Expenses of Collections. Likewise, loan agreements may ordinarily require the borrower in default to pay reasonable costs actually incurred by the lender in collecting the debt, on the ground that charges contingent on the borrower's actions are not subject to usury provisions.[80] There are, however, two problem situations. First, collection charges arising from the activity of in-house counsel may be deemed to be interest.[81] Second, if the parties enter into a new or modified agreement in which the lender forbears exercising his right to accelerate the indebtedness under the original contract, the authorities are divided on the question of whether the lender may charge the borrower with the amount spent for collection, without having such charges construed as interest.[82]

Interest Due Upon Acceleration. In order to preserve its security as to the entire loan, a commercial lender will invariably include in the mortgage note a provision that allows the entire indebtedness to be declared immediately due and payable when the borrower is in default.[83] Acceleration of the date on which repayment of principal is due necessarily shortens the period of the loan. Unless a corresponding reduction of the amount of interest is made, acceleration of repayment may cause the rate of interest to be increased, possibly to a level above the lawful maximum.

If the acceleration provision additionally provides for adjustment of the interest so that the rate will not exceed the lawful contract rate, there can be no usury problem. Absent such an express saving provision in the

---

[78] See, e.g., Hayes v. First Nat'l Bank of Memphis, 256 Ark. 328, 332, 507 S.W.2d 701, 704 (1974); Union Bank v. Kruger, 11 Wash. App. 622, 628, 463 P.2d 273, 277 (1969). But see Thrift Funds of Baton Rouge, Inc. v. Jones, 274 So. 2d 150, 161 (La. 1973), *cert. denied* 414 U.S. 820 (1974) (applying Louisiana statute under which damages for delay in the performance of an obligation to pay money are called interest); Bank v. Phelps & Bigelow Windmill Co., 96 Tenn. 361, 368, 34 S.W. 516, 517 (1896) (provision for payment of 10 percent interest after maturity held to be usurious).

[79] See ¶ 5.02[3][b].

[80] Peyser v. Cole, 11 Ore. 39, 46, 4 P. 520, 523 (1884); 91 *C.J.S.* "Usury" § 53 (1955).

[81] Thompson v. Chemical Bank, 84 Misc. 2d 721, 731, 375 N.Y.S.2d 729, 740 (1975). But cf. National Bank of Westchester, 58 App.2d, 593, 395 N.Y.S.2d 487, 489 (1977).

[82] 52 A.L.R.2d 703 (1957). Compare Kent v. Phelps, 2 Day 483 (Conn. 1807), with Bank of Pocahontas v. Browning, 111 Va. 237, 239 68 S.E. 1000,1001 (1910).

[83] See discussion at ¶ 3.08[4][g].

of the reported expenses.[72] Charges that are unreasonable, or greater than the usual compensation for the services performed, are viewed as evidence of usurious intent.[73]

In many jurisdictions, the borrower's prior written assent to payment of closing fees and expenses is essential for such charges to fall outside the ambit of the usury statutes.[74]

[6] Taxes

Loan agreements that prescribe the maximum lawful rate of interest and additionally require the mortgagor to pay taxes assessed against the mortgaged property, have uniformly withstood the raising of usury as a defense.[75] Similar agreements that require the mortgagor to pay taxes assessed against the loan, mortgage bond, or other interest of the lender have been held not to create usurious transactions in a majority of states.[76]

[7] Prepayment Penalty

A penalty for the privilege of repaying the loan before the time specified by the agreement ordinarily cannot make an otherwise lawful loan usurious. Because prepayment is an option of the borrower, the related penalty is not an amount that the borrower is liable to pay absolutely. One of the elements necessary for a transaction to be usurious is therefore lacking.[77]

[8] Charges Upon Default

Late Payment Charges. Most courts will allow the lender to assess a reasonable charge for late payments, without regard to usury restric-

---

[72] Continental Nat'l Bank v. Fleming, 170 Mich. 624, 625, 134 N.W. 656, 657 (1912); 91 *C.J.S.* "Usury" § 48a (1955).

[73] Chakales v. Djiovanides, 161 Va. 48, 87, 170 S.E. 848, 861 (1933); Hobart v. Michaud, 174 Minn. 474, 478, 219 N.W. 878, 879 (1928).

[74] See 45 *Am. Jur. 2d* "Interests & Usury" § 207 (1967).

[75] 21 A.L.R. 797, 880 (1922).

[76] See cases collected in 21 A.L.R. 797, 883, 53 A.L.R. 743, 756, and 105 A.L.R. 795, 812.

[77] See ¶ 5.02[3][b].

[4] Construction Loan Fees

Construction lenders have developed the expertise to monitor the construction work and will authorize disbursement only as the project progresses to predetermined stages and remains free of mechanics' liens. Supervision of the actual construction is not considered a routine function in the business of lending money; the costs of carrying out the supervisory activities are not classed among general overhead expenses. Accordingly, for usury purposes, charges imposed on the borrower to cover the costs of monitoring the construction are not taken into account.[67]

[5] Closing Expenses

As noted,[68] the usual and reasonable expenses incident to closing a mortgage loan are not subject to usury restrictions because these charges do not represent compensation for the use of money.[69] This general rule applies to legal fees for title examination and preparation of necessary papers, costs of appraisals, recording fees, and similar expenses.[70] These specific activities or services are distinguished from routine, overhead functions for which a charge, other than an interest, would not be allowed.[71]

Decisions supporting the exclusion of closing costs from the usury limitations are predicated on the good faith of the lender; this is reflected by its actual performance of the related services and payment

---

[67] Real Estate Trustee v. Rebham, 139 A. 351 (Md. 1927):

If, for example, a mortgagee is required to perform continuing duties in the application of the loan to the cost of building or other operations, over which he is intended to have supervision, a service would thus be contemplated for which a commission, fairly proportionate to its value, could be charged without being subject to the suspicion that it was an effort to circumvent the law against usury.

Id. at 353.

[68] ¶ 5.02[4][a].

[69] Union Central Life Ins. Co. v. Edwards, 219 Ky. 748, 751, 294 S.W. 502, 504 (1927); 91 *C.J.S.* "Usury" § 48 (1955).

[70] See cases collected in 21 A.L.R. 797 (1922), and the supplemental annotations in 53 A.L.R. 743 (1922), 63 A.L.R. 823 (1929), and 105 A.L.R. 795 (1936).

[71] See ¶ 5.02[4][a]. In distinguishing between overhead activities and specific services performed by the borrower, the judicial opinions do not consider whether the services are of benefit to the borrower. Thus, a developer may be required to pay for a survey or an appraisal, for example, even though he knows quite well both the value and the boundaries of his property.

[3] Brokerage and Other Fees Paid to Intermediaries

A broker who makes a loan with his own funds is, in most cases, subject to the same limitations as other lenders; accordingly, general service or origination fees will be considered interest for the application of usury restrictions.[63]

Where a broker or loan correspondent arranges for his client to obtain a loan from a lender, it is generally held that the broker's commission, even if termed an origination fee and based on the amount of the loan, is not part of the interest paid by the borrower.[64] However, in some jurisdictions, if the broker is an agent of the lender, the broker's service fee will be imputed to the lender; the fee received by the broker will be added to the interest paid or to be paid to the lender in determining whether the loan is usurious.[65]

A further complication may arise if the broker gives any part of his fee to the lender. In some states, the amount received by the lender will be added to the interest on the loan. But in other jurisdictions, the lender may exact part of the broker's fee as a condition to making the loan, without the fee or even the portion received by the lender characterized as interest.[66] The reasoning is simply that the borrower's agreement to pay a commission to his agent-broker is not altered or affected by the broker's agreement to split his fee with the lender.

---

business." Vee Bee Service Co. v. Household Fin. Corp., 51 N.Y.S.2d at 590.

There are a number of mostly older decisions to the effect that a lender who incurs costs in obtaining the money with which to make a loan may charge these costs to the borrower, in addition to interest. The rule in these cases is quite limited; only the incidental costs of the lender and not the interest he may have to pay to obtain the money may be passed on to the ultimate borrower. Moreover, these precedents cannot reasonably be construed as authority for institutional lenders to charge their customers the costs incurred in raising the capital necessary to carry on their lending business. See generally *45 Am. Jur. 2d.* "Interest and Usury" § 208 (1967); 91 A.L.R.2d 1389, 1392 (1963).

[63] See cases collected in 52 A.L.R.2d 703 (1957). See also Webb Southern Trust Co., 227 Ky. 79, 82, 11 S.W.2d 988, 989 (1928) (temporary advance by correspondent to get the loan closed held not to be loan by broker).

[64] See, e.g., Kline v. Mathewson, 384 Pa. 298, 302, 121 A.2d 577, 578 (1956); Webb v. Southern Trust Co., 227 Ky. 79, 82, 11 S.W.2d 988, 989 (1928); Talbott v. Manard, 106 Tenn. 60, 64, 59 S.W. 340, 342 (1900).

[65] See e.g., Ahrens v. Kelly, 88 N.J. Eq. 119, 123, 101 A. 571, 572 (1917), *aff'd* 89 N.J. Eq. 586, 105A. 237, 238, (1918) (per curiam). The unlikely situation in which the lender does not know of the service fee paid by the broker is a special case. Absent knowledge of the fee, the lender cannot have the necessary intent to collect excessive interest. See ¶ 5.02[1].

[66] See, e.g., Pushee v. Johnson, 123 Fla. 305, 308, 166 So. 847, 848, (1936); Patterson v. Blomberg, 196 N.C. 433, 434, 146 S.E. 66, 67 (1929); Jones v. Phillippe, 135 Ark. 578, 582, 206 S.W. 40, 42 (1918); 52 A.L.R.2d 703 (1967).

[1] Commitment Fees

A true commitment fee cannot make a loan usurious. The consideration paid to a lender for his promise to make the future loan on agreed terms cannot rationally be equated with compensation for the use of money. Perhaps because the distinction between the commitment fee and the interest is so evident, the issue has scarcely been litigated.[59]

[2] Origination or Service Fees

As in the case of commitment fees, the status of loan origination or service charges (usually a percentage of the loan amount) depends on whether or not these charges are to be characterized as interest. The courts have uniformly concluded that origination fees, paid to the lender[60] and intended to cover the lender's general overhead costs in making the loan, must be included in the amount of interest in determining whether the loan is usurious.[61] This conclusion follows not so much from the literal definition of interest as from the realistic judicial view of money lending as a business, in which the loan is the product to be acquired by the client at the price of the agreed upon amount of interest. In this light, interest is viewed as proper compensation to the lender for all normal or routine activities in making the loan, that is, carrying on the business of lending money. Conversely, any additional payment for such routine activities is deemed to be interest. In following this rationale, the courts implicitly have redefined interest to mean compensation not only for the actual use of the loaned money, but also for the normal costs of operating a money lending business.[62]

---

[59] There appears, in fact, to be but one relevant decision. In Pivot City Realty v. State Sav. & Trust Co., 88 Ind. App. 222, 230, 162 N.E. 27, 30 (1928), a 2 percent charge to cover the lender's expense of having the money for the loan on hand, so that the loan could be funded immediately upon the borrower's request, within a stated period as had been agreed, was held not to be interest for the application of the usury statute.

[60] Service fees paid to a party other than the immediate lender are discussed as brokerage fees at ¶ 5.03[3].

[61] See, e.g., Grady v. Price, 94 Ariz. 252, 256-257, 383 P.2d 173, 176 (1963); Vee Bee Serv. Co. v. Household Fin. Corp., 51 N.Y.S.2d 590, 612 (Sup. Ct.) aff'd without opinion 269 App. Div. 772, 55 N.Y.S.2d 570 (1944); Real Estate Trustee v. Rebham, 139 A. 351, 353 (Md. 1927).

[62] A literal interpretation of interest as compensation for the use of loaned money would not, of course, include the expenses of maintaining offices, processing loan applications, servicing the loan, etc. Nevertheless, the decisions expressly insist that "overhead expenses" be included in the amount of interest. "A lender may not exact extra charges...beyond the statutory rate, to reimburse it for a part of its general overhead expenses of carrying on its lending

lawful rate imposed by local law, there are some cases indicating that the usury restriction will apply.[54] However, the following suggestions are possible ways to avoid the usury problem. First, the mortgage or deed of trust note could provide that in the event the automatic rate increase causes the VRM interest rate to exceed the maximum lawful rate, the borrower would automatically have the right to prepay the mortgage indebtedness. Since the rate increase would arguably depend upon a contingency within the control of the borrower, the usury law should not apply.[55] Alternatively, there might be some way to provide for "averaging" the interest rate over the entire loan term to eliminate peaks in the automatic rate increases. This would include a proviso for reducing these increases if the average rate should approach the maximum rate allowed by local law.[56]

¶ 5.03 STATUS OF CUSTOMARY LOAN CHARGES

In contrast to the complexity of the modern mortgage loan transaction, the typical usury statute speaks simply of interest on loans.[57] The question naturally arises as to the status of the many and varied charges imposed on the borrower in the course of the commercial real estate lending cycle. In the context of usury, there is no overall theory or generally applicable criterion by which particular charges to the borrower can be characterized. Some legislatures have enacted provisions expressly governing the more common lender services and fees.[58] The courts, in deciding cases in which loan charges are alleged to be usurious, have found many of these charges beyond the scope of usury restrictions, but on various grounds. The following sections summarize the judicial decisions, in the absence of express statutory direction, as to customary fees in commercial loan transactions.

---

[54] E.g., Aztec Properties v. Union Planters Nat'l Bank, 530 S.W.2d 756, 761, (Tenn. 1975); Olwine v. Torrens, 236 Pa. Super. Ct. 51, 56, 344 A.2d 665, 668 (1975). But cf. American Century Mtge. Investors v. Regional Center, 529 S.W.2d 578, 584 (Tex. 1975), where the fact that the loan agreement specified interest at 4½ percent above prime rate did not establish a prima facie showing of usury where agreement provided that interest was not to exceed maximum rate permitted by law.

[55] See discussion at ¶ 5.02[3].

[56] See American Century Mtge. Investor v. Regional Center, 529 S.W.2d 578 (Tex. 1975).

[57] See ¶ 5.02[4][a].

[58] See Table 3 in Appendix A.

Surprisingly, in many jurisdictions the loan agreement rate may give the lender the right to receive interest in advance,[49] provided that the total amount of the interest does not exceed the amount allowed by statute. Moreover, in some jurisdictions, an agreement in advance for the payment of compound interest will not make the loan usurious, even though the stated rate of simple interest is the maximum permitted by law.[50]

[c] Interest Rate Escalator Clauses

During the recent inflationary years, lenders have found themselves burdened with long-term mortgage investments having yields well below the current market rates. Adopting a "never again" attitude, some have responded to the problem by insisting on nonassumption clauses or due-on-sale acceleration provisions and by making variable rate mortgage loans.[51] A device of similar purpose and recent origin is an escalator provision that ties the loan interest rate to the maximum lawful rate; the face rate automatically changes to the new maximum if and when the state legislature acts to allow higher rates of interest. The escalator clause device has not yet come under the scrutiny of many courts. In fact, there is only one reported case, and it is of limited general relevance. In *Campbell v. Gawart*,[52] the court could not give effect to the escalator provision because the statute that increased the lawful interest rate was limited, by its terms, to future loan transactions.

[d] Variable-Rate Mortgage

The "variable-rate mortgage" (VRM) is a long-term mortgage loan with an interest rate that fluctuates up or down in response to changes in the money market as reflected by some internal standard (e.g., the rate of interest currently being paid by the lender to its depositors) or external standard (e.g., the Consumer Price Index or the rate being paid on U.S. Government securities). This device has recently become popular with savings and loans and other long-term lenders in the home-building industry because it enables them to earn higher interest charges when their short-term borrowings become costlier.[53] If an automatic rate increase causes the interest rate on a VRM to exceed the maximum

---

[49] 91 *C.J.S.* "Usury" § 34 (1955).
[50] *Id.* § 36a.
[51] See discussion at ¶¶ 3.04[3], 3.04[8].
[52] 46 Mich. App. 529, 533, 208 N.W.2d 607, 610 (1973).
[53] See discussion at ¶ 3.04[3][c].

similar costs for specified services. The courts will, of course, look behind the mere label that the lender may use to describe a particular charge or fee where there is reason to believe that the charge represents interest disguised as a fee for services.

Additional charges closely related to the use of borrowed money, such as commitment fees and late payment penalties, are not so clearly free of usury implications.[46]

[b] How Interest Is Computed

The lawful contract rate of interest is the maximum permissible annual percentage rate. Generally, in testing a contract for usury, the courts will take into consideration the entire period of the loan; for example, discounts and other add-ons are normally apportioned over the contract term of the loan.[47] In the case of installment loans, the amount of interest that may be collected without violation of the usury statute is calculated by applying the lawful contract rate to the actual declining balance of principal, not by applying the lawful contract rate to the total principal for the entire period of the loan.[48]

---

[46] These charges are considered at ¶ 5.03.

[47] E.g., French v. Mortgage Guar. Co., 16 Cal. 2d 26, 30, 104 P.2d 655, 658 (1940) (per curiam); Home Sav. & Loan Ass'n v. Bates, 76 N.M. 660, 663, 417 P.2d 798, 820 (1966).

[48] 91 *C.J.S.* "Usury" § 29 (1955).

The significant difference in total interest depending on the method of calculation can be appreciated by an example. Consider a seven-year loan of $10,000 at 6 percent interest, with constant payments:

(1) Interest computed on declining balance:
   The annual percentage rate is 6 percent.
   The monthly payment will be $146.09.
   The borrower will receive $10,000 and pay a total of $12,271.56, of which $10,000 is repayment of principal and $2,271.56 is the interest.

(2) Interest computed on total principal for entire period:
   (a) Add-on method:
       Total interest = 6% of $10,000 x 7 years
                     = $4,200.
       The borrower will receive $10,000 upon signing a note for $14,200, which he will repay in 83 installments of $169.05 and a final payment of $168.85.
   (b) Discount method:
       Total interest = 6% of $10,000 x 7 years
                     = $4,200.
       The borrower will receive $5,800 upon signing a note for $10,000 which he will repay in 83 installments of $119.05 and a final payment of $118.85.

An example is *Thomassen v. Carr*,[43] a California case in which the lender had made a loan to a land speculator of dubious solvency, taking as security a mortgage that was subordinate to the lien of the construction loan. In addition to repayment of principal, the lender was to receive 30 percent of the net profits from the operation and sale of the property. Because the borrower had an absolute obligation to repay the principal, investment or "risk of principal" concepts were not applicable. Nevertheless, the court held that the loan agreement was within the law because the payment of interest was subject to a substantial and bona fide contingency, the earning of profits. The lender who had assumed the risk of receiving less than the law allowed was therefore found entitled to receive more, in spite of the general usury limitations.

[4] Exaction of Greater Compensation as Interest Than Is Allowed by Law

The typical usury statute provides that all contracts for the loan or forbearance of required payment of money at a rate of interest greater than the "lawful contract rate" are usurious. Many of the statutes also specify a "legal rate" of interest. The "legal rate" is simply that rate of interest that the law supplies when a loan agreement fails to specify the interest rate. Because lenders invariably prescribe the interest rate in instruments such as mortgages and deeds of trust, in the area of commercial finance the "legal rate" has little or no relevance to usury.

[a] Legal Definition of Interest

Interest is defined almost universally as compensation for the use of borrowed funds;[44] by negative inference, usury restrictions do not extend to other kinds of compensation received by a lender, even though they are received in connection with a loan. Reasonable fees for specific services rendered or arranged by the lender pose no usury problems because they do not represent compensation for the use of money.[45] Found within this category are charges for appraisals, credit reports or surveys, premiums for hazard or title insurance, attorneys' fees for searching title and preparing necessary instruments, recording fees, and

---

[43] 250 Cal. App. 2d 341, 351, 58 Cal. Rptr. 297, 303 (1967).

[44] See, e.g., Jersey City v. Zink, 133 N.J.L. 437, 441, 44 A.2d 825, 828 (1945); Comm'r v. Meyer, 139 F.2d 256, 259 (6th Cir. 1943); Weinrich v. Hawley, 236 Iowa 652, 659, 19 N.W.2d 665, 669 (1945).

[45] Union Central Life Ins. Co. v. Edwards, 219 Ky. 748, 751, 294 S.W. 502, 504 (1927); 105 A.L.R. 795 (1936).

the funding of a loan.[37] If, for example, the lender's return of capital and interest income is to be funded from the lender's share of business profits as an "arm's-length" partner or joint venturer, the usury limitations are totally inapplicable.[38] Where there is ample security for the loan or where the contingency affecting the repayment is improbable, the transaction will be deemed usurious.[39]

[b] Payment of Interest

An agreement that provides for payment of interest at the maximum lawful rate, as well as for the payment of additional interest, is not usurious if the additional payment depends upon a contingency within the borrower's control.[40] For example, this exception is important where prepayment charges cause the lender to receive compensation above the statutory limit.[41] Because the prepayment charges become due only upon the borrower's election to repay the loan before maturity, the usury problem is generally avoided—although the lender does receive compensation at a level above the usury ceiling.

A further and very significant exception to usury coverage allows compensation of the lender at a level above the statutory limit where there is a bona fide risk of his receiving less than the statutory limit.[42]

---

[37] Ambrose v. Alioto, 65 Cal. App. 2d 362, 367, 150 P.2d 502, 504 (1944). According to the court, the excessive premium is regarded as compensation for the hazard and not for the forbearance. *Id.* at 504.

[38] 91 *C.J.S.* "Usury" § 26 (1955). See discussion at ¶¶ 5.05[8], 11.02[3][c].

[39] See Wooton v. Coerber, 213 Cal. App. 2d 142, 159, 28 Cal. Rptr. 635, 645 (1963) (repayment contingent on sale of property at adequate price). As enunciated by Judge Learned Hand, the litmus test for identifying advances that are free of usury restrictions is "whether the principal is put at any genuine hazard." The impact must be "to imperil the principal not upon a merely colorable hazard but upon a genuine one." Provident Life & Trust Co. v. Fletcher, 237 F. 104, 109 (S.D.N.Y. 1916). See also 16 A.L.R.3d 477.

[40] 91 *C.J.S.* "Usury" § 31 (1955).

[41] Lyons v. National Sav. Bank, 280 App. Div. 339, 340, 113 N.Y.S.2d 695, 696 (1952). But see Atlantic Life Ins. Co. of Richmond v. Wolff, 54 A.2d 641, 643 (D.C. 1947) (dictum that prepayment fee may render loan usurious if total amount of interest received by lender exceeds lawful amount of interest he could have received had there been no prepayment).

[42] The principle is set forth in the *Restatement of Contracts.* Where the promise (made in consideration of a loan) is conditioned upon a contingency that may provide the lender with a profit in excess of the maximum statutory limit, the loan is not usurious if the repayment would be materially less than the maximum statutory limit if the contingency did not occur. *Restatement of Contracts* § 527 (1932); 91 *C.J.S.* "Usury" § 25 (1955).

restricted to consumer transactions or to transactions involving personal property. The time-price exception has been applied to remove installment land contracts from the reach of usury statutes[31] and to uphold purchase money deeds of trust[32] requiring installment payments that would clearly be usurious if the transaction had been structured as an interest-bearing loan. For example, in a leading case decided in New York, *Mandelino v. Fribourg*,[33] the New York Court of Appeals held that a purchase money mortgage requiring payment of seven percent was not a "loan" within the ambit of the New York usury statute, which imposed a maximum rate of six percent per annum. The court relied on the principle, adopted in earlier decisions, that a normal purchase money mortgage is not a loan, but is merely noncash consideration paid by the purchaser. The court cited Professor Williston's conclusion that where property is sold "the parties may agree that the price, if paid after a certain time, shall be a sum greater by more than legal interest than the price payable at an earlier day."[34] However, in the area of commercial real estate finance, the doctrine of time-price differential is principally of interest in connection with the sale-leaseback method of financing. The sale-leaseback as a technique for evading usury restrictions is examined in ¶ 5.05[4].

[3] Borrower's Absolute Obligation to Repay

[a] Repayment of Principal

The basic rule to follow is that usury restrictions do not apply if the principal sum loaned is repayable only upon a bona fide contingency.[35] Similarly, if the principal is subject to a substantial agreed-upon risk, the question of usury does not arise.[36] The rationale is that advancing money as an investment, subject to a risk of loss, is distinguishable from

---

credit sales. Hare v. General Contract Purchase Corp., 220 Ark. 601, 610, 249 S.W.2d 973, 979 (1952), is the leading case. See Note, "Judicial and Legislative Treatment of 'Usurious' Credit Sales," 71 Harv. L. Rev. 1143-1157 (1958); Shanks, "Practical Problems in the Application of Archaic Usury Statutes," 53 U. Va. L. Rev. 327, 343 (1967).

[31] Bailey v. Inman, 224 N.C. 571, 573, 331 S.E.2d 769, 770 (1944).

[32] Graeme v. Adams, 64 Va. (23 Gratt.) 225, 287, (1873); Evans v. Rice, 96 Va. 50, 30 S.E.463, 466 (1898).

[33] 23 N.Y.2d 145, 151, 242 N.E.2d 823, 826, 295 N.Y.S.2d 654, 658 (1968).

[34] 6 Williston, *Contracts* § 1685, at 721 (3d ed. 1972).

[35] See 45 *Am. Jur. 2d* "Interest and Usury" § 156 (1967); 91 *C.J.S.* "Usury" § 24 (1955).

[36] 91 *C.J.S.* "Usury" § 25 (1959).

to the extension of an existing indebtedness. The surprisingly difficult task is to describe what is meant by a loan in the context of usury law. Under the doctrine of time-price differential, a transaction that might intuitively be thought of as a sale accompanied by a loan may be viewed by the courts simply as a sale. The doctrine is well stated by the Virginia Supreme Court:

> Usury can only attach to loan of money; or to the forbearance of a debt. It is well settled that on a contract to secure the price or value...of property sold, the contracting parties may agree upon one price if cash be paid, and upon as large an addition to the cash price as may suit themselves, if credit be given; and it is wholly immaterial whether the enhanced price be ascertained by the simple addition of a lumping sum to the cash price, or by a percentage thereon. In neither case is the transaction usurious. It is neither a loan nor the forbearance of a debt, but simply the contract price of...property sold.[27]

The doctrine of time-price differential allows the owner of property to sell it at such a price and under such terms as he deems fit, free from the onus of usury restrictions, provided only that the sale be bona fide.[28]

In distinguishing between the additional amount paid in an installment purchase and the interest paid on a loan, (both of which charges are based on the time-value of money), the doctrine of time-price differential is a monument to the elevation of form over substance. It stands in sharp contrast to the judicial rhetoric in the usury cases, stating unequivocally that such decisions must be based on the substance of the disputed transactions. Nevertheless, the "substance over form" rhetoric cannot be ignored; the courts do look critically at the facts and circumstances of property transfers in order to determine whether there has been a bona fide sale as distinguished from a lease, or a transfer or conveyance merely to secure a loan.[29]

The doctrine of time-price differential is regularly applied to installment sales,[30] especially sales of consumer goods, but is not

---

[27] Graeme v. Adams, 64 Va. (23 Gratt.) 225, 234, 14 Am. Rep. 430, 436 (1873).

[28] 91 *C.J.S.* "Usury" § 18a (1955).

[29] *Id.* § 18b. See also Manufacturers Nat'l Bank of Detroit v. Burlison, 69 Mich. App. 570, 576, 245 N.W.2d 350, 353 (1976); State Wholesale Supply Inc. v. Allen, 30 N.C. App. 272, 281, 227 S.E.2d 120, 126 (1976); First Nat'l. Bank in Albuquerque v. Danek, 89 N.M. 623, 627, 556 P.2d 31, 35 (1976).

[30] See Brooks v. Auto Wholesalers, Inc., 101 A.2d 255, 259 (D.C. 1953); Lincoln Loan Serv. Inc. v. Motor Credit Co., 83 A.2d 230, 231 (D.C. 1951). However, there is a trend in the direction of holding usury laws applicable to

limited to agreements in which the unlawful interest rate is intended by the lender. An honest mistake of fact, such as miscalculation of the amount of interest due or of the period of the loan, may be found to rebut the presumption of unlawful intent.[20] Such factual errors usually absolve the lender from the penalties of usury, especially if they involve small amounts or are promptly corrected by the lender.[21] Similarly, if a third party or intermediary exacts additional charges from the borrower, either intentionally or by mistake, but with the result that interest is paid at an usurious rate, an unlawful intent will ordinarily not be imputed to the lender if it did not know of the additional charges.[22] On the other hand, a lender who interprets the law incorrectly does so at his own peril. Courts have held that a mistake of law does not disprove unlawful intent.[23] These decisions underscore the general rule that an intent to require interest above the lawful limit is sufficient to sustain a usury claim or defense.[24] Because an actual intent of the lender to violate the law is not essential, a mere disclaimer of such intent in the terms of the loan agreement cannot rescue the lender from the penalties of a transaction that is objectively usurious.[25] Exculpatory provisions that limit the liability for interest charges to the maximum amount allowed by law cannot be relied on to avoid usury problems, but have been given effect by some courts.[26]

[2] Loan or Forbearance of Money or Its Equivalent

It is, of course, simply a matter of definition that usury, which relates to the rate of interest, can attach only to the making of a loan or

---

[20] Annot., 11 A.L.R.3d 1498, 1501, § 2a (1967).

[21] *Id.* at 1516.

[22] *Id.* at 1524; 45 *Am. Jur. 2d* "Interest and Usury" § 225 (1969).

[23] 11 A.L.R.3d 1498, 1507.

[24] See note 16 *supra.*

[25] "[The lender] cannot charge usurious interest and then escape the penalties by disclaiming an intention to do what they had plainly done...If such a disclaimer clause were given full effect under this record, the usury laws would become meaningless." Terry v. Teachworth, 431 S.W.2d 918, 926 (Tex. 1968). See also 45 *Am. Jur. 2d* "Interest and Usury" § 161; 109 A.L.R. 1471 (1937).

[26] The following reduction of interest clause operated to negate usurious intent in Pan-American Life Ins. Co. v. Boyd, 124 S.W.2d 917, 920 (Tex. Civ. App. 1938); "[A]ny of said contracts for interest shall be held subject to reduction to the amount allowed under said usury laws as now or hereafter construed by courts having jurisdiction." Accord, Nevels v. Sarris, 127 Tex. 190, 197, 102 S.W.2d 1046, 1049-1050 (1937). Ironically, when the lender includes such a provision in an instrument, he may be conceding by implication that the compensation at issue is subject to usury restraints, when the compensation (for example, additional compensation in a mortgage note expressed as a percentage of the borrower's profits) may not be within the scope of the usury statutes.

(1) An unlawful intent on the part of the lender,
(2) An agreement to lend money or its equivalent or to forbear required repayment for a period of time,
(3) An absolute obligation to pay, on the part of the borrower, and
(4) The exaction of greater compensation than is allowed by the applicable law.[12]

Although usury is now governed almost entirely by state statutes,[13] the elements of common-law usury are considered by most courts in interpreting, and especially in defining, the scope or reach of the relevant statutes.[14]

To counsel for lenders and developers, where statutory exemptions do not apply, the separate elements of the usury defense will suggest what financing schemes may escape usury restrictions.[15]

[1] Unlawful Intent

To support a claim for usury, a general intent to charge more than the lawful rate for the use of money is sufficient;[16] an actual subjective intent to violate the law is not required.[17] A loan agreement requiring interest at a level above the lawful limit is almost uniformly held to be sufficient evidence of unlawful intent.[18] For this reason, it is often said that an unlawful intent will be presumed conclusively from an instrument that shows a usurious interest rate on its face.[19] However, this statement of the rule in terms of a conclusive presumption must be

---

[12] 91 *C.J.S.* "Usury" §§ 13-16, 24, 28 (1955). Cf. *In re* Bibbey, 9 F.2d 944, 947 (D. Minn. 1925).

[13] See Table 3 in Appendix A.

[14] See cases cited in 45 *Am. Jur. 2d* "Interest and Usury" § 111, at 97 ns. 12, 13 (1969).

[15] See discussion at ¶ 5.05.

[16] 45 *Am. Jur. 2d* "Interest and Usury" § 160 (1969).

[17] *In re* Dane's Estate 551 App. Div. 2d 220, 390 N.Y.S.2d 249, 250 (1976); Ferguson v. Tanner Dev. Co., 541 S.W.2d 483, 492 (Tex. 1976). However, the requirement in Florida is "a corrupt purpose in the lender's mind to get more than the legal interest for money lent." I.R.E. Financial Corp. v. Cassel, 335, So. 2d 598, 600 (Fla. 1976). Perhaps from a policy perspective the required intent should be geared expressly to the purpose of the statutes. For example, if the basic purpose is penal, the intent of a lender who receives usurious interest is obviously significant; but if the purpose is remedial, that is, to protect the borrowers, the lender's intent appears irrelevant. It is not surprising that in applying small-loan or similar remedial statutes, courts have not been swayed by lack of intent as a defense. See Annot., 11 A.L.R.3d 1498, 1501 (1967).

[18] Holt v. Rickett, 143 Ga. App. 337, 340, 238 S.E.2d 706, 708 (1977). See also cases cited in 45 *Am. Jur. 2d* "Interest and Usury" § 160, at 130 n.1. (1969).

[19] 91 *C.J.S.* "Usury" § 14(c) (1955).

adoption of the Uniform Consumer Credit Code,[10] which effectively regulates consumer credit transactions while leaving most business loans free of governmental control.[11]

Finally, effective April 1, 1980, under Title V of the Depository Institutions Deregulation and Monetary Control Act of 1980, state usury ceilings on first mortgage loans involving residential real estate, including apartment house loans, by federally insured savings and loan associations (12 U.S.C. § 1724, as amended); by national and federally insured state-chartered commercial and mutual savings banks (12 U.S.C. § 1811, as amended); by mortgage bankers; and by HUD-approved lenders under the National Housing Act are permanently preempted, without limitation as to the amount of interest that may be charged to borrowers, unless an affected state reestablishes the ceiling within three years. As to "business and agricultural loans", including residential real estate loans that are not secured by first liens, state usury ceilings on loans in excess of $25,000 made by any institution or individual will be preempted for three years, subject to a right of affected states to override the preemption. A federal usury ceiling of five percentage points above the discount rate in the Federal Reserve district where the institution or individual lender is located will apply to such loans. In order for a state to override any of the two preemptions discussed above, it must provide an explicit statement that the state is overriding such preemption under the Act in its state law or constitution.

¶ 5.02 ELEMENTS OF USURY

At common law, usury is a defense that must be asserted affirmatively and proved by clear and convincing evidence of the following four elements:

---

[10] The U.C.C.C. in draft form was approved by the House of Delegates of the ABA in August 1969 and has since been praised by numerous commentators, including Hershman, "Usury and the Tight Mortgage Market—Revisited," 24 Bus. Law. 1121-1141 (1969); Danford, Jr., "Usury: Applicability to Collateral Fees and Charges," 16 S.D. L. Rev. 52, 75-76 (1971); and Benfield, note 2 *supra*, at 873.

[11] Generally, a "consumer loan" is one incurred "primarily for a personal, family, household or agricultural purpose." U.C.C.C. § 3.104. The U.C.C.C. provides for a maximum rate on consumer loans, equal to 6 percent or twice the Federal Reserve discount rate. See also Uniform Land Transactions Act § 3-403, which would exempt business and commercial real estate loans from usury ceilings.

of artificial barriers. In the case of the home-building industry, the combination of usury restrictions and regulation of the supply of money by the Federal Reserve can create a shortage of funds for the lending institutions that invest most heavily in home mortgages,[5] with a resulting falloff in production and employment in the construction industry.[6]

Recognizing that the historical pattern of interest regulation was not compatible with the economic realities of a functioning money market, Western Europe long ago overcame its traditional aversion to moneylending and repealed its usury restrictions.[7] In this country, however, the anachronistic, patch-quilt system of regulation survives, as can be seen in the Table of Usury Statues in Appendix A. All states impose interest rate ceilings. Moreover, the penalties for usury are severe, ranging from forfeiture of the excess or usurious interest to loss of the entire mortgage principal and interest, to even criminal sanctions.[8]

An encouraging note is the emerging trend toward redirecting usury regulations at the consumer, not the commercial market. Significant in this regard is the action of several states to expand the exception for corporate borrowers to include other types of commercial entities.[9]

In addition, proponents of reform, including the American Bar Association, have been successful in their efforts to encourage wider

---

[5] Mortgage rates must be high enough to enable the thrift institutions to compete effectively for savings, and reduction in their loanable funds caused by disintermediation has been most severe in those states where the legislatures have lagged in adjusting the general usury statutes. See discussion at ¶ 2.02[1].

[6] See Cooper, "A Study of Usury Laws in the United States to Consider Their Affect on Mortgage Credit and Home Construction Starts: A Proposal for Change," 8 Am. Bus. L.J. 165-189 (1970).

[7] England began the trend toward repeal in 1854. Usury Law Repeal Act, 17 & 18 Vict., c. 90 (1854).

[8] See Table 3 in Appendix A. In at least one state, Texas, the borrower apparently has the right to recover twice the amount of all interest "contracted for" in violation of the usury statute, even if the loan is not actually funded. Tex. Rev. Civ. Stat. Ann. Art. 5069-1.06(1) (1971).

[9] For example, the State of Washington, in 1972, amended its statute to include Massachusetts trusts, associations, limited partnerships, and real estate development loans to individuals above $100,000 within the coverage of the corporate exception, so that a developer may now seek financing in the market place regardless of his organizational structure. Wash. Rev. Code Ann. § 19.52.080 (1975). Another example is Indiana, which prior to repealing all usury restrictions, Pub. L. 366, § 10(1), 1971 Ind. Acts, had amended the statute to exclude from usury restrictions all partnerships, limited partnerships, joint ventures, and trusts. Ind. Code Ann. § 19-12-101 (Cum. Supp. 1970) (repealed 1971).

¶ 5.01 RELEVANCE OF USURY IN TODAY'S REAL ESTATE MARKET

Most jurisdictions limit the amount of interest that may be charged— even for business loans[1]—and in many cases the amount is limited to a maximum rate that is unrealistically low in light of the national money market. This economic regulation, effected through state statutes notably lacking in uniformity, has little or no real relation to moral beliefs or to the popular notion of usury, with its connotations of grasping lenders and victimized borrowers. Nevertheless, the underlying rationale for the regulation of interest rates has always been, and still is, that the necessitous borrower must be protected from the overreaching and hardhearted usurer, who would otherwise exact an unconscionable charge for the use of his funds.[2] The evidence accumulated to date, however, suggests that it is the profit-motivated commercial borrower and not the individual with personal needs who is subject to the protective constraints of the usury statutes.[3]

For more than a decade, inflationary pressures have spawned a tight mortgage market. Local usury laws with low ceilings on the mortgage interest rate have forced many individual developers and partnership syndicates to adopt cumbersome circumvention devices in order to obtain necessary financing. In some instances they have even been forced to abandon otherwise sound real estate ventures. Although the overall impact of the general usury statutes is less than might be imagined,[4] they do operate to force syndicate developers into incorporation against their "tax will," to effect a cash flow from states with low ceilings into those with higher maximum rates and to create other kinds

---

[1] See Table 3, Analysis of State Usury Statutes, in Appendix A.

[2] From earliest times, moneylending has been subject to control by society, primarily on religious and moral grounds. For an excellent discussion of the history of usury laws, see Benfield, "Money, Mortgages, and Migraine—The Usury Headache," 19 Case W. Res. L. Rev. 819, 822 (1968).

[3] *Id.* at 835. The evidence suggests that less than one-half of the total amount of lending in this country is subject to usury restrictions— unfortunately, the wrong half. For, as Professor Benfield points out, the one area in which control of rates by statute is clearly needed is that of the small consumer loan, which is frequently the least regulated. In fact, nearly all secured consumer debt other than home mortgage loans is either subject to special rates of interest, much higher than the general lawful contract rate, or is not limited because the doctrine of time-price differential or some other exception is applicable.

[4] According to Professor Benfield, only about one-third of commercial real estate loans are subject to usury restrictions, even though loans to unincorporated organizations represent a large portion of the total. Benfield, note 2 *supra*, at 854.

Chapter 5

USURY AND THE MORTGAGE MONEY MARKET

Page

¶ 5.01 Relevance of Usury in Today's Real Estate Market 5- 2

¶ 5.02 Elements of Usury 5- 4
    [1] Unlawful Intent 5- 5
    [2] Loan or Forbearance of Money or Its Equivalent 5- 6
    [3] Borrower's Absolute Obligation to Repay 5- 8
        [a] Repayment of Principal 5- 8
        [b] Payment of Interest 5- 9
    [4] Exaction of Greater Compensation as Interest Than Is Allowed by Law 5-10
        [a] Legal Definition of Interest 5-10
        [b] How Interest Is Computed 5-11
        [c] Interest Rate Escalator Clauses 5-12
        [d] Variable-Rate Mortgage 5-12

¶ 5.03 Status of Customary Loan Charges 5-13
    [1] Commitment Fees 5-14
    [2] Origination or Service Fees 5-14
    [3] Brokerage and Other Fees Paid to Intermediaries 5-15
    [4] Construction Loan Fees 5-16
    [5] Closing Expenses 5-16
    [6] Taxes 5-17
    [7] Prepayment Penalty 5-17
    [8] Charges Upon Default 5-17

¶ 5.04 Statutory Exemptions 5-19
    [1] Corporate Exemption 5-21
    [2] Exemptions Available to Limited Partnerships 5-22
    [3] FHA Mortgage Exemption 5-22

¶ 5.05 Circumvention Devices 5-23
    [1] Conflicts of Law 5-23
    [2] Sale of Mortgage Note at Discount; Estoppel; Holder in Due Course 5-25
    [3] Incorporation of the Borrower 5-27
    [4] Sale and Leaseback 5-32
    [5] Installment Land Contract 5-33
    [6] Sale and Repurchase of Realty 5-34
    [7] Wraparound Mortgage 5-35
    [8] Contingent Compensation and Equity Participations by Lenders 5-38

the permanent lender.[221] Otherwise, the borrower might "shop around" for a lower permanent interest rate and, if the rates drop low enough, be willing to forfeit his security deposit in order to obtain a lower long-term rate from some other permanent lender. However, the original permanent lender has the right to specifically enforce the agreement.[222]

The buy-sell agreement can be "preclosed." This means that the permanent lender first approves the form of the construction loan note and mortgage before the construction loan is closed and the buy-sell agreement is executed, and actually takes an assignment of these instruments when the permanent loan is closed.[223] The alternative would be for both the construction and permanent lenders to close their respective loans "on their own (note and mortgage) papers," which is simply referred to as the "non-preclosed" form of buy-sell agreement.

The advantages in using the pre-closed approach are: (1) the lien priority of the construction mortgage automatically inures to the benefit of the permanent lender, as assignee, which is of particular importance in a jurisdiction with a strong mechanics' lien statute; (2) by collapsing the two closing transactions into one, the parties may avoid extra taxes and attorneys' and recording fees; (3) the use of integrated loan documents enables the permanent lender to approve much of the documentation early in the lending cycle, while the parties still have time to resolve their differences.

By contrast, the parties may prefer that the permanent lender refinance the construction loan indebtedness for the amount authorized in the permanent commitment and close the permanent loan on its own forms of note and mortgage because (1) the permanent lender may wish to avoid usury disabilities that are not covered by title insurance since interim lenders, as a practical matter, will not warrant against them; (2) the construction lender may insist that the construction loan be closed on its own papers, which it feels are better suited to the law of the particular jurisdiction than the standard "integrated" forms proferred by the permanent lender; or (3) occasionally, the borrower is fearful that prior approval of the documentation by the permanent lender will delay the closing of the construction loan and his receipt of the first construction disbursements, and accordingly, he may resist use of the preclosed form of buy-sell agreement.

---

[221] See *Fourth* paragraph of Form 4.2 in Appendix B.
[222] See *Ninth* paragraph of Form 4.2 in Appendix B.
[223] See Section No. 4 of Form 4.2 in Appendix B.

funds.[217] In regard to the latter, if the developer has defaulted and the partially completed improvements are rapidly deteriorating, the lender should consider the safer, albeit more costly, alternative of arranging for a court-appointed receiver to take possession and have the certificates of indebtedness added to secure additional loan payments made by it to complete, manage, and protect the property.

¶ 4.05 BUY-SELL AGREEMENT AND THE FINAL TAKEOUT STAGE

Finally, when construction of the project has been completed in accordance with the building loan agreement and the terms and conditions of the takeout commitment have been met, the permanent loan is closed, and the proceeds are used to satisfy the construction loan indebtedness. The requirements and mechanics involved in closing the permanent loan are discussed in Chapter 3.

Frequently, prior to closing the construction loan, the borrower, the construction lender, and the permanent lender will execute what is known as a buy-sell agreement. The purpose of this tripartite agreement is to bind all three parties to one another by privity of contract and by granting one another the right of specific performance.[218] In the sample buy-sell agreement, Form 4.2, the permanent lender covenants to the construction lender that if all the conditions of its permanent commitment have been met, it will purchase the construction loan for the full permanent loan amount or for the "floor" amount if the loan is a "platform" loan and if one of the requirements for maximum funding (e.g., rent-roll requirement) has not been met.[219] Absent this language, the construction lender would probably have no recourse against the permanent lender as a third-party beneficiary in the event the permanent lender failed to honor its commitment to the borrower, since the status of the construction lender would be merely that of an "incidental beneficiary."[220]

In exchange, the construction lender and borrower covenant that they will not accept payment of the construction loan from anyone but

---

[217] See discussion at ¶ 4.02[6][a][ii].

[218] See *Ninth* paragraph of Form 4.2, a sample buy-sell agreement in Appendix B.

[219] See *First* paragraph of Form 4.2 in Appendix B, and discussion at ¶ 3.04[2].

[220] E.g., Republic Nat'l Bank v. National Bankers Life Ins. Co., 427 S.W.2d 76, 82 (Tex. 1968).

value. Also, to raise additional capital, cut construction costs, or meet zoning or other local law objections, the property's usage could be converted (e.g., apartment building into condominiums) or additional land could be put to productive use. Perhaps the permanent lender could be persuaded to increase the amount of the takeout commitment if rentals are proceeding ahead of schedule or might be willing to go along with either secondary financing or split financing (e.g., a subordinated sale-leaseback of the land) to enable the developer to obtain additional funding.

Once a decision to work out the loan has been made, the construction lender, itself, might be willing to make a financial contribution to the project in conjunction with the efforts of others. For example, it might agree to absorb a portion of the cost overruns, increase the loan amount, waive or defer interest payments, or offer to furnish gap or standby financing if, because of a default, the developer must seek permanent financing from a different permanent lender.

Finally, short of foreclosure, the construction lender may go into possession and complete construction of the project.[214] As a result of its entry into possession, the construction lender can collect the rentals, oversee the progress of construction, and prevent a financially distressed developer from misappropriating loan funds for its personal use. If the lender must expend additional loan funds to complete the project, most building loan agreements also provide that the lender can treat these funds as additional indebtedness of the borrower, secured by the lien of the lender's first mortgage even though such amounts, when added to the monies already disbursed, exceed the original loan amount.[215]

However, in some lien theory states, executory agreements conferring the right of possession to a mortgagee in the event of default are unenforceable.[216] In addition, mortgagees in possession are subject to very strict fiduciary duties with respect to managing the property and accounting to the owner-developer for collected income. By entering into possession, the lender may also incur obligations to mechanics' lienors, local governmental authorities, and tenants, and thus may become vulnerable to tort liability. Moreover, if additional loan funds are voluntarily disbursed in excess of the original loan amount, such advances may be regarded as "optional" advances and junior in lien priority to intervening liens filed prior to the advancement of these

---

[214] See Article 23(B) of Form 4.1, and Article 7.1.3 of Form 3.4 in Appendix B.
[215] See Article 23(B) of Form 4.1 in Appendix B.
[216] See discussion at ¶ 3.08[4][g].

proceedings, with or without the appointment of a receiver.[210] However, few partially completed projects sell for their pro rata value at foreclosure, and the lender may be forced to accept a sacrifice price and seek a deficiency judgment against the developer-borrower or any guarantors on the note, if such remedy is allowed under local law. To avoid such a "knockdown" sale at foreclosure, the lender might prefer to bid in at the foreclosure sale, take title, and complete the improvements with its own funds. Thereafter, the construction lender could recoup its total outlay of capital by obtaining the permanent loan proceeds, as assignee of the takeout commitment, and could thereafter sell the property subject to the permanent mortgage.[211]

Alternatively, where the borrower-developer is unable to raise the additional funds needed to complete construction or to satisfy lien claims, the construction lender may be able to rescue a problem loan from foreclosure and preserve its ability to assign the loan to the permanent lender by procuring the necessary "work-out" capital from other interested parties who may be either legally obligated or economically impelled to make up the shortfall in funds. For example, if the developer is not acting as the contractor, the building loan agreement may require that the contractor complete the work called for under the construction contract with the remaining undisbursed construction loan funds.[212] In addition, the surety company may be obligated under its payment-performance bond to complete construction free of mechanics' liens, or the title company may be required to pay these liens.[213] Forfeiture of existing equity capital and the deleterious tax impact of foreclosure may prompt investors to furnish the work-out funds even if they are not liable, as limited partners, for the debts of the partnership and are not obligated, under the partnership agreement, to make additional capital contributions. Sometimes construction cost overruns can be funded by junior lienholders, such as a subordinated land purchase-money mortgagee or holders of mechanics' liens, whose interests could be extinguished at foreclosure by construction loan participants or the unsecured creditors of the developer, by the builder's risk insurer (to the extent that problems such as vandalism may have resulted in casualty losses), or by raising equity capital if accelerated depreciation is available and the property can be syndicated for its tax-shelter

---

[210] See Article 24 of Form 4.1 in Appendix B, and the discussion of foreclosure at ¶ 3.08[4][g].
[211] See discussion at ¶ 3.04[10].
[212] See Article 4(R) of Form 4.1 in Appendix B.
[213] See discussion at ¶¶ 4.02[6][b][i], 4.02[8][b].

legislature attempted to negate the results of *Connor* by enacting legislation aimed at insulating lenders from this type of liability.[206] However, although the *Connor* result is currently commanding little support, it could represent the harbinger of a future judicial leap toward lender liability; accordingly, cautious lenders should avoid cozy business relationships and joint-venture-type undertakings with inexperienced undercapitalized developers, and should include in their building loan agreements language to the effect that the right of inspection is solely for the benefit of the lender, and that any failure to disapprove a contractor, subcontractor, or the plans and specifications shall not constitute a warranty or representation that any of the persons not so disapproved are in fact qualified or that the plans and specifications not so disapproved are in fact the basis for sound construction.

[8] Construction Lender's Remedies Against Defaulting Developer

A material and actionable default by the developer under the building loan agreement can occur under a variety of circumstances: cost overruns, strikes or material shortages, insolvency of the developer or general contractor, diversion of loan funds by the developer, failure to obtain either blanket permanent financing for a rental project or separate permanent financing for each condominium or single-family unit, problems that postpone anticipated cash or equity inflows during the construction period, or the developer's failure to obtain building permits or certificates of occupancy or to otherwise comply with local law regulations.[207]

In the event of such default under either the building loan agreement or the cross-defaulted note and construction mortgage,[208] the construction lender may be forced to solicit a deed in lieu of foreclosure from the defaulting developer[209] or may have to institute foreclosure

---

[206] Cal. Civ. Code § 3434 (West, as added Sept. 4, 1969).

[207] For a good general discussion of how lenders deal with problem loans, see Roberts, *Working Out the Construction Mortgage Loan,* 5 Real Est. Rev. 50-57 (1975).

[208] See discussion at ¶ 4.03[2][a].

[209] To avoid redemption statutes and the procedural delays caused by foreclosure, the lender may be able to effectuate a quick takeover of the property by negotiating for a deed in lieu of foreclosure in exchange for some release of liability. However, if mechanics' liens have been filed, title would be conveyed subject to any such liens even though they could be extinguished at foreclosure were the lender to preserve its lien priority over the liens by maintaining its status as mortgagee. In addition, if the mortgagor-developer becomes bankrupt, the trustee in bankruptcy might be able to recapture the property.

plans and specifications and to make periodic inspections, the defendant had sufficient control to prevent the harmful conduct that was reasonably foreseeable in light of the inexperience and thin capitalization of the developer-borrowers.

If, as has been suggested,[202] the defendant's participation in, and control over, the enterprise in the *Connor* case was no greater than what is usual for the typical tract construction lender, it would be foolhardy to construe the decision too narrowly. However, while attempts have been made to follow the *Connor* result in other jurisdictions[203] and to extend by analogy the *Connor* rationale to situations involving subcontractors,[204] so far, none have succeeded. Indeed, in 1969 the California Court of Appeals distinguished the facts in the *Connor* case by holding in favor of the defendant construction lender,[205] and the California

---

[202] See J. Mosk's dissenting opinion, *Id.* at 876, 447 P.2d at 623, 73 Cal. Rptr. at 383; Comment, "New Liability in Construction Lending: Implications of Connor v. Great Western Savings and Loan," 42 U. So. Calif. L. Rev. 353, 354 (1969).

[203] E.g., Callaizakis v. Astor Dev. Co., 4 Ill. App. 3d 163, 172, 280 N.E.2d 512, 518 (1972); Flamingo Drift Fishing, Inc. v. Nix, 251 So.2d 316, 318 (Fla. 1971). In both cases the *Connor* rationale was rejected on the ground that the lender's inspection activities were not made for the benefit of the home buyers. But cf. Jemison v. Montgomery Real Estate & Co., 396 Mich. 106, 108, 240 N.W.2d 205 (1976), *rev'd* 47 Mich. App. 731, 743, 210 N.W.2d 10, 15 (1973) (facts appear at 210 N.W.2d 10) (held cause of action existed for fraudulent misrepresentation in sale of uninhabitable house based on *Connor* rationale); Morroco v. Felton, 112 N.J. Super. 226, 234-235, 270 A.2d 739, 743 (1970), where court suggested by way of dictum that mortgagee liability for maintaining decent dwellings may exist based on *Connor* rationale.

[204] For example, in First Nat'l State Bank of N.J. v. Carlyle House, Inc., 102 N.J. Super. 300, 324, 246 A.2d 22, 35 (1968), *aff'd* 107 N.J. Super. 398, 285 A.2d 545 (1969), counsel for unpaid subcontractors argued that the rationale in *Connor* should impel the court to declare that the construction lender that had advanced monies to a speculative undercapitalized developer owed a duty to the subcontractors to see that the owner or contractor properly disbursed loan funds earmarked for the payment of their claims as subcontractors. In rejecting the analogy, the New Jersey Superior Court stated, "The ordinary subcontractor who contemplates contracting with an undercapitalized developer has a number of checking procedures customarily available to him. Generally, he can inquire of other contractors. ...Therefore, he is far better prepared to assess his risks of dealing with the undercapitalized developer than the homeowner. ..." *Id.* at 316-317, 246 A.2d at 31. However, in dicta the court indicated that it might be receptive to the *Connor* rationale if the home buyers rather than subcontractors were urging its acceptance by the court. See also Lampert Yards, Inc. v. Thompson-Wetterling Constr. & Realty, Inc., 302 Minn. 83, 92, 233 N.W.2d 418, 424 (1974).

[205] Bradler v. Craig, 274 Cal. App. 2d 466, 477, 79 Cal. Rptr. 401, 409 (1969).

the replacement of defective materials that may become necessary in the future[197]; (2) a certificate of substantial completion executed by the developer's architect and, in some cases, by the lender's draw inspector or supervising engineer as well, along with certificates of occupancy indicating that the construction and use of the improvements comply with all zoning and other local law regulations; (3) all the necessary approvals required by state and federal regulatory agencies; and (4) where there is a permanent takeout, a letter from the permanent lender stating that the improvements have been properly constructed and that its takeout commitment is still in force and effect.[198] Where the project is a shopping center, the lender should also condition its final advance on acceptance of the premises by the major tenants.

[7] Construction Lender's Liability for Construction Defects

In 1968, the California Supreme Court, in an opinion written by Chief Justice Traynor, held that a construction lender has the duty to protect prospective buyers of new homes from construction defects, notwithstanding the fact that the lender neither owned nor constructed the improvements.[199] In the *Connor v. Great Western Savings & Loan Ass'n* case, the defendant-lender supplied virtually all the construction financing to an inexperienced and undercapitalized developer, whose failure to install properly designed foundations in individual dwellings caused them to collapse. The court held that while the business relationship between the defendant and the developer did not constitute a joint venture, the defendant nonetheless had "become much more than a lender content to lend money at interest on the security of real property," in part because of the protective financing measures it had imposed on the borrower-developer.[200] For example, the court cited the fact that the defendant had not only received interest on its construction loan, but had also received a substantial fee for making the loan, a 20 percent capital gain for "warehousing" the land, and protection from loss of profits in the event an insufficient number of persons made commitments to buy homes or any of the home buyers sought permanent financing elsewhere.[201] In rejecting the lack-of-privity defense of the defendant, the court implied that because of its right to approve the

---

[197] Copies of these final lien waivers will also be sent to the title company so that it can issue its final policy.
[198] See Article 19(I) of Form 4.1 in Appendix B.
[199] Connor v. Great W. Sav. & Loan Ass'n, 69 Cal. 2d 850, 880, 447 P.2d 609, 626, 73 Cal. Rptr. 369, 386 (1968).
[200] *Id.* at 864, 447 P.2d at 616, 73 Cal. Rptr. at 376.
[201] *Id.* at 865, 866, 447 P.2d at 616, 617, 73 Cal. Rptr. at 376, 377.

artifically kept alive and further jeopardize the lender's ability to recoup its loan investment.[195] Moreover, unless the building loan agreement specifies that the obligation of the developer to make interest payments is not predicated upon the disbursement of these funds by the lender, the developer could argue that such failure to fund under the interest code would force them into default and would thus constitute a breach of contract by the lender.

Throughout construction of the project, tempers on occasion flare, disputes arise, and developers in their off-moments sometimes want to fire their once-favorite architect or contractor, or even give up on the project and convey it to a third party. However, during construction, lenders usually take a very dim view of any proposed changes other than those that relate to the actual completion of construction. The lender naturally prefers that the architect who drafted the plans and specifications supervise the construction on behalf of the developer, since someone who has a first-hand familiarity with the plans and specifications is always in a better position to have them implemented. Moreover, any contractor who is thrown off the job-site during a dispute may hold up construction by filing a lien on the project or by not relinquishing the building permits. Consequently, the lender will insist upon a high degree of control if any of the foregoing types of changes are proposed by the developer.[196]

[6] The Final Loan Advance

Prior to the final loan advance, the construction loan administrator will require the following: (1) a final lien waiver from the contractor and subcontractors covering all labor and materials furnished or to be furnished so that no liens may be claimed for follow-up repairs or for

---

[195] During the 1973-1974 real estate crunch, some REITs and other lenders kept accruing interest on problem loans in order to reflect these payments as income on their income statements and thereby exposed their officers to claims by shareholders and beneficiaries that the former had not discharged their management duties in good faith and with reasonable diligence. For example, this problem arose where a cost overrun was projected for a particular trade item (e.g., wood siding, precast concrete) that would not be utilized and funded until some time in the future. In such case, if a cost overrun did occur, the lender would still keep the loan current by disbursing remaining loan funds allocable to current expenditures, a practice which some loan officers refer to as the "ostrich approach."

[196] See Article 15 of Form 4.1 in Appendix B, which, in the colorful jargon of real estate professionals is called the "status quo" or "don't rock the boat" clause.

permanent lender inasmuch as such approval is required under the terms of its takeout commitment.[192] In addition, if the lender consents to any such change order, it may require the developer to deposit additional equity funds to cover any extras or cost overruns.[193] During the 1973-1974 real estate shake-out, if construction lenders had more carefully monitored their disbursements under this language in the building loan agreement, many of the cost overruns by defaulting developers would have been prevented.

If, however, a change order produces a cost overrun on a particular item, the developer may be able to avoid an additional cash outlay if the construction lender is willing to reallocate funds from other items listed in the cost breakdown or (if the developer is not the contractor) in the construction contract so that the net change will not result in additional dollar requirements beyond those committed by the construction lender. The building loan agreement will list by code categories loan funds earmarked to pay both hard construction costs ("construction funds") and soft nonconstruction costs such as construction period interest, hazard insurance premiums and architect's fees ("non-construction funds").[194] Most construction lenders treat construction loan interest as a fundable soft cost during the construction period and will disburse loan funds to the developer so that it can remit these amounts back to the lender as interest payments. However, a prudent construction lender should demand the right to discontinue such disbursements for soft costs such as construction period interest and should reserve the right to reallocate such funds toward the payment of hard construction cost overruns. Otherwise, if the developer is not required to fund the interest payments with nonloan sources, a loan headed for default could be

---

[192] One practical problem in receiving the permanent lender's approval is that permanent lenders traditionally move very slowly in this area. Some construction lenders and borrowers have been successful with inserting a clause in the buy-sell agreement which provides that the change order is approved unless the permanent lender raises objections within a designated period of time. See discussion at ¶ 3.04[11] and condition 5 of Form 3.1 in Appendix B.

[193] See Article 7 of Form 4.1 in Appendix B.

[194] These cost breakdowns contained in the building loan agreement, which is signed by the developer and the general contractor, are but internal yardsticks that enable the developer to keep track of the remaining loan funds allocable to each cost item and the lender to closely monitor monthly loan disbursements. For example, even where hard construction costs are buttoned down by the terms of the construction contract, contingencies beyond the control of the contractor, such as strikes or shortages of materials, may cause cost overruns for the developer. As a result, the remaining undisbursed loan funds may become insufficient in amount to cover the balance of the projected construction costs. See Exhibits A and B of Form 4.1 in Appendix B.

behalf of the mortgagor and to furnish adequate proof of the sums paid and the purpose of the disbursement.[185]

Likewise, in *Fulmer Building Supplies, Inc. v. Martin*[186] a construction lender, to protect its loan funds, bypassed the developer and made loan payments directly to the contractor even though the subcontractors, as holders of mechanics' liens, were first entitled to payment. After the contractor failed to pay the subcontractors, the subcontractors sued the lender for the amount of the diverted funds and the lender defended on the ground that the South Carolina statute automatically confers lien priority for all construction loan advances.[187] The court, holding in favor of the subcontractors, stated:

> When the mortgagee assumed absolute control of the disbursement of the proceeds of the construction loan, it occupied the same position as the owner with respect to the duties and obligations imposed by statute as to the payment of the remaining funds after the perfection of the mechanic's lien.[188]

[5] Cost Overruns and Other Changes During Construction Period

Both the construction and permanent lenders' determination of the loan amount and value of the security is based in part on a careful examination of the plans and specifications submitted by the developer's architect.[189] Therefore, the construction lender will require its approval of any change order that provides for extra work or materials, or alters the plans and specifications in a manner that could result in additional costs or in a significant change in the improvements.[190] Ordinarily, these change orders must be approved by the architect and the lender's draw inspector or supervising engineer, and then examined for adherence to proper construction standards and existing building codes. A prudent construction lender should also require the consent of the bonding company.[191] Any significant changes should also be approved by the

---

[185] 283 Minn. 527, 529, 167 N.W.2d 66, 68 (1969) (per curiam). Implicit in the court's decision is the analogy to a mortgagee in possession who must account to the mortgagor for the rentals and other income earned from the property. See the discussion at ¶ 3.08[4][g].

[186] 251 S.C. 353, 360, 162 S.E.2d 541, 544 (1968).

[187] S.C. Code §§ 29-5-50, 29-5-70.

[188] 251 S.C. at 359, 162 S.E.2d at 544.

[189] See discussion at ¶ 3.04[11].

[190] See Article 4(R) and Article 7 of Form 4.1 in Appendix B.

[191] See discussion at ¶ 4.02[8][b].

discussed earlier, loan advances can in some states be made to the title company that acts as the disbursing agent of the lender.[181]

Frequently, the construction lender will reserve the right to make disbursement checks jointly payable to the developer and the contractor, or to the contractor and the subcontractors, or even the right to make payments directly to each subcontractor.[182] The lender's purpose in obtaining control over the payment of disbursements is to protect itself against forged lien waivers[183] and to forestall the improper diversion of construction loan funds from the subcontractors by either the developer or the general contractor. However, if the construction lender makes payments directly to the subcontractors, it may unwittingly become liable to the Internal Revenue Service and to the subcontractors for any unpaid or unwithheld FICA taxes.[184]

In addition, there is case law suggesting that when a lender steps into the shoes of another party in the project, the lender must assume all of the responsibilities of that party to others and, protect the interests of the party whose perogatives it has preempted. For example, in *M.S.M. Corp. v. Knutson Co.* the construction lender, bypassing the developer, made loan advances directly to the contractor and was held liable, as a fiduciary, to the developer for loan funds diverted by the lender to satisfy an unrelated debt owed to it by the contractor, even though the developer owed the contractor an amount far in excess of the diverted amounts. In so holding, the Minnesota court stated that:

> When a mortgagee undertakes to disburse funds for a mortgagor under a construction contract, a fiduciary relationship arises. Under such circumstances, the mortgagee has the duty not only to apply all of the proceeds to the use of the mortgagor without diverting them for unrelated obligations incurred by contractors or subcontractors, but also to account for all of the sums expended on

---

[181] See discussion at ¶ 4.02[6][b][i].

[182] See Article 19(K) of Form 4.1 in Appendix B.

[183] Dishonest and financially distressed contractors sometimes will forge lien waivers or procure them by defrauding the subcontractors. Forged waivers are obviously invalid; however, genuine waivers cannot be repudiated by subcontractors even if they were paid for their labor and materials with the worthless checks of a fraudulent contractor where the construction lender has relied on such waivers in making loan disbursements. E.g., St. Louis Flexicure Inc. v. Lintzenich, 414 S.W.2d 787, 791 (Mo. 1967) (per curiam); George M. Morris Constr. Co. v. Four Seasons, 90 N.M. 654, 659, 567 P.2d 965, 970, (1977).

[184] I.R.C. § 3505.

the existence and amount of said cost overrun would for purposes of litigation be predicated on the opinion of an independent third party.

Also, most lenders resist making any disbursements for stored materials in light of the dangers posed by possible thefts or damage caused by the elements. However, there are several avenues open for compromise, depending on the strength and the experience of the developer. For example, the lender and the developer can fix a maximum monthly dollar amount for stored materials, or can perhaps arrange a time schedule for incorporating stored materials into the project. In the event the lender does agree to fund stored on-site materials, a special endorsement to the builder's risk insurance policy for fire, damage, and theft of the stored material should be procured from the casualty company since some policies exclude such materials from coverage. Where the materials will not be stored at the project site and the lender is still willing to pay for such materials, it should insist that the materials be stored in a bonded warehouse and should carefully perfect its lien on the materials under the Uniform Commercial Code.

In addition, the building loan agreement frequently will contain a statement specifying that any request for an advance by the developer constitutes an affirmation that all of the representations and warranties made at the time the agreement was executed remain true and correct, unless the developer says otherwise. The developer must thus be very careful to review these representations at the time of each advance.

Finally, some developers, after having executed the building loan agreement, fail to take down construction advances and instead shop around for short-term credit that may be extended to them on more favorable terms on the security of the building loan agreement. To avoid this practice, construction lenders sometimes insert a clause in the loan agreement requiring the developer to pay interest on the amount of loan proceeds to which he would have been entitled on the basis of the completed construction, whether or not the loan advance is actually made, or else must provide that such a failure to take down loan funds constitutes a default.

[4] Payment of Loan Advances

When the construction loan administrator has received the report of the developer's architect, and perhaps its own inspector's affidavit as well as the updated file report, it will make the next loan advance and credit the funds to the account of either the developer (to whom the funds belong) or the general contractor, as the developer directs. As

structed within the lot or easement lines. The title company then certifies that there are no encroachments or violations of "set back" line restrictions.

As a general rule, lenders will require between a 5 and 15 percent holdback or retainage of construction loan funds, which amount is released along with the final loan advance upon completion of the project. So, for example, a 10 percent holdback means that for each 90 cents of construction loan proceeds, the lender expects to receive performance of at least one dollar of value.[178] However, some lenders are willing to decrease the retainage by one-half upon completion of 50 percent of the project. Many developers are also successful in having the retainage released upon completion of construction within a specific construction code instead of having to wait for completion of the entire project. In the event the developer is unable to impose holdbacks of like amounts on the contractor and subcontractors, it will be forced to fund the difference out of its own funds. In additon, prior to each loan advance, the construction lender may require that the reserves available for the completion of the improvements, whether in the form of undisbursed loan funds or the developer's equity, be sufficient to complete construction. The developer's architect is sometimes required to certify that this requirement has been met.[179] Frequently, this predisbursement requirement will be waived by lenders, especially when the project being financed is relatively small, since such cost audits tend to be expensive and time-consuming. However, if at any time the lender discovers that these reserves have been depleted because of cost overruns, it will require the developer to deposit sufficient equity funds, which when added to the remaining balance of undisbursed loan funds, will cover the remaining cost of construction.[180] However, in the event the lender concludes that there are sufficient funds to complete the project, and the developer objects to such a conclusion, a possible compromise would be for the parties to agree to a binding cost audit to be performed by an independent party, during which time disbursements and construction would continue. To protect the lender, the developer would be required to deposit by means of a letter of credit, cash, or a certificate of deposit, a sum sufficient to cover any deficiency amount revealed by such audit. This objective approach could also benefit the lender in the event there is a default based on a cost overrun;

---

[178] See discussion at ¶ 4.02[8][a], and see also Article 19(J) of Form 4.1 in Appendix B.
[179] See Article 19(C) of Form 4.1 in Appendix B.
[180] See Article 4(S) of Form 4.1 in Appendix B.

materials furnished by them to the date of the affidavit, and contains recitals by the contractor and subcontractors (partial lien waivers) to the effect that they waive their lien rights for work and materials for which they have received payments. The loan administrator or his draw inspector will then examine the dollar amounts recited in both the affidavit and lien waivers along with copies of receipted work and purchase orders. Any discrepancies are investigated to make certain that loan funds have not been improperly diverted from the subcontractors by the developer or general contractor, and the loan administrator will check the billings and lien waivers to make certain that the payments are up-to-date and in conformity with the payment schedules in the building loan agreement.[175]

Second, prior to each loan advance, the developer's architect will inspect the work progress on the site and will match the payment request with the work completed to make certain that neither the general contractor nor the subcontractors receive payment for work that has not been done. He will also certify that the work was performed in a timely first-class manner in accordance with the previously approved plans and specifications.[176] Many, if not most, lenders will also employ, at the developer's expense, their own draw inspectors, (licensed engineers or architects specializing in this area), to further certify these matters if the lender believes that such corroboration is necessary.

Third, after receiving the partial lien waivers, the title company will continue its search to the date of the proposed advance and will issue an endorsement to the title policy or "bring to date a letter" certifying that no liens or encumbrances have been filed against the project since the previous advance.[177] In compliance with the lender's commitment, the building loan agreement may also require the developer to furnish a "date-down" survey to insure that the improvements are being con-

---

[175] See Articles 19(D) and 14(J) and Exhibits A and B of Form 4.1 in Appendix B.

[176] The developer's architect should report the results of his inspection on the AIA Application and Certification of Payment Due form (G-702). These certificates vary somewhat in reporting work items, depending on the type of project and construction requirements as per the general construction contract and the initial breakdown of approved construction costs. They also contain relevant costs of the various trade areas involved in the project and relate both to the dollar amount of work completed and the percentage of completion in all areas. A certificate is issued, with the approval of the contractor and developer added, along with the developer's certification that all subcontractors have been paid. See also Article 19(F) of Form 4.1 in Appendix B.

[177] See discussion at ¶ 4.02[6][b][i], and Article 4(d) of Form 4.1 in Appendix B.

stipulated period of time is a material default.[173] Indeed, during the 1973-1974 real estate shake-out, delays in construction and cost overruns were, along with monetary defaults, the most common grounds for foreclosure by construction lenders. Accordingly, in his negotiations with the construction and permanent lenders, the developer's attorney should demand realistic time limits and attempt to procure the so-called "Act of God" clause, a clause that allows for extensions in the event of strikes or other causes of delay beyond the control of the developer. However, the construction lender should resist any attempt to have this protective language inserted in its building loan agreement unless the permanent lender agrees to incorporate the same in its takeout commitment.

[3] Predisbursement Requirements

As each phase of construction is completed, the lender's loan administrator advances loan funds to pay for the finished work. However, he must make certain that the work conforms to the plans and specifications, that it is being done on schedule and free of mechanics' liens, and that sufficient undisbursed loan proceeds remain to fund the remaining costs of construction. If these objectives are not met, the basic conditions of the takeout commitment will not be satisfied, and the construction lender will not be able to assign its loan to the permanent lender once the construction is completed. Although the methods employed by lenders for making disbursements vary, the following are typical of predisbursement requirements that must be met prior to each new loan advance in which the developer is not acting as the general contractor.

First, upon notification that construction has progressed to the next planned stage, the developer, after receiving the contractor's requisition for payment, will submit its formal request for payment to the construction lender.[174] As an alternative to the "stage of completion" method of payment, the developer will request his "draws" on a monthly basis, after finishing a designated percentage of the total work to be completed under the contract. The lender will require that the request for payment be accompanied by an affidavit of the contractor that identifies all the subcontractors, indicates the nature and dollar amounts of labor and

---

[173] E.g., Metropolitan Life Ins. Co. v. Hall, 10 N.Y.S. 196, 198, (1890); Emigrant Ind. Sav. Bank v. Willow Builders, 290 N.Y. 133, 145, 48 N.E.2d 293, 299 (1943).

[174] The developer should use AIA Form G-702 or a modified version thereof for payment.

developers should spend as much time reviewing and drafting this important document as they do the mortgage and note. The building loan agreement should be drafted so that it conforms to the method of construction disbursements employed by the lender, as modified by changes requested by the developer based on the characteristics of the particular project. Unfortunately, some lenders utilize methods of disbursements which, while satisfactory, are nonetheless incompatible with their standard form of building loan agreement that may have been copied from another lender's form, notwithstanding differences in their methods of disbursement.

[2] Borrower's Initial Representations and Warranties

Most building loan agreements contain a warranty by the borrower-developer to the lender that the latter's loan advances will at all times be accorded lien priority over any intervening liens.[168] However, such lien priority may depend on circumstances beyond the developer's control. For example, if under the building loan agreement the lender's discretionary authority to make loan advances is not geared to some objective criteria, such optional advances may in some states be junior in lien priority to any intervening mechanics' liens.[169] Accordingly, reliance on this warranty by the construction lender is misplaced if it fails to utilize title insurance or some other protective device against mechanics' liens.[170] Also, under this warranty the lender is not obligated to continue making disbursements if it cannot be assured of a first and prior lien for its loan advances, and in the so-called priority states the lender will require the developer to warrant that no work has commenced upon the land prior to the recording of the construction loan mortgage.[171]

In addition, the developer will be required to warrant that it will commence, continue, and complete construction within stipulated time limits and in a first-class workmanlike manner, in accordance with the approved plans and specifications and in conformity with private and local law restrictions.[172] Most lenders apply general "rule of thumb" criteria in deciding when a project should be completed (e.g., garden apartments: twelve to fourteen months; shopping centers: twelve to fourteen months); however, failure to complete construction within the

---

[168] See Article 3 of Form 4.1 in Appendix B.
[169] See discussion at ¶ 4.02[6][a][ii].
[170] Discussed earlier in ¶ 4.02[6][b].
[171] See discussion at ¶ 4.02[6][a][i] and Article 3 of Form 4.1 in Appendix B.
[172] See Article 6 of Form 4.1 in Appendix B.

its portfolio. A compromise solution would be to limit the prohibition of cash payouts to the construction period only, or merely to prohibit cash payouts from the construction loan proceeds.[167]

¶ 4.04 DISBURSEMENT OF CONSTRUCTION LOAN FUNDS UNDER BUILDING LOAN AGREEMENT

After the borrower-developer has met all of the closing requirements, the loan has closed, and perhaps a preliminary loan advance has been made to fund certain soft costs (e.g., land acquisition cost, recording fees, real estate taxes, and legal fees), the next stage of the lending cycle is that in which the improvements are constructed with loan funds advanced periodically by the construction lender.

During this hiatus period for the developer's attorney, if all goes well, the lender's servicing department or loan administrator takes over and, in collaboration with the developer's architect and title company, starts to disburse in accordance with its internal administrative procedures as reflected in and, if necessary, modified by the terms and conditions of its building loan agreement.

[1] Function of Building Loan Agreement

The building loan agreement, unique to construction financing, identifies all of the collateral and supportive documents such as construction contracts, cost breakdowns, and payment and performance bonds. It stipulates the conditions for when and how construction is to commence, continue, and be completed. While the basic mortgage instrument secures the construction loan indebtedness and sets forth the terms and conditions of default, the building loan agreement is concerned with the day-to-day turmoil and activity encountered during the construction period. It attempts the formidable task of giving the lender control over construction, without unduly impeding its progress.

During construction and prior to any default, the building loan agreement is the operative document. Hence, counsel for lenders and

---

against the limited partners for a return of their capital contributions. Kittredge v. Langley, 252 N.Y. 405, 421, 169 N.E. 626, 632 (1930) (by implication); Engleman v. Malchow, 91 Cal. App.2d 341, 345, 205 P.2d 413 (1949); Whitley v. Klauber, 417 N.Y.S.2d 959, 963 (1979). For an analagous situation involving a suit against shareholders of an insolvent corporation requiring the tendering of all unpaid stock subscriptions, see Fulton v. Abramsohn, 369 S.W.2d 815, 819 (Tex. Civ. App. 1963).

[167] See Article 5.6 of Form 3.4 in Appendix B.

[c] Release Clause

If the secured property consists of condominium units, a clause must be properly drafted providing for the release of condominium units from the lien of a construction mortgage to enable the developer to sell the units; the clause should be inserted in either the building loan agreement or the mortgage. Lenders basically prefer to insert the provision in the building loan agreement, while developers' attorneys are more comfortable with the provision in the mortgage since the release clause stipulates how units are to be released from the lien of the mortgage. A sample release clause reads as follows:

> Providing mortgage is not in default, Mortgagee will release from time to time any condominium unit(s) from the lien of this mortgage upon payment of 85 percent of the sales price.

Also, in the event the project consists of condominiums, developer's counsel should consider changing the standard provision found in the mortgage instrument from, that upon foreclosure, at the option of the mortgagee, the property can be sold en masse or in parcels, to a requirement that the property be offered for sale as units for a designated period of time to reflect its nature as a condominium.[165]

[d] Prohibition of Cash Distributions

Some cautious construction lenders will also demand a provision in the construction loan mortgage stating that during the term of the construction loan the mortgagor, if it be a corporation, will not declare and pay out any dividends, or, if it be a partnership, will neither distribute any of its cash earnings nor distribute any return of capital to the partners.[166] While such a provision may be appropriate for a corporation or a partnership formed specifically for the purpose of owning and developing this particular project, it should not apply to an already-established corporation or partnership with other properties in

---

[165] See Article 7.2 of Form 3.4 in Appendix B.

[166] Under Uniform Limited Partnership Act § 26, "a contributor, unless he is a general partner, is not a proper party to proceedings by or against a partnership, except where the object is to enforce a limited partner's right against or liability to the partnership." Courts have generally interpreted this language to mean that a creditor of a limited partnership cannot, at law, directly sue limited partners for a return of their capital contributions withdrawn from the limited partnership but must instead bring a complicated and costly creditor's suit in equity, or have the partnership adjudicated a bankrupt so that a trustee in bankruptcy can bring an action, on behalf of the partnership, directly

$500,000 gap amount, after assigning the $2 million first mortgage note to the permanent lender once construction is completed, and if such secondary financing is permitted by the permanent lender.[159]

[2] Construction Mortgage

With few exceptions, the construction loan mortgage or deed of trust contains the same provisions included in the permanent loan mortgage.[160]

[a] Cross-Default Provisions

The construction mortgage should identify and incorporate by reference all the terms and conditions of the building loan agreement and specify that any default in the building loan agreement constitutes a default under the terms of the mortgage. Conversely, any default under the note or mortgage should cause a default under the loan agreement.[161]

[b] Future Advance Clause

In the recent past, many lenders have experienced substantial cost overruns ranging as high as 50 percent of the original cost. In some states such as Maryland, any additional money loaned by the lender above the face amount of the original note secured by a first deed of trust would be subordinate to any intervening mechanics' liens.[162] However, in other states such as Florida, any funds advanced by the lender in excess of the secured first mortgage amount would be accorded first lien priority over all intervening mechanics' liens, providing the original construction mortgage contained a clause stating that future advances up to a stated maximum amount (for example, 150 percent of the original amount) could be made by the lender.[163] Accordingly, in drafting a construction mortgage it is imperative that the applicable state law be scrutinized to determine how, if possible, such future advances can be protected against loss of lien priority.[164]

---

[159] See discussion at ¶ 4.02[1].
[160] See Form 3.4 in Appendix B.
[161] See Articles 1(o), 1(t), and 6.2 of Form 3.4, and Article 24 of Form 4.1 in Appendix B.
[162] Md. Real Prop. Code Ann. § 7-102 (1974).
[163] Fla. Stat. Ann. § 697.04 (West Supp. 1979).
[164] See also discussion of "dragnet clauses" at ¶ 3.08[4][a].

course even if no assignment had been recorded and payment has been made to the construction lender, as holder of record, since the borrower-developer can protect himself by demanding production of the note as a precondition to payment.[154] However, if the note contains language that the borrower promises to pay the face amount or so much thereof as may be advanced thereunder, it would be nonnegotiable since it would not constitute a promise to "pay a sum certain"[155] and the developer would be able to assert the ordinary contract defenses against any assignee of the construction lender. To protect itself against such claims, the permanent lender will normally require in its takeout commitment an estoppel affidavit signed by the developer-borrower stating the amount unpaid on the note at the time of assignment and that no defenses or setoffs exist with respect thereto.[156]

Also, if the construction note is assigned to a permanent lender or some other assignee, the construction lender will customarily absolve itself from any secondary liability by endorsing the note "without recourse."[157] Ordinarily, the construction lender will also require that all parties who are secondarily liable on the construction note (e.g., guarantors, prior endorsers) waive those formal requirements that must be met[158] before suit can be brought against them.

Normally, the developer-borrower cannot prepay the construction loan where the construction lender has executed a buy-sell agreement with the permanent lender. Also, if the construction loan is to be satisfied by the proceeds of a permanent takeout commitment, the construction lender should protect itself against nonperformance of the commitment by providing for an option to call the loan, if the note is not funded by the permanent lender on or prior to the expiration date of its takeout commitment.

Finally, a second note payable either to the construction lender or to an interim lender may be used to evidence a contingent debt or "gap" commitment which would normally be cross-defaulted to the first deed of trust note during the construction period. For example, if the developer needs $2.5 million to complete construction and the permanent lender's takeout commitment is for only $2 million, the construction lender might be willing to accept a secondary lien position for the

---

[154] See City Bank v. Plank, 143 Wis. 653, 661, 124 N.W. 1000, 1003 (Wis. 1910).
[155] U.C.C. § 3-106.
[156] See condition 14 of Form 3.1, a sample permanent commitment, and Form 3.11, a sample estoppel certificate in Appendix B.
[157] U.C.C. § 3-414.
[158] U.C.C. §§ 3-501 et seq. See Form 3.3 in Appendix B.

[1] Construction Loan Note

The note and mortgage, fully discussed in Chapter 3,[147] will be examined here only in reference to problems and language in these instruments that are particularly germane to construction financing and, except as otherwise noted, reference will be made to the sample note and deed of trust in Appendix B (Forms 3.3 and 3.4) since each incorporates the standard requirements imposed by both the construction lender and the permanent lender.

Ordinarily, the payment provisions in the construction loan note will provide for payment of interest only, and, they set a maturity date for repayment of principal geared to the expiration date of the permanent lender's takeout commitment.[148]

In some jurisdictions (such as Maryland and Ohio), "judgment by confession" language in a mortgage note is enforceable so that, in the event of a default by the borrower, the lender can immediately obtain judgment and a judgment lien on the borrower's other assets by merely certifying the fact of default to the court. However, if the borrowing entity is a partnership, all the partners must execute the note in order for the confessed judgment to be effective against the partnership.[149]

If the construction note is negotiable[150] and the deed of trust or mortgage is assigned to the permanent lender when the permanent loan is closed, the permanent lender could qualify under the Uniform Commercial Code for "holder-in-due-course" status if he is not too "closely connected"[151] to the construction lender-transferor and if the permanent lender meets the value, good faith, and notice requirements of the Code.[152] In such event, the developer would be precluded from asserting failure, lack of consideration, or any of the other ordinary "personal" contract defenses against the permanent lender as assignee of the note.[153] For example, the developer, as borrower, would be precluded from claiming that less than the face amount of the note had been disbursed to it by the construction lender prior to the assignment of the loan. In addition, a claim by the borrower that the construction loan indebtedness has already been paid would also be a "personal" defense, unenforceable against the permanent lender as a holder in due

---

[147] See discussion at ¶ 3.08.
[148] See discussion at ¶ 4.02[3].
[149] See Farm Bureau Agricultural Credit Corp. v. Dicke, 29 Ohio App. 2d 1, 277 N.E.2d 562 (1972); Shafer Bros. v. Kite, 406 A.2d 673, 678 (Md. 1979).
[150] See discussion at ¶ 3.08.[3].
[151] E.g., Unico v. Owens, 50 N.J. 101, 126, 232 A.2d 405, 418 (1967).
[152] U.C.C. § 3-302.
[153] U.C.C. § 3-305.

of the lending cycle, when the construction loan is assigned to the permanent lender. At the closing, the developer and the lender will also execute the building loan agreement, which implements the predisbursement and closing requirements set forth in the loan commitment and also, as discussed in ¶ 4.04, establishes the legal and operational framework for the disbursements of loan proceeds during the construction period.

Over the years, construction lenders have developed essentially two varying approaches with respect to their additional requirements for closing the construction loan as embodied in their standard forms of loan commitment and building loan agreement. Some lenders prefer to expedite the closing by initially concerning themselves with only the soft costs of construction (such as the purchase price of the raw land and the construction loan interest) and the start-up costs of carrying the project until a positive cash flow is achieved. Under this approach, the initial closing requirements are limited to execution of the loan documents; the building loan agreement without the trade payments breakdown and schedule for withdrawals; the title binder; evidence of hazard and public liability insurance; a report indicating satisfactory soil conditions; satisfactory evidence of water, sewer, and utility hookups; satisfactory evidence of compliance with zoning regulations; and a takeout commitment from a permanent lender.

Other more cautious or conservative lenders are of the opinion that their maximal exposure to risks during the construction loan period occurs neither at the front end when the soft costs are closed, nor at the final takeout stage, but rather during the interim, when the improvements are being constructed. Accordingly, proponents of this latter approach believe that precautionary steps should be taken at this early juncture to obviate to the maximum extent possible any risks associated with the funding of the "hard costs" of bricks and mortar during the construction period. Therefore, under this approach, the construction lender will not close the construction loan until both the foregoing and the following additional requirements are met: (1) the plans and specifications must be reviewed and approved by the construction and permanent lenders; (2) the construction contract must be approved and executed by the developer and the contractor; (3) the trade payments breakdown must be approved by the construction lender and incorporated in the building loan agreement; and (4) the developer must have obtained the necessary building permits.

required, be assigned to the construction lender as additional collateral for the loan.[142]

(5) The developer execute a buy-sell agreement with both the construction and permanent lenders.[143]

(6) The permanent lender agree to assign its commitment, if required, to the construction lender during the term of the construction loan, and the developer agree neither to assign the construction loan commitment nor to further encumber or transfer title to the property prior to final disbursement without the prior written consent of the construction lender.[144]

(7) The developer's attorney, if requested, furnish an attorney's opinion that the making and acquiring of the loan will not constitute "doing business" for purposes of state taxation or qualification, and that the loan will not be usurious or otherwise illegal or unenforceable under applicable local law.

(8) The developer agree to pay all the expenses of closing the loan and assigning it to the permanent lender.[145]

(9) Finally, the developer agree to forfeit its "good faith" security deposit or to pay some other agreed-upon amount of liquidated damages if a default should occur under the terms of the loan commitment.[146]

¶ 4.03 CLOSING THE CONSTRUCTION LOAN

After negotiation and acceptance of the commitment are finalized, the initial settlement or closing of the construction loan occurs when the construction loan note is executed and the construction mortgage or deed of trust is executed and recorded. The lender's loan commitment may also require the execution and recordation of certain collateral security documents, such as an assignment of lease instrument and chattel mortgage in the form of a UCC financing statement.

If required by the loan commitment, the developer, construction lender, and permanent lender will also execute a buy-sell agreement. This agreement is discussed in ¶ 4.05 because it relates to the final stage

---

[142] See discussion at ¶ 3.04[16], and also see Article 9 of Form 3.4, and Article IV(F) of Form 4.1 in Appendix B.

[143] See discussion at ¶¶ 3.04[14], 4.05.

[144] See discussion at ¶ 3.04[10], and also Article 15 of Form 4.1 in Appendix B.

[145] See discussion at ¶ 3.04[15], and also Article 4(K) of Form 4.1 in Appendix B.

[146] See discussion at ¶ 3.06.

under Section 507(b) to the extent the protection proves to be inadequate after the fact. This claim even has priortity over the administration expenses of a superseding liquidation. In essence, it affords a super priority to post-petition creditors over every other allowable claim for administration expenses.

See ¶ 3.08[4][i] for a discussion of mortgagee's right to rents from mortgaged income-producing property constituting a part of the mortgagor's bankrupt estate.

[13] Other Terms and Conditions of Commitment

In other respects, the terms and conditions in the construction loan commitment are essentially the same as those required of the borrower-developer by the permanent lender in its permanent loan commitment.[138] For example, the construction loan commitment will ordinarily require that:

(1) The developer furnish satisfactory written evidence that all utilities (including water, sewer, gas, electricity, and telephone) will be available in sufficient quantity and quality to service the project once it is completed.[139]

(2) The developer furnish satisfactory written evidence (e.g., building permits, certificates of occupancy) that the construction and intended use of the improvements comply with building codes, zoning ordinances, and other applicable local, state, and federal law regulations.[140]

(3) The preliminary survey (prepared and certified by a licensed surveyor) be approved by the construction lender; the final plans and specifications be approved by the developer, the contractor, and both the construction and permanent lenders; and prior to the final construction advance, that the final survey be approved by both the construction and permanent lenders.[141]

(4) Any existing and future leases and franchise agreements, if

---

[138] See discussion at ¶ 3.04.

[139] As a result of utility shortages and no-growth moratoria in many communities, lenders are becoming concerned about the availability of utility services to a new project. Also see Article 4(D) of Form 4.1 in Appendix B.

[140] See discussion at ¶ 3.04[9], and also see Articles 4(C) and 4(P) of Form 4.1 in Appendix B.

[141] See discussion at ¶¶ 3.04[11], 3.04[15], and also see Articles 4(B), 4(E), and 4(M) and 19[E] of Form 4.1 in Appendix B.

undivided interest would realize significantly less for the estate than the sale of the entire property free of the other co-owners' interests,[130] and the benefit to the estate of the sale outweighs any detriment to the other co-owners.[131] This seemingly onerous provision is somewhat mitigated by Section 363(i), which gives the co-owner the right to purchase the entire property at the same price as offered in the sale.

Section 363(k) allows a mortgagee, in bidding for the estate's mortgaged property, to offset the amount of the debt against the purchase price. Section 363(l) permits a trustee or estate to use, sell, or lease such property despite provisions in the loan documents that would terminate or modify debtor's interest in the security property upon the debtor's insolvency, etc., or the transfer of the debtor's property.

Finally, Section 364 allows the Bankruptcy Court to authorize the trustee to obtain secured credit when the trustee has been unable to obtain unsecured credit. Subsection (c) of Section 364 authorizes the obtaining of credit and the incurring of debt with some special priority.[132] Furthermore, after notice and hearing, such secured credit may be secured by lien on property of the estate that is equal to or even superior to an already existing lien held by a lender.[133] This right is tempered somewhat by Section 364(d)(1)(B), which requires that adequate protection be provided for the holder of the lien on the property upon which such senior or equal lien is to be secured. Significantly, the burden of proof regarding adequate protection is placed upon the trustee.[134] Section 361 specifies three types of adequate protection: (1) the making of periodic cash payments to any party to the extent that either a stay under Section 362 or the granting of any lien under Section 364 results in an impairment of the value of such party's interest in the property,[135] (2) the provision of an additional or substitute lien to the extent of any decrease in the value of such party's interest,[136] or (3) the granting of other relief which will result in the realization by the aggrieved party of the "indubitable equivalent" of such party's interest in the property.[137] The practitioner should note that where the court has made a mistake in determining that adequate protection was given and the party in interest is damaged, the creditor is given a first priority administrative expense

---

[130] *Id.* § 363(h)(2).
[131] *Id.* § 363(h)(3).
[132] *Id.* §§ 364(c)(1), 364(c)(2), § 364(c)(3).
[133] *Id.* § 364(d).
[134] *Id.* § 364(d)(2).
[135] *Id.* § 361(1).
[136] *Id.* § 361(2).
[137] *Id.* § 361(3).

contract, notwithstanding a prior default or language to the contrary in the lease or contract, and provides adequate assurance of future performance by the assignee. The requirement that adequate assurance of future performance be given to the other party is new. However, upon such assignment, the trustee and estate are relieved from liability for breach occurring thereafter.[126] The other limitation on assumption under this section of benefit to lenders concerns contracts to make loans to the debtor. While a lender under this section is relieved of its obligation to make a loan,[127] it is not clear under the Code whether the trustee could require the construction lender to continue to disburse to the trustee or his assignee.

The new Code also offers protection to a tenant if his landlord's or sublessor's trustee rejects a lease. Under Section 365(h), the tenant, upon such rejection, may remain in possession for the balance of the term (and any renewal or extension not requiring the landlord's consent) of the lease and may offset against future rents any damages suffered by such tenant for nonperformance of any of the landlord's obligations under the lease. This provision eliminates the fears that plagued many leasehold mortgagees based on what happened during the Penn Central bankruptcy proceedings.

[vi] Right to Sell, Lease, or Mortgage Debtor's Property. A trustee or the debtor in possession has the right to use, sell, or lease the property (other than cash collateral) of the debtor in the ordinary course of the debtor's business without notice of hearing,[128] even if such property is secured by mortgages. However, there are limitations placed upon the trustee; for example: (1) the creditor seeking relief from the automatic stay, (Section 362) will have the determination of the "adequate protection" issue resolved before the trustee has the chance to use, sell, or lease in the ordinary course where no notice and hearing is required; (2) the order authorizing the operation of the business may contain limitations upon the right of the trustee to sell, use, or lease; (3) where the property is "cash collateral," specific protective provisions apply. Furthermore, Sections 363(g) and 363(h) of the new Code allow a sale to include both the debtor's interest and the interest of any co-owner having an undivided interest in the property, such as the interest of a tenant in common, joint tenant or tenant by the entirety, where partitioning of the property is impracticable[129] or the sale of the debtor's

---

[126] *Id.* § 365(K).
[127] *Id.* § 365(c)(2).
[128] *Id.* § 363(c)(1).
[129] *Id.* § 363(h)(1).

ing from such default.[120] He must further provide adequate assurance of future performance under the contract or lease.[121] In addition, the following four special conditions, set forth in Section 365(b)(3), must be satisfied to demonstrate adequate assurance of future performance in shopping center leases:

(1) adequate assurance of the source of rent and other consideration due under such lease;
(2) adequate assurance that any percentage rent due under such lease will not substantially decline;
(3) adequate assurance that assumption or assignment of such lease will not breach substantially any provision, such as a radius, location, use or exclusivity provision in any other lease; and
(4) adequate assurance that assumption or assignment of such lease will not disrupt substantially any tenant mix or balance in such shopping center.

Moreover, Sections 365(b) and 365(e) disallow default provisions triggered by insolvency or commencement of the bankruptcy proceedings and prohibit any termination of the lease based on the insolvency or bankruptcy of a tenant. In a Chapter 7 case (liquidation), the trustee must decide within sixty days after the order for relief to either assume or reject the lease or contract,[122] but under Chapter 11, such assumption or rejection can occur at any time prior to confirmation of the plan.[123] However, any party to the contract or lease can move to shorten the time period for such assumption or rejection. If not assumed within such period, the lease or contract will be deemed rejected by the trustee.[124]

This powerful right to assume contracts or leases is somewhat limited by Section 365(c). That section provides that a contract or unexpired lease of the debtor may not be assumed or assigned where applicable local law excuses a party other than the debtor from accepting performance or rendering performance to either the trustee or an assignee of the trustee (essentially personal service contracts), and the party refuses to consent to such assumption or assignment.[125] However, subject to the foregoing exception, the trustee may assign the lease or

---

[120] *Id.* § 365(b)(1)(B).
[121] *Id.* § 365(b)(1)(C).
[122] *Id.* § 365(d)(1).
[123] *Id.* § 365(d)(2).
[124] *Id.* § 365(d)(2).
[125] *Id.* § 365(c)(1)(B).

[iv] Automatic Stay. Section 362(a) of the new Code provides for the automatic stay of any foreclosure proceeding and any action to obtain possession of the property. The only relevant proceeding that is not so stayed is the commencement of any action by the Secretary of Housing and Urban Development to foreclose a mortgage, where such mortgage is insured under the National Housing Act and covers property consisting of five or more living units. Section 362(d) provides relief from the automatic stay by allowing any creditor to file a complaint seeking annulment, termination, or modification of the automatic stay; such creditor must, however, show in a hearing that cause for relief exists. Cause includes lack of adequate protection of the creditor's interest,[116] lack of any equity of the debtor in the property,[117] and no need for the property in the reorganization. Where the debtor's property is a hotel or motel, it would seem that such property[118] would, per se, be required for a reorganization; by contrast, where the property is inventoried for sale, such as homes or condominium units, and there is no equity, a strong case could be made to lift the stay since this property would not be needed for a reorganization of the debtor's business as a seller of realty. In addition, another cause for relief—which has been cited in the older cases, but not explicitly mentioned in the new Act—is that there is no prospect for adoption of a successful plan. Significantly, Section 362(e) shortens and clearly designates the time period for the hearing on relief from the stay that the preliminary hearing must be held within thirty days after request for relief, although there is no requirement that the court rule within any given period. Where the stay is continued after the preliminary hearing, the final hearing must be commenced within thirty days after the preliminary hearing.

[v] Expanded Power of Trustee Regarding Executory Contracts and Unexpired Leases. Section 365 of the new Code, together with Section 363, contain the area of greatest substantive change in bankruptcy law. Subject to the Bankruptcy Court's approval, a trustee may assume or reject any executory contract or unexpired lease with the provision that if there has been a default in said lease or executory contract, the trustee must cure or provide adequate assurance to the landlord that the default will be promptly cured[119] or must provide a prompt-fashion compensation for any actual out-of-pocket loss result-

---

[116] *Id.* § 362(d)(1).
[117] *Id.* § 362(d)(2)(A).
[118] *Id.* § 362(d)(2)(B).
[119] *Id.* § 365(b)(1)(A).

installments of $1 million each have a present value greater than or equal to the $4 million value of the real estate? The answer to that question depends on the discount rate, which is determined by a court. The court, in determining the applicable discount rate, must estimate the market rate of interest that would have been paid by the debtor in light of the inherent risks of business. Essentially, this discount rate reduces the money to be paid in the future to an amount of money with a stated present value. If the present value of $5 million, because of the discount rate, is lower than the value of the real estate, the plan cannot be confirmed. Obviously, the discount rate selected by the court is critical to both the lender and the debtor and will undoubtedly be an area of dispute in these reorganization cases.

[iii] Treatment of Nonrecourse Claims as Recourse. To prevent a debtor from unfairly cashing out a nonrecourse secured creditor where the value of the real estate is less than the value of the indebtedness, Section 1111(b)(2) allows the nonrecourse loan to be treated as recourse, which does give protection to permanent lenders, who frequently make nonrecourse loans. However, if the borrowing entity is a limited partnership and the general partners are deemed to be personally liable for the mortgage indebtedness of the partnership, the Internal Revenue Service might attempt to prevent the investor-limited partners from deducting tax losses in excess of their equity investments,[114] notwithstanding that mortgage indebtedness is a nonrecourse obligation under state law.[115] This imputed deficiency claim is lost where the real estate is sold pursuant to a plan, or where the lender elects to treat the entire allowed claim as secured pursuant to Section 1111(b)(2). The rationale for not allowing a recourse claim where the real estate is to be sold is based on the supposition that the lender, under Section 363(k), can bid in the amount of the outstanding indebtedness and will either be paid that amount or receive the real estate at the sale.

---

[114] See discussion at ¶¶ 1.05[4][b], 4.02[5]. To ameliorate this potential problem, borrower's counsel might attempt to secure a waiver from the lender of its right to elect such treatment under Section 1111(b)(2) on behalf of his then-solvent client while negotiating the terms of the loan commitment and mortgage.

[115] See generally, ABA Committee on Developments in Business Financing, "Structuring and Documenting Business Financing Transactions Under the Federal Bankruptcy Code of 1978," 35 Bus. Law. 1645, 1650 (1980).

fair and equitable with regard to any class that is impaired.[109] As for secured creditors, in order for the plan to be fair and equitable it must fulfill at a minimum one of the following three conditions:

(1) That the holder of each claim retain the lien securing such claim, whether the property subject to such lien is retained by the debtor or transferred to another entity, to the extent of the allowed amount of such claim,[110] and additionally that each holder of a claim (of such class) receive, on account of such claim, deferred cash payments totaling at least the allowed amount of such claim, which payments have a value, as of the effective date of the plan, at least equal to the value of such holder's interest in the estate's interest in such property[111];

(2) Subject to Section 363(k) of the new Code, that upon the sale of any property free and clear of the lien securing such claim, such lien will attach to the proceeds of such sale and be treated in accordance with the above paragraphs[112];

(3) That each such holder of a claim of such class realize the "indubitable" equivalent of such claim,[113] which, based on legislative history, could be a replacement lien on similar collateral or the collateral itself.

Example of the cramdown provision. To further clarify how this cramdown provision works, let us assume the following facts in a Chapter 11 reorganization: There is a $5 million mortgage on real estate having a fair market value of $4 million. A plan is proposed that calls for the mortgagee to receive, without interest, $4 million in five equal annual installments of $800,000. The mortgagee objects to the plan. While the plan does give the mortgagee the amount of its secured claim, which is $4 million, nevertheless, the present value of the five payments in the absence of interest payments constitutes a lesser amount. Hence, the plan is not fair and equitable. Now let us assume that given this situation the mortgagee elects to treat its claim as totally secured, and a plan is proposed to pay the mortgagee without interest a total of $5 million in five equal annual installments of $1 million. Clearly, the payments equal the amount of the secured claim—but do the five

---

[109] *Id.* § 1129(b)(1).
[110] *Id.* § 1129(b)(2)(A)(i)(I).
[111] *Id.* § 1129(b)(2)(A)(i)(II).
[112] *Id.* § 1129(b)(2)(A)(ii).
[113] *Id.* § 1129(b)(2)(A)(iii).

In the case of secured real estate financing, the new Act in a Chapter 11 reorganization requires the fragmenting of an allowed claim into secured and unsecured unless the secured lender elects under Section 1111(b)(2), in which case, the lender will hold a secured claim equal to the total amount of its debt. An example of this would be a mortgage securing an outstanding indebtedness of $5 million on real estate worth only $4 million. The secured claim would be equal to the $4 million value of the real estate, the unsecured claim would be $1 million, unless the lender elects to treat the entire claim as secured, in which case the secured claim would be $5 million. In the event of such an election, the lender would waive any right to a deficiency judgment. Whether a secured creditor should elect to treat the entire claim as a secured claim depends on the circumstances. Obviously, if the election were made, the lender could not be cashed out for less than the mortgage indebtedness, irrespective of the value of the real estate. Moreover, the lender would be able to retain a mortgage on the real estate for the outstanding indebtedness. However, the lender could be forced to accept extended payments for a recast mortgage loan with a present discounted value that would be no greater than the value of the mortgage property. A mortgage lender may wish not to elect where its debtor has assets in addition to the mortgaged real estate or where the secured lender, because of the size of the unsecured claim, could control the voting of the unsecured creditors in such class and hence be able to effectively block any unfavorable reorganization plan.

The debtor is given the exclusive right to file a plan of reorganization within the first 120 days after the commencement of the proceeding.[105] Whether or not a trustee has been appointed, any creditor or creditors committee can file a plan after 120 days.[106] Any proposed plan must file a claim or interest in a class having similar claims and interests.[107] A plan will be accepted if it is approved by at least two-thirds (in amount) and claim more than a simple majority (in number) of the creditors of each class.[108] Even where a class of creditors has not accepted the plan, the plan can be confirmed if the "cramdown" provisions of Section 1129(b) of the new Code are satisfied. In order for a plan to be approved over the objections of creditors, it must not discriminate unfairly; e.g., the dissenting class must be paid in full before any junior class can participate in the plan, and the plan must be

---

[105] *Id.* § 1121(b).
[106] *Id.* § 1121(c).
[107] *Id.* § 1122.
[108] *Id.* § 1126(c).

filed by creditors. To commence an involuntary suit, the new Code requires three petitioning creditors (only if there are less than twelve creditors), and the amount of noncontingent claims must now aggregate at least $5,000 more than the value of any lien.[97] Petitioning creditors must establish only that the debtor is not paying his debts as they become due. This provision represents a significant departure from previous law concerning the grounds for involuntary bankruptcy, which required not only balance sheet insolvency but an act of bankruptcy. The new Act abolishes the concept of acts of bankruptcy, and the only basis for an involuntary proceeding is either (1) the inability of the debtor to meet its debts, or (2) the fact that a custodian, such as an assignee for the benefit of creditors, took charge of all the debtor's property within 120 days of the filing of the petition.[98] Should the creditor's petition be dismissed, the Bankruptcy Court may award the debtor costs, attorney's fees, and proximate damages; if there is a finding of bad faith, punitive damages may also be awarded.[99] Furthermore, in answering the petition, the debtor can request the court to require the petitioning creditors to post bond.[100]

Once a proceeding is commenced, the debtor will be allowed to remain in possession and continue to operate the business, unless the court determines upon request of a party in interest that a trustee should be appointed for cause.[101] In the absence of a lender proving that the debtor has milked or stolen from the property, a debtor will stay in possession of the property. When a court, after request by a creditor to appoint a trustee, denies such request, the moving creditor can still request the court to order the appointment of an examiner to investigate the debtor when such debtor's unsecured debts exceed $5 million.[102] The Act mandates the appointment of a creditors committee, usually consisting of the seven creditors holding the largest unsecured claims.[103] However, the new Act authorizes the court to change the size or membership of the committee if the membership is not representative of the different kinds of claims or interests to be represented by the committee.[104]

---

[97] Bankruptcy Reform Act of 1978, § 303(b).
[98] *Id.* § 303(h)(2).
[99] *Id.* §§ 303(i)(1), 303(i)(2).
[100] *Id.* § 303(e).
[101] *Id.* § 1104.
[102] *Id.* § 1104(b).
[103] *Id.* § 1102.
[104] *Id.* § 1102(c).

became effective October 1, 1979 and applies to all bankruptcy cases filed on or after that date. Pending cases are not covered, but will be governed by the law as it existed prior to the 1978 Act. Procedurally, the bankruptcy process was simplified and time parameters on the Bankruptcy Court of benefit to the creditors have been provided. The severe and unfair cramdown provision of the former Chapter XII was eliminated; it was replaced by the new cramdown provision which is fairer and more limited in scope. However, the election treatment regarding claims and the determination of present value in a plan will require a plethora of complicated maneuverings on the part of the lender and the debtor.

The debtor, barring fraud or gross incompetency (difficult to prove), remains in control of the business. And, under certain circumstances, lenders can have their senior lien position become a junior lien. The automatic stay is now almost ironclad, preventing a lender from foreclosing or attempting to obtain possession of the property of the debtor.

Lenders should be aware of the major changes affecting real estate, summarized in the following discussion.

[i] Broadening of Bankruptcy Jurisdiction. Section 105 of the 1978 Act is an omnibus provision phrased in such general terms as to be the basis for a broad exercise of power in the administration of a bankruptcy case. What every practitioner learned as the gray line between summary and plenary jurisdiction can be forgotten for those cases filed after October 1, 1979. Where, for example, under the old Act the trustee in bankruptcy had to bring suit in a state court against limited partners of the bankrupt partnership for return of their capital contributions, the new Code grants the Bankruptcy Court jurisdiction to hear such a suit.

[ii] Reorganization of the Rehabilitation Chapters. Except for municipalities (Chapter 9) and individuals with regular income (Chapter 13), all reorganizations are now governed by a new Chapter 11, which combines Chapters VIII, X, XI, and XII of the old Act and ends the need for litigation over what type of reorganization is appropriate.

However, what practitioners learned regarding the old Chapters X, XI, and XII should not be totally discarded. Aside from the numerous cases proceeding under these old chapters, many of the provisions of the new Chapter 11 reflect various doctrines that are peculiar to each of the old chapters. A knowledge of how these doctrines operated, along with the legislative history of the new Act, will be important to the practitioner litigating a case under new Chapter 11. A proceeding under new Chapter 11 may be voluntarily commenced by the debtor or may be

[12] Bankruptcy of Borrower

[a] Language of the Loan Commitment

By its language, the construction lender's loan commitment will ordinarily terminate at the option of the lender if the borrower-developer should become bankrupt or insolvent during the commitment stage. Insolvency of the developer is also an event of default, which entitles either the construction or permanent lender to accelerate the indebtedness or exercise its other default remedies.[95]

The following is an example of the type of language demanded by lenders in their loan commitments:

> Upon Borrower's committing an act of bankruptcy, making a general assignment for the benefit of creditors, or if there is filed by or against Borrower a petition in bankruptcy, or for the appointment of a receiver, or if there commences under any bankruptcy or insolvency law proceedings for Borrower's relief or for the composition, extension, arrangement or adjustment of any of Borrower's obligations or property, or if there occurs the taking of possession of, or assumption of control of all or any substantial part of the property of Borrower's business by any government or governmental agency, then any commitment issued pursuant to this application shall be voidable at the option of Lender. The conditions of this paragraph shall apply also to any person named as a prospective endorser, guarantor, or surety in connection with the proposed transaction.

While sound lending practice demands that the lender be entitled to declare a default upon the bankruptcy or insolvency of the borrower, the language in the sample loan commitment clause affording this right in the event of the insolvency of *any* guarantor is onerous to the developer where there are several guarantors on the note. Accordingly, the developer should attempt to limit the operation of this language to the insolvency of either a key guarantor or to only a certain number of them.

[b] Implications of the Bankruptcy Reform Act of 1978 for Real Estate Financing

The Bankruptcy Reform Act of 1978,[96] a major revision to the Bankruptcy Code, is at best a mixed blessing for the lender. The Act

---

[95] See Articles 6.5 and 6.6 of Form 3.4, and Article 23 of Form 4.1 in Appendix B.

[96] Pub. L. 95-598, (codified in 11 U.S.C. §§ 1 et seq.).

normally requires that the amount be written for the loan amount; however, this policy contains a very complex, and little understood, clause which can jeopardize complete recovery by the borrower and the lender in the event of partial loss. This condition, known as the provisional limit of liability clause, states:

> The limit of liability applicable to property under this form is provisional. It is a condition of this insurance, wherein the rate and premium are based on an average amount of liability during the period of construction, that at any date while this policy is in force, the actual limit of liability under this form is that proportion of the provisional limit of liability that the actual value of the described property on that date bears to the value at the date of completion, but shall not in any case exceed the provisional limit of liability. Furthermore, in consideration of the reduced rate at which this policy is written, it is a condition of this insurance that in the event of loss, the Company shall be liable for no greater proportion thereof than the provisional limit of liability under this form bears to the value of the described property at date of completion. If this form applies to two or more items, the foregoing shall apply separately to each such item.

Under this provision, assume that a policy is written in the amount of $3 million in respect to which a partial loss of $1 million arises. If, upon completion, the property would be worth $4 million, under this condition the provisional amount of insurance would be written at 25 percent less than the complete value and, accordingly, only $750,000 could be recovered on the policy, leaving an uninsurable loss of $250,000. In effect, this is a hidden coinsurance clause that can have devastating effects. The clause itself is ambiguous, contradicts the other terms of the policy, and, in light of increased inflation, poses a potentially severe problem that cannot be ignored by lenders and developers. In the event the insurance company is not willing to delete this clause, lenders and developers should carefully consider requiring a reporting policy since it does not contain this provision.

Liability during construction is normally insured against by means of a "comprehensive general liability" policy, which includes exclusions from coverage that must also be carefully scrutinized.[94]

---

[94] For a discussion of co-insurance clauses and loss payable clauses (including the standard or union mortgage clause), see discussion at ¶ 3.04[12].

Borrower shall provide insurance in form and with companies approved by Lender, with standard mortgagee clause, covering, as a minimum, the hazards covered by an "all risks of physical loss" policy, including collapse, with loss payable to Lender. All policies must contain waivers of the right of subrogation. Borrower must provide evidence of the existence of contractor's and owner's liability insurance and workmen's compensation insurance in form and with insurers satisfactory to Lender. If property is damaged, Lender shall not be required to advance money thereafter unless such damage is repaired or arrangements satisfactory to Lender shall have been made for such repair.[91]

During the course of construction, employees and third parties can be injured and the property can be damaged as a result of fire, lightning, windstorm, hail, or explosion. The various endorsements under a standard builder's "all-risk" insurance policy protect the developer, the contractor, and the lender against these perils—except damage from an explosion of a steam boiler—but usually exclude from coverage losses arising from: (1) riot, civil commotion, and riot attending a strike; (2) earthquake, landslide, and mud flow; (3) flood, surface water, and overflowing of streams[92]; (4) sewer backup; (5) percolating water; (6) error, omission in design, specifications, workmanship, and materials[93]; (7) deterioration, rust-settling, and cracking; (8) explosion of steam boiler; and (9) nuclear damage.

The form of the policy can be either "reporting" or "nonreporting." The reporting type of policy increases coverage as the construction progresses; the property is always insured in an amount equal to the actual cost of construction. The sole disadvantage with this type of policy consists of the administrative chore of making certain that proper endorsements have been issued to raise the amount of coverage to reflect the actual capital investment of the developer. By contrast, the nonreporting policy is written for an agreed upon provisional fixed amount so that endorsements are needed as construction continues. Most construction lenders normally require this type of policy since it obviates the need to monitor their coverage under the policy. The lender

---

[91] Also see Article 4(G) of Form 4.1, and Article 4.5 of Form 3.4 in Appendix B and discussion at ¶3.04[12].

[92] If the proposed project is located in a floodplains area, a special flood insurance endorsement is available and should be required.

[93] For example, if a building collapses because of defects in construction, recovery is precluded because of this so-called errors and omissions exclusion; however, if the contractor is bondable, the performance bond issued by a surety company would insure the parties against collapse.

[9] Execution of Building Loan Agreement

The construction loan commitment will require the developer to execute the lender's standard form of building loan agreement as modified by the terms of its commitment.[88] For the sake of convenience, the building loan agreement separately incorporates in massive detail the terms and conditions designed to assure the lender that the improvements will be constructed in a timely manner in accordance with approved plans and specifications, that sufficient funds will be at hand at all times to complete the project and pay off the claims of the mechanics and materialmen, and that the lender will be protected to the maximum extent possible from the other risks and problems that may arise during the course of construction.

[10] Approval of Architect and Payment of Fees

The construction lender will ordinarily require its approval of the architect or engineer designated by the developer to make the construction and development inspections. Sometimes the lender will employ its own "draw" or "progress" inspector, or will select an independent inspector to make such inspections or to corroborate the findings of the developer's architect. The developer will be required to pay the costs of such inspections. In addition, some lenders also require, prior to the closing of the construction loan, a statement from the architect that his fee has been paid in full or that the fee will be subordinated to the lien of the construction mortgage.[89] It is certainly reasonable for a construction lender to request that at the loan closing the architect be paid for preparing the plans and specifications so that the architect is foreclosed from claiming a prior lien for services rendered before work on the project has commenced.[90] However, it is unreasonable for the lender to insist that the developer pay the architect for inspection services yet to be rendered; any such requirement should be resisted by the developer as being contrary to sound business practice.

[11] Builder's Risk Insurance

The following language exemplifies the lender's requirements as to the hazard insurance that will be contained in its loan commitment:

---

[88] See discussion of the sample building loan agreement at ¶ 4.04[1].
[89] See Article 4(R) of Form 4.1 in Appendix B.
[90] See discussion at ¶ 4.02[6][a].

transfer large accounts and deposits to the bank in return for the issuance of the letter of credit and future business. In issuing the letter of credit, the bank normally requires collateral such as a certificate of deposit ranging anywhere from 10 to 20 percent of the face amount of the letter of credit. It also requires that the borrower agree to indemnify the bank for any loss sustained by it in the transaction. The rate is normally higher than the bond rate and ranges anywhere from 2 to 3 percent of the letter of credit amount per annum.

[e] Contractor's Guarantee

In addition to requiring payment and performance bonds, another area of protection that lenders have been resorting to is use of a direct agreement between the general contractor and the construction lender. In consideration of the lender's agreement to disburse by check advances made jointly payable to the contractor and the borrower, the contractor agrees (1) that in the event of default by the developer under the loan documents, he will upon demand by the lender complete the work called for under the construction contract for the then-remaining undisbursed portion of the construction funds allocated to pay for costs of construction under the construction contract; and (2) to exculpate the construction lender from personal liability under the construction contract.[87] The contractor, in such agreement, further agrees not to perform any extra work nor to deviate from the approved plans and specifications, without first obtaining the prior written consent of the construction lender. The problem with this type of agreement concerns the contractor's bonding company. Several bonding companies have told contractors that if such agreements are executed, it will affect their bonding line with the bonding company. This is based on the notion that such agreements would increase their liability as contractors. Nevertheless, the authors have been successful in persuading bonding companies to allow contractors to execute these contractors' agreements, provided, however, that the contractor's agreement contain language requiring that the construction lender add to the construction funds those amounts, if any, that (1) shall equal any amount of the construction loan proceeds diverted from the work by the developer, (2) shall equal the amount by which the contract sum specified in the construction contract has been increased by authorized change-order work or other authorized extra work, and (3) shall represent the cost to repair or complete any work that has been lost or damaged through theft or casualty to the extent not covered by insurance.

---

[87] See Article 4(R) of Form 4.1 in Appendix B.

[c] Construction Disbursement Programs

As an alternative to the performance bond, title companies in the early 1970s introduced the Construction Disbursement Program, whereby the title company guarantees that the project will be completed for the contract sum. This program is the equivalent of the old completion bond since the written insurance guarantees, albeit indirectly, completion of the project as opposed to a performance bond that does not guarantee completion of the project, but merely guarantees that the contractor will perform his work. To insure completion of the project for the stipulated sum, title companies under this program closely monitor, although without assuming any liability, construction, and disbursements. Such ongoing review is in direct contrast to the surety company's practice of not concerning itself with the project after issuance of the bonds, unless demand is made upon it based upon a contractor's default. The problem with this program for the title companies has been their exorbitant costs and their lack of sufficient and competent staffs to minimize their losses, which have far exceeded their profits. Accordingly, this program has been phased out by most title companies. There is certainly a need for such a program for construction lenders making loans on a national basis. Whether in fact this program will some day be revived by title or other companies remains to be seen.[86]

[d] Letters of Credit

A somewhat more unusual alternative is a bank's letter of credit. It is unusual in that most banks hesitate to write a letter of credit in excess of a half million dollars, and, by contrast, to a payment and performance bond, the bank is obligated under an irrevocable and unconditional letter of credit to pay upon the mere tendering of the sight draft to the bank. However, where the obligee is to be either HUD or some local housing and development authority, the amount to be insured frequently is less than the contract price. In the situation where a surety company will not issue a bond because the owner-builder or the owner and contractor are related, the letter of credit becomes the only practical solution for the construction lender.

In today's cautious real estate market, a bank is only willing to issue a letter of credit to (1) an established and knowledgeable real estate customer of the bank, or (2) a nonbank customer who is willing to

---

[86] Dwyer, "New Protection for Construction Lenders," 3 Real Est. Rev. 76-79 (Fall 1973).

project will cost $1 million to complete and the developer defaults by not supplying the remaining $200,000 of construction funds, the construction lender must step in and stand ready to disburse the additional funds to the contractor; otherwise, the lender will lose its coverage under the bond. The rationale for the restriction holds that the bonding of the contractor is based upon the creditworthiness of the contractor and not the developer, and therefore the surety company is in no position to guarantee the latter's performance under the construction contract. Defenses against the construction lender under this clause may also arise when the general construction contract with the contractor does not include all the work to be performed on the project. For example, if the site or foundation work is being done by the developer, itself, or through a separate contract, the surety company may claim that the contractor's ability to perform was hampered by the failure, delay, or improper performance of the other work. Or, the surety company may claim that the contractor's performance was frustrated by the developer's delays in approving necessary change orders or payments to subcontractors, or perhaps by the developer's misrepresentations as to soil and other site conditions.

However, in the past, attorneys for construction lenders have been able to provide some solace for their clients by insisting that the payment and performance bonds contain the following self-explanatory language, which to some extent protects lenders against the "Los Angeles" clause and the other defenses available to surety companies:

> It is understood that Owner's default under the building contract shall not terminate the Surety's liability unless the Owner's default remains uncured for 30 days following written notice to Lender. It is specifically agreed that no change, extension of time, alteration, addition or modification of the construction agreement or any accommodation or accommodations extended by obligee to the principal for any reason or reasons whatsoever shall, in any way, affect Surety's obligations under this bond, and said Surety hereby waives notice of any such change, extension of time, alterations, additions and modifications of said construction agreement (whether in writing or otherwise); and further waives notice of any accommodation or accommodations extended by obligee to principal. No dealings, negotiations or other acts of the principal and obligee or between them, pertaining to said construction agreement and any work done in connection therewith and the work to be performed thereunder, shall in any manner affect Surety's obligations under this bond.

for any amount above the contract price. However, arrangements may be negotiated upon payment of an additional premium, that permit change-order increases in excess of the original contract price.

Another factor that both lenders and developers sometimes overlook is the fact that the underpinning for coverage under the performance bond is the construction contract, not the lender's building loan agreement. For example, if the surety issued a bond relying on a holdback of 15 percent by the developer pursuant to the construction contract, and the lender has been retaining only 10 percent of the loan funds pending completion of construction, the surety will not be responsible for the balance in the event of a default by the contractor. Also, to preserve performance bond protection under the building loan agreement, the developer must not be allowed to make progress payments to the contractor in advance of the dates stipulated in the construction contract.[82] Moreover, if the developer and construction lender lose their protection under the performance bond, the surety company may claim by subrogation the liens and rights against the property held by the subcontractors who were paid for their services and materials pursuant to the terms of a payment bond.[83] Consequently, a prudent construction lender should not approve any change order without the surety company's consent and should carefully review the building loan agreement to be sure that it conforms where applicable to the terms and conditions of the construction contract.[84] However, some surety companies will permit change orders up to a certain dollar amount or percentage of the contract amount without requiring their approval.

A final stumbling block with respect to recovery under these bonds is that when the lender is named as co-obligee, most surety companies insert the so-called "Los Angeles clause" in the bonds. This clause, variously phrased,[85] states that the surety's obligation to the construction lender is conditional on the owner-developer, or in the event of default, the construction lender performing the owner's obligations under the construction contract. For example, if an 80 percent financed

---

[82] See generally 17 *Am. Jur. 2d* "Contractors' Bonds" § 31 (1966). E.g., National Sur. Co. v. Long, 79 Ark. 523, 532, 96 S.W. 745, 747 (1906).

[83] E.g., Atlantic Coast Brewing Co. v. Clement, 59 N.J.L. 48, 35 A. 647, 649 (1896). Cf. Roland v. Lindsey, 104 Ark. 49, 58, 146 S.W. 115, 118 (1912).

[84] See Article 4(N) of Form 4.1 in Appendix B.

[85] An example of language used in such clauses is the following: "Any failure by either or both of the obligees to make payments to the principal [contractor], strictly in accordance with the terms of said contract, shall automatically relieve the principal and the surety from their obligations to perform hereunder."

surety company. Essentially, the surety company could argue that the failure of its bonded subcontractor to perform arose from the failure of the other subcontractors to perform their work as required.

Where a lender requires a payment and performance bond, to obtain maximum coverage lender's counsel should carefully review the construction contract and the payment and performance bonds to make certain that (1) no price increase for allowance items and change orders can be authorized without the prior written approval of the lender and the surety company; (2) the contractor be required to "sign off" or approve the plans and specifications, the site plan, and the soils engineering report; (3) the contractor be required to give the lender written notice in the event of default by the developer and reasonable time to investigate, and at the lender's option a right to cure the developer's default; (4) the construction contract cover all work so that the entire project can be bonded; (5) the lender require an endorsement from the surety company allowing the lender to release the developer from liability, provided such release does not prejudice the right of the surety company against the developer; and (6) the surety company review and approve the building loan agreement.

In exchange for items (5) and (6), sophisticated surety companies are requiring that they review the construction lender's documents and receive an agreement that the construction lender will not decrease the amount of loan funds set aside for payment due the general contractors.

Even with proper coverage, however, enforcement of these bonds by the construction lender is sometimes difficult because of certain constraints imposed by the bonding companies, as well as defenses that may arise against the lender. Frequently, the identification of the bonded work tends to be skeletal, making reference only to the names of the parties and the date of the contract, which terms are invariably modified during the course of construction through change orders requested and approved by the developer, the contractor, and the lender.[80] However, the performance bond is written to cover a specific construction contract as originally drafted and with a coverage amount geared to the original contract price. Accordingly, unless the contractor has specifically assumed the risk of a cost overrun,[81] or the increase in the contract price was caused by (or on the account of) the contractor, the owner-developer and the lender cannot look to the surety company

---

[80] See discussion at ¶ 4.04[5].

[81] Some forms of dual-obligee performance bonds automatically permit changes in plans which do not increase the cost of work beyond a stipulated percent (e.g., 10 percent) of the original contract amount.

[b] Payment and Performance Bonds

Combined payment and performance bonds were once a popular means used by both developers and construction lenders to protect themselves against defaults by a contractor and the filing of mechanics' liens. Currently, similar protection is afforded by separate payment bonds[78] and performance bonds, issued for a single combined premium and usually written for the amount of the construction contract. In the case of a standard AIA performance bond, the bonding company, as surety, guarantees the developer-owner, as obligee, that the contractor, as principal obligor, will meet its obligations under the construction contract. Accordingly, if the contractor defaults, the surety company promises the developer that it will step in and complete the project according to the terms of the construction contract. In order for a construction lender to be entitled to recover in the event of a contractor's default, the lender must be designated as co-obligee on the bond; the owner's form of bond without dual-obligee language states that no party other than the owner may derive benefit from it.

However, surety companies are usually willing to insure only well-established creditworthy general contractors who are often able to obtain a "bonding line" (similar to a general line of credit from a bank). A bonding company agrees to bond the contractor on any projects undertaken by it up to a certain coverage amount. Frequently, it is difficult to obtain coverage for a small general contractor, especially on his first project, unless the principals of the contractor are solvent enough to individually guarantee their company's performance. Consequently, some construction lenders will waive this bonding requirement since they are unable to procure it on a small project and do not wish to antagonize the large developer, possibly an important depositor, by forcing him to pay for the cost of the bond.[79] In a case where the general contractor is not bondable and the lender will not waive its bonding requirement, it is sometimes possible, if the subcontractors have the requisite financial strength, to fragment the original contract into separate but direct contracts for their services or supplies (e.g., for the plumbing, roofing, dry wall) and obtain bonds on these contracts.

One problem of concern to the developer and the lender with regard to bonding major subcontractors as opposed to bonding general contractors is the "integration and reliance" defense available to the

---

[78] See discussion at ¶ 4.02[6][b][ii].

[79] Bonding rates, as of this writing, are approximately $12 per thousand for the first $500,000 of coverage, $7.25 per thousand for the next $2 million, $5.75 per thousand for the next $2.5 million, $5.25 per thousand for the next $2.5 million, and $4.80 per thousand thereafter.

the basis of such architect's certification, the remaining construction cost, plus other cost items in connection with completing the project, exceed the remaining undisbursed proceeds of the loan. Disbursements shall be made once each month upon approved AIA form of requisition certified by architect. Disbursements may be conditioned upon satisfactory evidence of proper application of all prior disbursements. The final 10 percent shall be disbursed only upon completion of the project (including, but not limited to, on-site improvements and all utilities), to the written satisfaction of Lender and Permanent Lender and furnishing of releases of all mechanics' and materialmen's liens. The Building Loan Agreement shall contain other provisions customarily required by Lender and a default thereunder shall be a default under the Mortgage.

Quite often, the permanent mortgage to be placed upon completion is for an amount larger than the temporary construction loan, and the developer intends to pay these subcontractors and materialmen the balance due them from this source. Where this is not the case, however, the lender should inquire further as to how the balance of the contracts will be funded. Where holdbacks are excessive (more than 10 percent, for example), this immediately raises questions concerning the ability of the contractors, subcontractors, and materialmen to continue to carry out their contractual obligations, unless, of course, they are solvent, well-known firms. Similar doubts arise where these parties accept the developer's notes or an equity interest in lieu of cash payments. A general approach followed in these cases is that holdbacks, agreements for deferment of payments, acceptance of notes, and the like should not be for an amount greater than the portion of the contract price that represents the profit of the subcontractor or materialman. In any event, the developer must satisfy the lender that it will be able to meet all project costs—both direct and indirect—necessary to complete the project. The developer is often required either to (1) deposit with the lender an amount equal to the difference between the estimated cost of completion of construction of the improvements as determined by the lender and the amount of the construction loan that remains to be disbursed, or (2) pay for construction costs in that amount so that the amount of the construction loan that remains to be disbursed shall be sufficient to complete the construction of the improvements.[77]

---

[77] See Articles 4(S) and 19(C) of Form 4.1 in Appendix B.

[8] Assurances That Project Will Be Completed

[a] Holdback of Loan Funds

While the net worth of a developer is taken into account,[75] the construction lender's primary concern is to determine whether the developer will have sufficient equity funds, over and above the amount of the construction loan, available to complete the job. When the source of these funds is not readily apparent from an examination of the figures shown on the developer's financial statements, a further inquiry will usually disclose one or more of the following facts: (1) the cost estimate of the lender's appraiser does not coincide with the developer's, the latter's estimate being lower; (2) the developer is imposing "holdbacks" on his contractor or, if he is acting as his own contractor, on his subcontractors or materialmen, (i.e., he is withholding a portion of their contract price); or (3) the developer-contractor is paying for a portion of the work and material by giving his notes or by conveying ownership interests in the project.

With respect to the first possibility, the lender's representatives generally will be working on the basis of standard figures, while the developer uses actual figures where he has firm contracts. If the developer is acting as his own contractor, or if he is doing a portion of the work himself, the disparity in costs generally will be due to the fact that the developer, for purposes of cost estimates, is not allowing himself a normal profit. This is significant to the lender, for if the developer defaults and the lender must complete the project, it may have to relet these contracts to third parties at a cost that will include these profits and hence will increase the cost of completion.

Holding back a portion of the amounts due contractors, subcontractors, and materialmen is a common practice in the building industry, and a construction loan should be structured so that there is a holdback of loan funds until the completion of construction to pay for these retentions and to avoid mechanics' liens.[76] The following provision providing for a 10 percent holdback of funds pending final completion of construction typifies the type of language contained in most construction loan commitments:

> The Borrower will execute a Building Loan Agreement under which Lender will disburse 90 percent of the value of the work completed and approved for payment by an architect satisfactory to Lender, provided Lender may withhold disbursement at any time when, on

---

[75] See discussion at ¶ 4.02[5].
[76] See Article 19(I) & (J) of Form 4.1 in Appendix B.

any right to liens on the property is valid against subcontractors if this no-lien stipulation agreement is executed and recorded at the time the original construction contract is executed, and no prior performance has been rendered by any subcontractor.[71]

[7] Approval of Contractors and Building Contract

Frequently, the commitment will require that both the contractor and the form and substance of the building contract be approved in writing by the construction lender.[72] Accordingly, before a developer enters into a construction contract, it should attempt to procure the lender's approval of both the contract and the contractor. In the event the contract must be executed prior to such approval, the developer should insert an escape clause stating that the contract is subject to approval of the construction lender and in the event said contract is not approved, the contract shall be null and void without liability to either party. Obviously, the purpose of this requirement is to make certain that the contemplated project will not be built by a contractor with whom the lender has had problems in the past, or by a contractor who is known by the lender to have performed poorly on other projects.

While the lender will review the construction contract, a developer should make certain that the terms of the construction contract comply with the conditions for disbursement as well as other terms contained in the building loan agreement. For example, construction contracts normally provide for a retainage or holdback of part of each construction disbursement. This insures that the project will be completed properly and free of liens. Therefore, the retainage amounts called for in the construction contract and subcontracts should correspond to the holdback amounts provided for in the building loan agreement and other loan documents; otherwise, the developer may be forced to make out-of-pocket disbursements during the term of the loan.[73] Conversely, the contractor and subcontractors should be entitled under the construction contracts to receive holdback amounts pursuant to the same terms and conditions that are imposed by the building loan agreement, and the dates for commencement and completion of construction should be identical in both documents. Finally, the construction contract should incorporate the construction lender's requirement that the contractor's lien be made subordinate to the lien of the construction mortgage.[74]

---

[71] See Article 4(N) of Form 4.1 in Appendix B.
[72] See Imperial House of Ind. v. Eagle Sav. Ass'n, 376 N.E.2d 537 (1978).
[73] See Article 19[I] of Form 4.1 in Appendix B.
[74] See Article 3 of Form 4.1 in Appendix B.

As a control device, the title company may also require of the construction lender that it be allowed to disburse construction funds directly to the parties involved. As an extra precaution, many title companies will disburse directly to the subcontractors rather than to the developer or general contractor.[68] Customarily, the title company will insist upon receiving a list of contractors and subcontractors and make additional disbursements ("progress payments") only after receiving partial lien waivers and examining the land records to be sure that no liens have been filed. Even though architect's certificates will be furnished as construction progresses, many title companies will also make periodic inspections of the premises before disbursing the loan proceeds.[69] Finally, many title companies will require the construction lender and developer to stipulate in writing that the title company be in no way responsible for any deficiencies in the quality or the quantity of the work completed on the project, nor be responsible for the sufficiency of funds available for the completion of the project, as of the date of each disbursement.

[ii] Labor and Material Payment Bond. As additional protection against mechanics' liens, the construction lender may also require that the general contractor be covered by a labor and material payment bond from a surety company, on forms approved by the American Institute of Architects (AIA). With such a bond, if the general contractor, as principal obligor, defaults in paying its subcontractors and suppliers, the bonding company, as surety, is bound to the developer, as obligee, to pay these parties in accordance with the terms of the construction contract so that neither mechanics' liens nor materialmen's liens will be filed against the property. The construction lender will also require that it be named as co-obligee to insure that the benefit of the bond to it is direct rather than indirect. Customarily, separate payment and performance bonds are issued for a single one-time premium, and both are subject to the same constraints and pitfalls discussed at ¶ 4.02[8][b].[70]

[iii] Developer-Contractor Agreement. In a few states, a recorded agreement between an owner and a contractor that purports to waive

---

[68] See discussion at ¶ 4.04[4].

[69] See discussion at ¶ 4.04[3], and paragraph 19(D) and 14 of Form 4.1 in Appendix B.

[70] An additional problem concerning the use of payment bonds is determining whether certain items (e.g., tires supplied for a truck used by the general contractor) are covered by the bond. See Note, "Labor and Material Surety Bonds in Pennsylvania: What Is the Test," 33 U. Pitt. L. Rev. 430 (1971). See also paragraph 4(O) of Form 4.1 in Appendix B.

Finally, the following Endorsement D is used mainly in states where the construction lender's lien priority cannot be forfeited on the basis of subsequent action, except perhaps by its failure to comply with local law or the provisions of its building loan agreement[66]:

> The Company hereby insures against loss or damage by reason of loss of priority of the lien of the insured mortgage over any lien imposed by law for services, labor, or material heretofore or hereafter furnished.

In addition to retrenching from full mechanics' lien coverage, title companies have also been demanding additional safeguards to reduce their coverage risks, especially in cases where there is no initial lien priority for the mortgage being insured. Designation of the title company as co-obligee on the surety bond posted by the general contractor provides only partial protection for the title company.[67] Accordingly, the title company would prefer to be named as obligee on a special corporate surety bond in a form that insures the title company against any loss it may sustain as the result of its insurance against mechanics' liens. However, in such event, the surety company will demand security from the developer-borrower and charge the regular premium. Consequently, developers should object to paying an extra premium for reinsuring the title insurer, especially if the developer has already paid the premium for a completion and performance bond.

Absent a corporate surety bond, the title company may alternatively require that the developer indemnify the title company for any loss arising from its issuance of insurance coverage against mechanics' liens. In that regard, the title company may attempt to have cash or its equivalent escrowed to support the indemnity agreement, using the rationale that if a financially distressed developer is unable to pay mechanics and materialmen, chances are that he will also fail to meet his obligation, as indemnitor, to the title company.

---

[66] According to Lawyers Title Insurance Corporation, the list includes Delaware, Florida, Louisiana, and Maryland.

[67] Even if the coverage amount is adequate, the surety bond may not cover all mechanics and materialmen, and most such bonds contain the so-called Los Angeles clause, which exculpates the surety company from liability if the developer does not comply with the terms of the building contract. See discussion at ¶ 4.02[6][b][ii]. In addition, the title company must concern itself with litigation costs associated with defending the lien priority of the insured mortgage and the marketability of the title in the event that mechanics' liens are filed. See Bowling, note 60 *supra*, at 35.

invoices, etc., as a condition precedent to issuing each endorsement as the construction progresses. However, the lender will not be covered as to future construction and is only protected against lack of priority due to diversion of funds with respect to disbursements already made for work in place as of the date of the endorsement. In addition, the language exculpates the title company from liability if the lender loses lien priority because it fails to make disbursements in compliance either with local law or its own building loan agreement.

The following Endorsement B applies mainly to priority states where the construction lender's initial lien priority (by recording prior to commencement of construction) can be lost with respect to disbursements deemed to be optional and not obligatory[64]:

> The Company hereby insures against loss or damage by reason of loss of priority of the lien of the insured mortgage over any lien imposed by law for services, labor or material heretofore or hereafter furnished for that portion of the proceeds of the loan secured by said mortgage now or hereafter disbursed in compliance with a legal obligation to disburse contained in a written agreement which must exist at the date of this endorsement.

Under this language, the construction lender is covered as to future construction, and its obligatory advances are protected against mechanics' liens whenever filed.

Endorsement C is designed for use in those states in which the construction mortgage is accorded lien priority over a mechanics' lien only as to disbursements made by the construction lender prior to the filing of a mechanics' lien. [65] The endorsement reads in part as follows:

> The Company hereby insures against any loss or damage by reason of loss of priority of the lien of the insured mortgage over any lien imposed by law for services, labor or material heretofore or hereafter furnished for that portion of the proceeds of the loan secured by said mortgage now or hereafter disbursed prior to the filing of any assertion of any such lien or right thereto in the public records or thereafter disbursed with the written consent of the Company.

---

[64] According to Lawyers Title Insurance Corporation, all the priority states listed in note 37 *supra* fit this description, except for Delaware, Florida, Louisiana, and Maryland.

[65] According to Lawyers Title Insurance Corporation, the list includes the District of Columbia, Kentucky, New Jersey, North Dakota, South Carolina, and South Dakota.

liens and by checking the public records before issuing the policy.[61] However, in response to competitive pressures and the desire to obtain title insurance for the entire project, title companies began to issue item (7) coverage to construction lenders before the statutory period had expired, resulting in their assumption of the risk of future loss of lien priority over mechanics' liens for future work performed by mechanics and materialmen who might not be paid in the future. Consequently, title companies were forced to rely upon matters beyond their control, such as their future ability to obtain genuine lien waivers from the general contractor and subcontractors, and the lender's assurances that it would take the necessary steps required by local law (e.g., drafting building loan agreements to provide for obligatory advances) to obtain lien priority.[62]

However, because of large losses, within recent years title companies have begun to substantially curtail their coverage, especially in nónpriority states and to insist upon additional safeguards. Specifically, most title companies are in the process of replacing item (7) coverage with a construction loan policy (ALTA Construction Loan Policy 1975) and its accompanying endorsements, tailored to the law in a particular jurisdiction. For example, in states where the construction lender cannot safely rely on local law to obtain lien priority,[63] the title company will only furnish limited coverage based on standard Endorsement A (Form 91-116, revised March 1976), which reads in part as follows:

> The Company hereby insures against loss or damage by reason of the lack of priority of the lien of the insured mortgage over any lien imposed by law for services, labor or material, for that portion of the cost thereof the payment for which the insured has disbursed funds, and which services, labor or material were furnished prior to .... for an improvement on the land.

This language permits the insurer to impose whatever requirements it deems necessary to assure itself that mechanics and materialmen have been paid as of a certain date. For example, the title company may require lien waivers, affidavits, construction schedules, receipts and

---

[61] Bowling, "Lenders and Title Insurers Must Work Together," CXL American Banker 32 (Oct. 20, 1975).

[62] *Id.*

[63] Based on memorandum prepared on June 5, 1978 by Mr. John Goode, counsel for Lawyers Title Insurance Corporation, Richmond, Va., the following states fit within this high-risk assumption category: Alabama, Alaska, Colorado, Illinois, Indiana, Maine, Michigan, Missouri, Montana, Oregon, Texas, Virginia, and Wyoming.

loan proceeds even if the borrower-developer has defaulted.[59] However, certain time requirements must generally be met, and some statutes deny enforcement if a payment bond has been filed.

[b] Protection for the Construction Lender Against Mechanics' Liens

Since the statutory and case law is neither well settled nor uniform, lenders, to a large extent, have protected themselves against mechanics' liens by means of title insurance and payment and performance bonds.

[i] Title Insurance. Generally, the construction loan commitment will contain the following requirement:

> *Title Insurance.* Lender shall receive full-coverage mortgagee title insurance issued by a company or companies approved in writing by Lender and Permanent Lender. Unless otherwise specified, such insurance shall be in the standard ALTA form and shall include, among other things, insurance against filed and unfiled mechanics' and materialmen's liens and shall be subject only to such encumbrances, easements, defects, and objections as may be approved in writing by the Lender and Permanent Lender. As a condition to each advance, such insurance shall be extended by endorsement to cover such advance.[60]

Title insurance companies have traditionally offered broad protection to construction lenders on the basis of item (7) of the standard A.L.T.A. Loan Policy (revised Oct. 17, 1970), which insures the lender against loss by reason of: "any statutory lien for labor or materials which now has gained or hereafter may gain priority over the lien of the insured mortgage..." except for liens arising from subsequent improvements that are not financed by means of the insured mortgage. However, the drafters of this provision originally contemplated its purpose as the protection of a permanent lender once the improvements were completed. The title company could thus minimize its risk assumption by awaiting the expiration of the statutory period for filing mechanics'

---

[59] E.g., Cal. Civ. Code §§ 3156-3172 (West 1971); Wash. Rev. Code Ann. § 60.04.210; Tex. Rev. Civ. Stat. Ann. Art. 5463 (Vernon Cum. Supp. 1978); see generally Comment, "Mechanics Liens: The 'Stop Notice' Comes to Washington," 49 Wash. L. Rev. 685 (1974).

[60] See also Articles 4(A) and 19(D) of Form 4.1 in Appendix B.

no party to a contract should be forced to declare the other party in default and thereby discourage performance of a contract.[54] However, a minority of case law decisions holds that in such situations the nature of the advances remains obligatory.[55]

[iii] Equitable Lien Doctrine and the "Stop Notice" Statute. Construction lenders should be aware of the so-called equitable lien doctrine (that has gained special prominence in California), to the effect that a mechanic's lien claimant can claim priority to undisbursed construction loan funds after the borrower has defaulted, even though such claimant has waived or otherwise been deprived of his statutory lien rights against both the funds and the real estate.[56] However, the more traditional view followed in most jurisdictions holds that there exists no duty at equity on the part of the construction lender to protect contractors against the default or insolvency of the developer. For example, the Supreme Court of Wisconsin reaffirmed the traditional rule by stating: "In the ordinary case of a first mortgage..., there exists no duty on the part of the mortgagee to disclose pending or threatening defaults to contractors."[57] The court, in reviewing the status of a ten percent holdback of funds retained by the construction lender, held that the undisbursed funds were not trust funds nor did they belong in any way to the subcontractors, based upon either a third-party beneficiary or escrow theory.[58]

Likewise, in a few jurisdictions, statutory relief is afforded to an unpaid mechanic's lien claimant by permitting him to enforce his otherwise unenforceable claim against the undisbursed construction

---

Allied Constr. Co., 347 Pa. 312, 323, 97 A.2d 802, 807 (1953); Elmendorf-Anthony v. Dunn, 10 Wash. 2d 29, 43, 116 P.2d 253, 259 (1941); see also 80 A.L.R.2d 179, 199-203.

[54] Kratovil, *Modern Mortgage Law and Practice* § 211 at 135 (4th ed. 1972).

[55] E.g., Landers-Morrison-Christenson Co. v. Ambassador Holding Co., 171 Minn. 445, 454, 214 N.W. 503 (Minn. 1927); Hyman v. Hauff, 138 N.Y. 48, 57, 33 N.E. 735, 738 (1893); see also 80 A.L.R.2d 179, 199-203.

[56] E.g., Swinerton Walberg Co. v. Union Bank, 25 Cal. App. 3d 259, 268, 101 Cal. Rptr. 665, 671 (1972) (involving a general contractor, as claimant); see Lefcoe & Schaffer, "Construction Lending and the Equitable Lien," 40 Calif. L. Rev. 439 (1967); see 4 A.L.R.3d 848 (1974).

[57] Mortgage Associates, Inc. v. Monona Shores, Inc., 47 Wis. 2d 171, 185, 177 N.W.2d, 340, 349 (1970).

[58] *Id.* at 198-199, 177 N.W.2d at 352. See also Lampert Yards, Inc. v. Thompson-Wetterling Constr. & Realty Inc., 302 Minn. 83, 92, 233 N.W.2d 418, 424 (Minn. 1974).

final clause of the note is that if there were no events of default, the mortgagee was obligated to continue making advances under the note."[48]

The cogency of the majority view is supported by the fact that business reality and sound lending practice dictate inclusion of such conditions for performance and events of default in a building loan agreement[49] or other security instrument. Indeed, all well-drafted contracts contain such conditions. Moreover, some express language merely acknowledges what the law already implies; namely, that if one party to a contract fails to perform in a reasonable manner, the other party is excused from his obligation to perform.[50] However, to the chagrin of the authors and certain other commentators,[51] a minority of jurisdictions hold that such conditional, albeit necessary, language will cause future advances to be regarded as optional. For example, in *J.I. Kislak Mortgage Corp. v. William Matthews Builder Inc.,* a Superior Court of Delaware held construction loan advances to be optional where the building loan agreement provided that no disbursements would be made by the mortgagee until the borrower furnished satisfactory evidence that prior advances had been disbursed fully and properly to mechanics and materialmen.[52]

To make matters worse for the construction lender, the case law in a majority of jurisdictions suggests that if a default by the borrower actually does occur, and the mortgagee nonetheless disburses, such action will convert what would otherwise be deemed an obligatory advance into an optional advance even though the lender is economically compelled to continue the disbursements until the project is completed.[53] This rule has been severely criticized on the rationale that

---

[48] 85 N.M. 560, 564, 514 P.2d 611, 615 (1973).

[49] See ¶ 4.04[3].

[50] *Restatement (Second) of Contracts* § 262 (1973).

[51] E.g., Kratovil & Werner, "Mortgages for Construction and the Lien Priorities Problem—The 'Unobligatory' Advance," 41 Tenn. L. Rev. 311, 314-315 (1974).

[52] 287 A.2d 686, 689, *aff'd* 303 A.2d 648, 651 (Del. 1973). See also New York & Suburban Fed. Sav. & Loan Ass'n v. Fi-Pen Realty Co., 133 N.Y.S.2d 33, 35 (N.Y. Sup. Ct. 1954), where it was held that a provision in the building loan agreement nullifying the lender's obligation to disburse in the event of a default by the mortgagor rendered optional the advances thereunder; Community Lumber Co. of Baldwin Park v. California Pub. Co., 215 Cal. 274, 278, 10 P.2d 60, 62 (1932).

[53] E.g., Yost-Linn Lumber Co. v. Williams, 121 Cal. App. 571, 576, 9 P.2d 324, 326, (1932); New York & Suburban Fed. Sav. & Loan Ass'n v. Fi-Pen Realty Co., 133 N.Y.S.2d 33, 35, (N.Y. Sup. Ct. 1954); Housing Mfg. Corp. v.

Consequently, in some of the priority states the initial priority of the previously recorded construction mortgage may be lost to the extent that the mortgagee makes advances that it is not obligated to make.

The so-called open-end mortgage[44] and certain building loan agreements provide for "optional" future advances where the decision if and when to make such disbursements is expressly within the sole discretion of the lender. For example, in *National Bank of Washington v. Equity Investors,* the Washington Supreme Court held construction mortgage advances to be optional where the lender's building loan agreement left the loan funds under the control of the lender "to be advanced at such times and in such amounts as the lender shall determine." Also, the customary requirement that the work be done in a "good and workmanlike manner" was predicated upon the subjective opinion of the lender, not on a determination by third parties.[45] Likewise, if the provisions in the building loan agreement or mortgage are overly general and vague, it has been argued that the agreement is unenforceable for want of certainty, in which event future advances might be deemed optional and not obligatory.[46]

However, if the building loan agreement and other security instruments merely impose conditions precedent to the making of future advances, and list those events of default that would render inoperative the lender's obligation to make such advances, the majority view is that such conditions precedent or subsequent will not render the advances optional if they are spelled out with reasonable particularity.[47] For example, in *House of Carpets, Inc. v. Mortgage Investment Co.,* the New Mexico Supreme Court ruled construction loan advances to be obligatory where the advances were to be made pursuant to a certain time schedule, and the construction loan note stipulated that the mortgagee would be under no obligation to disburse if the borrower were in default under any of the terms and conditions of the mortgage. In so holding, the court noted: "The inference to be drawn from this

---

[44] Such mortgages secure not only the original indebtedness but also any future advances that the mortgagee elects to make; however, the mortgagee has no legal obligation to advance additional funds. The advantage to the borrower is that he can obviate the alternative of seeking more expensive short-term secondary financing and thereby avoid the expenses involved in executing a new mortgage with the secondary lender.

[45] 88 Wash. 2d 886, 898, 506 P.2d 20, 28 (1973); see also Imhoff v. Title Ins. Co., 113 Cal. App. 2d 139, 145, 247 P.2d 851, 856 (1952).

[46] See Wayne Bldg. & Loan Co. v. Yarborough, 11 Ohio St. 2d 195, 221, 228 N.E.2d 841, 858 (1967).

[47] 80 A.L.R.2d 179, 197-198.

Form 4.1.) For example, the lender should require photographs and affidavits from the borrower and contractor signifying that construction has not begun and that materials have not been delivered to the site, and should verify these facts by means of an on-site inspection of the premises.

In other jurisdictions, such as the District of Columbia and New York, a building loan mortgage will be afforded priority over mechanics' liens only as to disbursements made prior to the filing of any mechanic's lien.[40] In states like Virginia, mechanics' liens automatically have priority as to the improvements, but not the land.[41]

Finally, lenders and developers should be aware of the prevailing rule that a subcontractor or supplier who satisfactorily performs his services is entitled to a lien even if the general contractor is in default under the construction contract.[42]

[ii] Doctrine of "Obligatory" vs. "Optional" Advances. Perhaps the greatest area of confusion concerns the doctrine of "obligatory" versus "optional" advances. This, broadly speaking, states that if the mortgagee is obligated to make future advances, a recorded construction mortgage will be accorded lien priority over any subsequent mechanics' liens even though some of the loan proceeds are disbursed after a mechanic's lien has been attached to the mortgaged premises. Conversely, if the mortgagee's future advances are optional, its mortgage lien will be prior only as to those advances made up to the time of notice of the attachment of the mechanic's lien. The rationale for the doctrine is that if the future advance is obligatory, the obligation of the mortgagee is fixed at the time the mortgage is executed, and the fact that the money is not handed over until some later time is irrelevant.[43]

---

[40] D.C. Code Encycl. § 38-109 (West); prior recordation of the mortgage is *not* required: Waco Scaffold & Shor. Co. v. 424 Eye St. Ass'n, 355 A.2d 780, 784 (D.C. 1976). Under New York law, such prior advances are entitled to lien priority over mechanics' liens (regardless of when the building loan mortgage is recorded) only if (1) the building loan contract contains a covenant whereunder the mortgagor undertakes to receive loan advances in trust to pay for labor and materials before doing anything else with the money and (2) the contract is filed with the county clerk. N.Y. Lien Law § 13 (McKinney 1966).

[41] Va. Code Ann. § 43-21 (1976). For a more in-depth discussion of mechanics' liens priorities under state law, see Osborne, Nelson & Whitman, *Real Estate Finance Law* § 12.4 (1979).

[42] See Reiger v. Schulte & Eicher, 151 Ky. 129, 136, 151 S.W. 395, 398 (1912); Woodson Bend, Inc. v. Masters Supply, Inc., 571 S.W.2d 95, 102 (Ky. 1978). 1978).

[43] Osborne, *Handbook on the Law of Mortgages* § 114 (2d. ed. 1970).

its purchase of the construction loan, the permanent lender will require that the property be paid for and free of any prior liens.[33]

[i] Lien Priorities Under State Law. Rules governing the relative lien priorities between mechanics' liens and construction mortgages vary widely from state to state; accordingly, it is necessary for the construction lender to be aware of the statutory and case law in its particular jurisdiction.[34] For example, while in a few states like Florida a mortgage lien takes precedence over any subsequently filed mechanics' liens,[35] in many jurisdictions (so-called priority states) like Minnesota,[36] all mechanics' liens relate back to the commencement of construction. Accordingly, in the latter jurisdictions the construction mortgage will be accorded lien priority only if the mortgage is recorded and becomes a lien on the real estate before any construction begins.[37] However, while the date on which the construction mortgage is recorded can be accurately determined, case law in these priority states has rendered ambiguous the phrase "commencement of construction."[38] Generally, to constitute "commencement of construction" for purposes of this rule, the work must be of such a conspicuous and substantial nature as to be reasonably apparent to all that the owner is constructing improvements on the site and intended to do so at the time the initial work began. Delivery of materials or off-site preparations such as the completion of an engineering study or the drafting of an architect's plans and specifications generally do not constitute commencement of construction.[39] However, a prudent construction lender will demand evidence that the site was vacant at the time the mortgage was recorded. (See Article 3 of

---

[33] See discussion at ¶3.04, and "THE SECURITY" language of Form 3.1 and second paragraph of Form 3.2 in Appendix B.

[34] See generally, Casner, *American Law of Property* § 16.06 F (1952); Annot., 80 A.L.R.2d 179, 197-198 (1961); Bowling, "Lenders and Title Insurer Must Work Together," C&L American Banker 32-48 (Oct. 20, 1975).

[35] Fla. Stat. Ann. § 713.07(3) (West 1969).

[36] Minn. Stat. Ann. § 514.05 (West Cum. Supp. 1978).

[37] Based on a survey of statutory and case law in each state, Lawyers Title Insurance Corporation is of the opinion that subject to certain conditions the following states and the District of Columbia give priority to mortgages recorded prior to commencement of construction: Arkansas, Arizona, California, Connecticut, Delaware, Florida, Georgia, Hawaii, Idaho, Iowa, Kansas, Kentucky, Louisiana, Maryland, Massachusetts, Mississippi, Minnesota, Nebraska, Nevada, New Hampshire, New Mexico, New Jersey, New York, North Carolina, North Dakota, Ohio, Oklahoma, Pennsylvania, Rhode Island, South Carolina, South Dakota, Tennessee, Utah, Vermont, Washington, West Virginia, and Wisconsin. See notes 63-66 *infra*.

[38] See Annot., 1 A.L.R.3d 822.

[39] *Id.* at 824.

entity is a limited partnership, the investor partners may not be able to deduct tax losses in excess of their equity investments if the general partner or partnership is personally liable on the construction loan note. However, since the real estate cannot generate depreciation deductions until after the improvements are constructed and become income-producing, the prospect of large tax losses for the limited partners during the construction period is unlikely, especially in light of the present tax rules, which require amortization of such front-end items as prepaid interest and construction period interest and taxes.[31]

[6] Lien Priority Over Land Mortgages and Mechanics' Liens

The construction lender will require that all existing mortgage indebtedness be satisfied and that all recorded liens be expunged prior to the closing of the construction loan, except that most lenders will advance to the borrower from the first draw whatever funds are needed to pay off the existing land mortgage, or the remaining purchase price payable for the land. Most lenders will not even accept a subordination of an existing mortgage, fearing that the junior lienholder might somehow be offensive to the permanent lender and/or disrupt the subsequent loan disbursement procedure.[32]

[a] Problems of Mechanics' and Materialmen's Liens

The greatest problem facing the construction lender as opposed to the permanent lender is protecting the lien priority of its loan disbursements against intervening mechanics' and materialmen's liens. Prudent construction lenders never fund the entire loan amount to the developer at the outset of the project; the future improvements and not the land represent the principal security for the loan. However, once construction has begun and various subcontractors furnish labor (mechanics) or supply materials (materialmen), their liens, when subsequently perfected, may intervene between the time the construction mortgage is given and recorded, and the time the loan funds are actually disbursed. If such intervening liens are accorded lien priority over the construction loan disbursements, and the construction lender is relegated to the status of a junior lienor, its security interest would be seriously threatened if the incomplete project should be sold at foreclosure. Moreover, prior to

---

[31] See discussion of nonrecourse financing at ¶ 1.05[4][b], and changes affecting construction loan borrowers under the 1976 Tax Reform Act at ¶ 1.05[2][d].

[32] See discussion at ¶ 3.04[7], and Article 5.4 of Form 3.4, and "THE SECURITY" language of Form 3.1 in Appendix B.

balance.[30] Accordingly, some banks will offer construction loans at below-market rates to developers who maintain balances comparable to those of business customers. Most commercial banks charge an interest rate geared to a floating prime or dealer commercial paper rate, and with the introduction of the computer in the bank's servicing department, floating prime is adjusted daily with each change in the prime rate.

Many developers attempt to negotiate a ceiling on the maximum rate charged; however, commercial bankers, who in the recent past have seen the prime rate fluctuate in and out of the double-digit range, often refuse to place a cap or ceiling on the interest rate. However, where the project consists of a residential condominium or multi-family housing (the "bread and butter" specialities of the savings and loan industry), a savings and loan association, sometimes acting as both the construction lender and the permanent lender, will settle for a fixed interest rate during the construction period. A savings and loan association is willing to do this for two reasons: (1) since its deposits are essentially long-term savings deposits, its cost of lending money is not, in the short run, tied to fluctuations in the prime rate[30a]; (2) it is essentially interested in making the permanent loan and, as an inducement, is sometimes willing to charge the borrower a lower interest rate for the construction financing.

Finally, most REITs charge more for construction financing than do banks and savings and loan associations (S&Ls), since REITs depend largely on bank borrowings as a funding source for obtaining their loanable funds.

[5] Recourse Financing

Recognizing that it is the rental income stream and not the solvency of the borrower that primes most mortgages, most permanent lenders will accept nonrecourse financing by accepting the inclusion of an exculpatory provision in the permanent mortgage or deed of trust note. However, since the construction lender cannot be protected by the value of the real estate until the raw land is transformed into income-producing property, it will generally insist that the construction loan be guaranteed by the borrower and/or other guarantors. If the borrowing

---

[30] For example, a one-year construction loan for $200,000, with an average outstanding balance of 50 percent, or $100,000, at an interest rate of 10 percent plus a 1.5 percent fee would yield a 13 percent (rather than 11.5 percent) gross yield to the bank.

[30a] This may no longer be the case as S&Ls are now competing with the money market funds, which are pegged to prime rate fluctuations.

If the construction loan amount justified by the value of the real estate and the amount of the takeout commitment is insufficient to cover the total land and construction costs, the developer must look outside the real estate for additional value. For example, the difference might be funded by equity capital, in which event the construction lender may require that those funds be used prior to any loan disbursement. Another solution might be to offer the construction lender additional protection in the form of a letter of credit, third-party guarantee, or some other outside collateral to secure the difference between the developer's projected costs and the original loan amount. Or, perhaps the developer might be able to obtain a "bridge" loan or some other interim secondary financing until he can refinance the permanent mortgage for a larger loan amount after the real estate has increased in value.[27] However, any such secondary financing would have to be approved by both the construction lender and the permanent lender.[28]

[4] Rate of Interest

Since the permanent takeout commitment is the funding source for payment of the construction loan, there is no amortization of principal during the term of the construction loan. Only monthly interest is payable and, in most cases, an interest reserve is built into the construction loan considered a "soft" cost of construction by the construction lender, the permanent lender, and the developer.[29]

Since demand deposits represent the least expensive funding source for commercial banks, the banks tend to give preferential treatment, both as to interest rates and availability of funds, to borrowers who maintain high average balances. Since the bank balances maintained by leverage-minded developers are usually smaller than those of business customers and the risks entailed in construction lending are so high, loan rates offered to real estate borrowers by commercial banks tend to be substantially higher than those offered on prime business loans. In part, this differential is effectuated by charging real estate borrowers front-end fees—in addition to the contract interest rate—that are computed as a percentage of the total amount to be advanced, rather than as a percentage of the average amount of the outstanding loan

---

[27] See discussion at ¶ 7.04[2].
[28] See discussion at ¶ 3.04[7], and Article 5.4 of Form 3.4 and Article 15 of Form 4.1 in Appendix B.
[29] See discussion at ¶ 4.04[5].

tial period of time. A cautious construction lender even with the safest takeout commitment and a most creditworthy developer will always satisfy itself that the proposed project is economically viable from a cost and market standpoint.[23]

[3] Loan Amount and Repayment of Principal

As noted earlier, unless the construction lender is also supplying the permanent financing, it will customarily rely upon a permanent lender's takeout commitment as the source of repayment of its construction loan. In such instances, the term of the construction loan will mature upon the expiration date of the takeout commitment, and there will be no amortization or repayment of principal during the term of the construction loan.

In addition, the amount of the construction loan will be geared to the amount of the permanent takeout commitment, provided that such loan amount does not exceed the lender's maximum loan-to-value ratio[24] and is justified based on the lender's determination of the value of the project upon completion.[25] Consequently, if the takeout commitment provides for the funding of a floor or minimum amount upon completion of construction, and a contingent or ceiling amount upon the achievement of a specified rent-roll or other requirement, most construction lenders will refuse to lend more than the floor amount in order to avoid the problem of gap financing (discussed earlier) that would arise if the requirement in the takeout commitment is not met.[26]

Some construction lenders will not lend more than the total estimated cost of construction, including both the "hard costs" of bricks and mortar and the "soft costs" of construction (e.g., construction period interest, cost of land, insurance premium, architect's fees), and the start-up costs of carrying the property until a positive cash flow is achieved. The rationale for this constraint is that the developer should not be able to mortgage out any money from the project until it is satisfactorily completed and the mortgage assigned to the permanent lender. However, other less conservative lenders take the position that there is nothing objectionable about letting developers mortgage out by contributing their overhead and profit to equity if the end result is an economically sound project.

---

[23] See discussion at ¶ 3.04[7].

[24] See discussion at ¶ 2.02[2][d].

[25] The mortgage loan appraisal procedure based on a capitalization of the estimated income from the project is discussed at ¶ 3.04[1].

[26] See discussion at ¶¶ 4.02[1], 3.04[2].

including the square footage of the improvements, floor plan arrangements, data on the installation and location of elevators and plumbing, heating, electrical, and air-conditioning facilities, and all the other details of construction; (4) the proposed rent-roll or list of prime leases indicating the identities of the tenants, rentals, and lease terms; and (5) a pro forma operating statement for the project, estimating its future operating income and expenses.

The application also requires the developer to furnish a cost breakdown, indicating the costs for the raw land, land improvements, construction costs of the proposed buildings, equipment and furnishing costs, architect's fees, permanent financing fees, and legal fees. All of these costs should be buttoned down with firm bids by the time of commitment, and in many cases, the first progress payment or draw under the building loan agreement is conditioned upon approval of such contracts.[21] If the developer is purchasing and not leasing the fee,[22] some construction lenders will insist upon receiving a copy of the contract, stipulating the purchase price, they do not want to advance to the developer on the first draw more than is needed to either satisfy the purchase price or to pay off any existing land mortgage. If the developer has owned the land for some time, some cautious lenders are not willing to fund to the developer the present fair market value of the land. Accordingly, this matter should be negotiated as a special condition in the commitment. One compromise may be for the lender not to reimburse the developer for the cost of the land until construction is completed or upon the funding of the permanent loan.

Finally, the lender wants to know the exact identity and organizational form of the borrower (corporation, partnership, land trust, etc.), and is also interested in the history and reputation of the developer, together with financial details. The lender will want to know whether the developer has the requisite equity funds, or secondary financing (if allowed)[23] to complete the project, what experience he has had in developing and managing income-producing properties, and whether he is solvent enough to "carry" the project if unusual construction problems (e.g., strikes or bankruptcy of subcontractors) arise. However, it is important to realize that a developer, no matter how solvent, could rarely afford to carry a large multimillion dollar project for a substan-

---

[21] See discussion at ¶ 4.02[7], and also Article 4(N) of Form 4.1 in Appendix B.
[22] See discussion of leasehold financing and split financing at ¶¶ 6.01, 8.09.

hazard insurance, preliminary survey, preliminary title report, the leases with prime tenants, the standard form of lease agreement to be executed with secondary tenants, the soils report, the architect's certification that recommendations contained in the soils report have been incorporated in the plans and specifications, the partnership agreement or articles of incorporation, and the form opinion letter of borrower's counsel regarding compliance with zoning and EPA-related environment regulations.[18]

Frequently, the commitment of the permanent lender will provide for the "holdback" of loan proceeds pending satisfaction of occupancy, completion, or rental achievement requirements. For example, the permanent takeout commitment may impose a leasing requirement that provides for the funding of a "floor" or minimum loan amount upon completion of construction and a "ceiling" or maximum loan amount upon the achievement by the developer of a stipulated rent-roll within a few months thereafter.[19] As a result, the construction lender must assure itself that there is ample time within which to rent the project, and that the project is capable of generating the specified rent-roll. However, if practical, a cautious construction lender should agree to lend no more than the floor amount; otherwise, if the rent-roll requirement is not met, and the permanent lender refuses to fund the "gap" amount, the construction lender may be forced to retain and subordinate its mortgage lien on such amount until, and unless, the developer is able to meet the leasing requirement or obtain gap financing to fund the remaining balance of the construction loan.[20]

[2] Facts About Project, Borrower, and Other Backup Data

The first portion of the application or application-commitment is generally informational and includes both the terms of the loan and a description of the contemplated project. In regard to the latter, the developer will be asked to furnish both a legal and street description of the property and to briefly describe the proposed or existing improvements. As backup data, the lender will want: (1) an area property map showing the location of the property relative to the rest of the community; (2) a site plan describing the configuration of the site, how much land is being utilized, and the location of the improvements located or to be located on the site; (3) a copy of the plans and specifications

---

[18] See discussion at ¶ 4.05.
[19] See discussion at ¶ 3.04[2].
[20] *Id.*

[1] Conformity with Requirements in Permanent Mortgage Loan Commitment

Of paramount concern to the construction lender is that the terms and conditions of the permanent lender's takeout commitment are complied with. Otherwise, once the construction period is over, the construction lender may be faced with the "Hobson's" choice of converting the construction loan into a long-term permanent one if the lender wishes to avoid a forced sale at foreclosure and the developer is unable or unwilling to find either interim[16] or permanent financing elsewhere. Accordingly, the construction loan commitment, the building loan agreement, and the construction deed of trust will all require that the borrower agree to comply with all the requirements of the permanent commitment.[17]

In addition, the construction lender should carefully scrutinize the requirements of the permanent loan commitment. The commitment of the permanent lender will frequently impose certain lease requirements. If, for example, the permanent lender requires that satisfactory net leases containing escalation clauses be executed with certain high-credit tenants as a precondition to closing a shopping center loan, the construction loan commitment should specifically incorporate this requirement, and, if possible, these leases with prime tenants should be executed and approved by the permanent lender before disbursement of the construction loan begins. Likewise, the plans and specifications, dates for commencement and completion of construction, and the beginning date for loan amortization should conform to the terms stipulated and agreed upon in the permanent commitment. Also, the construction lender should determine whether the expiration date set forth in the takeout commitment will give the developer sufficient time to complete the project. In that regard, the possibilities of delay caused by strikes, weather, shortages, or tenants' requirements should prompt the developer and construction lender to request of the permanent lender that a grace period be included to cover such contingencies.

Generally, by using a "pre-closed" form of buy-sell agreement, the construction lender will be able, before disbursements begin, to obtain the permanent lender's approval of the note and mortgage, or deed of trust, and most of the collateral items and documents, such as the

---

[16] If a developer finds himself in a situation where his construction loan is due but is unable to obtain permanent financing, he may try to obtain interim financing to bridge the time gap until he is able to get the permanent financing. See discussion at ¶ 7.04[2].

[17] See Article 4(M) of Form 4.1, a sample building loan agreement, and Article 4.12 of Form 3.4, a sample deed of trust in Appendix B.

commercial banks have begun to make open-end construction loans and are sometimes converting these loans upon completion of construction into permanent standby loans with five-to-ten-year terms. Such loans provide for a fixed rate of interest or a floating rate geared to prime, with a ceiling, and typically require the borrower to also pay additional interest in the form of a substantial equity kicker. In lieu of the prearranged permanent takeout commitment, these lenders look to prepayment of the open-end construction financing or standby loan when the mortgaged property is sold, or to when some permanent lender, such as an insurance company, makes an "on-the-spot" purchase of the loan (called "spot-funding") when it finds itself in a liquid position and wants to "open the window" and make a last minute addition to its mortgage loan investment portfolio. In fact, with the shortening of the terms and general unavailability of long-term lending at fixed rates, the large national banks may, by the use of the equity kicker, become the "long-term" interim lender to maintain construction financing.

Occasionally, a developer may be able to obtain construction financing based on a mere nonfundable 'standby' commitment. Also, when money is tight, a very solvent developer with heavy bargaining clout may be able to demand construction financing without a takeout commitment (in other words, an open-end commitment) so that he can take advantage of lower permanent mortgage interest rates in the future. Sometimes a construction lender will also waive the takeout requirement if the developer is able to furnish the construction lender with a guarantee of repayment based on outside collateral owned by the borrower or some affiliated entity.

¶ 4.02 TERMS AND CONDITIONS OF CONSTRUCTION FINANCING AS DETERMINED BY CONSTRUCTION LOAN APPLICATION-COMMITMENT

While many, if not most, lenders use separate loan applications and commitment forms, the recent trend among lenders has been to employ a single form that integrates the terms and conditions of both documents. References will be made in the ensuing discussion to both the sample building loan agreement (Form 4.1) and the sample deed of trust (Form 3.4). The latter incorporates the lender's requirements for both a permanent loan and a construction loan, and can consequently be used to secure either type of loan indebtedness. To avoid redundancy, the following discussion will emphasize only those terms and conditions in the loan commitment that are unique to construction lending and have not already been covered in Chapter 3.

operating successfully beyond contemplated projections. Any increase in market value because of inflation was reflected in the amount of the permanent loan, which was based on a loan-to-value ratio.

(3) As opposed to the normal bank construction loan of eighteen months, the construction loan issued by the REIT would have about a sixty-month term, with interest perhaps only during the first twenty-four months and with very nominal amortization during the last thirty-six months. This extended term allowed a developer not only to complete the project but also to bring it on stream and produce a positive cash flow. Unfortunately, many REITs that engaged in construction lending without a takeout are now in financial difficulty, caused in part by this lending approach and by market conditions. Most REITs made loans at a floating rate over prime. When prime reached 12 percent, many loans had rates of 16 to 17 percent, and few properties could carry such a rate. REITs with their backs to the wall either had to recast the term of the loan or take over the property.[15] Whether the REITs that survived will once again make such construction loans remains to be seen. However, a continuance of this type of loan will be on a sharply reduced basis.

In more recent times, with the continued unavailability of the "forward" permanent takeout commitment (one that is prearranged prior to obtaining construction financing) from insurance companies, many large "money-center" commercial banks are increasingly making open-end construction loans without a backup permanent takeout, or are making such construction loans in conjunction with fundable standby commitments.[15a] Since federally chartered or national commercial banks are permitted, provided that they receive no interest or estate in real property,[15b] to demand additional interest in the form of an equity kicker geared to a percentage of the borrower's gross or net income from the mortgaged property, some of the larger national

---

[15] Shulkin, Commercial Bank Construction Lending, Federal Reserve Bank of Boston Research Report No. 47 (1970). The author's correct observation that the demand for bank construction financing is generally inelastic was not applicable to construction loans made by REITs, since, as opposed to the eighteen-month bank construction loan, interest on the REIT loan fully funded for a sixty-month term could be astronomical!

[15a] See discussion at ¶ 3.07[2].

[15b] See Comptroller of the Currency Interpretive Ruling 7.7312 under the Federal Reserve Act. See also the discussion of equity kickers at ¶ 3.04[3].

Chapter 3 at ¶ 3.04, let us assume that on January 1, 1979, Dan Development Co. obtains from Ace Insurance Co. its commitment to make a permanent $2 million mortgage loan on or before March 1, 1981. This is the first stage. Ordinarily, the second stage in the lending cycle occurs when the borrower, on the strength of the permanent takeout commitment, obtains a construction loan commitment from a commercial bank or other interim lender (unless the same lender is furnishing both the construction and permanent financing). Dan Development obtains a $2 million construction loan. Third, the construction loan is closed when the construction loan note, mortgage, and building loan agreement are executed by the borrower. In some instances, all three parties, the borrower, the construction lender, and the permanent lender also execute a buy-sell agreement (as in our hypothetical case, prior to March 29, 1979) as required by both the permanent and the construction loan commitments.[11] After the construction loan mortgage and collateral security documents are recorded, the fourth stage begins, at which time the construction lender starts to disburse the loan and construction commences (as in our hypothetical case, on or before March 29, 1979), pursuant to both commitments and in accordance with the building loan agreement.[12] Fifth and last, when the project is completed and all the terms of the takout commitment have been met, the permanent loan is closed when the construction loan is assigned to the permanent lender, pursuant to the buy-sell agreement (as in our hypothetical case,[13] on or before March 1, 1981).

[3] Open-end Construction Lending Without Permanent Takeout

In 1968,[14] unhampered by state banking law, REITs began making a substantial volume of construction loans without a backup permanent takeout. While the interest rates were higher than those charged by commercial banks, there were several advantages in procuring a loan from a REIT:

(1) The lead time for commencing and completing commitments was shortened by deleting the time spent on shopping and procuring a takeout;
(2) A developer had more leverage in obtaining a permanent loan on a completed project. Indeed, the permanent loan could be larger than a prior commitment takeout if the project was

---

[11] See discussion at ¶¶ 3.04[4], 4.05.
[12] See discussion at ¶ 4.04.
[13] See discussion at ¶ 4.05.
[14] See discussion at ¶ 2.05[5].

whether the project is being completed on schedule and in accordance with approved plans and specifications, and if progress payments are being used properly to pay off the claims of subcontractors furnishing either labor (mechanics) or materials (materialmen). In that regard, construction lenders have become specialists in dealing with such unique and complex problems as cost overruns, mechanics' and materialmen's liens, and construction delays caused by labor shortages or shortages of materials.

[1] Takeout Commitment as Bridging Mechanism

Because construction and permanent financing are for the most part supplied by two different lending groups, a device called the "permanent takeout commitment" has evolved. A permanent lender agrees to purchase the construction loan from the construction lender and issue its long-term mortgage to the developer, once construction is completed and the real estate becomes income-producing. From the perspective of the construction lender, the takeout commitment obviates the need to commit its loan funds on a long-term basis and eliminates the economic risk that the completed project cannot be sold or rented because of market changes, improper pricing, etc. Conversely, the permanent lender is relieved of dealing with those risks— cost overruns, mechanics' liens, strikes, and shortages of materials—that arise during the construction period and winds up with a long-term loan investment secured by the rental income stream from the completed property. Consequently, with few exceptions, if the construction lender is not also supplying the permanent financing,[8] the construction lender will demand that the developer secure a takeout commitment from an approved permanent lender as a precondition to supplying the construction financing for the project.[9] In that regard, construction lenders should be aware at all times of the availability of takeout financing, compliance with the requirements of the permanent lender contained in the latter's takeout commitment, and such problems as use of "gap financing" by the borrower during a development or "rent-up" period.[10]

[2] Construction Financing as Second Stage in Commercial Lending Cycle

Customarily, there are five essential stages in the financing of new income-producing real estate. Returning to our hypothetical case in

---

[8] *Id.*
[9] But see discussion at ¶ 4.01[3].
[10] See discussion at ¶ 3.04[2].

Commercial banks constitute the principal source of short-term construction financing of commercial real estate where the developer has a "takeout" commitment from a permanent lender. By April 1, 1978, construction loan holdings by commercial banks amounted to $22 billion or 37 percent of the total holdings by all major private lending groups.[2] Most commercial banks derive their loanable funds from short-term demand and time deposits, which are subject to the vagaries of seasonal fluctuations and swings in the business cycle.[3] Therefore, banks prefer to engage in short-term construction financing because of their need to maintain liquidity to meet unexpected drains on their cash deposit reserves. By contrast, permanent lenders, such as life insurance companies and savings and loan associations, are able to concentrate on long-term mortgage lending because their funding sources are of a more stable and permanent nature.[4] Also, some commercial banks and mortgage companies prefer to make short-term loans and maintain a brisk turnover in their real estate loan portfolio so that, as "loan correspondents" for permanent lenders, they can earn origination fees on construction loans sold and assigned to the permanent lender. In addition, these correspondents will receive a yearly servicing fee (ranging between one-quarter to one-half of one percent of the face amount of the committed loan) from the permanent lender as compensation for collecting and remitting to the permanent lender the net mortgage payments, after payment of taxes and insurance premiums, with the escrows collected by the correspondent from the borrower and maintained as balances by the correspondent.[5]

In addition, construction lenders such as commercial banks and short-term REITs[6] and lenders supplying the construction and permanent financing on a single project[7] have developed the requisite expertise to monitor the construction activities of a developer and determine

---

[2] See Exhibit 2.1 in Chapter 2.

[3] See discussion at ¶ 2.02[2][a].

[4] The chief sources of loanable funds for life insurance companies are regular repayments of existing investments and insurance premiums, which for the most part are of a semipermanent contractual nature. See discussion at ¶ 2.02[1][a].

[5] See discussion at ¶ 2.02[3].

[6] Since 1974, most short-term construction and development (C&D) REITs that specialize in construction financing have substantially curtailed their lending activities.

[7] Savings and loan associations, long-term mortgage REITs, and, recently, a few daring insurance companies, such as Equitable Life Assurance Society and Prudential Insurance Company, have on occasion supplied construction financing to borrowers as an inducement to obtaining the permanent financing on a project.

         [ii] Reorganization of the Rehabilitation Chapters.... 4-38
         [iii] Treatment of Nonrecourse Claims as Recourse.... 4-42
         [iv] Automatic Stay............................... 4-43
         [v] Expanded Power of Trustee Regarding Executory
             Contracts and Unexpired Leases................ 4-43
         [vi] Right to Sell, Lease, or Mortgage Debtor's
             Property 4-45
      [13] Other Terms and Conditions of Commitment............. 4-47
¶ 4.03 Closing the Construction Loan 4-48
      [1] Construction Loan Note............................... 4-50
      [2] Construction Mortgage............................... 4-52
         [a] Cross-Default Provisions 4-52
         [b] Future Advance Clause............................ 4-52
         [c] Release Clause 5-53
         [d] Prohibition of Cash Distributions.................. 4-53
¶ 4.04 Disbursement of Construction Loan Funds Under
      Building Loan Agreement.................................. 4-54
      [1] Function of Building Loan Agreement.................... 4-54
      [2] Borrower's Initial Representations and Warranties 4-55
      [3] Predisbursement Requirements 4-56
      [4] Payment of Loan Advances........................... 4-59
      [5] Cost Overruns and Other Changes During
         Construction Period 4-61
      [6] The Final Loan Advance 4-63
      [7] Construction Lender's Liability for
         Construction Defects................................. 4-64
      [8] Construction Lender's Remedies Against
         Defaulting Developer................................ 4-66

¶ 4.05 Buy-Sell Agreement and the Final Takeout Stage 4-69

¶ 4.01 ROLE OF CONSTRUCTION FINANCING IN COMMERCIAL LENDING CYCLE

In this country, most institutional lenders specialize in either short-term construction financing or long-term permanent financing because of differences in their funding sources, external regulation of their investment portfolios,[1] and the fact that different problems and risk factors arise during the construction period and thereafter when the completed property is being rented and managed by the borrower-developer.

---

[1] For example, local law in most jurisdictions forbids life insurance companies from making construction loans unless made in conjunction with permanent financing. E.g., N.Y. Ins. Law § 81(6)(a)(3) (McKinney Supp. 1979).

Chapter 4
CONSTRUCTION FINANCING

	Page
¶ 4.01 Role of Construction Financing in Commercial Lending Cycle	4- 2
[1] Takeout Commitment as Bridging Mechanism	4- 4
[2] Construction Financing as Second Stage in Commercial Lending Cycle	4- 4
[3] Open-end Construction Lending Without Permanent Takeout	4- 5
¶ 4.02 Terms and Conditions of Construction Financing as Determined by Construction Loan Application-Commitment	4- 7
[1] Conformity With Requirements in Permanent Mortgage Loan Commitment	4- 7
[2] Facts About Project, Borrower, and Other Backup Data	4- 9
[3] Loan Amount and Repayment of Principal	4-11
[4] Rate of Interest	4-12
[5] Recourse Financing	4-13
[6] Lien Priority Over Land Mortgages and Mechanics' Liens	4-14
[a] Problems of Mechanics' and Materialmen's Liens	4-14
[i] Lien Priorities Under State Law	4-15
[ii] Doctrine of "Obligatory" vs. "Optional" Advances	4-16
[iii] Equitable Lien Doctrine and the "Stop Notice" Statute	4-19
[b] Protection for the Construction Lender Against Mechanics' Liens	4-20
[i] Title Insurance	4-20
[ii] Labor and Material Payment Bond	4-24
[iii] Developer-Contractor Agreement	4-24
[7] Approval of Contractors and Building Contract	4-25
[8] Assurances That Project Will Be Completed	4-26
[a] Holdback of Loan Funds	4-26
[b] Payment and Performance Bonds	4-28
[c] Construction Disbursement Programs	4-32
[d] Letters of Credit	4-32
[e] Contractor's Guarantee	4-33
[9] Execution of Building Loan Agreement	4-34
[10] Approval of Architect and Payment of Fees	4-34
[11] Builder's Risk Insurance	4-34
[12] Bankruptcy of Borrower	4-37
[a] Language of the Loan Commitment	4-37
[b] Implications of the Bankruptcy Reform Act of 1978 for Real Estate Financing	4-37
[i] Broadening of Bankruptcy Jurisdiction	4-38

any corporate parent guarantees are required and that appropriate corporate resolutions are appended to each lease.

☐ The lender will require forms from the tenants indicating their legal acceptance of the premises and establishing the lease and rent commencement dates. These must be obtained when construction is completed.

☐ A final inspection of the property must be made and a certificate of completion furnished to the lender. A letter must be obtained from the appraiser indicating that the project meets the conditions of his original appraisal. The appraiser may also need leasing data if he conditioned the value estimate on anticipated rents.

☐ If some portion of construction is delayed, you may have to prepare and execute an escrow agreement so that funds may be held in escrow until all work is completed.

☐ A satisfactory hazard insurance policy, with the first annual premium paid, must be obtained and delivered to the permanent lender. The loan commitment must be checked to determine the minimum insurance company rating acceptable to the lender.

☐ Obtain copies of occupancy permits issued by the local authority when construction is completed. Also, it is advisable to obtain letters from the utility companies confirming that service is available and acknowledging payment by the mortgagor of applicable initial charges.

☐ Prepare and execute any joint-use documents that may be required if the project was built in stages, with an earlier phase financed by a different lender.

☐ Take steps to dedicate roads or other land to the state, if such action is required. This type of situation is time-consuming, and you must allow for any delays.

☐ Obtain the required evidence from the appropriate state commission that the mortgagor is authorized to do business in the state and that its charter is current.

☐ File environmental impact statements if they are required. Find out if pertinent obligations assumed by the developer have been met.

☐ Check to see if other miscellaneous documents are required for your specific closing. Examples might include a common-wall agreement, keyman insurance, off-site easements, or, if the lender wants his security instrument subordinated to certain leases, a subordination agreement.[345]

---

[345] See Waldron, "Conscientious Effort Needed for Timely Closings on Income Loans," 36 *The Mortgage Banker* 15, 16, 18 (1976).

within two weeks before closing. Other permanent lenders require their in-house appraiser to inspect the property also. The developer's attorney should make certain that these arrangements have been made by the permanent lender so as not to hold up the closing. The last divisional category are documents to be prepared by the attorney for the developer, for example, the attorney's opinion letter.[342] He should make certain that drafts of these closing requirements are prepared and submitted to the permanent lender's counsel for its review well in advance of the closing date.

Where the permanent lender is purchasing the construction lender's documents by assignment, the permanent lender will require, in addition to the foregoing documents and the assignment of the loan documents, an acknowledgment from the construction lender that the loan is current and not in default, as well as an estoppel certificate from the borrower.[343]

Finally, three or four days before the settlement date, counsel for the permanent lender will frequently submit a closing disbursement instruction letter to the title company or some other outside closing agent.[344]

[3] Checklist for Closing Permanent Loan

- ☐ The mortgagor should review the note, security instrument, lease assignments, and guaranty (all prepared by the lender) prior to closing. Do this early, because review of these documents may require some time.
- ☐ Obtain the title insurance binder and boundary survey, making sure the title company supplies photocopies of any easements, covenants, or restrictions of record. The lender will need these to prepare the security instrument and to assess the effects of any encumbrance or exceptions.
- ☐ Request, at least 45 days before closing, the building location survey, which also should depict the location of all easements. The lender also may want a certification that the engineer is covered by errors and omissions (E&O) insurance.
- ☐ Gather the fully executed leases for review by the lender early. Use and occupancy clauses, renewal options, percentage rents, common areas contributions, etc., may require modifications which take time to discuss, negotiate, and put into effect. Check to see if

---

[342] A sample letter is at Form 3.9 in Appendix B.
[343] A sample estoppel certificate is at Form 3.11 in Appendix B.
[344] A sample letter is reproduced at Form 3.8 in Appendix B.

[2] Documentation at Closing

The next division of work encompasses certain loan closing documents, such as the certified inventory statement, tenants' acceptance letters, architect's certificate, and estoppel certificates prepared by the permanent lender's counsel.[339] These documents, together with the assignment of leases and notices of assignment,[340] must be executed at or near the time of closing by third parties unrelated to the developer. Many times, a tenant will take weeks before executing such an acceptance letter. It would be embarrassing for the attorney representing the developer to tell his client that the closing cannot take place until the architect, who drafted the plans and specifications, returns from a three-month vacation in the Amazon, and executes the architect's certificate. Before the occupancy leases (and in the case of a leasehold mortgage, the ground lease, as well) are executed, the developer's attorney should obtain early approval from the permanent lender so that the lender, prime tenants, and ground lessor will be able to work out their differences and avoid any delay in the closing of the permanent loan. Another area which he must coordinate carefully are those closing documents to be prepared by third parties—the hazard insurance policy, the title policy, and the survey. It is appropriate and beneficial for the developer's attorney to send a copy of that part of the permanent commitment pertaining to the requirements for title insurance, hazard insurance, and survey to the respective parties so that they can become completely familiar with what is required of them by the permanent lender. With regard to the title company, the developer's attorney should make certain that months in advance a title binder is sent to the permanent lender so that the permanent lender may review it and, where necessary, require endorsements to make certain that there will be no surprises or problems with the final title insurance policy to be issued at the closing. By using a pre-closed form of buy-sell agreement, the developer's attorney will be able to obtain early approval of the note and mortgage (or deed of trust) and most of the collateral documentation, such as the hazard insurance policy and the preliminary title report.[341]

Sometimes there may be a breakdown in communications between the real estate department and the office of the general counsel of the permanent lender because many permanent lenders require the real estate department to review and make a final inspection of the property

---

[339] See Forms 3.7, 3.10, 3.11 and 3.13 in Appendix B. See discussion of these documents at ¶ 3.04.

[340] Discussed at ¶ 3.08[4][i]. See Forms 3.5 and 3.6 in Appendix B.

[341] See discussion at ¶ 4.05.

of the permanent commitment, he should be aware of the various parties involved in the permanent loan closing and develop a working relationship with them. Many times, a permanent closing will be helped along by the title company which often acts as escrow agent for the permanent lender, by counsel for the construction lender (who is interested in seeing that the loan funds supplied by the construction lender are repaid as quickly as possible), and last but not least, by counsel for the permanent lender.

Many permanent lenders will use their in-house staff of attorneys to close the loan. Some will rely completely on special and local counsel, and others, in effect, will use their in-house corporate attorneys together with special and local counsel selected by the permanent lender. There are advantages and disadvantages to each of three methods employed by the permanent lender. In the case where the permanent lender is using its in-house staff of attorneys only, the borrower does not have to pay the out-of-pocket legal fees incurred by the permanent lender. Just as important, the in-house attorney is very experienced in the loan closing procedures. Generally, special counsel can be helpful when an unusual question or problem arises with regard to local law. However, many of these attorneys have long represented the interests of the permanent lender and are just as familar with the closing requirements and procedures involved with the closing as would be an in-house attorney for the permanent lender. The obvious disadvantage in using special counsel is that the legal fees must be paid for by the developer. More importantly, since there is one more person who must be satisfied that the closing requirements have been met and the funding is in proper order, there is the possibility of a loan closing being unduly dragged out, creating expense and ill will on the part of all. One adage that should faithfully be kept is that the developer's attorney should not wait until the last minute and hope that the permanent loan will close itself. Even when started well in advance, permanent loan closings tend to be postponed and extended.

In most permanent loan closings, there is a division of responsibility required by the permanent lender's counsel. Usually, it is the responsibility of the permanent lender's counsel to prepare the loan documents, although in some cases the permanent lender will require that the title company prepare the documents; accordingly, the developer's attorney should be friendly, but as persistent as possible and make certain that the permanent loan documents are prepared several months in advance. This will give the attorney and his client an opportunity to review the documents and request changes where necessary and appropriate.

(f) Mortgagor represents and warrants that all improvements and leased space demised and let pursuant to each lease covering the whole or any part of said premises have been completed to the satisfaction of the lessee, that lessee has accepted possession of such leased space and is open for business, that all rents and other charges due and payable under any such lease have been paid, that none has been prepaid, except as expressly described under such lease, and that there is no existing default or breach of covenant or condition on the part of the lessee under any such lease.

(3) Mortgagor will give Mortgagee immediate notice by certified mail of any notice of default or notice of cancellation received from any tenant.

(4) Any default in any of the terms, conditions or covenants in any assignment of lessor's interest in leases given as additional security for this loan shall constitute an event of default hereunder.

(5) All representations made by it in the several occupancy leases are true.

(6) It will not expand or extend the Shopping Center except with the written consent of the Mortgagee.

(7) It will not construct, restore, add to or alter any building or other improvement in the Shopping Center or any extension thereof, nor consent to or permit any such construction, restoration, addition or alteration without Mortgagee's written consent unless it is legally obligated to do so by an express provision in one of the several leases, and even in the latter event to obtain Mortgagee's prior written approval of such construction, restoration, addition or alteration or of the form and substance of any consent it proposes to give.

(8) It will grant no parking rights in the Shopping Center other than those provided for in existing leases except with Mortgagee's written consent.

¶ 3.09 CLOSING THE PERMANENT LOAN

[1] Parties at Closing

The primary concern of the attorney representing the developer is to orchestrate a permanent loan closing as smoothly and efficiently as possible. In many cases, the developer is paying a higher rate of interest on the construction loan and can save a substantial amount of funds by closing quickly on the permanent loan. From the outset, upon issuance

[5] Special Mortgagor's Rider for Shopping Center Loans

In the case of a permanent mortgage loan to be secured by a shopping center, the lender will frequently insist that the following special provisions be attached as a rider to the regular mortgage or deed of trust form.[338]

Mortgagor covenants and agrees:

(1) That Mortgagee shall have access to and the right to inspect said premises at all reasonable times.
(2) (a) To faithfully perform the lessor's covenants under any subsiding and future leases affecting said premises, and neither do, nor neglect to do, nor permit to be done, anything other than pursuing the enforcement of the terms of such leases in the exercise of the lessor's remedies thereunder following default on the part of any lessee in the performance of its proscribed obligations, which may cause the modification or termination of any of said leases, or of the obligations of any lessee or any person claiming through such lessee, or which may diminish or impair the value of any lease, or the rents provided for therein, or the interest of the lessor or of Mortgagee therein or thereunder;
   (b) To permit no assignment of any of said leases or any subletting thereunder, unless the right to sublet or assign is expressly reserved by the lessee, nor to anticipate for more than one month any rents that may become collectible under such lease;
   (c) That mortgagor will not execute a mortgage or create or permit a lien which may be or become superior to any subsisting leases affecting said premises;
   (d) To notify Mortgagee promptly of any accidental damage to said premises in excess of $1,000;
   (e) That if any part of the automobile parking areas included within said premises is taken by condemnation or before said areas are otherwise reduced, Mortgagor will provide parking facilities in kind, size, and location to comply with all leases, and before making any contract therefor will furnish to Mortgagee satisfactory assurance of completion thereof free of liens and in conformity with all governmental zoning ordinances and regulations;

---

[338] Some of these provisions are included in Form 3.5 in Appendix B.

mortgagee might be turning an absolute assignment into a mere conditional pledge.[333] This would defeat the mortgagee's subsequent right to the rents against a trustee in bankruptcy or some other intervening claimant.

[j] Miscellaneous Covenants

A variety of clauses is included in a final section titled "miscellaneous covenants." They stipulate what loan expenses must be paid by the mortgagor; that certain actions by the mortgagee will not constitute any warranty or representation; the way in which notices will be given; and the beneficiary's right to perform certain obligations. Also included are clauses dealing with covenants running with the land; the application of the terms of the security documents to all successors and assigns; severability modification counterparts; applicable law; no release in the case of default; the nature of the loan; status of any clauses that would invalidate the document; headings; and deed to secure future advances[334]; and use of the trust.

Beneficiary's Right to Perform the Obligations. This provision allows the mortgagee to perform cetain obligations of the mortgagor and to add the cost incurred in curing the mortgagor's default to the outstanding indebtedness of the mortgage loan. Normally, at common law, any amount the mortgagee expended for taxes and insurance premiums (if the mortgage requires the mortgagor to keep the premises insured) due and owing on the property could be added to the mortgage indebtedness.[335] However, the mortgagee should be aware that in certain states, any sums expended to protect the property could be subordinate to any intervening mechanic's liens.[336]

Covenants Running With the Land. The reasoning behind the inclusion of this provision holds that there is some doubt among authorities as to whether a covenant to insure runs with the land.[337]

---

[333] See Malsman v. Brandler, 230 Cal. App. 2d 922, 924, 41 Cal. Rptr. 438, 440 (1964).

[334] See discussion of this clause at ¶ 4.03[2][b].

[335] Osborne (1970), note 188 *supra* §§ 172, 173.

[336] E.g., Horrigan v. Wellmuth, 77 Mo. 542, 546 (1883); Sidenberg v. Ely, 90 N.Y. 257, 267 (1882); see also Osborne, (1970), note 188 *supra*, § 173.

[337] See Burby, *Real Property* 154 (3rd ed. 1965).

executing and cannot convey ipso facto to the mortgagee the right to rents, which is an incident of title; a contrary holding, the court said, would subvert the rule followed in New York that a mortgage is merely a lien and cannot operate as a transfer of title. Consequently, such an assignment would become effective only upon foreclosure or upon the appointment of a receiver.[331]

It should also be noted that when a mortgagor is contemplating bankruptcy in a state which allows the activation of an assignment of leases and rents, the mortgagee must move quickly to perfect its assignment effectively; otherwise, the trustee in bankruptcy may get to the rents first and collect them for the account of the mortgagor.[332] The same problem might also arise in the event of default, where junior security holders, judgment creditors, or other assignees intervene before the first mortgagee takes action to activate its assignment of leases and rents.

Finally, it is important to note that in some states, such as Maryland, the phrase "additional security" is customarily placed in the assignment of lease and rents to avoid paying an additional transfer tax. By inserting this language as a concession to the mortgagor, the

---

[331] 62 Misc. 2d 391, 396, 308 N.Y.S.2d 436, 441 (1970).

[332] Prior to the Bankruptcy Reform Act of 1978 the majority of the federal circuit courts of appeal permitted the mortgagee to take the same steps to activate its lien on the rents and profits from mortgaged income-producing property constituting a part of the mortgagor's bankrupt estate as would have been allowed under state law had there been no bankruptcy. Comment, "The Mortgagee's Right to Rents & Profits Following Petition in Bankruptcy," 60 Iowa L. Rev. 1388, 1399 (1975). This majority rule has been confirmed by the Supreme Court in Butner v. United States, 99 S. Ct. 914, 919 (1979). Accordingly, the attorney for the mortgagee should research the applicable state law to determine what steps might be necessary to enforce and protect the mortgagee's right to collect the rents upon default under its assignment of rents and leases. However, assuming such compliance with local law, is the mortgagee entitled to rents during a bankruptcy reorganization? The Supreme Court in the *Butner* decision did not address this issue. However, in light of the emphasis on a debtor-in-possession and trustee's right to sell and lease the property under § 365(c)(2) of the Bankruptcy Reform Act of 1978, a likely approach with respect to disposition of rents during reorganization would be the way in which the First Circuit resolved the matter in *In re* Colonial Realty Inv. Co., 516 F.2d 154 (1975), under prior bankruptcy law. In that case involving a Chapter XII proceeding, the court dispossessed a mortgagee in possession, notwithstanding that Massachusetts law treated a mortgagee as the legal owner of the mortgaged property but held that while rental income from secured property could be used to defray expenses other than those like operating costs, taxes, mortgage payments that directly benefit the mortgagee, such other expenses must be reasonably expected to be of some benefit to the mortgagee in order to be charged against the rental income. *Id.* at 164.

mortgagee's simply serving notice on the tenants to pay rent.[329] However, courts in many lien-theory states have held that such a clause only creates a security interest, and further affirmative action is required of the mortgagee before he can collect the rents; that is, he must either take possession of the property himself or get a receiver appointed.[330] For example, in *Ganbaum v. Rockwood Realty Corp.,* it was held in New York, a lien-theory state, that an assignment of rents is not self-

---

[329] E.g., Randel v. Jersey Mortgage Inv. Co., 306 Pa. 1, 7, 158 A. 865, 866 (1932).

[330] The U.S. district court for Missouri stated:

After default the mortgagee has the right to possession of the mortgaged property for the purpose of collecting the rents and profits and applying them to the discharge of the mortgage debt, but that he is not entitled to the rents "until the mortgagee enters into the actual possession or takes some equivalent action." *In re* Stuckenberg, 374 F. Supp. 15, 17 (E.D.Mo.), aff'd 505 F.2d 1250 (8th Cir. 1974).

In applying California state law, the U.S. Court of Appeals for the Ninth Circuit, *In re Ventura-Louise Properties,* said:

Where a mortgage includes the rents as a portion of the property pledged to secure the debt (additional security as alleged by appellee here), only a security interest passes, and until the mortgagee (lender) obtains lawful possession, the mortgagor (debtor) in possession may collect the rents as they fall due. To perfect a claim to the rents thereto the mortgagee must actually acquire possession of the mortgaged property by consent or lawful procedure, or secure the appointment of a receiver.

In distinguishing the earlier case of *In re Hotel St. James, Co.,* which disallowed a mortgagee's right to the rents, the court noted that the pledge clause in the *Hotel St. James* mortgage failed to use the word "assignment" or "transfer" or any other indication that an assignment of the rents had actually taken place. Courts in other jurisdictions have also held that the mortgagee must take some affirmative or overt action such as taking possession or having a receiver appointed as a precondition to its collection of rents under the assignment instrument. See, e.g., Bornstein v. Somerson, 341 So. 2d 1043, 1049 (Fla. 1977); Wuorinen v. City Fed. Sav. & Loan Ass'n, 52 Wis. 2d 722, 730, 191 N.W. 2d, 27, 31 (1971); Dick & Reuteman Co. v. Jem Realty Co., 225 Wis. 428, 437, 274 N.W. 416, 422 (1937); Hall v. Goldsworthy, 136 Kan. 247, 254, 14 P.2d 659, 662 (1932).

It requires the mortgagee's prior written consent to any amendment, modification, termination, or surrender of the lease; prepayment in excess of one month's rent or subordination of the lease to any lien subordinate to the mortgage. It also provides that, in the event of tenant's default under the lease, the mortgagee shall be entitled to the proceeds of any settlement or collection on any judgment secured by the mortgagor. It also requires the mortgagee's participation or consent to any unilateral proceeding on the lease which might lead to termination.

The three-party agreement may toll the running of the statute of limitations until the mortgagee has actual notice of tenant's default under the lease; may include any use and occupancy payments and damages caused by rejection of the lease by a trustee in bankruptcy, as well as condemnation award proceeds; and may include provisions for additional amortization of the mortgage by the mortgagor in the event of premature termination of the lease and the mortgagor's inability, within a reasonable time, to secure a creditworthy replacement tenant paying substantially equivalent rent.

In utilizing the three-party agreement, the mortgagee may subject to the lien of the first mortgage all the mortgagor's rights as lessor under existing, as well as future, leases and make it a default under the mortgage for the mortgagor, as landlord, to default under the lease or under the three-party agreement.

(4) By far the most prevalent type of assignment is that exemplified by the sample assignment instrument (discussed below), which furnishes the lender with almost the same protection of an absolute *in praesenti* assignment without depriving the mortgagor of his control of the income from the property prior to any default.[328] As noted earlier, the mortgagor, while irrevocably assigning all of its title and interest to the leases and the income derived therefrom to the mortgagee, retains a present license to collect the rents and income for so long as there is no default. In the event of default, the license terminates and the mortgagee is entitled to collect the rents.

However, the enforceability of such a provision in the mortgage itself or in a separate assignment instrument depends upon local law. In title-theory states and most lien-theory states, an assignment of leases and rents empowers the mortgagee to collect rents accruing prior to the foreclosure sale on the theory that they are part of the security for the mortgage indebtedness. Some courts in these states have held that accrued rent can be assigned automatically, like any other "chose in action"; accordingly, the assignment is activated on default by the

---

[328] Reproduced at Form 3.5 in Appendix B.

obtaining the rental income? The answers to these questions are found in the applicable state law, and the nature of the particular assignment in question. There are essentially four methods of assignment:

(1) The simplest and least effective is a mere pledge of rents contained within the mortgage. A pledge of rents is viewed by most state courts as but incidental security and something less than an assignment.[326]

(2) At the other extreme is the absolute and unconditional *in praesenti* assignment of rents and income, which is effective and recorded on the closing of the first mortgage loan. In this type of assignment, the mortgagor, during the term of the mortgage, actually assigns the income stream directly to the mortgagee, who applies it to the debt service, sometimes with the proviso that absent default any rents not so used will be turned over to the mortgagor. This would protect the mortgagee against cancellation or adverse modifications of the leases by the mortgagor and his tenants, and would eliminate the difficulties of activiating a non-*in praesenti* assignment (as discussed below) in order to protect the permanent lender, as first mortgagee, against the claims of junior security holders, judgment creditors, and other assignees that may have intervened after the loan closing but prior to such activation of the non-*in praesenti* assignment. However, these assignments are atypical and are used only in special circumstances due to a serious practical problem—namely, the mortgagor's objection to loss of control over the income from his property prior to default. For example, this absolute assignment frequently appears in connection with real estate projects where the primary security is a valuable lease, and the underlying property secured by the mortgage is merely incidental to the lender's security.[327]

(3) Another approach that is beginning to appear in high-credit lease situations is the three-party agreement, signed by the mortgagee, the mortgagor, and the tenant, and recorded when the lease is recorded.

---

[326] In a leading case, Paramount Bldg. & Loan Ass'n v. Sacks, 107 N.J. Eq. 328, 332, 152 A. 457, 459 (1930), the Court of Chancery held that a mortgagee is not entitled to rents accruing prior to demand, entry into possession, or appointment of receiver, where rents are merely pledged and not assigned. The court stated:
> There is a marked difference between a pledge and an assignment. Ordinarily, a pledge is considered as a bailment, and delivery of possession, actual or constructive, is essential, but transfer of title is not. On the other hand, by assignment, title is transferred, although possession need not be.

Id. at 331-332, 152 A. at 458.

[327] See discussion of high-credit lease financing at ¶ 8.05.

this "anti-milking" clause was designed to prevent a recurrence of what happened in the 1930's, when mortgagors facing foreclosure accepted lump-sum payments from tenants in exchange for canceling their lease obligations. The purpose today is to prevent the landlord-mortgagor from eliminating rental income on which the lender relied in making the loan for a given amount. Moreover, cancellation or modification of a prime lease by the mortgagor could inadvertently violate a co-tenancy requirement or could cause some default under the lease agreements with secondary tenants.

To further protect the rental stream from these high-credit leases, the mortgagor also covenants and agrees to perform faithfully his obligations as landlord (Section 11 of sample assignment), and agrees not to consent to any assignment or subletting without the mortgagee's consent (Section 10 of sample assignment). Otherwise, the leasehold could be transferred to a substitute tenant who is a poor credit risk.[323]

Notice to Tenants. Upon recordation of the assignment of leases and rents, all subsequent tenants of the premises are put on notice that their leases cannot be altered, modified, or changed without the prior written consent of the mortgagee, and that an alteration, modification, or change without the mortgagee's consent will be of no force and effect. The tenant is also made aware that the mortgagor-landlord cannot collect rents in advance and that if a tenant pays rent in advance and the mortgagor defaults, the mortgagee, upon obtaining possession or title, can collect those rents as due and owing from the tenant.[324] For those leases that are prior to the recordation of the assignment of leases and rents, a mortgagee will require the tenant to execute an attornment agreement[325] whereby the tenant agrees that it will not modify or alter the lease without obtaining the consent of the mortgagee and that, in the event of default and foreclosure, it will attorn to the mortgagee as its new landlord.

Right to Collect the Rents Prior to Foreclosure. In a judicial foreclosure, where the actual foreclosure might take several months, if not a year or more after the initial default, lenders are always concerned about immediately securing the rental income stream. What right does the mortgagee have after default but prior to foreclosure to secure the rental income stream against the mortgagor, its creditors, and perhaps a trustee in bankruptcy of the mortgagor who is also interested in

---

[323] The enforceability of this type of assignment is discussed below.
[324] See notice form at Form 3.6 in Appendix B.
[325] See attornment form at Form 6.4 in Appendix B.

¶ 3.08[4][i]

This assignment of everything issuing out of the property with specified exceptions is *in praesenti* on its face, but made subject to a license granted by the assignee to the assignor to collect and receive all of the rents, as provided in the assignment. The license is specifically stated to be in effect only so long as there is no default by the assignor in the payment of any indebtedness or any other obligation of the note and mortgage or deed of trust or under the leases. The license permits the licensor to collect—but not prior to accrual—all of the rents arising out of the leases or any renewals, extensions, or replacements thereof. The assignor covenants that he shall receive such rents and hold them as a trust fund to be applied as required by the assignee and lists the order of priority in which the rents received are paid out, i.e., first for the payment of taxes and assessments on the real estate before penalty or interest is due; second, to pay premiums of insurance and actual cost of maintenance and repairs, i.e., operating cost requirements; third, to satisfy obligations of the landlord specifically set forth in the lease; and finally, to the payment of debt service, i.e., the interest and principal as it becomes due on the note and mortgage or deed of trust. The assignment instrument provides that immediately upon or at any time after default in the payment of any indebtedness secured by the note and mortgage or in the performance of any obligation, condition, or warranty contained in the note and mortgage or in the leases, the assignee may, without notice, terminate the license without taking possession of the mortgaged premises and may demand, collect, receive, sue and levy against the rents in its own name and, after deducting required expenses of operation, may apply the net proceeds together with any funds previously deposited by the assignor with the assignee to the mortgage indebtedness in such order as the assignee may determine.

It also provides that the assignee, immediately upon default, may accelerate the indebtedness, exercise all of the remedies set forth in the note and mortgage, and, without regard to the adequacy of the security or solvency of the assignor and without any action or proceeding and without regard to the assignor's possession, may enter upon, take possession of, manage and operate the mortgaged premises, modify, cancel or enforce any lease, and do such other acts as the assignee deems proper to protect the security of the mortgage as fully as the assignor could have done if the assignor had remained in possession.

In Section 7 of Form 3.5, the assignment instrument, the mortgagor covenants and agrees not to accept rents in advance and not to cancel or modify any of the specified leases or their terms and conditions without the prior written consent of the mortgagee.[322] Historically,

---

[322] See also clause 2(a) of the additional mortgagor's convenants at ¶ 3.08[5].

response, mortgagees and beneficiaries under mortgages and deeds of trust began to insist upon a clause, which only operates conditionally to assign rents and leases in the event of a default.[320] This remedy is superior to taking possession in that the mortgagee avoids the onerous accounting requirements which burden a mortgagee in possession. Moreover, in those instances (e.g., shopping center and office building loans) where the lender's appraisal-underwriting process is based on an evaluation of certain high-credit tenants, and the security for the loan is the value attributable to the long-term rental obligations of these tenants, lenders have begun to use a separate "assignment of lessor's interest in lease" instrument,[321] covering these specified leases as a concomitant to the assignment of rents clause contained in the mortgage.

Both the mortgage clause and the separate assignment instrument perform three functions in today's lending cycle:

(1) They prevent the mortgagor from materially affecting or altering the leases without the prior written consent of the mortgagee; the rental income stream that primes the mortgage will not thus be abated or otherwise threatened.
(2) They place certain tenants on notice that the lease cannot be modified without the prior written consent of the mortgagee.
(3) They constitute a possible method of enabling the mortgagee to collect the rents after default, but prior to foreclosure.

Protecting the Lease Security. The assignment of lessor's interest in lease instrument (Form 3.5 in Appendix B) is an assignment of both leases and rents in present terms. The leases are identified in an attached schedule. The assignment includes, as well all future leases, subleases, extensions, renewals, and replacements; all guaranties of tenants' performance; the immediate and continuing right to collect and receive all of the rents presently due or which may become due from the mortgaged premises, including minimum rent, additional rent, percentage rent, and deficiency rent. The assignment also covers liquidated damages, proceeds payable under any policy of insurance covering loss of rents or damage to the premises and any and all rights and claims of any kind that the assignor may have against any tenants under the leases or against any subtenants or occupants, excepting only sums which by the express provisions of any of the leases are payable to a governmental authority or to any person other than the landlord under the lease.

---

[320] See Article 9 of Form 3.4 in Appendix B.
[321] See Form 3.5 in Appendix B.

Waiver of Redemption, Notice, Marshaling, Etc. Such a waiver of notice as appears in Article 7.8 of the sample document is enforceable; consequently, the borrower should attempt to obtain a modest grace period even though most lenders are reluctant to go beyond the language in Article 6.2.

Tender of Payment of Default. This clause, inserted for the lender's benefit, attempts to prevent a mortgagor from trying to circumvent the penalty for prepayment of his loan by allowing the loan to go into default and, upon acceleration, coming in with another mortgage and paying off the loan.[317]

[h] Condemnation

The condemnation clause generally provides that the mortgagor will inform the mortgagee of any proceedings under eminent domain that will affect the property, and that the mortgagee will be entitled to any payments arising out of the proceeding. The provisions are not as onerous as they first appear, inasmuch as at common law the mortgagee's rights in mortgaged land taken by eminent domain follow the award and attach to it since the award equitably stands in the place of the land taken.[318] The authorities are divided on whether a mortgagee is a necessary party to a condemnation suit. For the most part, however, that issue is now governed by statute.[319]

[i] Assignment of Leases and Rents

In earlier times, lenders placing mortgages upon commercial realty soon realized that an important element of the security for their loans was the rental income derived from occupancy tenants. However, in some early cases, courts held that mortgage encumbered only the land and improvements; not the issues and rents derived from them. In

---

[317] See discussion at ¶ 3.04[5].

[318] E.g., Calumet River Ry. v. Brown, 26 N.E. 501, 503 (1891), *In re* City of New York, 266 N.Y. 26, 31, 193 N.E. 539 (1934); Chicago Title & Trust Co. v. City of Chicago, 321 Ill. App. 271, 277, 52 N.E.2d 1019, 1021 (1944). Cf. *In re* Braddock Ave., 251 App. Div. 669, 674, 297 N.Y.S. 301, 307 (1937), where the court made analogy to the mortgagee's rights in an action for waste and held that the mortgagee was only entitled to the provable impairment of his security in the property. But see Stopp v. Wilt, 177 Ill. 620, 624, 52 N.E. 1028, 1030 (1899), where condemnation award proceeds turned over to mortgagor because he was required to restore the premises which would not cause any diminution in value of the mortgagee's security interest.

[319] Osborne (1970), note 188 *supra*, § 136.

Sophisticated lenders almost invariably include in their mortgages a "pledge of income and receivership" provision whereby in an action to foreclose, the mortgagee, upon the mortgagor's default, is entitled, without notice, to the appointment of a receiver without proving the inadequacy of the security. It appears, however, that such contractual language is generally not controlling if the security is plainly adequate, based on the maxim at equity, that a court will not exercise its discretion in favor of a party who stands in no need of aid.[310]

However, such income and receivership clause in the mortgage is nevertheless valuable because it may save the mortgagee the trouble of valuation by affidavit[311]; moreover, courts when in doubt are sometimes favorably influenced by these clauses and, indeed, state statutes sometimes mandate enforcement of these clauses.[312] Also, notwithstanding potential constitutional law problems, there have been case decisions involving sophisticated borrowers in commercial transactions that have upheld the "waiver of notice" language in such clauses.[313] The provision stipulating the appointment of a receiver should, however, be drafted in conformity with the applicable state statute, if any.[314] The mortgage lender should also insist upon a separate assignment of leases and rents. The following clauses are also of particular importance in providing for default remedies.

Separate Sales. A provision regarding separate sales[315] seeks to overcome the rule in some jurisdictions that if the secured property is divisible, only so much of it shall be sold as shall be reasonably necessary to pay off the mortgage indebtedness.[316]

---

[310] E.g., Aetna Life Ins. Co. v. Broeker, 166 Ind. 576, 580, 77 N.E. 1092, 1093 (1906); Althausen v. Kuhn, 222, Ill. App. 324, 328 (1921); see also 2 Glenn, *Mortgages* § 175.1 (1943). But see Turner v. Superior Court, 72 Cal. App. 3d 804, 814, 140 Cal. Rptr. 475, 484 (1977); Osborne, et al., note 221 *supra*, § 438.

[311] 2 Glenn, *Mortgages* § 175.1.

[312] E.g., N.Y. Real Prop. Law § 254(10) (McKinney 1968); see Home Title Ins. Co. v. Scherman Holding Corp., 240 App. Div. 851, 267 N.Y.S. 84 (1933) (per curiam).

[313] E.g., Massachusetts Mut. Life Ins. Co. v. Avon Assocs. Inc., 83 Misc. 2d 829, 833, 373 N.Y.S.2d 464, 469 (1975); United States v. Mountain Village Co., 424 F. Supp. 822, 830 (D. Mass. 1976).

[314] E.g., Cal. Civ. Proc. Code § 564(2) (West); Minn. Stat. Ann. § 576.01(1) (West Supp. 1977).

[315] See Article 7.2 of Form 3.4 in Appendix B.

[316] E.g., Blazey v. Delius, 74 Ill. 299, 303 (1874); Griffin v. Reis, note 188 *supra*, 68 Ind. 9 (1879); See also Osborne (1970), note 188 *supra*, § 325.

right of possession in the event of default.[304] Since even in a title theory jurisdiction mortgagee's real interest in the property is that of a secured creditor, the mortgagee in possession becomes subject to strict fiduciary duties with respect to the management of and income from the property before any income can be applied to satisfy the mortgage indebtedness. Hence, this remedy is ordinarily used by lenders as a last resort.

Right to Receiver. By definition, a "receiver" is a third party appointed by a court, usually at the behest of the mortgagee and as an incident to judicial foreclosure. This third party collects rents, makes repairs, and otherwise takes possession and control of the property in order to preserve and protect the security interest of the mortgagee. Lenders generally prefer this remedy over obtaining possession as mortgagee; it is generally more expeditious and obviates some of the strict accounting responsibilities and potential tort-contract liabilities associated with being a mortgagee in possession.[305]

In jurisdictions following the title theory of mortgages, the principal impediment to the appointment of a receiver by a court of equity has been the notion that, in contrast to lien-theory jurisdictions, the mortgagee already has an adequate remedy at law, namely, the bringing of an action in ejectment to obtain possession.[306] By contrast, in lien theory jurisdictions, the chief obstacle to enforcement is "that a mortgagee is not entitled to a receiver if the security is adequate and no waste is threatened...the mortgage being but a lien, the mortgagor is entitled to possession."[307] Accordingly, in both title- and lien-theory jurisdictions, the mortgagee must demonstrate that the security is, or will be, inadequate relative to the amount of the indebtedness[308] and, in some jurisdictions, certain additional exigencies (e.g., insolvency of the mortgagor, loss or waste of the security) must also be present.[309]

---

[304] E.g., Barson v. Mulligan, 191 N.Y. 306, 315, 84 N.E. 75, 83 (1908); Holmes v. Gravenhorst, 263 N.Y. 148, 152, 188 N.E. 285, 287 (1908) (dictum). But see, e.g., Rives v. Mincks Hotel Co., 167 Okla. 500, 504, 30 P.2d 911, 915 (1934). See also Osborne, et al., note 221 *supra*, § 4.27.

[305] See generally Osborne, et al., note 221 *supra*, § 4.36

[306] E.g., Williams v. Robinson, 16 Conn. 517, 525 (1844).

[307] Dart v. Western Sav. & Loan Ass'n, 103 Ariz. 170, 173, 438 P.2d 407, 409 (1968).

[308] 2 Glenn, *Mortgages* § 173 (1943).

[309] E.g., First Nat'l Bank of Joliet v. Illinois Steel Co., 174 Ill. 140, 155, 51 N.E. 200, 204 (1898) (title theory); Mutual Benefit Life Ins. Co. v. Frantz, Klodt & Son, Inc., 306 Minn. 244, 249, 237 N.W.2d 350, 354 (1975) (lien theory).

observe certain safeguards during the initial application stage and the actual execution of the loan documents. These safeguards are: (1) During the application stage, the lender's commitment should provide that, in the event of default, a power of sale foreclosure will be instituted, and that as a condition of making the loan, the borrower in the deed of trust should be required to waive any and all rights arising under the due-process clause of the Fourteenth Amendment in regard to prior notice and a proper hearing. (2) The power-of-sale language contained in the deed of trust should be revised to refer specifically to a waiver by the mortgagor of any rights to notice and a proper hearing arising from the Fourteenth Amendment. At the closing, it may also be prudent for the lender to receive a letter from the borrower's counsel, advising the lender that borrower's counsel has informed his client of the power-of-sale provision and the effect of waiving rights under the due-process clause of the Fourteenth Amendment. Finally, as an extra precaution, prior to the foreclosure sale the lender might consider giving *actual* notice to the defaulting borrower. A statement by the lender disclaiming any intention on its part to forgo its right to full enforcement of the waiver provision should accompany the notice.

Mortgagee's Entry Into Possession. Under Article 7.1.2 of the sample deed of trust, the mortgagee may enter the mortgaged premises and take possession of them in the event of a default by the grantor. In jurisdictions following the title theory of mortgages, the mortgagee or beneficiary theoretically has the legal right to possession from the time the mortgage or deed of trust is executed.[300] By contrast, in lien-theory states, the mortgagor retains the legal right to possession before and after default and until foreclosure and the expiration of the redemption period.[301] While a few lien states refuse to recognize executory agreements allowing the mortgagee to take possession and collect rents,[302] most jurisdictions, including New York, permit such an entry. Entry is based on the mortgagor's consent under an express provision in the mortgage or separate assignment of lease instrument[303] conferring the

---

[300] E.g., Darling Shop v. Nelson Realty Co., 262 Ala. 495, 504, 79 So. 2d 793, 800; Cook v. Curtis, 125 Me. 114, 115, 131 A. 204, 206 (1925); Weathersbee v. Goodwin, 95 S.E. 491, 495 (N.C. 1918). In the so-called intermediate jurisdiction, the mortgagee is entitled to possession after default. E.g., Wells v. Kemme, 145 Ga. 17, 88 S.E. 562 (1916).

[301] E.g., Woodman of the World Life Ins. Soc'y v. Sears, Roebuck & Co., 294 Minn. 126, 137, 200 N.W.2d 181, 184 (1973).

[302] Osborne, et al., note 221 *supra*, at 117, n.36.

[303] Discussed at ¶ 3.08[4][i].

instrument. For example, in reviewing whether plaintiff had waived by contract the right to prior actual notice and an opportunity to be heard, the court in *Turner v. Blackburn* noted that the power-of-sale provision in the preprinted deed of trust was in very small print and further noted:

> Defendants have made no showing that plaintiff was actually aware or made aware of the legal significance of that language. Nor does the deed of trust even allude to the right to a prior hearing.[294]

However, in the *Garner* case, the court noted that "constitutional rights, including the right to a hearing, may be waived...a contractual waiver meets constitutional requirements only if it is voluntarily, intelligently, and knowingly made."[295] More importantly, the court approved a distinction for these purposes between an uninformed homeowner and a professional real estate broker: "While this phrase (power of sale) might be quite meaningless to the unsophisticated, it is not unreasonable to charge businessmen with knowledge of their own vernacular."[296] Also instructive on the question of waiver is *United States v. White*,[297] a case involving foreclosure proceedings instituted by the Farmers Home Administration (FmHA) against some unsophisticated borrowers. In holding that the borrowers had not made a "voluntary and intelligent waiver of their...due process rights," the court emphasized the fact that there was substantial inequality or bargaining power between the parties, that the borrowers probably did not understand the language in the deed of trust, and that the standardized deed of trust form was not subject to alteration, thus making the loan documents essentially a "contract of adhesion."[298] However, in another case involving a homeowner, *Hoffman v. Hud*,[299] the court held that the borrowers had waived their right to a hearing by their failure to respond to five notices of delinquency sent monthly to them by the lender prior to foreclosure.

In conclusion, although some circuit courts have held that the Fourteenth Amendment is not involved in foreclosures by power of sale, other circuits have yet to be heard on this issue; moreover, state courts might find that due-process requirements are mandated by the particular phraseology of their state statutes or constitutions. Consequently, while commercial real estate transactions can, in all probability, still obtain the benefits of a quick foreclosure by power of sale, they should

---

[294] 389 F. Supp. at 1260-1261.
[295] 382 F. Supp. at 380-381.
[296] *Id.* at 381.
[297] 429 F. Supp. 1245, 1253 (N.D. Miss. 1977).
[298] *Id.* at 1251-1252.
[299] 519 F.2d 1160, 1166 (5th Cir. 1975).

bids, and the court held that these powers constituted the requisite state action necessary to trigger the protection of the due-process clause of the Fourteenth Amendment. While refusing to find the North Carolina statute illegal per se, the court held,

> that defendants are barred by the fourteenth amendment from working a deprivation of the mortgagor's property without prior notice and an opportunity for a timely hearing unless it is clear that those rights have been expressly waived.[290]

Also, in a case involving commercial real estate, a U.S. district court in *Garner v. Tri-State Dev. Co.*,[291] found sufficient state action in the Michigan power-of-sale statute to hold that the due-process clause of the Fourteenth Amendment applied. The Michigan statute differed from the North Carolina statute involved in *Turner v. Blackburn* in that no report or certificate was required to be filed with a state court in order to effectuate or confirm the foreclosure. The court, nevertheless, found sufficient state action: "When statuatory provisions encourage private activity, state action may be present." The court further said:

> A seizure will be upheld though there is no prior hearing if (1) it is made under judicial supervision and (2) a hearing is provided on the underlying issue immediately after the seizure...The procedure used has no provision for a hearing before or immediately after the seizure. In fact the seizure is final, and no hearing need ever be afforded.[292]

The court rejected the defendant's claim that the mortgagor received notice of the foreclosure sale. The court observed, that "notice refers to notice of the hearing...notice of the auction may enable plaintiffs to affect the sale price, but would offer no opportunity for them to contest the fact of default."[293] However, it is the authors' opinion that since the facts appear similar to those in the *Northrip* case (decided one year later by the court of appeals in the same circuit), the validity of this decision now appears questionable.

Lastly, assuming that state action is present, a few recent decisions have addressed the question of whether a mortgagor can waive whatever due-process rights exist by stipulation in the mortgage or deed of trust

---

[290] *Id.* at 1260.
[291] 382 F. Supp. 377, 381 (E.D. Mich. 1974).
[292] *Id.* at 380.
[293] *Id.*

that the state statute imposed minimum notice-and-sale requirements, since the power-of-sale remedy, as characterized by the court, was but a private remedy bargained for by the parties. Also, in *Levine v. Stein*, the Fourth Circuit, in a per curiam decision, held that the Virginia statute requiring the trustee, after the sale had been completed, to return an account of the sale to the commissioner of accounts in the court where the instrument had been recorded, did not involve sufficient state action to come under Fourteenth Amendment scrutiny.[286] Finally, in *U.S. Hertz, Inc. v. Niobrara Farms*,[287] the California Supreme Court held that state action was not involved, and suggested, in the alternative, that the statute had not violated the trustor's due-process rights under the Fourteenth Amendment—even though only record, and not personal, notice had been required by the statute. The court stated:

> Under the provisions of the Civil Code, Section 2924, there is no immediate seizure of the property, nor any immediate impairment of the debtor's right in respect to the property. He is given, by the statute, a minimum of ninety (90) days in which he can refinance or sell the property, or more to the point, if he disputes the facts set forth in the notice of default, or has some legal or equitable defense to foreclosure, he may within the statutory period institute an action to enjoin the sale and thereby obtain the judicial hearing contemplated by the cases cited.[288]

However, in a case arguably involving greater state involvement than existed in the foregoing cases, a district court in the Fourth Circuit held in *Turner v. Blackburn*[289] that the due-process rights of the mortgagor had been violated. In that case, the North Carolina statute, distinguishable from the Virginia statute, according to the Fourth Circuit in *Levine*, vested deputy clerks of the local court with inter alia contempt power to enforce complete and correct sale reports by trustees. They were also given the right to accept or reject foreclosure

---

[286] 560 F.2d 1175, 1176 (4th Cir. 1977).

[287] 41 Cal. App. 3d 68, 87, 116 Cal. Rptr. 44, 57 (1974).

[288] *Id.* at 57. Other cases holding that statutes authorizing extrajudicial foreclosure involve private contractual rights and do not constitute sufficient state action to warrant Fourteenth Amendment scrutiny include: Armenta v. Nussbaum, 519 S.W.2d 673, 679 (Tex. 1975); Federal Nat'l Mortgage Ass'n v. Howlett, 521 S.W.2d 428, 440 (Mo. 1975); Kennebee, Inc. v. Bank of the West, 88 Wash. 2d 718, 726, 565 P.2d 812, 819 (1977); Cramer v. Metropolitan Sav. & Loan Ass'n, 401 Mich. 252, 262, 258 N.W.2d 20 (1977), *cert. denied* 436 U.S. 958 (1978); Charmicor, Inc. v. Deaner, 572 F.2d 694, 696 (9th Cir. 1978); Global Indus., Inc. v. Harris, 376 F. Supp. 1379, 1386 (N.D. Ga. 1974); Lawson v. Smith, 402 F. Supp. 851, 856 (N.D. Cal. 1975).

[289] 389 F. Supp. 1250, 1263 (W.D.N.C. 1975).

mortgage foreclosure practices attacked here. The power of sale was created, not through governmental enactment, but by private consensual agreement. We recognized long ago that a deed of trust "provides the remedies for its own enforcement."[280]

The court continued,

> Even assuming *arguendo* the presence of governmental action, we cannot conclude that the statutes on their face violate the due process clause of the fifth amendment. In essence, the challenged statutes recognize the right of private individuals contractually to create power of sale clauses which operate as a waiver of certain potential pre-foreclosure rights. The facial validity of these statutes is controlled by *D.H. Overmyer Co. v. Frick Co.*, 405 U.S. 174, 92 S. Ct. 775, L. Ed. 2D 124 (1972);...(in that case), the Supreme Court concluded that statutes permitting the inclusion of confession of judgment provisions in debt instruments were not unconstitutional *per se*.[281]

The Georgia Supreme Court followed this line of reasoning in upholding a power-of-sale provision in a 1975 case.[282] The court held that the power of sale is a purely contractual agreement between two parties in the exercise of their private property rights, and that statutory regulation of the power-of-sale procedure does not constitute significant state action where the power-of-sale language is contained in a private contract between the parties.

In *Northrip v. Federal National Mortgage Ass'n*[283] the Sixth Circuit held that although a deputy sheriff had conducted the sale pursuant to Michigan's foreclosure-by-advertisement statute and the registrar of deed had been involved in transferring title, their presence did not constitute state action under the Fourteenth Amendment. As an aside, the court also noted that the power-of-sale remedy contained in a mortgage had been recognized by Michigan courts as a common-law device long before the first statute dealing with the subject was ever enacted.[284] Also, the Fifth Circuit in *Barrerra v. Security Bldg. & Inv. Corp.*[285] found no state action to be involved by virtue of the mere fact

---

[280] 509 F.2d at 513.
[281] 509 F.2d at 515.
[282] Coffey Enterprises Realty & Dev. Co. v. Holmes, 233 Ga. 937, 948, 213 S.E.2d 882, 890 (1975).
[283] 527 F.2d 23, 33 (6th Cir. 1975), *rev'g* 372 F. Supp. 594, 600 (E.D. Mich. 1974).
[284] *Id.* at 27.
[285] 519 F.2d 1166, 1171 (5th Cir. 1975).

months after notice of default is given. Like judicial foreclosure, the mortgagee is entitled to receive a deficiency decree,[275] and while the conduct of the sale is determined by provisions in the mortgage rather than by a court, many state statutes (e.g., the New York one)[276] impose strict requirements governing the notice and conduct of the sale. Failure to satisfy these requirements may enable a court to set aside the sale. One major difference between a sale by the mortgagee under a power of sale and a sale by a trustee under a deed of trust is that the mortgagee is not an independent party with fiduciary responsibilities to the debtor, and hence is not allowed to bid in at the sale under a power that it exercises.[277] In states that allow the power of sale the mortgagee can obtain possession of the property; thus, the rights to a receiver or to collect rents pursuant to an assignment of leases are not as important as they otherwise might be.

However, within the last few years, suits by mortgagors and trustors have been instituted that question whether the power of sale, sanctioned by many state statutes, violates the due-process clause of the Fourteenth Amendment. While the outcome has been mixed, most courts addressing this issue have held that the requisite governmental or state action did not exist. They were thereby precluded them from resolving the question as to whether the due-process standard can be met when the particular state statute involved requires neither actual notice nor a hearing for the benefit of the mortgagor or trustor prior to the foreclosure sale. For example, in *Bryant v. Jefferson Federal Savings & Loan Ass'n*,[278] the plaintiff challenged the constitutionality of the District of Columbia's extrajudicial mortgage foreclosure procedures. Relying on *Sniadach v. Family Finance Corp.*,[279] the plaintiff claimed that a power of sale contained in a deed of trust violated the due-process clause of the Fourteenth Amendment. The court, in denying plaintiff's allegations, stated,

> The due process clause is a limitation on governmental, not private action...There is no significant governmental involvement in the

---

[275] E.g., Commercial Centre Realty Co. v. Superior Court, 59 P.2d 978, 983 (Cal. 1936).

[276] N.Y. Real Prop. Acts. & Proc. Law §§ 1401-1461 (McKinney 1979).

[277] E.g., Mills v. Mutual Bldg. & Loan Ass'n, 216 N.C. 664, 674, 6 S.E.2d 549, 555 (1940).

[278] 509 F.2d 511, 516 (D.C. Cir. 1974).

[279] 395 U.S. 337, 359 (1969). In *Sniadach,* the court held that the Wisconsin prejudgment garnishment of wages procedure, which did not require notice and a prior hearing, violated the due-process clause of the Fourteenth Amendment.

(1) Preliminary title search to determine the proper parties plaintiff and defendant;
(2) Filing of the foreclosure bill of complaint and lis pendens notice;
(3) Service of process;
(4) A hearing before a master in chancery who reports to the court;
(5) Notice of and issuance of a certificate after sale;
(6) Report of the sale;
(7) Judicial determination of the mortgagor's rights, if any, to surplus;
(8) Possible redemption from the sale by the mortgagor or other affected party; and
(9) Finally, the entry of a decree for deficiency judgment[272] in a jurisdiction that does not prohibit deficiency judgments.[273]

In Florida, one construction lender foreclosing on some condominium projects found that it could take, in some instances, three to four months merely to serve all the parties of record, let alone docket the cases. Accordingly, during the 1973–1974 crisis in the real estate market, many mortgagees were forced to come to an agreement by way of cash, a deed in lieu of foreclosure, or release of personal liability in order to accomplish a quick take-over of the property to protect it from waste and deterioration. Upon instituting a suit to foreclose, most mortgagees in their petition request the appointment of a receiver pending the sale of the property.

The mortgagor's equity of redemption or interest in the land can also be extinguished by power of sale contained in the mortgage, unless such use as a method of foreclosure is barred by statute.[274] This is a relatively speedy, nonjudicial procedure in which the property is sold at either a private or public sale usually held between three weeks and two

---

[272] See Osborne (1970), note 188 *supra*, § 318. Interestingly, a respectable albeit dated survey suggests that only one percent of foreclosed properties were ever redeemed and only 7 percent of the dollar amount of deficiency judgments were ever realized by mortgagees. Prather, "A Realistic Approach to Foreclosure," 14 Bus. Law. 132, 135 (1958).

[273] Some states have statutes that prohibit or restrict the granting of deficiency judgments. E.g., Cal. Civ. Proc. Code § 726 (West Supp. 1971). In New York, special motion must be made for a deficiency judgment, and the amount thereof is limited to the excess of the outstanding indebtedness (plus amounts due on all prior liens and encumbrances) with interest over either the market value of the property or its foreclosure sale price, whichever excess amount is less. N.Y. Real Prop. Acts. & Proc. Law § 1371(2) (McKinney 1979).

[274] E.g., Iowa Code Ann. § 654.1 (West 1950).

calculating the amount of any deficiency.[265] In some other states, there has been legislation tending toward the same objective.[266] In New York, while the mortgagee may sue on the debt rather than foreclose,[267] the mortgagee cannot prosecute the two actions concurrently.[268] Once a foreclosure action has been commenced, the mortgagee must obtain leave of the court before instituting an action on the debt.[269] Conversely, no action to foreclose may be commenced when a final judgment was previously rendered in an action to recover any part of the debt unless an execution has been returned wholly or partially unsatisfied.[270] However, since both actions are theoretically distinct, the right to foreclose survives when an action on the debt is barred by the statute of limitations.[271]

Judicial Foreclosure vs. Foreclosure Under Power of Sale. The long-established judicial foreclosure action in equity is generally used in a majority of states and is available in all. Among its salient features are the mortgagee's frequently exercised power to purchase, statutory redemption from the foreclosure sale in some jurisdictions, and a decree for a deficiency with the sale price conclusively determining the value of the property (except in a few states having anti-deficiency judgment statutes). While it is perhaps the best method for producing firm titles, it is complex, expensive, and time-consuming. A typical action in equity involves the following procedural steps:

---

[265] Cal. Civ. Proc. Code §§ 580, 725a, 726 (West). Also, Nevada follows the one-action rule by giving the mortgagee the same option. Nev. Rev. Stat. § 40.430(1975). See Paramount Ins., Inc. v. Rayson & Smitley, 86 Nev. 644, 651, 472 P.2d 530, 535 (1970), in which the court states:

> It is apparent the one-action rule was legislatively adopted to change the common law rule which permitted a creditor to pursue either the remedy of sale of the land or suit on the note, or both at once.

Id. at 650, 472 P.2d at 533. See also Bank of Italy Nat'l Trust & Sav. Ass'n v. Bentley, 217 Cal. 644, 654 20 P.2d 940, (1933).

[266] E.g., Wis. Stat. Ann. §§ 846.01, 846.04 (West 1977); Ind. Code Ann. §§ 34-2-29-1, 32-8-16-1 to 32-8-16-10 (Burns 1972). One curiosity has been the state of New Jersey. In that state, where the indebtedness is evidenced by a note secured by a mortgage, the mortgagee may institute a suit on the note without first foreclosing on the mortgage. However, where the indebtedness is evidenced by a bond, an action must first be brought to foreclose on the mortgage. See Schwartz v. Bender Invs. Inc., 58 N.J. 444, 446, 279 A.2d 100, 102 (1971) (per curiam).

[267] See Hebrew Children's Home, Inc. v. Walter, 168 Misc. 117, 5 N.Y.S.2d 228 (1938) (per curiam).

[268] N.Y. Real Prop. Acts Proc. Law § 1301 (McKinney 1979).

[269] *Id.*

[270] *Id.*

[271] See Cracco v. Cox, 414 N.Y.S.2d 404, 406 (1979).

money only.[262] Consequently, absent such a provision, a default in one or more installments will not cause the remaining indebtedness to mature. And some courts have held that, in an action to foreclose for a partial default, the secured property is indivisible and must hence be sold in its entirety, but is *not* free and clear of the remaining indebtedness. To make matters worse, the mortgagee is barred from later using foreclosure again for the remaining balance.[263]

Personal Suit on The Note. "The holder of a note secured by deed of trust or mortgage has traditionally had the right to sue on the note alone, to foreclose on the property, or to join these proceedings in one action."[264] Yet since the real security for most permanent commercial real estate loans is the rental income stream from the realty, rather than the solvency of the developer, many of these loans are today nonrecourse. In this event a personal suit on the note is not available to the mortgagee. However, in the case of certain high-risk or "specialty" loans requiring a high level of management skill, such as loans to hotel and motel developers, the permanent lenders usually require personal liability. Almost all construction lending is based on recourse financing.

This historic right to sue on the note has however, recently been restricted in those jurisdictions following the "one-action rule" or a milder variant of it. This rule permits enforcement of a mortgage debt only by an action to foreclose and is based on two reasons: first, to protect the mortgagor against duplicitous actions which, while theoretically distinct, involve the same issues and litigants; second, to compel the mortgagee to exhaust his agreed-upon security before attempting to reach the mortgagor's other assets. California was the first state to alter the mortgagee's traditional remedy by requiring that the mortgagee rely upon his security before enforcing the debt. The statute gives the mortgagee an option with respect to foreclosure. Upon default, the mortgagee can foreclose quickly through a private power of sale if no deficiency judgment is sought. Alternatively, it can obtain a deficiency judgment by using judicial foreclosure, which involves a single proceeding; the sale of the security is first accomplished, and a judgment for the amount of any remaining deficiency is then rendered. The procedure also permits a fair determination of market value for purposes of

---

[262] 4 Corbin, *Contracts* § 965 (1964).
[263] See Osborne (1970), note 188 *supra,* § 325. For a discussion of "due on sale" and "due on encumbrancing" acceleration clauses, see ¶¶ 3.04[7], 3.04[8].
[264] E.g., Foster Lumber Co. v. Weston Constructors, Inc. 33 Colo. App. 436, 521, P.2d 1294, 1297 (1974).

accelerate.[256] And, in the absence of language to the contrary in the mortgage, waiver will not result due to a subsequent default in payment because the mortgagee failed to accelerate on a prior default,[257] nor will waiver result even if the mortgagee accepts a late payment after acceleration[258] unless, in some jurisdictions,[259] the mortgagee has in the past consistently accepted such late payments.

In the event of a default by the mortgagor, the mortgagee may wish to pursue a course of action less drastic than accelerating the indebtedness and instituting foreclosure in the event that the entire indebtedness is not paid. Accordingly, debt-acceleration clauses are almost invariably "optional" and not mandatory. Formal notice is not required to render such "optional" clause operative absent language to the contrary—a "grace period"—in the mortgage instrument. However, the mortgagee must perform some overt act evidencing his intention to take advantage of the acceleration provision, such as formally instituting foreclosure proceedings before the mortgagor tenders what is due; otherwise, the mortgagee will lose his right to accelerate for that particular default.[260] Accordingly, to avoid this uncertainty as to whether the tender by the mortgagor is timely[261] or not, most lenders, prior to exercising their right to accelerate, will transmit written notice by registered mail of their intention to do so within a stipulated period of time. However, a prudent borrower should not rely upon such dubious notice but should require that notice and a reasonable grace period to cure both monetary (e.g., five to ten days) and nonmonetary defaults (e.g., fifteen to twenty days) be spelled out in the debt-acceleration clause.

A major reason for such clauses the doctrine of anticipatory breach that does not apply to the breach of a contract for the payment of

---

[256] E.g., Saunders v. Stradley, 25 Md. App. 85, 98, 333 A.2d 604, 612 (1975).

[257] See Dunn v. Barry, 35 Cal. App. 325, 328, 169 P. 910, 912 (1917). See also Osborne, et al., note 221 *supra*, at 437.

[258] See Robinson v. Miller, 317 Ill. 501, 510, 148 N.E. 319, 323 (1925); Odell v. Hoyt, 73 N.Y. 343, 347 (1878); 5 A.L.R. 437 (1920); see also Osborne, et al., note 221 *supra*, at 437.

[259] See Scelza v. Ryba, 169 N.Y.S.2d 462, 465 (Sup. Ct. 1957); Short v. A.H. Still Inv. Co., 206 Va. 959, 966, 147 S.E.2d 99, 105 (1966); Annot., 97 A.L.R.2d 997 (1964); see also Rosenthal, "The Role of Courts of Equity in Preventing Acceleration Predicated Upon a Mortgagor's Inadvertent Default," 22 Syracuse L. Rev. 897, 907 (1971); Osborne, et al., note 221 *supra*, at 437.

[260] See United States Sav. Bank v. Continental Arms, Inc., 338 A.2d 579, 582-583 (Del. 1975); Spires v. Lawless, 493 S.W.2d 65, 73 (Mo. 1973); see also Osborne, et al., note 221 *supra* at 436.

[261] See Lowry v. Northwestern Sav. & Loan Ass'n, 542 S.W.2d 546, 549 (Mo. 1976).

outstanding indebtedness has recently been modified in some respects.[255] Subject to these exceptions, the mortgagor generally cannot reinstate the loan by curing the particular default once the mortgagee has elected to

---

the mortgagee has waived the right to accelerate or has so acted as to have misled the mortgagor into a reasonable belief that the acceleration remedy would not be exercised with respect to an existing default. See also Comer v. Hargrave, 93 N.M. 170, 598 P. 2d 213 (1979), where the Supreme Court of New Mexico held in a simultaneous suit on the note and mortgage where the note contained a grace period but the mortgage did not, that the mortgagor was entitled to a grace period. In addition, the mortgagor was required to give notice of its intention to accelerate before commencing foreclosure.

[255] An increasing number of states have enacted amelioratory legislation. For example, the Colorado Code requires that

> Whenever the default or violation in the terms of the note and deed of trust or mortgage being foreclosed is nonpayment of any sums due thereunder, the owners of the property being foreclosed or parties liable thereon shall be entitled to cure said defaults if...the owners or parties pay to the officer conducting the sale all delinquent principal and interest payments...plus all costs, expenses, late charges, attorney's fees.

Colo. Rev. Stat. § 38-39-118(1)(a) (1978 Supp.). See Cal. Civ. Code Ann. § 2924c (West 1974); Penn. Stat. Ann., Tit. 41, § 404 (Purdon 1974); Ill. Rev. Stat., Ch. 95, § 57 (1976).

In some instances courts have showed leniency with respect to nondebt payment defaults. For example, in denying acceleration based on nonpayment of taxes and insurance premiums, which defaults were subsequently cured prior to foreclosure, a New Jersey court recently held: "The failure to pay taxes or to maintain insurance does not impair the security of the mortgagee if those defaults are corrected promptly, i.e., before the institution of foreclosure proceedings. On the other hand, a default in the payment of interest or principal is *ipso facto* an impairment of security and a violation of the principal condition of the mortgage conveyance." Kaminski v. London Pub., 123 N.J. Super. 112, 120, 301 A.2d 769, 771 (App. Div. 1973) (per curiam).

In other recent instances courts have shown an increasing willingness to ameliorate the harsh consequences of acceleration because of various mitigating and truly equitable circumstances. See Bisno v. Sax, 175 Cal. App. 2d 714, 721, 346 P.2d 814, 818 (1960), where acceleration was denied because it was based on a one-day delay in making a payment and time was not declared to be of essence in the note or mortgage; Middlemist v. Mosier, 151 Colo. 113, 114, 377 P.2d 110 (1963), where acceleration was denied because it was based on inadvertent failure by mortgagor to properly endorse check for single monthly payment; Rockaway Park Series Corp. v. Hollis Automotive Corp., 206 Misc. 955, 957, 135 N.Y.S.2d 588, 590 (1954), where foreclosure was based on housing code violations in existence several years before mortgagor purchased the premises and mortgagee had taken no previous action; Federal Home Loan Mortgage Corp. v. Taylor, 318 So. 2d 203, 209 (Fla. 1975), where acceleration was denied because it was based on a technical default of one month's installment that could have arisen from lack of communication between mortgagor and mortgagee. See also Rosenthal, "The Role of Courts of Equity in Preventing Acceleration Predicated Upon a Mortgagee's Inadvertent Default," 22 Syracuse L. Rev. 897 (1971); Osborne, et al., note 221 *supra*, at 438

some jurisdictions, the mortgagor or grantor has the right of statutory redemption after the sale, and in most jurisdictions, the mortgagee or beneficiary will be entitled to a deficiency judgment if the borrower has not been exculpated from personal liability.

In addition to the foregoing, the mortgagee may possess a number of ancillary remedies: (1) a right to step into possession of premises[249]; (2) a right to receive an assignment of rents, or in the case of a shopping center or other loan involving high-credit leases, to receive an assignment of specified leases with prime tenants[250]; (3) a right to appoint a receiver pending the foreclosure decree and sale; and (4) a right to accept a deed in lieu of foreclosure. Since a detailed treatment of these remedies is beyond the scope of this treatise, each will be discussed only briefly.

Acceleration of the Indebtedness. Unlike some rent-acceleration clauses in lease agreements, the prevailing view is that a debt-acceleration clause is enforceable. It is neither a forfeiture against a mortgagor who fails to promptly pay the debt or who commits some other actionable default[251] nor a penalty, since the mortgagor has already received his consideration (the loan proceeds), and acceleration is simply a contract matter determining when the debt is payable.[252] Hence, the general rule holds that no relief will be afforded to the mortgagor; he must pay the entire indebtedness or face foreclosure, even when a default occurs by reason of his negligence or mistake, or by accident.[253] However, some equity courts have refused to foreclose a mortgage when an acceleration of the indebtedness would be inequitable or unjust and the circumstances would render the acceleration unconscionable.[254] Moreover, the right of a mortgagee to accelerate the entire

---

[249] See Articles 7.1.2 and 7.1.3 of Form 3.4 in Appendix B.

[250] See Article 9 of Form 3.4 and Form 3.5 in Appendix B and discussion at ¶ 3.08[4][i].

[251] For example, debt acceleration has been permitted for non-debt-service-related defaults such as failure to pay taxes. Neubauer v. Smith, 40 App. Div. 2d 790, 791, 337 N.Y.S.2d 592, 594 (1972) (per curiam); First Nat'l Bank of Atlanta v. Blum, 141 Ga. App. 485, 489, 233 S.E.2d 835, 838 (1977); Eisen v. Kostakos, 116 N.J. Super. 358, 371, 282 A.2d 421, 428 (1971).

[252] E.g., Graf v. Hope Bldg. Corp., 254 N.Y. 1, 15, 171 N.E. 884, (1930); Verna v. O'Brien, 78 Misc. 2d 288, 291, 356 N.Y.S.2d 929, 933 (1974); Paydan, Inc. v. Agia Kipiaki, Inc., 130 N.J. Super. 141, 150, 325 A.2d 838 (1974).

[253] Osborne (1970), note 188 *supra*, at § 326.

[254] See, e.g., Kreiss Potassium Phosphate Co. v. Knight, 98 Fla. 1004, 1012, 124 So. 751, 756 (1929), where the mortgagee had periodically accepted late payments in exchange for an exorbitant rate of interest, and the value of the improved security exceeded twelve times the amount of the debt, the court held that it would be unconscionable to permit foreclosure upon acceleration where

never been enacted, this "boiler plate" provision remains in New York and elsewhere.

Foreclosure of Other Liens. Article 6.9 in the sample document, which holds that the foreclosure of a junior, subordinated, or senior mortgage holder—existing without the beneficiary's consent—will also cause default, is exceptional. No secondary lender, upon advice of counsel, would place secondary financing behind such a provision; any enforcement of the junior lender's rights and remedies could trigger an acceleration of the first indebtedness. If a default arises under a junior mortgage, most junior lenders would normally want to foreclose quickly and cure any default by the borrower reaching the senior mortgage.

Conversely, at common law a senior encumbrancer cannot, against his will, be made a party to foreclosure.[246] For one thing, a junior mortgagee's security is the property subject to the first mortgage; hence, that is all that can be sold when he forecloses his junior lien. Also, the theory is that a senior mortgagee should be able to select his own time for selling and not be forced to realize his claim in what he regards as an unfavorable market. Moreover, he may want to hold onto his investment if the foreclosure of the junior lien takes place before the senior lien matures.

[g] Default Remedies

Overview of Mortgagee's Default Remedies. Several remedies are available to the mortgagee or deed of trust beneficiary in the event of default by the mortgagor or grantor. Most mortgages and deeds of trust contain acceleration clauses empowering the mortgagee or beneficiary to accelerate the outstanding indebtedness.[247] And, in the event of recourse financing, either sue upon the personal covenants in the note or foreclose upon the property. The so-called one-action rule, which permits enforcement of a mortgage debt only by an action to foreclose, is followed in California and a few other states. In most jurisdictions, both actions can be pursued concurrently, but only one judgment can be taken for the outstanding amount of indebtedness. If the mortgagee decides to foreclose, it then has the option of using judicial foreclosure or the less expensive and time-consuming remedy of an out-of-court foreclosure under a power of sale contained in the mortgage. This is analogous to a sale by a trustee in a deed-of-trust jurisdiction.[248] In

---

[246] E.g., Jerome v. McCarter, 94 U.S. 734, 748 (1976).
[247] See Article 7.1.1 of Form 3.4 in Appendix B.
[248] See Article 7.1.4 of Form 3.4 in Appendix B.

Ownership. This clause prohibits the transfer of the property without the prior written consent of the mortgagee.[244]

[f] Events of Default

This section identifies the standard conditions triggering default, including default in payment or performance of obligations; false representations by the mortgagor, rendering of a final judgment that is not discharged; voluntary or involuntary bankruptcy; and dissolution of the borrowing entity.

Bankruptcy. Institutional lenders lost some of their confidence, as first mortgagees, during the 1973-1974 recession when, in the wake of rampant foreclosures, they were confronted with the specter of "cramdowns" in Chapter 12 proceedings and were compelled to modify their loan terms and accept effective subordination of their position as first mortgagees. This has prompted lenders to tighten the bankruptcy language in both their commitment letters and debt-acceleration clauses in their mortgage forms.[245] Today's lenders are demanding language that defines insolvency as an event of default with greater particularity and that permits them to terminate their obligation to fund the loan not only if the borrower should become insolvent but also if any prime tenant, whose lease has been assigned as additional security, should become the subject of any bankruptcy, reorganization, or insolvency proceeding. The ambit of the "no material change" clause in the permanent commitment letter has also been expanded to cover not only bankruptcy prior to the date of closing but also to cover any significant financial change which may, in the reasonable judgment of the lender, bring about bankruptcy revealed by audited financial statements required of the borrower prior to the funding date.

Taxation of Mortgage. Whoever said the history of mortgage documentation is boring? In Article 6.8 of Form 3.4 is found the "Brundage" clause, so called because in 1888 one brazen assemblyman from upstate New York sponsored a bill that would have required local tax assessors in New York to tax property owners only on the net worth value of the property and mortgagees on the remainder. This touched off a panic among lenders, and even though legislation of this sort has

---

[244] See Article 5.7 of Form 3.4 in Appendix B. This "due on sale" clause is discussed at ¶ 3.04[8].

[245] See Article 6.5 of Form 3.4 in Appendix B, and discussion of bankruptcy at ¶ 4.02[12].

mortgagor is legal on its face, the beneficiary or mortgagee need not contest its legality at its own expense or let it go unpaid at its peril.[240]

Maintenance of Books and Records. Article 4.15 of the sample deed of trust empowers the mortgagee to inspect and audit the books and records of the mortgagor to assure compliance with its requirement that the borrower pay "additional compensation" over and above the regular amount of interest.[241]

[e] Negative Covenants

Negative covenants stipulate certain acts that cannot be accomplished.[242] The mortgagor or grantor agrees not to violate any building codes or local municipal ordinances; not to alter the premises or commit waste; and not to replace fixtures and personalty without the written consent of the mortgagee or beneficiary unless these items are replaced with appropriate substitutes of equal value.

Other Liens. This section of the mortgage/deed of trust also usually includes a statement which prevents other liens from being filed on the secured property even though they are subordinate to the mortgage or deed of trust. However, the article in the sample document is objectionable to the borrower because it is so all-inclusive.[243]

No Dividend by Grantor. Article 5.6 of Form 3.4 contains a stringent requirement that should only be accepted by the borrower with respect to a construction loan mortgage where the mortgagor's sole asset is the 100 percent financing provided by the construction loan. A clause of this type is inappropriate for a permanent loan mortgage.

This provision, as stated in the sample document, should not be accepted by any borrower owning other projects and assets, especially if ongoing financing with a rollover of equity is being contemplated. A possible compromise would be language to the effect that no loan funds could be used to fund either dividends or a return of capital or, alternatively, that the original dividend-capital distribution restriction would expire at the end of the construction period.

---

[240] Osborne (1970), note 188 *supra,* § 173 (by implication).
[241] See discussion at ¶ 3.04[3][a].
[242] See Article 5 of Form 3.4 in Appendix B.
[243] See the discussion at ¶ 3.04[7].

insurance proceeds, the business investment of the mortgagor will effectively be destroyed. Moreover, such a demand is inherently unfair to the mortgagor because the mortgagor had bargained for maintaining a loan for a stated period of time; the lender should not have the right to unilaterally deprive a borrower, who is willing to restore the premises, from the use of such loaned funds unless it can show that its security will be impaired.[237] The plight of the mortgagor is further exacerbated because, while the insurance proceeds may reduce the mortgage debt pro tanto, the mortgagee is not obligated to reduce or postpone subsequent amortization payments absent a "partial prepayment" provision in the commitment.[238]

Consequently, as long as the premises can properly be restored, whether to restore or to repay the loan indebtedness should be not the mortgagee's but the mortgagor's election. Many lending institutions, while not automatically willing to give the mortgagor the option described above, do allow a provision whereby the mortgagor can request that the proceeds be used for restoration of the premises. While such a position is tolerable, counsel for the mortgagor should be very careful with language similar to that as set forth in Article 4.6 of Form 3.4. In this section, the grantor is required, at the behest of the mortgagee, to restore the premises, even if the funds received from the insurance proceeds are not enough to complete restoration. Any right to restore the premises should be predicated upon sufficient funds being realized under the insurance policy. However, the mortgagor should anticipate that the lender will require control over when and how disbursements will be made and should anticipate protection for itself against mechanics' liens.[239]

Contest of Tax Assessment, Etc. This provision merely acknowledges the common-law rule that if a tax contested by the grantor or

---

[237] The closest decision to acknowledge this line of reasoning involved an insured house covered by a deed of trust containing phraseology of similar import to the language in Article 5.6 where the defendant purchase-money mortgagee refused to permit the insurance proceeds to be used for restoration. The California Court of Appeal, in *Schoolcraft v. Ross*, held that such refusal violated an "implied covenant of good faith and fair dealing" that exists in every contract and held that notwithstanding language to the contrary in the deed of trust, the lender could not cut off the borrower's right to use the loan funds unless it can show that the security will be impaired. 81 Cal. App. 3d 75, 79-82, 146 Cal. Rptr. 57, 59-60 (1978).

[238] A provision of this type is described at ¶ 3.04[5].

[239] Also see discussion of the standard mortgagee loss payable clause at ¶ 3.04[12][b].

or incompetent management of the mortgaged property. Waste will be redefined more broadly in future mortgage forms, and attempts will be made to impose escrow requirements, not just for taxes and insurance premiums, but for replacement reserves to prevent the developer from "milking" income from the property that should be applied toward its maintenance and preservation. Obviously, attorneys representing developers should be alert to these likely changes and be ready to formulate an appropriate bargain posture based on the specific strengths of the client's circumstances.

Insurance. The "standard mortgage" payable clause[235] is one under which the mortgagee or beneficiary will receive the hazard insurance proceeds in the event of a fire or some other casualty. The mortgagor or grantor should not have any problems with this customary provision. However, a mortgagor may not want to agree to the inclusion of the adjunct provision providing that, in the event the premises are destroyed by fire and the mortgagee receives the insurance proceeds, the mortgagee is entitled at its option to apply the proceeds as a credit in the inverse order of maturity upon the indebtedness, with any remaining balance to be given to the mortgagor, or, if it so elects, to make the funds available to the mortgagor for restoration of the premises. The problem is not so much with the option itself, but with who has the right to elect the option. In Article 4.5 of Form 3.4, the mortgagee, in its sole discretion, has the right either to use the funds for a repayment of its loan or to give the funds to the mortgagor for restoration purposes. In some jurisdictions, the mortgagee automatically has this right, absent language in the mortgage to the contrary.[236] If the mortgagor has a thriving business and, for example, owns a shopping center or an office building, and the mortgagee insists upon repayment of its loan with the

---

[235] See Article 4.5 of Form 3.4 and Form 3.12 in Appendix B. See also discussion at ¶ 3.04[12].

[236] At common law the mortgagee probably has the option of not paying the proceeds over to the mortgagor for restoration of the premises absent an agreement to the contrary. Fergus v. Wilmarth, 117 Ill. 542, 548, 7 N.E. 508, 509 (1886). See Osborne, et al., note 221 *supra*, at 149. By statute in New York the lender has a qualified and limited right to do so. N.Y. Real Prop. Law § 254.4 (McKinney Supp. 1978). Moreover, in many jurisdictions (notably Michigan) the mortgagee is entitled to the insurance proceeds notwithstanding that the mortgagor has restored the premises with its own funds. Pink v. Smith, 281 Mich. 107, 113, 274 N.W. 727, 730 (1937); Price v. Harris, 251 Ark. 793, 795, 475 S.W.2d 162, 164 (1972). And, the mortgagee has this right even if the value of the uninjured portion of the security exceeds the balance of the mortgage indebtedness. E.g., Kintzel v. Wheatland Mut. Ins. Ass'n, 203 N.W.2d 799, 812 (Iowa 1973).

could compel the beneficiary to continue to make advances to protect its security interest, which could raise the loan amount beyond the maximum legal loan to appraised value ratio.

Repair. The beneficiary's or mortgagee's right to compel the owner to keep the premises in good repair depends upon a provision to that effect in the mortgage or deed of trust. The mortgagee would otherwise have to prove that the mortgagor's failure to repair would so impair the security as to justify an action for waste.[231]

In general, courts are reluctant to enforce "repair covenants" either by a damage action or by foreclosure and tend to strictly construe such clauses.[232] For example, in *United States v. Angel,* the court refused to accelerate the debt—of about $1 million—and foreclose a mortgage containing a repair and anti-waste provision because the U.S. Government, as mortgagee, had not proven sufficient impairment in the value of the security (a low-income housing project estimated by the mortgagor to be worth at least $7 million), notwithstanding that the mortgagor had been guilty of over 1,000 housing and health code violations.[233] Indeed, in the case of "amelioratory waste," courts generally have held that damage and debt-acceleration actions based on repair covenants are unforceable, unless, after the existing improvements are demolished, the market value of the substitute property is lower than the original property. This is notwithstanding the fact that the mortgagee forgoes control over the development and construction of the new property and is compelled to accept, as security, different improvements. These improvements may be less economical and secure than what was bargained for when the loan was first underwritten by the mortgagee.[234]

In light of the difficulties experienced by lenders in enforcing anti-waste and repair convenants in the mortgage, various approaches have been and will be attempted to address the problems posed by amateurish

---

[231] E.g., Cahn v. Hewsey, 8 Misc. 384, 388, 29 N.Y.S. 1107, 1109 (1894). See generally Leipziger, "The Mortgagee's Remedies for Waste," 64 Calif L. Rev. 1086 (1976).

[232] Osborne, et al., note 221 *supra,* at 139, § 4.11.

[233] 362 F. Supp. 445, 447 (E.D. Pa. 1973); see also Krone v. Goff, 53 Cal. App. 3d 191, 198, 127 Cal. Rptr. 390, 394 (1975), where the California Court of Appeal held that a damage action for waste based on a repair covenant would not lie even though the mortgagor commited financial waste and refused to make earthquake repairs ordered by the City of Los Angeles because the mortgagor, himself, had not commited any unreasonable or tortious acts which had impaired the security.

[234] Osborne, et al., note 221 *supra,* at 138, § 4.11.

mortgage, it will not be covered by the trust or mortgage, which is a lien only on the property owned by the borrower at the time he executed the security instrument. However, in most jurisdictions, if the grantor or mortgagor expressly warrants title, the lien of the mortgage or deed of trust will cover the after-acquired property under an estoppel theory.[225]

[d] Affirmative Covenants

The section of the mortgage/deed of trust dealing with affirmative covenants lists those standard affirmative covenants that the grantor or mortgagor agrees to observe throughout the period of the loan.[226] In the mortgage/deed of trust under study, the grantor covenants that he will maintain the borrowing entity's existence throughout the term of the loan, that he will comply at all times with all laws now or hereafter passed concerning the property, that he will pay the mortgage loan as it comes due and payable, and that he will maintain and restore the premises in case they need repair. Article 4.5 of Form 3.4 is the covenant whereby the grantor agrees to maintain hazard insurance at all times in an amount acceptable to the mortgagee on the insured premises.

Often, through mistakes in drafting, conditions and convenants of the original commitment letter are left out of the mortgage loan provisions. To prevent such an oversight from occurring, an article such as Article 4.12 in Form 3.4 incorporates all of the terms and conditions of the commitment into the mortgage.

The following provisions are of particular importance:

Payment of Local Taxes. Compliance with this provision is of special concern to the mortgagee or beneficiary since, in most jurisdictions, a tax lien for unpaid local taxes is paramount to the lien of an existing mortgage.[227] Accordingly, the beneficiary herein expressly[228] reserves the right to pay taxes on behalf of the grantor and to seek immediate recoupment or treat the advances together with interest thereon as additional mortgage indebtedness.[229] Alternatively, the beneficiary may exercise his right to accelerate.[230] If not, a defaulting grantor

---

[225] E.g., Bayler v. Commonwealth, 40 Pa. 37, 45 (1861); see also Osborne (1970), note 188 *supra,* § 38.

[226] See Article 4 of Form 3.4 in Appendix B.

[227] Osborne (1970), note 188 *supra,* § 221.

[228] At common law, the mortgagee has the right to pay taxes and add the amount to the mortgage debt even absent such a provision. E.g., People v. Pierce, 186 Misc. 285, 290, 64 N.Y.S.2d 251, 255 (App. Div. 1946).

[229] See Article 10.4 of Form 3.4 in Appendix B.

[230] See Article 7.1.1 of Form 3.4 in Appendix B.

acquired title to the after-acquired property. Most commentators seemingly are of the opinion, based on a title search burden rationale, that while the original mortgagee's interest is of record, it would be outside the subsequent taker's chain of title.[222] In other words, a subsequent taker need not trace the prior mortgages on the property because the original mortgagee's interest would not defeat his own.

[b] Grant

In this clause,[223] the grantor or the mortgagor, as the case may be, grants, bargains and sells, assigns, conveys, etc., to the trustee or to the mortgagee the estate to be encumbered by the deed of trust or mortgage.

[c] Representations and Warranties

Standard representations and warranties upon which a mortgagee relies in making the mortgage loan should be included in this section.[224] For instance, the grantor or mortgagor represents and warrants that its borrowing entity, whether a corporation or a limited partnership, is duly formed, organized, and filed under the laws of the state in which it is doing business; that the loan documents being executed by the borrowing entity are being done within the power of the corporation or the limited partnership; that all necessary governmental approvals have been obtained; and that the making of this loan does not violate any provision of law or any order of any court. In the sample deed of trust, the grantor also warrants to the beneficiary that all relevant data supplied by it to the beneficiary—in order to induce the beneficiary to make a loan—are true and correct and material in all respects. The grantor further warrants that all of the real estate taxes, as well as federal, state, county, and municipal income taxes, have been paid, and that at the time of the making of the loan there is no pending litigation against the property or the grantor.

Mortgaged Property and Other Property. It should be noted that absent a provision warranting the grantor's title in fee simple to the land, and good and marketable title to the fixtures and personalty, the grantor or mortgagor does not impliedly warrant title. If he should subsequently acquire the property described in the deed of trust or

---

[222] Osborne, et al., note 221 *supra*, at 583 to 585, § 9.3; 3 *Glenn on Mortgages* § 418 (1948).

[223] See Article 2 of Form 3.4 in Appendix B.

[224] See Article 3 of Form 3.4 in Appendix B.

After-Acquired Property Clause. An after-acquired property clause is used to create an equitable lien upon both the real and personal property subsequently acquired by the mortgagor with the exception of improvements put on the land.[217] The theory, applied in most jurisdictions, is that the clause is in substance a promise that the after-acquired property shall be made subject to the lien of the mortgage. The promise warrants specific performance when the mortgagor later acquires the property described in the clause.[218] However, in some states, such as New Jersey, the clause is enforceable only if the new property bears a functional relationship to the property originally mortgaged.[219] In other states, the clause is effective without the mortgagee actually taking possession or obtaining a supplemental mortgage only if the mortgagor is a railroad or public utility company.[220]

However, a problem frequently addressed by the commentators[221] is how to resolve certain troublesome questions involving claims of lien priority as between real estate mortgagees invoking their rights under these clauses and those obtaining a security or ownership interest in the after-acquired property before or after it became mortgaged. For example, if the after-acquired property covered by the original mortgage is later sold or mortgaged by the borrower to a subsequent purchaser or mortgagee, can it be said that the subsequent taker has record or inquiry notice of the original mortgagee's equitable lien under the recording statutes? Under the grantor-grantee index in a particular jurisdiction, it would be necessary for the subsequent taker to check every mortgage that the borrower may have previously executed—without the aid of a legal description of the subsequently acquired property—before he

---

[217] Clearly, to the extent that the subsequent improvements on the property that is originally mortgaged are fixtures, the mortgagee should be able to enjoy the benefit of these additions without the need to resort to use of the after-acquired property clause.

[218] 3 *Glenn on Mortgages* § 412 (1943); Cunningham & Tischler, "Equitable Real Estate Mortgages," 17 Rutgers L. Rev. 679, 719 (1963) (hereinafter cited as Cunningham).

[219] E.g., Williamson v. New Jersey So. R.R., 29 N.J. Eq. 311, 337 (E. & A. 1878); See Cunningham, note 218 *supra*, at 718; 3 *Glenn on Mortgages* § 414 (1943).

[220] Cunningham, note 218 *supra*, at 718; 3 *Glenn on Mortgages* §§ 421-423 (1943). See Franklin v. Community Federal S&L Ass'n, 478 F. Supp. 22 (E.D. Mo. 1979), where the court held that an after-acquired clause secures only real estate, fixtures, and attachments, and not any after-acquired consumer goods.

[221] See Osborne, Nelson & Whitman, *Real Estate Finance Law* 583-585, § 9.3 (1979) (hereinafter cited as Osborne, et al.), 3 *Glenn on Mortgages* § 418 (1943).

The Hawaii Supreme Court in *Akamine & Sons, Ltd. v. American Security Bank*[212] stated it would only enforce a dragnet clause if the additional indebtedness related to the same transaction. If it did not, such a dragnet clause would be against public policy in the state of Hawaii and would therefore not be enforceable. This "relation back" or "arising from the same indebtedness" test was further clarified by the Kansas Supreme Court in 1974, in the case of *Emporia State Bank & Trust Co., v. Mounkes*.[213] That court held that, "In the absence of clear, supportive evidence of a contrary intention a mortgage containing a dragnet type clause will not be extended to cover future advances unless the advances are of the same kind and quality or relate to the same transaction or series of transactions as the principal obligation secured or unless the document evidencing the subsequent advance refers to the mortgage as providing security therefor."[214] However, some states continue to adhere to the traditional mortgage law on the subject. For example, in a 1974 case the Georgia Supreme Court held, "Deeds to secure debt with open end or dragnet clauses continue to be effective so long as there exists indebtedness between the grantor and grantee."[215]

Nevertheless, as can be seen by the foregoing case law, any prudent mortgage lender should not rely upon the dragnet clause to secure additional indebtedness not related to the original secured indebtedness. As a minimum precaution, since such clauses are strictly construed against the party preparing the deed of trust,[216] the note evidencing subsequent indebtedness should specifically state that the indebtedness is secured by an already existing deed of trust, and the contract should show that the dragnet clause was a clearly understood and bargained-for element in the original deed of trust instrument. Finally, a conservative lender should insist upon a new deed of trust being executed with respect to the new indebtedness.

---

deed of trust did not cover judgments that a third party obtained against the mortgagors, and which were assigned to the mortgagee. Moreover, where there are several mortgagors, a dragnet clause does not reach other individually owned property of any of the mortgagors unless the dragnet clause specifically refers to "the mortgagor or either or any of them." See Holiday Inns v. Susher-Schaefer Inv. Co. 77 Mich. 658, 259 N.W.2d, 179 (1977).

[212] 50 Hawaii 304, 317, 440 P.2d 262, 268 (1968).
[213] 214 Kan. 178, 184, 519 P.2d 618, 623 (1974).
[214] *Id.* at 184, 519 P.2d at 623.
[215] Citizens & So. DeKalb Bank v. Hicks, 232 Ga. 244, 245, 206 S.E.2d 22, 24 (1974); see also Bryant v. Branch, 235 S.E.2d 688, 692 (Ga. 1977); Lanney v. Producers Livestock Credit Corp., 463 P.2d 491, 495 (Wyo. 1970); First Nat'l Bank v. Rozelle, 493 F.2d 1196, 1203 (10th Cir. 1974).
[216] E.g., Boyett v. Carden, 347 So. 2d 759, 761 (Fla. App. 1977).

However, based perhaps on historical favoritism toward purchase-money security interests, the Code, as amended in 1972, accords automatic lien priority as to a fixture claim if the security interest is a purchase-money security interest. Such interest is perfected by a "fixture filing" before the goods were affixed to the premises so as to become fixtures, or within ten days thereafter.[205] Lien priority over a real estate mortgage also extends, under the Code, to factory, office, and consumer-appliance fixtures that are readily removable, such as office machines, ranges, air conditioners, and refrigerators, if before the goods become fixtures, the security interest in such item is perfected by any method permitted under the Code.[206]

Indebtedness and the Dragnet Clause. The definition of indebtedness in Article 1 of the sample deed of trust (Form 3.4) includes not only the principal and interest due under the note, but also includes all other indebtedness of the borrower to this lender. The instant real estate security thus automatically secures other, usually unspecified, debt of the mortgagor that it may already owe or will owe in the future to this particular mortgagee. This is the dragnet clause which, while traditionally valid under mortgage law, has come under increasing attack by various state courts. In *Brose v. International Milling Co.,* a 1964 case, an Iowa court held, "Such provisions (dragnet clause) are not favored and should be closely scrutinized, but it will be enforced to the extent it appears to have been within the intent of the parties."[207] Another state court noted, "By their broad and general terms they enwrap the unsuspecting debtor in the folds of indebtedness embraced and secured in the mortgage which he did not contemplate."[208] A 1966 Texas decision held that the Anaconda clause is generally unenforceable unless the debts it purports to secure were in the contemplation of the parties at the time the mortgage was created.[209] In addition, there has also been some recent case law focusing on the intent of the parties and other traditional elements of contract law,[210] and limiting the reach of such clauses.[211]

---

[205] *Id.* § 9-313(4)(a) (1972).

[206] *Id.* § 9-313(4)(c) (1972). Also see generally Quinn, *UCC Commentary and Law Digest* § 9-313[A], (1978).

[207] 256 Iowa 875, 882, 129 N.W.2d 672, 675 (1964).

[208] Berger v. Fuller, 180 Ark. 372, 377, 21 S.W.2d 419, 421 (1929).

[209] Wood v. Parker Square State Bank, 400 S.W.2d 898, 911 (Tex. 1966).

[210] E.g., Freese Leasing, Inc. v. Union Trust & Sav. Bank, 253 N.W.2d 921, 927 (Iowa 1977). Kimball Foods, Inc. v. Republic Nat'l Bank of Dallas, 557 F.2d 491, 515 (5th Cir. 1977).

[211] In Pongetti v. Bankers Trust Sav. and Loan Ass'n, 368 So. 2d 819, 824 (Miss. 1979), the Supreme Court of Mississippi held that a dragnet clause in a

Usury Clause. An exculpatory provision absolving the lender beforehand from any intention to violate the local usury laws is often used. Although it is not harmful, reliance upon it is misplaced since it is usually held to be without curative effect.[202]

[4] The Mortgage/Deed of Trust

There are as many and as varied deeds of trust and mortgages as there are attorneys. However, the standard sample deed of trust, Form 3.4 (see Appendix B), was selected for analysis and commentary because it integrates the requirements of the construction lender (as discussed in Chapter 4) and those of the permanent lender. It is well detailed and employs a definitional format which goes beyond that contained in the typical real estate mortgage.

[a] Definitions

The first article of the document[203] defines the terms used throughout the deed of trust or mortgage—beneficiary, buildings, construction lender, events of default, fixtures, grantor, impositions, indebtedness, the land, leases, maturity date, and the mortgaged property. In the event of litigation, a deed of trust or mortgage with clearly defined terms is very helpful. Particular attention should be given to the following points when drafting the document.

Fixtures. Conflicts in lien priority frequently arise, especially in the case of apartment building loans, between a real estate mortgagee and a creditor claiming a security interest in chattels called "fixtures" (e.g., elevators, refrigerators) that become attached to the real estate. Under the Uniform Commercial Code, a security interest in such chattels— except for ordinary building materials incorporated into a structure like lumber and bricks—can be created by filing a "financing statement," which briefly describes the collateral, is signed by both the borrower and the secured party, and otherwise conforms to the requirements of U.C.C. § 9-402. As to fixtures, the general rule governing lien priority under the Code, as amended in 1972, is that any antecedent chattel security interest in fixtures will prevail over a real estate mortgage only if the prior chattel claim was filed before the real estate mortgage was recorded.[204] Under standard conveyancing legal theory, such prior filing would put a subsequent mortgagee on notice of the prior claim.

---

[202] See discussion at ¶ 5.02[1].
[203] See Article 1 of Form 3.4 in Appendix B.
[204] U.C.C. § 9-313(4)(b) (1972).

[3] The Note

The note,[193] not the deed of trust or mortgage, is the legal evidence of indebtedness. It must spell out the terms of payment, such as loan amount, rate of interest, and amortization period.[194] Thus, any prepayment privilege should be inserted in the note rather than in the deed of trust or mortgage.[195] Also, if there is a provision for "additional compensation" or some other "equity kicker," such provision should also be inserted in the note.[196]

Acceleration Upon Default. The lender must spell out its right to accelerate upon a default, including its, or subsequent holder's, right to apply any payments received to principal or interest as it elects, without notice to the borrower.[197] Penalty interest is usually charged as well, and is due and payable upon default. Since the payment of penalty interest is a contingency within the control of the borrower, such payment is not considered "interest" under local usury law.[198]

Assignment of a Construction Note. If the construction note is negotiable, and the note is assigned to the permanent lender when the permanent loan is closed, the permanent lender can qualify for "holder-in-due-course" status under the Uniform Commercial Code if it meets the value, good-faith, and notice requirements of the Code.[199] In such event, the permanent lender would take the construction note free from all "personal defenses," such as lack or failure of consideration, for example, when the borrower claims that the construction lender failed to make the loan, or that the loan has been paid.[200]

The note is usually drafted so that all parties who are secondarily liable—prior endorsers, guarantors—waive those formal UCC requirements (such as presentment, notice of protest, etc.) that must be met before suit can be brought against them. Also, if a construction note is assigned to a permanent lender or some other assignee, the construction lender will customarily absolve itself from any secondary liability by indorsing the note "without recourse."[201]

---

[193] For sample note, see Form 3.3 in Appendix B.
[194] See discussion of these terms at ¶ 3.04.
[195] See discussion of prepayment privilege at ¶ 3.04[5].
[196] See discussion of equity kickers at ¶ 3.04[3][a].
[197] See ¶ 3.08[4][g] for further discussion of acceleration and other default remedies.
[198] See discussion of usury and interest at ¶ 5.03[8].
[199] U.C.C. § 3-104(2).
[200] See discussion at ¶ 4.03[1].
[201] *Id.*

trustee may be *said* by the courts to gain title, yet he will be denied those incidents of title, notably the right to possession, that the courts in that state have decided should not be given to the mortgagee as additional protection for collecting his debt.[188]

The most important difference between the two security devices lies in the remedies afforded to the lender once the borrower defaults. By using a deed of trust, the lender can avoid the expense and delay of judicial foreclosure and statutory redemption; the lender can direct the trustees to carry out the terms of the trust by selling the property free of judicial interference.[189] However, to a large extent, even this difference vanishes in those mortgage jurisdictions permitting foreclosure under a power of sale contained in the mortgage.[190]

[2] Use of Uniform Documents

Most mortgage forms used by institutional lenders across the country could consist of uniform covenants. Convenants geared to local law would be needed only in such matters as debt acceleration and remedies on default, effect of future advances, and waiver of dower and curtesy. Of benefit to the conventional mortgage market is a joint effort by Fannie Mae and Freddie Mac to develop a single set of multi-family mortgage documents acceptable to both organizations for all fifty states. These will help to standardize mortgage documentation and will ultimately homogenize mortgage law throughout the country. The story of this effort and the documentation resulting therefrom is well told in an article written by James E. Murray, General Counsel of FNMA and Henry L. Judy, General Counsel of FHLMC.[191]

Since the note and the deed of trust or mortgage are so fundamental, the following discussion is designed to familiarize the reader with the standard language contained in these documents. The major provisions will be briefly explained or commented upon.[192]

---

[188] Osborne, *Handbook on the Law of Mortgages* § 17 (2d ed. 1970) (hereinafter cited as Osborne (1970)).

[189] *Id.*

[190] See discussion at ¶ 3.08[4][g].

[191] Murray & Judy, "The Federal National Mortgage Association and Federal Home Loan Mortgage Corporation Uniform Multi-family Mortgage Instruments," 33 Bus. Law. 2302 (1978).

[192] References are given to the appropriate sections of sample mortgage/deed of trust, Form 3.4 in Appendix B.

Since the loan term and lock-in period are so brief, the developer may seek this type of financing because he believes that long-term interest rates will drop in a few years, or in the case of new construction, that once construction is completed and the property is "on stream," he will be able to refinance or obtain a more attractive long-term loan than would otherwise have been possible at the time the standby was negotiated.

Alternatively, fundable standby takeouts have been used in instances where one real estate company takes over another to obtain the latter's real estate holdings. This is with the expectation that with better management it can increase the rentals from the acquired property. Accordingly, the acquiring entity negotiates a fundable standby loan based on current rental income streams, but nevertheless anticipates that in time, with better management, the income stream can be increased so that it will be able to secure a larger and more attractive conventional long-term mortgage loan. But if for some reason the increased income stream is not achieved, the company's fallback position is that it can request that the standby loan be funded, knowing that the existing rental income stream would be able to carry the standby loan.

¶ 3.08 DRAFTING THE MORTGAGE/DEED OF TRUST

[1] Definition of Mortgage/Deed of Trust

The mortgage is the basic security instrument-document; its definitional elements include: "a debt or obligation to be secured, due from the mortgagor to the mortgagee, a right to foreclose, and the reciprocal [borrower's] right to redeem...."[187] In addition to the ordinary mortgage, many states such as California and Virginia use a device called the deed of trust, sometimes called "trust deed mortgage." It consists of a conveyance of certain real property by the borrower ("grantor" or "trustor") to a person who is usually a third party ("trustee") to hold the property in trust as security for the payment of a debt to the lender ("beneficiary"),

Since courts recognize the true function of the deed of trust as a security device, they generally have refused to follow the usual trust doctrines and, as with the mortgage, they accord to the deed of trust only those incidents which they feel are necessary for security purposes. For example, in a lien theory state (where, as opposed to the situation in a title theory state, the mortgagor is regarded as retaining legal title) the

---

[187] R.H. Macy & Co. v. Bates, 280 App. Div. 292, 296, 114 N.Y.S.2d 143, 146 (1952).

whereas neither the borrower nor the lender expects or desires the standby loan ever to be funded. The standby commitment is made by one lender to assure a bank or some other lender to whom the developer has applied for a construction loan, that if a permanent takeout is not secured by the developer, the standby will be converted to a permanent takeout. To lessen the chance of the loan being called, the interest rate may be substantially above the market rate, and the constant may be exorbitant and unrealistic. Some require that, while the commitment is for perhaps a five-year period, the loan can only be funded in a given month, which, needless to say, makes funding very difficult. Another customary condition of funding is that the borrower must notify the standby lender of its intention to seek funding well in advance, say, 120 days, of the funding date. Many lenders, fearful of being called upon to fund,[185] have used the pretext of not receiving commitment renewal fees or closing in time in order to cancel the commitment. To date, few, if any, of the great number of standby loans issued have ever been funded. Surprisingly, there has been little litigation in this area.[186] However, it is the authors' opinion that no pattern of decision will emerge, as each case will be decided on totally different facts.

[2] The "Fundable Standby"

Recently, a new type of standby, the "fundable" or "bankable" standby, has appeared on the real estate financing scene. Such companies as General Electric Credit Corporation, the Aetna Business Corporation, US Life Real Estate Services Corp., and CIT Corporation are in the business of making fundable or bankable standby loans with the expectation of actually funding the standby loan commitment. Essentially, this type of commitment carries a higher interest rate, usually three to four points higher than a comparable conventional long-term mortgage loan. Moreover, the term of the loan, when funded, ranges only from two to seven years, *but* the constant is *affordable*, since amortization is based on a twenty-five or thirty-year term with a balloon at the end. The lock-in period usually lasts only one or two years.

---

[185] As market interest rates began to skyrocket in 1974, standby rates negotiated several years prior became more attractive, and banks with unviable completed projects started pressuring standby lenders to fund.

[186] See Hawkins v. First Fed. Sav. & Loan Ass'n, 291 Ala. 257, 262, 280 So. 2d 93, 97 (1973) (where standby lender successfully insisted that standby fee be forfeited because loan did not close at scheduled closing date even though building permit problem cured shortly after deadline date).

Moreover, it would seem that specific performance should be available to a borrower who cannot get financing within a reasonable time for the project to go forward as anticipated because the money market is so tight at a particular time that there is no money available elsewhere at a price the borrower could afford. The legal remedy of damages would not be possible because the unavailability of another loan actually prevents proof of loss of his bargain with the permanent lender; his ability to prove consequential damage would be limited by the requirements of specific proof and foreseeability. Finally, observe that later in the commercial lending cycle, each party becomes entitled to specific performance by virtue of express language in the buy-sell agreement.[183]

¶ 3.07 THE STANDBY "LOAN COMMITMENT"

[1] The Regular Standby

The inherent risks associated with construction lending are such that construction lenders view the permanent takeout commitment as the singular guaranty of payment at the end of the construction period. In addition, as noted earlier, nationally chartered banks are not subject to the requirements associated with a real estate loan if they lend against a takeout commitment.[184] Permanent financing is, therefore, ordinarily a condition precedent to obtaining a commitment from a construction lender. Accordingly, if the developer is not able to secure a permanent takeout commitment, it may be necessary for him to obtain a "standby commitment" in order to qualify for construction financing. The standby commitment seems to be similar to the permanent commitment. However, no two commitments could be more dissimilar. A permanent commitment is granted with the expectation of funding the loan,

---

Selective Builders Inc. v. Hudson City Sav. Bank, 349 A.2d 564, granted this relief to the borrower against a permanent lender even though the borrower had not fully completed construction by the date specified in the permanent commitment, on the grounds that the contract had not expressly stated that "time is of the essence." Moreover, since the lender did not object to the construction delays in a timely manner, he was estopped from claiming that these delays had caused a default. For a general discussion, see Groot "Specified Performance of Contracts to Provide Permanent Financing," 60 Cornell L. Rev. 718, 736-742 (1975). Mehr & Kilgore, "Enforcement of the Real Estate Loan Commitment: Improvement of the Borrower's Remedies," 24 Wayne L. Rev. 1011 (1978).

[183] See discussion at ¶ 4.05.
[184] See note 2 *supra,* and discussion at ¶ 2.02[2][d].

agreed that, if this application is approved and the loan committed without material change (material change is defined as a change in the loan amount, rate, term, guaranty, or prepayment provisions as set forth on page 1 of the application), the loan must be settled within .days after Borrower is notified of the commitment, and construction of the project must be commenced within . . . . .days after settlement or the good-faith deposit will be forfeited as liquidated damages to the Lender for Borrower's failure to consummate the transaction and the commitment shall become void.

The major problem with this type of clause is that the parties may disagree over what is a "material change" justifying a return of the good-faith deposit. Certainly, this phrase must be spelled out with great particularity, and the borrower should attempt to include all the terms and conditions of special benefit to him within the ambit of "material change." This language should not be confused with what is known as the "no material change" condition in the commitment, which requires the borrower to certify at or prior to closing that there has been no material change in the representations made in the application (e.g., in his or her tenants' financial condition) and that no judicial or administrative action is pending, which, if adversely determined, could adversely affect the loan or the secured property.[180]

While in theory a contract to lend money is not specifically enforceable[181] by either party, money damages being regarded as an adequate remedy, the lender might argue for specific performance on the rationale that the security for the loan is unique (e.g., borrower's reputation as builder, his credit standing, particular piece of property involved) and, as previously indicated, his actual money damages may be difficult to ascertain. However, there does not appear to be any case law supporting specific performance for the lender. Similarly, the borrower might argue that a loan commitment from a particular well-known lender has a unique value that is difficult to measure in monetary terms because many potential benefits for the borrower are so intangible. For example, a respected lender's expressed willingness to invest in the borrower's project may enable the borrower to exact more favorable terms from both the interim lender and the major tenants.[182]

---

[180] See Section 4(b) of Form 3.2 and condition 10 of Form 3.1 in Appendix B.
[181] 5A Corbin, *Contracts* § 1152 (1964).
[182] A few courts have recently granted specific performance to the borrower. E.g., Cuna Mut. Ins. Soc'y v. Dominguez, 9 Ariz. App. 172, 175, 450 P.2d 413, 416 (1969); Vandeventer v. Dale Constr. Co., 271 Ore. 691, 695, 534 P.2d 183, 185 (1975). Indeed, in 1975 the Superior Court of New Jersey, in

constitutes the agreed-upon amount of liquidated damages to which the lender is entitled if the borrower should go elsewhere for his loan if interest rates soften or if he should otherwise default. Since in most loan transactions it is quite difficult to measure the lender's actual cost of holding funds available and preparatory expenses for a particular loan closing,[176] courts have enforced such clauses when the amount of liquidated damages is reasonable.[177] There is also case law holding that when the borrower is prevented from closing the loan by the commitment date, impossibility of performance cannot be raised as a legal defense by the borrower in an action to recover a commitment fee forfeited to the lender.[178] Conversely, if the lender defaults under the terms of the commitment and the loan fails to close, the lender is liable to the borrower for all damages reasonably foreseeable at the time the commitment was executed, including the cost of obtaining new financing, and the difference between the interest at the contract rate and the rate of interest the borrower must pay in the open market.[179] Recovery for such items as loss of prospective tenants or prospective sales would probably be barred as too speculative.

Applications of some lenders also contain language which reads as follows:

> There is enclosed with this application a check in the amount of $ ....payable to Lender as a good-faith deposit which will be returned immediately to Borrower in the event this application is not approved as submitted. It is understood and

---

[176] Theoretically, the amount of damage would be the difference, reduced to present value, between the total interest on the committed amount at the contract rate and the total interest on the committed amount at the market rate and perhaps such consequential damages as could be proved by the lender as reasonably contemplated or foreseeable.

[177] E.g., Boston Rd. Shopping Center, Inc. v. Teachers Ins. & Annuity Ass'n of America, 13 App. Div. 2d 106, 111, 213 N.Y.S.2d 522, 528 (1961), aff'd 11 N.Y.2d 831, 227 N.Y.S.2d 444, 445 (1962); White Lakes Shopping Center v. Jefferson Standard Life Ins. Co., 208 Kan. 121, 128, 490 P.2d 609, 615 (1971); Lowe v. Massachusetts Mut. Life Ins. Co., 54 Cal. App. 3d 718, 743, 127 Cal. Rptr. 23, 37 (1976).

[178] See Hawkins v. First Fed. Sav. & Loan Ass'n, 291 Ala. 257, 262, 280 So. 2d 93, 97 (1973), wherein the city refused to issue a building permit, thus preventing the borrower from closing, and the court distinguished between impossibility created by a subsequent change in the law (valid defense) and impossibility due to the unfavorable exercise of discretion by local officials acting under existing law (invalid defense).

[179] E.g., Stanish v. Polish Roman Catholic Union of America, 484, F.2d 713, 726 (7th Cir. 1973); Pipkin v. Thomas & Hill, Inc., 33 N.C. App. 710, 722, 236 S.E.2d 725, 733.

mortgagee without an agreement between the mortgagee, the landlord-mortgagor, and the tenant, specifying the payment to be made on the exercise of the option, and providing that the proceeds shall be held to further secure the mortgage indebtedness. If the lease should be subordinate to the mortgage, the lease should provide that if the tenants should acquire title to the mortgaged premises, the lease shall not merge into the fee and the tenant shall assume the mortgage since the tenant will be taking the place of the prior mortgagor from whom the tenant acquired the title.

[9] Financing

A useful provision for the developer to incorporate in every prime lease is one that would enable him to make future changes to satisfy any permanent mortgagee—at least to the extent that the mortgagee may reasonably require—in order to secure financing of the proposed development. An additional stipulation would be that if the landlord cannot secure his financing within a specified period because the tenant will not modify its lease as required by mortgagee, then the landlord may terminate the lease within a specified number of days after the landlord has requested such changes from the tenant.[173]

¶ 3.06 REMEDIES FOR BREACH OF MORTGAGE LOAN COMMITMENT

Generally, the amount of the "good-faith" or security deposit is about 2 percent of the loan amount. The borrower should attempt to furnish this in the form of a letter of credit or certificate of deposit so that he can either avoid a tie-up of funds, or at least earn some interest on his outlay of cash.[174]

In contrast to the application fee,[175] the refundable "good-faith" security or "standby" deposit, sometimes called the "commitment fee,"

---

[173] Also see ¶ 3.08[5] for additional requirements with respect to shopping center loans.

[174] See section 2 of Form 3.2, and conditions 18 and 19 of Form 3.1 in Appendix B.

[175] Such fee is usually expressed as a fractional percentage (generally one percent) of the loan and is paid simultaneously with the submission of the application. In some cases, the application fee is also regarded as the consideration paid by the borrower to compensate the lender for the opportunity cost and administrative expense of processing the loan application and keeping sufficient loan funds on hand to fund the loan.

should agree not to subordinate its rights under the lease, except to the holder of the first mortgage. The tenant should also agree that its rights to any proceeds of hazard insurance, condemnation, or damages for change of grade shall be subordinate to the rights of the holder of the first mortgage. A permanent lender will often insist that it be given the unilateral right to subordinate its first mortgage to any subsequent lease, or, alternatively, that all the junior high-credit tenants execute attornment agreements with the lender. This problem often arises when the parties use a pre-closed form of buy-sell agreement, and the construction loan mortgage is assigned to the permanent lender. Since the permanent mortgage will automatically have lien priority over leases executed and recorded after the construction loan mortgage, these valuable leases could inadvertently be wiped out at foreclosure.[171]

As a quid pro quo for requiring attornment agreements, the developer should insist that the permanent lender agree to execute "non-disturbance" agreements with the major tenants, who will probably insist that the cross-obligations between themselves and the permanent lender be a "two-way street."

[7] Assignment

Assignment by a prime tenant must be prohibited without the consent of the landlord, and under the mortgage, this right of approval must be reserved to the mortgagee. Any assignment must be for a similar use and not conflict with any co-tenancy or exclusive-use privilege contained in the other leases. Also, no right to discontinue doing business at the leased premises should be afforded under the lease.[172] The right to preclude assignment must not be based on a standard of reasonableness, but must be at the absolute discretion of the lessor. On assignment, the obligation of the original tenant to meet the lease obligations should survive.

[8] Option to Purchase

If the lease is superior in lien priority to the mortgage and contains an option of first refusal right to purchase the leased premises, it too may prime the mortgage; hence, the lease cannot be approved by the

---

[171] See discussion at ¶ 4.05.

[172] The case law has not supported specific performance actions to enforce this covenant. See Price v. Herman, 81 N.Y.S.2d 361, 363, *aff'd* 87 N.Y.S.2d 221 (1949); Securities Builders v. Southwest Drug Co., 244 Miss. 877, 886, 147 So. 2d 635, 639 (1962).

assignment or subletting is permitted, the lender will insist that an appropriate alternative rent be imposed on the substitute tenant, whose sales volume may be lower than that of his predecessor.

[5] Alterations

Both the lender's standard form of deed of trust and assignment of lease instrument[167] prohibit major alterations by tenants without the lender's consent; the property might otherwise be exposed to mechanics' or materialmen's liens, and the rights of other tenants, such as parking ratios, might be violated. The lender will normally approve the request if the alteration is funded by the tenant and subject to posting a completion bond with adequate protection against mechanics' and materialmen's liens. The lease may require the landlord to fund a portion of the alteration cost if, for example, the tenant's gross sales exceed a stated minimum, but the mortgagee may not legally be able to comply in the event it takes over at foreclosure if the additional investment exceeds the maximum legal loan-to-value ratio. Consequently, any lease agreement giving tenants the right to alter or expand their premises should put them on notice of any prerogatives reserved by the lender.

[6] Subordination of Lease to Mortgage

In many deed of trust jurisdictions, such as California, and in a few states where the mortgage form is used,[168] any lease subsequent or subordinated by agreement to a mortgage will be automatically extinguished at foreclosure absent an "attornment" agreement executed by the tenant.[169] Consequently, a lease provision which automatically subordinates the lease to *any* mortgage without the mortgagor's and permanent lender's consent[170] is objectionable to the permanent lender holding the first mortgage, since in such jurisdictions a second mortgage by foreclosing, could inadvertently or purposely eliminate a prime tenant whose lease primes the first mortgage. Accordingly, the tenant

---

[167] See Article 5.2 of Form 3.4, and Form 3.5 in Appendix B.

[168] E.g., McDermott v. Burke, 16 Cal. 580, 590 (1860). But the majority rule is that where a lease is subsequent to the mortgage, the lessee must be joined in at the foreclosure action in order to extinguish his lease. E.g., Metropolitan Life Ins. Co. v. Childs Co., 230 N.Y. 285, 296, 130 N.E. 295, 299 (1921); Davis v. Boyajian, Inc., 11 Ohio Misc. 97, 102, 229 N.E.2d 116, 119 (1967). It is well settled that a lease prior to a mortgage is unaffected by foreclosure.

[169] See Form 3.14 in Appendix B.

[170] See Sections 7 and 10 of Form 3.5 in Appendix B.

of other tenants, control of the pricing and merchandising policies of other tenants, and limitations on the location of the other tenants in the shopping center or other premises.[163]

Sometimes, the mortgagor, as landlord, will covenant that neither it nor its assigns will lease property within a certain radius of the center. However, in the event the mortgagee is forced to take over at foreclosure, it might be powerless to enforce the restriction since it would relate to property located beyond the mortgaged premises. Consequently, the lender may want the tenant to waive its enforcement rights or, at a minimum, to limit its remedy to damages or injunctive relief in the event the mortgagee takes over as landlord.

Finally, some leases contain a co-tenancy requirement whereby secondary tenants receive a covenant from the mortgagor that certain prime tenants, with customer-drawing power, shall stay in continuous operation for time periods co-terminous with the lease terms of the dependent secondary tenants. The lender might require estoppel letters[164] ensuring that this condition be met. In addition it might ask that these secondary tenants waive their cancellation rights with respect to certain contingencies specified in the co-tenancy clause, over which it has no control, such as a major default by or bankruptcy of those prime tenants. Alternatively, the lender might insist that the provision not apply to temporary closings for repairs, etc., or that the landlord be permitted to supply comparable prime tenants, as substitutes, within a reasonable time to satisfy the restriction.

[4] Percentage Rental

Another provision frequently encountered in shopping center leases calls for additional rent in the form of a designated percentage of the tenant's gross or net sales. Such provision is analogous to an "additional compensation" clause in a mortgage or deed of trust note[165] and should be accompanied by an "audit" provision permitting an independent inspection of the tenant's books and records.[166] In the event an

---

[163] See Consent Decrees in *In re* Tyson's Corner S.C., Dkt. No. 8886 (F.T.C., May 3, 1974); and *In re* Gimble Bros., Dkt. No. 8885 (F.T.C., July 30, 1973).

[164] See Form 3.11 in Appendix B.

[165] See ¶ 3.04[3][a].

[166] See Article 4.15 of Form 3.4 in Appendix B. It is imperative that the definition of the percentage rental base be tightly drafted; otherwise, needless litigation may ensue. See, for example, Hempstead Theatre Corp. v. Metropolitan Playhouse, Inc., 6 N.Y.2d 311, 322, 160 N.E.2d 604, 610, 189 N.Y.S.2d 837, 845 (1959); Mutual Life Ins. Co. of N.Y. v. Tailored Woman, 309 N.Y. 248, 258, 128 N.E.2d 401, 406 (1955).

restoration period. In case of partial condemnation, most lenders will not tolerate a tenant's right to cancel unless it is geared to some reasonable percentage of area taken. Most will also insist that a portion of the proceeds sufficient to counteract the diminution in rent be applied to reduce the mortgage indebtedness, that the rent reduction be geared to some objective standard (e.g., "in proportion to the space taken"), and that the tenant not be allowed to share in the proceeds except to the extent of its loss of improvements and fixtures.

[3] Radius Restrictions, Exclusive-Use Clauses, and Co-tenancy Requirements in Shopping Center Leases

Often, an overanxious developer will be careless about granting exclusives in his effort to attract high-credit tenants into a shopping center. Accordingly, any lawyer reviewing shopping center leases for the permanent lender will be confronted with the onerous task of trying to reconcile overlapping exclusive-use clauses. Carefully worded and narrowly defined, specific-use clauses will help ameliorate such conflicts, and most lenders will require that, at a minimum, the tenants' remedies be limited to damages or injunctive relief; otherwise, a court may treat breaches of such clauses as material enough to warrant cancellation of the lease agreements.

The clause should contain a covenant by the lessee to the effect that under applicable zoning regulations, the premises can be used for the purposes for which leased, and that the tenant waives any right of cancellation if it cannot be so used during the term of the lease. The clause should not contain any warranty against future zoning changes.

Federal and state antitrust laws have recently been applied to both exclusive use and radius restrictions on the ground that such provisions, especially "no discounter" clauses, are illegal restraints of competition. The courts have generally tested lease restriction against a standard of reasonableness.[162]

The consent decrees which the Federal Trade Commission has secured in these cases generally strike down veto power over the identity

---

[162] E.g., Dalmo Sales Co. v. Tyson's Corner Regional Shopping Center, 308 F. Supp. 988, 995 (1970), aff'd 429 F.2d 206, 209 (D.C. Cir. 1970). See generally Note, "The Antitrust Implications of Restrictive Covenants in Shopping Center Leases," 86 Harv. L. Rev. 1201 (1973); Halper, "The Antitrust Laws Visit Shopping Center 'Use Restrictions'," 4 Real Estate L.J. 3 (1975). Note also the tax consequences to a lessee-covenantor who assigns or subleases his leasehold estate in a shopping center and demands a covenant not to compete of the assignee or sublessee. See Madison, "Tax Treatment of Covenants Not to Compete," 24 U. Miami L. Rev. 1 (1969).

[2] Default and Termination Provisions

Foremost among the lender's requirements is that the lease contain adequate termination and default provisions. Under an assignment of lease instrument,[157] the landlord-mortgagor may not, without the mortgagee's consent, cancel any lease assigned to the lender as additional collateral in the event of the tenant's default. However, if such consent is given and the lease is canceled, it should contain a "survival of liability" clause; otherwise, the landlord may be precluded from recovering as damages the difference, if any, between the contract rental and rental from a substitute tenant during the balance of the original lease term.[158]

Secondly, in the mortgage or deed of trust form there is a provision requiring the mortgagor to perform faithfully all of his covenants, as landlord, in the lease agreement.[159] However, the value of this provision to the mortgagee depends upon a requirement in the lease agreement that the tenant provide prompt notice of any default to the mortgagee. The mortgagee would also like an opportunity to cure any such default within a reasonable time. Some chain leases give the tenant the right to cancel for any default by the landlord; however, most lenders will insist that the cancellation privilege be waived with respect to those defaults which the mortgagee cannot cure, such as, for example, the insolvency of the mortgagor. Absent these protections, the tenant could threaten the security for the loan by canceling the lease or abating rent in the event of a serious default by the landlord-mortgagor.

The lender would object, however, to a lease provision enabling the tenant to cure the landlord's mortgage defaults and be reimbursed by paying less rent. Such rental offsets could be used to pay off a junior mortgage and deprive the first mortgagee of the security to which he is primarily entitled.

Finally, some chain leases authorize the tenant to cancel in the event of fire destruction or condemnation, no matter how small the damage or the taking. The lender will object to this language; however, in most cases it will agree to use the insurance proceeds, to which it is entitled under a "standard mortgage clause,"[160] to restore the premises rather than to reduce the mortgage indebtedness.[161] It will also agree to a rent reduction proportionate to the tenant's loss of space, during the

---

[157] See Form 3.5 in Appendix B.
[158] Friedman, *Preparation of Leases* 46 (1969).
[159] See Section 4.7 of Form 3.4 in Appendix B.
[160] See Form 3.12 in Appendix B.
[161] See Article 4.5 of Form 3.4 in Appendix B and discussion at ¶ 3.08 [4][d].

work with developer's lawyers in the drafting of the leases or in advising them as to their specific requirements. Correspondence should be promptly initiated by developer's counsel while the lease negotiations are under way. Unfortunately, the developer is frequently so anxious to secure the major leases in order to assure the financing that the developer's lawyer is often faced with a "fait accompli" in the form of a completed lease. He must then try to persuade the lender's lawyers that the lease provides the necessary assurances that the rental stream will continue for the term of the loan, or must face the onerous task of cajoling the tenant to modify the lease in order to satisfy the permanent mortgagee. Occasionally, the lender's lawyers are able to persuade a major tenant to sign a side letter providing that as long as the lender has an interest in the property, the lease shall be deemed modified as required by the lender. In some instances, these leases are sufficiently long-term to liquidate the loan indebtedness by the loan maturity date. The perspicacious lender must also visualize itself as having to live with these lease provisions in the event it steps in as owner-landlord after a serious default by the mortgagor.

Consequently, when negotiating occupancy lease terms with prime tenants, the developer must be mindful of the following lender's requirements; these are designed to protect the rental income stream from cancellation or abatement. Otherwise, the developer or its attorney may be caught in the middle on the closing date between a permanent lender insisting upon changes in the lease and a prime tenant, with equal bargaining clout, who refuses to renegotiate a lease executed months or even years ago.

[1] Rent Provisions

The permanent lender's attorney wants to see an *express* covenant to pay specific rent at specific times in advance (e.g., "Tenant covenants and agrees to pay...") rather than a mere reservation of rent (e.g., "the rent shall be..."); otherwise, if the original tenant has the right to assign the lease, his obligation to pay rent will not survive an assignment.[156] Also, the lender will demand a prescribed minimum rent to cover the tenant's aliquot share of debt service, and if there is a security deposit, that the mortgagee will not be liable to the lessee for such deposit in the event the mortgagee should acquire possession or title to the mortgaged premises after default by the mortgagor-lessor.

---

[156] E.g., Fanning v. Stimson, 13 Iowa 42 (1862); Kimpton v. Walker, 9 Vt. 191 (1837). But see Samuels v. Ottinger, 169 Cal. 209, 146 P. 638 (1915).

"due on sale" clauses will continue to force purchasers to refinance at market rates. Likewise, there will be a continuation of "due on encumberance"provisions enabling lenders to renegotiate higher loan rates if the developer should seek additional financing to expand or renovate the mortgaged premises. These latter clauses will also be used by lenders to reduce the increasing risk of a reduction or mortgaging out of the developer's equity participation, a trend which has recently become worrisome to lenders.

¶ 3.05 ANALYSIS OF SHOPPING CENTER AND OTHER HIGH-CREDIT LEASES BY PERMANENT LENDER

In our hypothetical case involving a mortgage loan on a garden apartment complex, the Ace Insurance Co.'s appraisal-underwriting process involved an evaluation of the projected aggregate rental flow from the short-term occupancy leases, which are regarded as fundable by the lender. However, in the case of certain loans—those involving shopping centers, office buildings with long-term tenants, warehouses and other industrial facilities, and urban-renewal projects master-leased to a local housing authority—the security for the loan is the value attributable by the lender's appraiser to the rental obligations of specified high-credit tenants. Accordingly, in such loan transactions, the lender will want to evaluate the credit standing of each major or "prime" tenant. Also, the lender will demand, as a nonnegotiable condition of the commitment, the right to approve the form and substance of each lease, including the term, the tenants, and the rent payable, since it will expect the rental income stream from these leases to pay off the debt service on the loan. The other standard requirements in the commitment letter as to occupancy leases are that each prime lease be assigned to the lender as additional security and that the assignment be recorded and notice of the assignment served on the tenant; that the lease be in full force and effect; that there be no rental offsets or claims or defenses to enforcement; that the tenant shall have accepted its premises, confirmed commencement of its lease term, acknowledged that it is in occupancy and paying rent on current basis; and that satisfactory evidence be submitted to the lender as to all of the foregoing.[155] Before the leases are executed and delivered, the developer's lawyer should initially familiarize himself with the lender's requirements as to leases. Lender's lawyers welcome the opportunity to

---

[155] See Forms 3.5, 3.6, 3.7, Section 4(a) of Form 3.2 and "Occupancy Leases" paragraph of Form 3.1 in Appendix B.

constancy of interest rates, but also the term of the mortgage investment in light of the recent uncertainties caused by inflation.

Also, many life insurance companies are finding themselves in a liquidity bind. There has been an unprecedented drain on their reserves, caused by policy loans, which suddenly seem very inexpensive as compared with other consumer credit. Insurers have also found themselves unable to liquidate bonds in their portfolios due to collapsing bond prices in early 1980. These events point to the following trends for the 1980s, assuming inflation remains a problem. The large life insurance companies will want to commit most of their loans to projects in which they have some type of equity position, such as equity kickers, convertible debt options, or joint venture interests; the terms of such loans will still be ten to fifteen years amortized on a thirty-to-thirty-five year schedule, with a balloon payment. Indeed, at present several large insurance companies have a policy of making a mortgage loan only when they are able to obtain an equity interest in the property and some are even demanding a controlling interest in such joint ventures.[153a] There will be a smaller amount allocated to straight conventional loans, and the terms will probably be in an even shorter range of between five to seven years. One exception to the foregoing trends will be loans to the large, first-class developers whose projects, even on a straight conventional loan basis, will receive special treatment because of the quality of the projects and the developers.

With the allocation of greater funds to equities by the large life insurance companies, the small to medium-size companies will initially find higher quality properties on which to make loans. They may also get somewhat higher interest rates due to lack of competition from the large life insurance companies. To take up this loan slack, the market may even see more loan participations between groups of smaller life insurance companies. This will enable them to fund the larger loans, formerly the exclusive domain of the large insurers. However, if the large life insurance companies are successful in their equity programs (which means the ability to acquire the equity position and make a substantial return on that equity position), the smaller life insurance companies will eventually venture into the equity side of financing.

In addition, the more conservative lenders are becoming more active in issuing short-term fundable standby commitments. They are also imposing stiff prepayment penalties and lock-in periods to discourage borrowers from refinancing elsewhere.[154] If permitted by local law,

---

[153a] See discussion at ¶ 11.02. Henry, "Insurer's Role as Investor Shifts and Grows," N.Y. Times, May 24, 1981, Sec. 8 at 1, col. 1.

[154] See ¶ 3.04[5].

parcel not be prejudiced by the releases by giving tenants of the main parcel the right to terminate their leases or offset rental if, for example, a tenant on the main parcel has parking rights on the fringe area which the developer agreed to keep in repair, and the lender could not enforce this obligation because its mortgage no longer covers this area. The occupancy leases of the main parcel should require appropriate provisions to prevent their cancellation or modification by anything that happens on the fringe parcel, reserving only rights of injunction or damages against the developer.

[17] No Material Change Between Date of Final Commitment and Funding

This is a difficult condition for a construction lender to accept. It will do so only if it is satisfied with the permanent lender's past performance. For one thing, the developer and his construction lender must be definitely satisfied that the representations made in the application will be met. Any material variation in the financial condition of the developer or of the property prior to the closing date will extricate the permanent lender from its commitment. Estimates made in the application should therefore be conservative. Also, any deterioration in the financial affairs of the developer or of the high-credit tenants that could create serious doubts as to solvency, would constitute in effect an escape clause for the permanent lender. In that regard, it might well be useful for the developer, in negotiating the commitment, to try to obtain language providing for substitution of an insolvent tenant with one just as creditworthy as the original tenant was when the commitment was first issued.[152]

[18] Joint Venturing Requirement by Permanent Lenders and Other Trends in Permanent Financing

Institutional lenders have become disenchanted with fixed-rate long-term mortgage instruments as inflation has eroded their fixed rate of investment return and has increased their capital costs and overhead expenses while permitting borrowers to repay their loan indebtedness with cheaper dollars. One response, as noted earlier, was to begin to demand, during periods when mortgage money was in short supply, equity "kickers" in the form of additional interest geared to the borrowers' annual gross or net income and equity participations as joint ventures.[153] In addition, lenders have begun to question not only the

---

[152] See condition 10 of Form 3.1 in Appendix B.
[153] See discussion at ¶ 3.04[3][a].

title insurer obtain co-insurance or reinsurance of a portion of the amount of the title coverage, the identity of acceptable co-insurers or reinsurers and the amounts required to be co-insured or reinsured should be ascertained from lender's counsel in advance. Bids for the coverage can then be obtained. Most lenders will require the ALTA standard form of title insurance, but will permit the borrower to select the company from an approved list. A few lenders will allow the borrower to receive a premium or commission when payable by a third party, but none will agree to pay such charges themselves. Obviously, in a jurisdiction where title insurance is not available, the lender will be satisfied with an abstract and an attorney's opinion.[150]

Finally, the permanent lender will require that the borrower agree to pay all costs and expenses required to satisfy the conditions of the commitment and close the permanent loan, including: the fees and expenses of local counsel when employed; title examination, insurance, and survey costs; recording and filing fees; and mortgage taxes. While the requirement is probably not negotiable, the developer may request the lender's permission to negotiate the fees and charges that are negotiable (e.g., fixed fees for counsel and inspection services), prior to the issuance of the commitment.[151]

[16] Plot Size, Description of the Improvements, Location

The commitment should meticulously specify the identity and extent of the real property to be mortgaged. The developer's lawyer must protect the ability of his client to retain the right to sell, lease, or develop those areas that may be on the fringe of the area to be mortgaged or that may be necessary for the granting of an appurtenant easement to the main parcel to be mortgaged. Any site plan submitted to the lender should clearly specify those areas not included, with a legend to that effect. If the lender's appraisal requires additional land to support the requested loan, a provision should be negotiated permitting releases on prepayment; of principal to certain stipulated figures. The release provision, if possible, should call for reduction of amortization after prepayment; otherwise, the lender's mortgage on the main parcel will normally provide that prepayments be applied against installments due in the inverse order of maturity, and the benefit of the prepayment in terms of increased cash flow will be lost to the developer. Also, the prepayment penalties should not apply to this type of prepayment. The lender's lawyer will, of course, insist that the mortgage on the main

---

[150] See Section 4(f) of Form 3.2, and condition 11 of Form 3.1 in Appendix B.
[151] See Section 8 of Form 3.2, and condition 17 of Form 3.1 in Appendix B.

By using a pre-closed form of buy-sell agreement, the developer will be able to obtain early approval of the note and mortgage, or deed of trust, and most of the collateral documents, such as the hazard insurance policy and the preliminary title report.[147]

[14] Buy-Sell Agreement

A standard requirement in the permanent takeout commitment is that the borrower obtain a construction loan satisfactory to the permanent lender from an interim lender. Normally, the borrower must obtain the construction loan commitment within a few months after the permanent loan application is accepted or the permanent commitment letter is issued. Frequently, the permanent lender will also require the borrower to enter into a buy-sell agreement with the interim lender, thus assuring the permanent lender of its right to purchase the construction loan.[148]

[15] Survey, Title Insurance, and Closing Costs

Within a reasonable time prior to the closing of the permanent loan, the borrower must furnish the permanent lender with a survey of a licensed surveyor prepared after completion of the improvements, and the survey must be satisfactory to the lender and the title company. Most title companies will demand compliance with certain minimum detail requirements (standardized by the American Land Title Association (ALTA) and American Congress on Surveying and Mapping), such as the showing of: interior lot lines, if any; dimensions and location of improvements; parking areas; easements; and identity of and distances to the nearest streets and intersections.[149]

Next, title insurance, in form and issued by a title company satisfactory to the lender, must be delivered to the lender insuring it in the amount of the loan, as the holder of indebtedness secured by a valid first mortgage or deed of trust, subject only to such exceptions waived by the lender's attorneys. If, prior to the issuance of the commitment letter, the developer intends to obtain a preliminary title commitment from a title insurance company, he should seek approval of the title company from the lender's counsel. Since the premium payable for the title policy will be affected by the lender's requirements that the lead

---

[147] See discussion at ¶ 4.05.

[148] See discussion of the buy-sell agreement at ¶ 4.05; Section 1(b) of Form 3.2; condition 23 of Form 3.1 and Form 4.2 in Appendix B.

[149] See Section 4(f) of Form 3.2, and condition 13 of Form 3.1 in Appendix B.

Under this clause and language in the mortgage or deed of trust, the policy must name the lender as beneficiary as its interest may appear.[142] In addition, the standard mortgage clause establishes an independent contract between the mortgagee and the insurer apart from the insurer's contract with the mortgagor. This further protects the mortgagee's security interest. Consequently, if the latter contract is terminated, the mortgagee's contract, subject to the foregoing terms and conditions, remains in effect. In addition, if the mortgagor defaults and the mortgaged property is purchased by the mortgagee at the foreclosure sale, the mortgagee is still covered under the standard mortgage clause with respect to a subsequent casualty loss, since the word "mortgagee" is merely a term of convenience and does not preclude the separately insured lender from receiving insurance proceeds in its capacity as purchaser.[143] In addition, if the lender fails to notify the insurer in a timely manner about the foreclosure sale, the lender's rights will not be forfeited since its acquisition of title to the insured property is generally deemed to be a risk-free increase of its interest rather than a change of ownership.[144] However, where there is a loss and a subsequent foreclosure ensues (in respect to which the mortgagee bids in the full amount of the mortgage indebtedness), recovery by the mortgagee for the loss under the policy has been denied based on a theory of no double recovery.[145]

[13] Approval of Security Documents

The permanent lender will also require that the form and substance of each loan and security document be approved by its attorneys.[146] A too literal construction of this requirement would probably render the commitment contract illusory; accordingly, a standard of reasonableness should apply.

---

[142] See "insurance" provision (Article 4.5) of Form 3.4 in Appendix B.

[143] Shores v. Rabon, 251 N.C. 790, 793, 112 S.E.2d 556, 562 (1960), *aff'd per curiam*, 253 N.C. 428, 117 S.E.2d 1 (1960).

[144] *Id.* But cf. Consolidated Mortgage Corp. v. American Security Ins. Co. 69 Mich. App. 251, 257, 244 N.W.2d 434, 437 (1976), where the insurer was exculpated from liability since the casualty loss took place after the mortgagor's period of redemption had expired and the lender continued to have insurance coverage at low rates by failing to notify the insurer of the foreclosure notwithstanding that the risk to the insurer increased immediately thereafter when the property was vacated by the mortgagor.

[145] E.g., Northwestern Nat'l Ins. Co. v. Mildenberger, 359 S.W.2d 380, 387 (Mo. 1962); Smith v. General Mortgage Corp., 73 Mich. App. 720, 730, 252 N.W.2d 551, 556 (1977); Whitestone Sav. & Loan Ass'n v. Allstate Ins. Co., 28 N.Y.2d 332, 343, 270 N.E.2d 694 (1971). The special insurance considerations of the construction lender are discussed at ¶ 4.02[11].

[146] See condition 1 of Form 3.1 in Appendix B.

For example, if the owner-insured of a building having an actual cash value of $100,000 carries $80,000 insurance and suffers a $40,000 casualty loss, the insurance carrier would pay $80,000/80,000 of the $40,000 loss, or $40,000. By contrast, if the owner carries only $50,000 insurance because he knows that most losses are partial, his premium will be less but the insurer would only pay $50,000/80,000 of the $40,000 loss, or $25,000.

It should be remembered that this clause only penalizes the policyholder who carries insufficient insurance. It does not limit the amount of coverage, so that if sufficient insurance is taken out, the policy will pay dollar for dollar any loss up to the face amount. Also, the owner-insured should not reduce his coverage amount in order to reduce his premium costs in a value-sliding market; the insurer, under most policies, will determine the loss on the basis of repair and replacement cost, which may be increasing notwithstanding a decline in the market value of the property.

[b] Loss Payable Clauses

There are essentially, two types of loss payable clauses: the simple or open mortgage clause and the standard or union mortgage clause. Under the simple mortgage clause, the mortgagee is designated as the party to receive the insurance proceeds as its interest may appear. Any recovery is limited to the amount of the mortagee's interest in the property. More importantly, the right of the mortgagee to recover is predicated on the mortgagor's underlying contract with the insurer, which. if terminated, will prevent recovery by the mortgagee.

The standard mortgage clause, required by the permanent lender,[141] provides the following:

> Loss or damage, if any, under this Policy, shall be payable to [the mortgagee]...as its interest may appear, and this insurance...shall not be invalidated by any act or neglect of the mortgagor or owner...nor by foreclosure...nor by any change in the title or ownership of the property, nor by the occupation of the premises for purposes more hazardous than are permitted by this policy; provided, that in case the mortgagor or owner shall neglect to pay any premium due under this policy, the mortgagee shall, on demand, pay the same...also, that the mortgagee shall notify this Company of any change of ownership or occupancy or increase of hazard....

---

[141] See Form 3.12 in Appendix B.

On the other hand, it enables a lender who has lost faith in the viability of the project to make unreasonable and unforseeable demands on the developer for changes in construction. Accordingly, the borrower should be prepared for a thorough "going-over" by the lender's appraiser prior to closing and should be mindful that lenders in the past have been allowed to cancel commitments solely because the construction was below standard. Finally, in the case of a shopping center loan, the lender will often insist on approving plans and specifications covering all tenant improvements, whether or not the premises are rented at the time of loan closing, since at this stage the lender will only see plans for "stripped down" space.

[12] Satisfactory Hazard Insurance

The lender will insist on approving the form and substance of the hazard insurance policy. Normally, if the policy is written at 80 percent "co-insurance," the lender will also require a coverage amount equal to the loan amount, plus the value of the fixtures and personal property, as determined by its mortgage loan manager, based on a certified inventory statement furnished by the borrower.[140]

If the developer has a single major tenant, the tenant may be a self-insurer, in which event provision for this should be made in the application-commitment.

[a] Co-insurance Clause

Simply stated, a co-insurance clause requires that the owner-insured become a co-insurer with respect to partial losses if the property is underinsured. Insurance companies have incorporated this clause in policies in order to equalize the distribution of premium costs among all policyholders by penalizing those who are underinsured. The clauses generally used are 80, 90, or 100 percent average clauses, and the typical 80 percent co-insurance clause reads in part, "This company shall not be liable for a greater proportion of any loss or damage to the insured property than the sum hereby insured bears to 80 percent of the actual cash value of said property at the time such loss shall happen, nor for more than the proportion that this policy bears to the total insurance thereon." For this purpose, "actual cash value" usually refers to replacement value, less depreciation.

---

[140] See Form 3.13, a sample certified inventory statement, in Appendix B. See also Section 4(d) of Form 3.2; condition 2 of Form 3.1; and Article 4.5 of Form 3.4.

Insurance Co. will also insist on receiving from its appraiser a report confirming that construction has been completed in a good, workmanlike manner and in accordance with the plans and specifications.[139]

In the absence of these commencement-completion dates, Dan Development Co. could "shop around" for a more favorable mortgage loan. However, this matter should be negotiated because delays in completion may provide the lender with an opportunity to reconsider its commitment to fund, or at least tempt him to do so, if interest rates have escalated since the date of the commitment letter. A force majeure provision should therefore be insisted upon by the developer that permits extension of completion date for at least a specified maximum period of time in the event of delays caused by strikes, etc. These are beyond the reasonable control of the developer, and are necessary even if the developer should have to pay a reasonable nonrefundable extension fee.

The commitment will also prohibit any changes in the final plans and specifications without the lender's written prior approval. No sophisticated construction lender would risk any changes without prior approval. It would make it too easy for the permanent lender to avoid the commitment if no longer satisfied with the project. Obviously, the lender's determination of the loan amount and the value of the security is based in part on its scrutiny of the plans and specifications. Accordingly, it wants to be assured that it will receive exactly what it bargained for. Moreover, notwithstanding compliance with the plans and specifications, if the materials and workmanship are shoddy, the real security for the loan (namely, the future rental income) shrinks, the landlord's covenants are more apt to be breached, and the property will bring less at foreclosure. Hence, the commitment also requires certain minimum standards of construction by employing much the same kind of language found in general construction contracts. Language such as "first-class equipment" may be objectified by referring to actual specifications, or the equivalent, to avoid a potential conflict over the meaning of such ambiguous language. One type of commitment form also requires that "any work or materials not directly stated in the plans and specifications but necessary for carrying out the intention thereof are to be implied." The need for this particular language is debatable. Its purpose is to protect the lender against the lack of specificity sometimes found in plans and specifications. Otherwise, when the work is later inspected and found wanting by the lender, the developer may argue that the construction literally complies with the approved plans and specifications, even if it is deficient in one important aspect or another.

---

[139] See Section 4(c) of Form 3.2, and condition 4 of Form 3.1 in Appendix B.

permit an assignment of the commitment to the construction lender so that the borrower may obtain interim financing.[138]

Even those lenders that permit a sale of the mortgaged property do not want a substitute borrower until the loan is closed and construction completed, since the commitment is being made to some degree in reliance on the borrower's reputation as a competent and trustworthy developer. The exception arises because in the event of default and acceleration, the construction lender may prefer to complete the construction of the improvements itself, rather than have the partially completed improvements sold for a sacrifice price at foreclosure. After construction is completed, the interim lender could recoup its outlay of funds by obtaining the permanent loan proceeds and selling the property, subject to the permanent mortgage.

Recently, however, some permanent lenders have ceased allowing an assignment of their commitment to the interim lender and will only allow an assignment of the loan proceeds if the borrower should meet the terms of the commitment. Such right to assign may, however, be illusory if the permanent commitment provides that the bankruptcy of the borrower will trigger termination of the commitment.

[11] Timely Completion of Improvements in Accordance With Approved Plans and Specifications

In our hypothetical case, Ace Insurance Co. will require that construction commence on or before a certain date (e.g., March 29, 1979) and be completed well in advance (e.g., January 1, 1981) of the date for closing the permanent loan (March 1, 1981). In addition, prior to construction, final plans and specifications for the improvements prepared by a licensed professional engineer or registered architect will be approved by the lender. This section of the commitment letter frequently cautions the developer that start of construction prior to such approval will be at the developer's risk and that receipt of reports from the inspecting architect will not be deemed such approval. It also requires receipt of a subsoil investigation "satisfactory" to the lender, prepared by a qualified soil engineer and accompanied by a certification by the architect and the soil engineer that the latter's recommendations have been included in the design of the improvements. The requirements of plans, specifications, soil engineer recommendations, and certifications are not negotiable, and a sophisticated construction lender will have seen to their compliance. Immediately prior to the closing, Ace

---

[138] See condition 16 of Form 3.1 in Appendix B.

pursuant to Section 208 of the Clean Water Act.[133] The receipt of water-pollution control grants from the federal government will soon be contingent upon local land-use control mechanisms being enacted that incorporate this water-pollution control planning.[134]

In addition, a goodly number of states have enacted coastal zone management statutes which give state agencies either absolute or qualifed control of development in the designated coastal zone and include far more than the kind of land-use control inherent in zoning. The most notable example of state control of coastal zone land use is the wide control exercised by the California coastal zone commissions. In New York, control of development in coastal areas is exercised by the State Department of Environmental Conservation under the aegis of the State Tidal Wetlands Act.[135] Under that state's Freshwater Wetlands Act,[136] the State Department of Environmental Conservation exercises similar control over many categories of development proximate to freshwater streams and lakes.[137]

[d] Developer's Reliance on Lender's Knowledge of Local Law

Finally, the developer should seek to eliminate from the commitment language to the effect that the loan or the lender's making of it complies with local law on the ground that the lender is in the best position to know whether the regulatory statutes governing the lender's investment portfolio permit it to make such a loan. This language in the commitment may also refer to the question of usury and, if nonnegotiable, the developer should determine the possibility and cost of obtaining a title company usury endorsement.

[10] Assignment of Commitment

Generally, the permanent lender will prohibit an assignment of the commitment without its prior written consent. However, most will

---

[133] *Id.*

[134] 33 U.S.C. § 1288

[135] N.Y. Envir. Conserv. Law §§ 25-0101 to 25-0602 (McKinney Supp. 1979).

[136] N.Y. Envir. Conserv. Law §§ 24-0101 to 24-1303 (McKinney 1979).

[137] Other federal and state environmental legislation mandate controls with respect to: (1) miscellaneous water-pollution discharges such as ocean dumping (Marine Protection, Research and Sanctuaries Act of 1972; 33 U.S.C. §§ 1401 et. seq.); (2) public water systems (Safe Drinking Water Act, 42 U.S.C. §§ 1401 et. seq.), (3) motor vehicle and aircraft emissions (Clean Air Act §§ 202-209, 42 U.S.C. §§ 7521-7570 (1977), and Clean Air Act §§ 231-234, 42 U.S.C. §§ 7571-7574 (1977)); (4) activities on federal and state lands, in marine sanctuaries and affecting fish and wildlife; (5) use of dangerous substances; and (6) noise control.

states, these plans include preconstruction review of proposed residential, commercial, and industrial land uses and provide that state approval is a precondition to the proposed land use.[125] Frequently, large shopping centers and office developments are considered "indirect sources" of air pollution and are subject to modification or even disapproval due to the capacity or location of the proposed accessory parking facilities.[126] Control over such land uses is based on the theory that by inducing traffic to it, a parking lot is indirectly responsible for the air pollution generated by the automobiles that park there!

The Federal Water Pollution Control Act Amendments of 1972[127] prohibit the discharge of any pollutants from a "point source" (any discernible, confined, and discrete conveyance, including any pipe, ditch, channel, tunnel, conduit, well, etc.)[128] into navigable waters, except as authorized by a permit issued under a regulatory scheme entitled the "National Pollutant Discharge Elimination System (NPDES)."[129] The NPDES permit must be obtained from the EPA, unless the state in which the discharge will take place has established its own permit program and such a program is not inadequate in the opinion of the EPA. For example, the State of Virginia has established its own program, administered by the State Water Control Board (SWCB) and NPDES permits issued by the SWCB implement provisions of the Virginia State Water Control Law[130] as well as the permit provision of the Federal Water Pollution Control Act. Water-pollution control permits are required in connection with the discharge of water from private residential sewage treatment facilities as well as from industrial and commercial uses.[131] The runoff from rainstorms is sometimes subject to the water-pollution permit requirements of the Federal Clean Water Act.[132] Under that Act, the federal government or delegated state agencies have the authority to issue or deny discharge permits based on chemical or ecological standards. Specific land uses are permissible only to the extent that necessary discharge permits can be secured. In addition, local land-use control plans are being developed

---

[125] "Indirect Sources of Air Contamination," 46 NYCRR 203.
[126] *Id.*
[127] 33 U.S.C. §§ 1251 et seq. (Supp. V. 1975).
[128] 33 U.S.C. §§ 1311-1314 (1948, as amended).
[129] 33 U.S.C. § 1342.
[130] Va. Code Ann. §§ 62.1-44.2 et seq. (1980 Supp.).
[131] 33 U.S.C. § 1342.
[132] See generally, 33 U.S.C. §§ 1251 et seq.

In those states where the environmental impact statement requirement is more than a procedural requirement, substantive land-use decision-making is changing to accommodate newly described environmental issues. Under many of these statutes, the opportunity has been provided to challenge proposed land uses because of the lack of "standing" requirements. That is, any party alleging an interest in the environment has standing to challenge an administrative decision merely upon the allegation that the land-use decision in question "may have" an effect on the environment.

The federal Clean Air Act and Clean Water Act[118] is beginning to directly affect land use. In addition, federal jurisdiction is asserted over specific land uses impacting on, among other things, navigable waters (the Corps of Engineers permits),[119] national parks, forests, grazing land, seashores, and wildlife refuges (Department of Interior approvals)[120] and designated historic and archaeological sites (the National Register of Historic Places).[121]

Under the Clean Air Act, all new "major sources" of air pollution require preconstruction permits.[122] A major source or major modification of an existing source is defined according to the amount of pollutants discharged into the air during a specific period of time. The thresholds are not high, and many types of commercial and industrial developments ruction permits.[122] A major source or major Irattained federally mandated ambient air quality conditions, new major sources of air pollution are required to demonstrate trade-offs of pollutants from other sources as a condition to the issuance of the requisite federal preconstruction permit.[123]

The Federal Clean Air Act is administered through a delegation of authority to state environmental officials in many states.[124] In most states, implementation plans and transportation control plans have been prepared that set forth specific regulatory measures, which will be taken by the states to enforce the provisions of the Clean Air Act. In many

---

[118] 42 U.S.C. §§ 7401 et seq. (1955); 33 U.S.C. §§ 1251 et seq. (1948).

[119] 33 U.S.C. § 1344 (1948, as amended).

[120] 42 U.S.C. §§ 1701 et seq.

[121] 16 U.S.C. §§ 470 et seq. (1966, as amended).

[122] 42 U.S.C. § 7475. The Clean Air Act (42 U.S.C. §§ 7401-7642, as amended by the Clean Air Act Amendments of 1977, Pub. L. No. 95-95, 91 Stat. 735) promulgates a regulatory system based on a state-administered preconstruction permit requirement in respect to which EPA is required to establish ambient air quality needed to protect the public health and to prevent significant deterioration of the air quality in regions where air quality standards are being currently maintained.

[123] 42 U.S.C. § 7503 (1955, as amended 1977).

[124] 42 U.S.C. § 7410.

[c] Environmental Restrictions

Reflective of the enactment of various recent environmental controls is the appearance of a condition that has become incorporated in the standard forms of commitment letters issued by permanent and construction loan lenders, to the effect that the borrower furnish satisfactory evidence that all improvements, and their use, comprising the security for the loan comply with all applicable environmental restrictions imposed by federal, state, and local law.

The National Environmental Policy Act of 1969 (NEPA)[110] requires federal governmental agencies to prepare an "Environmental Impact Statement" with respect to any "major *Federal* actions significantly affecting the quality of the human environment."[111] Recent examples of actions held to be "major Federal actions" are:

(1) A $3.5 million HUD loan for construction of a sixteen-story high-rise apartment building in Portland, Oregon, an area containing no high-rise projects.[112]
(2) Initiatives by the Navy to construct 600 multi-family residential units on 81 acres of land in an ecologically sensitive area.[113]
(3) The transfer of 10,200 acres of national forest land in exchange for 20,500 privately held acres of Montana woodlands, in anticipation of some recreational land development.[114]

The governmental agencies, in turn, normally require the land developer or other private party involved to prepare a comprehensive and expensive backup study as the matrix for their own independent EIS. As a consequence, these environmental impact statement requirements of the federal government[115] and of at least thirty states[116] have complicated, delayed, and increased the costs of land development[117] and have injected economic and social issues into the land-use control decision-making process, heretofore regarded as extraneous by land developers and lenders.

---

[110] 42 U.S.C. §§ 4331 et seq. (1970).

[111] 42 U.S.C. § 4332-(c) (emphasis added).

[112] San Francisco Tomorrow v. Romney, 472 F.2d 1021, 3 ELR 20124 (9th Cir. 1973).

[113] Fort story—its Future? v. Schlesinger, 5 ELR 20038 (E.D. Va. 1974).

[114] National Forest Preservation Group v. Butz, 485 F.2d 408, 3 ELR 20783 (9th Cir. 1973).

[115] 42 U.S.C. § 4322(2)(c).

[116] E.g., Va. Code Ann. §§ 10-17.107 to 10-17.112 (1978 replacement vol.).

[117] Council of Environmental Quality, *Environmental Quality (8th Annual Report 1977)* 119-121, 130-135; see, e.g., N.Y. Envir. Conserv. Law Art. 8 (McKinney Cum. Supp. 1979); Virginia, Ch. 384 (March 15, 1973).

to the Zoning Board of Appeals from the building department's issuance of a building permit, with respect to a party who had objected to the issuance, would be computed as running from the date of decision by the building department of which the objector had notice, rather than from the date the permit was issued. Under the rule in the *Pansa* case, it would appear that the builder and the lender who are relying on the issuance of the building permit, and the lapse of time for appeal from the building department's decision to grant the permit, must also make sure that neighbors who might object have had actual notice of the decision of the building department or other administrative bodies concerned.

Also, in a few jurisdictions, certificates are not issued, and in some areas a zoning change revokes or cancels a previously issued permit, even though the developer and the mortgagee have relied on the prior zoning, to their detriment.[108]

[b] Rezoning and Variances

Because zoning of use, height, bulk, and area is in most cases predicated on a master plan, the process of rezoning to obtain a zoning change is beset with difficulty; hence, the more likely approach is to obtain a variance based on practical difficulty and unnecessary hardship in utilizing the land as zoned, or some form of special permit achieved by way of "trade-offs" with the zoning authority.

However, reliance on a variance or rezoning may be misplaced since it may turn out to be "spot zoning," which is vulnerable to attack by adjoining land owners.[109] Consequently, where the lender feels there may be a zoning problem, the developer should be prepared to pay for zoning insurance (issued by title companies in some states as a zoning and building endorsement of the title policy) or for an opinion of local counsel in jurisdictions where such insurance is not available.

---

[108] 82 *Am. Jur. 2d* "Zoning and Planning," §§ 237-241 (1976).

[109] In French v. Zoning Bd. of Adjustment, 408 Pa. 479, 184 A.2d 791 (1962), a residents association objected to the issuance of a permit for the development of certain premises such as an A&P supermarket, a use permissible in an A-commerical district, which the particular parcel had been zoned for in the city zoning map for the past twenty-eight years. The court held the original A-commercial zoning was spot zoning and invalid. Since the use to which the property had been put for twenty-eight years was a nonconforming use that had been discontinued, the property could be developed only for conforming residential use.

restrictions is not an encumbrance, a zoning violation may be, and an existing zoning violation may render, the title unmarketable.[103] In any event, to invest in an unmarketable title may fall below the level of prudence required of fiduciaries. However, the issuance of a certificate of occupancy does not totally protect the lender since it is not binding if issued on the basis of the borrower's misrepresentations or by a governmental agency without the authority to do so.

Moreover, even if permits are granted by the duly constituted authority, they may be revoked if invalidly issued, even though the builder receiving the permit made no misrepresentation and incurred substantial expense in reliance thereon.[104] The danger is that there may be no time limitation for the revocation of invalidly issued permits. In *S.B. Garage Corp. v. Murdock*,[105] the revocation took place twenty years after issuance of the certificate of occupancy. However, had the adminisrative officer refused to issue the certificate and had an appeal been taken to the administrative agency at the next level, which reversed the building department, the expiration on time to appeal from that body to the courts would have, thereafter, made the certificate unassailable. In jurisdictions, this rule has been mitigated. In New York, a certificate of occupancy issued for a multiple dwelling is not revocable against a purchaser who, in good faith, purchases a multiple dwelling or lends money secured by a mortgage on a multiple dwelling for which a certificate of occupancy has been issued, even though invalidly.[106] This amelioration of the general rule applies only to multiple dwellings, but not to commercial or industrial property. Another limitation on the vulnerability in New York, with respect to certificates of occupancy, is that they may not be attacked collaterally, but only by a direct proceeding for revocation brought in the administrative agency and in the courts.

One other noteworthy caveat in relying on certificates of occupancy or building permits is the matter of jurisdiction of the agency to bind those objecting to the issuance of the permit or certificate. A decision of the New York Court of Appeals is instructive. In *Pansa v. Damiano*,[107] the court held that the thirty days allowed by the ordinance for appeal

---

[103] 107 Pa. Super. 588, 164 A. 111 (1933). See also Dunham, "Effect on Title of Violations of Building Covenants and Zoning Ordinances," 27 Rocky Mt. L. Rev. 265, 262-264 (1956).

[104] See annotations at 6 A.L.R.2d 960 (1949).

[105] 185 Misc. 55, 55 N.Y. Supp. 2d 456 (1945).

[106] N.Y. Mult. Dwell. Law § 301-5 (McKinney 1974); N.Y. Mult. Resid. Law § 302-5 (McKinney 1952).

[107] 14 N.Y.2d 356, 200 N.E.2d 563 (1964).

be rendered unenforceable.[99] Likewise, if the lender stipulates in the "due on sale" clause that "its consent shall not unreasonably be withheld," it may be compelled to prove economic impairment to justify an increase in the interest rate in a jurisdiction where such proof would otherwise not be necessary.

[9] Compliance With Local Law

The typical application-commitment requires the borrower to furnish evidence, satisfactory to the lender, certifying that all improvements and their use comply with all applicable environmental, floodplain, zoning, and building laws and requirements.[101]

[a] Issuance of Building Permit and Certificate of Occupancy

Normally, permits are required to commence construction, and the lender will require a certificate of occupancy or statement by the local governing authorities that, as of the end of construction, both the construction and the intended use of the improvements comply with applicable zoning and subdivision ordinances. Some lenders also require the borrower to furnish a similar statement signed and certified by the borrower's architect. Lawyers for permanent lenders are mindful that any illegal use of the improvements could be enjoined by a court order, which could result in an abatement of the rental income stream from the property. Under such circumstances, the borrower might not be able to meet his obligations under the mortgage.

Zoning violations may also render the real estate ineligible for investment under the constraints imposed by the investment codes that govern the lending financial institutions. All states generally follow the rule that, for investment by life insurance companies, the title must be unencumbered, with certain exceptions.[102] While the existence of zoning

---

[99] E.g., First So. Fed. Sav. & Loan Ass'n of Mobile v. Britton, 345 So. 2d 303-304; Bellingham First Fed. Sav. & Loan Ass'n v. Garrison, 87 Wash. 2d at 439, 553 P.2d at 1091 (dictum). But cf. Stith v. Hudson City Sav. Inst., 63 Misc. 2d at 864, 866-867, 313 N.Y.S.2d at 804, 807 (interest-rate justification for clause need not be stipulated). See also Dunn, "Selected Current Legal Issues in Mortgage Financing," 13 Real Prop., Prob. & Tr. J. 832 (1978). See Article 5.7 of Form 3.4 in Appendix B.

[100] See Silver v. Rochester Sav. Bank, 424 N.Y.S.2d 945 (1980).

[101] See Section 4(c) of Form 3.2, and conditon 12 of Form 3.1 in Appendix B. For a discussion of the kinds of constraints imposed by local usury laws, see Chapter 5.

[102] See ¶ 2.02[1][d].

that the enforceability of a "due on sale" clause in a note or deed of trust should not depend on whether there has been an outright sale (where legal title and possession are transferred), but on whether an institutional lender can demonstrate that enforcement is reasonably necessary to protect itself against impairment of its security or the risk of default.[94] In applying the two-factor test formulated in the *Tucker* case, the court first noted that a nonassumption clause in a deed of trust could have an inhibitory, or even prohibitory, effect on a proposed transfer if the purchaser is unwilling or unable to procure refinancing, at current rates, elsewhere.[95] The court then rejected the defendant-lender's contention that the risk of waste and default is greater in an outright sale than in a transfer where the seller retains neither possession nor legal title because the outright sale buyer, in order to pay off the seller's equity, may make a large down payment on the property, thereby creating an equity interest in the property, which is sufficient to provide an adequate incentive not to commit waste or permit the property to depreciate. Moreover, the buyer in such an outright sale may be at least as good, if not a better credit risk than the original borrower/seller.[96] Finally, the court rejected the defendant's argument that the lender's interest in maintaining its loan portfolio at current interest rates justifies enforcement of a "due on sale" clause with the rationale that such economic risks caused by an inflationary economy are inherent in every lending transaction and are foreseeable by lenders who can and do "take into account their projections of future economic conditions when they initially determine the rate of payment and interest on these long-term loans."[97] The court also noted that now that lenders can adjust their yields by use of a variable-rate mortgage, automatic enforcement of the "due on sale" clause is not the only method by which lenders can protect themselves against increases in the cost of their loan funds.[98]

Finally, from the perspective of the lender, if, in addition to providing protection for the security, the underlying *economic* purpose of the "due on sale" clause is to advance the financial interest of the lender (by requiring payment of an assumption fee or an increased rate of interest), such latter purpose should be openly stated and be a bargained-for element in the loan commitment or loan documents in any jurisdiction that sanctions such purpose; otherwise, as some decisions have indicated such lack of statement of purpose, the clause may

---

[94] *Id.* at 953, 582 P.2d at 977, 148 Cal. Rptr. at 386
[95] *Id.* at 950, 582 P.2d at 974-975, 148 Cal. Rptr. at 383.
[96] *Id.* at 952, 582 P.2d at 975-976, 148 Cal. Rptr. at 384-385.
[97] *Id.* at 952, 582 P.2d at 976, 148 Cal. Rptr. at 385.
[98] *Id.,* n. 11.

showing of reasonableness and hold on a case-by-case basis that a "due on sale" clause may be invoked only where a sale threatens the legitimate security interests of the lender.[88]

In that regard, the California Supreme Court in a benchmark decision, *Tucker v. Lassen Savings & Loan Ass'n*,[89] specified the following legitimate security interests of the lender to be protected by a "due on sale" clause: (1) preserving the security from waste or depreciation; and (2) guarding against "moral risks," that is, the risk of having to resort to the security because of default.[90] In applying a two-factor test, the court in *Tucker* questioned not only the lender's justification for the restriction, but also considered the "quantum of restraint," that is, the actual practical effect upon alienation which would result from its enforcement.[91] In that case, an attempt by a lender to enforce an automatic "due on sale" provision in a deed or trust note, after the borrower had entered into an installment land contract with its tenants, was held to be an unreasonable restraint on alienation; the lender made no effort to demonstrate how such a sale would impinge upon its legitimate security interest and did not show that the arrangement in any way endangered its primary recourse against the borrower for payment of the note.[92]

In a subsequent decision, *Wellenkamp v. Bank of America*,[93] while the California Supreme Court conceded that retention of possession and legal title were significant factors in its earlier decisions involving installment land contracts *(LaSala* and *Tucker)*, it nevertheless ruled

---

[88] E.g., Clark v. Lachenmeier, 237 So. 2d 583, 585 (Fla. 1970), wherein a Florida appellate court refused to allow a mortgagee to foreclose, based on a sale where no harm actually resulted to the mortgagee from the conveyance. In Baltimore Life Ins. Co. v. Harn, 15 Ariz. App. 78, 81, 486 P.2d 190, 193 (1971), an Arizona court likewise held that the lender must show the reasonableness of its action, namely, that the security would be impaired by the sale. Other decisions holding the same include: Tucker v. Pulaski Fed. Sav. & Loan Ass'n, 252 Ark. 849, 869, 481 S.W.2d 725, 737 (1972); Nichols v. Ann Arbor Fed. Sav. & Loan Ass'n, 73 Mich. App. 163, 174, 250 N.W.2d 804, 809 (1977); Bellingham First Fed. Sav. & Loan Ass'n v. Garrison, 87 Wash. 2d 437, 443, 553, P.2d 1090, 1093 (1976); Sanders v. Hicks, 317 So. 2d 61, 64 (Miss. 1975); Fidelity Land Dev. Corp. v. Rieder & Sons Bldg. & Dev. Co., 151 N.J. Super. 502, 514, 377 A.2d 691, 693 (1977) (per curiam).

[89] 12 Cal. 3d 629, 526 P.2d 1169, 116 Cal. Rptr. 633 (1974), also cited in notes 73 and 86 *supra*. Accord, Wellenkamp v. Bank of America, 582 P.2d 970, 148 Cal. Rptr. 379 (1978).

[90] *Id.* at 639, 526 P.2d at 1175, 116 Cal. Rptr. at 639. Accord, First So. Fed. Sav. & Loan Ass'n of Mobile v. Britton, 345 So. 2d at 304.

[91] *Id.* at 636, 526 P.2d at 1173, 116 Cal. Rptr. at 637.

[92] *Id.* at 640, 526 P.2d at 1176, 116 Cal. Rptr. at 640.

[93] 21 Cal. 3d 943, 958, 582 P.2d 970, 980, 148 Cal. Rptr. 379, 389 (1978).

current trend in judicial thinking appears unsettled as to whether a "due on sale" clause can be used by lenders merely to obtain a one-time assumption fee or can be used to increase the interest rate to the prevailing current market rate.[86] Otherwise, there is a split in the case authority; courts in some jurisdictions like New York go along with almost automatic enforcement of these clauses,[87] while others require a

---

on sale" clause was void at its inception; Coast Bank v. Minderhout, 61 Cal. 2d 311, 317, 392 P.2d 265, 268, 38 Cal. Rptr. 505, 509 (1964), wherein Justice Traynor persuasively argues against absolute prohibition of such restraints.

[86] The mortgagee's right to accelerate the loan indebtedness under a "due on sale" clause as a device to protect its economic position during a period of inflationary pressures and rising interest rates has been expressly approved by some recent case law decisions. See Cherry v. Home Sav. & Loan Ass'n, 276 Cal. App. 2d at 578, 81 Cal. Rptr. at 138; Century Fed. Sav. & Loan Ass'n v. Van Glahn, 144 N.J. Super. 48, 55, 364 A.2d 558, 562 (1976); Mutual Fed. Sav. & Loan Ass'n v. Wisconsin Wire Works, 71 Wis. 2d 531, 539, 239 N.W.2d 20, 24 (1976); Miller v. Pacific First Fed. Sav. & Loan Ass'n, 86 Wash. 2d 401, 405, 545 P.2d 546, 549 (1976); Malouff v. Midland Fed. Sav. & Loan Ass'n, 181 Colo. 294, 300, 509 P.2d 1240, 1245, (1973); Gunther v. White, 489 S.W.2d 529, 532 (Tenn. 1973); Crockett v. First Fed. Sav. & Loan Ass'n, 289 N.C. 620, 631, 224 S.E.2d 580, 587 (1976); Stith v. Hudson City Sav. Inst., 63 Misc. 2d 863, 867, 313 N.Y.S.2d 804, 809 (1970). Tieree v. Aps Co. 382 So. 2d 485 (Ala. 1980).

By contrast, other courts have recently expressed a contrary opinion. For example, in the *Tucker* case (note 89 *infra*), the California Supreme Court stated, "[W]e reject the suggestion that a lender's interest in maintaining its portfolio at current interest rates justifies the restraint imposed by the exercise of a 'due-on' clause." 12 Cal. 3d at 639, 526 P.2d at 1175, 116 Cal. Rptr. at 639, 640. Accord, Patton v. First Fed. Sav. & Loan Ass'n, 48 Ariz. 473, 478-479, 578 P.2d 152, 157 (1978); Nichols v. Ann Arbor Fed. Sav. & Loan Ass'n, 73 Mich. App. 163, 174, 250 N.W.2d 804, 809 (1977). In rejecting such use of the "due-on-sale" clause to advance the financial interest of the lender by requiring the payment of a penalty or an increase in interest rate, some courts have been influenced by the fact that such use of the clause was not a bargained for element in the loan contract. E.g., First So. Fed. Sav. & Loan Ass'n of Mobile v. Britton, 345 So. 2d 300, 304 (Ala. 1977). But cf. Stith v. Hudson City Sav. Inst., 63 Misc. 2d at 865, 313 N.Y.S. 2d at 807 (interest-rate justification for clause need not be spelled out in the acceleration clause).

[87] E.g., Mutual Real Estate Trust v. Buffalo Sav. Bank, 90 Misc. 2d 675, 680, 395 N.Y.S.2d 583, 586 (1977), wherein the court held that the refusal of a lender to consent to sale of the property to a financially responsible purchaser was not, per se, an unconscionable or inequitable exercise of the acceleration option. In Baker v. Loves Park Sav. & Loan Ass'n, 61 Ill. 2d 119, 126, 333 N.E.2d 1, 5 (1975), the Supreme Court of Illinois explicitly rejected a "reasonableness" test on the rationale that when land titles are involved, more certainty and greater predictability are required. See generally cases cited in the first paragraph of note 86 *supra*.

the lender with money to loan but at a less favorable interest rate.[81] However, this argument ignores the protections afforded to lenders by their right to demand a prepayment penalty and by their practice of demanding call options prior to maturity of the loan.

At common law, restraints on the alienation of property were viewed with disfavor.[82] An argument can be made that the "due on sale" clause is not really a direct restraint; the developer can choose to sell the property if he is willing to accept the consequences of having the mortgage loan accelerated. The opposing view is that in difficult times, when money is scarce, a "due on sale" clause demanding payment of the debt effectively prohibits the alienation of property by the borrower-seller. Alternatively, if a prospective purchaser may not assume the existing mortgage without paying the current market rate of interest, such clause may cause the purchaser to demand a lower purchase price or even to walk away from the transaction.[83]

If, as is suggested earlier, one purpose of the clause is to convert a fixed-interest-rate mortgage into a variable-rate mortgage (VRM), the borrower might attempt to negotiate a true variable interest rate formula, which rate goes *down* as well as up, in exchange for eliminating the lender's right to accelerate upon a sale of the property. On the other hand, if the lender's real concern is the reputation and skill of the substitute owner, the borrower might suggest a compromise clause giving the lender the right to accelerate only when the transferee is not reasonably satisfactory to the lender or when it fails to meet its normal credit standards.

In the past, courts have traditionally taken the position that a "due on sale" clause in a mortgage is not a direct restraint on alienation[84] or, if so, insufficient to render the clause void where the mortgagor's ability to dispose of the property is not absolutely restricted.[85] However, the

---

[81] This view prompted the California Appellate Court in Cherry v. Home Sav. & Loan Ass'n, 276 Cal. App. 2d 574, 578, 81 Cal. Rptr. 135, 138 (1969), to reject the contention that the refusal of a mortgagee to consent to an assumption of the existing indebtedness without demanding a higher rate of interest must be governed by a standard of reasonableness. But see the *LaSala* case, note 74 *supra*, and *Tucker* case, note 89 *infra*.

[82] 3 Simes & Smith, *The Law of Future Interest* § 1117 (2d ed. 1956).

[83] Volkmer, "The Application of the Restraints on Alienation Doctrine to Real Property Security Interests," 58 Iowa L. Rev. 747, 774 (1973).

[84] E.g., Jones v. Sacramento Sav. & Loan Ass'n, 248 Cal. App. 2d 522, 529, 56 Cal. Rptr. 741, 745 (1967).

[85] E.g., Peoples' Sav. & Loan Ass'n v. Standard Indus., Inc., 22 Ohio App. 2d 35, 38, 257 N.E.2d 406, 408 (1970), wherein the court held that a mortgagee has a right to maintain a degree of control over the financial responsibility and identity of a subsequent purchaser and rejected outright the position that the "due

foreclosure of the junior mortgage may terminate the occupancy leases on which the first mortgage relies.[78] Such subordination should be precluded in the occupancy leases, in any event at the outset of the negotiation of the occupancy leases. Alternatively, the developer may offer a "first refusal" to the first mortgagee in the event the developer should at any time seek additional financing. While not as good to the first mortgagee as a "due on encumbrance" acceleration, it may be persuaded that it would thereby get as good an opportunity at the additional financing as anyone else and get its chance first. The very existence of first refusal tends to discourage competition. The developer may also argue that the validity of "due on" clauses, particularly as they preclude junior financing, is questionable in light of the foregoing discussion of the relevant case law.[79] In conclusion, this is one area in which the borrower should be steadfast.

[8] Right to Sell Mortgaged Property

Recently, some real estate lenders in commercial transaction have insisted on prohibiting the developer from selling without the prior written consent of the lender. If the property is sold without the lender's consent, the lender, at its option, has the right to accelerate the maturity date of the loan.[80] The reasons for this are several and unrelated. One reason is that, in part, a loan is made to a developer in reliance upon his expertise with respect to a particular property. A lender is apprehensive that in any sale the new owner might not have the necessary operational ability to manage the property and that the income would deteriorate and its loan might go into default. Sometimes, because of liquidity problems, the lender would prefer to have the loan paid off. Other lenders view the prohibition of sale as a triggering device to enable them to review their loan portfolio and to discard any unattractive loans or use the prohibition to demand the market rate of interest during a period of rising interest rates. In the lender's view, such posture is defensible because of the dual risk it must bear: In periods of inflation and rising interest rates, it cannot increase its interest rate under the typical self-amortizing fixed-rate loan, even though its capital and overhead costs are rising, and the cost of repayment becomes cheaper for the borrower; in periods of lower interest rates the borrower may prepay the loan by refinancing elsewhere at a lower rate, thus leaving

---

[78] See discussion at ¶ 3.05[6].
[79] Also see discussion at ¶ 3.04[8].
[80] See Section 5 of Form 3.2 and Article 5.7 of Form 3.4 in Appendix B.

standard of reasonableness in deciding whether to enforce such a provision in either a mortgage or deed of trust.[73] For example, in 1971, the California Supreme Court, in *LaSala v. American Savings & Loan Ass'n*,[74] reviewed a first deed of trust that contained a provision stating, "Should Trustor sell, convey, transfer, dispose of or further encumber said property, or any part thereof, or any interest therein, or agree to do so without the written consent of Beneficiary being first obtained, then Beneficiary shall have the right, at its option, to declare all sums secured hereby forthwith due and payable."[75] The trustor subsequently, without consent of the beneficiary, placed a second trust on the property. The first trust beneficiary, receiving knowledge of the second trust, sent a form letter notifying the trustor of its right to accelerate, but agreed to waive its right in return for a fee of $150 and an increase in the interest rate from 6 percent to 9 percent. The court ruled that a "due on encumbrance" clause (in contrast to a "due on sale" provision)[76] would be tested by a reasonableness standard: If the property is jeopardized by the additional financing, or no equity remains, such a clause will be upheld and enforced. Holding against the lender, the court said, "When such enforcement is not reasonably necessary to protect the security, the lender's use of the clause to exact collateral benefit must be held as unlawful restraint on alienation."[77] The authors are of the opinion that other states will follow the approach of the California Supreme Court; accordingly, it is to the lender's advantage to define and set forth the conditions under which junior financing will be prohibited.

One practical solution that should be acceptable to both the lender and the developer would be to allow junior financing where it does not exceed, when aggregated with the first mortgage, a certain percentage, e.g., 90 percent, of the value as determined by an independent appraiser satisfactory to the lender.

The developer could also agree to eliminate the obvious prejudice to the first mortgagee if the occupancy leases permit the tenant to subordinate to junior mortgages, which create the possibility that

---

[73] 69 A.L.R.3d 713, 736, (1976).

[74] 5 Cal. 3d 864, 884, 489 P.2d 1113, 1126, 97 Cal. Rptr. 849, 862 (1971).

[75] *Id.* at 869, 489 P.2d at 1115, 97 Cal. Rptr. at 51.

[76] However, the *LaSala* approach was elucidated and expanded by the same court in Tucker v. Lassen Sav. & Loan Ass'n, 12 Cal. 3d 629, 636, 526 P.2d 1169, 1173, 116 Cal. Rptr. 633, 637 (1974) in a case involving a "due on sale" clause, and reflected an effort by the court to unify its law with respect to all "due on" clauses. See discussion of the *Tucker* case at ¶ 3.04[8]. The explanation in *LaSala* and *Tucker* makes it clear that the burden is on the lender to show that acceleration is reasonable.

[77] 5 Cal. 3d at 882, 489 P.2d at 1125, 97 Cal. Rptr. at 861.

selves with subsequent junior financing. In fact, most permanent lenders looked favorably on such junior financing. It indicated increased value, and a second mortgagee, to insure its security, would have to keep the permanent first loan current so as to avoid a foreclosure on the first loan, which could extinguish the junior lienor's position.

However, in the last few years many lenders have been fettering and limiting this right by requiring a "due on encumbrance" clause in the mortgage or deed of trust instrument.[70] The reasons expressed by the lenders vary. Some lenders are concerned with the borrower overburdening the property with financing that could turn a viable project into an uneconomical one; this could change a current loan into a problem loan in their portfolio. Other lenders like the fact that the equity cushion is increasing behind their secured first position, in effect converting a nonrecourse loan into a recourse one, since in an economic downturn a borrower would not as quickly walk away where there was equity in the property, no matter how frozen. Still, lenders, having found themselves in lengthy litigation with junior mortgagees, are wary of allowing junior financing, since it represents an additional party who could complicate foreclosure litigation or bankruptcy proceeding.[71]

Another related reason for the lenders' reluctance to allow junior financing is that while permanent lenders will frequently permit nonrecourse financing, the security may become subject to junior liens for which the developer has assumed personal liability. When the property becomes financially troubled, the developer may seek first to satisfy creditors who can sue him personally, while the first mortgage is permitted to run delinquent. To avoid this de facto subordination of the first mortgage, the permanent lender may require a "due on encumbrance" clause, or it may accept a limited exculpation provision, i.e., exculpation conditioned upon the party in whose favor the exculpation runs not having incurred personal liability for the repayment of an inferior lien.

Although lenders have traditionally enjoyed the common-law right to prohibit junior financing,[72] the emerging trend is for courts to apply a

---

[70] See Section 5 of Form 3.2 and Article 5.4 of Form 3.4 in Appendix B. In their loan documents, several lenders prohibit junior financing outright while others require the prior written consent of the lender. One insurance company, New York Life, allows traditional junior financing but prohibits wraparound financing, which appears to be a manifestation of the company's dislike of another lender profiting from the attractive first financing.

[71] See discussion at ¶¶ 3.03[2], 4.02[5].

[72] E.g., Baker v. Loves Park Sav. & Loan Ass'n, 61 Ill. 119, 126, 333 N.E.2d 1, 6 (1975).

opinion that in the near future they will eventually lose the fight to keep no-interest escrow deposits.[66] Some foresee this result based on the industry's realization that it might be good public relations to voluntarily absorb the costs associated with payment of interest to borrowers.[67] Consequently, the developer is currently in a better bargaining position to negotiate for the payment of interest on such deposits. Obviously, from the perspective of the lender, the escrow clause in its deed of trust should provide that no trust or pledge[68] is intended and should contain a waiver by the borrower of its right to such earnings unless prohibited by local statutory law.

[7] Lien Priority and Prohibition of Junior Financing

For a borrower locked into a permanent loan, the right to put subordinate financing on the property becomes, if not a financial necessity, highly desirable. Over time, as the equity in the property increases by a decrease in the first mortgage indebtedness, coupled with appreciation in property value, subordinate financing is the only way, other than a sale, to translate that equity into tax-free cash. In fact, even in the event of a sale of the property, the purchaser will probably need purchase-money financing or some other subordinate financing. Moreover, a prohibition against junior financing puts the permanent lender in a position to renegotiate a higher loan interest rate whenever the developer seeks to obtain additional leverage or funds with which to finance an expansion or renovation of the mortgaged premises.

Until recently, with the exception of a few lenders—including one major insurance company[69]—permanent lenders did not concern them-

---

Ann. § 49-2(a) (1975); Neb. Rev. Stat. §§ 45-105.05-.06 (1976); Mass. Gen. Laws Ann., Ch. 183 §§ 61 (1973); N.H. Rev. Stat. Ann. § 384:16-c (1974); Minn. Stat. Ann. § 47.20 (Supp. 1976). Also, statutes in several jurisdictions require, in the case of residential leases, that interest be paid on security deposits. E.g., Va. Code Ann. § 55-248.11 (Mich. Supp. 1978).

[66] See Comment, "Payment of Interest on Mortgage Escrow Accounts: Judicial and Legislative Development," 23 Syracuse L. Rev. 845 (1972).

[67] *Id.* at 871.

[68] See Madsen v. Prudential Fed. Sav. & Loan Ass'n, 558 P.2d 1337, 1341 (Utah 1977), where the mortgagors were successful in advancing a pledge theory based on "payments are hereby pledged" language contained in the deed of trust.

[69] Counsel for Teachers Life Insurance Company, concerned with inherent problems involved in relationships with subordinate lienors, as a condition of allowing such subordinate financing, requires that the junior mortgagee execute a document setting forth the rights of the lenders with respect to condemnation, fire proceeds, foreclosure, etc.

nized, based upon the apparent unambiguity of such language, it has been held that the accompanying language "without interest" relieves the mortgagee of any obligation of accounting, notwithstanding the presence of the trust relationship.[58]

Other judicial challenges against nonpaying escrow arrangements have been mounted based on various theories including truth-in-lending,[59] antitrust,[60] and constructive trust based on unjust enrichment[61]; however, these efforts by litigation-prone borrowers have all failed, with one notable exception. In the case of *Derenco, Inc. v. Benjamin Franklin Fed. Sav. & Loan Ass'n*,[62] the Oregon Supreme Court acknowledged itself to be the first court of last resort to hold, after trial, that the federally chartered mortgagee has a "quasi-contractual" obligation to account to the mortgagor for income earned on escrow funds beneficially belonging to the mortgagor. Otherwise, in the opinion of the court, the "defendant [mortgagee] would be unjustly enriched if allowed to retain the net proceeds generated by these funds."[63] However, this opinion is of limited precedential value inasmuch as its rejection of the federal preemption theory appears questionable.[64] In addition, the case appears distinguishable from most commercial loan transactions in that it involved a contract of "adhesion," with unsophisticated borrowers (homeowners), and the deed of trust form did not expressly absolve the mortgagee from any duty to pay earnings on the escrow accounts.

However, because real estate borrowers have become so undaunted in their litigation efforts and because the legislative response has become so favorable to their side,[65] many lenders are privately expressing the

---

[58] Marsh v. Home Fed. Sav. & Loan Ass'n, 66 Cal. App. 3d 674, 688, 136 Cal. Rptr. 180, 187 (1977).

[59] E.g., Moore v. Great W. Sav. & Loan Ass'n, 513 F.2d 688, 691 (9th Cir. 1975).

[60] Spens v. Citizens Fed. Sav. & Loan Ass'n, 364 F. Supp. 1161, 1165 (N.D. Ill. 1973).

[61] Brooks v. Valley Nat'l Bank, 113 Ariz. 168, 174, 548 P.2d 1166, 1171 (1976); Carpenter v. Suffolk Franklin Sav. Bank, 346 N.E.2d 892, 900 (Mass. 1976).

[62] 281 Ore. 533, 577 P.2d 477, 492 (1977) *cert. denied* 99 S. Ct. 733 (1978).

[63] *Id.*, 577 P.2d at 492.

[64] See Dunn, "Selected Current Legal Issues in Mortgage Financing," 13 Real Prop. Prob. & Tr. J. 812, 819 (1978).

[65] Several states have enacted statutes regulating escrow deposits and frequently requiring mortgagees to pay interest on escrow accounts. E.g., N.Y. Banking Law § 14-b (McKinney 1974). See Jamaica Sav. Bank v. Lefkowitz, 390 F. Supp. 1357, 1364 (E.D.N.Y. 1975), *aff'd without opinion* 423 U.S. 802 (1975), which held that the New York statute is constitutional under the Fourteenth Amendment. Ore. Rev. Stat. §§ 86.240, 86.245; Conn. Gen. Stat.

[6] Required Tax and Insurance Escrows

The typical application-commitment requires the borrower to pay, on the first of each month, debt-service installments and deposits of one-twelfth of the annual taxes and insurance premiums, as estimated by the lender or its servicing agent, so that sufficient escrow funds can be accumulated to pay for such charges when they become due. Customarily, the lender does not pay interest on such deposits.[50]

In recent years, there has been an increasing amount of litigation, usually of the class action variety, by mortgagors against mortgagees. This has been designed to compel mortgagees to pay interest on these escrow accounts or otherwise account to mortgagors for the income earned by mortgagees from their use of these funds. There is certainly no dearth of commentary on this issue.[51] To date, the most prevalent approach utilized by mortgagors has been to characterize the escrow agreement as an express trust based on the notion that a trust is created "where the mortgagor pays funds to a bank with an expressed purpose that the funds shall be used for a particular purpose."[52] Or, based on the "in trust" language contained in the mortgage instrument,[53] mortgagors argue that under traditional trust-law theory the lender, as trustee, is obligated to render an accounting of profits from the trust (escrow) assets to the mortgagor as beneficiary.[54] However, the judicial response so far has been to deny the existence of a trust based on a distinction between "general" and "special deposits,"[55] with the conclusion being that the parties did not intend such a relationship,[56] notwithstanding their use of the phrase "in trust" in the escrow clause of the mortgage instrument.[57] Moreover, even where an express trust has been recog-

---

[50] See Section 5 of Form 3.2, "the loan" section of Form 3.1; Article 4.13 of Form 3.4 in Appendix B.

[51] See generally Comment, "Payment of Interest on Mortgage Escrow Accounts: Judicial and Legislative Developments" 23 Syracuse L. Rev. 845 (1972) (hereinafter cited as "Escrow Accounts"); Note, "Tax and Insurance Escrow Accounts in Mortgages—The Attack Passes On," 41 Mo. L. Rev. 13 (1976).

[52] Carpenter v. Suffolk Franklin Sav. Bank, 262 Mass. 770, 777, 291 N.E.2d 609, 614 (1973); Buchanan v. Brentwood Fed. Sav. & Loan Ass'n, 457 Pa. 135, 144, 320 A.2d 117, 124 (1974).

[53] E.g., Brooks v. Valley Nat'l Bank, 113 Ariz. 169, 173, 548 P.2d 1166, 1170 (1976).

[54] Id.

[55] Carpenter v. Suffolk Franklin Sav. Bank, 346 N.E.2d 892, 899 (Mass. 1976); Durkee v. Franklin Sav. Ass'n, 17 Ill. App. 3d 978, 981, 309 N.E.2d 118, 120 (1974).

[56] 346 N.E.2d at 899.

[57] Brooks v. Valley Nat'l Bank, 113 Ariz. at 174, 548 P.2d at 1171 (1976).

apply the insurance proceeds toward payment of the outstanding mortgage indebtedness instead of permitting the mortgagor to use the proceeds for restoration of the premises. Alternatively, an involuntary prepayment may occur as a consequence of a condemnation of the property where the mortgagee applies the condemnation proceeds to satisfy the mortgage indebtedness.[45] In either event, it has been held that the mortgagee is not entitled to exact a prepayment penalty since the mortgagor is not voluntarily exercising its bargained-for privilege to prepay.[46] However, lenders will sometimes require language authorizing collection of the penalty in the event of any prepayment, whether it be voluntary or involuntary. In such an event, the borrower could theoretically argue, that in the case of a casualty loss, the mortgagee is compelling the prepayment since it always has the option of allowing the mortgagor to use the insurance proceeds to repair and restore the premises. In any event, the authors are of the opinion that borrower's counsel should insist that the prepayment penalty be waived as to both condemnation as well as fire insurance proceeds. Incidentally, the same rationale should apply with respect to proceeds realized by the permanent lender in exercising his call option.[47]

In the event of a partial prepayment or the lender's receipt and retention of fire insurance or condemnation proceeds as a credit against the outstanding indebtedness, the borrower might be required to pay the same monthly debt service absent a provision permitting a pro rata reduction in payments over the same term as applied to the original loan amount.[48]

Since voluntary prepayment is a contingency within the borrower's control, the prepayment actually is generally not treated as additional interest subject to local usury law.[49]

---

[45] See Article 8.1 of Form 3.4 in Appendix B.

[46] Compare Chestnut Corp. v. Bankers Bond & Mortgage Co., 395 Pa. 153, 157, 149 A.2d 48, 50 (1959) (involving fire destruction), with Dekalb County v. United Family Life Ins. Co., 235 Ga. 417, 420, 219 S.E.2d 707, 710 (1975); Associated Schools, Inc. v. Dade County, 209 So. 2d 489, 490 (Fla. 1968) (per curiam); and Silverman v. State, 48 App. Div. 2d 413, 415, 370 N.Y.S.2d 234, 237 (1975) (all three cases involving condemnation of mortgaged property).

[47] See discussion of call options at ¶ 3.04[4].

[48] See "insurance provision" in Article 4.5 of Form 3.4 in Appendix B.

[49] E.g., Bell Bakeries, Inc. v. Jefferson Standard Life Ins. Co., 245 N.C. 408, 419, 96 S.E.2d 408, 415 (1957); Dezell v. King, 91 So. 2d 624, 627 (Fla. 1956). Prepayment penalty provisions have also been unsuccessfully challenged as constituting unenforceable penalties bearing no reasonable relationship to the injury to the lender caused by the prepayment. See Lazzareschi Inv. Co. v. San Francisco Sav. & Loan Ass'n, 22 Cal. App. 3d 303, 311, 99 Cal. Rptr. 417, 421 (1971). Also, see discussion at ¶ 5.03[7].

year beginning with the fifteenth loan year thereafter. The prepayment charges are to be computed on the unpaid principal balance at the time of such prepayment. It is understood and agreed that the fourteenth loan year stated herein commences on the expiration of the thirteen years from the date of the first required amortization payment.

It is of great importance to the developer to secure a reasonable prepayment privilege because the lack of such right may seriously affect his ability to refinance, which could thwart a subsequent expansion of the mortgaged premises or adversely affect a subsequent sale because of the inability of the purchaser to finance a portion of the purchase price attributable to the developer's equity. Such lack of reasonable prepayment privilege could also prevent refinancing when the developer desires to cash out his equity position. It could even adversely affect his tax-shelter situation when nondeductible mortgage amortization starts to exceed deductible depreciation on the property, which is the time for the developer to refinance or sell.[42]

The developer should first try to negotiate a noncumulative right to make an annual payment not in excess of a specified percentage of the original loan, which can often be secured without a prepayment fee. He should then negotiate for further prepayment at a reasonable price because, when the occasion arises, the "free" prepayment may be added to the penalty prepayment to achieve the prepayment requirement necessary for the developer to obtain refinancing. Prepayment penalties are regarded as interest for income tax purposes. In this regard, the developer should be cautioned to do his tax planning before the commitment is fully executed. Any retroactive reallocation or recharacterization of prepayment fees and other loan costs for tax purposes may be regarded with disfavor by the IRS.[43]

A lender will often insert a clause providing, "in case notice of prepayment shall be given, the amount of the prepayment shall become due on the date of prepayment specified in the notice." This means that the borrower, by giving notice, commits himself to the prepayment on a specified date; failure to do so would constitute a default under the mortgage or deed of trust. Otherwise, the lender would not be able to plan ahead for the reinvestment of the prepayment funds with any degree of certainty.

As noted elsewhere,[44] in the event the premises are destroyed by fire or some other casualty, the lender will frequently reserve the right to

---

[42] See discussion at ¶ 1.05[2][a].
[43] See discussion at ¶ 12.01[4].
[44] See authors' comment in respect to Article 4.5 of Form 3.4 in Appendix B at ¶ 3.08[4][d].

reason being that a lender is entitled to receive the anticipated rate of return.[39] In the past, some borrowers faced with a lender reluctant to accept prepayment, have tried various means, such as defaulting on the loan, to force the lender to accelerate.[40] The developer, having arranged more favorable financing, would buy the property at the foreclosure sale or redeem it, as the case might be. However, there is case law suggesting that a borrower cannot force the lender to accelerate by defaulting, on the rationale that, since the right to accelerate contained in a mortgage or deed of trust is for the sole benefit of the mortgagee, it is not self-executing and merely confers upon the mortgagee the right to accelerate at his option.[41]

The following prepayment provision is typical in that it provides for an initial "lock-in" period during which no prepayment will be allowed, followed by a prepayment penalty that scales down each year beyond the fourteenth loan year. This permits the lender to recoup his overhead expenses prior to prepayment, and it discourages refinancing by the borrower when the market interest rates drop below the interest rate on the existing mortgage.

> No privilege is reserved to prepay principal during the first thirteen loan years. Beginning with the fourteenth loan year, and upon sixty days written notice, privilege is reserved to pay the loan in full on any interest date, upon payment of a prepayment charge of 5 percent if the loan is paid in full during the fourteenth loan year, such prepayment charge to decline one-quarter of one percent per

---

[39] Saunders v. Frost, 22 Mass. (5 Pick.) 259, 274, 16 A.D. 394 (1827). See also Hartford Life Ins. Co. v. Randall, 283 Ore. 297, 583 P.2d 1126, 1128 (1978), in which the Oregon Supreme Court upheld a clause prohibiting repayment of principal for eleven years as not a restraint on alienation that is void as against public policy.

[40] To avoid this problem, Teachers Life Insurance Company has the following provision:

> Upon any default by Grantor and following the acceleration of maturity as herein provided, a tender of payment of the amount necessary to satisfy the entire indebtedness secured hereby made at any time prior to foreclosure sale (including sale under power of sale) by the Grantor, its heirs, successors or assigns, shall constitute an evasion of the prepayment terms hereunder and be deemed to be a voluntary prepayment thereunder and any such payment to the extent permitted by law will, therefore, include the premium required under the prepayment privilege, if any, contained in the Note secured hereby or if at the time there be no payment privilege then such payment will, to the extent permitted by law, include a premium of five percent (5%) of the then principal balance.

Whether a court would uphold such a provision remains to be seen.

[41] E.g., Peter Fuller Enterprises, Inc. v. Manchester Sav. Bank, 102 N.H. 117, 123, 152, A.2d 179, 183 (1959).

the term, the lower the constant and the higher the annual return and vice versa. In light of the recent uncertainties caused by inflation, many permanent lenders have become disenchanted with long-term amortization periods; thus, at the present time, any reliance on rules of thumb regarding amortization periods would be misplaced. Until recently, an excellent term would have been thirty to thirty-five years, and an unfavorable one ten years, with the average commercial loan for apartment, shopping center, and office buildings being twenty-three to twenty-eight years, and for hotels and motels fifteen years. When a lender is insisting upon an uneconomical term, a compromise, which has worked in many cases, is to accept the shorter term, but cast the amortization on a longer payout with a "balloon" payment at the end of the term. An example of this would be a $5 million loan at 9½ percent interest. At a straight *fully* amortized fifteen-year term, the constant of 12.54 percent would require annual debt service of $627,000. With the same fifteen-year loan amortized on a twenty-five-year basis, there would be a constant of only 10.41 percent, making for an annual amortization of $524,500. In fact, a number of insurance companies are currently writing such commitments (e.g., for a fifteen-year term with a twenty-five-year payout) with "balloon" payments at the end of the term. From the developer's viewpoint, the shorter term should not be of much concern, since (1) the property will normally not be owned that long, and (2) the payments of principal will have increased with the decrease in interest payments and deductions, making refinancing an attractive avenue.[37a]

Other life insurance companies are experimenting with call options, whereby, for example, a twenty-five-year loan could be called in at the lender's option during the fourteenth to sixteenth years. This alternative is less desirable than the previous approach in that it leads to an air of financial uncertainty for the developer about whether the mortagage will reach its full term. This could also prove to be a problem in the event the owner were attempting to sell the property or arrange wraparound financing. At the very least, any call provision should give the borrower sufficient notice that the lender intends to exercise the option.[38]

[5] Prepayment Privilege

Under basic property law, in the absence of any language in the loan documents, a lender does not have to accept a prepayment, the

---

[37a] Indeed, this short-term rollover balloon mortgage along with "bullet loans" (short-term interest only loans), may possibly become the permanent lending norm in the current inflationary period.

[38] See condition 22 of Form 3.1 in Appendix B.

¶ 3.04[4]

In addition, the graduated payment mortgage (GPM) and the flexible loan insurance program (FLIP) recast the borrower's monthly debt-service payments for the convenience of the borrower. Under the GPM, the interest rate is fixed but, in contrast to the standard constant payment mortgage, the monthly debt service increases at a graduated rate over the term of the loan. Use of the FLIP effectuates early reduced debt-service payments by reallocating portions of the borrower's initial down payment.

Use of these inflation-related devices, however, poses certain serious legal issues yet to be resolved. For example, to date, only a few states have enacted enabling statutes authorizing lenders to utilize the VRM[34]; thus, VRMs may be in violation of local usury law,[35] absent a specific exemption. In addition, VRM notes are nonnegotiable under the Uniform Commercial Code because they do not represent a promise to pay a certain sum of money[36]; an increase in the instrument could constitute an "optional advance" and, as such, be subordinate in lien priority to sums advanced by junior mortgages under the doctrine of obligatory versus optional advances.[37]

[4] Amortization Period

Almost as important as the rate is the term of the loan. The longer

---

rollover mortgage is provided by the FHLBB:
Tables show mortgage rates and monthly payments on a $75,000, 30-year rollover mortgage with an initial rate of 12.5 percent that is renegotiated (or "rolled over") every three years. The rate may rise or fall by a maximum of 5 percentage points over the life of the mortgage, and the rate can fluctuate by no more than 1.5 percentage points during each renegotiation. Assume the rate rises or falls by the maximum allowed at each renegotiation.

If Rates Go UP:			If Rates Go DOWN:		
	Mortgage Rate	*Monthly Payment*		*Mortgage Rate*	*Monthly Payment*
Year 1	12.5%	$ 800.44	Year 1	12.5%	$800.44
Year 4	14.0%	$ 885.95	Year 4	11.0%	$717.16
Year 7	15.5%	$ 970.21	Year 7	9.5%	$640.76
Year 10	17.0%	$1,052.57	Year 10	8.0%	$573.01
Year 13	17.5%	$1,078.92	Year 13	7.5%	$553.37

For further discussion of the impact of rollover mortgages, see N.Y. Times, May 31, 1980, at L-30. Levin & Roberts, "Future Forms of Financing-Lending Devices Addressed to Inflation and Tight Money," in *Financing Real Estate During the Inflationary 80s,* at 31-51 (1981).

[34] E.g., Cal. Civ. Code § 1916.5, (West Supp. 1970); Wis. Stat. § 215.21(3)(6).

[35] See discussion at ¶ 5.02[4][c].

[36] See U.C.C. § 3-106.

[37] See discussion at ¶ 4.02[6][a][ii].

mortgages were extensively used only in California. Critics of this measure are questioning the Board's authority to authorize such instruments and argue that they will add substantially to the cost of home ownership.[31]

The following is a brief description of the various inflation-related mortgage devices:

(1) *Variable-rate mortgage (VRM):* The interest rates vary with an index that reflects changes in market rates of interest subject to certain restrictions designed to reduce the uncertainties involved.[32]

(2) *Roll-over mortgage (ROM):* This is a short-term loan with a long amortization period; payments and interest rates are periodically recast in line with prevailing market conditions.[33]

(3) *Constant payment and dual-rate VRMs:* These are but variants of the VRM. Under the former type, the monthly payments are constant but the maturity date varies with interest rate changes; the latter calls for two variable interest rates, one which determines interest on the outstanding principal and the other which determines the monthly payment.

(4) *Price level adjusted mortgage (PLAM):* While the interest rate remains constant, both the monthly payments and the outstanding principal balance are adjusted with reference to a price index.

(5) *Shared appreciation mortgages (SAM):* This is in exchange for granting a high loan-to-value (e.g., 90 percent) loan and a lengthy amortization period (e.g., 30 years) geared to a certain percentage (e.g., one-third) of the total appreciation in the value of the realty.

---

[30] Miller, "Home Loan Institutions Win Right to Charge Variable Levels on Mortgages for Housing," N.Y. Times, May 31, 1979 at A1, col. 4. (hereinafter cited as Miller).

[31] *Id.*

[32] The Bank Board also approved the creation of a nationwide index to measure increases in the cost of funds that will be used to permit changes in mortgage interest rates. At present, each of the twelve regional bank boards sets mortgage ceilings based on the cost of funds in their areas. Increases in mortgage rates will be limited to half a percentage point in any single year and to 2.5 percentage points over the life of the mortgage. There is no maximum decrease. Miller, note 29 *supra,* at D13.

[33] Federally chartered savings and loans are permitted to "roll over" or adjust mortgage rates every three, four, or five years. The maximum increase or decrease is one-half a percentage point a year and 5 percentage points over the life of a mortgage. The lender must automatically renew the loan, even if the borrower has been delinquent in making payments. The following example of a

mortgaged real estate to the developer, who then makes debt-service payments directly to the mortgage lender. The lender obtains a first lien on the property and also takes an assignment of the lease or sale contract as additional collateral for the loan. The purpose of the municipality acting as a conduit is to qualify the mortgage interest for tax-free treatment under I.R.C. § 103. In addition, because the interest income is exempt from federal and sometimes state taxation, the lender will frequently reduce the interest rate by 15 to 25 percent below the market rate for conventional loans. Moreover, the Internal Revenue Service will allow the developer to enjoy the full tax benefits of legal ownership.[27]

[c] Variable-Rate Mortgages, Joint Venturing, and Other Inflation-Related Financing Devices

Inflation has been of special concern to savings, loan associations, and mutual savings banks because of disintermediation, caused, in large measure, by Federal Reserve anti-inflation monetary measures that drive interest rates up in the short-term money market against which the thrifts must compete for loanable funds.[28] In addition, a sizeable portion of their investment portfolios consist of long-term, low-rate mortgages made years ago. Because of higher and variable interest rates now paid to depositors with the new money market certificates tied to treasury bills, both the earnings ability and lending capacity of thrift organizations have seriously eroded with respect to both single-family and multi-family residential loans. In response to their predicament, in 1976 the Federal Home Loan Bank Board (FHLBB) authorized a three-volume study entitled *The Alternative Mortgage Instruments Research Study.*[29] This study explores the variable-rate mortgage and other related mortgage forms that are designed to be more flexible and responsive to the needs of both the lender and the borrower during periods of inflation. Moreover, on May 31, 1979 it was announced that the FHLBB had decided, effective July 1, 1979, to permit federally chartered savings and loan associations to offer variable-rate mortgages in the interest of promoting "more stable mortgage flows, greater stability in housing markets, and a greater ability of savers of member associations to earn higher returns on their deposits."[30] Previously, floating-rate

---

[27] The tax-exempt mortgage is more fully discussed at ¶ 8.06.
[28] See discussion at ¶¶ 2.01[1][b], 2.02[3].
[29] *The Alternative Mortgage Instruments Research Study, (AMIRS), Federal Home Loan Bank Board* (Kaplan, ed. 1977); see generally Cowan & Foley, "New Trends in Residential Mortgage Finance," 13 Real Prop. Prob. & Tr. J. 1075 (1978).

income will decrease the potential sale price of the property.[24] Nevertheless, many permanent lenders are attracted to this method since it is fairly easy to ascertain gross income, and the method is an additional hedge against inflation. If the lender will not compromise on the gross income concept, an attempt should be made by the developer to negotiate a floor amount below which the equity participation will not attach. In effect, the floor or ceiling, depending on position, should cover projected operating expenses and debt service with, perhaps, some cushion. Gross or net income should be clearly defined, if not limited, in scope. Finally, if the gross or net income subject to participation is to include both the fixed-minimum and a percentage rental, then those terms should exclude charges for common-area maintenance and security, merchants' association dues, utility charges, rental of equipment, and other pass-through income items not directly related to charges for occupancy of the space. It is also questionable as to whether income obtained through the operation of escalation clauses should be included.

Percentage of Net Income. This is both a more refined and a fairer method of achieving a true equity participation. It allows a sharing in the profit only when net income exceeds all expense and debt service. A practical problem for the lender is the fact that this method is more difficult to police in ascertaining true expenses; however, the lender in the permanent commitment can insist upon annual audited financial statements of the property.[25]

In either case, it is imperative for the developer to discuss with his accountant and lawyer the existing participation submitted by the lender. Some lenders will waive the existing participation in exchange for an above-market fixed rate. Such a trade-off might be worthwhile to a developer desirous of syndicating, as most syndicators do not prefer equity participation.[26]

[b] Low-Interest Financing With Tax-Exempt Mortgages

The tax-exempt mortgage is essentially an industrial revenue bond structured as a tripartite mortgage loan to a municipality that net leases (with a purchase option) or sells, on the installment basis, the

---

[24] See Miller & Kates, "How to Value Real Estate Subject to an Equity Participation," 2 Real Estate Rev. 89 (1972).

[25] See "audit provision" in Article 4.15 of Form 3.4 in Appendix B, a sample deed of trust.

[26] The status of these "equity kickers" under local usury laws is discussed at ¶ 5.05[8]. See also discussion at ¶ 8.08.

requiring some type of equity kicker. Whether the equity kicker will be reinstated only when permanent financing is difficult to obtain, or whether it will become standard in light of the effect of inflation's eroding the fixed-mortgage rate of return remains to be seen. Nevertheless, the equity kicker is a fact of life and must be negotiated carefully. An equity kicker or participation is a method by which the lender shares in a percentage of the income derived from the property in addition to the fixed-interest rate. There are three types of equity participation: (1) percentage of gross income; (2) percentage of net income; and (3) joint venture position. Since joint venturing by permanent lenders is covered in Chapter 11, the following is an analysis of items (1) and (2).

Percentage of Gross Income. If, in our hypothetical case, Ace Insurance Co. insists upon receiving an equity kicker geared to gross income, the commitment letter might include the following typical condition:

> *Additional Compensation.* In addition to payments of the fixed monthly installments as herein above provided, the mortgagor shall pay us annually, as additional compensation, within thirty days after the expiration of each fiscal year of the mortgagor, a sum equal to 25 percent of the amount, if any, by which the gross income from the Real Property in such fiscal year shall exceed $402,190. Additional compensation for any partial fiscal year shall be pro rated. The term "gross income" as used herein shall mean the total revenue derived from the Real Property by the owner thereof as rental for the use of occupancy of apartments and parking facilities, and as charges, if any, for heating, air conditioning, and utilities, without any deductions whatsoever except that (1) tax increases after the first full year in which the Property shall be assessed as a completed building and (2) insurance premium increases after the first year in which the Property shall be occupied as a completed building shall be deducted from gross income before computing the additional compensation.

By acquiring a right to a percentage of the gross income collected, a lender is reaping all of the benefit and is in effect isolating its position and yield from market conditions at the expense of the developer. Bearing in mind the recent inflationary spiral, gross income can increase substantially, while the developer receives a smaller share of income after taxes because of rising operating expense and taxes. Since market value is dependent on a capitalization of net income, any decrease in net

In the event of a platform loan, the construction lender will ordinarily limit its loan to the floor amount; accordingly, in its negotiations with the permanent lender, Dan Development Co. should explore the possibility of paying an additional fee, at its option, to fund the $400,000 gap if the rent-roll requirement is not met. Another trade-off to solve the gap problem might be to offer the permanent lender additional protection by way of a personal guaranty or letter of credit covering all, or a stated portion, of the gap loan, to be in effect until the gap is filled by the subsequent achievement of the higher rent or until the loan has been amortized down to the platform figure. Alternatively, the developer might agree to execute and guarantee a so-called master lease covering all, or a stated portion, of the leasing gap. Also, in the event the leasing requirement cannot be eliminated, the developer must carefully negotiate how the rent-roll requirement is to be satisfied. For example, do the tenants merely have to execute the leases and pay rent, or must they be in occupancy, as well? Another gap situation may arise if the developer decides not to complete construction, for example, not to adapt open spaces for tenant occupancy until the tenant has been secured and the lease terms fixed. In such an event, the permanent lender will require a holdback of mortgage funds to assure lien-free completion. As an alternative to this arrangement, the developer may negotiate in the commitment that the permanent lender substitute an irrevocable letter of credit for the cash holdback or a personal guaranty to complete the construction "lien free" if the mortgage is otherwise without personal recourse.

[3] Rate of Interest

[a] "Equity Kickers"

Just a few years ago, the only advice given to developers and other borrowers on this topic would have to negotiate the most favorable rate. In 1969, when capital dried up, lenders began writing commitments

---

occupancy at the time of closing of the loan in an amount of $8,500,000 or more, you will be required to place in escrow an amount equal to $13 for each square foot of unfinished leaseable space which amount shall be released from such escrow as and when such space is completed to our satisfaction. No interest shall be payable on such escrow funds by the escrowee. The release of these funds from escrow shall be in increments of not less than $50,000. All of the work for which the funds in escrow are held shall be completed by May 1, 1982, and if such work is not completed by that date, the said funds shall be applied to the unpaid principal sum of the loan in the inverse order of maturity. If not less than 95% of the rentable space in this building is fully completed and ready for occupancy on or before May 1, 1982, the balance remaining in escrow will be released.

and principal shall be $14,258.20, and (2) the balance of $400,000 is to be advanced if and when said leasing requirements have been met, but not later than July 1, 1981, and the monthly payments shall be increased at the time of such advance to an amount sufficient to completely amortize the loan by the maturity date.

Recently, the floor-ceiling rent-roll requirement has become a floor with intermediate multi-platforms, resulting in a final ceiling. This multi-tiered refinement of the platform loan occurred in response to the developer's concern that in large-scale projects the gap between the floor and ceiling could involve millions of dollars. This staged approach shortens the time needed to bridge the gap and allows additional funding, even if the requirements for reaching the ceiling cannot be met.[23]

---

[23] For example, the following multi-tiered platform loan condition appeared in a commitment letter issued by an insurance company based in New York, involving a sizeable office building loan:

(A) for a loan of $8,800,000, leases for a term of 5 years or more for an aggregate annual rental of not less than $1,258,808, excluding parking income, derived from not more than 90,758 square feet of net rentable office space.

(B) for a loan of $8,500,000, leases for a term of 5 years or more for an aggregate annual rental of not less than $1,212,936 excluding parking income, derived from not more than 90,388 square feet of net rentable office space.

If by May 1, 1981 neither (A) nor (B) has been satisfied, the loan is to be closed as a 2 payment loan; e.g., the amount of $7,700,000 is to be paid out not later than May 1, 1981 subject, however, to full completion of the building and not less than 50% of the rentable space being fully completed and ready for occupancy, and subject also to compliance with all of the other applicable terms and conditions of this commitment. The monthly installments of principal and interest on a loan of $7,700,000 will be $64,955. If less than 50% of the aforesaid tenant finishing has not been completed, you will be required to place in escrow an amount equal to $14.50 for each square foot of the unfinished space, which amount will be released from such escrow when not less than 50% of the tenant finishing in the building has been completed to our satisfaction. Thereafter, if by March 1, 1982 either condition (A) or condition (B) has been satisfied, and provided the loan is not then in default, the additional amount of either $1,100,000 or $800,000, as the case may be, is to be advanced not later than March 1, 1982. If by March 1, 1982, the requirement of condition (B) has been satisfied, but the requirement of condition (A) has not been satisfied, the second advance of $800,000 shall nevertheless be increased by $100,000 for each $15,500 of rental income which has been achieved in excess of $1,212,936 provided the total rental achieved is derived from not more than 90,000 square feet of net rentable office space. The monthly installment of interest and principal shall be increased at the time of the second advance to the amount required to amortize the loan in full by maturity.

If full completion of the improvements has not been accomplished to the extent that some rentable space is not fully finished for tenant

loan is insufficient in amount to take out the construction loan because the construction lender has funded cost overruns resulting from change orders, the construction lender must be willing to take a subordinated loan for the difference; otherwise, the developer will be forced to obtain gap financing from some other source. For example, if the project is being syndicated, the limited partners might be required to fund additional capital contributions simultaneously to cover the gap with the closing of the permanent loan. Any financing approach used by the developer to eliminate the gap in funds should be arranged prior to his acceptance of the permanent mortgage loan commitment—not when the permanent loan is being closed.

In the example given earlier, the security for the $2 million mortgage loan to Dan Development Co. is a proposed garden apartment project. In this kind of multi-unit residential loan, the permanent lender's appraisal-underwriting process involves an evaluation of the projected aggregate rental flow or "rent-roll" from the short-term occupancy leases. Frequently, the lender will impose a leasing requirement whereby the loan amount is two-tiered, and the borrower's entitlement to the maximum loan amount is dependent upon his achievement of a stipulated rent-roll amount when the project is completed. If the leasing requirement is not met by the closing date, such a "platform" loan is funded only at the lesser, or "floor," amount; normally the borrower is given a few months after the closing date to meet the leasing requirement and receive the "ceiling" amount.

If the hypothetical $2 million loan to Dan Development Co. were a platform loan, a typical leasing requirement in the commitment letter would read as follows:

> *Leasing Requirements.* The annual rental from not more than 77 percent of the rooms in the buildings of the Real Property on an unfurnished basis shall be not less than $326,160, and the space rented shall be rented on a basis so that if the buildings were 100 percent rented, the annual rental would be at least $423,360. Such rooms shall be occupied by tenants on a current rent-paying basis under written leases or rental agreements having terms of not less than one year. The mortgagor shall deliver to us a rent-roll certified to be correct and indicating the apartments of which said rooms comprise the total rooms relied upon to satisfy this condition.
>
> No rental concessions to tenants shall have been made and said certificate should so state. If by March 1, 1981 said annual rental has not been achieved on the foregoing basis, the loan is to be closed as a two-payment loan, i.e., (1) the amount of $1.6 million is to be paid out not later than March 1, 1981 without said leasing requirement, in which event the monthly installments of interest

appraiser's report in deciding what the value of the property and resultant loan amount will be. While "cost" and "market" are correlative approaches used by appraisers to corroborate final value, the primary method used in appraising income-producing real estate is the "income approach." Under this approach, the estimated annual net income, before debt-service expenses, is divided by a selected rate of capitalization, generally defined as the rate of return on one's equity investment that will attract a prudent investor to the project.[21] For mortgage loan appraisal purposes, the overall capitalization rate is initially based on certain factors known at the time of appraisal: the loan-to-value ratio, market interest rate, and maximum loan amortization period. Assumptions are also made concerning how long one owner is likely to own the property ("income projection term") and whether the market value will increase or decline over the projection term. Based on a certain expected equity yield and rate of depreciation, the appraiser will finally compute the capitalization rate by using the Ellwood Tables[22] or other standardized formula. While the methodologies of appraisers may vary somewhat in applying this income approach, their common objective is to arrive at a high enough capitalization rate and low enough loan amount so that the subject property will "pay for itself," or generate annual net income sufficient in amount to cover the annual debt-service payments.

[2] Gap Financing Problem Caused by Construction Cost Overruns or by Platform Loan

While the loan amount must be realistic and must conform to acceptable appraisal techniques, it should be sufficient to enable the developer to meet his construction costs since the construction lender will ordinarily refuse to lend more than the permanent takeout amount. Consequently, in today's inflationary market the developer's construction costs should be determined with firm bids, and most of the prefinancing requirements (e.g., trade payments, construction surveys, title work, and architectural rendering of plans and specifications) should be completed to avoid unnecessary and costly delays. If the permanent

---

[21] Accordingly, the lower the risk and capitalization rate, the higher the value of the property, and vice versa. For example, high-risk property with a net income of $2,000 requiring a 20 percent return or capitalization rate would be valued at $10,000 (5 times earnings), whereas low-risk property with the same net income capitalized at 10 percent (10 times earnings) would be appraised at $20,000.

[22] Ellwood, "Appraisal for Mortgage Loan Purposes," in Friedman, *Encyclopedia of Real Estate Appraising* 681 (1959).

carefully examine its provisions, being alert to any that may provide the lender with an opportunity to renegotiate the terms as a condition of funding or that may require unanticipated expenditures by the developer.

The lender may be acting in good faith and may simply be using such "escape" clauses in the commitment to strengthen its security position pursuant to its original expectations; these may not have been adequately communicated to the developer at the time the commitment was negotiated. Alternatively, these additional unanticipated requirements at the time of funding may be imposed because of a substantial change in the money markets, such as a sharp rise in market interest rate between the dates of commitment and funding, and may reflect an act of bad faith on the part of the lender. Fortunately, this rarely occurs.

The following is a provision-by-provision analysis, with cross-references to the sample agreements found in Appendix B, of each major term and condition in the permanent mortgage loan commitment or application-commitment. For purposes of illustration, let us assume the following hypothetical facts: a builder, Dan Development Co., has applied to the Ace Insurance Co., on January 1, 1979 for a permanent loan of $2 million with interest at 9.75 percent per year and a term of twenty-five years, to be repaid in equal monthly payments of $17,822, such payments to be applied first to payment of interest and the balance to reduction of principal. A buy-sell agreement must be executed on or before March 29, 1979. The security is a proposed garden apartment project containing 360 units and recreational facilities to be constructed by the developer on a 16.7-acre site. If approved, the permanent loan is scheduled to close on or before March 1, 1981.

[1] Loan Amount Based on Appraised Value

Permanent lenders are required by external regulation[19] and by internal policy to limit the amount of their first mortgage loan to a certain percentage, usually 75 to 80 percent, of the value of the property. In our example, if Ace Insurance Co. were chartered in New York, its maximum loan-to-value ratio would be 75 percent,[20] so that it could make a first mortgage loan of $2 million only if the project has an appraised value of $2,666,666.

The permanent lender's loan committee will receive an appraisal report from the borrower; however, it will rely primarily upon its own

---

[19] Except for REITs, the investment portfolios of permanent lenders are tightly regulated by federal or local law. See discussion at ¶ 2.02.

[20] N.Y. Ins. Law ¶ 81.6(a) (McKinney Supp. 1980).

¶ 3.04 TERMS AND CONDITIONS OF PERMANENT FINANCING

The mortgage loan application prepared by the developer, with an assist from the mortgage loan processor, is not binding upon the lender until accepted in writing. While the broker, mortgage banker, or loan processor is generally familiar with the lender's requirements and guidelines, such financing terms can be quite unexpectedly changed by a lender if market or internal conditions warrant. The loan application is reviewed by several other people and committees before it is approved, and it is subject to changes, of a possibly material nature, depending upon the situation. Aside from the conditions for the actual funding of the loan, careful attention should be given to the method of repayment (e.g., constant monthly installments, interest only for a specified number of years, etc.) and other terms of the loan.

Essentially, the lender's position in negotiating the commitment or application-commitment is to make sure that, at the time of funding, the property constitutes sound security for the loan. The lender thus sets certain conditions that the property must meet at the time of funding. The property should be completed within the prescribed time limits in a "good, substantial and workmanlike manner," fully equipped with first-class equipment, and built in accordance with the approved plans and specifications. The property should be paid for and free of liens. Title to the property should be good, marketable and insured, without unauthorized exceptions. The property should be fully qualified for the purposes contemplated when the commitment was issued; e.g., it is fully in compliance with all applicable law and regulations for which all required governmental permits have been properly issued. The leasing must have been achieved in conformity with the commitment by means of lease forms which had been approved, and the lessees must have no defenses or offsets to the obligations undertaken by them in the leases. All required hazard insurance should be secured in amounts and with companies approved by the lender. There must be no material change in the financial condition of the mortgagor or of the tenants (e.g., no bankruptcy, reorganization, or other insolvency proceedings), or in the condition of the property—it must be determined that property damage has been satisfactorily repaired and no condemnation proceedings are pending as of the date the commitment was made.

The negotiating position of the developer and his construction lender is to make as certain as possible that the permanent loan will close when the property has been completed, and that prior to closing, they will not be faced with the imposition of unanticipated requirements that permit the permanent lender to reconsider its decision to fund the loan. Before the commitment is accepted, the developer's lawyer should

[2] Identity of Borrower and Other Backup Data

The permanent lender is interested in the facts relating to the project as reflected by the projected cost figures, plans and specifications, copies of any ground lease, principal occupancy leases, and so on. The permanent lender's appraiser and the borrower's appraiser will submit reports containing such items as a plot plan; typical floor plan; city, neighborhood, and site data; strip map with zoning areas; demand and competition data; analysis of comparable rents or leases; tax and insurance data; and a detailed estimate of land value and project value based on an analysis of the projected income and expenses. The permanent lender will also want to know whether the loan will be direct or will be purchased by assignment, whether the mortgage is to be a first lien on the fee title or on a leasehold, and where the property is located, including a plot plan showing easements, a legal description, and a strip map showing surrounding improvements. The lender is also interested in the history and reputation of the developer, together with financial details. Lawyers for the permanent lender are prone to point out how frequently lack of information or misinformation on these items can cause delay in closing the permanent loan.

The lender wants to know the exact identity and organizational form of the borrower; corporation, partnership, land trust, etc. If the borrowing entity is a corporation, most lenders will ask if the corporation is stock or nonstock, and will ask for the names and addresses of the principal stockholders and directors. If the loan is being made to a corporation yet to be formed, the commitment will be made to the individual incorporators; otherwise, the borrowers could avoid the contract by simply refusing to incorporate. From the borrower's perspective, it should be clear that the lender will agree to the assignment of the commitment to the corporation as soon as it comes into existence.

If the borrowing entity is a limited partnership, the principals should seriously consider the tax importance of having an exculpatory provision in the mortgage or deed of trust note; otherwise, the investor partners may not be able to receive tax losses in excess of their equity investments.[18] The permanent lender will usually agree, since it is generally the rental income stream from the property, not the solvency of the borrower, which primes the mortgage.

---

[18] See discussion at ¶ 1.05[5][b].

specified amount of money upon stated conditions; this creates a binding contract the very instant the offer is accepted by the lender.[13]

Frequently, the application is followed by a more detailed commitment letter that acts as the lender's formal acceptance of the borrower's offer. However, if possible, the borrower's attorney should examine the proposed lender's commitment form before his client files the application; if the lender's commitment tracks the application without change, the issuance of the commitment may be an acceptance of an offer, and there is then and thereby a contract.[14] Conversely, if the terms and conditions set forth in the commitment letter vary materially from those stipulated in the application, the commitment merely constitutes a counteroffer from the lender that requires acceptance by the borrower before a contract arises. To correct this problem and at the same time obviate a needless time-consuming step, at present, many lenders use a single, integrated document that incorporates all the terms and conditions of both the application and commitment letter.[15]

Normally, the broker, mortgage correspondent, or the lender's loan processor will give the borrower the lender's current guidelines as to the probable rate, yield, and term of the mortgage. If the developer feels uncomfortable with a provision in the application, he should not count on the lender's real estate or finance committee to modify or delete the objectionable terms. It should be resolved during the application stage, for if the application is accepted without change, the offer is binding, and if it is breached by the borrower, forfeiture of a good-faith deposit will result.

Finally, from the lender's perspective, if a well-tested standard form is not used, the application should contain concise language and should include all the essential conditions—agreement to lend a specified amount, identity of borrower, loan terms, method of repayment, prepayment privilege, if any, description of security, etc. Otherwise, any vague language will be construed against the lender[16] and the agreement may be unenforceable for want of certainty in its terms.[17]

---

[13] See St. Paul Corp. v. Manufacturers Life Ins. Co., 262 Md. 192, 255, 278 A.2d 12, 18 (1971) (by implication).

[14] See a sample commitment at Form 3.1 in Appendix B.

[15] See a sample application-commitment at Form 3.2 in Appendix B.

[16] E.g., Leben v. Nassau Sav. & Loan Ass'n, 46 App. Div. 2d 830, 831, 337 N.Y.S.2d 310, 313 (1972).

[17] Gay v. Grace, 433 F.2d 14 (5th Cir. 1970) (per curiam); Willowood Condominium Ass'n, Inc. v. HNC Realty Co., 531 F.2d 1249, 1253 (5th Cir. 1976).

directly approaching the permanent lender itself. As previously discussed in Chapter 2,[11] the choice of a permanent lender will depend upon which type of lender specializes in the sort of permanent financing being sought. Such loan preferences are a function of each lender's historical habit, the source and stability of its funding sources, external regulation, market competition, and a host of other factors. For example, if the security for the loan is a large piece of income-producing property such as an office building, a shopping center, or an apartment building, the permanent lender will probably be a life insurance company. Under local law, insurance companies can only invest in mortgages on income-producing property; they prefer large loans to reduce their overhead-per-loan costs. They have also recently begun to shy away from multi-unit residential loans in rent-control jurisdictions. By contrast, if the collateral for the loan is a small or medium-size apartment building, the permanent lender will probably be a savings and loan association or, in the Northeast, a mutual savings bank. On the other hand, if the real security priming the permanent mortgage is not occupancy rental but land in the process of being developed, or perhaps management skill (hotels, motels, mobile home parks), the developer may go to a less-regulated but more daring lender such as a REIT. Unlike most other permanent lenders, a long-term mortgage REIT will not deny such "specialty" loans, but will charge more, since it must pay more for its long-term funding than its competitors.

¶ 3.03 FUNCTION OF MORTGAGE LOAN APPLICATION-COMMITMENT

The application, normally on the lender's standard printed form, serves three functions: (1) it is a request by way of a written offer for the contemplated loan; (2) it identifies the borrower and gives the lender the basic facts and backup data supporting the loan application; and (3) it sets the legal and business parameters for the permanent loan, and to some extent, for the construction loan as well, because the permanent lender may refuse to purchase the construction loan pursuant to the buy-sell agreement unless the terms and conditions in the permanent mortgage loan commitment letter have been satisifed.[12]

[1] A Written Offer

While the application, as stated above, is usually on the lender's printed form, it represents a legal offer from the developer to borrow a

---

[11] See discussion at ¶ 2.02.
[12] See discussion at ¶ 4.02[1].

to ten-year standby loan. As another alternative, the borrower may merely obtain a nonfundable standby commitment as a prelude to obtaining construction financing.[5] Generally, the commercial bank or other interim lender will rely upon the permanent takeout (frequently pursuant to a buy-sell agreement[6] among itself, the borrower, and the permanent lender), and will sell the loan to the permanent lender once the terms of the permanent commitment are met and the project is completed and income-producing.[7]

After the project has been operating for a while, the developer-borrower may sometimes seek additional working capital by "mortgaging out" or refinancing the existing loan for a longer term with the same or other permanent lender.[8] Alternatively, if the prepayment penalty is steep, the interest rate on the existing loan is low, or the developer wants to increase its financial leverage, the developer may seek a second or third mortgage from a secondary lender with the legal authority and temerity to make such high-risk loans, provided that the first mortgage does not prohibit such junior financing. For such financing, the developer may go to some audacious commercial bank or, if necessary, to a more willing, and more expensive, lender such as a finance company, industrial corporation, or private syndicate.[9]

If the improvements are overdepreciated, the developer might instead obtain the necessary capital by means of a sale-and-leaseback arrangement with some institutional lender or investor that is either exempt (e.g., college) or quasi-exempt (e.g., insurance company) from income taxation. By selling the real estate and leasing it back, the developer might obtain more working capital and tax deductions than by retaining the fee and refinancing the first mortgage.[10]

¶ 3.02 SELECTING THE PERMANENT LENDER

A developer can obtain a permanent loan commitment either with the aid of an intermediary, such as a mortgage broker or banker, or by

---

[5] See ¶ 3.07 for a discussion of standby loan commitment. See also the discussion at ¶ 4.01[3].

[6] See discussion at ¶¶ 4.01[2], 4.05.

[7] However, REITs have sometimes supplied both the construction and permanent financing and recently a few daring insurance companies (e.g., Metropolitan Life Insurance Co., Aetna Life & Casualty Co., and Connecticut General Life Insurance Co.) have started to follow suit. Carberry, "Certain Major Life Insurance Companies Quietly Step Up Lending for Construction," Wall St. J., May 15, 1979, at 23, col. 1.

[8] See ¶ 7.02.

[9] See ¶ 7.03.

[10] See ¶ 6.04.

In classic post-war financing, the search for real estate financing began with the permanent mortgage loan commitment. The reasons for this, although historical, are still relevant. The majority of commercial banks, which do most of the construction financing, lend money on short-term deposits. Accordingly, suitable real estate lending is thought of as short term and is designed to maintain liquidity and turnover in the banks' real estate portfolio. Commercial banks, REITs, and other construction lenders have developed the requisite expertise to monitor the construction activity of the developer and determine whether the project is being completed on schedule in accordance with approved plans and specifications. They also determine whether or not progress payments are being used properly to pay off subcontractors and materialmen. However, in light of the risks inherent in construction lending, construction lenders view the permanent takeout commitment as a guarantee of the proverbial "light at the end of the tunnel."[2] In addition, nationally chartered banks are not subject to the requirements associated with a real estate loan if they lend against a permanent commitment.[3] Consequently, permanent financing has ordinarily been a condition precedent to obtaining construction financing.[4] However, in some recent instances, the borrower has been able to obtain an open-end construction loan without a backup permanent takeout from a large commercial bank. A loan of this sort is sometimes convertible to a five-

---

[2] Indeed, some states, such as New York, exempt construction lenders with a takeout from the real estate loan limitation. Section 103(4)(a) of the New York Banking Law states that construction lenders are limited to three-fourths of the appraised value, but Section 103(4)(d), a savings clause, states that "in no event shall a loan be considered a loan upon the security of real estate...(iv) where there is a binding and valid commitment or agreement by a financially responsible lender, purchaser or other financially responsible party either directly with the lending bank or trust company or which is for the benefit of, or has been assigned to, the lending bank or trust company and pursuant to which commitment, agreement or assignment, the lender, purchaser or other party is required to advance to the lending bank or trust company within thirty months from the date of such commitment or agreement the full amount of the loan to be made..." N.Y. Banking Law § 103(4) (McKinney Supp. 1980).

[3] A national bank loan to finance construction of commercial and industrial buildings, maturing in sixty months, is not a real estate loan if a valid and binding agreement is present from a financially responsible lender. 12 U.S.C. § 371(c).

[4] To generate loans, real estate investment trusts will often make construction loans without takeouts. Savings and loan associations frequently make combination construction-permanent loans. Life insurance companies also use this arrangement occasionally. See discussion at ¶¶ 4.01, 4.01[3].

purchase the fee, he must obtain leasehold mortgage financing to fund the cost of constructing the improvements.

☐ *Consider the need for gap financing.* It may be necessary for the developer to seek secondary financing to compensate for the difference between the amount of the permanent first mortgage financing and his equity money. Familiarity with the lending practices and investment constraints imposed on each permanent group, as well as with the types of secondary financing available, will aid the developer in the search for optimum financing.

☐ *Investigate legal questions that could delay or prevent purchase or use of the real estate.* This includes checking for any zoning or title problems associated with the property, as well as checking for environmental constraints that may exist under either federal or local law.[1]

[2] Review of the Commercial Lending Cycle

The customary lending cycle for most ventures involving income-producing real estate can be diagrammed as shown in Exhibit 3.1.

EXHIBIT 3.1. The Lending Cycle

1—Commitment obtained from permanent lender

2—Commitment obtained from construction lender

3—If pre-closed buy-sell agreement: permanent lender approves ground lease (if any), prime occupancy leases, and security documents

4—Construction loan closes; disbursements begin.

5—Construction completed in accordance with construction loan agreement; construction lender protects itself against mechanics' liens

6—Permanent loan closed when commitment conditions met; construction note and mortgage assigned to permanent lender

---

[1] See discussion at ¶ 3.04(a).

¶ 3.01 Pre-financing Considerations

Prior to their attempt to obtain financing, the promoters of a new real estate project must select the ownership entity or syndicate best suited for the dual purpose of raising the venture capital and securing the financing needed to develop or acquire the real estate (see Chapter 1). They must also make basic decisions concerning which parcel of land should be acquired, and must decide the financial feasibility of the project. Although these latter decisions are outside the scope of this book, they are briefly described here because they so greatly affect the ultimate financing arrangement.

[1] Pre-financing Checklist

☐ *Select the real estate to be developed.* In the case of newly constructed real estate, the construction site is chosen based on a marketing survey of factors, such as consumer demand; population, neighborhood, and tax-rate trends; and rent and vacancy levels of comparable properties. If the property is undeveloped, an engineering study should be done to discover the availability of utilities and to ascertain whether there are any insurmountable problems with soil conditions, surface water, or any other topographical features of the construction site. For already developed real estate, the considerations include the competitiveness of the location, the quality of tenants and lease terms, the physical condition, the need for future repairs, and the "free and clear rates of return," net income before tax or finance charges divided by purchase price, as projected by the sellers.

☐ *Estimate the rate of equity return to investors.* For developed realty, the purchaser's attorney, accountant, or financial adviser should closely examine the past rent schedules and operating records and canvass available financing in order to estimate the future cash flow and after-tax income from the property. In construction of new real estate, the developer must estimate the time, land, construction, and financing costs and must decide whether the project is feasible; that is, can he achieve a "break-even" level of income needed to meet tax, debt service, and "front-end" payments on a cash basis, at a level of risk acceptable to the investors.

☐ *Consider financing the land separately.* The developer of new real estate must decide whether to finance his land costs by means of a deferred purchase-money mortgage, land development loan, or some variant of split-financing. If he decides to ground lease and not

[15] Survey, Title Insurance, and
    Closing Costs 3- 47
[16] Plot Size, Description of the Improvements,
    Location 3- 48
[17] No Material Change Between Date
    of Final Commitment and Funding 3- 49
[18] Joint Venturing Requirement
    by Permanent Lenders and Other
    Trends in Permanent Financing........................ 3- 49

¶ 3.05 Analysis of Shopping Center and Other
    High-Credit Leases by Permanent Lender 3- 51
    [1] Rent Provisions 3- 52
    [2] Default and Termination Provisions..................... 3- 53
    [3] Radius Restrictions, Exclusive-Use
        Clauses, and Co-tenancy Requirements
        in Shopping Center Leases 3- 54
    [4] Percentage Rental 3- 55
    [5] Alterations... 3- 56
    [6] Subordination of Lease to Mortgage 3- 56
    [7] Assignment 3- 57
    [8] Option to Purchase 3- 57
    [9] Financing.. 3- 58

¶ 3.06 Remedies for Breach of Mortgage Loan Commitment 3- 58

¶ 3.07 The Standby "Loan Commitment"............................ 3- 61
    [1] The Regular Standby................................... 3- 61
    [2] The "Fundable Standby" 3- 62

¶ 3.08 Drafting the Mortgage/Deed of Trust...................... 3- 63
    [1] Definition of Mortgage/Deed of Trust.................. 3- 63
    [2] Use of Uniform Documents 3- 64
    [3] The Note 3- 65
    [4] The Mortgage/Deed of Trust............................ 3- 66
        [a] Definitions.. 3- 66
        [b] Grant 3- 70
        [c] Representations and Warranties 3- 70
        [d] Affirmative Covenants 3- 71
        [e] Negative Covenants................................. 3- 75
        [f] Events of Default.................................. 3- 76
        [g] Default Remedies................................... 3- 77
        [h] Condemnation 3- 92
        [i] Assignment of Leases and Rents.................... 3- 92
        [j] Miscellaneous Covenants 3-100
    [5] Special Mortgagor's Rider for Shopping Center Loans.... 3-101

¶ 3.09 Closing the Permanent Loan 3-102
    [1] Parties at Closing..................................... 3-102
    [2] Documentation at Closing 3-104
    [3] Checklist for Closing Permanent Loan 3-105

Chapter 3

PERMANENT FINANCING

		Page
¶ 3.01	Pre-financing Considerations	3- 3
	[1] Pre-financing Checklist	3- 3
	[2] Review of the Commercial Lending Cycle	3- 4
¶ 3.02	Selecting the Permanent Lender	3- 6
¶ 3.03	Function of Mortgage Loan Application-Commitment	3- 7
	[1] A Written Offer	3- 7
	[2] Identity of Borrower and Other Backup Data	3- 9
¶ 3.04	Terms and Conditions of Permanent Financing	3- 10
	[1] Loan Amount Based on Appraised Value	3- 11
	[2] Gap Financing Problem Caused by Construction Cost Overruns or by Platform Loan	3- 12
	[3] Rate of Interest	3- 15
	[a] "Equity Kickers"	3- 15
	[b] Low-Interest Financing With Tax-Exempt Mortgages	3- 17
	[c] Variable-Rate Mortgages, Joint Venturing, and Other Inflation-Related Financing Devices	3- 18
	[4] Amortization Period	3- 20
	[5] Prepayment Privilege	3- 21
	[6] Required Tax and Insurance Escrows	3- 25
	[7] Lien Priority and Prohibition of Junior Financing	3- 27
	[8] Right to Sell Mortgaged Property	3- 30
	[9] Compliance With Local Law	3- 35
	[a] Issuance of Building Permit and Certificate of Occupancy	3- 35
	[b] Rezoning and Variances	3- 37
	[c] Environmental Restrictions	3- 38
	[d] Developer's Reliance on Lender's Knowledge of Local Law	3- 41
	[10] Assignment of Commitment	3- 41
	[11] Timely Completion of Improvements in Accordance With Approved Plans and Specifications	3- 42
	[12] Satisfactory Hazard Insurance	3- 44
	[a] Co-insurance Clause	3- 44
	[b] Loss Payable Clauses	3- 45
	[13] Approval of Security Documents	3- 46
	[14] Buy-Sell Agreement	3- 47

Because approval of a loan by a permanent lender usually takes the form of a commitment to make the loan at a future date, subject to compliance with specified conditions in the commitment letter, the process of originating the loan may encompass the negotiation of the contractual terms and subsequently the preparation of documents attesting full compliance, prior to disbursement of funds. In the interim, the mortgage banker may be called on to arrange financing during the construction phase of the project, on terms that will facilitate or at least not impede the changeover to the permanent financing. The mortgage banker may receive a portion of the permanent lender's commitment fee for his work leading up to formal commitment. A more substantial source of income for the mortgage banker is the fee he will receive for servicing the loan, after the funds are disbursed. In consideration of an annual fee of perhaps one and one-quarter percent of the face amount of the loan, the mortgage banker will collect the mortgage payments and remit them to the lender, insure that taxes and insurance premiums are paid and that sufficient funds are placed in escrow to cover future payments, and take further action that may be required to protect the lender's interest. The mortgage banker, in carrying out his servicing tasks, is in the best position to watch over the security of the investment; he has immediate notice of defaults in loan payments and expenses, and by virtue of his local position can best monitor local market conditions, inspect the property, review the records of the project, counsel the developer, and thus give the lender timely notice of potential or actual problems that may make the investment less sound.

Many mortgage bankers maintain a close professional relationship with the permanent lenders, with the result that their opinions are sought after and highly respected. In the case of a marginal loan and when funds for permanent loans are tight, a strong endorsement from a respected mortgage banker can make a difference as to whether the loan application is accepted or rejected. The developer must understand, however, that the mortgage banker represents the interests of the permanent lender. However, the relationship between developer and mortgage banker, whether continuing or for a single project, is intended to yield mutual benefits by fostering the success of the enterprise.

D.C. mortgage banker, represents as a correspondent Union Dime Savings Bank, Aetna Life Insurance Company, John Hancock Mutual Life Insurance Company, Nationwide Life Insurance Company, and Life of Virginia. Similarly, Kesslering-Netherton, a Louisville-based mortgage banking firm, represents Aetna and New York Life.

¶ 2.03 THE ROLE OF MORTGAGE BROKERS AND MORTGAGE BANKERS

[1] The Mortgage Broker

The mortgage broker, either a corporation or an individual, is a specialist in compiling the financial details of a real estate project into a loan summary package that is suitable for review and evaluation by prospective lenders. As an agent of the developer, the mortgage broker will present the loan summary package to mortgage bankers and lenders throughout the country, whom he expects on the basis of his knowledge and experience to be interested in making a loan of the indicated type, rate of return, and level of risk. In his role as intermediary between borrower and lender, the mortgage broker is part of the dynamic system by which available funds become distributed to areas of demand. The mortgage broker, however, remains responsible to the developer throughout negotiations and loan origination, and accordingly looks to the developer for his fee. Mortgage brokers do not usually involve their own funds or credit in originating loans, nor do they generally assume continuing responsibilities to either party in the transaction.

[2] The Mortgage Banker

The mortgage banker plays one of the most important roles in commercial real estate financing—that of local correspondent for institutional lenders.[100] The mortgage banking function, in broad terms, includes the preparation of a descriptive and comprehensive loan package for submission to the permanent lender, the origination of the loan, and, if approved, the subsequent servicing of the mortgage throughout its term of amortization. Although this function may be carried out by a field office of the permanent lender or by a commercial bank correspondent, it is more commonly delegated to mortgage bankers, also known as mortgage companies, with whom the lender has established a continuing correspondent relation.[101]

---

[100] However, in the case of insurance companies, the mortgage banking industry at present is facing a loss of business. Some insurance companies have terminated their correspondent relationships with commercial banks and other mortgage bankers. Moreover, while insurance companies have increased their joint venture activities, the correspondent is not entitled to a fee under most correspondent agreements with respect to real property acquisitions. It remains to be seen whether mortgage bankers will be able to effectuate similar arrangements with pension funds and other lending groups that have recently become more active in their mortgage lending activities.

[101] Most mortgage bankers represent several lenders, such as a savings bank and insurance companies. For example, B.F. Saul Company, a Washington,

and the obligation of Freddie Mac to redeem at par after fifteen years. Unlike Fannie Mae, Freddie Mac does not conduct an auction; it quotes the price it will pay on an "over-the-counter" basis in response to offers from sellers telephoned or mailed to its regional offices.[98]

[c] Government National Mortgage Association

Ginnie Mae, before it was rechartered in 1969, was Fannie Mae's special assistance program through which the government financed moderate-income housing, housing for the elderly, and housing rehabilitation. This was accomplished by buying, at par and with funds supplied by the Treasury, mortgages originated by private lenders who made the loans with a view to selling them to Fannie Mae. Since 1969, when Ginnie Mae was constituted as a separate corporation in HUD, it has been conducting two multibillion dollar secondary financing programs: (1) Under the so-called Tandem program, Ginnie Mae buys mortgages at par from originating sellers and resells them at a discount to Fannie Mae. The difference is funded by a federal government subsidy which reduces borrowing costs when interest rates soar and thereby assures home loans for moderate-income families. For example, a lender who originates a mortgage loan at the FHA 75 percent rate might sell the mortgage at par to Ginnie Mae; the latter would then resell the mortgage to Fannie Mae at a discount, which would raise the effective interest to its then-market rate at the expense of the U.S. Treasury. (2) Ginnie Mae's other secondary financing program is a guaranteed mortgage-backed securities program, whereby mortgage bankers originate HUD and VA mortgages, put them together in a package, and issue debentures against the package (with a debt service corresponding to the debt service on the underlying pooled mortgages). Ginnie Mae guarantees the debt service on the debentures and markets the debentures that are purchased on the basis of competitive bidding by investment house syndicates, often at premium prices.

The success of these secondary financing programs has generated interest in similar programs by commercial banks, notably Bank of America, which has successfully marketed (without government backing) packages of mortgage-backed securities taken out of the bank's own portfolio. However, the steep rise in interest rates would militate strongly against such a program at this time.[99]

---

[98] See Strine, note 14 *supra,* at 1023-1031. Also see Brinkerhoff, "Urban Lending Initiatives and the Secondary Mortgage Market: FHLMC," in *1978 FNMA General Counsel's Conference* 27-34.

[99] See Strine, note 14 *supra,* at 1013-1023.

Home Loan Mortgage Corporation (Freddie Mac), and the Government National Mortgage Association (Ginnie Mae).

[a] Federal National Mortgage Association

Fannie Mae was created in the Great Depression and was designed to give liquidity to FHA-insured mortgages, which were then regarded with some suspicion. In its latest incarnation, Fannie Mae, as a consequence of the enactment of Title VIII of the Housing and Redevelopment Act of 1968, has become a private corporation, but five of its fifteen board members are appointed by the President of the United States, and HUD retains general regulatory power over Fannie Mae. It is funded by sale of common stock (purchase of which is required of mortgagees using FNMA services), retained earnings on its mortgage portfolio, and borrowing. It borrows by issuing debentures, short-term discount notes, and mortgage-backed bonds; its debentures and short-term discount notes have "federal agency" status, which makes them relatively riskless and eligible as investments for trusts, as collateral for Treasury tax and loan accounts, as purchases by the Open Market Committee of the Federal Reserve banks, etc. Its mortgage commitment system is conducted on an "auction" basis by periodic announcements of the total volume of forward commitments to purchase mortgages, for delivery at the seller's option, within four months and within twelve months. In each auction the prices of the mortgages it buys are based on the lowest bid. Fannie Mae deals primarily in government-insured mortgages, but it also buys conventional mortgages. Its purchases and sales run into billions of dollars.[97]

[b] Federal Home Loan Mortgage Corporation

Freddie Mac was created by Congress in 1970 to broaden the secondary market, primarily in the area of conventional residential mortgages for financial institutions having federally insured deposits. Originally funded by a $100 million stock purchase by the Federal Home Loan banks, it secures its funds for the purchase of mortgages by reselling mortgages and by issuing its own debt in various forms. For example, it offers participating interests in specific mortgages acquired by it and similar interests in a pool of mortgages as bonds that provide payments of semiannual interest, periodic amortization of principal,

---

[97] See generally Murray, "FNMA: Perspectives on a Unique Institution," in *1978 FNMA General Counsel's Conference* 3-17.

[6] Pension Funds and Other Lenders

Among the secondary sources of funds for real estate financing are the private noninsured pension funds, state and local government credit agencies and retirement funds, large industrial corporations, syndicates, and individuals. In recent years, the pension funds have experienced a tremendous increase in their asset size commensurate to their growth in numbers and contribution receipts from employers, unions, and employees. Pension funds do not have the cash flow problems of the depository-type lenders and, in contrast to life insurance companies, pay benefits to all members on a piecemeal basis. Therefore, in cases where the funds are not administered and invested by an insurance company (under annuity contracts) or some other intermediary, their liability structure is ideally suited to long-term mortgage lending. In the past, these funds have invested primarily in government securities and corporate bonds, but recently have entered the mortgage market by purchasing VA- and FHA-guaranteed loans.

While some pension funds directly acquire real estate investments, the majority purchase real estate by means of "commingled funds" sponsored by commercial banks, insurance companies and investment advisers. In 1980, pension funds held only about 1.25 percent of their approximately $600 billion worth of assets in real estate. However, in December of 1980 tax legislation was enacted that permits qualified pension trusts to acquire mortgaged real estate without subjecting the rental income to taxation as unrelated business income.[94] As a result, some experts are now predicting that investments in real estate by pension funds could more than double in the next few years.[95] The Employee Retirement Income Security Act of 1974 (ERISA) and its regulations also govern, among other matters, the types of investments that may be made by pension funds.[96]

[7] The Secondary Mortgage Market

In addition to the conventional (primary) sources of mortgage credit described in this chapter, the federal government created a so-called secondary mortgage market to keep the housing market alive when private-conventional mortgage credit dries up, by chartering the Federal National Mortgage Association (Fannie Mae), the Federal

---

[94] See I.R.C. § 512(b)(4); I.R.C. § 514(c) as amended by the Miscellaneous Revenue Act of 1980, Pub. L. 96-605, § 110(a), 94 Stat. 3525 (Dec. 28, 1980).

[95] See Sloane, "A Flow of Pension Funds Into Properties Is Foreseen," N.Y. Times, Feb. 1, 1981, Sec. 8, at 1, col. 3.

[96] 29 U.S.C.A. §§ 1001 *et seq.*

involving a project in respect to which it supplied the construction financing and frequently involving single-family home tracts that required extensive development prior to construction of houses.

Probably the chief advantage in borrowing from REITs is that their portfolios, unlike those held by the more traditional lenders, are relatively free of external regulation (except for the tepid diversity requirements of I.R.C. § 856), and REITs have become perhaps the most flexible, diversified, and innovative of all the major lending groups. For example, about 10 percent of their loan portfolio is represented by short- and intermediate-term first mortgages on completed properties. These mortgages have maturities of less than ten years and typically require little or no amortization. Developers generally use this type of financing for the following reasons: (1) to provide the time required to build up a successful operating history, which will enable it to procure better long-term financing than was initially available; (2) in the hope of obtaining less expensive permanent financing in the future when present long-term rates are historically high; or (3) as gap financing in the event the developer is unable to procure a takeout commitment for its REIT-financed construction loan. Furthermore, a few REITs specialize in junior mortgages, including wraparound mortgages.[92] Moreover, some also act as joint venturers with developers who are hard-pressed for capital and unable to obtain the requisite amount of construction financing. Finally, along with life insurance companies, REITs participate as purchaser-lessors in sale-and-leaseback arrangements. Often, the REIT will subordinate its fee interest to that of a leasehold mortgagee in exchange for receiving from the owner of the leasehold improvements (frequently an apartment building or shopping center) a share of the gross rental receipts and perhaps a share in any subsequent refinancing proceeds.

Except for local usury restrictions and securities laws, REIT lending is virtually free of state regulation. The Internal Revenue Code does impose certain minimal diversity requirements on their portfolios, as provided in I.R.C. § 856; however, the only requirement of real significance in regard to portfolio composition is that at the end of each quarter, 75 percent of the REIT's total assets must consist of real estate (including mortgages), cash, cash items, and government securities.[93]

---

[92] For discussion of wraparound mortgages, see ¶ 7.04[3].

[93] I.R.C. § 856(c)(5). Certain income source limitations are also imposed by I.R.C. § 856(c), which are designed, inter alia, to prevent the REIT from dealing or trading in properties.

with federal insurance. However, the loan portfolios of these federally insured mutuals are still regulated by state and not federal law. Yet, indirectly, the federal government has affected the investment flows of these lenders by imposing ceilings on the deposit interest rates payable by thrift institutions. This was first done in 1966, and since then the differential between rates payable by thrift lenders as compared to commercial banks on time-savings deposits has narrowed significantly, reducing their competitive edge in attracting deposit inflows.[90]

State statutes permit maximum loan-to-value ratios ranging between 60 and 90 percent of appraised value, with the higher ratios allowable for self-amortizing and single-family residential loans. Like S&Ls and insurance companies, the mutuals are generally confined to first mortgage loans. However, their amortization requirements are usually less rigid, and in contrast to insurance companies, they may invest in unimproved property. A very general synopsis of these constraints and the main features of a representative statute, that of New York, are summarized in Exhibit 2.5.

[5] Real Estate Investment Trusts

As previously noted, long-term mortgage and equity REITs have fared reasonably well since 1971. However, failure of builders to pay off construction loans and pressures from bank creditors has resulted since 1974 in disastrous times for the large part of the REIT industry active in short-term construction and development (C&D) mortgage lending. Accordingly, the C&D trusts have, for the most part, ceased making new loan commitments; even the long-term mortgage trusts have curtailed their lending because the rates on long-term mortgages have been low relative to the cost of their long-term bank borrowings. The impact of recent developments has also seriously eroded the ability of REITs to raise equity capital, as reflected by a 72.5 percent drop (from 62.35 to 16.87) in the National Association of Real Estate Investment Trusts (NAREIT) share price index in one year alone—namely, 1974.[91]

First mortgage construction loans are the most prevalent type of REIT loan acquisition. In contrast to life insurance companies, these lenders will sometimes provide both the permanent and construction financing, or act as interim lender even without a standby or takeout commitment for the long-term financing. In their heyday, REITs were also active in making first mortgage development or land loans, usually

---

[90] *Id.* at 36.
[91] By July 1979, the index had rebounded to 35.26. National Ass'n of Real Estate Investment Trusts, *REIT Fact Book,* 19 (1979).

of mortgage funds at mutuals increased from $1.8 billion in 1970 to $5.5 billion by the end of 1972. Conversely, during April to October 1974, as short-term interest rates peaked, the industry experienced an unprecedented $3.7 billion outflow (exclusive of interest) in deposits, and reduced its mortgage acquisitions by over $4 billion. By year-end 1978, the net inflow of mortgage funds had increased to a near record $6.3 billion.[85]

As regards to loan terms, mutual savings banks have in recent years charged less interest on conventional home mortgages than both S&Ls and commercial banks, but have been less competitive than S&Ls with respect to loan maturity dates and loan-to-value ratios.[86]

[b] Loan Allocation by Function and Property Type

Mutual savings banks are not only a major source of home mortgage lending, but also constitute a significant source of long-term apartment loan financing. Furthermore, some of the larger mutuals in New York City and other urban centers concentrate on both nonresidential and multi-family mortgage acquisitions. Their multi-family loan holdings totaled $16.5 billion at year-end 1978, which represented about a one-fifth market share. Their market share of net acquisitions of multi-family loans has been about 15 percent when funds were plentiful, but slipped to about 11-13 percent when mortgage credit was tight.[87] In addition, mutuals have furnished about 9-10 percent of new loan funds for nonresidential properties, and within recent years have been allocating equal shares of their portfolios to both multi-family and commercial loans.[88] As indicated earlier, they make few construction loans; during 1978, 77.5 percent of their gross mortgage acquisitions were long-term residential loans, 10.8 percent were long-term commercial real estate loans, and only 11.7 percent were construction loans.[89]

[c] Regulation of Mortgage Loan Portfolio

The confinement of savings banks to the Northeastern section of the nation is mainly attributable to state restrictions, which have prevented geographical extension of the industry. Alone among the nation's depository institutions, mutual savings banks are exclusively state-chartered and regulated, with the exception of those operating

---

[85] *Id.* at 8.
[86] *Id.* at 50.
[87] *Id.* at 49.
[88] See 66 F.R.B., note 40 *supra,* at A41.
[89] *Mutual Savings Fact Book,* note 4 *supra,* at 48.

most funds. In contrast to their in-state holdings, most of their outside holdings are in VA and FHA loans.[81]

[a] Source of Funds

The composition of the mutual savings banks' liability structure has remained the same and consists chiefly of ordinary demand deposits, special high-yield time or term accounts, and, recently, "NOW" accounts (interest-bearing savings accounts with negotiable order of withdrawal provisions). These liabilities—like savings shares at S&Ls—are held mainly by individuals and have a low rate of withdrawal. Consequently, savings banks are more capable of holding long-term assets than are commercial banks and have channeled their loanable funds almost exclusively into long-term mortgage loans, which at year-end 1978 represented about 60 percent of their total assets.[82] However, as previously noted, within recent years these institutions have done a considerable amount of portfolio-switching between mortgages and corporate bonds depending on capital market conditions. The latter type investment represented about 14 percent of their total assets at year-end 1976.[83] In overall diversity, their portfolios lie somewhere between those of commercial banks and those of the relatively specialized S&Ls.

Unlike other intermediaries, mutual savings banks have no capital stock and have not made extensive use of borrowings for liquidity or asset-expansion purposes.[84] However, these banks have provided protection for depositors by maintaining strong reserve positions and virtually all bank deposits are insured mainly by the FDIC and in Massachusetts by Mutual Savings Central Fund, Inc. Accordingly, these lenders sharply curtail their mortgage acquisitions when net deposit inflows and/or mortgage repayments slacken during periods of reduced household saving and severe disintermediation. For example, deposit gains reached unprecedented levels in 1971 and 1972, reflecting the favorable competitive yield position of savings accounts and the high marginal propensity to save among households. As a result, the annual net flow

---

[81] *Mutual Savings Fact Book,* note 4 *supra,* at 49-50.

[82] *Id.* at 12.

[83] *Id.*

[84] During the 1974 period of massive disintermediation, for instance, borrowings and mortgage warehousing averaged only 0.7 percent of total savings bank deposits. Nevertheless, external liquidity facilities are available to savings banks in New York at the Savings Banks Trust Company and in Massachusetts at the Mutual Savings Central Fund, Inc. Moreover, 85 savings banks were members of the FHLBB system at year-end 1978 and had access to the credit facilities of the system. *Id.* at 9.

In general, state-chartered S&Ls are fettered with the same kind of regulatory constraints as are the federals and for the most part make the same kinds of loans; however, there is usually a greater emphasis on single-family home mortgages with state associations. The New York statute is fairly representative of those imposed by the other states, and the salient provisions are also summarized in Exhibit 2.5.

[4] Mutual Savings Banks

A mutual savings bank is owned and operated for the benefit of its depositors, and all earnings after taxes and operating expenses (except for additions to protective reserves) are returned to them as savings account interest or dividends. Depositors, however, usually have no voting rights and are technically regarded as creditors of these institutions. Management often is vested in a self-perpetuating board of trustees. As their name implies, these banks are mutual organizations founded originally with a community-minded purpose, and accordingly are more sensitive to local financing needs than most other lender groups. Most such banks are geographically concentrated in the capital surplus areas of the Middle Atlantic and New England: Massachusetts has the greatest number followed by New York, Connecticut, Maine, and New Hampshire. However, as of 1978, 53.9 percent of total mutual savings bank deposits were concentrated in New York State, and the banks in the New York City metropolitan area held 44.8 percent of all savings in the state.[78] Their limited numbers and geographical presence belies their influence in the mortgage market for various reasons. First, their average asset size is about three times greater than that of S&Ls[79] (their closest counterpart in the mortgage market); they hold a much larger percentage of assets in mortgage loans than do commercial banks and insurance companies;[80] and they constitute the largest nationwide source of federally underwritten mortgage funds. Most banks confine their lending periphery to within a few miles of their home office, and venture elsewhere after local needs have been met and if market conditions so warrant. However, out-of-state lending programs have expanded recently as a result of legislative changes in some states. As of year-end 1978, about one-third of total bank mortgage holdings were in outside properties, with California, Texas, and Florida securing the

---

[78] *Mutual Savings Fact Book,* note 4 *supra,* at 45.

[79] *Id.* at 13.

[80] The mortgage loan-to-total-assets ratio for mutuals, insurance companies, and commercial banks were 60 percent, 28.4 percent, and 15 percent, respectively, at year-end 1978. 66 F.R.B., note 40 *supra,* at A18, A29.

EXHIBIT 2.5. Regulation of New York Savings and Loan Associations and Mutual Savings Banks

(continued)

N.Y. Savings & Loans	N.Y. Savings Banks
• **Improved:** 80% of appraised value; 75% of appraised value if value of improvements does not equal value of land alone but improvements are capable of producing sufficient income to cover debt service and operating expenses. N.Y. Bank. Law § 380-1(b)(1) (McKinney 1971). Full repayment required in forty years if installment payments are monthly and constant in amount (N.Y. Bank. Law § 380-1(a)(2) (McKinney Supp. 1979).	• **Improved:** 75% of appraised value. No amortization requirements. N.Y. Bank. Law § 235-6(a) (McKinney Supp. 1979).
• **Unimproved:** 60% of appraised value; 70% of appraised value if improved with streets, sewers, etc., preliminary to construction of permanent structures. Full repayment generally required in five years; plat must be filed. Amortization requirements for 60% loan same as for improved property. N.Y. Bank. Law § 380-1(b)(1) (McKinney 1971).	• **Unimproved:** "Unimproved property" is real property the value of which has not been enhanced by a permanent structure or other facilities capable of producing income and that has an appraised value of not less than 20% of the property to be mortgaged. N.Y. Bank. Law § 235-5-a(b) (McKinney 1971). 60% of appraised value; 70% of appraised value if improved with streets, sewers, etc. Full repayment required in five years. Property must be in state; plat must be filed. N.Y. Bank. Law § 235-5-a(a) (McKinney 1971).
• **Residential:** 95% of appraised value with term equal to 75% of remaining useful life of dwelling or forty years, whatever is less, if owner-occupied and situated in state or in adjoining state and within 50 miles from principal office of association. N.Y. Bank. Law § 380.1-a (McKinney Supp. 1979).	• **Residential:** 95% of appraised value with term equal to 75% of remaining useful life of dwelling or forty years, whichever is less. N.Y. Bank. Law § 235-6(b) (McKinney Supp. 1979).

* Requirements apply only to loans made to nonmember borrowers.

SOURCE: Savings and loan associations' investment portfolios are regulated by N.Y. Banking Law § 380 (McKinney 1971); savings banks' portfolios are regulated by N.Y. Banking Law § 235 (McKinney 1971 & Supp. 1979).

EXHIBIT 2.5. Regulation of New York Savings and Loan Associations and Mutual Savings Banks

N.Y. Savings & Loans	*N.Y. Savings Banks*
• **Leaseholds:** Same as Improved (see below), except that unexpired term shall not be less than fifteen years, including approved option to renew. Full repayment within period not exceeding four-fifths of unexpired lease term. N.Y. Bank. Law § 380-1(d) (McKinney Supp. 1979).	• **Leaseholds:** Same as Improved (see below). (1) Leasehold must have unexpired term of twenty-one years including renewal options. (2) Loan must be completely amortized within four-fifths of term of lease, including renewal options. (3) If under construction, no principal payments required for shorter of three years or construction period. N.Y. Bank. Law § 235-6(i) (McKinney 1971).
• **Construction:** Same as Improved (see below), except that first periodic payment may be deferred to maximum of three years after first construction advance. In such event, the repayment period is measured from time amortization commences. N.Y. Bank. Law § 380-1(a)(5) (McKinney Supp. 1979).	• **Construction:** May invest in construction loans when the building under construction will constitute a permanent improvement with a value of more than 25% total value of property as improved. Improvements must be capable of producing income sufficient to pay all costs of operation and maintenance, taxes, and the permanent loan. N.Y. Bank. Law § 235-6(c) (McKinney 1971).
• **Participations:** May participate in making authorized loan, but participation must not be subordinate to other interests. N.Y. Bank. Law § 380-c (McKinney Supp. 1979).	• **Participations:** May participate in loans per N.Y. Banking Law § 235-8 (4)(a), and in loans for improved realty in which it is individually authorized to invest. Participations cannot exceed 10% of assets or surplus of the bank. N.Y. Bank. Law § 235-6(h) (McKinney Supp. 1979).
• **Leeway clause:** None.	• **Exceptions:** Nonconforming investments. May invest up to 2% of its assets or 20% of its net worth in nonconforming investments, including real estate loans. Limited to one percent of its assets or 10% of its net worth to any investment or issuer. N.Y. Bank. Law § 235-29(a) (McKinney 1971).
• **Lien requirements:** First lien required unless prior mortgages held by same association. N.Y. Bank. Law § 380-4(a) (McKinney 1971).	• **Lien requirements:** First lien, except that a percentage of assets may be placed in nonconforming investments (see Exceptions, above). N.Y. Bank. Law § 235-5(a) and § 235-6 (McKinney 1971).

[vii] Leeway Authority for Residential Loans. A federal association may invest an amount not exceeding 5 percent of its assets in loans secured by residential real estate that otherwise do not comply with the regulations discussed above. In addition, an association may invest an amount not exceeding the greater of its surplus, undivided profits and reserves, or 5 percent of its assets in unsecured residential real estate loans where the lender relies substantially for repayment on either the borrower-developer's general credit standing or other assurance of repayment on either the borrower-developer's general credit standing or other assurance of repayment such as a third-party guaranty.[77b]

[viii] Mobile Home Financing. Federal associations may invest up to 20 percent of assets in mobile home chattel paper which either (1) finances the acquisition of inventory by a mobile home dealer, or (2) finances the retail purchase of a mobile home for the borrower or his relative. Investment in retail purchase mobile home chattel paper is limited to a twenty-year or less loan repayment period.[77c]

[ix] Urban Renewal Loans and Investments. Federal associations may invest in real property or interests in real property located within any urban renewal area as defined in Section 110(a) of the Housing Act of 1949, as amended, and in loans secured by liens on such properties. Investments in real property may not exceed the amount of qualified appraisal plus settlement costs. Loans must be in accord with requirements applicable to types of loan by virtue of other applicable provisions except certain specified exceptions.[77d]

[x] Participation Loans. Subject to certain restrictions, federal associations may participate with or purchase and sell participations in real estate loans of a type the association otherwise may make.[77e]

[77b] 12 C.F.R. § 545.6-5.
[77c] 12 C.F.R. § 545.7-6.
[77d] 12 C.F.R. § 545.6-10.
[77e] 12 C.F.R. § 545.6(a); 545.6(c).

To Individuals. Single-family owner-occupied home loans must not exceed 75 percent of value and must be repayable within fifteen years, with interest payable at least semiannually. In addition the loan contract must provide for monthly debt service payments that are sufficient to amortize at least 30 percent of the original principal amount before the end of the loan term.

With respect to loans both to builders and individuals if the lien of any portion of the secured property is released the loan balance must be reduced by the amount attributable to the released portion. Also, the time for payment may be extended for up to three years with respect to currently appraised property if the interest on the loan is current and the outstanding loan balance has been reduced to an amount not in excess of 75 percent of the current value of the secured property.[75]

[v] Land Acquisition and Development Loans

Land Only. Federal associations may lend up to 66⅔ percent of the value (as a completed project) of unimproved land intended primarily for residential usage. Such loans may be made for terms up to three years and interest must be payable at least semiannually.[76]

Development Loans. Loans to finance development of land for residential usage (including recreational or other facilities in an integrated development plan) shall not exceed 75 percent of the value of secured property (as a completed project) and must be repayable within five years, with interest payable at least semiannually.[77]

The release-of-lien and loan-extension rules that apply to loans on improved building lots and sites also apply to both land acquisition and development loans.

[vi] Loans on Cooperatives.

Subject to the restrictions discussed above relating to home loans federal associations may make permanent loans on individual cooperative housing units secured by the borrower's stock interest in the cooperative housing corporation and by an assignment to the association of the borrower's interest in the proprietary lease issued by the corporation.[77a]

---

[75] 12 C.F.R. §§ 545.6-2(e)(1), 545.6-2(e)(3).
[76] 12 C.F.R. § 545.6-2(c).
[77] 12 C.F.R. § 545.6-2(d).
[77a] 12 C.F.R. § 545.6-2(a)(6).

buildings. Such loans may be made with terms up to thirty years with interest payable at least semiannually. Similarly secured loans that are not fully amortized are subject to a maximum loan-to-value ratio of 75 percent. Nonamortized loans (no principal payments are made until the end of the loan period) may be made with terms up to five years and partially-amortized loans require debt service payments sufficient to satisfy a thirty-year amortization schedule. In the case of HUD-approved loans to construct or renovate low-rent housing the maximum loan terms and loan-to-value ratios are less rigorous.[70]

[iii] Commercial Real Estate Loans. Federal associations may make first mortgage loans up to 90 percent of value on improved commercial or industrial-type realty for terms up to thirty years with interest payable at least semiannually. However, construction loans and nonamortized loans must not exceed 75 percent of value and must be repayable within five years. Partially-amortized loans require debt service payments sufficient to satisfy a thirty-year amortization schedule.[71]

In the case of leasehold mortgage loans a commercial real estate loan is considered to be secured by a first lien if: (1) the leasehold estate is automatically renewable for five years after maturity of the loan, or renewable at the option of either the borrower or the lender, and (ii) in the *event of default the real estate* could be used to satisfy the loan obligation with the same priority as a first mortgage or first deed of trust in the jurisdiction where the real estate is located.[72]

Such commercial loans may not exceed in the aggregate 20 percent of an association's assets.[73]

[iv] Loans on Improved Building Lots and Sites

To Builders. Federal associations may make loans to builders up to 75 percent of value on residential real estate containing offsite or other improvements, or on residential real estate in the process of being improved by buildings for terms up to three years, with semiannual interest payments beginning not more than one year after the initial disbursement. Construction loans shall not exceed 75 percent of the value of the property and must be repaid in three years, with interest payable at least semiannually.[74]

---

[70] 12 CFR. §§ 545.6-2(b), 545.6-9.
[71] 12 C.F.R. § 545.6-6(a).
[72] 12 C.F.R. § 545.6-6(c). See ¶¶ 6.02 and 6.03 for discussion of leasehold mortgage loans.
[73] 12 C.F.R. § 545.6-6(b).
[74] 12 C.F.R. §§ 545.6-2(e)(2), 545.6-2(f)(1).

Federal S&Ls may make loans secured by savings accounts up to 100 percent of the withdrawal value thereof. These may be used to purchase real estate or for any other purpose. In addition, they are authorized to make mortgage loans upon various terms depending upon the type of real estate collateral, function, and geographical situs of the secured property. The following is a summary of the regulatory provisions affecting federal S&Ls that are presently in force that reflect changes made by Title IV of the Depository Institutions Deregulation and Monetary Control Act of 1980. Adopted March 31, 1980, the statute amends 12 U.S.C. § 1464 by providing new investment authority to federally chartered S&Ls, which include the following: (1) authorization to make residential real estate loans to the same extent as national banks, (2) removal of first lien restrictions on residential real estate loans and authorization of second mortgage loans, and (3) substitution of a 90 percent loan-to-value requirement in place of the current $75,000 limit on residential real estate loans.

[i] Home Loans. Federal associations may make loans secured by mortgages on homes (one-to-four family) or combination of home and business property with fully amortized (all principal payments are made by the end of the loan term) loan periods of up to forty years and a maximum loan-to-value ratio of 90 percent. Loans up to 95 percent may be made under certain conditions and are generally limited to loans secured by owner-occupied residences where the loan contract requires monthly prepaid and prorated escrows for payment of the annual property taxes and assessments on the property and, where the loan balance exceeds 90 percent of value, such balance over 80 percent is insured or guaranteed by a qualified private mortgage insurance company or secured by a pledged savings account.[67] Home loans that are not fully amortized (some principal payments are not made until the end of the term) are subject to a maximum loan-to-value ratio of 60 percent and, along with non-monthly-installment loans, are subject to stricter term-of-years limitations.[68] Also, the new FHLBB regulations authorize and regulate the use by federal associations of variable-rate mortgages and other inflation-related mortgage devices.[69]

[ii] Apartment-Type Loans. Federal associations may lend up to 90 percent of value on loans secured by mortgages on apartment-type

---

[67] 12 C.F.R. §§ 545.6-2(a)(1), 545.6-2(a)(2).
[68] 12 C.F.R. §§ 545.6-2(a)(3), 545.6-2(a)(4).
[69] 12 C.F.R. § 545.6-4. See discussion at ¶ 3.04[3][c].

acquisitions by S&Ls is so large, they have been the principal supplier of long-term apartment loans, with their market share usually ranging between 30 and 40 percent when credit is plentiful.[61] But when the S&Ls have been pinched for funds because of reduced savings inflows and disintermediation, their market share has fallen below 25 percent, including a low of 18.1 percent in the fourth quarter of 1974.[62] In addition, S&Ls accounted for about 20 percent of net acquisitions of commercial property loans during 1977-1979. As was the case for multi-family loans, the market shares of nonresidential loan acquisitions by the thrifts and commercial banks dwindled during periods of credit stringency (e.g., years 1970 and 1974) while the proportion held by life insurance companies expanded to above 30 percent.[63]

In the case of S&Ls, the rates of withdrawal from savings accounts are much lower than those from checking and time-savings accounts of commercial banks but higher than withdrawal rates at life insurance companies and REITs. Consequently, the portfolios of S&Ls contain a larger percentage of long-term mortgages than those of commercial banks but a smaller percentage as compared to life insurance companies. As of the first quarter of 1978, their long-term mortgage holdings represented 90 percent of their total mortgage portfolios.[64]

[d] Regulation of Mortgage Loan Portfolio

Like the commercial banking system, the S&L industry has a dual system of chartering and regulation. State associations are chartered under state statutes and are supervised and examined by state S&L departments. Federal associations are chartered under the provisions of the Home Owners' Loan Act of 1933,[65] as amended, and are subject to supervision and regulation by the FHLBB. As of year-end 1978, there were 2,723 state-chartered and 2,000 federally chartered S&Ls. Nevertheless, the assets of the federals amounted to $298.2 billion at year-end 1978, or 56.9 percent of the total assets figure.[66] Some state associations have joined the federal system for the privilege of borrowing from the FHLBB, but for these hybrid associations, the major regulatory reins are held by their state supervisors.

---

[61] HUD Study, note 49 *supra,* at 85.
[62] Based on data appearing in 66 F.R.B., note 40 *supra,* at A41.
[63] HUD Study, note 49 *supra,* at 86.
[64] Based on data appearing in Exhibit 2.1.
[65] 12 U.S.C.A. §§ 461 et seq.; 18 U.S.C.A. §§ 433, 493, 657, 709, 1006, 1014 (1964).
[66] *Savings & Loan Fact Book,* note 6 *supra,* at 48-51.

term interest rates accelerated to record levels during mid-1973, new net savings showed a complete reversal flowing out of S&Ls at an annual rate of $7.3 billion during the third quarter.

Savings deposits rebounded with the economy from 1975 to 1977; however, new record levels in open market interest rates (especially for six-month Treasury bills and other short-term securities) over the past years have again caused a severe disintermediation problem for savings associations. This is reflected by the fact that savings gains through May of 1978 were only 59.1 percent of the level achieved during that period in the previous year. To raise additional funds, associations have recently increased their outside borrowings (FHLBB advances increased from $19.9 billion in 1977 to $32 billion at year-end 1978) and introduced high-cost money market certificates to compete with open market interest rates. Although both mortgage rates and savings rates have risen during the current period of high inflation, savings rates have risen for the entire stock of savings, while mortgage rates have increased only for new loans. Notwithstanding present efforts to ameliorate this problem by increasing their secondary mortgage market operations and by developing new variable-rate mortgage instruments, S&Ls have been experiencing serious problems in both asset and liability management, and their income statements have started to reflect the inherent problem of a business that borrows short and lends long.[58]

[b] Loan Terms

Because of the higher interest rates paid to depositors, the S&Ls traditionally charge higher interest rates than commercial banks and other depository-type lenders for permanent financing. With respect to conventional single-family mortgages, the S&Ls charge higher interest rates but offer higher loan-to-value ratios and longer maturities than do the other major residential lenders.[59]

[c] Loan Allocation by Function and Property Type

In contrast to the so-called diversified lenders, the mortgage portfolios of S&Ls have for the most part been confined to residential loans, especially the higher-yielding conventional loans. As of the first quarter of 1980, 87 percent of net long-term mortgage loan acquisitions by S&Ls were secured by single-family dwellings with only 4 percent representing apartment house loans.[60] However, since the volume of

---

[58] *Savings & Loan Fact Book,* note 6 *supra,* at 58, 72, 84, 89.
[59] *Mutual Savings Fact Book,* note 4 *supra,* at 50.
[60] HUD News, note 48 *supra,* at Table 3.

property are accorded the same quasi-exempt status provided the bank has a firm takeout commitment from a responsible permanent lender.[54]

Any national bank may make nonconforming real estate loans if the total unpaid amounts do not exceed 10 percent of the amount that a national bank may invest in conforming real estate loans.[55] Such total amount of real estate loans permitted cannot exceed the amount of the bank's capital stock plus surplus, or the amount of its time and savings deposits, whichever is greater.[56]

[3] Savings and Loan Associations

[a] Source of Funds

As the largest supplier of long-term, single-family and apartment house loans in the country, the S&Ls occupy a pivotal position in the nation's residential mortgage structure. The funds that S&Ls place in new mortgage loans originate from three major sources (1) net new savings, which is simply gross savings minus withdrawals, held mainly by individuals in the form of savings deposits and certificates of deposit; (2) mortgage loan repayments and sales of mortgages in the secondary market; and (3) FHLBB advances and other borrowings. Since World War II, the mortgage repayment rate (as measured by inflows from mortgage loan portfolios in relation to total loans outstanding) has dropped, portending a potential long-term decline in lending capacity and earnings ability.[57] However, since 1960 the decline has stabilized and, as previously noted, has been somewhat countercyclical. Likewise, the variability in savings inflows has been extremely volatile and countercyclical within the past decade, in response to changes in net household saving and in instances where disintermediation has been severe. For example, net new savings at insured institutions during the first half of 1973 flowed in at the annual rate of $19.8 billion. As short-

---

[54] 12 U.S.C.A. § 371(c) (Supp. 1980).
[55] 12 U.S.C.A. § 371(f) (Supp. 1980).
[56] 12 U.S.C.A. § 371(a)(3) (Supp. 1980).
[57] Several factors have combined to force the ratio downward. The decline in the relative importance of construction lending has reduced the volume of builders' payoffs of short-term loans. Longer loan maturities and the accompanying slower repayment of principal also lower the repayment ratio. Reduced real estate activity can play a part too; when sales decline, so do loan payoffs. Periods of high mortgage interest rates also adversely affect repayments by causing home buyers to assume sellers' lower-rate existing loans (if the mortgage instrument does not prohibit such assumption) rather than to take out new loans. *Savings & Loan Fact Book,* note 6 *supra,* at 78.

provisions of the Federal Reserve Act, as amended. Some state banks have opted to become Federal Reserve member banks and/or operate with Federal Deposit Insurance. However, all state banks—regardless of what form of federal control they have accepted—are required to be chartered and regulated by their respective state authorities. Accordingly, there is a dual but separate regulation of real estate investments. National banks must comply with the Federal Reserve Act and interpretive regulations thereunder promulgated by the Comptroller (as summarized below), and state-chartered banks must adhere to the constraints imposed by their respective state laws as summarized in Appendix A, Table 2.

In 1974, the Federal Reserve Act was revised and made less restrictive. Previously, national banks could only make first mortgage loans on improved realty with loan-to-value ratios ranging from 50 to 80 percent depending on loan maturities and amortization requirements. The statute, as amended, now permits the following loans upon both unimproved and improved realty or upon a leasehold where the lease does not expire within ten years after the maturity date of the loan, without regard to lien priority:

(1) 66⅔ percent of appraised value if property is unimproved;
(2) 75 percent of appraised value if property is improved by off-site improvements (such as streets, water, sewers, etc.) or in process of being improved by building(s); and
(3) 90 percent of appraised value if such property is improved by a building or buildings.

However, if any such loan exceeds 75 percent or if the secured property is a one-to-four-family dwelling, the entire principal must be amortizable within a thirty-year period.[52] Moreover, the outstanding balance on loans secured by junior liens when added to the amount unpaid upon prior mortgages cannot exceed in the aggregate 20 percent of the bank's capital and surplus.[53]

Construction loans with maturities of not more than five years made by national banks to fund the construction of residential or farm buildings may at the option of the bank be treated as less regulated commercial loans rather than as real estate loans whether or not the loan is secured by a mortgage on the land site. Likewise, construction loans with maturities up to five years on industrial and commercial

---

[52] 12 U.S.C.A. § 371(a)(1) (Supp. 1980).
[53] 12 U.S.C.A. § 371(a)(3) (Supp. 1980).

Curiously, the proportion of total acquisitions allocable to construction loans was somewhat higher when credit was tight (in 1970 and 1974) than when credit was plentiful. This *cyclical pattern* suggests to market analysts that construction credit differs from long-term mortgage credit not only with respect to loan terms (higher interest rates, shorter repayment periods, and lower loan-to-value ratios) and sources of repayment (takeout long-term loan as opposed to income of borrower) but also with respect to availability. One obvious explanation is the time lag between the first stage in the commercial lending cycle (permanent commitment) and the second stage when construction financing is being sought. For example, the downtrend in construction financing for multi-family and nonresidential properties did not commence until the second and third quarters of 1974, respectively; whereas, the downturn for long-term net acquisition started in the second quarter of 1973.[49] A second factor may be that diversified construction lenders such as banks may prefer short-term over long-term commitments when short-term rates are rising faster than long-term rates in a tightening money market. Accordingly, in such a market they may be more willing to lend short notwithstanding the absence of a permanent takeout commitment.

Unlike long-term mortgage loans, which have been attractive to a wide array of lenders, many of whom regard mortgage loan acquisitions as an alternative to corporate bonds and other long-term security investments, construction loans are generally provided only by lenders that, apart from their other capabilities, have developed the requisite skill to handle the complex problems arising in this phase of real estate financing. As discussed in Chapter 4, these specialists are generally aware of, and hence attempt to make appropriate allowance for, such unique problems as cost overruns, mechanics' and materialmen's liens, construction delays from labor strikes or material shortages, delays in construction completion, availability of "takeout" permanent financing and compliance with the requirements of the permanent lender, and use of "gap financing"[50] during a development or "rent-up" period.

[d] Regulation of Mortgage Loan Portfolio

The commercial banking system in this country has two segments—national and state banking.[51] National banks are chartered, supervised, and regulated by the Comptroller of the Currency pursuant to the

---

[49] HUD Study at 81, 106.
[50] See discussion at ¶ 3.03[3][b].
[51] See generally Brown, *The Dual Banking System in the United States* (1968).

commercial banks charge an interest rate set over floating prime, and with the introduction of the computer in the banks' servicing departments, floating prime is adjusted daily with each change in the prime rate. With respect to large construction loans (loan amounts exceeding $500,000), the average term to maturity is less than two years.[44] Commercial banks are also a source of permanent financing for income properties. In connection with these long-term loans, commercial banks tend to charge more interest than insurance companies but less than S&Ls, which must pay more for their use of deposits. However, because of their short-term liability structure and fluctuations in their borrowing costs, most banks are reluctant to lend long unless they receive a floating interest rate. The commercial banks' other loan terms on income properties also tend to be more liberal than those offered by S&Ls. For example, national banks may now grant 90 percent thirty-year loans on improved realty,[45] whereas federal S&Ls are limited to 75 percent twenty-five-year loans.[46] On the state regulatory level, the modal maximum loan-to-value ratio for S&Ls and insurance companies is only about 75 percent, and their amortization requirements are more stringent. Finally, state-chartered banks are subject to less severe lien requirements than are S&Ls and constitute a larger source of secondary (junior mortgage) financing.[47]

[c] Loan Allocation by Function and Property Type

As indicated in Exhibit 2.1 at page 2-8, banks represent the second largest source of long-term mortgage financing, both residential and commercial, and by far the largest source of both land development financing and construction financing for commercial, multi-family, and industrial properties. Moreover, commercial banks have more diversified property-type portfolios than other lender groups. During the first quarter of 1980, 4 percent of net long-term mortgage acquisitions by banks were multi-family loans; 32 percent were commercial nonresidential loans; 58 percent were one-to-four-family home loans; and 6 percent were loans made to acquire farm properties.[48]

During 1970-1977, commercial banks' market share of construction loan holdings varied between 40 and 50 percent, and these loans accounted for about one third of their total new mortgage acquisitions.

---

[44] *Id.* at A26.

[45] 12 U.S.C.A. § 371(a)(1) (Supp. 1978).

[46] 12 C.F.R. §§ 545.6-1(c)(1), 545.6-1(c)(2).

[47] See summaries of state regulatory statutes, Table 1 in Appendix A.

[48] HUD, HUD News, Release No. 80-186, at Table 3 (June 12, 1980) (hereinafter cited as HUD News).

While real estate loans still occupy a modest percentage (16 percent) of their investment portfolio, the dollar volume of mortgage debt outstanding ($246 billion by year-end 1979) held by banks is second only to S&Ls.[41] Moreover, the impact of commercial banks on the mortgage market far surpasses their relative loan share because of their vital function as both loan intermediaries and servicing agents. Besides placing mortgages for their own account, they originate and act as servicing agents on loans later sold in the secondary market to life insurance companies and other lenders. They also supply interim credit and "warehouse" loans[42] for mortgage companies and REITs.

[a] Source of Funds

Both state and national banks obtain their loanable funds chiefly from (1) demand and time deposits, (2) advances from the Federal Reserve and other borrowings, (3) mortgage repayments, and (4) bank capital. As previously noted, the amount that commercial banks lend also depends in large measure on the credit and monetary policies of the Federal Reserve and tends to be countercyclical in relation to swings in the business cycle. When short-term interest rates are high, banks are also affected by disintermediation but less so than the thrift institutions. Commercial banks have the shortest term liability structure of all financial institutions. As of March 1980, demand deposits accounted for about 34 percent of their liabilities to depositors; the remainder was in time and savings deposits.[43] Bank capital (assets less liabilities) amounted to only about 7 percent of their total resources. Furthermore, because demand deposits experience wide cyclical and seasonal variations, banks must be prepared to meet large drains on their deposits and consequently on their reserves as well. For this reason, banks in general tend to lend mortgage money on a short- or intermediate-term basis.

[b] Loan Terms

Banks charge less for short-term construction financing than do REITs, which depend largely on bank borrowings for funding. Most

---

[41] *Id.* at A20, A41.

[42] A mortgage company procures a revolving line of credit from a bank, and as particular loans are closed and recorded, they are pledged as collateral by the mortgage company for its bank borrowings. The loans are held by the bank pending reassignment to a permanent lender; accordingly, the role of the bank in storing mortgages becomes that of a "warehouser."

[43] 66 F.R.B., note 40 *supra,* at A16.

presumably to achieve portfolio diversification. For example, under Section 81(6)(a) of the New York Insurance Law, conventional mortgage loans may not exceed 50 percent of the company's assets.

(2) *Individual loan limit.* Somewhat more common are provisions limiting the amount a life insurance company can invest on the security of a single parcel or property. Under Section 81(6)(a), loans upon any one property if in excess of $30,000 are limited to 2 percent of the company's assets.

(3) *Leeway or "basket" clause.* Most statutes permit a small percentage of the total assets of a life insurance company to be placed in nonconforming mortgage loans that would otherwise be ineligible under the statute. While these percentages may be small (e.g., 4 percent in New York) the asset size of insurance companies is so large that the actual dollar amount available for investment under these clauses can be quite substantial. Accordingly, if a prospective borrower has sufficient bargaining clout, he may be able to procure loan terms more liberal than those specified in the statute, or perhaps even obtain a loan on property that would not otherwise qualify. Even a loan applicant without a strong track record might attempt to fit himself within such a basket clause, going by the maxim "nothing ventured, nothing gained."[39]

[2] Commercial Banks

Commercial banks constitute the principal source of interim short-term construction financing where the developer has a "takeout" commitment from a permanent lender. They are also by far the largest financial intermediaries in both numbers and assets. By March 1980, commercial banks owned assets totalling $1,364 billion, with both national and state banks sharing equally. Spread throughout the nation, a total of 14,609 banks concentrate on local lending[40]; however, a network of approximately 30,000 branch banks has enabled the larger ones to extend their lending periphery to entire metropolitan areas and in some instances to entire states. In addition, several large money market banks, in New York City and elsewhere, make participation loans with small local banks throughout the country when the requested construction loan amounts exceed these local banks' legal maximum for individual loans.

---

[39] See N.Y. Ins. Law § 81(17) (McKinney Supp. 1979). In New York the percentage is 4 percent of the insurer's admitted assets.

[40] Board of Governors of Federal Reserve System, 66 F.R.B. No. 5, at A16 (May 1980) (hereinafter cited as 66 F.R.B.).

(2) *Loan-to-value ratio and amortization requirements.* The most common maximum loan-to-value ratio, expressed as a percentage of appraised value, is 75 percent; frequently, the principal amount must be amortized within a designated period of time. In New York, the maximum ratio is 75 percent for commercial and apartment building loans if the principal is scaled down to two thirds of its appraised value within thirty-five years, with interest-only payments allowed for five years. Apparently, the notion is that a minimum 25 percent value hedge is necessary if the property should go to foreclosure. And, while the debt service payments are usually constant, the income-generating capacity and economic useful life of an office building, shopping center, or apartment building may not always exceed thirty-five years.[36]

(3) *Leasehold loans.* Some states specify lower loan-to-value ratios and stricter amortization requirements for leasehold loans as compared to mortgages covering a fee interest. In New York, a 75 percent leasehold loan is permitted if the loan is fully amortizable within the lesser of four fifths of the unexpired leasehold term or forty years with interest-only payments for five years. The unexpired term of the leasehold must be no less than twenty-one years, including enforceable renewal options.[37]

Another restriction imposed under New York law is that the underlying fee may not be subject to any prior lien. Otherwise, the subordinate leasehold estate could be wiped out at foreclosure and the insurance company would lose its security for the loan. Moreover, since the security for the loan is a defeasible estate that could, for example, be extinguished in the event of a default under the terms of the ground lease by the mortgagor-ground lessee, the insurance company will normally insist that certain protective provisions be inserted in the ground lease.[38]

The following are the significant quantitative constraints on mortgage loans by life insurance companies:

(1) *Overall limit on mortgage loans.* A few states have established limits on the total mortgage holdings of a life insurance company,

---

[36] See N.Y. Ins. Laws § 81(6)(a) (McKinney Supp. 1979).

[37] *Id.* The purpose of this latter restriction is not clear; perhaps the notion is that a short payout period to pay, in effect, for the construction or acquisition of expensive leasehold improvements may pose too great a risk of economic collapse for the developer-borrower. If so, then one wonders why the same limitation does not apply to fee mortgages.

[38] See discussion at ¶ 7.01[3]; N.Y. Ins. Law § 81(6)(a) (McKinney Supp. 1979).

industry. Since the New York statute has been followed as a prototype for most state statutes elsewhere, the following overview will refer to the provisions of that statute.[34]

The Armstrong Committee Report indicates that the primary motivation behind the state-imposed constraints on life insurance company investment policy is to protect policyholders' equity from management incompetence, dishonesty, and speculative excess. To accomplish this, state laws have urged "safety of principal" upon life insurance companies as their primary investment objective. This "safety" objective is enforced by means of two kinds of constraints (1) qualitative limits that regulate, on the basis of risk standards, the kinds of realty permissible as collateral for mortgage loans, and (2) quantitative restraints that limit the proportion of assets companies can place in mortgage loans and other specified investments that have the effect of guarantying a minimum amount of portfolio diversification.

The following qualitative constraints apply to mortgage loans made by life insurance companies:

(1) *First mortgage loans upon improved realty located in the United States.* The majority of jurisdictions require that the company hold as security for the loan property that is both improved and unencumbered.[35] In addition, most insurance companies will demand that a conditional assignment of rentals be made to them as additional collateral for the loan. Obviously, by being a senior lienholder the company will be in a better position to be made whole again than it would as a junior lienholder if the property should go to foreclosure.

---

[34] For a more detailed analysis of these regulatory provisions and for a tabular summary of major provisions in nineteen other representative states, see Table 1 in Appendix A.

[35] See Va. Code Ann. § 38.1-207(1). See also N.Y. Ins. Law § 81(6)(a) (McKinney Supp. 1979). In 1973, the statute was amended to include second mortgages within authorized reserve investments. Under New York law, the definition of "improved" property includes land, "upon which there . . . . is in the process of construction a substantial building." Accordingly, insurance companies in New York are allowed to make construction loans. Unfortunately, the legislative history is not instructive on what the underlying rationale is for these provisions. The probable explanation is that improved income-producing realty is less speculative than vacant land, is easier to appraise based on a capitalization of earnings test, and generates net rental income capable of meeting the borrower's debt-service requirements. In that regard, insurance company appraisers use a high enough capitalization rate, which yields a low enough loan amount to assure their companies that the estimated net income from the property after all other carrying expenses have been met will be sufficient to cover the project's debt-service requirements.

during 1974-1978 their market share of net acquisitions of nonresidential mortgage loans (one third) has remained about the same.

[d] Regulation of Mortgage Loan Portfolio

Mortgage loans and other investments by life insurance companies are subject to tighter regulatory constraints than are the portfolios of other lender groups, and as a result insurance companies experience somewhat of a competitive disadvantage. For example, whereas mortgage loans by New York insurance companies are subject to quantitative restraints, the S&Ls have been unrestricted as to the proportion of assets they may hold in conventional mortgage loans. Furthermore, in most jurisdictions, life insurance companies, which are chartered and regulated by state law, may finance only the acquisition of improved property, whereas thrift institutions, commercial banks, and REITs are not so fettered. In contrast to commercial banks and REITs, life insurance companies are also frequently prohibited from acquiring junior mortgages and are constrained by relatively low loan-to-value ratios (60 to 75 percent) and stricter amortization requirements.

The need for *some* governmental regulation is not difficult to comprehend[33]: Most policyholders do not regard their premium payments as money invested and subject to loss or decrease in value; they are rarely interested in the investment practices of the company or in the selection of the management, even if they are entitled to elect the governing board. Moreover, broad participation in life insurance programs by the general public, who as consumers are unsophisticated in the ways of the business world, further suggests the need for some governmental regulation of these companies, which serve a concededly quasi-public function. However, if this be the rationale for regulation, then a fortiori, depositors at banks and thrift organizations should be afforded even more protection, and yet the investment portfolios of these depository institutions are subject to a lesser degree of regulation. As is often the case, this paradox has historical roots. Apparently, the investment restrictions of life insurance companies now prevalent in every state date back to the flurry of legislation induced by the revelations of widespread management abuses found among New York life insurance companies in 1905 by the Armstrong Committee, which had been commissioned by the New York legislature to investigate the

---

[33] The history and meaning of statutory regulation of investment policies is explored in depth in Jones, *Investment Policies of Life Insurance Companies* 74-124 (1968).

accuracy with which these companies can predict their future cash flows.[29] This is a function of both the regularity of repayments on existing investments and the semipermanent contractual nature of most insurance premiums. It is this cash flow feature that in large measure explains why insurance companies are able to concentrate on long-term mortgage lending. Moreover, local law in some jurisdictions, such as Virginia, prohibits companies from lending mortgage money on unimproved realty even when improvements are contemplated. And, in those jurisdictions like New York, which permit construction loans, most companies are disinclined to rely on local agents to monitor construction and decide the delicate question of when to make progress payments to the borrower-builder. The foregoing helps explain why construction loans accounted for only 5.6 percent of the total loan amount committed by fifteen major life insurance companies during the first quarter of 1978.[30] Life insurance companies specialize in long-term loans on nonresidential properties. Of the total loan amount committed in the first quarter of 1978 for multi-family and nonresidential mortgages, 70 percent was for repayment of a construction loan and for the permanent financing of newly completed property; 9 percent was for the purchase of existing property; 3.6 percent was for the purchase of new property; and 7.2 percent was for the refinancing of an existing mortgage.[31] As to loan allocation by property type during 1979, 10.6 percent of the total loan amount committed was for apartment buildings; 16.3 percent was for shopping centers; 38.7 percent was for office buildings; 11.4 percent was for commercial and industrial warehousing facilities; 1.2 percent was for manufacturing plants; and 14.3 percent was for hotels and motels.[32] In recent years, portfolio switching by life insurance companies from apartment house loans to commercial-industry property loans has been steadily increasing because of rent control and rent stabilization, either real or threatened. However,

---

[29] This assumption came into serious question, however, during the second quarter of 1980 when insurance companies faced a severe disintermediation problem caused by an unprecedentedly high level of loans by policyholders and by a loss of managed pension funds. See "Cash Crunch at Equitable Life" 101-10 Fortune 13 (May 19, 1980)

[30] American Council on Life Insurance, "Mortgage Commitments on Multi-family and Nonresidential Properties Reported by 15 Insurance Companies First Quarter 1978," Inv. Bull. No. 778, at Table H (July 11, 1978) (hereinafter cited as Inv. Bull.). The study deals exclusively with commitments of $100,000 and over on multi-family and nonresidential mortgages made by fifteen reporting life insurance companies.

[31] *Id.*

[32] Inv. Bull. No. 805, note 30 *supra,* at Table L.

EXHIBIT 2.4. Purpose of Insurance Company Mortgage Loans, Fourth Quarter 1979

(Commitments of $100,000 and Over on Multi-family and Nonresidential Mortgages Made by 20 Life Insurance Companies)

(continued)

Major Property Type Purpose of Loan	No. of Loans	Amount Committed ($000)	Loan Amount ($000)	Interest Rate (by #)	Interest Rate (by $)	Loan/ Value	Averages Capitalization Rate	Debt Coverage	Percent Constant	Term (Yrs./ Mos.)
Construct the property securing the mortgage	4	4,150	1,038	11.56	11.52	73.9	10.0	1.11	12.3	7/6
Purchase of existing property	22	18,872	858	11.06	11.42	70.8	10.3	1.21	12.1	21/10
Refinance	3	7,700	2,567	11.12	11.54	77.0	11.5	1.25	12.1	21/8
Institutional and recreational*	**9**	**$30,000**	**$3,333**	**11.69%**	**11.59%**	**70.6%**	**12.0%**	**1.20%**	**12.4%**	**17/9**
Repay construction loan and provide long-term financing for a newly completed property	3	19,500	6,500	11.42	11.62	50.4	12.5	1.38	12.4	23/4
Purchase of existing property	5	7,500	1,500	11.80	11.35	84.6	11.3	1.00	12.3	15/0

*The subtotals represent all the loans within the major property categories; the components do not necessarily add to the subtotals, because purpose categories with only a few loans are not shown separately.

SOURCE: American Council on Life Insurance, Investment Bull. No. 805, Table N (April 15, 1980)

EXHIBIT 2.4. Purpose of Insurance Company Mortgage Loans, Fourth Quarter 1979

(Commitments of $100,000 and Over on Multi-family and Nonresidential Mortgages Made by 20 Life Insurance Companies)

Major Property Type / Purpose of Loan	No. of Loans	Amount Committed ($000)	Loan Amount ($000)	Averages						
				Interest Rate (by #)	Interest Rate (by $)	Loan/ Value	Average Capitalization Rate	Debt Coverage	Percent Constant	Term (Yrs./ Mos.)
Apartments—Conventional*	**42**	**$217,695**	**$5,183**	**11.04%**	**11.22%**	**73.9%**	**11.0%**	**1.28%**	**11.6%**	**20/5**
Repay construction loan and provide long-term financing for a newly completed property	34	186,815	5,495	10.98	11.23	73.8	10.9	1.29	11.5	20/7
Refinance	6	25,455	4,242	11.39	11.22	73.9	11.1	1.27	12.0	20/0
Commercial retail*	**68**	**$313,074**	**$4,604**	**10.91%**	**10.82%**	**73.5%**	**10.7%**	**1.28%**	**11.6%**	**20/8**
Repay construction loan and provide long-term financing for a newly completed property	59	260,124	4,409	10.83	10.65	74.8	10.7	1.26	11.6	21/2
Purchase of existing property	5	11,900	2,380	11.00	11.14	70.3	11.1	1.36	11.7	18/2
Office buildings*	**128**	**$673,217**	**$5,260**	**10.85%**	**10.78%**	**73.7%**	**10.6%**	**1.26%**	**11.6%**	**22/0**
Repay construction loan and provide long-term financing for a newly completed property	115	619,007	5,383	10.84	10.78	73.9	10.5	1.25	11.5	22/3
Construct the property securing the mortgage	3	27,250	9,083	10.42	10.28	70.9	10.4	1.38	10.9	23/4
Purchase of existing property	4	4,040	1,010	10.91	10.92	67.8	10.9	1.37	11.8	20/0
Refinance	3	7,000	2,333	10.67	10.81	68.8	11.0	1.40	11.5	26/0
Commercial service*	**119**	**$132,382**	**$1,112**	**10.78%**	**10.82%**	**71.9%**	**10.2%**	**1.22%**	**11.6%**	**22/2**
Repay construction loan and provide long-term financing for a newly completed property	88	99,660	1,132	10.66	10.63	72.3	10.1	1.22	11.4	23/2

EXHIBIT 2.3. Insurance Company Mortgage Loans by Size Within Major Property Type, Fourth Quarter 1979 (Commitments of $100,000 And Over On Multi-family and Nonresidential Mortgages Made by 20 Life Insurance Companies)

(continued)

Major Property Type Loan Size	No. of Loans	Amount Committed ($000)	Loan Amount ($000)	Interest Rate (by #)	Interest Rate (by $)	Averages Loan/Value	Capitalization Rate	Debt Coverage	Percent Constant	Term (Yrs./Mos.)
Industrial										
Less than $1 million	66	101,401	1,536	10.86	10.84	73.8	10.8	1.27	11.6	21/9
$1 million–$3,999,000	28	16,186	578	10.77	10.78	72.7	10.6	1.26	11.6	20/2
$4 million–$7,999,000	35	61,515	1,758	10.94	10.94	75.1	10.9	1.27	11.6	22/10
$8 million and over	1	4,500	4,500	*	*	*	*	*	*	*
	2	19,200	9,600	*	*	*	*	*	*	*
Hotels and motels										
$1 million–$3,999,000	29	342,587	11,813	11.38	11.25	71.8	12.6	1.44	12.3	18/1
$4 million–$7,999,000	11	24,837	2,258	11.62	11.64	71.1	13.1	1.47	12.9	19/5
$8 million and over	5	31,250	6,250	11.20	11.14	71.5	12.5	1.46	12.1	15/0
	13	286,500	22,038	11.25	11.22	72.6	12.2	1.39	11.9	18/2
Multiple property complex	1	11,000	11,000	*	*	*	—	—	—	*
TOTAL	462	1,821,356	3,942	10.91	10.95	73.0	10.7	1.27%	11.7	21/0

* Data not shown where there are fewer than three loans.

NOTE: Averages for capitalization rate and particularly for debt coverage ratio and percent constant may represent a fewer number of loans than the total for the specified category.

SOURCE: American Council on Life Insurance, Investment Bull. No. 805 (April 15, 1980) (Table M).

EXHIBIT 2.3. Insurance Company Mortgage Loans by Size Within Major Property Type, Fourth Quarter 1979

(Commitments of $100,000 And Over On Multi-family and Nonresidential Mortgages Made by 20 Life Insurance Companies)

Major Property Type Loan Size	No. of Loans	Amount Committed ($000)	Loan Amount ($000)	Averages						
				Interest Rate (by #)	Interest Rate (by $)	Loan/ Value	Capital- ization Rate	Debt Cover- age	Percent Constant	Term (Yrs./ Mos.)
Apartments—Conventional	**42**	**$ 217,695**	**$5,183**	**11.04%**	**11.22%**	**73.9%**	**11.0%**	**1.28**	**11.6%**	**20/5**
Less than $1 million	1	925	925	*	*	*	*	*	*	*
$1 million–$3,999,000	23	54,740	2,380	10.95	10.94	72.9	10.8	1.29	11.6	21/4
$4 million–$7,999,000	13	64,230	4,941	11.12	11.12	73.9	11.0	1.28	11.6	17/8
$8 million and over	5	97,800	19,560	11.22	11.45	78.1	11.4	1.26	11.7	22/6
Commercial retail	**68**	**313,074**	**4,604**	**10.91**	**10.82**	**73.5**	**10.7**	**1.28**	**11.6**	**20/8**
Less than $1 million	10	5,590	559	11.05	10.96	74.3	10.4	1.21	11.8	20/6
$1 million–$3,999,000	43	87,361	2,032	10.83	10.82	71.0	10.7	1.32	11.6	19/10
$4 million–$7,999,000	8	44,173	5,522	11.38	11.32	83.6	11.7	1.23	12.2	21/10
$8 million and over	7	175,950	25,136	10.71	10.68	76.0	10.2	1.22	11.1	24/7
Office buildings	**128**	**673,217**	**5,260**	**10.85**	**10.78**	**73.7**	**10.6**	**1.26**	**11.6**	**22/0**
Less than $1 million	32	17,313	541	10.96	10.92	73.3	10.6	1.22	12.0	22/4
$1 million–$3,999,000	53	111,979	2,113	10.91	10.94	73.2	10.6	1.28	11.6	21/10
$4 million–$7,999,000	21	115,125	5,482	10.62	10.62	75.3	10.4	1.27	11.1	22/8
$8 million and over	22	428,800	19,491	10.78	10.78	74.1	10.6	1.29	11.2	21/5
Commercial services	**119**	**132,382**	**1,112**	**10.78**	**10.82**	**71.9**	**10.2**	**1.22**	**11.6**	**22/2**
Less than $1 million	73	39,182	537	10.75	10.79	71.6	10.1	1.22	11.7	23/10
$1 million–$3,999,000	42	74,400	1,771	10.83	10.84	71.4	10.1	1.22	11.5	19/9
$4 million–$7,999,000	4	18,800	4,700	10.79	10.80	83.2	11.4	1.22	11.5	17/6
Institutional and recreational	**9**	**30,000**	**3,333**	**11.69**	**11.59**	**70.6**	**12.0**	**1.20**	**12.4**	**17/9**
Less than $1 million	4	2,600	650	12.00	12.00	90.9	11.3	1.00	12.4	15/0
$1 million–$3,999,000	2	4,000	2,000	*	*	*	*	*	*	*
$4 million–$7,999,000	2	10,900	5,450	*	*	*	*	—	*	*
$8 million and over	1	12,500	12,500	*	*	*	—	—	*	*

* Data not shown where there are fewer than three loans.

EXHIBIT 2.2. Insurance Company Mortgage Loans by Property Type, Year 1979

(Commitments of $100,000 and Over on Multi-family and Nonresidential Mortgages Made by 20 Life Insurance Companies)

(continued)

Property Type	No. of Loans	Amount Committed ($000)	Loan Amount ($000)	Interest Rate (by #)	Interest Rate (by $)	Loan/Value	Capitalization Rate	Debt Coverage	Percent Constant	Term (Yrs./Mos.)	Percentage Distribution (by Loan Amount)
						Averages					
Industrial warehouse	341	513,820	1,507	10.31	10.28	74.0	10.6	1.28	11.3	22/2	4.8
Manufacturing plant	90	126,080	1,401	10.26	10.26	73.6	10.3	1.27	11.1	22/8	1.2
Other industrial	10	22,119	2,212	10.16	10.25	78.9	10.3	1.14	11.1	22/0	0.2
Hotel	82	1,308,672	15,959	10.80	10.75	72.2	11.9	1.39	11.8	18/0	12.2
Motel	53	221,210	4,174	11.02	10.98	71.8	12.6	1.47	12.4	17/7	2.1
Multiple property complex	9	266,675	29,631	10.24	10.18	70.6	10.3	1.30	10.6	27/7	2.5
Total	**2,637**	**$10,761,541**	**$ 4,081**	**10.36%**	**10.36%**	**74.1%**	**10.5%**	**1.26**	**11.3%**	**21/5**	**100.0%**

* Data not shown where there are fewer than three loans.
** Less than 0.05 percent.

NOTE: Averages for capitalization rate and particularly for debt coverage ratio and percent constant may represent a fewer number of loans than the total for the specified category.

SOURCE: American Council on Life Insurance, Investment Bull. No. 805, Table L (April 15, 1980)

EXHIBIT 2.2. Insurance Company Mortgage Loans by Property Type, Year 1979

(Commitments of $100,000 and Over on Multi-family and Nonresidential Mortgages Made by 20 Life Insurance Companies)

Property Type	No. of Loans	Amount Committed ($000)	Loan Amount ($000)	Averages								Percentage Distribution (by Loan Amount)
				Interest Rate (by #)	Interest Rate (by $)	Loan/ Value	Capital- ization Rate	Debt Cover- age	Percent Con- stant	Term (Yrs./ Mos.)		
Conventional elevator apartment	42	$ 285,161	$ 6,790	10.51%	10.79%	71.6%	10.8%	1.28	11.7%	17/10		2.6%
Conventional non-elevator apartment	262	858,903	3,278	10.41	10.41	74.4	10.5	1.27	11.1	21/0		8.0
Retail—less than 5 stores	77	143,236	1,860	10.32	10.33	74.2	10.6	1.28	11.4	22/11		1.3
Shopping center—5 or more stores	306	1,754,739	5,734	10.28	10.25	74.3	10.3	1.26	11.1	20/8		16.3
Supermarket	12	38,223	3,185	10.55	10.58	83.4	11.2	1.17	11.8	21/4		0.4
Department store	29	100,034	3,449	10.03	9.99	83.0	10.5	1.14	11.1	25/8		0.9
Automobile sales and service	1	355	355	*	*	*	*	*	*	*		**
Other sales and service	8	7,291	911	10.59	10.41	77.0	10.5	1.22	11.6	26/1		0.1
Office building	698	4,041,954	5,791	10.30	10.25	74.7	10.3	1.26	11.1	21/6		37.6
Medical office building	53	115,792	2,185	10.35	10.24	74.4	10.4	1.25	11.2	22/5		1.1
Parking garage	3	10,800	3,600	10.54	10.08	72.7	11.2	1.31	12.5	20/0		0.1
Restaurant	15	12,926	862	10.38	10.15	80.7	10.9	1.18	11.7	22/4		0.1
Commercial warehouse	455	705,654	1,551	10.36	10.32	73.3	10.0	1.21	11.3	21/9		6.6
Truck terminal	5	4,450	890	10.70	10.75	71.4	11.1	1.27	12.4	19/0		**
Other commercial	60	125,322	2,089	10.40	10.37	72.6	10.8	1.29	11.2	21/4		1.2
Religious	1	4,900	4,900	*	*	*	*	—	*	*		**
Educational	5	4,350	870	11.65	11.30	87.6	11.2	1.07	12.1	15/0		**
Hospital and institutional	8	32,625	4,078	10.84	11.24	62.2	12.0	1.58	12.1	16/11		0.3
Social and recreational	2	12,600	6,300	*	*	*	*	*	*	*		0.1
Nursing homes	10	43,650	4,365	10.60	10.54	53.0	13.0	2.08	11.7	20/2		0.4

of financing terms, and the non-depository nature of the flow of funds into the life insurance industry.[26]

[b] Loan Terms

Most life insurance companies charge a non-refundable commitment fee (usually one percent), lend near or at the maximum loan-to-value ratio (75 percent in most jurisdictions), are strict about permitting prepayment of the loan balance prior to maturity,[27] and charge less interest on long-term income property loans than do banks and savings and loans, since these latter lenders, especially the S&Ls, pay more for their long-term funding. During 1979, the average loan amount, average interest rate, average loan-to-value ratio, average capitalization rate (net stabilized earnings divided by property value), average percent constant (annual level debt service payment, per $100 of debt), and average maturity term for commitments of $100,000 and over on loans made by a representative sample of the larger life insurance companies were as shown in Exhibit 2.2.

[c] Loan Allocation by Function and Property Type

The majority of lender groups participate in all three functional segments of the mortgage market: They originate long-term loans in the primary market, purchase long-term loans in the secondary market, and make short-term construction loans. A few of them also make land loans. In addition, these lender groups, especially the so-called diversified ones (commercial banks and insurance companies), invest in all four property-type mortgages: one-to-four-family; multi-family; non-residential commercial, and farm loans.[28] For more detailed information on the size and purpose of insurance company mortgage loans, see Exhibits 2.3 and 2.4.

One important factor distinguishing insurance companies' loan operations from those of commercial banks and thrift institutions is the

---

[26] See *Insurance Co. Study,* note 23 *supra,* at 6.

[27] As of the date of this writing, most large insurance companies, such as New York Life Insurance Company, are insisting on lock-in periods (no right to prepay) of about ten years, followed by prepayment periods with penalties that de-escalate in amount as the date of prepayment approaches maturity. Also, many of these companies at present are insisting on the right to call in the loan ("call options") approximately during the fifteenth loan year, with respect to most mortgage loans. See also discussion at ¶ 3.03[3][d].

[28] See Exhibit 2.1.

policy. In large measure, this explains why insurance companies are responsible for so many of the trend-setting innovations and complexities that have come about in real estate financing during the past twenty-five years. For example, in recent years these lenders have popularized the sale-and-leaseback[24] as a nondebt financing device, and in the latter tight-credit half of the 1960s introduced the concept of mortgagees taking a participatory interest in contingent earnings—the so-called "equity kicker." Also, about the same time, a few insurance companies began to acquire equity interests in property as a hedge against inflation by entering into joint ventures with developers. Several companies now have a policy of making a mortgage loan only when they are to obtain an equity interest in the property, and some are even demanding a controlling interest in such joint ventures.[24a] Moreover, life insurance companies have led the way in using private investment funds to recycle the inner-city slums of this country. By the end of 1971, the insurance industry had already committed $1.8 billion in mortgage money to this task. Most of the funds generated below-market yields and went into FHA-insured mortgage programs.

[a] Source of Funds

Life insurance companies derive most of their loanable funds from premium receipts[25] and mortgage repayments. As previously noted, fluctuations in the business cycle have only a moderate degree of influence on the repayment rates for commercial real estate mortgages. Similarly, while life insurance companies experience some disintermediation and cyclical variability in their premium inflows, the business cycle effect on loanable funds is relatively small in comparison with the magnitude of changes in depository flows to banks and S&Ls. This is because of the semipermanent nature of this type of savings commitment by policyholders, which tends to stabilize the annual premium volume, especially in the case of annuities. Yet, the available statistics indicate that since the mid-1960s, when the investment patterns of life insurance companies began to change, income property mortgage commitments have been curtailed by cyclical periods of credit restraint in much the same way as residential mortgage financing by thrift institutions despite the different type of collateral involved, the different kind

---

[24] See discussion at ¶ 6.04.

[24a] See discussion at ¶ 11.02. Henry, "Insurer's Role As Investor Shifts and Grows," N.Y. Times, May 24, 1981, Sec. 8, at 1, col. 1.

[25] In 1978, premium receipts from policyholders accounted for 73 percent of industry income. *Life Insurance Fact Book,* note 7 *supra,* at 56.

other hand, developers will attempt wherever possible to get fixed-rate mortgages without equity kickers.[21] The softness of the market and the degree (and fear) of continued inflation will basically determine which side will win and when.

Pension funds are also entering the real estate market more and more, both as lenders and as leveraged and unleveraged investors. Likewise, foreign pension funds and foreign investors from all over the world are investing in all types of real estate from raw acreage to multimillion dollar office buildings. This influx of money bidding for real estate market products will probably force commercial real estate market prices up faster than the Consumer Price Index for a number of years to come.

¶ 2.02 MORTGAGE LENDERS

[1] Life Insurance Companies

With assets of about $389.9 billion at year-end 1978, life insurance companies constitute the principal source of permanent financing for office buildings, shopping centers, and other nonresidential income-producing realty.[22] Moreover, the average loan size on multi-family and nonresidential mortgages for insurance companies (about $3,942,000 during the fourth quarter of 1979) is much larger than for other lending groups, since the bulk of the industry-wide nonresidential lending is done by the asset-swollen giants (i.e., Prudential, Metropolitan, New York Life), which prefer large loans to reduce their overhead per-loan costs and to take advantage of "economies of scale."

In contrast to S&Ls and mutual savings banks, insurance companies lend over a wide geographical area by relying on an extensive network of loan correspondents and to some degree, as do commercial banks, on branch offices. Indeed, between 1950 and 1970, nearly four-fifths of the total dollar volume of mortgage commitments were related to income properties located in regions other than the Northeast, where nearly all of the larger reporting life insurance companies were domiciled, according to a Federal Reserve study on the lending practices of insurance companies.[23]

Guided by some of the ablest real estate lawyers in the country, insurance companies have pursued an aggressive mortgage placement

---

[21] See discussion of equity kickers at ¶ 3.04[3][a].
[22] *Life Insurance Fact Book,* note 7 *supra,* at 68.
[23] Board of Governors of Federal Reserve System, *Mortgage Commitments on Income Properties: A New Series for 15 Life Insurance Companies, 1951-1970,* at 9 (1973) (hereinafter cited as *Insurance Co. Study*).

market, particularly during tight money periods, since these federally chartered institutions are not restricted by state usury ceilings. On March 31, 1980, President Carter signed the Depository Institutions Deregulation and Monetary Control Act of 1980, which, among many things, provided for the gradual phase-out of the Federal Reserve's Regulation Q by 1985. This would mean an eventual free market for interest rates, and will probably cause a minimum of disintermediation between commercial banks and thrift institutions in the future.

In the 1980s, an expanding governmental presence is expected to accelerate the pace of structural change within the mortgage market. Federal government programs for the financing of residential real estate development and ownership through subsidization of housing for the poor, and insurance of residential mortgages covering all but luxury housing have mushroomed to proportions undreamed of when the United States Housing Act of 1937 initiated many of these programs.[16] Similarly, during the past decade there has been an explosive growth in the secondary residential mortgage market.[17] At the federal level, substantial efforts will continue to utilize such grants as the Community Block Grant[18] and the Urban Development Action Grant[19] programs to leverage private investment in the rehabilitation and renewal of land development (including industrial and commercial facilities) in the inner and downtown city areas. Paralleling these developments, though on a more modest scale, has been the continued rapid growth in efforts of state housing finance agencies to lend directly to sponsors of low-to-moderate-income multi-family housing and to lend indirectly by purchasing mortgage pools and using tax-exempt bond proceeds to provide single-family mortgage funds.[20]

On the private side, there will be an increasing effort by lenders to make their mortgages variable, with equity kickers. Also, there will be a greater effort to be involved in joint ventures with developers. On the

---

[16] For example, at present more than forty separate programs are being administered by the Department of Housing and Urban Development (HUD), which has a total budget of well over $33 billion, outstanding FHA insurance in excess of $100 billion, and guarantees of mortgage-backed securities approaching $65 billion. HUD Budget Tables, 5 BNA Housing & Dev. Rep. 822-830 (1978). See Salsich, "New Government Programs for Residential Real Estate Financing," 13 Real Prop. Prob. & Tr. J. 1055 (1978) (hereinafter cited as Salsich).

[17] For example, the mortgage portfolio of FNMA is now close to $40 billion. See discussion at ¶ 2.02[7].

[18] Housing and Community Development Act of 1977, Pub. L. 95-128, § 103(a), 91 Stat. 1113 (1977) (codified in 42 U.S.C.A. §5303(e)).

[19] Housing and Community Development Act of 1977, § 119.

[20] See Salsich, note 16 *supra,* at 1065-1068.

low-income versus luxury housing; urban versus rural real estate; private versus public ownership; improved versus unimproved land; rental versus special-purpose-use property (e.g., churches, bowling alleys), etc. It may be difficult for the borrower to discern the penchants of a particular lender before an application is made.

[3] Factors Contributing to a Restructuring of the Market

Observers of the mortgage market should always be alert to the quiet evolution that is changing its structure, and the role of mortgage lending institutions themselves. A few examples illustrate the types of changes that are under way. In mid-1974, government and private groups joined forces to form Automated Mortgage Market Information Network (AMMINET), a nationwide computerized system for communicating mortgage market information. This system has the potential for placing the mortgage market on a national footing analogous to the market for stocks and bonds. Another innovation occurred in late 1975 when a California S&L successfully marketed a public offering of mortgage-backed bonds for the first time.[14] Pursuant to Federal Home Loan Bank Board (FHLBB) authority,[15] California Federal Savings and Loan Association, the largest federally chartered S&L, issued $50 million worth of 9⅛ percent mortgage-backed bonds. The bonds were offered without SEC registration under an exception that applied because the bonds were sold only through registered brokers and dealers, and were secured by a pool of U.S. Government securities and by a pool of FHA-insured and VA-guaranteed notes and mortgages covering residential real estate located in California. In that same year, there was also the successful inauguration of trading in mortgage futures on the Chicago Board of Trade. This provides opportunities for either hedging or speculating in interest rate changes. In 1978, the 13,000 federal credit unions were authorized for the first time to make home loans (with loan-to-value ratios up to 95 percent) to credit union members, which could become an important factor in the mortgage

---

[14] See Adams, "The Thrifts Seek Capital With Mortgage-Backed Bonds," 6 Real Est. Rev. 38 (1976); Strine, "New Commercial Devices—Mortgage-Backed Securities," 13 Real Prop., Prob. & Tr. J. 1011, 1038 (1978) (hereinafter cited as Strine).

[15] On April 24, 1975, the regulations of the FHLBB were amended to authorize certain insured savings and loan associations to issue mortgage-backed bonds. Eligibility requirements include *inter alia* satisfaction of certain tests by a particular institution as to net income, ratio of problem loans to total assets, and provision for loss reserves. 40 Fed. Reg. 17982 (1975).

being sought. Such loan preferences are a function of each lender's historical habit, external regulation, the source and stability of its funding sources, and a host of other factors. For example, if the security for the loan is a large piece of income-producing commercial property, such as an office building or shopping center, the permanent lender will frequently be a life insurance company. The reason for this is that most insurance companies legally can invest in mortgages secured by income-producing property and they prefer larger loans to reduce their overhead per loan costs. Of course, they also have the requisite funds to invest. If the security priming the mortgage is not income-producing but, instead, is land in the process of being developed or involves unique management skills (hotels, motels, mobile home parks), the developer will often be forced to go to a less regulated institutional lender, such as a real estate investment trust. Unlike most other permanent lenders, a mortgage REIT will not shy away from such "specialty" loans, but charges more because it must pay more than its competitors for long-term funding.

The next customary stage in the lending cycle is when the borrower, on the strength of the permanent mortgage loan (or "takeout") commitment, obtains a short-term, interest-only construction loan from an interim lender, such as a commercial bank.[12] Unlike the permanent lender, the construction lender must have the requisite expertise to monitor the construction activity of the borrower and to determine whether the project is being completed on schedule in accordance with approved plans and specifications. It must also determine whether the progress payments or construction loan disbursements are being properly used to pay the subcontractors and materialmen. Since the short-term rates charged by banks and other construction lenders are geared to the "prime rate," the cost of construction financing will respond much more quickly to shifting market conditions and fluctuate within a wider band than the interest cost charged for long-term permanent financing. Occasionally, a lender, such as a REIT or a large commercial bank, will supply both the interim and permanent financing; otherwise, the construction loan will be sold (often by prearrangement under a tripartite agreement between the borrower, permanent lender, and construction lender—called the "buy-sell" agreement) to the permanent lender once the project is completed.[13]

The diversity within the mortgage market is also reflected by preferences among lenders for mortgages on new versus old structures;

---

[12] See Chapter 4 for a discussion of the construction loan.

[13] See ¶ 4.05 for a discussion of the buy-sell agreement. See also discussion at ¶ 4.01[3].

[2] Summary of the Lending Cycle

Unlike the stock market, the primary mortgage market is not a series of organized forums but a time-place continuum of interrelated lending points where bargains are struck by borrowers and lenders as to loan amounts and interest rates. However, to some degree (see Exhibit 2.1) the market can be divided into sub-markets according to the type of lender and depending upon the risk, duration, situs, and type of property securing the loan.

EXHIBIT 2.1. Commercial and Multi-family Mortgage Breakdown ($ millions)

Group	Land and Development Loan Holdings	Construction Loan Holdings			Long-Term Mortgage Holdings		
		Total***	Multi-family	All Non-residential*	Total***	Non-Farm, Non-residential*	Conventional Multi-family
Commercial banks	$ 4,182	$30,698	$4,797	$14,983	$214,860	$ 60,298	$ 6,084
S&Ls	5,351	20,519	3,220	3,538	453,208	31,483	32,448
REITs	546	1,248	433	586	2,926	1,795	880
Mutual savings banks	233	1,722	776	445	97,637	15,366	11,957
Life insurance companies	458	672	31	639	117,885	70,319	17,482
Mortgage companies	521	2,554	727	906	7,326	1,260	400
Total for all groups**	**$11,291**	**$57,413**	**$9,984**	**$21,097**	**$893,842**	**$180,521**	**$69,251**

* Principally commercial and industrial.
** Five minor HUD-designated groups not shown.
*** Total includes one- to four-family home and farm loans.

SOURCE: U.S. Department of Housing and Urban Development Release No. 80-186, Table 1 (June 12, 1980).

In the case of new construction, once the borrowing entity is selected, the developer often embarks upon his journey through the commercial lending cycle by approaching a permanent lender, sometimes with the aid of an intermediary, such as a mortgage broker, banker, or correspondent in order to obtain a permanent or long-term loan commitment.[11] In either case, the choice of a lender will depend upon which lender specializes in the permanent financing of the type

---

[11] See Chapter 3 for a discussion of the permanent loan.

for heat, light, and power, have increased at a faster rate than rentals.[10] Further, unfavorable demographic trends and the tendency for more rent-control legislation have caused the recent slump in conventional multi-family starts to drag on notwithstanding periodic softenings in mortgage rates.

Similarly, recent events have shown that the demand for single-family and condominium housing soared to new heights as the market prices for housing began to outstrip the double-digit inflation rates of the 1978-1979 period. Only incredibly high mortgage rates of 19 to 20 percent dampened the demand in early 1980. Demand for housing units tends to remain slack as mortgage rates begin to fall after a high mark, and only begins to firm as rates start to rise again after apparently having "bottomed out."

Another factor inherent in the demand for residential housing is consumer confidence, especially in an inflationary economy. If housing is perceived as a "good investment" in comparison to other investments, the demand for housing will remain strong, except in the face of unusually high interest rates.

---

[10] According to Anthony Downs, senior fellow of the Brookings Institution, Washington, D.C., speaking on November 15, 1978 at the National Association of Realtors convention in Honolulu, Hawaii, conventionally financed apartment buildings are becoming even scarcer, notwithstanding a 10 to 15 percent rent rise during 1978, because rent increases are still not keeping pace with mortgage rates and other operating costs. For example, based on data involving 440 unfurnished apartments in 144 cities located throughout the United States and Canada, it was reported that during 1975 rentals increased 4.3 percent while operating expenses increased 6.8 percent; and during 1976 the comparable figures were 6.4 percent and 6.5 percent, respectively. According to Mr. Downs, most rental markets are dominated by small-scale landlords who are fearful of charging "what the market will bear" and who are nervous about the prospect of rent control. According to Phillip Kozloff, president of Citicorp Real Estate Inc., the problem in the apartment house market is also attributable to the fact that while rental vacancies are at their lowest rate since just after World War II, they declined only slightly in 1978—from 5.1 percent at the beginning of the year to 5.0 percent at the end. Moreover, the decline was concentrated in small towns and rural areas, not in metropolitan areas. During 1978, about 225,000 unsubsidized rental starts were recorded, and Mr. Kozloff estimates even lower figures in the short-form future. Mortgage & Real Est. Exec. Rep., April 15, 1979, at 1, 2. However, notwithstanding this lag in conventional multi-family starts, experts such as Robert J. Mylod, president of Advance Mortgage Corporation, anticipate that the *overall* multi-family sector, which has been lagging for five years, should increase dramatically (approximately 30 percent, to over 700,000 starts during 1979) because of increases in construction of both high-rise condominiums and subsidized rental units. Mortgage & Real Est. Exec. Rep. at 1, (March 15, 1978).

aries reallocate investment funds into mortgages and other capital investments.

It is this countercyclicality that has led to four recent credit crunches for real estate borrowers: first in 1966, then in 1969-1970, next in 1973-1974, and finally in 1978-1979. Each occurred when the American economy was approaching full capacity and short-term interest rates began to outpace long-term rates. Conversely, the largest real estate boom in history started during the 1970-1971 recession when real GNP had dropped from 724.7 billion in 1969 to 715.9 billion by the last quarter of 1970.

[c] Demand "Passive" Relative to Supply

While the amount and cost of mortgage money flowing into the real estate sector is determined by counterfluctuations, it also depends to some extent on the collective demand for credit on the part of real estate borrowers.

In general, business borrowers enjoy a preferential claim to available funds because they tend to be such large and regular depositors. Thus, real estate borrowers fare better not when real estate demand is strong but when business demand is weak.

Real estate developers have traditionally leveraged their investments to a much greater degree than their rivals in the business sector. Often a one- or two-point increase in mortgage rates will decrease an investor's rate of equity return to a point of unprofitability. Therefore, a real estate borrower or developer remains out of the mortgage market (if he can) during high rates, since the projects he had in mind have become financially unfeasible. Therefore, levels of real estate construction activity depend more upon the availability and cost of mortgage money than upon market demand for space. The serious real estate slump of 1973-1974 and the high failure rate among developers and investors, coupled with the Tax Reform Act of 1976 (1976 TRA),[9] have caused many real estate developers and investors to be more concerned about a project's economic viability and less concerned about tax benefits.

Still, real estate investors like to leverage to the hilt if they can make a reasonable economic return on their equity. But, with heavy leverage, debt service payments are such a large percentage of total annual cash requirements that mortgage credit demand will continue to be extremely interest-elastic.

Other factors have recently tended to affect the demand for mortgage financing. In recent years, maintenance costs, as well as costs

---

[9] See discussion at ¶ 1.05[2][c].

corporate and U.S. long-term bonds, since bonds tend to be more liquid and entail less administrative expense. However, when loanable funds are in short supply and business demands intensify, corporate bond rates start to rise at a faster rate than contract yields on mortgages. Within recent times, diversified lenders, such as insurance companies and mutual savings banks, have switched a large portion of their portfolios from mortgages to bonds.[7] However, even with record high bond yields, institutional lenders have become somewhat reluctant to invest in long-term bonds because of their fear that rampant inflation will erode the fixed yield from bonds and that falling bond prices may prevent them from liquidating their assets without incurring substantial portfolio losses.[8]

Conversely, during a period of economic decline and impending recession, the business demand for short-term credit to finance inventories and output-producing capital goods slackens. During this time, demand for credit falls relative to household saving, which causes money market and corporate bond rates to fall faster than long-term mortgage yields. Moreover, the Federal Reserve often increases bank credit, which drives down money market interest rates even further. As short-term rates fall faster than long-term rates, a form of disintermediation-in-reverse occurs as both households and financial intermedi-

---

acted to make these financial institutions more competitive with the open market. And, during the last few years open market interest rates, particularly for short-term securities, have increased so fast (six-month Treasury bill interest rates increased at an average of eighteen basic points per month during 1977 and 1978) that in 1978 S&Ls were first authorized to pay their depositors Treasury bill rates on six-month certificates of deposit. Yet during the 1978-1979 period, savings and time deposit flows dropped sharply; for example, net new savings gains at federally insured S&Ls totalled only $10.1 billion for the first five months of 1978 compared to $17.1 billion for the same period during 1977. United States League of Savings Ass'ns, *Savings and Loan Fact Book '79*, at 58-60 (hereinafter cited as *Savings & Loan Fact Book*).

[7] For example, the fact that the traditional higher-yield differential in favor of mortgages reversed itself during the early 1970s helps explain why acquisitions by insurance companies of corporate bonds increased fivefold between 1969 and 1978, whereas the rate of mortgage acquisitions only doubled during the same period. Similarly, acquisitions by mutual savings banks of corporate securities increased sixfold between 1965 and 1978 while mortgage acquisitions only doubled in amount. See American Council on Life Insurance, *Life Insurance Fact Book '79*, at 72 (hereinafter cited as *Life Insurance Fact Book*); *Mutual Savings Fact Book*, note 4 *supra*, at 10.

[8] See Seligman, "The Revolt of the Lenders," 101-6 Fortune 57 (March 24, 1980).

as the economy reaches full capacity. During an economic expansion period, the demand for short-term credit by business borrowers, combined with Federal Reserve anti-inflation monetary measures, drives up the money market rate structure faster than both savings and time-deposit rates and the long-term capital market structure, of which mortgage credit is a part. In response, both households and financial intermediaries[5] tend to invest in these higher-yielding assets and cause an outflow of available mortgage money. This process is referred to as disintermediation.[6]

The capital assets themselves can also cause additional disintermediation from the mortgage market. Traditionally, a rate spread has existed between the higher-yielding mortgage and the lower-yielding

---

[5] Most of these depositories—especially the savings and loans (S&Ls)—borrow short to lend long. This means that while they compete in the market for short-term funds (demand deposits and savings accounts with fluctuating rates), these funds are invested primarily in long-term, fixed-rate mortgages and securities. Accordingly, if these institutions increase their rates to meet open market competition, they must apply the increase to all deposits. Yet, higher rates of return can be obtained only on new mortgages and other investments.

When short-term rates exceed mortgage and other long-term capital yields (as in 1974), it becomes foolish to lend long. Accordingly, during a period of economic expansion and inflation when short-term rates are relatively high, the diversified lending institutions (commercial banks, mutual savings banks and insurance companies) within regulatory statute limits, prefer to acquire more short-term obligations and to reinvest the liquidation proceeds back into the money market as the rates go higher. For example, in 1973, the three-month Treasury bill rate was 4.07. It jumped to 7.04 in 1974 and to 7.88 in 1975. Undoubtedly, this was a contributory factor in explaining why income property mortgage commitments by life insurance companies dropped in total amount committed from $4.85 billion in 1973 to $2.60 billion in 1974. However, the flight of capital from the home mortgage is to some degree ameliorated by federal "intermediation" in the form of direct mortgage acquisitions by federally sponsored agencies, such as the FNMA and loans to member S&Ls by the Federal Home Loan Bank Board (FHLBB) system. See discussion at ¶ 2.02[7].

[6] When short-term rates rise high enough relative to long-term capital market rates during periods of economic overexpansion, loanable funds are diverted en masse from the thrift institutions. For example, deposit flows decreased and holdings of direct market instruments by households increased as yields on open market instruments exceeded those on savings deposits, as in the 1971-1972, 1975-1976, and 1978-1979 periods. Conversely, savings flows increased in 1966, 1969, and during the 1973-1974 period as deposit rates climbed above market rates.

Under the Interest Rate Adjustment Act, the FHLBB in 1966 was granted the power to fix the maximum rates payable by S&Ls on various types of savings accounts. Until that time only commercial banks had been subject to savings rate controls. However, fearing sizeable deposit outflows from associations and banks to money market instruments as a result of quickly rising short-term market rates, both the Federal Reserve Board and the FHLBB in 1973

important source of net savings is the consumer or household sector, which has generated between 66 and 80 percent of gross national savings in recent years.[4]

Historically, real aggregate income and household income both rise, as does the nation's gross national product (GNP), in a growing economy. As household income increases, so will household saving, because a household's propensity to save an extra dollar of disposable income increases percentagewise as the household has more and more income left over after paying for needed goods and services. Conversely, as national income declines, as in a recession, or in a rampaging inflation, real household income and gross saving tend to fall, since households collectively must use a greater percentage of their incomes to meet current needs. Likewise, when households buy a disproportionate amount of capital goods, as when automobile sales are unusually high, their rate of net savings tends to decrease. It is primarily this net savings inflow by households that directly fuels the total credit system, and indirectly fuels the mortgage market.

However, for these funds to flow into the mortgage market, household savings deposits must be made into the financial intermediaries: commercial banks, mutual savings banks, savings and loans (S&Ls), life insurance companies, pension trusts, and real estate investment trusts (REITs). In turn, the financial intermediaries themselves must decide what portion of the investment reserves (from deposits, retained earnings and loan payments) to allocate to mortgages.

If households tend to emphasize other investments, such as savings bonds, stocks, or other securities, and if the financial intermediaries themselves also favor nonmortgage instruments to invest in, there can be a dramatic removal of funds available to make mortgage loans.

[b] Countercyclical Mortgage Credit Supply

Historically, mortgage credit and construction begin to rise as a *percentage* of GNP during economic downswings and begin to decline

---

to expand working capital and replace capital goods. Most of the remainder is invested in the short-term money market, often pending some anticipated capital outlay, and does not flow into the long-term mortgage market. Also, both federal and local governments within recent times have been net borrowers because of deficit spending. Although, certain federal agencies, such as the Government National Mortgage Association (GNMA) and the Federal National Mortgage Association (FNMA), extend direct credit to the residential mortgage market by underwriting or purchasing mortgages in the secondary mortgage markets. See discussion at ¶ 2.02[7]

[4] National Ass'n of Mutual Savings Banks, *1979 National Fact Book of Mutual Savings Banking* 43 (hereinafter cited as *Mutual Savings Fact Book*).

       [7] The Secondary Mortgage Market 2-44
          [a] Federal National Mortgage Association 2-45
          [b] Federal Home Loan Mortgage Corporation 2-45
          [c] Government National Mortgage Association........... 2-46

¶ 2.03   The Role of Mortgage Brokers and Mortgage Bankers 2-47
       [1] The Mortgage Broker 2-47
       [2] The Mortgage Banker 2-47

¶ 2.01 THE STRUCTURE OF THE MORTGAGE MARKET

[1] Cost and Availability of Mortgage Credit

The cost and availability of mortgage credit at any moment in time depends on (1) the size of the savings inflow into the total credit stream; (2) the competition between real estate and business/government sectors indirectly in the short-term money market and directly in the long-term capital market for their fair share of credit; (3) the role that the federal government chooses to play at any given time in regulating both credit for new real estate development and the secondary residential mortgage market[1]; and (4) the demand for credit by real estate developers, owners, and investors.

[a] Savings-Based Supply of Total Credit

Picturing the total supply of credit as a stream, the size of this stream flowing into the mortgage sector will initially depend upon the amount of net national savings, which in all its forms constitutes the ultimate financing source for real estate and all other capital formation in the economy.[2] Accordingly, one key to understanding the availability of mortgage money in broad terms is to understand what variables affect the ebb and flow of net national saving, especially that portion generated by household saving.

Gross savings by household is the amount of after-tax disposable income left over after expenditures for current consumption needs, and net savings is the balance of gross savings remaining after expenditures for the purchase of such durables as automobiles and refrigerators. While business and government sectors contribute to the gross savings inflow, both sectors are primarily net borrowers.[3] By far, the most

---

    [1] See discussion at ¶ 2.02[7].

    [2] An example of this correlation is that from 1973 to 1974 net national saving dropped from $128.4 billion to $95.8 billion and the net flow of mortgage funds decreased from $70.2 billion to $52.5 billion!

    [3] Businesses generate a large amount of internal savings in the form of retained earnings and depreciation allowances, but the preponderant part is used

Chapter 2
TYPES OF LENDERS

	Page
¶ 2.01 The Structure of the Mortgage Market	2- 2
[1] Cost and Availability of Mortgage Credit	2- 2
[a] Savings-Based Supply of Total Credit	2- 2
[b] Countercyclical Mortgage Credit Supply	2- 3
[c] Demand "Passive" Relative to Supply	2- 6
[2] Summary of the Lending Cycle	2- 8
[3] Factors Contributing to a Restructuring of the Market	2-10
¶ 2.02 Mortgage Lenders	2-12
[1] Life Insurance Companies	2-12
[a] Source of Funds	2-13
[b] Loan Terms	2-14
[c] Loan Allocation by Function and Property Type	2-14
[d] Regulation of Mortgage Loan Portfolio	2-22
[2] Commercial Banks	2-25
[a] Source of Funds	2-26
[b] Loan Terms	2-26
[c] Loan Allocation by Function and Property Type	2-27
[d] Regulation of Mortgage Loan Portfolio	2-28
[3] Savings and Loan Associations	2-30
[a] Source of Funds	2-30
[b] Loan Terms	2-31
[c] Loan Allocation by Function and Property Type	2-31
[d] Regulation of Mortgage Loan Portfolio	2-32
[i] Home Loans	2-33
[ii] Apartment-Type Loans	2-34
[iii] Income-Producing Business Property and Church Loans	2-34
[iv] Loans on Developed Building Lots and Sites	2-34
[v] Land Acquisition and Development Loans	2-34
[4] Mutual Savings Banks	2-39
[a] Source of Funds	2-40
[b] Loan Allocation by Function and Property Type	2-41
[c] Regulation of Mortgage Loan Portfolio	2-41
[5] Real Estate Investment Trusts	2-42
[6] Pension Funds and Other Lenders	2-44

¶ 1.08 COMMON-LAW LAND TRUST

One of the earliest forms of real estate syndication was the common-law land trust, still popular today in Illinois and a few other states. Since title to the realty is held by the trustees, the trust device provides both a convenient and anonymous method for holding the title; thus, difficulties upon the death of a beneficiary or the transfer of his interest to a minor are avoided. In addition, trust ownership offers investors the ability to relegate management decisions to the trustees and, at the same time, immunizes the beneficiaries from personal liability. However, much of trust device's utility is negated by the fact that its corporate attributes, which make it desirable for nontax purposes, also, for the reasons discussed in ¶ 1.05[4][a], make it vulnerable to tax treatment as a corporation.[211]

---

[211] See Morrissey v. Comm'r, 296 U.S. 344, 362 (1935).

tant factor, de-incorporate so that the participants as partners can take advantage of the depreciation losses. Finally, the use of security deposits or escrow arrangements rather than advance rentals and selection of a proper fiscal year can be used as devices to prolong the election period if this is necessary in order to permit a loss pass-through near, or at the end of the construction period.[208]

¶ 1.07 REAL ESTATE INVESTMENT TRUSTS

As previously noted, equity REITs have fared reasonably well since 1971 despite disastrous times for the large part of the REIT industry active in short-term construction and development lending.[209] REITs derive their existence from a 1960 IRC amendment permitting them to pay out cash flow distributions to trust shareholders without the imposition of a corporate tax. This is provided that they pay out at least 95 percent of their taxable earnings. Such trusts are to real estate what mutual funds are to stocks and bonds because of the Code requirement that a qualified REIT have at least 100 share or certificate holders. As a result of this requirement, and because of tighter SEC regulations (due to the inavailability of the "private offering" exemption), REITs are not well suited for small syndications; however, they still serve an important role in the raising of large amounts of equity capital. In contrast to a public limited partnership, a REIT cannot pass through losses to the equity owners. However, most REIT shares are traded at public exchanges or are redeemable, whereas limited partners must usually invoke their own resources to dispose of their investment shares. The chief disadvantage in using this type of ownership entity is probably the myriad Code requirements that are designed to ensure passive investment income for the trust as well as a maximum amount of portfolio diversification.[210]

---

methods. During this period, the higher net-after tax corporate income would be available to service the corporate debt.

The corporation could then be liquidated tax-free under Section 333, and the shareholders would obtain a new basis for the property equal to the adjusted basis of stock. Collapsible corporation status would be avoided by holding the property in corporate form for three years after completion of the construction. See I.R.C. § 341(d)(3).

[208] For a comprehensive treatment on Subchapter S corporations, see Grant, *Subchapter S Taxation* (1974).

[209] See discussion of REITs as lenders in ¶ 2.02[5].

[210] I.R.C. § 856.

percent of its gross receipts from passive income—rents, royalties, dividends, and interests.[203]

The purpose of the latter limitation is to restrict the use of Subchapter S to corporations having substantial amounts of operating, rather than investment income.[204] Under the regulations, the term "rents" does not include payments for the use of space where significant services are rendered to the lessee, other than those which are customarily rendered where rental of space is the principal activity. For example, the supplying of maid service constitutes a significant service, whereas the furnishing of utilities and cleaning services would not be so regarded.[205]

Accordingly, in the case of income-producing property, use of the Subchapter S corporation would be confined to ownership of hotels, motels, apartment buildings where hotel-like services are rendered, warehouses, and parking lots. However, even if the passive-income test is satisfied, a shareholder's portion of the corporation's net operating loss is limited to the sum of his adjusted basis of the shareholder's stock and amount of debt owed by the corporation to the shareholder.[206] Consequently, if the venture is highly leveraged the shareholder, unlike a limited partner in the case of nonrecourse financing, will be severely limited in his ability to take advantage of tax shelter losses.

This form of ownership entity may, however, be appropriate for holding unimproved land or for obtaining a tax-shelter loss while income-producing property is being constructed; in both instances there would be expenses but not gross receipts. In both cases, the participants will be protected against unlimited liability and, in jurisdictions with stringent usury laws, be in a better position to obtain mortgage financing while at the same time be able to deduct mortgage interest and other carrying charges. In the latter case, once the construction is completed, the enterprise could convert to a non-Subchapter S corporation for the continued operation of the property,[207] or if depreciation is an impor-

---

[203] I.R.C. § 1372(e)(5).

[204] See Bittker & Eustice, note 109 *supra*, at 718.

[205] Reg. § 1.1372-4(b)(5)(vi). Significant services were held not to be provided where a Subchapter S corporation operating an office building furnished maids, porters, elevator operators, a maintenance man, a secretary, and a night watchman, and leased some of its space for a barber shop, a drugstore, and a lunch counter. Bramlette Bldg. Corp. v. Comm'r, 424 F.2d 751, 754 (5th Cir. 1970). See also City Markets, Inc. v. Comm'r, 433 F.2d 1240, 1242 (6th Cir. 1970).

[206] I.R.C. § 1374(c)(2).

[207] After the construction period terminates, the corporation could operate as a taxable entity for three years, avoiding taxation by use of rapid depreciation

9. *Election by investors for tax treatment as mere co-owners*	Election in certain partnerships is available to avoid partnership tax provisions (I.R.C. § 761(a))	Not available
10. *Cancellation of syndicate indebtedness to third parties as capital gain rather than ordinary income*	Decrease in investor's share of partnership liabilities is equivalent to cash distribution (I.R.C. § 752(b)); cash distributions reduce investor's basis or, if zero, are treated as capital gain (I.R.C. §§ 731(a), 733). Case law supports capital gain treatment of reduced syndicate liabilities, as opposed to ordinary income treatment under I.R.C. § 16(a)(12)	Election is available under I.R.C. § 108 to avoid ordinary income from reduction if indebtedness, if basis reduction is made pursuant to I.R.C. § 1017	No special provisions
11. *Tax-free reorganization*	No specific Code provisions, but case law support tax-free exchange of partnership interests, of similar type, and with essentially the same kind of losses, under I.R.C. § 1031	Transfer of assets permitted under I.R.C. § 368, without recognition of gain or loss	No specific Code provision

EXHIBIT 1.1. Comparison of Different Forms of Real Estate Syndicates
(continued)

II. TAX FACTORS	Limited Partnership	Corporation	REIT
3. Operating losses	Pass-through to partners; useful as offset to investors' other income, to extent of basis in partnership interest, which may be increased by partner's share of syndicate nonrecourse liabilities; limited carryback and carryforward (I.R.C. §§ 172, 702(a)(8), 704(d))	No pass-through to shareholders unless corporation is a Subchapter S corporation under I.R.C. § 1372	No pass-through to beneficiaries; limited deduction if REIT is taxed directly (I.R.C. § 857(b)(2)(E))
4. Capital losses	Pass-through to partners; useful, to extent of basis in partnership interest as offset to capital gain and to ordinary income up to $3,000 (I.R.C. § 1211(b)(2)); carryforward (I.R.C. § 1212(b))	No pass-through to shareholders; limited carry back and carryforward (I.R.C. § 1212(a))	No pass-through to beneficiaries
5. Accumulation of taxable income	No adverse tax consequences; partners are taxed as to proportionate shares, whether or not distributed	Possible penalty tax (I.R.C. § 531)	The REIT will be taxed if income is not distributed promptly (I.R.C. § 857)
6. Liquidation	Limited tax consequences (I.R.C. §§ 708(b), 731(a)(2), 732(b))	Complex rules (I.R.C. §§ 331 et seq.)	No special provisions for REIT as such
7. Pension, profit-sharing, and other fringe benefits	Very limited as to deductible contributions	Liberal deductions allowed	Very limited
8. Sale of interest at total or partial loss	Generally, capital loss	Generally, capital loss but exception of ordinary loss for some small businesses (I.R.C. § 1244)	Generally, capital loss

	Limited Partnership	Corporation	REIT
C. Limitations on Activities or Transactions:			
1. Permissible ownership of interest in syndicate by syndicator-promoter	No limitations; promoters may be general or limited partners	No restrictions	Syndicators can own investment shares, provided the disqualifying limit of 50% ownership by five or less beneficiaries is not exceeded
2. Usury restrictions vary according to state law. See usury chart in Appendix A.			
3. Enforcement of securities regulations to sale or promotion of investment shares	While in theory, applicability is the same, less extensive than for corporate stock	Generally is rigid, subject to statutory exceptions and exclusions	While in theory, applicability is same, may be less extensive than for corporate shares, if trust is not a corporation
4. Restrictions on investments and investment income	None	None	Qualifying restrictions (I.R.C. § 856(c))
II. TAX FACTORS			
1. Taxation of syndicate income; double taxation	Income is not taxed to the syndicate; no double taxation; partners are taxed as to their distributive shares	Corporate income is taxed to the corporation; earnings and profits distributed as dividends are taxed to the shareholders, except for repayment of debts to creditor-shareholders	Income is not taxed to the REIT, provided 90% of taxable income is distributed (95% after 1979) (I.R.C. § 857(a)(1)); prompt distribution of earnings is necessary to avoid an excise tax (I.R.C. § 4981)
2. Capital gains	Retain their character in the hands of the investors (I.R.C. § 702(b))	No pass-through; dividends from earnings and profits represent ordinary income to the shareholders, even if occasioned by corporate capital gains (I.R.C. § 301)	Net capital gains if distributed retain their character in the hands of the beneficiaries (I.R.C. § 857(b)(3)(B))

EXHIBIT 1.1. Comparison of Different Forms of Real Estate Syndicates

NON-TAX FACTORS	Limited Partnership	Corporation	REIT
A. Qualification:			
1. Number of investors; extent of ownership	No requirements	No requirements	At least 100 (I.R.C. § 856(a)(5)); if five or less beneficiaries own more than 50% of the trust, directly or indirectly, the trust will not qualify as a REIT
2. Organizational form of syndicate and of investors	Generally, no requirements; possible tax complications if general partner is a corporation	No requirements	An unincorporated association will not qualify unless it would otherwise be taxable as a domestic corporation; trusts and corporations (other than banks and insurance companies) may qualify (I.R.C. § 856(a))
B. Characteristics of Syndicate:			
1. Continuity of life	Dissolution is not brought about by death or retirement or incapacity of limited partner(s)	Syndicate not affected by substitutions of shareholders	Status is not affected by substitutions of beneficiaries, but may be lost if income source tests are not met (I.R.C. §§ 856(a)-856(c))
2. Management	Centralized	Centralized	Centralized, but management rental of property is restricted (I.R.C. § 856(d))
3. Limited liability for investors	Yes	Yes	Yes
4. Liquidity of investment shares; alienability; value as collateral	Normally, not easily transferred; lower value as collateral than corporate shares	Generally liquid, totally alienable without restriction and valuable as collateral	Normally, totally alienable but not as salable as corporate shares or as valuable as collateral
5. Diversified investments	Possible, but not usual	Usually	Usually

[d] No Limitation on "Investment Interest"

The limitation on investment interest rule[198] is only applicable to noncorporate taxpayers.

[e] Corporation Survives Stock Ownership Changes

Under I.R.C. § 708(b)(1), a partnership shall be deemed terminated if, within a twelve-month period, there is a sale or exchange of 50 percent or more of the total interest in partnership capital and profits. Accordingly, if a majority interest is sold, minority partners could be subjected to adverse tax consequences over which they have no control, including the following:

(1) Since termination has the effect of closing the partnership's taxable year, more than twelve months of partnership income may be "bunched" into a single taxable year of the partner;[199]
(2) Termination will cause the continued business to be treated as a new partnership taxpayer; however, accelerated depreciation is available only for property "the original use of which commences with the taxpayer."[200]
(3) Termination will cause a constructive distribution of all partnership property taxable under I.R.C. §§ 731 and 751.

¶ 1.06 SUBCHAPTER S CORPORATION

By use of a Subchapter S[201] corporation, the co-venturers can enjoy the nontax advantages associated with corporate ownership, as well as the right to share losses and utilize other tax advantages available to partnerships. However, its use as a real estate ownership vehicle is severely limited by the requirements that the corporation not have more than one class of stock and not have more than fifteen stockholders, each of whom must be individuals,[202] and must not receive more than 20

---

[198] See discussion at ¶ 1.05[2][d].

[199] I.R.C. § 706(c). Under I.R.C. § 706(a), a partner must include in his taxable year all partnership gain or loss for any taxable year of the partnership ending with or within the taxable year of such partner.

[200] I.R.C. § 167(j)(2); Reg. § 1.167(j)-1(a)(2)(ii).

[201] A Subchapter S or small business corporation is a creature of statute and is governed by I.R.C. §§ 1372 et seq.

[202] Revenue Act § 341, amending I.R.C. § 1371(a). The law also permits a husband and wife to be counted as one shareholder regardless of how they hold their stock. Revenue Act § 342, amending I.R.C. § 1371(c).

without subjecting themselves to double taxation and the other tax disadvantages often associated with the use of the corporate form.

[a] Lower Tax Rate

Alternatively, to the extent that a corporation is capable of retaining its earnings without running afoul of the accumulated earnings and personal holding company provisions, incorporation may result in a lower current tax rate on the income generated by a real estate operation. While corporate income is now taxed at graduated rates of up to a maximum of 46 percent on taxable income in excess of $100,000,[193] individuals are taxed at progressive rates up to a maximum of 70 percent, or 50 percent in the case of "personal service[194] income." However, since in most cases corporate earnings must be disgorged in the form of dividends subject to a second layer of income tax, the aggregate double tax rate will probably be higher than the single tax rate payable by individual partners.

[b] Flexibility in Choice of Tax Year

Another tax advantage in using the corporate form is that while a corporate taxpayer is relatively free to select its taxable year,[195] a partnership may not change to, or adopt, a taxable year other than that of all its principal partners, unless it establishes a business purpose for the discrepancy.[196]

[c] Greater Fringe Benefits for Employees

As previously pointed out, certain fringe benefits available to corporate employees are not available to individual proprietors or partners.[197]

---

[193] 1976 TRA changed the corporate tax rate for 1975-1977 only, to the following: 20 percent on the first $25,000; 22 percent on the next $25,000; and 48 percent on the remainder. For tax years beginning after 1978, the normal tax, surtax, and surtax exemption system is replaced under the 1978 Revenue Act by a graduated tax rate structure which taxes the first four $25,000 increments of corporate income at rates of 17 percent, 20 percent, 30 percent, and 40 percent; and taxes the remainder (in excess of $100,000) at a flat rate of 46 percent. Revenue Act § 301, amending I.R.C. § 11.
[194] I.R.C. § 1348.
[195] I.R.C. § 441.
[196] I.R.C. § 706(b)(1).
[197] See note 36 *supra*.

such disallowed loss can, in a limited way, be carried forward against future partnership profits. Any loss disallowed under I.R.C. § 704(d) is allowed as a deduction at the end of any succeeding taxable year of the partnership, to the extent that the partner's adjusted basis for his partnership interest at the end of such year exceeds zero. In any succeeding year in which the partnership recognizes taxable income, the adjusted basis of each partner's interest in the partnership will be increased by the allocable share of such taxable income. If partnership distributions during such year do not otherwise reduce each partner's adjusted basis, the previously disallowed losses can be used to offset such taxable income. However, in order for the loss to be carried forward in this manner, it is essential for tax purposes that the partnership be continued and that the limited partner remain a partner.

[5] Tax Advantages of Incorporation

To reiterate, the individual or partnership form is preferable in most cases that involve income-producing realty because fast depreciation and other front-end losses can be passed through to the equity owners during the early years of the venture. By contrast, only straight-line depreciation can be used to shelter a shareholder's dividend income, and, except for Subchapter S corporations, losses cannot be passed through to investors. In addition, once the venture "turns the tax shelter corner" and starts making a taxable profit, the shareholders, unlike partners, must face double taxation.

However, any perfunctory choice made against corporate ownership is precarious. Frequently, for example, a rental operation is incorporated. Salaries paid to insiders, together with other projected operating expenses and a meager amount of depreciation, may be just enough to shelter operating income without generating losses. By planning an I.R.C. § 337[192] liquidation, the investors could also avoid double taxation when they sell the property and liquidate the venture. Accordingly, the investors could avoid personal liability and take advantage of corporate attributes, such as avoidance of usury restrictions,

---

[192] I.R.C. § 337(a) permits a corporation to sell its property free of taxation (except recapture of depreciation) if (1) the corporation adopts a plan of complete liquidation; (2) it distributes all of its assets (less those retained to meet liabilities) in complete liquidation within the twelve-month period beginning with the date of adopting the plan; and (3) the property sold is other than inventory or installment obligations. If these requirements are met, gain or loss will be recognized only at the shareholder level. Such gain or loss will ordinarily be capital in nature and will be measured by the difference between the fair market value of the property received and the shareholder's adjusted basis in his stock. I.R.C. § 331(a).

(b) The loan can be closed by the trustee of a land trust that can be used to hold the property for the benefit of the partnership.

(c) Regulation § 1.752-1(e) permits a limited partner to increase his basis by his share of *recourse* liabilities to the extent he is obligated to make additional contributions to the partnership; accordingly, the limited partners could agree to become liable to the partnership for additional capital contributions if a stipulated contingency should occur (e.g., in the event the partnership assets are insufficient to satisfy the mortgage indebtedness), to the extent by which future tax losses are expected to exceed the limited partner's tax basis in his partnership interest. In exchange, the limited partners would receive some *quid pro quo* from the general partners, or the general partners might agree to indemnify or reimburse the limited partners for any amount paid. This arrangement should withstand a "substance over form" attack by the Commissioner. The obligation of the limited partners would have economic reality if the general partners and partnership became insolvent. Analogously, a general partner is regarded as personally liable for the debts of the partnership for purposes of determining whether the entity lacks the corporate attribute of limited liability, and as such is more likely to be regarded for tax purposes under the Reg. § 7701 as a partnership and not a corporation.[190]

(d) Another and safer technique would be to provide for personal liability with respect to only a portion of the total indebtedness to the mortgage lender. Since Reg. § 1.752-1(e) limits nonrecourse liabilities to those situations in which no partner has any personal liability, the financing could be structured as two separate debts, one recourse for 10 percent and the other nonrecourse for 90 percent. The lender should not object if both mortgages are recorded simultaneously so that its lien priority could not be disturbed by any intervening lienors.[191]

If none of the above approaches is feasible, it should be remembered that if a limited partner's loss is disallowed under I.R.C. § 704(d),

---

tion of a limited partner to contribute capital and his obligation under an agreement to indemnify the general partner. Similarly, a distinction can be drawn between a debt in respect to which the general partner is personally liable in his individual capacity and a debt of the partnership in respect to which he is personally liable in his capacity as a general partner.

[190] Reg. § 301.7701-2(d).
[191] See McKee, Nelson & Whitmire, *Federal Taxation of Partnerships and Partners* ¶ 8.02[4] (1977).

to cover debt service and the enumerated operating expenses listed above.

Upon careful reading, such a clause is not onerous, nor is it a disguised method of achieving a recourse loan through the back door. It merely states that if there is an income stream from the property, then the partnership-borrower had better apply it to the payment of taxes, insurance, operating expenses, and the amounts due under the mortgage. If the borrower does not, it is liable to the mortgagee for the diversion of funds.

However, there is a problem with regard to this language. Traditionally, as discussed earlier, nonrecourse financing has always been a key to limited partnership syndications in that a pro rata amount of the mortgage indebtedness can be passed through to increase the basis of each limited partner's interest. However, the aforementioned Reg. § 1.752-1(e) states, "however, where none of the partners have any personal liability with respect to a partnership liability (as in the case of a mortgage on real estate acquired by the partnership without the assumption by the partnership or any of the partners of *any liability on the mortgage*), then all partners, including limited partners, shall be considered as sharing such liability under Section 752(c)...." The use of the words "of any liability on the mortgage" is disturbing. Clearly, in this situation, to the extent that there is a positive cash flow from the project, the partnership under the term of the mortgage is required and liable to account to the mortgagee for this income stream. Counsel to a limited partnership as a borrowing entity faced with this hybrid language might insist upon a private ruling to insure that, under this provision, the nonrecourse financing is not jeopardized.

If the lender will not agree to the exculpation of the general partners as discussed above, the following *untested* procedures might be considered:

(a) A related party, such as a parent corporation, could guarantee the mortgage indebtedness for the benefit of the subsidiary-general partner. A similar and less cautious technique would be for the general partners or a nominee corporation to purchase the property and assume an existing mortgage, or, in the event of new construction or refinancing, become personally liable for a new mortgage. In both cases, the property can then be conveyed to the partnership, subject to the mortgage but not assumed by the partnership.[189]

---

[189] Cf. Rev. Rul. 69-223, 1969-1 C.B. 184, wherein the Service takes a "form over substance" approach by drawing a distinction between the obliga-

the mortgage or deed of trust note. Or, if the property to be acquired is subject to an existing mortgage, the partnership could take the property "subject to the mortgage" and not "assume" the mortgage by means of an assumption agreement. In this way, the general partners will not be personally liable at local law based on privity of contract. Several years ago, lender's counsel was concerned about the fact that nonrecourse language might impair the lender's right to foreclose. Counsel added additional language whereby it was agreed under the mortgage that the nonrecourse paragraph would not in any way impair the lien of the mortgage upon the property covered thereunder. It would also not prevent the failure to make any payment of principal or interest or failure to perform all other obligations under said note and mortgage from being a default under the mortgage.

After the 1973-1974 real estate recession, even traditional lenders began to hedge on the meaning of nonrecourse financing. Specifically, some lenders viewed with growing alarm the proliferation of limited partnership or nominee, straw corporations, able to freely leave projects, or for tax reasons, to avoid depreciation recapture, fight a lender's foreclosure suit. Lenders have sought to curtail the broad nonrecourse scope in two separate areas. The first area was not only to limit personal liability merely against the partners of a partnership, but to also have recourse against any assets owned or subsequently owned by the partnership, all of which assets to be pledged to repayment of the indebtedness. The second area of curtailment has to do with the definition of "nonrecourse." Lenders in corporate boardrooms increasingly came to the decision that nonrecourse meant the lender would have no recourse against the partnership-borrower for income not generated from the project. It did not mean that a borrower would not be liable to a lender under a covenant not to commit waste contained in a mortgage, nor did it mean that a mortgagor could milk the property or divert the income stream and then, in the event of default, disappear. To guard against this practice, some lenders have added the following clarifying paragraph to the nonrecourse provision:

> Notwithstanding the foregoing limitation of liability and nonsuit, the mortgagor shall be liable for a proper accounting of all income and rents collected to the end that all monies collected in any month shall be first applied to debt service on this mortgage, taxes, insurance, operating expenses, reasonable repairs, and maintenance expenditures. The purpose of this indemnification is to prevent the mortgagor from taking monies collected in a given month and creating deficits or expenses which would otherwise have been covered out of monies collected without rendering the mortgagor liable for any deficit where such monies collected are not sufficient

The avowed rationale for the difference in result is that when recourse financing is used, the general partner is obligated to outsiders for the entire mortgage liability; a limited partner is liable only to the extent of his actual capital investment. However, given the reasoning behind the *Crane* doctrine, it is questionable whether this distinction may not make any sense. As previously noted, the *Crane* doctrine acknowledges the meaninglessness of distinguishing between a personal and nonpersonal liability mortgage. In addition, a limited partner like L in our example, might feel essentially the same economic compulsion to have the mortgage debt paid in order to keep his share of the partnership property. Moreover, he should be as entitled to depreciation benefits as an individual who acquires property subject to a nonpersonal liability mortgage.

In any event, this basis rule—which still applies to real estate partnerships—is especially important for the leveraged tax-shelter syndicate because: (1) the syndicate frequently generates depreciation losses during the early years, and (2) cash flow in excess of taxable partnership income is commonplace during the early years. Yet, since the cash investment by the limited partners is often very small relative to debt financing, the limited partner's basis may be reduced to zero, absent a liability "add-on" to basis.

[iii] Tax Planning To Avoid Basis Problem. As indicated in ¶¶ 3.03[2] and 4.02[5], nonrecourse financing on permanent mortgages, as opposed to construction mortgages, is the rule rather than the exception. It is ordinarily the income stream and not the solvency of the obligor-developer that primes the mortgage, especially when the loan amount is large. Traditionally, the permanent lender regards the improved real estate as the real security for its loan; accordingly, in most cases the lender will agree that in the event of default and foreclosure it will only seek recourse against the real estate and will not seek a deficiency judgment against the general partners. To accomplish this objective, simple nonrecourse language such as "the borrower shall not be personally liable hereunder" or "in the event of default, mortgagee will look solely to the property and not seek a deficiency judgment against the borrower,"[188] or another phrase of similar import should be inserted in

---

[188] Obviously, in a jurisdiction that does not recognize deficiency judgments this latter language is not appropriate. In a jurisdiction which follows the "one-action" rule like California, this language would suffice since the lender cannot sue upon the note or debt but must bring a foreclosure action (or sale by deed-of-trust trustee) along with an action for deficiency judgment if that be necessary. However, in other jurisdictions such "no deficiency judgment" language arguably may not suffice since, if the lender elects not to foreclose but to sue on the note, arguably personal liability still exists.

basis for purposes of the loss limitation rule of I.R.C. § 704(d), even if the property is acquired by means of nonrecourse financing.[187]

> *Example.* Returning to our tax-shelter example where *G* is a general partner and *L* is a limited partner in a partnership formed to acquire an apartment building costing $1 million, each makes a cash contribution of $100,000, and the partnership obtains a mortgage in the amount of $800,000 to fund the balance of the construction costs. Under the terms of the partnership agreement, they are to share profits equally, but *L*'s liabilities are limited to the extent of his contribution. Neither the partnership nor either of the partners assumes any liability on the mortgage.
>
> *Result.* The basis for *G*'s and *L*'s partnership interest is increased from $100,000 to $500,000, since each partner's share of the partnership liability has increased by $400,000. However, had *G* assumed personal liability by not insisting upon an exculpatory provision in the mortgage note, the basis for *G*'s interest would have increased by $800,000, and *L*'s basis would have remained at $100,000.
>
> Returning to our hypothetical example at ¶ 1.05[2][b], this failure to increase *L*'s basis could be disastrous. Since each year *L*'s basis is being reduced by his share of losses and tax-free cash flow under I.R.C. § 705, his basis would be reduced to zero by year number seven, assuming his net cash yield remains at $18,894 per annum. Consequently, he would thereafter be precluded from deducting his share of losses under I.R.C. § 704(d) and would not start realizing gain on the distribution of cash flow. If the financing had been nonrecourse, his tax basis at the end of year number seven would be a huge $389,387.

---

covered by the partnership at-risk rules are now covered by the new expanded version of the specific at-risk rules under I.R.C. § 465, the partnership at-risk rules of I.R.C. § 704(d) were repealed, effective for taxable years beginning after December 31, 1978. The Act extended the at-risk rules to all activities *other than the holding of real property* (except for mineral property). It also provided that any losses which were disallowed for a taxable year pursuant to the partnership at-risk rules of I.R.C. § 704(d) would be treated as if they had been disallowed by the specific at-risk rule of I.R.C. § 465 and, as a consequence, would be treated as a deduction in the first taxable year beginning after December 31, 1978. Revenue Act §201, amending I.R.C. §§ 465, 704 (d). See discussion of the at-risk rules at ¶ 1.05[2][d].

[187] See also discussion of at-risk activities under new I.R.C. § 465 in text at ¶ 1.05[2][d].

respect to a partnership liability—as in the case of nonrecourse financing—then all partners, including limited partners, shall be considered as sharing such liability in the same proportion as they share profits. Under the 1976 TRA and 1978 Revenue Act, this special rule still exists for limited partners in partnerships that hold real property other than mineral property.[186] However, limited partners in partnerships that engage in certain non-real estate activities may no longer increase their

---

[186] I.R.C. § 704(d), providing that a partner's distributive share of partnership loss shall be allowed only to the extent of the adjusted basis of such partner's interest in the partnership, was amended by inclusion of the following sentence, effective for partnership taxable years beginning after December 31, 1976:

For purposes of this subsection, the adjusted basis of any partner's interest in the partnership shall not include any portion of any partnership liability with respect to which the partner has no personal liability. The preceding sentence shall not apply with respect to any activity to the extent that Section 465 (relating to limited deductions to amounts of risk in case of certain activities) applies nor shall apply to any partnership the principal activity of which is investing in real property (other than mineral property). 1976 TRA, Pub. L. 94-455, § 213(e), 90 Stat. 1548.

An important aspect of this amended basis rule was that it applied to both general and limited partnerships and to both general and limited partners. Accordingly, even a general partner in a limited partnership to which this provision applied would not have been able to deduct losses against his share of nonrecourse partnership liabilities unless the "principal activity" of the partnership was "investing in real property (other than mineral property)." However, neither the Code nor the temporary regulations defined these phrases. A strict construction of the former might have required the use of separate partnerships for new real estate activities and the fragmentation of existing multi-activity partnerships. Moreover, a literal construction of the latter phrase might not have exculpated most real estate tax-shelter partnerships which own improved realty such as an apartment house or a shopping center, since such property would arguably be used in a trade or business and not simply as a passive investment for the production of income. Cf. § 1221(2) and Rothenberg, 48 T.C. 369 (1967); and compare § 162(a) with §§ 212(1), 212(2); Higgens v. Comm'r, 312 U.S. 212 (1941). Also query whether the literal language of I.R.C. § 704(d) would have applied to dealer partnerships holding raw land and other realty for sale to customers. However, this interpretational problem may have been resolved in that Congress enacted H.R. 6715, a technical amendment of I.R.C. § 704(d), which provided that a partnership could qualify for the exception to the amended basis rule if substantially all of its activities related to the holding of real property (other than mineral property) for sale or rental, and made it clear that active as well as passive rental operations were excepted. However, a few less serious ambiguities would still have remained unresolved. See Madison, "New Developments in the Taxation of Real Estate Partnerships," 12 Real Prop., Prob. & Tr. J. 728-740 (Winter 1977).

However, under the 1978 Revenue Act, since all the activities previously

equity capital; and (3) creditors making nonrecourse loans not to receive as the result of making the loan any interest "other than as a secured creditor." This last requirement may well affect institutional lenders, who, when mortgage money is tight, often demand a joint venture position. Moreover, if the phrase "other than as a secured creditor" is read too cursorily by the Service, other kinds of "equity kickers"—such as a percentage of the borrower's gross or net income—may be in jeopardy as well. Also, Rev. Proc. 75-16[180] sets forth a checklist of required information that must be submitted with requests for rulings.[181]

[b] Tax Shelter Basis Problem Caused by Recourse Financing

[i] **General Rule.** In both general and limited partnerships, a partner is not permitted to deduct his share of partnership losses to the extent that it exceeds the basis in the partnership interest.[182] In addition, any "cash flow" sheltered from partnership taxation is treated in the hands of a distributee partner as a return of his capital, and as such, reduces his adjusted basis in the partnership interest.[183] Ordinarily, these rules will not adversely affect a general partner in a leveraged partnership; his adjusted basis not only includes the amount of cash and adjusted basis of property contributed, but also includes his share of partnership liabilities under I.R.C. § 752.

This occurs because of the so-called *Crane* doctrine first enunciated in *Crane v. Comm'r*,[184] which provides that when property is acquired for cash and a mortgage, the cost tax basis of the property includes the mortgage indebtedness whether or not the purchaser is personally liable under the mortgage.[185] Under I.R.C. § 752 the position of a general partner under the *Crane* doctrine is identical to that of someone who individually purchases an undivided interest in the property.

[ii] **Special Basis Rule for Limited Partner.** Under Reg. § 1.752-1(e), a limited partner's share of partnership recourse liabilities for the purpose of increasing his adjusted basis shall not exceed the amount of future capital contributions that he is obligated to make. However, where none of the partners has any personal liability with

---

[180] 1975-1 C.B. 676.

[181] For a more detailed discussion of the "association" question, see Madison, *22nd Annual Tax Conference,* Marshall-Wythe School of Law, College of William & Mary 19-27 (1977).

[182] I.R.C. § 704(d).

[183] I.R.C. §§ 705(a)(2), 733.

[184] 331 U.S. 1 (1947). See also discussion of *Crane* doctrine at ¶ 12.01[3].

[185] See discussion of *Crane* doctrine at ¶ 12.01[3].

sell or right-of-first-refusal provision, such attribute is accorded less weight than full free transferability in any determination of classification. However, in most cases a buy-sell agreement will only restrict the alienability of a general partner's interest, and in a partnership where the limited partners own substantially all the profits and capital, such restriction on the general partner's interest would probably be disregarded.

Ruling Policy. Notwithstanding the detailed definitional description of the various corporate attributes, total reliance thereon for ruling purposes would be misplaced; the regulations state that other factors may be relevant in arriving at any classification determination and that such determination will depend upon the particular circumstances of each case.[177] Moreover, if a tax ruling is not obtained, a legal opinion as to partnership status is required by federal and/or state regulatory authorities, and such ruling will aid the sponsors in marketing investment shares.

In Rev. Proc. 72-13,[178] the Service indicates that it will issue a classification ruling with respect to a limited partnership having a corporation as its sole general partner only if: (1) the limited partners do not own more than 20 percent of the general partner's stock; and (2) the corporate general partner has a net worth of at least 15 percent of total contributions to the partnership, or $250,000—whichever is less, or, where contributions are $2,500,000 or more, at least 10 percent of total contributions. The rationale for the stricter standard involving a partnership with a corporate general partner is presumably to deny favorable partnership tax treatment for an organization whose individual members, like stockholders, would be shielded from outside liability to creditors.[178a]

Additionally, Rev. Proc. 74-17[179] requires: (1) general partners in *all* limited partnerships to have in the aggregate at least a one percent interest in each material item of income, deduction, etc. (computed by ignoring limited partnership interests owned by general partners); (2) the total losses to be claimed in the first two years not to exceed the invested

---

[177] Reg. § 301.7701-2(a)(1). However, the Tax Court in *Larson* indicated by way of dictum that such other characteristics (e.g., whether partnership interests are promoted and marketed in a manner similar to corporate securities; whether limited partners are required personally to sign the partnership certificates) will not be given controlling weight unless their materiality is unmistakeable. 66 T.C. at 185.

[178] 1972-1 C.B. 735

[178a] See note 168a *supra*.

[179] 1974-1 C.B. 438.

depreciation, operating, and other losses to which the basis limitation applies.

Free Transferability of Interests. The regulations provide that free transferability in the corporate sense exists "if each of its [the organization's] members owning substantially all of the interests in the organization have the power, without the consent of other members, to substitute for themselves in the same organization a person who is not a member of the organization." Moreover, for this power of substitution to exist, "the member must be able, without the consent of other members, to confer upon his substitute *all* of the attributes of his interest in the organization."[173] Under U.L.P.A. § 19 an assignee does not become a "substituted limited partner" entitled to demand an accounting and/or inspection of partnership books unless all the remaining partners consent, or unless the assignor is so empowered by the certificate to convey this right.

Draftsmanship suggestions: Based on the foregoing, if the limited partners own a substantial share of partnership profits and capital, the partnership agreement should provide that any assignee cannot become a full limited partner unless all or a specified percentage of the general partners and/or limited partners agree. However, caution should be taken that the consent clause does not state that "such consent may not unreasonably be withheld." Such was the case in the *Larson* decision. The court held that such an atypical circumscription of consent would be based on a standard of reasonableness and would not abolish free transferability of interests.[174] The automatic right to become a substituted limited partner should certainly not be specified in the certificate filed with the local authorities. Conversely, if the general partners own the substantial interests, the agreement should provide that in the event a general partner retires or withdraws from the partnership, the remaining general partners, or perhaps a majority thereof, must consent to any substitution in the event the partnership is not dissolved as a consequence of such substitution.[175]

Finally, the regulations recognize that a "modified" form of free transferability exists if each member can transfer his entire interest only after he has first offered such interest to the other members at its fair market value.[176] If such modified transferability exists, based on a buy-

---

[173] Reg. § 301.7701-2(e)(1)(emphasis added).

[174] 66 T.C. at 183.

[175] Reg. § 301.7701-2(e)(1) provides that free transferability is not present if, under local law, a transfer of a member's interest results in the dissolution of the old organization and the formation of a new one.

[176] Reg. § 301.7701-2(e)(2).

a "mutual agency" theory. Accordingly, this corporate attribute would appear to be present in a limited partnership if the general partner has no substantial assets even if not a mere "dummy." However, the *Larson* court, siding with the taxpayer, construed this language literally and held that limited liability did not exist because the general partner had not been a dummy of the limited partners, even though it did not own substantial assets during the years in issue.[169]

While the regulations do not define "substantial assets," they state that the test is met even if the assets of such general partner are insubstantial relative to the total undertaking of the partnership.[170] Moreover, an indemnity agreement whereby the limited partners agree to reimburse the general partner for payments made to outsiders will not negate personal liability so long as the general partner remains liable at local law to outside creditors, notwithstanding such agreement.[171] Accordingly, it is appropriate for the tax adviser representing a general partner not to object to language in the partnership agreement under which the limited partners agree to reimburse the general partner for amounts paid over and above his proportionate ratio for sharing partnership losses and liabilities.

Finally, if the partnership is forced to use nonrecourse financing in order to assure the limited partners of an increased tax basis in their partnership interest, a basis needed to absorb their distributive share of basis-reducing tax-free distributions of cash or losses, this should not automatically impose the corporate attribute of limited liability on the partnership; the general partner still remains personally liable for the tort and other contract obligations of the partnership.[172] The problem might be more acute if the partnership owned unimproved land, since potential tort and contract liability other than mortgage debt is arguably marginal. However, the need for increasing the tax bases of the limited partners is less, since non-income-producing property does not generate

---

noted by the court: "Otherwise the statutory requirement of at least one general partner with general liability [U.L.P.A. § 1] in a limited partnership can be circumvented or vitiated by limited partners operating the partnership through a corporation with minimum capitalization and therefore minimum liability." 526 S.W.2d at 546. But see Western Camps v. Riverway Ranch Enterprises, 70 Cal. App. 3d 714, 138 Cal. Rptr. 918 (1977); Frigidaire Sales Corp. v. Union Properties, Inc. 88 Wash. 2d 400, 562 P.2d 244 (1977).

[169] 66 T.C. at 181.
[170] Reg. § 301.7701-2(d)(2).
[171] Reg. § 301.7701-2(d)(1).
[172] See discussion at ¶ 1.05[4][b].

more than 60 percent, or must they own less than 40 percent to render their interest insubstantial? Unfortunately, the only example in the regulations suggests the obvious: 94 percent of the ownership is substantial.[163] On this point, perhaps one must of necessity be guided by the informal past experience of tax practitioners, apparently that the Internal Revenue Service will conclude that limited partners do *not* own substantially all of the interests if the general partners own a 20 percent or greater interest in partnership capital or profits.[164] In a Court of Claims case, *Zuckman v. United States*,[165] the court concluded that centralized management did not exist since the general partner owned a 62 percent interest in the partnership. Finally, if, as is often the case, the general partners are to receive an extra share of capital or profits once the limited partners recoup their capital outlay, the tax adviser should be alerted to the fact that the 20 to 40 percent requirement could inadvertently be met by the general partners.

Limited Liability. In contrast to centralized management, limited liability would appear to be the corporate characteristic easiest to avoid; by definition, the general partners are personally liable to outsiders.[166] Under the regulations, an organization does not possess limited liability so long as *any* member is personally liable for the debts of, or claims against, the organization.[167] However, in the case of a limited partnership the regulations further provide that limited liability does exist "with respect to a general partner when he has no substantial assets other than his interest in the partnership, which could be reached by a creditor of the organization *and* when he is merely a "dummy" acting as the agent of the limited partners."[168] Taken literally, this sentence appears to be meaningless since, if the general partner were merely an agent controlled by the limited partners, the organization would probably be treated at local law as a general partnership, and not as a limited partnership,[168a] thus exposing all the partners to personal liability under

---

[163] Reg. § 301.7701-3(b)(2), Ex. (1).

[164] E.g., Willis, *Partnership Taxation* ¶ 57.06 (2d ed. 1976); "Points to Remember No. 5," 25 Tax Law. 179 (1971).

[165] 524 F.2d 729 (Ct. Cl. 1975).

[166] U.L.P.A. §§ 1, 9.

[167] Reg. § 301.7701-2(d)(1).

[168] Reg. § 301.7701-2(d)(2)(emphasis added).

[168a] *See* U.L.P.A. § 7, which provides that a limited partner shall not become liable as a general partner unless he takes part in control of the business. In Delancey v. Fidelity Lease Ltd., 526 S.W.2d 543 (Tex. 1975) the limited partners, who were officers of the corporate general partner, were held liable for breach of partnership lease agreement on grounds that they had participated in the control of the business both in their individual and corporate capacities. As

Centralization of Management. Of all the disqualifying corporate attributes, this would appear to be the most difficult to avoid. By definition, the general partners must have the "exclusive authority" to make management decisions on behalf of the limited partners.[158] Otherwise, the limited partners who choose to partake in management decision-making would be exposed to outside contract and tort liability.[159] However, in addition to the "exclusive authority" definition of centralized management, the regulations also curiously state that while a limited partnership subject to the ULPA generally does *not* have centralized management, "centralized management ordinarily does exist in such limited partnership if *substantially all* the interests in the partnership are owned by the limited partners."[160] Obviously, in most limited partnerships, particularly public ones, the limited partners do own a substantial portion of the capital and/or profit share, since use of the limited partnership is ordinarily designed toward raising a maximum (not minimum) amount of venture capital from outside investors who then become the limited partners. This sentence in the regulations is apparently an attempt to correlate the present regulations with the regulations under the 1939 Revenue Code[161] as well as prior case law, notably *Glendser Textile Co.*,[162] which defined centralized management as management in a representative capacity.

However, what does the term "substantial" mean? Is centralized management avoided only if a substantial share is owned by the general partners, or is it sufficient for the general partners to own so much that the balance owned by the limited partners is "insubstantial"? For example, if, as is suggested in *Glendser Textile,* five-twelfths, or approximately 40 percent, is substantial, must the limited partners own no

---

[158] Reg. § 301.7701-2(c) defines centralized management as the "concentration of continuing exclusive authority to make independent business decisions on behalf of the organization that do not require ratification by members of such organization."

[159] U.L.P.A. § 7.

[160] Reg. § 301.7701-2(c)(4)(emphasis added).

[161] Reg. § 39.3797-4.

[162] 46 B.T.A. 176, 183 (1942), *acq.* In *Glendser Textile*, the Board of Tax Appeals held that general partners collectively owning a 5/12 interest in the partnership were not analagous to corporate directors and did not manage in a representative capacity, since by owning such a sizeable interest they presumably were acting mainly for their own benefit and not as representatives of the limited partners. Accordingly, by negative inference the regulations suggest that this corporate attribute may be avoided if the limited partners do not own a "substantial" share of profits and/or capital. This view is confirmed by dictum in the *Larson* case. 66 T.C. at 177.

whether a dissolution, in its technical sense, occurs. Is the organization as *originally* constituted replaced with an organization having a different, albeit slightly so, constituency if any of the specified contingencies should occur? This view was confirmed by the Tax Court in the case of *Philip G. Larson*,[154] which is on appeal before the Ninth Circuit.

Draftsmanship suggestions: Curiously, the regulations set forth a less-than-full dissolution test in respect to limited partnerships: "If the retirement, death, or insanity of a general partner of a limited partnership causes a dissolution of the partnership, *unless the remaining general partners agree to continue the partnership or unless all remaining members agree to continue the partnership*, continuity of life does not exist."[155] By contrast, U.L.P.A. § 20 states that a dissolution takes place "unless the business is continued by the remaining general partners (a) under a right to do so stated in the certificate, or (b) with the consent of all members." Consequently, the partnership agreement could contain language permitting the limited partnership to forgo dissolution if a majority of general partners agree.[156] A fortiori, the more constraining and less desirable alternative of having all partners agree to a continuation, should eliminate continuity of life, and the regulations so suggest.[157] Finally, the last alternative, automatic continuation by virtue of a right to do so stated in the certificate, is probably the least desirable, since the regulations do not expressly exculpate this least flexible of alternatives.

---

[154] 66 T.C. 159 (1976), *acq.* 1979-1 C.B. 1. (a reviewed decision with six dissents after withdrawal of November 1975 opinion in favor of the government). In that benchmark decision, a California limited partnership agreement provided that the partnership would be dissolved on the bankruptcy of the general corporate partner. The court held that even though such bankruptcy would probably not terminate the partnership since a general partner could be replaced by a bare majority of the limited partners, continuity of life did not exist because a technical dissolution would occur. *Id.* at 175.

[155] Reg. § 301.7701-2(b)(1)(emphasis added).

[156] Observe that the quoted "unless..." clause modifies the phrase "causes a dissolution..." and not the phrase "continuity of life does not exist." In addition, by negative inference, a majority would appear sufficient since "all" modifies "members" but not the phrase "general partners" in Reg. § 301.7701-2(b)(1).

[157] The regulations state that a limited partnership subject to the ULPA lacks continuity of life presumably because U.L.P.A. § 20 requires the consent of all members to continue absent an agreement to the contrary. Reg. § 301.7701-2(b)(3). See Ltr. Rul., Feb. 12, 1954 ¶ 76,585 P-H Fed. 1954.

partnership as an "association" taxable as a corporation under Reg. §§ 301.7701-2 through 301.7701-4. If a tax-shelter enterprise is so characterized, partners in a limited partnership then lose the loss pass-through advantage and are subjected to double taxation and all the other tax disadvantages associated with using the corporate form of ownership. To return to our tax-shelter example,[149] the $23,643 loss in the first year could not be passed through to L and G; in addition, only $16,430 of the cash outflow to these constructive shareholders would be sheltered from ordinary income treatment. Under the regulations, if the organization bears a closer resemblance to a corporation, it will be treated as such for tax purposes, notwithstanding its local law denomination as a partnership.[150] The regulations delineate six basic corporate characteristics: (1) having associates; (2) the objective to carry on a business and divide the gains therefrom; (3) the continuity of life; (4) the centralization of management; (5) limited liability; and (6) free transferability of interests.

Since the first two characteristics are common to both corporate and partnership organizations, an unincorporated organization will be taxed as a corporation only if it possesses more than two of the remaining four corporate attributes.[151]

Continuity of Life. An organization has continuity of life if the death, insanity, bankruptcy, retirement, or expulsion of any member will not cause a dissolution of the organization. The converse is also true; if "any member has the power under local law to dissolve the organization, the organization lacks continuity of life."[152] Of most significance is the way in which the regulations define "dissolution": "an alteration of the identity of an organization by reason of a change in the relationship between its members as determined under local law."[153] Thus, the regulations seem to apply a "form over substance" approach; namely, that continuity of life does not necessarily depend upon whether the organization continues. What is determinative is

---

responsibility to an executive committee. However, since each partner may nonetheless bind the other if he acts within the scope of his authority, such delegation probably does not constitute "centralized management", and the regulations so suggest. Reg. § 301.7701-2(c)(4). Accordingly, this pitfall is mainly associated with using the limited but not general partnership as the ownership vehicle.

[149] See ¶ 1.05[2][b].
[150] Reg. § 301.7701-1(c).
[151] Reg. § 301.7701-2(a)(2).
[152] Reg. § 301.7701-2(b).
[153] Reg. § 301.7701-2(b)(2).

accordingly, an ordinary rather than a capital loss.[143] However, if at the time of abandonment or forfeiture a partner's tax basis in his interest includes his share of partnership liabilities, his withdrawal will cause him to receive a construction distribution of cash equal to the decrease in his share of liabilities,[144] which, under the regular liquidation rules, will be treated as capital gain or loss from the sale or exchange of his partnership interest.[145] On the other hand, corporate stock that becomes worthless produces only a capital loss, except where stock in an affiliated corporation[146] or "Section 1244 stock" is involved.[147]

[4] Tax Pitfalls of Limited Partnership

To take advantage of losses that can be used to shelter a limited partner's outside ordinary income, such as salaries and dividends, the planner *must* take precautionary measures to ensure: (1) tax treatment of the entity as a partnership and not as an "association" taxable as a corporation, and (2) a maximum amount of adjusted basis for each limited partner's interest in the partnership, inasmuch as this amount is the ceiling for taking his share of partnership losses.

[a] Possible Taxation as an Association

The first tax pitfall to be overcome in order to utilize the limited partnership[148] form effectively, is to avoid characterization of the

---

[143] See Gaius G. Gannon, 16 T.C. 1134, 1139 (1951), *acq.* 1951-2 C.B. 2; Palmer Hutcheson, 17 T.C. 14, 20 (1951), *acq.* 1951-2 C.B. 2. Cf. Edward F. Neubecker, 65 T.C. 577, 586 (1975), where the partnership agreement contained no forfeiture provision and the taxpayer received property other than cash, unrealized receivables, or inventory upon dissolution of the partnership. This prompted the Tax Court to hold that the taxpayer did not secure any recognizable loss under I.R.C. § 731(a)(2).

[144] See I.R.C. § 752(b).

[145] See I.R.C. §§ 731(a), 741. See Andrew O. Stilwell, 46 T.C. 247 (1966); and Edward Pietz, 59 T.C. 207 (1972), where liabilities of the withdrawing partner were either paid off or assumed.

[146] I.R.C. § 165(g)(3).

[147] In general, losses from the sale or exchange of I.R.C. § 1244 stock issued by small business corporations are treated as ordinary rather than capital losses, thus partially avoiding the I.R.C. § 1211 limitations on capital losses. The 1978 Revenue Act increased the ordinary loss limitation from $25,000 to $50,000 and amended several aspects of I.R.C. § 1244 to permit more taxpayers to take advantage of the special loss treatment. Revenue Act § 345, amending I.R.C. § 1244.

[148] Normally, a general partnership possesses none of these four attributes except that sometimes a large partnership will delegate broad administrative

[ii] Flexibility in Determining Compensation Income. Another related advantage is that while a partnership is relatively free to determine the amount of its deductible guaranteed payments to a service partner, excessive salaries paid by a corporation to shareholders or their relatives could be treated as a nondeductible constructive dividend.[138]

[iii] No Penalty Tax Problem. Since under the "conduit theory," partners are taxed on the undistributed as well as the distributed earnings of the partnership, a partnership is subject neither to the personal holding company tax[139] nor accumulated earnings tax.[140]

[iv] Section 1237 Subdivision Rule. This Code section, which applies only to noncorporate taxpayers, sets forth straightforward rules which, if complied with, save the seller of subdivided real property from being presumptively treated as a dealer whose gains would otherwise be taxed at ordinary income rates rather than capital gain rates. To qualify, an individual or partnership must hold the subdivided property for at least five years and make no "substantial" improvements other than such "necessary" improvements as roads or sewage facilities. By contrast, similarly situated corporate taxpayers must deal with the imbroglio of case law that interprets the various "holding for sale" provisions of the Code.[141]

[v] Ordinary Loss Deduction Upon Worthlessness of Partnership Interest. Generally, the gain or loss on the sale of a partnership interest in a noncollapsible partnership, is treated as arising from the sale or exchange of a capital asset.[142] Consequently, if a partner sells his partnership interest at a loss, he will receive capital loss treatment. However, there is case law holding that if a partner abandons his partnership interest, or if it is forfeited pursuant to a partnership agreement, the loss does not arise from a sale or exchange and is,

---

[138] See generally Bittker & Eustice, note 109 *supra*, ¶ 7.05, at 7-39. While it is true that guaranteed payments by a partnership are likewise subject to the standard of reasonableness imposed by I.R.C. § 162(a), any excessive payment treated as a constructive distribution of profits to a payee partner would presumably reduce the other partner's distributive shares of partnership income. See note 134 *supra*.

[139] I.R.C. §§ 541 et seq.

[140] I.R.C. §§ 531 et seq.

[141] E.g., I.R.C. §§ 1221(1), 1231(b)(1), 337(b)(1). See discussion at ¶ 9.05[1].

[142] I.R.C. § 741.

prior to the due date, without extension, of the tax return for the year in question. For example, the partnership agreement could be amended to permit a retroactive allocation of depreciation or gain or loss on contributed property. However, in prior years, tax-shelter limited partnerships, relying upon a literal interpretation of the Code and the *Norman Rodman*[132] decision, have been allocating a full share of the partnership losses for the entire year to those limited partners joining in for tax purposes at the close of the year. In 1976, the *Rodman* decision was reversed by the Second Circuit, and, in addition, the 1976 TRA provides that income, loss, and special items can be allocated to a partner only insofar as the allocation reflects the period of time that he has been a partner.[133]

[c] Miscellaneous Tax Advantages of Partnerships

[i] Opportunity to Reduce Compensation Income of Partner Who Contributes Services and Not Property to the Partnership. A guaranteed payment made to a service partner as compensation for services rendered is deductible by the partnership if it qualifies as an ordinary and necessary business expense deduction under I.R.C. § 162(a).[134] Since the partnership business expense deduction is allocable in part to the service partner, his taxable compensation income will accordingly be offset by his pro rata share of the deduction.[135] Moreover, some authorities suggest that the service partner's compensation income could be totally eliminated by allocating the entire deduction to him, provided that the entire cost of his services is charged solely to his capital account.[136] By contrast, payments made to shareholders for services rendered to the corporation are fully taxable as ordinary compensation income to the recipient.[137]

---

[132] Rodman v. Comm'r, T.C. Memo. 1973-277 (1973), *rev'd in part* 542 F.2d 845 (2d Cir. 1976). See also Rev. Rul. 77-119, 1977-1 C.B. 761.

[133] 1976 TRA, Pub. L. 94-455, § 213(c)(1), 90 Stat. 1547-48, amending I.R.C. § 706(c)(2)(B).

[134] See 1976 TRA, Pub. L. 94-455, § 213(b), 90 Stat. 1547, amending I.R.C. § 707(c); Reg. § 1.707-1(c).

[135] In all the examples in Reg. § 1.707-1(c), the recipient of the guaranteed payment receives his pro rata share of the partnership deduction.

[136] E.g., Cowan, "Receipt of a Partnership Interest for Services," 32 N.Y.U. Inst. on Fed. Tax., Pt. II, 1521-1522 (1974). See discussion of special allocations at ¶ 1.05[3][b].

[137] See the *comment* to Section 3.2 of Form 1.1 in Appendix B for tax planning suggestions on how to structure payments made to a service partner as compensation for his promotorial and managerial services rendered to the partnership.

service partners' capital contributions, but instead favor allocating an extra share of the residual net assets of the partnership once the partnership is liquidated and the debt claims and capital account claims of the investor partners have been satisfied. Again, such arrangements would have an economic reality independent of their tax consequences.

[ii] Allocation of Depreciation or Gain or Loss on Contributed Property. A related consideration arises when one partner contributes property to the partnership with a carryover basis[129] less or greater than its fair market value. In the absence of a special agreement to the contrary, gain or loss or depreciation, with respect to contributed property, is allocated to partners in the same manner as if such property had been purchased by the partnership.[130] In response to the inequity created by any such general allocation, I.R.C. § 704(c)(2) permits the partners to allocate depreciation or gain or loss, with respect to contributed property, "so as to take account of the variation between the bases of the property to the partnership and its fair market value at the time of contribution."

Example. Suppose in an equal AB partnership A contributes $35,000, and B contributes depreciable realty with a basis of $25,000 and worth $35,000 in lieu of cash. If the partnership sells the property for $37,000, there is an *economic* gain to the partnership of $2,000, one half allocable to A and one half to B. However, since the partnership receives a carryover basis of $25,000, the $10,000 balance of the *taxable* gain is charged in equal amounts to A and B. Thus B will derive a tax benefit at the expense of A, since A will be taxed on $6,000 of gain even though A realized an economic gain of only $1,000. However, by special agreement, the tax consequences of the pre-contribution appreciation can be allocated to B, so that A would report only $1,000 of taxable gain, while B would be charged with the remaining $11,000. Similarly, a special allocation of depreciation can be arranged so that A's and B's tax and economic consequences coincide.[131]

[iii] Retroactive Amendment of Partnership Agreement. The flexibility and tax-planning significance of the partnership allocation provisions are further enhanced by I.R.C. § 761(c), which permits the partners to retroactively amend the partnership agreement at any time

---

[129] Under I.R.C. § 723, the partnership receives the contributing partner's basis with respect to contributed property.
[130] I.R.C. § 704(c)(1).
[131] Reg. § 1.704-1(c)(2) Ex.(1).

partnership income is allocated to *A* with the understanding that a comparable amount of income will be restored to *B* or loss charged to *A* in subsequent tax years. This will redress any imbalance in their income shares, and capital accounts, caused by the allocation. This issue was confronted by the Tax Court in *Jean V. Kresser*[125]; the taxpayer lost, since he failed to prove that there was a modification of the oral partnership consented to by all the partners. However, based on dictum in the case,[126] some planners have argued that I.R.C. § 704(b), when read literally, could be the basis for undermining a special allocation of constituent income or loss items, but not the basis for challenging an allocation of bottom-line profits or losses. However, the 1976 TRA amendment of I.R.C. § 704(b) clearly suggests that the reverse is now true.[127]

Nevertheless, certain allocations encountered most frequently in limited partnerships are still considered safe by the experts. They include a special allocation to the investor partners, who provide all of the capital: (1) all the start-up losses generated by such *front-end* items as interest, taxes, sales tax, construction loan points, or standby fees, and (2) early depreciation losses, frequently accompanied by a provision that once the partnership "turns the corner" they shall receive all bottom-line profits until they have recouped the losses previously charged to them. This is a customary business arrangement, even absent a tax motivation.[128]

Alternatively, the limited investor partners might receive all the profits and cash flow until they recoup their capital contributions. At that time, the general service partners would be permitted to share in the profits, cash flow, and losses of the partnership. Some planners prefer not to allocate any share of these items that is disproportionate to the

---

[125] 54 T.C. 1621, 1632 (1970).

[126] The Tax Court commented: "We are faced with the petitioner's troublesome argument that Sec. 704(b)(2) applies only to 'items' of income, etc., dealt with in pars. (1) through (8) of Sec. 702(a) and does not govern par. (9) relating to the composite of all the partnership's income (sometimes referred to as its 'ordinary income') which is here involved. . . ." *Id.* at 1631 n.5.

[127] I.R.C. § 704(b)(2), as amended by 1976 TRA, now expressly refers to a "share" of income or loss, as well as an "item" thereof, thereby precluding the argument raised by the taxpayer in the *Kresser* case.

[128] See Town & Country Plymouth Inc. v. United States, 20 A.F.T.R.2d 5823 (D.C. Cal. 1967), which supports such allocations of front-end losses to investors supplying all of the capital. See 1 Willis, *Partnership Taxation* 320 (2d ed. 1976); remarks by Richard Leder, note 123 *supra*, at 1552. For a general discussion on how to compensate general partners for their promotorial and managerial services, see the *comment* to Section 3.2 of Form 1.1 in Appendix B.

$500,000, and *A* only $300,000. As a result, *A* would sustain the full economic loss associated with taking the extra $100,000 of depreciation.

While it is true that *A* would only suffer economic harm on the loss but not on the gain side, the possibility of either contingency occurring reflects economic reality. Indeed, the regulations only require that the special allocation "may actually affect the dollar amount of the partners' shares."[122] Also, while *A*'s economic loss may not equal his tax loss if the building sells for more than $800,000, the regulations again do not require a coincidence of *A*'s tax and economic consequences. Consequently, some commentators[123] feel that such allocations should prevail, especially in view of the new language in I.R.C. § 704(b).[124]

wa However, to the chagrin of tax planners, *Stanley C. Orrisch* was so vague in its facts that the decision by the Tax Court obfuscates the issue. In that case, there was no written partnership agreement, and the court had doubts about what the parties intended. Accordingly, under the hypothetical facts stated above, the court struck down the special allocation in favor of *A*, since *A* failed to prove that he would have been required to pay, in liquidation, the amount of any deficit in his capital account. *A* could also not prove that he would have received a proportionately smaller share of partnership assets (by reason of the depreciation deductions) had the gain on sale of the partnership property been less than the specially allocated depreciation deductions.

Allocation of "Bottom-Line" Profit or Loss. Suppose that in an equal *AB* partnership *A* has a sizable net operating loss carryover due to expire by the end of his current tax year. In response, *A* and *B* agree to amend the partnership agreement; as a result, all of the current year's

---

[122] Reg. § 1.704(b)(2); S. Rep. No. 938, 94th Cong., 2d Sess. 100 (1976).

[123] E.g., remarks by Richard Leder, reported in 32 N.Y.U. Inst. on Fed. Tax., Pt. II, 1554 (1974). But see McKee, "Partnership Allocations in Real Estate Ventures: Crane, Kresser and Orrisch," 30 Tax L. Rev. 20 (1974).

[124] Under prior law, I.R.C. § 704(b) provided that a special allocation will prevail unless the "principal purpose...is the avoidance or evasion of any tax." However, 1976 TRA § 213(d), which amended I.R.C. § 704(b), expressly acknowledges the test to be whether the allocation has "substantial economic effect." See I.R.C. § 704(b)(2). While the Senate Committee report states that other factors set forth under the present regulations (Reg. § 1.704-1(b)(2))— such as the overall tax consequences of the allocation—might be relevant, the change in I.R.C. § 704(b) infers that the predominant consideration is one of economic viability and not tax avoidance. See S. Rep. No. 938, 94th Cong., 2d Sess. 100 (1976).

that for ten years the entire amount of straight-line depreciation ($200,000) has been allocated to *A,* who is in a higher tax bracket than *B.* Each year the partnership's net cash flow and net taxable income, exclusive of depreciation, has been fully distributed in equal amounts to both partners. Accordingly, by the end of the tenth year *B's* capital account would remain the same at $500,000, and *A's* account would have $300,000 (capital contribution less depreciation taken). Suppose that in the eleventh year the partners decide to sell the building and liquidate the partnership. What results?

Results. Let us assume *A* insists that in any business reckoning he be treated the same as *B.* So, for example, if the building were sold without tax gain for its adjusted basis, $800,000, *A* and *B* would each receive $400,000 at liquidation, notwithstanding the disparity in their capital accounts. Once this happens, the special allocation of extra depreciation to *A* loses economic reality, since it would have no bearing on the number of dollars that *A* and *B* receive. By contrast, if the capital account balances were scrupulously respected, so that at liquidation *A* receives only $300,000 and *B* receives $500,000, the allocation should be recognized as having substantial economic effect. However, if *A* were in a 50 percent bracket, he would be foolish to give up $100,000 of proceeds in exchange for extra depreciation of $100,000, worth at most $50,000 to him.

Suppose, instead, that *A* and *B* agree that any gain on the sale of the partnership property would first be charged back to *A's* account to the extent of the depreciation allocated to him; the gain or sales proceeds would be shared equally. (This is essentially what happened in the *Stanley C. Orrisch* case.) Thus, if the building were sold at a price equal to or greater than its original cost, for example, at a selling price of $1,100,000, $200,000 of the $300,000 gain would be charged back to *A*, and the balance of the gain, $100,000, would be split evenly so that *A* and *B* would end up with equal capital accounts, or $550,000 each. Consequently, the $1,100,000 sales proceeds would be divided equally. The only impact of the allocation would be to permit *A*, in a higher bracket, to trade ordinary income (extra depreciation deductions) for extra capital gain.

However, the crucial point is that if the building were sold for its adjusted basis, $800,000, or less, and the sale or liquidation proceeds were allocated according to their capital accounts, *B* would get

capital accounts will differ in dollar amount. On the other hand, if the agreement provides that A and B's distributive shares of partnership income shall be the first $10,000 of interest and dividend income, respectively, with the balances to be divided equally, the allocation will fail, since it's principal purpose is to allocate tax-exempt interest to A, the higher-bracket partner, and is accordingly but a tax avoidance fiction devoid of any economic reality.

Accordingly, if in a real estate partnership there is an allocation of "bottom-line" profits or losses disproportionate to capital contributions, or the ratio for sharing profits and losses varies from year to year, or certain constituent items such as capital gains are all allocated to one class of partners, these arrangements will be recognized if they reflect business and economic reality. Specifically, in most instances this means that the special allocation must be reflected in the capital accounts of the partners prior to and at liquidation, that cash flow is apportioned in the same manner as taxable income or loss, and that in later years there are no subsequent adjustments to offset the effects of the allocation.[120]

Special Allocation of Depreciation. Since tax shelter depends so thoroughly on depreciation deductions, the potential of a special allocation of extra depreciation to a high-bracket partner represents a distinct advantage in using the partnership mode of ownership. However, the following example, based on a decision by the Tax Court, *Stanley C. Orrisch*,[121] is instructive about what precautions must be taken to avoid the potential entanglements inherent in any such allocation plan.

> *Facts.* Assume that A and B each contribute $500,000 to the equal AB partnership. This partnership uses the $1 million to construct an office building with a fifty-year useful life and zero salvage value, on land leased to the partnership. Further assume

---

[120] For example, in the case of Leon A. Harris, 61 T.C. 770 (1974), the Tax Court sustained the special allocation to a partner of a loss incurred upon the sale of an interest in a shopping center, when the entire sales proceeds were distributed to that partner and his capital account was charged with the entire loss on the sale. See also Sellers v. Comm'r, 36 T.C.M. 305 (1977), wherein the partner in a Virginia limited partnership agreed orally to allocate all partnership losses to the limited partners and the special allocation was disallowed since there was no showing that the partners, in fact, intended that the limited partners bear the economic burden of the specially allocated losses; Smith v. Comm'r, 331 F.2d 298 (7th Cir. 1964); Town & Country Plymouth, Inc. v. United States, 67-2 U.S.T.C. ¶ 9680 (C.D. Cal. 1967).

[121] 55 T.C. 395 (1970), *aff'd per curiam* 31 AFTR 2d 73, 1069 (9th Cir. 1973).

ment. For example, a consenting corporation would not be able to receive nonrecognition treatment when such assets are sold in contemplation of a twelve-month liquidation under I.R.C. § 337. The rationale appears to be that charging a collapsible corporation with the gain inherent in such assets, whether it be capital or ordinary in nature, obviates converting the selling shareholder's gain into ordinary income.

[b] Flexibility in Allocation of Income or Loss

[i] **Special Allocations.** Since the corporation is a tax entity distinct from its shareholders, the composite nature of its income or loss of income is of no direct concern to shareholders whose entitlement to a share of profits depends upon the amount, and not the nature, of the constituent income and deduction items. Conversely, I.R.C. § 704(b), as amended by the 1976 TRA, applies the aggregate theory. Partners in their partnership agreement can allocate among themselves a specific share or item of partnership income or loss (such as bottom-line profits or losses, depreciation, or capital gains or losses) provided that the special allocation has "substantial economic effect," or when the allocation "*may* actually affect the dollar amount of the partners' shares of the total partnership income or loss independently of tax consequences."[118] If the agreement is silent as to a partner's share of income, loss, or constituent item, or, in the alternative, if a special allocation is devoid of economic substance, the partner's share will be determined by his "interest in the partnership" based on all facts and circumstances, including his interest in profit and losses, his interest in cash flow, and his rights to distribution upon liquidation.[119]

"*Substantial Economic Effect.*" While example (3) in Reg. § 1.704 (b)(2) does not involve real estate, it provides a simple and concise illustration of this phrase. In the example, the partners in an equal *AB* partnership agree to invest surplus partnership funds in equal dollar amounts of municipal bonds and stock. They agree that *A* is to receive all the tax-exempt interest income and gain or loss from the tax-exempt bonds, and *B* is to receive all the dividend income and gain or loss from the corporate stock. Even though the allocation benefits *A*, in a higher tax bracket than *B*, it has substantial economic effect for the partners, since the respective amounts of partnership income credited to their

---

[118] Act of Oct. 4, 1976, Pub. L. 94-455, § 213(d), 90 Stat. 1548, amending I.R.C. § 704(b); Reg. § 1.704-1(b)(2).

[119] S. Rep. No. 938, 94th Cong., 2d Sess. 100 (1976).

their gain on a sale of stock, liquidation, or distribution taxed as ordinary income, unless at least one of the following is satisfied:

(1) A shareholder will not be subjected to collapsible treatment unless he owns, directly or indirectly,[112] more than 5 percent in value of the outstanding stock.[113] Unfortunately, most corporate dealers and developers are closely held.

(2) Nor shall collapsible treatment apply to shareholder gain recognized during a taxable year unless more than 70 percent of such gain is attributable to "Section 341 assets," collapsible property such as inventory items and unrealized receivables.[114] However, most corporate dealers are likely to own little if any rental property or other noncollapsible assets, such as securities, during the taxable year involved.

(3) A corporation will not be deemed collapsible if at the time of sale, liquidation, or distribution, the corporation has realized a "substantial" part of the taxable income to be derived from its constructed or purchased properties. In the past, the Service sided with the Third Circuit in holding that collapsibility is avoided only when a sufficiently large amount (e.g., 85 percent) is realized; the remaining unrealized portion is thus *not* substantial.[115] However, in Rev. Rul. 72-48 the Service decided to support the view held by the Fifth Circuit that realization of a substantial part of net income, e.g., one-third, will suffice.[116]

(4) A shareholder can escape the taint of collapsibility if the gain on his stock is realized more than three years after the corporation completes its construction or purchase of collapsible property.[117]

(5) A final and less convoluted escape hatch is I.R.C. § 341(f), which allows the shareholder to sell his stock at capital gain rates if the corporation consents to have gain recognized on its "subsection (f) assets," including land and income-producing realty, when it disposes of such assets—even though such disposition would otherwise qualify for nonrecognition treat-

---

[112] The attribution rules of I.R.C. § 544(a) relating to personal holding companies apply.

[113] I.R.C. § 341(d)(1).

[114] I.R.C. § 341(d)(2).

[115] Rev. Rul. 62-12, 1962-1 C.B. 321; Accord, Abbott v. Comm'r, 28 T.C. 795, 809 (1957), *aff'd* 258 F.2d 537, 543 (3d Cir. 1958).

[116] Rev. Rul. 72-48, 1972-1 C.B. 102. Accord, Comm'r v. Kelley, 293 F.2d 904 (5th Cir. 1961).

[117] I.R.C. § 341(d)(3).

[ii] Corporate Tax Planning. While the collapsible rules affecting partnerships apply only to "dealer" realty and are governed by flat mathematical tests, the rules applicable to corporations are based on subjective intent and cover rental real estate as well. The collapsible corporation concept focuses upon whether the corporation is formed or utilized principally for the construction or production of property or purchase of ordinary income assets with a *'view'* to a sale of stock by its shareholders, or whether it is formed with a view to liquidation, or distribution to its shareholders *before the corporation realizes a substantial part of the taxable income* to be derived from the property and there is a realization by the shareholders of the gain attributable to such property.[108]

Unfortunately, the conditional part of the definition offers little solace to stockholders of most corporations owning rental realty because of the heavy allocation of deductible expenses, such as depreciation and mortgage interest, to the early years of the venture. However, Congress enacted I.R.C. § 341(e) as a remedial provision because the definition of a collapsible corporation was felt to be so far-reaching as to penalize stockholders of corporations investing in rental property. These would otherwise have been entitled to capital gains treatment.[109] Generally speaking, if a shareholder of an otherwise collapsible corporation sells his stock or receives a liquidating distribution, his gain will be capital gain if the unrealized appreciation in the corporation's "ordinary income" or "subsection (e)" assets is not more than 15 percent of the corporation's net worth. Since such assets are in the nature of inventory items, and trade or business property is not included—absent special circumstances—stockholders of corporations owning rental realty are absolved from collapsible treatment. However, an important exception occurs when a stockholder owning more than 5 percent in value of the stock is himself in the business of selling realty. He cannot insulate himself from dealer status by incorporating and selling stock rather than selling the property himself.[110] Furthermore, if any such stockholder owns more than 20 percent of the stock, then *none* of the stockholders will be extricated from collapsible treatment under I.R.C. § 341(e).[111]

If the corporation is engaged in the business of constructing or developing and selling real estate, its stockholders run the risk of having

---

[108] I.R.C. § 341(b)(1).

[109] See Bittker & Eustice, *Federal Income Taxation of Corporations and Shareholders* ¶ 12.07, at 12-26 (4th ed. 1979) (hereinafter cited as Bittker & Eustice).

[110] See I.R.C. § 341(e)(1)(B).

[111] I.R.C. § 341(e)(1)(C). See Bittker & Eustice, note 109 *supra*, ¶ 12.07.

of 20 percent based on leveraged *cost* may represent a 100 percent or more profit return to the investors based on their *equity*.

> *Example.* Returning to the previous example, if the $100,000 purchase price for the lots were funded by $20,000 cash and an $80,000 purchase money mortgage and sold for $120,000, the lots would not be collapsible assets since the 120 percent appreciation test would not be met. Accordingly, the percentage return to the partners, before taking operating expenses into account, would be 100 percent, based on their cash investment.

If, on the other hand, a profit margin exceeding 20 percent of total cost is contemplated, the following devices can be used to circumvent both the 120 percent and 10 percent tests for appreciated inventory:

(1) The appreciation percentage could be reduced in the aggregate to 120 percent or less by simply having the partnership purchase additional unimproved lots as inventory.

(2) To accomplish the same objective, some of the lots could be sold on account and converted into trade account receivables. Since these resultant receivables, themselves, would be regarded as inventory items,[106] they would reduce the ratio of the market value of inventory items to their tax basis.

(3) If the lots or other inventory items represent more than 10 percent of the aggregate value of all partnership property other than cash, this ratio can be diluted by using partnership cash or loans to purchase short-term marketable securities. These can then be disgorged after the partner sells or liquidates his partnership interest.

(4) A final escape hatch would exist if the partnership owned assets other than collapsible items. Namely, the regulations permit an arm's-length allocation as to that portion, if any, of the sale price that represents the selling partner's interest in the collapsible items. The rationale for respecting such allocation is the antithetical tax interests of the selling and purchasing partner.[107]

---

[106] I.R.C. § 751(d)(2) includes as "inventory" any property other than a capital or Section 1231 asset, and I.R.C. § 1221(4) excludes from the definition of "capital asset" any accounts or notes receivable acquired for services rendered or from the sale of inventory or property held for sale in the ordinary course of a trade or business.

[107] Reg. § 1.751(a)(2).

$500,000; (2) unrealized receivables worth $100,000, with a zero tax basis, and (3) improved lots held for sale worth $200,000, which cost $100,000 to acquire and develop (tax basis of $100,000). Partner L has an adjusted or tax basis in his partnership interest (in capital and profits) of $300,000, equal to his capital contributions less withdrawals in excess of profits, and sells his one-half interest for its fair market value of $650,000, equal to one-half of market value of partnership net assets.

Results. Of the $350,000 gain chargeable to L on the sale of his partnership interest, $50,000 is allocable to his one-half share of unrealized receivables and is taxable as ordinary income. Since the value of the lots ($200,000) exceeds 120 percent of their bases to the partnership ($100,000) and constitutes more than 10 percent of the value of total partnership assets, they constitute substantially appreciated inventory. Consequently, L will be charged with an additional $50,000 of ordinary gain equal to his share of appreciation in the value of the lots; the remainder of the gain ($250,000) allocable to his share of the rental property will be capital gain.[104]

In addition, if a partner in a collapsible partnership receives either a current or liquidating distribution of more or less than his pro rata share of tainted assets, the transaction is treated under I.R.C. § 751(b) as a taxable constructive sale or exchange of such assets between the partnership and the distributee-partner. This could result in ordinary income treatment for either the partner or partnership, since the normal distribution rules would not apply.[105]

Since a partnership-owning inventory or "dealer" realty is not regarded as collapsible unless the aggregate fair market value of the tainted property exceeds 120 percent of its cost or other basis to the partnership, collapsible treatment may be avoided because the syndicate's profit margin, based on total cost, may be less than 20 percent. Realistically, this constraint is less onerous than it appears. Most subdivision operations are quite leveraged. For example, a profit

---

[104] For simplicity's sake, the taxable gain in this hypothetical case is fragmented (allocated) in part to unrealized receivables and substantially appreciated inventory; however, the regulations require that the selling price and transferor's adjusted basis of his partnership interest be fragmented in this manner. Reg. § 1.751-1(a)(2). Consequently, there could be taxable gain attributable to a collapsible asset even though loss was incurred on the sale of the partnership interest, as, for example, where depreciation in the value of a noncollapsible asset (e.g., capital asset) exceeds the appreciation or gain inherent in the partnership's collapsible assets. See 1 Willis, *Partnership Taxation* § 27.13 (2d ed. 1976).

[105] Reg. § 1.751-1(b).

[i] Partnership Tax Planning. I.R.C. § 751(a) provides that when a partner sells his interest, the amount of the sales proceeds allocable to either "unrealized receivables" or "substantially appreciated inventory" will be accorded ordinary income and not capital gains treatment. Instead of the sale by a partner being viewed as the sale of a partnership interest (capital asset), the partner is deemed to have sold his share of the receivables and inventory (ordinary income assets), even though in the latter case the partner is not, himself, a dealer. The first type of collapsible or "tainted" asset refers to receivables in exchange for the past or future delivery of goods or services by a cash-basis partnership. It also refers to certain income recapture items that include potential depreciation recapture income.[99] The second type refers to "inventory" items only if their aggregate fair market value exceeds (1) 120 percent of the adjusted basis to the partnership of such property, and (2) 10 percent of the fair market value of all partnership property, *other than cash*.[100] Moreover, under the rule applicable to inventory items, if a partnership syndicate owns for investment and not as inventory some income-producing property—an apartment building or a shopping center—a selling partner who is not, himself, a dealer for tax purposes[101] will not be charged with ordinary gain no matter how much the realty has appreciated in value.[102] By contrast, if the partnership itself is a subdivider or dealer that holds improved lots or other appreciated realty as inventory for sale to customers, or if the partnership owns some other property which is neither a capital asset nor a Section 1231 asset, the collapsible rules will apply to all partners, including those who are themselves investors and not dealers.[103]

Facts. Investors L and G are equal partners in a cash-basis partnership. They own the following assets free and clear: (1) five-year-old rental property subject to straight-line depreciation, with a market value of $1 million and a tax basis to the partnership of

---

[98] See I.R.C. § 334(a) (formerly § 113(a)(15) of the 1939 Internal Revenue Code.

[99] I.R.C. § 751(c). See note 49 *supra*. Under Reg. § 1.751-1(c)(4)(ii), any "potential Section 1250 income" is the amount which would be reportable as ordinary income if the partnership had sold the Section 1250 property at its fair market value.

[100] I.R.C. § 751(d)(1).

[101] I.R.C. § 751(d)(2)(D). See discussion on tax definition of a "dealer" at ¶ 9.05 [1].

[102] As noted above, in the case of depreciable real property subject to accelerated depreciation, any potential depreciation recapture income under I.R.C. § 1250 would be treated as an "unrealized receivable" and as such could generate ordinary income to the selling partner.

[103] I.R.C. § 751(d).

prior law the credit was limited to tangible personal property, excluding a building and its structural components; however, the Revenue Act of 1978 extends the investment credit to expenditures incurred after October 31, 1978 to rehabilitate buildings used for non-lodging purposes; these buildings must have been in use for at least twenty years prior to rehabilitation.[95]

[3] Other Tax Advantages of Partnership Over Incorporation

Planners sometimes overlook the relative ease with which the real estate dealer or service partnership can avoid collapsible treatment. By contrast, the insidious collapsible corporation rules are much more difficult to circumvent and apply under certain circumstances to rental real estate as well. Another major advantage is the flexibility accorded to partners, but not shareholders, in allocating shares or items of partnership income and loss among themselves, even when such allocations are influenced by tax motives.

[a] Collapsible Provisions Less Stringent

Essentially, both collapsible provisions for partnerships and corporations[96] are designed to prevent conversion, into preferred capital gain, of what would otherwise be ordinary dealer or service income. For example, prior to inclusion of these provisions in the 1954 Code, a partnership or corporation would be formed to improve and sell land, or, as a cash-basis taxpayer, to provide services on account. Instead of selling the improved lots at ordinary income rates—or in the latter case, realizing ordinary income upon collection of the receivables—the partners or shareholders would sell their appreciated equity interests to outsiders at capital gains rates. The purchasing partners[97] or stockholders[98] would then immediately liquidate the partnership or corporation and receive a stepped-up basis in the inventory or receivables equal to the cost of their partnership interest or stock. Finally, they would incur little if any ordinary gain on the immediate sale or collection of the distributed property, since the fair market value of the property would approximately equal the cost basis of what was paid for the partnership interest or stock.

---

[95] Revenue Act § 311, amending I.R.C. § 46; Revenue Act § 312, amending I.R.C. § 46(a); and Revenue Act § 315, amending I.R.C. § 48(a) and adding I.R.C. § 48(g).

[96] I.R.C. §§ 751 et seq. and I.R.C. §§ 341 et seq., respectively.

[97] See I.R.C. § 732(b) (formerly § 113(a)(13) of the 1939 Internal Revenue Code.

directly or indirectly by five or fewer individuals.[92] On June 5, 1979, because these rules are so complex, the Treasury finally published a detailed set of Proposed Regulations.

Had income-producing realty been included within the at-risk provisions, the result to tax shelters would have been disastrous. For example, returning to our illustration of tax shelters[93], L, the limited partner, would be considered at-risk only to the extent of his $100,000 contribution, even though the partnership had obtained an $800,000 no-personal-liability mortgage. Consequently, L's at-risk amount which, like adjusted basis, is reduced each year by the amount of loss taken, would be reduced to zero by the end of the seventh tax year. Thereafter, L would be precluded from deducting his share of partnership losses unless he increased his at-risk amount. Consequently, since the at-risk provisions do not apply to real estate, except for mineral leases, it would appear that real estate, when compared to other tax shelters, has fared reasonably well under recent tax legislation.[94]

Investment Credit Liberalized. To further induce capital formation, the regular investment tax credit rate equal to 10 percent of the taxpayer's investment costs, scheduled to decrease to 7 percent on January 1, 1981, has been made permanent, and the "used-property" and "tax liability" limitations have been liberalized. In addition, under

---

property available as living accommodations shall be treated as part of the activity of holding such real property. For example, this exception is intended to exclude from application of the at-risk rule situations where a taxpayer owns and operates a hotel or motel. In such instances, the making available of personal property such as furniture and services in conjunction with the renting of the hotel or motel room are to be considered incidental to making real property available as living accommodations. Similarly, providing personal property and services in renting a furnished apartment are to be considered incidental to making real property available as living accommodations. In situations where trade or business involves both the holding of real property (other than mineral property) and the provision of personal property and services that are not incidental to making real property available as living accommodations, the holding of the real property will be treated as a separate activity that is not subject to the at-risk rule; the remainder of the trade or business will be treated as a separate activity (or separate activities) to which the at-risk rule would apply. In these situations, an allocation of the receipt, income, deductions, and basis of the activities would be made. Staff of Joint Comm. on Taxation, 96th Cong., 1st Sess., *General Explanation of the Revenue Act of 1978*, at 132 (Comm. Print 1979).

[92] Revenue Act § 202, amending I.R.C. § 465(a).

[93] See ¶ 1.05[2][b].

[94] See ¶ 1.05[4][b] for a discussion of a preexistent tax pitfall similar to the at-risk rule involving *recourse* financing by a limited partnership.

relatively small capital contributions, but also his much greater amount share of any nonrecourse mortgage liability.[89] Now such a partner is at-risk only for loans to which he is personally liable or has pledged outside property.[90]

The 1978 Revenue Act revised at-risk rules by extending them to all activities involving a trade or business, or the production of income other than the holding of real property (except for mineral property)[91] and equipment leasing by closely held corporations. Under the 1976 TRA, the rules applied to all taxpayers other than regular corporations, that is, corporations that are not Subchapter S corporations or personal holding companies. Under the 1978 Revenue Act, the rules also apply to closely held corporations where 50 percent or more of the stock is held

---

[89] Discussed at ¶ 1.05[4][b].

[90] Under the at-risk rule, a taxpayer's loss for any taxable year from covered activities is limited to the amount the taxpayer has placed at risk and could actually lose from this activity. Initially, the amount at risk is generally the sum of (1) the taxpayer's cash contributions to the activity, (2) the adjusted basis of other property contributed to the activity, and (3) amounts borrowed for use in the activity with respect to which the taxpayer has personal liability for repayment. Generally, this amount is increased by the taxpayer's share of income, and it is decreased by his share of losses and withdrawals from the activity.

The taxpayer is not generally considered at risk with respect to the proceeds (or his share of the proceeds) of a nonrecourse loan used directly or indirectly to finance his participation in the activity, unless he has pledged property (other than property used in the activity) to secure the nonrecourse indebtedness. Additional rules are provided to prevent avoidance of this rule by cross-collateralization of property involved in two different activities and borrowing from related persons or other participants in the same tax-shelter activity. Also, a taxpayer is not considered at risk to the extent his economic participation is protected from loss by guarantees, repurchase agreements, or insurance (except casualty insurance). I.R.C. § 465(b); Prop. Reg. § 1.465-6 (1979).

Losses that may not be deducted for any taxable year because of the at-risk rule are deferred and may be deducted in any subsequent year in which this at-risk limitation does not prevent the deduction. I.R.C. § 465(a)(2). Under a literal interpretation of prior law, the at-risk rules may have only required the taxpayer to be at risk at the end of the taxable year for which losses are claimed. Thus, arguably, subsequent withdrawals of amounts originally placed at risk may have been made without the recapture of previously allowed losses. However, to conform to the purpose of the at-risk rules, the Revenue Act of 1978 requires the recapture of previously allowed losses when the at-risk amount is reduced below zero. Revenue Act § 203, adding I.R.C. § 465(e).

[91] Revenue Act § 201, adding I.R.C. § 465(c)(3)(D)(i). In the case of activities to which the Act extends application of the at-risk rule, the holding of real property (other than mineral property) is to be treated as a separate activity, and the at-risk rule is not to apply to losses from this activity. For purposes of this exclusion, personal property and services that are incidental to making real

An investor realizing net long-term capital *losses* may continue to offset 50 percent of such losses against ordinary income (up to $3,000 a year with the excess carried over), even though only 40 percent of net gains would be taxed.

For corporate taxpayers, the alternative tax on capital gains was reduced from 30 percent to 28 percent, effective for sales occurring; installment payments received after 1978 and the untaxed portion remain subject to the corporate minimum tax.[85]

At-Risk Provisions Inapplicable to Real Estate. Perhaps of most significance to the real estate investor seeking a tax haven is not what the Tax Reform Act did, but what it failed to do concerning income-producing real estate. In the past, the House Ways and Means Committee recurringly attempted to curtail real estate and other shelters by eliminating so-called artificial accounting losses. Under the proposed system known as limitation on artificial accounting losses (L.A.L.), both accelerated depreciation and construction period costs could not exceed the annual income from the activity to which they relate.[86] For example, returning to the illustration of tax shelters,[87] the partnership has under present law a first-year tax loss of $23,643 that can be passed through to L and G. Under L.A.L., the syndicate's net related income would be $1,357, a net rent of $100,000 minus total interest and straight-line depreciation of $98,643. Accordingly, the partnership would only be able to deduct $1,357 of accelerated depreciation. The remaining first year loss of $23,643, albeit worth $11,822 in tax savings to L and G would be deferred, perhaps indefinitely, until the project produced sufficient taxable income to absorb the loss.

At the behest of the Senate Finance Committee, Congress abandoned L.A.L. and settled for the relatively mild curbs previously described, along with something new, the so-called at-risk provisions, which under the 1976 TRA were aimed primarily at tax shelters other than real estate, farming, oil and gas exploitation, production and distribution of films and tapes, and equipment leasing.[88] Briefly, new I.R.C. § 465 prevents certain investors from deducting losses in excess of their economic or at-risk investment. Under prior law, a limited partner in such highly leveraged enterprises could deduct losses each year up to the amount of his adjusted basis. This included not only his

---

[85] Revenue Act § 403, amending I.R.C. § 1201(a).
[86] See S. Rep. No. 938, 94th Cong., 2d Sess. 39 (1976).
[87] See ¶ 1.05[2][b].
[88] I.R.C. §§ 464, 465, as added by 1976 TRA, Pub. L. 94-455, § 204, 90 Stat. 1531.

To discourage individual taxpayers with substantial earned income from investing in tax shelters, the Tax Reform Act of 1969 introduced into the Code the 50 percent maximum tax rate on earned income of individuals. The benefits of the provision were lost to the extent that a taxpayer had tax preference items in excess of $30,000 in any one year, or an average exceeding $30,000 over five taxable years.[79] The 1976 TRA eliminated the $30,000 floor and expanded the definition of earned income.[80] Consequently, every dollar of tax preference now reduces the amount of earned income that qualifies for the maximum tax whether or not the taxpayer is required to pay any minimum tax on such preference items. However, with respect to gains from sales or exchanges occurring after October 1978, the Revenue Act of 1978 eliminated the capital gains deduction preference item as a reduction in the amount of personal service income eligible for the 50 percent maximum tax ceiling. [81]

Capital Gains Provisions Liberalized. The Revenue Act of 1978 ushered in substantive changes in the treatment of long-term capital gains for both corporate and noncorporate taxpayers. Commencing on November 1, 1978, 60 percent of net long-term capital gains are allowed as a deduction for noncorporate taxpayers.[82] Additionally, the 25 percent alternative capital gains tax available to individual taxpayers was repealed as of January 1, 1979.[83] As noted earlier, a companion section of the Act substantially altered the minimum-maximum tax provisions with respect to capital gains treatment; it created a new alternative minimum tax. The increase in the noncorporate capital gains deduction from 50 to 60 percent is based on the assumption that lower capital gains taxes will increase sales of appreciated assets, which will in turn offset much of the revenue loss from the tax cut and will stimulate capital investment and more tax revenues by improving the mobility of capital. This change, together with the modifications in the minimum tax, decreases the highest capital gains tax rate from about 49 percent to 28 percent. Given these changes, Congress decided that repeal of the alternative tax would both simplify the tax law and contribute to tax equity.[84]

---

[79] I.R.C. § 1348.
[80] 1976 TRA, Pub. L. 94-455, § 302, amending I.R.C. §§ 1304(b)(5), 1348.
[81] Revenue Act § 441, amending I.R.C. § 1348(b)(2)(B).
[82] Revenue Act § 402, amending I.R.C. § 1202.
[83] Revenue Act § 401, amending I.R.C. § 1201(b).
[84] Staff of Joint Comm. on Taxation, 96th Cong., 1st Sess., *General Explanation of the Revenue Act of 1978*, at 251, 252 (Comm. Print 1979).

tax had adversely affected capital formation, and that the purpose of the minimum tax could be better effectuated—in the case of capital gains—by imposing an alternative minimum tax on capital gains, payable only to the extent that it exceeds an individual's regular tax liability. By eliminating capital gains as an item of tax preference under the present minimum tax, and by enacting an alternative minimum tax applicable to capital gains and adjusted itemized deductions, Congress anticipated that capital formation would be facilitated, and that every individual would pay at least a reasonable minimum amount of tax with respect to large capital gains.[77] The new alternative minimum tax has as its base taxable income plus the amount of the new 60 percent long-term capital gain deduction, plus excess itemized deductions as redefined by the Act. The base is reduced by an exemption of $20,000, and the residual is taxed incrementally as follows: 10 percent on the first $40,000; 20 percent on the next $40,000; and 25 percent on the remainder. However, the new alternative minimum tax is only payable to the extent that it exceeds the taxpayer's regular tax liability, plus the revised 15 percent add-on minimum tax.[78] The latter, with respect to the other items of tax preference, has been retained under the Revenue Act of 1978. Accordingly, taxpayers paying high regular taxes generally will not be subject to any alternative minimum tax. Thus, they will have no disincentive, attributable to the minimum tax, for making capital gain investments. However, this new provision will insure that those high-income individuals currently paying low regular taxes due to large amounts of preference items will bear their fair share of the tax burden if they should sustain large amounts of capital gain.

> *Example.* In 1979, Mr. Owner has $100,000 taxable income, including taxable portion of capital gain, plus $10,000 of excess depreciation accelerated over straight-line, plus $50,000 of untaxed long-term gain. He pays no 15 percent minimum tax because the $10,000 minimum-tax deduction offsets the excess depreciation tax preference. In calculating his alternative minimum tax, he adds taxable income, $100,000, to untaxed gain, $50,000, for a total of $150,000. The $20,000 exemption reduces this to $130,000, on which the alternative tax would be $24,500—10 percent on $40,000, 20 percent on the next $40,000, plus 25 percent on the balance of $50,000. Since this is less than the regular tax liability on his $100,000 of taxable income, no minimum alternative tax is payable.

---

[77] Staff of Joint Comm. on Taxation, 96th Cong., 1st Sess. *General Explanation of the Revenue Act of 1978*, at 262 (Comm. Print 1979).

[78] Revenue Act § 421(a), adding I.R.C. § 55, amending I.R.C. § 58(c).

In addition, under present law, the deductible amount of investment interest by noncorporate taxpayers is $10,000 plus net investment income, exclusive of long-term capital gain. Less stringent rules apply to interest paid or accrued on investment indebtedness incurred to acquire a 50 percent or more interest in a partnership or corporation.[73]

Special Depreciation for Rehabilitating Low-Income Housing. To further stimulate the rehabilitation of low-income rental housing, the rule that permits depreciation of rehabilitation expenditures over a special sixty-month amortization period has been renewed, under the Revenue Act of 1978, until December 31, 1981. In addition, the Revenue Act of 1978 provides that rehabilitation expenditures made pursuant to a binding contract entered into before January 1, 1982 will still qualify for the special five-year depreciation write-off; this is permitted even though the expenditures are not made until after December 31, 1981.[74] There is a per-unit expenditure limit of $20,000, and the definition of "low-income rental housing" is geared to the Leased Housing Program under Section 8 of the Housing Act of 1937.[75]

Mini-Maxi Tax Tightened. The minimum tax on tax preference items was introduced into the Code by the Tax Reform Act of 1969. Its format is a compromise between those who believed that an additional tax should be paid by any taxpayer who receives excessive advantage from certain tax deductions (regardless of the amount of regular income tax paid by such taxpayers), and those who believed that the additional tax should only be borne by taxpayers whose regular tax liabilities are unduly reduced by the use of so many "tax preference items." Effective for taxable years beginning in 1976, the additional minimum tax rate of 10 percent on tax preference items (including accelerated depreciation, the excluded portion of capital gains [50 percent prior to 1979 and 60 percent thereafter], excess investment interest, and certain excess itemized deductions) was increased to 15 percent. In addition, the exemption was deliberalized for individual taxpayers. It is now $10,000, or one-half the regular tax, whichever is greater.[76]

However, in enacting the Revenue Act of 1978, Congress believed that in the case of capital gain, the present 15 percent add-on minimum

---

[73] 1976 TRA, Pub. L. 94-455, § 209, 90 Stat. 1542, amending I.R.C. § 163(d).

[74] Revenue Act of 1978, Pub. L. 95-600, § 367, 92 Stat. 2857 (hereinafter cited as Revenue Act) amending I.R.C. § 167(k).

[75] 1976 TRA, Pub. L. 94-455, § 203, 90 Stat. 1530, amending I.R.C. § 167(k).

[76] 1976 TRA, Pub. L. 94-455, § 301, 90 Stat. 1549, amending I.R.C. §§ 56, 57, 58.

the repayment period—which may be as long as thirty or forty years.[66c] Consequently, under this interpretation, the ten-year amortization of construction period interest could be postponed for the cash-basis borrower to the later years of the permanent loan.[66d]

Recapture of Accelerated Depreciation. Under present law, full recapture of post-1975 accelerated depreciation in excess of the straight-line amount is required with respect to residential realty.[67] However, in the case of "low-income housing,"[68] an owner can escape full recapture if the property is sold after the first 100 months (8⅓ years). Thereafter, there will be a one percent reduction in recapture for each month the realty is held; there will consequently be no recapture once it is held a minimum of 200 months (16⅔ years). In the case of commercial realty, full recapture is still required under present rules.[69]

Limitations on Prepaid and Investment Interests. Cash-basis taxpayers must now deduct prepaid interest ratably over the period of the loan.[70] In prior years, the Service permitted prepayment by cash-basis taxpayers for not more than twelve months beyond the close of the current year, if the prepayment did not result in a material distortion of income.[71] The new rule applies to loan processing fees or "points," with the exception that points paid on a home mortgage generally can still be currently deducted.[72]

[66c] See discussion at ¶¶ 2.02[1][b], 2.02[2][b], 2.02[3][b], 2.02[4][b].

[66d] See Feder, "Financing Real Estate Construction: The IRS Challenge to Construction Period Deductions," 8 J. Real Est. Tax. 3, 18-20 (1980).

[67] Act of Oct. 4, 1976, Pub. L. 94-455, § 202, 90 Stat. 1527, amending I.R.C. § 1250.

[68] I.R.C. § 1250(a)(1)(B). See note 66 *supra*.

[69] The current recapture rules are summarized in note 49 *supra*.

[70] I.R.C. § 461(g), as added by Act of Oct. 4, 1976, Pub. L. 94-455, § 208, 90 Stat. 1541. See ¶ 12.01[1][b].

[71] See Rev. Rul. 68-643, 1968-2 C.B.76.

[72] I.R.C. § 461(g)(2). As to construction period interest, the prepaid interest rules are to be applied to interest first (before the construction period interest and taxes rules) to determine the period to which the interest relates. If, under the prepaid interest provisions, interest is treated as allocable to the construction period, the ten-year amortization rule is then to apply to that portion of the interest. In effect, for the purposes of this provision, the interest is treated as paid or incurred in the year to which it is allocated under the prepaid interest rules. An exception occurs when construction period interest is also investment interest.

¶ 1.05[2][d]

operations until 1982, the next $10,000 deduction would not begin until 1982.

However, the transitional rules are less stringent for residential property, especially "low-income housing"; interest and taxes on a newly constructed apartment building financed under Sections 221(d) or 236 of the National Housing Act would be currently deductible when paid during construction, if such low-income housing project were begun prior to 1982.[66]

co In the case of new construction of income-producing real estate, the developer-borrower will frequently obtain a short-term, interest-only construction loan from an interim lender, such as a commercial bank. It will then have the construction loan repaid with the proceeds of a permanent loan, once the project is completed and the terms of the permanent mortgage loan commitment have been satisfied.[66a] It is often the case that the developer borrows from the construction lender the funds needed to pay interest on the construction loans. If the borrower is a cash-basis taxpayer, he may not treat such interest as paid for tax purposes until the principal of the construction loan is repaid. If a cash-basis developer-borrower has the construction period interest added to the principal of the construction loan note and, as is frequently the case, uses the permanent loan proceeds to pay the principal of the construction loan, the Service would argue that the construction period interest should not be deemed paid, for purposes of I.R.C. § 189, until the end of the construction period when the construction loan is repaid. Consequently, amortization would not commence under I.R.C. § 189 until that year.[66b] Therefore, most principal is repaid toward the end of

---

[66] I.R.C. § 189, as added by Act of Oct. 4, 1976, Pub. L. 94-455, § 201(a), 90 Stat. 1525. For a complete description of other categories qualifying as "low-income housing," see I.R.C. § 1250(a)(1)(B), which is incorporated by definitional reference in new I.R.C. § 189(e)(5). Included among these other categories are (1) properties financed under certain state and local programs; (2) dwelling units in housing where occupants qualified for rent subsidies under Section 8 of the Housing Act of 1937 or under similar state or local subsidies; (3) properties qualifying for rehabilitation expense depreciation deductions under I.R.C. § 167(k); and (4) properties with loan or mortgage insurance under Title V of the Housing Act of 1949.

[66a] See discussion at ¶¶ 2.01[2], 4.01.

[66b] In some cases the construction lender sells the loan note (and related documents) to the permanent lender pursuant to a buy-sell agreement. In a Technical Advice Memorandum (Ltr. Rul. 8017007) the Service reached the questionable conclusion that the arrangement results in only a single loan to the borrower, the principal of which would be repaid only as amortization of the principal of the loan occurred. If this contention were correct the loan used to pay construction period interest would be repaid, in part, with each principal payment. Theoretically, amortization under I.R.C. § 189 could not begin until that date. *Id.*

nue Act of 1978 has revised the pattern of the Tax Reform Acts of 1969 and 1976 by creating new incentives for real estate investment, notably by reducing the capital gains tax for investors. Of greatest significance for the real estate tax shelter is not what the 1978 Act does, but what it omits to do; it neither imposes new restrictions on the use of accelerated depreciation nor extends the depreciation recapture rules (as did the previous two tax reform acts); it also does not extend the so-called at-risk rules to real estate.

Construction Period Interest and Taxes. Under prior law, amounts paid for interest and taxes attributable to the construction of real property were allowable as a current deduction, except to the extent the taxpayer elected to capitalize these items as carrying charges.[64] However, in enacting I.R.C. § 189, Congress took the position that the prior rule was contrary to the fundamental accounting principle of matching income and expenses, the feeling being that construction period interest and taxes are expenditures that relate to the production of rental income over the life of the building. They should thus not be allowed as current deductions during the construction period when there is no income being generated from the property.[65]

Under present law, construction period interest and taxes are to be capitalized in the year during which they are paid or incurred, and they are to be amortized over a ten-year period. A portion of the amount capitalized may be deducted for the taxable year in which it was paid or incurred. The remainder must be amortized over the balance of the amortization period beginning with the year in which the real property is first placed in service or is ready for sale. However, for taxable years beginning in 1976, separate transitional rates apply for nonresidential real estate, residential real estate, and government subsidized low-income housing. In the case of nonresidential realty, costs paid or accrued in 1977 must be spread ratably over a five-year amortization period; for 1978, over a six-year period; for 1979, over a seven-year period; for 1980, over an eight-year period; for 1981, over a nine-year period; and for 1982 and thereafter, over a ten-year period.

Example. A shopping center or office building developer who pays $80,000 of construction period taxes in 1980 can deduct $10,000 in 1980. He then can deduct $10,000 in each of the following seven years. But if construction delays postpone rental

---

[64] I.R.C. § 266.
[65] Staff of Joint Comm. on Taxation, 94th Cong., 2d Sess., *General Explanation of the Tax Reform Act of 1969*, at 26 (Comm. Print 1976).

interest,[59] ground rent, and, during the construction period, certain other interim expenses such as sales and use taxes on machinery and construction materials that have been billed to the owner.[60] The corporate form is consequently more frequently used, especially where projected dealer gain is taxable at a rate exceeding the flat rate charged to corporations. In this case, the investors are in a high ordinary income tax bracket, and the collapsible corporation and double taxation problems can be avoided or at least minimized.[61]

[d] Post-1976 Tax Legislation

An increasing concern with inflation, accompanied by publicity concerning wealthy taxpayers who paid little, if any, taxes, culminated in the Tax Reform Act of 1969. The Act limited the tax advantages of investing in real estate by restricting the use of accelerated depreciation,[62] tightening up the depreciation recapture rules,[63] and introducing the "mini-maxi" tax. Notwithstanding its adverse impact on real estate, the House Ways and Means Committee continued to attempt to curtail real estate and other shelters by eliminating so-called artificial accounting losses, but Congress settled for the relatively milder at-risk provisions, which are primarily aimed at tax shelters other than real estate. While the other restrictions under the Tax Reform Act of 1976 (1976 TRA) have undoubtedly deterred real estate investment to some degree (especially because of the requirement that construction period interest and taxes be amortized ultimately over a ten-year period), it appears that tax-shelter investment in real estate, particularly investment in low-income housing limited partnerships, has fared reasonably well as opposed to other kinds of tax-shelter investments. Moreover, the Reve-

---

provide financing are currently deductible as a business expense. Rev. Rul. 56-136, 1956-1 C.B. 92. Other costs incurred to acquire a mortgage loan such as legal appraisal fees, broker's commissions, survey, and title costs are generally treated as capital expenditures, amortizable (on a straight-line basis) over the term of the loan. See ¶ 12.01[1][a].

[59] As a general rule, a deduction is allowed for "all interest paid or accured within the taxable year on indebtedness." I.R.C. § 163(a). Under I.R.C. § 461(g), taxpayers on the cash-basis method (like accrual-basis taxpayers) must amortize all payments of interest over the period to which they relate. See ¶ 12.01[1][b]. As to construction period interest, see note 72 *infra*.

[60] Rev. Rul. 58-292, 1958-1 C.B. 106; Joe Stout, 31 T.C. 1199 (1959); see also Herbert Shainberg, 33 T.C. 241 (1959).

[61] See discussion at ¶¶ 1.05[3][a], 1.05[5][a].

[62] See note 47 *supra*.

[63] See note 49 *supra*.

and the percentage allocable to nondeductible amortization increases. Returning to our tax shelter example, the annual amount of depreciation deduction, interest deduction, and amortization would be $36,755, $67,316, and $14,896, respectively, by the close of tax year number seven.

To some degree, the problem of the disappearing shelter can be mitigated by refinancing the mortgage to de-escalate the amount of nondeductible amortization, or by selling the over-depreciated property and then using the proceeds to fund the acquisition of some substitute property. This would start the depreciation cycle anew since the partnership would obtain a new depreciation basis equal to the cost of the newly acquired property. In addition, to the extent that the depreciation recapture provision in I.R.C. § 1250 is not applicable, any gain realized on the disposition would be treated as long-term capital gain. Therefore, ordinary depreciation losses taken during the early years of ownership are effectively converted into deferred long-term capital gain.[56]

[c] Nondepreciable Property

In the case of non-income-producing property (for example, undeveloped realty held by a speculator, or improved real estate in the process of being constructed or held primarily for sale to customers), the property is not subject to depreciation. Accordingly, the only potential deductions available either to shelter ordinary dealer income or to generate losses during the construction period are real estate taxes,[57] "front end" loan expenses such as loan commitment or standby fees and loan processing fees ("points"),[58] current but not prepaid

---

[56] See note 49 *supra*.

[57] See I.R.C. § 164; Reg. § 1.164-1. A cash-basis taxpayer may deduct property taxes in the year paid. As to accrual-basis taxpayers, the Service generally favors the assessment of the tax as the accrual event. Rev. Rul. 71-46, 1971-1 C.B. 63. But cf. Rev. Rul. 56-145, 1956-1 C.B. 612; Keil Properties, Inc., 24 T.C. 113 (1955), *acq.* (proper date to allow accrual was the lien and not the assessment date). See also Rev. Rul. 73-64, 1973-1 C.B. 70, which provides that accrual is allowed on the lien date for real property, and on the assessment date for personal property. However, I.R.C. § 189 requires that construction period taxes be amortized. See discussion at ¶ 1.05[2][d].

[58] Loan processing fees or "points" are deductible as interest if the payment is solely for the use of forebearance of money, and is not merely a charge for specific services. See Rev. Rul. 69-188, 1969-1 C.B. 54. However, points (other than those incurred upon the purchase or improvement of a personal residence) are treated as prepaid interest deductible over the term of the loan. The deductibility of points as prepaid interest is discussed at ¶ 12.01[1][b].

Commitment and standby fees paid to procure a lender's commitment to

Accordingly, while the syndicate may disburse $17,787 as a tax-free return of capital,[55] these same partners can avail themselves of a $23,643 tax loss to offset their ordinary income from outside sources such as salaries and dividends. The total amount of tax shelter for the first year is therefore approximately $42,000. *This paradox is explained by the fact that deductible depreciation exceeds nondeductible mortgage amortization by nearly $42,000.*

Assuming that both *G* and *L* are in a 50 percent tax bracket and have sufficient outside income to absorb their losses, the partners' collective cash return in the dramatic first year would be $17,787, and their tax savings $11,822. Their total after-tax cash return would be $29,609, or about 15 percent of their net $200,000 investment. Moreover, when the equity buildup attributable to mortgage amortization is taken into account the true economic return is even higher. Obviously, had the syndicate purchased rather than leased the land, it would also have received the benefit of appreciation in land value in times of inflation.

By contrast, if the corporate form were used, the corporation could use accelerated depreciation to both shelter the cash inflow of $17,787 and to produce an internal loss of $23,643; however, its earnings and profits, if totally disgorged as a dividend distribution, would only be reduced by straight-line depreciation ($25,000). Thus, only $16,430 of the cash outflow to shareholders would be sheltered from ordinary income treatment. Furthermore, only the corporation can avail itself of the $23,643 loss that cannot be passed through to its shareholders.

In addition, if the property were owned by a partnership and hypothetically worth $1,200,000 after having been completely constructed and rented, the syndicate might "mortgage out" by refinancing at the same 80 percent loan-to-value ratio for $960,000 and distributing the $160,000 of excess mortgage proceeds to the partners as a tax-free return of capital. However, if the corporate form were used, the distributee-shareholders would be taxed (in this example) to the extent the corporation had accumulated (prior) earnings and profits.

However, "all that glitters is not gold." Notice that the amount of the depreciation deduction and resultant shelter will decrease each year as the depreciable basis of the property declines by the amount of the accelerated depreciation taken the year before. Also, under a customary constant payment mortgage arrangement, the shelter will decrease as the percentage of each payment allocable to deductible interest decreases,

---

[55] While each distributee-partner's tax basis in his partnership interest (including his share of the firm's liabilities) would be reduced by the amount of cash received, he would not be taxed on the distribution unless his share exceeded his basis at the time of distribution. I.R.C. §§ 705, 731, 752.

How a Tax Shelter Works. The following example illustrates how a tax shelter works for a partnership as opposed to a corporation.

Facts. Assume that a limited partnership is formed by G, the general partner, and L, the limited partner, to construct at a cost of $1 million an apartment building on ground-leased land. Each partner contributes $100,000 equity capital in exchange for a 50 percent interest in partnership profits or losses and capital. The balance of the construction cost is funded by a twenty-five-year unsubordinated first leasehold mortgage of $800,000, which is self-liquidating and has a 10.28 percent annual constant, with fixed annual payments of $82,213 to be applied first to interest at 9¼ percent on the unpaid balance and then to amortization or repayment of principal. Second, assume the venture yields a free and clear return[54] of 10 percent, or $100,000 net rent after paying all expenses other than income taxes and mortgage payments. Last, assume that the building has a useful life of forty years, with a zero salvage value, and since it qualifies as "residential rental property," the partnership is entitled to use for tax purposes the 200 percent declining balance of accelerated depreciation.

Results. For the first year of operations the cash flow and tax results are as follows:

Cash Flow

Net operating income		$100,000
Mortgage interest	$73,643	
Mortgage amortization	8,570	
		82,213
		$17,787

Taxable Income

Net operating income		$100,000
Mortgage interest	$73,643	
Accelerated depreciation	50,000	
		123,643
		($ 23,643)

Burge, 28 T.C. 46 (1957), *aff'd* 253 F.2d 765 (4th Cir. 1958); Rev. Rul. 57-357, 1957-2 C.B. 900, *but declared obsolete in* Rev. Rul. 72-621, 1972-2 C.B. 612. See discussion at ¶ 1.05[3][a].

[54] This phrase, in the parlance of real estate developers, refers to net income before tax and finance charges divided by purchase or construction cost. See Wendt & Cert, *Real Estate Investment and Taxation* 19-24 (1969), for a description of customary rates of return for various kinds of income-producing realty.

[b] Income-Producing Property

From a tax perspective, in most cases the partnership form is clearly preferable when the syndicate owns some income-producing real estate.

Depreciation and Taxation of Unsheltered Income. First, accelerated depreciation will shelter the venture's cash flow, and since a partnership is not, in itself, regarded as a separate tax entity, such an individually owned syndicate may serve as a "conduit" through which depreciation losses may pass to the constituent proprietors. Moreover, any realized income not sheltered, and therefore recognized for tax purposes, will be exposed to only a single layer of taxation. By contrast, the interposition of the corporate form will eliminate or diminish these advantages, since a corporation is regarded as a tax entity separate and distinct from its owners. Accordingly, while accelerated depreciation may shelter the corporation's income, only the corporation itself, and not its shareholders, may make use of its losses, which must be carried forward or backward to other taxable years.[50] Moreover, only ordinary or straight-line depreciation is available to shareholders to shelter the amount of ordinary dividend income.[51] In addition, operating income not sheltered by depreciation will be subjected to double taxation on both the corporate and shareholder level.

Mortgaging Out. Especially if construction is involved, another shelter mechanism available for investor-partners is the so-called mortgaging-out or windfall financing device. This results from mortgage refinancing in excess of current indebtedness, once construction has been completed and/or the land has appreciated in value.[52] The excess may be distributed tax-free, since the placement of a mortgage—even in excess of the tax basis of the property—merely represents a borrowing of money; it does not in itself constitute a taxable event. By contrast, if a corporation owns the property, such distribution would be taxable to shareholders as a dividend to the extent that the corporation already has earnings and profits.[53]

---

[50] I.R.C. § 172. However, losses can be passed through to shareholders of a Subchapter S corporation. I.R.C. § 1374. See ¶ 1.06.

[51] I.R.C. § 312(k)(1).

[52] For further discussion of the tax implications, see ¶ 12.01[4].

[53] Even if at the time of distribution the corporation has no earnings and profits but a mortgage loan exceeds in amount the adjusted basis of the secured property, such excess will itself be treated temporarily as earnings and profits and constitute a taxable dividend if the loan is insured or guaranteed by the FHA or other U.S. agency. See I.R.C. § 312(j). To make matters worse, the corporation may be treated as collapsible under I.R.C. § 341. See Raymond

which may be claimed on the full leveraged cost of the acquired property and not merely the equity investment, frequently results in an excess of deductible depreciation over nondeductible mortgage amortization and capital expenditures[48] during these early years of operation. Since depreciation deductions do not reflect actual expenditures of cash, but nondeductible amortization payments and capital expenditures do, any excess of depreciation permits a cash return to investors in excess of their taxable income; in tax law parlance, a "tax-free return of capital." Indeed, it is not uncommon for an economically profitable real estate operation to shelter its entire cash flow from taxation. Moreover, if the syndicate is a partnership, it may also produce tax losses which distributee-investors may use to offset their ordinary income from other sources, such as salaries and dividends. The property can later be sold, and the excess of sale price over the remaining depreciated basis will be treated as long-term capital gain, with the exception that excess depreciation is recaptured as ordinary income.[49]

---

[48] Recurring expenses paid or incurred to maintain the improvements in functioning condition are currently deductible; by contrast, capital expenditures made to increase the value or prolong the useful life of the property must be added to its cost basis. Hence, they are only deductible indirectly as depreciation over the remaining useful life of the income-producing improvements. Compare I.R.C. § 162 with I.R.C. § 263.

[49] The depreciation deduction reduces ordinary income and also reduces the tax basis of the property. If the property is sold at or above its cost, the taxpayer is in effect taxed on the depreciation previously taken, since it has reduced his basis; however, absent corrective legislation, this gain would be long-term capital gain under I.R.C. § 1231 if the property is used in a trade or business and held for nine months in tax year 1977 or for one year in tax years beginning in 1978. In 1964, the law was amended to convert this long-term capital gain to ordinary income to the extent of the depreciation taken in excess of straight-line depreciation; however, the law provided that this "depreciation recapture" would decline by one percent per month after the property had been "held" twenty months, with the result that there would be no recapture and the gain would be long-term capital gain in its entirety after the property had been held for ten years. This rule was continued in effect by the 1969 Act only with respect to new residential rental property financed pursuant to Sections 221(d)(3) or 236 of the National Housing Act or similar state or local programs. For other residential rental property, the recapture would decline by one percent per month after the property had been held 100 full months, so that there would be no recapture if the property were sold after being held sixteen years and eight months. All other real estate would be subject to full recapture of "excess" depreciation regardless of the length of time held. I.R.C. § 1250(a)(1)(C). See ¶ 1.05[2][d] for an outline of changes under recent tax legislation.

[2] Tax Sheltering of Investor's Income

[a] In General

To obtain financial leverage, a partnership or corporation will customarily fund its acquisition or improvement of income-producing real estate by means of high-ratio[46] and constant-payment long-term mortgage financing. Because such mortgages provide for low amortization of principal in the earlier years, use of accelerated depreciation,[47]

---

[46] An institutional lender, when allowed by local law, will generally loan between 75 to 80 percent of the appraised value of the income-producing property comprising the security for the loan, except that the loan-to-value ratio may be higher when FHA insurance is available to protect the lender. As to local law restrictions, see discussion at ¶ 2.02. But this value is not determined by analyzing costs; rather, it is determined by discounting future net rental income at a fixed capitalization rate. Since a lender will advance a certain percentage of the discounted future income stream regardless of the syndicate's construction cost, the equity requirement and capacity for leverage will vary substantially, depending upon the cost efficiency of the developer. Also, a syndicate can usually increase its leverage by means of secondary financing, or refinancing if the outstanding principal indebtedness declines at a faster rate than does the income stream that primes the mortgage.

[47] The Tax Reform Act of 1969 restricted the use of the 200 percent declining balance and sum-of-the-years digits methods of accelerated depreciation to *new* residential rental housing, defined as buildings in which 80 percent of the income is from residential units. I.R.C. § 167(j)(2). The fastest write-off allowable for other *new* real property is the 150 percent declining balance method. I.R.C. § 167(j)(1)(B). Only straight-line depreciation can be utilized on *used* realty except for used residential rental housing where the 125 percent declining balance method may be used if the remaining useful life at acquisition is twenty years or more. I.R.C. § 167(j)(5).

> *Example:* The *ABC* Corporation constructs an apartment building having a useful life of fifty years, with zero salvage value. Under straight-line depreciation, a deduction of 2 percent (100% ÷ 50) per annum may be taken, and under the 150 percent declining balance depreciation, a deduction of 3 percent [(100% ÷ 50) × 150%] per annum on the decreasing basis may be taken. Under the double-declining balance method, the depreciation deduction allowed is 4 percent per annum [(100% ÷ 50) × 200%] on the decreasing basis; and the use of the sum-of-the-years digits method produces a depreciation deduction in the first year of 3.92 percent (50/1275). Thus, the accelerated methods of depreciation, particularly the double-declining balance and sum-of-the-years' digits methods, produce much greater depreciation over the first few years of the property's useful life. However, in contrast to straight-line depreciation, the amount of the accelerated depreciation deduction will decrease each year as the depreciable basis of the property declines by the amount of the accelerated depreciation taken the year before.
>
> Observe that the shifting of deductible depreciation to the earlier years of the operation's life span is augmented by the fact that since mortgage payments are constant, deductible interest is high and nondeductible amortization is low at the beginning of the payout period.

exempt for some other reason, the syndicators will probably be forced to utilize a nominee or "straw" corporation, or to employ some other circumvention device. In today's money market, the interest rate on the mortgage would otherwise probably exceed the maximum contract rate allowable by local law.[44] Finally, real estate securities are equally regulated in today's investment market, whether the issuer is a corporation or a partnership syndicate.[45]

---

any banks, including those in New York City, will value for credit purposes an investment unit in a noncorporate real estate syndicate for more than a fraction of its real worth. Interview with Robert Weaver, Vice-President, Mortgage and Real Estate Department, Citibank N.A., in July, 1979.

[44] See discussion of usury laws in Chapter 5.

[45] In the past, compliance by real estate partnership syndicates with the Securities Act of 1933 had been limited because of ambiguity in construing the term "security" (Section 2(1) of the Act) and because of the SEC's failure to accommodate its registration process and enforcement mechanism to the unique problems of real estate syndication. At present, it is clear that participation units in a limited partnership or REIT, like corporate stock, fall within the pale of the statute. Subsumed under the definition of "security" is the term "investment contract" which, according to current judicial and administrative thinking, is, as a matter of economic reality, indistinguishable from a partnership or trust share. Furthermore, had these modern forms of syndicate shares existed at the enactment date, Congress would undoubtedly have expressly included them within the definition of "security." Otherwise, these investors would be precluded from full disclosure and SEC protection merely because these forms of investment are somewhat novel. SEC v. W.J. Howey Co., 328 U.S. 293, 302 (1946); Hirsch v. duPont, 396 F. Supp. 1214, 1220, 1227 (S.C. N.Y. 1975), aff'd 553 F.2d 750 (2d Cir. 1977) (limited partner's but not general partner's interests are securities for purposes of antifraud provision of federal securities laws) (dictum); Goodman v. Epstein, 582 F.2d 388, 406 (7th Cir. 1978), (limited partner's interests in limited partnership under Illinois law were "securities" within the protective scope of federal securities laws); Securities Act Release No. 4877 (1967), at 1, 17 C.F.R. § 231.4877. The SEC has also ruled that the federal securities laws apply to REITs Release Nos. 33-4298, 34-6419, and IC-3140, 25 Fed. Reg. 12177 (Nov. 18, 1960).

Nevertheless, an issuer can avoid registration under the following exemptions:

(1) Private offerings to a limited number of offerees. Securities Act of 1933, § 4(2); Rule 146, Securities Act Release No. 5487 (April 23, 1974).

(2) Intrastate offerings. Securities Act of 1933, § 3(a)(11); Rule 147, Securities Act Release No. 5450 (Jan. 7, 1974).

(3) Offerings of not more than $1,500,000 under Regulation A by filing a short-form registration statement at any regional SEC office. Securities Act of 1933, § 3(b); Reg. A (17 C.F.R. §§ 230.251–230.264).

(4) Exemption of certain limited offers and sales by closely held issuers. Securities Act of 1933, § 3(b); Rule 240, Securities Act Release No. 4552 (Nov. 6, 1962).

agement,[39] automatic continuity of existence[40] and minimization of title-holding problems[41] are also inherent in using the limited partnership or trust as the ownership vehicle.

However, two distinct advantages of the corporate form remain, especially when the mortgage money market is tight: the inimitable liquidity of publicly held corporate stock and the corporation's exemption from local usury restrictions. In contrast to corporate shares, investment units in a limited partnership syndicate are not readily marketable because of self-imposed constraints of alienability legalized under the ULPA[42] and because of an absence of formal secondary markets for trading shares.[43] In addition, whereas the corporation, as a borrowing entity, is exempt from usury restrictions in most jurisdictions, the limited partnership is not. Accordingly, if the loan is not

---

[39] See note 35 *supra.*

[40] While the death or withdrawal of a partner causes the dissolution of a general partnership *absent an agreement to the contrary*, the ULPA provides that a limited partnership shall not be dissolved by the death or withdrawal of a limited or even general partner if in the latter case the certificate so provides or if the remaining members agree. U.P.A. § 31; U.L.P.A. §§ 20, 21.

[41] A partnership, whether it be general or limited, can, like a corporation, hold title to real estate in its own name. U.P.A. § 3(3).

[42] While U.L.P.A. § 19 permits a limited partner to freely assign his interest, the assignor cannot convey to his assignee his full privileges as a limited partner unless the assignor is empowered to do so under the certificate, or unless the remaining members agree. For example, if the assignee does not become a "substituted limited partner," he may share in future profits but may not ask for an inspection of partnership books or seek an accounting of partnership transactions. U.L.P.A. § 19(3). In addition, the articles of limited partnership customarily place restrictions on the class of persons in respect to which an interest can be assigned to achieve certain business or legal objectives. For example, the transferee often is required to be twenty-one years of age or older, a resident of the state in which the partnership is doing business, or subject to approval by the general partners. See note 30 *supra,* at 277, for an example of such restriction.

[43] While a few publicly held real estate limited partnerships, like American Housing Partners (underwritten by E.F. Hutton), maintain an after-market for shares at the issue price, the cashing in of a syndicate unit is almost always made expensive and cumbersome. Otherwise, an excessive number of redemptions could force the syndicate to maintain a level of reserves which could decimate its leveraging ability and unduly dilute the rate of equity return for its investors. See Benzer, note 33 *supra*; Roulac, *Real Estate Syndication Digest—Principles & Application* 90 (2d ed. 1973). Consequently, a limited partner must ordinarily invoke his own resources to sell or exchange his investment share. In this respect, his plight resembles the liquidity bind faced by shareholders in a closely held corporation. A correlative disadvantage is that for credit purposes, the collateral value of the partnership interest is quite low. While the maximum loan-to-value ratio for high-grade common stocks is apparently about 75 percent and for AAA municipal bonds about 80 percent, it is doubtful whether

available to shareholder-investors, especially with regard to construction projects. In addition, corporate ownership offers investors the ability to relegate management decisions and title-handling problems to the agents of the corporation. It also offers promotors the ability to reach a wide variety of investors in order to secure the necessary venture capital. In addition, use of the corporate form permits the participants to take full tax advantage of pension, profit-sharing, and other fringe benefit plans allowed to employees. Yet these factors have become less significant in our present era of maximum public liability insurance,[35] nonrecourse financing,[36] and liberalized fringe benefits for individual employers.[37] Moreover, limited liability,[38] easy access to investors, centralized man-

---

[35] This type of expensive insurance protects the insured against tort liability imposed by local law for damages due to personal injuries or property damage caused by the negligence of the insured.

[36] Nonrecourse financing refers to a loan arrangement whereby the debtor is not personally liable for repayment of the indebtedness and, if the loan is secured, recourse may only be had by the lender against the secured property. See discussion at ¶ 1.05[4][b].

[37] Certain fringe benefits available to corporate employees are not available to individual proprietors or partners. For example, a corporate employer can provide group term life insurance, sick pay, and death benefits on a tax-free basis; a partnership cannot. However, under the Pension Reform Act of 1974, treatment of corporate employees has become less preferential, relative to partners. For example, self-employed individuals, including partners, may now deduct up to $7,500 per annum or, if less, 15 percent of earned income for amounts contributed to qualified "Keogh" plans. Previously, the limits were $2,500 and 10 percent, respectively.

[38] However, in exchange for this limitation of liability, U.L.P.A. § 7 requires that a limited partner forgo participation in the control of the business; otherwise, he can become liable to outside creditors. While neither the statute nor the underlying case law defines the threshold limits to which a limited partner may go without being regarded as partaking in control, the case decisions do clearly suggest that a limited partner can safely engage in a limited degree of management activity. For example, a limited partner can certainly give advice when solicited by the general partner. E.g., Silvola v. Rowlett, 129 Colo. 522, 529, 272 P.2d 287, 291 (1954), wherein a limited partner, as shop foreman, occasionally discussed major matters with the general partner. He can occasionally perform ministerial functions, especially when the business is undergoing a crisis period. E.g., Grainger v. Antoyan, 48 Cal. 2d 805, 313 P.2d 848, 854 (1957), wherein a limited partner, as sales manager, sometimes signed checks but had no authority to hire personnel, purchase inventory, or set prices. And, in some jurisdictions, the limited partner can by statute vote on matters of vital concern to all the partners. For example, Cal. Corp. Code § 15507 (West 1977) permits limited partners to vote on such important matters as appointment or removal of general partners, termination of the partnership, amendment of the partnership agreement, and sale of substantially all of the firm's assets.

partnership taxation. However, as a consequence of some well-publicized failures caused by careless accounting and management practices, the limited partnership lost ground to the corporate type of syndicate during the early 1960s.[31] Yet, the limited partnership form of ownership has rebounded since the late 1960s, notwithstanding some curtailment of the tax shelter device imposed by the Tax Reform Acts of 1969 and 1976.[32] Today, especially with the recent decline in popularity of the equity real estate investment trusts, the limited partnership is one of the most prevalent forms of ownership for real estate investors both on[33] and off[34] Wall Street. For this reason, the following will deal primarily with the limited partnership as compared to the corporation.

[1] Legal and Financing Considerations

Traditionally, the main incentive for selecting corporate rather than partnership ownership has been the limited tort and contract liability

---

[31] The bankruptcy of Louis J. Glickman in 1963 is a prime example.

[32] In contrast to the Tax Reform Acts of 1969 and 1976, the Revenue Act of 1978 created new incentives for real estate investment, notably, by reducing the capital gains tax, by not further restricting the use of accelerated depreciation, and by not extending the at-risk rules to real estate. See discussion at ¶ 1.05[2][d].

[33] Since 1972, some of the nation's largest brokerage houses, such as Merrill Lynch, Pierce, Fenner & Smith, Kidder Peabody & Co., and E.F. Hutton & Co., have been underwriting limited partnership offerings at prices the public can afford. While the Tax Reform Act of 1969 provided impetus for public syndicators to invest in new residential construction, especially federally subsidized housing, such limited partnership syndicates have, to a lesser extent, also invested in commercial income-producing properties. Typical of the public syndications is a 1979 $60 million offering in unit denominations of $5,000, offered by a syndicate known as JMB Income Properties VI. This offering was marketed by Merrill Lynch to fund the acquisition of the Century City Office Building in Los Angeles. The syndicators estimate that for $5,000, each of the 6,000 limited partners will get a $300 a year net cash flow, most of which will be sheltered by depreciation deductions. It is also anticipated that in seven to twelve years the partnership can be liquidated at twice the original cost of the acquired properties and that the investors' gains will be taxed at capital gain rates. Only 78.3 percent of each $5,000 unit ($3,915) was used for equity—the balance was used to pay for commissions, fees, and other "front-end loads." See Fierro, "Many Become Limited Partners as Push for Investors Widens," N.Y. Times, Feb. 24, 1980, Sec. 8 at 1, col. 2. See also Benzer, "Real Estate Syndicates," N.Y. Times, March 19, 1972, Part III, at 2, col. 5.

[34] Most public real estate syndications are registered with the SEC; however, those that are sold intrastate or meet the requirements for exemption as private offerings are not regulated by the agency. The National Association of Securities Dealers estimates that in 1979 there were seventy-four offerings totalling $910 million. See Fierro, note 33 *supra*.

debts[28] and priority over general partners as to income and recapture of capital when accounts are settled, in the event the partnership is dissolved.[29] Moreover, recognizing that the limited partnership is but a close alternative to the corporation, in 1976 the National Conference of Commissioners on Uniform State Laws promulgated a Revised Uniform Limited Partnership Act that borrows many corporate law provisions, eliminates some troublesome questions under the old Act,[29a] and makes the limited partnership a less cumbersome type of ownership entity for real estate investors. Furthermore, the Internal Revenue Service has indicated that limited partnerships organized under the new Act should receive essentially the same tax treatment that was afforded to partnerships organized under the old Act.[29b] At present, three states have adopted the new ULPA,[29c] and it is anticipated that others will follow.

¶ 1.05 PARTNERSHIP VS. INCORPORATION

Because the limited partnership combines the tax advantages of partnership ownership with the legal and business advantages of incorporation, it is the most popular choice for real estate investors. Both private or "closely held" and public limited partnerships became very popular during the 1950-1960 decade, with the latter reaching its peak in 1961 when syndicate "units" costing $39 million were sold to acquire a major New York City office building.[30] This upsurge in popularity came about largely because of high federal income tax rates following World War II, as well as the 1954 Internal Revenue Code, which, to a large extent, extricated taxpayers from the imbroglio of pre-1954 Code

---

sublease the realty on a long-term net rental basis to insiders, for example, to the syndicate promoters themselves or their wholly owned affiliate. However, the general partners, exclusively, will make important policy and nonmanagement decisions such as if and when to lease, mortgage, refinance, or sell the realty.

[28] U.L.P.A. § 7.

[29] U.L.P.A. § 23.

[29a] For example, Section 303(b) of the revised ULPA supplies "safe harbor" provisions delineating activities that would not of themselves constitute an improper exercise of control by the limited partners under Section 7 of the old Act, so that these activities could be exercised without exposing the limited partners to unlimited liability. See note 37 *infra*. For an excellent general discussion of the new Act, see Kessler, "The New Uniform Limited Partnership Act: A Critique," XLVII Fordham L. Rev. 159 (1979).

[29b] *Id.* at 160. See also Rev. Rul. 79-106, 1979-12 I.R.B. 21.

[29c] Ark. Stat. Ann. §§ 65-501—566 (Supp. 1979); Conn. Gen. Stat. Ann. §§ 34-9-34-37 (West); Act of March 6, 1979, Ch. 153, §§ 17-14-201-17-14-1104, 1979, Wyo. Sess. Laws 357.

[30] 1 Roulac, *Syndication Landmarks* 19 (PLI 1974).

dissolves the partnership. However, this oft-cited advantage of the limited partnership is somewhat illusory; the case law clearly suggests that such continuity can also be effectuated by special agreement among the partners in a general partnership, without contravening the statute.[24]

A major disadvantage in the limited partnership form is the fact that while a limited partner's interest can automatically be transferred to his legal representative if any of these involuntary contingencies should occur, the interest is not very marketable, especially as, during latter years, tax shelter benefits start diminishing at an accelerated rate. Consequently, a nearly insolvent estate or legal representative may be forced into a real liquidity bind. By contrast, when a partner in a general partnership, or a general partner in a limited partnership, dies or becomes insolvent or legally incapacitated, his interest is customarily liquidated under a "buy-sell" or "first refusal" provision in the partnership agreement. Under the former, the interest of such partner is either sold to the remaining partners or retired by means of a liquidating distribution from the partnership, at a prearranged formula price, which may later be determinative of value for federal estate tax purposes.[25] Otherwise, the interest of the deceased or incapacitated partner might be sold to a stranger at a sacrifice price or passed on to an heir or devisee whose intrusion into the management decision-making process could spell disaster for the remaining partners.[26]

Nevertheless, if unsophisticated or numerous investors are involved, the limited partnership is still the more appropriate organizational entity. The investors, as limited partners, can relegate unwelcome management responsibilities to the promoter-general partners.[27] In exchange, they will receive limitation of personal liability for partnership

---

[24] The modern view adopted by several case decisions and, in a number of states, by statute, is that a partnership is not necessarily dissolved by the death or withdrawal of a partner if the agreement so provides. E.g., Zeibak v. Nasser, 12 Cal. 2d 1, 20, 82 P.2d 375, 384 (1938); Storer v. Ripley, 12 Misc. 2d 662, 178 N.Y.S.2d 7 (1958); Cal. Corp. Code § 15031(4) (West); Tex. Rev. Civ. Stat. Ann. Art. 6132b, § 31(4) (Vernon).

[25] However, the buy-sell restriction must apply during the lifetime of the deceased partner as well as upon his demise. E.g., Lomb v. Sugden, 82 F.2d 166, 168 (2d Cir. 1939).

[26] See Section 5.2(2) of Form 1.1, a sample limited partnership agreement in Appendix B, for an illustration of a typical buy-sell provision and Section 5.1(2) for an illustration of a typical right-of-first-refusal provision.

[27] While U.L.P.A. § 7 mandates that management authority be relegated to the general partners, the general partners seldom retain responsibility for ordinary management decisions. For example, the syndicate will frequently delegate management control to outsiders, perhaps to a real estate concern for a prearranged fee or percentage of the profits, or sometimes to the previous owner under a sale-and-leaseback arrangement. Alternatively, the syndicate might

purchase an equity interest in the secured property either immediately or upon substantial completion of the improvements. In most instances, this shift from a fixed-rate mortgage loan to a fluctuating equity investment occurs during a period of inflation, when mortgage money is tight and interest rates are high, or when common stock prices are falling. At such times, these lenders or their subsidiary corporations will acquire such a joint venture position either as a hedge against inflation, as a device to circumvent interest rate ceilings imposed by local usury laws, or as merely an alternative to investments such as stocks and bonds, which at the time look less attractive.[19]

¶ 1.04 GENERAL VS. LIMITED PARTNERSHIP

A general partnership is the ownership vehicle often preferred by a relatively small and intimate group of sophisticated insiders who do not depend upon outside sources for venture capital. The members are willing to forgo the automatic limited liability advantage of being limited partners in exchange for control over policy decisions[19a] and some liquidity for their estates in the event of their demise.

An oft-cited advantage of the limited partnership is its "continuity of enterprise." Unlike the tenancy in common and joint venture forms, the death, bankruptcy, incompetency, or withdrawal of an individual partner, whether general or limited, does not affect the real property directly. Under the Uniform Partnership Act (UPA), each partner's interest in the partnership is an interest in personalty, and the partner has no direct proprietary interest in the real property.[20] Death, insanity, or withdrawal of a limited partner does not dissolve a limited partnership. In the case of a general partner it will, unless the limited partnership certificate specifically gives the general partners the right to continue the business or gives the remaining partners consent to their doing so.[21] By contrast, under the UPA, the death, bankruptcy, incompetency,[22] and perhaps withdrawal[23] of a partner in a general partnership

---

[19] See ¶ 11.02 for detailed discussion of joint ventures between developers and institutional investors.

[19a] Uniform Limited Partnership Act § 7 (hereinafter cited as ULPA) provides that a "limited partner shall not become liable as a general partner, unless, in addition to the exercise of his rights and powers as a limited partner, he takes part in control of the business." See note 37 *infra*.

[20] U.P.A. §§ 8, 25(6), 26.

[21] U.L.P.A. §§ 20, 21.

[22] U.P.A. §§ 31(4), 31(5), 32(1)(a).

[23] Crane & Bromberg, note 17 *supra*, § 78(e).

(4) Perhaps the most constraining disadvantage is definitional, imposed by the Treasury regulations, which define the term "partnership" so broadly that it includes any joint ownership in which the co-owners actively carry on a trade, business, financial operation, or venture, and divide the profits thereof.[13]

Example. A and B are co-owners of an apartment building, are leasing space, and are providing services to the occupants indirectly, through an agent. Even though A and B regard themselves as tenants in common and are denominated as such at local law, for tax purposes they will be treated as partners of the *AB* partnership. By contrast, had they merely leased the building to self-sufficient tenants under a net-lease arrangement, passive co-owners A and B would be treated as tenants in common and not as partners.[14]

Curiously, the Code provides that an organization can, at the behest of all its members, "elect out" of partnership treatment if it is formed for "investment purposes and not for the active conduct of a business."[15] But why should such election be necessary if the ownership entity is passive and does not engage in substantive management activity? Perhaps the real function of this Code section is to permit passive owners to switch back to tenancy-in-common treatment after organizing and reporting their income as partners.[16]

¶ 1.03 JOINT VENTURES

A joint venture is distinguishable from the ordinary partnership in that it is generally formed to carry out a single undertaking rather than an indefinite number of transactions; it is also frequently of short duration.[17] However, in all essential aspects it is either analogized or simply treated as a partnership under local law and is subsumed for tax purposes under the definition of a partnership.[18] As a concomitant to making a permanent mortgage loan commitment, life insurance companies and other institutional lenders will often obtain the right to

---

[13] Reg. § 1.761-1(a).
[14] *Id.*
[15] I.R.C. § 761(a).
[16] An election must be made no later than the time prescribed for filing a partnership return for that tax year for which the exclusion is desired. Reg. § 1.761-2(b)(1).
[17] Crane & Bromberg, *Law of Partnership* § 35 (1968).
[18] I.R.C. § 7701(a)(2).

be separately charged with capital gain, since the nature of his gain would not to any extent depend upon the status of colleagues.
(3) No partnership return is required for a tenancy in common. Thus, if a tenant is audited, it is less likely that his co-owner will be audited, since there is no return filed that links them to one another.

[b] Disadvantages

The following are the disadvantages of a tenancy in common as compared to both partnership and corporate taxations:

(1) Each tenant must separately report only his proportionate part of net operating income or net gain from the sale or exchange of property. For example, if one tenant pays a larger share of the total expenses, he is entitled to deduct only his pro rata share. The excess payment is treated as an advance to his co-owners.[10]

(2) A corollary disadvantage lies in the fact that tenants in common, unlike partners and joint venturers,[11] may not reallocate income and deduction items, such as depreciation, in a ratio at variance with their interest in the commonly owned property.

(3) In the event of the death, insolvency, incompetency, or retirement of a tenant in common, title to his share of the realty may pass to his heir or devisee, creditor, court-appointed trustee, or assignee, as the case may be. By contrast, if property is taken in the name of a partnership, legal title in specific partnership property remains unencumbered if the remaining partners should agree to continue the partnership, subject, of course, to the rights of the former partner's legal representative or assignee to his share of the partnership profits and surplus.[12]

---

the Service and courts will necessarily scrutinize and be guided by the backgrounds of all the partners in determining the tax status of the partnership.
[10] E.g., Estate of Eugene Merrick Webb, 30 T.C. 1202 (1958), *acq.* 1959-2 C.B. 7.
[11] See I.R.C. §§ 704(b), 704(c).
[12] Uniform Partnership Act §§ 8, 25(2), 27(1) (hereinafter cited as UPA).

I.R.C. § 1372. By contrast, Subchapter K of the Internal Revenue Code dealing with partnerships, sidesteps the conflict and applies whichever approach produces the most desirable result. For example, to permit flexible arrangements among partners, the Code permits partners to make special allocations of deductions and income items[5] (the aggregate approach) and yet recognizes most partner-partnership dealings[6] for tax purposes (the entity approach). At the other end of the spectrum is the tenancy in common, with respect to which the aggregate approach is strictly applied.

[a] Advantages

The following are the advantages of the tenancy in common as compared to both partnership and corporate taxation:

> (1) Any election affecting the computation of taxable income may be made separately by each tenant. For example, one co-owner may capitalize carrying charges and/or claim accelerated depreciation while another may elect to currently deduct or "expense" such charges[7] and/or claim straight-line depreciation.[8]
>
> (2) Association with dealers in a new partnership or joint venture may taint partnership income. An investor partner, along with all the other partners, may thus be charged with dealer gain (i.e., ordinary income as opposed to capital gain).[9] The same investor, as a tenant in common, would

---

[5] I.R.C. § 704(b). See discussion at ¶ 1.05[3][b].

[6] I.R.C. § 707(a).

[7] I.R.C. § 266. Taxes, mortgage interest, and other carrying charges that are otherwise currently deductible may, at the option of the taxpayer, be charged to the taxpayer's capital account and be added to the taxpayer's cost or other tax basis in the real property. If the latter alternative is adopted, the taxpayer would, by means of a depreciation deduction, be able to indirectly write off the cost of these items over the useful life of the property. Reg. § 1.266-1. However, Tax Reform Act of 1976, Pub. L. 94-455, § 201, 90 Stat. 1525 (hereinafter cited as 1976 TRA) added I.R.C. § 189, which eliminates a current deduction for property construction period interest and taxes.

[8] See note 47 *infra,* for example illustrating difference between straight-line and accelerated depreciation.

[9] I.R.C. § 702(b) is ambiguous, but the weight of authority suggests that the nature of each partner's distributive share of gain or loss is determined by reference to the tax status of the partnership and not the partner. E.g., Hyman Podell, 55 T.C. 429, 434 (1970). See also Reg. § 1.702-1(b). However, in the case of a newly formed partnership that has acted neither as an investor nor dealer,

¶ 1.02 TENANCY IN COMMON

[1] Nontax Considerations

Tenancy in common is the simplest but rarest form of co-ownership because the right of partition and the requirement of unanimous consent for decision-making[2] renders this mode of operation too cumbersome to manage except in small, closely knit groups whose purpose is solely to maintain the property and collect the rental income. Moreover, upon the death of one of the co-owners, title to the property may be clouded by an unsettled estate, since all of the co-owners are ordinarily required under state law to execute the deed of conveyance at the time of transfer.[3] Nevertheless, this form of organizational entity does have its advantages. For example, in contrast to the general partnership form, the tenancy in common provides for continuity of enterprise beyond the death of any co-owner. It also permits free transferability of the ownership shares.[4] However, on balance, the problems of control, partition, title transfer, and death of a co-owner will generally dissuade large or less-than-intimate groups of investors from selecting this type of ownership entity, unless there is some compelling tax advantage.

[2] Tax Considerations

To appreciate the tax advantages and disadvantages inherent in this form of ownership, one must first understand the conflict in the tax law between the so-called aggregate and entity approaches. In determining tax consequences, an ownership entity can be treated as an aggregate of equity participants who pool their assets and resources for some common purpose. Under this aggregate approach, the entity is merely treated as a nontaxable conduit by which tax consequences flow directly to each constituent member. By contrast, under the entity approach, for tax purposes the organization itself is treated as an entity that is separate and distinct from its participants; accordingly, separate tax consequences accrue to both the entity and its members. For example, the entity approach applies to corporate taxation and accounts for the double taxation problem faced by shareholders other than those owning stock in a small business corporation (Subchapter S corporation) under

---

[2] 4A *Powell on Real Property* ¶ 6.08, at 633 (rev. ed. 1968). To some degree, this problem can be ameliorated by an agreement among the co-owners for centralized management. However, such an agreement may cause the entity to more closely resemble an association taxable as a corporation under Reg. § 301.7701-2(e).

[3] E.g., Haviland v. Haviland, 130 Iowa 611, 615, 105 N.W. 354, 355 (1905).

[4] See discussion at ¶ 1.04.

       [4] Tax Pitfalls of Limited Partnership 1-44
           [a] Possible Taxation as an Association 1-44
           [b] Tax Shelter Basis Problem Caused by
               Recourse Financing 1-52
               [i] General Rule 1-52
               [ii] Special Basis Rule for
                   Limited Partner 1-52
               [iii] Tax Planning to Avoid Basis Problem............ 1-55
       [5] Tax Advantages of Incorporation 1-59
           [a] Lower Tax Rate..................................... 1-60
           [b] Flexibility in Choice of Tax Year 1-60
           [c] Greater Fringe Benefits for Employees................ 1-60
           [d] No Limitation on "Investment Interest" 1-61
           [e] Corporation Survives Stock Ownership
               Changes 1-61
¶ 1.06 Subchapter S Corporation................................. 1-61
¶ 1.07 Real Estate Investment Trusts 1-67
¶ 1.08 Common-Law Land Trust................................. 1-68

¶ 1.01 DYNAMICS OF THE SELECTION PROCESS

In real estate ventures, the most important pre-financing consideration[1] is the decision as to which type of ownership entity is best suited for the dual purpose of raising the venture capital and securing the debt financing needed to fund the acquisition and/or improvement of the real estate. The choice is broad as to the ownership vehicle. It includes use of the tenancy in common, joint venture, general partnership, limited partnership, corporation, land trust, or real estate investment trust. The limited partnership has generally been the entity most preferred by investors because it best combines the tax advantages of individual ownership with the nontax advantages of corporate ownership. However, any such determination should always involve the careful balancing of the specific competing tax, financing, and legal attributes that characterize each form of entity. Unfortunately, this balancing process is complicated by the truism that what is otherwise suitable from a legal or financing standpoint is often intolerable from a tax perspective, or vice versa. Accordingly, in selecting the optimum alternative no fewer than three horses must be harnessed, one of which—tax—is always on the run!

---

[1] For a brief discussion of other salient pre-financing considerations, see ¶ 3.01.

Chapter 1

SELECTION OF OWNERSHIP ENTITY

		Page
¶ 1.01	Dynamics of the Selection Process	1- 2
¶ 1.02	Tenancy in Common	1- 3
	[1] Nontax Considerations	1- 3
	[2] Tax Considerations	1- 3
	[a] Advantages	1- 4
	[b] Disadvantages	1- 5
¶ 1.03	Joint Ventures	1- 6
¶ 1.04	General vs. Limited Partnership	1- 7
¶ 1.05	Partnership vs. Incorporation	1- 9
	[1] Legal and Financing Considerations	1-10
	[2] Tax Sheltering of Investor's Income	1-14
	[a] In General	1-14
	[b] Income-Producing Property	1-16
	[c] Nondepreciable Property	1-19
	[d] Post-1976 Tax Legislation	1-20
	[3] Other Tax Advantages of Partnership Over Incorporation	1-30
	[a] Collapsible Provisions Less Stringent	1-30
	[i] Partnership Tax Planning	1-31
	[ii] Corporate Tax Planning	1-34
	[b] Flexibility in Allocation of Income or Loss	1-36
	[i] Special Allocations	1-36
	[ii] Allocation of Depreciation or Gain or Loss on Contributed Property	1-41
	[iii] Retroactive Amendment of Partnership Agreement	1-41
	[c] Miscellaneous Tax Advantages of Partnerships	1-42
	[i] Opportunity to Reduce Compensation Income of Partner Who Contributes Services and Not Property to the Partnership	1-42
	[ii] Flexibility in Determining Compensation Income	1-43
	[iii] No Penalty Tax Problem	1-43
	[iv] Section 1237 Subdivision Rule	1-43
	[v] Ordinary Loss Deduction Upon Worthlessness of Partnership Interest	1-43

cial and industrial properties, and the even more complex relationship of holders of fee and leasehold mortgagees to their mortgagors. Nevertheless, not only has the doctrine of unconscionability, as enunciated in the Uniform Commercial Code in all its sphinx-like reticence, been translated to the different realm of landlord and tenant law by the *Restatement* and, even more so, by the Uniform Residential Landlord and Tenant Act, but to the whole realm of real property law with the approval, in February 1978, by the American Bar Association (by a close vote), of the Uniform Land Transactions Act (ULTA), largely premised on the Uniform Commercial Code. ULTA permits a court to find the agreement, or a term in the agreement, in any real property transaction unconscionable, including the creation and enforcement of consensual security interests. ULTA practically eliminates the statute of frauds. It introduces into the law of real estate an entirely new concept, that of allowing a party to avoid its obligations under a contract because performance has become "impracticable by the occurrence of a contingency the risk of which the parties did not assume would be borne" by that party. The comments would include as a contingency covered by this section (2-407 of ULTA) fluctuations in market value.

However, the impact of public law has been exceedingly influential not only in inhibiting or regulating real estate transactions but also in facilitating and promoting real estate development by engaging or assisting in the financing and subsidization of residential land development and by establishing a secondary market for single- and multifamily residential mortgage loans.

In conclusion, we have closed the ring from public to private to public law in eight centuries, from the feudal period preceding the Magna Carta and the establishment of the inviolability of the freehold estate to the decision of the United States Supreme Court in recent months sustaining New York City's Landmarks Preservation Act as applied to Grand Central Station.

Maitland, in his classic *Constitutional History of England* sums it all up (page 155): "If we examine our notion of feudalism does it not seem then, that land law is not private law, that public law is land law, that public and political rights and duties of all sorts and kinds are intimately and quite inextricably blended with rights in land?" And if we examine our notions of real property law today, do we not come to the same conclusion?

If this very brief perusal of real property law history succeeds in relating the past to the contemporary real estate transactions analyzed in sharp detail in this volume, it will have served its purpose.

Mendes Hershman

insurance company, commercial bank, savings and loan association, mutual savings bank, pension fund, or real estate investment trust are a product of unique external constraints imposed by local law. Examples are state usury restrictions on rates that lenders can charge real estate borrowers for the use of borrowed funds, and state regulatory statutes that impose both qualitative and quantitative limitations on loans that a lender can acquire for its investment portfolio.

A recent emerging trend toward consumerism and socialization of the law is causing attorneys for developers and lenders to adjust their common-law thinking with respect to the rights of real property owners. An example of the former is the Real Estate Settlement Procedures Act, which was enacted by Congress for the purpose of aiding home buyers by requiring that settlement costs and practice information be made available to buyers so that they would be in a better position to shop around for settlement services and make knowledgeable decisions on transfer costs. In addition, the Act reduces the buyer's acquisition costs by prohibiting referral fees and the amount lenders may require in the form of escrow deposits. An example of the latter trend toward the socialization of real property law is the so-called doctrine of unconscionability and its potential erosion-of-contract impact on property law in the context of commercial real estate transactions. The *Restatement of Property Law Second*, adopted by the American Law Institute in May 1976, after setting up an obligation of the landlord to keep leased property in repair, provides in Section 5.6 that "the parties to a lease may agree to increase or decrease what would otherwise be the obligations of the landlord with respect to the condition of the leased property and may agree to expand or contract what would otherwise be the remedies available to the tenant for the breach of those obligations, and those agreements are valid and binding on the parties to the lease unless they are unenforceable in whole or in part because they are unconscionable or significantly against public policy." The comment to Section 5.6 tells us that "an agreement is unconscionable when it would shock the conscience if enforced." The comment further states that although in the interests of certainty the provisions of written leases should not be disregarded lightly, certain facts could be considered in determining whether an agreement in a lease is in all or in part unenforceable because unconscionable and lists certain criteria. Section 2-302 of the Commercial Code defines "unconscionability" in terms of itself, as does the use of the term in the *Restatement*, that is, that a contract is unconscionable if a court finds it so—an exercise in tautology.

It would seem that a rule of a law that is not illuminating in connection with commercial sales is not particularly fitted to be translated to the completely different realm of estates for terms of years and fees, to the relationship of landlord and tenant, particularly of commer-

new towns and communities. As if such esoteric and ethereal concepts as a fee simple interest in delineated air space were not enough, a new concept of condominium time-sharing, wherein a group of individuals purchases blocks of time in a condominium, has been introduced to cure an ailing resort condominium market. Essentially, one purchaser has the use of Blackacre condominium for every first and second weekend in June while a subsequent purchaser has the use of that same Blackacre condominium for every third and fourth weekend in June *in futuro*. Is this an innovative concept or a mere variant of the historical fee estate and future interest? In either event, "tis such stuff that dreams are made of."

If the income stream from a building can be carved up, why can't the use and ownership of the building be similarly carved? Why not take a skyscraper and on the first floor have a leased mezzanine for commercial shopping and above that have an office space. For those who wish to own their office space, an office condominium for several floors could also be carved out. And since we are contemplating an office condominium, why not have a residential condominium above that for those who prefer to own air they breathe and several floors of apartment-leased space for the perennial would-be renters. Interesting? Yes. Creative? Yes. Novel? Yes. Unheard of? No. It has already been done and done successfully. How different is this concept from the Roman concept of property that was based not upon fee simple ownership, but upon the right to use or possess property for a given period of time?

Finally, the simple entrepreneurial developer back in the 1900s, doing business either as a sole proprietor, partnership, or corporation, has diversified its nature and now may instead be a limited partnership syndicate, a Subchapter S corporation, a real estate investment trust, an offshore trust, or a pension fund, and the cast of characters continues to expand.

Recent Impact of Public Law

While real estate financing was becoming increasingly complex, a similar evolutionary process was taking place in the public law sector. Tax law as well as the securities laws have become major influences in determining the forms in which land will be acquired and developed. Building code, planning, zoning, subdivision, and environmental laws and regulations at several governmental levels will determine to a substantial degree whether and where the land may be developed, for what uses, and to what design. Not only the securities laws but also the disclosure requirements of the Interstate Land Sales Full Disclosures Act affect the marketing of the land and improvements as developed. The lending practices of a mortgage lender, whether it be a life

out in multi-layered fashion of interests or estates in the cash flow from the real estate, known in the trade not as estates but as "positions." For example, in large developments such as office structures, it was not uncommon for the fee title to be vested in A or a subsidiary of A who had purchased the land from B and then leased it back to B under a long-term net "ground lease." The improvements were constructed by B, whose leasehold interest was subjected to a leasehold mortgage given to finance the construction, with title to the structures remaining in B for the term of the lease. The buildings were subleased by B under a long-term net lease, known in the trade as a "sandwich lease," to a public or private limited partnership; then sub-subleased under a long-term net "operating" lease to a real estate management company that actually operated the building, and finally, sub-sub-subleased to the actual occupants. The sandwich and operating leases in turn were encumbered by leasehold mortgages. What was sold or mortgaged in each instance was not a segment of the physical real estate nor was the segmentation in time, as in the case of state limitations, but interests in a cash flow (cast in the form of estates for years), interests generated to a large degree by a perceived need for tax shelter. Because of the changing perception of their needs by the owners of these interests, ground leases, sandwich leases, and operating leases have been sold just as frequently as, and probably more frequently than, the fee title to these properties. The conveyancing of these interests or "positions," just as the initial acquisition of land and construction of the buildings, is in almost every case made possible by mortgage financing.

Real estate development and financing became increasingly complex in other areas as well. In Chicago, with much of the prime space encumbered by railroad tracks, the concept of erecting buildings over the air rights either leased, sold, or conveyed by easement became popular. The basic building, by using reinforced steel, became the skyscraper. The entry into the automobile age created the regional shopping center that we know today. This shopping center, with its many tenants and competing rights and uses, called for complicated cross and reciprocal easement agreements to govern this newly created commercial community. These reciprocal easement agreements also became of great value to developers and attorneys planning industrial and office parks.

In another area of real estate, various state governments, borrowing on the Puerto Rican concept, enacted condominium statutes. These condominium statutes enable a developer to convey a fee simple interest in air defined and delineated by ceiling and wall dimensions!

The legal planning tools that were developed in constructing shopping centers, industrial and office parks, and residential subdivisions are the same tools used today to produce planned unit developments and

to the buildings in order to allow a simultaneous rental deduction for the leased land and still be entitled to a depreciation for the buildings.

Mortgage financing was also becoming more sophisticated. One hundred percent financing based on a high-credit lease was introduced. A developer would enter into a triple-A net lease with the tenant obligated to pay rents at all times and without the right to cancel or terminate the lease. The lender, in making the loan, would receive the rental payments directly from the tenant under a present and absolute assignment of lease agreement. In effect, the lender would be making a loan against the lease instead of placing a mortgage on the real estate. Another innovative device was the wraparound mortgage, borrowed from Canada, whereby a mortgagor executes a promissory note that includes the outstanding balance of the first mortgage, together with the funds to be advanced under the secondary wrap mortgage. The end result was a higher yield to the wraparound mortgagee.

Post World War II

In the late 1930s and early 1940s, real estate development and financing sprouted wings. The real property lawyer in the middle ages often encountered the need for complex and skillful draftsmanship for carving out ownership interests in time, what we would today call estate planning—the limitations of life estates, remainders vested and contingent, reverters and the possibilities of reverter or rights of reentry, springing and shifting uses, and all except rights of reentry within the strictures of the rule against perpetuities. And it was the genius of one William Zeckendorf who came up with a real estate device as creative and complicated as our seventeenth century ancestors developed. Zeckendorf, with his "pineapple theory," stood the layering of future interests and estates on its head. He turned Blackacre into a sheaf of securities and made real property law close kin to corporation law. Not caring or even aware of the durational estate concept, Zeckendorf was concerned with carving up the present income derived from Blackacre to enable as many diverse parties as possible to share in varying proportions of risk. An example of this technique is the syndication of the Hotel taft in New York City. This hotel, having a profit of $2.2 million a year, was sold to a syndicate for $18 million. The syndicate immediately leased the hotel to a second syndicate under a net lease calling for an annual rent of $1,950,000. This valuable lease was sold to Zeckendorf Hotel Corporation, which in turn sold the lease to a third syndicate, the Hotel Taft Company, which in turn subleased back to Zeckendorf Hotel Corporation. In effect, three ownership entities, together with the mortgagee, were sharing in an income stream.

After World War II, this concept became refined as real estate became segmented—both horizontally and vertically—with a carving

the mortgage companies, such as S.W. Strauss, and the title companies to allow for payment of interest, taxes, etc., and simply remit the proportionate amount of the total debt payable to the investor. Title companies then became guarantors of the debt to make it easier to market them, and many of these guaranteed mortgages were purchased by life insurance companies, creating an even greater flow of mortgage money. Mortgages in those days were short term, usually renewed and not self-amortized. (The self-amortizing mortgage did not come into vogue until the 1930s with the Federal Housing Authority.) The debt often exceeded the value of the properties that secured the debt, and toward the end of the 1920s the mountain of debt exceeded the capacity of the borrowers to meet their obligations. In time, many of these investors learned that even a secured position on overvalued land did not make for a safe investment.

Triggered in part by the stock market crash late in 1929, the real estate market fell apart by 1932, and the Great Depression was on. Between 1930 and 1935 more than a million American families lost their homes despite moratoria of mortgage foreclosures, and the first major intervention of the federal government into the real estate market followed. The National Housing Act of 1934 introduced the federally insured self-liquidating mortgage, guaranteeing to lenders that the government would bear any loss from a defaulted loan. And to make it easy to borrow, it raised the permissible loan to 90 percent of loan-to-value ratio, instead of the then-conventional amount of 50 to 60 percent. High loan-to-value ratios have characterized federally backed mortgages ever since, reaching 100 percent in the Veterans Administration loans of the 1950s, and in the Section 221 d-3 program of the 1960s, enacted to stimulate nonprofit groups to produce "moderate" income housing.

After the Great Depression that dampened debt-syndication, the next wave of syndication began with ownership entities. Groups of investors would form a limited partnership or some other ownership vehicle in order to acquire commercial real estate for investment purposes. In time, this type of syndication became one step removed from direct ownership through the use of tiered limited partnerships, whereby various and separate limited partnerships would join together to own a portion of an income stream. During this same period, greater use was made of an old financing technique known as leasehold mortgage financing which, coupled with the ground lease concept, ushered in the use and popularity of sale-leasebacks, where an owner of improved real estate would sell the real estate and retain possession under a long-term lease. A variation of the sale-leaseback was created solely for tax purposes whereby the owner of the realty would sell only the land, which he would then rent back, while reserving fee simple title

Public law has again become the major determinant of the text and prospects of real property law and has become a major *pre-financing* influence in determining the ways in which land may be acquired, developed, and financed. A brief excursion into the history of modern land development and finance should suffice to make the point.

The 1920s and the Great Depression

In the early 1900s, real estate financing consisted of a basic note or bond and mortgage. Many wizened attorneys still remember when a real estate practitioner was relegated to the back of the office while his colleagues up front practiced more glamorous specialties like corporate law. Since real estate ultimately led to a shovel and dirt, it was thought of as less sophisticated and challenging than stocks and securities. This was a far cry from the property attorney of the 1600s who was dealing with and creating complicated layering of estates. In the early 1900s, one could not find a real estate transaction as complex as a seventeenth century devise of "Blackacre to A for life, then if B reaches twenty-one upon the death of A, Blackacre to B for life, then Blackacre in fee simple to C and his heirs but should Georgetown University become a public institution then to D and his heirs." This durational aspect of carving up ownership by estates was not of great importance to the real estate practitioner of the early 1900s. Rather, the emphasis was placed upon the present use and ownership of a building. For the most part, commercial buildings were built by and used by the owner. But in time, with the introduction of the federal income tax and accounting concepts such as off-sheet balance financing, investors soon realized that real estate was an excellent way to make a profit by owning property for the beneficial use of others. The deferral of construction and the rapid urbanization of the population during World War I created a pent-up demand for new residential as well as commercial construction. A real estate boom followed, exerting great pressures for mortgage loans. The normal sources for such funds were the commercial banks for construction or interim financing and the life insurance companies for major residential and commercial financing; thrift institutions financed single-family homes. Restrictions on lending, such as a loan-to-value ratio then just beginning to move up from 50 percent and limitations on the percentage of total assets that an insurance company could invest in mortgages diverted builders to other resources. The consequence was large-scale syndications of mortgages, managed by mortgage companies and title companies. In the early 1920s, thousands of would-be small investors looked to the secured position of a mortgage creditor and purchased interests in bonds secured by mortgages or deeds of trust on real estate. Large-scale syndications thus originated not on the equity side, but on the debt side of the balance sheet. These investors relied on

chiefs and the grasping cunning of the baser sort." And they are still working today toward the satisfaction of this permanent social need—the exact definition of proprietary rights.

What is perhaps the most fascinating aspect of real property law is how a concept appears and then reappears centuries later in a new context and, indeed, crosses the sea to offer a new solution to a contemporary problem, much like a theme that weaves its way through a symphony.

Within the strictures of this space let me pose an illustration of this historical phenomenon that may be of considerable utilitarian value in the legislative and judicial solutions to legal problems affecting land development and finance.

Feudal land law made little distinction between public and private law. Land was held through a wholly personal relationship between the lord of the land and his knight tenant. The private right of the tenant in the land, which he expected to hold for his lifetime and which his lord expected to dispose of as he wished later, was accepted by the knight as a privilege. In exchange for this privilege, the lord of the manor, the public authority of that day, could exact the means for discharging public functions such as the defense of the realm at home and military adventures abroad, the administration of justice, and the even more mundane supplying of food for his lordship's groaning board. The design by ingenious common-law real property lawyers of remedies for the protection of the tenant's interest in the real property led to the gradual metamorphosis of that personal relationship into a system of freehold and nonfreehold estates transferable, devisable, and mortgageable.

The transformation of tenure from a personal relationship to an institutionalized, judicially enforced system of interests in real estate was indeed complete when, in the eighteenth century, Blackstone could write in his *Commentaries* that "regard of the law of private property is so great...that it will not authorize the least violation of it, not even for the general good of the whole community," and the elder Pitt could utter with rhetorical flourish that "the poorest man in his cottage could defy the king—storms may enter, the rain may enter—but the King of England may not enter."

Since the eighteenth century, however, the rise of a powerful mercantile class, the industrial revolution, the great migrations to centers of population, and worldwide wars and threats of war have brought us to a present-day situation when not only may government enter that humble cottage, but may and has determined, for presumably the general good of the whole community, where and how it may be built, financed, taxed, or taken.

INTRODUCTION: PUBLIC LAW AS A MAJOR PRE-FINANCING INFLUENCE ON LAND DEVELOPMENT AND FINANCE

> "Let us now peruse our ancient authors for out of the old fields must come the new corn"
> —Lord Chief Justice Sir Edward Coke (1552-1634)

Justice Holmes tells us that "the rational study of law is still to a large extent the study of history." In no branch of the law is this more evident than in the law governing the development and financing of real property.

There is more than an intellectual exercise in a retrospect of real property law. It is a storied tapestry woven by kings and knights, judges and lawyers, depicting the great contests and controversies of Anglo-American history in which real property law has been the field of battle. It is great drama, still unfinished, and in which trumpets that heralded the first act echo to this very day.

The role of the lawyer in this drama, while muted, has been more significant than that of the captains and the kings who strode across the stage of history in a clatter of arms and have since departed.

H.G. Wells, in his work, *Wealth and Happiness of Mankind*, summing up his defense of these "gentlemen of the long robe," the conveyancers haunted by the spirit of righteousness, writes: "The illumination they shed may not always have been a beacon, but at any rate the wick never ceased altogether to glow, and down the centuries we see a succession of these unloved men boring away in their tedious frowsty courts, really struggling in that dim medieval light to import some semblance of justice, some thought for the common weal, into the limitless greed of robber barons, the unqualified imperative of feudal

11.1	Loan Participation Agreement	App. B-242
11.2	Separate Noteholder's Agreement	App. B-246
11.3	Master Mortgage Warehouse Security Agreement and Financing Statement	App. B-248
11.4	Joint Venture Agreement	App. B-261
	Security Agreement and Financing Statement	App. B-00
11.4	Joint Venture Agreement	App. B-00

Table of Statutes Cited .... **T- 1**
Table of Regulations and Rulings .... **T- 7**
Table of Cases **T-11**

Index .... **I- 1**

Appendix A
ANCILLARY DATA

		Page
Table 1	State Statutory Limitations on Commercial Bank Real Estate Loans	App. A- 2
Table 2	Mortgage Debt Outstanding	App. A-12
Table 3	Analysis of State Usury Statutes	App. A-15

Appendix B
SAMPLE FORMS AND AGREEMENTS

Form		Page
1.1	Limited Partnership Agreement—Annotated	App. B- 2
3.1	Permanent Mortgage Loan Commitment—Annotated	App. B- 26
3.2	Permanent Mortgage Loan Application-Commitment—Annotated	App. B- 36
3.3	Note	App. B- 43
3.4	Mortgage/Deed of Trust—Annotated	App. B- 44
3.5	Assignment of Lessor's Interest in Lease	App. B- 69
3.6	Notice of Lease Assignment	App. B- 75
3.7	Tenant's Acceptance Letter	App. B- 76
3.8	Closing Disbursement Letter to Title Company	App. B- 77
3.9	Attorney's Certification	App. B- 81
3.10	Architect's Certificate	App. B- 82
3.11	Mortgagor's Estoppel Affidavit	App. B- 83
3.12	Standard Mortgage Clause	App. B- 83
3.13	Certified Inventory	App. B- 85
3.14	Attornment and Nondisturbance Agreement Between Mortgagee and Occupancy Subtenants	App. B- 86
4.1	Building Loan Agreement	App. B- 87
4.2	Buy-Sell Agreement	App. B-106
6.1	Attornment and Nondisturbance Agreement Between Ground Lessor, Tenant and Mortgagee	App. B-110
6.2	Ground Lease on Unsubordinated Fee	App. B-112
6.3	Ground Lease Option and Development Agreement: Involving Ground Lease on Unsubordinated Fee	App. B-175
6.4	Land Purchase-Leaseback Transaction Sales Contract	App. B-177
8.1	Three-Cornered Exchange Agreement	App. B-185
9.1	Bond and Agreement Procedures for Residential Development	App. B-197
9.2	Set-Aside Letter	App. B-206
9.3	Master Development Loan Agreement	App. B-207
10.1	Master Deed for Condominium	App. B-223
10.2	Construction Loan Commitment Letter for Condominium Financing	App. B-232

	[b] Points and Discount	12-3
	[2] The Cost of Lending	12-4
	[a] Fees and Payments by the Mortgagee	12-4
	[b] Fees, Points, and Discount to the Mortgagee	12-5
	[3] The Crane Doctrine	12-5
	[a] Determination of Cost Tax Basis	12-5
	[b] Effects in Nonrecourse Financing	12-6
	[4] Mortgaging Out	12-7
¶ 12.02	Tax Consequences During the Mortgagor-Mortgagee Relationship	12-9
	[1] Mortgagee's Tax Treatment of Mortgage Payments	12-9
	[a] Distinction Between Interest and Principal	12-9
	[b] Mortgages Purchased at Discount	12-10
	[2] Mortgagor's Tax Treatment of Mortgage Payments	12-11
	[a] Interest vs. Principal	12-11
	[b] Investment Interest Limitations	12-12
	[3] Mortgagee's Expenses	12-13
	[4] Assignment of Rents to Mortgagee	12-14
¶ 12.03	Tax Consequences of Mortgagor's Default	12-15
	[1] Overview	12-15
	[2] Compromise of Mortgage Indebtedness	12-15
	[a] Consequences to Mortgagor	12-15
	[i] Debt Cancellation, Settlement at Discount	12-15
	[ii] Restructuring of the Debt	12-18
	[b] Consequences to Mortgagee	12-18
	[i] Timing of the Deduction	12-19
	[ii] Deduction Equals Mortgagee's Basis in the Debt	12-19
	[iii] Nature of the Loss: Business vs. Nonbusiness Debt	12-21
	[c] Tax Planning	12-24
	[3] Voluntary Conveyance to Mortgagee, Deed in Lieu of Foreclosure, Abandonment	12-24
	[a] Consequences to Mortgagor	12-24
	[b] Consequences to Mortgagee	12-28
	[c] Planning the Voluntary Conveyance	12-29
	[4] Foreclosure Sales	12-30
	[a] Consequences to Mortgagor	12-30
	[b] Consequences to Mortgagee	12-33
	[i] Foreclosure Sale to Third Party	12-33
	[ii] Foreclosure Sale to Mortgagee	12-36
	[5] Mortgagee's Disposition of Property Acquired From Mortgagor	12-45
	[6] Loss of a Second Mortgage	12-46
¶ 12.04	Disposition of Mortgaged Property	12-47
	[1] Sales and Taxable Exchanges	12-47
	[2] Transfers to Other Entities	12-48
	[3] Gifts, Abandonment	12-49

[3] Business and Legal Reasons for Loan Participations 11- 3
[4] "Warehousing" Mortgage Loans 11- 5
[5] Permanent Loan Participations 11- 7
[6] Legal Pitfalls 11- 7
    [a] No "Privity" Between Participant
    and Borrower 11- 7
    [b] Bankruptcy of the Borrower or Lead
    Lender 11- 9
    [c] Piggyback Protection From Usury Laws
    Unlikely for Loan Participants 11-10
    [d] Lead Lender's Compliance With
    Securities Laws 11-11
[7] The Loan Participation Agreement 11-11
[8] Separate Notes Secured by One Mortgage 11-12

¶ 11.02 Joint Ventures Between Institutional Lenders
and Developers 11-13
[1] Historical Development as Hedge Against
Inflation for Institutional Lenders 11-13
[2] Legal Definition 11-16
[3] Concerns of Co-Venturers 11-17
    [a] Psychological Barriers 11-17
    [b] Problems for Institution Acting as
    Both Co-Venturer and Permanent Lender 11-18
    [c] Usury Considerations 11-20
[4] Selecting the Ownership Entity 11-21
    [a] General vs. Limited Partnership 11-21
    [b] Indirect Subsidiary Investment in Joint
    Ventures 11-22
[5] Analysis of Joint Venture Agreement 11-23
    [a] Allocation of Capital Contributions 11-24
    [b] Allocation of Control 11-25
    [c] Default Remedies 11-27
    [d] Buy-Sell Agreement and Transfer
    of Venture Interest 11-28
    [e] Dissolution 11-29
    [f] Tax Considerations 11-29
[6] Summary of Problems Inherent in
Joint Venturing 11-30
[7] Renewed Interest in Institutional
Joint Ventures 11-31

Chapter 12

TAX ASPECTS OF MORTGAGE FINANCING

Page

¶ 12.01 Tax Consequences of a Mortgage on Real Property 12- 2
[1] The Cost of Obtaining a Mortgage Loan 12- 2
    [a] Fees 12- 2

[b] New Accrual Rules for Sales of Depreciable
Property Between Related Parties 9-36
[6] Liberalization of Rules for Like-Kind Exchanges
Coupled with Installment Sales 9-37
[7] Using the Deferred-Payment Method to Report Gain 9-38

¶ 9.05 Capital Gain Treatment for the Investor-Subdivider
Under I.R.C. § 1237 9-41
[1] Tax Status as Dealer vs. Investor 9-41
[2] Statutory Relief for the Investor-Subdivider 9-42

Chapter 10

CONDOMINIUM AND COOPERATIVE FINANCING

Page

¶ 10.01 Legal Structure of Condominium Ownership 10- 1

¶ 10.02 Condominium Financing 10- 5
[1] Subdivision and Condominium
Financing Distinguished 10- 5
[2] Construction Financing 10- 6
    [a] Underwriting Analysis 10- 6
    [b] State and Federal Regulation 10- 8
    [c] Presale and Release Requirements 10-11
    [d] Construction Lender's Review of
        Condominium Documents 10-13
[3] Permanent Financing 10-15
    [a] Sources of Permanent Mortgage Funds 10-15
    [b] Permanent Lender's Considerations 10-16
    [c] Permanent Lender Checklist for
        Review of Condominium Project 10-19
    [d] Permanent Loan Documentation 10-21
[4] Phasing 10-22
[5] Condominium Conversion of Rental Units 10-23

¶ 10.03 Cooperative Financing 10-25

Chapter 11

LOAN PARTICIPATIONS AND JOINT VENTURES BY INSTITUTIONAL LENDERS

Page

¶ 11.01 Loan Participations 11- 2
[1] Definition 11- 2
[2] Participant Lenders in Construction Financing 11- 3

Chapter 9

SUBDIVISION FINANCING

		Page
¶ 9.01	Nature of Subdivision Financing	9- 2
	[1] Purchase-Money Financing	9- 3
	[a] Prepayment and Default Provisions	9- 3
	[b] Exculpatory Clauses	9- 4
	[c] Release Provisions	9- 5
	[d] Subordination of Purchase-Money Financing	9- 7
	[2] Financing by Institutional Lender	9- 9
	[3] Approvals and Requirements for Closing Land Development Loan	9- 9
	[4] Loan Documentation	9-12
¶ 9.02	Title X Financing	9-13
¶ 9.03	Effect of Interstate Land Sales Full Disclosure Act on Subdivision Financing	9-14
	[1] Purpose of the Act	9-14
	[2] Compliance Procedures	9-17
	[3] Exemptions	9-17
	[4] Concerns of the Lender	9-19
	[a] Protection of Security Interest	9-19
	[b] Direct Liability Under the Act	9-19
¶ 9.04	Seller's Use of Installment Method for Reporting Income (I.R.C. § 453) Under Installment Sales Revision Act of 1980	9-21
	[1] Overview of Changes	9-22
	[2] Requirements for Using Installment Method Under New Law	9-23
	[a] Timely Election Need No Longer Be Filed	9-23
	[b] Limitations on Payments by Purchaser in Year of Sale Eliminated	9-23
	[i] Two Payment Rule Eliminated	9-23
	[ii] 30 Percent Limitation on Payments in Year of Sale Eliminated	9-24
	[c] Use of Escrow Arrangements and Third-Party Guarantees Under the New Law	9-28
	[3] Illustration of How to Report Gain Under Installment Method	9-32
	[4] Sale or Other Disposition of Installment Obligations Under New Law	9-33
	[a] General Rule	9-33
	[b] Cancellation of Installment Obligation, by Gift or Bequest, Is a Disposition	9-34
	[c] Distribution of Installment Obligation Pursuant to Section 337 Liquidation Allowed Under New Law	9-35
	[5] Sales to Related Parties Restricted	9-36
	[a] Restrictions on Intra-Family Transfers of Appreciated Property	9-36

	[ii] State Recording and	
	Disbursement Statutes	7-17
	[iii] Title Insurance	7-17

¶ 7.05 Documentation for Secondary Financing 7-18
       [1] Protection of Junior Lender 7-19
       [2] Protection of Senior Lender 7-20

¶ 7.06 Statutory and Common-Law Rights of Junior Mortgagee 7-21

Chapter 8

SPECIAL TYPES OF HIGH-RATIO FINANCING

Page

¶ 8.01 Introduction 8- 2

¶ 8.02 Tax-Free Exchange of Real Estate 8- 2
       [1] Techniques to Boost Depreciation Deduction 8- 5
       [2] Requirements for Tax-Free Exchange 8- 6
       [3] Effect of "Boot" and Mortgage on Computation of Gain or Loss 8- 8
       [4] Three-Cornered Exchange 8-10

¶ 8.03 Installment Land Contract 8-13

¶ 8.04 Purchase-Money Mortgage 8-14

¶ 8.05 High-Credit Lease Financing 8-14
       [1] Developer's Considerations 8-17
       [2] Lease Provisions Required by Lender 8-17
           [a] Rental Obligation and Term 8-17
           [b] Insurance Against Casualty Loss 8-18
           [c] Condemnation 8-18
           [d] Buy-Out by Tenant 8-19
           [e] Assignment of Lease to Lender 8-19
           [f] Subordination of Mortgage to Lease 8-19
       [3] Planning Considerations 8-19

¶ 8.06 Low-Cost, High-Ratio Financing With Tax-Exempt Mortgages 8-20

¶ 8.07 "Piggyback" Mortgage Loans 8-23
       [1] Loan Participation 8-23
           [a] Lender's Concerns 8-24
           [b] Borrowers' Considerations 8-24
       [2] Collateralized Mortgage Loan 8-24

¶ 8.08 Participation by Lender—The "Equity Kicker" 8-25

¶ 8.09 Component or Split Financing 8-25
       [1] Sale-Leaseback Plus Leasehold Mortgage 8-26
       [2] Fee Mortgage Plus Leasehold Mortgage 8-27
       [3] Purchase and Installment Sale-Buyback 8-29

    [3] Tax Pitfalls Inherent in Sale-Leaseback 6-24
        [a] Loss Disallowed "Exchange" 6-24
            [i] Case Law Interpretations of "Exchange" 6-25
            [ii] Tax Planning.............................. 6-26
        [b] Treatment as Disguised Loan...................... 6-27
            [i] *Frank Lyon Co. v. United States* 6-28
            [ii] Tax Planning.............................. 6-29
        [c] Reallocation of Leaseback Rental.................. 6-30
        [d] Treatment as Disguised Purchase 6-31
    [4] Illustration of Leaseback Flexibility 6-31
    [5] Component, or "Split," Financing 6-36

Chapter 7

SECONDARY FINANCING

                                                                                                 Page

¶ 7.01   Introduction... 7- 2

¶ 7.02   Advantages Over Refinancing a First Mortgage 7- 2

¶ 7.03   Lenders and Loan Terms.................................. 7- 3

¶ 7.04   Special Types of Secondary Financing 7- 5
        [1] Purchase-Money Mortgage............................ 7- 5
            [a] Legal Definition 7- 5
            [b] Use to Facilitate Purchase Transaction 7- 6
                [i] High-Ratio, Low-Cost Financing
                    for Purchasers 7- 6
                [ii] Closing With Less Cash at
                    Higher Price.................................. 7- 6
            [c] Considerations of Purchase-Money Mortgagor 7- 8
                [i] Concerns as Ordinary Mortgagor................. 7- 8
                [ii] Subordination of Purchase-Money
                    Obligation to Development Loan 7- 8
                [iii] Release of Purchase-Money
                    Mortgage Lien 7-10
            [d] Considerations of Purchase-Money Mortgagee 7-10
                [i] Right to Deficiency Judgment................... 7-10
                [ii] Concerns When Purchase-Money
                    Mortgage Subordinated to
                    Development Loan 7-11
                [iii] Tax Considerations of Seller-
                    Mortgagee.................................... 7-11
            [e] Example: Purchase-Money Financing
                in Today's Complex Real Estate Market................ 7-12
        [2] Gap Financing...................................... 7-13
        [3] Wraparound Mortgage 7-15
            [a] Additional Covenants 7-16
            [b] Legal Problems................................. 7-17
                [i] Usury.. 7-17

TABLE OF CONTENTS

[5] Installment Land Contract 5-33
[6] Sale and Repurchase of Realty 5-34
[7] Wraparound Mortgage 5-35
[8] Contingent Compensation and Equity Participations
  by Lenders... 5-38

Chapter 6

LEASEHOLD AND LEASEBACK FINANCING

Page

¶ 6.01 Leasehold vs. Fee Mortgage Financing...................... 6- 2
    [1] Tax and Business Considerations........................ 6- 2
    [2] Regulatory Considerations 6- 3

¶ 6.02 Leasehold Mortgage on Subordinated Fee:
The "Streamlined" Mortgage............................... 6- 4
    [1] Advantage to Developer 6- 4
    [2] Subordination of Ground Leases and Attornment......... 6- 5
        [a] Subordination of Ground Lease 6- 6
        [b] Attornment by Subtenants 6- 7
    [3] Advantage to Fee Owner 6- 7
    [4] Protection for Fee Owner............................. 6- 8

¶ 6.03 Leasehold Mortgage on Unsubordinated Fee:
Lender's Requirements..................................... 6- 8
    [1] Fee Owner Cannot Mortgage the Fee.................... 6- 9
    [2] Right to Assign Leasehold Estate 6-10
    [3] Future Improvements 6-11
    [4] Antimerger Provision 6-11
    [5] Broad "Use" Clause and Mortgagee Consent to Change
      in Lease Terms 6-11
    [6] Application of Hazard Insurance Proceeds............... 6-12
    [7] Allocation of Condemnation Award..................... 6-12
    [8] Default Provisions 6-13
    [9] Changes in Ground Rent 6-13
    [10] Outline of Minimum Ground lease Requirements
      for Benefit of Leasehold Mortgagee..................... 6-14

¶ 6.04 Sale-and-Leaseback Financing vs. Debt Financing 6-17
    [1] Land But Not Improvements.......................... 6-18
        [a] Depreciation 6-18
        [b] Drafting Approaches............................. 6-19
        [c] Title Problems 6-19
    [2] Land and Improvements.............................. 6-20
        [a] Position of Seller-Lessee.......................... 6-21
            [i] Business Considerations 6-21
            [ii] Tax Considerations 6-23
        [b] Position of the Purchaser-Lessor 6-23
            [i] Business Considerations 6-23
            [ii] Tax Considerations 6-24

¶ 4.05   Buy-Sell Agreement and the Final Takeout Stage 4-69

Chapter 5

USURY AND THE MORTGAGE MONEY MARKET

	Page
¶ 5.01 Relevance of Usury in Today's Real Estate Market	5- 2
¶ 5.02 Elements of Usury	5- 4
[1] Unlawful Intent	5- 5
[2] Loan or Forbearance of Money or Its Equivalent	5- 6
[3] Borrower's Absolute Obligation to Repay	5- 8
[a] Repayment of Principal.............................	5- 8
[b] Payment of Interest	5- 9
[4] Exaction of Greater Compensation as Interest Than Is Allowed by Law	5-10
[a] Legal Definition of Interest	5-10
[b] How Interest Is Computed	5-11
[c] Interest Rate Escalator Clauses	5-12
[d] Variable-Rate Mortgage.............................	5-12
¶ 5.03 Status of Customary Loan Charges	5-13
[1] Commitment Fees	5-14
[2] Origination or Service Fees	5-14
[3] Brokerage and Other Fees Paid to Intermediaries	5-15
[4] Construction Loan Fees	5-16
[5] Closing Expenses	5-16
[6] Taxes	5-17
[7] Prepayment Penalty....................................	5-17
[8] Charges Upon Default	5-17
¶ 5.04 Statutory Exemptions	5-19
[1] Corporate Exemption	5-21
[2] Exemptions Available to Limited Partnerships	5-22
[3] FHA Mortgage Exemption..............................	5-22
¶ 5.05 Circumvention Devices	5-23
[1] Conflicts of Law	5-23
[2] Sale of Mortgage Note at Discount; Estoppel; Holder in Due Course...................................	5-25
[3] Incorporation of the Borrower	5-27
[4] Sale and Leaseback	5-32

TABLE OF CONTENTS

	[iii] Equitable Lien Doctrine and the "Stop Notice" Statute	4-19
	[b] Protection for the Construction Lender Against Mechanics' Lien	4-20
	[i] Title Insurance	4-20
	[ii] Labor and Material Payment Bond	4-24
	[iii] Developer-Contractor Agreement	4-24
[7]	Approval of Contractors and Building Contract	4-25
[8]	Assurances That Project Will Be Completed	4-26
	[a] Holdback of Loan Funds	4-26
	[b] Payment and Performance Bonds	4-28
	[c] Construction Disbursement Programs	4-32
	[d] Letters of Credit	4-32
	[e] Contractor's Guarantee	4-33
[9]	Execution of Building Loan Agreement	4-34
[10]	Approval of Architect and Payment of Fees	4-34
[11]	Builder's Risk Insurance	4-34
[12]	Bankruptcy of Borrower	4-37
	[a] Language of the Loan Commitment	4-37
	[b] Implications of the Bankruptcy Reform Act of 1978 for Real Estate Financing	4-37
	[i] Broadening of Bankruptcy Jurisdiction	4-38
	[ii] Reorganization of the Rehabilitation Chapters	4-38
	[iii] Treatment of Nonrecourse Claims as Recourse	4-42
	[iv] Automatic Stay	4-43
	[v] Expanded Power of Trustee Regarding Executory Contracts and Unexpired Leases	4-43
	[vi] Right to Sell, Lease, or Mortgage Debtor's Property	4-45
[13]	Other Terms and Conditions of Commitment	4-47

¶ 4.03 Closing the Construction Loan 4-48
    [1] Construction Loan Note 4-50
    [2] Construction Mortgage 4-52
        [a] Cross-Default Provisions 4-52
        [b] Future Advance Clause 4-52
        [c] Release Clause 4-53
        [d] Prohibition of Cash Distributions 4-53

¶ 4.04 Disbursement of Construction Loan Funds Under Building Loan Agreement 4-54
    [1] Function of Building Loan Agreement 4-54
    [2] Borrower's Initial Representations and Warranties 4-55
    [3] Predisbursement Requirements 4-56
    [4] Payment of Loan Advances 4-59
    [5] Cost Overruns and Other Changes During Construction Period 4-61
    [6] The Final Loan Advance 4-63
    [7] Construction Lender's Liability for Construction Defects 4-64
    [8] Construction Lender's Remedies Against Defaulting Developer 4-66

¶ 3.08　Drafting the Mortgage/Deed of Trust 3- 63
　　　　[1] Definition of Mortgage/Deed of Trust 3- 63
　　　　[2] Use of Uniform Documents 3- 64
　　　　[3] The Note 3- 65
　　　　[4] The Mortgage/Deed of Trust 3- 66
　　　　　　[a] Definitions 3- 66
　　　　　　[b] Grants 3- 70
　　　　　　[c] Representations and Warranties 3- 70
　　　　　　[d] Affirmative Covenants 3- 71
　　　　　　[e] Negative Covenants 3- 75
　　　　　　[f] Events of Default 3- 76
　　　　　　[g] Default Remedies 3- 77
　　　　　　[h] Condemnation 3- 92
　　　　　　[i] Assignment of Leases and Rents 3- 92
　　　　　　[j] Miscellaneous Covenants 3-100
　　　　[5] Special Mortgagor's Rider for
　　　　　　Shopping Center Loans 3-101

¶ 3.09　Closing the Permanent Loan 3-102
　　　　[1] Parties at Closing 3-102
　　　　[2] Documentation at Closing 3-104
　　　　[3] Checklist for Closing Permanent Loan 3-105

Chapter 4

CONSTRUCTION FINANCING

Page

¶ 4.01　Role of Construction Financing in Commercial Lending Cycle .. 4- 2
　　　　[1] Takeout Commitment as Bridging Mechanism 4- 4
　　　　[2] Construction Financing as Second Stage in
　　　　　　Commercial Lending Cycle 4- 4
　　　　[3] Open-end Construction Lending Without
　　　　　　Permanent Takeout 4- 5

¶ 4.02　Terms and Conditions of Construction Financing as
　　　　Determined by Construction Loan Applicant-Commitment 4- 7
　　　　[1] Conformity With Requirements in Permanent Mortgage
　　　　　　Loan Commitment 4- 7
　　　　[2] Facts About Project, Borrower, and Other Backup
　　　　　　Data 4- 9
　　　　[3] Loan Amount and Repayment of Principal 4-11
　　　　[4] Rate of Interest 4-12
　　　　[5] Recourse Financing 4-13
　　　　[6] Lien Priority Over Land Mortgages and Mechanics'
　　　　　　Liens 4-14
　　　　　　[a] Problems of Mechanics' and Materialmen's Liens 4-14
　　　　　　　　[i] Lien Priorities Under State Law 4-15
　　　　　　　　[ii] Doctrine of "Obligatory" vs. "Optional"
　　　　　　　　　　Advances 4-16

TABLE OF CONTENTS

	[c] Variable-Rate Mortgages, Joint Venturing, and Other Inflation-Related Financing Devices	3- 18
[4]	Amortization Period	3- 20
[5]	Prepayment Privilege	3- 21
[6]	Required Tax and Insurance Escrows	3- 25
[7]	Lien Priority, and Prohibition of Junior Financing	3- 27
[8]	Right to Sell Mortgaged Property	3- 30
[9]	Compliance With Local Law	3- 35
	[a] Issuance of Building Permit and Certificate of Occupancy	3- 35
	[b] Rezoning and Variances	3- 37
	[c] Environmental Restrictions	3- 38
	[d] Developer's Reliance on Lender's Knowledge of Local Law	3- 41
[10]	Assignment of Commitment	3- 41
[11]	Timely Completion of Improvements in Accordance With Approved Plans and Specifications	3- 42
[12]	Satisfactory Hazard Insurance	3- 44
	[a] Co-insurance Clause	3- 44
	[b] Loss Payable Clauses	3- 45
[13]	Approval of Security Documents	3- 46
[14]	Buy-Sell Agreement	3- 47
[15]	Survey, Title Insurance, and Closing Costs	3- 47
[16]	Plot Size, Description of the Improvements, Location	3- 48
[17]	No Material Change Between Date of Final Commitment and Funding	3- 49
[18]	Joint Venturing Requirement by Permanent Lenders and Other Trends in Permanent Financing	3- 49

¶ 3.05 Analysis of Shopping Center and Other High-Credit Leases by Permanent Lender ... 3- 51
    [1] Rent Provisions ... 3- 52
    [2] Default and Termination Provisions ... 3- 53
    [3] Radius Restrictions, Exclusive-Use Clauses, and Co-tenancy Requirements in Shopping Center Leases ... 3- 54
    [4] Percentage Rental ... 3- 55
    [5] Alterations ... 3- 56
    [6] Subordination of Lease to Mortgage ... 3- 56
    [7] Assignment ... 3- 57
    [8] Option to Purchase ... 3- 57
    [9] Financing ... 3- 58

¶ 3.06 Remedies for Breach of Mortgage Loan Commitment ... 3- 58

¶ 3.07 The Standby "Loan Commitment" ... 3- 61
    [1] The Regular Standby ... 3- 61
    [2] The "Fundable Standby" ... 3- 62

[3] Savings and Loan Association 2-30
  [a] Source of Funds 2-30
  [b] Loan Terms 2-31
  [c] Loan Allocation By Function and
      Property Type 2-31
  [d] Regulation of Mortgage Loan Portfolio 2-32
      [i] Home Loans 2-33
      [ii] Apartment-Type Loans 2-34
      [iii] Income-Producing Business Property and
            Church Loans 2-34
      [iv] Loans on Developed Building Lots and Sites ... 2-34
      [v] Land Acquisition and Development Loans 2-34
[4] Mutual Savings Banks 2-39
  [a] Source of Funds 2-40
  [b] Loan Allocation by Function and
      Property Type 2-41
  [c] Regulation of Mortgage Loan Portfolio 2-41
[5] Real Estate Investment Trusts 2-42
[6] Pension Funds and Other Lenders 2-44
[7] The Secondary Mortgage Market 2-44
  [a] Federal National Mortgage Association 2-45
  [b] Federal Home Loan Mortgage Corporation 2-45
  [c] Government National Mortgage Association 2-46

¶ 2.03 The Role of Mortgage Brokers and Mortgage Bankers 2-47
  [1] The Mortgage Broker 2-47
  [2] The Mortgage Banker 2-47

Chapter 3

PERMANENT FINANCING

Page

¶ 3.01 Pre-financing Considerations 3- 3
  [1] Pre-financing Checklist 3- 3
  [2] Review of the Commercial Lending Cycle 3- 4

¶ 3.02 Selecting the Permanent Lender 3- 6

¶ 3.03 Function of Mortgage Loan Application-Commitment 3- 7
  [1] A Written Offer 3- 7
  [2] Identity of Borrower and Other Backup Data 3- 9

¶ 3.04 Terms and Conditions of Permanent Financing 3- 10
  [1] Loan Amount Based on Appraised Value 3- 11
  [2] Gap Financing Problem Caused by Construction
      Cost Overruns or by Platform Loan 3- 12
  [3] Rate of Interest 3- 15
      [a] "Equity Kickers" 3- 15
      [b] Low-Interest Financing With
          Tax-Exempt Mortgages 3- 17

              [iv] Section 1237 Subdivision Rule 1-43
              [v] Ordinary Loss Deduction Upon
                    Worthlessness of Partnership Interest 1-43
        [4] Tax Pitfalls of Limited Partnership 1-44
              [a] Possible Taxation as an Association 1-44
              [b] Tax Shelter Basis Problem Caused by
                    Recourse Financing 1-52
                    [i] General Rule 1-52
                    [ii] Special Basis Rule for
                          Limited Partner.......................... 1-52
                    [iii] Tax Planning to Avoid Basis Problem 1-55
        [5] Tax Advantages of Incorporation 1-59
              [a] Lower Tax Rate...................................... 1-60
              [b] Flexibility in Choice of Tax Year 1-60
              [c] Greater Fringe Benefits for Employees................ 1-60
              [d] No Limitation on "Investment Interest" 1-61
              [e] Corporation Survives Stock Ownership
                    Changes 1-61

¶ 1.06   Subchapter S Corporation.................................. 1-61

¶ 1.07   Real Estate Investment Trusts 1-67

¶ 1.08   Common-Law Land Trust................................. 1-68

Chapter 2

TYPES OF LENDERS

Page

¶ 2.01   The Structure of the Mortgage Market...................... 2- 2
        [1] Cost and Availability of Mortgage Credit 2- 2
              [a] Savings-Based Supply of Total Credit 2- 2
              [b] Countercyclical Mortgage Credit Supply 2- 3
              [c] Demand "Passive" Relative to Supply 2- 6
        [2] Summary of the Lending Cycle.......................... 2- 8
        [3] Factors Contributing to a Restructuring
              of the Market 2-10

¶ 2.02   Mortgage Lenders... 2-12
        [1] Life Insurance Companies 2-12
              [a] Source of Funds 2-13
              [b] Loan Terms 2-14
              [c] Loan Allocation by Function
                    and Property Type 2-14
              [d] Regulation of Mortgage Loan Portfolio................ 2-22
        [2] Commercial Banks..................................... 2-25
              [a] Source of Funds 2-26
              [b] Loan Terms 2-26
              [c] Loan Allocation by Function
                    and Property Type 2-27
              [d] Regulation of Mortgage Loan Portfolio............... 2-28

TABLE OF CONTENTS

Introduction .... **xxvii**

Chapter 1

SELECTION OF OWNERSHIP ENTITY

		Page
¶ 1.01	Dynamics of the Selection Process	1- 2
¶ 1.02	Tenancy in Common	1- 3
	[1] Nontax Considerations	1- 3
	[2] Tax Considerations	1- 3
	[a] Advantages	1- 4
	[b] Disadvantages	1- 5
¶ 1.03	Joint Ventures	1- 6
¶ 1.04	General vs. Limited Partnership	1- 7
¶ 1.05	Partnership vs. Incorporation	1- 9
	[1] Legal and Financing Considerations	1-10
	[2] Tax Sheltering of Investor's Income	1-14
	[a] In General	1-14
	[b] Income-Producing Property	1-16
	[c] Nondepreciable Property	1-19
	[d] Post-1976 Tax Legislation	1-20
	[3] Other Tax Advantages of Partnership Over Incorporation	1-30
	[a] Collapsible Provisions Less Stringent	1-30
	[i] Partnership Tax Planning	1-31
	[ii] Corporate Tax Planning	1-34
	[b] Flexibility in Allocation of Income or Loss	1-36
	[i] Special Allocations	1-36
	[ii] Allocation of Depreciation or Gain or Loss on Contributed Property	1-41
	[iii] Retroactive Amendment of Partnership Agreement	1-41
	[c] Miscellaneous Tax Advantages of Partnerships	1-42
	[i] Opportunity to Reduce Compensation Income of Partner Who Contributes Services and Not Property to the Partnership	1-42
	[ii] Flexibility in Determining Compensation Income	1-43
	[iii] No Penalty Tax Problem	1-43

SUMMARY TABLE OF CONTENTS

Table of Contents ix

Introduction xxv

Chapter 1 —Selection of Ownership Entity 1-1

Chapter 2 —Types of Lenders 2-1

Chapter 3 —Permanent Financing 3-1

Chapter 4 —Construction Financing 4-1

Chapter 5 —Usury and the Mortgage Money Market 5-1

Chapter 6 —Leasehold and Leaseback Financing 6-1

Chapter 7 —Secondary Financing 7-1

Chapter 8 —Special Types of High-Ratio Financing 8-1

Chapter 9 —Subdivision Financing 9-1

Chapter 10—Condominium and Cooperative Financing 10-1

Chapter 11—Loan Participations and Joint Ventures
            by Institutional Lenders 11-1

Chapter 12—Tax Aspects of Mortgage Financing 12-1

Appendix A—Ancillary Data .... App. A-1

Appendix B—Sample Forms and Agreements .... App. B-1

Tables T-1

Index I-1

PREFACE

tion, Mendes Hershman, in his inimitable style, does discuss a major pre-financing consideration; namely, the tremendous impact public law has made in the realm of land development and finance.)

We would like to thank the many people who have played an important role in the preparation of these materials. First and foremost we are grateful to Mendes Hershman (under whose tutelage we learned to "ply our trade") for his valuable contributions and commentary. A large part of this work has been done at the Marshall Wythe School of Law at the College of William & Mary in Williamsburg, Virginia, and although its name does not appear on the title page, we feel a special sense of gratitude to Dean Spong and the staff there. The research and staff support and other working conditions at Fordham University Law School have also been excellent, and for this we would like to thank Dean McLaughlin, the administration, and staff. We are particularly grateful for the high level of research support received from Peter Chin of the New York Bar and Roger Cornelier of the Virginia Bar. Our special thanks go also to Jack Feder at Lane & Edson, Washington, D.C., for the contribution of his tax expertise to Chapter 12 of the book, and to John W. McClean, Vice President of Commercial Real Estate Loans Administration at The First National Bank of Maryland. Last, but far from least, we would like to thank Alvin Arnold and Harold Lubell for their invaluable assistance in developing the book; and, for their fine editorial assistance, Annette Gonella and Mary Martinez.

MICHAEL T. MADISON
JEFFRY R. DWYER

New York, N.Y.
March 1981

speaking, to explain the "how" of financing real estate without discussing the "why" of investing in real estate. On a more practical level, the most important decision made in the initial stages of a real estate venture — and one made primarily on the basis of tax shelter considerations — is which type of ownership entity is best suited for the dual purpose of raising the venture capital and securing the financing needed to fund the acquisition and/or improvement of the real estate. Moreover, such pre-financing decision is bound to have serious spillover effects in the financing area. For example, if the choice is that of a limited partnership, the developer must then utilize nonrecourse financing as opposed to recourse financing; otherwise, the limited partners could be deprived of their ability to deduct tax losses in excess of their actual economic investment in the partnership. In addition, tax considerations and planning suggestions are presented throughout the book. For example, in the discussion of prepayment penalty provisions in Chapter 3, we point out that such penalties are regarded as deductible interest payments for income tax purposes, and the developer's adviser is cautioned to do his tax planning before the permanent loan commitment is fully executed because any retroactive reallocation or recharacterization of prepayment fees asnd other loan costs for tax purposes will be regarded with disfavor by the I.R.S. Another example is the discussion in Chapter 12 concerning the tax consequences to both the developer and lender during the mortgagor-mortgagee relationship, including default by the developer-mortgagor.

The organization of the book reflects the fact that in the real world of real estate finance the attorney, banker, broker or other real estate professional must, in a chronological fashion (albeit with certain variations or short cuts), wade his way through the legal, business, and tax complexities of the real estate financing cycle. For example, in most cases involving the financing of income-producing property, the developer, after selecting the most appropriate form of ownership entity, will next seek a loan commitment from a permanent lender. Then, on the strength of such commitment, construction financing is obtained from a commercial bank or other interim lender whose loan will be "taken out" and purchased by the permanent lender once the project is completed and producing rental income. This is provided that the other requirements of the permanent loan commitment have been met. Accordingly, the foregoing topics are covered in order by Chapters 1, 2, 3, and 4. Also, we have, for the most part, ignored both pre-financing and post-financing considerations on the premise that, with the exception of the discussion in Chapter 1 dealing with selection of the ownership entity, they are beyond the legitimate scope of any treatise on real estate financing and are amply covered elsewhere. (However, in the introduc-

example, absent language permitting a pro rata reduction in monthly payments, the borrower might be required to pay the original amounts over the original loan term even though the original loan amount has been reduced as a consequence of fire loss and the lender's retention of the insurance proceeds.

Also, based on our experience in representing large institutional lenders, we have attempted throughout the text to highlight those provisions that are probably negotiable and those that are not. For example, the reader representing the borrower-developer is made aware that, in the event the premises are destroyed by fire or some other casualty, the lender will frequently reserve the right to apply the insurance proceeds toward payment of the outstanding mortgage indebtedness instead of permitting the mortgagor to use the proceeds for restoration of the premises. However, the reader is also told that, if pressed, most lenders will agree to have such proceeds used for restoration purposes, on the condition that they retain control over when and how disbursements will be made and that they be protected against mechanics' liens.

As to audience, we have attempted to address not only the concerns of the developer-borrower and his attorney, but also those of the lender and his counsel, as well as the other interested parties to a particular transaction. To those readers who might have preferred a more comprehensive treatment of one subject area or another, we stress our intention to present the material in a way that will be of optimal usefulness to the greatest number of readers.

The subject matter of the book reflects our opinion, already expressed, that this is an area of law in which freedom of contract is virtually unhampered and in which the parties are, in most cases, represented by counsel. Accordingly, we have emphasized only those aspects of law (e.g., judicial attacks against due-on-sale or encumbrance clauses and extra-judicial foreclosure arrangements) that may supersede the written word and have virtually ignored those areas like the doctrine of "equitable mortgages" that only apply in the absence of such formal agreement. Also, little discussion is devoted to either single-family residential financing or federally subsidized multi-family residential financing on the premise that the former is well within the expertise of most practitioners while the latter has so many special aspects as to be beyond the scope of this book.

Most of the standard treatises fail to integrate tax aspects of real estate financing into their discussion even though the emerging trend is for firms and corporations to demand such dual expertise of their attorneys. The rationale for such trend is clear: tax shelter considerations play such a dominant role in real estate investment decisions involving income-producing property that it is difficult, conceptually

PREFACE

The purpose of this treatise on real estate finance law is to fulfill a need that in our opinion is not being met by any of the available literature. Most texts tend to ignore the transactional context in which legal issues and business problems arise, as well as the documentation techniques that can be used to prevent many problems before they occur. Real estate finance is an area in which freedom of contract virtually reigns supreme. In most instances, general rules of law apply only in the absence of agreement to the contrary. Moreover, the interested parties (e.g., the developer, the permanent and construction lenders, fee owner, prime occupancy tenants) are almost invariably represented by legal counsel. Since this is the case, their transactional rights and responsibilities are usually governed by means of the "written word," embodied in some fairly standardized form of agreement that is custom-tailored to the particular transaction. This is especially true where the financing of income-producing property is involved, since the borrower is likely to be negotiating with a sophisticated institutional lender.

At the other end of the spectrum are those books that do address the practical problems but tend to be too forms-oriented and sometimes lack the legal scholarship and depth of analysis necessary to prepare the practitioner for the problems he will encounter in the complex area of law.

Our goal has been to provide a scholarly and authoritative treatise on the law of modern real estate financing, and at the same time to convey to our readers the creativity involved in this highly transactional area of the law. Accordingly, when we discuss the law, ample citations and legal analyses are provided. But we have attempted, where possible, to make the relevant documentation the matrix for our discussion.

Since the planner aims not only to solve present problems but also to anticipate issues that might arise in the future and to devise means of avoiding them, we have attempted to point out, where feasible, the pitfalls and legal consequences of one approach or another in the documentation. To illustrate, in the discussion in Chapter 3 concerning the terms and conditions of permanent financing (as determined by the permanent lender's take-out commitment letter) we discuss the general rules of law (i.e., in the absence of any language in the mortgage note, a lender does not have to accept a prepayment of the mortgage indebtedness). However, of equal importance to the reader is seeing what a typical prepayment penalty provision looks like and knowing that, for

To my children, Eve Tova and Joshua Avram Madison

Michael T. Madison

To Karen and our children, Amanda and Jason

Jeffry R. Dwyer

Copyright © 1981 by

WARREN, GORHAM & LAMONT, INC.
210 SOUTH STREET
BOSTON, MASSACHUSETTS 02111

ALL RIGHTS RESERVED

No part of this book may be reproduced in any form, by photostat, microfilm, xerography, or any means, or incorporated into any information retrieval system, electronic or mechanical, without the written permission of the copyright owner.

ISBN 0-88262-516-0

Library of Congress Catalog Card No. 8053430

This educational publication is designed to present information to professionals as an aid to independent research and preparation of materials. It is not to be regarded as providing opinion or advice for any individual case.

This publication is not intended to render legal, accounting, or other professional services or advice. The appropriate professional should be consulted for any such services or advice.

PRINTED IN THE UNITED STATES OF AMERICA

THE LAW OF REAL ESTATE FINANCING

WITH TAX ANALYSIS, PLANNING, AND FORMS

MICHAEL T. MADISON
Professor of Law, Fordham University
Member of the New York Bar

JEFFRY R. DWYER
Member of the New York and
District of Columbia Bars

WARREN, GORHAM & LAMONT
Boston
New York

THE LAW OF REAL ESTATE FINANCING

WITH TAX ANALYSIS, PLANNING AND FORMS

1982 Supplement

MICHAEL T. MADISON
Professor of Law, Fordham University
Member of the New York Bar

JEFFRY R. DWYER
Member of the New York and
District of Columbia Bars

WARREN, GORHAM & LAMONT
Boston • New York

Copyright © 1982 by
WARREN, GORHAM & LAMONT, INC.
210 SOUTH STREET
BOSTON, MASSACHUSETTS 02111

ALL RIGHTS RESERVED

No part of this book may be reproduced in any form, by photostat, microfilm, xerography, or any other means, or incorporated into any information retrieval system, electronic or mechanical, without the written permission of the copyright owner.

ISBN 0-88262-809-7

Library of Congress Catalog Card No. 80-53430

This educational publication is designed to present information to professionals as an aid to independent research and preparation of materials. It is not to be regarded as providing opinion or advice for any individual case.

This publication is not intended to render legal, accounting, or other professional services or advice. The appropriate professional should be consulted for any such services or advice.

PRINTED IN THE UNITED STATES OF AMERICA

HOW TO USE THIS SUPPLEMENT

This first supplement updates *The Law of Real Estate Financing* with significant developments that have occurred since the publication of the main volume. This supplement is both a means of keeping the main volume current and a reference to recent events in its own right. In addition to updating materials in the main volume, the supplement discusses significant new developments in the following areas:

- An expanded discussion of the impact of the Economic Recovery Tax Act of 1981 with respect to tax rates, depreciation, recapture, calculation of earnings and profits, the mini-tax, regular and rehabilitation investment credits, and liberalized tax rules for low-income housing.

- The impact of recent changes in lending activities of pension funds, life insurance companies, credit corporations, and other lending groups, the effect of liberalizing regulations on federally chartered savings and loan associations, and recent proposals for saving them from financial decline; the effect of liberalizing the taxing of debt-financed income and the impact of regulations under the Employee Retirement Income Security Act of 1974 (ERISA) on the investment activities of pension funds.

- An expanded discussion of recent inflation-inspired trends and techniques in post-construction financing, including an examination of legal and tax issues faced by developers and lenders with respect to the use of the convertible mortgage, the variable rate mortgage, and other new alternative mortgage instruments, as well as an analysis of the new convertible debt Treasury Regulations under Internal Revenue Code § 385.

- An analysis of new SEC Regulation D, governing the issuance of private offerings of corporations and limited partnerships.

- The impact of the Foreign Investment Real Property Tax Act (FIRPA) on foreign investment in U.S. real property.

- Cases subsequent to *Wellenkamp v. Bank of America* dealing with due-on-sale clauses, including a discussion of the federal preemption doctrine.

- A discussion of loan workouts as a remedy for defaults by mortgagors, and the impact that the Bankruptcy Reform Act of 1978 has thereon.
- A discussion of Title V of the Depository Institutions Deregulation and Monetary Control Act of 1980; that is, the federal usury preemption statute and the state overrides permitted by the statute.
- A new line of cases decided after *Frank Lyon Co. v. United States* on the tax aspects of sale-leaseback financing.
- An expanded discussion of equity participation and the problems lenders and developers must face in transacting joint venture arrangements.
- Samples of the most current financing forms, added to Appendix B.

Both the main volume and the supplement follow the same sequence, and each entry in the supplement is keyed to a chapter, paragraph (¶), and specific page number of the main volume. When using the main volume, you can quickly determine whether or not there have been post-publication developments by locating the corresponding paragraph in the supplement.

To further ensure access to the author's treatment of post-publication developments, this supplement contains a Cumulative Index and Cumulative Tables, which refer to materials published in both the main volume and the supplement. These tables supersede those in the main volume.

PREFACE

Page vi:

Add new text following runover paragraph.

Over the past few years, institutional lenders have become increasingly reluctant to invest in long-term fixed rate mortgages without substantial protections against inflation and volatile interest rates. Accordingly, traditional long-term lenders such as insurance companies are increasingly demanding full equity participations, renegotiation of interest rates within acceptable intervals of time, more stringent call options, and shorter loan periods. There has also been an increase in construction lending without takeout commitments, although this may be a temporary phenomenon. Consequently, to some extent the term "permanent financing" has recently become a misnomer and the dichotomy between post-construction (or "permanent") financing and construction financing has recently become less clear. However, the organization of the book reflects the dichotomy on the premise that the pattern of the post-World War II real estate financing cycle—though varied somewhat—essentially remains the same, and if the economy should normalize, these variations, which are discussed in Chapters 2, 3, 4, and 11, could become somewhat less pronounced.

Moreover, even if the dichotomy fails entirely, the rules and planning suggestions in Chapter 3 [Post-Construction ("Permanent") Financing] remain relevant with respect to short- and long-term post-construction loans and to loans where the same lender provides both the construction and post-construction financing.

TABLE OF CONTENTS

Chapter 1

SELECTION OF OWNERSHIP ENTITY

		Page
¶ 1.04	General vs. Limited Partnership	S1- 1
¶ 1.05	Partnership vs. Incorporation	S1- 2
	[1] Legal and Financial Considerations	S1- 2
	[2] Tax Sheltering of Investor's Income	S1- 4
	[b] Income-Producing Property	S1- 4
	[d] Post-1967 Tax Legislation	S1-12
	[3] Other Tax Advantages of Partnership Over Incorporation	S1-34
	[b] Flexibility in Allocation of Income or Loss	S1-34
	[i] Special Allocations	S1-34
	[4] Tax Pitfalls of Limited Partnership	S1-34
	[b] Tax Shelter Basis Problem Caused by Recourse Financing	S1-34
	[ii] Special Basis Rule for Limited Partner	S1-34
	[5] Tax Advantages of Incorporation	S1-35
	[a] Lower Tax Rate	S1-35
¶ 1.06	Subchapter S Corporation	S1-35

Chapter 2

TYPES OF LENDERS

¶ 2.01	The Structure of the Mortgage Market	S2- 1
	[1] Cost and Availability of Mortgage Credit	S2- 1
	[b] Countercyclical Mortgage Credit Supply	S2- 1
	[2] Summary of the Lending Cycle	S2- 2
	[3] Factors Contributing to a Restructuring of the Market	S2- 3
¶ 2.02	Mortgage Lenders	S2- 4
	[1] Life Insurance Companies	S2- 4
	[a] Source of Funds	S2- 4
	[2] Commercial Banks	S2-12
	[a] Source of Funds	S2-12
	[b] Loan Terms	S2-13

	Page
[3] Savings and Loan Associations	S2-13
[a] Source of Funds	S2-13
[e] Federal Assistance to Savings and Loan Industry [New]	S2-13
[6] Pension Funds and Other Lenders	S2-16
[8] Foreign Investments in U.S. Real Estate [New]	S2-22
¶ 2.03 The Role of Mortgage Brokers and Mortgage Bankers	S2-29
[1] The Mortgage Broker	S2-29
[2] The Mortgage Banker	S2-32

Chapter 3

POST-CONSTRUCTION ("PERMANENT") FINANCING
[Revised Title]

¶ 3.01 Pre-financing Considerations	S3- 2
[2] Review of the Commercial Lending Cycle	S3- 2
¶ 3.03 Function of Mortgage Loan Application-Commitment	S3- 2
[1] A Written Offer	S3- 2
¶ 3.04 Terms and Conditions of Post-Construction ("Permanent") Financing [Revised Heading]	S3- 2
[3] Rate of Interest	S3- 2
[c] Variable-Rate Mortgages and Other Residential Inflation-Related Mortgage Devices [Revised Heading]	S3- 2
[d] Convertible Mortgages, Bullet Loans, Rollover Mortgages, and Other Commercial Inflation-Related Mortgage Devices [New]	S3-12
[5] Prepayment Privilege	S3-13
[8] Right to Sell Mortgaged Property	S3-13
[9] Compliance With Local Law	S3-19
[a] Issuance of Building Permit and Certificate of Occupancy	S3-19
[12] Satisfactory Hazard Insurance	S3-20
[b] Loss Payable Clause	S3-20
[18] Joint Venturing Requirement, Convertible Mortgages, and Other Trends in Permanent Financing [Revised Heading]	S3-20
¶ 3.06 Remedies for Breach of Mortgage Loan Commitment	S3-28
¶ 3.07 The Standby "Loan Commitment"	S3-29
[2] The "Fundable Standby"	S3-29
¶ 3.08 Drafting the Mortgage/Deed of Trust	S3-29
[4] The Mortgage/Deed of Trust	S3-29
[a] Definitions	S3-29
[g] Default Remedies	S3-33
[i] Assignment of Leases and Rents	S3-35

SUPPLEMENT TABLE OF CONTENTS

Chapter 4

CONSTRUCTION FINANCING

		Page
¶ 4.02	Terms and Conditions of Construction Financing as Determined by Construction Loan Application-Commitment	S4-1
	[4] Rate of Interest	S4-1
	[6] Lien Priority Over Land Mortgages and Mechanics' Liens	S4-2
	[a] Problems of Mechanics' and Materialmen's Liens	S4-2
	[i] Lien Priorities Under State Law	S4-2
	[ii] Doctrine of "Obligatory" vs. "Optional" Advances	S4-3
	[8] Assurances That Project Will Be Completed	S4-3
	[e] Contractor's Guarantee	S4-3
	[12] Bankruptcy of Borrower	S4-3
	[b] Implications of Bankruptcy Reform Act of 1978 for Real Estate Financing	S4-3
	[14] Checklist of Construction Loan Agreement Terms [New]	S4-4
¶ 4.03	Closing the Construction Loan	S4-5
	[2] Construction Mortgage	S4-5
	[d] Prohibition of Cash Distributions	S4-5
¶ 4.04	Disbursement of Construction Loan Funds Under Building Loan Agreement	S4-6
	[8] Construction Lender's Remedies Against Defaulting Developer	S4-6
¶ 4.05	Buy-Sell Agreement and the Final Takeout Stage	S4-6

Chapter 5

USURY AND THE MORTGAGE MONEY MARKET

¶ 5.01	Relevance of Usury in Today's Real Estate Market	S5-1
¶ 5.02	Elements of Usury	S5-3
	[4] Exaction of Greater Compensation as Interest Than Is Allowed by Law	S5-3
	[b] How Interest Is Computed	S5-3
	[d] Variable-Rate Mortgage	S5-3
¶ 5.03	Status of Customary Loan Charges	S5-4
	[1] Commitment Fees	S5-4
	[2] Origination or Service Fees	S5-4
	[3] Brokerage and Other Fees Paid to Intermediaries	S5-5
¶ 5.04	Statutory Exemptions	S5-5
	[1] Corporate Exemption	S5-5

		Page
¶ 5.05	Circumvention Devices	S5-5
	[1] Conflicts of Law	S5-5
	[4] Sale and Leaseback	S5-5
	[6] Sale and Repurchase of Realty	S5-6
	[8] Contingent Compensation and Equity Participation by Lenders	S5-6

Chapter 6

LEASEHOLD AND LEASEBACK FINANCING

¶ 6.03	Leasehold Mortgage on Unsubordinated Fee: Lender's Requirements	S6-1
	[8] Default Provisions	S6-1
¶ 6.04	Sale and Leaseback Financing vs. Debt Financing	S6-2
	[3] Tax Pitfalls Inherent in Sale-Leaseback	S6-2
	[a] Loss Disallowed "Exchange"	S6-2
	[i] Case Law Interpretations of "Exchange"	S6-2
	[b] Treatment as Disguised Loan	S6-3
	[ii] Subsequent Case Law on Sale-Leasebacks [New]	S6-3
	[e] Treatment as Non-Profit-Motivated Transaction [New]	S6-5

Chapter 8

SPECIAL TYPES OF HIGH-RATIO FINANCING

¶ 8.06	Low-Cost, High-Ratio Financing With Tax-Exempt Mortgages	S8-1

Chapter 9

SUBDIVISION FINANCING

¶ 9.04	Seller's Use of Installment Method for Reporting Income (I.R.C. § 453) Under Installment Sales Revision Act of 1980	S9-1
	[1] Overview of Changes	S9-1
	[2] Requirements for Using Installment Method Under New Law	S9-2
	[b] Limitations on Payments by Purchaser in Year of Sale Eliminated	S9-2
	[ii] 30 Percent Limitation on Payments in Year of Sale Eliminated	S9-2

SUPPLEMENT TABLE OF CONTENTS

                                                                                                     Page

[4] Sale or Other Disposition of Installment Obligations Under the New Law S9-2
    [bb] Pledge of Installment Obligation as Security for Loan, Not a Disposition [New] S9-2
[5] Sales to Related Parties Restricted S9-3
    [a] Restriction on Intra-Family Transfers of Appreciated Property S9-3

Chapter 10

CONDOMINIUM AND COOPERATIVE FINANCING

¶ 10.02   Condominium Financing S10-1
         [5] Condominium Conversion of Rental Units S10-1

Chapter 11

LOAN PARTICIPATIONS AND JOINT VENTURES BY INSTITUTIONAL LENDERS

¶ 11.01   Loan Participations S11-1
         [6] Legal Pitfalls S11-1
             [d] Lead Lender's Compliance With Securities Laws S11-1
¶ 11.02   Joint Ventures Between Institutional Lenders and Developers S11-2
         [4] Selecting the Ownership Entity S11-2
             [c] Tenancy in Common [New] S11-2
         [5] Analysis of Joint Venture Agreement S11-2
             [a] Allocation of Capital Contributions S11-2
         [6] Summary of Problems Inherent in Joint Venturing ... S11-4

Chapter 12

TAX ASPECTS OF MORTGAGE FINANCING

¶ 12.01   Tax Consequences of a Mortgage on Real Property S12-1
         [3] The *Crane* Doctrine S12-1
             [b] Effects in Nonrecourse Financing S12-1
         [5] Distinction Between Debt and Equity [New] S12-2
             [a] Tax Treatment of Lender as Partner or Creditor .. S12-3
             [b] Status of Corporate Borrowers Under I.R.C. § 385 .... S12-5

		Page
¶ 12.03	Tax Consequences of Mortgagor's Default	S12-5
	[1] Overview	S12-5
	[3] Voluntary Conveyance to Mortgagee, Deed in Lieu of Foreclosure, Abandonment	S12-6

Appendix A

ANCILLARY DATA

		Page
Table 1	State Limitations on Commercial Bank Real Estate Loans, August 31, 1981	S.App. A- 2
Table 2	Mortgage Debt Outstanding	S.App. A-10
Table 3	Analysis of State Usury Statutes	S.App. A-11
Table 4	Real Estate Holdings of the 97 Largest Pension Funds [New]	S.App. A-17

Appendix B

SAMPLE FORMS AND AGREEMENTS

Form		Page
3.15	Shared Appreciation Mortgage Provisions for Sharing Cash Flow, Capital Appreciation, and Net Sale Proceeds	S.App. B- 1
3.16	Contingent Interest Provisions Based on Gross Receipts	S.App. B- 4
3.17	Due-on-Sale Clause Limited to Arm's-Length Transactions	S.App. B- 6
3.18	FHLMC-FNMA Due-on-Sale Clause	S.App. B- 8
4.3	Construction Mortgage Loan Commitment	S.App. B- 9
4.4	CD Method of Computing Construction Loan Interest	S.App. B-15
4.5	Conversion to Eurodollar Method of Computing Construction Loan Interest (LIBOR)	S.App. B-16
11.5	Letter of Intent for Leveraged Equity Joint Venture	S.App. B-19

Cumulative Table of Statutes .... T- 1
Cumulative Table of Regulations and Rulings .... T- 9
Cumulative Table of Cases T-13

Cumulative Index .... I- 1

Chapter 1

SELECTION OF OWNERSHIP ENTITY

		Page
¶ 1.04	General vs. Limited Partnership	S1- 1
¶ 1.05	Partnership vs. Incorporation	S1- 2
	[1] Legal and Financing Considerations	S1- 2
	[2] Tax Sheltering of Investor's Income	S1- 4
	[b] Income-Producing Property	S1- 4
	[d] Post-1967 Tax Legislation	S1-12
	[3] Other Tax Advantages of Partnership Over Incorporation	S1-34
	[b] Flexibility in Allocation of Income or Loss	S1-34
	[i] Special Allocations	S1-34
	[4] Tax Pitfalls of Limited Partnership	S1-34
	[b] Tax Shelter Basis Problem Caused by Recourse Financing	S1-34
	[ii] Special Basis Rule for Limited Partner	S1-34
	[5] Tax Advantages of Incorporation	S1-35
	[a] Lower Tax Rate	S1-35
¶ 1.06	Subchapter S Corporation	S1-35

¶ 1.04 GENERAL VS. LIMITED PARTNERSHIP

Page 1-7:

Change last sentence of note 19a to read as follows.

    [19a] See note 38 *infra*.

Page 1-9:

Change second sentence of note 29a to read as follows.

    [29a] See note 38 *infra*.

¶ 1.05 PARTNERSHIP VS. INCORPORATION

[1] Legal and Financing Considerations

Page 1-13:

Add to note 45 after Goodman v. Epstein citation.

[45] , *cert. denied* 440 U.S. 939 (1978).

Add at end of note 45.

[45] On March 8, 1982, the Securities and Exchange Commission promulgated Regulation D, S.E.C. Release No. 33-6389. This regulation rescinds Rules 146, 240, and 242 governing the issuance of private offerings, and replaces those rules with three new rules, Rules 504, 505, and 506, which will substantially liberalize the rules pursuant to which private offerings are made. See 12 C.F.R. §§ 230.501–230.506 (March 8, 1982).

General. Regulation D is effective on April 15, 1982, and Rule 146 and the other rules replaced by Regulation D will be rescinded effective June 30, 1982. Offerings commenced before April 15, 1982 may continue beyond June 30, 1982 in reliance on the existing rules. Offerings commenced after April 15, 1982 may only rely on the existing rules if sales are completed by June 30, 1982. The new rules are not mutually exclusive. That is, if one attempts to qualify under one of the new rules in Regulation D, and does not, but in fact qualifies under one of the other new rules, the transaction will still be exempt. Moreover, although Regulation D repeals Rules 146, 240, and 242, it does not eliminate exempt transactions that qualify as private placements under Section 4(2) of the Securities Act, but that do not meet the provisions of Regulation D.

Except in limited circumstances, the existing prohibitions on general solicitation and advertising continue in connection with all Regulation D offerings.

Reports of sales are required for Rule 504, Rule 505, and Rule 506 transactions. Reports must be filed with the SEC fifteen days after the first sale and every six months thereafter, until the offering is complete, and then thirty days after the last sale.

Coordination with state "Blue Sky" requirements. The Rule recites that the SEC has been working with the North American Securities Administrators Association to coordinate the federal and state system of regulating exempt offerings, and it is anticipated that the states will adopt complementary provisions over the next year or two. In the meantime, bear in mind that each state may continue to assert its own requirements for exemption or registration of private offerings, as the states have done in the past.

Rule 506—replacement for Rule 146. Rule 506 is the successor to Rule 146. It permits sales to thirty-five purchasers, plus an unlimited number of "accredited investors." Each *purchaser* under Rule 506 who does not meet the "accredited investor" criteria must be qualified as a person who has such knowledge and experience in financial and business matters that he is capable of evaluating the merits and risks of the prospective investment (either alone or with his purchaser representative). However, non-accredited investors no longer need meet a financial suitability test for federal purposes. Only the suitable requirements imposed on broker-dealers and state blue sky laws will establish minimum financial suitability standards for non-accredited purchasers. The sophistication and net worth tests at the offeree stage have been eliminated; *only actual purchasers need be qualified.*

Rule 505—replacement for Rule 242. Rule 505, which replaces old Rule 242, is now an alternative to Rule 146 [506] offerings. An advantage of Rule 505 over Rule 506 is that even non-accredited investors need not meet any suitability standard other than that imposed by broker-dealers and by state blue sky laws. (However, the requirements for the type of information that must be furnished to non-accredited investors, as discussed below, are equally applicable to both Rules 505 and 506.) The utility of Rule 505 (and Rule 504, discussed below) may be limited in that securities sold in a transaction designed to qualify under Rule 505 may not be paid for in installments. Thus, unless the Federal Reserve Board exempts Rule 504 and Rule 505 offerings from its restrictions on extensions of credit (Regulations T, C, U, and X), such offerings must be "single pay." Under Rule 505, sales of securities of any issuer over a twelve-month period may not exceed $5 million. Old Rule 242 was not available to limited partnerships, but that restriction has been removed in Rule 505. A transaction under Rule 505 may have thirty-five purchasers, plus an unlimited number of "accredited investors."

Rule 504—replacement for Rule 240. Rule 504 replaces Rule 240 and is available for offerings of $500,000 or less, with no limit on the number of investors. In Rule 504 offerings, no offeree or purchaser financial or sophistication requirements (other than the suitability requirements imposed on broker-dealers and by state blue sky laws) are imposed, and no information requirements are specified. However, as with Rule 505, there can be no installment payments for securities. A Rule 240 prohibition against the payment of brokerage commissions has been removed. Rule 504 will permit small transactions to go forward with only a minimum of documentation.

The "accredited investor" concept. The concept of "accredited investor" is central to Regulation D. Eight categories of accredited investors are listed:

(1) Any employee benefit plan within the meaning of Title I of the Employee Retirement Income Security Act of 1974 with total assets in excess of $5 million;

(2) Any private business development company as defined in Section 202(a)(22) of the Investment Advisers Act of 1940;

(3) Any organization described in I.R.C. § 501(c)(3) with total assets in excess of $5 million;

(4) Any director, executive officer, or general partner of the issuer of the securities being offered or sold, or any director, executive officer, or general partner of a general partner of that issuer;

(5) Any person who purchases at least $150,000 of the securities being offered, where the purchaser's total purchase price does not exceed 20 percent of his or her net worth at the time of sale, or joint net worth with that person's spouse. This means a $750,000 net worth for a $150,000 purchase. Payment must be made in: (a) cash, (b) securities for which market quotations are readily available, (c) an unconditional obligation to pay cash or securities for which market quotations are readily available, which obligation is to be discharged within five years of the sale of the securities to the purchaser, or (d) the cancellation of any indebtedness owed by the issuer to the purchaser;

(6) Any natural person whose individual net worth, or joint net worth with that person's spouse, at the time of his purchase exceeds $1 million;

(7) Any natural person who had an individual income in excess of $200,000 in each of the two most recent years and who reasonably expects an income in excess of $200,000 in the current year;

(8) Any entity in which all of the equity owners are accredited investors under paragraph (1), (2), (3), (4), (5), (6), or (7) above.

The most important definitions for most syndicators are in subsections (5), (6), and (7). Several points should be noted:

a. Purchasers who qualify under subsections (6) and (7) need not purchase any minimum amount, yet are still considered accredited investors;

b. The net worth provisions of subsections (5) and (6) do not exclude homes, home furnishings, or automobiles; and

c. The income test in subsection (7) is essentially for gross, rather than taxable, income.

If an offering is sold *exclusively* to accredited investors, no information requirements are specified by the Regulation.

Information requirements. For offerings of up to $5 million sold to both accredited and non-accredited investors under Rules 506 and 505, the information set forth in Part I of Form S-18 must be provided to non-accredited investors. This information is similar to that which has customarily been provided in private placement memoranda, except that two-year financial statements for a partnership and its general partners must be provided, audited for the last year. The financial statements may be presented on an income tax basis rather than a GAAP reporting basis if undue effort or expense is entailed in obtaining GAAP-basis financials. In addition, issuers must continue to provide an opportunity to investors to ask questions and receive answers prior to the sale. For offerings over $5 million, Rule 506, the only rule available, requires presentation of the type of information that would be required by the registration statement the issuer would use for a registered offering.

[2] Tax Sheltering of Investor's Income

[b] Income-Producing Property

Pages 1-17 through 1-19:

Replace text starting on top of page 1-17 and ending after the first complete paragraph on page 1-19 with the following.

Facts. Assume that a limited partnership is formed by G, the general partner, and L, the limited partner, to construct an apartment building on some ground-leased land at a cost of $1 million. Each partner contributes $100,000 equity capital in exchange for a 50 percent interest in partnership profits or losses, and capital. The balance of the construction cost is funded by an unsubordinated fifteen-year first leasehold mortgage of $800,000 with a twenty-five-year amortization schedule and a 14.45 percent annual constant, with constant annual payment of $115,561 to be applied first to interest at 14 percent on the unpaid balance and then to amortization or repayment of principal. Assume the venture yields a free and clear return[54] of 15 percent (or $150,000 net rental income after payment of all expenses other than income taxes and mortgage payments divided by acquisition costs). Lastly, assume that the building has a useful life of forty years with zero salvage value, and since it qualifies "as low-income housing" the partnership is entitled to use for tax purposes the 200 percent declining balance method of accelerated depreciation over a fifteen-year cost recovery period.[54a]

---

[54] This phrase, in the parlance of real estate developers, refers to net income before tax and finance charges divided by purchase or construction cost. See Wendt & Cert, *Real Estate Investment and Taxation* 19-24 (1969), for a description of customary rates of return for various kinds of income-producing realty.

[54a] The present law replaces the prior framework for depreciation with the Accelerated Cost Recovery System (ACRS), which permits real estate investors to recover their capital costs for most tangible depreciable real property over predetermined recovery periods that are generally unrelated to, but shorter than, the useful life periods under prior law. Under the new system, most real property taxpayers may use the straight-line method of depreciation over a fifteen-year period (or optional thirty-five- and forty-five-year recovery periods), in which event the depreciation recapture rules would not apply. Alternatively, accelerated depreciation may be elected for use over the standard fifteen-year recovery period based on either the 175 percent declining balance method or, in the case of low-income housing, the 200 percent declining balance method, with a transition to the straight-line method in later years under either type of accelerated recovery schedule. Under either method of accelerated depreciation the depreciation recapture rules would apply. Accordingly, in the example, the partnership could deduct, as straight-line depreciation, $66,666 ($1/15$ or 6.7 percent of the $1 million construction cost) each year during the fifteen-year cost recovery period and thereby avoid decline in its depreciable basis and any recapture problem once the property is sold or exchanged by the partnership. However, since the property qualifies as low-income housing, the syndicate has elected to use accelerated depreciation on a declining basis and deduct $133,332 (200 percent $\times$ 6.7 percent = 13.3 percent of $1 million construction cost) for the first operational year but must face depreciation recapture as explained at note 56 *infra*. See I.R.C. § 168(b)(2), added by Section 201(a) of the Economic Recovery Tax Act of 1981 (hereinafter cited as ERTA), applicable to property placed in service after December 31, 1980, in taxable years ending after such date. For an excellent discussion of legislative history; specifically how ERTA was influenced by and resembles the Kemp-Roth rate reduction proposal and the so-called "10-5-3 depreciation" proposals, see Aronsohn, "Real Estate Investment and the Economic Recovery Tax Act of 1981," 8 J. Real Est. Tax. 291 (1981).

For the first year of operations the cash-flow and tax results are as indicated in the following table, depending on whether the syndicate elects to use straight-line or accelerated depreciation over the fifteen-year cost recovery period.

Cash Flow

Net operating income		$150,000
Mortgage interest	$111,762	
Mortgage amortization	3,799	
		115,561
Net cash flow		$ 34,439

Taxable Income—Straight-Line Depreciation

Net operating income		$150,000
Mortgage interest	$111,762	
Depreciation	66,666	
		178,428
Taxable income		$(28,428)

Taxable Income—Accelerated Depreciation

Net operating income		$150,000
Mortgage interest	$111,762	
Depreciation	133,332	
		245,094
Taxable income		$(95,094)

Accordingly, while the syndicate may disburse $34,439 as a tax-free return of capital,[54b] these same partners can avail themselves of a $95,094 tax loss to offset their ordinary income from outside sources such as salaries and dividends in the event the partnership elects to use accelerated depreciation. *This apparent paradox is explained by the fact that deductible depreciation exceeds nondeductible mortgage amortization by $129,533.*

Assuming both G and L are in a 50 percent tax bracket and have sufficient outside income to absorb their losses, the partners' collective cash return in the dramatic first year would be $34,439 and their tax savings $47,547 if they use accelerated depreciation, so that their total after-tax cash return would be $81,986 or about 41 percent of their net $200,000 investment. By contrast, under prior law, if the building

---

[54b] While each distributee-partner's tax basis in his partnership interest (including his share of partnership liabilities) would be reduced by the amount of the cash received, he would not be taxed on the distribution (on the notion that he is recouping a part of his investment cost) unless his share exceeded his basis at the time of distribution. I.R.C. §§ 705, 731, and 752.

qualified as "residential rental housing," the amount of accelerated depreciation in the first year would have been only $50,000 and would have generated a total after-tax[54c] return of $59,439 or about 30 percent on their $200,000 equity investment. Moreover, the true economic return is even higher when the equity buildup attributable to mortgage amortization is taken into account. Obviously, had the syndicate purchased and not leased the fee, it would also receive the benefit of appreciation in land value in times of inflation.

By contrast, if the corporate form were used, the corporation could use accelerated depreciation both to shelter the cash inflow of $34,439 and to produce an internal loss of $95,094; however, its earnings and profits, if totally disgorged as a dividend distribution, would only be reduced by straight-line depreciation over a thirty-five-year cost recovery period ($28,571).[54d] Thus, the corporation would have earnings and profits of $9,667 and only $24,772 of the cash outflow to shareholders would be sheltered from ordinary income treatment. Furthermore, only the corporation can avail itself of the $95,094 loss, which cannot be passed through to its shareholders.

In addition, if the property were owned by a partnership and hypothetically worth $1.2 million when completely constructed and rented, the syndicate might "mortgage out" by refinancing at the same 80 per-

---

[54c] Under prior law, depreciation of income-producing property was determined under I.R.C. § 167 by estimating the property's useful life under a facts and circumstances test or by using Treasury guidelines prescribed under Revenue Procedure 62-21, 1962-2 C.B. 2,418, which ranged from forty years for apartment buildings to sixty years for warehouses. Accordingly, since the apartment building in the example has a useful life of forty years with a zero salvage value, the partnership would have been able to deduct, as straight-line depreciation, $25,000 ($1/40$ or 2½ percent of the $1 million construction cost) each year during the forty-year useful life of the building. Alternatively, had the building qualified as "residential rental housing" the partnership could have elected the 200 percent declining balance method to double the rate of depreciation to 5 percent and deduct $50,000 for the first year of opperation. Such use of accelerated depreciation produces much greater depreciation at the beginning of the property's useful life. However, in contrast to straight-line depreciation, all or part of the depreciation would be recaptured as ordinary income under I.R.C. § 1250 when the property is sold or exchanged. Also, the amount of the deduction decreases each year as the depreciable basis of the property declines by the amount of the accelerated depreciation taken the year before. For example, by the end of the seventh year of operation, depreciation would have de-escalated to $36,755 under prior law had the syndicate opted for accelerated depreciation, whereas under the straight-line method the annual amount of depreciation would have remained at $25,000.

[54d] See the discussion that follows, entitled "Calculating Corporate Earnings and Profits," this Supplement.

cent loan-to-value ratio for $960,000 and distribute the $160,000 of excess mortgage proceeds to the partners as a tax-free return of capital. By contrast, if the corporate form were used, the distributee-shareholders would be taxed (in this example) to the extent the corporation had accumulated (prior) earnings and profits.[55]

However, if L and G elect to use accelerated depreciation, observe that the amount of the depreciation deduction and resultant shelter will decrease each year as the depreciable basis of the property declines by the amount of the accelerated depreciation taken the year before. Also, under a customary constant-payment mortgage arrangement, the shelter will decrease as the percentage of each payment allocable to deductible interest decreases and the percentage allocable to nondelictible amortization increases. For example, as the following chart shows, by the end of Year 7, depreciation would be approximately $56,500, interest $106,805, and amortization $8,756; and by the end of Year 15, depreciation would be $45,470, interest $88,897, and amortization $26,663.

To some degree the problem of the disappearing shelter can be mitigated by refinancing the mortgage to de-escalate the amount of nondeductible amortization, or by selling the overdepreciated property and using the proceeds to fund the acquisition of some substitute property. This would start the depreciation cycle anew since the partnership would obtain a new depreciation basis equal to the cost of the newly acquired property. In addition, to the extent that the depreciation recapture provision, I.R.C. § 1250, is not applicable, any gain realized on the disposition would be treated as long-term capital gain. Therefore, ordinary depreciation losses taken during the early years of ownership are effectively converted into deferred long-term capital gain.[56]

---

[55] See ¶ 12.01[4].

[56] Under prior law, if a taxpayer utilized accelerated depreciation on real estate (other than subsidized low-income rental housing) used in its trade or business and after one year sold the property, that portion of the gain equal to the excess depreciation over the straight-line amount would have been recaptured as ordinary income regardless of how long it was held prior to sale. Only the balance of the long-term gain would be treated as Section 1231 gain and taxed at the preferential long-term capital gain rate. Accordingly, in the example, had the partnership deducted $50,000 of accelerated depreciation during its first operational year and sold its leasehold improvement, the building, at the end of its second operational year, for its original cost at a taxable gain of $97,500 (amount realized of $1 million less adjusted basis of $902,500), the excess of accelerated depreciation of $97,500 ($50,000 for Year 1 plus 5 percent of $950,000 (or $47,500) for Year 2) over the $50,000 straight-line amount, equal to $47,500 would have been recaptured as ordinary income under I.R.C. § 1250, and the $50,000 balance of the gain would have been taxed at the long-term capital gain rate. Had the property qualified under

Following is a chart, of the type likely to be found in a prospectus prepared by syndicators to attract potential investors, that outlines the projected tax benefits (and costs) to L and G over a fifteen-year period on the assumption that the annual net operating income of $150,000 remains the same during the entire period.

Observe that since G and L are in a 50 percent tax bracket, their tax savings would be $47,547 in the first year; however, by Year 9 the "crossover" point is reached and the tax shelter disappears because the declining excess of deductible depreciation over nondeductible mortgage amortization ($33,903) can be used to shelter all but $536 of the $34,439 cash flow, but once so expended there is nothing remaining of the excess (shelter) to generate any tax losses to the partners.

---

prior law as subsidized low-income housing, the amount of depreciation subject to recapture as ordinary income would have been phased out by one percent for each month the property had been held in excess of 100 months. Consequently, the partnership would have been able to fully escape recapture had the property been held at least 200 months (16⅔ years) prior to its sale or exchange.

Under the present system for depreciation, the phase-out recapture rule for subsidized low-income rental housing remains the same. However, if nonresidential real property is depreciated over the ACRS fifteen-year cost recovery period, the *full amount* of accelerated depreciation (and not just the excess over the straight-line amount) would be recaptured as ordinary income. By contrast, only the excess over the fifteen-year straight-line amount would be recaptured in the case of all residential real property. Accordingly, in the example, if the syndicate were to sell the property, at the end of its second operational year, for its original cost at a taxable gain of $248,599 (amount realized of $1 million less adjusted basis of $751,401), the excess of accelerated depreciation of $248,599 ($133,332 for Year 1 plus 13.3 percent of $866,668 (or $115,267) for Year 2) over the $133,332 fifteen-year straight-line amount, equal to $115.267 would be recaptured as ordinary income and the $133,332 balance of the gain would be taxed as long-term capital gain. However, if the straight-line method had been chosen, the entire gain of $248,599 would be taxed at the long-term capital gain rate regardless of whether the real property is residential or commercial in nature.

In addition, under the present recapture rules, component depreciation has been eliminated so that a taxpayer may no longer assign a separate useful life to the short-lived components of a building (such as wiring, plumbing, and heating systems) to reduce the composite life for the entire building. However, a taxpayer may elect to use accelerated depreciation for a substantial improvement to the building even if the straight-line method was used for the rest of the building, or vice versa. In such event, all gain on a subsequent disposition of the entire building would be treated first as ordinary income to the extent of all accelerated depreciation previously taken. The remainder of the gain would be capital gain. See I.R.C. §§ 1245 and 1250, as amended by ERTA § 204, applicable to property disposed of after December 31, 1980.

¶ 1.05[2][b] REAL ESTATE FINANCING S1-10

Year	Interest	Principal	Cash Flow*	Straight-Line Depreciation	Taxable Income (Loss)	Accelerated Depreciation	Taxable Income (Loss)	Tax Savings for 50% Bracket Investors Straight-Line Depreciation	Tax Savings for 50% Bracket Investors Accelerated Depreciation
1	111,762	3,799	34,439	66,666	(28,428)	133,332	(95,094)	14,214	47,547
2	111,195	4,366	34,439	66,666	(27,861)	115,555	(76,750)	13,930	38,375
3	110,543	5,018	34,439	66,666	(27,209)	100,148	(60,691)	13,604	30,345
4	109,794	5,767	34,439	66,666	(26,460)	86,795	(46,589)	13,230	23,294
5	108,932	6,629	34,439	66,666	(25,598)	75,222	(34,154)	12,799	17,077
6	107,942	7,619	34,439	66,666	(24,608)	65,191	(23,133)	12,304	11,566
7	106,805	8,756	34,439	66,666	(23,471)	56,500	(13,305)	11,735	6,652
8	105,496	10,065	34,439	66,666	(22,162)	48,967	(4,193)	11,081	2,096
9	103,994	11,567	34,439	66,666	(20,660)	45,470**	536	10,330	(268)
10	102,266	13,294	34,439	66,666	(18,932)	45,470	2,264	9,466	(1,132)
11	100,280	15,281	34,439	66,666	(16,946)	45,470	4,250	8,473	(2,125)
12	97,999	17,561	34,439	66,666	(14,665)	45,470	6,531	7,332	(3,265)
13	95,375	20,186	34,439	66,666	(12,041)	45,470	9,155	6,020	(4,577)
14	92,362	23,199	34,439	66,666	(9,028)	45,470	12,168	4,514	(6,084)
15	88,897	26,664	34,439	66,666	(5,563)	45,470	15,633	2,781	(7,816)

* Assuming that venture generates $150,000 net rental income each year after payment of all expenses other than income taxes and mortgage payments
** Switch over to straight-line depreciation

Also, if *L* and *G* elect to use accelerated depreciation rather than straight-line depreciation (as in the example), they would obtain more tax benefits in the early years (e.g., $133,332 depreciation in the first year) but each year the depreciation deduction would decline and by Year 6 the partners would start obtaining less tax benefits. Additionally, when residential property is sold under the recapture rules, the partners would lose the benefit of converting their *excess* depreciation deductions into long-term capital gain (except, as in our example, for one percentage point per month because of the recapture phase-out rule for subsidized low-income housing) and in the case of non-residential property *none* of the prior depreciation would be converted into long-term capital gain.

Page 1-19:

Add new text at end of first full paragraph.

Calculating Corporate Earnings and Profits. In calculating its taxable income, a corporation is subject generally to the same depreciation rules as an individual taxpayer. However, in determining whether a corporate distribution to its shareholders is taxable as a dividend or as a return of capital, the rule is that such distributions are taxable as dividends only to the extent that the distribution is out of the corporation's *current or accumulated earnings and profits.* In determining what are "earnings and profits" under prior law, a corporation was required to use straight-line depreciation over the useful life of the property (whether or not it used an accelerated method in determining the corporation's taxable income). In short, a corporation using accelerated depreciation may have had no taxable income (and so may not have paid any corporate income tax); nevertheless, because it was forced to use straight-line depreciation in computing earnings and profits, some or all of its distributions to its shareholders may have been taxable to them as dividends.

Under the Economic Recovery Tax Act of 1981, the rule relating to the use of straight-line depreciation in computing earnings and profits is unchanged. However, the recovery period (i.e., useful life) of the property being depreciated will be in accordance with the following table:

Extended Recovery Period

Property	Years
3-year property	5
5-year property	12
10-year property	25
15-year property	35

If the corporate taxpayer elects to use one of the longer recovery periods as described above in the discussion of depreciation, then such longer period must be used to compute earnings and profits.

The effect of this new rule will be to permit a larger amount of corporate distributions to be tax-free to shareholders and to that extent will make corporate ownership of real estate more attractive than in the past.

[d] Post-1976 Tax Legislation

Page 1-23:

Add new text before the first full paragraph.

Depreciation of Real Property. The rules concerning depreciation were formerly designed to allocate write-offs over the period the asset was used in business or for the production of income, so that deductions were matched with the income produced by the asset. ERTA makes a significant shift in emphasis. For property placed in service on or after January 1, 1981, deductions for depreciation may be taken over a set period that is shorter than the useful life of the asset. In other words, ERTA recognizes that depreciation write-offs should be related to replacement cost rather than original cost; the result of this will be a substantial increase in depreciation write-offs during the early years of ownership of depreciable property. The new depreciation system is known as the Accelerated Cost Recovery System (ACRS).

The new depreciation rules apply to most tangible depreciable real and personal property. However, the new rules do not apply to property that must be amortized, e.g., leasehold improvements and low-income rehabilitation expenditures.

Former IRS guideline lives for real property ranged from forty to sixty years, but actual lives may be shorter under a facts-and-circumstances approach. ERTA assigns real property a fifteen-year recovery period, but taxpayers may elect a thirty-five- or forty-five-year extended recovery period.

In choosing a depreciation method, taxpayers have the following options:

(1) *Accelerated Method.* If a taxpayer chooses accelerated depreciation, he must use the fifteen-year recovery period (not the thirty-five- or forty-five-year optional period). The accelerated method is either:

- The 175 percent declining balance method, changing to the straight-line method to maximize acceleration, for all types of real property other than low-income housing; or

- The 200 percent declining balance method, changing to straight-line, for low-income housing.

(2) *Straight-Line Depreciation.* The taxpayer may choose straight-line depreciation over either the fifteen-year period or one of the optional extended periods.

Composite depreciation is required under ERTA. Component depreciation (whereby different useful lives are assigned to components of the structure) no longer will be permitted.

However, a "substantial improvement" of a building is treated as a separate building. For example, the taxpayer may use a fifteen-year period for a substantial improvement even if the rest of the building is depreciable over a thirty-five- or forty-five-year period. In addition, an accelerated method can be used for the "substantial improvement" while the straight-line method is used for the rest of the building. An improvement is deemed substantial for this purpose if over a two-year period the improvement cost is at least equal to 25 percent of the adjusted basis of the building (disregarding adjustments for depreciation or amortization) as of the beginning of that two-year period, and the improvement is made at least three years after the building was placed in service.

A special rule allows a taxpayer to elect a new recovery period and a depreciation method for the first component placed in service after 1980 on a building owned before 1981, whether or not it is a substantial improvement.

Numerous components placed in service over a twenty-four-month period may in the aggregate exceed the 25 percent basis requirement. When the total exceeds 25 percent, the prior year's income tax return can be amended to reflect the more favorable alternative. Careful timing of the placement in service of components can enable a real estate investor to qualify for fast write-offs of additions or replacements made after January 1, 1981 to pre-1981 real estate.

ERTA contains some complex provisions intended to prevent a taxpayer from bringing pre-1981 real estate within the new ACRS in order to benefit from the fifteen-year recovery period. In essence, real property will not be eligible for the fifteen-year recovery period if:

(1) The taxpayer or someone related to the taxpayer owned the property at any time during 1980; or

(2) The property is transferred after 1980 and is then leased back to someone who owned the property in 1980 (or a related person); or

(3) The property is acquired in a tax-free exchange or other transaction that does not involve the recognition of tax in return for property the taxpayer (or a related person) owned in 1980.

The two methods of depreciation available to the real estate investor under the ACRS system, accelerated and straight-line, are discussed in greater detail below.

1. *Accelerated Depreciation.* A taxpayer electing accelerated depreciation under ERTA must use either the 175 percent declining balance method or the 200 percent declining balance method. ERTA eliminates the use of the following types of accelerated depreciation which were formerly available: 125 percent declining balance; 150 percent declining balance (except for foreign real estate); and sum-of-the-years'-digits. ERTA also eliminates the distinction between new and used property. (These continue to apply to real estate placed in service prior to 1981; see Table 1.3.)

a. *175 Percent Declining Balance Method of Depreciation.* This method of accelerated depreciation, as noted above, may be used for either residential or nonresidential property, provided that a fifteen-year recovery period is used. It allows a rate of depreciation equal to one and three-quarters the straight-line rate. However, the rate is not applied to the original cost basis each year (as is the case with straight-line depreciation), but instead is applied to the declining balance (i.e., cost less accumulated depreciation for prior taxable years). Since the depreciation base is reduced to reflect prior depreciation, the amount claimed as a depreciation deduction is greater in earlier years and declines in each succeeding year of the fifteen-year recovery period.

ERTA authorizes the IRS to provide a table to be used in connection with the 175 percent declining balance method, which will incorporate a switch to the straight-line method at such time as will maximize the deduction.

b. *200 Percent Declining Balance Method of Depreciation.* This method of depreciation may be used for subsidized low-income housing. (Under former law, it was available for all new residential housing.) Commonly referred to as double declining balance (DDB), this method allows a rate of depreciation equal to twice the straight-line rate. As with 175 percent declining balance, the rate is not applied to the original cost basis each year but is applied to the declining balance. Low-income housing for the purpose of DDB depreciation is property described in Sections 1250(a)(1)(B)(i)–1250(a)(1)(B)(iv) of the Internal Revenue Code and includes:

- Housing financed under Section 221(d)(3) or 236 of the National Housing Act or under similar state or local laws; or

- Housing eligible for the sixty-month write-off rehabilitation expenditures; or

- Housing occupied by families subsidized under Section 8 of the United States Housing Act of 1937 or under similar laws; or

- Housing financed under Section 515 of the Housing Act of 1949.

2. *Straight-Line Depreciation.* Under the straight-line method, an equal amount is deducted each year over the life of the property.

TABLE 1.1: Depreciation and Recapture of post-1980 Real Estate[1]

Property Type	Recovery Period (Years)	Depreciation Method	Recapture[4]
Residential	15	SL[2] or 175% DB [3]	No / Excess depreciation
	35	SL	No
	45	SL	No
Nonresidential	15	SL or 175% DB [3]	No / All depreciation
	35	SL	No
	45	SL	No
Subsidized housing	15	SL or 200% DB [3]	No / Excess depreciation phased out[5]
	35	SL	No
	45	SL	No

1. Real estate outside the United States is depreciated over thirty-five years using the 150% declining-balance method.
2. SL = straight-line depreciation.
3. 175% DB or 200% DB = 175% or 200% declining balance method with a switch to the SL method at such time as will maximize the deduction.
4. Depreciation on any real estate (except subsidized housing) held for less than twelve months is subject to 100% recapture. For subsidized housing held less than twelve months, recapture is limited to depreciation in excess of straight-line.
5. Recapture of excess depreciation phased out at rate of one percent for each month over 100, with no recapture after 200 months (sixteen years and eight months).

Example 1. An investor acquires real estate for $100,000 in 1981. Twenty percent, or $20,000, is allocated to nondepreciable land; 80 percent, or $80,000, is allocated to depreciable improvements. The taxpayer elects the fifteen-year recovery period. Thus, the investor is entitled to deduct 6.67 percent of $80,000 ($5,336) each year during the initial fifteen years of ownership, at the end of which time the investor will have recouped, tax-free, his $80,000 investment in the improvements. (His tax basis is reduced by a similar amount.)

The annual deduction offsets taxable income of the investor (whether the taxable income arises from the real property itself apart from the depreciation deduction, or from an outside source). Further, the deduction is available regardless of how much or how little equity the investor puts up and whether or not he is personally liable on the mortgage securing the loan.

The use of straight-line depreciation illustrates all three elements of a tax shelter: deferral of taxes, benefits from leveraging, and conversion of ordinary income to capital gain. This can be illustrated by continuing the example to the point where the property is sold by the investor.

Example 2. Assume the investor sells the real estate after ten years, during which time he took total depreciation deductions of $53,360 (6.67 percent per year × 10 years × $80,000). If he is in the 50 percent bracket, this represents total tax savings of $26,680. At the end of ten years, he sells the property for $100,000, his original cost. His basis for tax purposes is $46,640 (cost of $100,000 − $53,360 of cumulative depreciation deductions). Thus his gain is $53,360—exactly the amount of cumulative depreciation, since the property was sold at a price equal to its original cost. Assuming the property is a capital asset in his hands, only 40 percent of this long-term gain is subject to tax, or $21,344. The amount of tax thus is $10,672 (50 percent of the 40 percent taxable portion of the gain).

Net result: The use of straight-line depreciation (combined with resale of the property at a price equal to its original cost) has enabled the investor to:

(1) Defer until the sale of the property a total of $10,672 in tax payments that otherwise would have been due in equal amounts during the ten years of ownership;
(2) Convert ordinary income of $53,360 (which would have been taxable to him over the ten-year period had he not

TABLE 1.2: Depreciation Methods

Year	Straight-Line (SL)		150% Declining		175% Declining*		200% Declining*	
	Annual Allowance	Adjusted Basis	Annual Allowance	Adjusted Basis	Annual Allowance	Adjusted Basis	Annual Allowance	Adjusted Basis
1	6.66	93.33	10.00	90.00	11.67	88.33	13.33	86.66
2	6.66	86.66	9.00	81.00	10.31	78.02	11.55	75.11
3	6.66	80.00	8.10	72.90	9.10	68.92	10.01	65.09
4	6.66	73.33	7.29	65.61	8.04	60.88	8.67	56.41
5	6.66	66.66	6.56	59.04	7.10	53.78	7.52	48.89
6	6.66	60.00	5.90	53.14	6.28	47.50	6.51	42.37
7	6.66	53.33	5.31	47.82	5.54	41.96	5.65	36.72
8	6.66	46.66	4.78	43.04	4.90	37.06	4.89	31.82
9	6.66	40.00	4.30	38.74	4.32	32.74	4.24	27.58
10	6.66	33.33	3.87	34.86	3.82	28.92	3.67	23.90
11	6.66	26.66	3.48	31.38	3.37	25.55	3.18	20.71
12	6.66	20.00	3.13	28.42	2.98	22.57	2.76	17.95
13	6.66	13.33	2.82	25.41	2.63	19.94	2.39	15.56
14	6.66	6.66	2.54	22.87	2.33	17.61	2.07	13.48
15	6.66	0.00	2.28	20.58	2.06	15.55	1.79	11.68

* The switchover to the SL method occurs at such time as will maximize the deduction.

utilized depreciation deductions) to capital gain of $53,360, thus realizing a savings of $16,008 (30 percent of the gain, which is the amount saved by paying a 20 percent capital gains rate instead of a 50 percent ordinary income rate); and
(3) If we assume that 80 percent of the total investment of $100,000 was represented by borrowed funds, achieve this tax saving on an equity investment of $20,000.

The use of straight-line depreciation remains the major advantage of real estate investing for the reasons shown above; and with the shortened recovery period to fifteen years under ERTA, the tax benefit is greater than ever before.

TABLE 1.3: Depreciation of Real Estate Owned Prior to 1981

Depreciation Method	*Applicable to*
1. 200% declining balance	1. New residential housing
2. Sum-of-the-years'-digits	2. New residential housing
3. 150% declining balance	3. All new property, commercial and industrial
4. 125% declining balance	4. Used residential rental housing with useful life of at least twenty years
5. Straight-line	5. All new or used property
6. Straight-line using sixty-month useful life	6. Low-income rental housing rehabilitation expenditures (subject to dollar limitations)

Page 1-23:

Replace paragraph entitled "Recapture of Accelerated Depreciation" with the following.

Recapture of Real Property Depreciation. Prior to ERTA, gain on the disposition of real property was treated (recaptured) as ordinary income rather than as capital gain to the extent that prior depreciation taken by the taxpayer exceeded what would have been allowable if straight-line depreciation had been used.

Under ERTA:

- The treatment of residential real property is unchanged (i.e., excess depreciation is recaptured).
- The treatment of nonresidential real property is unchanged if the straight-line depreciation method is used (i.e., no recapture will occur).

- The treatment for nonresidential real property depreciated under an accelerated method is changed. Beginning January 1, 1981, gain on the sale of such property is treated as ordinary income to the extent of all prior depreciation taken (not merely depreciation in excess of straight-line).

In determining whether real estate is used for a residential or nonresidential purpose, it is reasonable to assume the same rules will apply as were formerly used to distinguish residential and nonresidential property for purposes of allowable depreciation methods (which differed depending on the property use under former law). Under these rules, residential rental property includes single- and multiple-family housing, apartments, and similar structures used to provide living accommodations on a rental basis. A building or other structure will qualify as residential rental property if 80 percent or more of the gross rental income from the building or structure is rental income from dwelling units. Hotels, motels, inns, or other similar establishments are not treated as dwelling units if more than one-half of the units are used on a transient basis.

TABLE 1.4: Comparison of Old and New Recapture Rules

Types of Property	Recapture of Depreciation on Non-ACRS Real Estate	Recapture of Depreciation on ACRS Real Estate
• All residential and nonresidential real estate, without exception, if held for less than 12 months	• All depreciation, including straight-line	• Same
• All residential and nonresidential real estate except subsidized housing projects, if held for more than 12 months	• All depreciation in excess of straight-line	• Same for residential; for nonresidential, *all* depreciation is recaptured
• Subsidized housing projects, if held between 12 and 100 months	• All depreciation in excess of straight-line	• Same
• Subsidized housing, if held more than 100 months	• Recapture of excess depreciation phased out at rate of one percent for each month over 100, with no recapture after 200 months (16 years and 8 months)	• Same

Page 1-24:

Add new text after first full paragraph.

Rehabilitation Investment Credit. Under prior law, rehabilitation expenses for a nonresidential building at least twenty years old were eligible for the 10 percent investment tax credit (plus an additional energy credit). When the rehabilitation was of a certified historic structure, the taxpayer could elect, in lieu of the investment credit, a sixty-month amortization of such expenditures.

ERTA substitutes for both the 10 percent investment credit and the sixty-month amortization, a three-tier investment credit. The credit is:

(1) 15 percent for nonresidential structures at least thirty years old;

(2) 20 percent for nonresidential structures at least forty years old; and

(3) 25 percent for certified historic structures, whether residential or nonresidential.

Three conditions are attached to use of the investment credit for rehabilitation expenditures:

(1) *Straight-line depreciation.* The credit is available only if the taxpayer elects to use the straight-line method of cost recovery (depreciation) with respect to the rehabilitation expenditures.

(2) *Reduction of basis.* For rehabilitation investment credits *other than* the credit for certified historic rehabilitations, the basis of the property must be reduced by the amount of the credit. (Thus, upon sale of the property, additional gain will be realized.)

(3) *Substantial rehabilitation.* Finally, only a "substantial rehabilitation" qualifies for the investment credit. A building will be substantially rehabilitated if the rehabilitation expenses during the preceding two years are at least $5,000 *and* exceed the adjusted basis of the property as of the beginning of the period.

However, an investor may substitute a five-year period for the two-year period (thus making it much easier to qualify for the credit) if:

- Written plans and specifications exist for the entire rehabilitation process; and
- There is a reasonable expectation that the entire rehabilitation will be completed.

It is not clear whether the adjusted basis of the property at the beginning of the rehabilitation period refers to the adjusted basis of the improvements only or of the improvements plus land. If the latter, the floor for eligible rehabilitation expenditures can be reduced substantially by leasing rather than purchasing the land under the buildings.

Treasury regulations under the former rehabilitation credit presumably will continue to apply to the extent they do not conflict with the new law. Significant points covered by these provisions include the following:

☐ *Buildings eligible for credit.* Eligible buildings include factories, warehouses, office buildings, hotels, and retail and wholesale stores. Buildings used for residential purposes, such as apartments, are not eligible for the credit unless they are certified historic structures. The status of an eligible building is determined on the basis of its use when placed in service after the rehabilitation. For example, if an apartment building (not a historic structure) is rehabilitated for use as an office building, it is eligible for the credit.

☐ *External walls.* At least 75 percent of the external walls must be retained in order for the expenditures to qualify as a rehabilitation. However, existing walls can be resurfaced (new siding or facade applied) or reinforced and still permit the rehabilitation to qualify for the credit.

☐ *Rehabilitation of only a part of the building.* Where only a part of a building is rehabilitated, the rehabilitation expenditures will qualify for the credit if the part of the building that is rehabilitated constitutes a "major portion" of the building. Whether or not a portion constitutes a "major portion" depends on factors such as volume, floor space, and functional differences between the rehabilitated and unrehabilitated parts of the building. For example, where a substantial part of a building is used for retail stores and another part is used for warehousing, each part constitutes a major portion of the building for purposes of these provisions.

☐ *Definition of qualified rehabilitation expenditures.* The types of expenditures that qualify for the credit are interior or exterior renovation or restoration expenditures that materially extend the useful life of the building or significantly upgrade its usefulness. For example, expenditures for replacement of plumbing, electrical wiring, flooring, permanent interior partitions in walls, and heating or air-conditioning systems qualify when they are incurred in connection with a rehabilitation that materially extends the useful life of a building and significantly upgrades its usefulness. However, in order to exclude minor repairs or improvements, the expenditures must be of the type that would be capitalized rather than expensed and be incurred with respect to property with a useful life of at least five years.

☐ *Cost of acquiring or enlarging an existing building.* The cost of acquiring or enlarging an existing building is not considered a "qualified rehabilitation expenditure," nor are costs incurred in connection with certain facilities, such as parking lots, that are related to an existing building. If, in the course of a qualifying rehabilitation, the floor space of an existing building is increased by reason of interior remodeling, such increased floor space will not constitute an enlargement of the building.

Under the new rules, a lessee may qualify for the rehabilitation credit if the remaining term of the lease at completion of the rehabilitation (without regard to any renewal period) is at least fifteen years.

An owner may now claim the investment credit for rehabilitation expenditures to property leased to a tax-exempt organization or governmental unit (as to uses after July 29, 1980).

The new law applies to expenditures incurred after December 31, 1981. The old law continues to apply to rehabilitations begun prior to 1982 that qualify under the old law but not under the new law (e.g., rehabilitation of a twenty-year-old building). If a rehabilitation does qualify under the new law, expenditures incurred prior to 1982 qualify for a 10 percent credit while expenditures incurred thereafter receive the higher credit (15, 20, or 25 percent). For a certified historic structure, the election between the 10 percent credit or the sixty-month amortization applies to any pre-1982 expenditures, but only the 25 percent credit is available for expenditures in 1982 and thereafter.

Historic Structure Rehabilitations. As noted above, rehabilitations of historic structures are eligible for a 25 percent investment credit. Such rehabilitations must meet two requirements:

(1) *Certified historic structure.* First, the building itself must be a "certified historic structure." This is defined as a depreciable structure that is:

- Listed in the *National Register* (existing law); or

- Located in a historic district designated under estate or local statute containing standards satisfactory to the Secretary of the Interior (existing law); or

- Located in a Registered Historic District (changes existing law which provides that, in addition, the Secretary of the Interior must certify that the particular building is of historic significance to the district).

(2) *Certified rehabilitation.* Second, the rehabilitation must be certified by the Secretary of the Interior as being consistent with the historic character of the property or the district.

Impact of the Tax Credit Plus Depreciation. The new rehabilitation tax credit can have an enormous impact on an investment return because the credit is taken up front and so reduces the equity required, and the credit is a dollar-for-dollar offset against taxes, not merely a deduction. And the combination of the rehabilitation credit and the new fifteen-year recovery period can produce very large deductions as compared to former law, as is shown by this hypothetical case.

Example. In January 1981, a taxpayer purchases a fifty-year-old nonresidential building for the price of $1.2 million. Beginning in January 1982, he restores it, spending $2 million, and places the improvements in service in January 1983. He elects to use straight-line depreciation (SLD) over a fifteen-year period.

☐ *1981-1982 depreciation write-offs.* Assume that of the $1.2 million cost, $200,000 is allocated to nondepreciable land and $1 million to the depreciable structure. Under SLD, the annual depreciation deduction in 1981 and 1982 will be $66,667.

☐ *Rehabilitation tax credit.* In 1983, the taxpayer is entitled to a 20 percent tax credit of the $2 million rehabilitation cost, or $400,000.

☐ *1983 and subsequent depreciation.* In 1983, the depreciable basis of the building is increased by $1.6 million (the $2 million rehabilitation cost minus the $400,000 credit). So in 1983 and thereafter, the annual depreciation deduction using SLD will be $173,334.

As Table 1.5 shows, over the first three years, a 50 percent taxpayer realizes savings of $260,000 over and above that realized under former law. Note that the 15 percent minimum tax on preference income will not apply to the investment under the new law since SLD is used.

TABLE 1.5: Rehabilitation Tax Benefits Under ERTA

Depreciation 1981-1982 (6.67% annually on $1 million)	$133,334
Depreciation 1983 (6.67% on $2.6 million)	173,334
Total (3 years)	$306,668
Tax savings (50% tax bracket)	153,334
Rehab credit 1983 (20% of $2 million)	400,000
Total tax savings (3 years)	$553,334
Total 3-year tax savings under former law (40-year life; 150% depreciation; 15% minimum tax)	$291,666
Increased tax savings	$261,668

The magnitude of the tax savings shown in Table 1.5 can be appreciated even more by showing how they affect the return on investment even in today's high interest rate environment. Assume that at the completion of the rehabilitation, the fair market value of the property was $3.5 million, approximately 10 percent above the total investment in land and building of $3.2 million.

TABLE 1.6: Rehabilitation Property Investment

Total investment (land plus building)		$3,200,000
First mortgage (70% of $3.5 million; 14% interest; 15% constant)		2,450,000
Equity required		$ 750,000
Tax savings (3 years) (from Table 1)		553,000
Net equity		$197,000
Cash Flow		
Net operating income (10.5%)		$367,500
Debt service		367,500
Cash flow		0
Tax Gain (Loss)		
Net operating income		$367,500
Less: Interest	$343,000	
Less: Depreciation	173,000	
Total deductions		516,000
Net loss		($148,500)
Tax savings (50% bracket)		$ 74,250
Return on $197,000 investment		38%

On this amount, the investor obtains a first mortgage of $2.45 million (70 percent of value) at 14 percent interest and 15 percent constant. Assume also that the property throws off a net operating income exactly equal to the debt service of $367,500. This would require a free and clear return of 10.5 percent, which would seem a minimum expectation. As a result, zero cash flow is realized.

However, the large deductions for interest and depreciation will yield a taxable loss of $148,500 for the first year the rehabilitated property is in service. For an investor in the 50 percent bracket, this represents a 38 percent after-tax return on his net investment of $197,000 (after-tax savings in years 1 to 3). Since straight-line depreciation is used and amortization begins at one percent, the annual loss will decline very slowly during the fifteen-year recovery period. On the other hand, net operating income should increase in future years, creating a positive cash flow. And if interest rates decline so that the first mortgage can be refinanced, it is possible that the investor can mortgage out in a few years.

Add new text after second full paragraph.

ERTA has two provisions that benefit investors in low-income housing.

Under prior law, taxpayers must capitalize and amortize construction period interest and taxes. This rule is not applicable to low-income housing until 1982. The new law exempts low-income housing permanently from the requirement, which means that construction period interest and taxes in connection with low-income housing is immediately deductible.

Prior to ERTA, qualified low-income housing rehabilitation expenditures up to $20,000 per dwelling unit could be amortized over a sixty-month period. This fast write-off was intended to encourage such expenditures. The new law leaves the prior rule unchanged but adds a provision that the amount of expenditures eligible for the fast write-off may increase to $40,000 per unit if:

(1) The rehabilitation is part of a program under which tenants who demonstrate homeownership responsibilities may purchase their units at a price that limits the seller's profit; and

(2) The tenants occupy the units as their principal residence.

This provision applies to amounts paid or incurred in 1981 and thereafter. Rehabilitation expenditures will not qualify for the fast write-off if the sum of the expenditures for two consecutive years with respect to any dwelling unit is less than $3,000.

Example. In 1981, *L* incurs $1,200 of rehabilitation expenditures for a dwelling unit in a low-income housing project. The expenditures do not qualify for the sixty-month write-off since they are less than $3,000. In 1982, *L* spends an additional $1,500 for the same unit. Since the two-year total is $2,700—still less than $3,000—the expenditures do not qualify for the special write-off. In 1983, *L* completes the rehabilitation, putting in an additional $14,000. *L* may elect in 1983 to write off over sixty months the $1,500 of expenditures in 1982 and the $14,000 of expenditures in 1983 (since these together do not exceed the $20,000 ceiling).

No limit is imposed on the number of separate units that may be rehabilitated under this provision. Thus, if a taxpayer incurs the maximum amount of qualified expenditures ($20,000) for each of 100 units, the total of $2 million may be deducted over the sixty-month period.

Page 1-25:

Replace sentence beginning on line 13 with the following.

Under the Revenue Act of 1978, the base was reduced by an exemption of $20,000, and the residual was taxed incrementally as follows: 10 percent on the first $40,000; 20 percent on the next $40,000; and 25 percent on the remainder. Under ERTA, the top rate was reduced from 25 percent to 20 percent.

Page 1-26:

Add new text at end of first full paragraph.

Accelerated depreciation is valuable to taxpayers because it increases the amount of write-offs during the early years of property ownership. But using accelerated depreciation may have a cost, too. Prior to ERTA, excess depreciation (i.e., the amount of write-off in excess of that allowable using straight-line depreciation) was one of nine *tax preference items*. Such items were subject to a flat 15 percent minimum tax if the total of tax preference items exceeded in any year the greater of $10,000 or (a) one-half of regular income taxes in the case of non-corporate taxpayers, or (b) the full amount of regular income taxes in the case of regular corporations.

Under ERTA, the amount of depreciation that constitutes a tax preference is the excess of the depreciation actually taken by the taxpayer over the amount that would have been allowable using the straight-line method over the prescribed periods as set forth below:

	Prescribed Period
Property	Years
3-year property	5
5-year property	8
10-year property	15
15-year property	15
15-year personal property	22

Under prior law, every dollar of a taxpayer's preference items reduced the amount of personal service taxable income that was eligible for the maximum tax rate of 50 percent. This provision becomes irrelevant under ERTA since no income will be taxed at a higher rate than 50 percent.

Example. The owner of residential property with a depreciable basis of $1 million holds the property for five years, during which time he uses accelerated depreciation. His annual deductions, and the deductions that would have been taken if straight-line depreciation had been used, are as follows:

Accelerated	Straight-Line	Excess
$120,000	$ 66,600	$ 53,400
100,000	66,600	33,400
90,000	66,600	23,400
80,000	66,600	13,400
70,000	66,600	3,400
$460,000	$333,000	$127,000

Assume the taxpayer's regular tax is not in excess of $20,000 (since most of his income is sheltered by the depreciation write-offs). His exemption for preference income then will be $10,000 each year. The minimum tax of 15 percent on the balance of preference income (i.e., excess depreciation) will result in a minimum tax in each of the five years as follows:

Year	Minimum Taxes
1	$ 6,510
2	3,510
3	2,010
4	510
5	0
	$12,540

For a total minimum tax cost of $12,540, the investor is able to defer tax on the ordinary income sheltered by the excess depreciation until the property is sold. Thus, the investor can defer tax on $53,400 for four years, on $33,400 for three years, and so forth (except for the final year's excess depreciation, when no deferral occurs because the property is sold). Except for taxpayers in very low tax brackets, use of accelerated depreciation would be worthwhile.

However, if the property had been nonresidential, the opposite conclusion is likely to be reached, since the owner must not only pay minimum taxes of $12,540 but also will see an additional $333,000 of gain (i.e., that attributable to straight-line depreciation) converted from capital gain to ordinary income upon sale. The additional tax on sale alone is likely to be far greater than the savings achieved by deferring taxes through use of accelerated depreciation. Generally speaking, the longer nonresidential property is held, the more likely that accelerated depreciation will prove worthwhile.

Page 1-27:

Add new text and note 85a after second paragraph.

Over the years, Congress has seen fit to accord preferential tax treatment to long-term capital gain. However, in enacting the Economic Recovery Tax Act of 1981, Congress shifted its emphasis in tax policy somewhat by reducing the top marginal rate on ordinary income from 70 percent to 50 percent to encourage both the earning as well as the saving of after-tax income by high-bracket taxpayers.

The preferential treatment for long-term capital gain continues. Since the taxable 40 percent portion of long-term capital gain is now subject to the top 50 percent marginal rate, the effective maximum rate on long-term capital gain was reduced from 28 percent to 20 percent.

Consequently, because of this continuing (albeit reduced) differential in maximum rates for both kinds of income tax, planners for high-bracket real estate investors[85a] will continue their attempt to (1) defer

---

[85a] It is interesting that neither the Code nor the Treasury regulations define the phrase "investing in real property," and a literal construction might preclude ownership of improved realty such as an apartment house or a shopping center (without net leases) since such property would arguably be used in a trade or business and not simply as a passive investment for the production of income. Cf. I.R.C. § 1221(2) and George Rothenberg v. Comm'r, 48 T.C. 369 (1967); and compare I.R.C. § 162(a) with I.R.C. §§ 212(1) and 212(2). For our purposes let us be colloquial and assume that "investing" refers to both active as well as passive type activities.

the investor's recognition of ordinary income from the operation of the real property, and (2) convert into long-term capital gain income that would otherwise be taxed at ordinary income rates.

Page 1-30:

Add to end of paragraph entitled "Investment Credit Liberalized."

Prior to ERTA, the amount of the regular investment credit (expressed as a percent of the acquisition cost) was as follows:

Estimated Useful Life (Years)	Credit (%)
3-4	3⅓
5-6	6⅔
7 or more	10

Under ERTA, the amount of the investment credit for the four depreciation classes of personal property is as follows:

Recovery Period (Years)	Credit (%)
3	6
5, 10, and 15	10

The $100,000 ceiling for used property eligible for the investment credit was increased to $125,000 in 1981, and will be increased to $150,000 in 1985. There is no ceiling on the amount of new property eligible for the credit. The investment credit may be used to offset the first $25,000 of tax liability plus (beginning in 1982) 90 percent of any tax in excess of $25,000. Any unused investment credits under prior law may be carried back three years and forward seven years. Under ERTA, both the carryback and carryforward periods are extended to fifteen years. Unchanged is the pre-ERTA law that any such carryovers may be used first against a current year's tax limit, before the current year's credit is applied.

Energy Tax Credits. The Energy Tax Act of 1978, as amended in 1980, provides for two types of energy tax credit—one for business property and one for residential property.

1. *Business energy credit.* Business firms may claim a tax credit for certain energy-saving equipment placed in service between October 1, 1978 and January 1, 1983 (except for solar or wind energy property, for which the credit is available until January 1, 1986). The energy credit is in addition to the regular investment credit. The equipment must be of a kind eligible for depreciation or amortization and must have the useful life of three years or more.

CHECKLIST FOR THE AVAILABILITY OF THE INVESTMENT CREDIT

Description of Property	Qualifies for Credit?		
	Yes	No	Uncertain
1. Storage bins and farm silos	☐	☐	☐
2. Fences used in connection with raising livestock	☐	☐	☐
3. Water wells to provide water for raising poultry and livestock	☐	☐	☐
4. Paved barnyards	☐	☐	☐
5. Trailer park electrical hookups, plumbing hookups, and water wells	☐	☐	☐
6. Electrical, plumbing, and sprinkler systems in a factory	☐	☐	☐
7. Special electrical and plumbing installations for specific machinery	☐	☐	☐
8. Outdoor lighting for parking lots	☐	☐	☐
9. Wall-to-wall carpeting attached to wood strips by hooks	☐	☐	☐
10. Wall-to-wall carpeting glued to floor	☐	☐	☐
11. Sprinkler system in building	☐	☐	☐
12. Special fire extinguisher to protect against fire at location of hazardous item of equipment	☐	☐	☐
13. Expenditures for dismantling, transporting, and installing used Section 38 property	☐	☐	☐
14. Movable office partitions	☐	☐	☐
15. Ski chair-lift towers and loading ramps	☐	☐	☐
16. Amusement park rides	☐	☐	☐
17. Grading and ramps for amusement park rides	☐	☐	☐
18. Aircraft hangar	☐	☐	☐
19. Paving around aircraft hangar	☐	☐	☐

	Description of Property	Qualifies for Credit?		
		Yes	No	Uncertain
20.	Costs of excavating and grading paved areas	☐	☐	☐
21.	Orchard of citrus trees	☐	☐	☐
22.	Leased propane gas storage tanks, water heaters and water softeners	☐	☐	☐
23.	Computer, including software cost that is not separately stated	☐	☐	☐
24.	Roadways in manufacturing complex used by trucks transporting materials and finished products	☐	☐	☐
25.	Parking lot for employees and visitors	☐	☐	☐
26.	Canopies over loading or storage docks	☐	☐	☐
27.	Raised floor for installation of computer equipment in factory	☐	☐	☐
28.	Movable trailers used as on-site construction offices	☐	☐	☐
29.	Trailer mounted on permanent concrete block foundation	☐	☐	☐
30.	Furniture leased by taxpayer to tenants of apartment buildings	☐	☐	☐
31.	Automotive equipment used for performing maintenance services in apartment complex	☐	☐	☐
32.	"Butler building" for raw material storage	☐	☐	☐
33.	Lighting to illuminate the exterior of a building	☐	☐	☐
34.	Identity signs and "logo" symbols on retail establishments and restaurants	☐	☐	☐
35.	Outdoor-advertising billboards	☐	☐	☐
36.	Elevators in apartment buildings	☐	☐	☐
37.	Elevators and escalators in other types of buildings	☐	☐	☐

The property eligible for the credit must be one of the following:

- Alternative energy property (10 percent energy credit)
- Solar or wind energy property (15 percent energy credit)
- Specifically defined energy property (10 percent energy credit)
- Recycling equipment (10 percent energy credit)

Before a property owner purchases equipment that he believes will qualify for a tax credit, he should ask the seller whether the equipment has been certified by the Secretary of the Treasury. Under Internal Revenue Service proposed regulations, manufacturers can obtain IRS certification that their product meets the statutory requirements necessary to qualify for the credit. Lenders might also be interested in determining whether the property has been certified by Treasury as qualifying for the tax credit.

The law permits state and local governments to issue tax-exempt bonds to finance the construction of (1) solid waste disposal facilities, (2) steam generating facilities, (3) hydroelectric generating facilities, and (4) solar, wind, or geothermal energy projects. However, there are various limits on the amount of such bonds that may be issued and there are regulations governing the type of government guarantees to be provided bondholders.

2. *Residential Energy Credit.* Section 44C of the Code provides a tax credit for those homeowners and tenants who install energy-conserving devices in their dwellings. The credit is allowed for two types of expenditures: (1) qualified energy conservation expenditures—for insulation and other energy-conserving components such as storm windows, thermostats, and improved furnace ignition systems—for which the credit is 15 percent of the first $2,000 of qualifying expenditures; and (2) qualified renewable-energy-source expenditures—for such heating and cooling devices as solar, geothermal, and wind systems—for which the credit is 40 percent of the first $10,000 of qualifying expenditures.

Expenditures of both types qualify only if the affected dwelling is located in the United States and is used by the taxpayer as his principal residence; and prior expenditures on the same residence for which the taxpayer was allowed a credit reduce the dollar amount qualifying for the credit in later years. An additional condition, applicable only to conservation expenditures, is that construction of the dwelling must have been substantially completed before April 20, 1977. Without this limitation, I.R.C. § 44C would provide an incentive for the construction of poorly insulated houses, since the purchaser could then qualify for a subsidy by rectifying the deficiency. As amended in 1980, I.R.C. §

44C(1) allows credits to two or more persons with separate principal residences who share the expense of joint qualifying energy-conservation or renewable-energy-source installations serving both premises and (2) precludes "double dipping" by claims for credits for installations financed with subsidized government loans or nontaxable government grants.

The credit for a taxable year cannot exceed the taxpayer's tax liability (reduced by most other credits) and is not refundable, but unused credits can be carried forward to later taxable years.

In a recent Tax Court decision,[95a] a "total solar plant" was found to be a building in both appearance and function, and therefore not "tangible personal property" or Section 38 property qualifying for an investment credit under I.R.C. § 48(a)(1). The credit was denied for the equipment and distribution system comprising the total energy plant as a whole because its owner was not an independent supplier of energy services and its linkage with the apartment building that it served caused it to be a nonqualifying structural component.

Tax shelter opinions. The promoters of a tax-sheltered investment generally request the opinion of a tax attorney with respect to all relevant tax aspects in the proposed transaction. The provision of these "tax shelter opinions" has created considerable debate and controversy within the securities industry, the legal profession, and the Internal Revenue Service.

A tax opinion is often relied upon by prospective investors when analyzing their investment. The opinion, therefore, becomes very important to the successful marketing of a tax shelter investment. The lawyer issuing the tax shelter opinion has certain ethical responsibilities. The Internal Revenue Service has outlined its position with respect to these responsibilities in a proposed amendment to Circular 230,[95b] relating to rules governing practice before the Treasury Department. The American Bar Association has issued a Formal Opinion,[95c] which outlines the ethical considerations surrounding the issuance of a "tax shelter opinion."

Proposed Circular 230 generally requires (1) that the attorney address all material issues with regard to federal tax matters, (2) that the attorney take reasonable steps to insure that the facts are as represented, and (3) that the attorney issue an opinion only if it is more likely than not that the bulk of tax benefits on the basis of which the shelter has been promoted are allowable under the law.

[95a] James M. Samis v. Comm'r, 76 T.C. 609 (1981).
[95b] 1980-42 I.R.B. 23.
[95c] ABA Formal Opinion No. 346 (Revised) (Jan. 29, 1982).

Formal Opinion 346 provides generally (1) that the attorney must require full disclosure from the promoter, (2) that the attorney must inquire into any underlying information that makes little common sense or that is dubious, and (3) that the attorney must render a true opinion with respect to the probable outcome of all material tax issues. Formal Opinion 346 differs from proposed Circular 230 in that the former will allow a negative conclusion to be stated and provides that in rare instances it may be impossible to render a judgment on a particular issue.

Page 1-37:

Add at end of note 120.

[120] Durand Holladay v. Comm'r, 72 T.C. 571 (1979), *aff'd* 649 F.2d 1176 (5th Cir. 1981).

[3] Other Tax Advantages of Partnership Over Incorporation

[b] Flexibility in Allocation of Income or Loss

[i] Special Allocations

Page 1-39:

Add new note 124a at end of second full paragraph.

[124a] See Martin Magazine v. Comm'r, 37 T.C.M. 873 (1978), where an *Orrisch*-styled special allocation of depreciation did not have substantial economic effect and failed because the partnership agreement did not require equilibrium in the capital accounts of the partners at liquidation.

Page 1-46:

Add at end of note 154.

[154] The appeal to the Ninth Circuit was dismissed upon government motion on January 15, 1978.

[4] Tax Pitfalls of Limited Partnership

[b] Tax Shelter Basis Problem Caused by Recourse Financing

[ii] Special Basis Rule for Limited Partner

Page 1-54:

Replace last paragraph with the following.

Returning to our hypothetical example at ¶ 1.05[2][b], this failure to increase *L*'s basis could be disastrous. Since each year *L*'s basis is being reduced by his share of losses and tax-free cash flow under I.R.C. § 705, his basis would be reduced to zero by Year 2, assuming his net cash yield remains at $17,220 per annum. Consequently, he would thereafter be precluded from deducting his share of losses under I.R.C. § 704(d) and would not start realizing gain on the distribution of cash flow. If the financing had been nonrecourse, his tax basis at the end of Year 2 would be a huge $379,638.

[5] Tax Advantages of Incorporation
[a] Lower Tax Rate

Page 1-60:

Replace note 193 with the following.

[193] Under prior law, the corporate income tax was imposed at the following rates:

Taxable Income	Rate
Less than $25,000	17%
$25,000–$50,000	20%
$50,000–$75,000	30%
$75,000–$100,000	40%
Over $100,000	46%

The new law decreases the tax rates on the two lowest brackets, i.e., those imposing tax on taxable income below $50,000. The change will be in effect in 1982 and 1983.

The brackets below $50,000 are adjusted as follows:

Taxable Income	Rate
In 1982—	
Less than $25,000	16%
$25,000–$50,000	19%
1983 and later years—	
Less than $25,000	15%
$25,000–$50,000	18%

Replace seventh and eighth lines of ¶ 1.05[5][a] with the following.

individuals are taxed at progressive rates up to a maximum of 50 percent on earned as well as unearned income.

¶ 1.06 SUBCHAPTER S CORPORATION

Page 1-67:

Add at end of section.

In addition to the requirement that no more than 20 percent of its gross receipts be passive investment income, a Subchapter S corporation must meet the following requirements:

(1) The Subchapter S corporation may not have more than twenty-five shareholders. A husband and wife are counted as one shareholder, regardless of the manner in which they hold their stock.

(2) Only individuals, estates, grantor trusts, or voting trusts can be shareholders. A testamentary trust can be a shareholder only for the 60-day period after shares are transferred to it as a result of the death of a decedent. Nonresident aliens may not be shareholders.

(3) The corporation may issue only one class of stock.

(4) The corporation must obtain at least 20 percent of its gross receipts from sources within the United States.

Taxable income of the Subchapter S corporation is assigned to shareholders in proportion to stock ownership on the last day of the corporate tax year. Therefore, a tax-saving device commonly utilized is a shift of stock ownership near the end of the tax year to taxpayers in lower tax brackets. Loss, unlike income, is allocated to shareholders on a daily basis so that length of ownership affects allocation of losses.

Chapter 2
TYPES OF LENDERS

		Page
¶ 2.01	The Structure of the Mortgage Market	S2- 1
	[1] Cost and Availability of Mortgage Credit	S2- 1
	[b] Countercyclical Mortgage Credit Supply	S2- 1
	[2] Summary of the Lending Cycle	S2- 2
	[3] Factors Contributing to a Restructuring of the Market	S2- 3
¶ 2.02	Mortgage Lenders	S2- 4
	[1] Life Insurance Companies	S2- 4
	[a] Source of Funds	S2- 4
	[2] Commercial Banks	S2-12
	[a] Source of Funds	S2-12
	[b] Loan Terms	S2-13
	[3] Savings and Loan Associations	S2-13
	[a] Source of Funds	S2-13
	[e] Federal Assistance to Savings and Loan Industry [New]	S2-13
	[6] Pension Funds and Other Lenders	S2-16
	[8] Foreign Investments in U.S. Real Estate [New]	S2-22
¶ 2.03	The Role of Mortgage Brokers and Mortgage Bankers	S2-29
	[1] The Mortgage Broker	S2-29
	[2] The Mortgage Banker	S2-32

¶ 2.01 THE STRUCTURE OF THE MORTGAGE MARKET

[1] Cost and Availability of Mortgage Credit

[b] Countercyclical Mortgage Credit Supply

Page 2-6:

Add new text and note 8a at end of subsection.

As of this writing, the economy is undergoing a period of decline and yet some noted economists like Felix G. Rohatyn, a partner at Lazard Frères & Company, are predicting tighter credit and higher interest rates which could push the economy "into a nosedive" because of large projected federal budget deficits. The Reagan Administration's current estimate for 1983 is a budget deficit of $91.5 billion. However, a minority of experts predict that the projected deficits over the next few years will not necessarily lead to higher interest rates and greater inflation, on the theory that the tax reductions and other incentives provided by the Economic Recovery Tax Act of 1981 (if not rescinded) will generate enough savings to absorb the projected federal government borrowings without undue pressure on inflation or on interest rates. These experts often cite the fact that the two countries with the lowest inflation rates, West Germany and Japan, have deficits that, in contrast to the United States, represent a larger part of their gross national product.[8a]

[8a] Arenson, "Executives See Hard Times With Huge Budget Deficits," N.Y. Times, Feb. 8, 1982, at B-12, Col. 1.

[2] **Summary of the Lending Cycle**

Page 2-8:

Add new text and notes 13a-13j at end of subsection.

Over the last few years, the financing of commercial real estate has been in a state of flux in response to fundamental changes in both the economy and investment practices of the various lending groups. To some extent these changes have caused a restructuring of the customary lending cycle faced by real estate borrowers. Recently, life insurance companies[13a] and thrift organizations[13b] have become less active as "permanent" lenders while pension funds[13c] and credit corporations[13d] have become more active in post-construction financing. Indeed, the term "permanent financing" has recently become somewhat of a misnomer because high levels of inflation and volatile interest rates have caused life insurance companies and other traditional long-term lenders to become increasingly disenchanted with long-term fixed-rate mortgages. This has prompted insurance companies and other post-construction lenders to sometimes demand floating or adjustable interest rates and shorter loan periods. Also, in addition to obtaining a share of the prof-

---

[13a] See ¶ 2.02[1].
[13b] See ¶ 2.02[3][a].
[13c] See ¶ 2.02[6].
[13d] See ¶ 2.02[6].

its in the form of an "equity kicker," [13e] insurance companies and other post-construction lenders are frequently demanding equity interests by entering into joint ventures with developer-borrowers[13f] or insisting on mortgage loans that are convertible into an equity interest.[13g] As an alternative to forfeiting substantial equity and with the declining availability of forward or takeout commitments, some developers have obtained open-end construction financing without a backup permanent takeout commitment[13h] or in conjunction with a fundable standby commitment.[13i] Upon completion of construction, the developer-borrower under such loan arrangements has a few years to secure all of his tenants, produce a positive cash flow, and bring the project "on stream" so that he can refinance the loan for a longer term and under better loan terms, if, as anticipated, interest rates drop and/or the loan amount increases because of an inflationary increase in the market value of the property.[13j] As of this writing, however, commercial banks and other construction lenders are becoming increasingly reluctant to provide such open-end construction financing.

[13e] See ¶ 3.04[3][a].
[13f] See discussion of joint ventures at ¶¶ 2.02[1], 3.04[18], and 11.02[1].
[13g] See ¶ 3.04[18].
[13h] See ¶ 4.01[3].
[13i] See ¶ 3.07[2].
[13j] See generally Henry, "New Twists in Financing Change Builders' World," N.Y. Times, Nov. 29, 1981, Sec. 8 at 1, Col. 1.

[3] Factors Contributing to a Restructuring of the Market

Page 2-12:

Add new text at end of subsection.

A recently emerging trend is the development of a secondary market for investment interests in income-producing realty. If it continues as many developers and securities firms anticipate, the general investing public will be able to invest in real estate without the liquidity problems associated with owning a typical investment share in a publicly held limited partnership. The momentum toward popularizing such an investment medium will depend to a large extent on whether some standarized yardstick for evaluating real estate interests can be developed. A possibility would be the use of standardized partnership provisions comparable to the new standardized Fannie Mae instruments.

¶ 2.02 MORTGAGE LENDERS

[1] Life Insurance Companies

Page 2-13:

Add new text and notes 24b-24d at end of subsection.

Life insurance companies recently have become less active and more selective with respect to straight (non-equity-related) post-construction financing of income-producing real estate. Total "forward" or takeout commitments to supply post-construction financing decreased from $26.7 billion by the end of 1979 to $16.5 billion as of the end of 1980.[24b] However, insurance companies have expanded their joint venturing activities, especially "all equity" arrangements where no mortgages are involved, and are also actively engaging in direct acquisitions of real estate, subject to investment restrictions on real estate ownership.[24c] Perhaps the most notable recent move in this direction was the acquisition by the Metropolitan Life Insurance Company in July 1981 of the Pan American Building in New York for an estimated $400 million, reported to be the highest price ever paid for a single building. In addition, life insurance companies have recently expanded their pension fund management business to the extent that in many life insurance companies, pension assets represent as much as 50 percent or more of their total assets. The expanding nature of this management of pension funds by insurance companies has now produced a number of funds available for both mortgage investments and equity participations.[24d]

[24b] Henry, "Insurer's Role as Investor Shifts and Grows," N.Y. Times, May 24, 1981, Sec. 8 at 8, Col. 2.

[24c] See N.Y. Ins. Law § 81(7)(h) (McKinney Supp. 1982). Most large insurance companies conform to the New York statute (which regulates domestic life insurance companies and demands substantial compliance of companies doing business in New York), and the New York statute has been followed as a prototype for most states elsewhere. Under the New York statute, no more than 12½ percent of a company's assets can be invested in real estate ownership. By contrast, the statute permits 50 percent of assets to be invested in mortgages. *Id.* § 81(6).

[24d] See discussion at ¶ 2.02[6].

[a] Source of Funds

Page 2-13:

Add new text and note 26a at end of subsection.

To some extent, high short-term interest rates and the resultant disintermediation have caused a decline in liquidity inasmuch as they have produced a sharp increase in life insurance policy loans. Recently, policyholders have been borrowing against the cash value of their policies at interest rates of 5 to 8 percent for reinvestment at higher rates elsewhere. These policy loans, which account for nearly 9 percent of industry assets, have risen 89.1 percent since 1976 and are viewed as lost business by the insurance companies since only a small percentage of these loans are repaid before maturity and the proceeds become payable to the beneficiary at the time of the death of the insured. Historically, during inflationary times policyholders increase their coverage amounts to fulfill their security goals; however, recently the bulk of sold life insurance has been term, which does not build up industry cash reserves the way whole life insurance does. In addition, the cash reserves of insurance companies have declined because of lower repayment rates on existing mortgages, which reflects a decrease in refinancing of existing mortgages caused by the current high level of interest rates.[26a]

[26a] Noble, "Insurer's Shift on Investments," N.Y. Times, Dec. 19, 1981, at 23, Col. 2.

Page 2-15:

Replace Exhibit 2.2 with the following:

EXHIBIT 2.2. Insurance Company Mortgage Loans in Property Type, Year 1981

(Commitments of $100,000 and Over on Multi-family and Nonresidential Mortgages Made by 20 Life Insurance Companies)

Property Type	No. of Loans	Amount Committed ($000)	Loan Amount ($000)	Averages							Percentage Distribution (by Loan Amount)
				Interest Rate (by #)	Interest Rate (by $)	Loan/Value	Capitalization Rate	Debt Coverage	Percent Constant	Term (Yrs./Mos.)	
Apartment (conventional)											
Elevator	5	$ 12,240	$ 2,448	16.00%	15.90%	62.9%	12.5%	1.23	16.7%	5/10	0.4%
Nonelevator	7	25,965	3,709	14.55	14.12	64.1	12.4	1.42	15.7	6/8	0.8
Retail—less than 5 stores	34	18,981	558	14.01	13.35	70.8	11.2	1.32	14.7	14/5	0.6
Shopping center—5 or more stores	42	269,177	6,409	14.22	13.58	69.8	13.0	1.28	14.5	13/6	8.3
Supermarket	1	5,800	5,800	*	*	*	*	*	*	*	0.2
Department store	2	9,600	4,800	*	*	*	*	*	*	*	0.3
Other sales and service	1	800	800	*	*	*	*	*	*	*	**
Office building	199	2,137,720	10,742	14.07	13.70	72.1	13.0	1.29	14.3	18/8	65.5
Medical office building	9	20,999	2,333	14.76	15.09	67.9	12.7	1.25	14.8	6/6	0.6
Parking garage	4	3,399	850	16.50	15.82	71.2	12.7	1.30	15.3	5/0	0.1
Commercial warehouse	2	585	292	*	*	*	*	*	*	*	**
Restaurant	46	126,315	2,746	13.98	13.77	68.8	12.3	1.27	14.2	10/10	3.9
Truck terminal	1	1,550	1,550	*	*	*	*	*	*	*	**
Other commercial	6	11,280	1,880	15.58	15.72	73.4	14.6	1.26	15.8	6/0	0.3

Property Type	No. of Loans	Amount Committed ($000)	Loan Amount ($000)	Interest Rate (by #)	Interest Rate (by $)	Averages					Percentage Distribution (by Loan Amount)
						Loan/Value	Capitalization Rate	Debt Coverage	Percent Constant	Term (Yrs./Mos.)	
Industrial warehouse	82	138,790	1,693	14.96	14.90	67.7	13.4	1.32	15.4	15/2	4.3
Manufacturing plant	2	4,375	2,188	*	*	*	*	*	*	*	0.1
Other industrial	19	47,994	2,526	13.92	13.80	76.7	14.5	1.32	14.2	27/11	1.5
Hotel	24	342,285	14,262	14.68	14.48	64.6	13.6	1.45	15.1	13/6	10.5
Motel	4	21,800	5,450	15.79	15.99	66.5	15.3	1.50	16.0	8/11	0.7
Multiple property complex	3	62,650	20,883	14.75	15.58	71.4	13.2	1.23	15.1	24/0	1.9
Total [1]	493	$3,262,305	$ 6,617	14.32%	13.90%	70.3%	13.0%	1.30	14.6%	15/10	100.0%

* Data not shown for a limited number of loans.
** 0.05 percent or less.

[1] Interest rate was not available for all loans (35 loans in the amount of $117 million).

NOTE: Averages for capitalization rate, debt coverage ratio, and percent constant may represent a fewer number of loans than the total for the specified category.

SOURCE: American Council on Life Insurance, Investment Bull. No. 836 (April 1, 1982).

Page 2-17:

Replace Exhibit 2.3 with the following:

EXHIBIT 2.3. Insurance Company Mortgage Loans by Size Within Major Property Type, Fourth Quarter 1981

(Commitments of $100,000 and Over on Multi-family and Nonresidential Mortgages Made by 20 Life Insurance Companies)

Major Property Type Loan Size	No. of Loans	Amount Committed ($000)	Loan Amount ($000)	Interest Rate (by #)	Interest Rate (by $)	Loan/ Value	Capital-ization Rate	Debt Cover-age	Percent Con-stant	Term (Yrs./ Mos.)
						Averages				
APARTMENT—CONVENTIONAL				*%	*%	*%	*%	*	*%	*
$1 million–$3,999(000)	2	$ 4,120	$ 2,060	*	*	*	*	*	*	*
	2	4,120	2,060							
COMMERCIAL RETAIL[1]										
Less than $1 million	10	23,238	2,324	15.26	14.93	66.6	13.7	1.36	15.5	11/7
$1 million–$3,999(000)	1	808	808	*	*	*	*	*	*	*
$4 million–$7,999(000)	7	12,840	1,834	15.44	15.38	64.5	13.5	1.38	15.6	7/3
	2	9,590	4,795	*	*	*	*	*	*	*
OFFICE BUILDING										
Less than $1 million	34	257,654	7,578	14.56	14.39	69.8	13.3	1.32	14.7	14/1
	4	2,890	722	15.00	14.91	71.6	14.3	1.31	15.2	11/8
$1 million–$3,999(000)	16	29,207	1,825	14.52	14.59	72.4	13.5	1.26	14.7	10/10
$4 million–$7,999(000)	5	28,907	5,781	14.95	15.02	74.5	13.4	1.20	15.1	11/0
$8 million and over	9	196,650	21,850	14.25	14.26	61.8	12.4	1.47	14.4	22/9
COMMERCIAL SERVICE										
Less than $1 million	9	22,884	2,543	14.35	14.52	70.3	13.5	1.29	15.0	7/8
	1	650	650	*	*	*	*	*	*	*
$1 million–$3,999(000)	6	13,860	2,310	14.77	14.78	69.8	13.5	1.26	15.5	6/8
$4 million–$7,999(000)	2	8,374	4,187	*	*	*	*	*	*	*

Averages

Major Property Type Loan Size	No. of Loans	Amount Committed ($000)	Loan Amount ($000)	Interest Rate (by #)	Interest Rate (by $)	Loan/ Value	Capitalization Rate	Debt Coverage	Percent Constant	Term (Yrs./ Mos.)
INDUSTRIAL[1]	27	61,978	2,295	15.48	15.28	66.3	13.6	1.31	15.7	16/1
Less than $1 million	10	5,775	578	15.61	15.62	59.6	12.1	1.35	15.8	19/10
$1 million–$3,999(000)	11	24,875	2,261	15.60	15.51	69.4	14.7	1.33	15.9	11/7
$4 million–$7,999(000)	6	31,328	5,221	15.05	15.00	71.8	13.3	1.22	15.3	18/4
HOTEL AND MOTEL	5	77,100	15,420	15.37	15.58	59.5	13.7	1.71	15.6	16/2
$8 million and over	5	77,100	15,420	15.37	15.58	59.5	13.7	1.71	15.6	16/2
Total	**87**	**$446,974**	**$ 5,138**	**14.98%**	**14.77%**	**67.4%**	**13.4%**	**1.34**	**15.2%**	**13/8**

* Data not shown for a limited number of loans.

[1] Interest rate was not available for all loans.

NOTE: Averages for capitalization rate, debt coverage ratio, and percent constant may represent a fewer number of loans than the total for the specified category. Nonrefundable fees were reported in connection with 11% of the number and 16% of the amount committed. The comparable shares by property type ran 10% and 3% for retail stores, 15% and 12% for office buildings, 11% and 3% for commercial service properties, and 60% and 51% for hotels and motels.

SOURCE: American Council on Life Insurance, Investment Bull. No. 836 (April 1, 1982).

Page 2-19:

Replace Exhibit 2.4 with the following:

EXHIBIT 2.4. Purpose of Insurance Company Mortgage Loans, Fourth Quarter 1981

(Commitments of $100,000 and Over on Multi-family and Nonresidential Mortgages Made by 20 Life Insurance Companies)

Major Property Type Purpose of Loan	No. of Loans	Amount Committed ($000)	Loan Amount ($000)	Averages						
				Interest Rate (by #) *%	Interest Rate (by $) *%	Loan/ Value *%	Capital- ization Rate *%	Debt Cover- age	Percent Con- stant *%	Term (Yrs./ Mos.)
APARTMENT—CONVENTIONAL Purchase of existing property, property improvement	2	$ 4,120	$ 2,060	*	*	*	*	*	*	*
COMMERCIAL RETAIL[1]	10	23,238	2,324	15.26	14.93	66.6	13.7	1.36	15.5	11/7
Repay construction loan and provide long-term financing	5	14,905	2,981	14.92	14.73	68.2	13.6	1.33	15.1	17/5
Purchase of existing property	5	8,333	1,667	15.69	15.51	64.9	13.9	1.41	15.9	5/10
OFFICE BUILDING **	34	257,654	7,578	14.56	14.39	69.8	13.3	1.32	14.7	14/1
Repay construction loan and provide long-term financing	22	197,992	9,000	14.30	14.54	69.0	12.8	1.32	14.5	15/10
Purchase of existing property	8	11,670	1,459	15.56	15.56	74.3	15.2	1.30	15.8	12/0
COMMERCIAL SERVICE	9	22,884	2,543	14.35	14.52	70.3	13.5	1.29	15.0	7/8
Repay construction loan and provide long-term financing	6	18,906	3,151	14.50	14.45	70.0	13.3	1.26	15.2	8/0
Purchase of existing property	3	3,978	1,326	14.04	14.82	70.9	13.8	1.37	14.4	7/0

Averages

Major Property Type Purpose of Loan	No. of Loans	Amount Committed ($000)	Loan Amount ($000)	Interest Rate (by #)	Interest Rate (by $)	Loan/ Value	Capital- ization Rate	Debt Cover- age	Percent Con- stant	Term (Yrs./ Mos.)
INDUSTRIAL[1]	27	61,978	2,295	15.48	15.28	66.3	13.6	1.31	15.7	16/1
Repay construction loan and provide long-term financing	7	24,415	3,488	14.57	14.38	75.2	14.4	1.29	14.8	26/5
Purchase of existing property	16	34,108	2,132	15.93	16.05	62.8	13.3	1.35	16.2	11/0
Purchase of new property	4	3,455	864	15.75	15.81	64.6	12.7	1.23	15.9	18/8
HOTEL AND MOTEL										
Repay construction loan and provide long-term financing	5	77,100	15,420	15.37	15.58	59.5	13.7	1.71	15.6	16/2
Total	**87**	**446,974**	**5,138**	**14.98**	**14.77**	**67.4**	**13.4**	**1.34**	**15.2**	**13/8**
Loans with Net Leases (included above)										
Commercial Retail	1	3,200	3,200	*	*	*	*	*	*	*
Office Building	1	1,335	1,335	*	*	*	*	*	*	*
Industrial	11	15,560	1,415	15.75	15.76	56.7	12.2	1.36	15.9	13/5
Total Net Leases	**13**	**$ 20,095**	**$ 1,546**	**15.66%**	**15.67%**	**56.8%**	**11.8%**	**1.34**	**15.8%**	**12/1**

* Data not shown for a limited number of loans.
** The subtotals represent all the loans within the major property categories; the components do not necessarily add to the subtotals because purpose categories with only a few loans are not shown separately.

[1] Interest rate was not available for all loans.

NOTE: Averages for capitalization rate, debt coverage ratio, and percent constant may represent a fewer number of loans than the total for the specified category.

SOURCE: American Council on Life Insurance, Investment Bull. No. 836 (April 1, 1982).

[2] Commercial Banks

[a] Source of Funds

Page 2-26:

Add new text and notes 43a-43c at end of subsection.

Recently, a growing source of investment activity for commercial banks has been their management of pension fund assets through commingled funds. Competing with insurance companies for these pooled investments, large financial-center banks have become successful at attracting these funds. Some smaller regional banks have had greater difficulty entering the field because they cannot immediately provide the same diversification offered by banks and insurance companies with more national expertise.

Bank-sponsored funds are organized in two ways as provided in regulations promulgated by the Comptroller of the Currency. Under 12 C.F.R. § 9.18(a)(1), banks are authorized to invest funds they hold as fiduciaries in a "common trust fund" for collective investment and reinvestment. Like the insurance company's separate accounts, the fund is tax-exempt, in this instance under I.R.C. § 584, being treated in somewhat the same manner as a partnership, with income passed through to participants who may be either tax-exempt pension funds or any fund for which the bank serves as trustee, executor, guardian, or administrator.

The regulations place certain restrictions upon the advertising of funds organized under Section 9.18(a)(1).[43a] Moreover, the bank sponsor is required to maintain a proportion of the fund's portfolio in cash or readily marketable securities; specifically, withdrawals or admissions to the fund are prohibited if less than 40 percent of its assets after such transactions would be composed of such investments.[43b]

Section 9.18(a)(2) allows funds to be organized as a "group trust" under Revenue Ruling 56-267.[43c] That ruling held that tax-exempt employee pension plans that qualify under I.R.C. § 401(a) may pool their funds in group trusts without threatening their tax-exempt status. Funds qualifying under I.R.C. § 401(a) will often also qualify under I.R.C. § 584. Both Section 9.18(a)(1) and Section 9.18(a)(2) funds must file written plans with the Comptroller; "group trusts" are not subject to the restrictions on advertising or to the 40 percent cash or cash equivalent rule of Code Section 584 funds. But participation in the group

---

[43a] 12 C.F.R. §§ 9.18(b)(5)(iii) and 9.18(b)(5)(v) (1980).
[43b] 12 C.F.R. § 9.18(b)(9)(iii) (1980).
[43c] 1956-1 C.B. 206.

trust is strictly limited to qualified pension plans, thus excluding other tax-exempt funds such as college, church, or charitable endowments.

[b] Loan Terms

Page 2-27:

Add new text and notes 47a and 47b at end of subsection.

With the implementation of the Depository Institutions Deregulation and Monetary Control Act of 1980,[47a] the Office of the Comptroller of the Currency has promulgated its final regulations authorizing adjustable rate mortgages (e.g., variable rate and renegotiable rate mortgages) for national banks.[47b]

[47a] Pub. L. No. 96-221, 94 Stat. 132 (1980).
[47b] 12 C.F.R. Part 29 (Docket No. 81-10, effective March 31, 1981).

[3] Savings and Loan Associations

[a] Source of Funds

Page 2-31:

Add at end of note 58.

[58] ; "S&L's Net Worth Fell in December by $396 Million," Wall St. J., Jan. 29, 1982, at 10. The Federal Home Loan Bank Board reported that the net worth of the nation's federally insured savings and loans declined by $4.9 billion in 1981 compared with a $667 million increase in 1980. Withdrawals exceeded deposits by $25.49 billion in 1981, while in 1980 thrift institutions showed a net gain in deposits of $10.67 billion. The gain in deposits of $13.35 billion in 1981 represents the smallest expansion since 1970. Six-month money market certificates and "All-Savers" certificates showed big drops in popularity by the end of 1981. In addition, the total sum of committed mortgages fell by 28 percent in 1981.

Page 2-39:

Add new ¶ 2.02[3][e] following first full paragraph.

[e] Federal Assistance to Savings and Loan Industry [New]

As a result of Title II of the Depository Institutions Act, savings and loan associations have been forced to reduce their reliance upon deposits as a source of funds. The six-year phase-out of Regulation Q interest rate ceilings on deposit accounts and the creation of new accounts indexed to prevailing market rates of interest will erode any cost difference for S&Ls between savings deposits and other liabilities. In addition, competition among lenders for deposits has increased. To offset the loss, S&Ls are selling loans in the secondary mortgage market, deriving profits from origination and servicing fees, thereby increasing competition in the secondary market. Another way to raise needed capital is by outside borrowing. The Federal Home Loan Bank Board (FHLBB) has increased limits on outside borrowing by S&Ls from 15 percent of deposits to 50 percent of assets.[77f]

Title II of the Depository Institutions Act provides still another way to offset losses by giving S&Ls six years to offer the new consumer services described above. The problem S&Ls face is to obtain the capital needed to support these new consumer services. The six-month money market certificates, which are already decontrolled, and the large portion of deposits currently indexed to market rates intensify this problem. Furthermore, net income of S&Ls dropped sharply in 1981,[77g] due, in part, to the fact that the average portfolio yield of mortgages in S&Ls is approximately 9 percent.[77h]

The Depository Institutions Act has resulted in a large number of mergers between financially strong S&Ls seeking to increase their capital base, and between strong S&Ls and weak ones that could not survive alone. To date about 200 S&Ls have merged, and an additional 400 to 500 are expected to merge or fail by the end of 1982.[77i]

If interest rates remain as high as they are at present, it seems clear to some authorities that the FHLBB and federal government will need to provide financial aid to S&Ls in order to keep them afloat. Congressman Fernand J. St. Germain (D-R.I.), chairman of the House Banking Committee, has introduced a bill (H.R. 5568) to provide $7.5 billion in federal aid to troubled S&Ls and other lending institutions.[77j] S&Ls accepting government aid would have to use at least 50 percent of their

---

[77f] Naef & Leaman, "Deregulation and the Mortgage Lender—A Mixed Blessing," Mortgage Banker, June 1981 at 36, 41.

[77g] For income figures, see ¶ 2.02[2] note 38. In January 1982, the net worth of S&Ls dropped by another $864 million. "Net Worth of S&Ls Dropped in January Record $864 Million," Wall St. J., Feb. 26, 1982 at 8.

[77h] Naef & Leaman, note 77f *supra* at 43.

[77i] Noble, "New Bill Could Aid Savings Institutions," N.Y. Times, Feb. 23, 1982 at D6. A Brookings Institution study forecasts that more than 1,000 S&Ls would be forced to merge or fail by the end of 1983. Treasury Secretary Donald T. Regan disagrees with the study and its basic assumption that interest rates would stay above 15.5 percent through 1983.

For a discussion of the income tax consequences of a merger between S&Ls see Rocky Mt. Fed. Sav. & Loan Ass'n v. United States, 473 F. Supp. 779 (D. Wyo. 1979).

[77j] *Id.*

deposits for home mortgages and repay the government when their net worth rose.[77k] One possible result of massive funding of S&Ls might be the acceleration of inflation caused by the funding's impact on capital markets and the already huge federal budget deficit.[77l]

On February 25, 1982, the FHLBB proposed to expand the lending powers of the nation's 3,987 S&Ls so that they could compete more directly with commercial banks.[77m] There will be a sixty-day comment period, after which the FHLBB will decide what new powers S&Ls will be given. Objections have already been raised by the Senate Banking Committee, which has been considering the expansion of the S&Ls' powers, and by commercial banks. The chief objection is that Congress and not the FHLBB should be regulating the functions of S&Ls. Congressional legislation concerning the powers of S&Ls has been stalled, in part because of the criticisms by commercial banks. The FHLBB, therefore, feels this proposal is now necessary, and that it "dovetails" with legislative proposals. The proposal would allow S&Ls to set up subsidiaries, called services, to offer a broad range of new services, including mutual and money-market funds, commercial lending, leasing activities, and other business activities.

Another proposal, calling for $10 billion in assistance from the federal government, has been made jointly by the National Association of Mutual Savings Banks and the United States League of Associations. The three elements of the proposal are as follows:

(1) A $7.5 billion swap program in which lenders with at least 20 percent of their assets locked into fixed-rate residential

---

[77k] *Id.*

[77l] Naef & Leaman, note 77f *supra* at 43. This is why the present administration is against his proposal. The administration feels there is no crisis in the savings and loan industry because cash flow remains strong. To deal with balance sheet losses, the administration has proposed to require federal insurance agencies to provide additional capital to failing S&Ls through an exchange of promissory notes. The insurance agency would give a troubled S&L an I.O.U. that the S&L could call on if it ran out of funds. To balance its books, the insurance agency would take an I.O.U. of the same size from the troubled S&L. If the S&L remained solvent, the government would lose nothing. If the S&L failed, the government would then lose whatever cash it put out. Officials of the S&L industry feel that this remedy is inappropriate and inadequate, as a loss of business by S&Ls, not a weak cash flow, is the problem that the government must deal with. Bennett, "Ways to Save the Thrift Industry," N.Y. Times, March 1, 1982 at D1, D7.

[77m] Noble, "Amid Debate, U.S. Panel Asks Wider Powers for Thrift Units," N.Y. Times, Feb. 26, 1982 at D3; "Bank Board Moves to Allow S&Ls to Offer Commercial Loans, Money Market Funds," Wall St. J., Feb. 26, 1982 at 8.

mortgages paying less than 9 percent could exchange these mortgages for variable-rate, three-year debentures tied to the current rates on thirty-month Treasury securities. For example, if the mortgage rate is 8 percent and the thirty-month Treasury rate is 14 percent, the supplement would be 3 percent, being half the difference between 8 and 14, and the total cost to the S&L would be 11 percent.

(2) A $2.5 billion subsidy for mortgage buydowns, which would give consumers low-cost financing for three years. Under the plan, the S&Ls would offer home loans at a percentage point below market rates, and the subsidy would further reduce the rate by three percentage points. At the end of the three years, the interest rate would rise to the current market rate.

(3) A capital maintenance program, which would bolster the net worth of failing S&Ls.

It appears that the present Administration will object as strongly to this proposal as to other bail-out proposals. The proposal has not yet gained the approval of the congressional committees considering bank deregulation.[77n]

[77n] Noble, "Thrift Units Seeking U.S. Aid," N.Y. Times, March 4, 1982 at D12.

[6] Pension Funds and Other Lenders
Page 2-44:

Replace note 94 with the following.

[94] An otherwise tax-exempt organization under I.R.C. § 501 such as a pension fund is taxed on its unrelated business income. I.R.C. §§ 511(a)(1), 511(a)(2)(A), and 511(b). The general rule is that, like dividends and interest, rental income from real estate is investment income and is therefore excludable from unrelated business income. Accordingly, a pension fund is taxable on dealer income from the sale of realty but not taxed on true rental income or on gain from the sale of property that has been held for the production of income. However, rental income that includes charges for the active rendition of services to occupants (e.g., hotel or parking lot) does not qualify for the exclusion and may even taint the remainder of the related rental income. Tech. Advice Memo. 7921005 (1979); Reg. § 1.856-4(b)(1); Reg. 1.512(b)-1(C)(5); Rev. Rul. 72-331, 1972-2 C.B. 513. In addition, the rental exclusion is not available where the rental is geared in whole or in part to the lessee's gross or net income (or profits) as opposed to rental based on receipts or sales. I.R.C. § 512(b)(3)(B)(ii); Reg. § 1.512(b)-1(C)(2)(iii)(*b*). To minimize the risk of losing the exclusion in the case of realty with leases having typical percentage rental clauses, different percentages can be charged to the various tenants and fixed rentals can be combined with the percentage rentals.

Notwithstanding the rental exclusion, under prior law rental income was taxable if the property was acquired or improved with borrowed funds. This prior rule which taxed "debt-financed" income discouraged pension funds from investing in real estate because it precluded them from leveraging their acquisition and development costs. Commencing in 1981, the rule has been relaxed so that "acquisition indebtedness" will not include indebtedness incurred by a qualified pension trust in acquiring or improving any real property. But this relief provision will not apply if (1) the acquisition price is not a fixed amount determinable on the acquisition date, (2) the amount or timing of interest payments is geared to income produced by the property, (3) the trust leases the property back to the seller, (4) the trust acquires property from a person related to the plan under which the trust is organized, or (5) the seller provides nonrecourse financing either with debt subordination or with artificially low interest rates. I.R.C. § 514(c)(9), as added by the Miscellaneous Revenue Act of 1980, Pub. L. 96-605, § 110(a), 94 Stat. 3525. See I.R.C. § 512(b)(4).

Interest income from mortgage loan investments is likewise excluded from taxable unrelated business income if the interest is not tied to the income of some business entity. Points charged for making a loan are excludable interest, whereas loan origination fees paid to a pension fund in exchange for services are treated as taxable unrelated business income. The unrelated business income rule applies whether the pension fund is a general or limited partner. Rev. Rul. 79-222, 1979-2 C.B. 236. If the risk of income recognition is substantial, as for example where the debt-financed property is financed with low-interest nonrecourse financing or where percentage rents or contingent interest is geared to net or gross income, the pension fund might wish to avail itself of depreciation or other deductions available to a partnership in which it is a partner. See Abramson, "Tax Tools for Structuring Real Estate Investments in the Inflationary 80s," in *Financing Real Estate During the Inflationary 80s* 298-299 (ABA 1981).

Add at end of third sentence.

Also, pension and profit sharing plans do not pay taxes on the bulk of their income.

Add at end of note 95.

[95] Indeed, pension and profit sharing plans are quickly becoming a repository of enormous amounts of available investment funds. As of September 1981, 4 percent of the $393 billion in funds held by the 200 largest employee-benefit funds were invested in real estate. The largest real estate holdings were American Telephone & Telegraph with $1.2 billion, Exxon with $360 million, the Ohio Teachers Fund with $252 million, and General Electric with $242 million. For a list of the ninety-seven largest pension funds and the amount of their real estate investment, see Table 4 in Appendix A, this Supplement.

See also Davis, "Special Report: The Real Estate Financing Industry Today," Mortgage & Real Estate Executives Report, Feb. 1, 1982 at 4-5, which states that in 1981 all U.S. pension funds held an estimated 2 percent of their approximately $750 billion of total assets in real estate. Assets are expected to climb to $1 trillion by 1985.

Add new text at end of subsection.

Most pension funds are not able to assume major leasing risks. They therefore buy 100 percent leased facilities. Those pension funds that are willing to assume a share of the leasing risks are doing so for a greater share of the cash flow once the leasing of a project is completed.

Pension funds are currently involved in two vehicles of investment: joint ventures and convertible debt instruments. In joint ventures, the fund provides the majority of new funds needed to complete a project in exchange for an equity interest of 50 to 80 percent. The convertible debt instruments are usually convertible first or second mortgages under which the pension fund loans cash at an interest rate of 10 to 13 percent. The loan becomes convertible after a given period of time into a 50 to 80 percent ownership interest.

Bank trust departments have been involved in the real estate business for many years and are now taking a much more visible role. They control a substantial amount of capital and their activities include the funneling of foreign investments, direct investment, and the advising of both foreign and domestic pension funds. They will have a large role in the future real estate activity of pension funds.

Credit corporations, which are often the real estate subsidiaries of large industrial companies, are becoming more active in real estate financing. Despite high interest rates considered prohibitive by some developer-borrowers, these lenders have become a major source of long- and intermediate-term debt and possibly could replace life insurance companies as the principal source of post-construction financing. Unlike life insurance companies and other institutional lenders, their investment portfolios are not regulated by federal or local law, and the types of financing provided by credit corporations include the following:

(1) Standbys or letters of credit to be funded by third-party sources

(2) Construction lending without permanent takeouts

(3) Wraparound mortgages

(4) Land development and acquisition loans

(5) Large second-mortgage loans on real estate where the market value and cash flow have been substantially increased. This last service allows developers to draw down equity funds that are currently unrealized on appreciated property.

(6) Interim or "bullet" loans

(7) Sale-leaseback financing

(8) Joint venture financing, acting as both co-venturer and post-construction lender

The investment powers of the fiduciary under ERISA are subject to a "prudent man" rule[96a] and express prohibitions of certain classes of transactions.[96b]

The Department of Labor regulation on investment pension plan assets, promulgated under Section 404(a)(2)(B) of ERISA, took effect on July 23, 1979.[96c] The regulation's preamble states that even an investment that, standing alone, would have a relatively high degree of risk should not be deemed imprudent if it is reasonably designed as part of an overall plan to further the purposes of the employee benefit plan.[96d] On the other hand, an individual investment will not necessarily be deemed prudent simply because the plan's portfolio contains a favorable mix of risk and return. Instead, the test of prudent investment is whether the fiduciary has given "appropriate consideration" to those facts and circumstances relevant to the individual investment and the role it plays in the overall plan portfolio.[96e] "Appropriate consideration" is defined in the regulations to include the following:

(1) Fiduciary's determination that the individual investment, its risks of loss, and potential for gain are reasonably designed to further the purposes of the plan, and

(2) Consideration of the following factors:
 (a) the portfolio's degree of diversification,[96f]
 (b) the portfolio's liquidity and current return relative to the anticipated cash flow requirements of the plan, and
 (c) the portfolio's projected return.[96g]

The preamble states that the manager of a portfolio plan based upon an index shall be deemed a prudent investor if

---

[96a] ERISA § 404(a)(1)(B).
[96b] ERISA § 406.
[96c] 29 C.F.R. Part 2550 (1979).
[96d] 44 Fed. Reg. 37,222-37,224 (1979).
[96e] 29 C.F.R. § 2550.404a-1(b)(1) (1979).
[96f] Although ERISA requires the fiduciary to diversify the plan portfolio so as to spread and minimize risk, the degree of diversification required is not made clear. ERISA § 404(a)(1)(C). For a discussion of the diversification requirement see Strum, "The Roles of Life Insurance Companies and Pension Funds in Financing Real Estate in the 80s," in *Financing Real Estate During the Inflationary 80s*—(ABA 1981).
[96g] 29 C.F.R. § 2550.404a-1(b)(2) (1979).

(1) The index fund contains a "screen" or "filter" process by which investments in companies listed in the index are prevented or terminated by findings of adverse financial developments within those companies, and

(2) The index fund is reasonably designed to fulfill the fund manager's fiduciary obligations.[96h]

The Department of Labor states further in the preamble that the requirements of the "prudence" rule must be met by the plan's investment in the index fund as well as by the investments made by the index fund.[96i]

The preamble addresses the issue of the prudence of investments in small or newly formed companies and non-income-producing investments with high capital returns. It states that prudent investments do not always have to produce current income under all circumstances. However, the Department declined to include a list of permissible "prudent" investments for the reason that such a list could not possibly be complete.[96j]

Section 406 of ERISA and Section 4975 of the Internal Revenue Code prohibit certain classes of transactions between the employee benefit plan and disqualified parties termed "parties in interest." A "party in interest" is a disqualified party no matter how fair a particular transaction might be.[96k] The term "party in interest" covers the following:

(1) All fiduciaries including, but not limited to, any administrator, trustee, officer, custodian, counsel, or employee to or of the plan

(2) All persons providing services to the plan

(3) Employers, and 50 percent owners thereof, with employers on the plan

(4) All "relatives," including spouses, ancestors, lineal descendants, or spouses of lineal descendants, of any party described in (1), (2), and (3); any organization 50 percent or more controlled by any party described in (1), (2), and (3); and any highly compensated employee, director, officer, and 10 percent shareholders of any party described in (2) and (3).[96l]

[96h] 44 Fed. Reg. 37,224 (1979).
[96i] *Id.*
[96j] 44 Fed. Reg. 37,225 (1979).
[96k] ERISA §§ 406(a)(1)(E), 406(a)(2), and 407.
[96l] ERISA § 3(14); I.R.C. § 4975(e)(2).

The transactions from which a "party in interest" is prohibited include a direct or indirect

(1) Sale, exchange, or lease of property to a party in interest for less than adequate consideration, or from a party in interest for more than adequate consideration

(2) Extension of credit to a party in interest without the receipt of adequate security and a rate of interest consistent with fiduciary duties under Section 404 of ERISA, or from a party in interest with the provision of excessive security or a rate of interest too high to be consistent with fiduciary duties under Section 404

(3) Furnishing of goods, services, or facilities to a party in interest for less than adequate consideration or by a party in interest for more than adequate consideration

(4) Transfer or use of plan assets for the benefit of a party in interest for less than adequate consideration

(5) Acquisition or retention by the plan of excess employer securities[96m]

Also prohibited is fiduciary self-dealing with plan assets,[96n] and transactions on behalf of persons whose interests are adverse to the plan, its participants, or its beneficiaries.[96o]

A fiduciary causing the plan to participate in a prohibited transaction is personally liable for any loss incurred by reason of the resulting disqualification of the plan (i.e., damages to employees from lost or delayed benefit payments).[96p] However, a fiduciary is liable only if he knew or should have known that the transaction engaged in by the plan was prohibited.[96q] The tax penalty imposed on culpable "parties in interest" is not subject to a knowledge requirement.[96r] An initial excise tax of 5 percent of the "amount involved" in a prohibited transaction for each taxable year is imposed on a "party in interest" or other disqualified party.[96s] An additional tax of 100 percent of the "amount involved" is imposed if the violation is not corrected within ninety days of receipt of an appropriate notice from the IRS.[96t] The tax provisions

---

[96m] 29 U.S.C. §§ 1106(a)(1)(A)-1106(a)(1)(E) (1974).
[96n] ERISA §§ 406(b)(1) and 409(b)(3); I.R.C. §§ 4975(c)(1)(E)-4975(c)(1)(F).
[96o] ERISA § 406(b)(2).
[96p] ERISA § 409.
[96q] ERISA § 406(a)(1).
[96r] I.R.C. § 4975(a).
[96s] Id.
[96t] I.R.C. § 4975(b).

do not apply to a fiduciary unless he has acted as other than a fiduciary in the prohibited transaction.[96u] In other words, a prudent fiduciary who engages in a prohibited transaction only in his fiduciary capacity will not be liable either under ERISA or the tax provisions.[96v]

The transactions prohibited by ERISA are numerous, but so are the exemptions. The most important of these exemptions, themselves subject to numerous qualifications and restrictions, are:

(1) Interest-bearing, adequately secured loans by the plan to participants or beneficiaries, if generally available to all participants and beneficiaries

(2) Contracts for office space or legal and other services necessary to the establishment and operation of the plan, if the compensation does not exceed a reasonable amount

(3) Contracts with qualified insurers for life and health insurance and annuities at no more than adequate consideration

(4) Receipt of properly computed benefits as a participant or beneficiary of the plan—nothing could better illustrate the breadth of the concept of "disqualified person" than the need to exempt employees receiving pensions and other benefits under the plan

(5) Receipt of reasonable compensation for services rendered and reimbursement of proper expenses in the performance of duties for the plan[96w]

A presumption of guilt attaches to any transaction involving an employee benefit plan that is not a contribution to provide employee benefits. The definitions of "party in interest" and "prohibited transaction," as well as the exemptions, must be fully understood before it is safe to decide that the presumption of guilt can be rebutted.

[96u] I.R.C. §§ 4975(a) and 4975(b).
[96v] Kroll & Tauber, "Fiduciary Responsibility and Prohibited Transactions Under ERISA," 14 Real Prop., Prob. & Tr. J. 657, 672 (1979).
[96w] 29 U.S.C. § 1108 (1974).

Page 2-46:

Add new ¶ 2.02[8].

[8] Foreign Investments in U.S. Real Estate [New]

Foreign investment in real estate has become a growing source of real estate equity capital (and to a lesser extent, debt financing) in the

United States.[99a] Although New York City has acquired a reputation as a haven for foreign real estate investment, other large metropolitan areas such as Washington, D.C., Houston, Dallas, and Denver have also become magnets for foreign investment.[99b] These new sources of capital include banks, pension funds, investment groups, and private individuals. While a few work directly in the domestic marketplace (e.g., Phillips Pension Fund, P.G.G.M., Olympia York), most foreign investors choose instead to deal with money-center bank trust departments, their own representatives, domestic representatives under foreign names, or companies that specialize in respresenting foreign investors in the acquisition of real estate (e.g., Savage/Fogarty Companies in Washington, D.C.). The climate of non-socialistic political stability in the United States coupled with devaluation of the dollar in relationship to foreign currencies and limited taxation of foreigner's investment income by the United States has attracted foreign investors to investment in U.S. real estate even at what appears to be a nominal or low cash-on-cash rate of return. Another attraction is that comparatively few restrictions on development exist in the United States.[99c] Moreover, the commercial real estate market in Europe is severely depressed and at present cannot absorb the available investment capital.

In the recent past, foreign investors have favored the acquisition of leveraged, leased real estate because of the lack of long-term mortgage financing in their own countries. While foreign investors have shown a preference for sole ownership, their participation in joint ventures has increased because of competition with domestic investors for real estate equities.[99d] They have also displayed a flair for the innovative, as exemplified by the acquisition in November 1980 of voting control in Mortgage Investors of Washington (a Washington, D.C., based real estate investment trust) by a consortium of European institutional investors.[99e]

Planning considerations with respect to foreign investment in U.S.

[99a] The National Association of Realtors estimates that direct foreign investment in real estate amounts to $53 billion. The Homer Hoyt Institute in Washington estimated all foreign investment in real estate at an amount between $125 billion and $188 billion. See Henry, "Foreign Investors Take a Look Beyond New York," N.Y. Times, Feb. 3, 1982 at A25.

[99b] In fact, some foreign investors are avoiding New York City because of a fear that the city will eventually be overbuilt, causing rents to come down. See *id.*

[99c] *Id.*

[99d] For a discussion of planning considerations unique to joint ventures with foreign investors, see Richards, Real Estate Counsel, Contract and Closing for the Foreign Investor," 14 Real Prop., Prob. & Tr. J. 757 (1979).

[99e] Wall St. J., Nov. 21, 1980 at A6.

realty are based on the impact of certain nontax federal and state regulations as well as the impact of the Foreign Investment in Real Property Tax Act (FIRPA).[99f]

Federal law requires the disclosure of foreign ownership interests in agricultural realty.[99g] State laws also contain disclosure requirements as well as substantive restrictions on investment in privately owned real estate.[99h] FIRPA significantly changes the rules for taxing foreign investments in U.S. real estate and applies to all investments made after June 18, 1980.[99i] The principal purpose of the statute is to achieve parity between foreign investors and U.S. investors with respect to capital gain treatment on the sale of real estate.

Two important changes effected by the passage of FIRPA are the elimination of the "trade or business" distinction and the "information return" requirement.

A nonresident individual or corporation carrying on a trade or business in the United States has always been taxed on trade or business income, as has a U.S. resident. However, prior to FIRPA, the foreignor who disposed of a U.S. real property interest unconnected with a trade or business was not taxed. The effect of FIRPA is to eliminate this distinction. As a result, any capital gain or loss realized by a foreign investor is now subject to the same tax rules and rates that apply to a U.S. investor. One difference in tax treatment exists in those situations in which a U.S. taxpayer might have had to pay the alternative minimum tax (AMT). Instead of paying the AMT, nonresident aliens are subject to tax at a minimum rate of 20 percent (if that tax would produce a tax higher than the one under the regular method). Gross rental income from a U.S. real estate investment that is not effectively connected with the conduct of a U.S. trade or business will continue to be taxed at a

---

[99f] Foreign Investment in Real Property Tax Act of 1980, Pub. L. 96-499, 94 Stat. 2682, 26 U.S.C.A. §§ 861, 871, 882, 897, 6039C, 6652 (West Supp. 1982).

[99g] The two main laws requiring disclosure of ownership are the International Investment Survey Act of 1976, Pub. L. 94-472, 90 Stat. 2059, 22 U.S.C. §§ 3101-3108, and the Agricultural Foreign Investment Disclosure Act of 1978, Pub. L. 95-460, 92 Stat. 1263.

[99h] A summary of state laws affecting foreign investment of real estate appears in ALI-ABA Course of Study Material 3555, *Foreign Investment in U.S. Real Estate* 505 (Jan. 1981).

[99i] If a conflict exists between FIRPA and a treaty with a foreign nation concerning tax treatment of its citizens, the treaty will control as to any gain recognized by a foreign investor before January 1, 1985. After that time, FIRPA will apply. What FIRPA does not do is impose restrictions on the extent of ownership of U.S. realty by foreigners, nor does it impose any withholding requirement on the sales proceeds received by a foreign seller.

flat 30 percent rate (or lower treaty rate, if applicable).[99j] As under prior law, the nonresident alien may elect to subject his net income to tax rates applicable to U.S. citizens rather than the 30 percent or treaty rate.[99k]

FIRPA requires an annual information return by partnerships and corporations having foreign investors. The return must include certain information with respect to any foreign investor who holds a pro rata share exceeding $50,000 in any "United States real property interest."[99l] Partnerships can exempt themselves from this disclosure requirement by giving the IRS a tax security insuring payment of any future taxes imposed on foreign investors.[99m]

FIRPA applies to any disposition of a "United States real property interest" (USRPI) by a foreign investor or by any domestic investor that is a "United States real property holding corporation" (RPHC). The statute, of course, provides definitions of both USRPI and RPHC.

The statutory definition of USRPI is very broad and includes:

(1) Direct ownership of U.S. real estate, including fee and leasehold interests, options to acquire real estate, and furnishings and other personal property associated with the use of real property. While fixed-interest-rate mortgages are not included in the definition, it is not clear whether participating mortgages are included. This may be clarified when the Treasury issues its regulations.[99n]

(2) Indirect ownership of U.S. real estate through interests held by a partnership, trust, or estate. Accordingly, amounts received from the sale or exchange of an interest in a partnership, trust, or estate that is attributable to a USRPI held by the entity will be deemed to be received from the sale of the USRPI.[99o]

A similar "look-through" approach is applied to distribution from a real estate investment trust (REIT). Distributions to a foreigner that are allocable to sales or exchanges of a USRPI by the REIT are subject to taxation.[99p]

[99j] I.R.C. § 871(a)(1)(A).

[99k] Reg. § 1.871-10.

[99l] The FIRPA definition of "United States real property interest" (USRPI) is discussed below in this section.

[99m] The information return rules can be found in I.R.C. § 6039C entitled "Returns With Respect to United States Real Property Interests."

[99n] I.R.C. §§ 897(c)(1)(A)(i), 897(c)(6)(A).

[99o] I.R.C. § 897(c)(1)(A)(ii).

[99p] I.R.C. §§ 897(a), 897(h).

FIRPA does not directly address the question of installment sales. Under rules that should continue to apply after the Act, gain from the sale of a U.S. real estate property reported under the installment method in taxable years after the year of sale is not taxable in the United States if the foreign investor is not engaged in a U.S. trade or business in those taxable years.[99q] This rule applies even if the property sold is used in a trade or business and the gain is effectively connected with that business. Foreign investors used to exploit this rule by selling a USRPI under the installment method and reporting most of the gain in years when the investor was not engaged in a U.S. trade or business.

Under the new law, this method of tax avoidance apparently will not succeed in the case of a USRPI. When gain is reported under the installment method, it presumably retains its character as gain from the disposition of a USRPI. I.R.C. § 897(a) provides that such gain is deemed to be effectively connected with a U.S. trade or business *engaged in during the taxable year that the gain is reported.* Under the rules that apply to installment sales, the gain will be taxable in the year reported because the taxpayer will be deemed to be engaged in a U.S. trade or business in that year.[99r]

Under pre-Act law, gain (or loss) from the sale or exchange of stock in a domestic corporation was generally not taxable to a foreign investor. When a foreign investor held stock in a domestic corporation that owned appreciated U.S. real property, the foreign investor could have realized the appreciation without incurring liability for U.S. tax in either of two ways: (1) The investor could cause the corporation to sell the property tax-free under I.R.C. § 337 [99s] and then could liquidate the corporation; capital gain realized by the stockholder from the liquidation would be tax-free. (2) The investor could sell the stock of the corporation and the capital gain would not be taxable.[99t]

The new law precludes a tax-free realization of the value of corporate-owned U.S. real property by devising the concept of a "real property holding corporation" (RPHC). A domestic corporation is an RPHC if the market value of its USRPIs amounts to 50 percent or

---

[99q] See Reg. § 1.864-3(b), Ex. (1); cf. Reg. § 1.871-7(d)(2)(iv), Ex. (1).

[99r] I.R.C. § 897(a).

[99s] I.R.C. § 337 provides that if a corporation sells property pursuant to a plan to completely liquidate within twelve months, generally no gain or loss is recognized on sales during the liquidation period.

[99t] Under pre-Act law, capital gain would not be taxable as a general rule unless the gain was effectively connected with a trade or business conducted in the United States or, in the case of an individual, unless the individual was present in the United States for more than 183 days during the taxable year. See I.R.C. §§ 871(a)(2), 871(b), 882.

more of the total market value of all its assets.[99u] Several rules apply in determining whether the "50 percent or more" test is met. All non-real estate or other liquid non-trade or business assets are excluded from the calculation; [99v] consequently, they cannot be used to circumvent RHPC status. If the corporation is a 50 percent or greater shareholder of one or more corporations owning U.S. real estate, the first corporation is deemed to own a pro rata share of such real estate.[99x] In addition, the IRS can look back five years prior to the time when the real property is disposed of to determine if a domestic corporation has an RPHC-tainted history. A corporation will have such history if it was an RPHC at any time during the five-year period terminating on the date of disposition (the "taint period").[99y]

Stock of a domestic corporation, *but not a foreign corporation,* that is an RPHC is a USRPI.[99z] Gain or loss from the sale of the stock of the corporation, or from its liquidation, will be gain or loss from the disposition of a USRPI. Consequently, although real property owned by the corporation can be sold tax-free under IRC § 337, a liquidation distribution of the sales proceeds will be taxable, as would a sale of the stock, so that at least a single U.S. income tax will be imposed on any gain. Under the new rules, a sale of an interest in a domestic corporation may be taxed even though at the time of the disposition the corporation is no longer an RPHC if the disposition occurred during the taint period. The new law provides three subsidiary rules relating to the assets of a corporation for the purpose of determining whether a corporation is an RPHC. First, the stock of a foreign corporation that is an RPHC is deemed to be a USRPI.[99aa] Thus, for example, if the only asset of a U.S. corporation is the stock of a foreign corporation that is an RPHC, the U.S. corporation will be an RPHC and its stock will be a USRPI.

Second, if a corporation holds a partnership interest, or is the beneficiary of an estate or trust, it shall be deemed to hold directly its proportionate share of USRPIs owned by the partnership, trust or estate.[99bb] The Act says nothing about the other assets owned by the partnership, estate, or trust. As a policy matter, the partners or beneficiaries should be deemed to own a proportionate share of all partnership, trust, or estate assets, not just its USRPIs. Ignoring other assets

---

[99u] I.R.C. § 897(c)(2).
[99v] I.R.C. § 897(c)(2)(B).
[99x] I.R.C. § 897(c)(5).
[99y] I.R.C. § 897(c)(1)(A)(ii).
[99z] *Id.*
[99aa] I.R.C. § 897(c)(4)(A).
[99bb] I.R.C. § 897(c)(4)(B).

unfairly weights the calculation against the taxpayer because the partnership interest owned by the corporation does not enter into the computation for determining whether the corporation is an RPHC.[99cc] Presumably, regulations will clarify this point as well as the method for calculating a "proportionate share" in the case of a partnership, estate or trust, i.e., whether by reference to interests in income, capital, or corpus or to all the facts and circumstances. Third, if a corporation, (X) owns a controlling interest in another corporation (Y), the stock held by X in Y is to be ignored, and X will be deemed to own a percentage of the assets of Y.[99dd]

Based on the foregoing, it appears that the new law permits one straightforward, simple way of avoiding RPHC status: Always maintain foreign real property or business property in a U.S. corporation that is worth substantially more than the USRPIs held by the corporation.[99ee] In this manner, the corporation will not be an RPHC. If the corporation is not an RPHC, the plans discussed above could be used to avoid U.S. taxes. For example, a Section 337 plan could be adopted pursuant to which the USRPI is sold. The proceeds of the sale and the foreign property could be distributed in liquidation of the corporation. Since the corporation is not an RPHC, the gain on liquidation would be tax-free in the United States. If such a plan is economically feasible, great care must be exercised to assure that the value of the corporation's USRPIs never exceeds 50 percent of the total value of the assets included in the RPHC computation.[99ff]

In addition, there are two types of transfers by RPHCs for which no tax will be imposed. The transfer of any stock regularly traded on an established securities market is exempt, provided its owner held 5 percent or less of a class of such stock.[99gg] Also exempt from FIRPA are sales of stock by corporations that have already disposed of all their U.S. real property interests and have paid the proper tax on those sales subject to FIRPA.[99hh] Moreover, an interest in a U.S. RPHC held solely as a creditor does not constitute a USRPI.[99ii]

[99cc] I.R.C. § 897(c)(2).

[99dd] I.R.C. §§ 897(c)(5)(i), 897(c)(5)(ii).

[99ee] If market value for purposes of the 50 percent rule refers to equity (and not value without regard to liabilities) of the real estate, the owner could refinance and obtain a larger mortgage on the U.S. property if it should appreciate in value.

[99ff] See Feder, "Planning Under the Foreign Investment in Real Property Tax Act of 1980," 59 Taxes 81, 84, 85 (1981).

[99gg] I.R.C. § 897(c)(3).

[99hh] I.R.C. § 897(c)(1)(B).

[99ii] I.R.C. § 897(c)(1)(A)(ii).

Finally, the new law also provides that whenever a foreign corporation distributes a U.S. real property interest to its stockholders (whether in liquidation or otherwise), the corporation must recognize gain on the distribution as if the corporation had sold the real property at its fair market value.[99jj] For example, suppose a foreign corporation with foreign investors buys U.S. real estate. After several years, the property greatly appreciates in value. The foreign investor then sells shares in the foreign corporation to a U.S. investor. The foreign investor has no tax obligation to the United States. However, if the U.S. investor subsequently has the corporation distribute the real estate to him, the corporation will be liable for a tax based on the full appreciation in the value of the real property since the date of its original acquisition.[99kk] Nor could the property be sold without tax under I.R.C. § 337.

Notwithstanding this recent growth in foreign investment, a cloud looms on the horizon. At present, governments in certain European countries (e.g., The Netherlands and Belgium) are considering the prohibition or restriction of overseas investment by their domestic pension funds in order to retard the flight of investment capital and to encourage investment in their local economies. Some observers are speculating that the next wave of foreign capital flowing into this country may come from affluent Asian countries like Malaysia and Hong Kong that have a British-styled pension fund system with large reserves available for overseas investment.

[99jj] I.R.C. § 897(d)(1).

[99kk] This means that at the time the U.S. owner purchases the stock in the foreign corporation, he should discount the price to reflect the future tax that will be payable as a result of the appreciation in value of the corporate real estate as of the time the stock is purchased.

¶ 2.03 THE ROLE OF MORTGAGE BROKERS AND MORTGAGE BANKERS

[1] The Mortgage Broker

Page 2-47:

Add new text and notes 99ll-99uu at end of subsection.

Several recent decisions serve as strong warnings to mortgage brokers against breaching the fiduciary duty owed their clients, and help define the scope of that duty. Mortgage brokers must make full and honest disclosures orally as well as in writing of all loan terms,[99ll] must inquire as to a prospective borrower's ability to make loan payments,[99mm] and, at least in some circumstances, offer the borrower advice on how to raise his income.[99nn]

In *Wyatt v. Union Mortgage Co.*,[99oo] plaintiffs, in response to television advertisements run by defendant-mortgage broker, came into defendant's office to seek a second mortgage on their home. Defendant's loan officer orally represented to plaintiffs that they could obtain a loan of $1,325 at 7 to 8 percent interest without any late payment charges until the payment was 10 days overdue. The loan officer further represented that a "small" balloon payment would be due after three years. Plaintiffs were then presented with a set of loan documents to sign. The terms in the loan documents included a 10 percent interest rate, a late payment charge to be imposed once payment was five days overdue, and a balloon payment of $950. When plaintiffs were late in making several payments, they were faced with a balloon payment of $1,340. Defendant refused to extend the loan, but renegotiated it for $2,000. Plaintiffs brought suit to enjoin defendant from foreclosing the mortgage. The California Supreme Court held that full and accurate disclosure of all loan terms in writing did not by itself satisfy defendant's fiduciary duty to plaintiffs. Defendant had the duty to provide plaintiffs with honest and complete oral disclosures as well. On these facts, the court found plaintiffs' reliance on defendant's expertise as reflected in the loan officer's statements to be reasonable.

In *Armstrong v. Republic Realty Mortgage Corp.*,[99pp] plaintiff requested defendant's services in arranging for $1.5 million in long-term financing. Defendant made these arrangements with a lender for whom defendant served as loan correspondent, and received a $14,000 fee from plaintiff. Defendant was also to receive periodic loan servicing fees from the lender. Although plaintiff was able to pay the "floor" portion of the three-stage loan commitment, it had difficulty with the second and third portions. Aware of this difficulty, plaintiff again contacted defendant and requested prepayment arrangements[99qq] and refinancing arrangements with another lender. Once again, defendant

---

[99ll] Wyatt v. Union Mortgage Co., 24 Cal. App. 3d 773, 598 P.2d 45, 157 Cal. Rptr. 392 (1979); Armstrong v. Republic Realty Mortgage Corp., 631 F.2d 1344 (8th Cir. 1980).

[99mm] Peirce v. Hom, 178 Cal. Rptr. 553 (Ct. App. 1981).

[99nn] *Id.*

[99oo] Note 99ll *supra.*

[99pp] *Id.*

[99qq] This occurred after plaintiff asked defendant to obtain extensions on the closing dates of the two remaining portions. After the extensions were obtained, plaintiff's problems continued, so it sought prepayment privileges.

acted for plaintiff. Fearing the loss in periodic loan servicing fees that prepayment would bring about, defendant entered into the following deal with the lender: Any prepayment fee that defendant would be able to negotiate with plaintiff in excess of $9000 would be split 50-50 between defendant and lender. Therefore, when plaintiff agreed to pay a fee of $18,000, defendant was made $4,500 richer.

Plaintiff sued defendant for breach of its fiduciary duty to it. The federal district court gave plaintiff a judgment of $14,000 in compensatory damages and $125,000 in punitive damages. The Eighth Circuit affirmed, finding that an agency relationship existed at the time plaintiff requested and defendant made the prepayment arrangements.[99rr] As an agent, whether paid or gratuitous,[99ss] defendant had the duty to place plaintiff's interest ahead of its own. It breached this duty once it agreed with the lender to share in a prepayment penalty.

Defendant could have avoided this liability, amounting to ten times the amount of damages suffered by plaintiff, had it advised plaintiff in advance that it would propose to the lender a prepayment penalty sufficient to cover defendant's lost periodic loan servicing fees. Defendant's wrongdoing, the court held, was not in using the prepayment fee to offset its losses, but in doing so behind the plaintiff's back.[99tt]

In *Peirce v. Hom*,[99uu] plaintiff, a 77-year-old widow, owned several mortgaged real properties. When the mortgage payments were subtracted from the total monthly rental income, plaintiff was left with scarcely enough to pay for the necessities of life. Defendant-mortgage broker arranged for junior loans for some of plaintiff's properties, all at interest rates above 10 percent, the then prevailing maximum rate allowed by the California Business and Professional Code. The loans contained large balloon payments, also prohibited by the Code. When plaintiff was unable to keep up with the payments on the loans negotiated by defendant, as well as on her other debts, the lenders foreclosed all mortgages negotiated for her by defendant. Having lost all of her properties, plaintiff brought suit against defendant on two grounds. The first ground was that violation of the Code amounted to a breach of the fiduciary duty owed plaintiff. The second ground was that de-

---

[99rr] There was a dispute between the parties as to whether the agency relationship ended once plaintiff accepted the loan commitment. Assuming arguendo that it did end, it was surely resumed once defendant agreed to make the prepayment arrangements.

[99ss] If it is assumed that the agency relationship ended when plaintiff accepted the loan commitment, the $14,000 broker's fee would not cover defendant's services in getting the lender to agree to prepayment, and, for those services, defendant would be plaintiff's gratuitous agent.

[99tt] 631 F.2d at 1349.

[99uu] Note 99mm *supra*.

fendant breached his fiduciary duty by failing to inquire as to the plaintiff's ability to repay the loans and to advise plaintiff on ways to raise more income (i.e., by selling some of the property).

The Court dismissed the first ground, finding no proof that defendant's violation of the Code caused plaintiff to lose her property. Finding that defendant breached his fiduciary duty on the second ground, and finding such breach to be the proximate cause of the loss of properties secured by the junior loans obtained by defendant, the Court awarded plaintiff the damages directly resulting from the breach.

[2] The Mortgage Banker

Page 2-48:

Add new text and note 102 at end of subsection.

If by chance a loan correspondent also acts as a mortgage broker and obtains a loan for a borrower from the lender with whom it has established the correspondent relationship, the mortgage broker-banker as a dual agent must be certain that its fiduciary responsibilities to and services for the lender and borrower do not conflict or overlap.[102]

---

[102] See Armstrong v. Republic Realty Mortgage Corp., note 99*ll supra*. In that case, Fortune-Tampa Co. sought to develop office and warehouse space for lease on a 6.5-acre tract in Tampa, Fla. The company needed $1.5 million in long-term financing. Fortune-Tampa asked the Republic Realty Mortgage Corp. to be its mortgage broker. Republic contacted Continental Assurance Co. (CAC), for which Republic served as a loan correspondent. Republic had Fortune-Tampa execute a loan application to CAC. Fortune-Tampa paid Republic a $14,000 broker's fee.

CAC then issued a loan commitment calling for a "platform" floor loan of $900,000 to be closed by August 1, 1974 and second- and third-tier loans of $225,000 and $360,000, respectively, which were each subject to the condition that tenant leases in the office-warehouse had to exceed specified annual dollar totals by a closing date of February 1, 1975. The commitments as to the second and third tiers were to expire if the conditions were not fulfilled by the closing date. Prepayment was prohibited over the first ten years and was allowable thereafter only with a 5 percent penalty reduced by one-half of one percent per year in years 12 through 20. Once the loan closed, Republic was to receive from CAC loan-servicing fees over the life of the loan.

Construction delays made it impossible for Fortune-Tampa to qualify for second- and third-tier loan funding. Fortune-Tampa asked Republic to seek an extension of the second- and third-tier loan closing date. Republic obtained a three-month extension to May 1, 1975. On April 28, 1975, CAC informed Fortune-Tampa through Republic that it would fund only the second-tier loan. Fortune-Tampa then sought permission to prepay the CAC loan so that it could obtain a first mortgage loan from an alternate source.

Fortune-Tampa again requested Republic to intervene on its behalf with

CAC. When the CAC executive agreed to permit prepayment with a one percent penalty, the Republic officer reminded him that under the commitment no prepayment was allowed during the ten-year lock-in period and that even in the eleventh year there would be a 5 percent penalty. The Republic officer suggested a 4 percent prepayment penalty to which the CAC executive replied that CAC would split with Republic any penalty that Republic could negotiate with Fortune-Tampa in excess of one percent. After some bargaining, CAC agreed to accept prepayment with a 2 percent penalty, or $18,000. Fortune-Tampa paid off CAC and CAC turned over $9,000 of the penalty to Republic.

Aggrieved by what had transpired, Fortune-Tampa brought an action in district court against CAC and against Republic for breaching its duty as an agent of Fortune. The district court awarded judgment for Fortune-Tampa against both defendants. The Republic judgment, $14,000 in compensatory damages and $125,000 in punitive damages, was appealed to the Eighth Circuit, which affirmed the decision and found that an agency relationship was established between Fortune-Tampa and Republic when the latter agreed to locate financing for the former. This agency relationship terminated when Fortune-Tampa accepted the loan commitment but was revived by the conduct of the parties following Fortune-Tampa's request that Republic obtain a closing date extension and permission to prepay from CAC; Republic breached this duty when it conspired to share in the prepayment penalty.

Chapter 3
POST-CONSTRUCTION ("PERMANENT") FINANCING
[Revised Title]

		Page
¶ 3.01	Pre-financing Considerations	S3- 2
	[2] Review of the Commercial Lending Cycle	S3- 2
¶ 3.03	Function of Mortgage Loan Application-Commitment	S3- 2
	[1] A Written Offer	S3- 2
¶ 3.04	Terms and Conditions of Post-Construction ("Permanent") Financing [Revised Heading]	S3- 2
	[3] Rate of Interest	S3- 2
	[c] Variable-Rate Mortgages and Other Residential Inflation-Related Mortgage Devices [Revised Heading]	S3- 2
	[d] Convertible Mortgages, Bullet Loans, Rollover Mortgages, and Other Commercial Inflation-Related Mortgage Devices [New]	S3-12
	[5] Prepayment Privilege	S3-13
	[8] Right to Sell Mortgaged Property	S3-13
	[9] Compliance With Local Law	S3-19
	[a] Issuance of Building Permit and Certificate of Occupancy	S3-19
	[12] Satisfactory Hazard Insurance	S3-20
	[b] Loss Payable Clause	S3-20
	[18] Joint Venturing Requirement, Convertible Mortgages, and Other Trends in Permanent Financing [Revised Heading]	S3-20
¶ 3.06	Remedies for Breach of Mortgage Loan Commitment	S3-28
¶ 3.07	The Standby "Loan Commitment"	S3-29
	[2] The "Fundable Standby"	S3-29
¶ 3.08	Drafting the Mortgage/Deed of Trust	S3-29
	[4] The Mortgage/Deed of Trust	S3-29
	[a] Definitions	S3-29
	[g] Default Remedies	S3-33
	[i] Assignment of Leases and Rents	S3-35

¶ 3.01 PRE-FINANCING CONSIDERATIONS

[2] Review of the Commercial Lending Cycle

Page 3-5:

Add at end of note 4:

[4] For discussion of how recent economic changes have restructured the customary lending cycle, see ¶ 2.01, this Supplement.

¶ 3.03 FUNCTION OF MORTGAGE LOAN APPLICATION-COMMITMENT

[1] A Written Offer

Page 3-8:

Add at end of note 16:

[16] , aff'd, 34 N.Y.2d 671, 356 N.Y.S.2d 46 (1973).

¶ 3.04 TERMS AND CONDITIONS OF POST-CONSTRUCTION ("PERMANENT") FINANCING [Revised Heading]

[3] Rate of Interest

[c] Variable-Rate Mortgages and Other Residential Inflation-Related Mortgage Devices [Revised Heading]

Page 3-19:

Add at end of note 32.

[32] The Comptroller of the Currency, with regard to commercial banks, has issued variable-rate mortgage regulations that would permit interest rates to rise up to one percent each six months or 2 percent annually with no limit on adjustments over the life of the loan. Interest rates charged must be based on one of three indices: the six-month Treasury bill rate, the yield on Treasury securities adjusted to a constant maturity of three years, or the Bank Board's average mortgage rate on previously occupied homes. The regulations became effective on March 27, 1981.

Page 3-19:

Add at end of enumeration (1).

The VRM is the simplest form of alternative mortgage instrument, and one that is sometimes used in commercial as well as residential mortgage transactions. Fluctuations in the interest rate are geared to a particular index and the regulations issued by the Comptroller of the Currency require national banks offering VRMs to disclose the following information to the borrower: the index used; a ten-year index showing index values on a semiannual basis; the frequency of interest rate adjustment; a description of the method by which interest rate changes will be implemented; a statement of fees; and a schedule of payments based on a $10,000 loan at the commitment rate, indicating what the payments would be if the rate should increase by ten percent. The regulations also require the lender to give the borrower thirty to forty-five days notice of any interest rate adjustment. Included in the notice must be the proposed interest rate together with changes in the index dictating the adjustment the monthly payment requires to fully amortize the loan at the new rate, and the fact that prepayment is permitted without penalty.[32a]

Interest rate changes may be implemented through changes in the monthly payment, the maturity date, or the principal amount of the indebtedness. Under the third method, any adjustment of the principal balance does not result in a change in the interest rate or loan term.[32b]

Prepayment penalties are often included in VRMs to discourage a borrower from converting his debt to a fixed-rate mortgage as soon as the VRM rate exceeds that of fixed-rate mortgages. The FHLBB and the Comptroller of the Currency have promulgated regulations permitting the borrower to prepay the loan without penalty during a period of time immediately following an interest rate increase.

Among the legal issues raised by the use of a VRM are:

[32a] *Id.* In Goebel v. First Fed. Sav. & Loan Ass'n of Racine, 266 N.W.2d 352 (Wisc. 1978), a case decided prior to the VRM regulations, a court refused to enforce a VRM clause in mortgages where information of the type required by the regulations was not disclosed to the borrowers and the loan documents did not expressly authorize adjustments in the monthly payments of interest.

[32b] One commentator presented the following illustration of this rate adjustment method: A twenty-five-year variable rate mortgage of $50,000 with an interest rate of 11 percent has a principal balance at the end of the year of $49,599.53. If the applicable index dictates an interest rate increase of one-half of one percent, the principal will be increased by one-half of one percent to $49,847.53. As a result, the monthly payment would rise slightly to $492.51, a much lower monthly payment than that obtained from directly raising the monthly payment to implement the interest rate adjustment. Strum, "Economics of Variable Rate Mortgages," in *Financing Real Estate During the Inflationary 80s* at 25-26 (ABA 1981).

A VRM structured so that interest rate adjustments affect the amount of the principal balance could not be used in those states that prohibit the capitalization of interest. See Partain v. First Nat'l Bank, 467 F.2d 167, 178 (5th Cir. 1972); Beneficial Fin. Co. v. Fusco, 160 Me. 273, 284, 203 A.2d 457 (1964).

(1) Would an upward rate adjustment that causes the interest rate to exceed the maximum rate allowed by local law render the loan usurious? [32c]

(2) Would a VRM structured so that interest rate adjustments affect amortization violate state statutes that prohibit capitalization of interest? [32d]

(3) Is a VRM a negotiable instrument under the Uniform Commercial Code? Since a VRM note is not a promise to pay a "sum certain," it apparently would not qualify for negotiability status under U.C.C. § 3-106.

(4) Would a new title insurance policy be required to protect the lender's lien priority? In contrast to a roll-over mortgage, the interest rate adjustment would occur automatically and not be considered a new loan for priority purposes if the loan documents are properly drafted.[32e] Specifically, the lender should include language in the loan documents obligating itself to add accrued but unpaid interest to the outstanding principal so that these amounts will be treated as obligatory rather than optional advances and thereby accorded lien priority over any intervening liens.[32f]

(5) If there are huge upward rate adjustments, could the borrower raise the doctrine of unconscionability as a defense in any action to enforce the loan obligation? [32g]

(6) Is it necessary to provide the borrower with a reasonable prepayment privilege? In the case of a residential VRM, Federal Home Loan Bank Board regulations permit the borrower to prepay without penalty during designated periods of time following any rate adjustment. In the case of commercial loans, a reasonably stringent prepayment penalty or lock-in period would be required to protect the lender against early refinancing by the borrower if interest rates should decline; however, there is a possibility that any stringent restriction might be viewed with judicial disfavor in light of the reasoning behind the FHLBB regulations.

[32c] See discussion at ¶ 5.02[4][d], this Supplement.

[32d] See Partain v. First Nat'l Bank, note 32b *supra;* Beneficial Fin. Co. v. Fusco, note 32b *supra.*

[32e] The American Land Title Association originated Endorsement Form 6, which can be utilized for a VRM.

[32f] See discussion at ¶ 4.02[6][a][ii], this Supplement.

[32g] See discussion at ¶¶ 3.04[3][c][5] and 3.04[18], this Supplement.

Page 3-19:

Add at end of enumeration (4)

The interest rate, which is nominal, might be as low as 4 percent. The major advantage of a PLAM is that initial payments are low because there is no necessity to charge an inflation premium. However, the borrower is assuming the risk that inflation will increase more rapidly than his income. PLAMs, which are used much more extensively in Brazil than in the United States, involve several legal problems.[33a]

The increase in principal due, which has been held to be interest for usury purposes, might be construed as an optional future advance and thus be denied priority as to intervening liens.[33b] A PLAM might be held to be in violation of the "gold clause resolution." The "gold clause," a common provision in nineteenth-century loan instruments, protected the lender against inflation by providing for payment in a fixed weight and amount of gold coins or its equivalent in currency. Congress passed a joint resolution in the 1930s declaring the gold clause void as against public policy. A recent case[33c] relied on this resolution in holding that a loan whose payments were based on the Consumer Price Index was void because a debt may not appreciate. The court found a gold-clause violation even though, at least for usury purposes, it treated the loan principal as interest.

Replace enumeration (5) with the following.

(5) *Shared appreciation mortgage (SAM):* In exchange for granting a high loan-to-value ratio (e.g., 90 percent) loan and a lengthy amortization period (e.g., thirty years), the borrower would pay the lender a certain percentage (e.g., 33⅓ percent) of the total appreciation in value of the periodically reappraised realty.

The loan typically provides for a fixed interest rate below the prevailing market rate and additional contingent interest based on an agreed-upon percentage of the appreciation in value of the

---

[33a] See ¶ 5.02[4][d], this Supplement, for a discussion of alternative mortgage instruments and potential usury problems. See also ¶ 3.04[18], this Supplement, for discussion of usury problems in connection with a mortgagee's option to purchase the mortgaged property under a convertible mortgage arrangement.

[33b] See Levin, note 33 *supra* at 50.

[33c] Aztec Properties, Inc. v. Union Planters Nat'l Bank, 530 S.W.2d 756 (Tenn. 1975), *cert. denied* 42 U.S. 975 (1976). This case involved a shared appreciation mortgage (SAM), but would be equally, if not more, applicable to a PLAM.

property securing the loan. The contingent interest usually becomes due at the earlier of maturity, full prepayment, sale of the property, or default. Occasionally, the lender will agree to permit the borrower to refinance with a new long-term, fixed-rate mortgage at the prevailing market rate.[33d]

SAMs are the newest and among the most speculative and controversial methods of alternative financing,[33e] especially in light of the fact that for the past fifteen years, the rate of appreciation of single-family housing has exceeded the average rate of salary increases for homeowners.[33f] In addition to the risks involved, there are a number of legal and practical problems associated with SAM financing.

Valuation. To resolve disputes concerning the amount of future appreciation, the mortgage may include a "full employment for appraisers" provision. Under this provision, each party would appoint an appraiser, and a third appraiser would be chosen by the first two. The appreciation in value would be determined by averaging the two closest appraisals.[33g]

The most difficult valuation problem is determining how much of the appreciation results from inflation, as opposed to capital improvements by the borrower.[33h] To obviate this problem, the parties might agree on a method that takes into account the borrower's proven expenses on capital improvements in determining the borrower's basis, without attempting to allocate appreciated value to those improvements.[33i]

[33d] A SAM typically includes the following additional terms and conditions: (1) a below-market fixed interest rate; (2) additional contingent interest at a rate determined by the percentage share of any appreciation and sufficient to produce a greater effective gross yield than that on a conventional fixed-rate mortgage; (3) a short-term loan with a longer amortization period; (4) due-on-sale and due-on-encumbrance clauses; (5) prepayment penalty, at least during the early years of the loan term; (6) a high loan-to-value ratio; and (7) appreciation to be determined either by the actual sales price or by appraisal, allowing the borrower to recoup the cost of capital improvements.

[33e] In September of 1980, the FHLBB proposed regulations, published in 45 Fed. Reg. 66,801 (1980), authorizing savings and loan associations to make SAMs.

[33f] For a nightmare scenario involving an $80,000 house appreciating to $125,000 in the course of five years, see Strum, note 32b *supra* at 27, 29.

[33g] In the case of nonresidential property, capitalization of rent increases is frequently utilized to determine the amount of appreciation. See Strum, note 32b *supra* at 28, 29.

[33h] See Levin, note 33 *supra* at 49.

[33i] A sample of an appraisal provision can be found in Appendix B, Form 3.15, this Supplement.

Unconscionability. A borrower might defend against a foreclosure action by claiming that the lender's rate of return is unconscionably high. To help avoid a challenge on the grounds of "unfair surprise," the lender should explain to the borrower his obligation to pay contingent interest as the property's value appreciated.[33j] A challenge on the grounds of oppressive behavior would be more difficult to circumvent because a finding of unequal bargaining power may be inevitable in some lending situations. The lender can somewhat reduce the likelihood of being challenged on grounds of oppression if it includes a savings clause disclaiming any intention on its part to overreach.[33k] However, no matter how fair the terms or how carefully the mortgage instrument is drafted, the lender must face the risk of an adverse judgment based on unconscionability from a court desiring to rescue an individual from having to sell his real estate.[33l]

Negative Amortization. When a SAM is structured so that contingent interest based on appreciation is added to the loan balance, a capitalization of interest might occur in contravention of those state statutes that prohibit the capitalization of interest.[33m] The use of complete refinancing instead of periodic adjustment of the loan balance might avoid such negative amortization.

Priority of Advances. The contingent interest when added to the loan balance could be treated as an optional advance lacking priority over intervening liens if the lender has the option to collect the contingent interest upon periodic appraisals.[33n] If no contingent interest accrues until maturity, this problem can be obviated. In addition, any SAM instrument should condition refinancing on the subordination or release of any intervening liens.

Negotiability. Notes secured by SAMs are not negotiable under U.C.C. § 3-106 since they do not contain a promise to pay a "sum certain." The buyer of such a note, therefore, cannot be a "holder in due course" and takes subject to all claims and defenses of the note's maker.[33o]

[33j] See Uniform Land Transactions Act § 1-311, Commissioner's Comment No. 1, 13 U.L.A. 539, 574 (1980); Alden & Benner, "Lenders May Face Legal Obstacles in Shared Appreciation Mortgages," Nat'l L.J., Feb. 15, 1982 at 18, 24; discussion at ¶ 3.04[18], this Supplement.

[33k] Levin, note 33 *supra* at 44.

[33l] Alden & Benner, note 33j *supra* at 24.

[33m] Partain v. First Nat'l Bank, note 32b *supra* at 178; Beneficial Fin. Co. v. Fusco, note 32b *supra* at 284.

[33n] See discussion at ¶ 4.02[6][a][ii], this Supplement.

[33o] See U.C.C. § 3-306.

Due-on-sale clause. The due-on-sale clause[33p] is an important provision in a SAM because a sale at an appreciated price is an appropriate event upon which to calculate the contingent interest. Some commentators are of the opinion that California and other states whose courts have held due-on-sale clauses to be unenforceable would not permit the lender to collect any contingent interest until the loan matures,[33q] while others believe that these same courts would uphold the contingent interest covenant in a SAM.[33r]

Foreclosure and clogging the equity of redemption. It is important that the loan documents define the lender's rights as those of a mortgagee and its right to a share of appreciation as "mortgage interest"; otherwise, the SAM borrower might contend at foreclosure that the lender merely has an equity interest in the property disguised in the form of a SAM mortgage.

Another defense against foreclosure is that the contingent interest covenant creates an illegal "clog" on the borrower's "equity of redemption."[33s] However, the doctrine does not apply when the right of redemption is available even when made more expensive by virtue of large accrued interest liabilities.

SAMs could also be challenged as usurious[33t] or in violation of the gold clause.[33u]

Federal regulations. The FHLBB has proposed regulations that would permit federal savings and loan associations to make SAMs.[33v] The regulations impose a 40 percent maximum on the amount of appreciation payable to the lender and establish maximum terms and amortization periods. The net appreciated value would be determined by subtracting from the market value[33w] of

---

[33p] See discussion at ¶ 3.04[8].

[33q] Levin, note 33 *supra* at 46. The authors cite the landmark decision of the Supreme Court of California, Wellenkamp v. Bank of America, 21 Cal. 3d 943, 948, 582 P.2d 970, 148 Cal. Rptr. 379 (1978), as a basis for this view. See discussion at ¶ 3.04[8], this Supplement.

[33r] Alden & Benner, note 33j *supra* at 19.

[33s] Case law prohibiting the mortgagee from obtaining a purchase option contemporaneously with the mortgage on "clogging" grounds include Barr v. Granaham, 255 Wis. 192, 38 N.W. 2d 705 (1949); Humble Oil & Ref. Co. v. Doerr, 123 N.J. Super. 530, 303 A.2d 898 (Ch. Div. 1973). See discussion at ¶ 3.04[18], this Supplement.

[33t] See discussion at ¶ 5.02[4][d].

[33u] See discussion in this subsection on price level adjustment mortgages (PLAMs).

[33v] See note 33e *supra*.

[33w] Under the regulations, the lender may choose either the net sales price or the appraised value as the property's market value.

the property. The borrower's basis in the property, the cost of capital improvements made by the borrower, and any appraisal costs.

The proposed regulations would preempt any conflicting state law that restricts the right of a federal savings and loan association to enter into a SAM transaction on grounds such as unconscionability, nonnegotiability under the U.C.C., the unreasonableness of due-on-sale clauses, and "clogging" of the borrower's equity of redemption. Substantial changes in the proposed regulations are anticipated.[33x]

Add new enumeration (6) after enumeration (5).

(6) *Renegotiable-Rate Mortgage* (RRM): In January 1980, the Federal Home Loan Bank Board proposed regulations to permit a new form of adjustable-rate mortgage that is similar to the variable-rate mortgage.[33y] Known as a "renegotiable-rate mortgage" (RRM), it is based upon a Canadian model and, in essence, provides long-term financing with an adjustment of the loan interest rate every three to five years. Each adjustment would be limited to one-half of one percent each year (1.5 percent over a three-year interval), with a maximum increase or decrease of 5 percent over the life of the mortgage, so that a mortgage with an original loan rate of 10 percent, for example, could vary between 5 and 15 percent.

The Canadian counterpart—which is about the only home financing available there—places no limit on changes in the interest rate. The loan takes the form of a mortgage, with payments based upon a twenty-five- or thirty-year rate, with the entire balance due at the end of the term of five or three years or even one year. At the end of that term, at least in theory, the borrower is free to obtain refinancing from another source, and the lender is free to turn down renewal if the borrower has not performed well or if funds are not available. Under the FHLBB proposal, the lender could not demand payment at the end of the term and must retain the loan as long as the borrower accepts the new "renegotiated" rate.

Recognizing that there will be little actual negotiation be-

[33x] As of this writing, the Bank Board has not acted on the proposed regulations.

[33y] 45 Fed. Reg. 1425 (1980).

tween borrower and lender at the end of the term, the regulations provide for maximum actual adjustments to be set by an index, and make downward adjustments mandatory, with upward adjustments optional. The proposal permits the lender to choose one of two indices at the time the loan is first made. The choices are either a lender's current market rate on similar loans or a national average contract rate for all major lenders on previously occupied houses, a figure reported monthly in the FHLBB *Journal*. If the index moves less than the maximum allowable adjustment during a loan term, the unused amount cannot be carried over to the next period. If the index moves more than the maximum adjustment, however, the regulations appear to permit the excess to be carried over. For example, if the index increases one percent during the first three-year period and 2.5 percent during the next period, the maximum rate increases would be one percent and 1.5 percent. If the index movements were reversed, however —2.5 percent and one percent—the loan could be increased 1.5 percent at each renewal for a total of 3 percent, with the unused one-half percent carrying over from the first renewal period.

The regulations require the lender to notify the borrower sixty days before the end of the loan term of any rate change if the loan is renewed. The borrower has the right to repay the mortgage without any penalty at the end of the first term, and no costs except for documentation may be charged for a renewal.

Page 3-20:

Add the following title to first paragraph.

> (7) *Graduated Payment Mortgage (GPM) and Flexible Loan Insurance Program (FLIP):*

Add after first paragraph:

> The FHLBB has promulgated regulations permitting federal savings and loan associations to make GPMs.[33z] The regulations impose restrictions on the size and frequency of payment graduations. The same legal issues affecting the use of VRMs, PLAMs, and SAMs (i.e., on the grounds of usury, unconscionability, non-negotiability, restraints on alienation, and "clogging the equity of redemption") apply to GPM transactions.
>
> Similar to GPMs are graduated payment adjustable mortgages (GPAMs). Payments are graduated as in GPMs, but in-

---

[33z] 12 C.F.R. § 545.6-4(b) (1980).

terest rates are adjusted in line with market rates as in VRMs. Because of their complexity, GPAMs will probably not be as well accepted as GPMs.

The FLIP loan is also known as the pledged account mortgage (PAM) because it uses the borrower's downpayment to create an interest-bearing savings account that is pledged as additional security for the mortgage loan. During the early years of the loan, the monthly payments consist of a combination of the borrower's reduced payments and withdrawals from the savings account. As the borrower's payments increase, the supplemental payments from the account decrease until the account has been exhausted (usually within five years). FLIPs have been approved for state-chartered lenders in at least twenty-seven states.

(8) *Deferred interest mortgage (DIM):* A DIM is a GPM in which a portion of the interest payments are deferred during the early part of the loan term and reallocated to the principal balance. The low initial interest rate increases within five or ten years.

(9) *Buy-down mortgages:* In a mortgage buy-down the seller or home builder obtains a loan at the current market rate and simultaneously loans the same amount to the buyer, while paying the buyer's loan interest charges for the first three to five years. The Federal Housing Administration (FHA) has announced that it will allow sellers to subsidize interest payments to the extent that it would reduce the buyer's mortgage rate by a maximum of three percentage points.[33aa]

(10) *Seller-seconds and "one, two, threes":* Under a seller-seconds plan (a variant of purchase-money mortgage financing), the buyer assumes the seller's existing mortgage, and the seller then takes back a second purchase-money mortgage for the unpaid balance at an interest rate below market value. Frequently, a balloon payment is due within three to five years on either the second mortgage or the entire purchase price.[33bb] The "one, two, three" is a seller-seconds

---

[33aa] "FHA to Allow Sellers to Subsidize Mortgages," Newsletter of the Society of Real Estate Appraisers, June 24, 1981 at 1.

[33bb] Frank, "If 'Creative' Buyers Can't Refinance, Associations Could Be Hurt, Too," Savings & Loan News, January 1982 at 71. See discussion of purchase-money financing at ¶ 9.01[1].

The mortgage assumption involved in this type of financing assumes the absence of any due-on-sale clause existing in the original mortgage. For a discussion of due-on-sale clauses and their enforceability see ¶ 3.04[8], this Supplement.

in which the buyer takes a second mortgage from the lender and a third mortgage from the seller.[33cc]

(11) *Blend:* Some savings associations are offering special refinancing packages to buyers of homes with existing low-rate mortgages. Under the most popular of these packages, the so-called blend arrangement, the association offers the buyer a combination of the old mortgage rate and the current higher rate.[33dd]

[33cc] Frank, note 33bb *supra* at 71-72.
[33dd] For examples of such plans, see *id.* at 74.

Add new ¶ *3.04[3][d].*

[d] Convertible Mortgages, Bullet Loans, Rollover Mortgages, and Other Commercial Inflation-Related Mortgage Devices [New]

With the possible exceptions of the variable-rate and renegotiable-rate mortgage, the relatively new inflation-related mortgage devices discussed at ¶ 3.04[3][c], this Supplement, are used almost predominantly in association with single-family residential financing. However, familiarity with these post-construction takeout devices is important for all real estate professionals, especially for the real estate developer and lender involved in either subdivision or condominium–cooperative development and financing. With the virtual demise of the long-term fixed rate mortgage, these residential mortgage devices (or variants thereof) could become more relevant to commercial real estate financing. At present, similar mortgage devices have become popular with respect to the financing of income-producing property such as the so-called bullet loan,[37a] convertible mortgage[37b] roll-over balloon mortgage[37c] and renegotiable-rate mortgage,[37d] which reflect an effort on the part of traditional long-term lenders like insurance companies to protect themselves against the ravages of inflation and volatile interest rates.

[37a] See discussion at ¶ 3.04[4].
[37b] See discussion at ¶ 3.04[18], this Supplement.
[37c] See discussion at ¶ 3.04[4]. Normally, the rollover mortgage has a long-term amortization schedule (e.g., twenty-five to thirty years) with a balloon payment required at the end of a short-term loan period (e.g., three to five years). While the lender is not obligated to renew the loan, the practice in most cases is for the lender to provide the refinancing at current loan terms.
[37d] See discussion at ¶ 3.04[3][c], this Supplement.

Page 3-21:

Renumber note 37a as 37e.

[5] Prepayment Privilege

Page 3-24:

Add at end of note 46.

⁴⁶ ; cf. Berenato v. Bell Sav. & Loan Ass'n, 276 Pa. Super. 599, 419 A.2d 620 (1980) (prepayment penalty enforceable where sale arranged by mortgagor's creditor did not render prepayment involuntary even though defaulting mortgagor had "no control over the sale").

Add new text and note 49a at end of subsection.

To date, when the mortgage instruments contain both a prepayment penalty and a valid due-on-sale clause, the courts have denied enforcement of the penalty on a sale by the mortgagor that accelerates the indebtedness. The rationale is that acceleration of the indebtedness by the mortgagee constitutes an involuntary prepayment and the election to accelerate renders the payment a "postpayment" (one made after maturity of the loan) that by definition is not a prepayment of the mortgage indebtedness.⁴⁹ᵃ

---

⁴⁹ᵃ E.g., Slevin Container Corp. v. Provident Fed. Sav. & Loan Ass'n, 98 Ill. App. 3d 646, 424 N.E.2d 939 (1981); see 86 A.L.R.3d 599, 605 (1978). See also Arend v. Great S. Sav. & Loan Ass'n, 611 S.W.2d 381 (Mo. Ct. App. 1981), where lender elected to rescind debt acceleration under due-on-sale clause and court held that subsequent prepayment by mortgagor necessitated payment of a prepayment penalty.

[8] Right to Sell Mortgaged Property

Page 3-31:

Add at end of note 84.

⁸⁴ After examining Section 404 of the *Restatement of Property* (1944), the Nebraska Supreme Court in Occidental Sav. & Loan Ass'n, 206 Neb. 469, 293 N.W.2d 843 (1980), concluded that a due-on-sale clause is not a direct restraint on alienation because in the opinion of the court such clause does not cause a forfeiture of title nor does it operate as a legal constraint on conveyance; it only causes debt acceleration and therefore the restraint, if any, attaches not to the conveyance of title but rather to the mortgage; accord, Mills v. Nashua Fed. Sav. & Loan Ass'n, 433 A.2d 1312 (N.H. 1981); Crestview Ltd. v. Foremost Ins. Co., 621 S.W.2d 816 (Tex. Civ. App. 1981).

Page 3-32:

Add at end of first paragraph of note 86.

[86] ; (in Tierce v. APS Co. the Supreme Court of Alabama declared the holding in the *Britton* case, *infra,* to be in error); Wekckhardt v. Wauwatosa Sav. & Loan Ass'n, 103 Wis. 2d 608, 309 N.W.2d 865 (Ct. App. 1981). Krause v. Columbia Sav. & Loan Ass'n, 631 P.2d 1158 (Colo. Ct. App. 1981); Parker v. Covington, 614 S.W.2d 810 (Tenn. Ct. App. 1981); Williams v. First Fed. Sav. & Loan Ass'n, 651 F.2d 910 (4th Cir. 1981); Sonny Arnold, Inc. v. Sentry Sav. Ass'n, 615 S.W.2d 333 (Tex. Civ. App. 1981) (court also noted that due-on-sale clause was not an invalid restraint on alienation).

Add at the end of note 87.

[87] New York has recently become less automatic in its enforcement of these clauses. In Silver v. Rochester Sav. Bank, 73 A.D.2d 81, 424 N.Y.S.2d. 945 (1980), the borrower-plaintiff constructed a bank building with a development loan from the bank-defendant on land owned by the borrower, and leased the property to the bank which was given a right of first refusal to purchase the property. The bank refused to consent to an assumption of the loan by a third-party purchaser unless the interest rate on the mortgage was increased notwithstanding a provision in the mortgage that the mortgagee would not unreasonably withhold its consent to any of the terms in the mortgage requiring the mortgagee's consent. The Appellate Division of the New York Supreme Court held that as a matter of law the lender could not arbitrarily withhold its consent solely to obtain a higher rate of interest when the bank had expressly agreed not to do so. In addition, to permit the bank to do so would have constituted a breach of the contract with the borrower because the reduced net income on the investment resulting from the higher mortgage interest rate would have produced a lower rate of return on the purchase price unless the seller-borrower reduced the purchase price which would have reduced the borrower's anticipated equity in the property. *Id.* at 85-86, 424 N.Y.S.2d at 948. The court also distinguished the decisions in Mutual Real Estate Trust v. Buffalo Sav. Bank, note 86 *supra,* and Stith v. Hudson City Sav. Inst., *supra,* based on the absence of a restriction on the lender's consent. 73 A.D.2d at 86, 424 N.Y.S.2d at 948. It appears that this decision will be of limited precedential value because of the special facts in the case and the court's noncommittal attitude on the question as to whether a due-on-sale clause is enforceable for interest rate adjustment purposes where the mortgage does not provide that the mortgagee shall not unreasonably withhold its consent.

Page 3-33:

Add at end of note 88.

[88] ; Warmack v. Merchants Nat'l Bank, 612 S.W.2d 733 (Ark. 1981).

Page 3-34:

Add new text and notes 99a-99aa following runover paragraph.

The lender in *Wellenkamp* was a financially strong institutional lender, and the borrower had purchased a single-family home. At issue in the California Court of Appeals[98a] was whether *Wellenkamp* also applies to a non-institutional seller of commercial real property who holds a second deed of trust securing a promissory note for part of the purchase price. The court held that *Wellenkamp* would not apply in such a situation, and that a due-on-sale clause would be enforceable.

The plaintiffs in *Dawn Investment Co.* purchased a ten-unit apartment building from the defendants. As part of the purchase price, plaintiffs gave defendants a promissory note for $34,000 secured by a second deed of trust. The mortgage contained a standard due-on-sale clause stating that "in the event of a sale, transfer, or change of ownership of title to the property . . . the unpaid balance of principal and interest due on the note . . . shall at the option of the holder . . . become immediately due and payable." Three years later, when plaintiffs sold the building, defendants sent a notice of intent to accelerate the balance on the loan. Plaintiffs, seeking to enjoin defendants from proceeding with a nonjudicial foreclosure, brought this action. Plaintiffs alleged in their complaint that "on information and belief" defendants constituted "an institutional lender." [98b]

The Court of Appeals first ruled on whether defendants constituted "an institutional lender." It held that plaintiffs' conclusion as to this was not supported by any evidence. Defendants consisted of husband, wife, and husband's mother, and "Dawn Investment Co." was merely a form of ownership by which defendants held title to their properties.[98c]

The court then stated that the *Wellenkamp* court expressly limited its ruling to institutional lenders, and did not express an opinion on due-on-sale clauses protecting private lenders.[98d] *Wellenkamp,* the

---

[98a] Dawn Inv. Co. v. Superior Court of Los Angeles County, 116 Cal. App. 3d 439, 172 Cal. Rptr. 142 (1981), *vacated* 30 Cal. 3d 695, 639 P.2d 974, 180 Cal. Rptr. 332 (1982).

[98b] 116 Cal. App. 3d at 444, 172 Cal. Rptr. at 143.

[98c] *Id.* at 445-446, 172 Cal. Rptr. at 144.

[98d] The court cited the following passage from *Wellenkamp* in support of its view:

"In the instant case the party seeking enforcement of the due-on-sale clause is an institutional lender. We *limit our holding accordingly.* We express no present opinion on the question whether a private lender, including the vendor who takes back secondary financing, has interests

court said, did not make due-on-sale clauses illegal or unenforceable for all purposes and in all situations; lenders can use these clauses to protect their interests when *Wellenkamp*-like facts are not present.[98e] The lender in *Wellenkamp* was a large bank with tremendous strength, resources, and bargaining power far superior to that of the individual homeowner seeking to avoid the disasterous choice between dispossession and costly refinancing. In contrast to this situation was the situation at bench in which defendants were not engaged in banking, mortgage financing, or any other institutional activity, and were about equal in bargaining power to plaintiffs. In addition, because plaintiffs purchased a commercial building with several apartments, the public policy favoring protection of a homeowner's equity does not play the role that it did in *Wellenkamp*.[98f] These plaintiffs, unlike owners of single-family homes, could meet their cost of acquisition and maintenance through rental income, thereby reducing the quantum of restraint the due-on-sale clause imposes.

The Court of Appeals was reversed a year later by the California Supreme Court, which held that *Wellenkamp* applies equally to private lenders and institutional lenders.[98g] It stated that the restraint on alienation imposed by either type of lender's enforcement of a due-on-sale clause would amount to the same thing: a prohibition on any sale or assignment of the property. It further stated that the private lender's security is in no greater need of the protection afforded by due-on-sale clauses than is that of the institutional lender.[98h] Private lenders, it stated, can obtain as much credit information about potential borrowers as can institutional lenders, if they use brokers. However, no mention of a broker was made under the facts of *Dawn Investment Co.* The Supreme Court rejected the defendants' argument that institutional lenders, unlike private lenders, can allocate the risk of loss over their multiple loan portfolios.[98i]

---

which might inherently justify automatic enforcement of a due-on-sale clause in his favor upon resale."

Id. at 446, 172 Cal. Rptr. at 144-445 (quoting Wellenkamp v. Bank of America, 21 Cal. App. 3d 943, 952 n.9, 582 P.2d 970, 976, 148 Cal. Rptr. 379, 385 (1978)).

[98e] *Id.* at 447, 172 Cal. Rptr. at 145.

[98f] *Id.*

[98g] 639 P.2d 974, 180 Cal. Rptr. 332 (Cal. 1982). For a different result, see Ceravolo v. Buckner, 444 N.Y.S.2d 861, 862-63 (Sup. Ct. 1981), where a New York court also was not influenced by the fact that the mortgagee was a private individual rather than an institutional lender. The court stringently applied the New York rule that due-on-sale clauses are enforceable even if the mortgagee's motive in enforcing the clause was to maintain mortgage funds at current interest rates. *Id.*

[98h] 639 P.2d at 976, 180 Cal. Rptr. at 334.

[98i] *Id.* at 977, 180 Cal. Rptr. at 335.

The court ruled that the *Wellenkamp* holding also applied to commercial property[98j] despite the footnote mention in *Wellenkamp* of the state public policy favoring the protection of a homeowner's equity.[98k] The Supreme Court also rejected defendants' argument that the risk of the purchaser's lack of creditworthiness justified any restraint on alienation. In rejecting this argument, the court reasoned that in most cases involving income-producing property it is the rental income stream, not the borrower's managerial ability, that primes the mortgage.[98l] However, this line of reasoning seems to ignore the fact that in the case of small rental properties (as was the case in *Dawn Investment Co.*) and so-called specialty properties such as motels and hotels, the managerial skill of the borrower is generally considered by lenders to be an important variable in the loan appraisal process.

Courts criticizing the legal reasoning in *Wellenkamp* have stated that due-on-sale clauses, when viewed in isolation, cannot be said to create direct restraints on alienation.[98m] Homeowners subject to these clauses are free to sell their homes and realize as much gain as homeowners holding unencumbered property. In fact, at least one court[98n] has pointed out that the seller of encumbered property enjoys a distinct economic advantage over the seller of unencumbered property during periods of rising interest rates.[98o] The majority opinion in *Wellenkamp* has also been criticized for protecting an economic advantage of borrowers over free-and-clear owners of property at the expense of a lender's contractual rights.[98p]

[98j] *Id.* at 978, 180 Cal. Rptr. at 336.

[98k] 21 Cal. App. 3d at 950 n.6, 582 P.2d at 975, 148 Cal. Rptr. at 384.

[98l] See 639 P.2d at 978, 180 Cal. Rptr. at 336.

[98m] Occidental Sav. & Loan Ass'n v. Venco Partnership, 206 Neb. 469, 471, 293 N.W.2d 843, 845 (1980); Williams v. First Fed. Sav. & Loan Ass'n, 651 F.2d 910, 923 (4th Cir. 1981).

[98n] 651 F.2d at 915 n.8; Wellenkamp v. Bank of America, 21 Cal. 3d 943, 954, 582 P.2d 970, 977, 148 Cal. Rptr. 379, 386 (1978) (Clark, J., dissenting).

[98o] The illustration presented in *Williams*, 651 F.2d at 915 n.8, is of a house whose market value would be $100,000 if unencumbered. If it was subject to an outstanding mortgage covering an unpaid balance of $50,000 payable over twenty-seven years at a rate of 10 percent, and if the mortgage obligation could be assumed, its present value to a purchaser seeking leverage would be $115,000.

[98p] 21 Cal. 3d at 954, 582 P.2d at 977, 148 Cal. Rptr. at 386 (Clark, J., dissenting). The court in *Williams* takes this logic one step further by stating in a footnote (651 F.2d at 924 n.29):

> "It is simply a misperception to eviscerate, as the California majority in *Wellenkamp* appears ready to eviscerate, as a restraint on alienation, a clause that only precludes the homeowner from realizing an additional and unbargained for economic advantage because interest rates have risen since the time when he secured, by mortgage or deed of trust, his promise to repay what he borrowed."

At present, the major conflict over due-on-sale clauses is in the federal versus state law arena and concerns the question as to whether federally chartered savings and loan associations can enforce these clauses by reason of the federal preemption doctrine even in jurisdictions like California where automatic enforcement of these clauses is contrary to state law. On May 3, 1976, the Federal Home Loan Bank Board promulgated regulations[98q] authorizing federal associations to employ such clauses on the basis of economic data suggesting that due-on-sale clauses were necessary to the survival of these institutions in light of the increasing rise in interest rates.

After *Wellenkamp* was decided, a U.S. District court, in *Glendale Federal Savings & Loan Ass'n v. Fox*,[98r] held that FHLBB regulations permitting federal savings and loan associations to include due-on-sale clauses in their loan contracts preempt California state law[98s] which limits the enforceability of such clauses. On the basis of federal legislative history and federal preemption case law, the court held that California law applied only to those loan instruments executed by savings and loan associations before June 9, 1976.[98t] Some state courts of California, however, have held that California law, as interpreted by *Wellenkamp,* is not preempted by the FHLBB regulations.[98u] With few exceptions,[98v] the *Glendale Federal Savings & Loan* decision has been upheld

---

[98q] 12 C.F.R. § 545. 8-3 (1980).

[98r] 481 F. Supp. 616 (C.D. Cal. 1979), appeal pending (9th Cir. 1979). In agreement with *Glendale,* but hesitant about its application to state-chartered savings and loan associations, is Williams v. First Fed. Sav. & Loan Ass'n, note 98m *supra.* In agreement with the more general proposition that state law may not interfere with the internal workings of federal savings and loan associations is Conference of Fed. Sav. & Loan Ass'ns v. Stein, 495 F. Supp. 12 (E.D. Cal. 1979), *aff'd* 604 F.2d 1256 (9th Cir.), *aff'd mem.* 445 U.S. 921 (1980). For a further discussion of this issue see Comment, "Due-on-Sale Clauses and Restraints on Alienation: Does *Wellenkamp* Apply to Federal Institutions?" 11 Pac. L.J. 1085 (1980).

[98s] Cal. Civ. Code § 711 (West 1954).

[98t] 481 F. Supp. at 632-633.

[98u] Wilhite v. Callihan, 121 Cal. App. 3d 627, 175 Cal. Rptr. 507 (1981); De la Cuesta v. Fidelity Fed. Sav. & Loan Ass'n, 121 Cal. App. 3d 328, 175 Cal. Rptr. 467 (1981), *hearing denied* (Cal., Aug. 26, 1981), *cert. granted* No. 81-750 (U.S., Jan. 25, 1981); Panko v. Pan Am. Fed. Sav. & Loan Ass'n, 119 Cal. App. 3d 916, 175 Cal. Rptr. 240 (1981). A closely connected issue also on appeal in *De la Cuesta* and *Panko* is whether a "law of jurisdiction" clause in the loan contract prevents the governance of the FHLBB regulations over California law. One recent New York decision, in addition to holding that FHLBB regulations preempt state law, held that a "law of jurisdiction" clause is to be read to mean the law of the state as preempted or supplemented by federal law. First Fed. Sav. & Loan Ass'n v. Jenkins, 441 N.Y.S.2d 373, 378-379 (Sup. Ct. 1981).

[98v] E.g., First Federal Sav. & Loan Ass'n v. Lockwood, 385 So. 2d 156 (Fla. Dist. Ct. App. 1980).

by courts that have considered the issue.[98w] In fact, on June 28, 1982, the United States Supreme Court reversed the anti-*Glendale* holding of the California Court of Appeals in *De la Cuesta v. Fidelity Federal Savings & Loan Ass'n.* Another recent development is pending legislation before Congress entitled the "Financial Institutions Restructuring and Services Act of 1981," which would expressly override any state law prohibition limiting the ability of federally insured lenders to enforce due-on-sale clauses.[98x]

While federally chartered savings and loans[98y] and national banks[98z] have been authorized to make adjustable-rate mortgages, these mortgages are not expected to lessen reliance on the rate adjustment purpose of the due-on-sale clause in the opinion of some commentators[98aa] because it will take years for long-term lenders to shift their portfolios into adjustable-rate instruments and there are constraints on how much these rates can be adjusted during any particular interval of time. However, the Federal Home Loan Mortgage Corporation ("Freddie Mac") recently indicated that it will not enforce due-on-sale clauses contained in nonassumable mortgages that it purchases from savings and loan associations and other institutional lenders in the secondary mortgage market.[98bb]

[98w] E.g., Price v. Florida Fed. Sav. & Loan Ass'n, 524 F. Supp. 175 (M.D. Fla. 1981); First Fed. Sav. & Loan Ass'n v. Peterson, 516 F. Supp. 732 (N.D. Fla. 1981); Dantus v. First Fed. Sav. & Loan Ass'n, 502 F. Supp. 658 (D. Colo. 1980); Bailey v. First Fed. Sav. & Loan Ass'n, 467 F. Supp. 1139 (C.D. Ill. 1979); Haugen v. Western Fed. Sav. & Loan Ass'n, 633 P.2d 497 (Colo. Ct. App. 1981).

[98x] S.1720, 97th Cong., 1st Sess. (1981).

[98y] FHLBB Resolution Nos. 79-303 and 80-231. See discussion at ¶¶ 2.02[3][a] and 3.04[3][c].

[98z] 12 C.F.R. Part 29 (Docket No. 81-10) (effective March 31, 1981).

[98aa] See Dunn & Nowinski, "Enforcement of Due-on-Transfer Clauses: An Update," 16 Real Prop., Prob. & Tr. J. 291, 313 (1981).

[98bb] See Henry, "Due-on-Sale Mortgages May Not Be," N.Y. Times, April 25, 1982, Sec. 8 at 1, col. 1.

[9] Compliance With Local Law

[a] Issuance of Building Permit and Certificate of Occupancy

Page 3-37:

Add at end of note 108:

[108] Under an innovative law recently enacted in California, which could be the precursor of similar legislation elsewhere, local governments may enter into "development agreements" with developers which will freeze the local governmental land-use regulations on parcels prior to the vesting of the de-

veloper's rights. 1979 Cal. Legis. Serv., Ch. 934, §§ 3357-3359. See Kramer, "Development Agreements: To What Extent Are They Enforceable?" 10 Real Est. L.J. 29 (1981).

[12] Satisfactory Hazard Insurance

[b] Loss Payable Clauses

Page 3-46:

Add at end of note 143.

[143] See 495 Corp. v. New Jersey Ins. Underwriting Ass'n, 173 N.J. Super. 114, 413 A.2d 630 (App. Div. 1980), where mortgagee acquired title by virtue of a deed in lieu of foreclosure and was entitled to collect under a standard mortgage clause when fire occurred after the conveyance of title to the mortgagee.

Page 3-49:

Replace present heading with the following.

[18] Joint Venturing Requirement, Convertible Mortgages, and Other Trends in Permanent Financing [Revised Heading]

Add new note at end of first sentence in subsection.

[152a] According to a recent Brookings Institute study of *real* value investment income earned by permanent lenders on fixed-rate, long-term mortgages during the last thirty years, the average contract interest rate was 9.34 percent for loans made from 1970 through 1975; however, after full repayment by 1979 (on the assumption that declining tax shelter benefits would prompt refinancing after about ten years), the average *real* interest earned was only 1.73 percent! Downs, "Real Interest Rates Short-Change Lenders," Nat'l Real Est. Inv., Oct. 1980, at 26.

Page 3-50:

Add new text and notes 153b-153y at end of first full paragraph.

Exemplifying this trend toward equity participation and fitting somewhere in the middle of the debt-equity spectrum between the equity kicker (on the debt side) and a joint venture interest (on the equity side) is a hybrid device called the "convertible mortgage" whereby the lender obtains, in addition to a fixed rate of interest and perhaps additional interest (in the form of an equity kicker), the additional right of converting the mortgage indebtedness into equity at some future date. In employing the convertible debt arrangement, the parties should pay special attention to (1) payment of interest, due-on-sale clause, prepayment privilege, and certain other loan terms; (2) the question of usury; (3) the doctrine of unconscionability; (4) whether the option may constitute a clog on the equity of redemption; (5) its status under the new Bankruptcy Law; and (6) federal tax implications, especially the status of the convertible mortgage under the new Treasury regulations for I.R.C. § 385.

Under a convertible loan arrangement, an institutional lender typically provides a developer with mortgage financing at below the market rate but receives the option to purchase all or a portion of the property after a stipulated period of time. By using the convertible mortgage, the developer is able to realize some appreciation in the value of the property without being taxed and at a below-market interest cost. He also retains full depreciation benefits during the option period, as well as a substantial portion of the cash flow. The following are two recent examples where convertible debt was used to finance real estate ventures.

The first venture was put together by Sonnenblick-Goldman Corp. and involved a shopping center owner and a foreign pension fund. The shopping center has a current market value of $77.5 million and is subject to an existing first mortgage of $44.5 million. Thus, the equity interest is $43 million. The pension fund will make a ten-year, standing second mortgage of $38 million (88 percent of the present equity) at 8 percent interest plus 88 percent of the center's cash flow after debt service on both the first and second mortgage. Thus, the owner keeps 12 percent of the cash flow plus management fees; in addition, the proceeds of both mortgages undoubtedly exceed his initial cost by a substantial amount. The lender has the right to buy the center after seven years at 14.28 times the owner's cash flow after service on the first mortgage. On the basis of present projections, that would make the total purchase price $44 million over the first mortgage (or $6 million in cash plus the $38 million second mortgage).

On the other hand, the shopping center owner also has the right to sell ("put") the property to the pension fund for $40 million if the latter does not exercise its conversion option. If neither party elects to buy or sell, then the second mortgage must be paid off. But the owner anticipates he can refinance the first mortgage at that time to raise sufficient funds.

The second convertible debt transaction involved General Motors Corp., which wanted to convert equity in an office building that it owned into cash which could be used in its automobile business. The following is a corporate version of the convertible mortgage. General Motors and Corporate Property Investors (CPI), a private real estate investment trust, entered into the following transaction involving GM's office tower on New York's Fifth Avenue. CPI bought from GM $500 million of

GM notes paying 10 percent interest and simultaneously received an option to buy the office building on January 2, 1991 for $500 million cash over an existing mortgage (with a present balance of about $50 million).

The building's present cash flow is estimated to be about $16 million, with most of the leases not due to expire until the second half of the decade, at which point rentals can be renegotiated. So CPI, as a lender rather than a buyer, receives far more in interest than it would in cash flow. At the same time, it has an interest in the property until 1991. It does lose the depreciation write-offs, but since many of CPI's shareholders are tax-exempt funds, this is not of major consequence. (GM will continue to pay the debt service on the existing mortgage.)

From GM's point of view, it realizes the $500 million in cash at once without having to pay any capital gains tax unless and until the option is exercised.

(1) *Loan Terms.*

(a) *Interest payments:* If the lender chooses not to exercise its conversion right, the lender might require a final interest payment equal to a percentage of the property's fair market value.

If the interest payments seem too great a burden on the cash flow during the early years of operation, the lender may be willing to capitalize a portion of the interest (negative amortization). However, if the capitalization of interest is treated as an "optional future advance," the lender might lose its priority over intervening creditors in the event of a foreclosure by the lender.

(b) *Loan term:* The lender could provide itself the opportunity to extend or call the loan upon sufficient written notice to the developer. It may also provide that the sale or refinancing of the premises triggers the maturity of the loan. Even though due-on-sale and due-on-refinancing clauses are invalid in many states,[153b] a special reason exists for upholding them in convertible loans. The lender may be relying on the developer's ability to operate the property so that its fair market value rises to the maximum extent possible. In addition, refinancing could significantly increase the risks to the equity position, which could threaten the lender's security interest.

(c) *Prepayment:* The lender could either impose a "lock-in" period and refuse prepayments or accept them subject to certain conditions. The lender could impose a substantial prepayment penalty over and above the final additional interest described above. The lender, however, may be unwilling to give up its conversion right no matter how

---

[153b] See discussion at ¶¶ 3.04[7] and 3.04[8].

huge a prepayment penalty it could collect. In addition, if the penalty is large enough, the borrower could argue that the arrangement is unconscionable. The lender could, in lieu of imposing a prepayment penalty, exercise its conversion right when the developer prepays. A disadvantage to the lender is that its hand is forced at a time chosen by the developer.[153c]

(d) *Control over leasing:* The lender, who is a potential owner under the convertible loan, is interested in a rental policy of maximizing rentals without impairing the future market value of the property. To ensure the existence of such a policy, the lender could demand approval power over leases materially deviating from a standard lease form it has approved in advance. However, unless the lender can establish an ownership interest in the rental property, it may have difficulty enforcing a "power of approval" clause.[153d]

(e) *Capital improvements:* The loan agreement should provide for how payments for significant maintenance and capital improvements are to be made. Payments can come from the cash flows, and can be allocated to the parties in proportion to their financial interests in the property, or can be the sole responsibility of the developer who can then raise the conversion price accordingly.

(2) *The Question of Usury.* The question of usury must be considered in a convertible loan transaction. In addressing this issue, two inquiries must be made: First, whether the value of the conversion right should be treated as additional interest, and second, whether the additional interest should be apportioned throughout the entire loan term or added onto the first year of the loan. There appears to be no precedent that is directly applicable; however, as to the first issue there is analogous case law suggesting that when the lender assumes a substantial risk of nonpayment of principal or of the full legal interest if the venture should fail, the lender would be able to charge interest in excess of the lawful maximum set by the local usury law.[153e] On the

---

[153c] See discussion at ¶ 3.04[5].

[153d] One possible solution is to have the developer give the lender an option to purchase the property under the same terms as contained in the convertible mortgage itself. The clause might be easier to enforce in an option contract than in a mortgage. See "Special Report: The Participating Convertible Loan," Mortgage & Real Est. Executives Rep., Dec. 15, 1981 at 1, 3.

[153e] See Thomassen v. Carr, 250 Cal. App. 2d 341, 58 Cal. Rptr. 297 (1967) (where the entire interest was at risk); Diversified Enterprises, Inc., v. West, 141 So. 2d 27 (Fla. Dist. Ct. App. 1962) (where both the principal and interest were at risk). See discussion at ¶ 5.05[8].

other hand, if in addition to charging a market rate of interest that is not subject to a bona fide contingency the lender demands and receives a bonus payment in the form of property at a price below its true value, such payment may be viewed as additional interest.[153f] However, there is a case law suggesting in the case of an option to purchase property, the value of the option *at the time it is granted* rather than the market value of the property at the time the option is exercised is the value of the bonus payment that will be taken into account (along with the stated interest) in determining whether the loan is usurious.[153g] As to the second issue, the general rule is that in testing a contract for usury the courts will take into consideration the entire period of the loan so that an option-styled bonus payment or collateral advantage (like discounts and other add-ons) will probably be apportioned over the contract term of the loan.[153h]

Based on the foregoing, in the case of a convertible mortgage, a court might be prompted to find that the option to purchase renders the loan usurious if (1) the stated interest rate is close to the market rate, especially if it is at or near the maximum set by the local usury statute; (2) the option price is a bargain price that is not related to the market value of the property at the time the option is exercised; (3) the appreciation in the value of the property exceeds normal appreciation due to inflation; and (4) there is substantial disparity in bargaining power (in favor of the lender) at the time the loan and option to purchase are arranged by the parties.

(3) *The Doctrine of Unconscionability.* As noted in the Introduction,[153i] the doctrine of unconscionability, as enunciated in U.C.C. § 2-302, has been incorporated into the Uniform Land Transactions Act (ULTA).[153j] The Act, which applies to consensual security interests, allows a party to avoid its obligations under a contract because performance has become "impracticable by the occurrence of a contingency the risk of which the parties did not assume would be borne" by the party and the comments would include within the ambit of "contingency," fluctuations in market value.[153k] Although the ULTA has yet to be adopted by state legislatures, some commentators are of the opinion that "unconscionability" as a legal concept may influence courts

---

[153f] See ¶ 5.05[8].

[153g] See Regents of Univ. of Cal. v. Superior Court of Alameda County, 17 Cal. 3d 533, 551 P.2d 844, 131 Cal. Rptr. 228 (1976).

[153h] See discussion at ¶ 5.02[4][b].

[153i] See p. xxxiii. See discussion at ¶ 3.04[3][c][5].

[153j] See Uniform Land Transactions Act § 1-311, 13 U.L.A. 539, 574 (1980).

[153k] *Id.* § 2-407, 13 U.L.A. at 626.

in their application of usury standards. Perhaps one explanation why courts have not expressly applied the doctrine to interest rates, unless the transaction was also a violation of usury law, is that the usury statutes and the exemptions thereunder constitute statements of public policy by state legislatures that courts are hesitant to override.[153l] Nevertheless, it appears possible that a borrower could raise the unconscionability issue in a transaction where the mortgagee obtains an option to purchase property that skyrockets in value so that the lender is not merely shielded from the effects of inflation but also receives a windfall while assuming no risks other than those that are traditionally associated with a mortgage loan.[153m]

There appears to be no precedent that is directly applicable, but the following case decision is instructive by analogy. In *Humble Oil & Refining Co. v. Doerr*,[153n] a case directly involving the rule against clogging a mortgagor's equity of redemption, an oil company brought an action for specific performance of its option to purchase service station property at any time for $150,000 under a "two-party" lease arrangement where the company leased the station from the defendant-owner at a rental equal to the debt-service payments on a mortgage loan obtained by the owner to finance construction of some new improvements on the land and the company then subleased the property back to the defendant for one year at the same rental. As collateral security the owner assigned its interest in the master lease to the construction lender. Additionally, there was a cross-default provision to the leases in the mortgage note, there was no obligation to sublease back to the mortgagor in the lease agreement, and the lease was entered into by the owner-mortgagor solely for the purpose of obtaining more favorable mortgage loan terms. The lease arrangement, in addition to the option feature, guaranteed the company-lessee with an outlet for its oil products, with little likelihood of any capital outlay, and, by taking the option, put the company in a favorable position where it had nothing to lose but much to gain if the value of the property exceeded the option price. The court held that even if the prohibition

---

[153l] See Kane, "The Mortgagee's Option to Purchase Mortgaged Property," in *Financing Real Estate During the Inflationary 80s* at 123, 126 (ABA 1981).

[153m] Suppose, for example, that a building originally cost $1 million and when the conversion right is exercised ten years later its worth rises to $3 million. An inflation rate of 8 percent would account for about half the gain; the other half would be due to the developer's management of the property. The developer could argue that the lender would be receiving a windfall if it benefitted from the "true growth" as well as from the growth due to inflation.

[153n] 123 N.J. Super. 530, 303 A.2d 898 (Ch. Div. 1973).

against options that clog the mortgagor's equity of redemption was not applicable, the option was not enforceable because in reality no lease was ever intended, the option was nothing more than a price paid for the mortgage, and "in the eyes of equity it [was] in fact unconscionable and oppressive." Since the property was worth $240,000 when the company sought to enforce the option, the company had superior bargaining power, and the rental under the master lease did not exceed the sublease rental, virtually all the benefits wrought by the transaction inured to the company.[153o]

(4) *Clogging the Equity of Redemption.* Another legal problem the lender faces when it obtains an option to purchase the mortgaged property is that the option may be invalidated on the grounds that it constitutes a clog on the mortgagor's traditional right at equity to redeem his property prior to a foreclosure decree by satisfying the outstanding mortgage indebtedness. By analogy, courts look askance at deeds in lieu of foreclosure and other transactions where the mortgagor loses his interest in the property because forfeiture is regarded with such judicial disfavor.[153p] For example, in the *Humble Oil & Refining Co.* case, the court held that the option to purchase was in essence an equitable mortgage securing the mortgagor's payment of the indebtedness that "clogged" the mortgagor's equitable right to redeem the property since on default the mortgagor would forfeit his interest at a fixed price as in the case of a prearranged deed in lieu of foreclosure.[153q] However, the court acknowledged that a different rule might apply where (1) the optionee has a right of first refusal,[153r] (2) the optionee is a true joint venturer, or (3) the option is granted in connection with a "three party" lease agreement.[153s]

[153o] *Id.* at 553-563, 303 A.2d at 910-915.

[153p] E.g., Carter Oil Co. v. Durvin, 376 Ill. 398, 34 N.E.2d 407 (1973). See Kane, note 153*l* supra at 127-139; discussion of judicial foreclosure at ¶ 3.08[4][g][iv], and adjustable-rate mortgages at ¶ 3.04[3][c](5).

[153q] 123 N.J. Super. at 544-550, 303 A.2d at 905-909.

[153r] But cf. Trecker v. Langel, 298 N.W.2d 289 (Iowa 1980), where the defendant obtained a thirty-year "preemptive right" (right of first refusal) to purchase eighty acres of farmland at $650 per acre and the court, citing *Restatement of Property* §§ 413(2)(a) and 406(c), held that the so-called option agreement was possibly in violation of the rule against perpetuities and definitely an illegal restraint on alienation because the property could be offered to the defendant at much less than its market value, which would discourage any sale of the property by the plaintiff. *Id.* at 291-292. As in *Humble Oil,* the court was influenced by the overreaching conduct of the right-holder. The lesson to be learned from the *Trecker* decision is that sloppy draftsmanship by the mortgagee could convert an otherwise enforceable option to purchase into an unenforceable preemptive right.

[153s] 123 N.J. Super. at 559-560, 303 A.2d at 913-914. See also Coursey v. Fairchild, 436 P.2d 35 (Okla. 1967) (where court found mortgagee's

(5) *Bankruptcy.* Under the Bankruptcy Reform Act of 1978, a lender's claim will be disallowed if the loan is found to be usurious. The principal problem with a mortgagee's option to purchase the mortgaged property (and sale-leaseback) appears to be the power of a trustee to reject any executory contract (or unexpired leasehold estate).[153t]

(6) *Federal Tax Implications.* Since the at-risk rules do not apply to real estate, an owner of leveraged income-producing property can deduct losses in excess of his equity investment by taking depreciation deductions on the full leveraged cost of the property even if its acquisition or construction was funded by nonrecourse financing. Accordingly, a notable tax difference between ordinary mortgage financing and a convertible debt or joint venture arrangement is that the owner-borrower is forced to forfeit depreciation deductions or, in the case of a partnership, to share the deductions with the lender-partner in accordance with the partnership agreement subject to the limitation that the allocation must have substantial economic effect.[153u] Moreover, if the owner elects to depreciate the property over the new ACRS straight-line fifteen-year period to avoid recapture problems, the amount of the deductions will remain constant and not decline over time so that any conversion prior to the end of the fifteen-year period could involve a substantial loss to the borrower in tax shelter benefits.[153v]

A fee mortgage coupled with a mortgagee's right to purchase or convert the loan indebtedness into equity resembles a sale-leaseback plus leasehold mortgage type of split financing[153w] except that the lender's equity capital is provided at or near the end of the loan term rather than at the beginning. In a sale-leaseback, if the option to repurchase stipulates an unusually low price and otherwise lacks the substantive appearance of a sale, the transaction may be treated by the IRS as a disguised sale and both a loss on the alleged sale and rental deductions on the leaseback may be disallowed to the "seller-lessee."[153x] Conversely, in the case of a convertible mortgage, the IRS might reclassify the convertible loan as a sale if the interest rate is below market and the option price is substantially less than either the indebtedness

---

taking of mineral rights on the mortgaged property to be a clogging of the equity of redemption). But cf. MacArthur v. North Palm Beach Util., Inc., 202 So. 2d 181 (Fla. 1967) (where court enforced mortgagee's option to purchase property but option was incidental to a sale and not the mortgage transaction); Smith v. Shattls, 66 N.J. Super. 430, 169 A.2d 503 (App. Div. 1961) (where court enforced option to purchase in mortgage that was supported by additional consideration).

[153t] See discussion at ¶ 4.02[12][b][v].
[153u] I.R.C. § 704(b). See discussion at ¶ 1.05[3][b].
[153v] See discussion at ¶ 1.05[2].
[153w] See discussion at ¶ 8.09[2].
[153x] See ¶ 6.04[3][b].

or current market value of the property—especially if there is non-recourse in excess of the market value of the property, since the lender would most certainly exercise the option and during the option period the real risk of gain or loss would arguably be on the lender. In such event, the lender would have to take the depreciation deductions and the borrower would be forced to report a gain on the constructive sale before the option is exercised. Returning to our example involving *General Motors Corp.* at ¶ 3.04[18], the transaction would appear to pass muster because though the interest rate is below market, it is not unreasonably low and the option price is above the current market value.

If the borrower is a corporation, the convertible mortgage transaction may run afoul of the new proposed debt-equity Treasury Regulations under I.R.C. § 385 where the principal value of the debt instrument is in the form of an equity return to the lender.[153y]

[153y] See discussion at ¶ 12.01[5].

¶ 3.06 REMEDIES FOR BREACH OF MORTGAGE LOAN COMMITMENT

Page 3-59:

Add to end of note 178.

[178] There is also case law holding that the doctrine of substantial performance of a contract is inapplicable to a loan commitment agreement. E.g., Johnson v. American Nat'l Ins. Co., 126 Ariz. 219, 613 P.2d 1275 (Ct. App. 1980), where the borrower was unsuccessful in obtaining refund of the commitment fee after failing to complete construction of an office building in a timely manner. But cf. Selective Builders Inc. v. Hudson City Sav. Bank, 137 N.J.Super. 500, 349 A.2d 564 (Ch. Div. 1975), where strict compliance with the terms of commitment was not required.

Add new note 178a at end of last sentence of runover paragraph.

[178a] See Butler v. Westgate State Bank, 226 Kan. 581, 602 P.2d 1276 (1979), where plaintiff-borrower was allowed to recover his out-of-pocket expenses but evidence of lost profits was held to be too speculative to comply with the rule that lost profits must be proved with reasonable certainty. But cf. Welch v. United States Bancorp Realty & Mortgage Trust, 286 Ore. 673, 596 P.2d 947 (1979), where the court held that the developer, in proving damages, was not confined to the cost of obtaining financing elsewhere but was entitled to recoup lost profits from the nonperformance of a development agreement with the lender-defendant to the extent that the damages were reasonably foreseeable, notwithstanding that the development plan involved a somewhat speculative business venture.

Page 3-61:

Add at end of Selective Builders cite in note 182.

[182] See First Nat'l Bank v. Commonwealth Fed. Sav. & Loan Ass'n, 610 F.2d 164 (3d Cir. 1979), where specific performance of a standby commitment for a long-term permanent loan on a shopping mall was granted to the borrower who had offered a bond guaranteeing completion of the allegedly minor unfinished work which the defendant-lender refused to accept. The court also noted that an award of damages would not have been susceptible to accurate calculation since the value of the mall was set by witnesses as between $1.5 million and $3.5 million. But cf. 805 Third Ave. Co. v. New York Life Ins. Co. and Metropolitan Life Ins. Co., N.Y.L.J., July 22, 1981, at 10, where the New York Supreme Court dismissed as premature a borrower's action for declaratory judgment or specific performance of a $65 million loan commitment. The borrower alleged anticipatory breach of the commitment but was unable to plead performance of the conditions precedent in the contract (e.g., completion of construction, execution of leases with certain tenants) because the time for performance had not yet arrived. In addition, the defendant's alleged breach was susceptible to a calculation of money damages. See also American Bancshares Mortgage Co. v. Empire Home Loans, Inc., 568 F.2d 1124 (5th Cir. 1978), where specific performance against permanent lender of its takeout commitment (under buy-sell agreement) denied to plaintiff-construction lender where plaintiff failed to establish that its remedy at law was inadequate.

¶ 3.07 THE STANDBY "LOAN COMMITMENT"

[2] The "Fundable Standby"

Page 3-62:

Change Aetna Business Corporation *to* Barclays American/Business Credit, Inc.

¶ 3.08 DRAFTING THE MORTGAGE/DEED OF TRUST

[4] The Mortgage/Deed of Trust

[a] Definitions

Page 3-67:

Add the following at end of note 205.

[205] But see U.C.C. § 9-313(6), which accords lien priority to a real estate construction mortgage or refinancing over a purchase-money security interest under certain circumstances.

Add at end of note 210.

[210] , aff'd 440 U.S. 715 (1978).

¶ 3.08[4][a]

Page 3-68:

Add new text and notes 216a-216i at end of page.

In a 4-3 decision, the New York Court of Appeals held that a dragnet clause is a continuing security for a floating debt up to the amount of the original loan.[216a] The mortgagors purchased a home and executed a $2,500 mortgage on the home. The mortgage contained a dragnet clause stating that the house, in addition to securing the $2,500 debt, was to stand as security for "any and all further loans or indebtedness owed or to be owed by the mortgagor to the mortgagee." The maximum debt to be secured by the home at any given time was to be $2,500.

Seven years after purchasing the home, the mortgagors borrowed $6,875 from the same mortgagee to purchase a parcel of land. The new mortgage instrument provided that the $6,875 was secured by the land and made no mention of the home. The mortgagors then conveyed the home to their mother, who paid the balance of the $2,500 loan in due course. When the sons fell behind in their payments on the land loan, the mortgagee foreclosed on the land. The mortgagee, left with a foreclosure deficiency of $3,000, notified the mother that she was liable for $2,500 under the dragnet clause.

When the mother refused to pay, the bank, seeking enforcement of the dragnet clause, brought a foreclosure action against the mother. The case was brought to the Court of Appeals after the trial court and Appellate Division held in favor of the mortgagee. In affirming the decision of the lower courts, the Court of Appeals held that the dragnet clause survived repayment of the original loan and extended to all other loans made by the mortgagee to the mortgagors. It based its holding on the technical distinction between a dragnet clause and a future advance clause. The distinction, it stated, was that a future advance clause contemplates actual loans to be made to the mortgagor in finite amounts, while a dragnet clause operates to secure loans of unspecified amounts which may or may not be made, providing a limit only on the amount of debt that may be secured at any one time. Once the Court of Appeals identified the loan provision as a dragnet clause instead of a future advance clause, it ended its analysis. Its analysis did not include the following important considerations:

(1) Whether the clause was ambiguous, and, therefore, whether any ambiguity should be resolved against the drafter.

(2) Whether dragnet clauses apply to subsequent debts that are separately secured

---

[216a] State Bank v. Fioravanti, 51 N.Y.2d 638 (1980).

(3) Whether transfer of the collateral to a third party may cut off the applicability of the dragnet clause

(4) Whether the original collateral could secure an unlimited number of debts over an unlimited period of time

In another recent decision,[216b] the Utah Supreme Court set forth factors that courts have considered in determining the applicability of dragnet clauses. They are as follows:

(1) The relationship between original and future debts and similarity in their character and type

(2) Separate security of the future debt

(3) Assignment of the future debt from a third party to the original lender

(4) Discharge of the entire original debt

(5) Transfer of the collateral on the original debt to a third party[216c]

A sixth factor, the contents of the security agreement in connection with a subsequent loan, played a large role in the Utah Supreme Court's decision. Not only did the security agreement fail to mention that the subsequent loan was secured by the original collateral, but it also contained an integration clause which recited that the security agreement contained the entire agreement between the parties.[216d]

The Supreme Judicial Court of Maine[216e] decided to look beyond the objective indicia cited by the Utah Supreme Court, and held that extrinsic evidence of the parties' intentions was admissible. The debtors, owners of a marina, borrowed $145,000 in 1976 from a bank in order to finance an inventory of boats. To secure the loan, the debtors executed a mortgage deed on land and buildings that they owned. The mortgage deed recited that it stood as security for the amount loaned and for all future advances made by the bank up to a total of $250,000. In 1977, the debtors borrowed $53,000 from the same bank on a promissory note that stated it was secured by a separate agreement, which did not, in fact, exist. In 1978, two more notes totaling $47,000 were given to secure two new loans. These notes stated that they were secured by the 1976 mortgage. When the bank demanded payment on the three notes and the demand was not met, the bank instituted an

---

[216b] First Sec. Bank v. Shiew, 609 P.2d 952 (Utah 1980).
[216c] *Id.* at 955.
[216d] *Id.* at 957.
[216e] Canal Nat'l Bank v. Becker, 431 A.2d 71 (Me. 1981).

action to foreclose the 1976 mortgage. The trial court held that the dragnet clause applied to the three notes and ordered foreclosure. The issue on appeal was whether extrinsic evidence could be admitted to interpret the dragnet clause. The bank argued that the dragnet clause was unambiguous and ought to stand alone in evidence. The court disagreed, stating that a dragnet clause is, by its very nature, ambiguous. The dragnet clause constitutes, at most, an offer by the mortgagor to extend the security of the mortgage to future advances as and if they are made. It becomes operative only when the mortgagee accepts the offer.[216f] Therefore, the court held, the parties' intentions must be considered both at the time of the original mortgage and upon the making of subsequent advances. Their intentions cannot be presumed solely by reason of the existence of the dragnet clause.[216g] The court then ordered the case remanded for further proceedings, as it was not clear from the trial record what the parties' intentions were. At the subsequent trial, the bank would bear the burden of showing that both parties intended the subsequent loans to be included within the dragnet clause.[216h]

To avoid a *Becker* outcome, the lender should spell out its precise intentions in the loan agreement with regard to the extension of collateral from one loan to another. More importantly, the lender's intentions regarding the collateral must again be made clear at the time any subsequent advance is made.

The lender should also spell out its intentions in loan agreements with joint borrowers, who may request additional advances as separate borrowers. To make a dragnet clause extend the whole mortgage security to the future debts of one of the joint borrowers, the language the lender should use in the dragnet clause is "made to the mortgagors, or either or any of them." This language enables the lender to avoid an adverse judgment as was the case in a recent decision by the Iowa Supreme Court.[216i] The defendants, husband and wife, jointly borrowed $69,000 from the plaintiff on a note secured by a mortgage on a seventy-nine-acre tract of land which they owned as tenants in common. The bank inserted a dragnet clause in the mortgage making the land security for future advances "made to the Mortgagors" of up to $31,000. Subsequently, the husband alone borrowed an additional $31,000. When the husband defaulted on the $31,000 loan, the bank declared the entire amount of the borrowers' debt immediately due and payable.

[216f] *Id.* at 73.
[216g] *Id.*
[216h] *Id.* at 75.
[216i] Farmers Trust & Sav. Bank v. Manning, 311 N.W.2d 285 (Iowa 1981).

The bank then brought an action seeking a foreclosure on the tract of land. The lower court held that while the entire $69,000 note was secured by the tract of land, the $31,000 in notes executed by the husband alone were secured by the land to the extent of the husband's interest therein. An appeal was taken to the Iowa Supreme Court because neither party was satisfied with the lower court's decision pertaining to the $31,000 debt. The bank claimed that the dragnet clause extended the security to all future loans made to either of the parties. The borrowers, on the other hand, claimed that the clause should be limited in scope to the loans made jointly to them. The Iowa Supreme Court read the language of the dragnet clause, "made to the Mortgagor," as referring to advances made to both borrowers jointly, and not to one or the other individually. An intention to apply the dragnet clause to advances made to either borrower separately would have been evidenced by "either or any of them" language. Accordingly, the lower court's judgment pertaining to the $31,000 debt was reversed, and the land was held not to secure any of that debt.

Page 3-69:

Add to note 220 after Franklin v. Community Federal S&L Ass'n cite.

[220], *rev'd on other grounds* 629 F.2d 514 (8th Cir. 1980).

[g] Default Remedies

Page 3-80:

Add at end of note 260.

[260]; but see Comer v. Hargrave, 93 N.M. 170, 598 P.2d 213 (1979) (acceleration denied where lender failed to provide borrower with notice of its intention to accelerate the loan indebtedness).

Page 3-86:

Add at end of note 286.

[286], *cert. denied* 434 U.S. 1046 (1978).

Add to note 288 after Federal Nat'l Mortgage Ass'n v. Howlett cite.

[288], *rehearing denied* 423 U.S. 1026 (1975).

Add at end of note 288.

[288] Garfinkle v. Superior Court, 578 P.2d 925 (Cal. 1978).

Page 3-90:

Add at end of note 304.

³⁰⁴ ; cf. Dime Sav. Bank v. Altman, 249 A.D. 174, 291 N.Y.S. 417 (1936), *aff'd* 275 N.Y. 62, 9 N.E.2d 778 (1937) (absent such express provision in the mortgage, mortgagee was held liable in damages for trespass after entering into possession against the vigorous protest of mortgagor); 107 Shore Road Corp. v. Gatnick Realty Corp., 40 Misc. 2d 455, 243 N.Y.S.2d 447 (Sup. Ct. 1963) (possession not granted where mortgage clause provided mortgagee with right to collect rents but not the right of possession).

Add at end of runover paragraph.

Finally, a leasehold mortgagee in possession of a leasehold estate must adhere to the requirements of the Uniform Commercial Code that protect the mortgagor's rights to the secured property.[304a]

[304a] E.g., E. Landau Indus., Inc. v. 385 McLean Corp., 58 Misc. 2d 725, 296 N.Y.S.2d 707 (Sup. Ct. 1969) (mortgage subject to U.C.C. Article 9). See Bowman, "Real Estate Interests as Security Under the U.C.C.: The Scope of Article Nine," 12 U.C.C.L.J. 99, 113-116 (1979).

Page 3-91:

Add to the end of note 316.

[316] See Metropolitan Life Ins. Co. v. Foote, 95 Mich. App. 399, 290 N.W.2d 158 (1980) (per curiam); Ames v. Pardue, 389 So. 2d 927 (Ala. 1980).

Page 3-92:

Add new text and note 317a at end of subsection.

Loan Workouts. Workouts are entered into with debtors by creditors who want to maximize their total recovery and avoid timely and costly bankruptcy proceedings. Three types of workouts are: extensions, compositions, and combinations. Creditors entering into an extension agree to reschedule debt payments to coincide with the debtor's cash flow or selling seasons. Payment in full will occur over the repayment period. In a composition, some or all creditors agree to reduce the amount of their debt, generally by pro rata reductions. In a combination, payments to some creditors are reduced, while payments to other creditors are deferred.

One advantage of a workout is that it permits a generally sound and well-managed business to continue, and gives it the opportunity to enjoy upward cycles or strong seasons for selling. The workout shields the business from the negative impact that formal bankruptcy proceedings may have on customers, employees, and trade. Another advantage of workouts is that they enable creditors to restructure their obligations so that a subsequent bankruptcy proceeding, if one is necessary, can be made shorter and less complex. Other advantages include the continued accrual of interest during a workout (which would be terminated by a bankruptcy proceeding), the speed, and the lower legal and accounting costs involved.

A problem the creditor participating in a workout often faces is the treatment of new advances as preferences or fraudulent transfers, making them recoverable by a trustee in bankruptcy in a subsequent proceeding. Fortunately for creditors, Section 67(d)(3) of the Bankruptcy Act has not been adopted by the Bankruptcy Code. Under Section 67(d)(3), new loans that were knowingly used to pay preferences could be attacked by the trustee in bankruptcy as fraudulent. To avoid preference treatment under Section 547(b) of the Bankruptcy Code, the creditor participating in a workout should have at least a reasonable expectation that a bankruptcy proceeding will not commence within ninety days. Payment terms to participating creditors should be tightened so that the forty-five-day preference exception under Section 547(c)(2) can be utilized. The extension of the ninety-day preference period to one year for "insiders" under Section 547(b) can be avoided as long as the participating creditors do not qualify as "insiders" under Section 101(25) of the Bankruptcy Code.[317a]

[317a] For a more detailed discussion of the impact of the Bankruptcy Code on loan workouts, see Yellin, "Workouts and the Bankruptcy Reform Act of 1978," in *The Bankruptcy Reform Act for Bank Counsel* 453-469 (Practicing Law Institute 1981).

[i] Assignment of Leases and Rents

Page 3-96:

Add at end of note 326.

[326] ; see Majestic Builders Corp. v. Harris, 598 F.2d 238 (D.C. Cir. 1979), where the court held assignment of rental language that granted the owners permission to continue to collect rents but terminated the permission upon default as to rents "due or collected thereafter" to be a mere pledge of rental income and ineffective to protect the mortgagee against the rights of a judgment creditor.

Page 3-98:

Add to note 330 following first sentence of third paragraph.

330 490 F.2d 1141, 1143 (9th Cir. 1974) (citing In re Hotel St. James, Co., 65 F.2d 82 (9th Cir. 1933)). By contrast, in the case of an absolute assignment (as opposed to an assignment of rents as additional collateral), in California the rents are regarded as immediately assigned to the mortgagee or deed of trust beneficiary upon execution of the mortgage or deed of trust, and upon a default the lender has the automatic right to receive the rents. See "Disposition of Rents After Mortgage Default," 16 Real Prop., Prob. & Tr. J. 835, 843 (1981). See Kinnison v. Guaranty Liquidating Corp., 18 Cal. 2d 256, 115 P.2d 450 (1941) (dictum). But cf. Malsman v. Brandler, 230 Cal. App. 2d 922, 41 Cal. Rptr. 438 (1964).

Add at the end of footnote 330.

330 ; Taylor v. Brennan, 621 S.W.2d 592 (Tex. 1981) (assignment characterized as a pledge and therefore conditional, not absolute); Levin v. Carney, 161 Ohio St. 513, 120 N.E.2d 92 (1954). However, even in some title-theory jurisdictions, the mortgagee is required to take some affirmative action to enforce a pledge or assignment of rents clause. See, e.g., Prusaczyk v. Kulo, 17 Conn. Supp. 348 (Super. Ct. 1951).

Page 3-99:

Add at the end of note 331.

331 See Nat'l Bank of N. Am. v. Tengard Realty Corp., 34 A.D.2d 934, 312 N.Y.S.2d 169 (1970). Even a mortgage clause that purports to assign the rents and leases as of the date of the mortgage requires some affirmative action on the part of the mortgagee. See, e.g., Kelley Bros. v. Primex Equities Corp., 46 Misc. 2d 255, 259 N.Y.S.2d 594 (Sup. Ct. 1965).

Chapter 4

CONSTRUCTION FINANCING

		Page
¶ 4.02	Terms and Conditions of Construction Financing as Determined by Construction Loan Application-Commitment	S4-1
	[4] Rate of Interest	S4-1
	[6] Lien Priority Over Land Mortgages and Mechanics' Liens	S4-2
	[a] Problems of Mechanics' and Materialmen's Liens	S4-2
	[i] Lien Priorities Under State Law	S4-2
	[ii] Doctrine of "Obligatory" vs. "Optional" Advances	S4-3
	[8] Assurances That Project Will Be Completed	S4-3
	[e] Contractor's Guarantee	S4-3
	[12] Bankruptcy of Borrower	S4-3
	[b] Implications of Bankruptcy Reform Act of 1978 for Real Estate Financing	S4-3
	[14] Checklist of Construction Loan Agreement Terms [New]	S4-4
¶ 4.03	Closing the Construction Loan	S4-5
	[2] Construction Mortgage	S4-5
	[d] Prohibition of Cash Distributions	S4-5
¶ 4.04	Disbursement of Construction Loan Funds Under Building Loan Agreement	S4-6
	[8] Construction Lender's Remedies Against Defaulting Developer	S4-6
¶ 4.05	Buy-Sell Agreement and the Final Takeout Stage	S4-6

¶ 4.02 TERMS AND CONDITIONS OF CONSTRUCTION FINANCING AS DETERMINED BY CONSTRUCTION LOAN APPLICATION-COMMITMENT

[4] Rate of Interest

Page 4-13:

Add new text at end of subsection.

Because of the recent increased spread between the prime rate and the cost of bank funds, certain money-center banks have been offering

¶ 4.02[6]

the following interest rate pricings (as alternatives to the float-above-prime method) with respect to construction loans:

(1) *CD Rates.* The certificate of deposit rate is the amount that the bank is paying on large certificates in the New York broker market. It is essentially the cost of "current funds," which can be substantially lower than the prime rate (see Appendix B).

(2) *Libor (London Inter Bank Offering Rate).* Libor is the rate of interest at which dollar deposits in the Eurodollar market would be offered by the commercial bank to major banks in the London market (see Appendix B).

(3) *Letter of Credit Backed Construction Loans.* In this case a bank receives funds from a pension fund at a fixed rate pegged above the T-bill rate backed by the bank's letter of credit. The bank loans this money to the borrower at a fixed albeit higher rate to allow for a spread of profit.

(4) *Matched Funding.* In the case of matched funding, the bank places a certificate of deposit at a fixed rate with an investor for a one- or two-year period. It then lends the money to the borrower at a higher rate, but allows the borrower to invest the funds in a Repo Account until the funds are drawn down monthly.

[6] Lien Priority Over Land Mortgages and Mechanics' Liens

Page 4-14:

Add new note 31a after comma in third line of subsection.

[31a] E.g., Woodmere N. Inv. Fund Ltd. v. Guardian Mortgage Investors, 393 So. 2d 563 (Fla. Dist. Ct. App. 1981), where the continued existence of a mechanic's lien justified the construction lender's nonperformance of a commitment letter even though the original $3.2 million loan had been drawn down and a written commitment for an additional $850,000 had been issued.

[a] Problems of Mechanics' and Materialmen's Liens

[i] Lien Priorities Under State Law

Page 4-15:

Add at end of note 37.

[37] But cf. Kilgore Hardware & Bldg. Supply Inc. v. Mullins, 387 So. 2d 834 (Ala. 1980) (unrecorded construction loan mortgage accorded lien priority over materialman's lien, where materialman knew of the existence of the mortgage prior to his delivery of materials even though mortgage was not recorded until after work had commenced). See Bank of Cave City v. Hill, 266 Ark. 727, 587 S.W.2d 833 (1979).

Add at end of note 39.

[39] Recent Michigan case law appears instructive on this issue. See Williams & Works, Inc. v. Springfield Corp., 408 Mich. 732, 293 N.W.2d 304 (1980), 81 Mich. App. 355, 265 N.W.2d 328 rev'g (1978) (off-site engineering services not sufficiently visible); Portage Realty Corp. v. Baas, 100 Mich. App. 260, 298 N.W.2d 892 (1980) (soil samples and topological surveys insufficiently visible on-site activity). But cf. Michigan Roofing & Sheet Metal, Inc. v. Dufty Road Properties, 100 Mich. App. 577, 298 N.W.2d 923 (1980) (*Williams & Works* decision distinguished where construction material visibly delivered to jobsite prior to execution and recordation of mortgage).

[ii] Doctrine of "Obligatory" vs. "Optional" Advances

Page 4-16:

Add at end of note 43.

[43] E.g., S & S Ceiling & Partition Co. v. Calvon Corp., 63 Ohio App. 2d 150, 410 N.E.2d 777 (1979).

[8] Assurances That Project Will Be Completed

[e] Contractor's Guarantee

Page 4-33:

Add at end of note 87.

[87] For an example of how a sloppily drafted completion assurance agreement can prevent indemnification and otherwise cause problems for the construction lender, see Modern Am. Mortgage Corp. v. Skyline Park, 614 F.2d 1009 (5th Cir. 1980).

[12] Bankruptcy of Borrower

[b] Implications of Bankruptcy Reform Act of 1978 for Real Estate Financing

Page 4-38:

Add note 96a to last sentence of subsection.

[96a] See discussion of loan work-outs and the Bankruptcy Reform Act at ¶ 3.08[4][g].

Page 4-38:

Add new ¶ 4.02[14].

[14] Checklist of Construction Loan Agreement Terms [New]

☐ Require borrower's warranty as to its title to the real estate and as to accuracy and sufficiency of plans and specifications.

☐ Require that lien of lender be paramount. Provide that no further advances will be made if interim title examination discloses intervening lien, and for title insurance covering each advance.

☐ Provide for advancing funds as work progresses—and for 10 percent retainage to assure complete performance:
  (a) Initial advance when building under roof, or 20 percent completed, or other requirement, with fact to be determined by lender's inspector;
  (b) Additional advances as work progresses—limit as to number by specifying percentages of completion or maximum number of draws, as above, subject to inspection by lender.

☐ Furnish lender with contractor's sworn statement setting forth names of subcontractors and amounts due, and showing total contract price. If borrower is not the builder, he should vouch for the accuracy of the sworn statement (at least as between himself and lender).

☐ Lender to be furnished by borrower with executed copies of all construction contracts and subcontracts, change orders, invoices, bids, estimates, and bonds required by lender; and lender is authorized to verify the foregoing.

☐ Require, prior to opening of loan deposit by borrower in cash or lien, waivers of difference between total cost and net amount of loan proceeds in order to assure that funds are available to complete the project.

☐ Determine method of charging and paying interest on the loan balance (that is, is interest to be charged on the entire balance set forth in the note from the date the funds are made available, or from the date of the first disbursement, or is the borrower required to pay interest only on amounts actually disbursed?).

☐ Require that waivers of lien (in form satisfactory to the lender) be presented in connection with each disbursement. If title coverage is being obtained, these may be presented to the title company.

☐ Indicate that no further advances need be made if it appears at any time that the lender does not have on hand sufficient funds to complete the construction.

☐ Provide for improvements to be completed in accordance with plans and specifications, with lender having the option to withhold further advances in the event of unauthorized deviations, change orders, or extras.

☐ Reserve right to inspect at reasonable times, and indicate affirmatively that inspections are solely for lender's benefit. Set forth that borrower has selected contractor, subcontractors, and materialmen, and that the lender has no responsibility for them or for the quality of their materials or workmanship.

☐ Set forth time for commencement and completion of construction.

☐ Place upon the borrower the burden of completing the project with reasonable diligence, and make it borrower's responsibility (whether or not he is the contractor) to complete free and clear of liens and in accordance with plans and specifications.

☐ Provide clearly that (1) lender is not the payout agent of borrower, but is checking and requiring documents (including lien waivers) solely for lender's protection; and (2) borrower has no right to rely on any procedures required by lender. It should affirmatively appear that the only consideration passing from lender to borrower is the loan proceeds.

☐ Provide that in the event lender requires payout orders executed by borrower prior to the making of any disbursement, any payouts made pursuant to such an order will, as between borrower and lender, be conclusively presumed to be proper disbursements of the loan proceeds.

☐ Remedies on default:
(a) Complete construction as attorney-in-fact for borrower, adding disbursements to balance due on loan
(b) Withhold disbursements
(c) Accelerate the debt and foreclose for balance disbursed

Courtesy of The Business Lawyer, Chicago, Ill.

¶ 4.03 CLOSING THE CONSTRUCTION LOAN

[2] Construction Mortgage

[d] Prohibition of Cash Distributions

Page 4-54:

Add to note 166 after Whitley v. Klauber cite.

[166] *aff'd* 51 N.Y.2d 555, 416 N.E.2d 569, 435 N.Y.S.2d 568 (1980).

¶ 4.04 DISBURSEMENT OF CONSTRUCTION LOAN FUNDS UNDER BUILDING LOAN AGREEMENT

[8] Construction Lender's Remedies Against Defaulting Developer

Page 4-67:

Add text and notes 211a-211c following runover paragraph.

The Wyoming Supreme Court[211a] recently held that when a loan is secured by both real estate and other property, the lender need not look to the other property before foreclosing on the realty. The plaintiff loaned defendants $70,000 to purchase and develop a parcel of land. Plaintiff took a mortgage on the land and, as additional security, a $10,000 certificate of deposit from defendants. Defendants made all monthly payments, but failed to pay property taxes and assessments, to discharge certain liens filed against the land, and to adequately insure the mortgaged land. Covenants requiring all of these payments of defendant existed in the mortgage documents.

The plaintiff declared the loan to be in default and brought an action for foreclosure on the land. The defendants' response was twofold: They argued that the loan was not in default, and that foreclosure on the land was not an available remedy because of the existence of the $10,000 certificate of deposit. Defendants lost on both counts.

The court held these encumbrances, small as they were in comparison to the value of the property, to constitute events of default justifying foreclosure.[211b] The court also held that plaintiff had a choice of remedies. It could either foreclose on the land or seize the $10,000 certificate of deposit. The court did not want to be put in the position of determining that certain breaches of the security agreement were too insubstantial to justify foreclosure.[211c]

[211a] *Foothill Indus. Bank v. Mikkelson,* 623 P.2d 748 (Wyo. 1981).
[211b] *Id.* at 754.
[211c] *Id.* at 756.

¶ 4.05 BUY-SELL AGREEMENT AND THE FINAL TAKEOUT STAGE

Page 4-69:

Add at end of note 219.

[219] If the conditions of the permanent loan commitment are not met prior to the takeout date, the interim lender would have no recourse against a permanent lender who refuses to purchase the interim loan. See, e.g., Texas Bank & Trust Co. v. Lone Star Life Ins. Co., 565 S.W.2d 353 (Tex. Civ. App. 1978).

Chapter 5
USURY AND THE MORTGAGE MONEY MARKET

		Page
¶ 5.01	Relevance of Usury in Today's Real Estate Market	S5-1
¶ 5.02	Elements of Usury	S5-3
	[4] Exaction of Greater Compensation as Interest Than Is Allowed by Law	S5-3
	[b] How Interest Is Computed	S5-3
	[d] Variable-Rate Mortgage	S5-3
¶ 5.03	Status of Customary Loan Charges	S5-4
	[1] Commitment Fees	S5-4
	[2] Origination or Service Fees	S5-4
	[3] Brokerage and Other Fees Paid to Intermediaries	S5-5
¶ 5.04	Statutory Exemptions	S5-5
	[1] Corporate Exemption	S5-5
¶ 5.05	Circumvention Devices	S5-5
	[1] Conflicts of Law	S5-5
	[4] Sale and Leaseback	S5-5
	[6] Sale and Repurchase of Realty	S5-6
	[8] Contingent Compensation and Equity Participation by Lenders	S5-6

¶ 5.01 RELEVANCE OF USURY IN TODAY'S REAL ESTATE MARKET

Page 5-4:

Replace first full paragraph with the following.

Finally, a federal preemption of state usury ceilings came into being on April 1, 1980 under Title V of the Depository Institutions De-

¶ 5.01

regulation and Monetary Control Act.[11a] This statute preempt's state statutory and constitutional usury provisions in loans made during the three-year period ending April 1, 1983. It preempts usury ceilings on residential first mortgages, loans by federally insured institutions, and business and agricultural loans.

The Depository Institutions Act permanently preempts from state usury ceilings "federally related loans" secured by first mortgages on residential real property. Loans are "federally related" when made by lenders that (1) are federally insured, guaranteed, assisted, or regulated, or are approved for participation in federal housing programs or in the federally authorized secondary mortgage market; (2) regularly arrange for installment credit or invest in more than $1 million in residential mortgages per year, and (3) are not individuals. Individual lenders who take back first mortgages on residential property are subject to a separate federal preemption law. That law is Section 327(d) of the Housing and Community Development Act of 1980. The Depository Institutions Act covers loans to purchase shares in cooperatives as well as home loans. It does not, however, cover discount points, prepayment fees, late charges, or other lending fees.

Loans by federally insured banks, savings and loan associations, and credit unions are also preempted from state usury ceilings. Instead, an alternative ceiling of one percent over the discount rate on ninety-day commercial paper in effect at the local Federal Reserve bank is imposed. Lenders covered under the Depository Institutions Act are permitted to charge the higher of this rate and the state usury ceiling. Federally insured lenders are subject to a forfeiture of the entire interest on the loan if they fail to comply with the Depository Institutions Act. In addition, the borrower can sue for twice any interest paid within two years after payment.

The Depository Institutions Act also preempts state usury ceilings on all business and agricultural loans of $25,000 or more until April 1, 1983. These loans are subject to an alternative federal ceiling, as are loans by federally insured lenders. This ceiling, however, is equal to 5 percent more than the discount rate on ninety-day commercial paper in effect at the local Federal Reserve bank. The penalties for violation are the same as for loans by federally insured lenders. On October 7, 1981, a bill concerning the application of the Depository Institutions Act to business and agricultural loans was introduced by Senator Edwin J. Garn (R-Utah), Chairman of the Senate Committee on Banking, Hous-

---

[11a] Pub. L. 96-221, 94 Stat. 132 (1980). For a discussion of Title IV of the Depository Institutions Act and the investment authority it grants to federally chartered savings and loan associations, see ¶ 2.02[3][d].

ing and Urban Affairs. The bill would eliminate the federal ceiling and make the federal preemption of state usury laws permanent.

The Depository Institutions Act provides that states have until April 1, 1983 to override the preemption of their usury ceilings. To date, ten states[11b] have done so.

The Arkansas Supreme Court ruled that the federal preemption statute was unconstitutional because it would result in interference by the federal government in state matters. The court subsequently reversed itself and acknowledged the impact that state regulation of interest rates may have on interstate commerce.[11c]

[11b] The seven states that overrode the preemption as to all loans are Colorado, Hawaii, Iowa, Kansas, Massachusetts, Nevada, and South Dakota. Three other states, Maine, Minnesota, and South Carolina, overrode the preemption only with respect to home mortgage and consumer loans.

[11c] McInnis v. Cooper Communities, Inc., No. 80-254 (Ark., Dec. 29, 1980), aff'd 271 Ark. 503, 611 S.W.2d 767 (1981).

¶ 5.02 ELEMENTS OF USURY

[4] Exaction of Greater Compensation as Interest Than Is Allowed by Law

[b] How Interest Is Computed

Page 5-13:

Add at end of note 49.

[49] But see Fausett & Co. v. G & P Real Est., Inc., 269 Ark. 481, 602 S.W.2d 669 (1980) (well-established rule permitting highest rate of interest in advance overruled).

[d] Variable-Rate Mortgage

Page 5-13:

Add to note 54 after Aztec Properties v. Union Planters Nat'l Bank cite.

[54] , cert. denied 425 U.S. 975 (1975).

Add to note 54 after Olwine v. Torrens cite.

[54] ; Kin-ark Corp. v. Boyles, 593 F.2d 361, 364 (10th Cir. 1979) where, in construing Texas law, a federal court held a loan to be usurious because a floating interest rate exceeded the maximum rate allowed by the Texas statute.

Add at end of footnote 56.

[56] Tanner Dev. Co. v. Ferguson, 561 S.W.2d 777, 781 (Tex. 1977); McConnell v. Merrill Lynch, Pierce, Fenner & Smith, Inc., 21 Cal. 3d 365, 378, 578 P.2d 1375, 146 Cal. Rptr. 371 (1978).

Add at end of subsection.

In those jurisdictions where a loan is not usurious if additional interest depends on a contingency outside of the lender's control,[56a] SAMs[56b] will probably be safe from a usury violation. On the other hand, some commentators see a usury problem in the notion that both parties anticipated that inflation would continue after the loan was made, and therefore the parties could reasonably foresee a usurious interest rate.[56c]

[56a] See note 40 *supra.* See also Arneill Rance v. Petit, 64 Cal. App. 3d 277, 134 Cal. Rptr. 456, 461 (1976); Beeler v. H & R Block, Inc., 487 P.2d 569, 573 (Colo. Ct. App. 1971).

[56b] See discussion at ¶ 3.04[3][c].

[56c] Strum, "An Introduction to Shared Appreciation Mortgages," in *Financing Real Estate During the Inflationary 80s* at 27, 30 (ABA 1981).

¶ 5.03 STATUS OF CUSTOMARY LOAN CHARGES

[1] Commitment Fees

Page 5-14:

Add at end of note 59.

[59] See People v. Central Fed. Sav. & Loan Ass'n, 46 N.Y.2d 41, 385 N.E.2d 555, 412 N.Y.S.2d 815 (1978).

[2] Origination or Service Fees

Page 5-14:

Add at end of note 61.

[61] ; see Abramowitz v. Barnett Bank, 394 So. 2d 1033 (Fla. Dist. Ct. App. 1981), where appellate court held that a $4,000 "point" charge made at loan closing, when added to the regular interest, was additional interest that rendered the loan usurious.

[3] Brokerage and Other Fees Paid to Intermediaries

Page 5-15:

Add at end of note 65.

[65] See North American Mortgage Investors v. Cape San Blas Joint Venture, 378 So. 2d 287 (Fla. 1979) (commission paid to lender's agent and loan extension fee held to be additional interest that rendered the loan usurious).

¶ 5.04 STATUTORY EXEMPTIONS

[1] Corporate Exemption

Page 5-21:

Add at end of note 97.

[97] See R. J. Carter Enterprises, Inc. v. Greenway Bank & Trust, 615 S.W.2d 826 (Tex. Civ. App. 1981), where court held that lender may, as a condition to making the loan, require that the loan be made to a corporation in order to obtain a higher interest rate; cf. Prestonview Co. v. State Mut. Investors, 581 S.W.2d 701 (Tex. 1980) (loan borrowed by corporation secured by property owned by a partnership held not to be loan to partnership since loan documents were executed by the corporation).

¶ 5.05 CIRCUMVENTION DEVICES

[1] Conflicts of Law

Page 5-24:

Add at end of note 109.

[109] ; Continental Mortgage Investors v. Sailboat Key, Inc., 395 So. 2d 507 (Fla. 1981), where court upheld a choice of law provision in case involving a Massachusetts REIT and a Florida developer, since the REIT with its only office in Massachusetts had sufficient nexus to Massachusetts; Sarlot-Kantarjian v. First Pa. Mortgage Trust, 599 F.2d 915 (1979).

[4] Sale and Leaseback

Page 5-33:

Change fourth line of first full paragraph to read as follows.

to the developer. Unless the sale is found to be a sham transaction, the rental

[6] Sale and Repurchase of Realty

Page 5-34:

Change third line from bottom of page to read as follows.

tion the sale of the property to the investor appears to be a sham transaction

[8] Contingent Compensation and Equity Participation by Lenders

Page 5-38:

Change third line of third paragraph to read as follows.

a sham arrangement whereby the investor pays less than what its

Chapter 6
LEASEHOLD AND LEASEBACK FINANCING

		Page
¶ 6.03	Leasehold Mortgage on Unsubordinated Fee: Lender's Requirements	S6-1
	[8] Default Provisions	S6-1
¶ 6.04	Sale and Leaseback Financing vs. Debt Financing	S6-2
	[3] Tax Pitfalls Inherent in Sale-Leaseback	S6-2
	[a] Loss Disallowed "Exchange"	S6-2
	[i] Case Law Interpretations of "Exchange"	S6-2
	[b] Treatment as Disguised Loan	S6-3
	[ii] Subsequent Case Law on Sale-Leasebacks [New]	S6-3
	[e] Treatment as Non-Profit-Motivated Transaction [New]	S6-5

¶ 6.03 LEASEHOLD MORTGAGE ON UNSUBORDINATED FEE: LENDER'S REQUIREMENTS

[8] Default Provisions

Page 6-13:

Add at end of note 24.

[24] The American Bar Association Real Property Probate and Trust Law Section in 1980 issued a Committee Report on Model Leasehold Encumbrance Provisions which espouses a "new lease" provision that would provide a leasehold mortgagee with the absolute right to step into the shoes of the defaulting ground lessee-borrower. Under this concept, the lender would have the right to obtain a new lease from the ground lessor, with substantially identical terms for the balance of the lease term, along with any right of renewal that was bargained for by the original ground lessee. However, the "new lease" concept does not address the problem of a rejection of such arrangement by a trustee in bankruptcy who has the power to reject any executory contract or unexpired lease of a debtor, notwithstanding the lender's potential status as a third-party beneficiary. Nor does the proposal address

the possible nugatory impact of the rule against perpetuities or the rights of intervening creditors or subsequent purchasers in the event the right to the new lease is construed as an option right of the leasehold mortgagee. See Levitan, "Leasehold Mortgage Financing: Reliance on the *New Lease* Provision," 15 Real Prop., Prob. & Tr. J. 413 (1980).

¶ 6.04 SALE AND LEASEBACK FINANCING VS. DEBT FINANCING

[3] Tax Pitfalls Inherent in Sale-Leaseback

[a] Loss Disallowed "Exchange"

[i] Case Law Interpretations of "Exchange"

Page 6-27:

Add new text and note 52a at end of subsection.

A recent case[52a] involves a taxpayer who avoided I.R.C. § 1031 in this exact manner. The taxpayer was a department store chain looking for space to lease for a new store. A developer of shopping malls offered to sell taxpayer a parcel of land from a shopping complex it was building. The taxpayer, however, wanted to lease rather than purchase the property so that it would have available capital with which to operate the store. For this reason, it entered into a sale-leaseback with Prudential Insurance Co. and then hired a construction firm to build the store. Under the sale-leaseback, Prudential agreed to buy the completed building and the land thereunder for $4 million, and then lease it back for thirty years at an annual rent of $360,000. After the sale-leaseback was entered into, construction was completed at a cost of $4.3 million. The taxpayer reported an ordinary loss of $300,000 for the year. The IRS disallowed the loss reduction on the ground that the sale-leaseback constituted a like-kind exchange within the meaning of I.R.C. § 1031. Taxpayer argued that the transaction was not a like-kind exchange because the lease itself had no capital value so that the transfer was a sale for cash only. The court ruled for the taxpayer. It held that whether the lease had capital value turned upon whether $4 million was close to the fair market value and whether $360,000 is not less than the fair rental value. Answering these inquiries in the affirmative, the court concluded that the lease itself had no capital value.

A secondary argument of the IRS—that the $300,000 excess cost

---

[52a] Milner & Co. v. Comm'r, 76 T.C. 1030 (1981).

was a premium for the lease and should therefore be amortized over the thirty-year period—was rejected. The court held that the $300,000 represented costs the taxpayer incurred to complete construction of the building. And since it found the lease to lack capital value, such amortization would not have been possible.

[b] Treatment as Disguised Loan

Page 6-29:

Change "**[ii] Tax Planning**" *to* "**[iii] Tax Planning**" *and insert new* ¶ 6.04[3][b][ii].

[ii] Subsequent Case Law on Sale-Leasebacks [New]

The case law after *Frank Lyon Co.* was decided has generally followed the *Frank Lyon Co.* definition of a bona fide sale-leaseback, i.e., a genuinely multiple-party transaction with economic substance based on business realities and nontax considerations. As did the court in *Frank Lyon Co.,* other courts have considered the arm's-length nature of the transaction, the gap between the sales price and the fair market value, the reasonableness of rents, and the apparent motives of both buyer-lessor and seller-lessee.

Carol W. Hilton[58a] involved a financing corporation that obtained a newly constructed department store in a sale-leaseback. The financing corporation was able to finance the purchase 100 percent by selling its corporate notes to some insurance companies. The notes were secured by a mortgage on the store and an assignment of the lease and rentals. After obtaining the store, the corporation conveyed it to a general partnership. Taxpayers, through a rather complicated web of limited partnerships, in some of which they were limited partners, acquired an interest in the general partnership. Claiming an interest in the department store as well, albeit indirect, the taxpayers reported deductions for depreciation and interest payments arising from their alleged acquisition and possession of the store.

The court, in applying the *Frank Lyon Co.* test, held the transaction not to be a bona fide sale-leaseback and disallowed the deductions.

[58a] 74 T.C. 305 (1980), *aff'd* 671 F.2d 316 (9th Cir. 1982). In *Hilton,* the Court relied to some extent upon the fact that the nonrecourse liability used in the purchase of the property exceeded the fair market value of the property. The court cited this as a factor indicating the lack of economic substance in the transaction. This issue is related to two other cases, *Crane* and *Est. of Franklin.* See ¶ 12.01[3] for a more complete discussion.

What the court found missing was a genuinely multiple-party concern about nontax economic considerations. The financing corporation entered the transaction for a nontax reason: to be assured of 100 percent financing from the insurance companies. There was evidence that the insurance companies would have financed only 75 percent of the store's fair market value had conventional refinancing been used by the financing corporation in lieu of the sale-leaseback. On the other hand, the general partnership stood only to gain a tax advantage from the sale-leaseback. At the time of the transaction, rents from the property were low and the cash flow was nominal. No evidence existed of any nontax interest on the part of the general partnership. So, of course, no such interest was evident on the part of the taxpayers.

David Narver[58b] involved a corporation that purchased a building and the land underlying it for $650,000. On the same day it purchased the property, the corporation sold the building but not the land to two limited partnerships for $1,800,000. The corporation was the sole general partner of both limited partnerships. The limited partnerships then leased the building to the corporation's subsidiary for rent that would exactly cover the partnerships' nonrecourse purchase obligation to the corporation. The Tax Court disallowed deductions claimed by the limited partners for depreciation and interest payments because no genuine sale was found to exist for two reasons: first, that buyer and seller were, in effect, the same party—the limited partnerships; and second, that the building's sales price was several times higher than its fair market value, which was estimated to be no greater than $412,000 by various expert witnesses. The court refused to give serious consideration to the $1,800,000 figure as any indication of the fair market value because the transaction was not at arm's length,[58c] and the parties did not have adverse economic interests.[58d] Finding that there was no sale, the court ruled that there was no actual investment on which depreciation deductions could be based,[58e] no genuine indebtedness, and therefore no genuine interest payments for which deductions could be claimed.[58f]

Schaefer v. Commissioner[58g] was similar to *Hilton v. Commissioner* in that the seller-lessee used the sale-leaseback for financing purposes while the buyer-lessor was motivated only by tax considerations.

[58b] 75 T.C. 53 (1980).

[58c] See John McShain, 71 T.C. 998 (1979); Scope v. Comm'r, 41 T.C.M. 304 (1980).

[58d] Campana Corp. v. Harrison, 114 F.2d 400 (7th Cir. 1940).

[58e] 75 T.C. at 98 (citing Manuel D. Mayerson, 47 T.C. 340, 350 (1966)).

[58f] 75 T.C. at 98 (citing the rule of Knetsch v. United States, 364 U.S. 361 (1960)).

[58g] 41 T.C.M. 100 (1980).

The seller had originally purchased hotel property for $20,000 in cash and a $180,000 installment note calling for annual payments of $10,000 plus interest. Business at the hotel was slow, so the seller had trouble making the annual payments and financing the hotel's operation. In order to obtain capital for loan payments and operation costs, the seller conveyed the hotel property to a friend via a sale-leaseback. What attracted the buyer to this transaction was the opportunity it would give him to shelter some income from taxation. The buyer allowed the seller to operate the hotel exactly as she did before the transaction occurred, and did not even look at the hotel property or its financial statements. The only involvement that the buyer had with the hotel was the receipt of $10,000 annually in rentals and the payment of $10,000 annually on the installment note. The buyer had a "put" option allowing him to resell the property at any time to the seller for $200,000, which was to include cash in the amount of the buyer's equity. After the sale-leaseback, the seller searched for, and subsequently found, a third party who would operate the hotel and have an option to purchase it. This option was exercised without the original buyer's consent. The seller and buyer reported depreciation deductions, operating losses, lease payments, and an investment tax credit.

The Tax Court disallowed the deductions, ruling that the sale-leaseback was not a sale but merely a financing arrangement with tax avoidance motivation. Buyer's tax avoidance motivation was not, by itself, the basis of the court's ruling.[58h] Far more important in the opinion of the court was the lack of a true sale. The buyer neither intended a sale, nor changed his position in any way. He clearly did not assume the burdens and risk of hotel ownership. No cash was invested in or earned by him from the hotel property because he was paying out $10,000 annually while receiving $10,000 annually, and had the opportunity to recapture his "equity" at any time under the terms of the sale-leaseback. On these facts, the court found a case against loss deductions even stronger than that presented in *Hilton*.

[58h] See United States v. Cumberland Pub. Serv. Co., 338 U.S. 451 (1950), holding that a tax avoidance motivation by itself would not vitiate a tax shelter.

Page 6-31:

Add new ¶ 6.04[3][e].

[e] Treatment as Non-Profit-Motivated Transaction [New]

Whenever a transaction is found not to have been entered into for profit, loss deductions will be subject to the limitations of I.R.C. § 183.

A transaction is not subject to the Section 183 limitations if it is apparent from surrounding facts and circumstances that profit making[65a] was intended. A reasonable expectation of profits is not required.

In *Langford v. Commissioner*,[65b] the taxpayers purchased a home and paid $7000 ($100 cash down, $700 in maintenance work, and $100 per month until the purchase price was fully paid). The seller leased back the house at a rent well below the fair rental value. The Tax Court found the transaction to be at arm's-length, and that the taxpayers intended to profit from it. The taxpayers were expecting the seller, who was advanced in years, to remain in the house for a sufficiently short time to permit them to resell and realize the anticipated appreciation. Consequently, the Tax Court allowed the taxpayers to take loss deductions, which would not be subject to I.R.C. § 183.

[65a] See Stanley A. Golanty, 72 T.C. 411, 425 (1979); Truette E. Allen, 72 T.C. 28 (1979); Herbert A. Dunn, 70 T.C. 715, 720 (1978), *aff'd* 615 F.2d 578 (2d. Cir. 1980); Edward B. Hager, 76 T.C. 759 (1981).

[65b] 42 T.C.M. 1165 (1981).

Chapter 8
SPECIAL TYPES OF HIGH-RATIO FINANCING

	Page
¶ 8.06 Low-Cost, High-Ratio Financing With Tax-Exempt Mortgages	S8-1

¶ 8.06 LOW-COST, HIGH-RATIO FINANCING WITH TAX-EXEMPT MORTGAGES

Page 8-23:

Add at end of section.

Recently, the administration has proposed tax changes, soon to be introduced in Congress, that would eliminate tax-exempt bond financing.[58a] In addition, a bill currently before the House of Representatives would phase out tax-exempt bond financing by 1984.[58b] The ostensible reason for the proposed legislation is that the revenue lost by virtue of tax-free treatment of these bonds under I.R.C. § 103 has been excessive. In addition, projects have been funded that were either economically unsound or, as in the case of fast-food franchises and discount stores, beyond the congressional intent for the program.

[58a] 10 CCH Stand. Fed. Tax Rep. ¶ 6156, at 70,845 (March 1982).
[58b] H.R. 4420, 97th Cong., 1st Sess. (1981).

Chapter 9
SUBDIVISION FINANCING

Page

¶ 9.04 Seller's Use of Installment Method for Reporting Income (I.R.C. § 453) Under Installment Sales Revision Act of 1980 .... S9-1
    [1] Overview of Changes S9-1
    [2] Requirements for Using Installment Method Under New Law S9-2
        [b] Limitations on Payments by Purchaser in Year of Sale Eliminated S9-2
            [ii] 30 Percent Limitation on Payments in Year of Sale Eliminated S9-2
    [4] Sale or Other Disposition of Installment Obligations Under the New Law S9-2
        [bb] Pledge of Installment Obligation as Security for Loan, Not a Disposition [New] S9-2
    [5] Sales to Related Parties Restricted S9-3
        [a] Restriction on Intra-Family Transfers of Appreciated Property S9-3

¶ 9.04 SELLER'S USE OF INSTALLMENT METHOD FOR REPORTING INCOME (I.R.C. § 453) UNDER INSTALLMENT SALES REVISION ACT OF 1980

[1] Overview of Changes

Page 9-22:

Add at end of note 56.

    [56] See generally Kurn & Nutter, "The Installment Sales Revision Act of 1980: In the Name of Simplification Has a Measure of Complexity Been Added?" 8 J. Real Est. Tax. 195 (1981).

[2] Requirements for Using Installment Method Under New Law

[b] Limitations on Payments by Purchaser in Year of Sale Eliminated

[ii] 30 Percent Limitation on Payments in Year of Sale Eliminated

Page 9-24:

Correct second from bottom line on page from "than 6 percent simple annual interest...." *to* "than 9 percent simple annual interest...."

Replace Reg. § 1.483-1 at end of note 64 with the following.

, or (3) 9 percent per annum simple interest for payments on account of a sale or an exchange of property entered into on or after July 1, 1981. Reg. § 1.483-1. On July 1, 1981, the IRS issued new regulations raising the imputed interest on property installment sales from 7 percent to 10 percent, which is to be compounded semiannually. The new rates were made retroactive to any contract entered into on or after September 29, 1980. In one situation, a maximum imputed interest rate of 7 percent is set by statute, notwithstanding the new minimum of 9 percent per annum simple interest. This situation is one meeting the following three requirements:

(1) The sale is of land not buildings;
(2) The sale is intrafamily; and
(3) The total annual sales between family members does not exceed $500,000.

[4] Sale or Other Disposition of Installment Obligations Under the New Law

Page 9-35:

Add new ¶ 9.04[4][bb].

[bb] Pledge of Installment Obligation as Security for Loan, Not a Disposition [New]

The Tax Court[97a] recently ruled that the assignment of an installment obligation to a bank to secure a loan was not a sale or other disposition, and, thus, the taxpayer realized no gain. The taxpayer, a partnership, sold real estate to a corporation for cash and an installment note for $788,000 secured by a deed of trust. On the same day, taxpayer obtained a loan equal in face value to the amount of the obligation evidenced by the installment note. This loan was secured with the collateral assignment of the installment obligation. The bank loan and

---

[97a] Schaeffer v. Comm'r, 41 T.C.M. 752 (1981).

installment obligation payments were scheduled in such a way that principal and interest payments on both were made at the same times and in approximately the same amounts. Moreover, taxpayer advised the corporate obligor to make its payments directly to the bank, which would apply them to the outstanding balance of the bank loan.[97b]

The IRS contended that the taxpayer's transaction effected a sale or other disposition of the installment obligation and that gain should therefore be recognized from the sale of the real property to the corporation in exchange for the installment note under the provisions of I.R.C. § 453B.[97c] The taxpayer contended that it merely pledged the obligation as security, and that such a pledge does not constitute a sale or other disposition. In its favorable ruling to the taxpayer, the Tax Court relied primarily on several of its previous decisions defining a sale or disposition as the relinquishment of incidents of ownership. The court found the mere entrustment of collateral that occurred here not to fit that definition. Other factors convincing the court that the taxpayer did not dispose of the obligations were the structuring of the transaction as a loan and the payment of state income tax by the taxpayer on interest received on the installment obligation. The court rejected an IRS argument that the installment obligation and bank loan, similar in face amount and payment schedule, were substantially identical and, therefore, the installment obligation was sold. Differences in term and interest rate were found to exist between the two. In addition, the court stated it would not find a sale or disposition even if the installment obligation and bank loan were substantially identical.

[97b] The partnership did it this way to prevent payments from getting entwined in one of the partner's impending bankruptcy proceedings.

[97c] I.R.C. § 453B was formerly I.R.C. § 453(d).

[5] Sales to Related Parties Restricted

[a] Restriction on Intra-Family Transfers of Appreciated Property

Page 9-36:

Replace last sentence with the following.

Effective for installment sales (first dispositions) after May 14, 1980, a resale of the property within two years will trigger recognition of the entire gain on the installment sale by the original seller.[101]

Formerly, if a seller canceled the installment payments to be made by a related buyer, the seller did not have to report the balance of the gain due under the installment sale. The Installment Sales Act makes the balance of the gain taxable. If the seller died before all installment payments were made and the obligations (an asset of the estate) were left to the related buyer, the remaining gain was never taxed prior to the Installment Sales Act. Under the Act, the remaining gain would be taxable.

Add at end of note 101.

[101] The two-year limit does not apply to the intra-family sale and resale of marketable securities. If the related buyer resells them at any time during the installment period, the original seller must report the balance of his gain at once.

Chapter 10
CONDOMINIUM AND COOPERATIVE FINANCING

	Page
¶ 10.02 Condominium Financing	S10-1
[5] Condominium Conversion of Rental Units	S10-1

¶ 10.02 CONDOMINIUM FINANCING

[5] Condominium Conversion of Rental Units

Page 10-25.

Add new note 63a at end of last sentence in subsection.

[63a] See Kramer, "Conversion of Rental Housing to Unit Ownership—A Noncrisis," 10 Real Est. L.J. 187 (1982); Kurtzon & Nekritz, "Going Condo: How to Represent Tenants in Condominium Conversions," 8 Barrister 15 (1980).

Chapter 11
LOAN PARTICIPANTS AND JOINT VENTURES BY INSTITUTIONAL LENDERS

		Page
¶ 11.01	Loan Participations	S11-1
	[6] Legal Pitfalls	S11-1
	[d] Lead Lender's Compliance With Securities Laws	S11-1
¶ 11.02	Joint Ventures Between Institutional Lenders and Developers	S11-2
	[4] Selecting the Ownership Entity	S11-2
	[c] Tenancy in Common [New]	S11-2
	[5] Analysis of Joint Venture Agreement	S11-2
	[a] Allocation of Capital Contributions	S11-2
	[6] Summary of Problems Inherent in Joint Venturing	S11-4

¶ 11.01 LOAN PARTICIPATIONS

[6] Legal Pitfalls

[d] Lead Lender's Compliance With Securities Laws

Page 11-11:

Add at end of note 30.

[30] But cf. American Fletcher Mortgage Co. v. United States Steel Credit Corp., 635 F.2d 1247 (7th Cir. 1980) (where loan participation involved commercial real estate and lender was not entitled to any share of borrower's profits but only regular interest, court held that participation was not a security under either the Federal Securities Laws or the Indiana Blue Sky Act), *cert. denied* 451 U.S. 911 (1981).

¶ 11.02 **JOINT VENTURES BETWEEN INSTITUTIONAL LENDERS AND DEVELOPERS**

[4] Selecting the Ownership Entity

Page 11-23:

Add new ¶ 11.02[4][c].

[c] **Tenancy in Common [New]**

Unless clearly specified to the contrary in an appropriate agreement, a title insurance company may choose to regard a joint venture as a tenancy in common. If one of the joint venturers (tenants in common) becomes insolvent, the consequences can be serious. For instance, the solvent venturer may not be able to obtain title insurance for a deed signed by himself. This may be true despite a joint venture agreement authorizing the solvent venturer to continue the venture.[88a]

[88a] Noel W. Nellis, "Pension Investment Funds in Realty," Practicing Law Institute Law Seminar, New York City, November 9-11, 1981.

[5] Analysis of Joint Venture Agreement

[a] **Allocation of Capital Contributions**

Page 11-25:

Add note 90a at the end of the first full paragraph.

[90a] A similar alternative gives the noncontributing venturer ninety days to repay the advance. If he pays, the advance is treated as a loan on which interest is due. Repayment is due on demand after the ninety days, or otherwise out of the net cash flow to which the non-contributing venturer is entitled. See Nellis & Hastie, "Real Estate Joint Ventures in the 80s," in *Financing Real Estate During the Inflationary 80s* at 214 (ABA 1981).

Add after first full paragraph.

Numerous formulae for recalculating the percentage interests in the venture exist. One method uses the initial capital contributions of the venturers.[90b] For example, assume a venture with a development cost of $100 which is owned 50-50 between the venturers, each of whom contributed $50 cash. Assume additional capital of $1 is re-

---

[90b] *Id.* at 214-215.

quired from each to complete the project, and one venturer fails to provide the dollar. The change in percentage interests on an initial capital contribution basis would reflect the value of the additional capital to the entire project cost. The percentage readjustment is as follows:

Contributing venturer's percentage interest:

$$\frac{50 + 1 + 1}{100 + 2} = \frac{52}{102} = 51\%$$

Noncontributing venturer's percentage interest:

$$\frac{50}{100 + 2} = \frac{50}{102} = 49\%$$

This formula is inappropriate for a highly leveraged venture; the readjustment would exclude the value of the project attributable to the leverage. For example, consider the same venture as in the example above (development cost of $100 owned 50-50 between the venturers). But assume that instead of making $50 cash contributions, each venturer contributes $10 in cash with the remaining $80 borrowed by the venture. Further assume (as in the earlier example) that additional capital of $1 is needed from each and that one venturer pays both dollars. In this example, the percentage readjustment should reflect the value of the additional capital to the invested cash only. The result: a substantially greater change in the percentage interest as follows:

Contributing venturer's percentage interest:

$$\frac{10 + 1 + 1}{20 + 2} = \frac{12}{22} = 55\%$$

Noncontributing venturer's percentage interest:

$$\frac{10}{20 + 2} = \frac{10}{22} = 45\%$$

In other formulae the percentage readjustments can be designed to reflect the value of the additional capital to the value of the project as determined either by an appraiser or by the contributing venturer.

A liquidated damages clause in the joint venture agreement is a good assurance of the enforceability of the formula selected. A workable clause would state that both parties recognize the difficulty in assessing damages attributable to the failure to make necessary capital contributions. Because of this, the clause continues, the parties have agreed on such an assessment in advance, which assessment is the appropriate formula.

[6] Summary of Problems Inherent in Joint Venturing

Page 11-30:

Add after first full paragraph.

Some institutional and foreign investors (and the number appears to be rising) will agree to contribute capital at the start of a project. The practical result is that they share the construction risk with the developer. Investors are willing to take these risks (sometimes known as "front-end deals") because their potential returns are designed to reflect the higher risk. A typical "front-end" investor may receive a cumulative preferred return on his contributed capital, *plus* 50 percent or more of the remaining cash flow—this in addition to a guarantee of a priority return of his capital when the development is sold, refinanced, or liquidated.[109a]

[109a] See Nellis & Hastie, note 90a *supra* at 205.

Chapter 12
TAX ASPECTS OF MORTGAGE FINANCING

		Page
¶ 12.01	Tax Consequences of a Mortgage on Real Property	S12-1
	[3] The *Crane* Doctrine	S12-1
	[b] Effects in Nonrecourse Financing	S12-1
	[5] Distinction Between Debt and Equity [New]	S12-2
	[a] Tax Treatment of Lender as Partner or Creditor	S12-3
	[b] Status of Corporate Borrowers Under I.R.C. § 385	S12-5
¶ 12.03	Tax Consequences of Mortgagor's Default	S12-5
	[1] Overview	S12-5
	[3] Voluntary Conveyance to Mortgagee, Deed in Lieu of Foreclosure, Abandonment	S12-6

¶ 12.01 TAX CONSEQUENCES OF A MORTGAGE ON REAL PROPERTY

[3] The *Crane* Doctrine

[b] Effects in Nonrecourse Financing

Page 12-7:

Add at end of note 29.

> [29] In John F. Tufts v. Comm'r, 70 T.C. 756, *rev'd* 651 F.2d 1058 (5th Cir. 1981), the Fifth Circuit Court of Appeals enunciated a doctrine of fair market value limitation based on Footnote 37 in *Crane*. In *Tufts,* a partnership acquired an apartment complex for a $1.8 million nonrecourse note and no cash. The property declined in value to $1.4 million, and the partnership sold its interest for no money but subject to the $1.8 million mortgage. The Commissioner claimed that this sale generated income for the partnership. The partnership claimed that the amount realized from the sale should be limited to the fair market value of the property by reason of Footnote 37 in *Crane*. Footnote 37 reads as follows:
>> Obviously if the value of the property is less than the amount of the mortgage, a mortgagor who is not personally liable cannot realize a

¶ 12.01[5]   REAL ESTATE FINANCING   S12-2

benefit equal to the mortgage. Consequently, a different problem might be encountered where a mortgagor abandoned the property or transferred it subject to the mortgage without receiving boot. That is not this case.

The court, in *Tufts,* stated that the issue presented was whether Footnote 37 created an exception to the *Crane* holding. The court concluded that such an exception did exist and ruled that the amount realized upon the sale of property encumbered by a nonrecourse liability cannot exceed the fair market value of the property.

See also Bittker, "Tax Shelters, Nonrecourse Debt, and the *Crane* Case," 33 Tax L. Rev. 277 (1978).

Page 12-8:

Add new ¶ 12.01[5].

[5] Distinction Between Debt and Equity [New]

As a hedge against inflation and volatile interest rates, lenders have and will continue to devise innovative methods and financing techniques to replace the long-term fixed-rate mortgage as the principal mode of real estate financing. The common characteristic of these various methods and combinations of methods that have been created in order to cope with inflation is equity participation. Some, like the equity kicker,[33a] are at the debt end of debt-equity spectrum; others, like the joint venture[33b] arrangement, represent a pure equity position; while still others, like the convertible mortgage[33c] and equity appreciation mortgage,[33d] are somewhere in the middle. Under a convertible mortgage, the lender has the right to convert some or all of the loan indebtedness into a partnership (equity) interest or the right to purchase part or all of the secured property.

When there is a substantial equity participation, one important issue is whether the relationship between the lender and borrower will be regarded for tax purposes as a debtor-creditor relationship or as an equity (partnership) relationship. As noted elsewhere,[33e] if the lender's investment is indebtedness, the interest paid by the borrower is deductible and the interest received by the lender is income, except when

---

[33a] See ¶ 3.04[3][a].
[33b] See ¶ 11.02.
[33c] See ¶ 3.04[18].
[33d] The loan documents provide that either upon a sale of the secured property or at periodic intervals the lender will receive additional interest equal to a percentage of the appreciation in the value of the property, and sometimes the value is to be paid by increasing the principal balance of the indebtedness.
[33e] See ¶¶ 12.01 and 12.02[1]-12.02[4].

interest paid by state or local governments meets the criteria under I.R.C. § 103.[33f] Moreover, if the lender is solely a creditor, the borrower can include the full amount of the loan indebtedness, whether recourse or nonrecourse, in its tax basis for purposes of computing depreciation.[33g] On the other hand, if the loan transaction is characterized by the IRS as a partnership, the so-called borrower must share such tax benefits as depreciation and investment tax credits with any lender who is constructively deemed to be a partner. Also, payments to the lender-partner by the borrower that are contingent upon net or gross income (equity kickers) will not be deductible and will be taxed as distributions from the partnership if the loan is made to the partnership in its capacity as a partner.[33h] In addition, foreign investors are subject to either no tax or a reduced tax rate on interest income but must pay a tax on partnership U.S. trade or business income and on capital gain from the sale of a U.S. interest in real estate.[33i] Moreover, if the transaction is a loan transaction with an interest add-on feature geared to refinancing or sale of the property, the borrower will receive ordinary deductions equal to the interest paid, which is beneficial especially in the case of a sale, which, unlike refinancing, is a taxable event.

Another significant issue involving any borrower that is a corporation, especially in the case of a convertible mortgage, is whether the loan transaction will be reclassified as equity under the new and formidable debt-equity regulations under I.R.C. § 385.

[a] Tax Treatment of Lender as Partner or Creditor

Whether the relationship between the lender and borrower is a debtor-creditor or partnership relationship depends upon the intentions of the parties[33j] as reflected by the particular facts and circumstances of the transaction. However, the following criteria are relevant in distinguishing a debtor-creditor relationship from that of a partnership relationship:

(1) Is there any characterization of intent in the documentation? However, this factor is far from conclusive.[33k]

[33f] See ¶ 8.06.
[33g] See ¶ 1.05[2][b].
[33h] See I.R.C. §§ 707(a) and 707(c); Pratt v. Comm'r, 505 F.2d 1023 (5th Cir. 1977); Rev. Rul. 81-300, 1981-2 C.B. —; Rev. Rul. 81-301, 1981-2 C.B. —.
[33i] See ¶ 2.02[8]; I.R.C. §§ 871(b), 875, 882, and 897(c)(1)(A).
[33j] See, e.g., Smith v. Comm'r, 313 F.2d 724 (8th Cir. 1963).
[33k] See discussion at ¶¶ 3.04[18] and 6.04[3][b].

(2) How are profits and losses shared and what are the respective contributions of capital and services by the parties?

(3) Who controls the final disposition of the property and other important policy decisions?

(4) If there is an option to purchase, does the option price fluctuate, is the borrower forced to share profits as well, and who bears the risk of appreciation or depreciation in the value of the property?

(5) Does the transaction have independent economic significance, or is tax avoidance the motivating reason for the transaction?

(6) In the case of nonrecourse financing, is the loan-to-value ratio reasonably low? [33l]

(7) Are the traditional indicia of indebtedness (e.g., fixed maturity date) employed by the parties?

In general, in the case of a straight equity kicker-styled loan, profit participation alone will create a partnership relationship.[33m] By analogy in the case of employment contracts, courts have generally held that profit sharing arrangements do not convert the employer-employee relationship into a partnership.[33n] If the loan is nonrecourse and the loan-to-value ratio is high, the lender arguably shares the risk of loss, especially if the value of the mortgaged property declines below the amount of the mortgage indebtedness and the lender contributes at least some equity capital.[33o] Also, in the case of a below-market rate of fixed interest, the IRS might argue that the bargain feature is really property contributed by the lender in exchange for its right to receive additional interest.[33p] Since the lender's interest return is dependent to some degree on the profitability of the enterprise, it may want to exercise some equity-type control over management decisions; however, the existence

---

[33l] See ¶ 12.01[3]; Hambeuchen v. Comm'r, 43 T.C. 77 (1964).

[33m] See Arthur Venneri Co. v. Comm'r, 340 F.2d 337 (Ct. Cl. 1965); Comm'r v. Williams, 256 F.2d 152 (5th Cir. 1958); Astoria Marine Constr. Co. v. Comm'r, 4 T.C.M. 278 (1943). See also Kena, Inc., 44 B.T.A. 217 (1941) (percentage of profits held to be interest).

[33n] See, e.g., Estate of Smith v. Comm'r, 313 F.2d 724 (8th Cir. 1963).

[33o] However, the nonrecourse nature of a loan will be respected and not treated as a capital contribution where the loan-to-value ratio is reasonable. See ¶ 12.01[3].

[33p] By analogy, under the proposed regulations under I.R.C. § 385, if a loan at a below-market rate is made to a corporation by a shareholder, the lender is regarded as making a capital contribution equal to the excess of the consideration paid over the market value of the instrument. Prop. Reg. § 1.385-6(c)(1).

of such controls could jeopardize the debtor-creditor status of the relationship.

[b] Status of Corporate Borrowers Under I.R.C. § 385

In the case of a loan made to a corporate borrower, the new (and highly complex) proposed regulations might reclassify the loan indebtedness as stock if, on the date of issue, less than 50 percent of the present discounted value of a "hybrid instrument" (a convertible mortgage, mortgage loan with equity kicker, or any other convertible instrument or instrument having contingent payments of principal or interest) issued in a proportionate manner is reflected in fixed payments of principal and interest.[33q] The same equity treatment will be accorded to the proportionate issuance of straight debt instruments with (1) excessive debt, (2) unreasonable interest and debt issued for property, or (3) unreasonable interest and debt payable on demand. In such event, payments of both fixed and contingent interest would be viewed as corporate distributions and would not be deductible from the borrower's operating income, and any payments to the lender on the sale of the property would not reduce the borrower's gain on the disposition.[33r] However, if the safe harbor rules do not apply, it might be possible to circumvent I.R.C. § 385 by using a loan to a partnership composed of the corporation and either its subsidiary or one of its shareholders.

[33q] See Prop. Reg. §§ 1.385-5(a), 1.385-5(d), and 1.385-4(c)(1).

[33r] See generally Bush, "The Debt-Equity Regulations: Do Stock Redemptions and Other Areas Require Special Attention?" 39 N.Y.U. Inst. on Fed. Tax. 1-1 (1981); Beghe, "Redrawing the Lines Between Corporate Debt and Equity Interests: The Proposed Regulations Under Section 385," 58 Taxes 931 (1980).

¶ 12.03 TAX CONSEQUENCES OF MORTGAGOR'S DEFAULT

[1] Overview

Page 12-15:

Add at end of note 79.

[79] For a discussion of the tax impact of the Bankruptcy Tax Act of 1980, Pub. L. 96-589, 94 Stat. 3389 (Dec. 24, 1980), see Sheinfeld & Caldwell, "The Bankruptcy Tax Act of 1980 and Its Effect on Real Estate," 9 J. Real Est. Tax. 3 (1981).

[3] Voluntary Conveyance to Mortgagee, Deed in Lieu of Foreclosure, Abandonment

Page 12-25:

Add to note 134 after "Aff'd *Millar v. Comm'r, 577 F.2d 212 (3d Cir.)*":

[134] , *cert. denied* 439 U.S. 1046 (1978).

Appendix A
ANCILLARY DATA

		Page
Table 1	State Limitations on Commercial Bank Real Estate Loans, August 31, 1981	S.App. A- 2
Table 2	Mortgage Debt Outstanding	S.App. A-10
Table 3	Analysis of State Usury Statutes	S.App. A-11
Table 4	Real Estate Holdings of the 97 Largest Pension Funds [New]	S.App. A-17

Pages App. A-1 through App. A-20.

Replace entire Appendix A with the following.

Table 1   REAL ESTATE FINANCING   S.App. A-2

TABLE 1. State Limitations on Commercial Bank Real Estate Loans, August 31, 1981

State	Maximum ratio of loan value	Maximum term	Loan limit: Aggregate—One borrower	FHA or VA insured or guaranteed loans exempt from loan restrictions
Alabama	....	....	....	Yes
Alaska	A. 80 percent B. 90 percent	A. 25 years B. 30 years	....	Yes
Arizona	....	....	One borrower: 15 percent	Yes
Arkansas	....	....	20% capital, surplus, and capital notes for one borrower.	Yes
California	A. 60 percent B. 90 percent C. 85 percent, construction loan	A. 10 years B. 30 years, equal monthly installments C. 60 months	Aggregate: 70 percent of savings and time deposits One borrower: 20 percent capital stock, surplus, capital notes and debentures	Yes
Colorado	A. 50 percent B. 90 percent C. 75 percent	A. 5 years B. 30 years, 35 years if for construction of one or more buildings; fully amortized C. 7 years, fully amortized	Aggregate: 100 percent capital surplus; 100 percent time and savings deposits or 25 percent interest bearing securities, whichever is greatest	Yes
Connecticut	A. 50 percent B. Construction loan, no limit C. 90 percent, not over $25,000 or 10% of capital, whichever is greater	A. .... B. 24 months (or 36 months with approval of Bank Commissioner) C. 40 years, fully amortized in equal at least semiannual payments	Aggregate: 25 percent of capital and surplus or 25 percent of commercial deposits, whichever is greater One borrower: Total liabilities, including mortgage loans, of any one obligor to bank cannot exceed 10% of the bank's capital, surplus, undivided profits and loss reserves	Yes
Delaware	....	....	25% of capital	Yes
Florida[1]	....	....	....	No

S.App. A-3 APP. A—ANCILLARY DATA Table 1

State				
Georgia	A. 75 percent loan to value B. 90 percent loan to value C. 100 percent loan to value, construction loan	A. 5 years, unamortized B. 30 years, fully amortized or 35 years with negative amortization in first 5 yrs. C. 24 months residential, 60 months commercial or industrial	Aggregate: With all other loans limited to 20% statutory capital base.	Yes
Guam	A. 80 percent		Aggregate: 75 percent of savings deposits plus 25 percent of bank's capital, surplus, and commercial deposits on obligations secured by real estate	Yes
Hawaii	A. 80 percent		Aggregate: 75 percent of savings deposit plus 25 percent of bank's capital, surplus and commercial deposits on obligations served by real estate	Yes
Idaho	90 percent	30 years	Aggregate: 100 percent capital and surplus or 60 percent time and savings deposit whichever is greater One borrower: 20 percent of aggregate paid-in capital and surplus of bank	Yes
Illinois			Aggregate: 15 percent capital and surplus unless qualified for excess in which case limitations; 50 percent of capital and surplus including all obligations of borrower	Yes
Indiana	A. 50 percent B. 66-2/3 percent C. 90 percent	A. 5 years B. 10 years, 40 percent amortized C. 30 years, fully amortized	Aggregate: 100 percent total sound capital, 40 percent total deposits over 75 percent time deposits, whichever is greatest	Yes
Iowa	A. 75 percent B. 90 percent	A. 25 years, equal and full amortization B. 30 years, fully amortized	One borrower: Bank loan limit prevails as to total indebtedness per borrower	Yes

Table 1 REAL ESTATE FINANCING S.App. A-4

TABLE 1 (continued)

State	Maximum ratio of loan value	Maximum term	Loan limit: Aggregate—One borrower	FHA or VA insured or guaranteed loans exempt from loan restrictions
Kansas	No specific restrictions	.....	.....	.....
Kentucky	General loan limits apply	.....	.....	Yes
Louisiana	No restrictions	.....	.....	No
Maine	No restrictions	.....	.....	Yes
Maryland	Subject only to bank's legal lending limit, limit of 10 percent of unimpaired capital and surplus	.....	.....	No
Massachusetts	A. 50 percent, improved farm land B. 50 percent, improved real estate C. 60 percent, improved real estate D. 80 percent, improved real estate	A. 3 years; 5 years if at least 2 percent per year of principal is repaid B. 5 years C. 3 years; 5 years if at least 2 percent per year of principal is repaid D. 25 years, fully amortized and at least 40 percent amortized within 10 years	Aggregate: 15% of total deposits	Yes
Michigan	A. 80 percent	A. 30 years	Aggregate: 70% time savings deposits. One borrower: 10%/20% Capital & surplus	Yes
Minnesota	A. 50 percent	.....	First mortgages on improved property in this state, or adjoining state within 20 miles of the principal bank office in excess of 50% of current appraisal included in lending limit of 20% capital and surplus, but not to exceed 25% of capital & surplus	Yes

S.App. A-5　　　APP. A—ANCILLARY DATA　　　Table 1

State			
Mississippi	Statutes are silent	....	One borrower: Shall not exceed 20 percent of aggregate paid-in capital and surplus of bank
Missouri	....	....	Aggregate: Real estate loans are treated like any other loan and are subject to usual legal loan limit.
Montana	....	2	2 ....
Nebraska	A. 75 percent, first lien and first mortgage	A. 5 years	Aggregate: 100 percent capital, surplus and undivided profits or 70 percent time and savings deposits or 20% total deposits, whichever is greater
	B. 80 percent, improved real estate, not a first mortgage	B. 10 years, fully amortized	One borrower: 25 percent capital, surplus, and capital notes or debentures
	C. 90 percent, improved real estate, first mortgage	C. 10 years, 60 percent balloon payment	
	D. 90 percent, improved real estate, first mortgage	D. 25 years, fully amortized	
	E. 95 percent, improved real estate, first mortgage	E. 30 years, fully amortized, excess over 70 percent must be insured by a private company	
Nevada	A. 80 percent	A. 30 years	One borrower: 25 percent of unimpaired capital and surplus
New Hampshire	A. 70 percent	....	Aggregate: limitation included 15 percent of capital and surplus
New Jersey	A. 90 percent	A. 40 years	Aggregate: 80 percent of time deposits
			One borrower: 10 percent of capital funds including capital stock, surplus, undivided profit, capital note. Contingency reserves and any non-allocated valuation reserves less tax liability which would occur if transferred from the reserve to undivided profits

Yes (Mississippi)
Yes (Missouri)
Yes (Montana)
Yes (Nevada)
Yes (New Hampshire)
Yes (New Jersey)

Table 1   REAL ESTATE FINANCING   S.App. A-6

TABLE 1 (*continued*)

State	Maximum ratio of loan value	Maximum term	Loan limit: Aggregate—One borrower	FHA or VA insured or guaranteed loans exempt from loan restrictions
New Mexico	A. 66-2/3 percent unimproved B. 75 percent partially or being improved C. 90 percent improved by building	A. 30 years, fully amortized B. 30 years, fully amortized C. 30 years, fully amortized	Aggregate: 100 percent time and savings deposits	Yes
New York	A. 66-2/3 percent unimproved real estate B. 75 percent improved real estate C. 80 percent improved or two family dwelling D. 95 percent appraised value, 1 or 2 family dwelling	A. .... B. .... C. .... D. 40 years	One borrower: 10 percent of capital funds of the bank	Yes
North Carolina	....	....	....	Yes
North Dakota	A. 90 percent	A. 30 years, fully amortized	Aggregate: 100 percent capital and surplus or 66-2/3 percent time and savings deposits, whichever is greater	Yes
Ohio	A. 66-2/3 percent unimproved real estate B. 75 percent, improved real estate C. 90 percent, improved real estate	A. 10 years B. 10 years C. 30 years, equal and full amortization	Aggregate: 10 percent of paid in capital, surplus, and capital securities	Yes
Oklahoma	A. 80 percent B. 85 percent C. 80 percent	A. 5 years B. 10 years, 40 percent amortized C. 25 years, fully amortized	Aggregate: 100 percent capital and surplus on 70 percent time and savings deposit, whichever is greater	Yes

Oregon	A. 80 percent B. 90 percent C. 90 percent D. 95 percent	A. 5 years B. 10 years, 40 percent amotized C. 30 years and 62 days, fully amortized D. 30 years and 62 days, fully amortized. Excess over 90% must be insured	Aggregate: 25 percent capital and surplus, plus 10 percent demand deposit, plus 75 percent time deposits One borrower: 25 percent capital and surplus, plus debentures over 5 years	Yes
Pennsylvania	A. 66-2/3 percent, improved real estate B. 80 percent, improved real estate C. 90 percent not over $40,000; one family dwelling D. 95 percent, provided that principal in excess of 75 percent is made in reliance upon a private company mortgage insurance or a guarantee acceptable to department E. 66-2/3 percent, unimproved real estate F. 75 percent, unimproved real estate provided that untilities, streets, etc. necessary for development have been completed	A. 10 years, unamortized B. 30 years, fully amortized C. 30 years, fully amortized D. 30 years, fully amortized E. 3 years F. 5 years	Aggregate: 100 percent capital, capital securities and surplus, or 70 percent of total time and savings deposits, whichever is greater One borrower: 10 percent capital surplus, undivided profits and capital securities	Yes
Puerto Rico				Yes
Rhode Island (applicable only to savings departments)	A. 50 percent, unimproved real estate B. 80 percent, improved real estate C. 90 percent, improved real estate	A. ... B. 30 years, fully amortized C. 30 years, fully amortized	Aggregate: 80 percent savings deposits, or up to 90 percent savings deposits with excess over 80 percent insured by U.S. government or a private insurer	No

Table 1   REAL ESTATE FINANCING   S.App. A-8

TABLE 1 (continued)

State	Maximum ratio of loan value	Maximum term	Loan limit: Aggregate—One borrower	FHA or VA insured or guaranteed loans exempt from loan restrictions
Rhode Island (cont.)	D. 90 percent, improved real estate in a residential neighborhood and designed for not more than 4 families	D. 30 years, fully amortized		
South Carolina	A. 90 percent, first lien improved real estate B. 66-2/3 percent, first lien improved real estate C. 75 percent, first lien improved real estate D. 75 percent, first lien improved real estate E. 90 percent, first lien improved real estate	A. 1 year B. 5 years C. 10 years, 40 percent amortized D. 15 years, 60 percent amortized E. 30 years, fully amortized	Aggregate: 50 percent capital plus; 50 percent deposits One borrower: Total of all loans cannot exceed 15 percent of capital stock, capital notes and debentures and surplus of the bank with the approval of two-thirds of the directors. However, loans to directors and officers of the bank are limited to 10 percent of these accounts	Yes
South Dakota	Statutes are silent			Yes
Tennessee			25% of capital, surplus & undivided profits	Yes
Texas	A. 60 percent B. 70 percent C. 90 percent	A. .... B. 15 years C. 40 years, fully amortized	Aggregate: 200% of capital and certified surplus	Yes
Utah			One borrower: 15 percent of capital and surplus	Yes
Vermont	A. 1-2 family units, 40 years maximum B. 90 percent	A. Regular and equal installments B. 40 years, fully amortized, at least semiannual payments		Yes

APP. A—ANCILLARY DATA   Table 1

	C. 80 percent	C. 40 years, fully amortized, payments made at least annually. Construction of primary residences: Monthly interest payments until 90 days after completion, then two years to amortize.	
	D. 90 percent, 95 percent if in state, 1 or 2 family dwelling	D. 40 years, fully amortized, payments made at least every 6 months	
Virginia	A. 50 percent	A.	Aggregate: 100 percent capital and surplus or 70 percent time and saving deposits, whichever is greater
	B. 90 percent	B. 40 years, 3½ percent amortized per year	
Washington	....	....	One borrower: Shall not exceed 15 percent of capital and surplus	Yes
West Virginia	....	....	10 percent of capital, surplus, undivided profits, and reserves	Yes
Wisconsin	....	....	Aggregate: 50 percent capital, surplus and deposits, but loans exceeding this limit may be authorized by directors of bank under certain conditions	Yes
Wyoming	A. 50 percent	A. 5 years	Aggregate: 10 percent capital and surplus or 70 percent deposits, whichever is greater but uninsured loan may not exceed 20 percent of capital, surplus and deposits	Yes
	B. 75 percent	B. 10 years, 40 percent amortized		
	C. 75 percent	C. 20 years, fully amortized		
	D. 90 percent	D. 30 years, fully amortized		

[1] By statute state banks may make real estate loans under the same restrictions as national banks.
[2] Same as national banks.

SOURCE: Conference of State Bank Supervisors, *A Profile of State-Chartered Banking* (9th ed.), December 1981.

Table 2   REAL ESTATE FINANCING   S.App. A-10

TABLE 2. Mortgage Debt Outstanding

(Millions of dollars, end of period)

	Type of holder, and type of property	1979	1980	1981	1980 Q4	1981 Q1	1981 Q2	1981 Q3	1981 Q4
1	All holders	1,326,916	1,446,074	1,543,771	1,446,074	1,467,370	1,497,061	1,523,522	1,543,771
2	1- to 4-family	878,938	960,344	1,018,472	960,344	972,556	990,862	1,007,529	1,018,472
3	Multifamily	128,850	137,163	144,267	137,163	138,544	140,100	141,675	144,267
4	Commercial	236,451	256,549	279,096	256,549	261,809	268,587	274,250	279,096
5	Farm	82,677	92,018	101,936	92,018	94,461	97,512	100,068	101,936
6	Major financial institutions	938,567	996,789	1,044,496	996,789	1,006,836	1,023,340	1,036,687	1,044,496
7	Commercial banks[1]	245,187	263,030	286,626	263,030	266,734	273,225	281,126	286,626
8	1- to 4-family	149,460	160,326	172,549	160,326	161,758	164,873	169,378	172,549
9	Multifamily	11,180	12,924	14,905	12,924	13,282	13,800	14,478	14,905
10	Commercial	75,957	81,081	90,717	81,081	83,133	86,091	88,836	90,717
11	Farm	8,590	8,699	8,455	8,699	8,561	8,461	8,434	8,455
12	Mutual savings banks	98,908	99,866	100,000	99,866	99,719	99,993	100,200	100,000
13	1- to 4-family	64,706	65,332	65,420	65,332	65,236	65,415	65,551	65,420
14	Multifamily	17,180	17,347	17,370	17,347	17,321	17,369	17,405	17,370
15	Commercial	16,963	17,127	17,150	17,127	17,102	17,149	17,184	17,150
16	Farm	59	60	60	60	60	60	60	60
17	Savings and loan associations	475,688	502,812	517,637	502,812	507,152	514,803	518,379	517,637
18	1- to 4-family	394,345	419,446	432,693	419,446	423,269	430,324	433,313	432,693
19	Multifamily	37,579	38,113	38,253	38,113	38,189	38,044	38,308	38,253
20	Commercial	43,764	45,253	46,691	45,253	45,694	46,435	46,758	46,691
21	Life insurance companies	118,784	131,081	140,233	131,081	133,231	135,319	136,982	140,233
22	1- to 4-family	16,193	17,943	17,966	17,943	17,847	17,646	17,512	17,966
23	Multifamily	19,274	19,514	20,101	19,514	19,579	19,603	19,592	20,101
24	Commercial	71,137	80,666	88,991	80,666	82,839	85,038	86,742	88,991
25	Farm	12,180	12,958	13,175	12,958	12,966	13,032	13,136	13,175
26	Federal and related agencies	97,084	114,300	126,186	114,300	116,243	119,124	121,772	126,186
27	Government National Mortgage Association	3,852	4,642	4,765	4,642	4,826	4,972	4,382	4,765
28	1- to 4-family	763	704	765	704	696	698	696	765
29	Multifamily	3,089	3,938	4,000	3,938	4,130	4,274	3,686	4,000
30	Farmers Home Administration	1,274	3,492	2,235	3,492	2,837	2,662	1,562	2,235
31	1- to 4-family	417	916	914	916	1,321	1,151	500	914
32	Multifamily	71	610	473	610	528	464	242	473
33	Commercial	174	411	506	411	479	357	325	506
34	Farm	612	1,555	342	1,555	509	690	495	342
35	Federal Housing and Veterans Administration	5,555	5,640	6,073	5,640	5,799	5,895	6,005	6,073
36	1- to 4-family	1,955	2,051	2,293	2,051	2,135	2,172	2,240	2,293
37	Multifamily	3,600	3,589	3,780	3,589	3,664	3,723	3,765	3,780
38	Federal National Mortgage Association	51,091	57,327	61,412	57,327	57,362	57,657	59,682	61,412
39	1- to 4-family	45,488	51,775	55,986	51,775	51,842	52,181	54,227	55,986
40	Multifamily	5,603	5,552	5,426	5,552	5,520	5,476	5,455	5,426
41	Federal Land Banks	31,277	38,131	46,446	38,131	40,258	42,681	44,708	46,446
42	1- to 4-family	1,552	2,099	2,788	2,099	2,228	2,401	2,605	2,788
43	Farm	29,725	36,032	43,658	36,032	38,030	40,280	42,103	43,658
44	Federal Home Loan Mortgage Corporation	4,035	5,068	5,255	5,068	5,161	5,257	5,433	5,255
45	1- to 4-family	3,059	3,873	4,018	3,873	3,953	4,025	4,166	4,018
46	Multifamily	976	1,195	1,237	1,195	1,208	1,232	1,267	1,237
47	Mortgage pools or trusts[2]	119,278	142,258	162,273	142,258	147,246	152,308	158,140	162,273
48	Government National Mortgage Association	76,401	93,874	105,790	93,874	97,184	100,558	103,750	105,790
49	1- to 4-family	74,546	91,602	102,750	91,602	94,810	98,057	101,068	102,750
50	Multifamily	1,855	2,272	3,040	2,272	2,374	2,501	2,682	3,040
51	Federal Home Loan Mortgage Corporation	15,180	16,854	19,843	16,854	17,067	17,565	17,936	19,843
52	1- to 4-family	12,149	13,471	15,888	13,471	13,641	14,115	14,401	15,888
53	Multifamily	3,031	3,383	3,955	3,383	3,426	3,450	3,535	3,955
54	Farmers Home Administration	27,697	31,530	36,640	31,530	32,995	34,185	36,454	36,640
55	1- to 4-family	14,884	16,683	18,378	16,683	16,640	17,165	18,407	18,378
56	Multifamily	2,163	2,612	3,426	2,612	2,853	3,097	3,488	3,426
57	Commercial	4,328	5,271	6,161	5,271	5,382	5,750	6,040	6,161
58	Farm	6,322	6,964	8,675	6,964	8,120	8,173	8,519	8,675
59	Individual and others[3]	171,987	192,727	210,816	192,727	197,045	202,289	206,923	210,816
60	1- to 4-family	99,421	114,123	126,064	114,123	117,180	120,639	123,465	126,064
61	Multifamily	23,249	26,114	28,301	26,114	26,470	27,067	27,772	28,301
62	Commercial	24,128	26,740	28,880	26,740	27,180	27,767	28,365	28,880
63	Farm	25,189	25,750	27,571	25,750	26,215	26,816	27,321	27,571

1. Includes loans held by nondeposit trust companies but not bank trust departments.
2. Outstanding principal balances of mortgages backing securities insured or guaranteed by the agency indicated.
3. Other holders include mortgage companies, real estate investment trusts, state and local credit agencies, state and local retirement funds, noninsured pension funds, credit unions, and U.S. agencies for which amounts are small or separate data are not readily available.

NOTE: Based on data from various institutional and governmental sources, with some quarters estimated in part by the Federal Reserve in conjunction with the Federal Home Loan Bank Board and the Department of Commerce. Separation of nonfarm mortgage debt by type of property, if not reported directly, and interpolations and extrapolations when required, are estimated mainly by the Federal Reserve. Multifamily debt refers to loans on structures of five or more units.

SOURCE: *Federal Reserve Bulletin,* 68 F.R.B. No. 3 at A41 (March 1982).

TABLE 3. Analysis of State Usury Statutes

State	Maximum contract rate [1] (Percent per year) Individual	Maximum contract rate [1] (Percent per year) Corporate	FHA and VA loans exempt	Other limitations on mortgage loans [2]	Other limitations on installment loans [3]	Banks exempt as licensed lenders for small loans
Alabama	18 [4]	18 [4]	X		6 percent per year, add-on (not over 11.1 percent per year), discount (not over 11.8 percent per year)	X
Alaska	(5)	(5)				
Arizona [6]	N/L	N/L	X	N/L	N/L	
Arkansas [8]	10	10				
California [7]	UCCC					
Colorado	N/L	N/L		N/L	18% for open end credit arising from retail sales of consumer goods on services	X
Connecticut						
Delaware	N/L	N/L	X	5 percentage points over FRS discount rate plus surcharge on unregulated lenders only		
Florida [9]	18	18 to $500,000	X	N/L		
Georgia [9]	16 [10]	N/L over $3000 for business purposes, corporate or not	X	2.50 points over monthly average yield on 20 year maturity US Government Bonds sold during second preceding month	9 percent per year, add-on; if less than $3000 and 36 months, 8 percent, add-on plus one-time fee of 8 percent on first $600 and 4 percent on excess	
Guam	UCCC	UCCC/24	X	Loans may be made to come under UCCC by agreement between the parties	36 percent to $660, 18 percent to $1100, 12 percent to $3300	

Table 3 REAL ESTATE FINANCING S.App. A-12

TABLE 3 (continued)

State	Maximum contract rate [1] (Percent per year) Individual	Maximum contract rate [1] (Percent per year) Corporate	FHA and VA loans exempt	Other limitations on mortgage loans [2]	Other limitations on installment loans [3]	Banks exempt as licensed lenders for small loans
Hawaii	11	11	X	N/L	1½ percent per month on unpaid balance for term up to 15 years.[12]	X
Idaho	UCCC/21		X	Loans made be made to come under UCCC by agreement of the parties	36 percent to $660 24 percent from $660 to $2,200 18 percent from $2,200 to $55,000 (or 21% overall)	
Illinois	N/L	N/L	X	N/L	N/L	
Indiana	UCCC/21	N/L	X		15% per year	X
Iowa	N/L	N/L		N/L	21% per year on closed-end credit	
Kansas	10	N/L	X	1½ percentage points above the "Freddie Mac"	UCCC/18	
Kentucky	8 [14]	N/L	X		8 percent per annum, discount with maturity up to 5 years and 32 days, only add-on up to 10 years and 32 days.	
Louisiana	8 [15]	N/L	X	12 percent on conventional obligations secured by immovable property	18 percent per year on unpaid balance or 36 percent per year on unpaid principal of $800 or less, 27 percent over $800 to $2000, 21 percent over $2000 to $3500 and 15 percent on excess.	X
Maine	N/L	N/L			Consumer credit—18 percent per year for loans repaid within 37 months, or 30% on first $540, 21% over $540 to $1800, 15% on amount over $1800	
Maryland	18 [9]	N/L (16)	X	First mortgages—N/L Second mortgages—16%	18 percent per year on unpaid balance	(16)

S.App. A-13 APP. A—ANCILLARY DATA Table 3

State				
Massachusetts	N/L	N/L		
Michigan	7 25% for unincorporated businesses	N/L	X	18 percent per year on second mortgages on owner-occupied property with up to 6 units	7% per year add-on or 1% above prevailing discount rate, 16.5% per annum or 1% above discount rate on motor vehicle loans credit card financing 1½% per month
Minnesota	8 [10]	N/L	X	25 percent per year until 12/31/81 on first mortgages and land contracts made by regulated lenders; other first mortgage loans & land contracts made by unregulated lenders, 11 percent per year	
Mississippi	10 [24]	15 [24]	X	Variable rate established monthly by Commissioner of Banks	12 percent per year or 4½% over the Federal Reserve Discount Rate, whichever is greater, up to $35,000 for term of 12 years, 32 days
Missouri	10 [17]	N/L	X	10% individual; 15% corporate [24]	Until 6/30/82: Loans under $2500; greater of 12% add-on, or 5% APR over discount. Over $2500: greater of 6% add-on, or 8% over discount (APR). After 6/30/82: 10% add-on if under $2500, 6% add-on if over $2500.
Montana	N/L	N/L	X [19]	20.04% on second mortgage loans secured by residential real estate	26.62% on first $800; 15% from $800 to $2500; 10% above $2500.
Nebraska	16	N/L	X		19 percent per year; single interest installment loans may draw 19% simple interest per annum or a minimum charge of $10.

Table 3   REAL ESTATE FINANCING   S.App. A-14

TABLE 3 (*continued*)

State	Maximum contract rate [1] (Percent per year) Individual	Corporate	FHA and VA loans exempt	Other limitations on mortgage loans [2]	Other limitations on installment loans [3]	Banks exempt as licensed lenders for small loans
Nevada	N/L	N/L	X		8 percent per year up to $500, 7 percent over $500 up to $1500; add-on	
New Hampshire	N/L	N/L				
New Jersey	16 [20]	50	X	17% for first lien on 1–6 family dwelling, a portion of which may be used for other than residential purposes	Negotiable up to 30%.	
New Mexico	N/L	N/L	X	N/L	N/L	
New York		N/L	X		6 percent per year, discounted	
North Carolina	[23]	N/L		N/L on single family dwelling first mortgage loan	See note 23.	
North Dakota	N/L	N/L			N/L	
Ohio	18 [25]	N/L	X	3 percentage points over 4th FR District discount rate		
Oklahoma	UCCC/21	N/L	X	45 percent per year	N/L	
Oregon	N/L	N/L	X	N/L		
Pennsylvania	6 [20]	N/L	X	Residential mortgages based on monthly index of long term U.S. government bonds for 2nd preceding month plus 2½ percent [30]	6 percent per year discount and 1 percent per month on revolving credit Alternatively, may charge Federal discount rate plus 5%.	
Puerto Rico	9	27	X	See note 27.	See note 27.	

APP. A—ANCILLARY DATA Table 3

Rhode Island	21	21 [13]	X	8 percent per year, add-on
South Carolina	18 APR [26]	N/L [28]		Revolving credit and bank credit cards—24% APR on balance up to $650, 18% over $650, until 7/1/82.
South Dakota	10	N/L	X	8 percent per year up to $1,000, 7 percent over $1,000 up to $15,000; add-on
Tennessee	10	10	X	6 percent per year, add-on or discount
Texas	24	28	X [19]	
Utah	UCCC/18	N/L	X	
Vermont	12 [29]			Retail installment contracts, bank credit cards or retail charge accounts, 18 percent up to $500 and 12 percent over $500. Interest calculated on actuarial method other installment loans 24% on first $100, 12% in excess of $1000
Virginia	8 [21]	N/L	X	N/L on non-agricultural loans secured by first mortgage on realty [31]
Washington	22	N/L		
West Virginia	8 [18]	N/L	X	1½ percent over the average yield of long term U.S. Govt. notes and bonds
Wisconsin	N/L	N/L	X	18%
Wyoming	UCCC/18	N/L		Consumer credit: 18 percent per year up to $1000 and 15 percent over $1000.

Key: N/L—No limit   UCCC—Uniform Commercial Credit Code

Table 3   REAL ESTATE FINANCING   S.App. A-16

TABLE 3 (*continued*)

UCCC rates are the following on supervised loans: Greater of 18 percent on all unpaid balances or total of 36 percent on balances $330 or less, 21 percent on over $330 and not over $1,000, 15 percent on over $1,000. UCCC rates apply to all loans under $25,000; no restrictions on loans greater than that.

[1] Maximum that may be set by contract between two parties, subject in a number of States to one or more exceptions listed either in the table or by footnote.

[2] General limitations applicable to mortgage loans and not subject to other statutory limitations.

[3] General limitations applicable to installment loans and not subject to other statutory limitations and in some states special limitations on loans to consumers; i.e., loans for the purchase of goods.

[4] No ceiling on loans over $5000.

[5] 5 percentage points above discount rate charged by 12th Federal Reserve district.

[6] 10 percent per annum, unless a different rate is contracted for in writing, in which case there is no limit.

[7] Banks and other regulated lenders are exempt from usury ceiling; 10% for non-regulatory lenders.

[8] Arkansas banks operate under the Depository Institutions Deregulation and Monetary Control Act of 1980.

[9] 1½ percent per month for revolving credit and credit card transactions.

[10] N/L over $100,000; can be 4½% over FR discount rate for any loan (except open-end credit, limited to 1½%).

[11] N/L on loans over $750,000.

[12] For the period June 1, 1980 to June 30, 1985, the maximum interest rate permitted on simple interest loans is 24% a year. Credit cards maximum rate is 18% a year. Discount rate, effective from June 1, 1980 to June 30, 1985 maximum rate increased— From: To:
                             12%   14% first 18 months.
                              9%   10½% next 12 months.
                              6%   7% next 12 months.
                              3%   3% next 6 months.

[13] On business loans over $25,000, rate is 10% above the 13-week alternate usury rate.

[14] May agree in writing to 4% in excess of 90-day commercial paper rate, or 10%, whichever is less; no limit on loans over $15,000.

[15] N/L over $25,000.

[16] N/L on business loans over $5,000; national banks are exempt from usury limitations on small loans if they qualify as licenses, state banks are not.

[17] N/L on business loans over $5,000 (or monthly index of U.S. Government long term bonds plus three percentage points).

[18] Or 1% above FR discount rate.

[19] FHA only.

[20] Or 1% above discount rate. Loans over $50,000 may go to 30%.

[21] N/L on loans over $5,000 for business purposes.

[22] Higher of 12% or 4% above average 26-week T-bill rate of preceding calendar month.

[23] For loans under $25,000, the Commissioner of Banks announces the maximum rate on the 15th of each month. The rate so announced will be the maximum rate in effect for the term of all loans made during the following calendar month. The rate is the higher of 16% or the non-competitive rate for six-month U.S. Treasury Bills in effect on the 15th of the month, rounded to the nearest ½ of 1% plus 6%.

[24] Through 6/30/82, limits are greater of limit shown or 5% over discount rate; for real estate loans, greatest of limit shown, 5% above discount, or 5% above 20 year bond index.

[25] 10% or 1½% per month. No limit on loans over $100,000 or if securities are pledged as collateral.

[26] for loans under $390—36%; $390-$1300—21%; over $1300—15%; or 18% APR on total loan.

[27] Variable rates subject to regulations of Usury Act No. 1, approved Oct. 15, 1973, as amended.

[28] For corporations with over $40,000 capital stock.

[29] N/L on loans for income producing business or activity.

SOURCE: Conference of State Bank Supervisors, *A Profile of State-Chartered Banking* (9th ed.), December 1981.

TABLE 4. Real Estate Holdings of the 97 Largest Pension Funds
[New]

FUNDS INVESTING IN REAL ESTATE		FUNDS INVESTING IN REAL ESTATE	
Fund/sponsor	($ mil)	Fund/sponsor	($ mil)
Alabama	50.9	Illinois State	2.8
Alaska	37.9	Inland Steel	47.0
Alcoa	78.0	International Harvester	157.0
American Can	28.0	International Paper	45.0
American Electric Power	8.2	ITT	29.0
Armco	90.6	Kennecott	24.0
Ashland Oil	23.7	Kentucky Employes	62.0
AT&T/Bell System	1,243.5	Eli Lilly	13.6
Baltimore Retirement	8.8	Los Angeles County	32.0
Bendix	142.2	Machinists' Nat'l Hq.	46.8
Boilermakers	103.0	Marine Engineers	62.0
Ca. Food Employes	13.4	Merck	7.7
Caterpillar	112.0	Minnesota Mining	6.9
Celanese	72.0	Minnesota State Board	31.0
Chrysler	87.0	Monsanto	98.0
Cities Service	6.1	Montana	4.1
Colorado Employes	20.1	Motorola	7.0
Conoco	65.3	National Steel	85.0
Continental Group	78.0	Nevada Employes	8.2
Crown Zellerbach	33.7	N.Y. State Teachers	15.0
Dana Corp.	41.0	Ohio School	41.0
Deere	9.3	Ohio Teachers	254.0
Dow Chemical	50.0	Operating Engineers	52.5
Dresser Industries	20.0	Oregon Employes	23
Eastern Airlines	92.0	Owens Illinois	82.0
Eastman Kodak	76.0	Pacific Gas	10.0
IBEW	66.0	Pan American Airways	11.0
Exxon	360.0	J. C. Penney	30.0
Firestone	9.5	Pennsylvania School	23.0
Ford	109.0	Phillips Petroleum	7.0
General Electric	242.0	PPG Industries	4.0
Goodrich	13.2	RCA	73.0
Goodyear	103.0	Republic Steel	8.2
Grumman	37.0	Reynolds Metal	29.7
Hercules	77.0	Safeway	13.5
Honeywell	62.4	San Francisco City	58.8
Hughes Aircraft	97.6	Shell Oil	186.0

Table 4 REAL ESTATE FINANCING S.App. A-18

FUNDS INVESTING IN REAL ESTATE		FUNDS INVESTING IN REAL ESTATE	
Fund/sponsor	**($ mil)**	**Fund/sponsor**	**($ mil)**
Southern Baptists	98.0	Union Oil	40.0
Southern Co.	2.0	United Methodist	9.0
Southern New England Tel.	9.6	United Nations	184.0
Standard Oil (Ca.)	137.0	United Technologies	54.0
Standard Oil (In.)	55.0	Upjohn	9.8
Sun Co.	107.0	Utah Employes	67.0
Teamsters (Central)	125.0	Virginia Supplemental	36.0
Teamsters (Western)	101.0	Warner Lambert	20.0
TVA	20.7	Westinghouse	140.0
Texas Instruments	40.0	Xerox	6.8
Textron	5.3	**Total**	**6,831.0**
TWA	85.0		

SOURCE: *Pensions and Investment Age,* January 18, 1982 at 53.

Appendix B
SAMPLE FORMS AND AGREEMENTS

Form		Page
3.15	Shared Appreciation Mortgage Provisions for Sharing Cash Flow, Capital Appreciation, and Net Sale Proceeds	S.App. B- 1
3.16	Contingent Interest Provisions Based on Gross Receipts	S.App. B- 4
3.17	Due-on-Sale Clause Limited to Arm's-Length Transactions	S.App. B- 6
3.18	FHLMC-FNMA Due-on-Sale Clause	S.App. B- 8
4.3	Construction Mortgage Loan Commitment	S.App. B- 9
4.4	CD Method of Computing Construction Loan Interest	S.App. B-15
4.5	Conversion to Eurodollar Method of Computing Construction Loan Interest (Libor)	S.App. B-16
11.5	Letter of Intent for Leveraged Equity Joint Venture	S.App. B-19

Page App. B-87:

Add new Forms 3.15-3.18.

Form 3.15

SHARED APPRECIATION MORTGAGE PROVISIONS FOR SHARING CASH FLOW, CAPITAL APPRECIATION, AND NET SALE PROCEEDS

I. DEFINITIONS

(a) "Premises" as used herein shall mean the building and underlying land described as follows:

. . . .

(b) "Positive Cash Flow" shall mean the total gross rents received by Borrower as lessor during the period of .... including, but not limited to, fixed rentals, parking rentals, rentals from concessions plus all other revenues derived from the "Premises" (all such rentals and revenues hereinafter called "Gross Receipts") minus all bona fide operating and business expenses and capital expenditures incurred by the Borrower in connection with Premises during the period of .... In determining "Positive Cash Flow," deductions from "Gross Receipts" shall include "Fixed Interest" and shall not include "Annual Additional Interest," "Final Additional Interest," income taxes, and expenses not incurred during the period of ....

(c) "Fixed Interest" shall include monthly payments of .... percent on the principal balance.

(d) "Annual Additional Interest" shall be due and payable in quarterly installments based on the "Positive Cash Flow." The method of payment shall be as described below.

(e) "Final Additional Interest" shall be due and payable at the maturity of the loan in an amount based on the fair market value or "Net Sale Proceeds" derived from the "Premises."

(f) "Net Sale Proceeds" shall mean the gross proceeds derived from the sale of the "Premises" minus the amount of unpaid principal balance on the first mortgage, charges, penalties and all reasonable costs incurred by the Borrower in connection with the sale.

II. ANNUAL ADDITIONAL INTEREST

The "Annual Additional Interest," due and payable in equal quarterly installments corresponding to the fiscal quarters, shall amount to .... percent of the "Positive Cash Flow." A determination shall be made within ...... days after the end of a fiscal year as to whether the sum of the quarterly installments equaled, exceeded or was identical to .... percent of the "Positive Cash Flow." If "Positive Cash Flow" exceeded the quarterly installments, the Borrower shall pay the difference immediately after receiving notice thereof. If the quarterly installments exceeded .... percent of the "Positive Cash Flow," the excess shall be credited to the next installment(s) of "Annual Additional Interest" due. However, if the installments paid for the final fiscal year exceeded .... percent of the "Positive Cash Flow," the excess shall be paid promptly to the Borrower upon payment of all sums due under the mortgage note.

III. FINAL ADDITIONAL INTEREST

Upon maturity of the mortgage, whether by reason of the due date, acceleration, refinancing, or otherwise, "Final Additional Interest" shall be due and payable equal to the following:

(a) If the maturity occurs within ...... years from the date hereof, "Final Additional Interest" shall amount to the greater of .... percent of the fair market value of the "Premises" as determined by an appraiser acceptable to both parties, *or* ...... times the highest annual debt service (to include "Fixed Interest" and "Annual Additional Interest") payable during any prior fiscal year.

(b) If the maturity occurs after ...... years from the date hereof, "Final Additional Interest" shall amount to the greater of .... percent of the fair market value of the "Premises," as determined by an appraiser acceptable to both parties, subtracting therefrom $........ plus an amount equal to the unpaid principal balance, *or* .... times the highest annual debt service (to include "Fixed Interest" and "Annual Additional Interest") payable during any prior fiscal year.

(c) If the appraisal by the appraiser referred to in paragraphs (a) and (b) above proves unsatisfactory to the Lender, the Lender may then appoint a second appraiser. If such appraiser and the original appraiser do not within thirty (30) days agree on an appraisal of the Premises, then a third appraiser shall be appointed by said appraisers to prepare a third appraisal. The fair market value shall be the (middle) (average) figure.

In the event there is a sale of the premises, the "Final Additional Interest" due shall be as follows:

(i) If the sale occurs within ...... years from the date hereof, the "Final Additional Interest" shall equal .... percent of "Net Sale Proceeds" after subtracting from such proceeds the unpaid principal balance.

(ii) If the sale occurs after ...... years from the date hereof, "Final Additional Interest" shall equal .... percent of "Net Sale Proceeds" after subtracting from such proceeds $ .... plus an amount equal to the unpaid principal balance.

IV. NO VIOLATION OF USURY LAW

It is not intended to charge interest at a rate in excess of the maximum rate of interest permitted to be charged to the Borrower under applicable law, but if, notwithstanding, interest in excess of said maximum rate shall be paid hereunder, the excess shall be, at the option of the Lender, either (a) retained by Lender as additional cash collateral for the payment of said principal sum, or the amount thereof outstanding, or (b) returned to the Borrower.

V. GOVERNING LAW

This instrument is made and delivered in the state of ...., where all payments shall be made. The parties agree that this instrument shall be construed in accordance with the laws, including the conflict of law rules, of the state of ....

Form 3.16

CONTINGENT INTEREST PROVISIONS BASED ON GROSS RECEIPTS

In addition to the principal and fixed interest provided for in this Agreement, the Borrower agrees to pay additional contingent interest accruing from January 1, 19..... Such contingent interest shall be based on .... percent of the differential of the Gross Receipts, defined in Paragraph 1 and the Base Amount, defined in Paragraph 4, and shall be paid in the manner set forth in the Mortgage in the following installments:

....
....
....

In addition, the following shall apply:

(1) "Gross Receipts" shall mean an amount equal to the aggregate of all fixed, minimum and guaranteed rents, overage rents, percentage or participation rents, and all rents and receipts from licenses and concessions, received by Mortgagor or the then owner of the mortgaged premises from the mortgaged premises, including all amounts received pursuant to escalation and contribution provisions contained in any and all occupancy leases and subleases and all income and revenue of a non-rental nature.

No deductions from Gross Receipts shall be allowed except for the following:

    (a) The differential of the Aggregate Expenses, defined in Paragraph 6 and the Base Aggregate Expenses, defined in Paragraph 7 of this Agreement; and

    (b) The unreimbursed capitalized cost of work performed to prepare the premises for new or renewed lease occupancy divided by the number of years in the fixed term (excluding renewal terms) of the lease.

(2) Gross Receipts shall not include the following:

....
....
....

(3) There shall be no duplication of "Gross Receipts" by reason of lease-sublease-sub-sublease arrangements. The calculation of the

amount of Gross Receipts shall include the aggregate amount of all rents, receipts, income, revenue and other amounts (except as above excluded) paid to Mortgagor or the then owner of the mortgaged premises by lessees, occupants and users of any part of the mortgaged premises without duplication.

(4) The Base Amount shall be $ . . . . . ., the cost of constructing the . . . . . . square feet contained in the . . . . . . floors of the building.

In the event that a condemnation results in the permanent reduction or the size of the buildings and improvements constructed on the mortgaged premises in excess of 25 percent of the gross leaseable area immediately prior to such taking, then said Base Amounts shall, effective for the Fiscal year next following the date upon which physical possession of the taken space is taken by the condemning authority, be reduced in the proportion that the amount of gross leaseable area of such buildings and improvements is reduced. In addition, for the last fiscal year occurring during the term of this Mortgage, if such last fiscal year be less than twelve (12) months, the said Base Amount (or any reduced Base Amount) shall be decreased pro rata.

(5) Notwithstanding anything herein or in any related loan document to the contrary, it is not the intention of the parties to charge, nor shall there at any time be charged any interest (whether fixed, contingent or otherwise) which would result in a rate of interest being charged which is in excess of the maximum rate permitted to be charged by law; and in the event that any sum in excess of the maximum legal rate of interest is paid or charged, the same, shall immediately upon discovery thereof, be deemed to have been a prepayment of principal (which prepayment shall be permitted, and be without premium or penalty) as of the date of such receipt, and all payments made thereafter shall be appropriately reapplied to interest and principal to give effect, to the maximum rate permitted by law, and after such reapplication, any excess payment shall be immediately refunded to Mortgagor.

(6) Aggregate Expenses shall include all real estate taxes, property insurance premiums and operating costs.

(7) Base Aggregate Expenses shall include the aggregate of $ . . . . per square foot of office space and $ . . . . per square foot of retail space in the building.

(8) The Mortgagee shall have the right at all reasonable times to inspect the books, papers and records of Mortgagor or all subsequent owners of the property for the purposes of ascertaining the amount of said Gross Receipts and of determining the correctness of any statement delivered to it by the Mortgagor or any subsequent owners of the property. Such inspection shall be made at the office of Mortgagor or at such other place as Mortgagor may designate provided Mortgagee approves same. If upon such inspection it is found that an error has occurred with

respect to the amount of Gross Receipts or Contingent Interest, the parties shall adjust any differences that shall have occurred by an appropriate payment to the Mortgagee. If the Mortgagee should find that any statement furnished by the Mortgagor or any subsequent owners of the property has materially understated such Gross Receipts or Continent Interest then Mortgagor or any subsequent owners of the property shall promptly, upon demand, reimburse the Mortgagee for any sums expended by the Mortgagee in making such inspections. The inspection on behalf of the Mortgagee may be made by an officer thereof or by any agent or accountant appointed for that purpose.

(9) It is agreed that the Mortgagee shall not be considered as a partner or joint venturer in the leases to the premises with the Mortgagor, his successors or assigns.

Form 3.17

DUE-ON-SALE CLAUSE LIMITED TO ARM'S-LENGTH TRANSACTIONS

I. *Definitions*

    A. "Mortgagee" shall mean the mortgagee named in this instrument during such time as it is the holder of the mortgage, and no other person or entity.

    B. "Mortgagor" shall mean the person or entity that is the owner from time to time, as the case may be, of the interest of the Mortgagor, as defined below.

    C. "Sale" shall mean a transfer of record of the Mortgagor's Interest, or any part thereof, as the result of an arm's-length contractual transaction with the Mortgagor for a price aggregating, in the event of a transfer of the whole Interest, a dollar amount greater than the principal sum due under this instrument at the time of the transfer, and in event of a transfer of a partial Interest, a dollar amount greater than the principal balance then due under this instrument proportionately attributable to the Interest sold when computed on the basis of the land area of the property.

    Without limiting the foregoing, and solely for the purpose of illustration, a Sale does not include the following:

        (1) Transfers to or from nominees or agents
        (2) Transfers to or from subsidiary or affiliated entities

(3) Transfers to a restructured limited partnership on the termination or continuance of a partnership according to the certificate of partnership on file
(4) Transfers between a partnership and its individual members
(5) Any transfer made to or among the parties interested in the transferor, including the transferor's stockholders, if a corporation, or the transferor's partners, if a partnership
(6) A corporate merger or consolidation
(7) A transfer that is, in substance, a security transaction, but only if made expressly subject to this mortgage
(8) Any transfer that is one of form only, irrespective of whether or not it comes within any of the foregoing exceptions or is in common use at the date of this instrument. A transaction that constitutes or is part of a scheme to circumvent the privileges of the Mortgagee under this Article, involving, for example, bad faith conduct of the Mortgagor, shall constitute a Sale. A lease or transfer or a nonpossessory interest (whether a license, easement, or otherwise) shall, subject to the requirement of the Mortgagor's good faith, not be considered a Sale.

D. "Interest of the Mortgagor" shall mean the present interest held by the Mortgagor in the property hereby mortgaged.

II. Subject to Paragraph III below, the principal sum secured by this mortgage shall, at the Mortgagee's option, become due and payable ...... days after a Sale, of the Interest of the Mortgagor. Mortgagee must, in order to exercise the option, give Mortgagor notice thereof before the expiration of said ...... (....)-day period. If less than ...... (......) days remain between the date of the notice by Mortgagee and the expiration of said ...... (......) days, the principal sum shall become due and payable ...... (......) days after the giving of notice. The ...... (......)-day period shall be measured from the date the transfer of title is recorded or from the date on which the transfer first became known to Mortgagee, whichever is later.

III. Mortgagor may, at its election, notify Mortgagee of a proposed Sale at any time, giving the name of the individual or group with whom, or with whose nominee, Mortgagor proposes to contract or has contracted, setting forth the proposed terms of the Sale, including the proposed settlement date, and confirming that the proposed Sale is a bona fide Sale. Within ...... (......) days after the date of the notice of a proposed Sale by Mortgagor, Mortgagee must notify Mortgagor of any objection to said Sale, which objection must in all circumstances be reasonable and stated with reasonable particularity. If Mortgagee shall, within the ...... (......)-day period, fail to notify Mortgagor of its objections or shall be unreasonable in the statement thereof in its notice, Mortgagor shall have the right to make the proposed Sale on the Terms of Sale stated in the notice to Mortgagee, and Mortgagee's right to accelerate the principal sum secured by the mortgage shall automatically lapse and be void.

IV. For those Sales for which the Mortagee has the option to accelerate the due date of the mortgage, Mortgagor shall have the privilege to prepay at its option the principal sum secured by this mortgage, without penalty but with accrued interest to the date of prepayment, on ...... (......) days notice to Mortgagee given at any time in the period beginning ...... (......) days before the date of the transfer and expiring ...... (......) days thereafter.

V. All time periods set forth in this Article are of the essence.

VI. Notices must be in writing, mailed by registered or certified mail, addressed to the parties at the respective addresses set forth for them in this mortgage or at such other address of which notification shall have been given in the manner stated in this mortgage for the giving of notices. As to registered mail, notice shall be deemed served when properly addressed and duly accepted for mailing as registered mail in a branch of the United States Post Office located in the City of ....; and as to certified mail, when duly deposited in a United States mailbox or at a branch United States Post Office located in the City of ...., properly addressed, with the postage duly prepaid.

Form 3.18

FHLMC-FNMA DUE-ON-SALE CLAUSE

If all or any part of the Property or an interest therein is sold or transferred by Borrower without Lender's prior written consent, excluding (a) the creation of a lien or encumbrance subordinate to this mortgage; (b) the creation of a purchase-money security interest for household appliances; (c) a transfer by devise, descent, or operation of law upon the death of a joint tenant; or (d) the grant of any leasehold interest of three (3) years or less not containing an option to purchase, Lender may, at Lender's option, declare all the sums secured by this mortgage to be immediately due and payable. Lender shall have waived such option to accelerate if, prior to the sale or transfer, Lender and the person to whom the Property is to be sold or transferred reach agreement in writing that the credit of such person is satisfactory to Lender and that the interest payable on the sums secured by this mortgage shall be at such rate as Lender shall request. If Lender has waived the option to accelerate provided in this Paragraph (17) [*omitted*] and if Borrower's successor in interest has executed a written assumption agreement accepted in writing by Lender, Lender shall release Borrower from all obligations under this mortgage and the Note.

If Lender exercises such option to accelerate, Lender shall mail Borrower notice of acceleration in accordance with Paragraph (14) [*omitted*] hereof. Such notice shall provide a period of not less than thirty (30) days from the date the notice is mailed within which Borrower may pay the sums declared due. If Borrower fails to pay such sums prior to the expiration of such period, Lender may, without further notice or demand on Borrower, invoke any remedies permitted by Paragraph (18) [*omitted*] hereof.

Page App. B-110:

Add new Forms 4.3-4.5.

Form 4.3

CONSTRUCTION MORTGAGE LOAN COMMITMENT

ABC Construction Lending Institution

COMMITMENT NO. ....
Date: ....
To: ....

This constitutes a commitment of ABC Construction Lending Institution (hereinafter referred to as ABC) to make a construction mortgage loan to the Borrower subject to the specific terms hereinafter set forth, to the "General Conditions of Construction Loan" and to the "Specific Conditions of Construction Loan" annexed hereto and made a part hereof:

Borrower(s): ....

Property and Improvements: ....

Qualified Loan Amount: The amount qualified for disbursement under the permanent loan commitment, but in no event greater than the Maximum Loan Amount.

Fm. 4.3 REAL ESTATE FINANCING S.App. B-10

Maximum Loan Amount: $..

Permanent Loan Commitment: Commitment No. ...... dated ......

Permanent Lender: ....

Variable Interest Rate: ....

Maturity Date: ....

Guarantor(s): ....

Nonrefundable Commitment Fee: $..................................

Inspecting Architect: ....

ABC Counsel: ....

Loan Officer: ....

    This commitment shall be considered null and void unless you indicate your acceptance by signing and returning the attached copy of this commitment to us together with the Nonrefundable Commitment Fee in care of the Loan Officer by no later than ....

BY: ABC Construction Lending Institution

AGREED TO AND ACCEPTED
THIS ...... day of ...... 19....
....
....
....

"General Conditions of Construction Loan"

ABC COMMITMENT NO. ....
Date: ....

    (1) The construction mortgage loan contemplated by this commitment to the Borrower shall be secured at all times by a first lien on the Property and Improvements and shall be in an amount not to exceed the Qualified Loan Amount.

    (2) This commitment and our obligation to make advances under the loan are subject to satisfaction of the terms hereof and to the Permanent Loan Commitment being in full force and effect at all times throughout the term of our loan.

    (3) The loan is to be evidenced by the Borrower's promissory note for the Maximum Loan Amount which shall bear a variable Interest Rate payable monthly and be due and payable in full at the Maturity Date and is to be secured by a mortgage which shall be a first lien on the fee simple title to the security with any ground lease or leases expressly subordinated, and additionally secured by (i) security agreements and

financing statements creating a first lien covering all supplies delivered and to be used in the construction of the Improvements to be financed hereby as well as all equipment and furnishings actually installed in the Improvements; it is understood and agreed that the inclusion of any and all non-fixture items is solely for the purpose of insuring completion of construction and compliance with the Permanent Loan Commitment and not for the purposes of producing income or return on investment; (ii) an assignment of rents and leases free of any prior interest in said rents and leases; (iii) a building loan agreement; (iv) the unconditional joint and several guaranty by the Guarantors of completion of construction and of repayment of the indebtedness; and (v) such other documents as are designated by ABC's Counsel (all hereinafter collectively referred to as the Loan Documents). The Loan Documents are to be satisfactory to us and our counsel both as to form and content.

(4) The improvements shall be constructed and the loan advanced in accordance with the terms of the building loan agreement, which, among other things, shall require the inspection of construction and approval of advances (to be made not more frequently than once monthly) by the Inspecting Architect, and the receipt and approval by us and our Counsel both as to form and content prior to the first advance (the initial closing) of the following:

(a) An appraisal, also to be approved by the Permanent Lender, prepared without cost to us by an appraiser acceptable to us and the Permanent Lender. The Qualified Loan Amount shall in no event exceed 75 percent of the value established by such appraisal;

(b) The undertakings of the general contractor, architect and engineer, if any, to continue performance on our behalf without additional cost in the event of a default under any of the loan documents;

(c) One set of final detailed plans and specifications for all construction, including borings and soil reports and evidence of permanent lender's acceptance thereof, designating the manufacturer and model number of all equipment (i) with the approval of the Borrower, Guarantors, Permanent Lender and Inspecting Architect noted thereon; (ii) bearing an endorsement by the appraiser that he has examined said plans and specifications and finds them to be in keeping with the basis on which he appraised the property for us; (iii) accompanied by a certification by an architect acceptable to us that the plans and specifications meet all applicable local zoning, building and other pertinent requirements of the public authorities having jurisdiction, including, but not limited to, compliance with the National Environmental Policy Act and any other applicable federal, state, municipal or local environmental impact or energy laws or regulations, and that the construction covered thereby is sound, of good design and satisfactory for the purpose intended; (iv) accompanied by a certification by a qualified professional engineer acceptable to us certifying on a basis of personal inspection, with supporting data (borings, soil reports, etc.) that what is planned and specified will be adequate, and (v) showing that the parking facilities will be constructed as required within the security. Any and all changes from the approved plans and specifications must be approved by us;

(d) The Loan Documents executed by all parties necessary to create the rights and duties respectively set out in each document;

(e) A detailed cost breakdown showing all costs of the proposed construction with the approval of the Inspecting Architect that the cost breakdown is reasonable and accurate being noted thereon;

(f) Current financial statements for the Borrower, Guarantors, general contractor and major subcontractors;

(g) Evidence that the Property is free and clear of all restrictions and encumbrances unless approved by us;

(h) Architects', contractors', subcontractors' and engineers' contracts relating to construction of the Improvements with parties acceptable to us and assignments of said contracts to us;

(i) Borrower's affidavit and opinion of Borrower's Counsel;

(j) Form lease to be used for all tenants;

(k) A policy of mortgagee's title insurance written by a title company or companies acceptable to us on the American Land Title Association 1970 Loan Policy form assignable to a permanent mortgagee;

(l) A current survey certified to us and the title insurer; a foundation survey will also be required when the foundation is completed and we reserve the right to call for interim surveys locating the improvements as construction progresses;

(m) Evidence of compliance with all laws, ordinances, rules, regulations and restrictions affecting the premises, the construction of the improvements and the consummation of the transaction, including but not limited to zoning, issuance of all building permits and licenses and availability of utility and municipal services;

(n) Such policies of builder's risk, liability, workmen's compensation and other insurance as we may require in forms, companies and amounts acceptable to us, including, but not limited to, collapse insurance;

(o) Evidence that sufficient funds have been made available by the Borrower in a manner satisfactory to us for the purpose of completing the improvements heretofore described;

(p) Evidence that the Borrower has purchased the land herein referred to and has fully paid for it;

(q) An assignment of the Borrower's rights under the Permanent Loan Commitment, with such assignment approved by the Permanent Lender;

(r) Evidence that all requirements of the Permanent Loan Commitment which can be satisfied prior to the initial closing have been complied with to the satisfaction of the Permanent Lender, including but not limited to approval by the Permanent Lender of the state of title and survey; that the Permanent Loan Commitment is in full force and effect, without modification, except as we may have approved in writing, and that the Permanent Lender has agreed to accept the certificate of the Inspecting Architect in satisfaction of any conditions of the Permanent Loan Commitment requiring certification as to performance of construction and completion of improvements in accordance with the plans and specifications;

(s) Evidence as to the Borrower's capacity and authority to take the loan and to execute the Loan Documents;

(t) Such other documents, instruments, opinions, and assurances as we may require including but not limited to 100 percent labor and material payment and performance bonds covering the general contractor and/or subcontractors in amounts and issued by companies satisfactory to us, in which we are to be named as dual obligee, assignments of specified leases and, at our option, an agreement by the Permanent Lender for the purchase of the note and mortgage;

(5) The loan shall be made without cost to us. The fees of our Counsel, the appraiser, the Inspecting Architect, title insurance premiums and charges, survey charges, mortgage and documentary stamp taxes, if any, recording charges, brokerage commissions and any other connected costs shall be payable by the Borrower and the Guarantors, and the Borrower and the Guarantors hereby jointly and severally agree to pay such fees and to indemnify us against claims of brokers arising in connection with the execution of this commitment by us or the consummation of the loan contemplated hereby, all regardless of whether the loan contemplated hereby closes.

(6) Our Counsel shall be satisfied that all fees and charges respecting the making of the loan will result in no exceeding of any applicable interest limitation of the jurisdiction in which the property securing the loan is located. The loan and our making of it shall be in all respects legal and shall not violate any applicable law or other requirement of any governmental authority.

(7) The improvements are to be constructed in accordance with the approved appraisal and final plans and specifications, and are to be completed, free of all liens, other than the lien of the construction mortgage contemplated hereby, not less than thirty days in advance of the Maturity Date of the Note.

(8) The proceeds of the loan shall be advanced (a) as construction progresses, but not more frequently than once a month, in amounts which at our election shall be 90 percent of either:

(a) The amount of the qualified loan multiplied by the percentage of completion of construction then attained; or
(b) The estimated total cost of construction of the improvements as determined at the time of each advance by the Inspecting Architect, (and/or, at our option, by our in-house architect) multiplied by the percentage of completion of construction then attained, less the difference between said estimated total cost of construction and the amount of the qualified loan.

less in each case, amounts theretofore advanced; and (b) in no event in an amount greater than the Qualified Loan Amount. Funds will be advanced for materials stored on-site only at our option.

(9) Each request for funds from the Borrower shall be on ABC's forms, duly approved for payment by the Contractor, Inspecting Architect and Borrower and accompanied by all documentation deemed necessary by us to substantiate the requested payment. Draw requests are to be sent to the Loan Officer in sufficient time to allow five (5) business days for processing and wiring of funds.

(10) By accepting this commitment, the Borrower agrees, at our request, to affix a sign approved by us, at a location on the premises satisfactory to us, which shall recite, among other things, that ABC is financing the construction.

(11) This commitment assumes the accuracy of all information, representations, exhibits and other matter submitted to us and presupposes no material adverse change in the state of facts indicated therein prior to any disbursement of funds hereunder.

(12) This commitment may be amended only by a writing executed by us and is not assignable without our prior written consent.

(13) After accepting this commitment, the Borrower is requested

to promptly get in touch with our Counsel for the purpose of arranging for the preparation of the Loan Documents and other items necessary for the initial closing.

(14) The initial closing shall be held on a date within forty-five (45) days from the date of the acceptance of this commitment, upon not less than five (5) days written notice to us, care of the Loan Officer. No such notice shall be effective to establish a closing date unless we shall have previously received and approved a current report of title and the requisite survey. Unless the initial closing is held within such forty-five (45)-day period, our obligation hereunder will, at our option, terminate.

COMMENT: See discussion of Construction Mortgage Loan Commitment at ¶ 4.02.

Form 4.4

CD METHOD OF COMPUTING CONSTRUCTION LOAN INTEREST

As used herein, the term "CD Rate" means the per annum rate of interest determined by the Bank (which determination shall be conclusive) on the basis of the per annum rate (rounded upwards to the nearest five one-hundredths of one percent (1/20%)) at which the Bank is paying on certificates of deposits of $1,000,000 or more in the New York broker market as determined by a quote from a major New York dealer, two (2) business days before the rate shall apply.

The CD Rate shall be applied to all or that portion of the unpaid principal balance as Promisor and the Bank shall have agreed plus such reserves, as determined by the Bank (which determination shall be conclusive), which the Bank must hold because of Regulation D of Board of Governors of the Federal Reserve System or any other regulation determined by a Governmental body in effect from time to time.

"Regulation D" shall mean Regulation D of the Board of Governors of the Federal Reserve System from time to time in effect and shall include any successor or other regulation of said Board of Governors relating to reserve requirements applicable to member banks of the Federal Reserve System. In addition, the Borrower agrees to pay to the Lender as additional interest such amounts as will compensate the Lender for any increase or decrease in the cost to Lender of making or maintaining the Loan hereunder, by reason of a change in any reserve, special deposit, or similar requirement with respect to assets of, deposits with or for the account of, or credit extended by, the Lender which are imposed on, or deemed applicable by, the Lender, under any law, treaty, rule, regulation (including, without limitation, Regulation D of the Board of Governors of the Federal Reserve System), any interpretation thereof by any governmental, fiscal, monetary or other authority charged with the administration thereof or having jurisdiction over such loan or the Lender, or any requirement imposed by any such authority, whether or not having the force of law. Such additional amounts shall be payable on demand.

If any payment to be made by Borrower to Lender under the Loan shall become due on a Saturday, Sunday or other day which is a legal holiday under the laws of the State of Maryland, the due date for such payment shall be extended to the next business day and the amount of such payment shall include interest accrued during such extension.

All interest shall be calculated on the basis of a 360-day year but shall be computed for the actual number of days in the period for which interest is charged.

Form 4.5

CONVERSION TO EURODOLLAR METHOD OF COMPUTING CONSTRUCTION LOAN INTEREST (LIBOR)

1. CONVERSION OF ADVANCES TO EURODOLLAR INCREMENTS, CONVERSIONS FROM EURODOLLAR INCREMENTS TO ADVANCES

1.1 From time to time, during the Availability Period and subject to the terms and conditions of this Agreement, the Venture may elect to convert all or part of the outstanding principal balance of the Advances to a Eurodollar Increment by giving to Agent an irrevocable written notice executed by both Venturers specifying (a) an Interest Period of any number of months greater than or equal to three (3) and less than or equal to twelve (12), with the actual length of each period to be determined in accordance with customary London inter-bank market practices and always ending on a Banking Day, provided that the last month ends before January 4, 1988; (b) the effective date for such conversion, which date must be a Banking Day after the Closing Date and before October 1, 1987, and which date must not be less than five (5) Banking Days nor more than fifteen (15) Banking Days after the date of receipt of such notice by Agent; and (c) the amount of such conversion, which amount must not be less than Five Million Dollars ($5,000,000). Upon receipt of a notice which complies with the requirements of Paragraph 1.1 hereof, Banks shall make the conversion on the Banking Day specified in the notice.

1.2 Each Bank's portion of each Eurodollar Increment shall be determined by application of the percentage set forth opposite such Bank's name in Paragraph 2.1 [*omitted*] to the amount of the Eurodollar Increment.

1.3 Unless the Venture has complied with the requirements of Paragraph 1.1 and provided Agent with the notice specified therein for another Eurodollar Increment, on the last day of each Interest Period respecting each Eurodollar Increment, such Eurodollar Increment shall be automatically converted to an Advance in the amount of such Eurodollar Increment. In the event Venture complies with the requirements of Paragraph 1.1 for Eurodollar Increments in connection with a current Eurodollar Increment whose Interest Period is maturing ("Maturing Eurodollar Increment"), such Maturing Eurodollar Increment shall continue as a new Eurodollar Increment in accordance with the provisions of this Article 1.

1.4 If for any reason (including, without limitation, the occurrence of any of the events specified in Paragraph 1.7) Agent receives all or part of the principal amount of a Eurodollar Increment other than on the last day of the Interest Period for such Eurodollar Increment, the Venture shall, on demand, pay Agent the amount (if any) by which (a) the additional interest which would have been payable on the amount so received had it been received on the last day of the Interest Period for such Eurodollar Increment exceeds (b) the interest which would have been recoverable by Agent by placing such amount on deposit in the London interbank market for a period starting on the date on which it was so received and ending on the last day of the Interest Period for such Eurodollar Increment.

1.5 Notwithstanding anything to the contrary contained in this Agreement, if at any time Majority Banks, in their sole and absolute discretion, determine that:

(a) Dollar deposits in the principal amount and for periods equal to the Interest Periods of a Eurodollar Increment are not available in the London interbank market;

(b) The Inter-bank Rate does not accurately reflect the cost to Majority Banks of making, continuing or converting to a Eurodollar Increment;

(c) any change in financial, political or economic conditions or currency exchange rates makes it impractical for Majority Banks to make, continue or convert to a Eurodollar Increment; or

(d) any change in applicable law or regulation or in the interpretation thereof makes it unlawful or impractical for Majority Banks to make, continue or convert to a Eurodollar Increment;

Agent shall promptly give notice thereof to the Venture, and upon the giving of such notice, Banks' obligation to continue or convert to a Eurodollar Increment shall immediately terminate.

1.6 Upon the giving of the notice referred to in Paragraph 1.5, the outstanding principal balance of all Eurodollar Increments shall be converted to Advances and shall be added to the outstanding principal balance of all Advances as of said conversion, and the resulting sum shall be payable and shall bear interest from the date of such conversion at the rate as specified in Paragraph 2.5 [omitted] for Advances.

1.7 The Venture shall reimburse or compensate each Bank, upon demand by Agent for such Bank, for all costs incurred, losses suffered or payments made by Agent or such Bank which are applied or allocated by Agent or such Bank to any Eurodollar Increment, all as determined in good faith by such Bank in its sole and absolute discretion, by reason of:

(a) any and all present or future reserve, deposit or similar requirements against (or against any class of, or change in, or in the amount of) assets or liabilities of such Bank imposed by any regulatory authority (including but not limited to Regulation D of the Board of Governors of the Federal Reserve System);

(b) any and all present and future taxes, duties, fees, withholdings or other charges referred to in Paragraph 2.16 [omitted];

(c) the maintenance of any reserves against the "Eurocurrency liabilities" under Regulation D of the Board of Governors of the Federal Reserve System;

(d) any measurement or analysis based on an excess above a specified base level of the amount of a category of deposits or other liabilities of such Bank which includes deposits by reference to which the Inter-bank Rate is determined or a category of extensions of credit or other assets of such Bank which includes a Eurodollar Increment, or restrictions on the amount of such a category of liabilities or assets which such Bank may hold;

(e) compliance by such Bank with any direction, requirement or request from any regulatory authority, whether or not having the force of law, in connection with the Loan or any part thereof.

Upon request of the Venture, such Bank through Agent shall provide the Venture with a written statement of the amount and basis of its request for reimbursement or compensation under this Paragraph, and such statement, absent manifest error, shall be conclusive and binding on the Venture.

Form 11.5

LETTER OF INTENT FOR LEVERAGED EQUITY JOINT VENTURE

Re: Letter of Intent for Proposed Office Development
Dear Institutional Investor:
   Set forth below is a summary of our discussions concerning the formation of a joint venture to develop an office building in ....
(street, city, state)

   (1) *The Project.* We have discussed plans to construct and develop a single office building containing .... (....) gross square feet on a site located .... The height of the building shall be approximately .... (....) stories above street level. As part of the development, the building presently standing on the site shall be acquired by the Developer and demolished. The underlying land shall then be converted to a plaza which shall be an integral part of the building.
   We have also discussed the construction of a covered parking structure to be built as part of the office development. We expect that the first phase of construction of the garage shall coincide with the construction of the office building to give the building tenants access to the parking facility when construction is finished.
   If sufficient financing is obtained, we plan to commence construction of the building on ...., 19.... and complete it .... (....) months later. The buildings shall be constructed by a contractor selected by the Developer and approved by the Institutional Investor.

   (2) *Building Name.* The building shall bear the name of either the Institutional Investor, an affiliate thereof, or some variation thereof which is mutually acceptable to the Developer and the Institutional Investor.

   (3) *Building Design.* The building shall be designed by a designer or architectural firm selected by the Developer and acceptable to the Institutional Investor. Once we agree upon those performance standards and budget limitations that we would expect the final building design to meet, we shall give the designer or architectural firm a substantial amount of latitude in the design. We would like the building to be constructed by the "fast track" method so that construction commences before final plans and specifications become available. Once preliminary plans progress to what is agreed to be a meaningful phase, the Developer shall

furnish an architectural model of the building. The Developer and the Institutional Lender shall then review the proposed design to establish that it meets their mutual standards and expectations.

(4) *Space Lease.* It is agreed that the Institutional Investor shall lease .... (....) rentable square feet of office space in the building. Any leased spaced not occupied by the Institutional Investor or its affiliates may be subleased to fulfill the rental commitment, provided that the subleases are drawn from tenants presently occupying the building now standing on the premises. Any space vacated by such tenants must be immediately occupied by the Institutional Investor, its affiliates, or by tenants of other building operated by the Institutional Investor so that vacancies which are created do not constitute office space that is competitive with space in buildings developed by the Developer. We have agreed that some of the more important terms in the space lease shall be the following:

   (a) The primary term shall be .... (....) years with mutually acceptable renewal options;
   (b) The per square foot rental rate shall be ....;
   (price term or method of determination)
   (c) Tenant shall pay all electric bills in addition to the basic rent;
   (d) The basic rent shall be subject to increases based upon the landlord's reasonable estimate of increased operating costs; and
   (e) The location of the leased space shall be subject to our mutual agreement and shall not unduly restrict leasing efforts relating to the building as a whole.

(5) *Ground Lease.* The Institutional Investor shall purchase the land constituting the building site from the Developer at a purchase price equal to Developer's cost of acquisition, and shall lease such land to the Developer under a long-term ground lease. To the extent the amount of the first mortgage loan for the building is reduced by virtue of the ground lease obligation, the Institutional Investor shall extend secondary financing to the development on mutually acceptable terms. We have agreed that some of the more important terms in the ground lease shall be the following:

   (a) The term of the lease shall be ....;
   (b) The ground rental rate shall be ....;
   (price term or method of determination)
   (c) The ground lease shall be adjusted after .... (....) years and shall thereafter be adjusted every .... (....) years based upon reappraisals of the land;

(d) The ground lessee has the right to mortgage or assign the leasehold estate without obtaining consent from the ground lessor; and
(e) The ground lessee shall have the right of first refusal to purchase the land should the ground lessor elect to sell the same.

(6) *Financing.* All forms of financing for the project shall be obtained by the Developer without liability on the part of the Institutional Investor. The Developer shall make all reasonable efforts to accommodate any financing which the Institutional Investor offers in connection with the project and on competitive terms.

(7) *Form of Ownership.* The project shall be developed by a limited partnership consisting of Developer and Insurance Company shall be the sole general partner and the Institutional Investor shall be one of several limited partners. Additional limited partners are to be chosen by the Developer. The limited partnership agreement forming the entity shall include, among other terms, the following:

(a) Only the general partner shall participate in the day-to-day management of the project;
(b) The general partner shall receive a development fee, leasing fee, and management fee in amounts approved of by the limited partners;
(c) Limited partners shall not be liable for partnership debts;
(d) No initial or additional contributions to the partnership's capital shall be required of the Institutional Investor; and
(e) Profits and losses shall be distributed among partners in accordance with the ratios of their respective partnership interests.

The Institutional Investor shall initially hold a .... percent (....%) limited partnership interest which shall possibly be increased to as much as a .... percent (....%) interest. Any increase in the percent interest shall be determined in the following way: ......
....

(8) *Conditions of Performance.* We agree that the Institutional Investor's obligations in connection with the project are expressly conditioned upon;

(a) Reimbursement of the Institutional Investor for all costs of acquiring and demolishing the building presently standing on the building site; and

(b) Regulatory approval by all necessary federal and state regulatory agencies of Institutional Investor's participation in the project.

(9) *Letter of Intent.* Both parties understand that this letter is not a legally binding agreement. A final agreement consisting of the terms set forth in this letter plus additional terms has not yet been reached, and shall not be reached until negotiations relating to the project have been concluded. Neither the expenditure of funds nor the undertaking of actions in furtherance of the project shall be partial performance of a binding agreement, nor shall it be the basis for any reliance upon the terms of this letter. The letter is nothing more than an expression of our present intentions and our willingness to continue in negotiations which we hope shall lead to an agreement.

If the foregoing correctly summarizes our discussions, please so indicate by signing this letter in the place provided below.

Very truly yours,

....
Developer

Approval

The foregoing letter of intent is an accurate expression of our present intentions, but is not yet a binding agreement this .... day of ...., 19.....

....
Institutional Lender

By: ....
Officer

CUMULATIVE TABLE OF STATUTES

[References are to paragraphs (¶) and to sample forms in Appendix B. References to the Supplement are preceded by "S."]

INTERNAL REVENUE CODE

I.R.C. §
- 11 .... 1.05[5][a] n.193
- 16(a)(12) .... 1.06 Ex. 1.8
- 38 .... S1.05[2][d]
- 44C .... S1.05[2][d]
- 44C(1) .... S1.05[2][d]
- 46 .... 1.05[2][d] n.95
- 46(a) .... 1.05[2][d] n.95
- 48(a) .... 1.05[2][d] n.95
- 48(a)(1) .... S1.05[2][d]
- 48(g) .... 1.05[2][d] n.95
- 55 .... 1.05[2][d] n.78, 9.04 n.55
- 56 .... 1.05[2][d] n.76, 8.02 n.4
- 57 .... 1.05[2][d] n.76
- 58 .... 1.05[2][d] n.76
- 58(c) .... 1.05[2][d] n.78
- 61(a) .... 12.01[2][b] n.16
- 61(a)(4) .... 12.02[1][a] n.34, 12.02[4] n.76
- 61(a)(12) ...... 12.03[2][a][i] n.80
- 83(b) ...... Form 1.1, Section 3.2A, Comment
- 103 .... 3.04[3][b], 8.06, S8.06
- 103(b)(6)(D) 8.06 n.55
- 108 .... 1.06 Ex. 1.8, 12.03[2][a][i] n.88
- 108(a) .... 12.03[2][a][i] n.87
- 111 .... 12.02[1][a] n.35, 12.03[4][b][i] n.178, 12.03[4][b][ii] ns. 221, 222
- 121 .... 10.01 n.3
- 121(d)(3) .... 12.03[4][b][ii] n.203
- 121(d)(4) .... 12.03[4][b][ii] n.203
- 162 .... 1.05[2][a] n.48, 12.01[1][a] n.1, 12.02[2][b] n.66, 12.03[2][b][iii] n.131
- 162(a) ... 1.05[3][c][i], S1.05[2][d] n.85a, 1.05[3][c][ii] n.138, 1.05[4][b][ii] n.186, Form 1.1, Section 3.2A, Comment
- 163(a) ... 1.05[2][c] n.59, 10.01 n.3,

I.R.C. §
12.02[2][a] n.55
- 163(d) .. 1.05[2][d] n.73, 8.05 n.39, 12.02[2][b] n.61
- 163(d)(1) .... 12.02[2][b] n.64
- 163(d)(2) .... 12.02[2][b] n.69
- 163(d)(3)(B) ..... 12.02[2][b] n.65
- 163(d)(3)(C) ..... 12.02[2][b] n.66
- 163(d)(3)(D) .... 12.02[2][b] n.62
- 163(d)(4)(A)(i) .. 12.02[2][b] n.67
- 163(d)(4)(A)(ii) .. 12.02[2][b] n.67
- 163(d)(4)(D) .... 12.02[2][b] n.63
- 163(d)(6)(B) .... 12.02[2][b] n.68
- 164 .... 1.05[2][c] n.57
- 164(a)(1) .... 10.01 n.3, 12.02[2][b] n.66
- 164(a)(2) .... 12.02[2][b] n.66
- 165 .. 10.01 n.3, 12.03[2][b][iii] n.131
- 165(a) .... 12.03[3][a] n.139
- 165(c)(1) .... 12.03[3][a] n.139
- 165(c)(2) .... 12.03[3][a] n.139
- 165(g) .... 12.03[2][b][iii], 12.03[2][b][iii] n.129, 12.03[4][b][i], 12.03[4][b][ii]
- 165(g)(2) ..... 12.03[4][b][i] n.176
- 165(g)(3) ...... 1.05[3][c][v] n.146
- 166 .. 12.02[2][b] n.66, 12.02[3] n.71, 12.03[2][a][ii] n.97, 12.03[2][b], 12.03[4][b][i]
- 166(a)(1) .... 12.03[2][b] n.98, 12.03[2][b][iii] n.122, Form 1.1, Section 2.7, Comment
- 166(a)(2) .... 12.03[2][b] n.98, 12.03[2][b][ii] n.111
- 166(b) .... 12.03[2][b] n.100, 12.03[2][b][ii] ns. 109, 110
- 166(d) .... 12.03[2][b][ii] n.121
- 166(d)(1)(A) .... 12.03[2][b] n.99, 12.03[2][b][iii] n.124
- 166(d)(1)(B) ... 12.03[2][b] n.101, 12.03[2][b][iii] n.123
- 166(d)(2) ...... 12.03[2][b] n.101, 12.03[2][b][iii] n.125

T-1

[*References are to paragraphs (¶) and to sample forms in Appendix B. References to the Supplement are preceded by "S."*]

I.R.C. §

166(e) ...... 12.03[2][b][iii] n.129, 12.03[4][b][i] n.176
167 .... S1.05[2][b] n.54c, 10.01 n.3, 12.02[2][b] n.66
167(j)(1)(B) ...... 1.05[2][a] n.47
167(j)(2) .... 1.05[2][a] n.47, 1.05[5][e] n.200
167(j)(5) .. 1.05[2][a] n.47, 8.02 n.4
167(k) .... 1.05[2][d] ns. 66, 74, 75
168(b)(2) ..... S1.05[2][b] & n.54a
169 .... 12.02[2][a] n.52
171 .... 12.02[2][b] n.66
172 .... 1.05[2][b] n.50, 1.06 Ex. 1.8
178 .... 6.01[1] n.1
183 .... S6.04[3][e]
189 .. 1.02[2][a] n.7, 1.05[2][c] n.57, 1.05[2][d], 1.05[2][d] n.66, 12.02[2][a] n.52
189(e)(5) .... 1.05[2][d] n.66
201(a) .... S1.05[2][d] n.54a
212 .... 12.01[1][a] n.1, 12.02[2][b] n.66
212(1) .... 1.05[4][b][ii] n.186, S1.05[2][d] n.85a
212(2) .... 1.05[4][b][ii] n.186, S1.05[2][d] n.85a
216 .... 10.03
263 .... 1.05[2][a] n.48, 12.01[2][a] n.15
265(2) 8.06 n.57
266 .. 1.02[2][a] n.7, 1.05[2][d] n.64
267 .... 6.04[3][c] n.63, 6.04[4] n.68, 12.03[4][a] n.159
267(a)(1) .... 12.03[4][a] n.159
267(b) .... 6.04[3][c] n.63
301 ...... 1.06 Ex. 1.8, 12.01[4] n.31
301(b)(1)(A) .... 5.05[3] n.142
301(c)(1) .... 5.05[3] n.143
301(c)(3)(A) .... 5.05[3] n.144
302(a) .... 5.05[3] n.148
311(d) .... 5.05[3] n.149
312(i) .... 12.01[4] n.31
312(j) .... 1.05[2][b] n.53
312(k)(1) .... 1.05[2][b] n.51
316 .... 5.05[3] n.143, 12.01[4] n.31
317(b) .... 5.05[3] n.148
331 .... 1.06 Ex. 1.8

I.R.C. §

331(a) ...... 1.05[5] n.192, 5.05[3] ns. 145, 153
331(a)(2) .... 5.05[3] n.148
333 .... 1.06 n.207, 5.05[3]
333(e)(1) .... 5.05[3] n.147
334(a) .... 1.05[3][a] n.98
336 .... 5.05[3] n.149
337 .... 1.05[3][a][ii], 1.05[5], S2.02[8] & n.99s, 5.05[3] n.152, 9.04[4][c]
337(a) .... 1.05[5] n.192
337(b)(1) ..... 1.05[3][c][iv] n.141
341 .... 1.05[2][b] n.53, 1.05[3][a] n.96, 1.05[3][a][ii]
341(b)(1) ...... 1.05[3][a][ii] n.108
341(d)(1) ..... 1.05[3][a][ii] n.113
341(d)(2) ..... 1.05[3][a][ii] n.114
341(d)(3) ..... 1.05[3][a][ii] n.117, 1.06 n.207
341(e) .... 1.05[3][a][ii]
341(e)(1)(B) .. 1.05[3][a][ii] n.110
341(e)(1)(C) .. 1.05[3][a][ii] n.111
341(f) .... 1.05[3][a][ii]
346 .... 5.05[3] n.148
351 .... 5.05[3] n.141, 9.04[2][b][ii] n.72, 9.04[5][b] n.104, 12.04[2], 12.04[2] n.249
357(c) .... 12.04[2] n.250
358(a) .... 9.04[2][b][ii] n.72
361 .... 4.02[12][b][vi]
362 .... 4.02[12][b][vi], 9.04[5][b] n.104
362(a) .... 4.02[12][b][iv], 9.04[2][b][ii] n.72
362(d) .... 4.02[12][b][iv]
362(e) .... 4.02[12][b][iv]
363 .... 4.02[12][b][v]
363(g) .... 4.02[12][b][vi]
363(h) .... 4.02[12][b][vi]
363(i) .... 4.02[12][b][vi]
363(k) .... 4.02[12][b][ii], 4.02[12][b][iii], 4.02[12][b][vi]
363(1) .... 4.02[12][b][vi]
364 .... 4.02[12][b][vi]
364(c) .... 4.02[12][b][vi]
364(d)(1)(B) ...... 4.02[12][b][vi]
365 .... 4.02[12][b][v]
365(b) .... 4.02[12][b][v]

CUMULATIVE TABLE OF STATUTES

[*References are to paragraphs (¶) and to sample forms in Appendix B. References to the Supplement are preceded by "S."*]

I.R.C. §

365(b)(3) .... 4.02[12][b][v]
365(c) .... 4.02[12][b][v]
365(e) .... 4.02[12][b][v]
365(h) .... 4.02[12][b][v]
368 .... 1.06 Ex. 1.8
385 .... S3.04[18], 11.02[4][b] n.86, S12.01[5], S12.01[5][a] n.33p, S12.01[5][b]
401(a) .... S2.02[2][a]
441 .... 1.05[5][b] n.195
453 ...... 7.04[1][d][iii], 8.03 n.28, 9.01[1][a], 9.04, 9.04[1], 9.04[2][b][ii] n.73, 9.04[2][c], 12.03[2][b][ii], 12.03[4][b][i], 12.03[4][b][ii]
453(b)(1) .... 9.04[2][a] n.58, 9.04[2][b][i] n.61, 9.04[2][b][ii] n.74
453(b)(2)(B) .... 9.04[2][b][ii], 9.04[2][b][ii] n.74
453(d) .... 5.05[3] n.151, 9.04[2][a] n.58, 9.04[4][c] n.98, S9.04[4][bb] n.97c
453(d)(1) .... 9.04[4][a] ns. 90, 92, 12.03[2][b][iii] n.128, 12.03[4][b][i] n.175
453(d)(2) .... 9.04[4][a] n.91
453(e) .... 9.04[5][a] n.101
453(f) .... 9.04[5][a] n.101
453(f)(3) .... 9.04[2][b][ii], 9.04[2][b][ii] n.65, 9.04[2][c]
453(f)(6) .... 9.04[6] n.107
453(g) .... 9.04[5][b] n.102
453(g)(2) .... 9.04[5][b]
453(h) .... 9.04[4][c] n.99
453(i)(2) .... 9.04[7] n.112
453B .... S9.04[4][bb] & n.97c
453B(f) .... 9.04[4][b] n.96
461(g) .. 1.05[2][c] n.59, 1.05[2][d] n.70, 12.01[1][b], 12.01[1][b] n.8, 12.02[2][a] n.57
461(g)(2) .... 1.05[2][d] n.72, 12.01[1][b] n.9
464 .... 1.05[2][d] n.88
465 ..... 1.05[2][d], 1.05[2][d] n.88, 1.05[4][b][ii] ns. 186, 187
465(a) .... 1.05[2][d] n.92
465(a)(2) .... 1.05[2][d] n.90

I.R.C. §

465(b) .... 1.05[2][d] n.90
465(c)(3)(D)(i) ... 1.05[2][d] n.91
465(e) .... 1.05[2][d] n.90
482 .... 6.04[3][c] n.61, 6.04[4] n.68
483 .... 9.04[2][b][ii], 9.04[2][b][ii] n.64
501 .... S2.02[6] n.94
501(a) .... S2.02[2][a]
501(c)(3) .... S1.05[1]
507(b) .... 4.02[12][b][vi]
511(a)(1) .... S2.02[6] n.94
511(a)(2)(A) .... S2.02[6] n.94
511(b) .... S2.02[6] n.94
512(b)(3)(B)(ii) .... S2.02[6] n.94
512(b)(4) ... 2.02[6] n.94, S2.02[6] n.94
514(c) .... 2.02[6] n.94
514(c)(9) .... S2.02[6] n.94
531 .... 1.05[3][c][iii] n.140, 1.06 Ex. 1.8
541 .... 1.05[3][c][iii] n.139
544(a) .... 1.05[3][a][ii] n.112
582 .... 12.03[4][b][i] n.176
582(a) .... 12.03[2][b][iii] n.129
584 .... S2.02[2][a]
591 .... 11.02[4][b] n.83
611 .... 12.02[2][b] n.66
691(a)(5) .... 9.04[4][b] n.97
702(a) .... 1.05[3][b][i] n.126
702(a)(8) .... 1.06 Ex. 1.8
702(b) .. 1.02[2][a] n.9, 1.06 Ex. 1.8, Form 1.1, Section 1.2, Comment
704(b) .. 1.02[2] n.5, 1.02[2][b] n.11, 1.05[3][b][i], 1.05[3][b][i] ns. 118, 124, S3.04[18] n.153t, Form 1.1, Section 3.2A, Comment
704(b)(1) .... 11.02[5][f] n.109
704(b)(2) .... 1.05[3][b][i] ns. 124, 126, 127, Form 1.1, Section 2.7, Comment
704(c) ... 1.02[2][b] n.11, Form 1.1, Section 3.2A, Comment
704(c)(1) ...... 1.05[3][b][ii] n.130
704(c)(2) .... 1.05[3][b][ii]
704(c)(3) .... Form 1.1, Section 2.5, Comment
704(d) .... 1.05[4][b][i] n.182, 1.05[4][b][ii], 1.05[4][b][ii]

REAL ESTATE FINANCING T-4

[References are to paragraphs (¶) and to sample forms in Appendix B. References to the Supplement are preceded by "S."]

I.R.C. §

n.186, 1.05[4][b][iii], 1.06 Ex. 1.8, 11.02[5][f] n.108, Form 1.1, Section 2.6A, Comment
705 ... S1.05[2][b] n.54b, 1.05[2][b] n.55, 1.05[4][b][ii]
705(a)(2) ...... 1.05[4][b][i] n.183
706(a) .... 1.05[5][e] n.199
706(b)(1) .... 1.05[5][b] n.196
706(c) .... 1.05[5][e] n.199
706(c)(2)(B) .. 1.05[3][b][iii] n.133
707(a) ...... 1.02[2] n.6, S12.01 [5] n.33h, Form 1.1, Section 4.3, Comment
707(b) .... Form 1.1, Section 2.5, Comment
707(b)(1) ... 6.04[3][c] n.63, Form 1.1, Section 3.2A, Comment
707(b)(2) ... 6.04[3][c] n.64, Form 1.1, Section 3.2A, Comment
707(c) .... 1.05[3][c][i] n.134, S12.01[5] n.33h, Form 1.1, Section 3.2A, Comment
708(b) .... 1.06 Ex. 1.8
708(b)(1) .... 1.05[5][e]
708(b)(1)(B) .... Form 1.1, Section 2.5, Comment
721 .... 9.04[5][b] n.104, 12.04[2] n.249
723 .... 1.05[3][b][ii] n.129, 9.04[5][b] n.104
731 .... S1.05[2][b] n.54b, 1.05[2][b] n.55, 1.05[5][e]
731(a) .... 1.05[3][c][v] n.145, 1.06 Ex. 1.8
731(a)(1) .... Form 1.1, Section 2.7, Comment
731(a)(2) ...... 1.05[3][c][v] n.143, 1.06 Ex. 1.8, Form 1.1, Section 2.7, Comment
732(b) .... 1.05[3][a] n.97, 1.06 Ex. 1.8
733 .... 1.05[4][b][i] n.183, 1.06 Ex. 1.8
736 .. Form 1.1, Section 5.1, Comment
736(a) .... Form 1.1, Section 5.1, Comment, Form 1.1, Section 5.2, Comment

I.R.C. §

736(b)(1) .... Form 1.1, Section 2.7, Comment
736(b)(2)(B) .... Form 1.1, Section 5.1, Comment
741 ...... 1.05[3][c][v] ns. 142, 145, Form 1.1, Section 5.1, Comment
741(a) .... Form 1.1, Section 2.7, Comment
743(b) .... Form 1.1, Section 5.1, Comment
751 ..... 1.05[3][a] n.96, 1.05[5][e], Form 1.1, Section 5.1, Comment
751(a) ..... 1.05[3][a][i], Form 1.1, Section 5.1, Form 1.1, Section 5.2
751(b) .... 1.05[3][a][i]
751(c) .... 1.05[3][a][i] n.99
751(d) .... 1.05[3][a][i] n.103
751(d)(1) ...... 1.05[3][a][i] n.100
751(d)(2) ...... 1.05[3][a][i] n.106, Form 1.1, Section 5.1, Form 1.1, Section 5.2
751(d)(2)(D) .. 1.05[3][a][i] n.101
752 ... S1.05[2][b] n.54b, 1.05[2][b] n.55, 1.05[4][b][i], Form 1.1, Section 2.7, Comment
752(a) .... 11.02[5][f] n.108
752(b) .... 1.05[3][c][v] n.144, 1.06 Ex. 1.8
752(c) .... 1.05[4][b][iii]
754 .... Form 1.1, Section 5.1, Comment, Form 11.4, Section 3.04
761(a) .. 1.02[2][b] n.15, 1.06 Ex. 1.8
761(c) .... 1.05[3][b][iii]
801 .... 11.02[4][b] n.82
802 .... 11.02[4][b] n.82
803 .... 11.02[4][b] n.82
804 .... 11.02[4][b] n.82
805 .... 11.02[4][b] n.82
806 .... 11.02[4][b] n.82
807 .... 11.02[4][b] n.82
808 .... 11.02[4][b] n.82
809 .... 11.02[4][b] n.82
810 .... 11.02[4][b] n.82
811 .... 11.02[4][b] n.82
812 .... 11.02[4][b] n.82
813 .... 11.02[4][b] n.82
814 .... 11.02[4][b] n.82
815 .... 11.02[4][b] n.82

CUMULATIVE TABLE OF STATUTES

[References are to paragraphs (¶) and to sample forms in Appendix B. References to the Supplement are preceded by "S."]

I.R.C. §

816	11.02[4][b] n.82
817	11.02[4][b] n.82
818	11.02[4][b] n.82
819	11.02[4][b] n.82
820	11.02[4][b] n.82
856	1.07 n.210, 2.02[5], 5.05[7]
856(a)	1.06 Ex. 1.8
856(a)(1)	11.02[5][b] n.95
856(a)(5)	1.06 Ex. 1.8
856(b)	1.06 Ex. 1.8
856(c)	1.06 Ex. 1.8, 2.02[5] n.93
856(c)(2)	5.05[7] n.177
856(c)(3)	5.05[7] n.177
856(c)(5)	2.02[5] n.93
856(d)	1.06 Ex. 1.8
856(d)(1)	11.02[5][b]
857	1.06 Ex. 1.8, 11.02[4][b] n.84
857(a)(1)	1.06 Ex. 1.8
857(b)(2)(E)	1.06 Ex. 1.8
857(b)(3)(B)	1.06 Ex. 1.8
871(a)(1)(A)	S2.02[8] n.99j
871(a)(2)	S2.02[8] n.99t
871(b)	S2.02[8] n.99t, S12.01[5] n.33i
875	S12.01[5] n.33i
882	S2.02[8] n.99t, S12.01[5] n.33i
897(a)	S2.02[8] & ns. 99p, 99r
897(c)(1)(A)	S12.01[5] n.33i
897(c)(1)(A)(i)	S2.02[8] ns. 99k, 99n
897(c)(1)(A)(ii)	S2.02[8] ns. 99l, 99o, 99p, 99y, 99z, 99ii
897(c)(1)(B)	S2.02[8] ns. 99r, 99hh
897(c)(2)	S2.02[8] ns. 99m, 99u, 99cc
897(c)(2)(B)	S2.02[8] ns. 99n, 99v
897(c)(3)	S2.02[8] ns. 99q, 99gg
897(c)(4)(A)	S2.02[8] n.99aa
897(c)(4)(B)	S2.02[8] n.99bb
897(c)(5)	S2.02[8] ns. 99o, 99x
897(c)(5)(i)	S2.02[8] n.99dd
897(c)(5)(ii)	S2.02[8] n.99dd
897(c)(6)(A)	S2.02[8] ns. 99k, 99n
897(d)(1)	S2.02[8] ns. 99s, 99jj
897(h)	S2.02[8] n.99p

I.R.C. §

1001	8.02 n.2, 12.01[3][a] n.22, 12.03[4][a] n.159, 12.03[5] n.235
1001(b)	12.01[3][a] n.25, 12.03[2][b][ii] n.114
1011	8.02 n.2, 12.01[3][a] n.22, 12.03[2][b][ii] n.112
1012	8.02 n.2, 12.01[3][a] n.22, 12.03[2][b][ii] ns. 112, 113
1014	Form 1.1, Section 5.2, Comment
1015	9.04[4][b] n.95
1017	1.06 Ex. 1.8, 12.03[2][a][i], 12.03[2][a][i] n.87
1031	1.06 Ex. 1.8, 6.04[2][a][ii], 6.04[3][a][ii], S6.04[3][a][ii], 6.04[4], 8.02n.1, 8.02[4], 8.02[4] n.24, 9.04[6] n.105, Form 8.1
1031(c)	6.04[4]
1031(a)	6.04[3][a], 8.02 n.2, 8.02[2], 8.02[2] ns. 15, 17
1031(b)	6.04[2][a][ii] n.41, 6.04[4] n.71, 8.02[3] n.19
1031(d)	6.04[4] ns. 70, 75, 8.02 n.2, 8.02[3] n.20
1034	10.01 n.3
1034(f)	12.03[4][b][ii] n.203
1034(i)	12.03[4][b][ii] n.203
1038	7.04[1][d][iii], 12.03[4][b][ii], 12.03[4][b][ii] ns. 203, 226
1038(a)	12.03[4][b][ii] ns. 202, 220
1038(b)	12.03[4][b][ii], 12.03[4][b][ii] ns. 202, 210
1038(b)(2)	12.03[4][b][ii] ns. 216, 217
1038(c)	12.03[4][b][ii] n.219
1038(d)(2)	12.03[4][b][ii] n.222
1111(b)(2)	4.02[12][b][ii], 4.02[12][b][iii], 4.02[12][b][iii] n.114
1129(b)	4.02[12][b][ii]
1201(a)	1.05[2][d] n.85, 6.04[4] n.69
1201(b)	1.05[2][d] n.83, 9.04 n.54
1201(c)	9.04 n.54
1202	1.05[2][d] n.82, 9.04 n.54
1211	1.05[3][c][v] n.147, 12.03[2][b][iii] n.123

[References are to paragraphs (¶) and to sample forms in Appendix B. References to the Supplement are preceded by "S."]

I.R.C. §

1211(b)(2) .... 1.06 Ex. 1.8
1212 .... 12.03[2][b][iii] n.123
1212(a) .... 1.06 Ex. 1.8
1212(b) .... 1.06 Ex. 1.8
1221 .... 6.04[4] n.68, 9.04 n.53, 12.02[1][b] n.43, 12.03[3][a] ns. 138, 148, 12.03[5] n.236
1221(1) ...... 1.05[3][c][iv] n.141, 9.05[1] n.115
1221(2) .... S1.05[2][d] n.85a, 1.05[4][b][ii] n.186
1221(4) .... 1.05[3][a][i] n.106
1223 .... 12.03[4][b][ii] n.225
1231 .... 1.05]2][a] n.49, S1.05[2][b] n.56, 1.05[3][a][i], 1.05[3][a][i] n.106, 6.04[2][a][ii], 6.04[3][a], 6.04[4], 6.04[4] n.68, 9.04 n.53, 12.03[3][a], 12.03[5], Form 1.1, Section 3.2A, Form 1.1, Section 3.2A, Comment
1231(b)(1) .... 1.05[3][c][iv] n.141, 9.05[1] n.115, 12.03[3][a] n.138, 12.03[5] n.238
1231(b)(1)(B) ...... 12.03[5] n.237
1232 .... 12.03[3][b] n.155
1232(a) .... 12.02[1][b] n.47
1232(a)(2)(A) .... 12.02[1][b] n.48
1232(a)(3)(A) .... 12.02[1][b] n.50
1232(a)(3)(B) .... 12.02[1][b] n.50
1232(a)(3)(E) .... 12.02[1][b] n.51
1232(b) .... 12.02[1][b] n.49
1237 ... 1.05[3][c][iv], 9.05, 9.05[2], 9.05[2] n.122, 10.02[1]
1237(a)(1) .... 9.05[2] n.119
1237(a)(2) .... 9.05[2] n.120
1237(a)(3) .... 9.05[2] n.121
1237(b)(1) .... 9.05[2] n.122
1239 .. 5.05[3] n.152, 6.04[3][c] n.64, 12.04[2] n.251
1239(a) .... 9.04[5][b]
1239(b) .... 9.04[5][b] n.103
1239(c) .... 9.04[5][b] n.103
1244 ... 1.05[3][c][v], 1.05[3][c][v] n.147, 1.06 Ex. 1.8
1245 .... S1.05[2][b] n.56
1250 .... 1.05[2][b], S1.05[2][b] & n.56, 1.05[2][d] n.67, 1.05[3][a][i] ns. 99, 102, 5.05[3]

I.R.C. §

n.150, 8.02 n.4, 9.04 n.52, 11.02[5][a] n.89
1250(a)(1)(B) .... 1.05[2][d] ns. 66, 68
1250(a)(1)(B)(i) ...... S1.05[2][b]
1250(a)(1)(B)(ii) ..... S1.05[2][b]
1250(a)(1)(B)(iii) .... S1.05[2][b]
1250(a)(1)(B)(iv) ..... S1.05[2][b]
1250(a)(1)(C) ..... 1.05[2][a] n.49
1304(b)(5) .... 1.05[2][d] n.80
1348 .... 1.05[2][d] ns. 79, 80, 1.05[5][a] n.194
1348(b)(2)(B) ..... 1.05[2][d] n.81
1371(a) 1.06 n.202
1371(c) 1.06 n.202
1372 ...... 1.02[2], 1.06 n.201, 1.06 Ex. 1.8
1372(c)(5) .... 5.05[3] n.124
1372(e)(5) 1.06 n.203
1374 .... 1.05[2][b] n.50
1374(c)(2) 1.06 n.206
1504(b) .... 11.02[4][b] n.85
4981 .... 1.06 Ex. 1.8
6031 .... Form 11.4, Section 3.04
7701 .... Form 1.1, Section 1.1, Comment
7701(a)(2) ..... 1.03 n.18, 11.02[2] n.60

UNIFORM LIMITED PARTNERSHIP ACT

U.L.P.A. §

1 .... 1.05[4][a] ns. 166, 168a, 11.02[4][a] n.78, Form 1.1, Section 2.6A, Comment
2 ... Form 1.1, Section 1.1, Comment
7 ..... 1.04 ns. 19a, 28, 1.05[1] n.38, 1.05[4][a] ns. 159, 168a, 11.02[4][a] n.75, Form 1.1, Section 2.6A, Comment, Form 1.1, Section 4.1, Comment
9 .... 1.05[4][a] n.166, Form 1.1, Section 4.2, Comment
13 .... 11.02[4][a]
17(1) ...... Form 1.1, Section 2.6A, Comment

[*References are to paragraphs (¶) and to sample forms in Appendix B. References to the Supplement are preceded by "S."*]

U.L.P.A. §

19 .... 1.05[1] n.42, 1.05[4][a]
19(3) ...... 1.05[1] n.42, Form 1.1,
    Section 4.4, Comment
20 .... 1.04 n.21, 1.05[1] n.40,
    1.05[4][a], 8.05 n.40,
    11.02[5][e] n.105
21 .... 1.04 n.21, 1.05[1] n.40,
    11.02[5][e] n.105
23 .... 1.04 n.29
26 .... 4.03[2][d] n.166
303(b) 1.04 n.29a

UNIFORM PARTNERSHIP ACT

U.P.A. §

2 .... 11.02[2] n.57
3(3) .... 1.05[1] n.41
6 .... 11.02[2] n.57
8 .... 1.02[2][b] n.12, 1.04 n.20
8(3) .... 11.02[2] n.54
15 .... 11.02[4][a] n.79
18(a) ...... Form 1.1, Section 2.6A,
    Comment
18(c) .... Form 1.1, Section 2.3,
    Comment, Form 1.1, Section 2.7,
    Comment

U.P.A. §

21 .... 11.02[2] n.56, Form 1.1,
    Section 4.3, Comment
22 .... 11.02[2] n.56
22(d) .... 11.02[5][c] n.98
25(2) .... 1.02[2][b] n.12
25(6) 1.04 n.20
26 .... 1.04 n.20
27(1) .... 1.02[2][b] n.12
31 ...... 1.05[1] n.40, 11.02[2] n.55,
    11.02[5][e] n.105
31(1)(b) .... Form 1.1, Section 1.4,
    Comment
31(2) .... Form 1.1, Section 1.4,
    Comment, Form 1.1, Section 6.1,
    Comment
31(4) 1.04 n.22, 8.05 n.40
31(5) 1.04 n.22
31(6) 8.05 n.40
32 .. Form 1.1, Section 6.1, Comment
32(1)(a) 1.04 n.22
38(1) .... 11.02[2] n.56
38(2) .... Form 1.1, Section 1.4,
    Comment, Form 1.1, Section 6.1,
    Comment
40(b) .. 11.02[3][b] n.62, Form 1.1,
    Section 2.3, Comment

CUMULATIVE TABLE OF REGULATIONS AND RULINGS

[References are to paragraphs (¶) and to sample forms in Appendix B. References to the Supplement are preceded by "S."]

TREASURY REGULATIONS

REG. §

1.108(a)-1(a)(1) .... 12.03[2][a][i] n.89
1.108(a)-1(a)(2) .... 12.03[2][a][i] ns. 88, 90
1.108(a)-2 ...... 12.03[2][a][i] n.93
1.162-11(b)(1) ..... 6.04[1][a] n.28
1.162-11(b)(2) .... 6.01[1] n.1
1.163-1(b) .... 12.02[2][a] n.53
1.164-1 .... 1.05[2][c] n.57
1.165-2 .... 12.03[3][a] n.139
1.166-1(a) .... 12.03[2][b] n.97
1.166-1(d) .... 12.03[3][b] n.150
1.166-1(d)(2)(i)(b) . 12.03[2][b][ii] n.113
1.166-1(e) .... 12.03[2][b][ii] n.110, 12.03[3][b] n.150, 12.03[4][b][i] n.174
1.166-2(a) .... 12.03[2][b][i] n.102, 12.03[4][b][i] n.180
1.166-2(b) .... 12.03[2][b][i] ns. 103, 181
1.166-2(c)(1) .. 12.03[2][b][i] n.104
1.166-2(c)(2) .. 12.03[2][b][i] n.104
1.166-5(a)(2) .. 12.03[2][b][ii] n.121
1.166-5(b) .... 12.03[2][b][iii] n.125, 12.03[4][b][i] n.173
1.166-5(d) .... 12.03[2][b][iii] n.126
1.166-6(a) .... 12.03[4][a][i] n.170, 12.03[4][b][i] n.183, 12.03[4][b][ii] ns. 185, 186
1.166-6(a)(1) .. 12.03[2][b][ii] n.110
1.166-6(a)(2) .. 12.03[4][b][i] n.174
1.166-6(b) .... 12.03[4][b][ii] ns. 185, 193
1.166-6(b)(1) .. 12.03[4][b][ii] n.196
1.166-6(b)(2) ...... 12.03[4][b][ii] n.195, 12.03[5] n.234

REG. §

1.166-6(c) .. 12.03[4][b][ii] ns. 193, 197, 12.03[5] n.233
1.167(a)-4 .... 6.01[1] n.1, 6.04[1][a] n.28
1.167(a)-8 .... 12.03[3][a] n.139
1.167(j)-1(a)(2)(ii) ..... 1.05[5][e] n.200
1.170A-4 .... 12.04[3] n.253
1.176-1(a) 8.05 n.39
1.266-1 .... 1.02[2][a] n.7
1.451-1 ...... 12.03[2][b][ii] n.116, 12.03[4][b][i] n.179
1.451-2 .... 9.04[2][c] n.76
1.453-1(b) .... 9.04[3] n.87
1.453-1(b)(1) .... 9.04[3] n.89
1.453-4(c) .... 9.04[2][b][ii] ns. 62, 73, 75, 9.04[3] n.88
1.453-6(a) .... 9.04[7] n.109, 12.03[2][b][ii] n.115
1.453-(6)(a)(2) ..... 9.04[7] n.108, 12.03[2][b][ii] n.118
1.453-6(b) .... 12.03[4][b][ii] n.229
1.453-6(c) .... 12.03[4][b][ii] n.229
1.453-8(b) .... 9.04[2][a] n.57
1.453-9 .... 12.03[4][b][ii] n.227
1.453-9(a) .... 9.04[4][a] n.92
1.453-9(b)(1) ...... 9.04[4][a] n.90
1.453-9(b)(2) ...... 9.04[4][a] n.91, 12.03[2][b][ii] n.117
1.461-1 .... 12.03[3][b] n.150
1.461-1(a)(2) ...... 6.04[3][c] n.59, 12.03[2][a][ii] n.96
1.483-1 .... 9.04[2][b][ii] n.64, S9.04[2][b][ii] n.64
1.512(b)-1(c)(2)(iii)(b) .. S2.02[6] n.94
1.512(b)-1(c)(5) ..... S2.02[6] n.94
1.702-1(b) .... 1.02[2][a] n.9, Form 1.1, Section 1.2, Comment, Form 1.1, Section 3.2A, Comment

[References are to paragraphs (¶) and to sample forms in Appendix B. References to the Supplement are preceded by "S."]

REG. §	REG. §
1.704-1 ..... Form 1.1, Section 3.2A, Comment	1.1031(d)-2 .... 8.02[1] n.7, 8.02[3] ns. 22, 23
1.704-1(b)(2) .... 1.05[3][b][i] ns. 118, 122, 124	1.1038-1(a) .... 12.03[4][b][ii] n.204
1.704-1(c)(2) .. 1.05[3][b][ii] n.131	1.1038-1(a)(2) ...... 12.03[4][b][ii] n.203
1.707-1(c) .... 1.05[3][c][i] ns. 134, 135, Form 1.1, Section 2.7, Comment, Form 1.1, Section 3.2A, Comment	1.1038-1(a)(3) ...... 12.03[4][b][ii] n.205
	1.1038-1(a)(3)(ii) .. 12.03[4][b][ii] n.208
1.721-1(b) .. Form 1.1, Section 3.2A, Comment	1.1038-1(a)(4) ...... 12.03[4][b][ii] n.209
1.721-1(b)(1) .... Form 1.1, Section 3.2A, Comment	1.1038-1(b)(1) ..... 12.03[4][b][ii] n.210
1.736-1(b)(1) .... Form 1.1, Section 5.1, Comment	1.1038-1(b)(2)(i) ... 12.03[4][b][ii] n.212
1.751-1(a)(2) .... 1.05[3][a][i] ns. 104, 107	1.1038-1(b)(2)(ii) .. 12.03[4][b][ii] ns. 213, 215
1.751-1(b) ...... 1.05[3][a][i] n.105	1.1038-1(b)(2)(iii) .. 12.03[4][b][ii] n.214
1.751-1(c)(3) .... Form 1.1, Section 5.1, Comment	1.1038-1(c)(3) ..... 12.03[4][b][ii] n.217
1.751-1(c)(4)(ii) ..... 1.05[3][a][i] n.99	1.1038-1(c)(4) ...... 12.03[4][b][ii] n.218
1.752-1(c) .... 12.04[2] n.250	1.1038-1(d) .... 12.03[4][b][ii] ns. 227, 228, 229
1.752-1(d) .... 12.04[2] n.250	
1.752-1(e) .... 1.05[4][b][ii], 1.05[4][b][iii], Form 1.1, Section 27, Comment	1.1038-1(f)(2) ...... 12.03[4][b][ii] n.221
1.761-1(a) .... 1.02[2][b] n.13	1.1038-1(f)(3) ...... 12.03[4][b][ii] n.222
1.761-2(b)(1) ...... 1.02[2][b] n.16	
1.856-1(b)(1) ..... 11.02[5][b] n.95	1.1038-1(g)(1) ...... 12.03[4][b][ii] n.219
1.856-1(d)(1) ..... 11.02[5][b] n.95	
1.856-4(b)(1) .... S2.02[6] n.94	1.1038-1(g)(3) ...... 12.03[4][b][ii] n.224
1.864-3(b) Ex. (1) .. S2.02[8] n.99q	
1.871-7(d)(2)(iv) Ex. (1) .. S2.02[8] n.99q	1.1372-4(b)(5)(vi) 1.06 n.205
	39.3797-4 .... 1.05[4][a] n.161
1.871-10 .... S2.02[8] n.99k	301.7701-1(c) ..... 1.05[4][a] n.150
1.1011-2 .... 12.04[3] n.253	301.7701-2 .... 1.05[4][a]
1.1011-2(a)(3) ...... 12.04[3] n.255	301.7701-2(a)(1) .. 1.05[4][a] n.177
1-1011-2(b) .... 12.04[3] n.254	301.7701-2(a)(2) .. 1.05[4][a] n.151
1.1011-2(c) .... 12.04[3] n.255	301.7701-2(b) ..... 1.05[4][a] n.152
1.1017-1(a)(1) .. 12.03[2][a][i] n.94	301.7701-2(b)(1) .... 1.05[4][a] ns. 155, 156
1.1017-1(a)(2) .. 12.03[2][a][i] n.94	
1.1017-1(b)(5) ... 12.03[3][a] n.137	301.7701-2(b)(2) .... 1.05[4][a] n.153
1.1031(a)-1(a) .... 8.02[2] n.18	
1.1031(a)-1(b) .... 8.02[2] ns. 8, 17	301.7701-2(b)(3) .... 1.05[4][a] n.157, Form 1.1, Section 1.4, Comment
1.1031(a)-1(c)(2) .... 6.04[2][a][ii] n.40, 8.02[2] ns. 9, 13	

T-11 CUMULATIVE TABLE OF REGS. AND RULINGS

[References are to paragraphs (¶) and to sample forms in Appendix B. References to the Supplement are preceded by "S."]

REG. §

301.7701-2(c) ..... 1.05[4][a] n.158,
  11.02[5][b] n.95
301.7701-2(c)(4) .... 1.05[4][a]
  ns. 148, 160
301.7701-2(d) ...... 1.05[4][b][iii]
  n.190
301.7701-2(d)(1) .... 1.05[4][a]
  ns. 167, 171, Form 1.1,
  Section 2.8, Comment
301.7701-2(d)(2) .... 1.05[4][a]
  ns. 168, 170
301.7701-2(e) .... 1.02[1] n.2
301.7701-2(e)(1) .... 1.05[4][a]
  ns. 173, 175
301.7701-2(e)(2) .. 1.05[4][a] n.176,
  Form 1.1, Section 5.1, Comment
301.7701-3 .... 1.05[4][a]
301.7701-3(b) .... Form 1.1, Section
  1.4, Comment
301.7701-3(b)(2) .. 1.05[4][a] n.163
301.7701-4 .... 1.05[4][a]

REVENUE RULINGS

REV. RUL.

55-234 .... 9.04[2][b][ii] n.70
55-429 .... 12.03[2][a][ii] n.95
56-136 .... 1.05[2][c] n.58,
  12.01[1][a] n.4
56-145 .... 1.05[2][c] n.57
56-267 .... S2.02[2][a]
56-396 .... 9.04[2][a] n.57
57-198 .... 12.02[2][a] n.58
57-357 .... 1.05[2][b] n.53,
  12.01[4] n.31
57-400 .... 12.01[2][a] n.14
58-292 .... 1.05[2][c] n.60
60-43 .... 6.04[3][a][i],
  6.04[3][a][i] n.49
60-52 .... 9.04[2][b][ii] n.66
61-217 .... 6.04[1][a] n.29
62-12 .... 1.05[3][a][ii] n.115
62-178 .. 6.01[1] n.1, 6.04[1][a] n.29
63-57 .... 12.02[1][a] n.36
64-31 .... 10.01 n.3
65-155 .... 9.04[6] ns. 105, 106
65-297 .... 9.04[2][a] n.57

REV. RUL.

67-188 .... Form 1.1, Section 1.2,
  Comment, Form 1.1,
  Section 3.2A, Comment
67-200 .... 12.03[2][a][i] n.89
67-255 .... 8.02[2] n.14
68-36 .... 8.02[1] n.6
68-246 .... 9.04[2][c] n.79
68-419 .... 12.03[2][a][ii] n.95
68-523 .... 12.03[2][b][ii] n.110,
  12.03[3][b] ns. 149, 155,
  12.03[4][b][i] n.177
68-643 .... 1.05[2][d] n.71,
  12.01[1][b] n.8
68-661 .... 12.03[5] n.238
69-77 .... 12.01[3][b] n.28
69-188 .... 1.05[2][c] n.58,
  12.01[1][b] ns. 5, 6
69-223 .... 1.05[4][b][iii] n.189
69-462 .... 9.04[2][b][i] n.59
70-56 .... 12.03[2][a][ii] n.96
70-540 . 12.01[2][b] ns. 17, 18, 19, 20
70-647 .... 12.02[1][a] n.38
70-697 .... 12.03[2][a][ii] n.96
71-46 .... 1.05[2][c] n.57
72-48 .... 1.05[3][a][ii],
  1.05[3][a][ii] n.116
72-100 .... 12.01[1][b] n.11,
  12.01[2][b] n.20
72-238 .... 12.03[2][b][iii] n.127,
  12.03[4][b][ii] ns. 185, 199
72-254 .... 11.02[5][b] n.95
72-543 .... 6.04[3][b] n.54
71-595 .... 9.04[2][b][i] n.59
72-331 .... S2.02[6] n.94
72-621 .... 1.05[2][b] n.53
73-45 .... 9.04[2][c]
73-64 .... 1.05[2][c] n.57
73-160 .... 12.03[2][a][ii] n.95
73-555 .... 9.04[2][b][ii] n.66
74-159 .... 12.03[5] ns. 237, 239, 241
74-395 .... 1.05[2][d] n.66b,
  12.01[1][a] n.4, 12.01[1][b] n.11
74-607 .... 12.01[2][b] ns. 17, 20
74-621 .... 12.03[2][b][ii] n.110
75-52 .... 11.02[5][b] n.96
75-99 .... 5.05[7], 7.04[3] n.23a
75-194 .... 12.04[3] n.253

[*References are to paragraphs (¶) and to sample forms in Appendix B. References to the Supplement are preceded by "S."*]

Rev. Rul.

75-291 .... 8.02[4] n.25
76-111 .... 12.03[3][a] ns. 133, 134, 136, 137, 147, 12.04[1] n.247
77-119 .... 1.05[3][b][iii] n.132
77-294 .. 9.04[2][c], 9.04[2][c] n.80
77-297 .... 8.02[4] n.25
78-135 .... 8.02[2] n.15
79-106 .... 1.04 n.29b
79-222 .... S2.02[6] n.94
80-126 .... 10.02[1] n.18a
81-301 .... S12.01[5] n.33h

REVENUE PROCEDURES

Rev. Proc.

62-21 .... S1.05[2][b] n.54c
72-13 .. 1.05[4][a], 11.02[4][a] n.76, Form 1.1, Section 1.1, Comment
74-17 .... 1.05[4][a]
75-16 .... 1.05[4][a]

CUMULATIVE TABLE OF CASES

[References are to paragraphs (¶) and to sample forms in Appendix B. References to the Supplement are preceded by "S."]

A

Abbott v. Comm'r .... 1.05[3][a][ii] n.115
Abramowitz v. Barnett Bank .... S5.03[2] n.61
Abramsohn, Fulton v. .... 4.03[2][d] n.166
Abramson, Comm'r v. ... 12.03[3][a] n.140, 12.03[4][a] n.158
Adams, Graeme v. ... 5.02[2] ns.27, 32
Aetna Life Ins. Co. v. Broeker ...... 3.08[4][g] n.310
Agee, Mallory v. 7.06 n.30
Agia Kipiaki, Inc., Paydan, Inc. v. .... 3.08[4][g] n.252
Ahrens v. Kelly .... 5.03[3] n.65
Ajax Constr. Co., Martin v. .. 5.05[2] n.117
A.J. Indus. v. U.S. ...... 12.03[3][a] ns.140, 142
Akamine & Sons, Ltd. v. American Security Bank .... 3.08[4][a]
Albany Car Wheel .. 12.01[3][b] n.29
Aldens v. Packel ...... 5.05[1] n.104
Alderson, James .... 8.02[4] n.25
Alioto, Ambrose v. .. 5.02[3][a] n.37
Allen v. Comm'r ... S6.04[3][e] n.65a
Allen, State Wholesale Supply Inc. v. .... 5.02[2] n.29
Allied Constr. Co., Housing Mfg. Corp. v. ...... 4.02[6][a][ii] n.53
Allstate Ins. Co., Whitestone Sav. & Loan Ass'n v. .... 3.04[12][b] n.145
Alstores Realty Corp. . 6.04[3][c] n.60
Althausen v. Kuhn .. 3.08[4][g] n.310
Altman, Dime Sav. Bank v. .... S3.08[4][g] n.304
Ambassador Holding Co., Landers-Morrison-Christenson Co. v. .... 4.02[6][a][ii] n.55
Ambrose v. Alioto ... 5.02[3][a] n.37
American Bancshares Mortgage Co. v. Empire Home Loans, Inc. S3.06 n.182
American Century Mortgage Investors v. Regional Center ..... 5.02[4][d] ns. 54, 56
American Fletcher Mortgage Co. v. United States Steel Credit Corp. .... S11.01[7][d] n.30
American Nat'l Ins. Co., Johnson v. S3.06 n.178
American Realty Trust v. U.S. .... 6.04[3][b] n.53
American Sav. & Loan Ass'n, LaSala v. .... 3.04[7], 3.04[7] n.76, 3.04[8], 3.04[8] n.81
American Security Bank, Akamine & Sons, Ltd. v. .... 3.08[4][a]
American Security Ins. Co., Consolidated Mortgage Corp. v. .... 3.04[12][b] n.144
Ames v. Pardue ... S3.08[4][g] n.316
Andrews v. Pond ...... 5.05[1] n.101
Ane, Ethel S. .... 12.02[4] n.78
Angel, U.S. v. .... 3.08[4][d]
Ann Arbor Fed. Sav. & Loan Ass'n, Nichols v. ...... 3.04[8] ns. 86, 88
Anover Realty Corp. . 12.01[1][a] n.1
Antoyan, Grainger v. ... 1.05[1] n.38
Aps Co., Tieree v. ..... 3.04[8] n.86
Arend v. Great S. Sav. & Loan Ass'n .... S3.04[5]
Armenta v. Nussbaum ... 3.08[4][g] n.288
Armstrong v. Republic Realty Mortgage Corp. .... S2.03[1] n.99ll, S2.03[2] n.102
Arneill Rance v. Petit .... S5.02[4][d] n.56a
Arnold, Sonny, Inc. v. Sentry Sav. Ass'n .... S3.04[8] n.86
Associated Schools, Inc. v. Dade County .... 3.04[5] n.46

T-13

[References are to paragraphs (¶) and to sample forms in Appendix B. References to the Supplement are preceded by "S."]

Astor Dev. Co.,
   Callaizakis v. ...... 4.04[7] n.203
Astoria Marine Constr. Co.
   v. Comm'r .... S12.01[5][a] n.33m
Atlantic Coast Brewing Co.
   v. Clement .... 4.02[8][b] n.83
Atlantic Life Ins. Co. of Richmond
   v. Wolff .... 5.02[3][b] n.41
Atlas Subsidiaries v.
   O.&O., Inc. .... 5.04[1] n.95
Auto Wholesalers, Inc.,
   Brooks v. .... 5.02[2] n.30
Avon Assocs., Inc., Massachusetts Mut. Life Ins. Co. v. .. 3.08[4][g] n.313
Aztec Properties v. Union Planters Nat'l Bank ..... S3.04[3][c] n.33c, 5.02[4][d] n.54, S5.02[4][d] n.54

B

Baas, Portage Realty Corp.
   v. .... S4.02[6][i] n.39
Bailey v. First Fed. Sav. & Loan
   Ass'n .... S3.04[8] n.98w
Bailey v. Inman .... 5.02[2] n.31
Baird, J.H. Publishing Co. ... 8.02[4] n.25
Baker v. Loves Park Sav. & Loan
   Ass'n .. 3.04[7] n.72, 3.04[8] n.87
Baltimore Baseball Co., Inc.
   v. U.S. .... 9.04[2][b][i] n.60
Baltimore Life Ins. Co.
   v. Harn .... 3.04[8] n.88
Bankers Bond & Mortgage Co.,
   Chestnut Corp. v. .... 3.04[5] n.46
Bankers Trust Sav. & Loan Ass'n,
   Pongetti v. ...... 3.08[4][a] n.211
Bank v. Phelps & Bigelow
   Windmill Co. .... 5.03[8] n.78
Bank of America, Wellenkamp
   v. ...... S3.04[3][c] ns. 33p, 33q, 3.04[8], 3.04[8] n.89, S3.04[8] & ns. 98d, 98n, 98p
Bank of Cave City
   v. Hill .... S4.02[6][a][i] n.37
Bank of Italy Nat'l Trust & Sav. Ass'n
   v. Bentley .... 3.08[4][g] n.265
Bank of Newberry ... 12.03[2][b][ii] n.121

Bank of Pocahontas
   v. Browning .... 5.03[8] n.82
Bank of the West, Kennebee,
   Inc. v. .... 3.08[4][8] n.288
Banks v. Walters ...... 5.05[4] n.159
Barigoni v. Hill ... 7.04[1][d][i] n.17
Barnett Bank, Abramowitz
   v. .... S5.03[2] n.61
Barr v. Granahan .. S3.04[3][c] n.33r
Barrerra v. Security Bldg. & Inv.
   Corp. .... 3.08[4][g]
Barry, Dunn v. .... 3.08[4][g] n.257
Barson v. Mulligan .. 3.08[4][g] n.304
Bass, Moody v. .... 5.05[1] n.109
Bates, Home Sav. & Loan
   Ass'n v. .... 5.02[4][b] n.47
Bates, R.H. Macy & Co. v. ... 3.08[1] n.187
Bayler v. Commonwealth .. 3.08[4][c] n.225
Beard Land Co., Lynn v. .... 9.03[1] n.26
Becker, Canal Nat'l Bank
   v. .... S3.08[4][a] & ns. 216e-216h
Becker v. Werner ...... 6.03[2] n.15
Beeler v. H & R Block,
   Inc. .... S5.02[4][d] n.56a
Beeler, Memphis Natural Gas
   Co. v. .... 11.02[2] n.57
Bell Bakeries, Inc. v. Jefferson Standard
   Life Ins. Co. .... 3.04[5] n.49
Bell Sav. & Loan Ass'n,
   Berenato v. .... S3.04[5] n.46
Bellingham First Fed. Sav. & Loan
   Ass'n v. Garrison .... 3.04[8] ns. 88, 99
Bender Invs. Inc.,
   Schwartz v. ..... 3.08[4][g] n.266
Beneficial Fin. Co.
   v. Fusco ..... S3.04[3][c] ns. 32b, 32d, 33m
Benjamin Franklin Fed. Sav. & Loan
   Ass'n, Derenco, Inc. v. .... 3.04[6]
Bentley, Bank of Italy Nat'l Trust &
   Sav. Ass'n v. .... 3.08[4][g] n.265
Berenato v. Bell Sav. & Loan
   Ass'n .... S3.04[5] n.46
Berenson, Arthur .... 12.03[6] n.243
Berger v. Fuller .... 3.08[4][a] n.208

CUMULATIVE TABLE OF CASES

[References are to paragraphs (¶) and to sample forms in Appendix B. References to the Supplement are preceded by "S."]

Bergin v. Robbins 7.06 n.35
Berkey v. Third Ave.
   Ry. .... 11.02[4][b] n.87
Bialock, Harry L. .... 12.03[3][a]
   ns. 136, 137
Bibbey, *In re* 5.02 n.12
Bickerstaff v. Comm'r ... 12.03[3][a] n.139
Biggs v. Comm'r .... 8.02[4] n.24
Bingham v. Comm'r .. 12.03[2][b][ii] n.110, 12.03[3][b] ns. 149, 152
Bisno v. Sax .... 3.08[4][g] n.255
Black, Leon S. . 12.03[2][b][iii] n.130
Black, Sr., Charles ...... 12.03[4][a]
   ns. 161, 164, 165
Blackburn, Turner v. ..... 3.08[4][g]
Blackstone Theatre Co. ... 12.01]3][a] n.24
Blazey v. Delius .... 3.08[4][g] n.316
Blomberg, Patterson v. ... 5.03[3] n.66
Bloomington Coca-Cola Bottling Co.
   v. Comm'r .... 8.02[3] n.19
Blossom, Harold .. 12.03[4][a] n.163
Blum, First Nat'l Bank of
   Atlanta v. ...... 3.08[4][g] n.251
Boag, Centex Homes
   Corp. v. 10.01 n.22
Boatman, Ralph A. ... 12.03[4][b][ii] n.230
Bokser v. Lewis .... 11.02[3][c] n.70
Bolger, David F. v. Comm'r .. 5.05[3], 5.05[3] n.138, 12.01[3][b]
Boone, Heubush v. .... 5.05[2] n.116
Borchard, Antone ...... 8.02[4] n.25
Borish, Rabinowitz v. ... 11.02[3][b] n.67
Bornstein v. Somerson .... 3.08[4][i] n.330
Boston Rd. Shopping Center, Inc. v.
   Teachers Ins. & Annuity Ass'n of
   America 3.06 n.177
Bower, Paul M.,
   Estate of .... 12.02[1][a] n.38
Boyajian, Inc., Davis v. . 3.05[6] n.168
Boyd, Pan-American Life Ins.
   Co. v. .... 5.02[1] n.26
Boyett v. Carden .... 3.08[4][a] n.216
Boyles, Kin-ark Corp.
   v. .... S5.02[4][d] n.54

Braddock Ave., *In re* .... 3.08[4][h] n.318
Bradler v. Craig ...... 4.04[7] n.205
Brager Bldg. & Land Corp.,
   U.S. v. n.125
Braley, E.R. .... 8.02[2] n.10
Bramlette Bldg. Corp.
   v. Comm'r 1.06 n.205
Branch, Bryant v. ... 3.08[4][a] n.215
Brandler, Malsman v. ..... 3.08[4][i] n.333, S3.08[4][i] n.330
Braniff Inv. Co. v. Robertson .. 5.03[8] n.88
Brekke, Warren
   v. Comm'r .... 6.04[3][c] n.62
Brennan, Taylor v. ... S3.08[4][i] n.330
Brentwood Fed. Sav. & Loan Ass'n,
   Buchanan v. .... 3.04[6] n.52
Britt v. U.S. .... 5.05[3] n.127
Britton, First So. Fed. Sav. & Loan
   Ass'n of Mobile v. .... 3.04[8]
   ns. 86, 90, 99
Broeker, Aetna Life Ins.
   Co. v. .... 3.08[4][g] n.310
Brooks v. Auto Wholesalers,
   Inc. .... 5.02[2] n.30
Brooks v. Valley Nat'l Bank .. 3.04[6]
   ns. 53, 57, 61
Brose v. International
   Milling Co. .... 3.08[4][a]
Brown, Calumet River
   Ry. v. .... 3.08[4][h] n.318
Brown v. Cardoza ..... 5.05[8] n.185
Brown v. Crawford .... 5.05[2] n.115
Brown, Home Credit Co. v. .. 5.03[8] n.87
Browning, Bank of
   Pocahontas v. .... 5.03[8] n.82
Brown, Meridan Bowling Lanes,
   Inc. v. .... 5.05[6] n.169
Bryant v. Branch .... 3.08[4][a] n.215
Bryant v. Jefferson Fed. Sav. & Loan
   Ass'n .... 3.08[4][g]
Bryce's Mountain Resort, Inc.,
   Hall v. .... 9.03[1] n.24
Buchanan v. Brentwood Fed. Sav. &
   Loan Ass'n .... 3.04[6] n.52
Buckley, Estate of .. 12.02[1][a] n.40
Buckner, Ceravolo v. ... S3.04[8] n.98g

[*References are to paragraphs (¶) and to sample forms in Appendix B. References to the Supplement are preceded by "S."*]

Buffalo Sav. Bank, Mut. Real Estate Trust v. .... 3.04[8] n.87, S3.04[8] n.87
Burge, Raymond .... 1.05[2][b] n.53, 12.01[4] n.31
Burke, McDermott v. .. 3.05[6] n.168
Burkhard Inv. Co. v. U.S. .... 8.02[2] n.11
Burlison, Manufacturers Nat'l Bank of Detroit v. .... 5.02[2] n.29
Burnet v. Logan ...... 9.04[7] n.107, 12.03[2][b][ii] n.118
Burnquist, Bert .... 12.03[3][a] n.145
Burr v. Capital Reserve Corp. .... 5.05[4] n.159
Burrows, Walter F. .. 12.03[6] n.244
Butler v. Westgate State Bank .. S3.06 n.178a
Butner v. U.S. .... 3.08[4][i] n.332
Butz, National Forest Preservation Group v. .... 3.04[9][c] n.114

C

Cahn v. Hewsey .... 3.08[4][d] n.231
California Pub. Co., Community Lumber Co. of Baldwin Park v. .... 4.02[6][a][ii] n.52
Callihan, Wilhite v. .. S3.04[8] n.98u
Calumet River Ry. v. Brown .... 3.08[4][h] n.318
Callaizakis v. Astor Dev. Co. ... 4.04[7] n.203
Calvon Corp., S & S Ceiling & Partition Co. v. .... S4.02[6][a][ii] n.43
Campana Corp. v. Harrison .... S6.04[3][b][ii] n.58d
Campbell v. Gawart ...... 5.02[4][c]
Canal Nat'l Bank v. Becker .... S3.08[4][a] & ns. 216e-216h
Cape San Blas Joint Venture, North Am. Mortgage Investors v. .... S5.03[3] n.65
Capital Coal Corp. v. Comm'r .... 12.03[2][a][i] n.82
Capital Reserve Corp., Burr v. .... 5.05[4] n.159
Capri, Inc. v. Comm'r .... 6.04[3][a] n.42

Carden, Boyett v. ... 3.08[4][a] n.216
Cardoza, Brown v. .... 5.05[8] n.185
Carlton v. U.S. .. 8.02[4] ns. 24, 25, 26
Carlyle House, Inc., First Nat'l State Bank of N.J. v. .... 4.04[7] n.204
Carney, Levin v. ... S3.08[4][i] n.330
Carpenter v. Suffolk Franklin Sav. Bank .. 3.04[6] ns. 52, 55, 61
Carr, Thomassen v. ...... S3.04[18] n.153e, 5.02[3][b], 5.05[8]
Carter Oil Co. v. Durbin ... S3.04[18] n.153p
Carter, R.J., Enter., Inc. v. Greenway Bank & Trust ...... S5.04[1] n.97
Carver v. U.S. .... 5.05[3] n.134
Cassel, I.R.E. Financial Corp. v. .... 5.02[1] n.17
Castner, George L., Co. .... 12.03[2][b][ii] n.116
Caswal Corp. v. Comm'r .... 5.05[3] n.134
Centex Homes Corp. v. Boag .. 10.01 n.22
Central Cuba Sugar Co. ... 12.02[1][a] n.37
Central Fed. Sav. & Loan Ass'n, People v. .... S5.03[1] n.59
Central Nat'l Bank, Lehigh Valley Trust Co. v. .... 11.01[7] n.30
Century Elec. Co. v. Comm'r .... 6.04[2] n.32, 6.04[3][a][i], 6.04[3][a][ii], 8.02[2] n.13
Century Fed. Sav. & Loan Ass'n v. Van Glahn .... 3.04[8] n.86
Ceravolo v. Buckner .. S3.04[8] n.98g
Chakales v. Djiovanides . 5.03[5] n.73
Chandler, Commercial Credit Plan v. .... 5.05[7] n.174
Charmicor, Inc. v. Deaner .... 3.08[4][g] n.288
Charnita, Hoffman v. .... 9.03[1] n.24
Charnita, Tober v. ...... 9.03[1] n.24
Chase Nat'l Bank, Dabney v. ...... 11.01[6][a] n.20
Chase Nat'l Bank v. Sweeney .... 7.04[1][a] n.8
Chemical Bank, NBI Mortgage Inv. Corp. v. .... 11.01[7] n.30

[References are to paragraphs (¶) and to sample forms in Appendix B. References to the Supplement are preceded by "S."]

Chemical Bank,
   Thompson v. .... 5.03[8] n.81
Cherry v. Home Sav. & Loan
   Ass'n .... 3.04[8] ns. 81, 86
Chestnut Corp. v. Bankers Bond &
   Mortgage Co. .... 3.04[5] n.46
Chicago, City of, Chicago Title & Trust
   Co. v. .... 3.08[4][h] n.318
Chicago Title & Trust Co. v. City of
   Chicago .... 3.08[4][h] n.318
Childs Co., Metropolitan Life Ins.
   Co. v. .... 3.05[6] n.168
Citizens Fed. Sav. & Loan Ass'n,
   Spens v. .... 3.04[6] n.60
Citizens Nat'l Bank,
   Heights v. .... 11.01[6] n.16
Citizens & So. DeKalb Bank
   v. Hicks .... 3.08[4][a] n.215
City Bank v. Plank .... 4.03[1] n.154
City Fed. Sav. & Loan Ass'n,
   Wuorinen v. ..... 3.08[4][i] n.330
City Investing Co.
   v. Comm'r .... 6.04[3][a][i],
            6.04[3][a][ii], 6.04[4]
City Markets, Inc. v. Comm'r ... 1.06 n.205
Clark, Gaither v. ...... 5.05[4] n.159
Clark v. Lachenmeier ... 3.04[8] n.88
Clarkson Coal Co. ... 12.03[4][b][ii] n.198
Clearwater Sav. & Loan Ass'n, County
   of Pinellas v. ...... 7.04[1][a] n.8
Clement, Atlantic Coast Brewing
   Co. v. .... 4.02[8][b] n.83
Clementson, William A. .... 12.02[4] n.77
Climate Control, Inc. ... 8.02[2] n.17
Coast Bank v. Minderhout ... 3.04[8] n.85
Coastwise Transp. Co.,
   Comm'r v. .... 12.03[2][a][i] n.84
Coddon, L.D., & Bros.,
   Inc. .... 12.03[2][a][i] n.84
Coe Laboratories, Inc. .... 6.04[3][c] n.60
Coerber, Wooton v. ... 5.02[3][a] n.39
Coffey Enterprises Realty & Dev. Co.
   v. Holmes .... 3.08[4][g] n.282
Cole, Peyser v. .... 5.03[8] n.80

Collazo, Gulf Petroleum,
   S.A. v. .... 11.01[6][b] n.26
Collins, Leland S. ... 12.03[3][a] n.134
Colonial Realty Inv. Co.,
   In re .... 3.08[4][i] n.332
Columbia Sav. & Loan Ass'n,
   Krause v. .... S3.04[8] n.86
Columbus & Greenville
   R.R. .... 12.01[3][b] n.29
Comer v. Hargrave ...... 3.08[4][g] n.254, S3.08[4][g] n.260
Commerce Farm Credit Corp.,
   Shropshire v. .... 5.03[8] n.87
Commercial Centre Realty Co. v.
   Superior Court .. 3.08[4][g] n.275
Commercial Credit Plan
   v. Chandler .... 5.05[7] n.174
Commonwealth Fed. Sav. & Loan
   Ass'n, First Nat'l State Bank
   v. S3.06 n.182
Community Bank .... 12.03[4][b][ii] ns. 185, 194, 195, 12.03[5] n.234
Community Fed. S&L Ass'n,
   Franklin v. ...... 3.08[4][a] n.219, S3.08[4][a] n.220
Community Lumber Co. of Baldwin
   Park v. California Pub.
   Co. .... 4.02[6][a][ii] n.52
Conestoga Transp.
   Co. .... 12.03[2][a][i] n.83
Conference of Fed. Sav. & Loan Ass'ns
   v. Stein .... S3.04[8] n.98r
Connor v. Great W. Sav. & Loan
   Ass'n .... 4.04[7], 4.04[7] ns. 199, 203, 204
Conover v. Hobart .... 5.05[2] n.112
Consolidated Mortgage Corp. v.
   American Security Ins.
   Co. .... 3.04[12][b] n.144
Continental Arms, Inc., United States
   Sav. Bank v. ..... 3.08[4][g] n.260
Continental Mortgage Investors v.
   Sailboat Key, Inc. .. S5.05[1] n.109
Continental Nat'l Bank
   v. Fleming .... 5.03[5] n.72
Cook v. Curtis ..... 3.08[4][g] n.300
Cooper Communities, Inc.,
   McInnis v. S5.01 n.11c

REAL ESTATE FINANCING T-18

[References are to paragraphs (¶) and to sample forms in Appendix B. References to the Supplement are preceded by "S."]

Costal Terminals Inc. v. U.S. ... 8.02[4] n.25
Coupe, Leslie Q. .... 8.02[4] ns. 25, 26
Coursey v. Fairchild ...... S3.04[18] n.153s
Covington, Parker v. ... S3.04[8] n.86
Cox, Cracco v. ..... 3.08[4][g] n.267
Craig, Bradler v. ...... 4.04[7] n.205
Cracco v. Cox ...... 3.08[4][g] n.267
Cramer v. Metropolitan Sav. & Loan Ass'n .... 3.08[4][g] n.288
Crane, Comm'r v. .. 12.03[3][a] n.145
Crane v. Comm'r ..... 1.05[4][b][i], 1.05[4][b][i] ns. 184, 185, 1.05[4][b][ii], S6.04[3][b][ii] n.58a, 8.02[3] n.21, 12.01[3][a], S12.01[3][b] n.29, 12.02[4] n.78, 12.03[2][a][i], 12.03[3][a], 12.03[3][a] ns. 133, 134, 143, 12.03[4][a] n.160, 12.04[1] ns. 246, 247
Crawford, Brown v. .... 5.05[2] n.115
Crenshaw v. U.S. .. Form 1.1, Sec. 5.1, Comment
Crestview Ltd. v. Foremost Ins. Co. .... S3.04[8] n.84
Crichton, Comm'r v. .... 8.02[2] n.12
Cripe, McCarty v. ...... 12.03[4][a] ns. 159, 164
Crouse v. Michell ...... 6.03[2] n.16
Crockett v. First Fed. Sav. & Loan Ass'n .... 3.04[8] n.86
Cuesta, Larson v. .... 12.03[4][b][ii] n.198
Culbertson, A.B. ... 12.02[1][b] n.43
Culbertson v. Comm'r .. 9.04[7] n.114
Cumberland Pub. Serv. Co., U.S. v. .... S6.04[3][b][ii] n.58h
Cuna Mut. Ins. Soc'y v. Dominguez 3.06 n.182
Curtis, Cook v. .... 3.08[4][g] n.300

D

Dabney v. Chase Nat'l Bank .... 11.01[6][a] n.20
Dade County, Associated Schools, Inc. v. .... 3.04[5] n.46
Dale Constr. Co., Vandeventer v. 3.06 n.182
Dallas Transfer & Terminal Warehouse Co. v. Comm'r ..... 12.03[2][a][i] n.81, 12.03[3][a] n.136
Dalmo Sales Co. v. Tyson's Corner Regional Shopping Center .. 3.05[3] n.162
Damiano, Pansa v. .... 3.04[9][a]
Danek, First Nat'l Bank in Albuquerque v. .... 5.02[2] n.29
Dane's Estate, *In re* .... 5.02[1] n.17
Dantus v. First Fed. Sav. & Loan Ass'n .... S3.04[8] n.98w
Darling Shop v. Nelson Realty Co. .... 3.08[4][g] n.300
Dart v. Western Sav. & Loan Ass'n .... 3.08[4][g] n.307
Dash, Hughes v. .... 11.02[4][a] n.77
Davies, Blanche F. ... 12.03[2][b][iii] ns. 130, 131
Davis v. Boyajian, Inc. .. 3.05[6] n.168
Davis, Mindlin v. .... 5.05[7]
Dawn Inv. Co. v. Superior Court of Los Angeles County ..... S3.04[8] & n.98a
Deaner, Charmicor, Inc. v. .... 3.08[4][g] n.288
Dean, J. Simpson .. 12.02[2][a] n.53
DeGrazia, Wong v. .. 6.04[1][c] n.30
Dekalb County v. United Family Life Ins. Co. .... 3.04[5] n.46
DeKorwin v. First Nat'l Bank .... 5.05[2] n.122
De la Cuesta v. Fidelity Fed. Sav. & Loan Ass'n ..... S3.04[8] & n.98u
Delancey v. Fidelity Lease Ltd. .... 1.05[4][a] n.168a
Delaney, Parker v. .. 12.01[3][a] n.25, 12.02[4] n.78, 12.03[3][a] ns. 133, 135, 143, 144
Delius, Blazey v. .... 3.08[4][g] n.316
Delman, Estate of .. 12.03[3][a] n.136
Dematteo, M., Constr. Co. v. U.S. .... 6.01[1] n.1
Dennis, Clement O. ..... 12.03[3][b] n.155
Depau v. Humphreys .. 5.05[1] n.101
Derby Realty ..... 12.03[4][a] n.166

[*References are to paragraphs (¶) and to sample forms in Appendix B. References to the Supplement are preceded by "S."*]

Derenco, Inc. v. Benjamin Franklin Fed. Sav. & Loan Ass'n .... 3.04[6]
Dezell v. King .... 3.04[5] n.49
Diamond, Harry H. ..... 12.03[4][a] ns. 161, 164, 165
Diamond, Sol .. Form 1.1, Sec. 3.2A, Comment
Dicke, Farm Bureau Agricultural Credit v. .... 4.03[1] n.149
Dick & Reuteman Co. v. Jem Realty Co. ...... 3.08[4][i] n.330
Dime Sav. Bank v. Altman ...... S3.08[4][g] n.304
Diversified Enter. Inc. v. West .... S3.04[18] n.153e
Djiovanides, Chakales v. .... 5.03[5] n.73
Dominguez, Cuna Mut. Ins. Soc'y v. 3.06 n.182
Dunn v. Barry ..... 3.08[4][g] n.257
Dunn, Elmendorf-Anthony v. .... 4.02[6][a][ii] n.53
Dobkin, Isidor v. Comm'r ...... 11.02[4][b] n.86
Doerr, Humble Oil & Ref. Co. v. .... S3.04[3][c] n.33r, S3.04[18] & n.153r
Dorminey, J.T. ..... 12.03[2][b][iii] n.125
Dufty Road Properties, Michigan Roofing & Sheet Metal, Inc. v. .... S4.02[6][i] n.39
Dunn v. Comm'r .. S6.04[3][e] n.65a
duPont, Hirsch v. ...... 1.05[1] n.45
Durbin, Carter Oil Co. v. .... S3.04[18] n.153p
Durey, Ludlow Value Mfg. Co. v. ...... 12.03[2][b][ii] n.121
Durkee v. Franklin Sav. Ass'n .... 3.04[6] n.55

E

Eagle Sav. Ass'n, Imperial House of Ind. v. .... 4.02[7]
Ebner, Minnie .... 9.04[2][b][ii] ns. 68, 70
Edwards Indus., Inc. .... 8.02[2] n.17
Edwards, Union Central Life Ins. Co. v. .... 5.02[4][a] n.45, 5.03[5] n.69

Effinger, *In re* ...... 11.02[3][b] n.62
805 Third Ave. Co. v. New York Life Ins. Co. S3.06 n.182
Eisen v. Kostakos .. 3.08[4][g] n.251
Electro-Chemical Engraving Co. v. Comm'r ...... 12.03[4][a] n.158
Eliasberg, Rabinowich v. . 5.04[1] n.97
Ellsworth, Tipton v. .... 5.03[8] n.89
Elmendorf-Anthony v. Dunn .... 4.02[6][a][ii] n.53
Ely, Sidenberg v. .... 3.08[4][j] n.336
Emigrant Ind. Sav. Bank v. Willow Builders .... 4.04[2] n.173
Empire Home Loans, Inc., American Banchares Mortgage Co. v. S3.06 n.182
Emporia State Bank & Trust Co. v. Mounkes .... 3.08[4][a]
Engleman v. Malchow .... 4.03[2][d] n.166
Ennis v. Comm'r .... 9.04[7]
Ennis, Estate of, v. Comm'r .. 9.04[7] n.111
Epstein, Goodman v. .... 1.05[1] n.45, S1.05[1] n.45
Equitable Life Assurance Soc'y v. Kerpel .... 5.05[7] n.174
Equity Investors, National Bank of Washington v. ...... 4.02[6][a][ii]
Erickson v. Minnesota & O. Power Co. .... 11.02[4][b] n.87
Erie Forge & Steel Corp., *In re* .... 11.01[6][b] n.21
Erwin, Wallerstein v. .... 11.02[3][b] n.63
Evans v. Rice .... 5.02[2] n.32
Exchange Nat'l Bank of Shreveport v. Head .... 8.09[3] n.78

F

Fabs v. Martin .... 5.05[1] n.101
Fairchild, Coursey v. ..... S3.04[18] n.153s
Family Fin. Corp., Sniadach v. ...... 3.08[4][g], 3.08[4][g] ns. 272, 279
Fanning v. Stimson .... 3.05[1] n.156
Farm Bureau Agricultural Credit v. Dicke .... 4.03[1] n.149

REAL ESTATE FINANCING

[References are to paragraphs (¶) and to sample forms in Appendix B. References to the Supplement are preceded by "S."]

Farmers Trust & Sav. Bank
  v. Manning .... S3.08[4][a] n.216i
Fausett & Co. v. G & P Real Estate,
  Inc. .... S5.02[4][b] n.49
FDIC Receiver v. Mademoiselle of
  Cal. .... 11.01[6][b] n.24
Federal Home Loan Mortgage Corp.
  v. Taylor .... 3.08[4][g] n.255
Federal Nat'l Mortgage Ass'n
  v. Howlett ...... 3.08[4][g] n.288,
                    S3.08[4][g] n.288
Federal Nat'l Mortgage Ass'n, Northrip
  v. .... 3.08[4][g]
Federal Sav. & Loan Ass'n
  v. Stein .... S3.04[8] n.98r
Feldman v. Urban Commercial
  Inc. .... 6.03[2] n.16
Felton, Morroco v. .... 4.04[7] n.203
Ferguson v. Tanner Dev. Co. . 5.02[1]
      n.17, S5.02[4][d] n.56
Fergus v. Wilmarth .. 3.08[4][a] n.236
Fidelity Fed. Sav. & Loan Ass'n,
  De la Cuesta v. .. S3.04[8] & n.98u
Fidelity Land Dev. Corp. v. Rieder &
  Sons Bldg. & Dev. Co. ..... 3.04[8]
                              n.88
Fidelity Lease Ltd., Delancey
  v. .... 1.05[4][a] n.168a
Fifth Avenue-14th St. Corp.
  v. Comm'r .... 12.03[2][a][i] n.84
Fioravanti, State Bank
  v. .... S3.08[4][a] n.216a
Fi-Pen Realty Co., New York &
  Suburban Fed. Sav. & Loan Ass'n
  v. .... 4.02[6][a][ii] ns. 52, 53
First Fed. Sav. & Loan Ass'n,
  Bailey v. .... S3.04[8] n.98w
First Fed. Sav. & Loan Ass'n, Crockett
  v. .... 3.04[8] n.86
First Fed. Sav. & Loan Ass'n,
  Dantus v. .... S3.04[8] n.98w
First Fed. Sav. & Loan Ass'n, Hawkins
  v. .... 3.06 n.178, 3.07[1] n.186
First Fed. Sav. & Loan Ass'n
  v. Jenkins .... S3.04[8] n.98u
First Fed. Sav. & Loan Ass'n
  v. Lockwood ...... S3.04[8] n.98v
First Fed. Sav. & Loan Ass'n, Patton
  v. .... 3.04[8] n.86

First Fed. Sav. & Loan Ass'n
  v. Peterson .... S3.04[8] n.98w
First Fed. Sav. & Loan Ass'n,
  Williams v. ... S3.04[8] ns. 86, 98m,
                       98o, 98p, 98r
First Fed. Sav. & Loan of Racine,
  Goebel v. ...... S3.04[3][c] n.32a
First Nat'l Bank of Atlanta
  v. Blum .... 3.08[4][g] n.251
First Nat'l Bank, DeKorwin
  v. .... 5.05[2] n.122
First Nat'l Bank, Partain
  v. .... S3.04[3][c] ns. 32d, 33m
First Nat'l Bank in Albuquerque
  v. Danek .... 5.02[2] n.29
First Nat'l Bank of
  Durant ..... 12.03[2][b][iii] n.131
First Nat'l Bank of Joliet v. Illinois
  Steel Co. .... 3.08[4][g] n.309
First Nat'l Bank of Lawrence
  County ...... 12.03[4][b][i] n.178
First Nat'l Bank of Memphis, Hayes
  v. .... 5.03[8] n.78
First Nat'l Bank of Omaha, Fisher
  v. .... 5.05[1] n.108
First Nat'l Bank v.
  Rozelle .... 3.08[4][a] n.215
First Nat'l State Bank v.
  Commonwealth Fed. Sav. & Loan
  Ass'n S3.06 n.182
First Nat'l State Bank of N.J. v. Carlyle
  House, Inc. .... 4.04[7] n.204
First Pa. Mortgage Trust,
  Sarlot-Kantarjian v. ..... S5.05[1]
                             n.109
First Sec. Bank v. Shiew .. S3.08[4][a]
                ns. 216b, 216c, 216d
First So. Fed. Sav. & Loan Ass'n of
  Mobile v. Britton ... 3.04[8] ns. 86,
                            90, 99
Fischer v. Woodruf 7.06 n.31
Fisher v. First Nat'l Bank of
  Omaha .... 5.05[1] n.108
Flamingo Drift Fishing, Inc.
  v. Nix .... 4.04[7] n.203
Fleming, Continental Nat'l Bank
  v. .... 5.03[5] n.72
Fletcher v. Tuscaloosa Fed. Sav. &
  Loan Ass'n .... App. A, Table 3

[*References are to paragraphs (¶) and to sample forms in Appendix B. References to the Supplement are preceded by "S."*]

Florida Fed. Sav. & Loan Ass'n, Price v. .... S3.04[8] n.98w
Flori Inv. Co., Gangadean v. . 5.04[1] n.95
Foote, Metropolitan Life Ins. Co. v. .... S3.08[4][g] n.316
Foothill Indus. Bank v. Mikkelson ..... S4.04[8] ns. 211a, 211b, 211c
Ford, Page v. ..... 7.04[1][d][i] n.18
Foreman, United Hous. Foundation, Inc. v. .... 10.02[2][b] n.32, 10.03 n.64
Foremost Ins. Co., Crestview Ltd. v. .... S3.04[8] n.84
Foster Lumber Co. v. Weston Constructors, Inc. . 3.08[4][g] n.264
495 Corp. v. New Jersey Ins. Underwriting Ass'n .. S3.04[12][b] n.143
Four Seasons, George M. Morris Constr. Co. v. ...... 4.04[4] n.183
424 Eye St. Ass'n, Waco Scaffold & Shor. Co. v. .... 4.02[6][a][i] n.40
Fox, Blaine S. ..... 12.03[3][a] n.145
Fox, Glendale Fed. Sav. & Loan Ass'n v. ...... S3.04[8] & n.98r
Fox, Golden States Lanes v. ... 5.05[4] n.157
Foxman, David ... Form 1.1, Sec. 5.1, Comment
Franklin v. Community Fed. S&L Ass'n .... 3.08[4][a] n.219, S3.08[4][a] n.220
Franklin Estate v. Comm'r .... S6.04[3][b][ii] n.58a, 12.01[3][b], 12.01[3][b] n.26
Franklin Sav. Ass'n, Durkee v. .... 3.04[6] n.55
Frantz, Klodt & Son, Inc., Mutual Benefit Life Ins. Co. v. . 3.08[4][g] n.309
Frazell, U.S. v. ... Form 1.1, Sec. 3.2A, Comment
Freeland, Estate of, v. Comm'r .... 9.05[1] n.116
Freeland, Eugene L. .... 12.03[3][a] n.147

Freese Leasing, Inc. v. Union Trust & Sav. Bank .... 3.08[4][a] n.210
French v. Mortgage Guar. Co. .... 5.02[4][b] n.47
French v. Zoning Bd. of Adjustment ...... 3.04[9][b] n.109
Frenzel v. Comm'r ... 6.04[3][b] n.53
Fribourg, Mandelino v. ...... 5.02[2]
Frick Co., D.H. Overmeyer Co. v. .... 3.08[4][g]
Fried Furniture Corp., *In re* . 11.01[6] n.16
Frigidaire Sales Corp. v. Union Properties, Inc. .. 1.05[4][a] n.168a
Frost, Sanders v. .... 3.04[5] n.39
Fuller, Berger v. .... 3.08[4][a] n.208
Fuller, Peter Enterprises, Inc. v. Manchester Sav. Bank .. 3.04[5] n.41
Fulmer Bldg. Supplies, Inc. v. Martin .... 4.04[4]
Fulton v. Abramsohn ..... 4.03[2][d] n.166
Fulton Gold Corp. .... 12.03[2][a][i] n.85
Fusco, Beneficial Fin. Co. v. .. S3.03[4][c] ns. 32b, 32d, 33m

G

Gaither v. Clark .... 5.05[4] n.159
Galloway v. Korzekwa . 11.02[2] n.58
Galvin v. Hudson ..... 12.03[4][b][i] n.177
Ganbaum v. Rockwood Realty Corp. .... 3.08[4][i]
G & P Real Estate, Inc., Fausett & Co. v. .... S5.02[4][b] n.49
Gangadean v. Flori Inv. Co. ... 5.04[1] n.95
Gannon, Gaius G. ..... 1.05[3][c][v] n.143
Garfinkle v. Superior Court .... S3.08[4][g] n.288
Garner v. Tri-State Dev. Co. .... 3.08[4][g]
Garrison, Bellingham First Fed. Sav. & Loan Ass'n v. .... 3.04[8] ns. 88, 99

[References are to paragraphs (¶) and to sample forms in Appendix B. References to the Supplement are preceded by "S."]

Gatnick Realty Corp., 107 Shore Road Corp. v. .... S3.08[4][g] n.304
Gawart, Campbell v. ..... 5.02[4][c]
Gay v. Grace .... 3.03[1] n.17
Gelber v. Kugelis Tavern, Inc. .... 5.04[1] n.95
General Am. Life Ins. Co. .... 12.02[2][a] n.59
General Capital Corp., Tei Serv. Co. v. .... 5.04[1] n.96
General Contract Purchase Corp., Hare v. .... 5.02[2] n.30
General Mortgage Corp., Smith v. .... 3.04[12][b] n.145
Generes v. U.S. ..... 12.03[2][b][iii] n.127
Gilford v. Comm'r . 12.03[4][a] n.164
Gimble Bros., *In re* .... 3.05[3] n.163
Girard Corn Exch. Bank .... 12.03[5] n.241
Girard, John Hancock Mut. Life Ins. Co. v. .... 11.01[2] n.9
Glahn, Van, Century Fed. Sav. & Loan Ass'n v. .... 3.04[8] n.86
Glendale Fed. Sav. & Loan Ass'n v. Fox .... S3.04[8] & n.98r
Glendser Textile Co. ..... 1.05[4][a], 1.05[4][a] n.162
Global Indus., Inc. v. Harris .... 3.08[4][g] n.288
Goebel v. First Fed. Sav. & Loan of Racine .... S3.04[3][c] n.32a
Goff, Krone v. ...... 3.08[4][a] n.233
Golanty v. Comm'r ..... S6.04[3][e] n.65a
Golden States Lanes v. Fox .. 5.05[4] n.157
Goldsworthy, Hall v. . 3.08[4][i] n.330
Goodman v. Comm'r .. 7.04[3] n.23a
Goodman v. Epstein .... 1.05[1] n.45, S1.05[1] n.45
Goodwin, Weathersbee v. ... 3.08[4][g] n.300
Gordon, Handy v. .... 6.02[1] n.6
Grace, Gay v. .... 3.03[1] n.17
Grady v. Price .... 5.03[2] n.61
Graeme v. Adams .. 5.02[2] ns. 27, 32
Graf v. Hope Bldg. Corp. ... 3.08[4][g] n.252

Grainger v. Antoyan .... 1.05[1] n.38
Granahan, Barr v. ... S3.04[3][c] n.33r
Gravenhorst, Holmes v. ... 3.08[4][g] n.304
Great S. Sav. & Loan Ass'n, Arend v. .... S3.04[5]
Great W. Sav. & Loan Ass'n, Connor v. ... 4.04[7], 4.04[7] ns. 199, 203, 204
Great W. Sav. & Loan Ass'n, Moore v. .... 3.04[6] n.59
Green, Comm'r v. ... 12.03[3][a] n.141
Greenberg, *In re* .... 5.04[1] n.95
Greenway Bank & Trust, R.J. Carter Enter., Inc. v. ...... S5.04[1] n.97
Gries, Robert H. .... 12.02[1][a] n.36
Griffin v. Reis ..... 3.08[4][g] n.316
Grigg v. Wobinson Furniture Co. . 5.04 n.90
Groves, George S. .. 12.02[1][a] n.36
Guaranty Bank & Trust Co. ... 5.05[1] n.101
Guaranty Liquidating Corp., Kinnison v. .... S3.08[4][i] n.330
Guardian Mortgage Investors, Woodmore N. Inv. Fund Ltd. v. .... S4.02[6] n.31a
Gulf Petroleum, S.A. v. Collazo .... 11.01[6][b] n.26
Gunther v. White ...... 3.04[8] n.86
Gutman, Theodore, Estate of .... 12.03[2][b][iii] n.127

H

Haden, W.D., Co. v. Comm'r . 8.02[4] n.24 12.03[3][b] n.151
Hadley Falls Trust Co. v. U.S. ....12.02[3] n.72, 12.02[4] n.75, 12.03[4][b][ii] n.185, 12.03[4][b][ii] n.198
Haering, Industrial Acceptance Corp. v. .... 11.01[2] n.10
Hager v. Comm'r .. S6.04[3][e] n.65a
Hagist Ranch Inc. v. Comm'r . 5.03[3] n.127
Hale v. Helvering . 12.03[3][b] n.155, 12.03[4][b][i] n.177

[*References are to paragraphs (¶) and to sample forms in Appendix B. References to the Supplement are preceded by "S."*]

Hall v. Bryce's Mountain Resort,
   Inc. .... 9.03[1] n.24
Hall v. Goldsworthy . 3.08[4][i] n.330
Hall, Metropolitan Life Ins. Co.
   v. .... 4.04[2] n.173
Hambeuchen
   v. Comm'r ..... S12.01[5][a] n.331
Hammel, Helvering v. ... 12.03[4][a]
   n.158
Hammond, James . 9.04[2][b][ii] n.70
Hancock, John Mut. Life Ins. Co.
   v. Girard .... 11.01[2] n.9
H & R Block, Inc., Beeler
   v. .... S5.02[4][d] n.56a
Handy v. Gordon .... 6.02[1] n.6
Hare v. General Contract Purchase
   Corp. .... 5.02[2] n.30
Hargrave, Comer v. ...... 3.08[4][g]
   n.254, S3.08[4][g] n.260
Harkelrode, Van Huffel v. ... 8.09[3]
   n.77
Harn, Baltimore Life Ins. Co.
   v. .... 3.04[8] n.88
Harris, Global Indus., Inc.
   v. .... 3.08[4][g] n.288
Harris, Leon A. ... 1.05[3][b][i] n.120
Harris, Majestic Builders Corp.
   v. .... S3.08[4][i] n.326
Harrison, Campana Corp.
   v. .... S6.04[3][b][ii] n.58d
Harrison, N. Lucille . 12.03[2][b][iii]
   n.131
Harrison Property Management Co.
   v. U.S. .... 5.05[3] n.134
Harris, Price v. ..... 3.07[4][d] n.236
Hartford Life Ins. Co.
   v. Randall .... 3.04[5] n.39
Hartman, William, & Son, Inc.,
   Reisman v. ...... 11.02[3][c] n.72
Hassen, E.E ...... 12.03[4][a] n.159
Hatridge v. Home Accident & Life Ins.
   Co. .... 5.05[7] n.174
Hauff, Hyman v. .. 4.02[6][a][ii] n.55
Haugen v. Western Fed. Sav. & Loan
   Ass'n .... S3.04[8] n.98w
Havemeyer, Doris D. . 12.03[4][b][i]
   ns. 181, 182
Haviland v. Haviland .... 1.02[1] n.3

Hawkins v. First Fed. Sav. & Loan
   Ass'n ... 3.06 n.178, 3.07[1] n.186
Hawkins, J.C. .... 12.03[4][a] n.166
Hawley, Weinrich v. ... 5.02[4][a] n.44
Hayes v. First Nat'l Bank of
   Memphis .... 5.03[8] n.78
Head, Exchange Nat'l Bank of
   Shreveport v. .... 8.09[3] n.78
Hebrew Children's Home, Inc.
   v. Walter .... 3.08[4][g] n.267
Heidler, McCown v. .... 9.03[1] n.22
Heights v. Citizens Nat'l
   Bank .... 11.01[6] n.16
Heinemann, William C., &
   Co. .... 12.03[4][b][i] n.184
Heiner v. Tindle .... 8.02[2] n.17
Helvering v. A.L. Killian
   Co. .... 12.03[2][a][i] n.84
Helvering v. F.&R. Lazarus &
   Co. .... 6.04[3][b] n.54
Helvering, Hale v. . 12.03[3][b] n.155,
   12.03[4][b][i] n.177
Helvering v. Hammel .... 12.03[4][a]
   n.158
Helvering v. Horst .... 12.02[4]
   ns. 77, 78
Helvering v. Midland Mut. Life Ins.
   Co. .... 12.03[4][b][i] n.179,
   12.03[4][b][ii] ns. 185, 186, 190
Helvering v. Missouri State Life Ins.
   Co. .... 12.03[3][b] n.153
Helvering v. New President
   Corp. .... 12.03[4][b][ii] n.193
Hempstead Theatre Corp.
   v. Metropolitan Playhouse,
   Inc. .... 3.05[4] n.166
Herbert's Estate v.
   Comm'r ..... 12.03[4][b][i] n.179
Herman, Price v. .... 3.05[7] n.172
Heubush v. Boone ..... 5.05[2] n.116
Hewsey, Cahn v. ... 3.08[4][d] n.231
Hicks, Citizens & So. DeKalb Bank
   v. .... 3.08[4][a] n.215
Hicks, Sanders v. .... 3.04[8] n.88
Higgens v. Comm'r .... 1.05[4][b][ii]
   n.186
Higginbotham-Bailey-Logan
   Co. .... 12.01[1][b] n.11,
   12.02[2][a] n.55

[*References are to paragraphs (¶) and to sample forms in Appendix B. References to the Supplement are preceded by "S."*]

Higgins v. U.S. ..... 12.03[2][b][iii] n.127
High Sky, Inc., Rockefeller v. .... 9.03[1] n.24
Hill, Bank of Cave City v. .... S4.02[6][a][i] n.37
Hill, Barigoni v. ... 7.04[1][d][i] n.17
Hill, Sherwin A. ... 12.03[4][a] n.168
Hilpert, Anna L. ...... 12.02[4] n.78
Hilton v. Comm'r .... S6.04[3][b][ii] & n.58a
Hirsch v. Comm'r .... 12.03[2][a][i] n.84
Hirsch v. duPont .... 1.05[1] n.45
HNC Realty Co., Willowood Condominium Ass'n, Inc. v. .... 3.03[1] n.17
Hobart, Conover v. .... 5.05[2] n.112
Hobart v. Michaud ..... 5.03[5] n.73
Hoffman v. Charnita .... 9.03[1] n.24
Hoffman, Comm'r v. .... 12.03[3][a] ns. 142, 145
Hoffman v. Hud .... 3.08[4][g]
Holiday Inns v. Susher-Schaefer Inv. Co. .... 3.08[4][a] n.211
Holladay, Durand .... S1.05[3][b][i] n.120
Holland Furnace Co., Mathis v. .... 5.03[8] n.85
Hollis Automotive Corp., Rockaway Park Series Corp. v. .... 3.08[4][g] n.255
Holmdel Village Shops, Inc., Monmouth Capital Corp. v. .... 5.04[1] n.96
Holmes, Coffey Enterprises Realty & Dev. Co. v. .... 3.08[4][g] n.282
Holmes v. Gravenhorst ... 3.08[4][g] n.304
Holt v. Rickett .... 5.02[1] n.18
Home Accident & Life Ins. Co., Hatridge v. .... 5.05[7] n.174
Home Credit Co. v. Brown ... 5.03[8] n.87
Home Fed. Sav. & Loan Ass'n, Marsh v. .... 3.04[6] n.58
Home Sav. & Loan Ass'n v. Bates .... 5.02[4][b] n.47

Home Sav. & Loan Ass'n, Cherry v. .... 3.04[8] ns. 81, 86
Home Title Ins. Co. v. Scherman Holding Corp. ... 3.08[4][g] n.312
Hope Bldg. Corp., Graf v. . 3.08[4][g] n.252
Hopkins, John R. ... 12.01[1][b] n.13
Horrigan v. Wellmuth ..... 3.08[4][j] n.336
Horst, Helvering v. .... 12.02[4] ns. 77, 78
Hotel Astoria, Inc. .... 12.03[2][a][i] n.85
Hotel St. James, Co., In re . 3.08[4][i] n.330, S3.08[4][i] n.330
House of Carpets, Inc. v. Mortgage Inv. Co. .... 4.02[6][a][ii]
Household Fin. Corp., Vee Bee Serv. Co. v. .... 5.03[2] ns. 61, 62
Housing Mfg. Corp. v. Allied Constr. Co. .... 4.02[6][a][ii] n.53
Howell, Charles M. ...... 12.02[1][a] n.35
Howell v. Comm'r ...... 9.05[1] n.116
Howlett, Federal Nat'l Mortgage Ass'n v. .... 3.08[4][g] n.288, S3.0[4][g] n.288
Howey, W.J., Co., SEC v. ... 1.05[1] n.45
Hoyt, Odell v. ...... 3.08[4][g] n.258
Hud, Hoffman v. .... 3.08[4][g]
Hudson City Sav. Bank, Selective Builders Inc. v. 3.06 n.182, S3.06 n.178
Hudson City Sav. Inst., Stith v. .... 3.04[8] ns. 86, 99, S3.04[8] n.87
Hudson, Galvin v. .... 12.03[4][b][i] n.177
Hughes v. Dash .... 11.02[4][a] n.77
Humble Oil & Ref. Co. v. Doerr .... S3.04[3][c] n.33r, S3.04[18] & n.153r
Humphrey v. Comm'r ..... 12.03[4][b][ii] n.189
Humphreys, Depau v. .. 5.05[1] n.101
Huntington Redondo Co. . 12.02[1][a] ns. 36, 37, 12.02[2][a] n.56

[*References are to paragraphs (¶) and to sample forms in Appendix B. References to the Supplement are preceded by "S."*]

Hutcheson, Palmer .... 1.05[3][c][v] n.143
Hyde, Gordon I. ...... 12.02[3] n.73
Hyman v. Hauff .. 4.02[6][a][ii] n.55

I

Illinois Steel Co., First Nat'l Bank of Joliet v. .... 3.08[4][g] n.309
Imhoff v. Title Ins. Co. .... 4.02[6][a][ii] n.45
Imperial House of Ind. v. Eagle Sav. Ass'n .... 4.02[7]
Industrial Acceptance Corp. v. Haering .... 11.01[2] n.10
Inland Properties, Inc., National Surety Corp. v. .... 5.05[1]
Inman, Bailey v. .... 5.02[2] n.31
International Milling Co., Brose v. .... 3.08[4][a]
Investing Co. v. Comm'r .... 6.04[3][a][i]
I.R.E. Financial Corp. v. Cassel .... 5.02[1] n.17

J

Jackson Inv. Co., Comm'r v. .... Form 1.1, Sec. 5.1, Comment
Jacobsen v. Woodmoor Corp. . 9.03[1] n.24
Jamaica Sav. Bank v. Lefkowitz .... 3.04[6] n.65
James Bros. Coal Co. .... 12.01[1][b] ns. 10, 11, 12.02[2][a] n.55
Jameson v. Warren .... 5.05[8]
Janisse v. Winston Instrument Co. .... 5.05[2] n.114
Janofsky v. Wernick ... 11.02[2] n.58
Jefferson Fed. Sav. & Loan Ass'n, Bryant v. .... 3.08[4][g]
Jefferson Standard Life Ins. Co., Bell Bakeries, Inc. v. ...... 3.04[5] n.49
Jefferson Standard Life Ins. Co., White Lakes Shopping Center v. 3.06 n.177
Jemison v. Montgomery Real Estate & Co. .... 4.04[7] n.203
Jem Realty Co., Dick & Reuteman Co. v. .... 3.08[4][i] n.330

Jenkins, First Fed. Sav. & Loan Ass'n v. .... S3.04[8] n.98u
Jenkins v. Moyse .... 5.04[1]
Jerome v. McCarter . 3.08[4][f] n.246
Jersey City v. Zink ... 5.02[4][a] n.44
Jersey Mortgage Inv. Co., Randel v. .... 3.08[4][i] n.329
Johnson, Joseph W. ... 12.04[3] n.252
Johnson v. American Nat'l Ins. Co. S3.06 n.178
Johnson, Pushee v. ..... 5.03[3] n.66
Johnston v. Comm'r ... 9.04[7] n.108
Jones Co., Comm'r v. .... 12.03[2][b][ii] n.115
Jones v. Kaufman ..... 5.05[2] n.122
Jones, Maxa v. ..... 11.02[3][b] n.67
Jones v. Phillippe .... 5.03[3] n.66
Jones v. Sacramento Sav. & Loan Ass'n .... 3.04[8] n.84
Jones, Thrift Funds of Baton Rouge, Inc. v. .... 5.03[8] n.78
Jones, Warren Co. v. Comm'r . 9.04[7] n.111

K

Kaminski v. London Pub. ... 3.08[4][g] n.255
Kanawha Valley Bank ..... 12.03[5] n.236
Kauaian Dev. Co., State Sav. & Loan Ass'n v. .... 10.01[2][b] n.37
Kaufman v. Comm'r .... 12.03[3][a] ns. 133, 137
Kaufman, Jones v. .... 5.05[2] n.122
Kawauchi v. Tabata ... 5.05[4] n.158
K-C Land Co. v. Comm'r .... 5.05[3] n.134
Keil Properties, Inc. .. 1.05[2][c] n.57
Motor Credit Co., Lincoln Loan Serv. Inc. v. .... 5.02[2] n.30
Kelley, Comm'r v. .... 1.05[3][a][ii] n.116
Kelley Bros. v. Primex Equities Corp. .... S3.08[4][i] n.331
Kelly, Ahrens v. .... 5.03[3] n.65
Kemme, Wells v. ... 3.08[4][g] n.300
Kena, Inc. v. Comm'r .. S12.01[5][a] n.33m

[References are to paragraphs (¶) and to sample forms in Appendix B. References to the Supplement are preceded by "S."]

Kennebee, Inc. v. Bank of the West . . . . 3.08[4][g] n.288
Kent v. Phelps . . . . 5.03[8] n.82
Kerpel, Equitable Life Assurance Soc'y v. . . . . 5.05[7] n.174
Kessing v. National Mortgage Corp. . . . . 11.02[3][c]
Kilgore Hardware & Bldg. Supply Inc. v. Mullins . . S4.02[6][a][i] n.37
Killian, A.L., Co., Helvering v. . . . . 12.03[2][a][i] n.84
Kimball Foods, Inc. v. Republic Nat'l Bank of Dallas . . 3.08[4][a] n.210, S3.08[4][a] n.210
Kimpton v. Walker . . . . 3.05[1] n.156
Kin-ark Corp. v. Boyles . . S5.02[4][d] n.54
King, Dezell v. . . . . 3.04[5] n.49
Kinnison v. Guaranty Liquidating Corp. . . . . S3.08[4][i] n.330
Kintzel v. Wheatland Mut. Ins. Ass'n . . . . 3.08[4][d] n.236
Kirby Lumber, U.S. v. . . . . 12.03[2][a][i] n.80
Kirk, J.J., Inc. . . . . . . 6.04[3][c] n.59
Kislak, J.I. Mortgage Corp. v. William Matthews Builder Inc. . . . . 4.02[6][a][ii]
Kite, Shafer Bros. v. . . . 4.03[1] n.149
Kittredge v. Langley . . . . . 4.03[2][d] n.166
Klauber, Whitley v. . . 4.03[2][d] n.166, S4.03[2][d] n.166
Klett v. Security Acceptance Co. . . . . 5.05[7] n.174
Kline v. Mathewson . . . . 5.03[3] n.64
Knetsch v. U.S. . . . . . S6.04[3][b][ii] n.58f
Knight, Kreiss Potassium Phosphate Co. v. . . . . 3.08[4][g] n.254
Knutson Co., M.S.M. Corp. v. . . . . 4.04[4]
Kohn v. Comm'r . . 12.03[3][b] n.151, 12.03[5] n.232
Korth v. Zion's Sav. Bank & Trust Co. . . . . 12.03[4][b][ii] n.193
Korzekwa, Galloway v. . . . . 11.02[2] n.58
Kostakos, Eisen v. . . 3.08[4][g] n.251

Krause v. Columbia Sav. & Loan Ass'n . . . . S3.04[8] n.86
Kreiss Potassium Phosphate Co. v. Knight . . . . 3.08[4][g] n.254
Kresser, Jean V. . . . . . . 1.05[3][b][i], Form 1.1, Sec. 2.7 Comment
Krone v. Goff . . . . . . 3.08[4][a] n.233
Kruger, Union Bank v. . . . 5.03[8] n.78
Kugelis Tavern, Inc., Gelber v. . . . . 5.04[1] n.95
Kuhn, Althausen v. . . . 3.08[4][g] n.310
Kulo, Prusaczyk v. . . . . . . S3.08[4][i] n.330

L

Lachenmeier, Clark v. . . . 3.04[8] n.88
Lakeland Grocery Co. . . . . . 12.03[2][a][i] ns. 81, 82, 12.03[3][a] n.136
Lampert Yards, Inc. v. Thompson-Wetterling Constr. & Realty Inc. . . . . 4.02[6][a][iii] n.58, 4.04[7] n.204
Landau, E., Indus. v. 385 McLean Corp. . . . . S3.08[4][g] n.304a
Landers-Morrison-Christenson Co. v. Ambassador Holding Co. . . . . 4.02[6][a][ii] n.55
Langel, Treker v. . . S3.04[18] n.153r
Langford v. Comm'r . . . . S6.04[3][e]
Langley, Kittredge v. . . . . . 4.03[2][d] n.166
Lanney v. Producers Livestock Credit Corp. . . . . 3.08[4][a] n.215
Larson v. Cuesta . . . . . 12.03[4][b][ii] n.198
Larson, Philip G. . . . . 1.05[4][a], 1.05[4][a] ns. 162, 177
LaSala v. American Sav. & Loan Ass'n . . . . 3.04[7], 3.04[7] n.76, 3.04[8], 3.04[8] n.81
Lassen Sav. & Loan Ass'n, Tucker v. . . . 3.04[7] n.76, 3.04[8] ns. 81, 86
Lawless, Spires v. . . . 3.08[4][g] n.260
Lawrence v. Shutt . . . . . 9.01[1][c] n.4
Lawson v. Smith . . . 3.08[4][g] n.288
Lay, Lyndell E. . . . . 1.05[2][d] n.66b, 12.01[1][a] n.1

[References are to paragraphs (¶) and to sample forms in Appendix B. References to the Supplement are preceded by "S."]

Lazarus, F.&R. & Co., Comm'r
 v. . . . . 6.01[1] n.1
Lazarus, F.&R. & Co., Helvering
 v. . . . . 6.04[3][b] n.54
Lazzareschi Inv. Co. v. San Francisco Sav. & Loan Ass'n . . . . 3.04[5] n.49
Leben v. Nassau Sav. & Loan Ass'n . . 3.03[1] n.16, S3.03[1] n.16
Leeds & Lippincott Co.
 v. U.S. . . . . 6.04[3][b] n.53
Lefkowitz, Jamaica Sav. Bank
 v. . . . . 3.04[6] n.65
Lehigh Valley Trust Co. v. Central Nat'l Bank . . . . 11.01[7] n.30
Lennon, Sisco-Hamilton Co.
 v. . . . . 11.02[4][b] n.87
Lenway, Fred H., & Co. . . 12.03[3][a] n.147
Leslie Co. v. Comm'r . . 6.04[3][a][ii] n.52
Levin v. Carney . . . S3.08[4][i] n.330
Levin v. Comm'r . . 6.04[2][a][i] n.36
Levine v. Stein . . . . 3.08[4][g]
Lewis, Bokser v. . . . . 11.02[3][c] n.70
Lewis, S. Rex . . . . 12.01[1][b] n.8
Liftin v. Comm'r . . 12.02[1][b] n.44
Lincoln Loan Serv. Inc. v. Motor Credit Co. . . . . 5.02[2] n.30
Lindsey, Roland v. . . . . 4.02[8][b] n.83
Lintzenich, St. Louis Flexicure Inc.
 v. . . . . 4.04[4] n.183
Litho, K.&L., Corp., Rochester Capital Leasing v. . . . . 5.05[1] n.106
Lockwood, First Fed. Sav. & Loan Ass'n v. . . . . S3.04[8] n.98v
Logan, Burnet v. . . . . 9.04[7] n.108, 12.03[2][b][ii] n.118
Lomb v. Sugden 1.04 n.25
London Pub., Kaminski
 v. . . . . 3.08[4][g] n.255
Lone Star Life Ins. Co., Texas Bank & Trust Co. v. S4.05 n.219
Long, National Sur. Co. v. . . 4.02[8][b] n.82
Lovejoy, Julia Stow . . . . . 12.01[1][a] ns. 1, 2
Loves Park Sav. & Loan Ass'n, Baker v. . . . . . . 3.04[7] n.72, 3.04[8] n.87
Lowe v. Massachusetts Mut. Life Ins. Co. 3.06 n.177
Lowry v. Northwestern Sav. & Loan Ass'n . . . . 3.08[4][g] n.261
L-R Heat Treatment
 Co. . . . . 12.01[1][b] n.5
Lubbock Hotel Co. v. Guaranty Bank & Trust Co. . . . . 5.05[1] n.101
Ludlow, Lewis . . . 9.04[2][b][ii] n.67
Ludlow Value Mfg. Co.
 v. Durey . . . . 12.03[2][b][ii] n.121
Lutz v. Schramm . . . . 12.03[3][a] ns. 133, 134, 135, 12.04[1] ns. 246, 248
Lynn v. Beard Land Co. . 9.03[1] n.26
Lyon, Frank Co.
 v. U.S. . . . . 6.04[3][a][ii] n.52, 6.04[3][b] n.53, 6.04[3][b][i], S6.04[3][b][ii]
Lyons v. National Sav.
 Bank . . . . 5.02[3][b] n.41

M

MacArthur v. North Palm Beach Utils., Inc. . . . . . . S3.04[18] n.153s
Macy, R.H., & Co. v. Bates . . . 3.08[1] n.187
Mademoiselle of Cal., FDIC Receiver
 v. . . . . 11.01[6][b] n.24
Madsen v. Prudential Fed. Sav. & Loan Ass'n . . . . 3.04[6] n.68
Magazine v. Comm'r . . S1.05[3][b][i] n.124a
Main & McKinney Bldg. Co. v.
 Comm'r . . . . 6.04[3][c] n.59
Main Properties, Inc. . . 12.03[2][a][i] n.81, 12.03[3][a] n.136
Majestic Builders Corp.
 v. Harris . . . . S3.08[4][i] n.326
Malat v. Riddell . . . . . . 9.05[1] n.115
Malchow, Engleman v. . . . 4.03[2][d] n.166
Mallory v. Agee 7.06 n.30
Malmstedt, Margaret
 E.J. . . . . 12.03[4][a] n.163
Malouff v. Midland Fed. Sav. & Loan Ass'n . . . . 3.04[8] n.86

REAL ESTATE FINANCING T-28

[References are to paragraphs (¶) and to sample forms in Appendix B. References to the Supplement are preceded by "S."]

Malsman v. Brandler ..... 3.08[4][i] n.333, S3.08[4][i] n.330
Manard, Talbott v. ..... 5.03[3] n.64
Manchester Sav. Bank, Peter Fuller Enterprises, Inc. v. ... 3.04[5] n.41
Mandelino v. Fribourg ...... 5.02[2]
Manhattan Mut. Life Ins. Co. .... 12.02[1][a] n.39, 12.03[3][b] n.153
Manning, Farmers Trust & Sav. Bank v. .... S3.08[4][a] n.216i
Manufacturers Life Ins. Co., St. Paul Corp. v. .... 3.03[1] n.13
Manufacturer's Life Ins. Co. ... 12.02[1][a] n.39, 12.03[3][b] n.153, 12.03[4][b][ii] n.190
Manufacturers Nat'l Bank of Detroit v. Burlison .... 5.02[2] n.29
Marcus, Leonard ... 12.01[3][b] n.29
Marsh v. Home Fed. Sav. & Loan Ass'n .... 3.04[6] n.58
Marshall, U.S. v. ... 9.04[2][b][ii] n.66
Marsh, Jordan, Co. v. Comm'r .... 6.04[3][a][i], 6.04[3][a][ii], 6.04[4], 8.02[2] n.13
Martin v. Ajax Constr. Co. .. 5.05[2] n.117
Martin, Fabs v. .... 5.05[1] n.101
Martin, Fulmer Bldg. Supplies, Inc. v. .... 4.04[4]
Martin v. Raleigh State Bank 7.06 n.28
Massachusetts Mut. Life Ins. Co. v. Avon Assocs., Inc. ... 3.08[4][g] n.313
Massachusetts Mut. Life Ins. Co., Lowe v. 3.06 n.177
Masters Supply, Inc., Woodson Bend, Inc. v. .... 4.02[6][a][i] n.42
Mathewson, Kline v. .... 5.03[3] n.64
Mathis v. Holland Furnace Co. .... 5.03[8] n.85
Matthews, William, Builder Inc., J.I. Kislak Mortgage Corp. v. .... 4.02[6][a][ii]
Maurer, J.A., Inc. .... 12.03[2][a][i] n.83
Maxa v. Jones ..... 11.02[3][b] n.67
May, Marvin M. .... 12.01[3][b] n.29

Mayerson, Manual ...... 12.01[3][b]
Mayerson v. Comm'r .. S6.04[3][b][ii] n.58e
McCarter, Jerome v. .... 3.08[4][f] n.246
McCarty v. Cripe ...... 12.03[4][a] ns. 159, 164
McConnell v. Merrill Lynch, Pierce, Fenner & Smith, Inc. .... S5.02[4][d] n.56
McCown v. Heidler .... 9.03[1] n.22
McDermott v. Burke .. 3.05[6] n.168
McInerney v. Comm'r .. 9.04[2][b][ii] n.72
McInnis v. Cooper Communities, Inc. S5.01 n.11c
McNeil, R.H. ..... 12.03[4][a] n.159
McShain v. Comm'r .. S6.04[3][b][ii] n.58c
Meador Brook Nat'l Bank v. Recile .... 5.05[1] n.108
Memphis Natural Gas Co. v. Beeler .... 11.02[2] n.57
Memphis Natural Gas Co. v. Pope .... 11.02[2] n.57
Mendham Corp. ... 12.04[1] ns. 246, 248
Mercantile Trust Co. of Baltimore .... 8.02[4] n.24
Merchant's Nat'l Bank of Commerce v. Comm'r ... 12.03[4][b][i] n.178
Merchant's Nat'l Bank of Mobile .... 12.02[1][b] n.43
Merchants Nat'l Bank, Warmack v. .... S3.04[8] n.88
Meridan Bowling Lanes, Inc. v. Brown .... 5.05[6] n.169
Merrill Lynch, Pierce, Fenner & Smith, Inc., McConnell v. .... S5.02[4][d] n.56
Merrit, Sr., J.H. ... 12.03[4][a] n.159
Metropolitan Life Ins. Co. v. Childs Co. .... 3.05[6] n.168
Metropolitan Life Ins. Co. v. Foote .... S3.08[4][g] n.316
Metropolitan Life Ins. Co. v. Hall .... 4.04[2] n.173
Metropolitan Mortgage Fund ...... 12.01[2][b] ns. 16, 19

[*References are to paragraphs (¶) and to sample forms in Appendix B. References to the Supplement are preceded by "S."*]

Metropolitan Playhouse, Inc., Hempstead Theatre Corp. v. .... 3.05[4] n.166
Metropolitan Properties Corp. .... 12.01[1][a] n.3
Metropolitan Sav. & Loan Ass'n, Cramer v. .... 3.08[4][g] n.288
Meurer Steel Barrel Co. .... 12.03[2][b][i] n.106
Meyer, Comm'r v. ... 5.02[4][a] n.44
Meyer, Rollin E. Estate v. Comm'r .... 8.02[2] n.15
Michaud, Hobart v. .... 5.03[5] n.73
Michell, Crouse v. ...... 6.03[2] n.16
Michigan Roofing & Sheet Metal, Inc. v. Dufty Road Properties .... S4.02[6][i] n.39
Middlemist v. Mosier ..... 3.08[4][g] n.255
Midland Fed. Sav. & Loan Ass'n, Malouff v. .... 3.04[8] n.86
Midland Life Ins. Co., Helvering v. . 12.03[4][b][ii] ns. 185, 186, 190
Midland Mut. Life Ins. Co., Helvering v. ... 12.03[4][b][i] n.179
Mikkelson, Foothill Indus. Bank v. ... S4.04[8] ns. 211a, 211b, 211c
Mildenberger, Northwestern Nat'l Ins. Co. v. .... 3.04[12][b] n.145
Miles, Tomlinson v. .... 5.05[3] n.127
Millar v. Comm'r .. 12.03[3][a] n.134, S12.03[3][a] n.134, 12.04[1] n.247
Millar, Gavin S. .... 12.03[3][a] ns. 134, 147, 12.03[4][a] ns. 158, 160, 12.04[1] n.247
Miller v. Pacific First Fed. Sav. & Loan Ass'n .... 3.04[8] n.86
Miller, Robinson v. ... 3.08[4][g] n.258
Miller v. Tiffany ...... 5.05[1] n.101
Miller v. Usry ...... 9.04[4][b] n.94
Miller v. Walser ...... 11.02[2] n.58
Mills v. Mutual Bldg. & Loan Ass'n .... 3.08[4][g] n.277
Mills v. Nashua Fed. Sav. & Loan Ass'n .... S3.04[8] n.84
Milner v. Comm'r .... S6.04[3][a][i] n.52a

Mincks Hotel Co., Rives v. . 3.08[4][g] n.304
Minderhout, Coast Bank v. ... 3.04[8] n.85
Mindlin v. Davis .... 5.05[7]
Minnesota & O. Power Co., Erickson v. .... 11.02[4][b] n.87
Mission Hill Dev. Corp. v. Western Small Business Inv. Co. ... 5.05[8] n.185, 11.02[3][c] n.70
Missouri Pac. R.R. v. U.S. .... 6.04[3][a][ii] n.52
Missouri State Life Ins. Co. v. Comm'r .... 12.02[3] n.72
Missouri State Life Ins. Co., Helvering v. .... 12.03[3][b] n.153
Mitchell, Clinton H. ... 9.04[6] n.106
Modern Am. Mortgage Corp. v. Skyline Park ... S4.02[8][e] n.87
Moline Properties, Inc. v. Comm'r .... 5.05[3]
Monaghan v. Comm'r .. 9.04[2][b][ii] n.70
Monmouth Capital Corp. v. Holmdel Village Shops, Inc. ... 5.04[1] n.96
Monona Shores, Inc., Mortgage Assocs., Inc. v. .... 4.02[6][a][iii] n.57
Montgomery, John E. ... 12.03[2][a][i] n.84
Montgomery Real Estate & Co., Jemison v. .... 4.04[7] n.203
Moody v. Bass .... 5.05[1] n.109
Moore, Comm'r v. ...... 6.01[1] n.1
Moore v. Great W. Sav. & Loan Ass'n .... 3.04[6] n.59
Morgan, J.I., Inc. ...... 8.09[3] n.79
Morris, Edna ...... 12.02[1][b] n.45
Morris, George M., Constr. Co. v. Four Seasons ..... 4.04[4] n.183
Morrissey v. Comm'r 1.08 n.211
Morroco v. Felton ..... 4.04[7] n.203
Mortgage Assocs., Inc. v. Monona Shores, Inc. ... 4.02[6][a][iii] n.57
Mortgage Inv. Co., House of Carpets, Inc. v. .... 4.02[6][a][ii]
Mortgage Guar. Co., French v. .... 5.02[4][b] n.47

[*References are to paragraphs (¶) and to sample forms in Appendix B. References to the Supplement are preceded by "S."*]

Mortgage Security Corp., Sharp
  v. .... 5.03[8] n.86
Morton v. Comm'r ..... 12.03[4][a]
  n.167
Mosier, Middlemist v. .... 3.08[4][g]
  n.255
Motor Prods. Corp. ... 12.03[2][b][ii]
  n.121
Mounkes, Emporia State Bank & Trust
  Co. v. .... 3.08[4][a]
Mountain Village Co., U.S.
  v. .... 3.08[4][g] n.313
Moyse, Jenkins v. .... 5.04[1]
M.S.M. Corp. v. Knutson
  Co. .... 4.04[4]
Mulligan, Barson v. . 3.08[4][g] n.304
Mullins, Kilgore Hardware & Bldg.
  Supply Inc. v. ... S4.02[6][a][i] n.37
Murdock, S.B., Garage Corp.
  v. .... 3.04[9][a]
Murray v. Comm'r .... 12.02[4] n.77
Murray, E.J. .... 12.02[4] n.75
Mutual Benefit Life Ins. Co.
  v. Frantz, Klodt & Son,
  Inc. .... 3.08[4][g] n.309
Mutual Fed. Sav. & Loan Ass'n
  v. Wisconsin Wire Works .. 3.04[8]
  n.86
Mutual Life Ins. Co. of N.Y.
  v. Tailored Woman .. 3.05[4] n.166
Mutual Real Estate Trust v. Buffalo
  Sav. Bank .... 3.04[8] n.87,
  S3.04[8] n.87

N

Narver v. Comm'r ... S6.04[3][b][ii]
Nashua Fed. Sav. & Loan Ass'n,
  Mills v. .... S3.04[8] n.84
Nassau Sav. & Loan Ass'n, Leben
  v. ..... 3.03[1] n.16, S3.03[1] n.16
Nasser, Zeibak v. 1.04 n.24
National Bankers Life Ins. Co.,
  Republic Nat'l Bank v. ... 4.05 n.220
National Bank of Commerce of San
  Antonio, Comm'r v. ... 12.03[3][b]
  n.152
National Bank of N. Am. v. Tengard
  Realty Corp. .... S3.08[4][i] n.331

National Bank of Washington
  v. Equity Investors .. 4.02[6][a][ii]
National Bank of
  Westchester .... 5.03[8] n.81
National Carbide Corp.
  v. Comm'r .... 5.05[3]
National Forest Preservation Group
  v. Butz .... 3.04[9][c] n.114
National Leasing Corp., Plummer
  v. .... 5.05[4] n.160
National Mortgage Corp., Kessing
  v. .... 11.02[3][c]
National Sav. Bank, Lyons
  v. .... 5.02[3][b] n.41
National Surety Corp. v. Inland
  Properties, Inc. .... 5.05[1]
National Sur. Co.
  v. Long .... 4.02[8][b] n.82
NBI Mortgage Inv. Corp. v. Chemical
  Bank .... 11.01[7] n.30
Nelson Realty Co., Darling Shop
  v. .... 3.08[4][g] n.300
Neubauer v. Smith .. 3.08[4][g] n.251
Neubecker, Edward F. .. 1.05[3][c][v]
  n.143
Nevels v. Sarris .... 5.02[1] n.26
Newhouse, George R. ... 12.02[1][a]
  n.39
New Jersey Ins. Underwriting Ass'n,
  495 Corp. v. ... S3.04[12][b] n.143
New Jersey So. R.R., Williamson
  v. .... 3.08[4][a] n.219
New McDermott, Inc. ... 12.02[2][a]
  n.53
New President Corp., Helvering
  v. .... 12.03[4][b][ii] n.193
New York, City of, *In re* .. 3.08[4][h]
  n.318
New York & Suburban Fed. Sav. &
  Loan Ass'n v. Fi-Pen Realty
  Co. ...... 4.02[6][a][ii] ns. 52, 53
New York Life Ins. Co., 805 Third
  Ave. Co. v. S3.06 n.182
Nichols v. Ann Arbor Fed. Sav. & Loan
  Ass'n .... 3.04[8] ns. 86, 88
Nichols v. Comm'r ... 12.03[4][b][ii]
  ns. 185, 190
Niobrara Farms, U.S. Hertz, Inc.
  v. .... 3.08[4][g]

CUMULATIVE TABLE OF CASES

[References are to paragraphs (¶) and to sample forms in Appendix B. References to the Supplement are preceded by "S."]

Nix, Flamingo Drift Fishing, Inc.
   v. .... 4.04[7] n.203
North Am. Mortgage Investors
   v. Cape San Blas Joint
   Venture .... S5.03[3] n.65
North Palm Beach Utils., Inc.,
   MacArthur v. .... S3.04[18] n.153s
Northridge Coop. Section No. 1 v. 32nd
   Ave. Constr. Corp. 10.03 n.64
Northrip v. Federal Nat'l Mortgage
   Ass'n .... 3.08[4][g]
Northwestern Nat'l Ins. Co.
   v. Mildenberger .. 3.04[12][b] n.145
Northwestern Sav. & Loan Ass'n, Lowry
   v. .... 3.08[4][g] n.261
Nussbaum, Armenta v. ... 3.08[4][g]
   n.288
Nye v. Comm'r ... 9.04[2][b][ii] n.72

O

O.&O., Inc., Atlas Subsidiaries
   v. .... 5.04[1] n.95
O'Brien, Verna v. ... 3.08[4][g] n.252
Occidental Sav. & Loan Ass'n v. Venco
   Partnership .. S3.04[8] ns. 84, 98m
Odell v. Hoyt ...... 3.08[4][g] n.258
Oden v. Comm'r .... 9.04[2][c] n.76
Olson, E.C. ..... 12.03[2][b][i] n.108
Olwine v. Torrens .... 502[4][d] n.54
107 Shore Road Corp. v. Gatnick
   Realty Corp. ... S3.08[4][g] n.304
O'Neill v. Comm'r .... 5.05[3] n.128
Orrisch, Stanley C. .... 1.05[3][b][i],
   S1.05[3][b][i] n.124a
Ott .... 12.03[2][b][i] n.105
Ottinger, Samuels v. ... 3.05[1] n.156
Overmeyer, D.H. Co.
   v. Frick Co. .... 3.08[4][g]
Owens, Unico v. ...... 4.03[1] n.151

P

Pacific First Fed. Sav. & Loan Ass'n,
   Miller v. .... 3.04[8] n.86
Packel, Aldens v. ..... 5.05[1] n.104
Page v. Ford ..... 7.04[1][d][i] n.18
Pan Am. Fed. Sav. & Loan Ass'n,
   Panko v. .... S3.04[8] n.98u

Pan-American Life Ins. Co.
   v. Boyd .... 5.02[1] n.26
Panko v. Pan Am. Fed. Sav. & Loan
   Ass'n .... S3.04[8] n.98u
Pansa v. Damiano .... 3.04[9][a]
Paramount Bldg. & Loan Ass'n
   v. Sacks .... 3.08[4][i] n.326
Paramount Ins., Inc. v. Rayson &
   Smitley .... 3.08[4][g] n.265
Pardue, Ames v. ... S3.08[4][g] n.316
Parker v. Covington ... S3.04[8] n.86
Parker v. Delaney .. 12.01[3][a] n.25,
   12.02[4] n.78, 12.03[3][a] ns. 133,
   135, 143, 144
Parkersburg State Bank
   v. U.S. ...... 12.03[5] ns. 239, 241
Parker Square State Bank, Wood
   v. .... 3.08[4][a] n.209
Partain v. First Nat'l
   Bank .... S3.04[3][c] ns. 32b, 32d,
   33m
Patterson v. Blomberg .. 5.03[3] n.66
Patton v. First Fed. Sav. & Loan
   Ass'n .... 3.04[8] n.86
Paydan, Inc. v. Agia Kipiaki,
   Inc. .... 3.08[4][g] n.252
Paymer v. Comm'r ... 5.05[3] n.128
Pender v. Comm'r .. 12.03[3][a] n.137
Peninsula Properties Co. ... 12.03[3][a]
   ns. 136, 137
Penn Athletic Club Bldg., Comm'r
   v. .... 12.02[4] n.75
Peoples' Sav. & Loan Ass'n
   v. Standard Indus., Inc. ... 3.04[8]
   n.85
Perry, *In re* .... 5.05[7] n.174
Peterson, First Fed. Sav. & Loan
   Ass'n v. .... S3.04[8] n.98w
Peterson, Seppala & Aho Constr. Co.
   v. 7.06 n.27
Petit, Arneill Rance v. ... S5.02[4][d]
   n.56a
Petit, William Justin ..... 12.02[1][a]
   n.39
Peyser v. Cole .... 5.03[8] n.80
Phelps, Kent v. .... 5.03[8] n.82
Philadelphia Park Amusement Co.
   v. U.S. .... 12.03[2][b][ii] ns. 115,
   119, 12.03[4][b][ii] n.197

[*References are to paragraphs (¶) and to sample forms in Appendix B. References to the Supplement are preceded by "S."*]

Phillippe, Jones v. ...... 5.03[3] n.66
Pierce, People v. ... 3.08[4][d] n.228
Pietz, Edward ... 1.05[3][c][v] n.145
Pinellas, County of v. Clearwater Sav. & Loan Ass'n .... 7.04[1][a] n.8
Pink v. Smith ...... 3.08[4][d] n.236
Pipkin v. Thomas & Hill, Inc. ... 3.06 n.179
Pivot City Realty v. State Sav. & Trust Co. .... 5.03[1] n.59
Plank, City Bank v. ... 4.03[1] n.154
Plummer v. National Leasing Corp. .... 5.05[4] n.160
Plunkett, Theodore R. ... 12.02[1][a] n.38
Podell, Hyman .... 1.02[2][a] n.9
Polin v. Comm'r .. 12.03[3][a] n.145
Polish Roman Catholic Union of America, Stanish v. 3.06 n.179
Pond, Andrews v. ..... 5.05[1] n.101
Pongetti v. Bankers Trust Sav. & Loan Ass'n .... 3.08[4][a] n.211
Pope, Memphis Natural Gas Co. v. .... 11.02[2] n.57
Portage Realty Corp. Baas .... S4.02[6][i] n.39
Portland Mfg. Corp. .. 12.03[2][b][i] n.108
Potter, W.H. .... 12.02[1][b] n.44
Pozzi v. Comm'r .... 9.04[2][c] n.76
Pratt v. Comm'r .... S12.01[5] n.33h
Prestonview Co. v. State Mut. Investors .... S5.04[1] n.97
Price v. Florida Fed. Sav. & Loan Ass'n .... S3.04[8] n.98w
Price, Grady v. .... 5.03[2] n.61
Price v. Harris ..... 3.08[4][d] n.236
Price v. Herman ...... 3.05[7] n.172
Primex Equities Corp., Kelley Bros. v. .... S3.08[4][i] n.331
Producers Livestock Credit Corp., Lanney v. .... 3.08[4][a] n.215
Provident Fed. Sav. & Loan Ass'n, Slevin Container Corp. v. . S3.04[5]
Provident Life & Trust Co. v. Fletcher .... 5.02[3][a] n.39
Prudential Fed. Sav. & Loan Ass'n, Madsen v. .... 3.04[6] n.68
Prusaczyk v. Kulo .. S3.08[4][i] n.330

Pulaski Fed. Sav. & Loan Ass'n, Tucker v. .... 3.04[8] n.88
Pushee v. Johnson ...... 5.03[3] n.66

R

Rabinowich v. Eliasberg . 5.04[1] n.97
Rabinowitz v. Borish .... 11.02[3][b] n.67
Rabon, Shores v. .. 3.04[12][b] n.143
Raleigh State Bank, Martin v. ... 7.06 n.28
Randall, Hartford Life Ins. Co. v. .... 3.04[5] n.39
Randel v. Jersey Mortgage Inv. Co. .... 3.08[4][i] n.329
Rayson & Smitley, Paramount Ins., Inc. v. .... 3.08[4][g] n.265
Reading Co. v. Comm'r ... 12.03[2][b][i] n.105
Real Estate Trustee v. Rebham .... 5.03[2] n.61, 5.03[4] n.67
Rebham, Real Estate Trustee v. ...... 5.03[2] n.61, 5.03[4] n.67
Recile, Meador Brook Nat'l Bank v. .... 5.05[1] n.108
Regals Realty Co. v. Comm'r . 8.02[2] n.17
Regents of Univ. of Cal. v. Superior Court of Alameda County .... S3.04[18] n.153g
Regional Center, American Century Mortgage Investors v. ... 5.02[4][d] ns. 54, 56
Reiger v. Schulte & Eicher .... 4.02[6][a][i] n.42
Reis, Griffin v. ..... 3.08[4][g] n.316
Reisman v. William Hartman & Son, Inç. .... 11.02[3][c] n.72
Republic Nat'l Bank v. National Bankers Life Ins. Co. ... 4.05 n.220
Republic Nat'l Bank of Dallas, Kimball Foods, Inc. v. .... 3.08[4][a] n.210, S3.08[4][a] n.210
Republic Realty Mortgage Corp., Armstrong v. ..... S2.03[1] n.99ll, S2.03[2] n.102

[References are to paragraphs (¶) and to sample forms in Appendix B. References to the Supplement are preceded by "S."]

Rhodes v. Comm'r ...... 12.03[3][a] n.139
Rice, Evans v. .... 5.02[2] n.32
Rice, *In re* .... 11.02[3][b] n.62
Richter v. Comm'r ...... 12.03[3][a] n.141
Rickett, Holt v. .... 5.02[1] n.18
Riddell, Malat v. ...... 9.05[1] n.115
Rieder & Sons Bldg. & Dev. Co., Fidelity Land Dev. Corp. v. ....3.04[8] n.88
Ripley, Storer v. 1.04 n.24
Rivers, Jr., E.D. ... 12.03[3][b] n.155
Riverway Ranch Enterprises, Western Camps v. .... 1.05[4][a] n.168a
Rives v. Mincks Hotel Co. . 3.08[4][g] n.304
Robbins, Bergin v. 7.06 n.35
Robertson, Braniff Inv. Co. v. .... 5.03[8] n.88
Robinson v. Miller .. 3.08[4][g] n.258
Robinson, Williams v. .... 3.08[4][g] n.306
Rochester Capital Leasing v. K.&L. Litho Corp. .... 5.05[1] n.106
Rochester Sav. Bank, Silver v. .... 3.04[8] n.100, S3.04[8] n.87
Rockaway Park Series Corp. v. Hollis Automotive Corp. . 3.08[4][g] n.255
Rockefeiler v. High Sky, Inc. .... 9.03[1] n.24
Rockwood Realty Corp., Ganbaum v. .... 3.08[4][i]
Rodman v. Comm'r ... 1.05[3][b][iii] n.132
Rodman, Norman .... 1.05[3][b][iii]
Rodney, Inc. v. Comm'r .. 12.02[2][a] n.54
Rogers v. Comm'r .... 9.04[2][b][ii] n.72, 12.03[3][a] n.137
Rogers, Henry, Estate of v. Comm'r ..... 9.04[2][b][ii] n.72
Rogers, John M. .. 8.02[4] ns. 25, 26
Roland v. Lindsey ... 4.02[8][b] n.83
Romero, Trinidad Indus. Bank v. .... 5.05[1] n.103
Romney, San Francisco Tomorrow v. .... 3.04[9][c] n.112

Rosson, Sullivan v. 7.06 n.35
Ross, Schoolcraft v. . 3.08[4][d] n.237
Rothenberg v. Comm'r .. S1.05[2][d] n.85a, 1.05[4][b][ii] n.186
Rowlett, Silvola v. ...... 1.05[1] n.38
Rozelle, First Nat'l Bank v. .... 3.08[4][a] n.215
Rubnitz, Alan A. .... 12.01[1][b] ns. 5, 10, 11
Ruby v. Warrior .... 5.03[8] n.89
Rushing v. Comm'r ...... 9.04[5][a]
Russell Inc. ...... 9.04[2][b][ii] n.72
Russo, Ann S. .... 12.03[3][a] n.147, 12.03[4][a] n.158
Ruth Iron Co. v. Comm'r .... 9.04[7] n.113
Ryba, Scelza v. ..... 3.08[4][g] n.259

S

Sacks, Paramount Bldg. & Loan Ass'n v. .... 3.08[4][i] n.326
Sacramento Sav. & Loan Ass'n, Jones v. .... 3.04[8] n.84
Sailboat Key, Inc., Continental Mortgage Investors v. .... S5.05[1] n.109
St. Louis Flexicure Inc. v. Lintzenich .... 4.04[4] n.183
St. Paul Corp. v. Manufacturers Life Ins. Co. .... 3.03[1] n.13
Samis v. Comm'r .. S1.05[2][d] n.95a
Samuels v. Ottinger .... 3.05[1] n.156
Sanders v. Frost ...... 3.04[5] n.39
Sanders v. Hicks .... 3.04[8] n.88
Sanders v. Stradley .. 3.08[4][g] n.256
S&L Blvd. Co. ...... 12.01[1][a] n.3
S&S Ceiling & Partition Co. v. Calvon Corp. .... S4.02[6][a][ii] n.43
Sandor, Andrew A. ... 12.01[1][b] n.8
San Francisco Indus. Park, Inc., *In re* .... 5.05[4] n.159
San Francisco Sav. & Loan Ass'n, Lazzareschi Inv. Co. v. .... 3.04[5] n.49
San Francisco Tomorrow v. Romney ...... 3.04[9][c] n.112
Sarlot-Kantarjian v. First Pa. Mortgage Trust .... S5.05[1] n.109

[*References are to paragraphs (¶) and to sample forms in Appendix B. References to the Supplement are preceded by "S."*]

Sarris, Nevels v. . . . . 5.02[1] n.26
Sax, Bisno v. . . . . . . 3.08[4][g] n.255
S.B. Garage Corp.
   v. Murdock . . . . 3.04[9][a]
Scelza v. Ryba . . . . . 3.08[4][g] n.259
Schaeffer v. Comm'r . . S6.04[3][b][ii], S9.04[4][bb] n.97a
Scherman Holding Corp., Home Title Ins. Co. v. . . . . . . 3.08[4][g] n.312
Scheuber v. Comm'r . . . 9.05[1] n.117
Schieffelin, Lucy S.,
   Estate of . . . . . 12.02[3] ns. 70, 72, 12.03[2][b][ii] n.120, 12.03[4][b][i] n.171
Schoellkopf, Buddy, Prods., Inc. . . . . 12.01[1][a] n.3
Schoolcraft v. Ross . . 3.08[4][d] n.237
Schramm Co., Lutz v. . . . 12.03[3][a] ns. 133, 134, 135, 12.04[1] ns. 246, 248
Schulte & Eicher,
   Reiger v. . . . . . . 4.02[6][a][i] n.42
Schultz, Neils . . . . . 12.03[4][a] n.164
Schwartz v. Bender Invs. Inc. . . . . 3.08[4][g] n.266
Scope v. Comm'r . . . . S6.04[3][b][ii] n.58c
Sears, Roebuck & Co., Woodman of the World Life Ins. Soc'y v. . . 3.08[4][g] n.301
Securities Builders v. Southwest Drug Co. . . . . 3.05[7] n.172
Securities Inv. Co. v. Finance Acceptance Corp. . . . 5.05[1] n.109
Securities Mortgage Co. . . 12.03[4][a] n.166, 12.03[4][b][ii] ns. 193, 195, 200
Security Acceptance Co., Klett v. . . . . 5.05[7] n.174
Security Bldg. & Inv. Corp., Barrerra v. . . . . 3.08[4][g]
SEC v. W.J. Howey Co. . 1.05[1] n.45
Selective Builders Inv. v. Hudson City Sav. Bank . . 3.06 n.182, S3.06 n.178
Sellers v. Comm'r . 1.05[3][b][i] n.120
Sentry Sav. Ass'n, Sonny Arnold, Inc. v. . . . . S3.04[8] n.86
Seppala & Aho Constr. Co. v. Peterson 7.06 n.27

Shafer Bros. v. Kite . . . . 4.03[1] n.149
Shainberg, Herbert . . 1.05[2][c] n.60
Shapfa Realty Corp. . 12.02[1][b] n.46
Sharp v. Mortgage Security Corp. of Am. . . . 5.03[8] n.86, 5.05[2] n.112
Shattls, Smith v. . . . . S3.04[18] n.153s
Shaw Constr. Co. v. Comm'r . . 5.05[3] n.125
Shelby Salesbook Co. v. U.S. . . . . 6.04[3][c] n.59
Sherman, Comm'r v. . . 12.03[2][a][i] n.84
Shiew, First Sec. Bank v. . . S3.08[4][a] ns. 216b, 216c, 216d
Sholund, Ronald W. . . . 9.04[2][b][ii] n.66
Shores v. Rabon . . 3.04[12][b] n.143
Shor, State Tax Commission v. . . . 10.03 n.64a
Short v. A.H. Still Inv. Co. . . . . 3.08[4][g] n.259
Shropshire v. Commerce Farm Credit Corp. . . . . . . 5.03[8] n.87
Shutt, Lawrence v. . . . . 9.01[1][c] n.4
Sidenberg v. Ely . . . . 3.08[4][j] n.336
Silver v. Rochester Sav. Bank . . . . S3.04[8] n.87
Silverman v. State . . . . . . 3.04[5] n.46
Silver v. Rochester Sav. Bank . . . . 3.04[8] n.100
Silvola v. Rowlett . . . . . . 1.05[1] n.38
Sisco-Hamilton Co. v. Lennon . . . . . . 11.02[4][b] n.87
Skaer, A.W. . . . . 12.03[2][b][i] n.108
Skyline Park, Modern Am. Mortgage Corp. v. . . . . S4.02[8][e] n.87
Slevin Container Corp. v. Provident Fed. Sav. & Loan Ass'n . . . S3.04[5]
Smith, Weldon D. . . 12.02[1][a] n.41
Smith v. Comm'r (1964) . . . . . . 1.05[3][b][i] n.120
Smith v. Comm'r (1963) . . . . S12.01[5][a] n.33j
Smith, Estate of v. Comm'r . . . . S12.01[5][a] n.33n
Smith v. General Mortgage Corp. . . . . 3.04[12][b] n.145
Smith, Lawson v. . . . 3.08[4][g] n.288
Smith, Neubauer v. . . 3.08[4][g] n.251

[*References are to paragraphs (¶) and to sample forms in Appendix B. References to the Supplement are preceded by "S."*]

Smith, Pink v. . . . . . . 3.08[4][d] n.236
Smith v. Shattls . . . . S3.04[18] n.153s
Sniadach v. Family Fin.
    Corp. . . . . . 3.08[4][g], 3.08[4][g]
        ns. 272, 279
Somerson, Bornstein v. . . . . 3.08[4][i]
        n.330
Sondeno v. Union Commerce
    Bank . . . . 11.01[6][c]
Sotar, Sam F. . . . . 12.03[2][a][ii] n.95
Southern Trust Co., Webb v. . . 5.03[3]
    ns. 63, 64, 5.05[2] n.113
Southwest Drug Co., Securities
    Builders v. . . . . 3.05[7] n.172
Spens v. Citizens Fed. Sav. & Loan
    Ass'n . . . . 3.04[6] n.60
Spires v. Lawless . . . . 3.08[4][g] n.260
Spivey v. Comm'r . 9.04[2][b][ii] n.71
Sprague v. U.S. . . . . 9.04[2][c]
Spreckles, Comm'r v. . . . 12.03[2][b][ii]
    n.110, 12.03[3][b] ns. 149, 152
Springfield Corp., Williams & Words,
    Inc. v. . . . . S4.02[6][i] n.39
Stamler v. Comm'r . . . . . 12.03[3][a]
    n.141
Standard Indus., Inc., Peoples' Sav. &
    Loan Ass'n v. . . . . 3.04[8] n.85
Stanish v. Polish Roman Catholic Union
    of America 3.06 n.179
Starker v. U.S. . . . . 8.02[4] n.24
Starr v. Comm'r . . . . 6.04[3][d] n.65
State Bank v. Fioravanti . . S3.08[4][a]
    n.216a
State Sav. & Loan Ass'n v. Kauaian
    Dev. Co. . . . . 10.01[2][b] n.37
State Sav. & Trust Co., Pivot City
    Realty v. . . . . 5.03[1] n.59
State Tax Commission v. Shor . . 10.03
    n.64a
State Wholesale Supply Inc.
    v. Allen . . . . 5.02[2] n.29
Stein, Conference of Fed. Sav. & Loan
    Ass'n's v. . . . . S3.04[8] n.98r
Stein, Federal Sav. & Loan Ass'n
    v. . . . . S3.04[8] n.98r
Stein, Levine v. . . . . 3.08[4][g]
Still, A.H., Inv. Co.,
    Short v. . . . . 3.08[4][g] n.259
Stillman v. Comm'r . . . . 5.05[3] n.134

Stilwell, Andrew O. . . . 1.05[3][c][v]
    n.145
Stimson, Fanning v. . . . 3.05[1] n.156
Stith v. Hudson City Sav.
    Inst. . . . . 3.04[8] ns. 86, 99,
    S3.04[8] n.87
Stokes v. Comm'r . . 12.03[3][a] n.145
Stonecrest Corp. . . . 9.04[2][b][ii] n.75
Stopp v. Wilt . . . . . . 3.08[4][h] n.318
Storer v. Ripley 1.04 n.24
Stout, Joe . . . . 1.05[2][c] n.60
Stradley, Sanders v. . . 3.08[4][g] n.256
Strong v. Comm'r . . . . . 5.05[3] n.128
Stuckerberg, *In re* . . . 3.08[4][i] n.330
Suffolk Franklin Sav. Bank,
    Carpenter v. . 3.04[6] ns. 52, 55, 61
Sugden, Lomb v. 1.04 n.25
Sullivan v. Rosson 7.06 n.35
Sun Oil Co. v. Comm'r . . . 6.04[3][b]
    n.53
Superior Court, Commercial Centre
    Realty Co. v. . . . . 3.08[4][g] n.275
Superior Court, Garfinkle
    v. . . . . S3.08[4][g] n.288
Superior Court of Alameda County,
    Regents of Univ. of Cal.
    v. . . . . S3.04[18] n.153g
Superior Court of Los Angeles
    County, Dawn Inv. Co.
    v. . . . . S3.04[8] & n.98a
Superior Court, Turner v. . . 3.08[4][g]
    n.310
Susher-Schaefer Inv. Co., Holiday
    Inns v. . . . . 3.08[4][a] n.211
Sweeney, Chase Nat'l
    Bank v. . . . . 7.04[1][a] n.8
Swinerton Walberg Co. v. Union
    Bank . . . . 4.02[6][a][iii] n.56

T

Tabata, Kawauchi v. . . . 5.05[4] n.158
Tailored Woman, Mutual Life Ins. Co.
    of N.Y. v. . . . . 3.05[4] n.166
Talbott v. Manard . . . . . . 5.03[3] n.64
Tanner Dev. Co.,
    Ferguson v. . . . . 5.02[1] n.17,
    S5.02[4][d] n.56
Taylor v. Brennan . . S3.08[4][i] n.330

[*References are to paragraphs (¶) and to sample forms in Appendix B. References to the Supplement are preceded by "S."*]

Taylor v. Comm'r ..... 5.05[3] n.127
Taylor, Federal Home Loan Mortgage Corp. v. .... 3.08[4][g] n.255
Taylor, W.F. .. 12.03[2][b][iii] n.130
Teachers Ins. & Annuity Ass'n of America, Boston Rd. Shopping Center, Inc. v. 3.06 n.177
Teachworth, Terry v. .... 5.02[1] n.25
Tel Serv. Co. v. General Capital Corp. .... 5.04[1] n.96
Tendler, Zandri v. 7.06 n.29
Tengard Realty Corp., National Bank of N. Am. v. .... S3.08[4][i] n.331
Terry v. Teachworth .... 5.02[1] n.25
Texas Bank & Trust Co. v. Lone Star Life Ins. Co. S4.05 n.219
Theatre Inv. Co. v. Comm'r .... 12.03[6] n.243
Third Ave. Ry., Berkey v. .... 11.02[4][b] n.87
Thomas v. Comm'r .. 12.03[2][b][iii] ns. 130, 131
Thomas & Hill, Inc., Pipkin v. .. 3.06 n.179
Thomassen v. Carr .... S3.04[18] n.153e, 5.02[3][b], 5.05[8]
Thompson v. Chemical Bank .. 5.03[8] n.81
Thompson-Wetterling Constr. & Realty Inc., Lampert Yards, Inc. v. .... 4.02[6][a][iii] n.58, 4.04[7] n.204
385 McLean Corp., E. Landau Indus. v. .... S3.08[4][g] n.304a
Thrift Funds of Baton Rouge, Inc. v. Jones .... 5.03[8] n.78
Tieree v. Aps Co. ...... 3.04[8] n.86
Tiffany, Miller v. ..... 5.05[1] n.101
Tindle, Heiner v. .... 8.02[2] n.17
Tipton v. Ellsworth .... 5.03[8] n.89
Title Ins. Co., Imhoff v. ...... 4.02[6][a][ii] n.45
Tober v. Charnita ...... 9.03[1] n.24
Tomlinson v. Miles .... 5.05[3] n.127
Torrens, Olwine v. ... 5.02[4][d] n.54
Town & Country Plymouth, Inc. v. U.S. .. 1.05[3][b][i] ns. 120, 128
Treker v. Langel .... S3.04[18] n.153r
Trinidad Indus. Bank v. Romero .... 5.05[1] n.103
Tri-State Dev. Co., Garner v. .... 3.08[4][g]
Tucker v. Lassen Sav. & Loan Ass'n .... 3.04[7] n.76, 3.04[8] ns. 81, 86
Tucker v. Pulaski Fed. Sav. & Loan Ass'n .... 3.04[8] n.88
Tufts v. Comm'r .. S12.01[3][b] n.29
Turner, Albert W. .... 9.04[6] n.106
Turner v. Blackburn ...... 3.08[4][g]
Turner v. Superior Court .. 3.08[4][g] n.310
Turney's Estate v. Comm'r ...... 12.03[3][a] n.136
Tuscaloosa Fed. Sav. & Loan Ass'n, Fletcher v. ...... App. A, Table 3
12701 Shaker Blvd. Corp. .... 12.01[1][a] n.3, 12.02[2][a] n.60
Tyson's Corner Regional Shopping Center, Dalmo Sales Co. v. .... 3.05[3] n.162
Tyson's Corner S.C., *In re* ... 3.05[3] n.163

U

Underhill, Wingate E. .. 12.03[2][b][ii] n.118
Unico v. Owens ...... 4.03[1] n.151
Union Bank v. Kruger .. 5.03[8] n.78
Union Bank, Swinerton Walberg Co. v. .... 4.02[6][a][ii] n.56
Union Central Life Ins. Co. v. Edwards ...... 5.02[4][a] n.45, 5.03[5] n.69
Union Commerce Bank, Sondeno v. .... 11.01[6][c]
Union Pac. R. Co., Comm'r v. ..... 12.03[3][a] n.138
Union Planters Nat'l Bank, Aztec Properties v. .... S3.04[3][c] n.33c, 5.02[4][d] n.54, S5.02[4][d] n.54
Union Properties, Inc., Frigidaire Sales Corp. v. .... 1.05[4][a] n.168a
Union Trust & Sav. Bank, Freese Leasing, Inc. v. .. 3.08[4][a] n.210

CUMULATIVE TABLE OF CASES

[*References are to paragraphs (¶) and to sample forms in Appendix B. References to the Supplement are preceded by "S."*]

Unique Art Mfg. Co. .... 12.03[3][a]
    ns. 136, 137
United Family Life Ins. Co., Dekalb
    County v. .... 3.04[5] n.46
United Housing Foundation, Inc.
    v. Foreman ..... 10.02[2][b] n.32,
    10.03 n.64
United Pac. Corp. .... 9.04[2][b][ii]
    n.75
United States Bancorp Realty
    & Mortgage Trust, Welch v. ... S3.06
    n.178a
U.S. Hertz, Inc. v. Niobrara
    Farms .... 3.08[4][g]
United States Sav. Bank v. Continental
    Arms, Inc. ...... 3.08[4][g] n.260
Urban Commercial Inc.,
    Feldman v. .... 6.03[2] n.16
Usry, Miller v. ...... 9.04[4][b] n.94

V

Valley Nat'l Bank, Brooks v. ... 3.04[6]
    ns. 53, 57, 61
Vancoh Realty Co. .... 12.03[4][b][i]
    n.183
Vandeventer v. Dale Constr.
    Co. 3.06 n.182
Van Huffel v. Harkelrode .... 8.09[3]
    n.77
Van Zandt, I.L.
    v. Comm'r .... 6.04[3][c] n.62
Vee Bee Serv. Co. v. Household
    Fin. Corp. ...... 5.03[2] ns. 61, 62
Venco Partnership, Occidental Sav.
    & Loan Ass'n v. .... S3.04[8] ns. 84,
    98m
Venneri, Arthur, Co.
    v. Comm'r .... S12.01[5][a] n.33m
Ventura-Louise Properties,
    In re .... 3.08[4][i] n.330
Verna v. O'Brien .... 3.08[4][g] n.252
Voight, F.J. ...... 9.04[2][b][ii] n.75

W

Waco Scaffold & Shor. Co. v. 424 Eye
    St. Ass'n ...... 4.02[6][a][i] n.40
Wagegro, E.G., Corp.
    v. Comm'r .... 9.04[2][b][ii] n.66

Walker, Kimpton v. .... 3.05[1] n.156
Wallerstein v. Erwin .... 11.02[3][b]
    n.63
Walser, Miller v. ...... 11.02[2] n.58
Walter, Hebrew Children's Home,
    Inc. v. .... 3.08[4][g] n.267
Walters, Banks .... 5.05[4] n.159
Walther v. Comm'r .. 12.02[2][a] n.53
Warmack v. Merchants Nat'l
    Bank .... S3.04[8] n.88
Warren, Jameson v. .... 5.05[8]
Warrior, Ruby v. ...... 5.03[8] n.89
Washington Inst. of Technology,
    Inc. .... 12.03[2][b][i] n.107
Watson, Katherine
    v. Comm'r .... 9.04[2][b][ii] n.66
Wauwatosa Sav. & Loan Ass'n,
    Wekchardt v. .... S3.04[8] n.86
Wayne Bldg. & Loan Co.
    v. Yarborough .. 4.02[6][a][ii] n.46
Weathersbee v. Goodwin .. 3.08[4][g]
    n.300
Webb, Eugene Merrick,
    Estate of .... 1.02[2][b] n.10
Webb v. Southern Trust Co. ... 5.03[3]
    ns. 63, 64, 5.05[2] n.113
Weiner v. Comm'r . 12.03[3][b] n.155
Weinrich v. Hawley .. 5.02[4][a] n.44
Weiss .... 12.03[2][b][i] n.106
Wekchardt v. Wauwatosa Sav. &
    Loan Ass'n .... S3.04[8] n.86
Welch v. United States Bancorp
    Realty & Mortgage Trust S3.06
    n.178a
Wellenkamp v. Bank of
    America .. S3.04[3][c] ns. 33p, 33q,
    3.04[8], 3.04[8] n.89,
    S3.04[8] ns. 98d, 98n, 98p
Wellmuth, Horrigan v. .... 3.08[4][j]
    n.336
Wells v. Kemme .... 3.08[4][g] n.300
Werner, Becker v. ...... 6.03[2] n.15
Wernick, Janofsky v. .. 11.02[2] n.58
West, Diversified Enter., Inc.
    v. .... S3.04[18] n.153e
West Coast Sec. Co. ... 12.03[2][b][iii]
    n.131
Western Camps v. Riverway Ranch
    Enterprises ..... 1.05[4][a] n.168a

[*References are to paragraphs (¶) and to sample forms in Appendix B. References to the Supplement are preceded by "S."*]

Western Fed. Sav. & Loan Ass'n,
  Haugen v. . . . . S3.04[8] n.98w
Western Sav. & Loan Ass'n,
  Dart v. . . . . 3.08[4][g] n.307
Western Small Business Inv. Co.,
  Mission Hill Dev. Corp. v. . . 5.05[8]
    n.185, 11.02[3][c] n.70
Westgate State Bank, Butler
  v. S3.06 n.178a
Weston Constructors, Inc., Foster
  Lumber Co. v. . . . 3.08[4][g] n.264
Westrom v. Comm'r . . 9.04[2][b][ii]
    n.67
Wheatland Mut. Ins. Ass'n,
  Kintzel v. . . . . 3.08[4][d] n.236
Whipple v. Comm'r . . 12.03[2][b][iii]
    n.127
White, Gunther v. . . . . . . 3.04[8] n.86
White Lakes Shopping Center
  v. Jefferson Standard Life
  Ins. Co. 3.06 n.177
Whitestone Sav. & Loan Ass'n
  v. Allstate Ins. Co. . . . . 3.04[12][b]
    n.145
White v. U.S. . . . . 3.08[4][g]
Whitley v. Klauber . . . . . . 4.03[2][d]
  n.166, S4.03[2][d] n.166
Wilhite v. Callihan . . . S3.04[8] n.98u
Wilkerson, Donald L. . . . . 1.05[2][d]
  n.66b, 12.01[1][b] ns. 7, 12
Williams, Comm'r v. . . . S12.01[5][a]
    n.33m
Williams v. First Fed. Sav. & Loan
  Ass'n . . S3.04[8] ns. 86, 98m, 98o,
    98p, 98r
Williams v. Robinson . . . . . 3.08[4][g]
    n.306
Williams v. U.S. . . . . . 9.04[2][c] n.76
Williams, Yost-Linn Lumber
  Co. v. . . . . 4.02[6][a][ii] n.53
Williams & Words, Inc. v. Springfield
  Corp. . . . . S4.02[6][i] n.39
Williamson v. New Jersey
  So. R.R. . . . . 3.08[4][a] n.219
Willow Builders, Emigrant Ind.
  Sav. Bank v. . . . . 4.04[2] n.173
Willowood Condominium Ass'n, Inc.
  v. HNC Realty Co. . . . 3.03[1] n.17
Wilmarth, Fergus v. . 3.08[4][a] n.236

Wilt, Stopp v. . . . . . . 3.08[4][h] n.318
Winston Instrument Co.,
  Janisse v. . . . . 5.05[2] n.114
Wisconsin Wire Works, Mutual Fed.
  Sav. & Loan Ass'n v. . . 3.04[8] n.86
Wobinson Furniture Co.,
  Grigg v. 5.04 n.90
Wolff, Atlantic Life Ins. Co.
  of Richmond v. . . . . 5.02[3][b] n.41
Wong v. DeGrazia . . . 6.04[1][c] n.30
Wood v. Parker Square State
  Bank . . . . 3.08[4][a] n.209
Woodman of the World Life Ins.
  Soc'y v. Sears, Roebuck
  & Co. . . . . 3.08[4][g] n.301
Woodmoor Corp.,
  Jacobsen v. . . . . 9.03[1] n.24
Woodmore N. Inv. Fund Ltd.
  v. Guardian Mortgage
  Investors . . . . S4.02[6] n.31a
Woodruf, Fischer v. 7.06 n.31
Woodsam Assocs. . 12.01[4] ns. 30, 33
Woodson Bend, Inc. v. Masters
  Supply, Inc. . . . . 4.02[6][a][i] n.42
Wooton v. Coerber . . 5.02[3][a] n.39
World Publishing Co.
  v. Comm'r . . . . 6.01[1] n.1
Wrenn v. Comm'r . 9.04[2][b][ii] n.72
Wuorinen v. City Fed. Sav. & Loan
  Ass'n . . . . 3.08[4][i] n.330

Y

Yarborough, Wayne Bldg. & Loan
  Co. v. . . . . 4.02[6][a][ii] n.46
Yost-Linn Lumber Co.
  v. Williams . . . . 4.02[6][a][ii] n.53
Yale Express Sys. Inc.,
  In re . . . . 11.01[6][b] n.21

Z

Zacek, Thomas . . . . 12.03[4][a] n.159
Zandri v. Tendler 7.06 n.29
Zeibak v. Nasser 1.04 n.24
Zink, Jersey City v. . . 5.02[4][a] n.44
Zion's Sav. Bank & Trust Co.,
  Korth v. . . . . . 12.03[4][b][ii] n.193
Zoning Bd. of Adjustment,
  French v. . . . . 3.04[9][a] n.109
Zuckman v. U.S. . . . . 1.05[4][a]

CUMULATIVE INDEX

[References are to paragraphs (¶) and to sample forms in Appendix B. References to the Supplement are preceded by "S."]

A

Abandonment, tax consequences
  partnership interest, 1.05[3][c][v]
  property, 12.03[3]
Accelerated Cost Recovery System (ACRS), S1.05 n.54a, S1.05[2][d]
Accelerated depreciation
  availability to completed project, 11.02[5] n.89
  under E.R.T.A., S1.05[2][d]
  nontransferable, 1.05[5][e]
  recapture, 1.05[2][a], 1.05[2][d], 5.05[3], 9.04
  sale-and-leaseback financing, 6.04[1][a]
  in tax-free exchanges, 8.02 n.4
  as tax shelter, 1.05[2], 8.05[3]
Acceleration of debt
  See also Prepayment
  based on borrower's default, 3.08[4][g], 3.08[4][i], 4.02[12][a]
  due-on-encumbrance, 3.04[7]
  due-on-sale, 3.04[8]
  interest rates in, 5.03[8]
  notice requirements, 3.08[4][g]
  penalty for sale of property, 3.04[8]
  repair/waste actions, 3.08[4][d]
  right exclusive to mortgagee, 3.04[5]
  wraparound borrower's rights in, 7.04[3][a]
Accounts and audits
  See also Taxes
  "equity kicker" lender requires, 3.04[3][a]
  of escrows held by lender, 3.04[6]
  of lender-developer ventures, 11.02[2], 11.02[5][b], 11.02[5][c]
  lender requires in asset swap, 7.04[1][e]
  lender checks developer's cash reserves, 4.04[3]
  purchase-money lender requires, 7.04[1][d][ii]
  of seller-lessee in sale-leaseback, 6.04[2][a][i]
  of shopping center tenants' books, 3.05[4]
Accredited investor, S1.05[1]
Advances of funds. *See* Building loan agreements
After-acquired property, 3.08[4][a], 3.08[4][c], 7.04[1][a]
Aged, housing for, 2.02[3][d][v]
Agency
  participation lenders' agreement, 11.01[8]
  relationship of corporation/principal, 5.05[3]
Agreements. *See* Commitments; Contracts
Air pollution. *See* Pollution
Allocations
  condominium sale proceeds, lender/developer, 10.02[2][c]
  contributed property, 1.05[3][b][ii]
  depreciation, 1.05[3][b], 11.02[5][f]
  "economic effect" required, 1.05[3][b][i]
  equity invested by co-venturers, 11.02[5][a]
  income or loss, 1.02[2], 1.05[3][b]
  of lender's income, 12.02[1]
  among limited partners, App. B, Fm. 1.1 (Secs. 2.5, 2.7, 3.1A Comment)
  loan allocations. *See* Mortgages, loan allocations
  in partnerships, 1.05[3][b]
  retroactive, 1.05[3][b][iii]
  to service partner, 1.05[3][c][i]

I-1

[References are to paragraphs (¶) and to sample forms in Appendix B. References to the Supplement are preceded by "S."]

Alterations. *See* Construction

Alternative mortgage instruments (AMIs). *See* Blends; Buy-down mortgages; Contingent interest mortgage; Deferred interest mortgage; Flexible loan insurance program; Graduated payment mortgage; "One, two, threes"; Price level adjusted mortgage; Renegotiable rate mortgages; Roll-over mortgages; Seller seconds; Shared appreciation mortgages; Variable-rate mortgages

Amortization
See also Payment of loans
allocation of interest/principal
for borrower's taxes, 12.02[2][a]
for lender's taxes, 12.02[1]
commercial bank loans, 2.02[2][d]
of fees/costs as deductions, 12.01[1], 12.01[2]
fundable standby commitments, 3.07[2]
in gap financing, 7.04[2]
high-credit lease accomplishes, 8.05[2][a]
leaseback rental geared to, 6.04[3][b] ns. 53, 54
insurance company loans, 2.02[1][d]
nondeductible, decreasing, 1.05[2][b]
permanent loans, 3.04[4]
in purchase-money mortgage, 7.04[1][b][ii]
restructuring to cure default, 12.03[2][a][ii]
sale-buyback installment contract, 8.09[3]
savings bank loans, 2.02[4][c]
S & L loans, 2.02[3][d]
seller's carryover basis in sale-leaseback, 6.04[4] n.70

Antitrust laws, lease restrictions, 3.05[3]

Apartments. *See* Multifamily housing

Apportionment. *See* Allocations

Appraisals and valuations
See also Loan-to-value ratio
as basis for depreciation, 12.01[3]
as basis of ground rent, 6.03[9]
as basis of sale-leaseback price, 5.05[4], 6.04[2][a][i], 6.04[3], 6.04[4]
"equity kicker" decreases values, 3.04[3][a]
as factor in lender-partner's usury, 11.02[3][c]
foreclosure bid price as, 12.03[5]
income approach, 3.04[1], 8.06
installment sale pricing, 9.04[1][b], 9.04[4]
as mortgagee's basis in property, 12.03[5]
by permanent lender, 3.03[2], 3.04[1], 3.09[2]
at permanent loan closing, 3.09[3]
role in voluntary conveyance/abandonment, 12.03[3]

Appreciation. *See* Capital gains

Architects
See also Engineers; Inspections
certificate, 3.09[2], 4.04[6], 6.03[6]
sample form, App. B, Fm. 3.10
change of, discouraged by lender, 4.04[5]
construction lender approval, 4.02[10]

Association, partnership taxed as, 1.05[4][a], 11.02[4][a]

Assumption of mortgages
due-on-sale clauses block, 3.04[8]
liability, effect on, 1.05[4][b][iii]

At-risk rule, 1.05[2][d], 1.05[4][b][ii] n.186

Attorney
certificate, sample form, App. B, Fm. 3.9
local counsel must approve leasehold mortgage, 6.03[10]
role at permanent loan closing, 3.09[1]

Attornment agreements
high-credit tenants, 3.05[6], 3.08[4][i]
sample form, App. B, Fms. 6.3, 6.4
subtenants, leasehold financing, 6.02[2][b]

Audits. *See* Accounts and audits

[References are to paragraphs (¶) and to sample forms in Appendix B. References to the Supplement are preceded by "S."]

B

Backup agreements, 8.05 n.34
Bad debts. *See* Worthless debts
Bank trust departments as lenders, S2.02[6]
Bankruptcy
   See also Bankruptcy Reform Act of 1978; Receivership; Trustees in bankruptcy
   cash collateral, 4.02[12][b][vi]
   effect on assignment of lease/rent, 3.08[4][i], 8.05[2][e]
   as an event of default, 3.08[4][f], 4.02[12][a]
   as evidence of worthless debt, 12.03[2][b][i]
   of fee owner, leasehold financing, 6.03 n.12, 8.09[2]
   general partnership, 1.04
   generally, 4.02[12]
   insolvent's gain from cancelled debt, taxability, 12.03[2][a][i], 12.03[3][a]
   involuntary, proceedings, 4.02[12][b][ii]
   in leasehold financing, 6.03[8], 6.03[10]
   in lender-developer ventures, 11.02[5][e]
   limited partnership, 1.04, 1.05[4][a]
   of mortgagor-landlord, 3.05[2]
   nonrecourse/recourse claims, 4.02[12][b][iii]
   participation loans, effect on, 11.01[6][b]
   protection of junior lender in, 7.05[1]
   sale of property, 4.02[12][b][vi]
   subdivision lender's rights, 9.01[3]
   tenancy in common, 1.02[2][b]
   terminates commitment, 3.04[10], 4.02[12][a], 4.02[12][b][v]
   trustees in, 4.02[12][b]
Bankruptcy Reform Act of 1978
   automatic stay, 4.02[12][b][iv]
   jurisdiction of court broadened, 4.02[12][b][i]
   loan workouts, S3.08[4][g]
   real estate financing implications, 4.02[12]
   reorganizations under, 4.02[12][b]

Banks
   See also Commercial banks; Lenders; Mutual savings banks; S & Ls
   letters of credit, requirements, 4.02[8][d]
   participations, business/legal reasons, 11.01[3]
   as seller in sale-leaseback, 6.04[3][b][i]
Basis
   cash plus mortgage as, 12.01[3], 12.01[4]
   effect of debt cancellation, 12.03[2][a][i]
   lender's
      in bad debt deduction, 12.03[2][b][ii], 12.03[4][b]
      increased by expense payments, 12.02[3], 12.03[4][b][i]
      in property acquired by default, 12.03[5]
   limited partners', App. B, Fm. 1.1 (Sec. 2.7 Comment)
   planning to avoid problems, 1.05[4][b][iii], 11.02[5][f]
   purchase-money lender, on reacquisition, 12.03[4][b][ii]
   Subchapter S shareholder, 1.06
   substituted, tax-free exchange, 8.02
   tax shelter problems, 1.05[2][b], 1.05[4][b]
Blanket mortgage
   in cooperative housing, 10.03
   release to protect condominium unit buyer, 10.02[2][c]
Blends, S3.04[3][c]
Bonds
   See also Surety bonds
   industrial revenue, tax exempt, 3.04[3][b], 8.06
   mortgage-backed, 2.01[3], 2.02[7]
   mortgages, competition with, 2.01[1][b]
   tax treatment of lender's gains, 12.02[1][b]
"Boot"
   in sale-leaseback, 6.04[2][a][ii], 6.04[3][a], 6.04[4]
   in tax-free exchange, 8.02[3]
Bridge loans. *See* Gap financing

[References are to paragraphs (¶) and to sample forms in Appendix B. References to the Supplement are preceded by "S."]

Brokerage fees. *See* Fees
Building contracts. *See* Construction contracts
Building loan agreements
  checklist for, 4.06
  cross-defaulted to construction mortgage, 4.03[2][a]
  disbursements under
    advance payments prohibited, 4.02[8][b]
    checklist for, 4.06
    comply with construction contract, 4.02[7], 4.02[8][b]
    construction lender approves, 4.03, 11.02[5][b]
    final advance, requirements, 4.04[6], 4.06
    lender makes directly, 4.04[4]
    ongoing requirements for, 4.04[3], 4.04[4]
    optional/obligatory, 4.02[6][a][ii], 4.02[6][b][i]
    reallocation of, 4.04[5]
    sample form, App. B, Fm. 3.8
    title company monitors, 4.02[6][b][i], 4.02[8][c]
  drafting, checklist, 4.06
  execution of, 4.02[9]
  function, contents, 4.04[1]
  sample form, App. B, Fm. 4.1
  surety company reviews, 4.02[8][b]
Building lots. *See* Land, improved
Buildings. *See* Construction; Rehabilitation; Repairs; Specific type of building
Business cycles
  effect on commercial banks, 2.02[2][a], 2.02[2][c]
  effect on credit market, 2.01
  effect on insurance funds, 2.02[1][a]
Buy-down mortgages, S3.04[3][c]
Buy-sell agreements
  in construction loan commitment, 4.02[13]
  lender-developer ventures, 11.02[5][c], 11.02[5][d]
  lender's right to buy construction loan, 3.04[14]
  partnerships, 1.04, 11.02[5][c], 11.02[5][d]
  partnerships, App. B, Fm. 1.1 (Sec. 5.2 Comment)
  pre-closed form, 3.04[13], 4.05
  sample form, App. B, Fm. 4.2
  tripartite, 4.05, 7.04[2]

C

Call options, 3.04[4], 3.04[5]
Cancellation of debt, 12.03[2], 12.03[3]
Capital. *See* Equity funds; Equity interest; Loans
Capital gains
  to borrower
    default conveyance, 12.03[3][a], 12.03[3][c]
    foreclosure sale, 12.03[4][a]
  collapsible property, sale, 1.05[3][a], 5.05[3]
  distributions
    borrower agrees not to pay, 3.08[4][f]
    of liquidating corporation, 5.05[3]
  excess depreciation as, 1.05[2][a], 1.05[2][b]
  fee plus leasehold mortgage to avoid, 8.09[2]
  in installment sales contract, 9.04
  to lender
    foreclosure sale, 12.03[4][b], 12.03[5]
  recent legislation, 1.05[2][d]
  in sale-leaseback "exchanges," 6.04[3][a]
  to sale-leaseback seller, 6.04[2][a][ii], 6.04[4]
  subdivision dealer/investor, 9.05
  taxation under E.R.T.A., S1.05[2][d]
  tax-free exchanges to defer, 8.02
Capital losses
  allocation, 1.05[3][b][i]
  bad debts as, 12.03[2][b][iii], 12.03[4][b]
  foreclosure sale
    to borrower, 12.03[4][a]
    to lender, 12.03[5]

[*References are to paragraphs (¶) and to sample forms in Appendix B. References to the Supplement are preceded by "S."*]

recent legislation, 1.05[2][d]
sale/abandonment of partnership interest, 1.05[3][c][v]
in sale-leaseback "exchanges," 6.04[3][a], 6.04[4]
to sale-leaseback seller, 6.04[2][a][ii], 6.04[3][c], 6.04[4]
sale of corporation as tax shelter, 5.05[3]

Capitalization rate. *See* Mortgages, loan terms

Cash flow
See also Operating income
partnership special allocations of income or loss, 1.05[3][b][i]
secondary lenders require, 7.03

Casualties
See also Force majeure; Insurance
losses excluded from insurance, 4.02[11]
prepayment in case of, 3.04[5]
tenant rights/obligations, 3.05[2]

Certificate of occupancy, 3.04[9][a], 3.09[3], 4.04[6]

Chain leases, 3.05[2]

Change orders. *See* Construction, cost overruns

Charities, 12.04[3]

Chattels. *See* Personal property

"Clogging the equity of redemption," S3.04[3][c], S3.04[18]

Closings
construction loan
developer pays costs, 4.02[13]
generally, 4.03
costs exempt from usury, 5.03[5]
permanent loan
checklist, 3.09[3]
costs of, 3.04[15]
documentation, 3.09[2]
parties; attorneys; timing, 3.09[1]
recording taxes in, 7.04[3][b][ii]
subdivision loans, 9.01[3]

Collapsible treatment
corporations, 12.01[4] n.31
corporations vs. partnerships, 1.05[3][a]

Subchapter S corporations, 1.06 n.207

Commercial banks
as financing source, 2.02[2], 4.01
interest rates; fees, 4.02[4]
loan allocations, 2.02[2][c]
loan terms, 2.02[2][b]
national, regulation, 2.02[2][d]
"one-stop" construction/permanent financing, 8.06
participation loans, role in, 11.01
regulation of portfolios, 2.02[2][d]
state laws, App. A, Table 1
role in refinancing REITs, 7.04[1][e]
sources of funds, 2.02[2][a]
state, regulation, 2.02[2][d]

Commitments
sale-and-leaseback transaction, 6.04
subdivision development loan, 9.01[1][d]

Commitments (Construction loan)
assignment prohibited, 4.02[13]
bankruptcy terminates, 4.02[12][a]
condominium, sample form, App. B, Fm. 10.2
data required by lender, 4.02[2]
drafting, checklist, 4.06
effect of borrower's bankruptcy, 4.02[12][b][v]
generally, 4.02
lender-developer ventures, conflicts, 11.02[3][b]
permanent commitment, conformance to, 4.02[1], 4.02[13]
sample forms, S.App. B, Fm. 4.3, Fm. 4.4, Fm. 4.5

Commitments (Permanent loan)
See also Applications
assignment of, 3.04[10], 4.02[13]
borrower's proof of local law compliance, 3.04[9]
breach of, remedies, 3.06
condominium financing, 10.02[2][a], 10.02[2][d]
effect of borrower's bankruptcy, 4.02[12][b][v]
estoppel affidavit in, 4.03[1]
form; function; contents, 3.03

[References are to paragraphs (¶) and to sample forms in Appendix B. References to the Supplement are preceded by "S."]

Commitments (Permanent loan) *(cont'd)*
  increasing to permit construction completion, 4.04[8]
  lender as co-venturer, conflicts, 11.02[3][b]
  maintenance of books and records, 3.08[4][c]
  no material changes after final, 3.04[17]
  plans/specifications in, 3.04[11]
  power-of-sale clause, 3.08[4][g]
  provisions incorporated into mortgage, 3.08[4][d]
  role in lending cycle, 3.01[2]
  sample form, App. B, Fm. 3.1
  standby commitments
    fundable or bankable, 3.07[2]
    regular, 3.07[1]
  terms and conditions, 3.04

Compensation. *See* Employees; Ordinary income

Component financing, 8.09

Comptroller of the Currency
  variable-rate mortgage regulations, S3.04[3][c]

Condemnation
  allocation in leasehold financing, 6.03[7], 6.03[10]
  clause in loan instrument, 3.08[4][h], 8.05[2][c]
  effect on junior mortgages, 7.05[2]
  in high-credit leases, 8.05[2][c]
  partial, effect on rent, 3.05[2], 8.05[2][c]
  prepayment penalty, 3.04[5]

Condominiums
  See also Construction financing, condominiums; Cooperative housing; Documentation; Master deeds (Condominiums); Permanent financing, condominiums
  in bankruptcy reorganization, 4.02[12][b][iv]
  bylaws of, 10.01, 10.02[1]
  common areas
    assessment control necessary, 10.02[3][b]
    defined, 10.01

  financing considerations, 10.02[1]
  lender may require reserves for upkeep, 10.02[3][d]
  permanent lender's checklist, 10.02[3][c]
  risk of tort liability to unit owners, 10.02[3][b]
  tax liability in income from, 10.02[3][b]
  defined, 10.01
  financing
    compared to subdivision, 10.02[1]
    construction lender restrictions on junior lender, 7.05[2]
    conversion from rental, 10.02[5]
    data basic to lenders available, 10.02[1]
    generally, 10.02
    loan commitment form, App. B, Fm. 10.2
    sales contract subordinated to construction loan, 10.02[2][d]
    sources for unit purchasers, 10.02[3][a]
  generally, 10.01, 10.02
  insurance required, 10.02[3][b]
  legal structure, 10.01, 10.02[1]
  management, 10.02[3][b]
  moratorium on conversion of rental units, 10.02[5]
  non-residential space
    construction lender's right to income from, 10.02[2][d]
    rental to businesses, 10.02[3][b]
  phase development, 10.02[1], 10.02[4]
  releases to sell separate units
    construction loan, 4.03[2][c]
    rental conversions, 10.02[5]
    second mortgages, 7.05[2]
    unit buyers protected, 10.02[2][c]
  rental feature changes legal status, 10.02[2][b]
  rental units converted to, 10.02[5]
  sale of units
    buyers' eligibility, 10.02[2][a]
    construction lender requires presale, 10.02[2][c]

[*References are to paragraphs (¶) and to sample forms in Appendix B. References to the Supplement are preceded by "S."*]

documents, 10.02[2][d]
government regulation, 10.02[2]
proceeds allocation to
   lenders/developers,
   10.02[2][c]
state/federal regulation, 10.01,
   10.02[1], 10.02[2][b]
time sharing device, 10.01, 10.02[1]
types of, 10.01, 10.02[1]
unit-owners
   interest conveyed by deed, 10.01
   tax advantages; rights, 10.01
   voting rights, 10.01
unit owners' associations
   consequences of incorporation,
   10.02[3][b]
   permanent lender's checklist,
   10.02[3][c]

Conflicts of law. *See* Foreign states

Construction
See also Building loan agreements;
   Contractors; Preconstruction
building loan agreement's function
   in, 4.04
completion, methods of assuring,
   4.02[8], 4.04[8]
compliance with local laws, 3.04[9],
   4.04[2]
cost overruns
   audit reveals, 4.04[3]
   gap financing for, 3.04[2]
   generally, 4.04[5]
   in lender-developer ventures,
     11.02[5][a]
   lien priority of loans for,
     4.03[2][b]
   surety bond provisions for,
     4.02[8][b]
costs
   data in construction loan
     application, 4.02[2]
   developer/lender arrangements to
     cover, 4.02[8][a]
   soft/hard, lender's risks, 4.03
defects, lender's liability, 4.04[7]
improvements by ground lessee,
   6.03[3], 6.03[10]
local law prohibits, remedies,
   7.04[1][c][i]
materials, stored, 4.04[3]
plans and specifications
   lenders' approval, 3.04[11],
     4.02[2], 4.02[13], 4.03
   work proceeds according to,
     4.04[3]
   standards required by lender,
     3.04[11], 4.04[2]
tenant alterations/improvements,
   3.04[11], 3.05[5]
timely completion, 3.04[11], 4.04[2]

Construction contracts
See also Building loan agreements;
   Contractors
construction lender's approval,
   4.02[7], 4.02[8][b], 4.03
fragmenting of to obtain bonding,
   4.02[8][b]
surety company approves, 4.02[8][b]

Construction financing
See also Applications; Building loan
   agreements; Commitments
   (Construction loan);
   Construction contracts; Gap
   financing; Fees; Holdbacks;
   Leasehold financing; Subdivision
   financing
amount of loan, 4.02[3]
availability cycles, 2.02[2][c]
closing the loan, 4.03
condominiums, 10.02[1], 10.02[2]
   additional costs included,
     10.02[2][a]
   insured by federal government,
     10.01
   lender approval of
     condominium/developer
     documents, 10.02[2][c],
     10.02[2][d]
   lender's liability for developer's
     malfeasance, 10.02[2][b]
   loan-to-value/loan sellout basis,
     10.02[2][a]
   lender's major risk, 10.02[1]
   lender's protective measures in
     foreclosure, 10.02[2][c],
     10.02[2][d]
   phase development, 10.02[4]
   restrictions on junior lender,
     7.05[2]
   safeguards necessary, 10.02[2][a]

[*References are to paragraphs (¶) and to sample forms in Appendix B. References to the Supplement are preceded by "S."*]

Construction financing *(cont'd)*
  specialized design may cause restrictions by lender, 10.02[2][c]
  defaulting developer, lender's remedies, 4.04[8]
  developer must pay interest on entire loan, 4.04[3]
  generally, 4.01-4.05
  interest rates, 4.02[4]
    CD rates, S4.02[4], S.App. B, Fm. 4.4
    letter of credit, construction loans backed by, S4.02[4]
    LIBOR rates, S4.02[4], S.App. B, Fm. 4.5
    matched funding, S4.02[4]
  investor-furnished work-out funds, 4.04[8]
  lender's liability for construction defects, 4.04[7]
  lender's remedies to cure default, 4.04[8]
  lender's two approaches to risks, 4.03
  lien priority problems. *See* Liens
  mortgage, 4.03[2]
  mortgage banker's role, 2.03[2]
  note, 4.03[1]
  open-end mortgage, 4.02[6][a][ii]
  participation loans, 11.01[2], 11.01[3]
  permanent commitment as basis, 3.01[2], 3.07[1], 4.01[1]
  permanent commitment lacking, 4.01[3]
  permanent lender's approval, 4.02[1], 4.05
  permanent lender's right to buy loan, 3.04[14], 4.05
  and purchase-money mortgages, 7.04[1][c], 7.04[1][d]
  repayment of loan, 4.02[3]
  sources
    commercial banks, 2.02[2], 4.01
    industrial revenue bonds, 8.06
    insurance companies, 2.02[1][c], 4.01
    REITs, 2.02[5], 4.01[3]
    savings banks, 2.02[4][a]
  standby commitment as basis, 3.07

  surety bonds, lender as co-obligee, 4.02[8][b]
  terms and conditions, 4.02
  checklist, S4.02[14]

Construction period
  borrowing entity forgoes cash distributions, 4.03[2][d]
  changes discouraged by lender, 4.04[5]
  depreciation deductions unavailable, 4.02[5]
  insurance, 4.02[11]
  interest and taxes, deduction, 1.05[2][d]
  lead lender services loan, 11.01[2]
  Subchapter S suitable, 1.06
  credit unions as source of, S2.02[6]

Contingent interest mortgage (CIM), S.App. B, Fm. 3.16

Continuity of enterprise
  corporate attribute, 1.05[4][a]
  corporations, 1.05[5][c]
  limited partnerships, 1.04, 1.05[1], 1.05[4][a]
  partnerships, 1.04
  tenancy in common, 1.02[1]

Contractors
  See also Mechanics' and materialmen's liens; Subcontractors
  change of, lender discourages, 4.04[5]
  construction lender approval, 4.02[7]
  construction stages, role in, 4.04[3]
  default. *See* Default and foreclosure
  guarantee to lender of project completion, 4.02[8][e]
  no-lien agreement with developer, 4.02[6][b][iii]
  payments to by lender, 4.04[4]
  surety bond against mechanics' liens, 4.02[6][b][ii]

Contracts
  See also Specific subjects
  executory
    in bankruptcy, 4.02[12][b][v], 6.03[8]
    conferring right of possession, 4.04[8]

CUMULATIVE INDEX

[References are to paragraphs (¶) and to sample forms in Appendix B. References to the Supplement are preceded by "S."]

loan application/commitment as, 3.03[1]
mortgagor-insurer-mortgagee, insurance clauses, 3.04[12][b]
power-of-sale clauses as, 3.08[4][g]
to loan money, enforceability, 3.06

Contributed property, allocation, 1.05[3][b][ii]

Control. *See* Management

Convertible mortgages
loan terms, S3.04[18]
pension funds as source of, S2.02[6]
tax implications, S3.04[18]
usury implications, S3.04[18]

Convertible participation loans, S3.04[3][a], S3.04[18]

Cooperative housing
advantages over condominiums, 10.03
permanent financing difficulties, 10.03
sources of financing, 10.03

Co-owners
See also Service partners
bankruptcy sale, rights in, 4.02[12][b][vi]
partners, outside activities, App. B, Fm. 1.1 (Sec. 4.3 Comment)
status change
general partnership, 1.04
lender-developer joint venture, 11.02[2]
limited partnership, 1.04, 1.05[4][a]
tenancy in common, 1.02[1], 1.02[2][b]

Corporations
See also Bonds; Dividends; Non-profit corporations; Securities; Stockholders
advantages, 1.05[1]
to avoid usury laws, 5.04[1], 5.05[3]
for nondepreciable property, 1.05[2][c]
allocations inappropriate, 1.05[3][b][i]
attributes of, 1.05[4][a]
capital-raising methods available to, 6.04[2][a][i]
collapsible provisions, 1.05[3][a]
condominium owners, liability risk, 10.02[3][b]
continuity of enterprise, 1.05[4][a], 1.05[5][c]
depreciation rules, effect on earnings and profits, S1.05[2][b]
disadvantages, 1.05[3][c]
disadvantages for income-producing property, 1.05[2][b], 8.05[3]
as general partners, 1.05[4][a], 11.02[2]
as joint venturers, 11.02[2]
as lenders, "doing business" problems, 11.01[3]
liquidation, tax advantages, 1.05[5], 5.05[3]
loan applications by, 3.03[2]
as mortgagee-buyer, foreclosure sale, 12.04[b][ii]
partnerships compared, 1.05
property transfers, tax effects, 12.04[2]
qualifications for tax-free sale, 5.05[3]
sale-leaseback advantages for, 6.04[4]
sale-leaseback deals within, 6.04[3][c] n.64
straw, to evade usury/tax laws, 5.05[3]
as structure of cooperative housing, 10.03
Subchapter S, 1.06, 5.05[3]
tax advantages, 1.05[5]
taxation of partnership as, 1.05[4][a]
taxation of partnership as, App. B, Fm. 1.1 (Sec. 1.1 Comment)

Correspondents
commercial banks as, 2.02[2]
construction lenders as, 4.01
insurance companies' relationships with mortgage bankers, 11.02[7]
of lender, as agents, 5.05[2], n.119
mortgage bankers as, 2.03[2]
role in participation loans, 11.01[2], 11.01[3]

[References are to paragraphs (¶) and to sample forms in Appendix B. References to the Supplement are preceded by "S."]

Cost tax basis. *See* Basis
Costs. *See* Construction; Fees; Front-end costs; Points
Co-tenancy
  modification of prime lease effects, 3.08[4][i]
  requirement in shopping center lease, 3.05[3]
Crane doctrine, 12.01[3]
Credit
  See also Mortgages
  generally, 2.01
Credit corporations as lenders, S2.02[6]
Credit unions, home loans by, 2.01[3], S2.02[6]
Cycles. *See* Business cycles; Lending cycle

D

Damages
  in bankruptcy proceedings, 4.02[12][b][ii]
  breach of loan commitments, 3.06, 4.02[13]
  fraudulent land sales, 9.03[1]
  repair/waste actions, 3.08[4][d]
  tenant assigns to lender, 3.08[4][i]
Dealers
  collapsible property, sale, 1.05[3][a]
  income, sheltering, 1.05[2][c]
  limited partners as, App. B, Fm. 1.1 (Sec. 1.3(1) Comment)
  subdivision seller as, 1.05[3][c][iv], 9.05
  tax-free exchange unavailable to, 8.02[2]
  tenant assigns to lender, 3.08[4][i]
Debt financing. *See* specific type
Declaration. *See* Master deed
Deductions
  See also Capital gains; Capital losses; Depreciation; Interest; Losses; Rents; Worthless debts
  available to cooperative housing shareholders, 10.03
  compensation of service partner, 1.05[3][c][i]
  deficiency judgment, 12.03[4][a]
  fees and costs, 12.01[1]

  leaseback rental payments, 6.04[2], 6.04[3]
  for lender
    bad debts, 12.03[2][b]
    expense in property upkeep, 12.02[3]
    on nondepreciable property, 1.05[2][c]
    prepayment/late payment penalties, 12.02[2][a]
    worthless debt, 12.03[2][b][i], 12.03[2][c]
Deeds of trust
  See also Mortgages
  defined, 3.08[1]
  drafting of, 3.08
  sample form, App. B, Fm. 3.4
Default and foreclosure
  See also Acceleration of debt; Bankruptcy
  abandonment of property, 12.03[3]
  alternative mortgage instruments, S3.04[3][c]
  assignment of leases/rents in event of, 3.08[4][i], 8.05[2][e]
  in bankruptcy, automatic stay, 4.02[12][b][iv]
  "clogging the equity of redemption," S3.04[3][c]
  condominiums
    lender may sell separate units, 4.03[2][c]
    lenders' protective measures, 10.02[2][a], 10.02[2][c], 10.02[2][d], 10.02[3][d]
    unit owner's responsibility, 10.02[3][d]
  construction delay as, 4.04[2]
  construction lender's remedies for default, S4.04[8]
  by contractors, surety bonds covering, 4.02[8][b]
  cooperative housing shareholders' liability in, 10.03
  cross-default provisions
    construction loan/building loan agreement, 4.03[2][a]
    junior/senior lenders, 7.05[1]
    purchase-money/land-development loans, 9.01[1][d]

[*References are to paragraphs (¶) and to sample forms in Appendix B. References to the Supplement are preceded by "S."*]

deed in lieu of foreclosure, 4.04[8], 12.03[3]
device to force refinancing, 3.04[5], 3.08[4][g]
effect on construction completion, 4.02[8][b], 4.02[8][e]
effect on hazard insurance, 3.04[12][b]
effect on leases, 3.05[2], 8.05[2][e]
effect on priority of mechanics' liens, 4.02[6][a]
events triggering, 3.08[4][f]
foreclosure sales
  borrower's right of redemption, 3.08[4][g], 12.03 [4][a], 1203[4][b][ii]
  tax consequences, 12.03[4]
  to mortgagee, 12.03[4][b][ii]
  to third party, 12.03[4][b][i]
holder in due course, 5.05[2]
insurance companies' protection against, 2.02[1][d], 8.05[2]
joint ventures; conflicts; remedies, 11.02[3][b], 11.02[5][c]
junior lender's rights, 7.06, 12.03[6]
leasehold-mortgagor, 6.02, 6.03
lender's remedies for default, 3.08[4][g], 3.08[4][i], 4.02[12][a], 4.04[8]
"marshaling of assets" option, 7.06
mortgagee's entry into possession, 3.08[4][g]
  construction incomplete, 4.04[8]
  disposition of property, 12.03[5]
  foreclosure sale, 12.03[4][b][ii]
  purchase-money lender, 7.04[1][d][iii]
notice requirements, 3.08[4][g]
"one-action rule," 3.08[4][g]
participation loans, 11.01[6][a], 11.01[7], 11.01[8]
partnerships, liability, 1.05[4][b][iii]
power of sale clause, 3.08[4][g]
in purchase-money financing, 12.03[4][b][ii]
in sale-leaseback, remedies, 6.04[2][b]
subdivisions
  of land developer exposes lender to liability, 9.03[4]
  lender's rights in, 9.01[3]

purchase-money financing, 9.01[1]
tax consequences, 12.03
by tenants, 3.08[4][i], 3.08[5], 4.02[12][b][v]
voluntary conveyance to mortgagee, 12.03[3]

Deferred interest mortgage (DIM), S3.04[3][c]

Deferred payment method, 9.04[4]
in bankruptcy, lender's rights, 4.02[12][b][ii]
as default remedy, 3.08[4][g]
foreclosure sales, 12.03[4]
generally, 12.03[4]
nonrecourse financing, 1.05[4][b][iii]
purchase-money mortgages, 7.04[1][a], 7.04[1][c][iii], 7.04[1][d][i]

Depository Institutions Deregulation and Monetary Control Act of 1980, 2.01[3], 2.02[3][d], 5.01

Deposits. *See* Security deposits

Depreciation
See also Accelerated depreciation; Basis
allocation in partnerships, 1.05[3][b], 11.02[5][f]
annual decrease of, 1.05[2][b]
under E.R.T.A., S1.05[2][b], S1.05[2][d]
improvements by ground lessee, 6.01[1]
inapplicable to construction loan, 4.02[5]
low-income housing rehabilitation, 1.05[2][d]
sale-buyback financing, 8.09[3]
sale-leaseback financing
  land and improvements, 6.04[2], 6.04[3], 6.04[4]
  land only, 6.04[1][a]
straight-line
  corporations must use in computing earnings and profits, 1.05[2][b]
  in tax-free exchange, 8.02
Subchapter S corporations, 1.06
tax-free exchange to boost, 8.02[1]
as tax shelter, 1.05[2], 8.05[1]

[*References are to paragraphs (¶) and to sample forms in Appendix B. References to the Supplement are preceded by "S."*]

Developers
  See also Construction financing; Contractors; Landlords; specific topic
  condominium, misuse of funds, 10.02[2][b]
  data on required by lenders
    construction, 4.02[2]
    permanent, 3.03[2]
  default. *See* Default and foreclosure
  equity fund problems during construction, 4.04[3]
  high-credit leases, advantages/ disadvantages to, 8.05[1]
  joint ventures with lenders, 11.02
  liability. *See* Liability
  mortgage brokers' services, 2.03[1]
  psychological barriers to joint ventures, 11.02[3][a], 11.02[5][b], 11.02[6]
  REIT financing, reasons for, 2.02[5]
  subdividers
    capital gains treatment, 9.05[2]
    data required by Interstate Land Sales Act, 9.03
  substitution of restricted by lenders, 3.04[10]

Development financing. *See* Construction financing; Land; Subdivision financing

Disbursements. *See* Building loan agreements; Subdivision financing

Discounts
  See also Secondary mortgage market
  tax treatment
    for borrower, 12.01[1][b], 12.03[2][a][i]
    for lender, 12.01[2][b], 12.02[1][b], 12.03[4][b][i]

Disintermediation
  commercial banks, 2.02[2][a]
  defined; examples, 2.01[1][b]
  S&Ls, 2.02[3][a]
  savings banks, 2.02[4][a]
  usury laws may cause, 5.01 n.5

Dividends
  construction loan forbids to corporate borrower, 4.03[2][d]
  distribution by non-liquidating corporation taxable, 5.05[3]
  grantor agrees not to pay, 3.08[4][e], 3.08[4][f]
  "mortgaging out" proceeds as, 1.05[2][b], 12.01[4]

Documentation
  condominiums, 10.01, 10.02[2][d], 10.02[3][d]
  construction lender requires, 4.04[6]
  construction loan closing, 4.03
  form/substance approved by lender, 3.04[13]
  integrated loan forms, 4.05
  land development loan, 9.01[4]
  lender's, to do business in state, 11.01[3]
  permanent loan closing, 3.09[2]
  for secondary financing, 7.05
  uniform mortgage covenants, 3.08[2]
  of worthlessness of debt/property, 12.03[2][b][i], 12.03[2][c], 12.03[3][c]

Double taxation
  corporations, income-producing property, 1.05[2][b], 1.05[5]

Dragnet clause, 3.08[4][a], 4.03[2][b] n.164

Due-on-encumbrance clause, 3.04[7]

Due-on-sale clause, 3.04[8]
  FHLMC-FNMA clause, S.App. B, Fm. 3.18
  limited to arm's-length transactions, S.App. B, Fm. 3.17
  in shared appreciation mortgage, S3.04[3][c]

Due process, power of sale may violate, 3.08[4][g]

E

Earned income, 1.05[2][d]
Easements, 3.09[3], 9.01[1][c]
Economic Recovery Tax Act of 1981 (E.R.T.A.)
  Accelerated Cost Recovery System (ACRS), S1.05n.54a, S1.05[2][d]
  capital gains tax, S1.05[2][d]
  depreciation, accelerated, S1.05[2][d]

[*References are to paragraphs (¶) and to sample forms in Appendix B. References to the Supplement are preceded by "S."*]

depreciation, recapture, S1.05[2][d]
depreciation, straight-line,
   S1.05[2][b], S1.05[2][d]
minimum tax, S1.05[2][d]
ordinary income, S1.05[2][d]
rehabilitation investment credit,
   S1.05[2][d]
Eminent domain. *See* Condemnation
Employees
See also Service partners
compensation, partnership vs.
   corporation, 1.05[3][c]
fringe benefits, 1.05[1], 1.05[5][c]
"End-loan" financing, 10.02[5]
Engineers
See also Architects; Inspections
construction lender approves,
   4.02[10]
errors and omissions insurance,
   3.09[3]
Environmental regulations
compliance; types, 3.04[9][c]
impact statement, 3.09[3], 9.02
Equity funds
developer's needs during
   construction, 4.04[3], 4.04[5]
required for tax basis, 12.01[3][b]
sources for to complete
   construction, 4.04[8]
Equity interest
allocation in lender-developer
   ventures, 11.02[5][a]
developer gives to cover construction
   costs, 4.02[8][a]
limited partnerships, App. B, Fm. 1.1
   (Secs. 2.3, et seq. Comments)
Equity kickers, 2.01[3], 11.02[1]
convertible participation loans,
   S3.04[3][a]
gross/net income percentages,
   3.04[3][a]
in high-ratio financing, 8.08
insurance companies' use of, 2.02[1],
   3.04[18]
in sale-buyback financing, 8.09[3]
usury implications, S3.04[3][a],
   5.05[8], 11.02[1]
Equity participation by lenders
See also Equity kickers; Joint
   ventures

joint ventures, 11.02
relationship between partners,
   S12.01[5]
risk compensation to lenders, 5.05[8]
status of corporate borrowers,
   S12.01[5][b]
tax treatment of partners,
   S12.01[5][a]
usury implications, 5.05[8]
Escrows
See also Security deposits
condominium security deposits,
   10.02[2][b] n.35
funds to complete construction,
   3.09[3]
in installment sales tax planning,
   9.04[1][c][i]
recommended for loan participations,
   11.01[6][b]
rents under assignment to lender,
   3.08[4][i]
repair/waste covenants, 3.08[4][d]
tax and insurance, held by lender,
   3.04[6], 7.04[1][c][i]
in three-cornered exchanges, 8.02[4]
wraparound mortgages, 7.04[3][a]
Estoppel certificates
for holder in due course, 5.05[2]
in permanent loan commitment,
   4.03[1]
permanent lender requires, 3.09[2]
sample form, App. B, Fm. 3.11
Exchanges
See also "Boot"
bad debt loss as, 12.03[2][b][iii]
among controlled entities, taxation,
   12.04[2]
default conveyance as, 12.03[3][a],
   12.03[3][c]
foreclosure sale as, 12.03[4][a],
   12.03[4][b][ii]
lender-REIT-new buyer, 7.04[1][e]
mortgaged property, tax effects,
   12.04[1]
in sale-leaseback, 6.04[2][a][ii],
   6.04[3][a], 6.04[4]
   three-cornered, 8.02[4]
   three-cornered, sample agreement,
     App. B, Fm. 8.1
two requirements for, 8.02[2]
within partnerships, 8.02[2]

REAL ESTATE FINANCING I-14

[References are to paragraphs (¶) and to sample forms in Appendix B. References to the Supplement are preceded by "S."]

Exclusive-use clauses, 3.05[3]
Exculpation
 See also Liability; Nonrecourse financing
 fee owner in leasehold financing, 6.02[3]
 intent in usury, 5.02[1]
 lender, under construction contract, 4.02[8][e]
 provision in mortgage
  limited partnership, 1.05[4][b][iii], 3.03[2], 7.04[1][c][i]
  limited to first loan, 3.04[7]
Executory interests, 6.04[1][b], 6.04[1][c]
Expenses. *See* Fees; specific subjects

F

Fair market value. *See* Appraisals and valuations
Family housing
 in bankruptcy reorganization, 4.02[12][b][iv]
 corporate ownership cancels usury exemption, 5.04 n.90
 defects in, lender's liability, 4.04[7]
 financing
  savings and loans, 2.02[3][c], 2.02[3][d]
  savings banks, 2.02[4]
  subdivisions, 9.01-9.05
Fannie Mae. *See* Federal National Mortgage Association
Federal government
 See also specific agencies and acts
 condominiums, regulation by, 10.02[2][b]
 effect on mortgage market, 2.01[3]
 environmental restrictions by, 3.04[9][c]
 secondary mortgage market created by, 2.02[7]
 Title X mortgage insurance, 9.02
 usury law preemption by, 5.01
Federal Home Loan Bank Board (FHLBB)
 due-on-sale clause, S.App. B, Fm. 3.18

 permits variable mortgages, 3.04[3][c]
 regulation of S&Ls, 2.02[3][d]
 renegotiable rate mortgage, S3.04[3][c]
Federal Home Loan Mortgage Corporation (FHLMC)
 due-on-sale clause, S.App. B, Fm. 3.18
 role in secondary mortgage market, 2.02[7][b]
 uniform mortgage documents by, 3.08[2], 10.02[1], 10.02[3][d]
Federal Housing Administration (FHA)
 permits buy-downs, S3.04[3][c]
Federal National Mortgage Association
 document standardization, 3.08[2]
 generally, 2.02[7][a]
 participation loans, 11.01[2]
Federal Reserve System, 2.02[2][d]
Fee owners
 bankruptcy of, 6.03 n.12, 8.09[2]
 prohibited to mortgage fee, 6.03[1]
 protection under leasehold financing, 6.02[4]
 reasons for using leasehold financing, 6.02[3]
 subordination to leasehold, 6.02
Fees
 application, 3.06
 assumption fee, 3.04[8]
 attorneys' liability for, 3.09[1]
 in bankruptcy proceedings, 4.02[12][b][ii]
 brokerage
  fiduciary duty as to, S2.03[1]
  tax treatment, 12.01[2][a]
  usury considerations, 5.03[3]
 closing, 3.04[15], 4.02[13]
 commitment
  borrower pays, 3.04[15], 4.02[13]
  as damages for breach of commitment, 3.06
  insurance companies, 2.02[1][b]
  mortgage bankers, 2.03[2]
  tax aspects, 12.01[1][a]
  usury implications, 5.02[4][a], 5.03[1]
 construction lender's front-end, 4.02[4]

[*References are to paragraphs (¶) and to sample forms in Appendix B. References to the Supplement are preceded by "S."*]

correspondents' yearly service, 4.01
deductibility, 1.05[2][c]
inspections of construction, 4.02[10]
origination, as interest, 5.03[2], 5.03[3]
reduce sale price, purchase-money foreclosure, 12.03[4][b][ii]
for services
  tax aspects, 12.01[1], 12.01[2]
  usury implications, 5.02[4][a], 5.03
tax aspects, 12.01[1][a]
FHA loans, exempt from usury, 5.04, 5.04[3]
FHA Model Condominium Act (1962), 10.01
Fiduciary duty of mortgage broker, S2.03[1]
Financial intermediaries. *See* Lenders
Financing. *See* Construction financing; High-ratio financing; Leasehold financing; Mortgages; Nonrecourse financing; Permanent financing; Prefinancing; Recourse financing; Refinancing; Sale and leaseback; Subdivision financing; type of property being financed
Fires. *See* Casualties
Fixtures. *See* Personal property
Flexible loan insurance program (FLIP), 3.04[3][c]
Floating debt. *See* Dragnet clause
Force majeure, 3.04[11], 4.04[2]
Foreclosure. *See* Default and foreclosure
Foreign Investment in Real Property Tax Act (F.I.R.P.A.), S2.02[8]
Foreign investments in U.S. real estate, S2.02[8]
Foreign states
Interstate Land Sales Act, 9.03
mutual savings banks loans, 2.02[4]
participation loans
  "doing business" problems, 11.01[3], 11.01[8]
  usury problems, 11.01[6][c]
in usury law circumvention, 5.05[1]
Forms
Architect's Certificate, App. B, Fm. 3.10
Assignment of Lessor's Interest in Lease, App. B, Fm. 3.5
Attorney's Certificate, App. B, Fm. 3.9
Attornment and Nondisturbance Agreement, App. B, Fm. 6.3, Fm. 6.4
Bond for Residential Development, App. B, Fm. 9.1
Building Loan Agreement, App. B, Fm. 4.1
Buy-Sell Agreement, App. B, Fm. 4.2
CD Method of Computing Construction Loan Interest, S.App. B, Fm. 4.5
Certified Inventory, App. B, Fm. 3.13
Closing Disbursement Letter to Title Company, App. B, Fm. 3.8
Construction Loan Commitment for Condominium, App. B, Fm. 10.2
Construction Mortgage Loan Commitment, S.App. B, Fm. 4.3
Contingent Interest Provision, S.App. B, Fm. 3.16
Due-on-Sale-Clause Limited to Arm's-Length Transactions, S.App. B, Fm. 3.17
FHLMC-FNMA Due-on-Sale Clause, S.App. B, Fm. 3.13
Ground Lease, App. B, Fm. 6.2, Fm. 6.5
Joint Venture Agreement, App. B, Fm. 11.3
Land Purchase-Leaseback Transaction Sales Contract, App. B, Fm. 6.1
Letter of Intent for Leveraged Equity Joint Venture, S.App. B, Fm. 11.5
Limited Partnership Agreement, App. B, Fm. 1.1
Loan Participation Agreement, App. B, Fm. 11.1
Master Deed for Condominium, App. B, Fm. 10.1
Mortgage Deed of Trust, App. B, Fm. 3.4

[*References are to paragraphs (¶) and to sample forms in Appendix B. References to the Supplement are preceded by "S."*]

Forms *(cont'd)*
   Master Development Loan Agreement, App. B, Fm. 9.3
   Mortgagor's Estoppel Affidavit, App. B, Fm. 3.11
   Note, App. B, Fm. 3.3
   Notice of Lease Assignment, App. B, Fm. 3.6
   Permanent Mortgage Loan Application-Commitment, App. B, Fm. 3.2
   Permanent Mortgage Loan Commitment, App. B, Fm. 3.1
   Separate Noteholder's Agreement, App. B, Fm. 11.2
   Set-Aside Letter, App. B, Fm. 9.2
   Shared Appreciation Mortgage Provisions, S.App. B, Fm. 3.15
   Standard Mortgage Clause, App. B, Fm. 3.12
   Tenant's Acceptance Letter, App. B, Fm. 3.7
   Three-Cornered Exchange Agreement, App. B, Fm. 8.1
Franchise agreements, 4.02[13]
Fraud and misrepresentation, land sales, 9.03[1]
Freddie Mac. *See* Federal Home Loan Mortgage Corporation (FHLMC)
Fringe parcels, 3.04[16]
Front-end costs
   See also Construction period
   allocation, 1.05[3][b][i]
   condominium developer recoups, 10.02[2][c]
   fee to construction lender, 4.02[4]
   in lender-developer ventures, 11.02[3][b], 11.02[5][a]
Future interests. *See* Executory interests

G

Gains. *See* Capital gains; Income
Gap financing
   avoiding; solutions, 3.04[2]
   described, 7.04[2]
   note, cross-defaulted to construction loan, 4.03[1]
   rental units converted to condominiums, 10.02[5]
Gifts, 12.04[3]
Ginnie Mae. *See* Government National Mortgage Association
"Gold clause resolution" and PLAMs, S3.04[3][c]
Government National Mortgage Association, 2.02[7][c]
Graduated payment adjustable mortgage (GPAM), S3.04[3][c]
Graduated payment mortgage (GPM), 3.04[3][c]
Grants, 3.08[4][b]
Ground leases
   See also Sale and leaseback
   effect of lessee's default, 6.02[4], 6.03[8]
   percentage rent, 8.09[1]
   provisions in, 2.02[1][d], 6.03, 8.09[1]
   rent, changes in, 6.03[9]
   sample option and development agreement, App. B, Fm. 6.2, Fm. 6.5
   subordination to leasehold mortgage, 6.02[2], 8.09[1]

H

Hazard insurance. *See* Insurance
High-ratio financing
   See also Equity kickers; Exchanges; Installment sales contracts; Junior mortgages; Leasehold financing; Leases; Leverage; Participation loans; Purchase-money mortgages; Sale and leaseback
   generally, 8.01-8.09
Historic structure rehabilitations, S1.05[2][d]
Holdbacks
   construction funds, 4.02[8][a], 4.04[3]
   construction commitment provides for, 4.02[9]

[*References are to paragraphs (¶) and to sample forms in Appendix B. References to the Supplement are preceded by "S."*]

construction contract/building loan agreement agree on, 4.02[7]
of permanent loan funds, 4.02[1]

Holder in due course
exemption from usury, 5.05[2]
permanent lender as, 3.08[3], 4.03[1], 9.03[4]

Holding period, 12.03[4][b][ii]

Home loans. *See* Family housing

Hotels and motels
in bankruptcy reorganization, 4.02[12][b][iv]
as financing risks, 7.02
financing sources, 3.02
Subchapter S suitable, 1.06

Housing
See also Condominiums; Cooperative housing; Low-income housing; Multifamily housing; One-to-four-family housing; Subdivision financing
for aged, 2.02[3][d][v]
demand for, 2.01[1]]c]
financing sources
federal purchase of mortgages, 2.02[7]
S&Ls, 2.02[3]
tax-free exchanges, 8.02[2]
trends in financing, 2.01[3]

Housing and Community Development Act of 1980, S5.01

I

Improvements. *See* Construction; Land

Income
See also Allocations; Capital gains; Cash flow; Employees, compensation; Equity kickers; Ordinary income
as basis of ground rent, 6.03[9]
investment income, defined, 12.02[2][b]
operating vs. investment income, 1.06
tax treatment
condominium commercial rentals, 10.02[3][b]
to lender, 12.01[2][b]

rents as "passive" income, 11.02[5][b]
tenants in common, 1.02[2]
unpaid rights, zero basis, 12.03[2][b][ii] n.110

Income-producing property
financing
insurance companies as source, 2.02[1], 11.02[1]
S&Ls as source, 2.02[3][d][iii]
tax shelters, 1.05[2][b]

Incorporation. *See* Corporations

Indebtedness, dragnet clause, 3.08[4][a]

Indemnity agreements, 1.05[4][a], 1.05[4][b][iii]

Industrial facilities, 8.06

Industrial revenue bonds. *See* Bonds

Insanity. *See* Co-owners, status change

Insolvency. *See* Bankruptcy

Inspections, construction, 4.02[10], 4.04, 4.04[7]

Installment sales contracts
See also Purchase-money mortgages; Sale and leaseback; Sale-repurchase financing
assignment to lender, dangers, 9.03[4], S9.04[4][bb]
bad debts, tax consequences, 12.03[2][b][ii], 12.03[2][b][iii]
foreclosure sale, tax effect, 12.03[4][b][i]
generally, 9.04
in high-ratio financing, 8.03
Installment Sales Revision Act of 1980, 9.04
land, usury exemption, 5.05[5]
in purchase-money financing, 12.03[4][b][ii]
in sale-buyback financing, 8.09[3]
sale-leaseback as "disguised," 6.04[3][d]
usury implications, 5.02[2], 5.04

Insurance
See also Life insurance companies; Title insurance
casualty
co-insurance clause, 3.04[12][a), 4.02[11]
construction period, 4.02[11]

[References are to paragraphs (¶) and to sample forms in Appendix B. References to the Supplement are preceded by "S."]

Insurance *(cont'd)*
  casualty *(cont'd)*
    in high-credit leases, 8.05[2][a], 8.05[2][b]
    leasehold financing, 6.02[4], 6.03[6], 6.03[10]
    lender approves, 3.04[12], 3.09[3], 4.02[11]
    loss payable clauses, 3.04[12][b]
    option to restore premises, 3.08[4][d]
    standard mortgage clause, App. B, Fm. 3.12
    stored materials coverage, 4.04[3]
  condominiums, 10.02[3][b]
  escrow accounts held by lender, 3.04[6]
  liability, 1.05[1]
  mortgage insurance
    private, 8.07[1][a]
    Title X, 9.02
  premiums
    borrower's default in paying, 3.08[4][g] n.255
    mortgagee pays; remedies, 3.08[4][j], 12.02[3]
  proceeds
    junior mortgagee assigns to senior, 7.05[2]
    mortgagee collects, 3.04[5], 3.04[12], 3.05[2], 3.08[4][d]
    tenant assigns to lender, 3.08[4][i]
  subdivisions; public liability, workmen's compensation, 9.01[3]
  zoning compliance, 3.04[9][b]
Interest
  See also Discounts; Interest rates; "Points"; Prepayment; Usury
  advance payment of, 5.02[4][b], 12.01[1][b]
  CD rates, S4.02[4], S.App. B, Fm. 4.4
  collection charges as, 5.03[8]
  compound, 5.02[4][b]
  computation methods, 5.02[4][b]
  construction loan, funding of, 4.04[5]
  contingent, gross receipts as basis, S.App. B, Fm. 3.16
  convertible participation loan, S3.04[3][a]
  deductibility, 12.02[2], 12.03[2][a][ii], 12.03[4][a]
    construction period, 1.05[2][d]
    "constructive" interest, 6.04[3][b]
    investment interest limitation, 12.02[2][b]
    nondepreciable property, 1.05[2][c]
    subsidiary pays to parent, 11.02[4][b]
  deferred, S3.04[3][c]
  discount on mortgage note sale as, 5.05[2]
  income from tax-exempt, industrial revenue bonds, 8.06
  as income to lender, 12.02[1], 12.03[3][b], 12.03[4][b]
  legal definition of, 5.02[4][a]
  LIBOR rates, S4.02[4], S.App. B, Fm. 4.5
  sale-repurchase payments as, 5.05[6]
  on tax/insurance escrows held by lender, 3.04[6]
  rates
    "averaging" to avoid usury, 5.02[4][d]
Interest rates
  "averaging" to avoid usury, 5.02[4][d]
  "bondable" net lease lowers, 8.05 n.36
  commercial banks, 2.02[2][b], 4.02[4]
  computation to avoid usury, 5.02[4][b]
  construction loans, 4.02[4]
  contingent, S3.04[3][c]
  in default-accelerated repayment, 5.03[8]
  Depository Institutions Deregulation and Monetary Control Act of 1980, S2.02[3][d]
  due-on-sale clause as device to raise, 3.04[8]
  effect of business cycles, 2.01[1][b]
  escalator clauses, 5.02[4][c], 7.04[1][e], 7.04[1][b][iii]
  federal regulation, 2.02[4][c]

CUMULATIVE INDEX

[References are to paragraphs (¶) and to sample forms in Appendix B. References to the Supplement are preceded by "S."]

free market, 2.01[3]
industrial revenue bonds, 8.06
insurance companies, 2.02[1][b]
"legal rate" defined, 5.02[4]
permanent financing, 3.04[3]
purchase-money mortgages, 7.04[1][b]
Regulation Q ceilings, phase-out of, S2.02[3][d]
REITs, 4.01[3]
renegotiable, S3.04[3][c]
S & Ls, 2.02[3][b], 3.04[3][c]
secondary mortgage market, 7.03
standby commitments, 3.07
subdivision financing, 9.01[1], 9.02
subsidy by Ginnie Mae, 2.02[7][c]
use of "due on sale" clause to raise, 3.04[8]
variable, 3.04[3][c]
Interim financing. *See* Gap financing
Interstate Land Sales Full Disclosure Act (ILSFDA)
applicable to condominium sales, 10.02[2][b]
liability of lender under, 9.03[4][b]
purpose and scope, 9.03
revisions and exemptions from, 9.03[3]
Interstate loans. *See* Foreign states
Inventory
certified, sample form, App. B, Fm. 3.13
mobile homes, loans for, 2.02[3][d][v]
sale, tax treatment, 1.05[3][a]
Investment interest limitations, 12.02[2][b]
Investment tax credit, 1.05[2][d], 1.05[5][d]

J

Joint venture
See also Equity participation by lenders
adverse publicity, 11.02[3][a], 11.02[4][b], 11.02[6]
agreement, 11.02[5]
calculating percentage interests, S11.02[5][a]
developer with REIT, 2.02[5]

lender-developer, 11.02
allocations of capital/control, 11.02[5]
dangers of liability to lender, 4.04[7]
dissolution, 11.02[5][c], 11.02[5][e]
history, 11.02[1], 11.02[7]
letter of intent to form, S.App. B, Fm. 11.5
leveraged equity, S11.02[6], S.App. B, Fm. 11.5
ownership vehicles suitable, 11.02[4]
pension fund participation in, S2.02[6]
as ownership entities, 1.03
sample agreement, App. B, Fm. 11.3
tenancy in common treatment, S11.02[4][c]
usury exemptions for, 5.04[2], 5.05[8], 11.02[3][c]
Junior mortgages
See also Gap financing; Liens, priority of; Purchase-money mortgages; Wraparound mortgages
advantages of, 7.02
basic requirements, 7.05
in condominium financing, 7.05[2]
default/foreclosure, effect, 12.03[6]
"first refusal" to first lender, 3.04[7]
foreclosure of as event of default, 3.08[4][f]
in high-ratio financing, 8.07[1]
lender's statutory/common law rights, 7.06
lender's protective covenants, 7.05[1]
loan allocations, 7.02
loan terms, 7.03
net cash flow coverage, 7.03
reasons for, 7.02
in rental unit conversions, 10.02[5]
restricted/prohibited by first lender, 3.04[7]
sources
commercial banks, 2.02[2][b], 7.03
credit unions, S2.02[6]

[*References are to paragraphs (¶) and to sample forms in Appendix B. References to the Supplement are preceded by "S."*]

Junior mortgages *(cont'd)*
  sources *(cont'd)*
    insurance companies, 2.02[1][d], 7.03
    S & Ls, 2.02[3][d]
    subordination demanded by senior lenders, 7.05[2]
  types of, 7.04
  wraparound payment method prudent, 7.05[1]
Jurisdiction
  borrower's choice of, 5.05[1]
  lender's "doing business" problems, 11.01[3]

L

Labor. *See* Employees; Mechanics' and materialmen's liens
Land
  See also Leasehold financing; Sale and leaseback; Subdivision financing
  "banking" of for future development, 9.01 n.1
  covenants running with, 3.08[4][j]
  financing sources
    commercial banks, 2.02[2][d], 4.02[2]
    insurance companies, 2.02[1][c], 2.02[1][d]
    REITs, 3.02
    S & Ls, 2.02[3][d][v]
  improved
    advantage of FHA usury exemption, 5.04[3]
    description, lender's requirements, 3.04[16]
    loans by S & Ls, 2.02[3][d]
    nonrecourse financing crucial, 9.01[1][b]
  limited partnership owns, 1.05[4][a]
  mortgage on, construction lender prohibits, 4.02[6]
  partial release of liens on, 7.04[1][c][iii]
  prefinancing considerations, 3.01[1]
  profit on, taxes, 1.05[3][a][i]
  reasons for leasing, 6.01[1]
  sales
    effect of market conditions, 9.01
    federal regulation, 9.03
    procedural steps, 9.01[4]
    site plans, 3.04[16], 4.02[2]
    Subchapter S suitable, 1.06
  subdivision
    bond assuring improvements, 9.01[1][c], 9.01[3]
    bond assuring improvements, sample, App. B, Fm. 9.1
    easement release agreements required, 9.01[1][c]
    hazards for developer/lender, 9.01
    requirements for development loan, 9.01[3]
Land trusts
  acting for partnership, 1.05[4][b][iii]
  generally, 1.08
Land use, 3.04[9][c], 9.01[3]
Landlords
  mortgagor's duties as, 3.05[2]
  obligations on lease assignments, 3.08[4][i]
  position under net/gross leases, 8.05
  shopping centers
    special mortgage riders, 3.08[5]
Late payment. *See* Default and foreclosure; Repayment of loans
Leasehold financing
  See also Fee owners; Ground leases; Sale and leaseback
  commercial banks, 2.02[2][d]
  fee mortgage combined with, 8.09[2]
  generally, 6.01-6.03
  insurance companies restricted in, 2.02[1][d], 6.01[2], 6.03[1]
  merger of fee/leasehold, 6.03[4], 6.03[10]
  subordinated fee
    advantages to developer, 6.02[1]
    fee owner's protections, 6.02[4]
    as high-ratio technique, 8.09[1]
    lender's requirements, 6.02
    two methods of subordination, 6.02[1]
  tax/business considerations, 6.01[1]
  unsubordinated fee
    assignment of estate, 6.03[2], 6.03[10]
    lender's requirements, 6.03

[References are to paragraphs (¶) and to sample forms in Appendix B. References to the Supplement are preceded by "S."]

Leases
See also Co-tenancy; Ground leases; Rents; Sale and leaseback; Shopping centers; Tenants
assignment
in bankruptcy, 4.02[12][b][v]
to lender, 3.05, 3.08[4][i], 4.02[13], 8.05[2], 8.06
notice of, sample, App. B, Fm. 3.6
restrictions, 3.05[7]
sample form, App. B, Fm. 3.5
in bankruptcy, 4.02[12][b][v], 4.02[12][b][vi]
"bondable," 8.05
in condominiums to commercial tenants, 10.02[3][b]
default provisions, 3.05[2]
exclusive, radius and co-tenancy clauses, 3.05[3]
high-credit
as high-ratio financing device, 8.05
lender's requirements, 3.05, 6.03[5], 8.05[2]
planning considerations, 8.05[3]
three-party agreements, 3.08[4][i]
junior mortgage subject to, 7.05[2]
modification or change in
clause in loan instrument, 3.08[4][i]
lender's financing requirements may cause, 3.05[9]
effect on investment interest limitation, 12.02[2][b]
net leases, 8.05
platform loans based on, 3.04[2]
purchase option in, 3.05[8], 8.05[2][d]
recreation, in condominiums, 10.02[1]
subordination
to junior mortgages, 3.04[7], 3.05[6], 8.05[2][f]
lender's requirements, 3.05[6]
termination
assignment of lease to control, 3.08[4][i]
in bankruptcy, 4.02[12][b][v]
effect of foreclosure, leasehold, 6.02[2][b]
effect of release of fringe parcels, 3.04[16]
effect of subordination, 3.05[6]
lender's requirements, 3.05[2], 3.05[9], 8.05[2]

Lenders. *See also* Equity kickers; Equity participation by lenders; Financing; Mortgages; specific class of lender
attorneys for, 3.09[1], 3.09[2]
bankruptcy of borrower, rights, 4.02[12][b][vi]
choice of by developer, 3.02
complete construction if developer defaults, 4.02[8][b], 4.04[8], 9.01[3]
construction/interim/permanent, assignment of commitments, 3.04[10]
construction, two approaches of, 4.03
disintermediation, effect on, 2.01[1][b]
"doing business" problems, 11.01[3]
joint ventures with developers, 11.02
lead lender. *See* Participation loans
liability of. *See* Liability
mortgage bankers' services to, 2.03[2]
mortgage liability, attitudes, 1.05[4][b][iii]
obligations of borrower performed by, 3.08[4][j]
preferences, habits, etc., 2.01[2]
property upkeep expenses of, 12.02[3]
psychological barriers to joint ventures, 11.02[3][a], 11.02[5][b], 11.02[6]
real estate personnel, duties, 3.09[2], 4.04
rights in subdivision set-asides, 9.01[3]
tax aspects of lending, 12.01, 12.02, 12.03
types of, 2.01-2.03
Lending cycle, 2.01[2], 2.02[2][c]
construction loan's role, 4.01
steps involved, 3.01[2]
Letters of credit
assuring project completion, 4.02[8][d]

REAL ESTATE FINANCING   I-22

[References are to paragraphs (¶) and to sample forms in Appendix B. References to the Supplement are preceded by "S."]

Letters of credit *(cont'd)*
  covering gap loans, 3.04[2], 4.02[3]
  lender requires of developer during construction, 4.04[3]
  use as security deposit, 3.06
Leverage
  See also High-ratio financing
  increasing by tax-free exchange, 8.02[1]
  mortgage demand caused by, 2.01[1][c]
  obtaining, 1.05[2][a]
  pitfalls in, 8.01
Liability
  See also Deficiency judgments; Exculpation; Insurance; Liens; Nonrecourse financing; Surety bonds
  bankruptcy trustee, 4.02[12][b][v]
  of buyer in asset swap agreement, 7.04[1][e]
  condominium developers/unit owners, 10.02[3][b]
  corporations, 1.05[1]
  land trust investors, 1.08
  lender's
    for construction defects, 4.04[7]
    for developer's malfeasance, 10.02[2][b]
    under Interstate Land Sales Act, 9.03[4][b]
    in joint ventures, 11.02[3][b], 11.02[4][a], 11.02[4][b]
    in leasehold financing, 6.03[2], 6.03[10]
    in participation loans, 11.01[6][d], 11.01[7]
    when acting as mortgagor, 4.04[5]
    when in possession of property, 4.04[8]
  limited, corporate attribute, 1.05[4][a]
  limited partnerships, 1.05[1], 1.05[4][a], Fm. 1.1 (Secs. 1.1, 2.6A Comment)
    for construction loan, 4.02[5]
  of original tenant for rent, 3.05[2]
  personal

  of cooperative housing shareholders, 10.03
  developer, sale-leaseback, Fm. 6.1 (Sec. 10 Comment)
  effect on cost tax basis, 8.02[3], 12.01[3], 12.01[4]
  effect on foreclosure sale gain/loss, 12.03[4][a]
  effect on gain/loss, defaulted property, 12.03[3]
  effect on interest deductibility, 12.02[2][a]
  for mortgage, 1.05[4][b], 3.04[7]
  lender's right to sue, 3.08[4][g], 11.01[8]
  partnerships, 1.04
  sale of property, tax effect, 12.04[1]
  secondary, on construction note, 4.03[1]
  of wraparound mortgagee, 7.04[3][a]
Liens
  See also Mechanics' and materialmen's liens; Mortgages; Surety bonds
  architect's fees, 4.02[10]
  covenants in loan instrument, 3.08[4][e]
  equitable lien doctrine, 4.02[6][a][iii]
  priority of
    after-acquired property, 3.08[4][a]
    condominiums, 10.02[2][c], 10.02[2][d], 10.02[3][d]
    construction loan/land mortgage, 4.02[6]
    construction loan/mechanics' liens, 4.02[6][a], 4.02[6][b], 4.04[2], 10.02[2][c]
    construction loan priority transfers to permanent lender, 4.05
    construction loan/purchase-money loan, 704[1][c][ii]
    cost-overrun loan/mechanics' liens, 4.03[2][b]
    fee mortgage/leasehold mortgage, 6.01[2], 6.03[1], 8.09[2]

[*References are to paragraphs (¶) and to sample forms in Appendix B. References to the Supplement are preceded by "S."*]

first/junior mortgages, 3.04[7], 7.04[1][a]
junior lenders in receivership, 7.06
lease/mortgage, 3.05[6], 3.05[8], 8.05[2][f]
mortgage/security interest in chattels, 3.08[4][a]
pre-bankruptcy/post-bankruptcy loans, 4.02[12][b][vi]
purchase-money mortgage/other claims, 7.04[1][a], 7.04[1][c][ii], 9.01[1][d]
on rents, 3.08[4][i]
wraparound mortgages, 7.04[3][b][iii]
reinstatement of junior, after foreclosure, 7.06

Life insurance companies
as condominium lenders, 10.02[5]
cooperative housing blanket loans by, 10.03
joint ventures with developers, 11.02
leasehold mortgages by, 8.09[2]
loan allocations, 2.02[1][c], 3.04[3][c], 11.01[5]
loan terms, 2.02[1][b], 3.04[3][c], 8.05[2]
as mortgage lenders, 2.02[1], 3.02, 8.05
regulation of portfolios, 2.02[1][d], 6.01[2], 6.03[1], 8.05, 11.02[1]
as sale-leaseback purchasers, 6.04[2], 11.02[1]
sources of funds, 2.02[1][a]
trend to outright property purchase, 11.02[7]

Limited partnerships
See also Co-owners; Management; Partnership agreements; Partnerships
additional contributions as loans/capital, App. B, Fm. 1.1 (Sec. 2.3 Comment)
advantages for income-producing property, 1.05[2][b]
buy-sell agreements, App. B, Fm. 1.1 (Sec. 5.2 Comment)
construction lender forbids cash distributions, 4.03[2][d]
corporation as general partner, 1.05[4][a], 11.02[2]
corporations compared, 1.05
a dealer/investor for tax purposes, App. B, Fm. 1.1 (Sec. 1.3(1) Comment)
general partnerships compared, 1.04
history, 1.05
lender-developer joint ventures as, 11.02[2], 11.02[4][a], 11.02[5]
mortgage liability, 1.05[4][b]
public sale of, 1.05
rulings as to tax status, 1.05[4][a]
special basis rules, 1.05[4][b][ii]
sample agreement, App. B, Fm. 1.1
tax pitfalls, 1.05[4]
taxation as a corporation, 1.05[4][a]
taxation as a corporation, App. B, Fm. 1.1 (Sec. 1.1 Comment)
term; duration, App. B, Fm. 1.1 (Sec. 1.4 Comment)
transfer of shares, 1.05[1]
transferability of interests, 1.05[4][a]
transferability of interests, App. B, Fm. 1.1 (Art. 4 Comments)
usury exemptions for, 5.04[2]

Loan applications
construction loan
  checklist, 4.06
  data required by lender, 4.02[2]
permanent loan
  clause on good faith deposit, 3.06
  fees, 3.06
  functions; data required, 3.03, 3.04
  sample form, App. B, Fm. 3.2

Loan sellout value, 10.02[2][a]

Loan-to-value ratio
See also High-ratio financing
appraisal as basis, 3.04[1], 6.04[2][a][i]
commercial banks, 2.02[2][b], 2.02[2][d]
in condominium financing, 10.02[2][a], 10.02[3][a]
construction loans, exemptions, 3.01[2]
for corporate borrowers, 6.04[4] n.66
first plus junior mortgages, 3.04[7]
under high-credit leases, 8.05

REAL ESTATE FINANCING I-24

[References are to paragraphs (¶) and to sample forms in Appendix B. References to the Supplement are preceded by "S."]

Loan-to-value ratio *(cont'd)*
  insurance companies, 2.02[1][b], 2.02[1][d], 6.04[2][a][i]
  leasehold mortgage, subordinated fee, 6.02[1]
  S & Ls, 2.02[3][d]
  savings banks, 2.02[4][c]
  second mortgages, 7.03
  subdivision financing, 9.01[1]
  in subordinated purchase-money mortgages, 7.04[1][d][ii]
  tax-exempt mortgages, 8.06
  Title X financing of subdivisions, 9.02
  in wraparound mortgages, 7.04[3]
Loan workouts, S3.08[4][g]
Loans
  See also Mortgages; Loan applications
  church properties, 2.02[3][d][iii]
  defined, in usury law, 5.02[2], 5.02[3][a]
  investments distinguished, 5.02[3][a]
  to limited partnership by partner, App. B, Fm. 1.1 (Sec. 2.7 Comment)
  origination or service fees, 5.03[2]
  sale-leaseback as "disguised" loan, 5.05[4], 6.04[3][b]
  time-price differential, 5.02[2]
Local law
  See also Certificate of occupancy; State regulation; Zoning
  developer's compliance with, 3.04[9], 4.02[13]
  lender's knowledge of, reliance on inadvisable, 3.04[9][d]
  subdivision requirements, 9.01[3]
Long-term financing. *See* Permanent financing
Losses
  See also Capital losses
  allocation, 1.05[3][b][i]
  artificial accounting, 1.05[2][d]
  bad debts, tax treatment, 12.03[2], 12.03[3], 12.03[4]
  dealer/investor status, 9.05[1]
  defaulted/abandoned property
    borrower's tax treatment, 12.03[3][a]
    lender's tax treatment, 12.03[3][b], 12.03[3][c], 12.03[4][b][ii]
  disallowed, carrying forward, 1.05[4][b][iii]
  foreclosure sale
    borrower's tax treatment, 12.03[4][a]
    lender's tax treatment, 12.03[4][b], 12.03[5]
  partnership, deductibility, 1.05[4][b]
  partnership, deductibility, App. B, Fm. 1.1 (Sec. 2.7 Comment)
  REIT shareholders, 1.07
  sale/abandonment of partnership interest, 1.05[3][c][v]
Lots. *See* Land
Low-income housing
  deductions, 1.05[2][d]
  rehabilitation, special depreciation, 1.05[2][d]

M

Management
  See also Service partners
  centralized, corporate attribute, 1.05[4][a], 11.02[5][b]
  condominiums, 10.02[3][b]
  improved, as basis of permanent loan, 3.07[2]
  land trusts, 1.08
  lender-developer ventures, 11.02[3][a], 11.02[4][a], 11.02[5][b]
  of mortgaged property, 3.08[4][d]
  partnerships, 1.04, 11.02[3][a]
Marshaling of assets, 7.06
Master deeds (Condominium)
  construction lender requires restrictions in, 10.02[2][d]
  establishes condominium entity, 10.02[2][c]
  permanent lender's checklist, 10.02[3][c]
  sample form, App. B, Fm. 10.1
Materialmen's liens. *See* Mechanics' and materialmen's liens
Maturity term. *See* Amortization
Mechanics' and materialmen's liens
  legal issues, checklist, 4.06

CUMULATIVE INDEX

[References are to paragraphs (¶) and to sample forms in Appendix B. References to the Supplement are preceded by "S."]

priority over construction loan
  condominiums, 10.02[2][c]
  cost overruns, 4.03[2][b]
  developer's warranty, 4.04[2]
  equitable lien doctrine; "stop
    notice" law, 4.02[6][a][iii]
  lender acting as mortgagor, 4.04[4]
  obligatory/optional advances
    doctrine, 4.02[6][a][ii],
    4.02[6][b][i]
  title insurance to protect lender,
    4.02[6][b][i]
  state laws, 4.02[6][a][i],
    4.02[6][b][i]
  surety bonds against, 4.02[6][b],
    4.02[8][b]
  for tenant's alterations, 3.05[5]
  waiver of, 4.02[6][b][i],
    4.02[6][b][iii], 4.04[3],
    4.04[4], 4.06
Mergers
  savings and loan associations,
    S2.02[3][d]
Minimum tax, 1.05[2][d]
Mobile home financing, 2.02[3][d][v], 3.02
Mortgage bankers
  generally, 2.03[2]
  "warehousing" of loans, 11.01[4]
Mortgage brokers, 2.03[1]
Mortgage Guaranty Insurance Corporation (MGIC), 10.02[3][c]
Mortgagee. *See* Lenders
Mortgages. *See also* Amortization;
  Applications; Closings;
  Commitments; Construction
  financing; Deeds of trust; Default
  and foreclosure; Documentation;
  Fees; Gap financing; Interest;
  Junior mortgages; Leasehold
  financing; Lenders; Liens;
  Loan-to-value ratio; Participation
  loans; Permanent financing;
  Purchase-money mortgages;
  Repayment of loans; Roll-over
  mortgages; Secondary mortgage;
  Subdivision financing;
  Variable-rate mortgages
  allocate interest/principal payments,
    12.02[1], 12.02[2][a]

availability, 2.01[1]
bankruptcy trustee's right to obtain,
  4.02[12][b][vi]
blanket mortgages, 10.02[2][c],
  10.03
bonds backed by, 2.01[3], 2.02[7]
cancellation/restructuring of,
  12.03[2]
collateralized loan, 8.07[2]
commitment letter incorporated into,
  3.08[4][d]
condominium, 10.02[3][d]
convertible, pension funds as source
  of, S2.02[6]
cooperative housing, 10.03
covenants
  affirmative, 3.08[4][d]
  miscellaneous, 3.08[4][j]
  negative, 3.08[4][e]
defined, 3.08[1]
definitions in, 3.08[4][a]
demand for, 2.01[1][c]
disposition of property, 12.04
drafting of, 3.08
effect of business cycles, 2.01[1][b],
  7.02[2]
effect on disposition of property,
  12.04
federal intermediation, 2.01[1][b]
  n.5
fee plus leasehold, 8.09[2]
form and substance approved by
  lender, 3.04[13]
futures trading in, 2.01[3]
grants, 3.08[4][b]
inflation-related types, 3.04[3][c]
insurance of. *See* Insurance
large
  insurance companies as source,
    2.02[1]
lessee assumes by purchase option,
  3.05[8]
loan allocations
  commercial banks, 2.02[2][c]
  insurance companies, 2.02[1][c]
  S & Ls, 2.02[3][c]
  savings banks, 2.02[4][b]
  commercial banks, 2.02[2][b]
loan terms, 3.04
  insurance companies, 2.02[1][b]

[References are to paragraphs (¶) and to sample forms in Appendix B. References to the Supplement are preceded by "S."]

Mortgages *(cont'd)*
  loan terms *(cont'd)*
    S & Ls, 2.02[3][b]
    savings banks, 2.02[4][a]
  market information (AMMINET), 2.01[3]
  market structure, 2.01
  note, function of, 3.08[3]
  obtaining, broker's role, 2.03[1]
  open-end, 4.02[6][a][ii]
  outstanding debt, App. A, Table 2
  sale-leaseback compared, 6.04[4]
  sample form, App. B, Fm. 3.4
  secured/unsecured claims in bankruptcy, 4.02[12][b][ii]
  servicing of. *See* Correspondents
  sources of, 2.02, 3.02, 11.01, 10.02[3][a]
  tax-exempt, 3.04[3][b], 8.06
  in tax-free exchanges, 8.02[3]
  uniform documents, use of, 3.08[2]
  "warehousing" of, 2.02[2], 11.01[4]
  warranties and representations, 3.08[4][c]

Mortgaging out
  construction lenders' attitudes, 4.02[3]
  tax shelter device, 1.05[2][b], 12.01[4]

Multifamily housing
  See also Condominiums; Cooperatives; Rehabilitation; Urban renewal
  certificate of occupancy, 3.04[9][a]
  conversion from rental to condominiums, 10.02[5]
  financing
    participation loans, 11.01[2]
    S & Ls, 2.02[3][c], 2.02[3][d]
    savings banks, 2.02[4][a]
  inflation's effect on supply, 2.01[1][c]
  uniform mortgage documents, 3.08[2]

Mutual savings banks
  geographical distribution, 2.02[4]
  loan allocations, 2.02[4][b]
  loan terms, 2.02[4][a]
  regulation of portfolios, 2.02[4][c]
  source of funds, 2.02[4][a]

N

National Credit Union Administration, S2.02[6]
Nondisturbance agreements. *See* Attornment agreements
Non-income-producing property, 1.05[2][c]
  See also Land
Non-profit corporations, usury exemption, 504[1]
Nonrecourse financing
  See also Liability
  bankruptcy changes to recourse claim, 4.02[12][b][iii]
  defined, 1.05[1] n.36
  by lenders, 1.05[4][b][iii]
  drafting techniques suggested, 1.05[4][b][iii]
  effect on "at risk" rule, 1.05[2][d] n.90
  effect on cost tax basis, 12.01[3][b], 12.03[2][a][i]
  liability, effect on, 1.05[4][a], 1.05[4][b][iii]
  need for in subdivision financing, 9.01[1][b]
  in purchase-money mortgages, 7.04[1][d][i]

Notes
  See also Bonds; Mortgages
  construction loan, 3.08[3], 4.03[1]
  developer's, use to cover construction costs, 4.02[8][a]
  function; contents, 3.08[3]
  participation loans
    payable to lead lender only, 11.01[1], 11.01[6][a], 11.01[7]
    separate notes, one mortgage, 11.01[8]
  personal suit on by lender, 3.08[4][g]
  sale at discount not usury, 5.05[2]
  sample form, App. B, Fm. 3.3

Nursing homes, 2.02[3][d][v]

O

Office building leases, 3.05
Office of Interstate Land Sales Registration (OILSR), 9.03[2]

[*References are to paragraphs (¶) and to sample forms in Appendix B. References to the Supplement are preceded by "S."*]

"One, two, threes," S3.04[3][c]
Ordinary income
    to borrower, cancelled debt; exceptions, 12.03[2][a][i], 12.03[3][a]
    collapsible property, sale, 1.05[3][a]
    dealer gain as, 1.02[2][a]
    deducting bad debts against, 12.03[2][b][iii]
    leaseback rents as, 6.04[2]
    to lender
        defaulted property conveyance, 12.03[3][b], 12.03[5]
        foreclosure sale, 12.03[4][b], 12.03[5]
        interest/discount gain, 12.02[1]
        purchase-money foreclosure, 12.03[4][b][ii]
    partnership, offsetting, 1.05[2]
    property transfers within entities, 12.04[2]
    sale-leaseback gain as, 6.04[3][c]
    subdivision profits as, 9.05
    taxation under E.R.T.A., S1.05[2][d]
Owners
    See also Co-owners; Developers; Fee owners; Ownership entities; Partnerships; specific topics, specific types of ownership
    lender's concern with change of, 3.04[8]
Ownership entity
    See also Continuity of enterprise
    generally, 1.01-1.08
    for high-credit lease financing, 8.05[3]
    for lender-developer ventures, 11.02[4]
    property transfers between, tax effects, 12.04[2]
    selection process, 1.01
    usury exemptions, 5.01

P

Parking lots
    condemnation, effect on, 8.05[2][c]
    environmental controls, 3.04[9][c]
    shopping centers, mortgage rider, 3.08[5]

    Subchapter S suitable, 1.06
Participation agreements, 11.01[6][a], 11.01[7]
Participation loans
    borrower's default/bankruptcy, 11.01[6][a], 11.01[6][b], 11.01[7], 11.01[8]
    business/legal reasons for, 11.01[3]
    construction financing, 11.01[2], 11.01[3]
    convertible, S3.04[3][a]
    defined, 11.01[1]
    generally, 8.07[1], 11.01
    lead lender
        bankruptcy of, 11.01[6][b], 11.01[7]
        fiduciary responsibility to participants, 11.01[6][a], 11.01[7]
    legal pitfalls, 11.01[6]
    life insurance companies, 3.04[3][c], 11.01[2], 11.01[5]
    permanent financing, 11.01[4]
    sample agreement, App. B, Fm. 11.1
    S&Ls, 2.02, [3][d][v], 11.01[2]
    securities law considerations, 11.01[6][d]
    separate notes, one mortgage, 11.01[8]
    separate notes, sample agreement, App. B, Fm. 11.2
    usury considerations, 11.01[6][c]
Partners. *See* Co-owners; Service partners
Partnership agreement
    aggregate approach, 1.02[2], 1.05[3][b][i]
    allocations
        contributed property, 1.05[3][b][ii]
        income; loss; depreciation, 1.05[3][b]
        retroactive, 1.05[3][b][iii]
    drafting suggestions
        continuity of life, 1.05[4][a]
        transferability of interests, 1.05[4][a]
    indemnity agreements in, 1.05[4][a]
    sample form, App. B, Fm. 1.1

REAL ESTATE FINANCING I-28

[References are to paragraphs (¶) and to sample forms in Appendix B. References to the Supplement are preceded by "S."]

Partnerships
See also Limited partnerships; Management; Service partners
advantages/disadvantages, 1.04, 1.05
advantages for income-producing property, 1.05[2][b], 8.05[3]
allocation of income or loss, 1.05[3][b]
basis problems, 1.05[4][b]
collapsible provisions, 1.05[3][a]
continuity of enterprise, 1.04, 1.05[1], 1.05[4][a]
corporations compared, 1.05
general vs. limited, 1.04
joint ventures as, 1.03
lender-developer joint ventures as, 11.02[2], 11.02[3][b], 11.02[4][a]
liquidation, 1.04
liquidation
  lender-developer ventures, 11.02[5][e]
  tax consequences, 1.05[5][e], 11.02[5][f]
liquidation; sale of share, taxes, 1.05[3][a][i], 1.05[3][b][i], 1.05[3][c][v]
net leases, tax effects, 8.05
property exchanges among members, 8.02[2]
property transfers within, taxation, 12.04[2]
retroactive amendment of, 1.05[3][b][iii]
sale-leaseback deals within, 6.04[3][c] ns. 63, 64
tax advantages, 1.05[3]
tenancy in common as, 1.02[2][b][4]
Payment of loans
See also Acceleration of debt; Amortization; Prepayment
decline in, reasons, 2.02[3][a]
late payment
  as default, 3.08[4][g]
  charges, deductibility, 12.02[2][a]
  charges for, as usury, 5.02[4][a]
Pension funds as lenders, 2.02[6], 11.01[2]
  bank-sponsored, S2.02[2][a]
  chart of real estate holdings of 97 largest, S.App. A, Table 4
  taxation of, S2.02[6]
  types of loans offered by, S2.02[6]
Permanent financing
See also Commitments (Permanent loan); Construction financing; Mortgages; Subdivision financing
borrower covenants to use original lender, 4.05
closing the loan, 3.09
condominiums
  documentation, 10.02[3][d]
  lender's checklist, 10.02[3][c]
  lender's concerns, 10.02[3][b]
  insured by federal government, 10.01
  legal complexities in, 10.02[1]
  sources for unit purchasers, 10.02[3][a]
cooperative housing, 10.03
drafting the loan instrument, 3.08
"floor"/"ceiling" amounts, 3.04[2], 4.02[1], 4.02[3]
forms, preclosed/unique, 4.05
generally, 3.01-3.09
junior loans, lender's protection against, 7.05[2]
lease requirements by lender, 3.05, 3.08[4][i]
lender also co-venturer, conflicts, 11.02[3][b]
lender approves construction changes, 4.04[5]
lender's defenses as holder in due course, 4.03[1]
lender's role in financing rental unit conversions, 10.02[5]
participation loans uncommon, 11.01[5]
sources
  commercial banks, 2.02[2][b], 2.02[2][c]
  insurance companies, 2.02[1][c]
  pension funds, 2.02[6]
  REITs, 2.02[5]
  S&Ls, 2.02[3][c]
  savings banks, 2.02[4][a]
terms and conditions, 3.04

[References are to paragraphs (¶) and to sample forms in Appendix B. References to the Supplement are preceded by "S."]

Permits
See also Certificate of occupancy; specific topics
building, 3.04[9], 4.03
cause of breach of commitment, 3.06 n.178
land development, 9.01[3], 9.01[4]
preconstruction, 3.04[9][c]
Personal holding company tax, 1.05[3][c][iii], 1.05[5][a]
Personal liability. *See* Liability
Personal property
See also Inventory
effect of "at risk" rule, 1.05[2][d] n.91
fixtures, defined in mortgage, 3.08[4][a]
insurance required by lender, 3.04[12]
mobile homes, 2.02[3][d][v]
stored materials, 4.04[3]
"Piggyback" mortgage loans, 8.07
See also Participation loans
Platform loans, 3.04[2], 4.02[1], 7.04[2]
Pledged account mortgage (PAM). *See* Flexible loan insurance program (FLIP)
Points
as deduction, 1.05[2][c], 1.05[2][d], 12.01[1][b]
as income to lender, 12.01[2][b]
as interest, 1.05[2][c], 12.01[1][b], 12.01[2][b]
Pollution, 3.04[9][c]
Preconstruction permits, 3.04[9][c]
Prefinancing
checklist of considerations, 3.01[1]
selection of ownership entity, 1.01
charges exempt from usury, 5.02[3][b], 5.03[7]
construction note, 4.03[1]
default as device to avoid penalties, 3.04[5], 3.08[4][g]
of interest, deductibility, 1.05[2][d], 12.01[1][b], 12.02[2][a]
lender terms
insurance companies, 2.02[1][b]
restrictions; penalties, 3.04[5], 3.04[16]
purchase-money mortgages, 7.04[1][b], 7.04[1][c][i], 9.01[1][a], 9.01[1][c]
releases additional land used as collateral, 3.04[16]
voluntary/involuntary, 3.04[5]
Prepayment
convertible participation loan, S3.04[18]
and due-on-sale clause, S3.04[5]
variable-rate mortgages, S3.04[3][c]
Price level adjusted mortgage (PLAM), 3.04[3][c]
Principal, repayment of. *See* Amortization; Repayment of loans
Private offerings, S1.05[1]
Profits. *See* Capital gains; Income
Promissory notes. *See* Notes
Property
See also Construction; Default and foreclosure; Exchanges; Income-producing property; Land; Non-income-producing property; Personal property; Purchase of property; Sale of property; specific type of property
after-acquired, 3.08[4][a], 3.08[4][c], 7.04[1][a]
bankruptcy trustee's right to sell, lease or mortgage, 4.02[12][b][vi]
described in construction loan application, 4.02[2]
disposition of
effect of mortgage, 12.04
tax treatment of lender, 12.03[5]
lender's upkeep expenses, tax treatment, 12.02[3]
"like kind" in exchanges, 8.02[2]
value
foreclosure bid price as, 12.03[4][b][ii]
sale-leaseback price, 5.05[4]
worthless, abandonment, 12.03[3]
Property Report, 9.03[2], 9.03[3]
Purchase-leaseback. *See* Sale and leaseback

REAL ESTATE FINANCING I-30

[References are to paragraphs (¶) and to sample forms in Appendix B. References to the Supplement are preceded by "S."]

Purchase-money mortgages
borrower's considerations, 7.04[1][c], 7.04[1][d][i]
cancellation of debt, 12.03[2][a][i]
capital gains treatment, 7.04[1][d][iii]
as high-ratio financing device, 7.04[1][b], 8.04
incident to asset swap financing, 7.04[1][e]
legal definition, 7.04[1][a]
lender's tax liability upon default, 12.03[4][b][ii]
liability to deficiency judgments, 7.04[1][d][i]
lien priority of, 7.04[1][a]
partial release of lien on, 7.04[1][c][iii]
in subdivision financing, 9.01[1]
   restrictions on development loan necessary, 9.01[1][d]
   risk to seller when subordinated, 9.01[1][b], 9.01[1][d]
subordinated
   borrower's considerations, 7.04[1][c][ii], 7.04[1][c][iii]
   lender's considerations, 7.04[1][d]
   to other financing, 7.04[1][c][ii], 7.04[1][d][ii]
terms, 7.04[1][b]
usury implications, 5.02[2]

Purchase of property
See also Buy-sell agreements; Default and foreclosure; Exchange of property; Purchase-money mortgages; Sale and leaseback; Sale of property
tenant's purchase option, 3.05[8], 8.05[2][d]
trend among lenders, 11.02[6]

R

Radius restrictions, 3.05[3]
Real estate investment trusts (REITs)
asset swap to avoid bankruptcy, 7.04[1][e]
developer's reasons for use, 2.02[5]
interest rates, 4.01[3]
as lenders, 2.02[5], 3.02, 5.05[7], 7.03
construction loans, 4.01, 11.01[2]
joint ventures with developers, 11.02[4][b], 11.02[5][b]
as ownership entities, 1.07

Real property taxes
construction period, deductibility, 1.05[2][d]
contesting of assessment, 3.08[4][d], 7.04[1][c][i]
cooperative housing shareholders' liability, 10.03
default in payments, 3.08[4][g] n.255
escrow accounts held by lender, 3.04[6]
exempt from usury, 5.03[6]
junior/senior lender, rights, 7.05[2], 7.06
mortgagee pays
   remedies, 3.08[4][d], 3.08[4][j], 12.02[3]
nondepreciable property, deductibility, 1.05[2][c]
split between owner/lender, 3.08[4][f]
tenant pays, 8.05

Recapture of accelerated depreciation, S1.05[2][d]

Receivership
preference rights of junior lenders, generally, 7.06
upon default, 3.08[4][g], 4.04[8]

Recourse financing
bankruptcy changes nonrecourse to, 4.02[12][b][iii]
basis problems caused by, 1.05[4][b]
construction lender requires, 4.02[5]

Refinancing
See also Junior mortgages; Mortgaging out; Sale and leaseback; Sale-repurchase financing; Wraparound mortgages
advantages of secondary loans over, 7.02
effect on purchase-money loan, 7.04[1][d][ii]
lenders' defenses against, 3.04[3][c]

[*References are to paragraphs (¶) and to sample forms in Appendix B. References to the Supplement are preceded by "S."*]

prepayment clause may block, 3.04[5]
restructuring by original lender, 12.03[2][a][ii]
use to decrease nondeductible amortization, 1.05[2][b]
Regulation. *See* Federal government; State regulation
Regulation Q
interest ceilings, phase-out of, S2.02[3][d]
Rehabilitation
See also Insurance, proceeds; Repairs
historic structures, S1.05[2][d]
investment credit under E.R.T.A., S1.05[2][d]
low-income housing, 1.05[2][d]
nonresidential buildings, 1.05[2][d]
Related parties
effect on "at risk" rule, 1.05[2][d] n.90
in foreclosure sale, 12.03[4][a] n.159
in sale-leaseback, 6.04[3][b], 6.04[3][c], 6.04[4]
Releases
in condominium financing, 4.03[2][c], 7.05[2], 10.02[2][c], 10.02[5]
of subdivided portions protects seller/developer, 9.01[1][c]
Renegotiable rate mortgages, S3.04[3][c]
Rents
See also Cash flow; Ground leases; Leases; Tenants
advance payments prohibited, 3.08[4][i]
assignment
insurance companies require, 2.02[1][d], 8.05
to lender, 3.08[4][i], 12.02[4], 8.05[2]
effect of default; casualty; condemnation, 3.05[2], 8.05[2]
ground rent, 6.03[9], 11.02[1]
in high-credit leases, 8.05
junior lender gets under receivership, 7.06
lender's license to collect, 3.08[4][i]
multifamily housing, 2.01[1][c]

original tenant covenants to pay, 3.05[1]
percentage of income as additional, 3.05[4], 11.02[1]
platform loans based on, 3.04[2], 4.02[1], 7.04[2]
pledge of, 3.08[4][i]
rent control, 2.01[1][c], 3.02
sale-leaseback payments
deductibility, 6.04[2], 6.04[3], 6.04[4]
fair market value of, 6.04[3][a], 6.04[3][b], 6.04[3][c], 6.04[4]
reallocation, 6.04[3][c]
usury implications, 5.05[4]
taxable to owner, 12.02[4]
Repairs
See also Rehabilitation
in high-credit leases, 8.05[2]
lender's expenses for, 12.02[3]
owner's duty; lender's remedies, 3.08[4][d]
Representations. *See* Warranties and representations
Residential property. *See* Housing
Restoration of property. *See* Insurance; Rehabilitation; Repairs
Restraints on alienation, 3.04[7], 3.04[8]
Restructuring of debt, 12.03[2]
Retirement. *See* Co-owners, status change
Revenue Act of 1978, 1.05[2][d]
Risk insurance. *See* Insurance
Roll-over mortgages (ROM), 3.04[3][c]
Rule against perpetuities, 6.04[1][c]
"Rule of validation," 5.05[1]

S

Sale-buyback. *See* Sale-repurchase financing
Sale and leaseback
See also Rents, sale-leaseback payments; Sale-repurchase financing
debt financing, compared to; mixed with, 6.04[4]
as disguised installment sale, 6.04[3][d]

[References are to paragraphs (¶) and to sample forms in Appendix B. References to the Supplement are preceded by "S."]

Sale and leaseback *(cont'd)*
  as disguised loan, 6.04[3][b]
  flexibility, 6.04[4]
  generally, 6.04
  insurance companies as buyers, 2.02[1], 6.04[2], 11.02[1]
  land and improvements
    purchaser's business/tax considerations, 6.04[2][b]
    seller's business/tax considerations, 6.04[2][a]
  land only, 6.04[1], 8.09[1]
  leasehold, valuation of, 6.04[3]
  long-/short-term results, 6.04[4]
  profit-motivated transaction, S6.04[3][e]
  REITs as buyers, 2.02[5]
  repurchase options, 5.05[4], 6.04[3][b], 6.04[3][d]
  sample form, App. B, Fm. 6.1
  tax advantages, 5.05[4], 6.04
  tax planning, 6.04[3][b][ii], S6.04[3][b][iii]
  tax pitfalls, 6.04[3]
  usury exemption requirements, 5.05[4]
Sale of property
  See also Buy-sell agreements; Condominiums; Default and foreclosure; Exchanges; Installment sales contracts; Purchase-money mortgages; Purchase of property; Sale and leaseback
  bad debt loss as, 12.03[2][b][iii]
  in circumvention of usury, 5.02[2]
  default conveyance as, 12.03[3][a]
  Interstate Land Sales Act, 9.03
  mortgaged, tax effects, 12.04
  partial, upon default, 3.08[4][g]
  restricted in joint venture, 11.02[5][d]
  restriction by lender, 3.04[8], 3.08[4][e]
Sale-repurchase financing
  tax advantages, 5.05[6]
  using installment buyback, 8.09[3]
  usury exemption requirements, 5.05[6]
Sales contracts
  See also Installment sales contracts

condominium lender may restrict or cancel, 10.02[2][d]
recommended for sale and leaseback, 6.04
subdivision lender may require, 9.01[2]
Savings, as source of mortgage money, 2.01[1][a], 2.02[3][a]
Savings and loan associations (S&Ls)
  condominium loans by, 10.02[3][a], 10.02[5]
  cooperative housing loans by, 10.03
  federal, regulation, 2.02[3][d]
  inflation-related mortgages, 3.04[3][c]
  loan allocations, 2.02[3][c]
  loan terms, 2.02[3][b], 2.02[3][d], 4.04[4]
  mergers between, S2.02[3][d]
  participation loans, 8.07[1], 11.01[2]
  proposals to aid, S2.02[3][d]
  regulation of portfolios, 2.02[3][d]
  shared appreciation mortgages, S3.04[3][c]
  sources of funds, 2.02[3][a]
  state regulation, 2.02[3][d]
Savings banks. *See* Mutual savings banks
Secondary mortgage lenders, 7.03
Secondary mortgage market
  See also Discounts
  generally, 2.02[7]
  usury implications, 5.05[2]
Second mortgages. *See* Junior mortgages
Securities (Real estate)
  condominiums as, 10.02[2][b]
  cooperative housing shares as, 10.03
  federal regulation, 1.05[1], 10.02[2][b]
  limited partnership shares as, 1.05[1]
  participation loan certificates as, 11.01[6][d]
  REIT, 1.07
  worthless, as tax loss, 12.03[2][b][iii], 12.03[4][b][i]
Security deposits
  condominiums, unit purchase, 10.02[2][b]
  for construction loan, 4.02[13]
  for permanent loan commitment, 3.06

[*References are to paragraphs (¶) and to sample forms in Appendix B. References to the Supplement are preceded by "S."*]

lessee's, lender not liable, 3.05[1]
Seller seconds, S3.04[3][c]
Service contracts, as lender's loan guarantee, 8.05 n.34
Service income. *See* Operating income
Service partners
   compensation; allocations, 1.05[3][c]
   compensation; allocations, App. B, Fm. 1.1 (Secs. 3.2, 3.4 Comment)
   taxation, 11.02[5][f]
   taxation, App. B, Fm. 1.1 (Secs. 3.1A, 3.2, 3.2A Comment)
Servicing agents. *See* Correspondents
Set-aside letters
   caveats for lender in, 9.01[3]
   sample form, App. B, Fm. 9.2
Shared appreciation mortgages (SAMs), S3.04[3][c], S.App. B, Fm. 3.15
Shopping centers
   See also Leases; Rents; Tenants
   industrial revenue bonds for, 8.06
   leases
      exclusives; radius rules; co-tenancy, 3.05[3]
      future performance in bankruptcy, 4.02[12][b][v]
      lender's requirements, 3.05
      percentage rental, 3.05[4]
   lender approves improvements
      by landlord, 3.08[5]
      by tenant, 3.04[11], 3.05[5]
   special mortgage riders for, 3.08[5]
Short-term financing
   See also Construction financing; Gap financing
   business cycles affect, 2.01[1][b]
   commercial banks as major source, 2.02[2]
   developers "shop" for, clause to avoid, 4.04[3]
Specific performance, 3.06, 4.05, 10.02[1], 11.02[3][b]
Split financing, 8.09, 11.02[1]
Standby commitments. *See* Commitments
State regulation
   See also Foreign states; Local law
   commercial banks, 2.02[2][d]
   commercial banks, App. A, Table 1

condominiums, 10.01, 10.02[1], 10.02[2][b]
corporations, determining tax status, 5.05[3]
of deficiency judgments, 3.08[4][g]
life insurance companies, 2.02[1][c], 2.02[1][d], 11.02[1]
environmental controls, 3.04[9][c]
interest on escrow accounts, 3.04[6]
mechanics'/materialmen's liens, priority of, 4.02[6][a][i]
mutual savings banks, 2.02[4][c]
of power of sale, 3.08[4][g]
possession of property after default, 3.08[4][g]
recording costs, wraparound notes, 7.04[3][b][ii]
REITs exempt, 2.02[5]
S&Ls, 2.02[3][d]
usury, 5.01, 5.04, 5.05[1], 5.05[7]
usury, App. A, Table 3
Stockholders
   cooperative housing corporations, 10.03
   ordinary income, avoidance, 1.05[3][a][ii]
Stocks. *See* Securities
Straight-line depreciation, S1.05[2][b], S1.05[2][d]
Subchapter S corporations, 1.06
Subcontractors
   See also Mechanics' and materialmen's liens
   bonding of, 4.02[8][b]
   construction stages, role in, 4.04[3]
   payments to by lender, 4.04[4]
Subdividers. *See* Developers
Subdivision financing
   See also Dealers; Developers; Land
   ample and extendable loan period desirable, 9.01
   development loan agreement, sample, App. B, Fm. 9.3
   disbursement procedure, 9.01[4]
   distinguished from condominiums, 10.02[1]
   documentation of land development loan, 9.01[4]
   generally, 9.01-9.05
   hazards for developer/lender, 9.01

REAL ESTATE FINANCING I-34

[References are to paragraphs (¶) and to sample forms in Appendix B. References to the Supplement are preceded by "S."]

Subdivision financing *(cont'd)*
  Interstate Land Sales Act, 9.03
  lender's lien priority, 9.01[1][d]
  local community requirements, 9.01[3]
  phase development, 9.01[1][d]
  purchase-money loans, 9.01[1]
  requirements for land development loan, 9.01[3]
  sources
    institutional lenders, 9.01[2]
    purchase-money mortgage lenders, 9.01[1]
    Title X-sponsored, 9.02
Subordinate financing. *See* Junior mortgages
Subsidiaries of lenders, 11.02[4][b]
Subsidies, interest rates, 2.02[7][c]
Surety bonds
  against contractor's default, 4.02[8][b]
  effect of contractor guarantee, 4.02[8][e]
  against mechanics' liens
    for construction lender/contractor, 4.02[6][b][ii], 4.02[8][b]
    for construction lender/title company, 4.02[6][b][i]
  guarantee subdivision improvements, 9.01[1][c], 9.01[3]
  guarantee subdivision improvements, sample agreement, App. B, Fm. 9.1
Surveys
  costs of, 3.04[15]
  lenders require, 4.02[13], 10.02[2][c], 9.01[3]
  at permanent loan closing, 3.09[2], 3.09[3]
  update of during construction, 4.04[3]

T

Takeout commitments. *See* Commitments (Permanent loan)
Tax avoidance
  See also Deductions; Tax shelters
  allocations, primary purpose, 1.05[3][b][i]
  sale and leaseback method, 5.05[4], 6.04[3][b][i]
  straw corporations, 5.05[3]
Tax basis. *See* Basis
Tax consequences
  mortgage on real property, 12.01
  mortgagor-mortgagee relationship, 12.02
  mortgagor's default, 12.03
Tax-exempt organizations
  quasi-exempt, joint venture vehicles, 11.02[4][b]
  as sale-leaseback purchasers, 6.04[2], 6.04[3]
Tax exemption
  industrial revenue bonds, 3.04[3][b], 8.06
Tax-free exchanges. *See* Exchanges
Tax-free return of capital, 1.05[2][b]
Tax planning
  corporations, 1.05[3][a][ii]
  debt restructuring agreement, 12.03[2][c]
  generally, 12.01-12.04
  high-credit lease financing, 8.05[3]
  partnerships, 1.05[3][a][i]
    avoiding basis problems, 1.05[4][b][iii]
  in sale-leaseback, 6.04[3][b][ii]
Tax preference items, 1.05[2][d]
  See also Capital gains
Tax rates, corporations, 1.05[5][a]
Tax Reform Act of 1969, 1.05[2][d]
Tax Reform Act of 1976, 1.05[2][d]
Tax shelters
  See also Deductions; High-ratio financing; Mortgaging out
  generally, 1.05[2][a]
  income-producing property, 1.05[2][b]
  investor income, 1.05[2]
  recent legislation, 1.05[2][d]
  sale of qualifying corporation, 5.05[3]
  tax opinion, S1.05[2][d]
Taxes
  See also Deductions; Double taxation; Income; Losses; Minimum tax; Real property taxes; Tax shelters
  accumulated earnings,

[References are to paragraphs (¶) and to sample forms in Appendix B. References to the Supplement are preceded by "S."]

1.05[3][c][iii], 1.05[5][a]
audit of taxpayer by IRS, 1.02[2][a], 6.04[2][a][ii]
condominium advantages, 10.01
effect of ownership entity selected, 1.01-1.08
FICA, lender's liability, 4.04[4]
generally, 12.01-12.04
lessee with "no competition" covenant, 3.05[3] n.162
recording taxes, state, 7.04[3][b][ii]
state, lender protected from, 4.02[13]
sale-leaseback's effect on, 6.01-6.04
Taxpayers. *See* Related parties; specific topics
Tenancy in common
bankruptcy sale, effect, 4.02[12][b][vi]
in condominium common areas, 10.01
non-tax factors, 1.02[1]
partnership, treatment as, 1.02[2][b][4]
tax considerations, 1.02[2]
advantages, 1.02[2][a]
aggregate/entity, 1.02[2]
disadvantages, 1.02[2][b]
Tenants
See also Attornment agreements; Co-tenancy; Leases; Rents; Shopping centers
acceptance letter, sample, App. B, Fm. 3.7
assignment of interest in lease, 3.08[4][i], 8.05
chain lease, rights/obligations, 3.05[2]
default by
bankruptcy trustee's duties, 4.02[12][b][v]
special mortgage rider, 3.08[5]
three-party agreement, 3.08[4][i]
major
acceptance by required for final advance, 4.04[6]
bankruptcy of, 3.08[4][f]
co-tenancy requirements, 3.05[3]
lender's requirements, 3.05, 8.05[2]
as self-insurer, 3.04[12]

purchase option, 3.05[8], 8.05[2][d]
remedies restricted, 3.05[3], 8.05[2][a]
rights in landlord's bankruptcy, 4.02[12][b][v]
subsequent, notice to, lease restrictions, 3.08[4][i]
substitution of after commitment, 3.04[17], 3.05[2], 3.05[4]
subtenants, leasehold financing, 6.02[2][b]
Title
effect on interest deductibility, 12.02[2][a]
to improvements made by ground lessee, 6.03[10]
in installment sale contract, 8.03, 8.09[3]
joint ventures, problems in holding, 11.02[2]
in purchase-money financing, 7.04[1][a], 12.03[4][b][ii]
in sale and leaseback, 6.04[1][c]
under deed of trust/mortgage, 3.08[1]
warranty to in loan instrument, 3.08[4][c]
zoning violations, effect, 3.04[9][b]
Title insurance
companies
closing disbursement letter to title company, sample, App. B, Fm. 3.8
Construction Disbursement Program, 4.02[8][c], 4.04[4]
indemnifications asked by, 4.02[6][b][i]
role at closing, 3.09[1]
condominiums, to protect lender, 10.02[2][c], 10.02[3][b]
in land development loan, 9.01[3]
for leasehold lender, 6.01[2]
lender's requirements, 3.04[15]
policy
ongoing update of during construction, 4.04[3]
permanent loan closing, 3.09[2], 3.09[3]
protecting construction lender from mechanics' liens, 4.02[6][b][i]

[References are to paragraphs (¶) and to sample forms in Appendix B. References to the Supplement are preceded by "S."]

Title insurance *(cont'd)*
  sale and leaseback, 6.04[1][c]
  sale and leaseback, App. B, Fm. 6.1 (Sec. II Comment)
  wraparound lender's needs, 7.04[3][b][i], 7.04[3][b][iii]
Title X financing, 9.02
Trust accounts. *See* Escrows
Trust deed mortgages. *See* Deeds of trust
Trust departments as lenders, S2.02[6]
Trustees in bankruptcy
  appointment, 4.02[12][b][ii]
  powers over leases and contracts, 4.02[12][b][v]
  right to sell, lease or mortgage property, 4.02[12][b][vi]

U

Unconscionability
  convertible participation loans, S3.04[18]
  shared appreciation mortgages, S3.04[3][c]
Underwriting standards
  condominium construction loan, 10.02[2][a], 10.02[2][c]
  land subdivision, 9.01[2]
Uniform Commercial Code, 3.04[3][c], 3.08[3], 3.08[4][a], 4.03[1], 4.04[3], 11.01[6][a]
Uniform Consumer Credit Code, 5.01
Uniform Limited Partnership Act, 1.04, 1.05, 4.03[2][d] n.166, 11.02[2], 11.02[4][a], 11.02[5][e]
Uniform Partnership Act, 1.04, 1.05, 11.02[2], 11.02[5][e]
Urban Development Action Grant (UDGA), 8.06
Urban renewal
  See also Rehabilitation
  insurance companies lead in, 2.02[1]
  master-leased projects, lender requirements, 3.05
  S & L financing, 2.02[3][d][v]
Usury
  circumvention devices, 5.04[1], 5.05
  conflicts of law, 5.05[1]
  convertible participation loans, S3.04[3][a]
  Depository Institutions Deregulation and Monetary Control Act, S5.01
  developer states loan is not, 4.02[13]
  elements of, 5.02
  estoppel against borrower, 5.05[2]
  exemptions from
    bona fide sale at discount, 5.05[2]
    closing costs, 5.03[5]
    compound interest, 5.02[4][b]
    corporations, 5.04[1]
    equity participation by lenders, 5.05[8], 11.02[3][c]
    expenses of collection, 5.03[8]
    federally chartered lenders, 2.01[3]
    high-risk investments, 5.02[3][a]
    holder in due course, 5.05[2]
    installment sales contracts, 5.05[5], 5.05[6]
    interest paid in advance, 5.02[4][b]
    interest subject to profits, 5.02[3][b]
    late payment charges, 5.03[8]
    loan prepayment charges, 5.02[3][b], 5.03[7]
    sale and leaseback, 5.05[4]
    statutory, 5.04
    taxes paid by mortgagor, 5.03[6]
  federal preemption of ceilings, 5.01
  fees as
    brokerage fees, 5.03[3]
    commitment fees, 5.03[1]
    service fees exempt, 5.02[4][a], 5.03[4]
    origination fees as interest, 5.03[2], 5.03[3]
  generally, 5.01-5.05
  Housing and Community Development Act of 1980, S5.01
  interest rate computation in, 5.02[4][b]
  interest rates in accelerated repayment, 5.03[8]
  "legal rate" of interest, 5.02[4]
  participation loans, one lender exempt, 11.01[6][c]

[*References are to paragraphs (¶) and to sample forms in Appendix B. References to the Supplement are preceded by "S."*]

penalties, 5.01
shared appreciation mortgages (SAMs), S5.02[4][d]
state statutes, 5.01, 5.04, 5.05[1], 5.05[7]
  analysis, App. A, Table 3
Subchapter S use, 1.06
title company endorsement advised, 3.04[9][d]
unlawful intent
  disguised loan, 5.05[4], 5.05[6]
  exculpatory provisions, 5.02[1]
  objectively determined, 5.02[1]
  variable-rate mortgages, 5.02[4][d]
  wraparound mortgages, 7.04[3][b][i]

V

Valuation. *See* Appraisals and valuations; Loan-to-value ratio
Variable-rate mortgages, 2.01[3]
  as alternative to due-on-sale clause, 3.04[8]
  Comptroller of the Currency regulations, S3.04[3][c]
  credit unions allowed to offer, S2.02[6]
  as inflation-related device, 3.04[3][c]
  prepayment, S3.04[3][c]
  usury considerations, 5.02[4][d]
Voluntary conveyance to mortgagee, 12.03[3], 12.03[4][b][ii]

W

Waivers
  bonding requirement, by construction lender, 4.02[8][b]
  in loan instruments, 3.08[4][g]
  of mechanics' liens, 4.02[6][b][i], 4.02[6][b][iii], 4.04[3], 4.04[4], 4.06
  by parties secondarily liable on construction note, 4.03[1]
Warehouses
  leases, lender's requirements, 3.05
  Subchapter S suitable, 1.06
"Warehousing" mortgage loans, 2.02[2], 11.01[4], 11.01[6][a] n.17

Sample form for, App. B, Fm. 11.3
Warranties and representations
  developer's, in building loan agreement, 4.04[2], 4.04[3]
  mortgage clauses, 3.08[4][c], 3.08[4][j]
  shopping center riders, 3.08[5]
Waste covenants, 1.05[4][b][iii], 3.08[4][d], 10.02[3][d]
Water pollution. *See* Pollution
Workouts, S3.08[4][g]
Worthless debts
  junior lender ascertains, 12.03[6]
  lender's tax deduction
    foreclosure, 12.03[4][b]
    purchase-money reacquisition, 12.03[4][b][ii]
    voluntary conveyance, 12.03[3][c]
Worthless property, 12.03[3]
Wraparound mortgages
  advantages for rental unit conversions, 10.02[5]
  advantages to lender, 5.05[7], 7.04[3]
  described, 5.05[7], 7.04[3]
  protective covenants for participants, 7.04[3][a], 7.04[3][b]
  subrogation in, 7.04[3][b][iii]
  terms, generally, 7.04[3]
  usury implications, 5.05[7], 7.04[3][b][i]

Y

Year
  See also specific topics
  corporation/partnership, 1.05[5][b]
  Subchapter S, 1.06

Z

Zoning
  coastal areas, 3.04[9][c]
  compliance; insurance, 3.04[9][b]
  considerations in land development, 9.01[3]
  lease clauses involving, 3.05[3]

THE LAW OF REAL ESTATE FINANCING

SPECIAL REPORT: IMPACT OF THE ECONOMIC RECOVERY TAX ACT OF 1981 ON REAL ESTATE INVESTMENTS

> The following brief synopsis of the effects of the Economic Recovery Tax Act of 1981 on real estate investments has been prepared by the publisher. A more detailed analysis will be provided by the authors in the forthcoming first supplement to this volume. For complete coverage of present and prior law, this summary should be used in conjunction with the main volume as indicated by the cross-references provided throughout.

In passing the Economic Recovery Tax Act of 1981, Congress has shifted the emphasis in tax policy towards encouraging capital investment. Real estate investors should be particularly pleased with the new depreciation rules, which in many cases will substantially increase depreciation write-offs. In addition, the increased investment credit for rehabilitation expenditures will undoubtedly stimulate a boom in older buildings and historic structures.

The following material briefly discusses the significant provisions of the new tax law for real estate investors. For general discussion of tax law affecting real estate investment, see ¶ 1.05[2] of this book.

Copyright © 1981 by Warren, Gorham & Lamont, Inc., 210 South Street, Boston, Mass. 02111

REDUCTIONS IN INDIVIDUAL RATES AND CAPITAL GAINS TAX

The new law provides for reductions in tax rates for all taxpayers on the following schedule (the figures are cumulative, i.e., the total reduction is 23 percent):

1981	1¼%
1982	10%
1983	19%
1984	23%

In addition, the top marginal rate is reduced from 70 to 50 percent in 1982. Thus, the maximum effective rate on long-term capital gains is reduced from 28 to 20 percent (the result of multiplying the 50 percent top rate by the 40 percent portion of long-term capital gains subject to tax).

Special Rule For 1981

In order not to discourage the realization of long-term gains for the balance of 1981, the law provides that the maximum 20 percent rate on net capital gains applies to sales or exchanges occurring after June 9, 1981 (even though the top marginal rate remains at 70 percent for the balance of this year).

REDUCTION IN CORPORATE RATES

Under present law, the corporate income tax is imposed at the following rates:

Taxable Income	Rate
Less than $25,000	17%
$25,000–$50,000	20%
$50,000–$75,000	30%
$75,000–$100,000	40%
Over $100,000	46%

The new law decreases the tax rates on the two lowest brackets, i.e., those imposing tax on taxable income below $50,000. The change will go into effect in 1982 and 1983.

The brackets below $50,000 will be adjusted as follows:

Taxable Income	Rate
In 1982—	
Less than $25,000	16%
$25,000–$50,000	19%
1983 and later years—	
Less than $25,000	15%
$25,000–$50,000	18%

See ¶¶ 1.05[2][d] and 1.05[5][a].

IMPUTED INTEREST RATES

If real estate is sold under an installment sales contract that provides for less than a fixed interest rate, a minimum portion of the installment payments must be treated as interest (such interest is called "imputed interest"). The rate formerly used for this purpose was 10 percent in the case of contracts that do not specifically provide for at least 9 percent interest.

The new law sets a maximum imputed interest rate of 7 percent on installment sales provided the following requirements are met:

(1) The sale is of land (not buildings);
(2) The sale is between members of the same family; and
(3) The total annual sales between the family members does not exceed $500,000. (The regular imputed interest rate applies to any sales above the ceiling.)

See ¶ 9.04.

DEPRECIATION DEDUCTIONS AND RECAPTURE

The rules concerning depreciation were formerly designed to allocate write-offs over the period the asset was used in business or for the production of income, so that deductions were matched with the income produced by the asset. The new law makes a significant shift in emphasis. For property placed in service during the current year, i.e., on or after January 1, 1981, deductions for depreciation may be taken over a set period that is shorter than the useful life of the asset. In other words, the new law recognizes that depreciation write-offs should be related to replacement cost rather than original cost; the result of this will be a substantial increase in depreciation write-offs during the early years of ownership of depreciable property. The new depreciation system is known as the Accelerated Cost Recovery System (ACRS).

The new depreciation rules apply to most tangible depreciable real and personal property. However, the new rules do not apply to property that must be amortized, e.g., leasehold improvements and low-income rehabilitation expenditures.

Depreciation Of Real Property

Former IRS guideline lives for real property ranged from forty to sixty years, but actual lives may be shorter under a facts-and-circumstances approach. The new law assigns real property a fifteen-year recovery period, but taxpayers may elect a thirty-five- or forty-five-year extended recovery period.

In choosing a depreciation method, taxpayers have the following options:

(1) *Accelerated Method.* If a taxpayer chooses accelerated depreciation, he must use the fifteen-year recovery period (not the thirty-five- or forty-five-year optional period). The accelerated method is either:

- The 175-percent declining balance method, changing to the straight-line method to maximize acceleration, for all types of real property other than low-income housing; or
- The 200-percent declining balance method, changing to straight-line, for low-income housing.

(2) *Straight-Line Depreciation.* The taxpayer may choose straight-line depreciation over either the fifteen-year period or one of the optional extended periods.

Observation. Composite depreciation is required under the new law. Component depreciation (whereby different useful lives are assigned to components of the structure) no longer will be permitted.

Recapture Of Real Property Depreciation

Prior to the 1981 law, gain on the disposition of real property was treated (recaptured) as ordinary income rather than as capital gain to the extent that prior depreciation taken by the taxpayer exceeded what would have been allowable if straight-line depreciation had been used.

Under the new law:

- The treatment of residential real property is unchanged (i.e., excess depreciation is recaptured).

- The treatment of nonresidential real property is unchanged if the straight-line depreciation method is used (i.e., no recapture will occur);

- The treatment for nonresidential real property depreciated under an accelerated method is changed. Beginning January 1, 1981, gain on the sale of such property is treated as ordinary income to the extent of all prior depreciation taken (not merely depreciation in excess of straight line).

See ¶ 1.05[2].

Calculating Corporate Earnings and Profits

In calculating its taxable income, a corporation is subject generally to the same depreciation rules as an individual taxpayer. However, in determining whether a corporate distribution to its shareholders is taxable as a dividend or as a return of capital, the rule is that such distributions are taxable as dividends only to the extent that the distribution is out of the corporation's *current or accumulated earnings and profits*. In determining what are "earnings and profits" under prior law, a corporation was required to use straight-line depreciation over the useful life of the property (whether or not it used an accelerated method in determining the corporation's taxable income). In short, a corporation using accelerated depreciation may have had no taxable income (and so may not have paid any corporate income tax); nevertheless, because it was forced to use straight-line depreciation in computing earnings and profits, some or all of its distributions to its shareholders may have been taxable to them as dividends.

Under the new law, the rule relating to the use of straight-line depreciation in computing earnings and profits is unchanged. However, the recovery period (i.e., useful life) of the property being depreciated will be in accordance with the following table:

Extended Recovery Period

Property	Years
3-year property	5
5-year property	12
10-year property	25
15-year property	35

If the corporate taxpayer elects to use one of the longer recovery periods as described above in the discussion of depreciation, then such longer period must be used to compute earnings and profits.

Observation. The effect of this new rule will be to permit a larger amount of corporate distributions to be tax-free to shareholders and to that extent will make corporate ownership of real estate more attractive than in the past. See ¶ 1.05[2][b].

Add-On Minimum Tax

Accelerated depreciation is valuable to taxpayers because it increases the amount of write-offs during the early years of property ownership. But using accelerated depreciation may have a cost too. Under prior law, excess depreciation (i.e., the amount of write-off in excess of that allowable using straight-line depreciation) was one of nine *tax preference items*. Such items were subject to a flat 15 percent minimum tax if the total of tax preference items exceeded in any year the greater of $10,000 or:

- One-half of regular income taxes in the case of non-corporate taxpayers, or
- The full amount of regular income taxes in the case of regular corporations.

Under the new law, the amount of depreciation which constitutes a tax preference is the excess of the depreciation actually taken by the taxpayer over the amount that would have been allowable using the straight-line method over the prescribed periods as set forth below:

Prescribed Period

Property	Years
3-year property	5
5-year property	8
10-year property	15
15-year property	15
15-year personal property	22

Observation. Under prior law, every dollar of a taxpayer's preference items reduced the amount of personal service taxable income that was eligible for the maximum tax rate of 50 percent. This provision becomes irrelevant under the new law since no income will be taxed at a higher rate than 50 percent. See ¶ 1.05[2][d].

REGULAR INVESTMENT CREDIT

The regular investment credit rules that apply primarily to acquisition of tangible personal property have been liberalized. See ¶ 1.05[2][d].

REHABILITATION INVESTMENT CREDIT

Under prior law, rehabilitation expenses for a nonresidential building at least twenty years old were eligible for the 10 percent investment tax credit (plus an additional energy credit). When the rehabilitation was of a certified historic structure, the taxpayer could elect, in lieu of the investment credit, a sixty-month amortization of such expenditures.

The new law substitutes for both the 10 percent investment credit and the sixty-month amortization, a three-tier investment credit. The credit is:

(1) 15 percent for nonresidential structures at least thirty years old;

(2) 20 percent for nonresidential structures at least forty years old; and

(3) 25 percent for certified historic structures, whether residential or nonresidential.

Conditions To Use Of Credit

Three conditions are attached to use of the investment credit for rehabilitation expenditures:

(1) *Straight-Line Depreciation*. The credit is available only if the taxpayer elects to use the straight-line method of cost recovery (depreciation) with respect to the rehabilitation expenditures.

(2) *Reduction of Basis*. For rehabilitation investment credits *other than* the credit for certified historic rehabilitations, the basis of the property must be reduced by the amount of the credit. (Thus, upon sale of the property, additional gain will be realized.)

(3) *Substantial Rehabilitation*. Finally, only a "substantial rehabilitation" qualifies for the investment credit. A building will be substantially rehabilitated if the rehabilitation expenses during the preceding two years are at least $5,000 *and* exceed the adjusted basis of the property as of the beginning of the period.

However, an investor may substitute a five-year period for the two-year period (thus making it much easier to qualify for the credit) if:

- Written plans and specifications exist for the entire rehabilitation process; and

- There is a reasonable expectation that the entire rehabilitation will be completed.

Historic Structure Rehabilitations

As noted above, rehabilitations of historic structures are eligible for a 25 percent investment credit. Such rehabilitations must meet two requirements:

(1) *Certified Historic Structure.* First, the building itself must be a "certified historic structure." This is defined as a depreciable structure which is:

- Listed in the *National Register* (existing law); or
- Located in a historic district designated under estate or local statute containing standards satisfactory to the Secretary of the Interior (existing law); or
- Located in a Registered Historic District (changes existing law which provides that, in addition, the Secretary of the Interior must certify that the particular building is of historic significance to the district).

(2) *Certified Rehabilitation.* Second, the rehabilitation must be certified by the Secretary of the Interior as being consistent with the historic character of the property or the district.

See ¶ 1.05[2][d].

LOW-INCOME HOUSING

The new law has two provisions that benefit investors in low-income housing.

Construction Period Taxes and Interest

Under prior law, taxpayers must capitalize and amortize construction period interest and taxes. This rule is not applicable to low-income housing until 1982.

The new law exempts low-income housing permanently from the requirement, which means that construction period interest and taxes in connection with low-income housing is immediately deductible.

Low-Income Housing Rehabilitations

Under present law, qualified low-income housing rehabilitation expenditures up to $20,000 per dwelling unit may be amortized over a sixty-month period. This fast write-off is intended to encourage such expenditures. The new law leaves the present rule unchanged but adds a provision that the amount of expenditures eligible for the fast write-off may increase to $40,000 per unit if:

(1) The rehabilitation is part of a program under which tenants who demonstrate homeownership responsibilities may purchase their units at a price that limits the seller's profit; and

(2) The tenants occupy the units as their principal residence.

This provision applies to amounts paid or incurred in 1981 and thereafter. See ¶ 1.05[2][d].